DP 2 No check figure
FSP Cash increased by $448.6 million.

8-1A Net accounts receivable, direct write-off method, $48,210; Net accounts receivable, allowance method, $45,140
8-2A 3. Net accounts receivable, $135,657; 4. Net accounts receivable, $136,400
8-3A Net accounts receivable, 19X7, $279,861
8-4A Note 3: Maturity value, $8,200; Less discount, $193; proceeds, $8,007
8-5A No check figure
8-1B Net accounts receivable, direct write-off method, $138,800; Net accounts receivable, allowance method, $129,900
8-2B 3. Net accounts receivable $160,601; 4. Net accounts receivable, $160,955
8-3B Net accounts receivable, 19X5, $163,651
8-4B Note 3: Maturity value, $8,400; Less discount, $271; proceeds, $8,129
8-5B No check figure
8-6B No check figure
DP 1 Net income, 19X3, $51,400
DP 2 No check figure
FSP Net Accounts Receivable at April 30, 1989, $307.3 million.

9-1A LIFO ending inventory, $25,609
9-2A FIFO inventory profit, $750
9-3A Gross margin: Average, $1,965; FIFO, $2,145; LIFO, $1,735
9-4A No check figure
9-5A Gross margin, $279,000
9-6A Net income: 19X1, $4 mil.; 19X2, $32 mil.; 19X3, $11 mil.
9-7A Estimated cost of ending inventory, $403,500
9-8A Ending inventory, at cost, $59,895
9-9A FIFO ending inventory, $1,080
9-1B LIFO ending inventory, $3,464
9-2B FIFO inventory profit, $285
9-3B Gross margin: Average, $54,520; FIFO, $55,170; LIFO, $53,870
9-4B No check figure
9-5B Gross margin, $154,000
9-6B Net income: 19X4, $31 mil.; 19X5, $34 mil.; 19X6, $39 mil.
9-7B Estimated cost of ending inventory, $367,400
9-8B Ending inventory, at cost, $37,281
9-9B FIFO ending inventory, $890
DP 1 Net income without purchase: FIFO, $42,000; LIFO, $37,000. Net income with purchase: FIFO, $42,000; LIFO, $25,000
DP 2 No check figure
FSP Total inventories at April 30, 1989, $344.7 million.

10-1A Depr.: Land improve., $2,805; Home office bldg., $22,459; Garage, $1,519; Furniture, $25,144
10-2A Depr. for 19X6: SL, $7,000; UOP, $7,560; Revenue Canada rate, $2,067

10- A No check figure
10-5A Cost of new truck, $18,578
10-6A No check figure
10-1B Depr.: Land improve., $2,277; Office bldg., $16,936; Storage bldg., $1,065; Furniture, $14,625
10-2B Depr. for 19X5: SL, $15,750; UOP, $11,250; Revenue Canada rate, $7,370
10-3B Depreciation expense, Dec. 31, 19X3, balance before closing, $3,916
10-4B No check figure
10-5B Cost of new truck, $16,807
10-6B No check figure
DP 1 Net income, Frycer Company $38,000 more than Bergdahl Company
DP 2 No check figure
FSP No check figure

11-1A No check figure
11-2A No check figure
11-3A Total liabilities, $283,926
11-4A Payroll Payable, $13,930
11-5A Total annual cost for employee, $53,337
11-6A 3. Cash payment, $13,557; 4. Cash payment, $8,816
11-7A Net pay, $1,767.76
11-1B No check figure
11-2B No check figure
11-3B Total liabilities, $317,035
11-4B Wage Expense, $15,640
11-5B Total annual cost for employee, $62,143.32
11-6B 3. Cash payment, $71,245; 4. Cash payment, $28,418
11-7B Net pay, $1,620.83
DP 1 No check figure
DP 2 No check figure
FSP No check figure

12-1A No check figure
12-2A No check figure
12-3A No check figure
12-4A Gross profit, installment method, $18,000
12-5A Net income, year 3, $60,200
12-6A Income, 19X8, percentage-of-completion method, $854,000
12-7A Correct net income, 19X5, $42,100
12-1B No check figure
12-2B No check figure
12-3B No check figure
12-4B Gross profit, installment method, $204,900
12-5B Net income, year 3, $105,830
12-6B Income, 19X6, percentage-of-completion method, $942,000
12-7B Correct net income, 19X9, $47,700
DP 1 Net income, $27,800
DP 2 No check figure
FSP No check figure

(continued on back cover)

FINANCIAL ACCOUNTING

Prentice-Hall Canada Series in Accounting

FINANCIAL ACCOUNTING

CANADIAN EDITION

Charles T. Horngren
Stanford University

Walter T. Harrison, Jr.
Baylor University

W. Morley Lemon
University of Waterloo

Prentice-Hall Canada Inc.
Scarborough, Ontario

Canadian Cataloguing in Publication Data

Horngren, Charles T., 1926–
    Financial accounting

(Prentice-Hall Canada series in accounting)
Canadian ed.

Contains financial accounting chapters from:
Horngren, Charles T., 1926–   . Accounting.
Canadian ed.
Includes index.
ISBN 0-13-318700-4

1. Accounting. I. Harrison, Walter T.   II. Lemon,
W. Morley, 1939–   . III. Title. IV. Series.

HF5635.H67 1991   657   C91-094099-1

Prentice-Hall, Inc., Englewood Cliffs, New Jersey
Prentice-Hall International, Inc., London
Prentice-Hall of Australia, Pty., Ltd., Sydney
Prentice-Hall of India Pvt., Ltd., New Delhi
Prentice-Hall of Japan, Inc., Tokyo
Prentice-Hall of Southeast Asia (Pte.) Ltd., Singapore
Editora Prentice-Hall do Brasil Ltda., Rio de Janeiro
Prentice-Hall Hispanoamericana, S.A., Mexico

ISBN 0-13-318700-4

Managing Editor: Yolanda de Rooy
Project Editor: David Jolliffe
Production Editor: Amy Lui-Ma
Art Director: Joe Chin
Production Coordinator: Crystale Chalmers
Paste-up Art: Brian Lehen   Shelley Parsons
Typesetting: Q Composition Inc.
Cover design: Bob Garbutt Productions
Cover art: Steuben crystal "Genesis" (designer: Donald Pollard;
    engraving designer: Terry Haas), 1959. Reproduced by
    permission of Steuben Glass, New York.

1 2 3 4 5 JDC 95 94 93 92 91

Printed and bound in Canada by John Deyell Company

Original U.S. edition published by Prentice-Hall Inc.,
Englewood Cliffs, New Jersey
Copyright © 1989 Prentice-Hall Inc.
This edition is authorized for sale in Canada only.

For our wives, Joan, Nancy and Margie

Brief Contents

Contents

4 Completing the Accounting
Cycle *131*

5 Merchandising and the Accounting
Cycle *175*

Part Two ————————————

*Introduction to Accounting
Systems* *225*

6 Accounting Information Systems *227*

Practice Set *275*

The Business Context of
FINANCIAL
ACCOUNTING

To enhance our presentation of accounting, we set out to create a business context for the student. As accounting educators, we know that students benefit from perceiving accounting as more than mere numbers set apart from the rest of their lives and education. We have constructed this business context in two ways.

(1) As often as possible, we have integrated real-world companies and their data into our text and assignment material. Students reading about companies familiar to them find the material more interesting and also develop a deeper appreciation for accounting's importance in today's business world. We have not used boxes to set aside this real-world material. Our references to the world of business are woven into our text narrative.

(2) When information drawn from real companies would be too advanced for introductory students, we have illustrated the accounting point at hand by using realistic examples, building a framework of relevance that makes learning the topic more inviting for the student.

The following list presents only a sampling of how our narrative creates a business context in Chapter 1, *Accounting and Its Environment*. This chapter contains many other realistic business examples. We invite readers to examine the chapter and other chapters to see how we incorporate the world of business throughout the entire book.

Chapter 1

pp. 1-2 A student's decision whether to attend college or university depends in part on accounting information, including the costs and benefits of various education choices.

p. 5 Investors and creditors use accounting information reported in *The Financial Post* and *The Globe and Mail*'s "Report on Business".

p. 7 Private accountants work for a local department store, the Swiss Chalet restaurant chain or Alcan Aluminium.

pp. 8-9 The three major accounting bodies in Canada are the Canadian Institute of Chartered Accountants, the Certified General Accountants Association of Canada and the Society of Management Accountants of Canada.

p. 11 London Life Insurance Co. and J.M. Schneider are leaders in budgeting. Hudson's Bay Co. and the Toronto-Dominion Bank have internal auditors.

p. 13 To illustrate the entity concept, the income from the pizzeria owner's personal business dealings is distinguished from the pizzeria's operations.

p. 16 Gary Lyon, CA, is introduced. His accounting practice is used to illustrate proprietorships throughout Chapters 1 through 4.

p. 25 Fast Apartment Locators, owned by Jill Smith, is the subject of a *Summary Problem for Your Review*, which asks students to record transactions and prepare financial statements.

p. 30 In Exercise 1-2, students use the accounting equation to analyze the first month's events for the medical practice of Gloria Hill, M.D.

p. 31 Exercise 1-5 uses the business of Fadal Travel Agency to focus on income statement preparation.

p. 32 Stevens Interiors in Problem 1-1A provides the data with which students analyze transactions and prepare financial statements.

p. 33 In Problem 1-2A, Zane Jones, a lawyer, opens up his own law office. Students are tested on the entity concept, transaction analysis, and the accounting equation using his business.

p. 41 *Decision Problem 1* centres on whether to loan money to Butler Department Store or Nielson Home Decorators.

p. 42 The *Financial Statement Problem* requires students to turn to the actual financial statements of John Labatt Limited, which appears in Appendix E, and asks them to write the accounting equation at April 30, 1989. Many chapters feature a *Financial Statement Problem*, which ties the chapter's topic directly to John Labatt's financial statements.

Charles T. Horngren is the Edmund W. Littlefield Professor of Accounting at Stanford University. A graduate of Marquette University, he received his M.B.A. from Harvard University and his Ph.D. from the University of Chicago. He is also the recipient of honorary doctorates from Marquette University and DePaul University.

A Certified Public Accountant, Horngren served on the Accounting Principles Board for six years, the Financial Accounting Standards Board Advisory Council for five years and the Council of the American Institute of Certified Public Accountants for three years. He is currently serving as a trustee of the Financial Accounting Foundation.

A member of the American Accounting Association, Horngren has been its President and its Director of Research. He received the Outstanding Accounting Educator Award in 1973, when the association initiated an annual series of such awards.

The California Certified Public Accountants Foundation gave Horngren its Faculty Excellence Award in 1975 and its Distinguished Professor Award in 1983. He is the first person to have received both awards.

In 1985 the American Institute of Certified Public Accountants presented its first Outstanding Educator Award to Horngren.

Professor Horngren is also a member of the National Association of Accountants, where he was on its research planning committee for three years. He was a member of the Board of Regents, Institute of Management Accounting, which administers the Certified Management Accountant examinations.

Horngren is the author of three other books published by Prentice Hall: *Cost Accounting: A Managerial Emphasis,* Seventh Edition, 1991 (with George Foster); *Introduction to Financial Accounting,* Third Edition, 1987 (with Gary L. Sundem); and *Introduction to Management Accounting,* Eighth Edition, 1990 (with Gary L. Sundem).

Charles T. Horngren is the Consulting Editor for the Prentice Hall Series in Accounting.

Walter T. Harrison, Jr., is Professor of Accounting and holds the
Peat Marwick-Thomas L. Holton Chair in Accounting at the
Hankamer School of Business, Baylor University. He received his
B.B.A. degree from Baylor University, his M.S. from Oklahoma
State University and his Ph.D. from Michigan State University.

Professor Harrison, recipient of numerous teaching awards from
student groups as well as from university administrators, has also
taught at Cleveland State Community College, Michigan State
University, the University of Texas and Stanford University.

A member of the American Accounting Association and the
American Institute of Certified Public Accountants, Professor
Harrison has served as Chairperson of the Financial Accounting
Standards Committee of the American Accounting Association and
on the Program Advisory Committee for Accounting Education
and Teaching.

Professor Harrison has published research articles in numerous
journals, including *The Accounting Review, Journal of Accounting
Research, Journal of Accountancy, Journal of Accounting and Public
Policy* and *Economic Consequences of Financial Accounting Standards.*
He has received scholarships, fellowships and research grants
from Price Waterhouse & Co., Deloitte Haskins & Sells and the
Arthur Young Tax Research Program.

W. Morley Lemon is Associate Professor of Accounting at the School of Accountancy, University of Waterloo. He received his B.A. from the University of Western Ontario, his M.B.A. from the University of Toronto and his Ph.D. from the University of Texas at Austin.

Professor Lemon has taught at the University of Texas, the University of Illinois, McMaster University and the University of Waterloo. In addition, he has taught and prepared courses for professional accountants and accounting students in Canada and the United States.

A member of the Institute of Chartered Accountants of Ontario, Professor Lemon was elected a Fellow by that body. He is also a member of the Canadian Academic Accounting Association and the American Accounting Association, and has served as Chairperson of and on committees for all three organizations.

Professor Lemon is the author of *Auditing: An Integrated Approach*, Canadian Fourth Edition, 1987 (with Alvin A. Arens and James K. Loebbecke), published by Prentice-Hall Canada Inc. He has co-authored a monograph published by the Canadian Academic Accounting Association, and has published articles in *CAMagazine, Contemporary Accounting Research*, and other professional and academic publications. He has received scholarships, fellowships and research grants from the Canadian Academic Accounting Association, Peat Marwick, and Ernst and Whinney.

Preface

In content and emphasis, instructors will find that **Financial Accounting** is in the mainstream for courses in introductory accounting. This book focuses on the most widely used accounting theory and practice. This text and its supplements supply the most effective tools available for learning fundamental accounting concepts and procedures.

Clarity and Accuracy

Two themes have directed our writing of this text: *clarity* and *accuracy*. We believe that we have produced the clearest prose, learning objectives, exhibits, definitions, and assignment material for courses in principles of accounting. Students will find this book easy to study. We have assumed that students have no previous education in accounting or business.

The contributions of technical reviewers, general reviewers, and class testers and their students have guided us in writing an accurate text. We and the publishers have sought input on our work from an unprecedented number of accounting educators and students in order to publish a book that meets your strict demands for accuracy.

Distinctive Features

Financial Accounting offers many features that make this text special and superior.

1. **Financial Accounting** has more — and better — exercises and problems on this subject than the leading competitors. Exercises and problems tie directly with the text in terminology, setup and difficulty level. They progress from simple to complex, from short to long.
2. The emphasis on real-world examples promotes student interest.
3. The two color design enlivens and eases learning. A strong program of visual features — exhibits and tables — helps reinforce the text.
4. An up-to-the-minute chapter on the statement of changes in financial position, Chapter 18, presents a framework for understanding both the concepts and procedures underlying the statement and its preparation.
5. Appendix A: Taxation in Canada provides a thorough introduction to taxation in Canada. There is a discussion of the preparation of a personal income tax return in which the various kinds of income and the major deductions are described. Corporate taxation is also discussed.

6. Appendix B: Accounting with Computers provides a useful introduction to computers as they apply to accounting. The appendix, which expands the discussion of computers in Chapter 6, includes a discussion of accounting software programs and of various modules, such as an accounts receivable module, that can be used by an entity to provide computerized accounting services.

7. Appendix C: Mathematical Presentations presents the mathematical operations essential to accounting. Students may refer to this appendix to refresh their knowledge of necessary math skills.

8. Appendix D: Reversing Entries offers instructors the opportunity to teach reversing entries. This appendix is presented in a standard text chapter format, complete with learning objectives and assignment material.

Chapter Organization

1. Each chapter begins with *Learning Objectives*, which also appear in the margin, keyed to the relevant chapter material.

2. Most chapters offer two *Summary Problems for Your Review*. Each *Summary Problem* includes its fully worked-out solution. These features, which generally appear at the halfway point and at the end of each chapter, provide students with immediate feedback and serve as key review aids.

3. Each chapter presents three important tools for student review. A text *Summary* recaps the chapter discussion. *Self-Study Questions* allow students to test their understanding of the chapter. The text that supports the answer is referenced by page number, and the answers appear on the last page of the chapter. *Accounting Vocabulary* presents the key terms introduced in the chapter, referenced by page number. A complete Glossary, also with terms keyed by page number, appears at the end of the book.

4. *Assignment Material* is more varied and plentiful than in competing texts. *Questions*, covering the major definitions, concepts, and procedures, may be assigned as homework or used to promote in-class discussion. **Financial Accounting** has more exercises and more problems than the competitors. *Exercises*, identified by topic area, cover the full spectrum of the chapter text. These "short problems" allow instructors to cover a wide range of topics in a limited time. *Problems*, also identified by topic area, come in A and B sets. The two sets allow instructors to vary assignments from term to term and to solve the A or B problem in class and assign the related problem for homework.

5. Each chapter presents two *Decision Problems*, which help students to develop critical thinking skills. Analysis, interpretation and determining a course of action are ordinarily required.

6. Most chapters feature a *Financial Statement Problem*. In these problems, the chapter's subject matter is directly linked to the actual financial statements of John Labatt Limited, which appear in Appendix E. As students progress through the course, they will grow increasingly comfortable with the real-world financial report of a large company.

The Supplements Package

We have a far-reaching, highly developed package of teaching and learning tools to supplement the text. A team of numerous contributors, editors and coordinators, and a multitude of reviewers devoted hundreds of hours to perfecting the supplements.

Resources for the Instructor

Annotated Instructor's Edition

Solutions Manuals (Volume I, Chapters 1–13 and Appendix D; Volume II, Chapters 12–26)

Test Bank

Computerized Test Bank

Solutions & Teaching Transparencies

Resources for the Student

Study Guide with Demonstration and Practice Problems (Volume I, Chapters 1–13; Volume II, Chapters 12–26)

Working Papers (Volume I, Chapters 1–13 and Appendix D; Volume II, Chapters 12–26)

PHACTS Videos

Manual and Computerized Practice Sets

Lotus 1-2-3 Templates for Selected Problems

Acknowledgments to the Canadian Edition _____

I would like first to thank Chuck Horngren and Tom Harrison for their encouragement and support.

Special thanks to Carol E. Dilworth for all her work. Thanks to Jack Hanna, University of Waterloo, for his help with the material in Chapter 17 on inflation accounting. Thanks also to Ralph Myers, Ryerson Polytechnical Institute, for his work on the appendix on income taxes and Peter H. Fuhrman, Fraser Valley College, for his work on the appendix on computers. The work of Melanie Russell on the Test Bank and Lynn Miske on the Solutions Manual is also appreciated.

I would also like to thank the following individuals for the invaluable assistance they provided in reviewing the text and supplements and for providing so many helpful suggestions:

Wayne A. Campbell
Ray Carroll
Johan de Rooy
Randy Dickson
Janet E. Falk
Harvey C. Freedman
John Glendenning
Maureen Labonté
Robert F. Madden
Allen McQueen
Michael A. Perretta
Gordon Rice
Al Scherbluk
Ralph H. Sweet
Nora Wilson
Leroy Wright

Thanks are extended to Robert G. Vaux, John Labatt Limited, for permission to use the John Labatt Limited annual report. Thanks are also due to John Labatt and National Trust for permission to use as exhibits a bond and a stock certificate, respectively issued by their companies, and Four Seasons Hotels Inc. and TransCanada PipeLines Limited for permission to use as illustrations management letters from their annual reports.

Publications from the Canadian Institute of Chartered Accountants, the Butterworths series on Financial Statement Presentation prepared by the partners of Price Waterhouse and edited by Christina Drummond, *The Financial Post*, *The Globe and Mail*, and financial statements issued by a large number of Canadian companies have been very helpful in the writing of this book.

I would like especially to acknowledge the people of Prentice-Hall Canada, especially the editorial work of David Jolliffe and the support of Yolanda de Rooy over the past months as the Canadian Edition took shape. I would also like to acknowledge the editorial support of Amy Lui-Ma and Marta Tomins. And I would like to thank Lu Mitchell, who was there at the start.

Finally, I thank my family for their encouragement and support.

W. Morley Lemon
Waterloo, Ontario
1991

PART ONE

The Basic Structure
of Accounting

1

Accounting and Its Environment

LEARNING OBJECTIVES

After studying this chapter, you should be able to

1 Define accounting

2 Identify users of accounting information

3 Identify different aspects of the accounting profession

4 Identify the three different types of business organizations

5 Apply accounting concepts and principles to business situations

6 Use the accounting equation to describe an organization

7 Use the accounting equation to analyse business transactions

8 Describe three financial statements

Accounting has been called "the language of business." Perhaps a better term is "the language of financial decisions." The better you understand the language, the better you can manage the financial aspects of living. Personal financial planning, investments, loans, car payments, income taxes, and many other aspects of daily life are based on accounting.

A recent survey indicates that business managers believe college students should spend more time and effort learning accounting than studying any other subject. Other surveys show that persons trained in accounting and finance make it to the top of their organizations in greater numbers than persons trained in any other field. Indeed, accounting is an important subject.

Decisions and Accounting

Do you make decisions that have a financial impact? Your answer is undoubtedly yes. Regardless of your roles in life — student, head of household, investor, manager, politician — you will find a knowledge of accounting helpful. The major purpose of this book is to help you learn to use accounting information to make informed decisions. Individuals who can do so have a great advantage over those who cannot.

As a student you must decide whether to attend a community college or a university. And how are you going to finance your education? To make these decisions, you weigh the costs and benefits of the various educational choices. These decisions are largely accounting matters. Accounting is also used to form a financial picture of complex businesses, such as Bell Canada Enterprises (BCE) and Canadian Pacific. Being able to understand their financial statements will help you make wise investment decisions.

<table>
<tr><td>OBJECTIVE 1
Define accounting</td></tr>
</table>

What Is Accounting?

Accounting is the system that measures business activities, processes that information into reports and financial statements, and communicates these findings to decision-makers. **Financial statements** are the documents that report on an individual's or an organization's business in monetary amounts.

Is the business making a profit? Should we start up a new line of stereo systems? Are sales strong enough to warrant opening a new branch outlet? The most intelligent answers to business questions may be found by using accounting information.

Decision-makers use the information to develop sound business plans. As new programs affect the business's activities, accounting takes the company's financial pulse beat. The cycle continues as the accounting system measures the results of activities and forwards the results to the decision-makers.

Bookkeeping is not accounting, as some people think, but only the clerical recording of the information that accountants use in their work. Bookkeeping is a procedural element of accounting as arithmetic is a procedural element of mathematics. Increasingly, people are using computers to do much of the detailed bookkeeping work at all levels—in households, business, and organizations of all types. Exhibit 1-1 illustrates the role of accounting in business.

EXHIBIT 1-1 *The Accounting System: the Flow of Information*

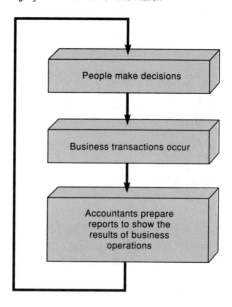

Users of Accounting Information _____

| **OBJECTIVE 2** |
| Identify users of accounting information |

Most of the material in this book describes business situations, but the principles of accounting are also important in the financial considerations of individuals. A range of people and groups use accounting information.

Household Members   "Ordinary" people use accounting information in day-to-day affairs to manage their bank accounts, evaluate job prospects, make investments, and decide whether to rent or buy a house.

Businesses   Managers of businesses use accounting information to set goals for their organizations, evaluate their progress toward those goals, and take corrective action if necessary. Decisions based on accounting information may include which building and equipment to purchase, how much merchandise inventory to keep on hand, and how much cash to borrow.

Investors and Creditors   Investors provide the money that businesses need to begin operations. To decide whether to help start up a new venture, potential investors evaluate what return they can reasonably expect on their investment. This means analysing the financial statements of the new business. Those people who do invest monitor the progress of the business by analysing the company's financial statements and by keeping up with its developments in the business press, for example, *The Financial Post, The Financial Times of Canada* and *Report on Business* published by *The Globe and Mail*. Accounting reports are a major source of information for the business press.

Before making a loan, potential lenders determine the borrower's ability to meet scheduled payments. This evaluation includes a projection of future operations, which is based on accounting information.

Government Regulatory Agencies   Most organizations face government regulation. For example, the provincial securities commissions in British Columbia, Alberta, Saskatchewan, Manitoba, Ontario and Quebec see that businesses, which sell their shares or borrow money from the public, disclose certain financial information to the investing public. The Ontario Securities Commission (OSC), like many government agencies, bases its regulatory activity in part on the accounting information it receives from the firms that it watches over.

Taxing Authorities   Local, provincial and federal governments levy taxes on individuals and businesses. The amount of the tax is figured using accounting information. Businesses determine their sales tax based on their accounting records that show how much they have sold. Individuals and businesses compute their income tax based on how much money their records show they have earned.

Nonprofit Organizations   Nonprofit organizations such as churches, hospitals, government agencies and colleges, which operate for purposes other than to earn a profit, use accounting information in much the same way that profit-oriented businesses do, that is, to manage and control their operations. Both profit organizations and nonprofit organizations deal with budgets, payrolls, rent payments, and the like — all from the accounting system.

Other users   Employees and labour unions may make wage demands based on the accounting information that shows their employer's reported income. Consumer groups and the general public are also interested in the amount of income that businesses earn. For example, during times of fuel shortages, consumer groups have charged that oil companies have earned "obscene profits." On a more positive note, newspapers may report "improved profit pictures" of major companies as the nation emerges from an economic recession. Such news, based on accounting information, is of widespread interest because it covers the economic activity that affects our standard of living.

The Development of Accounting Thought

The importance of accounting is further shown by the fact that its value was recognized early in the human evolution. Some scholars claim that writing arose in order to record accounting information. Account records date back to the ancient civilizations of China, Babylonia, Greece and Egypt. The rulers of these civilizations used accounting to keep track of the cost of labour and materials used in building structures like the great pyramids.

Accounting developed further as a result of the information needs of merchants in the city-states of Italy during the 1400s. In that busy commercial climate, the monk Luca Pacioli, a mathematician and friend of Leonardo da Vinci, published in 1494 the first known description of double-entry bookkeeping. Double-entry accounting, which we will look at in the next chapter, is practiced today in much the same way Pacioli described it nearly five hundred years ago.

The pace of accounting development increased during the Industrial Revolution of the eighteenth and nineteenth centuries as the economies of developed countries moved from handcraft industries to the factory system and mass-produced goods. Until this time, merchandise had been priced by merchants based on their hunches about cost, but the increased competition in the Industrial Revolution required merchants to adopt more sophisticated cost accounting systems. The specialized field of cost accounting emerged to meet managers' needs for accurate cost data.

In the nineteenth century, the growth of corporations, especially those in the railroad and steel industries, spurred the continuing development of accounting. The corporation owners — the shareholders — were no longer necessarily the managers of their business. Company management had to create accounting systems to report the business's operating results and financial position to the shareholders.

The role of government has led to still more accounting developments. When the federal government started collecting income tax, accounting supplied the concept "income." Also, as economic activities become more complex, government at all levels has assumed expanded roles in health, education, labour and economic planning. To ensure that the information that it uses to make decisions is reliable, government has required strict accountability in the business community.

The Accounting Profession

The accountability demanded of the business community is as complex as it is strict and nowadays requires the specialized skills of professional accountants. Today the field of accounting may be divided into several areas. The two general classifications are *public accounting* and *private accounting*. **Public accountants** are those who serve the general public and collect professional fees for their work, much as doctors and lawyers do. Their work includes auditing, income tax planning and preparation of returns, management consulting, and various accounting services. These specialized accounting services are discussed in the next section. Public accountants are a small fraction of all accountants.

Private accountants work for a single business, such as a local department store, the Swiss Chalet restaurant chain or Alcan Aluminium. Charitable organizations, educational institutions and government agencies also employ private accountants. The chief accounting officer usually has the title of controller, treasurer or chief financial officer. Whatever the title, this person usually carries the status of vice-president.

In Canada, accountants, both public and private, belong to one of three accounting bodies, which are responsible for professional standards and procedures: The Canadian Institute of Chartered Accountants, whose members are called Chartered Accountants (CA); the Certified General Accountants Association of Canada, whose members are called Certified General Accountants (CGA); and the Society of Management Accountants of Canada, whose members are called Certified Management Accountants (CMA). The role and activities of each of these bodies are discussed below.

Some public accountants pool their talents and work together within a single firm. Public accounting firms are called *CA firms*, *CGA firms* or *CMA firms*, depending on the accounting body from which the partners of the firm come. Public accounting firms vary greatly in size. Some are small businesses, and others are medium-sized partnerships. The largest firms are worldwide partnerships with over 2,000 partners. Such huge firms are necessary because some of their clients are so large and their operations are so complex. For instance, Price Waterhouse, one of the six largest international public accounting firms, has reported that its annual audit of one particular client would take one accountant 630,720 hours of effort—that equals 72 years of nonstop work! Another Price Waterhouse client owns 300 separate corporate entities. All their records are combined into a single set of financial statements. Such time-consuming tasks make a large staff of accountants a necessity.

The six largest accounting firms in the world are often called the Big Six. They represent the first five and eighth largest CA firms in Canada and are, in alphabetical order:

Arthur Anderson
Coopers & Lybrand
Deloitte & Touche (Samson Belair/
   Deloitte & Touche in Quebec)
Ernst & Young (formerly
   Clarkson Gordon)
Peat Marwick Thorne
Price Waterhouse

Although these firms employ only about 17 percent of the 45,000 CAs in Canada, they audit approximately 85 percent of the 1,000 largest corporations. The top partners in large accounting firms earn about the same amount as the top managers of large private businesses.

Exhibit 1-2 shows the accounting positions within public accounting firms

EXHIBIT 1-2 *Accounting Positions within Organizations*

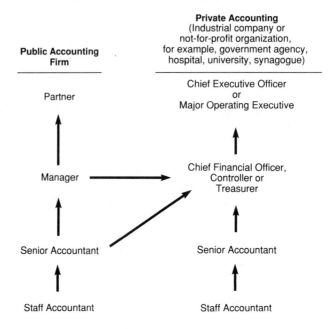

and other organizations. Of special interest in the exhibit is the upward movement of accounting personnel, as the arrows show. In particular, note how accountants may move from positions in public accounting firms to similar or higher positions in industry and government. This is a frequently traveled career path. Because accounting deals with all facets of an organization, such as purchasing, manufacturing, marketing and transportation, it provides an excellent basis for gaining broad business experience.

Accounting Organizations and Designations

The importance of accounting in today's business world has created the need for control over the professional, educational and ethical standards of accountants. Through statutes passed by provincial legislatures, the three accounting organizations in Canada have received the authority to set educational requirements and professional standards for their members and to discipline members who fail to adhere to their codes of conduct. The acts make them self-regulating bodies, just as provincial associations of doctors and lawyers are.

The *Canadian Institute of Chartered Accountants* (CICA), whose members are chartered accountants or CAs, is the senior accounting organization in Canada. Experience and education requirements for becoming a CA vary among the provinces. Generally, the educational requirement includes a university degree. All provinces, however, require that an individual, to qualify as a CA, pass a national four-day uniform final examination administered by the CICA. The province grants the right to use the professional designation CA.

CAs in Canada must earn their practical experience by working for a public accounting firm; subsequently, about half the CAs in Canada leave public practice for jobs in industry, government or education. A small number of CAs meet their experience requirements working for the federal or provincial governments. CAs in public accounting have the right to perform audits and issue opinions on the audited financial statements in all provinces in Canada.

CAs belong to a provincial institute (*Ordre* in Quebec) and through that body to the CICA. The provincial institutes have the responsibility for developing and enforcing the code of professional conduct which guides the actions of the CAs in that province.

The CICA, through the *Accounting Standards Committee (AcSC)* and the *Auditing Standards Committee (AuSC)* respectively, promulgates accounting standards (**Generally Accepted Accounting Principles** or **GAAP** which are discussed later in this chapter and Chapter 12) and auditing standards (**Generally Accepted Auditing Standards** or **GAAS**). These standards are enunciated in the *CICA Handbook*. Specific standards are italicized and called *recommendations*. Accounting recommendations are the standards or regulations that govern the preparation of financial statements in Canada. Steering committees of AcSC and AuSC publish accounting and auditing guidelines respectively; these do not have the force of recommendations, but simply provide guidance on specific issues. A third body, the *Public Sector Accounting and Auditing Committee (PSAAC)*, issues standards pertaining to public sector accounting and auditing. The CICA supports and publishes research relating primarily to financial reporting and auditing, and publishes a monthly professional journal *CAMagazine*.

The *Certified General Accountants Association of Canada (CGAAC)* is also regulated by provincial law. The experience and education requirements for becoming a CGA vary from province to province, but in all provinces the individual must either pass national examinations administered by the CGAAC in the various subject areas, or gain exemption by taking specified university courses. Certain subjects may only be passed by taking a national examination.

CGAs may gain their practical experience through work in public accounting, industry or government. They are employed in public practice, industry and government. Some provinces license CGAs in public practice, which gives them the right to conduct audits and issue opinions on financial statements, while some other provinces do not require a licence for them to perform audits.

The association supports research in various areas pertaining to accounting through the Canadian CGA Research Foundation. CGAAC publishes a professional journal entitled *CGA Magazine*.

The *Society of Management Accountants of Canada (SMAC)* administers the *Certified Management Accountant* program which leads to the Certified Management Accountant (CMA) designation. The use of this designation is similarly controlled by provincial law. Students generally must have a university degree, and must pass examinations in required subject areas as well as three uniform national exams administered by the SMAC at the end of the course. They must also meet experience requirements in order to earn the right to use the designation. CMAs earn their practical experience in industry or government, and are generally employed in industry or government although some CMAs are in public accounting. The Society promulgates standards relating to management accounting through the SMAC. The SMAC conducts and publishes research relating primarily to management accounting, and publishes a professional journal entitled *Cost and Management*.

The *Financial Executives Institute (FEI)* is an organization composed of senior financial executives from many of the larger corporations in Canada, who meet on a regular basis with a view to sharing information on how they can better manage their organization. Most of these executives have one of the three designations just discussed. It supports and publishes research relating to management accounting, and also publishes a journal, the *Financial Executive*.

The *Institute of Internal Auditors (IIA)* is a world-wide organization of internal auditors. It administers the examinations leading to and grants the Certified Internal Auditor (CIA) designation. Internal auditors are employees of an organization whose job is to review the operations, including financial operations, of the organization with a view to making it more efficient and effective.

Many Canadian internal auditors are members of Canadian chapters of the IIA. It supports and publishes research and conducts courses related in internal auditing. The IIA journal is *The Internal Auditor*.

The *Canadian Academic Accounting Association* (*CAAA*) directs its attention toward the academic and research aspects of accounting. A high percentage of its members are professors. The CAAA publishes a journal, *Contemporary Accounting Research*.

Specialized Accounting Services _____

Because accounting affects so many people in so many different fields, public accounting and private accounting include specialized services.

Public Accounting

Auditing is the most significant service that public accountants perform. An audit is the independent examination that assures the reliability of the accounting reports that management prepares and submits to investors, creditors, and others outside the business. In carrying out an audit, public accountants from outside a business examine the business's financial statements. If the public accountants believe that these documents fairly represent the business's operations, they offer a professional opinion stating that the firm's financial statements are in accordance with generally accepted accounting principles, which is the standard used by the profession. Why is the audit so important? Creditors considering loans want assurance that the facts and figures the business submits are reliable. Shareholders, who have invested in the business, need to know that the financial picture management shows them is complete. Government agencies need information from businesses.

Tax accounting has two aims: complying with the tax laws and minimizing taxes to be paid. Because combined federal and provincial income tax rates range as high as 47 percent for individuals and 46 percent for corporations, reducing income tax is an important management consideration. Tax work by accountants consists of preparing tax returns and planning business transactions in order to minimize taxes. Public accountants advise individuals on what types of investments to make, and on how to structure their estates and design their transactions.

Management consulting is the catchall term that describes the wide scope of advice public accountants provide to help managers run a business. As they conduct audits, public accountants look deep into a business's operations. With the insight they gain, they often make suggestions for improvements in cost accounting, budgeting and information systems design. (We discuss these areas of accounting in the next section.) Management consulting is the fastest-growing service provided by accountants.

Accounting services is also a catchall term used to describe the wide range of services related to accounting provided by public accountants. These services include bookkeeping, write-up work and preparation of financial statements on a monthly or annual basis. Some small companies have all their accounting done by a public accounting firm.

Private Accounting

Cost accounting determines and controls a business's costs. Traditionally, cost accounting has emphasized manufacturing costs, but it is increasingly concerned with the cost of selling the goods. Good cost accounting records guide managers in pricing their products to achieve greater profits. Also, cost accounting information shows management when a product is not profitable and should be dropped.

Budgeting sets sales and profit goals and develops detailed plans — called budgets — for achieving those goals. Many companies regard their budgeting activities as one of the most important aspects of their accounting systems. Some of the most successful companies in Canada have been pioneers in the field of budgeting, London Life Insurance Co. and J.M. Schneider Inc., the meat packing company, for example.

Information systems design identifies the organization's information needs, both internal and external. It then develops and implements a system to meet those needs. Accounting information systems help control the organization's operations. Flow charts and manuals that describe the various functions of the business and the placement of responsibility with specific employees are parts of system design.

Internal auditing is performed by a business's own accountants. Many large organizations — Ontario Hydro, Hudson's Bay Co. and the Toronto-Dominion Bank among them — maintain a staff of internal auditors. These accountants evaluate the firm's own accounting and management systems. Their aim is to improve operating efficiency, and to ensure that employees and departments follow management's procedures and plans.

The specialized functions that accountants perform are many and important. For convenience, we have grouped them under public accounting and private accounting. Exhibit 1-3 summarizes these specializations. They may also be grouped under the headings "financial accounting" and "management accounting."

EXHIBIT 1-3 Accounting

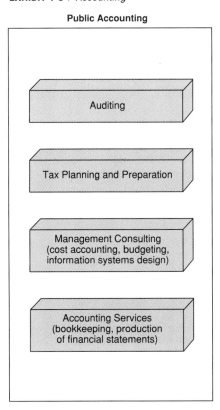

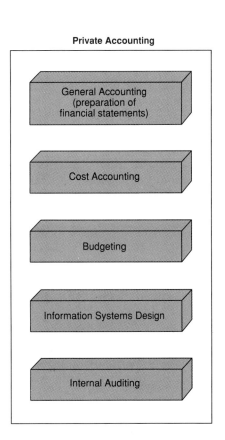

Financial accounting provides information to people outside the firm. Creditors and shareholders, for example, are not part of the day-to-day management of the company. Likewise, government agencies, such as Revenue Canada and the Alberta Securities Commission, and the general public are external users of a firm's accounting information. Chapters 2 through 19 of this book deal primarily with financial accounting.

Management accounting generates confidential information, including cost accounting information, for internal decision-makers, such as top executives, department heads, college deans and hospital administrators. Chapters 20 through 26 cover this aspect of accounting.

OBJECTIVE 4
Identify the three different types of business organizations

Types of Business Organizations

The accountants, who provide the private accounting services just described, provide them to three different kinds of businesses: proprietorships, partnerships and corporations. You should understand the characteristics of the three, since they have different forms of organization, and in some cases the accounting procedures depend on the organizational form. For example, the owners' interest is called capital for a proprietorship and partnership, and shareholders' equity for a corporation. Distributions to owners are called withdrawals in the case of a proprietorship or partnership, and dividends in the case of a corporation. Proprietorships and partnerships do not pay taxes on income while corporations do.

A **proprietorship** has a single owner, called the proprietor, who is usually also the manager. Proprietorships tend to be small retail establishments and individual professional businesses, such as those of physicians, lawyers and accountants. From the accounting viewpoint, each proprietorship is distinct from its proprietor. Thus the accounting records of the proprietorship do *not* include records of the proprietor's personal affairs.

A **partnership** joins two or more individuals together as co-owners. Each owner is a partner. Many retail establishments, as well as some professional organizations of physicians, lawyers and accountants, are partnerships. Most partnerships are small and medium-sized, but some are gigantic, running to more than 700 partners. We treat the partnership as a separate organization, distinct from the personal affairs of each partner.

A **corporation** is a business owned by **shareholders**. The business becomes a corporation when the federal or provincial government approves its articles of incorporation. A corporation is a legal entity, an "artificial person" that conducts its business in its own name. Like the proprietorship and partnership, the corporation is also an organization with existence separate from its owners.

Accounting Concepts and Principles

Accounting practices rest on certain guidelines. The rules that govern how accountants measure, process and communicate financial information fall under the heading GAAP, which stands for generally accepted accounting principles. Among these rules are the *entity concept, reliability* or *objectivity principle* and *cost principle.*

The Entity Concept

The most basic concept in accounting is that of the *entity*. An accounting entity is an organization or a section of an organization that stands apart from other organizations and individuals as a separate economic unit. From an accounting perspective, sharp boundaries are drawn around each entity so as not to confuse its affairs with those of other entities.

Consider a pizzeria owner whose bank account shows a $20,000 balance at the end of the year. Only half of that amount, $10,000, grew from the business's operations. The other $10,000 arose from the owner's sale of the family motorboat. If the owner follows the entity concept, he will keep separate the money generated by the business — one economic unit — from the money generated by the sale of an item belonging not to the business but to himself — a second economic unit. This separation makes it possible to view the business's operating result clearly. The owner knows that the pizzeria did not bring in much money. To turn his pizzeria into a more profitable business, he probably must make some operating changes.

Suppose he disregards the entity concept and treats the full $20,000 amount as income from the pizzeria's operations. He will be misled into believing that the business has performed twice as well as it has. The steps needed to improve the business will likely not be taken.

Consider Canadian Pacific Ltd. (CP), the fourth largest company in Canada with revenues exceeding $12 billion and assets exceeding $18 billion. CP has five divisions: Transportation (which includes CP Rail, CP Ships and CP Trucks), Energy (which includes PanCanadian Petroleum), Forest Products (which includes Great Lakes Forest Products), Real Estate and Hotels (which includes Marathon Realty and Canadian Pacific Hotels), and Manufacturing (which includes AMCA International and CP Telecommunications). Management of CP considers each company in each division to be a separate accounting entity. The divisions and the companies in them produce financial data so that the management of CP will know how each division and each company in that division is doing. If all the revenue data were combined in a lump-sum amount and suppose CP Ships were doing badly, management of CP would not know that was the case. And because management did not know what CP Ships situation was, they would not be able to suggest a solution to the problem. However, because the separate financial statements are prepared, CP management would know immediately if CP Ships or any other company in the group was having problems.

Other accounting entities include professional organizations such as a law firm, a doctor's practice, a hospital, a church or synagogue, a college or university, and a family household. Each entity may have a number of subentities. For example, family accounting for a household can be organized by expenditures. The household may break overall costs down into payments for food, housing, utilities, clothing, health care and recreation. To control these costs, the household may consider each category a subentity in its accounting.

In summary, business transactions should not be confused with personal transactions. Similarly, the transactions of different entities should not be accounted for together. Each entity should be evaluated separately.

The Reliability (or Objectivity) Principle

Accounting records and statements are based on the most *reliable data* available so that they will be as accurate and useful as possible. This is the reliability principle. Reliable data are verifiable. They may be confirmed by any independent observer. Ideally, then, accounting records are based on information that flows from activities that are documented by objective evidence. Without the reliability principle, also called the objectivity principle, accounting records would be based on whims and opinions and would be subject to dispute.

Suppose you start a stereo shop, and in order to have a place for operations, you transfer a small building to the business. You believe the building is worth $55,000. To confirm its value, you hire two real estate professionals, who appraise the building at $47,000. Is $55,000 or $47,000 the more reliable estimate of the building's value? The real estate appraisal of $47,000 is, because it is supported by independent, objective observation.

The Cost Principle

The *cost principle* states that assets and services that are acquired should be recorded at their actual cost, also called historical cost. Even though the purchaser may believe the price paid is a bargain, the item is recorded at the price paid in the transaction.

Suppose your stereo shop purchases some stereo equipment from a supplier who is going out of business. Assume you get a good deal on this purchase and pay only $2,000 for merchandise that would have cost you $3,000 elsewhere. The cost principle requires you to record this merchandise at its actual cost of $2,000, not the $3,000 that you believe the equipment to be worth.

The cost principle also holds that the accounting records maintain the historical cost of an asset for as long as the business holds the asset. Suppose your store holds the stereo equipment for six months. During that time, stereo prices increase, and the equipment can be sold for $3,500. Should its accounting value—the figure "on the books"—be the actual cost of $2,000 or the current market value of $3,500? According to the cost principle, the accounting value of the equipment remains at actual cost, $2,000.

As we continue to explore accounting, we will discuss other principles that guide accountants.

OBJECTIVE 6

Use the accounting equation to describe an organization

The Accounting Equation _____

Guided by GAAP such as these, accountants measure business activities and turn out financial statements that reflect these activities. Their basic tool for analysing business activities is the accounting equation developed by Luca Pacioli as the basis for double-entry bookkeeping. Recall that Pacioli was the 15th century monk who is considered the parent of modern accounting.

Every business transaction has at least two equal and opposite elements that effect both sides of the accounting equation equally: assets on the left of the equality and claims to assets, called equities, on the right of the equality. The accounting equation refers to each of these two elements.

The equality is fundamental to accounting and, as you will learn later in this course, applies to all of the different kinds of organization that exist and applies whether the organization is successful or not.

The accounting equation is

$$\textbf{Assets} = \textbf{Equities}$$

Assets are the economic resources a business owns that are expected to be of benefit in the future. Cash, office supplies, merchandise, furniture, land and building are examples.

Equities are the legal and economic claims to the assets. For example, a creditor who has loaned money to a business has a claim—a legal right, in fact—to a part of the assets until the business pays the debt. Also, the owner of the business has a claim to those assets that he or she has invested in the business. Equities logically divide into two categories: claims owing to people outside the business and claims held by people inside the business.

"Outsider" claims are economic obligations—debts—due to outsiders, and they are called **liabilities**. Debts owed to banks and lenders, for example, are liabilities. These outside parties are called *creditors*.

"Insider" claims belong to the owner of the business, and they are called **owner's equity**, or **capital**.

As a general rule, outsider claims in law rank ahead of insider claims on the assets of a business. In other words, owners have a residual claim on the assets of a company; assets are used first to pay the claim of outsider claimants (creditors) and then any remaining assets go to pay the claims of insider claimants (owners).

Adding these two categories, liabilities and owner's equity, to the accounting equation gives us:

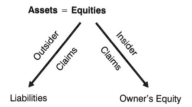

Liabilities plus owner's equity equals total equities, so we can express the accounting equation in its most common form and the one that we will use throughout the book:

$$\textbf{Assets} = \textbf{Liabilities} + \textbf{Owner's Equity}$$

Let us take a closer look at the elements that make up the accounting equation. Suppose you run a business that supplies meat to fast-food restaurants. Some customers may pay you in cash when you deliver the meat. Cash is an asset. Other customers may buy on credit and promise to pay you within a certain time after delivery. This promise is also an asset because it is an economic resource that will benefit you in the future when you receive cash from the customer. This promise is called an **account receivable**. If the promise that entitles you to receive cash in the future is written out, it is called a **note receivable**. All receivables are assets.

The fast-food restaurant's promise to pay you in the future for the meat it purchases on credit creates a debt for the restaurant. This liability is an **account payable**, which means the debtor (restaurant) does not give the creditor (meat seller) a written promise to pay, but accepts an invoice from the seller, which is an acknowledgement of the debt. The debt does not need to be supported by a written promise because it is backed up by the reputation and credit standing of the restaurant and its owner. A written promise of future payment is called a **note payable**. All payables are liabilities.

Owner's equity is the amount of the assets that remains after subtracting liabilities. A rearrangement of the accounting equation shows this relationship:

$$\text{Assets} - \text{Liabilities} = \text{Owner's Equity}$$

Accounting for Business Transactions

A business entity exists in the world and accordingly continues to be impacted by events occurring in that world. Some of these events, such as a sale of product, affect the entity and the accounting equation; such an event is called a **transaction**. Other events, such as election of a new mayor in a civic election, may affect the company but, for reasons explained below, do not affect the accounting equation and are ignored for accounting purposes.

In accounting terms, a transaction is any event that *both* affects the financial position of the business entity *and* may be reliably recorded. Many events may affect a company, including (1) elections, (2) economic booms and recessions, (3) purchases and sales of merchandise inventory, (4) payment of rent, (5) collection of cash from customers, and so on. However, the accountant recognizes only events with effects that can be measured reliably as transactions.

Which of the above five events would the accountant record? The answer is events (3), (4) and (5) because their dollar amounts can be measured reliably. Dollar effects of elections and economic trends cannot be measured reliably, so they would not be recorded even though they may affect the business more than events (3), (4) and (5).

To illustrate accounting for business transactions, let us assume that Gary Lyon has recently become a CA and opens his own accounting practice. Because the business has a single owner, it is called a proprietorship.

We now consider eleven events and analyse each in terms of its effect on the accounting equation of Gary Lyon's accounting practice. We believe that it is important for you to understand the accounting process, although at this point in your accounting education, you may not fully understand the terminology and concepts underlying that process. Of necessity, some of the transactions introduce further basic accounting terms, which are explained and examined in detail in subsequent chapters. Here they are presented to acquaint you with some of the fundamental accounting components of business transactions. Such analysis of transactions affecting a business is the essence of accounting.

Transaction 1   Gary Lyon invests $50,000 that he has just inherited from a grandparent to begin the business. Specifically, he deposits $50,000 in a bank account entitled Gary Lyon, CA. The effect of this transaction on the accounting equation of the business entity is

Assets			
		Type of Owner's	
Assets	**Liabilities +**	**Owner's Equity**	**Equity Transaction**
Cash		**Gary Lyon, Capital**	
(1) +50,000		+50,000	Owner investment

The first transaction increases both the assets, in this case Cash, and the owner's equity of the business, Gary Lyon, Capital. The transaction involves no liabilities of the business because it creates no obligation for Lyon to pay an outside party. To the right of the transaction we write "Owner investment" to keep track of the reason for the effect on owner's equity.

> **OBJECTIVE 7**
> Use the accounting equation to analyse business transactions

Note that the amount on the left side of the equation equals the amount on the right side. This equality must hold for every transaction.

Transaction 2   Lyon purchases land for a future office location, paying cash of $20,000. The effect of this transaction on the accounting equation is

	Assets			Liabilities +	Owner's Equity	Type of Owner's Equity Transaction
	Cash	**+**	**Land**		**Gary Lyon, Capital**	
(1)	50,000				50,000	Owner investment
(2)	−20,000	+	20,000			
Bal.	30,000		20,000		50,000	
		50,000			50,000	

The cash purchase of land increases one asset, Land, and decreases another asset, Cash, by the same amount. After the transaction is completed, Lyon's business has cash of $30,000, land of $20,000, no liabilities, and owner's equity of $50,000. Note that the sums of the balances (which we abbreviate "Bal.") on each side of the equation are equal. This equality must always exist.

Lyon operates his accounting practice out of a spare room in his home. The land is for an office building he hopes to build as his business grows.

Transaction 3   Lyon buys stationery and other office supplies, agreeing to pay $500 within thirty days. This transaction increases the assets and liabilities of the business. Its effect on the accounting equation is

	Assets					Liabilities +	Owner's Equity
	Cash	**+**	**Office Supplies**	**+**	**Land**	**Accounts Payable +**	**Gary Lyon, Capital**
Bal.	30,000				20,000		50,000
(3)			+500			+500	
Bal.	30,000		500		20,000	500	50,000
		50,500				50,500	

The asset affected is office supplies, and the liability is called an account payable. The term *payable* signifies a liability. Since Lyon is obligated to pay $500 in the future, but signs no formal promissory note, we record the liability as an Account Payable, not as a Note Payable. We say that purchases supported by the general credit standing of the buyer but not by written evidence are made on *open account*.

Transaction 4   The purpose of business is to increase owner's equity through **revenues**, which are amounts earned by delivering goods or services to customers. Revenues increase owner's equity because they increase the business's assets but not its liabilities. As a result, the owner's interest in the assets of the business increases.

Our illustration shows that Gary Lyon earns service revenue by providing professional accounting services for his clients. Assume he earns $5,500 and collects this amount in cash. The effect on the accounting equation is an increase in the asset Cash and an increase in Gary Lyon, Capital, as follows:

		Assets			Liabilities +	Owner's Equity	Type of Owner's Equity Transaction
	Cash	+ Office Supplies	+ Land	=	Accounts Payable	+ Gary Lyon, Capital	
Bal.	30,000	500	20,000		500	50,000	
(4)	+ 5,500					+ 5,500	Service revenue
Bal.	35,500	500	20,000		500	55,500	
		56,000				56,000	

This revenue transaction caused the business to grow, as shown by the increase in total assets and total equities.

Transaction 5   Lyon performs services for a client who does not pay immediately. In return for his accounting services, Lyon receives the client's promise to pay the $3,000 amount within one month. This promise is an asset, an account receivable to Lyon because he expects to collect the cash in the future. In accounting, we say that Lyon performed this service on *account*; that is, the client does not pay cash but has Lyon charge the fee for the service to the client's account receivable. When the business performs service for a client or a customer, the business earns revenue regardless of whether it receives cash immediately or expects to collect cash later. This $3,000 of service revenue is as real to Lyon's business as the $5,500 of revenue that he collected immediately in the preceding transaction. Lyon records an increase in the asset accounts receivable and an increase in owner's equity as follows:

			Assets				Liabilities +	Owner's Equity	Type of Owner's Equity Transaction
	Cash	+ Accounts Receivable	+ Office Supplies	+ Land	=		Accounts Payable	+ Gary Lyon, Capital	
Bal.	35,500		500	20,000			500	55,500	
(5)		+3,000						+ 3,000	Service revenue
Bal.	35,500	3,000	500	20,000			500	58,500	
		59,000						59,000	

Again, this revenue transaction caused the business to grow.

Transaction 6   In earning revenue a business incurs expenses. **Expenses** are decreases in owner's equity that occur in the course of delivering goods or services to clients. Expenses decrease owner's equity because they use up the business's assets. Expenses include office rent, salaries paid to employees, newspaper advertisements, and utility payments for light, electricity, gas, and so forth.

This transaction shows that during the month Lyon pays $2,700 in cash expenses: office rent, $1,100; employee salary, $1,200 (for a part-time assistant); and total utilities, $400. The effect on the accounting equation is

	Assets							**Liabilities +**	**Owner's Equity**	**Type of Owner's Equity Transaction**
	Cash	**+**	**Accounts Receivable +**	**Office Supplies +**	**Land**			**Accounts Payable +**	**Gary Lyon, Capital**	
Bal.	35,500		3,000	500	20,000	=		500	58,500	
(6)	− 2,700								− 1,100	Rent expense
									−1,200	Salary expense
									− 400	Utilities expense
Bal.	32,800		3,000	500	20,000			500	55,800	
	56,300							56,300		

Because expenses have the opposite effect of revenues, they cause the business to shrink, as shown by the smaller amounts of total assets and total equities.

Each expense can be recorded in a separate transaction or together, as shown here. Note that even though the figure $2,700 does not appear on the right-hand side of the equation, the three individual expenses add up to a $2,700 total. As a result, the "balance" of the equation holds, as we know it must.

Business people, Gary Lyon included, run their businesses with the objective of taking in more revenues than they pay out in expenses. An excess of total revenues over total expenses is called **net income, net earnings** or **net profit**. If total expenses are greater than total revenues, the result is called a **net loss**.

Transaction 7   Lyon pays $400 to the store from which he purchased $500 worth of office supplies in Transaction 3. In accounting, we say that he pays $400 *on account*, or on his account payable to the store (while the store receives the money on its account receivable). The effect on the accounting equation is a decrease in the asset Cash and a decrease in the liability Accounts Payable, as follows:

	Assets							**Liabilities +**	**Owner's Equity**
	Cash	**+**	**Accounts Receivable +**	**Office Supplies +**	**Land**			**Accounts Payable +**	**Gary Lyon, Capital**
Bal.	32,800		3,000	500	20,000	=		500	55,800
(7)	− 400							−400	
Bal.	32,400		3,000	500	20,000			100	55,800
	55,900							55,900	

The payment of cash on account has no effect on the asset Office Supplies because the payment does not increase or decrease the supplies available to the business.

Transaction 8   Lyon remodels his home at a cost of $30,000, paying cash from his personal funds. This event is a *nonbusiness* transaction. It has no effect on Lyon's accounting practice and therefore is not recorded by the business. It is a transaction of the Gary Lyon *personal* entity, not the Gary Lyon, CA *business* entity. We are focusing now solely on the business entity, and this event does not affect it. This transaction illustrates an application of the *entity concept*.

Transaction 9   In Transaction 5, Gary Lyon performed service for a client on account. Lyon now collects $1,000 from the client. We say that Lyon collected the cash *on account*. Lyon will record an increase in the asset Cash. Should he also record an increase in service revenue? No, because Lyon already recorded the revenue when he earned it in Transaction 5. The phrase "collect cash on account" means to record an increase in Cash and a decrease in the asset Accounts Receivable. The effect on the accounting equation is

		Assets					Liabilities +	Owner's Equity
	Cash	+ Accounts Receivable	+ Office Supplies	+ Land		=	Accounts Payable	+ Gary Lyon, Capital
Bal.	32,400	3,000	500	20,000			100	55,800
(9)	+ 1,000	− 1,000						
Bal.	33,400	2,000	500	20,000			100	55,800
			55,900					55,900

Total assets are unchanged from the preceding transaction's total. Why? It is because Lyon merely exchanged one asset for another. Also, total equities are unchanged.

Transaction 10   An individual approaches Lyon about selling a parcel of the land owned by the Gary Lyon, CA, entity. Lyon and the other person agree to a sale price of $6,000, which is equal to Lyon's cost of the land. Lyon's business sells the land and receives $6,000 cash, and the effect on the accounting equation is

		Assets					Liabilities +	Owner's Equity
	Cash	+ Accounts Receivable	+ Office Supplies	+ Land		=	Accounts Payable	+ Gary Lyon, Capital
Bal.	33,400	2,000	500	20,000			100	55,800
(10)	+ 6,000			− 6,000				
Bal.	39,400	2,000	500	14,000			100	55,800
			55,900					55,900

Transaction 11   Lyon withdraws $2,100 cash from the business for personal use. The effect on the accounting equation is

	Cash	Accounts + Receivable	Office + Supplies	+ Land		Accounts Payable	Gary Lyon, + Capital	Type of Owner's Equity Transaction
Bal.	39,400	2,000	500	14,000	=	100	55,800	
(11)	– 2,100						– 2,100	Owner withdrawals
Bal.	37,300	2,000	500	14,000		100	53,700	
	53,800					53,800		

(Assets header spans Cash + Accounts Receivable + Office Supplies + Land; Liabilities + Owner's Equity spans Accounts Payable + Gary Lyon, Capital)

Lyon's withdrawal of $2,100 in cash decreases the asset Cash and also the owner's equity of the business.

Does this withdrawal decrease the business entity's holdings? The answer is yes because the cash withdrawn is no longer available for business use after Lyon spends it on food, clothing, home mortgage payments, and so on. The withdrawal does *not* represent a business expense, however, because the cash is used for personal affairs unrelated to the business. We record the decrease in owner's equity in an account called Withdrawals. Another acceptable title is Drawing.

Exhibit 1-4 shows that owner investments and revenues increase owner's equity, while expenses as well as owner withdrawals decrease owner's equity. Owner withdrawals are those amounts removed from the business by the owner. Withdrawals are the opposite of owner investments. Expenses are the cost of doing business and the opposite of revenues.

EXHIBIT 1-4   *Transactions that Increase and Decrease Owner's Equity*

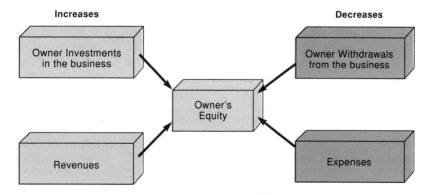

Exhibit 1-5 summarizes the eleven preceding transactions. Panel A of the exhibit lists the details of the transactions, and Panel B presents the analyses. As you study the exhibit, note that every transaction maintains the equality:

Assets = Liabilities + Owner's Equity

EXHIBIT 1-5   *Analysis of Transaction of Gary Lyon, CA*

Panel A: Details of Transactions

1.   Lyon invested $50,000 cash in the business.
2.   Paid $20,000 cash for land.
3.   Purchased $500 office supplies on account payable.
4.   Received $5,500 cash from clients for accounting fee revenue earned.
5.   Performed accounting service for a client on account, $3,000.
6.   Paid cash expenses: rent, $1,100; employee salary, $1,200; utilities, $400.
7.   Paid $400 on the account payable created in Transaction 3.
8.   Remodeled his personal residence. This is not a business transaction.
9.   Received $1,000 on the account receivable created in Transaction 5.
10. Sold land for cash equal to its cost of $6,000.
11. Withdrew $2,100 cash for personal living expenses.

Panel B: Analysis of Transactions

	Assets					Liabilities	Owner's Equity	Type of Owner's Equity Transaction
	Cash	+ Accounts Receivable	+ Office Supplies	+	Land	Accounts Payable +	Gary Lyon, Capital	
(1)	+50,000						+50,000	Owner investment
Bal.	50,000						50,000	
(2)	−20,000				+20,000			
Bal.	30,000				20,000		50,000	
(3)			+500			+500		
Bal.	30,000		500		20,000	500	50,000	
(4)	+ 5,500						+ 5,500	Service revenue
Bal.	35,500		500		20,000	500	55,500	
(5)		+3,000					+ 3,000	Service revenue
Bal.	35,500	3,000	500		20,000	500	58,500	
(6)	− 2,700						− 1,100	Rent expense
							− 1,200	Salary expense
							− 400	Utilities expense
Bal.	32,800	3,000	500		20,000	500	55,800	
(7)	− 400					−400		
Bal.	32,400	3,000	500		20,000	100	55,800	
(8)	Not a business transaction							
(9)	+ 1,000	−1,000						
Bal.	33,400	2,000	500		20,000	100	55,800	
(10)	+ 6,000				− 6,000			
Bal.	39,400	2,000	500		14,000	100	55,800	
(11)	− 2,100						− 2,100	Owner withdrawal
Bal.	37,300	2,000	500		14,000	100	53,700	

=

53,800   53,800

OBJECTIVE 8

Describe three financial statements

Financial Statements

The analysis of the transactions complete, what is the next step in the accounting process? How does an accountant present the results of the analysis? We now look at the **financial statements**. These business documents report financial information about the entity to persons and organizations both inside and outside the business.

The primary financial statements are the (1) balance sheet, (2) income statement, (3) statement of owner's equity, and (4) statement of changes in financial position. In this chapter, we discuss and illustrate the first three statements. We cover the statement of changes in financial position in Chapter 18.

The **balance sheet** lists all the *assets, liabilities* and *owner's equity* of an entity as of a specific date, usually the end of a month or a year. The balance sheet is like a snapshot of the entity. For this reason, it is also called the **statement of financial position**.

The **income statement** presents a summary of the *revenues* and *expenses* of an entity for a specific period, such as a month or a year. The income statement, also called the **statement of operations**, is like a moving picture of the entity's operations during the period. The income statement holds perhaps the most important single piece of information about a business — its net income, which is revenues minus expenses. If expenses exceed revenues, the result is a net loss for the period.

The **statement of owner's equity** presents a summary of the changes that occurred in the owner's equity of the entity during a specific period, such as a month or a year. Exhibit 1-4 shows how owner's equity may be changed in any of four ways. Increases in owner's equity arise from investments by the owner and net income earned during the period. Decreases result from withdrawals by the owner and from a net loss for the period. Net income or net loss comes directly from the income statement. Investments and withdrawals by the owner are capital transactions between the business and its owner, so they do not affect the income statement.

Each financial statement has a heading, which gives the name of the business — in our discussion, Gary Lyon, CA, the name of the particular statement, and the date or period covered by the statement. A balance sheet taken at the end of year 19X4 would be dated December 31, 19X4. A balance sheet prepared at the end of March 19X7 is dated March 31, 19X7. An income statement or a statement of owner's equity covering an annual period ending in December 19X5 is dated "for the year ended December 31, 19X5." A monthly income statement or statement of owner's equity for September 19X9 has in its heading "for the month ended September 30, 19X9" or simply "for the month of September 19X9."

Exhibit 1-6 illustrates all three statements. Their data come from the transaction analysis in Exhibit 1-5. We are assuming the transactions occurred during the month of April 19X1. Study the exhibit carefully, because it shows the relationships among the three financial statements.

Observe the following in Exhibit 1-6:

1. The *income statement* for the month ended April 30, 19X1
   a. Reports all *revenues* and all *expenses* during the period. Revenues and expenses are reported only on the income statement.
   b. Reports *net income* of the period if total revenues exceed total expenses, as in the case of Gary Lyon's accounting practice for April. If total expenses exceed total revenues, the result is a net loss.
2. The *statement of owner's equity* for the month ended April 30, 19X1
   a. Opens with owner's capital balance at the beginning of the period.
   b. Adds *investments by the owner* of the business and also adds *net income* (or subtracts *net loss*, as the case may be). Net income (or net loss) comes directly from the income statement, which includes the effect of all the revenues and all the expenses for the period (see the first arrow).
   c. Subtracts *withdrawals by the owner*.

EXHIBIT 1-6 Financial Statements of Gary Lyon, CA

Gary Lyon, CA
Income Statement
for the month ended April 30, 19X1

Revenues		
Service revenue..............................		$8,500
Expenses		
Salary expense	$ 1,200	
Rent expense	1,100	
Utilities expense	400	
Total expenses................................		2,700
Net income		$5,800

①

Gary Lyon, CA
Statement of Owner's Equity
for the month ended April 30, 19X1

Gary Lyon, capital, April 1, 19X1	$ 0	
Add: Investment by owner	50,000	
Net income for the month	5,800	←
	55,800	
Less: Withdrawals by owner.............	2,100	
Gary Lyon, capital, April 30, 19X1	$53,700	

②

Gary Lyon, CA
Balance Sheet
April 30, 19X1

Assets		Liabilities	
Cash................	$37,300	Accounts payable.....	$ 100
Accounts receivable ..	2,000	**Owner's Equity**	
Office supplies	500		
Land................	14,000	Gary Lyon, capital	53,700
		Total liabilities and	
Total assets	$53,800	owner's equity	$53,800

---

    d. Ends with owner's capital balance at the end of the period.

3. The *balance sheet* at April 30, 19X1, the end of the period
    a. Reports all *assets*, all *liabilities* and *owner's equity* of the business at the end of the period. No other statement reports assets and liabilities.
    b. Balances. That is, total assets equal the sum of total liabilities plus total owner's equity. This balancing feature gives the balance sheet its name. It is based on the accounting equation.
    d. Reports the owner's ending capital balance, taken directly from the statement of owner's equity (see the second arrow).

Summary Problem for Your Review

Jill Smith opens an apartment-locator business in a western city. She is the sole owner of the proprietorship, which she names Fast Apartment Locators. During the first month of operations, May 19X1, Smith engages in the following transactions:

a. Smith invests $20,000 of personal funds to start the business.
b. She purchases on account office supplies costing $350.
c. Smith pays cash of $8,000 to acquire a lot. She intends to use the land as a future building site for her business office.
d. Smith locates apartments for clients and receives cash of $1,900.
e. She pays $100 on the account payable she created in transaction b.
f. She pays $2,000 of personal funds for a vacation for her family.
g. She pays cash expenses for office rent, $400, and utilities, $100.
h. The business sells office supplies to another business for its cost of $150.
i. Smith withdraws cash of $1,200 for personal use.

Required

1. Record the preceding transactions in terms of their effects on the accounting equation of Fast Apartment Locators. Use Exhibit 1-5 as a guide.
2. Prepare the income statement, statement of owner's equity and balance sheet of the business after recording the transactions. Use Exhibit 1-6 as a guide.

SOLUTION TO REVIEW PROBLEM

Panel A: Details of Transactions

a. Smith invested $20,000 cash to start the business.
b. Purchased $350 in office supplies on account.
c. Paid $8,000 to acquire land as a future building site.
d. Earned service revenue and received cash of $1,900.
e. Paid $100 on account.
f. Paid for a personal vacation, which is not a business transaction.
g. Paid cash expenses for rent, $400, and utilities, $100.
h. Sold office supplies for cost of $150.
i. Withdrew $1,200 cash for personal use.

Panel B: Analysis of Transactions

	Assets				Liabilities +	Owner's Equity	Type of Owner's Equity Transaction
	Cash	+ Office Supplies +	Land		Accounts Payable	Jill Smith, Capital	
(a)	+20,000					+20,000	Owner investment
(b)		+350			+350		
(c)	− 8,000		+8,000				
(d)	+ 1,900					+ 1,900	Service revenue
(e)	− 100			=	−100		
(f)	Not a business transaction						
(g)	− 500					− 400	Rent expense
						− 100	Utilities expense
(h)	+ 150	−150					
(i)	−1,200					− 1,200	Owner withdrawals
Bal.	12,250	200	8,000		250	20,200	

Assets total: 20,450   Liabilities + Owner's Equity total: 20,450

Financial Statements of Fast Apartment Locators

Fast Apartment Locators
Income Statement
for the month ended May 31, 19X1

Revenues		
Service revenue...............................		$1,900
Expenses		
Rent expense.....................................	$400	
Utilities expense	100	
Total expenses..................................		500
Net Income		$1,400

Fast Apartment Locators
Statement of Owner's Equity
for the month ended May 31, 19X1

Jill Smith, capital, May 1, 19X1	$ 0
Add: Investment by owner	20,000
Net income for the month	1,400
	21,400
Less: Withdrawals by owner	1,200
Jill Smith, capital, May 31, 19X1	$20,200

① ②

Fast Apartment Locators
Balance Sheet
May 31, 19X1

Assets		Liabilities	
Cash..................	$12,250	Accounts payable.......	$ 250
Office Supplies.........	200	**Owner's Equity**	
Land..................	8,000		
		Jill Smith, capital	20,200
		Total liabilities and	
Total assets	$20,450	owner's equity	$20,450

Summary

Accounting is a system for measuring, processing and communicating financial information. As the "language of business," accounting helps a wide range of decision-makers.

Accounting dates back to ancient civilizations, but its importance to society has been greatest since the Industrial Revolution. Today, accountants serve as CAs, CGAs or CMAs in all types of organizations. They offer many specialized services for industrial companies, including general accounting, cost accounting, budgeting, system design and internal auditing. Accountants in public practice deal with auditing, tax planning and preparation, management consulting and accounting services.

The form of a business affects the accounting done for the business. The three basic forms of business organization are the proprietorship, the partnership and the corporation. Whatever the form, accountants use the entity concept to keep the business's records separate from the personal records of the people who run it.

Generally accepted accounting principles (GAAP) guide accountants in their work. Among these guidelines are the entity concept, reliability principle and cost principle.

In its most common form, the accounting equation is

Assets = Liabilities + Owner's Equity

Transactions affect a business's assets, liabilities and owner's equity. Therefore, transactions are analysed in terms of their effect on the accounting equation.

The *financial statements* communicate information for decision-making by the entity's managers, owners, employees and creditors and by government agencies. The *income statement* presents a moving picture of the entity's operations in terms of revenues earned and expenses incurred during a specific period. Total revenues minus total expenses equal net income. Net income or net loss answers the question: How much income did the entity earn, or how much loss did it incur during the period? The *statement of owner's equity* reports the changes in owner's equity during the period. The *balance sheet* provides a photograph of the entity's financial standing in terms of its assets, liabilities and owner's equity at a specific time. It answers the question: What is the entity's financial position?

Self-Study Questions

Test your understanding of the chapter by marking the correct answer for each of the following questions:

1. Accounting information is used by *(pp. 5, 6)*
   a. Businesses
   b. Governments and government agencies
   c. Household members
   d. All of the above
2. The organization that formulates generally accepted accounting principles is *(p. 8)*
   a. Ontario Securities Commission
   b. Public Accountants Council of Canada
   c. Canadian Institute of Chartered Accountants (CICA)
   d. Revenue Canada
3. Which of the following forms of business organization is an "artificial person" and must obtain legal approval from the federal government or a province to conduct business? *(p. 12)*
   a. Law firm   c. Partnership
   b. Proprietorship   d. Corporation

4. The economic resources that a business owns and expects to be useful to the enterprise are called *(p. 15)*
    a. Assets   c. Owner's equity
    b. Liabilities   d. Receivables

5. A business has assets of $140,000 and liabilities of $60,000. How much is its owner's equity? *(p. 15)*
    a. $0   c. $140,000
    b. $80,000   d. $200,000

6. The purchase of office supplies (or any other asset) on account will *(p. 18)*
    a. Increase an asset and increase a liability
    b. Increase an asset and increase owner's equity
    c. Increase one asset and decrease another asset
    d. Increase an asset and decrease a liability

7. The performance of service for a customer or client and immediate receipt of cash will *(p. 18)*
    a. Increase one asset and decrease another asset
    b. Increase an asset and increase owner's equity
    c. Decrease an asset and decrease a liability
    d. Increase an asset and increase a liability

8. The payment of an account payable (or any other liability) will *(p. 19)*
    a. Increase one asset and decrease another asset
    b. Decrease an asset and decrease owner's equity
    c. Decrease an asset and decrease a liability
    d. Increase an asset and increase a liability

9. The business document that reports assets, liabilities and owner's equity is called the *(p. 23)*
    a. Financial statement   c. Income statement
    b. Balance sheet   d. Statement of owner's equity

10. The financial statements that are dated for a time period (rather than a specific time) are the *(p. 23)*
    a. Balance sheet and income statement
    b. Balance sheet and statement of owner's equity
    c. Income statement and statement of owner's equity
    d. All financial statements are dated for a time period.

Answers to the Self-Study Questions are at the end of the chapter.

Accounting Vocabulary

Accounting, like many other subjects, has a special vocabulary. It is important that you understand the following terms. They are explained in the chapter and also in the glossary at the end of the book.

accounting *(p. 4)*
account payable *(p. 16)*
account receivable *(p. 15)*
assets *(p. 15)*
auditing *(p. 10)*
balance sheet *(p. 23)*
budgeting *(p. 11)*
capital *(p. 15)*
Certified General Accountant
  (CGA) *(p. 7)*
Certified Management
  Accountant (CMA) *(p. 7)*
Chartered Accountant (CA)
  (p. 7)

corporation *(p. 12)*
cost accounting *(p. 10)*
entity *(p. 13)*
equities *(p. 15)*
expenses *(p. 19)*
financial accounting *(p. 12)*
financial statements *(p. 22)*
generally accepted accounting
  principles (GAAP) *(p. 9)*
income statement *(p. 23)*
information systems design
  (p. 11)
internal auditing *(p. 11)*
liabilities *(p. 15)*

management accounting
  (p. 12)
net earnings *(p. 19)*
net income *(p. 19)*
net loss *(p. 19)*
net profit *(p. 19)*
note payable *(p. 16)*
note receivable *(p. 15)*
owner's equity *(p. 15)*
partnership *(p. 12)*
private accountant *(p. 7)*
proprietorship *(p. 12)*
public accountant *(p. 7)*
revenues *(p. 18)*

shareholders *(p. 12)*   statement of operations *(p. 23)*   transaction *(p. 16)*
statement of financial position   statement of owner's equity
   (p. 23)   *(p. 23)*

Assignment Material _____

Questions

1. Distinguish between accounting and bookkeeping.
2. Identify five users of accounting information and explain how they use it.
3. Where did accounting have its beginning? Who wrote the first known description of bookkeeping? In what year?
4. Name two important reasons for the development of accounting thought.
5. Name three professional titles of accountants. Also give their abbreviations.
6. What organization formulates generally accepted accounting principles? Is this organization a government agency?
7. Name the four principal types of services provided by public accounting firms.
8. How do financial accounting and management accounting differ?
9. Give the name(s) of the owner(s) of a proprietorship, a partnership and a corporation.
10. Why is the entity concept so important to accounting?
11. Give four examples of accounting entities.
12. Briefly describe the reliability principle.
13. What role does the cost principle play in accounting?
14. If *assets = liabilities + owner's equity*, then how can *liabilities* be expressed?
15. Explain the difference between an account receivable and an account payable.
16. What role do transactions play in accounting?
17. What is a more descriptive title for the balance sheet?
18. What feature of the balance sheet gives this financial statement its name?
19. What is another title of the income statement?
20. Which financial statement is like a snapshot of the entity at a specific time? Which financial statement is like a moving picture of the entity's operation during a period of time?
21. What information does the statement of owner's equity report?
22. Give two synonyms for the owner's equity of a proprietorship.
23. What piece of information flows from the income statement to the statement of owner's equity? What information flows from the statement of owner's equity to the balance sheet?

Exercises

Exercise 1-1 *Transaction analysis*

Indicate the effects of the following business transactions on the accounting equation. Transaction *a* is answered as a guide.

a. Paid $90 cash to purchase office supplies.
   Answer: Increase asset (Office Supplies).
               Decrease asset (Cash).

b. Performed legal service for a client and received cash of $2,000.

c. Paid monthly office rent of $700.

d. Invested cash of $1,800 in the business.

e. Performed legal service for a client on account, $650.

f. Purchased on account office furniture at a cost of $500.

g. Received cash on account, $400.

h. Paid cash on account, $250.

i. Sold land for $12,000, which was our cost of the land.

Exercise 1-2   *Transaction analysis, accounting equation*

Gloria Hill opens a medical practice to specialize in child care. During her first month of operation, January, her practice, entitled Gloria Hill, M.D., experienced the following events:

Jan. 6   Hill invested $135,000 in the business by opening a bank account in the name of Gloria Hill, M.D.

9   Hill paid cash for land costing $90,000. She plans to build an office building on the land.

12   She purchased medical supplies for $2,000 on account.

15   On January 15, Hill officially opened for business.

15–31   During the rest of the month she treated patients and earned service revenue of $6,000 to be billed to the provincial health plan.

15–31   She paid cash expenses: employee salaries, $1,400; office rent, $1,000; utilities, $300.

28   She sold supplies to another physician for cost of $500.

31   She paid $1,500 on account.

Required

Analyse the effects of these events on the accounting equation of the medical practice of Gloria Hill, M.D. Use a format similar to that of Exhibit 1-5 in the chapter with headings for Cash; Supplies; Land; Accounts Payable; and Gloria Hill, Capital.

Exercise 1-3   *Accounting equation*

Compute the missing amount in the accounting equation of each of the following three entities:

	Assets	Liabilities	Owner's Equity
Entity A	$?	$41,800	$26,400
Entity B	85,900	?	34,000
Entity C	63,700	29,800	?

Exercise 1-4   *Business organization, balance sheet*

Presented below are the balances of the assets and liabilities of Stark Delivery Service as of September 30, 19X2. Also included are the revenue and expense figures of the business for September.

Delivery service revenue	$3,500	Delivery equipment	$9,500
Accounts receivable	900	Supplies	600
Accounts payable	750	Note payable	5,000
D. Stark, capital	?	Rent expense	500
Salary expense	1,000	Cash	650

Required

1. What type of business organization is Stark Delivery Service? How can you tell?
2. Prepare the balance sheet of Stark Delivery Service as of September 30, 19X2. Not all amounts are used. Recall that only assets, liabilities and owner's equity appear on the balance sheet.

Exercise 1-5   *Income statement*

Presented below are the balances of the assets, liabilities, owner's equity, revenues and expenses of Fadal Travel Agency at December 31, 19X3, the end of its first year of business. During the year, W. Fadal, the owner, invested $20,000 in the business.

Note payable	$ 30,000	Office furniture	$ 45,000
Utilities expense	5,800	Rent expense	21,000
Accounts payable	3,300	Cash	3,600
W. Fadal, capital	27,100	Office supplies	4,800
Service revenue	108,000	Salary expense	29,000
Accounts receivable	9,000	Salaries payable	2,000
Supplies expense	4,000	Property tax expense	1,200

Required

1. Prepare the income statement of Fadal Travel Agency for the year ended December 31, 19X3. Not all amounts are used. Recall that only revenues and expenses appear on the income statement.
2. What was the amount of the proprietor's withdrawals during the year?

Exercise 1-6   *Business transactions*

For each of the following items, give an example of a business transaction that has the described effect on the accounting equation:

a. Increase an asset and increase owner's equity.
b. Increase an asset and increase a liability.
c. Increase one asset and decrease another asset.
d. Decrease an asset and decrease owner's equity.
e. Decrease an asset and decrease a liability.

Exercise 1-7   *Business organization, transactions and net income*

The analysis of the transactions that United Rentals engaged in during its first month of operations follows. The company buys equipment that it rents out to earn rent revenue. The owners of the business made only one investment to start the business and no withdrawals.

	Cash	+	Accounts Receivable	+	Rental Equipment	=	Accounts Payable	+	Partners' Capital
a.	+ 65,000								+ 65,000
b.					+ 100,000		+ 100,000		
c.	+ 1,600								+ 1,600
d.			+ 150						+ 150
e.	− 10,000						− 10,000		
f.			+ 850						+ 850
g.	+ 150		− 150						
h.	− 2,000								− 2,000

Required

1. What type of business organization is United Rentals? How can you tell?
2. Describe each transaction.
3. If these transactions fully describe the operations of United Rentals during the month, what was the amount of net income or net loss?

Exercise 1-8   *Accounting equation*

Milstead Supply balance sheet data, at May 31, 19X2 and June 30, 19X2, were as follows:

	May 31, 19X2	June 30, 19X2
Total assets	$150,000	$195,000
Total liabilities	109,000	131,000

Required

Below are three assumptions about investments and withdrawals by the owner of the business during June. For each assumption, compute the amount of net income or net loss of the business during June 19X2.

1. The owner invested $25,000 in the business and made no withdrawals.
2. The owner made no additional investments in the business but withdrew $12,000 for personal use.
3. The owner invested $8,000 in the business and withdrew $12,000 for personal use.

Exercise 1-9   *Transaction analysis*

Bliss Stone Masonry, a proprietorship, recorded the following events. State whether each event (1) increased, (2) decreased, or (3) had no effect on the total assets of the business. Identify any specific asset affected.

a. Paid cash on accounts payable.
b. Purchased machinery and equipment for a manufacturing plant; signed a promissory note in payment.
c. Ron, an employee, performed service for a customer on account.
d. Bliss, the owner, withdrew cash from the business for personal use.
e. Received cash from a customer on account receivable.
f. Bliss used personal funds to purchase a swimming pool for his home.
g. Sold land for a price equal to the cost of the land; received cash.
h. Borrowed money from the bank.
i. Purchased land for a future building site.
j. Bliss, increased his cash investment in the business.

Problems   (Group A)

Problem 1-1A   *Transaction analysis, accounting equation, financial statements*

Margaret Stevens owns and operates an interior design studio called Stevens Interiors. The following amounts summarize the financial position of her business on August 31, 19X2:

	Assets		=	Liabilities +	Owner's Equity
	Cash +	Accounts Receivable +	Land =	Accounts Payable +	Margaret Stevens, Capital
Bal.	1,250	1,500	12,000	8,000	6,750

During September 19X2, the following events occurred:

a. Stevens inherited $15,000 and deposited the cash in the business bank account.
b. Performed services for a client and received cash of $700.
c. Paid off the beginning balance of accounts payable, $8,000.
d. Purchased supplies on account, $500.
e. Collected cash from a customer on account, $800.
f. Invested personal cash of $1,000 in the business.
g. Consulted on the interior design of a major office building and billed the client for services rendered, $2,000.
h. Recorded the following business expenses for the month:
   1. Paid office rent, $900.
   2. Paid advertising, $100.
i. Sold supplies to another business for $150.
j. Withdrew cash of $1,800 for personal use.

Required

1. Record the effects of the above transactions on the accounting equation of Stevens Interiors. Adapt the format of Exhibit 1-5. You need to add a column for Supplies.
2. Prepare the income statement of Stevens Interiors for the month ended September 30, 19X2. List expenses in decreasing order by amount.
3. Prepare the statement of owner's equity of Stevens Interiors for the month ended September 30, 19X2.
4. Prepare the balance sheet of Stevens Interiors at September 30, 19X2.

Problem 1-2A *Entity concept, transaction analysis, accounting equation*

Zane Jones practiced law with a large firm, a partnership, for five years after graduating from law school. Recently he resigned his position to open his own law office, which he operates as a proprietorship. The name of the new entity is Zane Jones, Lawyer.

Jones recorded the following events during the organizing phase of his new business and its first month of operations. Some of the events were personal and did not affect his law practice. Others were business transactions and should be accounted for by the business.

May 4 Jones received $50,000 cash from his former partners in the law firm from which he resigned.

May 5 Jones deposited $50,000 cash in a new business bank account, entitled Zane Jones, Lawyer.

May 6 Jones paid $300 cash for letterhead stationery for his new law office.

May 7 Jones purchased office furniture for his law office. Jones agreed to pay the account payable, $5,000, within six months.

May 10 Jones sold 3,750 shares of National Trust stock, which he and his wife had owned for several years, receiving $75,000 cash from his stockbroker.

May 11 Jones deposited the $75,000 cash from sale of the National Trust stock in his personal bank account.

May 12 A representative of a large company telephoned Jones and told him of the company's intention to transfer its legal business to the new entity of Zane Jones, Lawyer.

May 29 Jones finished court hearings on behalf of a client and submitted his bill for legal services, $4,000. Jones expected to collect from this client within two weeks.

May 30 Jones paid office rent expense, $1,000.

May 31 Jones withdrew $2,500 cash from the business for personal living expenses.

Required

1. Classify each of the preceding events as one of the following:
   a. Personal transaction *not* to be accounted for by the proprietorship of Zane Jones, Lawyer.
   b. Business transaction to be accounted for by the proprietorship of Zane Jones, Lawyer.
   c. Business-related event but *not* a transaction to be accounted for by the proprietorship of Zane Jones, Lawyer.
2. Analyse the effects of the above events on the accounting equation of the proprietorship of Zane Jones, Lawyer. Use a format similar to Exhibit 1-5.

Problem 1-3A *Balance sheet*

The bookkeeper of Dorman Home Builders prepared the balance sheet of the company while the accountant was ill. The balance sheet contains numerous errors. In particular, the bookkeeper knew that the balance sheet should balance, so he plugged in the owner's equity amount needed to achieve this balance. However, the owner's equity amount is not correct. All other amounts are accurate.

Dorman Home Builders
Balance Sheet
for the month ended July 31, 19X3

Assets		Liabilities	
Cash	$ 2,000	Accounts receivable	$ 3,000
Office supplies	1,000	Service revenue	35,000
Land	22,000	Property tax expense	800
Advertising expense	500	Accounts payable	8,000
Office furniture	10,000	**Owner's Equity**	
Note payable	16,000		
Rent expense................	4,000	Owner's equity	8,700
Total assets	$55,500	Total liabilities..............	$55,500

Required

1. Prepare the correct balance sheet as of July 31, 19X3. Compute total assets and total liabilities. Then take the difference to determine correct owner's equity.
2. Identify the accounts listed above which should *not* be presented on the balance sheet and state why you excluded them from the correct balance sheet you prepared for 1.

Problem 1-4A *Business transactions and analysis*

Laiken Company was recently formed. The balance of each item in the company's accounting equation is shown below for May 10 and for each of nine following business days.

Required

Assuming a single transaction took place on each day, describe briefly the transaction that was most likely to have occurred from May 11. Indicate which accounts were affected and by what amount. No revenue or expense transactions occurred on these dates.

	Cash	Accounts Receivable	Supplies	Land	Accounts Payable	Owner's Equity
May 10	$ 6,000	$4,000	$1,000	$ 8,000	$4,000	$15,000
11	11,000	4,000	1,000	8,000	4,000	20,000
12	6,000	4,000	1,000	13,000	4,000	20,000
15	6,000	4,000	3,000	13,000	6,000	20,000
16	5,000	4,000	3,000	13,000	5,000	20,000
17	8,000	1,000	3,000	13,000	5,000	20,000
18	16,000	1,000	3,000	13,000	5,000	28,000
19	13,000	1,000	3,000	13,000	2,000	28,000
22	12,000	1,000	4,000	13,000	2,000	28,000
23	8,000	1,000	4,000	13,000	2,000	24,000

Balance sheet, entity concept

Jan Gibson is a realtor. She buys and sells properties on her own, and she also earns commission as a real estate agent for buyers and sellers. She organized her business as a proprietorship on November 24, 19X4. Consider the following facts as of November 30, 19X4:

a. Gibson owed $100,000 on a note payable for some undeveloped land that had been acquired by her business for a total price of $160,000.

b. Gibson's business had spent $15,000 for a Century 21 real estate franchise, which entitled her to represent herself as a Century 21 agent. Century 21 is a national affiliation of independent real estate agents. This franchise is a business asset.

c. Gibson owed $120,000 on a personal mortgage on her personal residence, which she acquired in 19X1 for a total price of $170,000.

d. Gibson had $10,000 in her personal bank account and $12,000 in her business bank account.

e. Gibson owed $1,800 on a personal charge account with Holt-Renfrew.

f. Gibson acquired business furniture for $17,000 on November 25. Of this amount, her business owed $6,000 on open account at November 30.

g. Office supplies on hand at the real estate office totaled at $1,000.

Required

1. Prepare the balance sheet of the real estate business of Jan Gibson, Realtor, at November 30, 19X4.
2. Identify the personal items given in the preceding facts that would not be reported on the balance sheet of the business.

Problem 1-6A   *Income statement, statement of owner's equity, balance sheet*

Presented below are the amount of (a) the assets and liabilities of Johnson Service Company as of December 31, and (b) the revenues and expenses of the company for the year ended on that date. The items are listed in alphabetical order.

Accounts payable	$ 19,000	Note payable	$ 85,000
Accounts receivable	12,000	Property tax expense	4,000
Advertising expense	11,000	Rent expense	23,000
Building	180,000	Salary expense	53,000
Cash	10,000	Salaries payable	1,000
Furniture	20,000	Service revenue	200,000
Interest expense	9,000	Supplies	3,000
Land	65,000		

The beginning amount of Ray Johnson, Capital, was $150,000. During the year Johnson withdrew $65,000 for personal use.

Required

1. Prepare the income statement of Johnson Service Company for the year ended December 31 of the current year.
2. Prepare the statement of owner's equity of the company for the year ended December 31.
3. Prepare the balance sheet of the company at December 31.

Problem 1-7A   *Transaction analysis for a large company*

A recent balance sheet of Scott, Boyle & Company, one of Canada's larger sellers of jeans and casual pants, is summarized below (in thousands):

Scott, Boyle & Company
Balance Sheet
November 25, 19XX

Assets		Liabilities	
Cash	$ 263,389	Notes payable	$ 83,361
Accounts receivable	339,798	Accounts payable	229,453
Merchandise inventories . . .	387,660	Other liabilities	300,847
Property, plant and equip. .	330,455		
Other assets	99,800	Total liabilities	613,661
		Owners' Equity	807,441
		Total liabilities and	
Total assets	$1,421,102	owners' equity	$1,421,102

During December, the company had the following transactions and events:

a. Received cash investments from owners, $18,000.
b. Received special equipment from an owner as an investment in the company. The value of the equipment was $40,000.
c. Borrowed cash, signing a note payable, $100,000.
d. Purchased equipment for cash, $125,000.
e. Purchased inventories on account, $90,000.
f. Paid cash on account (to reduce accounts payable), $54,000.
g. Sold equipment to another company on account, $14,000. The equipment had cost $14,000.
h. Discovered that the prime minister of Canada was going to wear Scott blue jeans while performing the ceremonial kick-off at the 19X1 Grey Cup.
i. Collected cash on account from customers, $84,000.

Required

1. Rounding all amounts to the nearest $1,000, analyse the December transactions of Scott, Boyle. Use a format similar to Exhibit 1-5.
2. Prove the assets = liabilities + owner equity after analysing the transactions.

(Group B)

Problem 1-1B   *Transaction analysis, accounting equation, financial statements*

Maury Cheng owns and operates an interior design studio called Cheng Designers. The following amounts summarize the financial position of his business on April 30, 19X5:

	Assets			= Liabilities	+ Owner's Equity
	Cash +	Accounts Receivable +	Land =	Accounts Payable +	Maury Cheng Capital
Bal.	720	2,240	23,100	4,400	21,660

During May 19X5, the following events occurred:

a. Cheng received $12,000 as a gift and deposited the cash in the business bank account.
b. Paid off the beginning balance of accounts payable, $4,400.
c. Performed services for a client and received cash of $1,100.
d. Collected cash from a customer on account, $750.
e. Purchased supplies on account, $120.
f. Consulted on the interior design of a major office building and billed the client for services rendered, $5,500.
g. Invested personal cash of $1,700 in the business.
h. Recorded the following business expenses for the month:
    1. Paid office rent, $1,200.
    2. Paid advertising, $860.
i. Sold supplies to another interior designer for cost of $80.
j. Withdrew cash of $2,400 for personal use.

Required

1. Record the effects of the above transactions on the accounting equation of Cheng Designers. Adapt the format of Exhibit 1-5. You need to add a column for Supplies.
2. Prepare the income statement of Cheng Designers for the month ended May 31, 19X5. List expenses in decreasing order by amount.
3. Prepare the statement of owner's equity of Cheng Designers for the month ended May 31, 19X5.
4. Prepare the balance sheet of Cheng Designers at May 31.

Problem 1-2B   *Entity concept, transaction analysis, accounting equation*

Rhonda Sperry practiced law with a large firm, a partnership, for ten years after graduating from law school. Recently she resigned her position to open her own law office, which she operates as a proprietorship. The name of the new entity is Rhonda Sperry, Lawyer.

Sperry recorded the following events during the organizing phase of her business and its first month of operations. Some of the events were personal and did not affect the law practice. Others were business transactions and should be accounted for by the business.

July 1   Rhonda sold 3,000 shares of Dofasco stock, which she had owned for several years, receiving $88,000 cash from her stockbroker.
July 2   Rhonda deposited the $88,000 cash from sale of the Dofasco stock in her personal bank account.

July   3   Rhonda received $135,000 cash from her former partners in the law firm from which she resigned.

July   5   Rhonda deposited $130,000 cash in a new business bank account entitled Rhonda Sperry, Lawyer.

July   6   A representative of a large company telephoned Rhonda and told her of the company's intention to transfer its legal business to the new entity of Rhonda Sperry, Lawyer.

July   7   Rhonda paid $550 cash for letterhead stationery for her new law office.

July   9   Rhonda purchased office furniture for the law office, agreeing to pay the account payable, $11,500, within three months.

July 23   Rhonda finished court hearings on behalf of a client and submitted her bill for legal services, $2,100. She expected to collect from this client within one month.

July 30   Rhonda paid office rent expense, $1,900.

July 31   Rhonda withdrew $3,000 cash from the business for personal living expenses.

Required

1. Classify each of the preceding events as one of the following:
    a. Personal transaction *not* to be accounted for by the proprietorship of Rhonda Sperry, Lawyer.
    b. Business transaction to be accounted for by the proprietorship of Rhonda Sperry, Lawyer.
    c. Business-related event but *not* a transaction to be accounted for by the proprietorship of Rhonda Sperry, Lawyer.
2. Analyse the effects of the above events on the accounting equation of the proprietorship of Rhonda Sperry, Lawyer. Use a format similar to Exhibit 1-5.

Problem 1-3B   *Balance sheet*

The bookkeeper of Reynolds Construction Company prepared the balance sheet of the company while the accountant was ill. The balance sheet contains numerous errors. In particular, the bookkeeper knew that the balance sheet should balance, so he plugged in the owner's equity amount needed to achieve this balance. However, the owner's equity amount is not correct. All other amounts are accurate.

<table>
<tr><td colspan="4" align="center">**Reynolds Construction Company**
Balance Sheet
for the month ended October 31, 19X7</td></tr>
<tr><td>**Assets**</td><td></td><td>**Liabilities**</td><td></td></tr>
<tr><td>Cash ....</td><td>$ 1,400</td><td>Notes receivable ....</td><td>$11,000</td></tr>
<tr><td>Advertising expense ....</td><td>300</td><td>Interest expense ....</td><td>2,000</td></tr>
<tr><td>Land ....</td><td>31,600</td><td>Office supplies ....</td><td>800</td></tr>
<tr><td>Salary expense ....</td><td>2,200</td><td>Accounts receivable ....</td><td>1,600</td></tr>
<tr><td>Office furniture.............</td><td>4,700</td><td>Note payable ....</td><td>20,000</td></tr>
<tr><td>Accounts payable ....</td><td>3,000</td><td>**Owner's Equity**</td><td></td></tr>
<tr><td>Utilities expense ....</td><td>1,100</td><td></td><td></td></tr>
<tr><td></td><td></td><td>Owner's equity ....</td><td>8,900</td></tr>
<tr><td>Total assets ....</td><td>$44,300</td><td>Total liabilities...............</td><td>$44,300</td></tr>
</table>

Required

1. Prepare the correct balance sheet as of October 31, 19X7. Compute total assets and total liabilities. Then take the difference to determine correct owner's equity.

2. Identify the accounts listed above that should *not* be presented on the balance sheet and state why you excluded them from the correct balance sheet you prepared for 1.

Problem 1-4B *Business transactions and analysis*

Miske Company was recently formed. The balance of each item in the company's accounting equation is shown below for February 8 and for each of nine following business days.

	Cash	Accounts Receivable	Supplies	Land	Accounts Payable	Owner's Equity
Feb. 8	$3,000	$7,000	$ 800	$11,000	$3,800	$18,000
9	5,000	7,000	800	11,000	3,800	20,000
10	6,000	6,000	800	11,000	3,800	20,000
13	6,000	6,000	1,100	11,000	4,100	20,000
14	3,000	6,000	1,100	11,000	4,100	17,000
15	1,900	6,000	1,100	11,000	3,000	17,000
16	7,900	6,000	1,100	5,000	3,000	17,000
17	7,000	6,000	1,100	5,000	2,100	17,000
20	6,800	6,000	1,300	5,000	2,100	17,000
21	1,700	6,000	1,300	10,100	2,100	17,000

Required

Assuming a single transaction took place on each day, describe briefly the transaction that was most likely to have occurred, beginning with February 12. Indicate which accounts were affected and by what amount. No revenue or expense transactions occurred on these dates.

Problem 1-5B *Balance sheet, entity concept*

Drew Beaty is a realtor. He buys and sells properties on his own, and he also earns commission as a real estate agent for buyers and sellers. He organized his business as a proprietorship on March 10, 19X2. Consider the following facts as of March 31, 19X2:

a. Beaty had $5,000 in his personal bank account and $9,000 in his business bank account.
b. Office supplies on hand at the real estate office totaled $1,000.
c. Beaty's business had spent $15,000 for an Electronic Realty Associates (ERA) franchise, which entitled him to represent himself as an ERA agent. ERA is a national affiliation of independent real estate agents. This franchise is a business asset.
d. Beaty owed $38,000 on a note payable for some undeveloped land that had been acquired by his business for a total price of $70,000.
e. Beaty owed $65,000 on a personal mortgage on his personal residence, which he acquired in 19X1 for a total price of $90,000.
f. Beaty owed $950 on a personal charge account with Eaton's.
g. He had acquired business furniture for $12,000 on March 26. Of this amount, Beaty's business owed $6,000 on open account at March 31.

Required

1. Prepare the balance sheet of the real estate business of Drew Beaty, Realtor, at March 31, 19X2.
2. Identify the personal items given in the preceding facts that would not be reported on the balance sheet of the business.

Problem 1-6B *Income statement, statement of owner's equity, balance sheet*

Presented below are the amounts of (a) the assets and liabilities of Bryant Repair Service as of December 31, and (b) the revenues and expenses of the company for the year ended on that date. The items are listed in alphabetical order.

Accounts payable	$ 14,000	Note payable	$ 31,000
Accounts receivable	6,000	Property tax expense	2,000
Building	18,000	Rent expense	14,000
Cash	4,000	Salary expense	38,000
Equipment	26,000	Service revenue	110,000
Interest expense	4,000	Supplies	13,000
Interest payable	1,000	Utilities expense	3,000
Land	8,000		

The beginning amount of Mike Bryant, Capital, was $12,000. During the year Bryant withdrew $32,000 for personal use.

Required

1. Prepare the income statement of Bryant Repair Service for the year ended December 31 of the current year.
2. Prepare the statement of owner's equity of the company for the year ended December 31.
3. Prepare the balance sheet of the company at December 31.

Problem 1-7B *Transaction analysis for an actual company*

A recent balance sheet of Xerox Canada Inc., the manufacturer of copiers and other office equipment, is summarized as follows, with amounts in thousands. For example, Cash of $26,660,000 is presented as $26,660.

Xerox Canada Inc.
Balance Sheet
December 31, 19XX

Assets		Liabilities	
Cash	$ 26,660	Notes payable	$ 198,550
Accounts receivable	146,690	Accounts payable	39,030
Merchandise inventories.....	146,980	Other liabilities	210,760
Land, buildings and equip....	265,970	Total liabilities.............	448,340
Other assets...............	395,370	**Owners' Equity**	533,330
		Total liabilities	
Total assets	$981,670	and capital..............	$981,670

During January, the company had the following transactions and events:

a. Received cash investment from owners, $37,000.
b. Purchased inventories on account, $400,000.
c. Paid cash on account (to reduce accounts payable), $136,000.
d. Sold inventory to another company on account, $670,000. The equipment had cost $670,000.

e. Learned that a CBC Television news program would show members of the House of Commons using Xerox copy machines as part of a Senate investigation. The value of this advertisement to the company is estimated to be $1,000,000.

f. Borrowed cash, signing a note payable, $550,000.

g. Purchased equipment for cash, $380,000.

h. Collected cash on account from customers, $289,000.

i. Received special equipment from an owner as an investment in the company. The value of equipment was $119,000.

Required

1. Rounding all amounts to the nearest $1,000, analyse the January transactions of Xerox. Use a format similar to Exhibit 1-5.

2. Prove that assets = liabilities + owner equity after analysing the transactions.

Decision Problems

1.   Using financial statements to evaluate a request for a loan

The proprietors of two businesses, Butler Department Store and Susan Nielsen Home Decorators, have sought business loans from you. To decide whether to make the loans, you have requested their balance sheets.

Butler Department Store
Balance Sheet
August 31, 19X4

Assets		Liabilities	
Cash	$ 1,000	Accounts payable	$ 12,000
Accounts receivable	14,000	Note payable	18,000
Merchandise inventory	85,000	Total liabilities	30,000
Store supplies	500		
Furniture and fixtures	9,000	**Owner's Equity**	
Building	90,000		
Land	14,000	Roy Butler, capital	183,500
		Total liabilities and	
Total assets	$213,500	owner's equity	$213,500

Susan Nielsen Home Decorators
Balance Sheet
August 31, 19X4

Assets		Liabilities	
Cash	$11,000	Accounts payable	$ 3,000
Accounts receivable	4,000	Note payable	18,000
Office supplies	1,000	Total liabilities	21,000
Office furniture	6,000	**Owner's Equity**	
Land	19,000		
		Susan Nielsen, capital	20,000
		Total liabilities and	
Total assets	$41,000	owner's equity	$41,000

Required

1. Based solely on these balance sheets, which entity would you be more comfortable loaning money to? Explain fully, citing specific items and amounts from the balance sheets.
2. In addition to the balance sheet data, what other financial statement information would you require? Be specific.

2. Using accounting information

A friend learns that you are taking an accounting course, knowing that you do not plan a career in accounting, and asks why you are "wasting your time." Explain to the friend

1. Why you are taking the course.
2. How accounting information is used or will be used:
    a. In your personal life.
    b. In your business life even though you plan to work in a hospital.
    c. In the business life of your friend, who plans to be a farmer.
    d. In the business life of another friend, who plans a career in sales.

Financial Statement Problem

Identifying items from a company's financial statements

This and similar problems in succeeding chapters focus on the financial statements of an actual company (John Labatt Limited). As each problem is solved, you will gradually strengthen your understanding of actual financial statements in their entirety.

  Referring to the John Labatt financial statements in Appendix E, answer the following questions:

1. How much did John Labatt's customers owe the company at April 30, 1989?
2. What were total assets at April 30, 1989? At April 30, 1988?
3. Write the company's accounting equation at April 30, 1989 by filling in the dollar amounts:

Assets = Liabilities + Shareholders' equity

  Note: Treat deferred taxes and convertible debentures as liabilities for purposes of this question.
4. Identify total revenues and net revenues for the year ended April 30, 1989. (Net revenues mean total revenues less certain subtractions.) What was subtracted from total revenues to get net revenues?
5. How much net income (net earnings) did John Labatt experience for the year ended April 30, 1989?

Answers to Self-Study Questions

1.	d	3.	d	5.	b	7.	b	9.	b
2.	c	4.	a	6.	a	8.	c	10.	c

2

Recording Business Transactions

Chapter 1 illustrates how to account for business transactions by analysing their effects on the accounting equation. Understanding how transactions affect this equation is fundamental to grasping accounting concepts. Yet if accountants simply analysed business activities transaction by transaction in this manner, their records and job would become unwieldy. In large business, such as a chain of department stores, hundreds or even thousands of transactions occur hourly. To manage and organize this voluminous accounting information, accountants combine the data on a daily, weekly or monthly basis. This chapter focuses on the methods accountants use to process, or record, information about business transactions.

The Account

OBJECTIVE 1
Define and use all new terms in the chapter

The basic summary device of accounting is the **account**. This is the detailed record of the changes that have occurred in a particular asset, liability or owner's equity during a period of time. For example, the account Cash for the period January 1 to December 31, 19X1 would include all transactions involving cash for that period. Each account appears on its own page. For convenient access to the information in the accounts the pages are grouped together in a single book called the **ledger**. When you hear reference to "keeping the books" or "auditing the books," the word *books* refers to the ledger. The ledger may be a bound book, a loose-leaf set of pages or a computer record.

In the ledger, the accounts are grouped in three broad categories, based on the accounting equation:

$$\text{Assets} = \text{Liabilities} + \text{Owner's Equity}$$

Assets

The following asset accounts are common to many firms. Remember that an asset is any economic resource that will benefit the business in the future.

Cash   The Cash account records a business's cash transactions. Cash means money and any medium of exchange that a bank accepts at face value. Cash includes currency, coins, money orders, certificates of deposit and cheques. The Cash account covers these items whether they are kept on hand, in a safe, in a cash register or in a bank.

Accounts Receivable   A business may sell its goods or services as we have seen, in exchange for a promise of future cash receipt. Such sales are made on credit, or on account. The Accounts Receivable account includes these amounts.

Notes Receivable   As indicated in Chapter 1, a business may also sell its goods or services in exchange for a promissory note, which is a written pledge that the customer will pay the business a fixed amount of money by a certain date. The Notes Receivable account is a record of the promissory notes that the business expects to collect in cash.

Prepaid Expenses   A business often pays certain expenses in advance. Prepaid expenses are assets because they will be of future benefit to the business. The ledger holds a separate asset account for each prepaid item. Prepaid Rent and Prepaid Insurance are prepaid expenses that occur often in business. Office Supplies are also considered prepaid expenses.

Land   The Land account is a record of the land that a business owns.

Building   The buildings (office, warehouse, garage, and the like) that a business owns and uses in its operations appear in the Building account.

Equipment, Furniture and Fixtures   A business has a separate asset account for each type of equipment—Office Equipment and Store Equipment, for example. The Furniture and Fixtures account shows the cost of this asset. Other asset categories and accounts will be discussed as needed. For example, many businesses have an Investments account for their investments in other companies.

Liabilities

Recall from Chapter 1 that a *liability* is a debt. A business generally keeps fewer liability accounts than asset accounts because a business's liabilities can be summarized under relatively few categories.

Accounts Payable   This account is the opposite of the Accounts Receivable account. The oral or implied promise to pay off debts arising from credit purchases of goods appears in the Accounts Payable account. Such purchases are said to be made on acount. Other liability categories and accounts are added as needed. Taxes Payable, Wages Payable and Salary Payable are accounts that appear in many ledgers.

Notes Payable   Notes Payable records the amounts that the business must pay because it signed a promissory note to purchase goods or services.

Owner's Equity

The claim that the owner has on the assets of the business is called *owner's equity*. In a proprietorship or a partnership, owner's equity is often split into separate accounts for the owner's capital balance and the owner's withdrawals.

Capital   This account shows the owner's claim to the assets of the business. After total liabilities are subtracted from total assets, the remainder is the owner's capital. The balance of the capital account equals the owner's investments in the business plus its net income and minus net losses and owner withdrawals. In addition to the capital account, the following accounts also appear in the owner's equity section of the ledger.

Withdrawals   When the owner withdraws cash or other assets from the business for personal use, its assets and its owner's equity both decrease. The amounts taken out of the business appear in a separate account entitled Withdrawals or Drawing. If withdrawals were recorded directly in the Owner's Equity account, the amount of owner withdrawals would be merged with owner investments. To separate these two amounts for decision-making, businesses use a separate account for Withdrawals. This account shows a *decrease* in owner's equity.

Revenues   The increase in owner's equity from delivering goods or services to customers or clients is called *revenue*. The ledger contains as many revenue accounts as needed. Gary Lyon's accounting practice would have a Service Revenue account for amounts earned by providing accounting service for clients. If the business loans money to an outsider, it will also need an Interest Revenue account. If the business rents a building to a tenant, it will need a Rent Revenue account. Revenue accounts are *increases* in owner's equity.

Expenses   The cost of operating a business is called *expense*. Expenses have the opposite effect of revenues, so they *decrease* owner's equity. A business needs a separate account for each category of its expenses, such as Salary Expense, Rent Expense, Advertising Expense, and Utilities Expense. Expense accounts are decreases in owner's equity.

Exhibit 2-1 shows how asset, liability and owner's equity accounts can be grouped into the ledger. Typically, each account occupies a separate sheet.

Double-Entry Bookkeeping

Accounting is based on double-entry bookkeeping, which means that accountants record the *dual effects* of a business transaction. We know that each transaction affects at least two accounts. For example, Gary Lyon's $50,000 cash investment in his accounting practice increased both the Cash account and the Owner's Equity account of the business. It would be incomplete to record only the increase in the entity's cash without recording the increase in its owner's equity.

Consider a *cash purchase of supplies*. What are the dual effects of this transaction? The purchase (1) decreases cash and (2) increases supplies. A *purchase of supplies on credit* (1) increases supplies and (2) increases accounts payable. A *cash payment on account* (1) decreases cash and (2) decreases accounts payable. All transactions have at least two effects on the entity.

EXHIBIT 2-1   *The Ledger (Asset, Liability and Owner's Equity Accounts)*

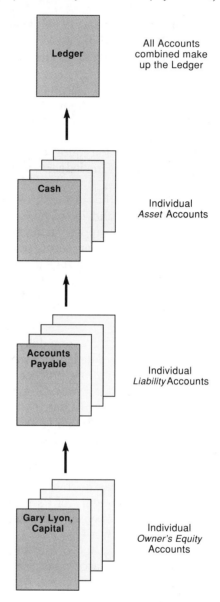

The T-Account

How do accountants record business transactions in the accounts? The account format used for most illustrations in this book is called the T-account. It takes the form of the capital letter "T". The vertical line in the letter divides the account into its left and right sides. The account title rests on the horizontal line. For example, the Cash account of a business appears in the following T-account format:

Cash	
Left side	**Right side**
Debit	*Credit*

The left side of the account is called the **debit** side, and the right side is called the **credit** side. Often beginners in the study of accounting are confused by the words *debit* and *credit*. To become comfortable using them, simply remember this:

debit = left side

credit = right side

Even though *left side* and *right side* may be more convenient, *debit* and *credit* are too deeply entrenched in accounting to avoid using.[1]

In everyday conversation, we sometimes use the word *credit* in a sense that is different from its technical accounting meaning. For example, we may praise someone by saying, "She deserves credit for her good work." In your study of accounting forget this general use. Remember that *debit means left side* and *credit means right side*. Whether an account is increased or decreased by a debit or credit depends on the type of account (see Exhibit 2-2).

Increases and Decreases in the Accounts

The type of an account determines how increases and decreases in it are recorded. Increases in *assets* are recorded in the left (the debit) side of the account. Decreases in assets are recorded in the right (the credit) side of the account. Conversely, increases in *liabilities* and *owner's equity* are recorded by credits. Decreases are recorded by debits.

This pattern of recording debits is based on the accounting equation:

Assets = Liabilities + Owner's Equity

Notice that assets are on the left of the equation while liabilities and owner's equity are on the right or opposite side. This explains why increases and decreases in assets are recorded in the opposite manner from liabilities and owner's equity. It also explains why liabilities and owner's equity follow the same pattern: they are on the same side of the equal sign. Exhibit 2-2 shows the relationship between the accounting equation and the rules of debit and credit.

To illustrate the ideas diagrammed in Exhibit 2-2, reconsider the first transaction from the preceding chapter. Gary Lyon invested the $50,000 he inherited in cash to begin his accounting practice. What accounts are affected? By what

EXHIBIT 2-2   *Accounting Equation and the Rules of Debit and Credit*

Accounting Equation	Assets		=	Liabilities		+	Owner's Equity	
Rules of Debit and Credit	Debit for Increase	Credit for Decrease		Debit for Decrease	Credit for Increase		Debit for Decrease	Credit for Increase

---

[1] The words *debit* and *credit* have a Latin origin (*debitum* and *creditum*). Pacioli, the Italian monk who wrote about accounting in the fifteenth century, used them.

amounts? On what side (debit or credit)? The answer is that Assets and Owner's Equity would increase by $50,000, as the following T-accounts show:

Assets	**= Liabilities +**	**Owner's Equity**
Cash		Gary Lyon, Capital

Debit for Increase 50,000			Credit for Increase, 50,000

The amount remaining in an account is called its *balance*. This initial transaction gives Cash a $50,000 debit balance and Gary Lyon, Capital, a $50,000 credit balance.

OBJECTIVE 2

Apply the rules of debit and credit

The second transaction presented in Chapter 1 is a $20,000 cash purchase of land. This transaction affects two assets: Cash and Land. It decreases Cash (a credit) and increases Land (a debit), as shown in the T-accounts:

Assets	**= Liabilities +**	**Owner's Equity**
Cash		Gary Lyon, Capital

Balance 50,000	Credit for Decrease, 20,000		Balance 50,000

Land	
Debit for Increase 20,000	

After this transaction, Cash has a $30,000 debit balance ($50,000 debit amount — $20,000 credit amount), Land's debit balance is $20,000, and Capital has a $50,000 credit balance.

Transaction 3 is a $500 purchase of office supplies on account. This transaction increases the asset Office Supplies and the liability Accounts Payable, as shown in the following accounts:

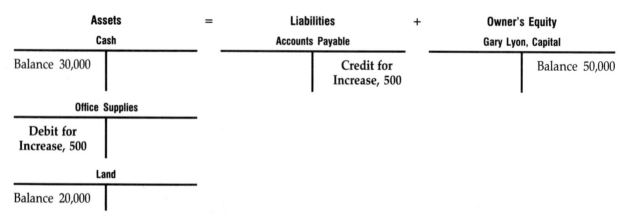

Accountants add accounts as needed. The process of writing a new T-account in preparation for recording a transaction is called *opening the account*. For Transaction 1, we opened the Cash account and the Gary Lyon, Capital account. For Transaction 2, we opened the Land account, and for Transaction 3, Office Supplies and Accounts Payable.

Accountants could record all transactions directly in the accounts as we have shown for the first three transactions. However, that way of accounting is not practical because it does not leave a clear record of each transaction. Suppose you need to know what account was debited and what account was credited in a particular transaction. Looking at each account in the ledger does not answer this question because double-entry accounting always affects at least two accounts. Therefore, you may have to search through all the accounts in the ledger to find both sides of a particular transaction. To avoid this waste of time, accountants keep a record of each transaction and then transfer this information into the accounts.

Recording Transactions in Journals ———————————————

To keep track of the individual transactions, accountants record transactions first in a book called the **journal**. A journal is a chronological record of the entity's transactions. In this section, we describe the recording process and illustrate how to use the journal and the ledger.

The recording process follows these five steps:

1. Identify the transactions from source documents, such as bank deposit slips, sales receipts and stubs.
2. Specify each account affected by the transaction and classify it by type (asset, liability or owner's equity).
3. Determine whether each account is increased or decreased by the transaction.
4. From the rules of debit and credit, determine whether to debit or credit the account.
5. Enter the transaction in the journal, including a brief explanation for the journal entry. It is customary to write the debit side of the entry first and the credit side next.

We have discussed steps 1, 2, 3 and 4. Step 5, "Enter the transaction in the journal," means to write the transaction in the journal. This step is also called "making the journal entry," "preparing the journal entry," or "journalizing the transaction." A major part of learning accounting is learning how to make journal entries.

Let us apply the five steps to journalize the first transaction of the accounting practice of Gary Lyon, CA — the $50,000 cash investment in the business.

> **OBJECTIVE 3**
> Record transactions in the journal

Step 1.   The source documents are the bank deposit slip and Lyon's $50,000 cheque, which is drawn on his personal bank account.

Step 2.   *Cash* and *Gary Lyon, Capital* are the accounts affected by the transaction. Cash is an asset account, and Gary Lyon, Capital is an owner's equity account.

Step 3.   Both accounts increase by $50,000. Therefore, debit Cash: it is the asset account that is increased. Also, credit Gary Lyon, Owner's Equity: it is the owner's equity account that is increased.

Step 4.   Debit Cash to record an increase in this asset account. Credit Gary Lyon, Capital to record an increase in this account.

Step 5. The journal entry is

Date	Accounts and Explanation	Debit	Credit
Apr. 2	Cash	50,000	
	Gary Lyon, Capital		50,000
	Initial investment by owner.		

Note that the journal entry includes (1) the date of the transaction, (2) the title of the account debited (placed flush left) and the total of the account credited (indented slightly), (3) the dollar amounts of the debit (left) and credit (right) — dollar signs are omitted in the money columns, and (4) a short explanation of the transaction.

A helpful hint: To get off to the right start when analysing a transaction, you should first pinpoint its effects (if any) on cash. Did cash increase or decrease? Then find its effect on other accounts. Typically, it is much easier to identify the effect of a transaction on cash than to identify the effect on other accounts.

The journal offers information that the ledger's T-accounts do not provide. Each journal entry shows the complete effect of a business transaction. Let us examine Gary Lyon's initial investment. The Cash account shows a single figure, the $50,000 debit. We know that every transaction has a credit, so in what account will we find the corresponding $50,000 credit? In this simple illustration, we know that the Capital account holds this figure. But imagine the difficulties an accountant would face trying to link debits and credits for hundreds of daily transactions — without a separate record of each transaction. The journal answers this problem and presents the full story for each transaction.

The journal can be a loose-leaf notebook or a bound book. Exhibit 2-3 shows how a journal page might look with the first transaction entered.

EXHIBIT 2-3 *The Journal*

	Journal		Page 6
Date	Accounts and Explanation	Debit	Credit
Apr. 2	Cash	50,000	
	Gary Lyon, Capital		50,000
	Initial investment by owner.		

Posting from the Journal to the Ledger

Posting means transferring the amounts from the journal to the appropriate accounts in the ledger. Debits in the journal are posted as debits in the ledger, and credits in the journal as credits in the ledger. The initial investment transaction of Gary Lyon is posted to the ledger as shown in Exhibit 2-4.

EXHIBIT 2-4   *Journal Entry and Posting to the Ledger*

Panel A: Journal Entry

Accounts and Explanation	Debit	Credit
Debit: Cash	50,000	
Credit: Gary Lyon, Capital		50,000
Initial investment by owner.		

Panel B: Posting to the Ledger

Cash

50,000

Gary Lyon, Capital

50,000

> **OBJECTIVE 4**
> Post from the journal to
> the ledger

Flow of Accounting Data

Exhibit 2-5 summarizes the flow of accounting data from the business transaction to the ledger.

EXHIBIT 2-5   *Flow of Accounting Data*

Transaction occurs.

↓

Source Documents prepared.

↓

Transaction *Analysis* takes place.

↓

Transaction entered in *Journal.*

↓

Amounts posted to *Ledger.*

Illustrative Problem

In this section, we illustrate transaction analysis, journalizing and posting. We continue the example of Gary Lyon, CA and account for six of his early transactions.

Transaction Analysis, Journalizing and Posting

1. *Transaction:* Lyon invested $50,000 to begin his accounting practice.

   Analysis: Lyon's investment in the business increased its asset cash; to record this increase, debit Cash.

   His investment also increased the owner's equity of the entity; to record this increase, credit Gary Lyon, Capital.

   Journal Entry:
   ```
   Cash .....................................  50,000
        Gary Lyon, Capital ..................          50,000
   Initial investment by owner.
   ```

   Ledger Accounts:

Cash		Gary Lyon, Capital	
(1) 50,000			(1) 50,000

2. *Transaction:* He paid $20,000 cash for land as a future office location.

   Analysis: The purchase increased the entity's asset land; to record this increase, debit Land.

   The purchase decreased cash; therefore, credit Cash.

   Journal Entry:
   ```
   Land .....................................  20,000
        Cash ................................          20,000
   Paid cash for land
   ```

   Ledger Accounts:

Cash		Land	
(1) 50,000	(2) 20,000	(2) 20,000	

3. *Transaction:* He purchased $500 office supplies on account.

   Analysis: The credit purchase of office supplies increased this asset; to record this increase, debit Office Supplies.

   The purchase also increased the liability accounts payable; to record this increase, credit Accounts Payable.

   Journal Entry:
   ```
   Office Supplies ...........................  500
        Accounts Payable ...................          500
   Purchased office supplies on account.
   ```

   Ledger Accounts:

Office Supplies		Accounts Payable	
(3) 500			(3) 500

4. *Transaction:* He paid $400 on the account payable created in the preceding transaction.

Analysis: The payment decreased the asset cash; therefore, credit Cash.

The payment also decreased the liability, accounts payable; to record this decrease, debit Accounts Payable.

Journal Entry:

Accounts Payable.........................	400	
Cash..............................		400

Paid cash on account.

Ledger Accounts:

Cash		Accounts Payable	
(1) 50,000	(2) 20,000	(4) 400	(3) 500
	(4) 400		

5. *Transaction:* He remodeled personal residence. This is not a business transaction of the accounting practice, so no journal entry is made.

6. *Transaction:* Lyon withdrew $2,100 cash for personal living expenses.

Analysis: The withdrawal decreased the entity's cash; therefore, credit Cash.

The transaction also decreased the owner's equity of the entity and must be recorded by a debit to an owner's equity account. Decreases in the owner's equity of a proprietorship that result from owner withdrawals are debited to a separate owner's equity account entitled Withdrawals. Therefore, debit Gary Lyon, Withdrawals.

Journal Entry:

Gary Lyon, Withdrawals	2,100	
Cash..............................		2,100

Withdrawal of cash by owner.

Ledger Accounts:

Cash		Gary Lyon, Withdrawals	
(1) 50,000	(2) 20,000	(6) 2,100	
	(4) 400		
	(6) 2,100		

As each journal entry is posted to the ledger, it is keyed by date or by transaction number. In this way, a trail is provided through the accounting records so that any transaction can be traced from the journal to the ledger, and, if need be, back to the journal. This linking allows the accountant to locate efficiently any information needed.

Ledger Accounts after Posting

We next illustrate how the accounts look when the amounts of the preceding transactions have been posted. The accounts were grouped under the accounting equation's headings.

Note that each account has a balance figure. This amount is the difference between the account's total debits and its total credits. For example, the balance in the Cash account is the difference between the debits, $50,000 and the credits, $22,500 ($20,000 + $400 + $2,100). Thus the balance figure is $27,500. The balance amounts are not journal entries posted to the accounts, so we set an account balance apart by horizontal lines.

If the sum of an account's debits is greater than the sum of its credits, that account has a debit balance, as the Cash account does here. If the sum of its credits is greater, that account has a credit balance, as Accounts Payable does.

Assets	=	Liabilities	+	Owner's Equity

Cash

(1)	50,000	(2)	20,000
		(4)	400
		(6)	2,100
Bal.	27,500		

Office Supplies

(3)	500	
Bal.	500	

Land

(2)	20,000	
Bal.	20,000	

Accounts Payable

(4)	400	(3)	500
		Bal.	100

Gary Lyon, Capital

	(1)	50,000
	Bal.	50,000

Gary Lyon, Withdrawals

(6)	2,100	
Bal.	2,100	

Trial Balance

A **trial balance** is a list of all accounts with their balances. It provides a check on accuracy by showing whether the total debits equal the total credits. A trial balance may be taken at any time the postings are up to date. Exhibit 2-6 is the trial balance of the general ledger of Gary Lyon's accounting practice after the first six transactions have been journalized and posted.

The word *trial* is well chosen. The list is prepared as a *test* of the accounts' amounts. The trial balance shows the accountant whether the total debits and total credits are equal. In this way it may signal accounting errors. For example, if only the debit (or only the credit) side of a transaction is posted, the total debits will not equal the total credits. If a debit is posted as a credit or vice versa, debits and credits will be out of balance. For example, if the $500 debit in Office Supplies is incorrectly posted as a credit, total debits will be $49,600

OBJECTIVE 5

Prepare a trial balance

EXHIBIT 2-6 *Trial Balance*

Gary Lyon, CA
Trial Balance
April 30, 19X1

	Balance	
Account Titles	Debit	Credit
Cash	$27,500	
Office supplies...................	500	
Land	20,000	
Accounts payable		$ 100
Gary Lyon, capital		50,000
Gary Lyon, withdrawals	2,100	
Total	$50,100	$50,100

and total credits will be $50,600. The trial balance alerts the accountant to such errors in posting.

Some errors may not be revealed by the trial balance. For example, a $1,000 cash payment for supplies may be debited to Office Furniture instead of to Office Supplies. This error would cause Office Furniture to be overstated and Office Supplies to be understated, each by $1,000. But these errors would offset each other (they are both asset accounts) so the trial balance would still show debits equal to credits. Also, if an accountant erroneously recorded a $5,000 transaction at only $500, the trial balance would show no error. However, total debits and total credits would both be understated by $4,500 (that is, $5,000 − $500).

Summary Problem for Your Review

On August 1, 19X5, Liz Shea, opens a business that she names Shea's Research Service. She will be the sole owner of the business, so it will be a proprietorship. During the entity's first ten days of operations, the following transactions take place:

a. To begin operations, Shea deposits $60,000 of personal funds in a bank account entitled Shea's Research Service.
b. Shea pays $40,000 cash for a small house to be used as an office. (Debit an asset account entitled Building.)
c. Shea purchases $450 in office supplies on credit (that is, on account).
d. Shea pays cash of $6,000 for office furniture. (Debit Office Furniture.)
e. Shea pays $150 on the account payable she created in transaction c.
f. Shea withdraws $1,000 cash for personal use.

Required

1. Prepare the journal entries to record these transactions. Key the journal entries by transaction number.
2. Post the entries to the ledger.
3. Prepare the trial balance of Shea's Research Service at August 10, 19X5.

SOLUTION TO REVIEW PROBLEM

Requirement 1

	Accounts and Explanation	Debit	Credit
1.	Cash..	60,000	
	Liz Shea, Capital.................................		60,000
	Initial investment by owner.		
2.	Building	40,000	
	Cash		40,000
	Purchased building for an office.		
3.	Office Supplies	450	
	Accounts Payable		450
	Purchased office supplies on account.		

4.	Office Furniture	6,000	
	Cash		6,000
	Purchased office furniture.		
5.	Accounts Payable	150	
	Cash		150
	Paid cash on account.		
6.	Liz Shea, Withdrawals	1,000	
	Cash		1,000
	Withdrew cash for personal use.		

Requirement 2

Assets

Cash

(1) 60,000	(2) 40,000		
	(4) 6,000		
	(5) 150		
	(6) 1,000		
Bal. 12,850			

Office Supplies

(3) 450	
Bal. 450	

Office Furniture

(4) 6,000	
Bal. 6,000	

Building

(2) 40,000	
Bal. 40,000	

Liabilities

Accounts Payable

(5) 150	(3) 450
	Bal. 300

Owner's Equity

Liz Shea, Capital

	(1) 60,000
	Bal. 60,000

Liz Shea, Withdrawals

(6) 1,000	
Bal. 1,000	

Requirement 3

Shea's Research Service
Trial Balance
August 10, 19X5

Account Title	Balance	
	Debit	Credit
Cash	$12,850	
Office supplies	450	
Office furniture	6,000	
Building.............................	40,000	
Accounts payable		$ 300
Liz Shea, capital.......................		60,000
Liz Shea, withdrawals	1,000	
Total	$60,300	$60,300

Details of Journals and Ledgers _____

In order to focus on the main points of journalizing and posting, we purposely omitted certain essential data. In actual practice, the journal and the ledger provide additional details that create a "trail" through the accounting records for future reference. For example, an accountant may need to verify the date of a transaction or to determine whether a journal entry has been posted to the ledger. Let us take a closer look at the journal and the ledger.

Journal   In Exhibit 2-7, Panel B presents the journal format most often used by accountants. The top of the journal holds the journal title. Note also that the journal page number appears in the upper-right corner.

As the column headings indicate, the *journal* displays the following information:

1. The *date*, which is most important because it indicates when the transaction occurred. The year appears first. It is not necessary to repeat it for each journal entry. The year appears only when the journal is started or when the year has changed. Note that the year appears with an X in the third column. We present the year in this way because the dates we choose are for illustration only. Thus 19X1 is followed by 19X2, and so on. We will use this format throughout the book. Like the year, the month is entered only once The second date column holds the day of the transaction. This column is filled in for every transaction.
2. The *account title* and explanation of the transaction. You are already familiar with this presentation from Exhibit 2-3.
3. The *posting reference*, abbreviated Post. Ref. How this column helps the accountant becomes clear when we discuss the details of posting.
4. The *debit* column, which shows the amount debited.
5. The *credit* column, which shows the amount credited.

Ledger   Panel C in Exhibit 2-7 presents the *ledger* in T-account format. Each account has its own page in the ledger. Our example shows Gary Lyon's Cash account. This account maintains the basic format of the T-account but offers more information.

The account title appears at the top of the page. Note also the account number at the upper-right column. Each account has its own identification number. We will look later at how accountants assign account numbers.

The column headings identify the ledger account's features, as follows:

1. The date.
2. The item column. This space is used for any special notation.
3. The journal reference column, abbreviated Jrnl. Ref. The importance of this column becomes clear when we go through the mechanics of posting.
4. The debit column, with the amount debited.
5. The credit column, with the amount credited.

Posting _____

We know that posting means moving information from the journal to the ledger accounts. But how do we handle the additional details that appear in the journal and the ledger formats that we have just seen? Exhibit 2-7 illustrates

EXHIBIT 2-7 *Details of Journalizing and Posting*

Panel A: Illustrative Transactions

Date	Transaction
April 2, 19X1	Gary Lyon invested $50,000 in his accounting practice.
3	Paid $500 cash for office supplies.

Panel B: Journal

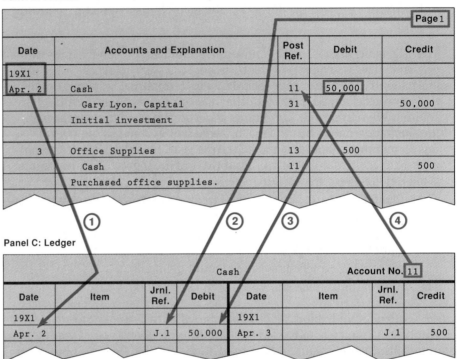

Date	Accounts and Explanation	Post Ref.	Debit	Credit
19X1				
Apr. 2	Cash	11	50,000	
	Gary Lyon, Capital	31		50,000
	Initial investment			
3	Office Supplies	13	500	
	Cash	11		500
	Purchased office supplies.			

Panel C: Ledger

Cash   Account No. 11

Date	Item	Jrnl. Ref.	Debit	Date	Item	Jrnl. Ref.	Credit
19X1				19X1			
Apr. 2		J.1	50,000	Apr. 3		J.1	500

Office Supplies   Account No. 13

Date	Item	Jrnl. Ref.	Debit	Date	Item	Jrnl. Ref.	Credit
19X1							
Apr. 3		J.1	500				

Gary Lyon, Capital   Account No. 31

Date	Item	Jrnl. Ref.	Debit	Date	Item	Jrnl. Ref.	Credit
				19X1			
				Apr. 2		J.1	50,000

the steps in full detail. Panel A lists the first two transactions of Gary Lyon, CA; Panel B presents the journal; and Panel C shows the ledger.

Since the flow of accounting data moves from the journal to the ledger, the accountant first records the journal entry, as shown in Panel B. The transaction data are given in Panel A, except for the Post. Ref. number. Let us trace the arrows to follow the details of posting.

Arrow 1 traces the date, Apr. 2, 19X1, from the journal to the ledger account Cash.

Arrow 2 begins at the journal's page number, Page 1, and ends in the journal reference column, Jrnl. Ref. of the ledger. The J.1 entry in that column stands for "Journal (page) 1." Why bother with this detail? If an accountant is using the Cash account and needs to locate the original journal entry, the journal page number tells where to look.

Arrow 3 indicates that the accountant records the debit figure, $50,000 in this journal entry, as a debit figure in the account.

Arrow 4 points to a posting detail. Once the accountant has recorded a dollar figure to the appropriate account, that account's number is entered in the journal's Post. Ref. column. This step indicates that all the information for that account has been posted from the journal to the ledger. A blank Post. Ref. column for an entry means that the entry has not yet been posted to the ledger account.

Having performed these steps for the debit entry, the accountant then posts the credit entry to the ledger. After posting, the accountant draws up the trial balance, as we discussed earlier.

Chart of Accounts

As you know, the general ledger contains the business's accounts grouped under the headings Assets, Liabilities, Owner's Equity, Revenues and Expenses. To keep track of their accounts, Organizations have a **chart of accounts**, which lists all the accounts and their account numbers. These account numbers are used as posting references, as illustrated by arrow 4 in Exhibit 2-7. It is easier to write the account number, 11, in the posting reference column of the journal than to write the account title, Cash. Also, this numbering system makes it easy to locate individual accounts in the ledger.

Assets are usually numbered beginning with 1, liabilities with 2, owner's equity with 3, revenues with 4, and expenses with 5. The second digit in an account number indicates the position of the individual account within the category. For example, Cash may be account number 11, which is the first asset account. Accounts Receivable may be account number 12, the second asset account. Accounts Payable may be account number 21, the first liability account. All accounts are numbered using this system.

Many organizations have so many accounts that they use three- or four-digit account numbers. For example, account number 101 may be Cash on Hand, account number 102 may be Cash on Deposit in Huron Bank, and account number 103 may be Cash on Deposit in the Bank of Manitoba.

The chart of accounts for Gary Lyon, CA appears in Exhibit 2-8. Notice that the account numbers jump from 13 to 17. Gary Lyon realizes that later on he may want to add other supplies accounts, for example, Tax Forms Supplies. Any additional supplies account would logically appear next to Office Supplies, and Tax Forms Supplies might be account number 14.

EXHIBIT 2-8 Chart of Accounts: Accounting Practice of Gary Lyon, CA

Balance Sheet Accounts

Assets	Liabilities	Owner's Equity
11 Cash	21 Accounts Payable	31 Gary Lyon, Capital
12 Accounts Receivable	22 Notes Payable	32 Gary Lyon, Withdrawals
13 Office Supplies		
17 Office Furniture		
19 Land		

Income Statement Accounts

	Revenues	Expenses
	41 Service Revenue	51 Rent Expense
		52 Salary Expense
		53 Utilities Expense

Normal Balances of Accounts

Accountants speak of an account's *normal balance*, which refers to the side of the account—debit or credit—where *increases* are recorded. This term also refers to the usual balance—debit or credit—in the account. For example, Cash and all other assets usually have a debit balance, so assets are *debit-balance* accounts. On the other hand, liabilities and owner's equity usually have a credit balance, so they are *credit-balance* accounts. Exhibit 2-9 illustrates the normal balances of assets, liabilities, and owner's equity.

An account that normally has a debit balance may occasionally have a credit balance. This indicates a negative amount of the item. For example, Cash will have a temporary credit balance if the entity overdraws its bank account. Similarly, the liability Accounts Payable (normally a credit balance account) will have a debit balance if the entity overpays its account. In other instances, the shift of a balance amount away from its normal column indicates an accounting error. For example, a credit balance in Office Supplies, Office Furniture or Buildings indicates an error because negative amounts of these assets cannot exist.

As we have explained, owner's equity usually contains several accounts. In total, these accounts show a normal credit balance for the owner's equity of the business. Each individual owner's equity account has a normal credit balance if it represents an *increase* in owner's equity, for example, the Capital account. However, if the individual owner's equity account represents a *decrease* in owner's equity, the account will have a normal debit balance, for example, the Withdrawals account.

EXHIBIT 2-9 Normal Balances of Balance Sheet Accounts

Assets	=	Liabilities	+	Owner's Equity
Normal Bal. Debit		Normal Bal. Credit		Normal Bal. Credit

Additional Owner's Equity Accounts: Revenues and Expenses

The owner's equity category, which may be subdivided into capital and withdrawals, includes two additional types of accounts: revenues and expenses. As we have discussed, **revenues** are increases in owner's equity that result from delivering goods or services to customers. **Expenses** are decreases in owner's equity due to the cost of operating the business. Therefore, the accounting equation may be expanded as follows:

$$\text{Assets} = \text{Liabilities} + \text{Owner's Equity}$$

$$\underbrace{\text{(Capital} - \text{Withdrawals)} + \text{(Revenues} - \text{Expenses)}}$$

Revenues and expenses appear in parentheses because their impact on the accounting equation arises from their effect on owner's equity. If revenues exceed expenses, the net effect—revenues minus expenses—is net income, which increases owner's equity. If expenses are greater, the net effect is a net loss, which decreases owner's equity.

We can now express the *rules of debit and credit* in final form as shown in Panel A of Exhibit 2-10. Panel B shows the *normal balances* of the five types of

EXHIBIT 2-10 *Rules of Debit and Credit and Normal Balances of Accounts*

Panel A: Rules of Debit and Credit

Assets		=	Liabilities		+	Capital	
Debit for Increase	Credit for Decrease		Debit for Decrease	Credit for Increase		Debit for Decrease	Credit for Increase

						Withdrawals	
						Debit for Increase	Credit for Decrease

						Revenues	
						Debit for Decrease	Credit for Increase

						Expenses	
						Debit for Increase	Credit for Decrease

Panel B: Normal Balances

Assets	Debit	
Liabilities		Credit
Owner's equity—overall		Credit
Capital		Credit
Withdrawals	Debit	
Revenue		Credit
Expenses	Debit	

accounts: (1) assets, (2) liabilities, (3) capital minus withdrawals, (4) revenues, and (5) expenses. Note that owner's equity is normally a credit because capital must exceed withdrawals (an owner of a company cannot withdraw more than the capital that has been put in) and revenues normally exceed expenses.

All of accounting is based on these five types of accounts. You should become very familiar with the related rules of debit and credit and the normal balances of accounts.

Typical Account Titles

Thus far we have dealt with a limited number of transactions and accounts to introduce key concepts. Businesses engage in more transactions, requiring more accounts. Additional transactions are recorded in the same manner, with accounts added to the analysis as needed. The following summary describes some of the more common accounts grouped by financial statement and account category. As you answer the exercises and problems in this and future chapters, you will find these descriptions useful.

Income Statement: Revenues and Expenses

Revenues
   Service revenue: Revenue earned by performing a service (accounting service by a CA firm, laundry service by a laundry, and so forth).
   Sales revenue: Revenue earned by selling a product (sales of hardware by a hardware store, food by a grocery store, and so forth).

Expenses
   Rent expense: Expense for office rent and the rental of office equipment or any other business asset.
   Salary expense: Expense of having an employee work for the business.
   Utilities expense: Expense of using electricity, water, gas, and other items provided by utility companies.
   Supplies expense: Expense of using supplies such as stationery, stamps, paper clips, staples, and so forth.
   Advertising expense: Expense of advertising the business.
   Interest expense: Expense of using borrowed money.
   Property tax expense: Expense for property tax on business land and buildings.

Balance Sheet: Assets, Liabilities and Owner's Equity

Assets
   Cash: Money on hand and in the bank.
   Accounts receivable: Claim on open account against the cash of a client or a customer. (Open account means that no written promise exists to support the receivable.)
   Note receivable: Claim against the cash of another party, supported by a promissory note signed by the other party. (All receivables are assets and any account with receivable in its title is an asset.)
   Merchandise inventory: Merchandise an entity sells in its business (such as clothing by a department store, stereos by a stereo shop, and so forth).
   Office supplies: Stationery, stamps, paper clips, staples, and so forth.

Office furniture: Desks, chairs, file cabinets, and so forth.

Office equipment: Typewriters, calculators and other equipment used in a business office.

Building: Building used in a business.

Land: Land on which a business building stands.

Liabilities

Account payable: Liability to pay cash to another party on open account.

Note payable: Liability to pay cash to another party, supported by a signed promissory note.

Salary payable: Liability to pay an employee for work. (Most liabilities have the word payable in the account title, and any account with payable in its title is a liability.)

Owner's Equity

Gary Lyon, Capital: The interest of the owner of the business in its assets. (This account title bears the name of the owner.)

Gary Lyon, Withdrawals: The owner's withdrawals of assets from the business for personal use.

Illustrative Problem _____

Let us account for the revenues and expenses of the accounting practice of Sally Gunz, Lawyer for the month of July 19X1. We follow the same steps illustrated earlier: analyze the transaction, journalize, post to the ledger, and prepare the trial balance. Revenue accounts and expense accounts work just like asset, liability, and owner's equity accounts. Each revenue and each expense account has its own page in the ledger and its own identifying account number.

Transaction Analysis, Journalizing and Posting

> **OBJECTIVE 6**
> Record revenues and expenses

1. *Transaction*: Sally Gunz invested $10,000 cash in a business bank account to open her law practice.

   Analysis: The asset cash is increased; therefore debit Cash.

   The owner's equity of the business increased; therefore, credit Sally Gunz, Capital

   Journal Entry:
   Cash 10,000
       Sally Gunz, Capital 10,000
   Invested cash in the business.

   Ledger Accounts:

Cash		Sally Gunz, Capital	
(1) 10,000			(1) 10,000

2. *Transaction*: Gunz performed service for a client and collected $3,000 cash.

   Analysis: The asset cash is increased; therefore, debit Cash.

   The revenue service revenue is increased; credit Service Revenue.

Journal Entry:	Cash	3,000
	Service Revenue	3,000
	Performed service and received cash.	

Ledger Accounts:

Cash		Service Revenue	
(1) 10,000			(2) 3,000
(2) 3,000			

3. *Transaction:* Gunz performed service for a client and billed the client for $500 on account receivable. This means the client owes the business $500 even though the client signed no formal promissory note.

   Analysis: The asset accounts receivable is increased; therefore, debit Accounts Receivable.

   The revenue service revenue is increased; credit Service Revenue.

Journal Entry:	Accounts Receivable	500
	Service Revenue	500
	Performed service on account.	

Ledger Accounts:

Accounts Receivable		Service Revenue	
(3) 500			(2) 3,000
			(3) 500

4. *Transaction:* Gunz performed accounting service of $700 for a client, who paid $300 cash immediately. Gunz billed the remaining $400 to the client on account receivable.

   Analysis: The assets cash and accounts receivable are increased; therefore, debit both of these asset accounts.

   The revenue service revenue is increased; credit Service Revenue for the sum of the two debit amounts.

Journal Entry:	Cash	300
	Accounts Receivable	400
	Service Revenue	700
	Performed service for cash and on account.	

   Note: Because this transaction affects more than two accounts at the same time, the entry is called a *compound entry*. No matter how many accounts a compound entry affects (there may be any number), total debits must equal total credits.

Ledger Accounts:

Cash		Accounts Receivable	
(1) 10,000		(3) 500	
(2) 3,000		(4) 400	
(4) 300			

Service Revenue	
	(2) 3,000
	(3) 500
	(4) 700

5. *Transaction:* Gunz paid the following cash expenses: office rent, $900; employee salary, $1,500; and utilities, $500.

   Analysis: The following expenses are increased: Rent Expense, Salary Expense, and Utilities Expense. They should each be debited. The asset cash is decreased; therefore, credit Cash for each of the three expense amounts.

   Journal Entry:

(a) Rent Expense	900	
Cash		900
(b) Salary Expense	1,500	
Cash		1,500
(c) Utilities Expense	500	
Cash		500

   Issued three cheques to pay cash expenses.

   Ledger Accounts:

Cash				Rent Expense		
(1) 10,000	(5a)	900		(5)	900	
(2) 3,000	(5b)	1,500				
(4) 300	(5c)	500				

Salary Expense		Utilities Expense	
(5) 1,500		(5) 500	

6. *Transaction:* Gunz received a telephone bill for $120 and will pay this expense next week.

   Analysis: Utilities expense is increased; therefore, debit this expense. The liability accounts payable is increased; credit this account.

   Journal Entry:

Utilities Expense	120	
Accounts Payable		120

   Received utility bill.

   Ledger Accounts:

Accounts Payable		Utilities Expense	
	(6) 120	(5) 500	
		(6) 120	

7. *Transaction:* Gunz collected $200 cash from the client established in Transaction 3.

   Analysis: The asset cash is increased; therefore, debit Cash. The asset accounts receivable is decreased; therefore, credit Accounts Receivable.

   Journal Entry:

Cash	200	
Accounts Receivable		200

   Received cash on account.

   Note: This transaction has no effect on revenue; the related revenue is accounted for in transaction 3.

   Ledger Accounts:

Cash			Accounts Receivable		
(1) 10,000	(5) 2,900		(3) 500	(7) 200	
(2) 3,000			(4) 400		
(4) 300					
(7) 200					

8. *Transaction:* Gunz paid the telephone bill that was received and recorded in transaction 6.

   Analysis: The liability accounts payable is decreased; therefore, debit Accounts Payable.

   The asset cash is decreased; credit Cash.

   Journal Entry:

   Accounts Payable.......................... 120

       Cash................................ 120

   Paid cash on account.

   Note: This transaction has no effect on expense because the related expense was recorded in transaction 6.

   Ledger Accounts:

Cash				Accounts Payable			
(1)	10,000	(5)	2,900	(8)	**120**	(6)	120
(2)	3,000	(8)	**120**				
(4)	300						
(7)	200						

9. *Transaction:* Gunz withdrew $1,100 cash for personal use.

   Analysis: The withdrawal decreased owner's equity; therefore, debit Sally Gunz, Withdrawals.

   The asset cash decreased; credit Cash.

   Journal Entry:

   Sally Gunz, Withdrawals 1,100

       Cash................................ 1,100

   Withdrew for personal use.

   Ledger Accounts:

Cash				Sally Gunz, Withdrawals		
(1)	10,000	(5)	2,900	(9)	**1,100**	
(2)	3,000	(8)	120			
(4)	300	(9)	**1,100**			
(7)	200					

Ledger Accounts After Posting

Assets

Cash					Accounts Receivable			
(1)	10,000	(5)	2,900		(3)	500	(7)	200
(2)	3,000	(8)	120		(4)	400		
(4)	300	(9)	1,100		Bal.	700		
(7)	200							
Bal.	9,380							

Liabilities

Accounts Payable			
(8)	120	(6)	120
		Bal.	0

Owner's equity

Sally Gunz, Capital				Sally Gunz, Withdrawals		
		(1)	10,000	(9)	1,100	
		Bal. 10,000		Bal.	1,100	

Revenue

Service Revenue			
		(2)	3,000
		(3)	500
		(4)	700
		Bal.	4,200

Expenses

Rent Expense			Salary Expense			Utilities Expense		
(5)	900		(5)	1,500		(5)	500	
Bal.	900		Bal.	1,500		(6)	120	
						Bal.	620	

Trial Balance

Sally Gunz, Lawyer
Trial Balance
July 31, 19X1

Account Title	Balance Debit	Balance Credit
Cash................................	$ 9,380	
Accounts receivable	700	
Accounts payable		$ 0
Sally Gunz, capital		10,000
Sally Gunz, withdrawals	1,100	
Service revenue		4,200
Rent expense	900	
Salary expense........................	1,500	
Utilities expense	620	
Total	$14,200	$14,200

Analytical Use of Accounting Information

What dominates the accountant's analysis of transactions: the accounting equation, the journal, or the ledger? The *accounting equation* is most fundamental. In turn, the ledger is more useful than the journal in providing an overall model of the organization. Accountants and other business persons must often make quick decisions without the benefit of a complete accounting system: journal, ledger, accounts and trial balance. For example, the owner of a company may be negotiating the purchase price of another business. In spur-of-the-moment analysis of the effects of transactions, accountants often skip the journal and go directly to the ledger. They compress transaction analysis, journalizing and posting into one step. This type of analysis saves time that may be the difference between a good business decision and a passed-up opportunity.

OBJECTIVE 7
Analyse transactions without a journal

Let us take an example to see how it works. For instance, the first revenue transaction—Lyon performed accounting service for a client and collected cash of $3,000—may be analysed be debiting the Cash account and crediting the Service Revenue account directly in the ledger in the following manner:

Cash	Service Revenue
3,000	3,000

With this short cut, the accountant can see immediately the effect of the transaction on both the entity's cash and its service revenue. Modern computer-assisted accounting systems often have this "journal-less" feature. These systems can also produce the essential data associated with individual transactions, such as the date, transaction amount and accounts affected.

Summary Problem for Your Review

The trial balance of Tomassini Computer Service Centre on March 1, 19X2, lists the entity's assets, liabilities and owner's equity on that date.

	Balance	
Account Title	Debit	Credit
Cash..................................	$26,000	
Accounts receivable	4,500	
Accounts payable		$ 2,000
L. Tomassini, capital		28,500
Total	$30,500	$30,500

During March the business engaged in the following transactions:

1. Tomassini borrowed $45,000 from the bank. He signed a note payable in the name of the business.
2. He paid cash of $40,000 to a real estate company to acquire land.
3. He performed service for a customer and received cash of $5,000.
4. He purchased supplies on credit, $300.
5. He performed customer service and earned revenue on account, $2,600.
6. He paid $1,200 on account.
7. He paid the following cash expenses: salaries, $3,000; rent, $1,500; and interest, $400.
8. He received $3,000 on account.
9. He received a $200 utility bill that will be paid next week.
10. Tomassini withdrew $1,800 for personal use.

Required

1. Open the following accounts, with the balances indicated, in the ledger of Tomassini Computer Service Centre. Use the T-account format.
   Assets: Cash, $26,000; Accounts Receivable, $4,500; Supplies, no balance; Land, no balance
   Liabilities: Accounts Payable, $2,000; Note Payable, no balance
   Owner's Equity: Larry Tomassini, Capital, $28,500; Larry Tomassini, Withdrawals, no balance
   Revenues: Service Revenue, no balance
   Expenses: Salary Expense, Rent Expense, Utilities Expense, Interest Expense, (none have balances)
2. Journalize the preceding transactions. Key journal entries by transaction number.
3. Post to the ledger.
4. Prepare the trial balance of Tomassini Computer Service Centre at March 31, 19X2.
5. Compute the net income or net loss of the entity during the month of March. List expenses in order from the largest to the smallest.

SOLUTION TO REVIEW PROBLEM

Requirement 1

Assets

Cash	Accounts Receivable	Supplies	Land
Bal. 26,000	Bal. 4,500		

Liabilities

Accounts Payable	Note Payable
Bal. 2,000	

Owner's Equity

Larry Tomassini, Capital	Larry Tomassini, Withdrawals
Bal. 28,500	

Revenues	Expenses

Service Revenue	Salary Expense	Rent Expense
	Utilities Expense	Interest Expenses

Requirement 2

	Accounts and Explanation	Debit	Credit
1.	Cash	45,000	
	Note Payable		45,000
	Borrowed cash on note payable.		
2.	Land...	40,000	
	Cash...		40,000
	Purchased land for cash.		
3.	Cash	5,000	
	Service Revenue		5,000
	Performed service and received cash.		
4.	Supplies...	300	
	Accounts Payable		300
	Purchased supplies on account.		
5.	Accounts Receivable	2,600	
	Service Revenue		2,600
	Performed service on account.		
6.	Accounts Payable....................................	1,200	
	Cash...		1,200
	Paid on account.		

7.	(a)	Salary Expense	3,000	
		Cash		3,000
	(b)	Rent Expense	1,500	
		Cash		1,500
	(c)	Interest Expense	400	
		Cash		400
		Issued three cheques to pay cash expenses.		

8.	Cash	3,000	
	Accounts Receivable		3,000
	Received on account.		

9.	Utilities Expense	200	
	Accounts Payable		200
	Received utility bill.		

10.	Larry Tomassini, Withdrawals	1,800	
	Cash...		1,800
	Withdrew for personal use.		

Requirement 3

Assets

Cash			
Bal.	26,000	(2)	40,000
(1)	45,000	(6)	1,200
(3)	5,000	(7a)	3,000
(8)	3,000	(7b)	1,500
		(7c)	400
		(10)	1,800
Bal.	31,100		

Accounts Receivable			
Bal.	4,500	(8)	3,000
(5)	2,600		
Bal.	4,100		

Supplies		
(4)	300	
Bal.	300	

Land		
(2)	40,000	
Bal.	40,000	

Liabilities

Accounts Payable			
(6)	1,200	Bal.	2,000
		(4)	300
		(9)	200
		Bal.	1,300

Note Payable			
		(1)	45,000
		Bal.	45,000

Owner's Equity

Larry Tomassini, Capital		
	Bal.	28,500

Larry Tomassini, Withdrawals		
(10)	1,800	
Bal.	1,800	

Revenues

Service Revenue			
		(3)	5,000
		(5)	2,600
		Bal.	7,600

Expenses

Salary Expense		
(7a)	3,000	
Bal.	3,000	

Rent Expense		
(7b)	1,500	
Bal.	1,500	

Utilities Expense		
(9)	200	
Bal.	200	

Interest Expense		
(7c)	400	
Bal.	400	

Requirement 4

Tomassini Computer Service Centre
Trial Balance
March 31, 19X2

Account Title	Balance	
	Debit	Credit
Cash.................................	$31,100	
Accounts Receivable	4,100	
Supplies.............................	300	
Land................................	40,000	
Accounts Payable		$ 1,300
Note Payable		45,000
Larry Tomassini, Capital		28,500
Larry Tomassini, Withdrawals	1,800	
Service Revenue		7,600
Salary Expense........................	3,000	
Rent Expense	1,500	
Interest Expense	400	
Utilities Expense	200	
Total................................	$82,400	$82,400

Requirement 5   Net income for the month of March

Revenues		
Service Revenue		$7,600
Expenses		
Salary Expense	$3,000	
Rent Expense.......................	1,500	
Interest Expense	400	
Utilities Expense	200	
Total expenses.........................		5,100
Net income		$2,500

Summary

The *account* can be viewed in the form of the letter "T." The left side of each account is its *debit* side. The right side is its *credit* side. The *ledger*, which contains a page for each account, groups and numbers accounts by category in the following order: assets, liabilities, owner's equity, revenues and expenses.

Assets and *expenses* are increased by debits and decreased by credits. *Liabilities, owner's equity* and *revenues* are increased by credits and decreased by debits. The side—debit or credit—of the account in which increases are recorded is that account's normal balance. Thus the normal balance of assets and expenses is a debit, and the normal balance of liabilities, owner's equity and revenues is a credit. An exception is the Withdrawals account, which is an owner's equity account with a normal debit balance. *Revenues*, which are increases in owner's equity, have a normal credit balance. *Expenses*, which are decreases in owner's equity, have a normal debit balance.

The accountant begins the recording process by entering the transaction's information in the *journal*, a chronological list of all the business's transactions. The information is then posted—transferred—to the *ledger* accounts. Posting references are used to trace amounts back and forth between the journal and the ledger. Businesses list their account titles and numbers in a chart of accounts.

The *trial balance* is a summary of all the account balances in the ledger. When *double-entry accounting* has been done correctly, the total debits and the total credits in the trial balance are equal.

We can now trace the flow of accounting information through these steps:

Business Transaction → Source Documents → Journal Entry → Posting to Ledger → Trial Balance

Self-Study Questions

Test your understanding of the chapter by marking the correct answer for each of the following questions:

1. An account has two sides called the *(p. 46)*
   a. Debit and credit
   b. Asset and liability
   c. Revenue and expense
   d. Journal and ledger

2. Increases in liabilities are recorded by *(p. 47)*
   a. Debits
   b. Credits

3. Why do accountants record transactions in the journal? *(p. 49)*
   a. To ensure that all transactions are posted to the ledger
   b. To ensure that total debits equal total credits
   c. To have a chronological record of all transactions
   d. To help prepare the financial statements

4. Posting is the process of transferring information from the *(p. 50)*
   a. Journal to the trial balance
   b. Ledger to the trial balance
   c. Ledger to the financial statements
   d. Journal to the ledger

5. The purchase of land for cash is recorded by a *(p. 52)*
   a. Debit to Cash and a credit to Land
   b. Debit to Cash and a debit to Land
   c. Debit to Land a a credit to Cash
   d. Credit to Cash and a credit to Land

6. The purpose of the trial balance is to *(p. 54)*
   a. Indicate whether total debits equal total credits
   b. Ensure that all transactions have been recorded
   c. Speed the collection of cash receipts from customers
   d. Increase assets and owner's equity

7. What is the normal balance of the Accounts Receivable, Office Supplies and Rent Expense accounts? *(p. 61)*
   a. Debit
   b. Credit

8. A business has Cash of $3,000, Notes Payable of $2,500, Accounts Payable of $4,300, Service Revenue of $7,000 and Rent Expense of $1,800. Based on these data, how much are its total liabilities? *(p. 63)*
   a. $5,500
   b. $6,800
   c. $9,800
   d. $13,800

9. The earning of revenue that is not received in cash is recorded by a *(pp. 63, 64)*
   a. Debit to Cash and a credit to Revenue
   b. Debit to Accounts Receivable and a credit to Revenue
   c. Debit to Accounts Payable and a credit to Revenue
   d. Debit to Revenue and a credit to Accounts Receivable

10. The account credited for a receipt of cash on account is *(p. 65)*
    a. Cash   c. Service Revenue
    b. Accounts Payable   d. Accounts Receivable

Answers to the Self-Study Questions are at the end of the chapter.

Accounting Vocabulary

account *(p. 43)*	debit *(p. 47)*	posting *(p. 50)*
chart of accounts *(p. 59)*	journal *(p. 49)*	trial balance *(p. 54)*
credit *(p. 47)*	ledger *(p. 43)*	

Assignment Material _____

Questions

1. Name the basic summary device of accounting. What letter of the alphabet does it resemble, and what are its two sides called?
2. Is the following statement true or false? Debit means decrease and credit means increase. Explain your answer.
3. Write two sentences that use the term *debit* in different ways.
4. What are the three *basic* types of accounts? Name two additional types of accounts. To which one of the three *basic* types are these two additional types of accounts most closely related?
5. Suppose you are the accountant for Smith Courier Service. Keeping in mind double-entry bookkeeping, identify the *dual effects* of Mary Smith's investment of $10,000 cash in her business.
6. Briefly describe the flow of accounting information. (Hint: See the diagram in the chapter summary.)
7. To what does the *normal balance* of an account refer?
8. Complete the table by indicating the normal balance of the five types of accounts.

Account Type	Normal Balance
Assets	_____
Liabilities	_____
Owner's Equity	_____
Revenues	_____
Expenses	_____

9. What does posting accomplish? Why is it important? Does it come before or after journalizing?
10. Label each of the following transactions as increasing owner's equity (+), decreasing owner's equity (−), or as having no effect on owner's equity (0). Write the appropriate symbol in the space provided.
    _____ a. Investment by owner   _____ e. Cash payment on account
    _____ b. Revenue transaction   _____ f. Withdrawal by owner
    _____ c. Purchase of supplies on   _____ g. Borrowing money on a note
               credit   payable
    _____ d. Expense transaction   _____ h. Sale of services on account
11. What four steps does posting include? Which step is the fundamental purpose of posting?

12. Rearrange the following accounts in their logical sequence in the ledger:

Notes Payable	Cash
Accounts Receivable	Jane East, Capital
Sales Revenue	Salary Expense

13. What is the meaning of the statement, Accounts Payable has a credit balance of $1,700?

14. Jack Brown Campus Cleaners launders the shirts of customer Bobby Baylor, who has a charge account at the cleaners. When Bobby picks up his clothes and is short on cash, he charges it. Later, when he receives his monthly statement from the cleaners, Bobby writes a cheque on Dear Old Dad's bank account and mails the cheque to Jack Brown. Identify the two business transactions described here. Which transaction increases Jack Brown's owner's equity? Which transaction increases Jack Brown's cash?

15. Explain the difference between the ledger and the chart of accounts.

16. Why do accountants prepare a trial balance?

17. What is a compound journal entry?

18. The accountant for Bower Construction Company mistakenly recorded a $500 purchase of supplies on account as a $5,000 purchase. He debited Supplies and credited Accounts Payable for $5,000. Does this error cause the trial balance to be out of balance? Explain your answer.

19. What is the effect on total assets of collecting cash on account from customers?

20. What is the advantage of analysing and recording transactions without the use of a journal? Describe how this "journal-less" analysis works.

Exercises

Exercise 2-1 *Analysing transactions*

Analyse the following transactions in the manner shown for the October 1 transaction:

Oct. 1 Paid monthly rent expense of $700. (Analysis: The expense rent expense is increased; therefore, debit Rent Expense. The asset cash is decreased; therefore credit Cash.)

    4 Received $350 cash on account from a customer.

    8 Performed service on account for a customer, $1,100.

   12 Purchased office furniture on account, $620.

   19 Sold for $19,000 land that had cost this same amount.

   24 Purchased building for $48,000; signed a note payable.

   27 Paid the liability created on October 12.

Exercise 2-2 *Journalizing transactions*

Garner Service Company engaged in the following transactions during March 19X3, its first month of operations:

Mar. 1 Lynn Garner invested $40,000 of cash to start the business.

    2 She purchased supplies of $200 on account.

    4 She paid $15,000 cash for land to use as a future building site.

    6 She performed service for customers and received cash, $2,000.

    9 She paid $100 on accounts payable.

   17 She performed service for customers on account, $1,600.

   23 She received $1,200 cash from customer on account.

   31 She paid the following expenses: salary, $1,200; rent, $500.

Required

Record the preceding transactions in the journal of Garner Service Company. Key transactions by date and include an explanation for each entry, as illustrated in the chapter.

Exercise 2-3 *Posting to the ledger and preparing a trial balance*

a. After journalizing the transactions of Exercise 2-2, post the entries to the ledger, using T-account format. Key transactions by date as in the following example. Label the balance of each account *Bal.*

Lynn Garner, Capital

	Mar. 1 40,000

b. Prepare the trial balance of Garner Service Company at March 31, 19X3.

Exercise 2-4 *Describing transactions and posting*

The journal of Scholes Company follows:

Journal   **Page 5**

Date	Accounts and Explanation	Post Ref.	Debit	Credit
Aug. 5	Cash		850	
	Sales Revenue			850
9	Supplies		270	
	Accounts Payable			270
11	Accounts Receivable		2,100	
	Sales Revenue			2,100
14	Rent Expense		900	
	Cash			900
22	Cash		1,400	
	Accounts Receivable			1,400
25	Advertising Expense		350	
	Cash			350
27	Accounts Payable		270	
	Cash			270
31	Utilities Expense........................		220	
	Accounts Payable			220

Required

1. Describe each transaction. Example: Aug. 5—Cash sale.
2. Post the transactions to the ledger using the following account numbers: Cash, 11; Accounts Receivable, 12; Supplies, 13; Accounts Payable, 21; Sales Revenue, 41; Rent Expense, 51; Advertising Expense, 52; Utilities Expense, 53. Use dates, journal references and posting references as illustrated in Exhibit 2-7. You may write the account numbers as posting references directly in your book unless directed otherwise by your instructor.

3. Compute the balance in each account after posting. The first debit amount of $850 is posted to Cash as an example:

Cash

Aug. 5 J.5 850	

Exercise 2-5   *Preparing a trial balance*

The accounts of Norman Realty Company are listed below with their normal balances at September 30, 19X4. The accounts are listed in no particular order.

Account	Balance
Ken Norman, capital	$48,800
Advertising expense	650
Accounts payable	1,300
Sales commission revenue	16,000
Land	23,000
Note payable	25,000
Cash	7,000
Salary expense	3,000
Building	45,000
Rent expense	2,000
Ken Norman, withdrawals	4,000
Utilities expense	400
Accounts receivable	5,500
Supplies expense	300
Supplies	250

Required

Prepare the company's trial balance at September 30, 19X4, listing accounts in proper sequence, as illustrated in the chapter. Supplies comes before Building and Land. List the expense with the largest balance first, the expense with the next largest balance second, and so on.

Exercise 2-6   *Journalizing transactions*

The first five transactions of Hoyt Repair Service have been posted to the company's accounts as follows:

Cash		Supplies		Equipment	
(1) 25,000	(3) 19,000	(2) 400		(5) 6,000	
(4) 7,000	(5) 6,000				

Land		Accounts Payable		Note Payable	
(3) 19,000			(2) 400		(4) 7,000

Stu Hoyt, Capital	
	(1) 25,000

Required

Prepare the journal entries that served as the sources for the five transactions. Include an explanation for each entry as illustrated in the chapter.

Exercise 2-7   *Preparing a trial balance*

Prepare the trial balance of Hoyt Repair Service at September 30, 19X4, using the account data from the preceding exercise.

Exercise 2-8   *Correcting errors in a trial balance*

The trial balance of Walker Enterprises at November 30, 19X9 does not balance.

Cash	$ 6,000	
Accounts receivable	2,000	
Supplies.	600	
Land.	46,000	
Account payable		$ 3,000
Claudia Walker, capital		42,000
Service revenue		6,500
Salary expense	1,700	
Rent expense	800	
Utilities expense	300	
Total.	$57,400	$51,500

Investigation of the accounting records reveals that the bookkeeper

a. Recorded a cash revenue transaction by debiting Cash for the correct amount of $5,000 but failed to record the credit to Service Revenue.

b. Posted a $1,000 credit to Accounts Payable as $100.

c. Did not record utilities expense or the related account payable in the amount of $200.

d. Understated Cash and Claudia Walker, Capital, by $400 each.

Required

Prepare the correct trial balance at November 30, complete with a heading.

Exercise 2-9   *Recording transactions without a journal*

Write the following T-accounts on a sheet of paper: Cash; Accounts Receivable; Office Supplies; Office Furniture; Accounts Payable; Lisa Lenski, Capital; Lisa Lenski, Withdrawals; Service Revenue; Salary Expense; Rent Expense.

Record the following transactions directly in the T-accounts without using a journal. Use the letters to identify the transactions.

a. Lisa Lenski opened an accounting firm by investing $10,000 cash and office furniture valued at $7,400.

b. Paid monthly rent of $1,500.

c. Purchased office supplies on account, $800.

d. Paid employee salary, $1,800.

e. Paid $400 of the account payable credited in *c.*

f. Performed accounting service on account, $1,700.

g. Withdrew $2,000 for personal use.

Exercise 2-10   *Preparing a trial balance*

After recording the transactions in Exercise 2-9, prepare the trial balance of Lisa Lenski, CGA at May 31, 19X7.

Problems

Problem 2-1A *Analysing and journalizing transactions*

Paramount Theatre Company owns movie theatres in the shopping centres of a major metropolitan area. Its owner, Robert Preston, engaged in the following personal and business transactions:

Dec. 1   Preston invested $100,000 personal cash in the business by depositing this amount in a bank account entitled Paramount Theatre Company.

2   Paid $55,000 cash to purchase land for a theatre site.

5   Borrowed $300,000 from the bank to finance the construction of the new theatre. Preston signed a note payable to the bank in the name of Paramount Theatre Company.

7   Received $20,000 cash from ticket sales and deposited this amount in the bank. (Label the revenue as Sales Revenue.)

10   Purchased supplies for the older theatres on account, $1,700.

15   Paid theatre employee salaries, $2,800, and rent on a theatre building, $1,800.

15   Paid property tax expense on theatre building, $1,200.

16   Paid $800 on account.

17   Withdrew $2,000 from the business to take his family to a nearby resort.

Required

1. Prepare an analysis of each business transaction of Paramount Theatre Company, as shown for the December 1 transaction:

Dec. 1   The asset Cash is increased. Increases in assets are recorded by debit; therefore, debit Cash.

The owner's equity of the entity is increased. Increases in owner's equity are recorded by credits; therefore, credit Robert Preston, Capital.

2. Prepare the journal entry for each transaction. Explanations are not required.

Paramount uses the following accounts: Cash; Supplies; Land; Accounts Payable; Notes Payable; Robert Preston, Capital; Robert Preston, Withdrawals; Sales Revenue; Salary Expense; Rent Expense; Property Tax Expense.

Problem 2-2A *Journalizing transactions, posting to T-accounts and preparing a trial balance*

Gwen Kraft opened a law office on September 3 of the current year. During the first month of operations, she completed the following transactions:

Sept. 3   Kraft transferred $25,000 cash from her personal bank account to a business account entitled Gwen Kraft, Lawyer.

4   Purchased supplies, $200, and furniture, $1,800, on account.

6   Performed legal services for a client and received $1,000 cash.

7   Paid $15,000 cash to acquire land for a future office site.

10   Defended a client in court, billed the client, and received his promise to pay the $900 within one week.

14   Paid for the furniture purchased September 4 on account.

15   Paid the secretary's salary, $600.

16   Paid the telephone bill, $120.

17   Received partial payment from client on account, $700.

20   Prepared legal documents for a client on account, $800.

24   Paid the water and electricity bills, $110.

28   Received $1,500 cash for assisting a client sell real estate.

30   Paid secretary's salary, $600.

30   Paid rent expense, $500.

30   Withdrew $2,000 for personal use.

Required

Open the following T-accounts on a sheet of paper: Cash; Accounts Receivable; Supplies; Furniture; Land; Accounts Payable; Gwen Kraft, Capital; Gwen Kraft, Withdrawals; Service Revenue; Salary Expense; Rent Expense; Utilities Expense.

1. Record each transaction in the journal, using the account title given. Key each transaction by date. Explanations are not required.
2. Post the transactions to the ledger, using transaction dates as posting references in the ledger. Label the balance of each account *Bal.*, as shown in the chapter.
3. Prepare the trial balance of Gwen Kraft, Lawyer, at September 30 of the current year.

Problem 2-3A   *Journalizing transactions, posting to ledger accounts and preparing a trial balance*

The trial balance of the accounting practice of Rob Cheng, CMA at February 14, 19X3, was

Rob Cheng, CMA
Trial Balance
February 14, 19X3

Account Number	Account	Debit	Credit
11	Cash	$ 4,000	
12	Accounts Receivable	11,000	
13	Supplies	800	
14	Land	18,600	
21	Accounts Payable		$ 3,000
31	Rob Cheng, capital		29,000
32	Rob Cheng, withdrawals	1,200	
41	Service revenue		6,200
51	Salary expense	1,600	
52	Rent expense	800	
53	Utilities expense	200	
	Total	$38,200	$38,200

During the remainder of February, Cheng completed the following transactions:

Feb. 15   Cheng collected $2,000 cash from a client on account.

16   Performed tax services for a client on account, $700.

18   Paid utilities, $300.

20   Paid on account, $1,000.

21   Purchased supplies on account, $100.

21   Withdrew $1,200 for personal use.

21   Paid for a swimming pool for private residence, $13,000.

22   Received cash of $2,100 for consulting work just completed.

28   Paid rent, $800.

28   Paid employees' salaries, $1,600.

Required

1. Record the transactions that occurred during February 15 through 28 in page 3 of the journal. Include an explanation for each entry.
2. Open the ledger accounts listed in the trial balance, together with their balances at February 14. Use the account format illustrated below. Enter *Bal.* (for previous balance) in the Item column, and place a check mark (✔) in the journal reference column for the February 14 balance, as illustrated for Cash:

Account   Cash   Account No. 11

Date	Item	Jrnl. Ref.	Debit	Credit	Balance	
Feb. 14	Bal.	✔			4,000	Dr.

Post the transactions to the ledger, using dates, account numbers, journal references and posting references.

3. Prepare the trial balance of Rob Cheng, CMA at February 28, 19X3.

Problem 2-4A   *Journalizing, posting to T-accounts and preparing a trial balance*

Flaten Delivery Service completed the following transactions during its first month of operations:

a. Dick Flaten, the proprietor of the business, began operations by investing $5,000 cash and a truck valued at $10,000 in the business.
b. Paid $200 cash for supplies.
c. Used a credit card to purchase $50 fuel for the delivery truck. (Credit Accounts Payable).
d. Performed delivery services for a customer and received $600 cash.
e. Completed a large delivery job, billed the customer $2,000, and received a promise to be paid the $2,000 within one week.
f. Paid employee salary, $800.
g. Received $900 cash for performing delivery services.
h. Purchased fuel for the truck on account, $40.
i. Received $2,000 cash from a customer on account.
j. Paid for advertising in the local newspaper, $170.
k. Paid utility bills, $100.
l. Purchased fuel for the truck, paying $30 with a credit card.
m. Performed delivery services on account, $200.
n. Paid for repairs to the delivery truck, $110.
o. Paid employee salary, $800, and office rent, $200.
p. Paid $120 on account.
q. Withdrew $1,900 for personal use.

Required

1. Record each transaction in the journal, using the account titles given. Key each transaction by letter. Explanations are not required.
2. Open the following T-accounts: Cash; Accounts Receivable; Supplies; Delivery Truck; Accounts Payable; Dick Flaten, Capital; Dick Flaten, Withdrawals; Delivery Service Revenue; Salary Expense; Rent Expense; Advertising Expense; Fuel

Expense; Repair Expense; Utilities Expense. Post the transactions to the ledger, keying transactions by letter. Label the balance of each account *Bal.*, as shown in the chapter. However, if an account has only one entry, it is not necessary to label the balance separately. If an account has a zero balance after posting, draw double underlines under the posted amounts.

3. Prepare the trial balance of Flaten Delivery Service, using the current date.

Problem 2-5A *Correcting errors in a trial balance*

The following trial balance does not balance:

Family Counseling Services Trial Balance June 30, 19X2		
Cash...............................	$ 2,000	
Accounts receivable	10,000	
Supplies.............................	900	
Office furniture	3,600	
Land................................	26,000	
Accounts payable		$ 4,000
Note payable		14,000
Lisa Vivaldi, capital....................		22,000
Lisa Vivaldi, withdrawals	2,000	
Counseling service revenue		6,500
Salary expense	1,600	
Rent expense	1,000	
Advertising expense	500	
Utilities expense	300	
Property tax expense	100	
Total...............................	$48,000	$46,500

The following errors were detected:

a. The cash balance is understated by $300.
b. Property Tax Expense of $500 is omitted from the trial balance.
c. Land should be listed in the amount of $25,000.
d. A $200 purchase of supplies on account was neither journalized nor posted.
e. A $2,800 credit to Counseling Service Revenue was not posted.
f. Rent Expense of $200 was posted as a credit rather than a debit.
g. The balance of Advertising Expense is $600, but it was listed as $500 on the trial balance.
h. A $300 debit to Accounts Receivable was posted as $30.
i. The balance of Utilities Expense is overstated by $70.
j. A $400 debit to the Withdrawal account was posted as a credit to Lisa Vivaldi, Capital.

Required

Prepare the correct trial balance at June 30. Journal entries are not required.

Problem 2-6A   *Recording transactions directly in the ledger; preparing a trial balance*

Peg Howison started a consulting service and during the first month of operations completed the following selected transactions:

a. Howison began the business with an investment of $15,000 cash and a building valued at $75,000.
b. Borrowed $30,000 from the bank; signed a note payable.
c. Purchased office supplies on account, $1,300.
d. Paid $18,000 for office furniture.
e. Paid employee salary, $2,200.
f. Performed consulting service on account for client, $2,100.
g. Paid $800 of the account payable created in *c*.
h. Received a $900 bill for advertising expense that will be paid in the near future.
i. Performed consulting service for customers and received cash, $1,600.
j. Received cash on account, $1,200.
k. Paid the following cash expenses:
   (1) Rent on land, $700.
   (2) Utilities, $400.
l. Withdrew $3,500 for personal use.

Required

1. Open the following T-accounts on a sheet of paper: Cash; Accounts Receivable; Office Supplies; Office Furniture; Building; Accounts Payable; Note Payable; Peg Howison, Capital; Peg Howison, Withdrawals; Service Revenue; Salary Expense; Advertising Expense; Rent Expense; Utilities Expense.
2. Record the following transactions directly in the T-accounts without using a journal. Use the letters to identify the transactions.
3. Prepare the trial balance of Howison Consulting Service at June 30, 19X3.

(Group B)

Problem 2-1B   *Analysing and journalizing transactions*

Roland Marks practices medicine under the business title Roland Marks, M.D. During April his medical practice engaged in the following transactions:

Apr. 1   Marks deposited $50,000 cash in the business bank account.
      5   Borrowed $20,000 from the bank for business use. Marks signed a note payable to the bank in the name of the business.
      9   Paid $25,000 cash to purchase land for an office site.
     10   Purchased supplies on account, $1,200.
     19   Paid $1,000 on account.
     30   Revenues earned during the month included $11,000 on account from the provincial health services plan.
     30   Paid employee salaries ($2,400), office rent ($1,500) and utilities ($400).
     30   Paid monthly rent on medical equipment, $700.
     30   Withdrew $4,000 from the business to take his family on a trip.

Required

1. Prepare an analysis of each business transaction of Roland Marks, M.D., as shown for the April 1 transaction:
   Apr. 1   The asset Cash is increased. Increases in assets are recorded by debits; therefore, debit Cash.

The owner's equity is increased. Increases in owner's equity are recorded by credits; therefore, credit Roland Marks, Capital.

2. Prepare the journal entry for each transaction. Explanations are not required.

Problem 2-2B   *Journalizing transactions, posting to T-accounts and preparing a trial balance*

Nancy Katz opened a law office on January 2 of the current year. During the first month of operations she completed the following transactions:

Jan. 2   Katz deposited $45,000 cash in a business bank account entitled Nancy Katz, Lawyer.

3   Purchased supplies, $300, and furniture, $2,100, on account.

4   Performed legal services for a client and received cash, $1,500.

7   Paid cash to acquire land for a future office site, $22,000.

11   Defended a client in court, billed the client, and received his promise to pay the $800 within one week.

15   Paid secretary salary, $650.

16   Paid for the furniture purchased January 3 on account.

17   Paid the telephone bill, $110.

18   Received partial payment from client on account, $400.

19   Prepared legal documents for a client on account, $600.

22   Paid the water and electricity bills, $130.

29   Received $1,800 cash for helping a client sell real estate.

31   Paid secretary salary, $650.

31   Paid rent expense, $700.

31   Withdrew $2,200 for personal use.

Required

Open the following T-accounts: Cash; Accounts Receivable; Supplies; Furniture; Land; Accounts Payable; Nancy Katz, Capital; Nancy Katz, Withdrawals; Service Revenue; Salary Expense; Rent Expense; Utilities Expense.

1. Record each transaction in the journal, using the account titles given. Key each transaction by date. Explanations are not required.

2. Post the transactions to the ledger, using transaction dates as posting references in the ledger. Label the balance of each account *Bal.* as shown in the chapter.

3. Prepare the trial balance of Nancy Katz, Lawyer at January 31 of the current year.

Problem 2-3B   *Journalizing transactions, posting to ledger accounts and preparing a trial balance*

The trial balance of the accounting practice of Ralph Cohen, CGA at November 15, 19X3 follows on the next page. During the remainder of November, Cohen completed the following transactions:

Nov. 15   Collected $4,000 cash from a client on account.

17   Performed tax services for a client on account, $1,200.

19   Paid utilities, $200.

21   Paid on account, $2,600.

22   Purchased supplies on account, $200.

23   Withdrew $2,100 for personal use.

23   Paid for the renovation of private residence, $55,000.

24   Received $1,900 cash for accounting work just completed.

30   Paid rent, $700.

30   Paid employees' salaries, $1,800.

Ralph Cohen, CGA
Trial Balance
November 15, 19X3

Account Number	Account	Debit	Credit
11	Cash	$ 5,000	
12	Accounts Receivable	8,000	
13	Supplies	600	
14	Land	38,000	
21	Accounts Payable		$ 4,400
31	Ralph Cohen, capital		45,000
32	Ralph Cohen, withdrawals	2,100	
41	Service revenue		7,100
51	Salary expense	1,800	
52	Rent expense	700	
53	Utilities expense	300	
	Total	$56,500	$56,500

Required

1. Record the transactions that occurred during November 16 through 30 in page 6 of the journal. Include an explanation for each entry.
2. Post the transactions to the ledger, using dates, account numbers, journal references and posting references. Open the ledger accounts listed in the trial balance together with their balances at November 15. Use the account format illustrated below. Enter Bal. (for previous balance) in the Item column, and place a check mark (✔) in the journal reference column for the November 15 balance, as illustrated for Cash:

Account   Cash   **Account No. 11**

Date	Item	Jrnl. Ref.	Debit	Credit	Balance	
Nov. 15	Bal.	✔			5,000	Dr.

3. Prepare the trial balance of Ralph Cohen, CGA at November 30, 19X3.

Problem 2-4B   *Journalizing, posting to T-accounts and preparing a trial balance*

Marquardt Appliance Delivery Service began operations during May of the current year. During a short period thereafter, the entity engaged in the following transactions:

a. Rube Marquardt, the owner, deposited $3,500 cash in a bank account entitled Marquardt Appliance Delivery Service and also invested in the business a delivery truck valued at $8,000.
b. Purchased $40 fuel for the delivery truck, using a business credit card.
c. Paid $100 cash for supplies.
d. Completed a delivery job and received cash, $700.
e. Performed delivery services on account, $3,200.

f. Purchased advertising leaflets for $200, cash.

g. Paid the office manager $950, salary.

h. Received $1,000 cash for performing delivery services.

i. Received cash from customer on account, $1,800.

j. Purchased used office furniture on account, $600.

k. Paid office utility bills, $120.

l. Purchased $70 fuel on account for the truck.

m. Completed a delivery job and received the customer's promise to pay the amount due, $500, within ten days.

n. Paid cash to creditor on account, $200.

o. Paid $250 for repairs to the delivery truck.

p. Paid office manager the salary of $950 and office rent of $250.

q. Withdrew $1,700 for personal use.

Required

1. Record each transaction in the journal, using the account titles given. Key each transaction by letter. Explanations are not required.

2. Open the following T-accounts: Cash; Accounts Receivable; Supplies; Delivery Truck; Office Furniture; Accounts Payable; Rube Marquardt, Capital; Rube Marquardt, Withdrawals; Delivery Service Revenue; Salary Expense; Rent Expense; Repair Expense; Advertising Expense; Utilities Expense; Fuel Expense. Post the transactions to the ledger, keying transactions by letter. Label the balance of each account *Bal.* as shown in the chapter. However, if an account only has one entry, it is not necessary to label the balance separately.

3. Prepare the trial balance of Marquardt Appliance Delivery Service using the current date.

Problem 2-5B   *Correcting errors in a trial balance*

The following trial balance does not balance:

Jackson Management Consulting Trial Balance October 31, 19X1		
Cash	$ 3,800	
Accounts receivable	2,000	
Supplies..............................	500	
Office furniture	2,300	
Land.................................	46,800	
Accounts payable		$ 2,000
Note payable		18,300
Pamela Jackson, capital		32,100
Pamela Jackson, withdrawals	3,700	
Consulting service revenue.............		4,900
Salary expense	1,000	
Rent expense	600	
Advertising expense	400	
Utilities expense	200	
Property tax	100	
Total.................................	$61,400	$57,300

The following errors were detected:

a. The cash balance is overstated by $400.
b. Office maintenance expense of $200 is omitted from the trial balance.
c. Rent expense of $200 was posted as a credit rather than a debit.
d. The balance of Advertising Expense is $300, but it is listed as $400 on the trial balance.
e. A $600 debit to Accounts Receivable was posted as $60.
f. The balance of Utilities Expense is understated by $60.
g. A $500 debit to the withdrawal account was posted as a credit to Pamela Jackson, Capital.
h. A $100 purchase of supplies on account was neither journalized nor posted.
i. A $4,800 credit to Consulting Service Revenue was not posted.
j. Office furniture should be listed in the amount of $1,300.

Required

Prepare the correct trial balance at October 31. Journal entries are not required.

Problem 2-6B *Recording transactions directly in the ledger; preparing a trial balance*

Jack Montague started a cable television service and during the first month of operations completed the following selected transactions:

a. Montague began the business with an investment of $30,000 cash and a building valued at $65,000.
b. Borrowed $25,000 from the bank; signed a note payable.
c. Paid $32,000 for transmitting equipment.
d. Purchased office supplies on account, $400.
e. Paid employee salary, $1,300.
f. Received $500 for cable TV service performed for customers.
g. Sold cable service to customers on account, $2,300.
h. Paid $100 of the account payable created in *d*.
i. Received a $600 bill for utility expense that will be paid in the near future.
j. Received cash on account, $1,100.
k. Paid the following cash expenses:
   (1) Rent on land, $1,000.
   (2) Advertising, $800.
l. Withdrew $2,600 for personal use.

Required

1. Open the following T-accounts: Cash; Accounts Receivable; Office Supplies; Transmitting Equipment; Building; Accounts Payable; Note Payable; Jack Montague, Capital; Jack Montague, Withdrawals; Service Revenue; Salary Expense; Rent Expense; Advertising Expense; Utilities Expense.

2. Record the following transactions directly in the T-accounts without using a journal. Use the letters to identify the transactions.

3. Prepare the trial balance of Montague Cable TV Service at January 31, 19X7.

Decision Problems

1. *Recording transactions directly in the ledger, preparing a trial balance and measuring net income or loss*

You have been requested by a friend named Milton Abel to give advice on the effects that certain business transactions will have on the entity he plans to start. Time is short, so you will not be able to do all the detailed procedures of journalizing and posting. Instead, you must analyse the transactions without the use of a journal. Abel will continue in the business only if he can expect to earn monthly net income of $2,750. Assume the following transactions have occurred:

a. Abel deposited $6,000 cash in a business bank account.
b. Borrowed $4,000 cash from the bank and signed a note payable due within one year.
c. Paid $300 cash for supplies.
d. Purchased advertising in the local newspaper for cash, $800.
e. Purchased office furniture on account, $1,500.
f. Paid the following cash expenses for one month: secretary salary, $1,400; office rent, $400; utilities, $300; interest, $50.
g. Earned revenue on account for one month, $3,300.
h. Earned revenue and received $2,500 cash.
i. Collected cash from customers on account, $1,500.
j. Paid on account, $1,000.

Required

1. Write on a sheet of paper the T-accounts needed for the analysis.
2. Recorded the transactions directly in the accounts without using a journal. Key each transaction by letter.
3. Prepare a trial balance at the current date. List expenses with the largest first, the next largest second, and so on. The business name will be Abel Apartment Locators.
4. Compute the amount of net income or net loss for this first month of operations. Would you recommend Abel continue in business?

2. *Using the accounting equation*

The following questions, while dealing with the accounting equation, are not related:

1. Explain the advantages of double-entry bookkeeping over single entry bookkeeping to a friend who is opening a used book store.
2. When you deposit money in your bank account, the bank credits your account. Is the bank misusing the word credit in this context? Why does the bank use the term credit and not debit?
3. Edward Phipps invested $20,000 in a pizza business. He bought all his equipment ($10,000) and supplies ($2,600) on account and started to sell "Edward's Wonderful Pizza" for cash from a rented store at a local mall. His prices were low and sales were $3,952 for the first month. Expenses were $1,769, to be paid the following month. He was pleased with his success and withdrew $23,000 to buy a sports car as a reward for his hard work. What would the balances be for the various asset, liability and owner's equity accounts at the end of the month? Are they different from normal balances described in the chapter? If so, why? (Hint: post the transactions to appropriately labelled T-accounts.)
4. Your friend asks, "When revenues increase assets and expenses decrease assets, why are revenues credits and expenses debits and not the other way around?" Explain to your friend why revenues are credits, and expenses are debits.

Financial Statement Problem

Journalizing transactions

This problem helps to develop skill in recording by using an actual company's account titles. Refer to the John Labatt financial statements in Appendix E. Assume John Labatt completed the following selected transactions during August, 1988:

Aug. 5   Earned revenues on account, $40,000.

9   Borrowed $500,000 by signing a note payable (long-term debt).

12   Purchased equipment on account, $70,000.

17   Paid $120,000, which represents payment of $100,000 on long-term debt plus interest expense of $20,000.

19   Earned revenues and immediately received cash of $16,000.

22   Collected the cash on account that was earned on August 5.

24   Paid rent of $14,000 for three months in advance.

29   Received a home-office electricity bill for $1,000, which will be paid in September. (This is a sales, selling and administration expense.)

30   Paid half the account payable created on August 12.

Required

Journalize these transactions using the following account titles taken from the financial statements of John Labatt: Accounts Receivable; Inventories; Prepaid Expenses; Buildings and Equipment; Bank Advances (Instead of showing Cash as an asset, John Labatt has netted [deducted] the balance of Cash [a debit] from Bank Advances [a credit] to show a smaller balance in the latter: note that no Cash account appears on the Balance Sheet); Accounts Payable; Non-convertible Long-term Debt; Gross Sales; Cost of Sales, Selling and Administration; Interest. Explanations are not required.

Answers to Self-Study Questions

1. a	5. c	8. b ($6,800 = $2,500 + $4,300)
2. b	6. a	9. b
3. c	7. a	10. d
4. d		

3

Measuring Business Income: The Adjusting Process

LEARNING OBJECTIVES

After studying this chapter, you should be able to

1 Distinguish accrual-basis accounting from cash-basis accounting

2 Explain and apply the revenue and matching principles

3 Make the typical adjusting entries at the end of the accounting period

4 Prepare an adjusted trial balance

5 Prepare the financial statements from the adjusted trial balance

The primary goal of business is to earn a profit. By providing food and other goods at a reasonable price, a grocery store benefits its customers. The benefit to the store owner is the excess of the business's revenues over its expenses—net income. Gary Lyon, the CA whose accounting practice we discussed in the earlier chapters, earns business income by providing accounting services for clients. Regardless of the type of activity, the profit motive increases the owner's drive to carry on the business.

At the end of each accounting period, the accountant prepares the entity's financial statements. The period may be a month, three months, six months or a full year. Whatever the length of the accounting period, the end product is the same—the financial statements. And the most important single amount in these statements is the net income or net loss—the profit or loss—for the period. A double-entry accounting system produces not only the income statement but the other financial statements as well.

An important step in financial statement preparation is the trial balance that we discussed in Chapter 2. The trial balance includes the effects of the transactions that occurred during the period: the cash collections, purchases of assets, payments of bills and sales of assets. To measure its income properly, however, a business must do some additional accounting at the end of the period to bring the records up to date before preparing the financial statements. This process is called *adjusting the books*. It consists of making special entries called *adjusting entries*. This chapter focuses primarily on these adjusting entries to help you better understand the nature of business income.

Accountants have devised concepts and principles to guide the measurement of business income. Chief among these are the concepts of accrual accounting, accounting period, revenue principle and matching principle. In this chapter, we apply these concepts and principles to measure the income and prepare the financial statements of Gary Lyon's business for the month of April.

Accrual-Basis Accounting versus Cash-Basis Accounting

There are two widely used bases of accounting: the accrual basis and cash basis. In **accrual-basis accounting**, an accountant recognizes the impact of a business event as it occurs. When the business performs a service, makes a sale or incurs an expense, the accountant enters the transaction into the books, whether or not cash has been received or paid. In **cash-basis accounting**, however, the accountant does not record a transaction until cash is received or paid. GAAP requires that a business use the accrual basis. This means that the accountant records revenues as they are *earned* and expenses as they are *incurred*—not necessarily when cash changes hands.

Using accrual-basis accounting, Gary Lyon records revenue when he performs services for a client on account. Lyon has earned the revenue at that time because his efforts have generated an account receivable, a legal claim against the client for whom he did the work.

By contrast, if Gary Lyon used cash-basis accounting, he would not record revenue at the time he performed the service. He would wait until he received cash. The client might pay cash for the service at the time the service is performed. If that happens (and he was using accrual accounting), Gary would also record the revenue, but no receivable would be recorded.

Why does GAAP require that businesses use the accrual basis? What advantage does accrual-basis accounting offer? Suppose Gary Lyon's accounting period ends after he has earned the revenue, but before he has collected the money due him. If he used the cash-basis method, his financial statements would not include this revenue or the related account receivable. As a result, the financial statements would be misleading. Revenue and the asset Accounts Receivable would be understated, and thus his business would look less successful than it actually is because his net income would be lower. If he wants to get a bank loan to expand his practice, the understated revenue and asset figures might hurt his chances.

Gary Lyon, using accrual-basis accounting, treats expenses in a like manner. For instance, salary expense includes amounts paid to employees plus any amount owed to employees but not yet paid. Lyon's use of the employee's service, not the payment of cash to the employee, brings about the expense. Under cash-basis accounting, Lyon would record the expense only when he actually paid the employee.

Suppose Gary Lyon owes his secretary a salary payment, and the financial statements are drawn up before Lyon pays. Expenses and liabilities would be understated and net income would be overstated, so that the business would look more successful than it really is. This misleading information would not be fair to potential creditors.

As these examples show, accrual accounting provides more complete information than does cash-basis accounting. This is important because the more complete the data, the better equipped decision-makers are to reach intelligent conclusions about the firm's financial health and future prospects. Three concepts used in accrual accounting are the accounting period, the revenue principle and the matching principle.

The Accounting Period

The only way to know for certain how successfully a business has operated is to close its doors, sell all its assets, pay the liabilities and return any leftover cash to the owner. This process, called liquidation, is the same as going out of business. Obviously, it is not practical for accountants to measure business income in this manner. Instead, businesses need periodic reports on their progress. Accountants slice time into small segments and prepare financial statements for specific periods. Until a business liquidates, the amounts reported in its financial statements must be regarded as estimates.

The most basic accounting period is one year, and virtually all businesses prepare annual financial statements. For slightly more than 60 percent of companies in a recent Canadian survey, the annual accounting period or *fiscal year* runs the calendar year from January 1 through December 31. The other companies in the survey use a fiscal year ending on some date other than December 31. The year-end date is usually the low point in business activity for the year. Depending on the type of business, the fiscal year may end on April 30, July 31 or some other date. Retailers are a notable example. Traditionally, they have used a fiscal year ending on January 31, because the low point in their business activity has followed the after-Christmas sales during January.

Companies cannot wait until the end of the year to gauge their progress. The manager of a business wants to know how well the business is doing each month, each quarter and each half year. Outsiders such as lenders also demand current information about the business. So companies also prepare financial statements for *interim* periods, which are less than a year. Monthly financial statements are common, and a series of monthly statements can be combined for quarterly and semiannual periods. Many of the discussions in this book are based on an annual accounting period. However, the procedures and statements can also be applied to interim periods as well.

Revenue Principle

The **revenue principle** tells accountants (1) *when* to record revenue and (2) the *amount* of revenue to record. When we speak of "recording" something in accounting, the act of recording the item naturally leads to posting to the ledger accounts and preparing the trial balance and the financial statements. Although the financial statements are the end product of accounting and what accountants are most concerned about, our discussions often focus on recording the entry in the journal because that is where the accounting process starts.

The general principle guiding *when* to record revenue is that revenue should be recorded when, but not before, it has been earned. In most cases, revenue is earned when the business has delivered a completed good or service to the customer. The business has done everything required by the agreement, including transferring the item to the customer. Two situations that provide guidance on when to record revenue follow. The first situation illustrates when *not* to record revenue. Situation 2 illustrates when revenue should be recorded.

Situation 1: Do not record revenue. A client of another CA expresses her intention to transfer her tax work to Gary Lyon. Should Lyon record any revenue based on this intention? The answer is no because no transaction has occurred.

Situation 2: Record revenue. Next month Gary Lyon consults with this client and tailors a business plan to her goals. After transferring the business plan to the client, Lyon should record revenue. If the client pays for this service immediately, Lyon will debit Cash. If the service is performed on account, Lyon will debit Accounts Receivable. In either case, Lyon should record revenue by crediting the Service Revenue account.

The general principle guiding the *amount* of revenue to record is record

OBJECTIVE 2
Explain and apply the revenue and matching principles

revenue equal to the cash value of the goods or the service transferred to the customer. Suppose that in order to obtain a new client, Gary Lyon performs accounting service for the cut-rate price of $500. Ordinarily, Lyon would have charged $600 for this service. How much revenue should Lyon record? The answer is $500 because that was the cash value of the transaction. Lyon will not receive the full value of $600, so that is not the amount of revenue to record. He will receive only $500 cash, and that pinpoints the amount of revenue earned.

Matching Principle

The **matching principle** is the basis for recording expenses. Recall that expenses, such as rent, utilities and advertising, are the costs of operating a business. Expenses are the costs of assets and services that are used up in the earning of revenue. The matching principle directs accountants (1) to identify all expenses incurred during the accounting period, (2) to measure the expenses, and (3) to "match" them against the revenues earned during that same span of time. To "match" expenses against revenues means to subtract the expenses from the revenues in order to compute net income or net loss.

There is a natural link between revenues and some types of expenses. Accountants follow the matching principle by first identifying the revenues of a period and the expenses that can be linked to particular revenues. For example, a business that pays sales commissions to its sales persons will have commission expense if the employees make sales. If they make no sales, the business has no commission expense. A merchandising business like a clothier or a hardware store has an expense called cost of goods sold. If sales are made, the entity has cost of goods sold. If there are no sales, there is none of this expense.

Other expenses are not so easy to link with particular sales. Monthly rent expense occurs, for example, regardless of the revenues earned during the period. The matching principle directs accountants to identify these types of expenses with a particular time period, such as a month or a year. If Gary Lyon employs a secretary at a monthly salary of $1,900, the business will record salary expense of $1,900 each month.

Because financial statements appear at definite intervals, there must be some cutoff date for the necessary information. Most entities engage in so many transactions that some are bound to spill over into more than a single accounting period. Gary Lyon prepares monthly statements for his business at April 30. How does he handle a transaction that begins in April but ends in May? How does he bring the accounts up to date for preparing the financial statements? To answer these questions, accountants use adjusting entries.

Adjustments to the Accounts

At the end of the period, the accountant prepares the financial statements. This end-of-the-period process begins with the trial balance that lists the accounts and their balances after the period's transactions have been recorded in the Journal and posted to the accounts in the ledger. Exhibit 3-1 is the trial balance of Gary Lyon's accounting practice at April 30, 19X1.

EXHIBIT 3-1   *Unadjusted Trial Balance*

Gary Lyon, CA
Unadjusted Trial Balance
April 30, 19X1

Cash.............................	$24,800	
Accounts receivable	2,250	
Supplies..........................	700	
Prepaid rent	3,000	
Furniture.........................	16,500	
Accounts payable		$13,100
Unearned service revenue...........		450
Gary Lyon, capital.................		31,250
Gary Lyon, withdrawals	3,200	
Service revenue		7,000
Salary expense	950	
Utilities expense	400	
Total............................	$51,800	$51,800

This *unadjusted* trial balance lists most, but not all, of the revenue and expenses of Lyon's accounting practice for the month of April (including some new accounts that will be explained later in this section). These trial balance amounts are incomplete because they omit certain revenue and expense transactions that affect more than one accounting period. That is why it is called an unadjusted trial balance. In most cases, however, we refer to it simply as the trial balance, without the "unadjusted" label.

Under the cash basis of accounting, there would be no need for adjustments to the accounts because all April cash transactions would have been recorded. However, the accrual basis requires adjusting entries at the end of the period in order to produce correct balances for the financial statements. To see why, consider the Supplies account in Exhibit 3-1.

Lyon's accounting practice uses supplies in providing accounting services for clients during the month. This reduces the quantity of supplies on hand and thus constitutes an expense, just like salary expense or rent expense. Gary Lyon does not bother to record his daily expense, and it is not worth his while to record supplies expense more than once a month. It is time-consuming to make hourly, daily or even weekly journal entries to record the expense incurred by the use of supplies. So how does he account for supplies expense?

By the end of the month, the Supplies balance is not correct. The balance represents the amount of supplies on hand at the start of the month plus any supplies purchased during the month. This balance fails to take into account the supplies used (supplies expense) during the accounting period. It is necessary, then, to subtract the month's expenses from the amount of supplies listed on the trial balance. The resulting new adjusted balance measures the cost of supplies that are still on hand at April 30. This is the correct amount of supplies to report on the balance sheet. Adjusting entries in this way brings the accounts up to date.

Adjusting entries assign revenues to the period in which they are earned and expenses to the period in which they are incurred. They are needed (1) to measure properly the period's income and (2) to bring related asset and liability accounts to correct balances for the financial statements. For example, an adjusting entry is needed to transfer the amount of supplies used during the period from the asset account Supplies to the expense account Supplies Expense. The adjusting entry updates both the Supplies asset account and the Supplies Expense account. This achieves accurate measures of assets and expenses. Adjusting entries, which are the key to the accrual basis of accounting, are made before preparing the financial statements.

The end-of-period process of updating the accounts is called *adjusting the accounts, making the adjusting entries* or *adjusting the books.* Adjusting entries can be divided into five categories:

1. Prepaid expenses
2. Depreciation
3. Accrued expenses
4. Accrued revenues
5. Unearned revenues

Some accountants would combine categories 1 and 2 and have only four categories of adjusting entries. They would argue that a fixed asset is a form of prepaid expense and that depreciation expense reflects the depletion of prepaid expense.

Prepaid Expenses

Prepaid expenses is a category of miscellaneous assets that typically expire or are used up in the near future. Prepaid rent, prepaid insurance and supplies are examples of prepaid expenses. They are called prepaid expenses because they are expenses that are paid in advance. Salary expense and utilities expense, among others, are *not* prepaid expenses unless they are paid in advance.

Prepaid Rent   Landlords usually require tenants to pay rent in advance. This prepayment creates an asset for the renter, because that person has purchased the future benefit of using the rented item. Suppose Gary Lyon prepays three months' rent on April 1, 19X1, after negotiating a lease for the office of his accounting practice. If the lease specifies monthly rental amounts of $1,000 each, the entry to record the payment for three months is a debit to the asset account, Prepaid Rent, as follows:

Apr. 1	Prepaid Rent ($1,000 × 3)	3,000	
	Cash...................................		3,000
	Paid three months' rent in advance.		

After posting, Prepaid Rent appears as follows:

Prepaid Rent	
Apr. 1 3,000	

The trial balance at April 30, 19X1 lists Prepaid Rent as an asset with a debit balance of $3,000. Throughout April, the Prepaid Rent account maintains this beginning balance, as shown in Exhibit 3-1.

At April 30, Prepaid Rent should be adjusted to remove from its balance the amount of the asset that has *expired*, which is one month's worth of the prepayment. By definition, the amount of an asset that has expired is *expense*. The adjusting entry transfers one third, or $1,000 ($3,000 × ⅓), of the debit balance from Prepaid Rent to Rent Expense. The debit side of the entry records an increase in Rent Expense and the credit records a decrease in the asset Prepaid Rent.

Apr. 30   Rent Expense ($3,000 × ⅓) 1,000
                 Prepaid Rent 1,000
              To record rent expense.

OBJECTIVE 3
Make the typical adjusting entries at the end of the accounting period.

After posting, Prepaid Rent and Rent Expense appear as follows:

Prepaid Rent				Rent Expense		
Apr. 1	3,000	Apr. 30	1,000	⟷ Apr. 30	1,000	
Bal.	2,000			Bal.	1,000	

Correct asset amount, $2,000 → | Total accounted for, $3,000 | ← Correct expense amount, $1,000

The full $3,000 has been accounted for: two thirds is asset and one third is expense. This is correct because two thirds of the asset remains for future use and one third of the prepayment has expired. Recording this expense illustrates the matching principle. The same analysis applies to a prepayment of three months' insurance premiums. The only difference is in the account titles, which would be Prepaid Insurance and Insurance Expense instead of Prepaid Rent and Rent Expense.

Supplies   On April 2, Gary Lyon paid cash of $700 for supplies.

Apr. 2   Supplies 700
                 Cash 700
              Paid cash for supplies.

Assume that Lyon purchased no additional supplies during April. The April 30 trial balance, therefore, lists Supplies with a $700 debit balance, as shown in Exhibit 3-1.

During April, Lyon used supplies in performing services for clients. The cost of the supplies used is the measure of *supplies expense* for the month.

Lyon does not keep a continuous record of supplies used each day or each week during April. To keep detailed records for so insignificant an asset would be impractical. Instead, to measure his firm's supplies expense during April, Gary Lyon counts the supplies on hand at the end of the month. This is the amount of the asset still available to the business. Assume the count indicates that supplies costing $400 remain. Subtracting the entity's $400 of supplies on hand at the end of April from the cost of supplies available during April ($700) measures supplies expense during the month ($300).

Cost of asset available during the period		Cost of asset on hand at the end of the period		Cost of asset used (expense) during the period
$700	−	$400	=	$300

The April 30 adjusting entry to update the Supplies account and to record the supplies expense for the month debits the expense and credits the asset, as shown on the next page.

Apr. 30   Supplies Expense ($700 – $400) 300
                    Supplies   300
                    To record supplies expense.

After posting, the Supplies and Supplies Expense accounts appear as follows:

Supplies				Supplies Expense	
Apr. 2	700	Apr. 30	300 ⟷ Apr. 30	300	
Bal.	400		Bal.	300	

Correct asset   → | Total accounted | ←   Correct expense
amount, $400 | for, $700 | amount, $300

The Supplies account enters the month of May with a $400 balance, and the adjustment process is repeated each month.

Depreciation and Plant Assets

The logic of the accrual basis is best illustrated by how businesses account for plant assets. **Plant assets** are long-lived assets, such as land, buildings, furniture, machinery and equipment. As one accountant said, "All assets but land are on a march to the junkyard." That is, all plant assets but land decline in usefulness as they age. This decline is an *expense* to the business. Accountants systematically spread the cost of each plant asset, except land, over the years of its useful life. This process is called the recording of **depreciation**. The concept underlying accounting for plant assets and depreciation expense is the same as for prepaid expenses. In both cases the business purchases an asset that wears out. As the asset becomes less and less useful, more and more of its cost is transferred from the asset account to the expense account. The only difference between prepaid expenses and plant assets is the length of time it takes for the asset to lose its usefulness. Prepaid expenses usually expire within a few months. Most plant assets remain useful for a number of years.

Consider Gary Lyon's accounting practice. Suppose on April 3, Lyon purchased furniture on account for $16,500.

Apr. 3   Furniture 16,500
                    Accounts Payable   16,500
                    Purchased office furniture on account.

After posting, the Furniture account appears as follows:

Furniture		
Apr. 3	16,500	

Using cash-basis accounting, Gary Lyon would enter in the ledger the entire $16,500 as an expense for April. As a result, his financial statements for that month would be extremely misleading. Income would be significantly understated. Also, the cash-basis approach fails to take into consideration that the asset will be of benefit to Gary Lyon in future accounting periods. After all, his furniture will remain useful for quite some time.

In accrual-basis accounting, an asset is recorded when the furniture is acquired. Then, a portion of the asset's cost is transferred from the asset account to Depreciation Expense each period that the asset is used. This method matches the asset's expense to the revenue of the period, which is an application of the matching principle. We discuss how accountants determine the amount of depreciation for each accounting period in Chapter 10. For now, we need concern ourselves only with the accounts involved in recording depreciation.

Let us assume the depreciation for the month of April is $275, computed by dividing the asset's cost ($16,500) by its useful life (60 months). Depreciation Expense for April is recorded by the following entry:

Apr. 30 Depreciation Expense 275
            Accumulated Depreciation — Furniture   275
            To record depreciation expense on furniture.

You may be wondering why Accumulated Depreciation is credited instead of Furniture. The reason is that the original cost of the plant asset is an objective measurement and that figure remains in the original asset account as long as the business uses the asset. Accountants may refer to that account if they need to know how much the asset costs. This information is useful in a decision about whether to replace the furniture and the amount to pay. The amount of depreciation, however, is an *estimate*. Accountants use the **Accumulated Depreciation** account to show the cumulative sum of all depreciation expense from the date of acquiring the asset.

Accumulated Depreciation is a **contra asset** account, which means an asset account with a credit balance. A **contra account** has two distinguishing characteristics: (1) it always has a companion account and (2) its normal balance is opposite that of the companion account. In this case, Accumulated Depreciation accompanies Furniture. It appears in the ledger directly after Furniture. Furniture has a debit balance, and therefore Accumulated Depreciation has a credit balance.

A business carries an accumulated depreciation account for each depreciable asset. If a business has a building and a machine, for example, it will carry the accounts Accumulated Depreciation — Building, and Accumulated Depreciation — Machine.

After posting the depreciation entry, the Furniture, Accumulated Depreciation and Depreciation Expense accounts are

Furniture		Accumulated Depreciation — Furniture		Depreciation Expense	
Apr. 3 16,500			Apr. 30 **275**	Apr. 30 275	
Bal. 16,500			Bal. 275	Bal. 275	

The balance sheet shows the relationship between Furniture and Accumulated Depreciation. The balance of Accumulated Depreciation is subtracted from the balance of Furniture. This net amount of a plant asset is called its **book value**, as shown below for Furniture:

Plant Assets

Furniture $16,500
Less: Accumulated Depreciation   275
Book Value $16,225

Suppose Lyon's accounting practice owns a building that cost $48,000, on which annual depreciation is $2,400. The amount of depreciation for one month would be $200 ($2,400/12) and the entry to record depreciation for April is

Apr. 30 Depreciation Expense 200
     Accumulated Depreciation — Building   200
   To record depreciation expense on building.

The balance sheet at April 30 would report Lyon's plant assets as shown in Exhibit 3-2.

EXHIBIT 3-2 *Plant Assets on the Balance Sheet*

Plant assets		
Furniture	$16,500	
Less: Accumulated Depreciation.........	275	$16,225
Building	48,000	
Less: Accumulated Depreciation.........	200	47,800
Book Value of Plant Assets		$64,025

Accrued Expenses

Businesses often incur expenses before they pay out the cash because payment is not due until later. Consider an employee's salary. The employer's salary expense and salary payable grow as the employee works, so the liability is said to *accrue*. Another example is interest expense on a note payable. Interest accrues as the clock ticks. The term **accrued expenses** refers to an expense that the business has incurred but has not yet paid.

It is time-consuming to make hourly, daily or even weekly journal entries to accrue expenses. Consequently, the accountant waits until the end of the period. Then an adjusting entry brings each expense (and related liability) up to date just before the financial statements are prepared.

Salary Expense Most companies pay their employees at set times. Suppose Gary Lyon pays his employee a monthly salary of $1,900, half on the 15th and half on the last day of the month. Here is a calendar for April that has paydays circled:

APRIL

S	M	T	W	T	F	S
					1	2
3	4	5	6	7	8	9
10	11	12	13	14	(15)	16
17	18	19	20	21	22	23
24	25	26	27	28	29	(30)

Assume that if either payday falls on a weekend, Lyon pays the employee on the following Monday. During April, Lyon paid his employee's first half-month salary of $950 on Friday, April 15 and recorded the following entry:

```
Apr. 15   Salary Expense  ...............................   950
               Cash  ..................................          950
          To pay salary.
```

After posting, the Salary Expense account is

Salary Expense

Apr. 15	950	

The trial balance at April 30 (Exhibit 3-1) includes Salary Expense, with its debit balance of $950. As April 30, the second payday of the month, falls on a Saturday, the second half-month amount of $950 will be paid on Monday, May 2. Without an adjusting entry, this second $950 amount is not included in the April 30 trial balance amount for Salary Expense. Therefore, at April 30, Lyon adjusts for additional *salary expense* and *salary payable* of $950 by recording an increase in each of these accounts, as follows:

```
Apr. 30   Salary Expense  ...............................   950
               Salary Payable..........................          950
          To accrue salary expense.
```

After posting, the Salary Expense and Salary Payable accounts appear as follows:

Salary Expense				**Salary Payable**		
Apr. 15	950				**Apr. 30**	**950**
Apr. 30	**950**				Bal.	950
Bal.	1,900					

The accounts at April 30 now contain the complete salary information for the month. The expense account has a full month's salary and the liability account shows the portion that the business still owes.

Lyon will record the payment of this liability on May 2 by debiting Salary Payable and crediting Cash for $950. This payment entry does not affect April or May expenses, because the April expense was recorded on April 15 and April 30. May expense will be recorded in a like manner. All accrued expenses are recorded with similar entries—a debit to the appropriate expense account and a credit to the related liability account.

Often a business's period-end will occur during a pay period. For example, Dr. Maria di Pietro's radiology practice has March 31 as its year end. In 1992, March 31 is a Tuesday. Maria pays her staff on Friday for the week ended on that day. Assume her weekly payroll is $1,800 in March, 1992. She will have to set up accrued salary payable of $720 ($1,800 $\times$ $\frac{2}{5}$) at her year end. When Maria pays her employees on Friday, April 3, 1992, the entry will debit Salary Expense for the balance of the week, debit Salary Payable for $720 and credit Cash for $1,800 as follows:

```
April 3   Salary Expense ($1,800 × ⅗) ...................   1,080
               Salary Payable...............................    720
                    Cash ...................................          1,800
          To pay salary.
```

Accrued Revenues

Businesses often earn revenue before they receive the cash for their work, because payment is not due until later. A revenue that has been earned but not yet received in cash is called an **accrued revenue**. Assume Gary Lyon is hired on April 15 by Guerrero Construction Co. Ltd. to perform tax services on an as-needed basis. Under this agreement, Guerrero will pay Lyon $500 monthly, with the first payment on May 15. During April, Gary Lyon will earn half a month's fee, $250. On April 30, he makes the following adjusting entry to record an increase in Accounts Receivable and Service Revenue:

Apr. 30	Accounts Receivable ($500 × ½)	250	
	Service Revenue		250
	To accrue service revenue.		

Recall that Accounts Receivable has an unadjusted balance of $2,250 and the Service Revenue unadjusted balance is $7,000 (Exhibit 3-1). Posting this adjustment has the following effects on these two accounts:

Accounts Receivable				Service Revenue		
	2,250					7,000
Apr. 30	**250**			**Apr. 30**		**250**
Bal.	2,500			Bal.		7,250

This adjusting entry is needed to update the accounts. It illustrates accrual accounting and the revenue principle in action. Without the adjustment, Lyon's financial statements would be misleading. All accrued revenues are accounted for similarly — by debiting a receivable and crediting a revenue.

Unearned Revenues

Some businesses collect cash from customers in advance of doing work for the customer. This creates a liability called **unearned revenue**. The liability arises because the business receiving cash in advance is obligated to provide a product or a service in the future. Only when the job is completed will the business have earned the revenue. Suppose Baldwin Computer Service Centre engages Lyon's services, agreeing to pay him $450 monthly, beginning immediately. If Baldwin makes the first payment on April 21, Lyon records this increase in the business's liabilities as follows:

Apr. 21	Cash..	450	
	Unearned Service Revenue		450
	Received revenue in advance.		

After posting, the liability account appears as follows:

Unearned Service Revenue		
	Apr. 21	450

Unearned Service Revenue is a liability because it represents Lyon's obligation to perform service for the client. The April 30 unadjusted trial balance (Exhibit 3-1) lists this account with a $450 credit balance prior to the adjusting entries. During the last 10 days of the month, Lyon will have earned one third

(10 days divided by April's total 30 days) of the $450, or $150. Therefore, he makes the following adjustments to decrease the liability, Unearned Service Revenue, and record an increase in Service Revenue:

Apr. 30   Unearned Service Revenue ($450 × ⅓)   150
    Service Revenue   150
    To record service revenue that was collected in
    advance.

This adjusting entry shifts $150 of the total amount from the liability account to the revenue account. After posting, the balance of Service Revenue is increased by $150 and the balance of Unearned Service Revenue has been reduced to $300.

Unearned Service Revenue					Service Revenue		
Apr. 30	**150**	Apr. 21	450				7,000
						Apr. 30	250
		Bal.	300			**Apr. 30**	**150**
						Bal.	7,400

Correct liability amount, $300 → | **Total accounted for, $450** | ← **Correct revenue amount, $150**

Accounting for all types of revenues that are collected in advance — insurance premiums, magazine subscriptions, and so on — follows the same pattern.

Summary of the Adjusting Process

Since one purpose of the adjusting process is to measure business income properly, each adjusting entry affects at least one income statement account — a revenue or an expense. The other side of the entry, a debit or a credit, as the case may be, is to a balance sheet account, an asset or a liability. This step updates the accounts for preparation of the balance sheet, which is the second purpose of the adjustments. No adjusting entry debits or credits Cash, because the cash transactions are recorded earlier in the period. The end-of-period adjustment process is reserved for the non-cash transactions that are required by accrual accounting. If an adjusting entry does debit or credit Cash, you will know that the entry is in error. Exhibit 3-3 summarizes the adjusting entries.

EXHIBIT 3-3   *Summary of Adjusting Entries*

Adjusting Entry	Type of Account Debited	Type of Account Credited
Prepaid expense, supplies	Expense	Prepaid expense, supplies
Depreciation	Expense	Accumulated depreciation
Accrued expenses	Expense	Payable
Accrued revenues	Receivable	Revenue
Unearned revenues	Unearned revenue	Revenue

Adapted from Beverly Terry.

Appendix D at the end of the book covers the adjusting process in more detail. It also discusses and illustrates an optional category of accounting entries known as reversing entries.

Posting the Adjusting Entries

Exhibit 3-4 summarizes the adjusting entries of Lyon's business at April 30. Panel A briefly describes the data for each adjustment, Panel B gives the adjusting entries, and Panel C shows the accounts. The adjustments are keyed by letter.

EXHIBIT 3-4   *Journalizing and Posting the Adjusting Entries*

Panel A: Information for Adjustments at April 30, 19X1

a. Accrued service revenue, $250.
b. Supplies on hand, $400.
c. Prepaid rent expired, $1,000.
d. Depreciation on furniture, $275.
e. Accrued salary expense, $950.
f. Amount of unearned service revenues that has been earned, $150.

Panel B: Adjusting Entries

a. Accounts Receivable	250	
Service Revenue		250
To accrue service revenue.		
b. Supplies Expense	300	
Supplies		300
To record supplies used.		
c. Rent Expense	1,000	
Prepaid Rent		1,000
To record rent expense.		
d. Depreciation Expense	275	
Accumulated Depreciation		275
To record depreciation on furniture.		
e. Salary Expense	950	
Salary Payable		950
To accrue salary expense.		
f. Unearned Service Revenue	150	
Service Revenue		150
To record unearned revenue that has been earned.		

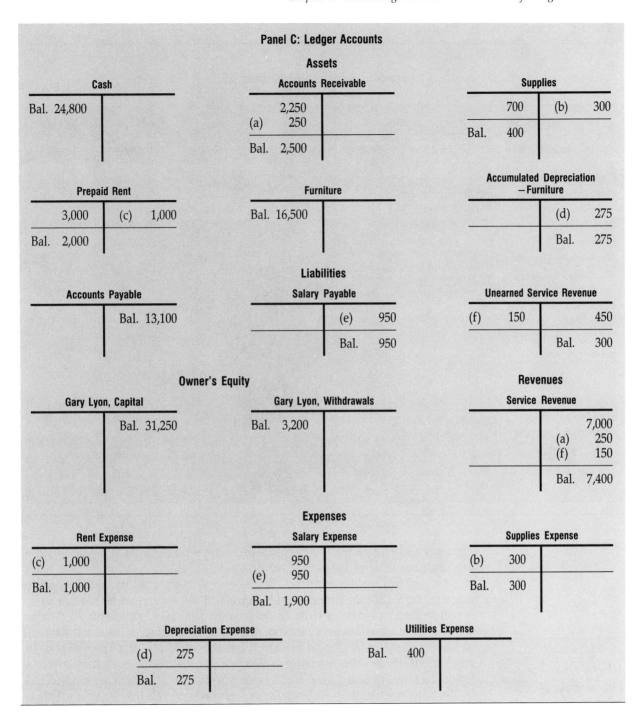

Panel C: Ledger Accounts

Assets

Cash			Accounts Receivable			Supplies		
Bal. 24,800			2,250			700	(b)	300
			(a) 250			Bal. 400		
			Bal. 2,500					

Prepaid Rent			Furniture			Accumulated Depreciation — Furniture		
3,000	(c)	1,000	Bal. 16,500				(d)	275
Bal. 2,000							Bal.	275

Liabilities

Accounts Payable			Salary Payable			Unearned Service Revenue		
	Bal.	13,100		(e)	950	(f) 150		450
				Bal.	950		Bal.	300

Owner's Equity

Gary Lyon, Capital			Gary Lyon, Withdrawals			**Revenues**		
	Bal.	31,250	Bal. 3,200			Service Revenue		
								7,000
							(a)	250
							(f)	150
							Bal.	7,400

Expenses

Rent Expense			Salary Expense			Supplies Expense		
(c)	1,000			950		(b)	300	
Bal.	1,000		(e)	950		Bal.	300	
			Bal.	1,900				

Depreciation Expense			Utilities Expense		
(d)	275		Bal.	400	
Bal.	275				

Adjusted Trial Balance

This chapter began with the trial balance before any adjusting entries — the unadjusted trial balance (Exhibit 3-1). Panel C in Exhibit 3-4 shows the account balances reflecting the adjusting entries. A useful step in preparing the financial statements is to list the accounts, along with their adjusted balances, on an **adjusted trial balance**. This document has the advantage of listing all the

EXHIBIT 3-5 *Preparation of Adjusted Trial Balance*

Gary Lyon, CA
Preparation of Adjusted Trial Balance
April 30, 19X1

Account Title	Trial Balance		Adjustments		Adjusted Trial Balance	
	Debit	Credit	Debit	Credit	Debit	Credit
Cash	24,800				24,800	
Accounts receivable	2,250		(a) 250		2,500	
Supplies	700			(b) 300	400	
Prepaid rent	3,000			(c) 1,000	2,000	
Furniture	16,500				16,500	
Accumulated depreciation				(d) 275		275
Accounts payable		13,100				13,100
Salary payable				(e) 950		950
Unearned service revenue		450	(f) 150			300
Gary Lyon, capital		31,250				31,250
Gary Lyon, withdrawals	3,200				3,200	
Service revenue		7,000		(a) 250		7,400
				(f) 150		
Rent expense			(c) 1,000		1,000	
Salary expense	950		(e) 950		1,900	
Supplies expense			(b) 300		300	
Depreciation expense			(d) 275		275	
Utilities expense	400				400	
	51,800	51,800	2,925	2,925	53,275	53,275

accounts and their adjusted balances in a single place. Exhibit 3-5 shows the preparation of the adjusted trial balance.

Each amount on the adjusted trial balance is computed by combining the amounts from the unadjusted trial balance and the adjustments. For example, Accounts Receivable starts with a debit balance of $2,200. Adding the $250 debit amount from adjusting entry *a* gives Accounts Receivable an adjusted balance of $2,450. Supplies begins with a debit balance of $700. After the $300 credit adjustment, its adjusted balance is $400. More than one entry may affect a single account, as is the case for Service Revenue. If accounts are unaffected by the adjustments, they show the same amount on both trial balances. This is true for Cash, Furniture, Accounts Payable and the Owner's Equity accounts.

OBJECTIVE 4

Prepare an adjusted trial balance

Preparing the Financial Statements from the Adjusted Trial Balance

The April financial statements of Gary Lyon, CA can be prepared from the information on the adjusted trial balance. The income statement comes from the revenue and expense accounts. The balance sheet reports the assets, liabilities and owner's equity. The statement of owner's equity shows the reasons

EXHIBIT 3-6   *Preparing the Financial Statements from the Adjusted Trial Balance*

Account Title	Adjusted Trial Balance	
	Debit	Credit
Cash	24,800	
Accounts receivable	2,500	
Supplies	400	
Prepaid rent	2,000	
Furniture	16,500	
Accumulated depreciation		275
Accounts payable		13,100
Salary payable		950
Unearned service revenue		300
Gary Lyon, capital		31,250
Gary Lyon, withdrawals	3,200	
Service revenue		7,400
Rent expense	1,000	
Salary expense	1,900	
Supplies expense	300	
Depreciation expense	275	
Utilities expense	400	
	53,275	53,275

Balance Sheet

Statement of Owner's Equity

Income Statement

for the change in the owner's capital during the period. Exhibit 3-6 shows how the accounts are distributed from the adjusted trial balance to these three financial statements.

Financial Statements

The accounts and amounts for the income statement and balance sheet may be taken from the adjusted trial balance. The adjusted trial balance also provides the data for the statement of owner's equity. Exhibits 3-7, 3-8 and 3-9 illustrate these three financial statements, best prepared in the order shown: the income statement first, followed by the statement of owner's equity and last, the balance sheet. The essential features of all financial statements are (1) the name of the entity, (2) the title of the statement, (3) the date or the period covered by the statement and (4) the body of the statement.

It is customary to list expenses in descending order by amount, as shown in Exhibit 3-7. However, Miscellaneous Expense, a catch-all account for expenses that do not fit another category, is usually reported last regardless of its amount.

Relationships among the Three Financial Statements _____

The arrows in Exhibits 3-7, 3-8 and 3-9 illustrate the relationship among the income statement, the statement of owner's equity and the balance sheet.

OBJECTIVE 5

Prepare the financial statements from the adjusted trial balance

EXHIBIT 3-7 Income Statement

Gary Lyon, CA
Income Statement
for the month ended April 30, 19X1

Revenue		
Service revenue		$7,400
Expenses		
Salary expense	$1,900	
Rent expense	1,000	
Utilities expense	400	
Supplies expense	300	
Depreciation expense	275	
Total expenses		3,875
Net income		$3,525

EXHIBIT 3-8 Statement of Owner's Equity

Gary Lyon, CA
Statement of Owner's Equity
for the month ended April 30, 19X1

Gary Lyon, capital, April 1, 19X1.....................................	$31,250
Add: Net income	3,525
	34,775
Less: Withdrawals	3,200
Gary Lyon, capital, April 30, 19X1..................................	$31,575

EXHIBIT 3-9 Balance Sheet

Gary Lyon, CA
Balance Sheet
April 30, 19X1

Assets			Liabilities		
Cash		$24,800	Accounts payable		$13,100
Accounts receivable ...		2,500	Salary payable		950
Supplies		400	Unearned service		
Prepaid rent..........		2,000	revenue............		300
Furniture	$16,500		Total liabilities		14,350
Less: Accumulated			**Owner's Equity**		
depreciation....	275	16,225	Gary Lyon, capital		31,575
			Total liabilities and		
Total assets...........		$45,925	owner's equity		$45,925

① ②

1. The income statement reports net income or net loss, figured by subtracting expenses from revenues. Revenues and expenses being owner's equity accounts, their net figure is then transferred to the statement of owner's equity. Note that in Exhibit 3-7 net income, $3,525, increases owner's equity in Exhibit 3-8. A net loss would decrease owner's equity.

2. Owner's equity is a balance sheet account, so the ending balance in the statement of owner's equity is transferred to the balance sheet. This amount is the final balancing element of the balance sheet. To solidify your understanding of this relationship, trace the $31,575 figure from Exhibit 3-8 to Exhibit 3-9.[1]

Microcomputers and the Accounting Process _____

Computers have been used by large businesses to account for their transactions for years, but most computers were bulky and expensive, and only large organizations could afford them. In recent years, small, more affordable microcomputers have caused a revolution in the computer industry. The term *microcomputer* simply means "small computer." Like the bigger computers, these machines handle electronically much of the work done by hand in the past. Their prices continue to fall, enabling more and more small businesses to own one. Names like Apple (a leading microcomputer company), IBM PC (International Business Machines Personal Computer), Tandy (a line of Radio Shack microcomputers) and Zenith (the CGA computer) have become almost household words.

Whether an accounting system is manual, as we have illustrated so far, or computerized, the steps in the accounting process are essentially the same: journalize transactions, post to the ledger, prepare the trial balance, make the adjustments and present the financial statements. Computers can perform mathematical operations fast and error-free. This ability comes in handy for such routine tasks as recording cash receipts and cash payments, and keeping track of accounts receivable and accounts payable. Posting, which requires no analysis, is also well suited for a computer. The computer can be programmed to print the trial balance and financial statements. Having the machine do these routine jobs saves time and so saves money.

What are a computer's limits? Computers are not people, so they cannot think. The adjusting entries illustrate the need for the type of analysis that requires the human touch. At the end of the period, the office manager may count the supplies on hand. The accountant then makes the necessary entry to adjust the Supplies and Supplies Expense accounts. A computer cannot

---

[1] You may be wondering why the total assets on the balance sheet ($45,925 in Exhibit 3-9) do not equal the total debits on the adjusted trial balance ($53,275 in Exhibit 3-6). Likewise, the total liabilities and owner's equity do not equal the total credits on the adjusted trial balance. The reason for these differences is that Accumulated Depreciation and Owner Withdrawals are *subtracted* from their related accounts on the balance sheet, but *added* in their respective columns on the adjusted trial balance.

perform these operations. It takes a human to count assets on hand and enter the data for the adjustments. If the system is computerized, the machine takes over and does the posting and statement preparation. In a manual system, these steps are done by hand.

It may be economical to use a computer for some of the adjusting entries. Depreciation, for example, is often a routine computation that a computer performs well. But it takes a human to do the thinking and program the machine to make the calculations. As we progress through the study of accounting, we will be discussing computer applications that fit the topics under discussion.

Summary Problem for Your Review

The trial balance of Sally's Service Company at December 31, 19X1, which is the end of its year-long accounting period, is presented in the following:

Sally's Service Company
Trial Balance
December 31, 19X1

Cash	$ 198,000	
Accounts receivable	370,000	
Supplies	6,000	
Furniture and fixtures	100,000	
Accumulated depreciation—furniture and fixtures		$ 40,000
Building	250,000	
Accumulated depreciation—building		130,000
Accounts payable		380,000
Salary payable		
Unearned service revenue		45,000
Sally Gunz, capital		293,000
Sally Gunz, withdrawals	65,000	
Service revenue		286,000
Salary expense	172,000	
Supplies expense		
Depreciation expense—furniture and fixtures		
Depreciation expense—building		
Miscellaneous expense	13,000	
Total	$1,174,000	$1,174,000

Data needed for the adjusting entries include

a.   Supplies on hand at year's end, $2,000
b.   Depreciation on furniture and fixtures, $20,000
c.   Depreciation on building, $10,000
d.   Salaries owed but not yet paid, $5,000
e.   Accrued service revenue, $12,000
f.   Of the $45,000 balance of unearned service revenue, $32,000 was earned during the year.

Required

1.   Open the ledger accounts with their unadjusted balances. Show dollar amounts in thousands, as shown for Accounts Receivable.

Accounts Receivable

370

2.   Journalize Sally's Service Company's adjusting entries at December 31, 19X1. Key entries by letter as in Exhibt 3-4.
3.   Post the adjusting entries.
4.   Write the trial balance on a sheet of paper, enter the adjusting entries and prepare an adjusted trial balance, as shown in Exhibit 3-5.
5.   Prepare the income statement, the statement of owner's equity and the balance sheet. Draw the arrows linking the three statements together.

SOLUTION TO REVIEW PROBLEM

Requirements 1 and 3

Assets

Cash		Accounts Receivable		Supplies		Furniture and Fixtures	
Bal. 198		370		6	(a) 4	Bal. 100	
		(e) 12		Bal. 2			
		Bal. 382					

Accumulated Depreciation—Furniture and Fixtures		Building		Accumulated Depreciation—Building	
	40	Bal. 250			130
	(b) 20				(c) 10
	Bal. 60				Bal. 140

Liabilities

Accounts Payable	
	Bal. 380

Salary Payable	
	(d) 5
	Bal. 5

Unearned Service Revenue	
(f) 32	45
	Bal. 13

Owner's Equity

Sally Gunz, Capital	
	Bal. 293

Sally Gunz, Withdrawals	
Bal. 65	

Revenues

Service Revenue	
	286
	(e) 12
	(f) 32
	Bal. 330

Expenses

Salary Expense	
172	
(d) 5	
Bal. 177	

Supplies Expense	
(a) 4	
Bal. 4	

Depreciation Expense— Furniture and Fixtures	
(b) 20	
Bal. 20	

Depreciation Expense— Building	
(c) 10	
Bal. 10	

Miscellaneous Expense	
Bal. 13	

Requirement 2

	19X1				
a.	Dec. 31	Supplies Expense ($6,000 – $2,000)	4,000	
		Supplies.		4,000
		To record supplies used.		
b.	31	Depreciation Expense—Furniture and Fixtures .	20,000	
		Accumulated Depreciation—Furniture and Fixtures		20,000
		To record depreciation expense on furniture and fixtures.		
c.	Dec. 31	Depreciation Expense—Building.	10,000	
		Accumulated Depreciation—Building		10,000
		To record depreciation expense on building.		

d.	31	Salary Expense	5,000
		Salary Payable	5,000
		To accrue salary expense.	
e.	31	Accounts Receivable	12,000
		Service Revenue	12,000
		To accrue service revenue.	
f.	31	Unearned Service Revenue	32,000
		Service Revenue	32,000
		To record unearned service revenue that has been earned.	

Requirement 4

Sally's Service Company
Preparation of Adjusted Trial Balance
December 31, 19X1
(amounts in thousands)

	Trial Balance		Adjustments				Adjusted Trial Balance	
	Debit	**Credit**	**Debit**		**Credit**		**Debit**	**Credit**
Cash	198						198	
Accounts receivable	370		(e)	12			382	
Supplies	6				(a)	4	2	
Furniture and fixtures	100						100	
Accumulated depreciation— furniture and fixtures		40			(b)	20		60
Building	250						250	
Accumulated depreciation—building		130			(c)	10		140
Accounts payable		380						380
Salary payable					(d)	5		5
Unearned service revenue		45	(f)	32				13
Sally Gunz, capital		293						293
Sally Gunz, withdrawals	65						65	
Service revenue		286			(e)	12		330
					(f)	32		
Salary expense	172		(d)	5			177	
Supplies expense			(a)	4			4	
Depreciation expense— furniture and fixtures			(b)	20			20	
Depreciation expense— building			(c)	10			10	
Miscellaneous expense	13						13	
	1,174	1,174		83		83	1,221	1,221

Requirement 5

Sally's Service Company
Income Statement
for the year ended December 31, 19X1
(amounts in thousands)

Revenues
    Service revenue $330
Expenses
    Salary expense $177
    Depreciation expense—furniture and fixtures   20
    Depreciation expense—building   10
    Supplies expense   4
    Miscellaneous expense   13
        Total expenses   224
Net income $106

Sally's Service Company
Statement of Owner's Equity
for the year ended December 31, 19X1
(amounts in thousands)

Sally Gunz, capital, January 1, 19X1 .... $293
Add: Net income   106
                                      399
Less: Withdrawals   65
Sally Gunz, capital, December 31, 19X1 .... $334

Sally's Service Company
Balance Sheet
December 31, 19X1
(amounts in thousands)

Assets			Liabilities		
Cash		$198	Accounts payable		$380
Accounts receivable		382	Salary payable		5
Supplies		2	Unearned service revenue ...		13
Furniture and fixtures	$100		Total liabilities		398
Less: Accumulated depreciation	60	40			
Building	250		**Owner's Equity**		
Less: Accumulated depreciation	140	110	Sally Gunz, capital		334
			Total liabilities and		
Total assets		$732	owner's equity		$732

Summary

In *accrual-basis accounting*, business events are recorded as they affect the entity. In *cash-basis accounting*, only those events that affect cash are recorded. The cash basis omits important events such as purchases and sales of assets on account. It also distorts the financial statements by labeling as expenses those cash payments that have long-term effects, like the purchases of buildings and equipment. Some small organizations use cash-basis accounting, but the generally accepted method is the accrual basis.

Accountants divide time into definite periods, such as a month, a quarter and a year, to report the entity's financial statements. The year is the basic *accounting period*, but companies prepare financial statements as often as they need the information. Accountants have developed the *revenue principle* to guide them in when to record revenue and the amount of revenue to record. The *matching principle* guides the accounting for expenses.

Adjusting entries are a result of the accrual basis of accounting. These entries, made at the end of the accounting period, update the accounts for preparation of the financial statements. One of the most important pieces of accounting information is net income or net loss, and the adjusting entries help measure the *income* of the period.

Adjusting entries can be divided into five categories: *prepaid expenses, depreciation, accrued expenses, accrued revenues* and *unearned revenues*. To prepare the *adjusted trial balance*, enter the adjusting entries next to the *unadjusted trial balance*. This document can be used to prepare the income statement, the statement of owner's equity and the balance sheet.

These three financial statements are related as follows: Income, shown on the *income statement*, increases owner's equity, which also appears on the *statement of owner's equity*. The ending balance of owner's equity is the last amount reported on the *balance sheet*.

Computers can aid the accounting process in a number of ways, chiefly by performing routine operations. Many adjusting entries, however, require analysis that is best done manually, without the computer.

Self-Study Questions

Test your understanding of the chapter by marking the correct answer for each of the following questions:

1. Accrual-basis accounting *(p. 90)*
   a. Results in higher income than cash-basis accounting
   b. Leads to the reporting of more complete information than does cash-basis accounting
   c. Is not acceptable under GAAP
   d. Omits adjusting entries at the end of the period
2. Under the revenue principle, revenue is recorded *(p. 91)*
   a. At the earliest acceptable time
   b. At the latest acceptable time
   c. After it has been earned, but not before
   d. At the end of the accounting period
3. The matching principle provides guidance in accounting for *(p. 92)*
   a. Expenses   c. Assets
   b. Revenues   d. Liabilities
4. Adjusting entries *(p. 93)*
   a. Assign revenues to the period in which they are earned
   b. Help to properly measure the period's net income or net loss
   c. Bring asset and liability accounts to correct balances
   d. All of the above

5. A law firm began November with supplies of $160. During the month, the firm purchased supplies of $290. At November 30, supplies on hand total $210. Supplies expense for the period is *(p. 95)*
   a. $210   c. $290
   b. $240   d. $450

6. A building that cost $120,000 has accumulated depreciation of $50,000. The book value of the building is *(p. 97)*
   a. $50,000   c. $120,000
   b. $70,000   d. $170,000

7. The adjusting entry to accrue salary expense *(p. 99)*
   a. Debits Salary Expense and credits Cash
   b. Debits Salary Payable and credits Salary Expense
   c. Debits Salary Payable and credits Cash
   d. Debits Salary Expense and credits Salary Payable

8. A business received cash of $3,000 in advance for revenue that will be earned later. The cash receipt entry debited Cash and credited Unearned Revenue for $3,000. At the end of the period, $1,100 is still unearned. The adjusting entry for this situation will *(p. 100)*
   a. Debit Unearned Revenue and credit Revenue for $1,900
   b. Debit Unearned Revenue and credit Revenue for $1,100
   c. Debit Revenue and credit Unearned Revenue for $1,900
   d. Debit Revenue and credit Unearned Revenue for $1,100

9. The links between the financial statements are *(p. 106)*
   a. Net income from the income statement to the statement of owner's equity
   b. Ending owner's equity from the statement of owner's equity to the balance sheet
   c. Both of the above
   d. None of the above

10. Accumulated Depreciation is reported on the *(p. 106)*
    a. Balance sheet   c. Statement of owner's equity
    b. Income statement   d. Both a and b

Answers to the self-study questions are at the end of the chapter.

Accounting Vocabulary

accrual-basis accounting *(p. 90)*
accrued expense *(p. 98)*
accrued revenue *(p. 100)*
accumulated depreciation *(p. 97)*
adjusted trial balance *(p. 103)*
adjusting entry *(p. 93)*

book value of a plant asset
    (p. 97)
cash-basis accounting *(p. 90)*
contra account *(p. 97)*
contra asset *(p. 97)*
depreciation *(p. 96)*

matching principle *(p. 92)*
plant asset *(p. 96)*
prepaid expense *(p. 94)*
revenue principle *(p. 91)*
unearned revenue
    (p. 100)

Assignment Material _____

Questions

1. Distinguish the accrual basis of accounting from the cash basis.
2. How long is the basic accounting period? What is a fiscal year? What is an interim period?

3. What two questions does the revenue principle help answer?
4. Briefly explain the matching principle.
5. What is the purpose of making adjusting entries?
6. Why are adjusting entries made at the end of the accounting period, not during the period?
7. Name five categories of adjusting entries and give an example of each.
8. Do all adjusting entries affect the net income or net loss of the period? Include in your answer the definition of an adjusting entry.
9. Why does the balance of Supplies need to be adjusted at the end of the period?
10. Manning Supply Company pays $1,800 for an insurance policy that covers three years. At the end of the first year, the balance of its Prepaid Insurance account contains two elements. What are the two elements and the correct amount of each?
11. The title Prepaid Expense suggests that this type of account is an expense. If so, explain why. If not, what type of account is it?
12. What is a contra account? Identify the contra account introduced in this chapter, along with the account's normal balance.
13. The manager of a Quickie-Pickie convenience store presents his entity's balance sheet to a banker to obtain a loan. The balance sheet reports that the entity's plant assets have a book value of $135,000 and accumulated depreciation of $65,000. What does *book value* of a plant asset mean? What was the cost of the plant assets?
14. Give the entry to record accrued interest revenue of $800.
15. Why is an unearned revenue a liability? Use an example in your answer.
16. Identify the types of accounts (assets, liabilities, and so on) debited and credited for the five types of adjusting entries.
17. What purposes does the adjusted trial balance serve?
18. Explain the relationship among the income statement, the statement of owner's equity and the balance sheet.
19. Bellevue Company failed to record the following adjusting entries at December 31, the end of its fiscal year: (a) accrued expenses, $500; (b) accrued revenues, $850; and (c) depreciation, $1,000. Did these omissions cause net income for the year to be understated or overstated and by what overall amount?
20. Identify several accounting tasks for which it is efficient to use a microcomputer. What is the basic limitation on the use of a computer?

Exercises

Exercise 3-1   *Applying accounting concepts and principles*

Identify the accounting concept or principle that gives the most direction on how to account for each of the following situations:

a. The owner of a business desires monthly financial statements to measure the progress of the entity on an ongoing basis.
b. Expenses of the period total $4,900. This amount should be subtracted from revenue to compute the period's income.
c. Expenses of $650 must be accrued at the end of the period to properly measure income.
d. A customer states her intention to shift her business to a travel agency. Should the travel agency record revenue based on this intention?

Exercise 3-2 *Journalizing adjusting entries*

Journalize the entries for the following adjustments at December 31, the end of the accounting period:

a. Employee salaries owed, $3,600
b. Prepaid insurance expired, $450
c. Interest revenue accrued, $5,000
d. Unearned service revenue earned, $800
e. Depreciation, $6,200

Exercise 3-3 *Analysing the effects of adjustments on net income*

Suppose the adjustments required in Exercise 3-2 were not made. Compute the overall overstatement or understatement of net income as a result of the omission of these adjustments.

Exercise 3-4 *Allocating prepaid expense to the asset and expense*

Compute the amounts indicated by question marks for each of the following Prepaid Rent situations. Consider each situation separately.

	Situation			
	1	**2**	**3**	**4**
Beginning Prepaid Rent......................	$ 900	$ 600	$ 300	$500
Payments for Prepaid Rent during the year ...	1,100	?	700	?
Total amount to account for	2,000	1,500	1,000	?
Ending Prepaid Rent	?	500	200	800
Rent Expense	1,600	1,000	?	300

Exercise 3-5 *Recording adjustments in T-accounts*

The accounting records of Manny Fernandez, Tailor include the following unadjusted balances at May 31: Accounts Receivable, $1,200; Supplies, $600; Salary Payable, $0; Unearned Service Revenue, $400; Service Revenue, $5,100; Salary Expense, $1,200; and Supplies Expense, $0.

Fernandez's accountant develops the following data for the May 31 adjusting entries:

a. Supplies on hand, $200
b. Salary owed to employee, $100
c. Service revenue accrued, $350
d. Unearned service revenue that has been earned, $250

Open the foregoing T-accounts and record the adjustments directly in the accounts, keying each adjustment amount by letter. Show each account's adjusted balance. Journal entries are not required.

Exercise 3-6   *Adjusting the accounts*

Complete the following adjusted trial balance by entering the adjustment amounts directly in the adjustment columns of the text. Service Revenue is the only account affected by more than one adjustment.

Austin Hill Travel Agency
Preparation of Adjusted Trial Balance
October 31, 19X2

Account Title	Trial Balance		Adjustments		Adjusted Trial Balance	
	Debit	*Credit*	*Debit*	*Credit*	*Debit*	*Credit*
Cash	3,000				3,000	
Accounts receivable	6,500				6,950	
Supplies	1,040				800	
Office furniture	19,300				19,300	
Accumulated depreciation		11,060				11,320
Salary payable						600
Unearned revenue		900				690
Capital		16,340				16,340
Owner's withdrawals	6,200				6,200	
Service revenue		11,830				12,490
Salary expense	2,690				3,290	
Rent expense	1,400				1,400	
Depreciation expense					260	
Supplies expense					240	
	40,130	40,130			41,440	41,440

Exercise 3-7   *Journalizing adjustments*

Make journal entries for the adjustments that would complete the preparation of the adjusted trial balance in Exercise 3-6.

Exercise 3-8   *Preparing the financial statements*

Refer to the adjusted trial balance in Exercise 3-6. Prepare Austin Hill Travel Agency's income statement and statement of owner's equity for the three months ended October 31, 19X2 and its balance sheet on that date. Draw the arrows linking the three statements.

Exercise 3-9   *Preparing the financial statements*

The accountant for Patrick Beckham, M.D. has posted adjusting entries *a* through *e* to the accounts at September 30, 19X2. All the revenues and expenses of the entity are listed here in T-account form.

Accounts Receivable	
23,000	
(e) 3,500	

Supplies	
4,000	(a) 2,000

Accumulated Depreciation— Furniture	
	5,000
	(b) 3,000

Accumulated Depreciation— Building	
	33,000
(c) 6,000	

Salaries Payable	
(d) 1,500	

Service Revenue	
	135,000
	(e) 3,500

Salary Expense	
28,000	
(d) 1,500	

Supplies Expense	
(a) 2,000	

Depreciation Expense— Furniture	
(b) 3,000	

Depreciation Expense— Building	
(c) 6,000	

Required

Prepare the income statement of Patrick Beckham, M.D. for the year ended September 30, 19X2. List expenses in order from the largest to the smallest.

Exercise 3-10   *Preparing the statement of owner's equity*

A. B. Leewright Company began the year with owner's equity of $85,000. On July 9, the owner invested $12,000 cash in the business. On September 26, he transferred to the company land valued at $19,000. The income statement for the year ended September 30, 19X5 reported a net loss of $28,000. During this fiscal year, the owner withdrew $1,500 monthly for personal use. Prepare the company's statement of owner's equity for the year ended September 30, 19X5.

Problems   *(Group A)*

Problem 3-1A   *Journalizing adjusting entries*

Journalize the adjusting entry needed on December 31, end of the current accounting period, for each of the following independent cases affecting Willis Engineering Company:

a.   Each Friday Willis pays its employees for the current week's work. The amount of the payroll is $2,500 per day for a five-day work week. The current accounting period ends on Thursday.

b.   Willis has received notes receivable from some clients for professional services. During the current year, Willis has earned accrued interest revenue of $8,575, which will be received next year.

c.   The beginning balance of Engineering Supplies was $3,800. During the year the entity purchased supplies costing $12,530, and at December 31 the inventory of supplies on hand is $2,970.

d.   Willis is conducting tests of the strength of the steel to be used in a large building, and the client paid Willis $27,000 at the start of the project. Willis recorded this amount as Unearned Engineering Revenue. The tests will take several months to complete. Willis executives estimate that the company has earned two thirds of the total fee during the current year.

e.   Depreciation for the current year includes: Office Furniture, $4,500; Engineering Equipment, $6,360; and Building, $3,790. Make a compound entry.

f. Details of Prepaid Insurance are shown in the following account:

Prepaid Insurance

Jan. 1 Bal. 2,400	
Apr. 30 3,600	
Oct. 31 3,600	

Willis pays semiannual insurance premiums (the payment for insurance coverage is called a *premium*) on April 30 and October 31. At December 31, $2,400 of the last payment is still in force.

Problem 3-2A   *Preparing the financial statements from an adjusted trial balance*

The adjusted trial balance of Sommerfeld Engineering Services at December 31, 19X8 follows:

Sommerfeld Engineering Services
Adjusted Trial Balance
December 31, 19X8

Cash	$ 8,340	
Accounts receivable	41,490	
Prepaid rent	1,350	
Supplies	970	
Equipment.......................................	55,690	
Accumulated depreciation — equipment.............		$ 7,240
Office furniture	24,100	
Accumulated depreciation — office furniture		18,670
Accounts payable................................		13,600
Unearned service revenue		4,520
Interest payable		2,130
Salaries payable		930
Note payable....................................		40,000
Lou Sommerfeld, capital..........................		36,380
Lou Sommerfeld, withdrawals	48,000	
Service revenue		197,790
Depreciation expense — equipment.................	11,300	
Depreciation expense — office furniture	2,410	
Salary expense	102,800	
Rent expense	12,000	
Interest expense	4,200	
Utilities expense	3,770	
Insurance expense	3,150	
Supplies expense	1,690	
Total	$321,260	$321,260

Required

Prepare Sommerfeld's 19X8 income statement, statement of owner's equity and balance sheet. List expenses in decreasing order on the income statement and show total liabilities on the balance sheet. Draw the arrows linking the three financial statements.

Problem 3-3A *Preparing an adjusted trial balance and the financial statements*

The unadjusted trial balance of Bette Kurtz, Consulting Psychologist at October 31, 19X2 and the related month-end adjustment data follow:

Bette Kurtz, Consulting Psychologist
Trial Balance
October 31, 19X2

Cash	$16,300	
Accounts receivable	8,000	
Prepaid rent	4,000	
Supplies	600	
Furniture	12,000	
Accumulated depreciation		$3,000
Accounts payable		2,800
Salary payable		
Bette Kurtz, capital		33,000
Bette Kurtz, withdrawals	3,600	
Consulting service revenue		7,400
Salary expense	1,400	
Rent Expense		
Utilities expense	300	
Depreciation expense		
Supplies expense		
Total	$46,200	$46,200

Adjustment data:

a. Prepaid rent expired during the month, $1,000
b. Supplies on hand at October 31, $400
c. Depreciation on furniture for the month, $250
d. Accrued salary expense at October 31, $300
e. Accrued consulting service revenue at October 31, $1,000

Required

1. Write the trial balance on a sheet of paper, using as an example Exhibit 3-4, and prepare the adjusted trial balance of Bette Kurtz, Consulting Psychologist at October 31, 19X2. Key each adjusting entry by the letter corresponding to the data given.
2. Prepare the income statement, statement of owner's equity and balance sheet. Draw the arrows linking the three financial statements.

Problem 3-4A *Analysing and journalizing adjustments*

Song Kim Sales Company's unadjusted and adjusted trial balances at December 31, 19X0 are shown on the next page.

Required

Journalize the adjusting entries that account for the differences between the two trial balances. The only account affected by more than one adjustment is Commission Revenue.

Song Kim Sales Company
Adjusted Trial Balance
December 31, 19X0

Account Title	Trial Balance		Adjusted Trial Balance	
	Debit	*Credit*	*Debit*	*Credit*
Cash	3,620		3,620	
Accounts receivable	11,260		12,090	
Supplies	1,090		780	
Prepaid insurance	2,200		1,330	
Office furniture	21,630		21,630	
Accumulated depreciation		8,220		10,500
Accounts payable		6,310		6,310
Salary payable				960
Interest payable				350
Note payable		12,000		12,000
Unearned commission revenue		1,440		960
Song Kim, capital		13,010		13,010
Song Kim, withdrawals	29,370		29,370	
Commission revenue		72,890		74,200
Depreciation expense			2,280	
Supplies expense			310	
Utilities expense	4,960		4,960	
Salary expense	26,660		27,620	
Rent expense	12,200		12,200	
Interest expense	880		1,230	
Insurance expense			870	
	113,870	113,870	118,290	118,290

Problem 3-5A *Journalizing and posting adjustments to T-accounts; preparing the adjusted trial balance and the financial statements*

The trial balance of Conrad Realty at August 31 of the current year is shown on the next page. The data needed for the month-end adjustments are as follows:

Adjustment data:

a. Prepaid rent still in force at August 31, $900
b. Supplies used during the month, $300
c. Depreciation for the month, $400
d. Accrued advertising expense at August 31, $110 (Credit Accounts Payable)
e. Accrued salary expense at August 31, $550
f. Unearned commission revenue still unearned at August 31, $1,670

Conrad Realty
Trial Balance
August 31, 19XX

Cash	$ 2,200	
Accounts receivable	23,780	
Prepaid rent..................................	2,420	
Supplies	1,180	
Furniture	19,740	
Accumulated depreciation		$ 3,630
Accounts payable		2,410
Salary payable................................		
Unearned commission revenue		2,790
Lou Conrad, capital		39,510
Lou Conrad, withdrawals	4,800	
Commission revenue		11,700
Salary expense................................	3,800	
Rent expense.................................		
Utilities expense	550	
Depreciation expense		
Advertising expense...........................	1,570	
Supplies expense		
Total	$60,040	$60,040

Required

1. Open T-accounts for the accounts listed in the trial balance, inserting their August 31 unadjusted balances.
2. Journalize the adjusting entries and post them to the T-accounts. Key the journal entries and posted amounts by letter.
3. Prepare the adjusted trial balance.
4. Prepare the income statement, statement of owner's equity and balance sheet. Draw the arrows linking the three financial statements.

Problem 3-6A *Journalizing and posting adjustments; preparing the adjusted trial balance and the financial statements*

The trial balance of King Carpet Cleaners at May 31, 19X3 is shown on the next page. The data needed to make the year-end adjustments are as follows:

Adjustment data:

a. At May 31 the business has earned $1,000 service revenue that has not yet been recorded.
b. Supplies used during the year totaled $5,650.
c. Prepaid rent still in force at May 31 is $330.
d. Depreciation for the year is $3,100.
e. King cleans the carpets of a large apartment complex that pays him in advance. At May 31 the entity has earned $3,600 of the unadjusted balance of Unearned Service Revenue.
f. At May 31 the business owes its employees accrued salaries of $1,300.

King Carpet Cleaners
Trial Balance
May 31, 19X3

Account Number			
101	Cash	$ 3,260	
112	Accounts receivable	4,700	
127	Supplies	7,700	
129	Prepaid rent.....................	1,430	
143	Cleaning equipment	28,300	
154	Accumulated depreciation		$ 12,550
211	Accounts payable		4,240
221	Salary payable		
243	Unearned service revenue		5,810
301	Thomas King, capital		7,080
311	Thomas King, withdrawals.........	34,800	
401	Service revenue...................		80,610
511	Salary expense....................	28,800	
513	Depreciation expense		
515	Supplies expense		
519	Rent expense		
521	Utilities expense	1,300	
	Total	$110,290	$110,290

Required

1. Open the accounts listed in the trial balance, inserting their May 31 unadjusted balances. The balances of the following accounts are unchanged since May 1: Supplies, Prepaid Rent, Accumulated Depreciation and Unearned Service Revenue.
2. Journalize the adjusting entries, using page 7 of the journal.
3. Post the adjusting entries to the ledger accounts, using all posting references.
4. Prepare the adjusted trial balance at May 31.
5. Prepare the income statement, statement of owner's equity and balance sheet. Draw the arrows linking the three financial statements.

(Group B)

Problem 3-1B   *Journalizing adjusting entries*

Journalize the adjusting entry needed on December 31, end of the current accounting period, for each of the following independent cases affecting Enfield Air Conditioning Contractors:

a. Enfield pays its employees each Friday. The amount of the weekly payroll is $1,800 for a five-day work week and the daily salary amounts are equal. The current accounting period ends on Monday.
b. Enfield has borrowed money by issuing notes payable. During the current year the entity has incurred accrued interest expense of $1,673 that it will pay next year.

c. The beginning balance of Supplies was $2,680. During the year the entity purchased supplies costing $8,180, and at December 31 the inventory of supplies on hand is $2,150.

d. Enfield is installing the air-conditioning system in a large building, and the owner of the building paid Enfield $12,900 at the start of the project. Enfield recorded this amount as Unearned Service Revenue. The installation will take several weeks to complete. Les Enfield, the owner, estimates that the company has earned one fourth of the total fee during the current year.

e. Depreciation for the current year includes: Office Furniture, $650; Equipment, $3,850; and Trucks, $10,320. Make a compound entry.

f. Details of Prepaid Rent are shown in the following account:

Prepaid Rent

Jan. 1	Bal.	600
Mar. 31		1,200
Sept. 30		1,200

Enfield pays office rent semiannually on March 31 and September 30. At December 31, $600 of the last payment is still an asset.

Problem 3-2B *Preparing the financial statements from an adjusted trial balance*

The adjusted trial balance of Gillen Tax Service at December 31, 19X6 is as follows:

<table>
<tr><td colspan="3" align="center">Gillen Tax Service
Adjusted Trial Balance
December 31, 19X6</td></tr>
<tr><td>Cash</td><td>$ 3,320</td><td></td></tr>
<tr><td>Accounts receivable</td><td>11,920</td><td></td></tr>
<tr><td>Supplies</td><td>2,300</td><td></td></tr>
<tr><td>Prepaid rent</td><td>600</td><td></td></tr>
<tr><td>Office equipment</td><td>23,180</td><td></td></tr>
<tr><td>Accumulated depreciation — office equipment</td><td></td><td>$ 6,350</td></tr>
<tr><td>Office furniture</td><td>17,680</td><td></td></tr>
<tr><td>Accumulated depreciation — office furniture</td><td></td><td>4,870</td></tr>
<tr><td>Accounts payable</td><td></td><td>3,640</td></tr>
<tr><td>Property tax payable</td><td></td><td>1,100</td></tr>
<tr><td>Interest payable</td><td></td><td>830</td></tr>
<tr><td>Unearned service revenue</td><td></td><td>620</td></tr>
<tr><td>Note payable</td><td></td><td>30,500</td></tr>
<tr><td>Monica Gillen, capital</td><td></td><td>6,090</td></tr>
<tr><td>Monica Gillen, withdrawals</td><td>44,000</td><td></td></tr>
<tr><td>Service revenue</td><td></td><td>124,880</td></tr>
<tr><td>Depreciation expense — office equipment</td><td>6,680</td><td></td></tr>
<tr><td>Depreciation expense — office furniture</td><td>2,370</td><td></td></tr>
<tr><td>Salary expense</td><td>39,900</td><td></td></tr>
<tr><td>Rent expense</td><td>14,400</td><td></td></tr>
<tr><td>Interest expense</td><td>3,100</td><td></td></tr>
<tr><td>Utilities expense</td><td>2,670</td><td></td></tr>
<tr><td>Insurance expense</td><td>3,810</td><td></td></tr>
<tr><td>Supplies expense</td><td>2,950</td><td></td></tr>
<tr><td>Total</td><td>$178,880</td><td>$178,880</td></tr>
</table>

Required

Prepare Gillen's 19X6 income statement, statement of owner's equity and balance sheet. List expenses in decreasing order on the income statement and show total liabilities on the balance sheet. Draw the arrows linking the three financial statements.

Problem 3-3B *Preparing an adjusted trial balance and the financial statements*

The unadjusted trial balance of Jack Ochs, Lawyer at July 31, 19X2 and the related month-end adjustment data are as follows:

Jack Ochs, Lawyer Trial Balance July 31, 19X2		
Cash..	$14,600	
Accounts receivable	11,600	
Prepaid rent	3,600	
Supplies..	800	
Furniture.......................................	16,000	
Accumulated depreciation......................		$ 4,000
Accounts payable		3,150
Salary payable		
Jack Ochs, capital		38,650
Jack Ochs, withdrawals	5,000	
Legal service revenue.........................		8,750
Salary expense	2,400	
Rent expense		
Utilities expense	550	
Depreciation expense		
Supplies expense..............................		
Total...	$54,550	$54,550

Adjustment data:

a. Prepaid rent expired during the month, $900
b. Supplies on hand at July 31, $500
c. Depreciation on furniture for the month, $350
d. Accrued salary expense at July 31, $200
e. Accrued legal service revenue at July 31, $700

Required

1. Write the trial balance on a sheet of paper similar to Exhibit 3-4 and prepare the adjusted trial balance of Jack Ochs, Lawyer at July 31, 19X2. Key each adjusting entry by the letter corresponding to the date given.
2. Prepare the income statement, statement of owner's equity and balance sheet. Draw the arrows linking the three financial statements.

Problem 3-4B *Analysing and journalizing adjustments*

Maddux Service Company's unadjusted and adjusted trial balances at April 30, 19X1 are as follows:

Maddux Service Company
Adjusted Trial Balance
April 30, 19X1

Account Title	Trial Balance Debit	Trial Balance Credit	Adjusted Trial Balance Debit	Adjusted Trial Balance Credit
Cash	8,180		8,180	
Accounts receivable	6,360		6,540	
Interest receivable			50	
Note receivable	4,100		4,100	
Supplies	980		290	
Prepaid rent	1,440		720	
Building	66,450		66,450	
Accumulated depreciation		14,970		16,070
Accounts payable		6,920		6,920
Wages payable				220
Unearned service revenue		670		110
Debra Maddux, capital		60,770		60,770
Debra Maddux, withdrawals	3,600		3,600	
Service revenue		9,940		10,680
Interest revenue				50
Wage expense	1,600		1,820	
Rent expense			720	
Depreciation expense			1,100	
Insurance expense	370		370	
Supplies expense			690	
Utilities expense	190		190	
	93,270	93,270	94,820	94,820

Required

Journalize the adjusting entries that account for the differences between the two trial balances. The only account affected by more than one adjustment is Service Revenue.

Problem 3-5B   *Journalizing and posting adjustments to T-accounts; preparing the adjusted trial balance and the financial statements*

The trial balance of Impala Realty at October 31 of the current year is shown on the next page. The data needed for the month-end adjustments are as follows:

Adjustment data:

a. Prepaid rent still in force at October 31, $650
b. Supplies used during the month, $440
c. Depreciation for the month, $700
d. Accrued advertising expense at October 31, $320 (Credit Accounts Payable)
e. Accrued salary expense at October 31, $180
f. Unearned commission revenue still unearned at October 31, $2,000

Impala Realty
Trial Balance
October 31, 19X2

Cash	$ 1,460	
Accounts receivable	14,750	
Prepaid rent	3,100	
Supplies.	780	
Furniture.	22,370	
Accumulated depreciation.		$11,640
Accounts payable		1,940
Salary payable		
Unearned commission revenue		2,290
Ellie Taft, capital		24,140
Ellie Taft, withdrawals	2,900	
Commission revenue		8,580
Salary expense	2,160	
Rent expense		
Utilities expense	340	
Depreciation expense		
Advertising expense	730	
Supplies expense.		
Total.	$48,590	$48,590

Required

1. Open T-accounts for the accounts listed in the trial balance, inserting their October 31 unadjusted balances.
2. Journalize the adjusting entries and post them to the T-accounts. Key the journal entries and posted amounts by letter.
3. Prepare the adjusted trial balance.
4. Prepare the income statement, statement of owner's equity and balance sheet. Draw the arrows linking the three financial statements.

Problem 3-6B   *Journalizing and posting adjustments; preparing the adjusted trial balance and the financial statements*

The trial balance of Apartment Cleaning Service at July 31, 19X3 is shown on the next page. The data needed to make the year-end adjustments are as follows:

Adjustment data:

a. At July 31 the business has earned $1,420 service revenue that has not yet been recorded.
b. Supplies used during the year totaled $3,060.
c. Prepaid rent still in force at July 31 is $1,040.
d. Depreciation for the year is $3,730.
e. The entity cleans the carpets of a large apartment complex that pays in advance. At July 31, the entity has earned $2,210 of the unadjusted balance of Unearned Service Revenue.
f. At July 31, the business owes its employees accrued salaries of $1,780.

Apartment Cleaning Service
Trial Balance
July 31, 19X3

Account Number			
101	Cash	$ 2,110	
121	Accounts receivable	6,200	
131	Supplies	3,400	
133	Prepaid rent.....................	1,890	
141	Cleaning equipment	36,200	
151	Accumulated depreciation		$ 14,360
201	Accounts payable		6,410
211	Salary payable		
221	Unearned service revenue		3,110
301	Alvin McKay, capital		14,310
302	Alvin McKay, withdrawals	40,100	
401	Service revenue...................		91,060
501	Salary expense....................	32,150	
504	Depreciation expense		
506	Supplies expense		
509	Rent expense.....................	6,000	
511	Utilities expense	1,200	
	Total	$129,250	$129,250

Required

1. Open the accounts listed in the trial balance, inserting their July 31 unadjusted balances. Date the balances of the following accounts as of July 31: Supplies, Prepaid Rent, Accumulated Depreciation and Unearned Service Revenue.
2. Journalize the adjusting entries, using page 4 of the journal.
3. Post the adjusting entries to the ledger accounts, using all posting references.
4. Prepare the adjusted trial balance at July 31.
5. Prepare the income statement, statement of owner's equity and balance sheet. Draw the arrows linking the three financial statements.

Decision Problems

1. Valuing a business based on its net income

Slade McQueen has owned and operated McQueen Medical Systems, a management consulting firm for physicians, since its beginning ten years ago. From all appearances the business has prospered. McQueen lives in the fast lane — flashy car, home located in an expensive suburb, frequent trips abroad and other signs of wealth. In the past few years, you have become friends with him and his wife through weekly rounds of golf at the country club. Recently, he mentioned that he has lost his zest for the business and would consider selling it for the right price. He claims that his clientele is firmly established and that the business "runs on its own." According to McQueen, the consulting procedures are fairly simple and anyone could perform the work.

Assume you are interested in buying this business. You obtain its most recent monthly trial balance, which follows. Assume that revenues and expenses vary little from month to month and April is a typical month.

McQueen Medical Systems
Trial Balance
April 30, 19XX

Cash	$ 7,700	
Accounts receivable	4,900	
Prepaid expenses	2,600	
Plant assets	252,300	
Accumulated depreciation		$189,600
Land	138,000	
Accounts payable		11,800
Salary payable		
Unearned consulting revenue		56,700
Slade McQueen, capital		148,400
Slade McQueen, withdrawals	9,000	
Consulting revenue		12,300
Salary expense	3,400	
Rent expense		
Utilities expense	900	
Depreciation expense		
Supplies expense		
Total	$418,800	$418,800

Your investigation reveals that the trial balance does not include the effects of monthly revenues of $1,100 and expenses totaling $2,100. If you were to buy McQueen Medical Systems, you would hire a manager so that you could devote your time to other duties. Assume this person would require a monthly salary of $2,000.

Required

1. Is this an unadjusted or adjusted trial balance? How can you tell?
2. Assume the most you would pay for the business is thirty times the monthly net income you could expect to earn from it. Compute this possible price.
3. McQueen states that the least he will take for the business is his ending owner's equity. Compute this amount.
4. Under these conditions, how much should you offer McQueen? Give your reasons.

2. Understanding the concepts underlying the accrual basis of accounting
The following are unrelated questions related to the accrual basis of accounting:

a. Some students believe the matching process means the matching of revenues to expenses. Explain why this definition is incorrect while the one in the chapter is correct.
b. It has been said that the only time a company's financial position is known is when the company is formed, and when it is wound up and its only asset is cash. Why do you think the statement might be true?
c. A friend suggests to you that the purpose of adjusting entries is to correct errors in the accounts. Is your friend's statement true? What is the purpose of adjusting entries if your friend is wrong?
d. The text suggested that furniture (and all the other plant assets that are depreciated) is a form of prepaid expense. Do you agree? Why do you think some accountants think it to be so?

Financial Statement Problem

This problem uses the financial statements and the notes to the financial statements in Appendix E. The notes are needed to avoid cluttering the financial statements (the balance sheet, for example) with excessive detail.

Journalizing and posting transactions, and tracing account balances to the financial statements

Prepaid expenses appear on the balance sheet in the John Labatt financial statements in Appendix E; note 7 in the financial statements gives details of the inventory amount on the balance sheet.

Required

1. Open T-accounts for Prepaid Expenses and for Containers. For each account, insert John Labatt's actual April 30, 1988 balance (in millions).
2. Journalize the following for fiscal 1989. Key entries by letter. Explanations are not required.
   Cash transactions (amounts in millions):
   a. Paid prepaid expenses of $18.7
   b. Purchased containers for $5.3
   Adjustments at April 30, 1989 (amounts in millions):
   c. Prepaid expenses expired $13.6 (Debit Administrative Expenses)
   d. Container inventory write-down to reflect containers which will not be returned and which were scrapped $13.8 (Debit Cost of Sales)
3. After these entries are posted, show that the balances in the two accounts opened in question 1 agree with their April 30, 1989 amounts on the balance sheet (Prepaid Expenses) and in note 7 (Containers). Key posted amounts by letter.

Answers to Self-Study Questions

1. b	6. b ($120,000 − $50,000 = $70,000)
2. c	7. d
3. a	8. a ($3,000 received − $1,100 unearned = $1,900 earned)
4. d	9. c
5. b ($160 + $290 − $210 = $240)	10. a

4

Completing the Accounting Cycle

You have studied how accountants journalize transactions, post to the ledger accounts, prepare the trial balance and the adjusting entries, and draw up the financial statements. One major step remains to complete the accounting cycle—closing the books. This chapter illustrates the closing process for Gary Lyon's accounting practice at April 30, 19X1. It also shows how to use two additional accounting tools that are optional. One of these optional tools is the accountant's work sheet. Building upon the adjusted trial balance, the work sheet leads directly to the financial statements, which are the focal point of financial accounting. The chapter also presents an example of an actual balance sheet to show how companies classify assets and liabilities in order to provide meaningful information for decision-making.

Overview of the Accounting Cycle

The **accounting cycle** is the process by which accountants produce an entity's financial statements for a specific period of time. For a new business, the cycle begins with setting up (opening) the ledger accounts. Gary Lyon started his accounting practice from scratch on April 1, 19X1, so the first step in the cycle was to open the accounts. After a business has operated for one period, however, the account balances carry over from period to period. Therefore, the accounting cycle usually starts with the account balances at the beginning of the period, as shown in Exhibit 4-1. The exhibit highlights the new steps that we will be discussing in this chapter.

The accounting cycle is divided into work that is performed during the period—journalizing transactions and posting to the ledger—and work performed at the end of the period to prepare the financial statements. A secondary purpose of the end-of-period work is to get the accounts ready for recording the transactions of the next period. The greater number of individual steps at the end of the period may seem to suggest that most of the work is done at the end. This is not the case. In actual practice, the recording and posting during the period takes far more time than the end-of-period work. Some of

OBJECTIVE 1

Give an overview of the accounting cycle

EXHIBIT 4-1 *The Accounting Cycle*

During the period	1. Start with the account balances in the ledger at the beginning of the period.
	2. Analyse and journalize transactions as they occur.
	3. Post journal entries to the ledger accounts.
End of the period	4. Compute the unadjusted balance in each account at the end of the period.
	5. Enter the trial balance on the work sheet, and complete the work sheet.
	6. Using the work sheet as a guide,
	a. Prepare the financial statements.
	b. Journalize and post the adjusting entries.
	c. Journalize and post the closing entries.
	7. Prepare the postclosing, or afterclosing, trial balance.

the terms in Exhibit 4-1 may be unfamiliar, but by the end of the chapter you will be able to follow the complete accounting cycle.

OBJECTIVE 2

Prepare a work sheet

The Accountant's Work Sheet _____

Accountants often use a **work sheet**, a columnar document that is designed to help move data from the trial balance to the finished financial statements. The work sheet provides an orderly way to compute net income and arrange the data for the financial statements. By listing all the accounts and their unadjusted balances, it helps the accountant identify the accounts needing adjustment. Although it is not essential, the work sheet is helpful because it brings together in one place the effects of all the transactions of a particular period. The work sheet aids the closing process by listing the adjusted balances of all the accounts. It also helps the accountant discover potential errors.

The work sheet is not part of the ledger or the journal, nor is it a financial statement. Therefore, it is not part of the formal accounting system. Instead, it is a summary device that exists for the accountant's convenience. There is no single correct way of preparing the work sheet.

Exhibits 4-2 through 4-6 illustrate the development of a typical work sheet for the business of Gary Lyon, CA. The heading at the top names the business, identifies the document and states the accounting period. A step-by-step description of its preparation follows. Observe that steps 1 through 4 yield the adjusted trial balance that was introduced in Chapter 3. Only step 5 is entirely new.

The steps introduced in Chapter 3 to prepare the adjusted trial balance were

1. Write the account titles and their unadjusted ending balances in the Trial Balance columns of the work sheet and total the amounts.
2. Enter the adjustments in the Adjustments columns and total the amounts.
3. Compute each account's adjusted balance by combining the trial balance and adjustment figures. Enter the adjusted amounts in the Adjusted Trial Balance columns.
4. Extend the asset, liability and owner's equity amounts from the Adjusted Trial Balance to the Balance Sheet columns. Extend the revenue and expense amounts to the Income Statement columns. Total the statement columns.

A new step to be introduced in this chapter is

5. Compute net income or net loss as the difference between total revenues and total expenses on the income statement. Enter net income or net loss as a balancing amount on the income statement and the balance sheet, and compute the adjusted column totals.

   1. *Write the account titles and their unadjusted ending balances in the Trial Balance columns of the work sheet and total the amounts.*   Of course, total debits should equal total credits as shown in Exhibit 4-2. The account titles and balances come directly from the ledger accounts before the adjusting entries. If the business uses a work sheet, there is no need for a separate trial balance. It is written directly onto the work sheet, as shown in the exhibit. Accounts are grouped on the work sheet by category and are usually listed in the order they appear in the ledger. By contrast, their order on the financial statements follows a different pattern. For example, the expenses on the work sheet in Exhibit 4-2 indicate no particular order. But on the income statement, expenses are ordered by amount with the largest first (see Exhibit 4-7).

   Accounts may have zero balances, for example, Accumulated Depreciation. All accounts are listed on the trial balance because they appear in the ledger. Electronically prepared work sheets list all the accounts, not just those with a balance.

   2. *Enter the adjusting entries in the Adjustments columns and total the amounts.* Exhibit 4-3 includes the April adjusting entries. These are the same adjustments that were illustrated in Chapter 3 to prepare the adjusted trial balance.

   How does the accountant identify the accounts that need to be adjusted? The accountant scans the trial balance and identifies accounts for which an adjustment must be made so that the balance will be correct on the financial statements. Cash needs no adjustment because all cash transactions are recorded as they occur during the period. Consequently, Cash's balance is up to date.

   Accounts Receivable is listed next. Has Gary Lyon earned revenue that he has not yet recorded? The answer is yes. Lyon provides professional service for a client who pays a $500 fee on the 15th of each month. At April 30, Lyon has earned half of this amount, $250, which must be accrued. To accrue this service revenue, Lyon debits Accounts Receivable and credits Service Revenue on the work sheet in Exhibit 4-3. A letter is used to link the debit and the credit of each adjusting entry. By moving down the trial balance, Lyon identifies the remaining accounts needing adjustment. Supplies is next. The business has used supplies during April, so Lyon debits Supplies Expense and credits Supplies. The other adjustments are analysed and entered on the work sheet as shown in the exhibit.

   The process of identifying accounts that need to be adjusted is aided by listing the accounts in their proper sequence. However, suppose one or more accounts is omitted from the trial balance. It can always be written below the first column totals, $51,800. Assume that Supplies Expense was accidentally omitted and thus did not appear on the trial balance. When the accountant identifies the need to update the Supplies account, he or she knows that the debit in the adjusting entry is to Supplies Expense. In this case, the accountant can write Supplies Expense on the line beneath the amount totals and enter the debit adjustment, $300, on the Supplies Expense line. Keep in mind that the work sheet is not the finished version of the financial statements, so the

EXHIBIT 4-2

Gary Lyon, CA
Work Sheet
for the month ended April 30, 19X1

Account Title	Trial Balance		Adjustments		Adjusted Trial Balance		Income Statement		Balance Sheet	
	Debit	Credit	Debit	Credit	Debit	Credit	Debit	Credit	Debit	Credit
Cash	24,800									
Accounts receivable	2,250									
Supplies	700									
Prepaid rent	3,000									
Furniture	16,500									
Accumulated depreciation		13,100								
Accounts payable										
Salary payable		450								
Unearned service revenue		31,250								
Gary Lyon, capital										
Gary Lyon, withdrawals	3,200									
Service revenue		7,000								
Rent expense										
Salary expense	950									
Supplies expense										
Depreciation expense										
Utilities expense	400									
	51,800	51,800								

EXHIBIT 4-3

Gary Lyon, CA
Work Sheet
for the month ended April 30, 19X1

Account Title	Trial Balance		Adjustments		Adjusted Trial Balance		Income Statement		Balance Sheet	
	Debit	Credit	Debit	Credit	Debit	Credit	Debit	Credit	Debit	Credit
Cash	24,800									
Accounts receivable	2,250		(a) 250							
Supplies	700			(b) 300						
Prepaid rent	3,000			(c) 1,000						
Furniture	16,500									
Accumulated depreciation				(d) 275						
Accounts payable		13,100								
Salary payable				(e) 950						
Unearned service revenue		450	(f) 150							
Gary Lyon, capital		31,250								
Gary Lyon, withdrawals	3,200									
Service revenue		7,000		(a) 250 (f) 150						
Rent expense			(c) 1,000							
Salary expense	950		(e) 950							
Supplies expense			(b) 300							
Depreciation expense			(d) 275							
Utilities expense	400									
	51,800	51,800	2,925	2,925						

order of the accounts on the work sheet is not critical. When the accountant prepares the income statement, Supplies Expense can be listed in its proper sequence.

After the adjustments are entered on the work sheet, the amount columns should be totaled to ensure that total debits equal total credits. This provides some assurance that each debit adjustment is accompanied by an equal credit.

3. Compute each account's adjusted balance by combining the trial balance and adjustment figures. Enter the adjusted amounts in the Adjusted Trial Balance columns.   Exhibit 4-4 shows the work sheet with the adjusted trial balance added.

This step is performed as it was in Chapter 3. For example, the Cash balance is up to date, so it receives no adjustment. Accounts Receivable's adjusted balance of $2,500 is computed by adding the trial balance amount of $2,250 to the $250 debit adjustment. Supplies' adjusted balance of $400 is determined by subtracting the $300 credit adjustment from the debit balance of $700. An account may receive more than one adjustment, as does Service Revenue. The column totals should maintain the equality of debit and credits.

4. Extend the asset, liability and owner's equity amounts from the Adjusted Trial Balance to the Balance Sheet columns. Extend the revenue and expense amounts to the Income Statement columns. Total the statement columns.   Every account is either a balance sheet account or an income statement account. The asset, liability and owner's equity accounts go to the balance sheet, and the revenues and expenses go to the income statement. Note that Gary Lyon, withdrawals, goes to the balance sheet because it is part of owner's equity. Debits on the adjusted trial balance remain debits in the statement columns, and likewise for credits. Each account's adjusted balance should appear in only one statement column, as shown in Exhibit 4-5.

The income statement indicates total expenses in the debit column ($3,875) and total revenues ($7,400) in the credit column. The balance sheet shows total debits of $49,400 and total credits of $45,875. The column totals should *not* necessarily be equal.

5. Compute net income or net loss as the difference between total revenues and total expenses on the income statement. Enter net income or net loss as a balancing amount on the income statement and on the balance sheet and compute the adjusted column totals. The amount should equal the difference between the debits and the credits on the balance sheet.   Exhibit 4-6 presents the completed work sheet, which shows net income of $3,525, computed as follows:

Revenue (total credits on the income statement) $7,400
Expenses (total debits on the income statement).   3,875
Net income $3,525

Net income of $3,525 is entered in the debit column of the income statement, and the income statement columns are totaled at $7,400. The net income amount is then extended to the credit column of the balance sheet. This is because an excess of revenues over expenses increases owner's equity, and increases in owner's equity are recorded by a credit. In the closing process, which we discuss later, net income will find its way into the owner's equity account.

If expenses exceed revenue, the result is a net loss. In that event, the accountant writes the words *Net loss* on the work sheet. The loss amount should be entered in the credit column of the income statement and in the debit column of the balance sheet. This is because an excess of expenses over revenue

EXHIBIT 4-4

Gary Lyon, CA
Work Sheet
for the month ended April 30, 19X1

Account Title	Trial Balance Debit	Trial Balance Credit	Adjustments Debit	Adjustments Credit	Adjusted Trial Balance Debit	Adjusted Trial Balance Credit	Income Statement Debit	Income Statement Credit	Balance Sheet Debit	Balance Sheet Credit
Cash	24,800				24,800					
Accounts receivable	2,250		(a) 250		2,500					
Supplies	700			(b) 300	400					
Prepaid rent	3,000			(c) 1,000	2,000					
Furniture	16,500				16,500					
Accumulated depreciation				(d) 275		275				
Accounts payable		13,100				13,100				
Salary payable				(e) 950		950				
Unearned service revenue		450	(f) 150			300				
Gary Lyon, capital		31,250				31,250				
Gary Lyon, withdrawals	3,200				3,200					
Service revenue		7,000		(a) 250 (f) 150		7,400				
Rent expense			(c) 1,000		1,000					
Salary expense	950		(e) 950		1,900					
Supplies expense			(b) 300		300					
Depreciation expense			(d) 275		275					
Utilities expense	400				400					
	51,800	51,800	2,925	2,925	53,275	53,275				

137

EXHIBIT 4-5

Gary Lyon, CA
Work Sheet
for the month ended April 30, 19X1

Account Title	Trial Balance Debit	Trial Balance Credit	Adjustments Debit	Adjustments Credit	Adjusted Trial Balance Debit	Adjusted Trial Balance Credit	Income Statement Debit	Income Statement Credit	Balance Sheet Debit	Balance Sheet Credit
Cash	24,800				24,800				24,800	
Accounts receivable	2,250		(a) 250		2,500				2,500	
Supplies	700			(b) 300	400				400	
Prepaid rent	3,000			(c) 1,000	2,000				2,000	
Furniture	16,500				16,500				16,500	
Accumulated depreciation				(d) 275		275				275
Accounts payable		13,100				13,100				13,100
Salary payable				(e) 950		950				950
Unearned service revenue		450	(f) 150			300				300
Gary Lyon, capital		31,250				31,250				31,250
Gary Lyon, withdrawals	3,200				3,200				3,200	
Service revenue		7,000		(a) 250 (f) 150		7,400		7,400		
Rent expense			(c) 1,000		1,000		1,000			
Salary expense	950		(e) 950		1,900		1,900			
Supplies expense			(b) 300		300		300			
Depreciation expense			(d) 275		275		275			
Utilities expense	400				400		400			
	51,800	51,800	2,925	2,925	53,275	53,275	3,875	7,400	49,400	45,875

EXHIBIT 4-6

Gary Lyon, CA
Work Sheet
for the month ended April 30, 19X1

Account Title	Trial Balance Debit	Trial Balance Credit	Adjustments Debit	Adjustments Credit	Adjusted Trial Balance Debit	Adjusted Trial Balance Credit	Income Statement Debit	Income Statement Credit	Balance Sheet Debit	Balance Sheet Credit
Cash	24,800				24,800				24,800	
Accounts receivable	2,250		(a) 250		2,500				2,500	
Supplies	700			(b) 300	400				400	
Prepaid rent	3,000			(c) 1,000	2,000				2,000	
Furniture	16,500				16,500				16,500	
Accumulated depreciation				(d) 275		275				275
Accounts payable		13,100				13,100				13,100
Salary payable				(e) 950		950				950
Unearned service revenue		450	(f) 150			300				300
Gary Lyon, capital		31,250				31,250				31,250
Gary Lyon, withdrawals	3,200				3,200				3,200	
Service revenue		7,000		(a) 250		7,400		7,400		
				(f) 150						
Rent expense			(c) 1,000		1,000		1,000			
Salary expense	950		(e) 950		1,900		1,900			
Supplies expense			(b) 300		300		300			
Depreciation expense			(d) 275		275		275			
Utilities expense	400				400		400			
	51,800	51,800	2,925	2,925	53,275	53,275	3,875	7,400	49,400	45,875
Net income							3,525			3,525
							7,400	7,400	49,400	49,400

decreases owner's equity, and decreases in owner's equity are recorded by a debit.

The balance sheet columns are totaled at $49,400. An out-of-balance condition indicates an error in preparing the work sheet. Common mistakes include arithmetic errors and carrying an amount to the wrong column — to the incorrect statement column, or extending a debit as a credit or vice versa. Columns that balance offer some, but not complete, assurance that the work sheet is correct. For example, it is possible to have offsetting errors. Fortunately, that is unlikely. Detecting and correcting errors will be discussed later in the chapter.

Summary Problem for Your Review

The trial balance of Sally's Service Company at December 31, 19X1, the end of its fiscal year, is presented below:

Sally's Service Company
Trial Balance
December 31, 19X1

Cash	$ 198,000	
Accounts receivable	370,000	
Supplies	6,000	
Furniture and fixtures	100,000	
Accumulated depreciation — furniture and fixtures		$ 40,000
Building	250,000	
Accumulated depreciation — building		130,000
Accounts payable		380,000
Salary payable		
Unearned service revenue		45,000
Sally Gunz, capital		293,000
Sally Gunz, withdrawals	65,000	
Service revenues		286,000
Salary expense	172,000	
Supplies expense		
Depreciation expense — furniture and fixtures		
Depreciation expense — building		
Miscellaneous expense	13,000	
Total	$1,174,000	$1,174,000

Data needed for the adjusting entries include

a. Supplies on hand at year end, $2,000
b. Depreciation on furniture and fixtures, $20,000
c. Depreciation on building, $10,000
d. Salaries owed but not yet paid, $5,000
e. Accrued service revenue, $12,000
f. Of the $45,000 balance of Unearned Service Revenue, $32,000 was earned during the year.

Required

Prepare the work sheet of Sally's Service Company for the year ended December 31, 19X1. Key each adjusting entry by the letter corresponding to the data given.

SOLUTION TO REVIEW PROBLEM

Sally's Service Company
Work Sheet
for the year ended December 31, 19X1

Account Title	Trial Balance Debit	Trial Balance Credit	Adjustments Debit	Adjustments Credit	Adjusted Trial Balance Debit	Adjusted Trial Balance Credit	Income Statement Debit	Income Statement Credit	Balance Sheet Debit	Balance Sheet Credit
Cash	198,000				198,000				198,000	
Accounts receivable	370,000		(e) 12,000		382,000				382,000	
Supplies	6,000			(a) 4,000	2,000				2,000	
Furniture and fixtures	100,000				100,000				100,000	
Accumulated depreciation— furniture and fixtures		40,000		(b) 20,000		60,000				60,000
Building	250,000				250,000				250,000	
Accumulated depreciation— building		130,000		(c) 10,000		140,000				140,000
Accounts payable		380,000				380,000				380,000
Salary payable				(d) 5,000		5,000				5,000
Unearned service revenue		45,000	(f) 32,000			13,000				13,000
Sally Gunz, capital		293,000				293,000				293,000
Sally Gunz, withdrawals	65,000				65,000				65,000	
Service revenue		286,000		(e) 12,000 (f) 32,000		330,000		330,000		
Salary expense	172,000		(d) 5,000		177,000		177,000			
Supplies expense			(a) 4,000		4,000		4,000			
Depreciation expense— furniture and fixtures			(b) 20,000		20,000		20,000			
Depreciation expense—building			(c) 10,000		10,000		10,000			
Miscellaneous expense	13,000				13,000		13,000			
	1,174,000	1,174,000	83,000	83,000	1,221,000	1,221,000	224,000	330,000	997,000	891,000
Net income							106,000			106,000
							330,000	330,000	997,000	997,000

OBJECTIVE 3

Use the work sheet to complete the accounting cycle

Using the Work Sheet _____

As illustrated thus far, the work sheet helps organize accounting data and compute the net income or net loss for the period. It also aids in preparing the financial statements, recording the adjusting entries and closing the accounts.

Preparing the Financial Statements

Even though the work sheet shows the amount of net income or net loss for the period, it is still necessary to prepare the financial statements. These statements report the entity's progress to outsiders such as creditors. The sorting of accounts to the balance sheet and income statement makes it easy to draw them up. The work sheet also provides the data for the statement of owner's equity. Exhibit 4-7 presents the April financial statements for the accounting practice of Gary Lyon, CA (based on the data from the work sheet in Exhibit 4-6).

The financial statements can be prepared directly from the adjusted trial balance as shown in Chapter 3. That is why completion of the work sheet is optional.

Recording the Adjusting Entries

The adjusting entries are a key element of accrual-basis accounting. They update the accounts and help distribute the revenues and expenses to the appropriate periods. It is convenient to use the work sheet to identify the accounts that need adjustments, and it is helpful to make the adjustments directly on the work sheet as shown in Exhibits 4-2 through 4-6. However, these work sheet procedures do *not* adjust the accounts. Recall that the work sheet is neither a journal nor a ledger. Actual adjustment of the accounts requires journal entries that are posted to the ledger accounts. Therefore, it is necessary to record the adjusting entries in the journal as shown in Panel A of Exhibit 4-8. Panel B shows the postings to the accounts, with Adj. denoting an amount posted from an adjusting entry. Only the revenue and expense accounts are presented here in order to focus on the closing process, which is discussed in the next section.

The adjusting entries could have been recorded in the journal as they were entered on the work sheet. However, it is not necessary to journalize them at that time. Most companies go ahead and prepare the financial statements immediately after completing the work sheet. They can wait to journalize and post the adjusting entries when they make the closing entries.

Delaying the journalizing and posting of the adjusting entries illustrates another use of the work sheet. Many companies journalize and post the adjusting entries (as in Exhibit 4-8) only once annually, at the end of the year. The need for monthly and quarterly financial statements, however, requires a tool like the work sheet. The entity can use the work sheet to aid in preparing interim statements without entering the adjusting entries in the journal and posting them to the ledger.

Closing the Accounts

Accountants use the term **closing the accounts** to refer to the step at the end of the period that prepares the accounts for recording the transactions of the next period. Closing the accounts consists of journalizing and posting the

EXHIBIT 4-7 *April Financial Statements of Gary Lyon, CA*

Gary Lyon, CA
Income Statement
for the month ended April 30, 19X1

Revenues		
Service revenue..		$7,400
Expenses		
Salary expense..	$1,900	
Rent expense..	1,000	
Utilities expense	400	
Supplies expense	300	
Depreciation expense	275	
Total expenses...		3,875
Net income		$3,525

Gary Lyon, CA
Statement of Owner's Equity
for the month ended April 30, 19X1

Gary Lyon, capital, April 1, 19X1	$31,250
Add: Net income	3,525
	34,775
Less: Withdrawals	3,200
Gary Lyon, capital, April 30, 19X1	$31,575

Gary Lyon, CA
Balance Sheet
April 30, 19X1

Assets			Liabilities		
Cash		$24,800	Accounts payable.......		$13,100
Accounts receivable ...		2,500	Salary payable		950
Supplies		400	Unearned service		
Prepaid rent..........		2,000	revenue		300
Furniture	$16,500		Total liabilities		14,350
Less: Accumulated					
depreciation....	275	16,225	**Owner's Equity**		
			Gary Lyon, capital		31,575
			Total liabilities and		
Total assets...........		$45,925	owner's equity		$45,925

closing entries. Closing sets the balances of the revenue and expense accounts back to zero in order to measure the net income of a single period. Recall that the income statement reports only one period's income. For example, net income for Journey's End Corp., owner of Journey's End motels, for 1989 relates exclusively to 1989. At July 31, 1989, Journey's End accountants close the company's revenues and expense accounts for that year. Because these

EXHIBIT 4-8   Journalizing and Posting the Adjusting Entries

Panel A: Journalizing   **Page 4**
Adjusting Entries

Apr. 30	Accounts Receivable	250	
	Service Revenue		250
30	Supplies Expense	300	
	Supplies		300
30	Rent Expense	1,000	
	Prepaid Rent		1,000
30	Depreciation Expense	275	
	Accumulated Depreciation		275
30	Salary Expense	950	
	Salary Payable		950
30	Unearned Service Revenue	150	
	Service Revenue		150

Panel B: Posting the Adjustments to the Revenue and Expense Accounts

Revenue   **Expenses**

Service Revenue			Rent Expense			Salary Expense	
	7,000		Adj. 1,000			950	
	Adj. 250					Adj. 950	
	Adj. 150		Bal 1,000				
						Bal. 1,900	
	Bal. 7,400						

Supplies Expense			Depreciation Expense			Utilities Expense	
Adj. 300			Adj. 275			400	
Bal. 300			Bal. 275			Bal. 400	

Adj. = Amount posted from an adjusting entry
Bal. = Balance

accounts are open for only one accounting period at a time, the revenue and expense accounts are called **temporary (nominal) accounts**. The owner's withdrawal account—though not a revenue or an expense—is also a temporary account, because it is important to measure withdrawals for a specific period. The closing process applies only to temporary accounts.

To better understand the closing process, contrast the nature of the temporary accounts with the nature of the **permanent (real) accounts**—the assets, liabilities and owner's equity. The permanent accounts are *not* closed at the end of the period, because they continue period after period and do not represent the transactions of a single period as temporary accounts do. Their balances are not used to measure income as temporary accounts are.

The permanent accounts represent the accumulated financial history of the entity; each account includes all the debits and credits to that account since the entity's start. Consider Cash, Accounts Receivable, Supplies, Buildings, Accounts Payable, Notes Payable and Gary Lyon, Capital. They represent assets, liabilities and capital that are on hand at a specific point in time. This is why their balances at the end of one accounting period carry over to become the beginning balances of the next period. For example, the Cash balance at December 31, 19X1 is also the beginning balance for 19X2.

Briefly, **closing entries** transfer the revenue, expense and owner withdrawal balances from their respective accounts to the owner's equity account. As you know, revenues increase owner's equity, and expenses and owner withdrawals decrease it. It is when we post the closing entries that owner's equity absorbs the impact of the balances in the temporary accounts. As an intermediate step, however, the revenues and the expenses are transferred first to an account entitled **Income Summary**, which is like a temporary "holding tank" used only in the closing process. Then the balance of Income Summary is transferred to owner's equity. The steps in closing the accounts of a proprietorship like Gary Lyon, CA, are as follows:

1. Debit each revenue account for the amount of its credit balance. Credit Income Summary for the sum of the revenues. This entry transfers the sum of the revenues to the credit side of the Income Summary.

2. Credit each expense account for the amount of its debit balance. Debit Income Summary for the sum of the expenses. This entry transfers the sum of the expenses to the debit side of the Income Summary.

3. Debit Income Summary for the amount of its credit balance (revenues minus expenses) and credit the Capital account. If Income Summary has a debit balance, then credit Income Summary for this amount and debit Capital. This entry transfers the net income or loss to the Capital account.

4. Credit the Withdrawals account for the amount of its debit balance as shown in the Balance Sheet column of the work sheet. Debit the Capital account of the proprietor. Withdrawals are not expenses and do not affect net income or net loss. Therefore this account is *not* closed to the Income Summary. This entry transfers the withdrawal amount to the debit side of the Capital account.

To illustrate, suppose Gary Lyon closes the books at the end of April. Exhibit 4-9 presents the complete closing process for Lyon's business. Panel A gives the closing journal entries, and Panel B shows the accounts after the closing entries have been posted.

The amount in the debit side of each expense account is its adjusted balance. For example, Rent Expense has a $1,000 debit balance. Also note that Service Revenue has a credit balance of $7,400 before closing. These amounts come directly from the adjusted balances in Exhibit 4-8.

Closing entry 1, denoted in the Service Revenue account Clo., transfers Service Revenue's balance to the Income Summary account. This entry zeroes out Service Revenue for April and places the revenue on the credit side of Income Summary. Closing entry 2 zeroes out the expenses and moves their total ($3,875) to the debit side of Income Summary. At this point, Income Summary contains the impact of April's revenues and expenses, and hence the month's net income ($3,525), which is denoted by Net inc. in the exhibit. Closing entry 3 closes the Income Summary account by transferring net income to the credit side of the Capital account.[1] The last closing entry (4) moves the owner withdrawals to the debit side of Capital, leaving a zero balance in the Withdrawals account.

---

[1] The Income Summary account is a convenience for combining the effects of the revenues and expenses prior to transferring their income effect to Capital. It is not necessary to use the Income Summary account in the closing process. Another way of closing the revenues and expenses makes no use of this account. In this alternative procedure, the revenues and expenses are closed directly to Capital.

OBJECTIVE 4
Close the revenue, expense and withdrawal accounts

EXHIBIT 4-9   *Journalizing and Posting the Closing Entries*

Panel A: Journalizing Closing Entries

Page 5

1.	Apr. 30	Service Revenue	7,400	
		Income Summary		7,400
2.	30	Income Summary	3,875	
		Rent Expense		1,000
		Salary Expense		1,900
		Supplies Expense		300
		Depreciation Expense		275
		Utilities Expense		400
3.	30	Income Summary ($7,400 — $3,875)...........	3,525	
		Gary Lyon, Capital....................		3,525
4.	30	Gary Lyon, Capital	3,200	
		Gary Lyon, Withdrawals..............		3,200

Panel B: Posting

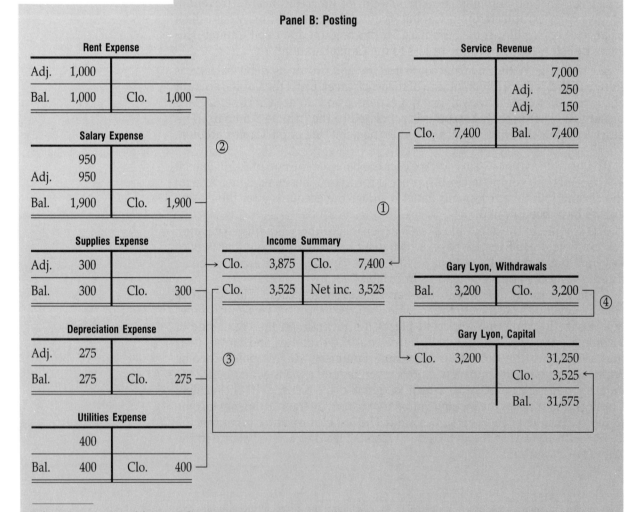

Adj. = Amount posted from an adjusting entry
Clo. = Amount posted from a closing entry
Bal. = Balance
Net inc. = Net income

After all the closing entries, the revenues, expenses and withdrawals accounts are set back to zero to make ready for the next period. The owner's Capital account includes the full effects of the April revenues, expenses and withdrawals. These amounts, combined with Capital's beginning balance, give this account an ending balance of $31,575. You should determine that this Capital balance agrees with the amount reported on the statement of owner's equity and on the balance sheet in Exhibit 4-7. Also note that the ending balance of Capital remains. We do not close it out, because it is a permanent account.

What would the closing entries be, if Lyon's business had suffered a net *loss* during April? Only closing entries 2 and 3 would be altered. Suppose April expenses totaled $7,700 and all other factors were unchanged. Closing entry 2 would transfer expenses of $7,700 to Income Summary, which would appear as follows:

Income Summary	
Clo. 7,700	Clo. 7,400
Net loss 300	

Closing entry 3 would then credit Income Summary to close its debit balance and to transfer the net loss to Capital as follows:

3.	Apr. 30	Gary Lyon, Capital	300	
		Income Summary		300

After posting, these two accounts would appear as follows:

Income Summary			Gary Lyon, Capital	
Clo. 7,700	Clo. 7,400	→ Clo. 300	31,250
Net loss 300	Clo. 300		

Finally, the Withdrawals balance would be closed to Capital, as illustrated in Exhibit 4-9.

Postclosing Trial Balance

The accounting cycle ends with the **postclosing trial balance** (see Exhibit 4-10). The postclosing trial balance is the final check on the accuracy of journalizing and posting the adjusting and closing entries. Like the trial balance that begins the worksheet, the postclosing trial balance is a list of the ledger's accounts and balances. This step ensures that the ledger is in balance for the start of the next accounting period. The postclosing trial balance is dated as of the end of the accounting period for which the statements have been prepared.

Note that the postclosing trial balance resembles the balance sheet. It contains the ending balances of the permanent accounts — the assets, liabilities and the owner's equity of the entity. No temporary accounts — revenues, expenses or withdrawal accounts — are included because their balances have been closed.

EXHIBIT 4-10   *Postclosing Trial Balance*

Gary Lyon, CA Postclosing Trial Balance April 30, 19X1		
Cash..	$24,800	
Accounts receivable	2,500	
Supplies..	400	
Prepaid rent..	2,000	
Furniture...	16,500	
Accumulated depreciation...........................		$ 275
Accounts payable		13,100
Salary payable		950
Unearned service revenue...........................		300
Gary Lyon, capital.................................		31,575
Total..	$46,200	$46,200

OBJECTIVE 5

Classify assets and liabilities as current or long-term

Classification of Assets and Liabilities

On the balance sheet, assets and liabilities are classified as either *current* or *long-term* to indicate their relative *liquidity*. **Liquidity** is a measure of how quickly an item may be converted to cash. Therefore, cash is the most liquid asset. Accounts receivable is a relatively liquid asset because the business expects to collect the amount in cash in the near future. Supplies are less liquid than accounts receivable, and furniture and buildings are even less so because of the difficulty of selling them, that is, turning them into cash. Supplies, such as pens and stationery are more easily sold than used office furniture or a building.

Users of financial statements are interested in liquidity because business difficulties often arise owing to a shortage of cash. How quickly can the business convert an asset to cash and pay a debt? How soon must a liability be paid? These are questions of liquidity. Balance sheets list assets and liabilities in the order of their relative liquidity.

Assets

Current Assets   **Current assets** are assets that are expected to be converted to cash, sold or consumed during the next 12 months or within the business's normal operating cycle if longer than a year. The *operating cycle* is the time it takes to go from cash to a receivable and back to cash. The operating cycle of a merchandising entity provides an illustration of the cash to cash idea embodied in the definition of the cycle. A company uses cash A to buy inventory which it then sells for a promise to pay or account receivable. When the account receivable is collected, the company will have cash B; it has gone from cash to cash. The time it takes to go from A to B is the operating cycle. A fast-food outlet has a very short operating cycle; a company that builds large office buildings will have an operating cycle that is several years long. For most businesses, the operating cycle is a few months. A few types of business have operating cycles longer than a year. Cash, Accounts Receivable, Notes Receivable and Prepaid Expenses are current assets. Merchandising entities such as Eaton's, The Bay and Zellers have an additional current asset, Inventory. This account shows the cost of goods that are held for sale to customers.

Long-Term Assets   **Long-term assets** are all assets other than current assets.

They are not held for sale, but rather they are used to operate the business. One category of long-term assets is plant assets or fixed assets. Land, Buildings, Furniture and Fixtures, and Equipment are examples of plant assets.

Liabilities

Financial statement users such as creditors are interested in the due dates of an entity's liabilities. The sooner a liability must be paid, the more current it is. Liabilities that must be paid on the earliest future date create the greatest strain on cash. Therefore, the balance sheet lists liabilities in the order in which they are due. Knowing how many of a business's liabilities are current and how many are long-term helps creditors assess the likelihood of collecting from the entity. Balance sheets usually have at least two liability classifications, *current liabilities* and *long-term liabilities*.

Current Liabilities   **Current liabilities** are debts that are due to be paid within one year or one of the entity's operating cycles if the cycle is longer than a year. Accounts Payable, Notes Payable due within one year, Salaries Payable, Unearned Revenue and Interest Payable owed on notes payable are current liabilities.

Long-Term Liabilities   All liabilities that are not current are classified as **long-term liabilities**. Many notes payable are long-term. Other notes payable are paid in installments, with the first installment due within one year, the second installment due the second year, and so on. In this case, the first installment would be a current liability and the remainder a long-term liability.

An Actual Classified Balance Sheet

Exhibit 4-11 is a classified balance sheet of Brampton Brick Limited. Brampton Brick combines all its plant assets under the title Fixed Assets.

As you study the balance sheet, you will be delighted at how much of it you understand. You have been exposed to the more common assets and liabilities reported by this actual company. You will note, however, that there are other accounts, such as Income Taxes Recoverable, Deferred Property Development Costs, Deferred Plant Start-up Costs, Minority Interest and Deferred Taxes, with which you will not be familiar. These accounts will become familiar to you as your study of financial accounting progresses.

Formats of Balance Sheets _____

The balance sheet of Brampton Brick shown in Exhibit 4-11 lists the assets at the top, with the liabilities and owner's equity (called shareholders' equity in Exhibit 4-11) below. This is the **report format**. The balance sheet of Gary Lyon, CA, presented in Exhibit 4-7 lists the assets at the left, with the liabilities and the owner's equity at the right. That is the **account format**.

Either format is acceptable. A recent survey of 600 companies indicated that 56 percent use the account format and 44 percent use the report format.

Detecting and Correcting Accounting Errors _____

You have now learned all the steps that an accountant takes from opening the books and recording a transaction in the journal through closing the books and the postclosing trial balance. Along the way, errors may occur. Accounting

EXHIBIT 4-11   *Classified Balance Sheet*

Brampton Brick Ltd.
Balance Sheet
December 31, 1988

	(dollar amounts in thousands)
Assets	
Current assets	
Cash and short-term investments	$ 116
Accounts receivable	6,664
Inventories	8,286
Income taxes recoverable	3,702
Other current assets	379
	19,147
Fixed assets, at cost (note 2)	64,515
Less: Accumulated depreciation	15,626
	48,889
Other non-current assets	
Deferred property development costs (note 3)	1,548
Deferred plant start-up costs (note 2)	704
Goodwill, less amortization of $146	2,284
Investments and other	19
	4,555
	$72,591
Liabilities and Shareholders' Equity	
Current liabilities	
Bank indebtedness (note 4)	$ 1,477
Accounts payable and accrued liabilities	5,001
Dividends payable	474
Long-term debt, current portion (note 5)	233
	7,185
Long-term debt, less current portion (note 5)	20,000
Minority interest	242
Deferred income taxes	7,324
	27,566
Shareholders' equity	
Capital stock (note 6)	24,970
Retained earnings	12,870
	37,840
	$72,591

errors include incorrect journal entries, posting mistakes, and transpositions and slides. This section discusses their detection and correction.

OBJECTIVE 6
Correct typical accounting errors

Incorrect Journal Entries   When a journal entry contains an error, the entry can be erased and corrected—if the error is caught immediately. Other accountants prefer to draw a line through the incorrect entry to maintain a record of all entries to the journal. After the incorrect entry is crossed out, the accountant can make the correct entry.

If the error is detected later, the accountant makes a *correcting entry*. Suppose Gary Lyon paid $5,000 cash for office furniture and erroneously debited Supplies as follows:

Incorrect Entry

May 13   Supplies   5,000
                 Cash   5,000
                 Bought supplies.

The debit to Supplies is incorrect, so it is necessary to make a correcting entry as follows:

Correcting Entry

May 15   Office Furniture   5,000
                 Supplies..............................   5,000
                 To correct May 13 entry.

The credit to Supplies in the second entry offsets the incorrect debit of the first entry. The debit to Office Furniture in the correcting entry places the purchase amount in the correct account.

Incorrect Posting   Sometimes an accountant posts a debit as a credit or a credit as a debit. Such an error shows up in the trial balance: total debits do not equal total credits.

Suppose a $100 debit to Cash is posted as a $100 credit. Cash and the trial balance's total debits are $200 too low and won't balance with the credits. The difference comes to $200. Whenever a debit or credit has been misplaced, the resulting difference is evenly divisible by 2, as is the $200 figure in our example. Dividing that difference by 2 yields the amount of the incorrect posting, which in this case we know to be $100. The accountant may then search the journal for the misplaced $100 entry and make the corrections.

Transpositions and Slides   A **transposition** occurs when digits are flip-flopped; for example, $85 is a transposition of $58. Transpositions cause errors that are evenly divisible by 9. In this particular case, the transposition causes a $27 error ($85 — $58), which is evenly divisible by 9 ($27/9 = $3).

A **slide** results from adding one or more zeroes to a number or from dropping off a zero, for example, writing $500 as $5,000 or vice versa. The difference of $4,500 ($5,000 — $500) is evenly divisible by 9 ($4,500/9 = $500).

Transpositions and slides occur in the transfer of numbers, for example, from the journal to the ledger or from the ledger to the trial balance.

Incorrect postings, transpositions and slides can be corrected by crossing out the incorrect amount and then inserting the correct amount in its appropriate place.

Microcomputer Spreadsheets _____

OBJECTIVE 7
Explain how a microcomputer spreadsheet can be used in accounting

Companies offer a variety of specialized computer programs known as **software** that require almost no computer programming expertise. Some software programs create an electronically prepared work sheet, also called a **spreadsheet**. The spreadsheet can be programmed to complete the work sheet after the accountant has entered the trial balance and the adjustment amounts. This is a big time-saver, because once the spreadsheet program is set up, it can be used over and over again without having to rewrite the account titles and do the arithmetic by hand. The spreadsheet can also be programmed to journalize and post the adjusting and closing entries, and prepare the financial statements directly from the data on the work sheet.

To illustrate how a spreadsheet can be programmed to complete the work sheet, let us focus on the Accounts Receivable account. Assume that the goal is to determine Accounts Receivable's balance sheet amount of $2,500. The Accounts Receivable line from Exhibit 4-4 follows:

Account Title	Trial Balance		Adjustments		Adjusted Trial Balance		Income Statement		Balance Sheet	
	Debit	*Credit*	*Debit*	*Credit*	*Debit*	*Credit*	*Debit*	*Credit*	*Debit*	*Credit*
Cash										
Accounts receivable	2,250		250		2,500				2,500	
Supplies										

How can the accountant use a spreadsheet program to accomplish this task? The spreadsheet appears on a video screen as a matrix of columns and lines, with no amounts or labels. Assume the spreadsheet provides a work space of 500 columns and 500 lines as follows:

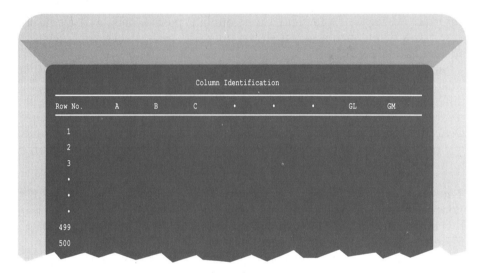

Using the keyboard of a microcomputer, the accountant can program the spreadsheet to resemble a work sheet. The columns are labeled to represent the work sheet columns, and the lines represent the accounts listed on the trial balance. It is also necessary to label the spaces where the dollar amounts go. The accountant may denote Accounts Receivable's unadjusted trial balance amount as w, a debit adjustment as x, a credit adjustment as y and Accounts Receivable's adjusted balance as z. Thus labeled, the partial spreadsheet appears on the video screen as follows:

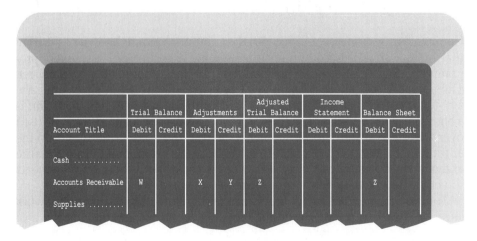

A fully computerized accounting system can transfer the account balances from the ledger to the trial balance. These amounts, plus or minus the adjustments, equal the adjusted balances. The accountant can program the computer to complete the work sheet as follows:

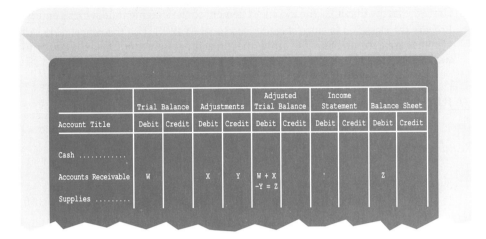

Gary Lyon can use the keyboard to enter the following values into the computer: w = $2,250; x = $250; and y = $0. The spreadsheet takes over and computes z = $2,500 for the adjusted trial balance and the balance sheet. The accountant gives the computer a print command, and it prints the completed work sheet as shown for Accounts Receivable at the beginning of this section. The other account balances are generated similarly.

As in a manual system, the completed work sheet yields the amounts for the adjusting entries, closing entries and financial statements. The beauty of the spreadsheet is that once the computer program is written, it can perform its task as often as desired with no arithmetic errors. As the business changes and new accounts are needed, the accountant can simply insert the new account titles and adapt the spreadsheet program accordingly.

Summary Problem for Your Review

Refer to the data in the earlier Summary Problem for Your Review, presented on p. 140.

Required

1. Journalize and post the adjusting entries. (Before posting to the accounts, enter their balances as shown in the trial balance. For example, enter the $370,000 balance in the Accounts Receivable account before posting its adjusting entry.) Key adjusting entries by letter, as shown in the work sheet solution to the first review problem. You can take the adjusting entries straight from the work sheet on p. 141.

2. Journalize and post the closing entries. (Again, each account should carry its balance as shown in the trial balance.) To distinguish closing entries from adjusting entries, key the closing entries by number. Draw the arrows to illustrate the flow of data,

as shown in Exhibit 4-9, p. 146. Indicate the balance of the Capital account after the closing entries are posted.

3. Prepare the income statement for the year ended December 31, 19X1. List Miscellaneous Expense last among the expenses, a common practice.

4. Prepare the statement of owner's equity for the year ended December 31, 19X1. Draw the arrow that links the income statement to the statement of owner's equity.

5. Prepare the classified balance sheet at December 31, 19X1. Use the report form. All liabilities are current. Draw the arrow that links the statement of owner's equity to the balance sheet.

SOLUTION TO REVIEW PROBLEM

Requirement 1

a.	Dec. 31	Supplies Expense	4,000	
		Supplies...............................		4,000
b.	31	Depreciation Expense—Furniture and Fixtures .	20,000	
		Accumulated Depreciation—Furniture and Fixtures		20,000
c.	31	Depreciation Expense—Building..............	10,000	
		Accumulated Depreciation—Building		10,000
d.	31	Salary Expense	5,000	
		Salary Payable		5,000
e.	31	Accounts Receivable	12,000	
		Service Revenue		12,000
f.	31	Unearned Service Revenue	32,000	
		Service Revenue		32,000

Accounts Receivable		Supplies		Accumulated Depreciation —Furniture and Fixtures	
370,000		6,000	(a) 4,000		40,000
(e) 12,000					(b) 20,000

Accumulated Depreciation —Building		Salary Payable		Unearned Service Revenue	
	130,000		(d) 5,000	(f) 32,000	45,000
	(c) 10,000				

Service Revenue		Salary Expense		Supplies Expense	
	286,000	172,000		(a) 4,000	
	(e) 12,000	(d) 5,000			
	(f) 32,000			Bal. 4,000	
		Bal. 177,000			
	Bal. 330,000				

Depreciation Expense —Furniture and Fixtures		Depreciation Expense —Building	
(b) 20,000		(c) 10,000	
Bal. 20,000		Bal. 10,000	

Requirement 2

1.	Dec. 31	Service Revenue..............................	330,000	
		Income Summary		330,000
2.	31	Income Summary.............................	224,000	
		Salary Expense.........................		177,000
		Supplies Expense		4,000
		Depreciation Expense — Furniture and Fixtures		20,000
		Depreciation Expense — Building		10,000
		Miscellaneous Expense..................		13,000
3.	31	Income Summary ($330,000 — $224,000)	106,000	
		Sally Gunz, Capital		106,000
4.	31	Sally Gunz, Capital	65,000	
		Sally Gunz, Withdrawals		65,000

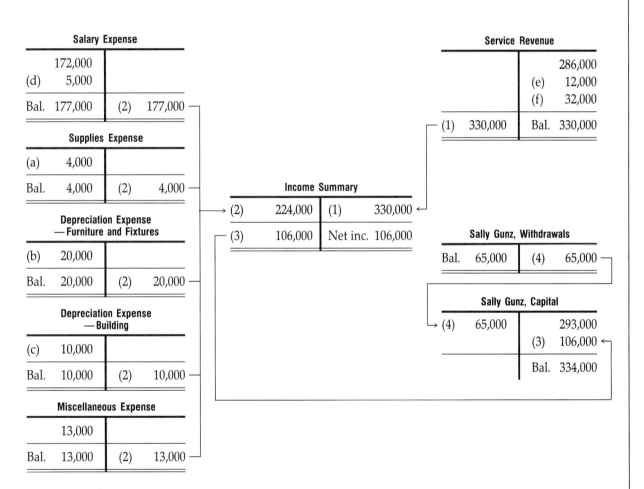

Requirement 3

Sally's Service Company
Income Statement
for the year ended December 31, 19X1

Revenues		
Service revenue		$330,000
Expenses		
Salary expense	$177,000	
Depreciation expense—furniture and fixtures ..	20,000	
Depreciation expense—building	10,000	
Supplies expense	4,000	
Miscellaneous expense	13,000	
Total expenses		224,000
Net Income		$106,000

Requirement 4

Sally's Service Company
Statement of Owner's Equity
for the year ended December 31, 19X1

Sally Gunz, Capital, January 1, 19X1	$293,000
Add: Net income	106,000
	399,000
Less: Withdrawals	65,000
Sally Gunz, Capital, December 31, 19X1	$334,000

Requirement 5

Sally's Service Company
Balance Sheet
December 31, 19X1

Assets

Current assets			
Cash			$198,000
Accounts receivable			382,000
Supplies			2,000
Total current assets			582,000
Plant assets			
Furniture and fixtures		$100,000	
Less: Accumulated depreciation		60,000	40,000
Building		250,000	
Less: Accumulated depreciation		140,000	110,000
Total plant assets		150,000	
Total assets			$732,000

Liabilities

Current liabilities	
Accounts payable	$380,000
Unearned service revenue	13,000
Salary payable	5,000
Total current liabilities	398,000

Owner's Equity

Sally Gunz, Capital	334,000
Total liabilities and owner's equity................	$732,000

Summary

The *accounting cycle* is the process by which accountants produce the financial statements for a specific period of time. The cycle starts with the beginning account balances. During the period, the business journalizes transactions and posts them to the ledger accounts. At the end of the period, the *work sheets* are prepared beginning with the trial balance; the accounts are adjusted on the work sheets to measure the period's income. The work sheet is a columnar document that summarizes the effects of all the activity of the period. It is neither a journal nor a ledger but merely a convenient device for completing the accounting cycle.

The work sheet has columns for the trial balance, adjustments, adjusted trial balance, income statement and balance sheet. It aids the adjusting process, and it is the place where the period's net income or net loss is first computed. The work sheet also provides the data for the financial statements and closing entries. However, it is *not* necessary. The accounting cycle can be completed from the less elaborate adjusted trial balance.

Revenues, expenses and withdrawals represent increases and decreases in owner's equity for a specific period. At the end of the period, their balances are closed out to zero and, for this reason, are called *temporary accounts*. Assets, liabilities and capital are not closed, because they are the *permanent accounts*. Their balances at the end of one period become the beginning balances of the next period. The final accuracy check of the period is the *postclosing trial balance*.

Four common accounting errors are *incorrect journal entries, incorrect postings, transpositions* and *slides*. Techniques exist for detecting and correcting these errors.

Microcomputer *spreadsheets* are extremely useful for tasks such as completing the accounting cycle. Their main advantage is that they can be programmed to print documents such as the work sheet and perform repetitious calculations without errors.

Self-Study Questions

Test your understanding of the chapter by marking the correct answer to each of the following questions:

1. The focal point of the accounting cycle is the *(p. 131)*
   a. Financial statements
   b. Trial balance
   c. Adjusted trial balance
   d. Work sheet

2. Arrange the following accounting cycle steps in their proper order *(p. 132)*:
   a. Complete the work sheet
   b. Journalize and post adjusting entries
   c. Prepare the postclosing trial balance
   d. Journalize and post cash transactions
   e. Prepare the financial statements
   f. Journalize and post closing entries

3. The work sheet is a *(p. 132)*
   a. Journal
   b. Ledger
   c. Financial statement
   d. Convenient device for completing the accounting cycle

4. The usefulness of the work sheet is *(p. 132)*
   a. Identifying the accounts that need to be adjusted
   b. Summarizing the effects of all the transactions of the period
   c. Aiding the preparation of the financial statements
   d. All of the above

5. Which of the following accounts is not closed? *(pp. 143, 144)*
   a. Supplies Expense
   b. Prepaid Insurance
   c. Interest Revenue
   d. Owner Withdrawals

6. The closing entry for Salary Expense, with a balance of $322,000, is *(pp. 145, 146)*
   a. Salary Expense.......................... 322,000
       Income Summary   322,000
   b. Salary Expense.......................... 322,000
       Salary Payable   322,000
   c. Income Summary 322,000
       Salary Expense   322,000
   d. Salary Payable 322,000
       Salary Expense   322,000

7. The purpose of the postclosing trial balance is to *(p. 147)*
   a. Provide the account balances for preparation of the balance sheet
   b. Ensure that the ledger is in balance for the start of the next period
   c. Aid the journalizing and posting of the closing entries
   d. Ensure that the ledger is in balance for completion of the work sheet

8. Which of the following accounts will appear on the postclosing trial balance? *(p. 147)*
   a. Building
   b. Depreciation Expense — Building
   c. Service Revenue
   d. Owner Withdrawals

9. The classification of assets and liabilities as current or long-term depends on *(p. 148)*
   a. Their order of listing in the general ledger
   b. Whether they appear on the balance sheet or the income statement
   c. The relative liquidity of the item
   d. The format of the balance sheet — account format or report format

10. Posting a $300 debit as a credit causes an error *(p. 151)*
    a. That is evenly divisible by 9
    b. That is evenly divisible by 2
    c. In the journal
    d. Known as a transposition

Answers to the self-study questions are at the end of the chapter.

Accounting Vocabulary

account format of the balance
  sheet *(p. 149)*
accounting cycle *(p. 131)*
closing entry *(p. 145)*
closing the accounts *(p. 142)*
current assets *(p. 148)*
current liabilities *(p. 149)*
income summary *(p. 145)*

liquidity *(p. 148)*
long-term assets *(p. 148)*
long-term liabilities *(p. 149)*
nominal account *(p. 144)*
permanent account *(p. 144)*
postclosing trial balance
  (p. 147)
real account *(p. 144)*

report format of the balance
  sheet *(p. 149)*
slide *(p. 151)*
software *(p. 151)*
spreadsheet *(p. 151)*
temporary account *(p. 144)*
transposition *(p. 151)*
work sheet *(p. 132)*

Assignment Material _____

Questions

1. Identify the steps in the accounting cycle, distinguishing those that occur during the period from those that are performed at the end.

2. Why is the work sheet a valuable accounting tool?

3. Name two advantages the work sheet has over the adjusted trial blance.

4. Why must the adjusting entries be journalized and posted if they have already been entered on the work sheet?

5. Why should the adjusting entries be journalized and posted before making the closing entries?

6. Which types of accounts are closed?

7. What purpose is served by closing the accounts?

8. State how the work sheet helps with recording the closing entries.

9. Distinguish between permanent accounts and temporary accounts, indicating which type is closed at the end of the period. Give five examples of each type of account.

10. Is Income Summary a permanent account or a temporary account? When and how is it used?

11. Give the closing entries for the following accounts (balances in parentheses): Service Revenue ($4,700), Salary Expense ($1,100), Income Summary (credit balance of $2,000), Rhonda McGill, Withdrawals ($2,300).

12. Why are assets classified as current or long-term? On what basis are they classified? Where do the classified accounts appear?

13. Indicate which of the following accounts are *current assets* and which are *long-term assets*: Prepaid Rent, Building, Furniture, Accounts Receivable, Merchandise Inventory, Cash, Note Receivable (due within one year), Note Receivable (due after one year).

14. In what order are assets and liabilities listed on the balance sheet?

15. Name an outside party that is interested in whether a liability is current or long-term. Why is this party interested in this information?

16. A friend tells you that the difference between a current liability and a long-term liability is that they are payable to different types of creditors. Is your friend correct? Include in your answer the definitions of these two categories of liabilities.

17. Give the name of the following accounting errors:
    a. Posted a $300 debit from the journal as a $300 credit in the ledger.
    b. Posted a $300 debit from the journal as a $3,000 debit in the ledger.
    c. Recorded a transaction by debiting one account for $3,100 and crediting the other account for $1,300.

18. How could you detect each of the errors in the preceding question?

19. Capp Company purchased supplies of $120 on account. The accountant debited Supplies and credited Cash for $120. A week later, after this entry has been posted to the ledger, the accountant discovers the error. How should he correct the error?

20. Briefly explain how a microcomputer spreadsheet can be programmed to complete the work sheet.

Exercises

Exercise 4-1   *Preparing a work sheet*

The trial balance of Alban's TV Repair Service follows on the next page.

Additional information at September 30, 19X6:

a. Accrued salary expense, $600
b. Prepaid rent expired, $900
c. Supplies used, $2,250
d. Accrued service revenue, $210
e. Depreciation, $70

Alban's TV Repair Service
Trial Balance
September 30, 19X6

Cash..	$ 1,560	
Accounts receivable	2,840	
Prepaid rent	1,200	
Supplies...................................	3,390	
Equipment	12,600	
Accumulated depreciation....................		$ 2,240
Accounts payable		1,600
Salary payable		
Ned Alban, capital.........................		16,030
Ned Alban, withdrawals	3,000	
Service revenue		7,300
Depreciation expense		
Salary expense	1,800	
Rent expense		
Utilities expense	780	
Supplies expense...........................		
Total.....................................	$27,170	$27,170

Required

Complete Alban's work sheet for September 19X6.

Exercise 4-2   *Journalizing adjusting and closing entries*

Journalize the adjusting and closing entries in Exercise 4-1.

Exercise 4-3   *Posting adjusting and closing entries*

Set up T-accounts for those accounts affected by the adjusting and closing entries in Exercise 4-1. Post the adjusting and closing entries to the accounts, denoting adjustment amounts by Adj., closing amounts by Clo. and balances by Bal. Double rule the accounts with zero balances after closing and show the ending balance in each account.

Exercise 4-4   *Preparing a postclosing trial balance*

Prepare the postclosing trial balance in Exercise 4-1.

Exercise 4-5   *Identifying and journalizing closing entries*

From the following selected accounts that Fortin Sales Company reported in its June 30, 19X4 annual financial statements, prepare the entity's closing entries.

Prepaid expenses	$ 600	Interest expense	$ 2,200
Service revenue	90,500	Accounts receivable	26,000
Unearned revenues	1,350	Salary payable	850
Salary expense	15,500	Depreciation expense	10,200
Accumulated depreciation	35,000	Rent expense	5,900
Supplies expense	1,400	A. Fortin, withdrawals	40,000
Interest revenue	700	Supplies	1,100

Exercise 4-6 *Identifying and journalizing closing entries*

The accountant for Trish O'Malley, Lawyer has posted adjusting entries *a* through *e* to the accounts at December 31, 19X2. All the revenue, expense and capital accounts of the entity are listed here in T-account form.

Accounts Receivable		Supplies		Accumulated Depreciation — Furniture	
23,000		4,000	(a) 2,000		5,000
(e) 3,500					(b) 3,000

Accumulated Depreciation — Building		Salary Payable		Trish O'Malley, Capital	
	33,000		(d) 1,500		49,400
	(c) 6,000				

Trish O'Malley, Withdrawals		Service Revenue		Salary Expense	
52,400			103,000	28,000	
			(e) 3,500	(d) 1,500	

Supplies Expense		Depreciation Expense — Furniture		Depreciation Expense — Building	
(a) 2,000		(b) 3,000		(c) 6,000	

Required

Journalize O'Malley's closing entries at December 31, 19X2.

Exercise 4-7 *Preparing a statement of owner's equity*

From the following accounts of Kathryn Hopkins Realty Company, prepare the entity's statement of owner's equity for the year ended December 31, 19X5.

Kathryn Hopkins, Capital			Kathryn Hopkins, Withdrawals		
Dec. 31 34,000	Jan. 1	35,000	Mar. 31 8,000	Dec. 31	34,000
	Mar. 9	28,000	Jun. 30 8,000		
	Dec. 31	43,000	Sept. 30 8,000		
			Dec. 31 10,000		

Income Summary		
Dec. 31 85,000	Dec. 31	128,000
Dec. 31 43,000		

Exercise 4-8 *Identifying and recording adjusting and closing entries*

The trial balance and income statement amounts are presented from the March work sheet of Tekell Service Company on the next page.

Account Title	Trial Balance		Income Statement	
Cash	$ 3,100			
Supplies	2,400			
Prepaid rent.......................	1,100			
Office equipment	36,800			
Accumulated depreciation		$ 6,900		
Accounts payable		10,600		
Salary payable......................				
Unearned service revenue		4,400		
Angela Tekell, capital.................		14,800		
Angela Tekell, withdrawals	1,000			
Service revenue......................		12,700		$16,000
Salary expense......................	3,000		$ 3,800	
Rent expense.......................	1,200		1,400	
Depreciation expense			400	
Supplies expense			1,700	
Utilities expense	800		800	
	$49,400	$49,400	$ 8,100	$16,000
Net income			7,900	
			$16,000	$16,000

Required

Journalize the adjusting and closing entries of Tekell Service Company at March 31.

Exercise 4-9   *Preparing a classified balance sheet*

Use the data in Exercise 4-8 to prepare Tekell Service Company's classified balance sheet at March 31 of the current year. Use the report format.

Exercise 4-10   *Correcting accounting errors*

Prepare a correcting entry for each of the following accounting errors:

a. Recorded a $400 cash purchase of supplies by debiting Supplies and crediting Accounts Payable.
b. Debited Office Furniture and credited Cash for a $2,300 credit purchase of office equipment.
c. Adjusted prepaid rent by debiting Prepaid Rent and crediting Rent Expense for $900. This adjusting entry should have debited Rent Expense and credited Prepaid Rent for $900.
d. Debited Salary Expense and credited Cash to accrue salary expense of $300.
e. Recorded the earning of $3,200 service revenue collected in advance by debiting Accounts Receivable and crediting Service Revenue.
f. Accrued interest revenue of $800 by a debit to Accounts Receivable and a credit to Interest Revenue.

(Group A)

Problem 4-1A   *Preparing financial statements from an adjusted trial balance; journalizing adjusting and closing entries*

The adjusted trial balance of Ikeda Service Company at June 30, 19X1, the end of the company's fiscal year, follows:

Ikeda Service Company
Adjusted Trial Balance
June 30, 19X1

Cash	$ 3,350	
Accounts receivable	11,470	
Supplies	1,290	
Prepaid insurance	1,700	
Equipment	55,800	
Accumulated depreciation — equipment		$ 16,480
Building	144,900	
Accumulated depreciation — building		16,850
Accounts payable		36,900
Interest payable		1,490
Wage payable		770
Unearned service revenue		2,300
Note payable, long-term		104,000
Gayle Ikeda, capital		37,390
Gayle Ikeda, withdrawals	52,300	
Service revenue		108,360
Depreciation expense — equipment	6,300	
Depreciation expense — building	3,470	
Wage expense	18,800	
Insurance expense	3,100	
Interest expense	11,510	
Utilities expense	4,300	
Property tax expense	2,670	
Supplies expense	3,580	
Total	$324,540	$324,540

Additional data at June 30, 19X1:

a. Supplies used during the year, $3,580
b. Prepaid insurance expired during the year, $3,100
c. Accrued interest expense, $680
d. Accrued service revenue, $940
e. Depreciation for the year: equipment, $6,300; building, $3,470
f. Accrued wage expense, $770
g. Unearned service revenue earned during the year, $6,790

Required

1. Prepare Ikeda's income statement and statement of owner's equity for the year ended June 30, 19X1 and the classified balance sheet on that date. Use the account format for the balance sheet.
2. Journalize the adjusting and closing entries.

Problem 4-2A   *Preparing a work sheet*

The trial balance of Schoepplein Painting Contractors at July 31, 19X3 follows on the next page.

Additional data at July 31, 19X3:

a. Accrued wage expense, $440
b. Supplies on hand, $14,740

c. Prepaid insurance expired during July, $500
d. Accrued interest expense, $180
e. Unearned service revenue earned during July, $4,770
f. Accrued advertising expense, $100 (Credit Accounts Payable)
g. Accrued service revenue, $1,100
h. Depreciation: equipment, $430; building, $270

Schoepplein Painting Contractors
Trial Balance
July 31, 19X3

Cash	$ 4,200	
Accounts receivable	37,820	
Supplies	17,660	
Prepaid insurance	2,300	
Equipment	32,690	
Accumulated depreciation—equipment		$ 26,240
Building	36,890	
Accumulated depreciation—building		10,500
Land	28,300	
Accounts payable		22,690
Interest payable		
Wage payable		
Unearned service revenue		10,560
Note payable, long-term		22,000
Leslie Schoepplein, capital		62,130
Leslie Schoepplein, withdrawals	4,200	
Service revenue		17,190
Depreciation expense—equipment		
Depreciation expense—building		
Wage expense	5,800	
Insurance expense		
Interest expense		
Utilities expense	270	
Property tax expense	840	
Advertising expense	340	
Supplies expense		
Total	$171,310	$171,310

Required

Complete Schoepplein's work sheet for July.

Problem 4-3A   *Taking the accounting cycle through the closing entries*

The unadjusted T-accounts of Julie Warner, M.D. at December 31, 19X2 and the related year-end adjustment data follow:

Cash	Accounts Receivable	Supplies
Bal. 7,000	Bal. 38,000	Bal. 9,000

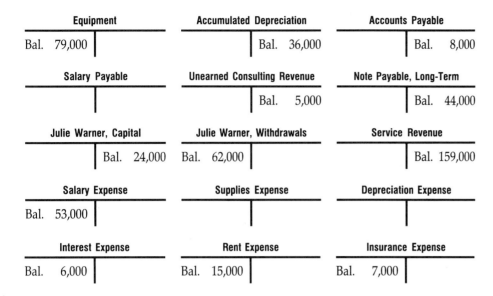

Equipment		Accumulated Depreciation		Accounts Payable	
Bal. 79,000			Bal. 36,000		Bal. 8,000

Salary Payable		Unearned Consulting Revenue		Note Payable, Long-Term	
			Bal. 5,000		Bal. 44,000

Julie Warner, Capital		Julie Warner, Withdrawals		Service Revenue	
	Bal. 24,000	Bal. 62,000			Bal. 159,000

Salary Expense		Supplies Expense		Depreciation Expense	
Bal. 53,000					

Interest Expense		Rent Expense		Insurance Expense	
Bal. 6,000		Bal. 15,000		Bal. 7,000	

Adjustment data at December 31, 19X2:

a. Supplies on hand, $1,000
b. Depreciation for the year, $9,000
c. Accrued salary expense, $2,000
d. Accrued service revenue, $1,000
e. Unearned consulting revenue earned during the year, $5,000

Required

1. Write the trial balance on a work sheet, and complete the work sheet. Key each adjusting entry by the letter corresponding to the data given.
2. Prepare the income statement, statement of owner's equity and classified balance sheet in account format.
3. Journalize the adjusting and closing entries.

✓ Problem 4-4A   *Completing the accounting cycle*

This problem should be used only in conjunction with Problem 4-3A. It completes the accounting cycle by posting to T-accounts and preparing the postclosing trial balance.

Required

1. Using the Problem 4-3A data, post the adjusting and closing entries to the T-accounts, denoting adjusting amounts by Adj., closing amounts by Clo. and account balances by Bal., as shown in Exhibit 4-9. Double underline all accounts with a zero ending balance.
2. Prepare the postclosing trial balance.

Problem 4-5A   *Completing the accounting cycle*

The trial balance of Vachon Realty at August 31, 19X9 and the data needed to make the month-end adjustments are as follows on the next page.

Adjustment data:

a. Prepaid insurance still in force at August 31, $1,190

b. Supplies used during the month, $140
c. Depreciation on building for the month, $130
d. Depreciation on furniture for the month, $370
e. Accrued salary expense at August 31, $460
f. Unearned commission revenue still unearned at August 31, $7,750

Vachon Realty
Trial Balance
August 31, 19X9

Account Number	Account Title	Debit	Credit
11	Cash	$ 6,800	
12	Accounts receivable	17,560	
13	Prepaid insurance........................	1,290	
14	Supplies	900	
15	Furniture	15,350	
16	Accumulated depreciation — furniture		$ 12,800
17	Building	89,900	
18	Accumulated depreciation — building		28,600
21	Accounts payable		6,240
22	Salary payable		—
23	Unearned commission revenue		8,900
31	R. Vachon, capital.......................		74,920
32	R. Vachon, withdrawals	4,800	
41	Commission revenue		7,800
51	Salary expense...........................	1,600	
52	Insurance expense	—	
53	Utilities expense	410	
54	Depreciation expense — furniture...........	—	
55	Depreciation expense — building	—	
56	Advertising expense......................	650	
57	Supplies expense	—	
	Total	$139,260	$139,260

Required

1. Open the accounts listed in the trial balance, inserting their August 31 unadjusted balances. Also open the Income Summary account, number 33. Date the balances of the following accounts as of August 1: Prepaid Insurance, Supplies, Building, Accumulated Depreciation — Building, Furniture, Accumulated Depreciation — Furniture, Unearned Commission Revenue and R. Vachon, Capital.

2. Record the trial balance on a work sheet and complete the work sheet of Vachon Realty for the month ended August 31 of the current year.

3. Prepare the income statement, statement of owner's equity and classified balance sheet in report format.

4. Using the work sheet data, journalize and post the adjusting and closing entries. Use dates and posting references. Use page 7 as the number of the journal page.

5. Prepare a postclosing trial balance.

Problem 4-6A *Preparing a classified balance sheet in report format*

The accounts of Matusak Sales Agency at December 31, 19X6 are listed in alphabetical order. All adjustments have been journalized and posted, but the closing entries have not yet been made. Prepare the company's classified balance sheet in report format at December 31, 19X6. Show total assets, total liabilities, and total liabilities and owner's equity.

Accounts payable	$ 3,100	Inventory	$ 6,600
Accounts receivable	4,600	Lou Matusak, capital,	
Accumulated depreciation—		December 31, 19X5	50,300
building	37,800	Lou Matusak, withdrawals	47,400
Accumulated depreciation—		Note payable, long-term	7,800
furniture	11,600	Note receivable, long-term	4,000
Advertising expense	2,200	Other assets	3,600
Building	84,400	Other current assets	1,700
Cash	4,500	Other current liabilities	4,700
Commission revenue	93,500	Prepaid insurance	1,100
Current portion of note payable	2,200	Rent expense	1,300
Current portion of note receivable	1,000	Salary expense	22,600
Furniture	22,700	Salary payable	1,900
Insurance expense	800	Supplies	2,500
Interest payable	600	Supplies expense	5,700
Interest receivable	200	Unearned commission revenue	3,400

Problem 4-7A *Analysing and journalizing corrections, adjustments, and closing entries*

Accountants for Mills Service Company, a proprietorship, encountered the following situations while adjusting and closing the books at December 31. Consider each situation independently.

a. The company bookkeeper made the following entry to record a $400 credit purchase of supplies:

> Nov. 12 Office Furniture 400
> Accounts Payable   400

Prepare the correcting entry, dated December 31.

b. A $750 debit to Cash was posted as a credit.
(1) At what stage of the accounting cycle will this error be detected?
(2) Describe the technique for identifying the amount of the error.

c. The $35,000 balance of Equipment was entered as $3,500 on the trial balance.
(1) What is the name of this type of error?
(2) Assume this is the only error in the trial balance. Which will be greater, the total debits or the total credits, and by how much?
(3) How can this type of error be identified?

d. The accountant failed to make the following adjusting entries at December 31:
(1) Accrued property tax expense, $600
(2) Supplies expense, $1,390
(3) Accrued interest revenue on a note receivable, $950
(4) Depreciation of equipment, $4,000
(5) Earned service revenue that had been collected in advance, $5,300
Compute the overall net income effect of these omissions.

e. Record each of the adjusting entries identified in item *d*.

f. The revenue and expense accounts after the adjusting entries had been posted were Service Revenue, $55,800; Salary Expense, $13,200; Rent Expense, $5,100; Advertising Expense, $3,550; Utilities Expense, $1,530; and Miscellaneous Expense, $1,190. Two balances prior to closing were J. E. Mills, Capital, $58,600; and J. E. Mills, Withdrawals, $30,000. Journalize the closing entries.

(Group B)

Problem 4-1B   *Preparing financial statements from an adjusted trial balance; journalizing adjusting and closing entries*

The adjusted trial balance of Chun Consultants at April 30, 19X2, the end of the company's fiscal year, follows:

Chun Consultants
Adjusted Trial Balance
April 30, 19X2

Cash	$ 2,370	
Accounts receivable	25,740	
Supplies	3,690	
Prepaid insurance	2,290	
Equipment	63,930	
Accumulated depreciation—equipment		$ 28,430
Building	74,330	
Accumulated depreciation—building		18,260
Accounts payable		19,550
Interest payable		2,280
Wage payable		830
Unearned service revenue		3,660
Note payable, long-term		77,900
Vivian Chun, capital		46,200
Vivian Chun, withdrawals	55,500	
Service revenue		99,550
Depreciation expense—equipment	6,700	
Depreciation expense—building	3,210	
Wage expense	29,800	
Insurance expense	5,370	
Interest expense	8,170	
Utilities expense	5,670	
Property tax expense	3,010	
Supplies expense	6,880	
Total	$296,660	$296,660

Additional data at April 30, 19X2:

a. Supplies used during the year, $6,880
b. Prepaid insurance expired during the year, $5,370
c. Accrued interest expense, $2,280
d. Accrued service revenue, $2,200
e. Depreciation for the year: equipment, $6,700; building, $3,210
f. Accrued wage expense, $830
g. Unearned service revenue earned during the year, $5,180

Required

1. Prepare Chun's income statement and statement of owner's equity for the year ended April 30, 19X2 and the classified balance sheet on that date. Use the account format for the balance sheet.
2. Journalize the adjusting and closing entries.

Problem 4-2B   *Preparing a work sheet*

The trial balance of Kowalski Realty Brokers at May 31, 19X2 follows:

Kowalski Realty Brokers
Trial Balance
May 31, 19X2

Cash	$ 1,670	
Notes receivable	10,340	
Interest receivable		
Supplies	560	
Prepaid insurance	1,790	
Furniture	27,410	
Accumulated depreciation — furniture		$ 1,480
Building	55,900	
Accumulated depreciation — building		33,560
Land	13,700	
Accounts payable		14,730
Interest payable		
Salary payable		
Unearned commission revenue		6,800
Note payable, long-term		18,700
John Kowalski, capital		34,290
John Kowalski, withdrawals	3,800	
Commission revenue		9,970
Depreciation expense — furniture		
Depreciation expense — building		
Salary expense	2,170	
Insurance expense		
Interest expense		
Utilities expense	490	
Property tax expense	640	
Advertising expense	1,060	
Supplies expense		
Total	$119,530	$119,530

Additional data at May 31, 19X2:

a. Accrued salary expense, $600
b. Supplies on hand, $410
c. Prepaid insurance expired during May, $390
d. Accrued interest expense, $220
e. Unearned commission revenue earned during May, $1,400
f. Accrued advertising expense, $60 (Credit Accounts Payable)
g. Accrued interest revenue, $170
h. Depreciation for May: furniture, $380; building, $160

Required

Complete Kowalski's work sheet for May.

Problem 4-3B   *Taking the accounting cycle through the closing entries*

The unadjusted T-accounts of Steve Deitmer, M.D. at December 31, 19X2 and the related year-end adjustment data follow:

Cash	Accounts Receivable	Supplies
Bal. 8,000	Bal. 44,000	Bal. 6,000

Equipment	Accumulated Depreciation	Accounts Payable
Bal. 57,000	Bal. 12,000	Bal. 4,000

Salary Payable	Unearned Consulting Revenue	Note Payable, Long-Term
	Bal. 2,000	Bal. 38,000

Steve Deitmer, Capital	Steve Deitmer, Withdrawals	Service Revenue
Bal. 41,000	Bal. 54,000	Bal. 133,000

Salary Expense	Supplies Expense	Depreciation Expense
Bal. 36,000		

Interest Expense	Rent Expense	Insurance Expense
Bal. 5,000	Bal. 12,000	Bal. 8,000

Adjustment data at December 31, 19X2:

a. Supplies on hand, $2,000
b. Depreciation for the year, $6,000
c. Accrued salary expense, $3,000
d. Accrued service revenue, $4,000
e. Unearned consulting revenue earned during the year, $2,000

Required

1. Write the trial balance on a work sheet and complete the work sheet. Key each adjusting entry by the letter corresponding to the data given.
2. Prepare the income statement, statement of owner's equity and classified balance sheet in account format.
3. Journalize the adjusting and closing entries.

Problem 4-4B   *Completing the accounting cycle*

This problem should be used only in conjunction with Problem 4-3B. It completes the accounting cycle by posting to T-accounts and preparing the postclosing trial balance.

Required

1. Using the Problem 4-3B data, post the adjusting and closing entries to the T-accounts, denoting adjusting amounts by Adj., closing amounts by Clo. and account balances by Bal., as shown in Exhibit 4-9. Double underline all accounts with a zero ending balance.
2. Prepare the postclosing trial balance.

Problem 4-5B *Completing the accounting cycle*

The trial balance of Houle Realty at October 31, 19X0 and the data needed for the month-end adjustments are as follows:

Houle Realty
Trial Balance
October 31, 19X0

Account Number	Account Title	Debit	Credit
11	Cash	$ 1,900	
12	Accounts receivable	12,310	
13	Prepaid insurance........................	2,200	
14	Supplies	840	
15	Furniture	26,830	
16	Accumulated depreciation — furniture		$ 3,400
17	Building	68,300	
18	Accumulated depreciation — building		9,100
21	Accounts payable		7,290
22	Salary payable		—
23	Unearned commission revenue		5,300
31	Y. Houle, capital		85,490
32	Y. Houle, withdrawals	3,900	
41	Commission revenue		8,560
51	Salary expense...........................	1,840	
52	Insurance expense	—	
53	Utilities expense	530	
54	Depreciation expense — furniture...........	—	
55	Depreciation expense — building	—	
56	Advertising expense......................	490	
57	Supplies expense	—	
	Total	$119,140	$119,140

Adjustment data:

a. Prepaid insurance still in force at October 31, $2,000
b. Supplies used during the month, $570
c. Depreciation on building for the month, $280
d. Depreciation on furniture for the month, $250
e. Accrued salary expense at October 31, $310
f. Unearned commission revenue still unearned at October 31, $4,700

Required

1. Open the accounts listed in the trial balance, inserting their October 31 unadjusted balances. Also open the Income Summary account, number 33. Date the balances of the following accounts as of October 1: Prepaid Insurance, Supplies, Building, Accumulated Depreciation — Building, Furniture, Accumulated Depreciation — Furniture, Unearned Commission Revenue and Y. Houle, Capital.
2. Record the trial balance on a work sheet and complete the work sheet of Houle Realty for the month ended October 31 of the current year.

3. Prepare the income statement, statement of owner's equity and classified balance sheet in report format.
4. Using the work sheet data, journalize and post the adjusting and closing entries. Use dates and posting references. Use 12 as the number of the journal page.
5. Prepare a postclosing trial balance.

Problem 4-6B   *Preparing a classified balance sheet in report format*

The accounts of Varma Travel Agency at March 31, 19X3 are listed in alphabetical order. All adjustments have been journalized and posted, but the closing entries have not yet been made. Prepare the company's classified balance sheet in report format at March 31, 19X3. Show total assets, total liabilities, and total liabilities and owner's equity.

Accounts payable	$ 2,700	Interest receivable	$ 800
Accounts receivable	11,500	Inventory	4,700
Accumulated depreciation —building	47,300	Bikash Varma, capital, March 31, 19X2	32,800
Accumulated depreciation —furniture	27,700	Bikash Varma, withdrawals	31,200
Advertising expense	900	Note payable, long-term	3,200
Building	55,900	Note receivable, long-term	6,900
Cash	1,400	Other assets	1,300
Commission revenue	71,100	Other current assets	900
Current portion of note payable	800	Other current liabilities	1,100
Current portion of note receivable	3,100	Prepaid insurance	600
		Rent expense	1,900
Furniture	43,200	Salary expense	17,800
Insurance expense	600	Salary payable	1,400
Interest payable	200	Supplies	3,800
		Supplies expense	4,600
		Unearned commission revenue	2,800

Problem 4-7B   *Analysing and journalizing corrections, adjustments, and closing entries*

The auditors of Lane Service Company, a proprietorship, encountered the following situations while adjusting and closing the books at February 28. Consider each situation independently.

a. The company bookkeeper made the following entry to record a $950 credit purchase of supplies:

Feb. 26   Supplies 950
              Cash 950

Prepare the correcting entry, dated February 28.

b. A $390 credit to Accounts Receivable was posted as $930.
   (1) At what stage of the accounting cycle will this error be detected?
   (2) Describe the technique for identifying the amount of the error.

c. The $5,630 balance of Utilities Expense was entered as $56,300 on the trial balance.
   (1) What is the name of this type of error?
   (2) Assume this is the only error in the trial balance. Which will be greater, the total debits or the total credits, and by how much?
   (3) How can this type of error be identified?

d. The accountant failed to make the following adjusting entries at February 28:
   (1) Accrued service revenue, $700
   (2) Supplies expense, $1,460
   (3) Accrued interest expense on a note payable, $520

(4) Depreciation of building, $3,300

(5) Earned service revenue that had been collected in advance, $2,700

Compute the overall net income effect of these omissions.

e. Record each of the adjusting entries identified in item *d*.

f. The revenue and expense accounts after the adjusting entries had been posted were Service Revenue, $95,330; Wage Expense, $29,340; Rent Expense, $6,180; Interest Expense, $4,590; Utilities Expense, $1,620; and Supplies Expense, $740. Two balances prior to closing were W. T. Lane, Capital, $75,150 and W. T. Lane, Drawing, $48,000. Journalize the closing entries.

Decision Problems

1. *Completing the accounting cycle to develop the information for a bank loan*

One year ago, your friend John T. Williams founded Williams Computing Service. The business has prospered. Williams, who remembers that you took an accounting course while in college, comes to you for advice. He wishes to know how much net income his business earned during the past year. He also wants to know what the entity's total assets, liabilities and capital are. His accounting records consist of the T-accounts of his ledger, which were prepared by an accountant who moved to another city. The ledger at December 31 of the current year is

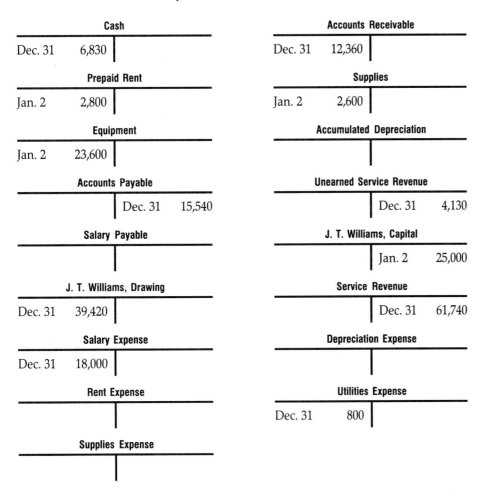

Williams indicates that at the year's end customers owe him $1,600 accrued service revenue, which he expects to collect early next year. These revenues have not been recorded. During the year he collected $4,130 service revenue in advance from customers, but he earned only $1,190 of that amount. Rent expense for the year was $2,400, and he used up $2,100 in supplies. Williams estimates that depreciation on his equipment was $5,900 for the year. At December 31, he owes his employee $1,200 accrued salary.

At the conclusion of your meeting, Williams expresses concern that his withdrawals during the year might have exceeded his net income. To get a loan to expand his business, he must show the bank that his capital account has grown from its original $25,000 balance. You and Williams agree that you will meet again in one week. You perform the analysis and prepare the financial statements to answer his questions.

2. Finding an error in the work sheets

You are preparing the financial statements for the year ended October 31, 19X5 for Ron Publishing Ltd., a weekly newspaper. You began with the trial balance of the ledger, which balanced, and then made the required adjusting entries. To save time, you omitted preparing an adjusted trial balance. After making the adjusting entries, you extended the balances from the trial balance adjusted for the adjusting entries to the income statement and balance sheet columns.

a. You added the debits and credits on the income statement and found that the credits exceeded the debits by $X. Did Ron Publishing have a profit or a loss based on your finding?

b. You entered the balancing amount from the income statement columns in the balance sheet columns and found the total debits did not equal the total credits in the latter. The difference between the debits and credits is twice the amount ($2X) you calculated in question a. What is the likely cause of the difference? What assumption have you made in your answer?

c. Assume no error was made in entering the balancing amount from the income statement columns to the balance sheet columns. The total debits do not equal the total credits in the balance sheet. You check the adding machine tape and find you have added the two columns in each of the income statement and balance sheet correctly. Where might you look for the error?

Financial Statement Problem

Using an actual balance sheet

This problem, based on John Labatt's balance sheet in Appendix E, will familiarize you with some of the assets and liabilities of this actual company. Answer these questions, using John Labatt's balance sheet:

1. Which balance sheet format does John Labatt use?

2. Name the company's largest current asset and largest current liability at April 30, 1989?

3. How much were total current assets and total current liabilities at April 30, 1989? Which had increased by the greater percentage during the year ended April 30, 1989: total current assets or total current liabilities?

4. John Labatt has two different categories of account receivable at April 30, 1989. What are they called and what amounts are due to John Labatt under each?

5. What is John Labatt's total long-term debt? How much is due in the year ended April 30, 1990?

6. Does John Labatt have cash on hand at April 30, 1989, or does the company have loans due to its bankers?

Answers to Self-Study Questions

1. a	3. d	5. b	7. b	9. c
2. d, a, e, b, f, c	4. d	6. c	8. a	10. b

5

Merchandising and the Accounting Cycle

LEARNING OBJECTIVES

After studying this chapter, you should be able to

1 Explain the operating cycle of a merchandising business

2 Account for the purchase and sale of inventory

3 Compute cost of goods sold and gross margin

4 Prepare a merchandiser's financial statements

5 Adjust and close the accounts of a merchandising business

6 Recognize different formats of the income statement

In the first four chapters we discussed accounting for a business that earns revenue by selling its services, using Gary Lyon, CA as our example. Service enterprises include Four Seasons Hotels, Canadian Airlines, physicians, lawyers, public accountants, the Edmonton Oilers hockey team, and the twelve-year-old who cuts lawns in your neighborhood. A *merchandising entity* earns its revenue by selling products, called *merchandise inventory* or, simply, *inventory*. A Canadian Tire store, a Loblaws grocery, a Woodwards department store and an ice-cream shop are merchandising entities. Exhibit 5-1 shows the income statement for an actual merchandising business. You will notice that this income statement differs from those you have seen thus far.

EXHIBIT 5-1   *A Merchandiser's Income Statement*

Prairie Supply Company Income Statement for the year ended December 31, 19X6		
Net sales revenue		$680,000
Cost of goods sold		370,000
Gross margin		310,000
Operating expenses		
Salary expense	$130,000	
Rent expense	60,000	
Insurance expense	18,000	
Depreciation expense	14,000	
Supplies expense	8,000	230,000
Net income		$ 80,000

The amounts that a merchandiser earns from selling its inventory before subtracting expenses is called **sales revenue**, often abbreviated as **sales**. The income statement in Exhibit 5-1 reports sales revenue of $680,000. The major revenue of a merchandising entity, sales revenue, represents the increase in owner's equity from delivering inventory to customers. The major expense of a merchandiser is *Cost of Goods Sold*. This expense's title is well chosen, because this account represents the cost to the entity of the goods (inventory) it has sold to customers. As long as inventory is held, it is an asset. Once a unit of inventory has been sold to the customer, it is no longer an asset; the unit's cost becomes an expense (cost of goods sold). The excess of Sales Revenue over Cost of Goods Sold is called **gross margin** or **gross profit**. This important business statistic is often mentioned in the business press because it helps measure a business's success. The higher the gross margin, the more successful a given business will usually be.

If a company can increase its gross margin and keep its operating expenses constant, it will be more profitable. Gross margin for a product may be increased by increasing the product's selling price or by reducing the cost of the product. For example, consider a blouse that The Bay purchases for $25 and sells for $49; the gross margin is $24. The Bay could increase the gross margin by purchasing the blouse for less than $25 and retaining the selling price of $49, or by continuing to buy the blouse for $25 but increasing the selling price to more than $49.

The following illustration will clarify the nature of gross margin. Consider a concession stand at a football game. Assume the business sells a soft drink for $1.00 and the vendor's cost is $.20. Gross margin per unit is $.80 ($1.00 − $.20), and the overall gross margin is $.80 multiplied by the number of drinks sold. If the concession stand sells 400 drinks on a Saturday afternoon, its gross margin on drink sales is $320 (400 × $.80). The gross margin on all sales, including hot dogs, popcorn and candy, is the sum of the gross margins on all the items sold. Petro-Canada's gross margin — and that of a Red and White grocery store, a neighborhood drug store and every other merchandiser — is computed in exactly the same way: Sales − Cost of Goods Sold = Gross Margin.

Margin in gross margin refers to the excess of revenue over expense. *Gross* indicates that the operating expenses (rent, depreciation, advertising, and so on) have not yet been subtracted. After subtracting all the expenses we have *net income*. Gross margin and net income are not accounts in the ledger, so we cannot make journal entries to them. Instead, we compute these amounts by subtracting one amount from another: Gross Margin − Operating Expenses = Net Income. Study Exhibit 5-1, focusing on the sales revenue, cost of goods sold and gross margin. Also note the separate category for operating expenses.

The Operating Cycle for a Merchandising Business _____

A merchandising entity buys inventory, sells the inventory to its customers and uses the cash to purchase more inventory to repeat the cycle. Exhibit 5-2 diagrams the flows of resources from *cash sales* and from *sales on account*. For a cash sale (item *a* in the exhibit) resources flow from cash to inventory, which is purchased for resale and back to cash. For a sale on account (item *b*) the cycle is from cash to inventory to accounts receivable and back to cash. This cycle is very important for two reasons: (1) it represents the major source of a business's cash, and (2) it explains a large portion of all business transactions.

EXHIBIT 5-2 *Operating Cycle of a Merchandiser*

OBJECTIVE 1
Explain the operating cycle of a merchandising business

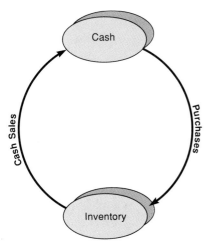

a. Purchase and Cash Sale

b. Purchase and Sale on Account

Purchase of Inventory

The flow of resources of a merchandising entity begins with the purchase of inventory, as Exhibit 5-2 shows. **Purchases**, in the accounting sense, are only those items of inventory that a firm buys to resell to customers in the normal course of business. For example, a stereo centre records in the Purchases account the price it pays for tape decks, turntables and other items of inventory acquired for resale. A bicycle shop records Purchases when it buys ten-speeds for its inventory. A grocery store debits Purchases when it buys canned goods, meat, frozen food, and so on.

The Purchase Invoice: A Basic Business Document

Business documents are the tangible evidence of transactions. As we trace the steps that Austin Sound takes in ordering, receiving and paying for inventory, we point out the roles that documents play in carrying on business.

1. Suppose Austin Sound wants to stock JVC brand turntables, cassette decks and speakers. Austin prepares a *purchase order* and mails it to JVC.
2. On receipt of the purchase order, JVC scans its warehouse for the inventory that Austin Sound ordered. JVC ships the equipment and mails the invoice to Austin on the same day. The **invoice** is the seller's request for payment from the purchaser. It is also called the *bill*.
3. Often the purchaser receives the invoice before the inventory arrives. Austin Sound does not pay immediately. Instead, Austin waits until the inventory arrives in order to ensure that it is (1) the correct type, (2) the quantity ordered and (3) in good condition. After the inventory is inspected and approved, Austin Sound pays JVC the invoice amount.

Exhibit 5-3 is a copy of an actual invoice from JVC to Austin Sound Stereo Centre. From Austin Sound's perspective, this document is a *purchase invoice*, whereas to JVC it is a *sales invoice*. The circled numbers that appear on the exhibit correspond to the following numbered explanations:

1.   The seller is JVC Maritimes Branch.
2.   The invoice date is 05/27/89. The date is needed for determining whether the purchaser gets a discount for prompt payment (see item 5 below).
3.   The purchaser is Austin Sound Stereo Centre. The inventory is invoiced (billed) and shipped to the same address, 305 West Mackenzie King Blvd., Halifax, Nova Scotia.
4.   Austin Sound's purchase order (P.O.) date was 05/25/89.
5.   Credit terms of the transaction are 3% 15, NET 30 DAYS. This means that Austin Sound may deduct 3 percent of the total amount due if Austin pays within 15 days of the invoice date, not the purchase order date. Otherwise, the full amount (net) is due in 30 days. (A full discussion of discounts appears in the next section.)
6.   Austin Sound ordered 6 turntables, 3 cassettes decks and 2 speakers.
7.   JVC shipped 5 turntables, no cassette decks and no speakers.
8.   Total invoice amount is $707.

EXHIBIT 5-3   *Business Invoice*

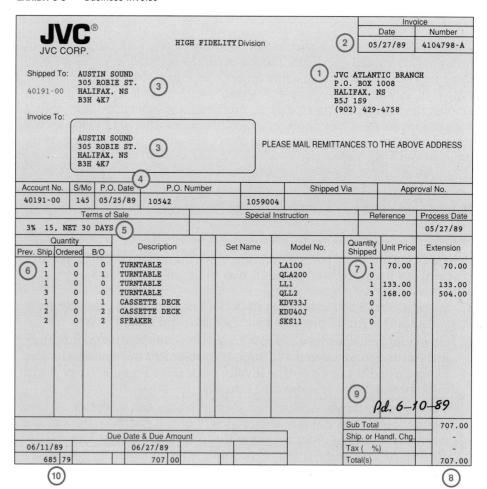

9. Austin Sound paid on 6-10-89. How much did Austin pay?
10. Payment occurred 14 days after the invoice date — within the discount period. Therefore, Austin Sound paid $685.79 ($707 minus the 3 percent discount).

Discounts from Purchase Prices

There are two major types of discounts from purchase prices: cash discounts (called purchase discounts) and trade discounts.

Purchase Discounts

Many businesses offer inventory purchase discounts to their customers. A **purchase discount** is a reduction in the cost of inventory that is offered by the seller as an incentive for the customer to pay promptly. JVC's credit terms of 3% 15 NET 30 DAYS can also be expressed as 3/15 n/30. Terms of simply n/30 indicate that no discount is offered and that payment is due within 30 days of the invoice date. Terms of eom mean that payment is due by the end of the month.

Let us use the Exhibit 5-3 transaction to illustrate accounting for a *purchase discount*. Austin Sound records this purchase on account as follows:

May 25	Purchases	707.00	
	Accounts Payable		707.00
	Purchased inventory on account.		

> **OBJECTIVE 2**
> Account for the purchase and sale of inventory

Since Austin Sound paid within the discount period, its cash payment entry is

June 9	Accounts Payable	707.00	
	Cash ($707.00 × .97)		685.79
	Purchase Discounts ($707.00 × .03)		21.21
	Paid on account within discount period.		

Purchase Discounts, which has a credit balance, is a contra account to Purchases. We show how to report Purchase Discounts on the income statement later in the chapter.

Alternatively, if Austin Sound pays this invoice after the discount period, it must pay the full invoice amount. In this case, the payment entry is

June 29	Accounts Payable...........................	707.00	
	Cash...................................		707.00
	Paid on account after discount period.		

Purchases can also be made for cash. Suppose Austin Sound had phoned JVC to place this order and had learned that the net cost would be $685.79. After mailing a cheque along with the purchase order, Austin Sound would record the cash purchase as follows:

May 25	Purchases	685.79	
	Cash...................................		685.79
	Cash purchase of inventory.		

In this case, Purchases is recorded at the net amount and there is no entry to Purchase Discounts.

Trade Discounts

A second type of discount is the **trade discount**, which works this way: the larger the quantity purchased, the lower the price per item. For example, JVC may offer no trade discount for the purchase of only one or two cassette decks and charge the list price (the full price) of $200 per unit. However, JVC may offer the following trade discount terms in order to persuade customers to buy a larger number of cassette decks:

Quantity	Trade Discount	Net Price Per Unit
Buy minimum quantity, 3 cassette decks	5%	$190 [$200 − .05($200), or $10]
Buy 4–9 decks	10%	$180 [$200 − .10($200), or $20]
Buy more than 9 decks	20%	$160 [$200 − .20($200), or $40]

Suppose Austin Sound purchases 5 cassette decks from this manufacturer. The cost of each unit is, therefore, $180. Purchase of five units on account would be recorded by debiting Purchases and crediting Accounts Payable for the total price of $900 ($180 × 5).

There is no trade discount account and no special accounting entry for a trade discount. Instead, all accounting entries are based on the net price of a purchase after subtracting the trade discount.

Purchase Returns and Allowances

Most businesses allow their customers to *return* merchandise that is defective, damaged in shipment or otherwise unsuitable. Or if the buyer chooses to keep damaged goods, the seller may deduct an *allowance* from the amount the buyer owes. Because returns and allowances are similar — they both decrease the buyer's debt — they are usually recorded in a single account, **Purchase Returns and Allowances**. This account is a contra account to Purchases. Later in the chapter, we show how to report this account on the income statement.

Suppose the $70 turntable purchased by Austin Sound (Exhibit 5-3) was not the turntable ordered. Austin returns the merchandise to the seller and records the purchase return as follows:

June 3	Accounts Payable	70.00	
	Purchase Returns and Allowances		70.00
	Returned inventory to seller.		

Now assume that one of the JVC turntables is damaged in shipment to Austin Sound. The damage is minor, and Austin decides to keep the turntable in exchange for a $10 allowance from JVC. To record this purchase allowance, Austin Sound makes this entry:

June 4	Accounts Payable	10.00	
	Purchase Returns and Allowances		10.00
	Received a purchase allowance.		

Observe that the return and the allowance had two effects. (1) They decreased Austin Sound's liability, which is why we debit Accounts Payable. (2) They decreased the net cost of the inventory, which is why we credit

Purchase Returns and Allowances. It would be incorrect to credit Purchases because Austin Sound did in fact make the purchase. Changes due to returns and allowances are recorded in the contra account.

During the period, the business records the cost of all inventory bought in the Purchases account. The balance of Purchases is a *gross* amount because it does not include subtractions for purchase discounts, returns or allowances. **Net purchases** is the remainder that is computed by subtracting the contra accounts as follows:

> Purchases (*debit* balance account)
> − **Purchase discounts** (*credit* balance account)
> − **Purchase returns and allowances** (*credit* balance account)
> _____
> = **Net purchases (a subtotal, not a separate account)**

Transportation Costs

The transportation cost of moving inventory from seller to buyer can be significant. The purchase agreement specifies FOB terms to indicate who pays the shipping charges. The term *FOB* stands for *free on board* and governs when the legal title to the goods passes from seller to buyer. Under *FOB shipping point* terms, title passes when the inventory leaves the seller's place of business. The buyer owns the goods while they are in transit, and therefore pays the transportation cost and is responsible for insurance. Under *FOB destination* terms, the seller pays transportation cost and is responsible for insuring the inventory while it is in transit.

	FOB Shipping Point	FOB Destination
When does title pass to buyer?	Shipping point	Destination
Who pays transportation cost?	Buyer	Seller

Generally, the buyer bears the shipping cost. The buyer debits Freight In (sometimes called Transportation In) and credits Cash or Accounts Payable for the amount. Suppose the buyer receives a shipping bill directly from the freight company. The payment entry is

March 3	Freight In	190	
	Cash		190
	Paid a freight bill.		

The seller sometimes prepays the transportation cost as a convenience and lists this cost on the invoice. The buyer would *not* debit Purchases for the combined cost of the inventory and the shipping cost. Rather, the buyer would debit Purchases for the cost of the goods and Freight In separately as follows:

March 12	Purchases	5,000	
	Freight In................................	400	
	Accounts Payable		5,400
	Purchased inventory on account plus freight.		

Purchase discounts and trade discounts are computed only on the cost of the inventory, *not* on the freight charges. Suppose the $5,000 credit purchase allows a $100 discount for early payment. The cash payment within the discount period would be $5,300 [net payment of $4,900 on the inventory ($5,000, less the $100 purchase discount), plus the freight charges of $400].

Sale of Inventory

The sale of inventory may be for cash or on account, as Exhibit 5-2 shows.

Cash Sale   A significant proportion of the sales of retailers like department stores, drug stores, gift shops and restaurants are for cash. A $300 cash sale is recorded by debiting Cash and crediting the revenue account, Sales Revenue, as follows:

Jan. 9	Cash	300	
	Sales Revenue		300
	Cash sale.		

Sale on Account   Most sales by wholesalers, manufacturers and retailers are made on account or on credit. A $5,000 sale on account is recorded by a debit to Accounts Receivable and a credit to Sales Revenue as follows:

Jan. 11	Accounts Receivable...........................	5,000	
	Sales Revenue............................		5,000
	Sale on account.		

The related cash receipt on account is journalized by the following entry:

Jan. 19	Cash	5,000	
	Accounts Receivable		5,000
	Collection on account.		

Sales Discounts, Sales Returns and Allowances

Sales Discounts and **Sales Returns and Allowances** are contra accounts to **Sales Revenue,** just as Purchase Discounts, and Purchase Returns and Allowances are contra accounts to Purchases. Let us take a sequence of the sale transactions of JVC. Suppose JVC uses one account for Sales Returns and Allowances.

On July 7, JVC sells stereo components with a list price of $8,000, subject to a 10 percent trade discount and credit terms of 2/10 n/30. JVC's entry to record this credit sale is based on the net amount after subtracting the trade discount as follows:

July 7	Accounts Receivable [$8,000 − .10($8,000)]	$7,200	
	Sales Revenue...........................		$7,200
	Sale on account.		

Assume the buyer returns goods that cost $600. JVC records the sales return and the related decrease in Accounts Receivable as follows:

July 12	Sales Returns and Allowances	600	
	Accounts Receivable......................		600
	Received returned goods.		

JVC grants a $100 sales allowance for damaged goods. JVC journalizes this transaction by debiting Sales Returns and Allowances and crediting Accounts Receivable as follows:

July 15	Sales Returns and Allowances	100	
	Accounts Receivable......................		100
	Granted a sales allowance for damaged goods.		

After the preceding entries are posted, Accounts Receivable has a $6,500 debit balance as follows:

Accounts Receivable

July 7	7,200	July 12	600
		15	100
Bal.	6,500		

On July 17, the last day of the discount period, JVC collects half ($3,250) of this receivable ($6,500 × ½ = $3,250). The cash receipt is $3,185 [$3,250 − (.02 × $3,250)], and the collection entry is

July 17	Cash	3,185	
	Sales Discounts (.02 × $3,250)	65	
	Accounts Receivable		3,250
	Cash collection with the discount period.		

Suppose JVC collects the remainder on July 28 (after the discount period), so there is no sales discount. To record this collection on account, JVC debits Cash and credits Accounts Receivable for the same amount as follows:

July 28	Cash	3,250	
	Accounts Receivable		3,250
	Cash collection after the discount period.		

NET SALES is computed in a manner similar to net purchases. We subtract the contra accounts as follows:

> **Sales revenue (*credit* balance account)**
> **− Sales discounts (*debit* balance account)**
> **− Sales returns and allowances (*debit* balance account)**
> _____
> **= Net sales (a subtotal, not a separate account)**

Cost of Goods Sold

Cost of goods sold is the largest single expense of most merchandising businesses. It is the cost of the inventory that the business has sold to customers. Another name for cost of goods sold is **cost of sales**. How is it computed?

Recall from Chapter 3 that supplies expense is computed as follows:

Beginning supplies
+ Supplies purchased during the period

= Supplies available for use during the period
− Supplies on hand at the end of the period

= Supplies expense

Cost of goods sold is computed this same way, as shown in Exhibit 5-4.

By studying the exhibit, you will see that the computation and the diagram tell the same story. That is, a company's goods available for sale during a period come from beginning inventory and the period's net purchases and freight costs. Either the merchandise is sold during the period or it remains on hand at the end. The merchandise that remains is an asset, Inventory, and the cost of the inventory that has been sold is an expense, Cost of Goods Sold.

Two main types of inventory accounting systems exist: the periodic system and the perpetual system. In this chapter, we illustrate the periodic inventory system because it highlights the relationship between inventory and cost of goods sold, as shown in Exhibit 5-4. This model for computing expense is used throughout accounting and is extremely useful for analytical purposes. Furthermore, the periodic system is used by many small businesses, such as the proprietorships we use as illustrations in the early chapters of this book. Chapter 9 illustrates the perpetual system.

EXHIBIT 5-4 *Measurement of Cost of Goods Sold*

Computation:

Beginning inventory
+ Net purchases
+ Freight in

= Cost of goods available for sale
− Ending inventory

= Cost of goods sold

Diagram:

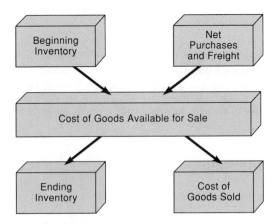

Under the periodic system, the business does not keep a running record of the cost of its inventory on hand. Instead, it counts the goods on hand at the end of each period to determine the inventory to be reported on the balance sheet. This ending inventory amount becomes the beginning inventory of the next period and is used to compute cost of goods sold for the income statement. Thus entries to the Inventory account are made only at the end of the period.

In this inventory system, cost of goods sold is *not* a ledger account like Salary Expense, Rent Expense and the other operating expenses. Instead, it is the cost left over when we subtract the cost of ending inventory from the cost of goods available for sale. Computationally, cost of goods sold is more complex than the other expenses.

Exhibit 5-5 summarizes the first half of the chapter by showing Austin Sound's net sales, cost of goods sold (including net purchases) and gross margin on the income statement.

> **OBJECTIVE 3**
> Compute cost of goods sold and gross margin

Note that arithmetic operations, addition and subtraction, move across the columns from left to right. For example, the figures for Sales Discounts and Sales Returns and Allowances appear in the left-most column. Their sum, $3,400, appears in the middle column, where it is subtracted from Sales Revenue. The net sales amount of $135,900 appears in the right-most column.

The contra accounts related to sales and purchases — discounts, returns and allowances, and the like — are frequently netted against their related accounts parenthetically. This netting of the contra amounts underscores an important fact: published financial statements usually report only *net* amounts for sales and purchases, because discounts and returns and allowances are relatively small in amount. For most businesses, these contra items are details of primary interest only to managers and therefore are not highlighted in the financial statements. Thus many accountants would report sales in our example as follows:

Net sales revenue (net of sales discounts, $1,400,
  and returns and allowances, $2,000) $135,900

EXHIBIT 5-5   *Partial Income Statement*

Austin Sound			
Income Statement			
for the year ended December 31, 19X6			
Sales revenue		$139,300	
Less: Sales discounts	$ 1,400		
Sales returns and allowances	2,000	3,400	
Net sales revenue			$135,900
Cost of goods sold			
Beginning inventory		$50,500	
Purchases	$89,300		
Less: Purchase discounts	$3,000		
Purchase returns and allowances . .	1,200	4,200	
Net purchases		85,100	
Freight in		5,200	
Cost of goods available for sale		140,800	
Less: Ending inventory		52,000	
Cost of goods sold			88,800
Gross margin			$ 47,100

Purchases can also be reported at its net amount in the following manner:

Cost of goods sold
Beginning inventory . . . . $ 50,500
Net purchases (net of purchase discounts, $3,000,
  and returns and allowances, $1,200)   85,100
Freight in   5,200
Cost of goods available for sale $140,800
Less: Ending inventory.   52,000
    Cost of goods sold . . . . $ 88,800

Summary Problem for Your Review

Brun Sales Company engaged in the following transactions during June of the current year:

June   3   Purchased inventory on credit terms of 1/10 net eom (end of month), $1,610.

       9   Returned 40 percent of the inventory purchased on June 3. It was defective.

       9   Sold goods for cash, $920.

      15   Purchased merchandise of $5,100, less a $100 trade discount. Credit terms were 3/15 net 30.

      16   Paid a $260 freight bill on goods purchased.

      18   Sold inventory on credit terms of 2/10 n/30, $2,200, less a $200 trade discount offered to customers who purchase in large quantities.

      22   Received damaged merchandise from the customer to whom the June 18 sale was made, $800.

      24   Owing to a cash shortage, had to borrow money from the bank to take advantage of the discount offered on the June 15 purchase. Signed a note payable to the bank for this amount.

      24   Paid supplier for goods purchased on June 15, less all discounts.

      28   Received cash in full settlement of the account from the customer who purchased inventory on June 18.

      29   Paid the amount owed on account from the purchase of June 3.

      30   Purchased inventory for cash, $900, less a trade discount of $35.

Required

1. Journalize the above transactions.
2. Assume the note payable signed on June 24 requires the payment of $95 interest expense. Was the decision wise or unwise to borrow funds to take advantage of the cash discount? Support your answer by comparing the discount earned to the interest paid.

SOLUTION TO REVIEW PROBLEM

Requirement 1

June 3	Purchases	1,610	
	Accounts Payable.......................		1,610
9	Accounts Payable ($1,610 × .40)................	644	
	Purchase Returns and Allowances		644
9	Cash.......................................	920	
	Sales Revenue		920
15	Purchases ($5,100 − $100)	5,000	
	Accounts Payable.......................		5,000
16	Freight In	260	
	Cash		260
18	Accounts Receivable ($2,200 − $200)	2,000	
	Sales Revenue		2,000
22	Sales Returns and Allowances	800	
	Accounts Receivable		800
24	Cash [$5,000 − .03($5,000)]	4,850	
	Note Payable		4,850
24	Accounts Payable	5,000	
	Purchase Discounts ($5,000 × .03)		150
	Cash ($5,000 × .97)		4,850
28	Cash [($2,000 − $800) × .98]....................	1,176	
	Sales Discounts [($2,000 − $800) × .02]	24	
	Accounts Receivable ($2,000 − $800)		1,200
29	Accounts Payable ($1,610 − $644)	966	
	Cash		966
30	Purchases ($900 − 35)	865	
	Cash		865

Requirement 2   The decision to borrow funds was wise, because the discount earned ($150) exceeded the interest paid on the amount borrowed ($95). Thus the entity was $55 better off as a result of its decision.

The Adjusting and Closing Process for a Merchandising Business

A merchandising business adjusts and closes the accounts much as a service entity does. The steps of this end-of-period process are the same: enter the trial balance on the work sheet and complete the work sheet to determine net income or net loss. The work sheet provides the data for preparing the financial statements and journalizing the adjusting and closing entries. After these entries are posted to the ledger, a post-closing trial balance can be prepared.

The Inventory account is the major difference between a merchandiser and a service entity. At the end of the period, before any adjusting or closing entries, the Inventory balance is still the cost of the inventory that was on hand at the beginning date. It is necessary to remove this beginning balance and replace it with the cost of the ending inventory. Some accountants view this process as the *adjustment* of the Inventory balance. Other accountants consider it as *closing* the beginning balance of Inventory and setting up the Inventory ending balance. Either method is acceptable as long as the financial statements report the

EXHIBIT 5-6   *Trial Balance*

Austin Sound
Trial Balance
December 31, 19X6

Cash	$ 4,850	
Accounts receivable	17,000	
Note receivable, current	10,000	
Interest receivable		
Inventory	50,500	
Supplies	650	
Prepaid insurance	1,200	
Furniture and fixtures	6,800	
Accumulated depreciation		$ 2,400
Accounts payable		7,000
Unearned sales revenue		2,000
Note payable, long-term		12,600
Interest payable		
W. Nelson, capital		65,900
W. Nelson, withdrawals	34,100	
Sales revenue		138,000
Sales discounts	1,400	
Sales returns and allowances	2,000	
Interest revenue		600
Purchases	89,300	
Purchase discounts		3,000
Purchase returns and allowances		1,200
Freight in	5,200	
Rent expense	8,400	
Depreciation expense		
Insurance expense		
Supplies expense		
Interest expense	1,300	
Total	$232,700	$232,700

Additional data at December 31, 19X6:

a. Interest revenue earned but not yet collected, $400

b. Supplies on hand, $100

c. Prepaid insurance expired during the year, $1,000

d. Depreciation, $600

e. Unearned sales revenue earned during the year, $1,300

f. Interest expense incurred but not yet paid, $200

g. Inventory on hand, $52,000

correct amounts for Inventory on the balance sheet and Cost of Goods Sold on the income statement. The closing entry approach is more popular, so we illustrate that approach in this book.

To illustrate a merchandiser's adjusting and closing process, let us use Austin Sound's December 31, 19X6 trial balance in Exhibit 5-6.

All the new accounts — Inventory, Freight In and the contra accounts — are highlighted for emphasis. However, Inventory is the only account that is affected by the new closing procedures. Note that additional data item g gives the ending inventory of $52,000.

Work Sheet of a Merchandising Business

The Exhibit 5-7 work sheet is similar to the work sheets we have seen so far, but a few differences appear. Note that this work sheet does not include

EXHIBIT 5-7   *Work Sheet*

Austin Sound
Work Sheet
for the year ended December 31, 19X6

Account Title	Trial Balance Debit	Trial Balance Credit	Adjustments Debit	Adjustments Credit	Income Statement Debit	Income Statement Credit	Balance Sheet Debit	Balance Sheet Credit
Cash	4,850						4,850	
Accounts receivable	17,000						17,000	
Note receivable, current	10,000						10,000	
Interest receivable			(a) 400				400	
Inventory	50,500				50,500	52,000	52,000	
Supplies	650			(b) 550			100	
Prepaid insurance	1,200			(c) 1,000			200	
Furniture and fixtures	6,800						6,800	
Accumulated depreciation		2,400		(d) 600				3,000
Accounts payable		7,000						7,000
Unearned sales revenue		2,000	(e) 1,300					700
Note payable, long-term		12,600						12,600
Interest payable				(f) 200				200
W. Nelson, capital		65,900						65,900
W. Nelson, withdrawals	34,100						34,100	
Sales revenue		138,000		(e) 1,300		139,300		
Sales discounts	1,400				1,400			
Sales returns and allowances	2,000				2,000			
Interest revenue		600		(a) 400		1,000		
Purchases	89,300				89,300			
Purchase discounts		3,000				3,000		
Purchase returns and allowances		1,200				1,200		
Freight in	5,200				5,200			
Rent expense	8,400				8,400			
Depreciation expense			(d) 600		600			
Insurance expense			(c) 1,000		1,000			
Supplies expense			(b) 550		550			
Interest expense	1,300		(f) 200		1,500			
	232,700	232,700	4,050	4,050	160,450	196,500	125,450	89,400
Net income					36,050			36,050
					196,500	196,500	125,450	125,450

adjusted trial balance columns. In most accounting systems, a single operation combines trial balance amounts with the adjustments and extends the adjusted balances directly to the income statement and balance sheet columns. Therefore, to reduce clutter, the adjusted trial balance columns are omitted. A second difference is that the merchandiser's work sheet includes inventory amounts (which are highlighted). Let us examine the entire work sheet.

Account Title Columns   The trial balance lists a number of accounts without balances. Ordinarily, these accounts are used only in the adjusting process. Examples include Interest Receivable, Interest Payable and Depreciation Expense. The accounts are listed in the order they appear in the ledger. This eases the preparation of the work sheet. If additional accounts are needed, they can be written in at the bottom of the work sheet before net income is determined. Simply move net income down to make room for the additional accounts.

Trial Balance columns   The trial balance amounts have not yet been adjusted and therefore are unsuitable for the financial statements. On the work sheet, we work toward the ending balance in each account. Examine the Inventory account. Its trial balance amount, $50,500, is the cost of the beginning inventory. The work sheet is designed to replace this outdated amount with the new ending balance, which in our example is $52,000 (additional data item g in Exhibit 5-6).

Adjustments Columns   The adjustments are similar to those discussed in Chapters 3 and 4. They may be entered in any order desired. The debit amount of each entry should equal the credit amount, and total debits should equal total credits.

Income Statement Columns   The income statement columns contain adjusted amounts for the revenues and expenses. Sales Revenue, for example, is $139,300, which includes the $1,300 adjustment. Revenues are credits on the income statement, and expenses are debits.

You may be wondering why the two inventory amounts appear in the income statement columns. The reason is that beginning inventory and ending inventory are part of the computation of cost of goods sold. Recall that beginning inventory is added to cost of goods amount sold and ending inventory is subtracted. Even though the resulting cost of goods sold does not appear on the work sheet, all the components of cost of goods sold are evident there. Placement of beginning inventory ($50,500) in the work sheet's income statement debit column has the effect of removing beginning inventory from assets and including it in the expense of cost of goods sold. Placing ending inventory ($52,000) in the credit column has the effect of subtracting ending inventory from the expense, cost of goods sold, and adding it to assets.

Purchases and Freight In appear in the debit column because they are added in computing cost of goods sold. Purchase Discounts and Purchase Returns and Allowances appear as credits because they are subtracted. Together, all these items are used to compute cost of goods sold, $88,800 on the income statement in Exhibit 5-5.

The income statement column subtotals on the work sheet indicate whether the business earned net income or incurred a net loss. If total credits are greater, the result is net income, as shown in the exhibit. Inserting the net income amount in the debit column brings total debits into agreement with total credits. If total debits are greater, a net loss has occurred. Inserting a net loss amount in the credit column would equalize total debits and total credits. Net income or net loss is then extended to the opposite column of the balance sheet.

Balance Sheet Columns   The only new item on the balance sheet is inventory. The balance listed is the ending amount of $52,000, which is determined by a physical count of inventory on hand at the end of the period, since Austin Sound is using the periodic system.

Financial Statements of a Merchandising Business

Exhibit 5-8 presents Austin Sound's financial statements. The *income statement* through gross margin repeats Exhibit 5-5. This information is followed by the **operating expenses**, which are those expenses incurred in the entity's major line of business — merchandising. Rent is the cost of obtaining store space for Austin Sound's operations. Insurance is necessary to protect the inventory. The business's store furniture and fixtures wear out. The cost of that wear is called depreciation. Supplies expense is the cost of stationery, mailing, packages, and the like, used in operations.

Many companies report their operating expenses in two categories. *Selling expenses* are those expenses related to marketing the company's products: sales salaries; sales commissions; advertising; depreciation, rent, utilities and property taxes on store buildings; depreciation on store furniture; delivery expense, and the like. *General expenses* include *office* expenses, such as the salaries of the company president and office employees who are not engaged in selling, depreciation, rent, utilities, property taxes on the home office building, and supplies.

Gross margin minus operating expenses equals **income from operations**, or **operating income**, as it is also called. Many businesspeople view operating income as the most reliable indicator of a business's success because it measures the entity's major ongoing activities.

The last section of Austin Sound's income statement is **other revenue and expense**. This category reports revenues and expenses that are outside the main operations of the business. Examples include gains and losses on the sale of plant assets (not inventory) and gains and losses on lawsuits. Accountants have traditionally viewed Interest Revenue and Interest Expense as "other" items, because they arise from loaning money and borrowing money — activities that are outside the scope of selling merchandise or, for a service entity, rendering services.

The bottom line of the income statement is net income, which includes the effects of all the revenues and gains less all the expenses and losses. We often hear the term *bottom line* used to refer to a final result. The term originated in the position of net income on the income statement.

A merchandiser's *statement of owner's equity* looks exactly like that of a service business. In fact, you cannot determine whether the entity is merchandising or service oriented from looking at the statement of owner's equity.

If the business is a merchandiser, the *balance sheet* shows inventory as a major asset. In contrast, service businesses usually have minor amounts of inventory.

EXHIBIT 5-8 *Financial Statements of Austin Sound*

Austin Sound
Income Statement
for the year ended December 31, 19X6

Sales revenue			$139,300
Less: Sales discounts.............................		$ 1,400	
Sales returns and allowances		2,000	3,400
Net sales			$135,900
Cost of goods sold			
Beginning inventory		50,500	
Purchases.......................................		89,300	
Less: Purchase discounts	$3,000		
Purchase returns and allowances...........	1,200	4,200	
Net purchases..................................		85,100	
Freight in.......................................		5,200	
Cost of goods available for sale		140,800	
Less: Ending inventory		52,000	
Cost of goods sold			88,800
Gross margin..			47,100
Operating expenses			
Rent expense		8,400	
Insurance expense.............................		1,000	
Depreciation expense		600	
Supplies expense		550	10,550
Income from operations			36,550
Other revenue and expense			
Interest revenue................................		1,000	
Interest expense		(1,500)	(500)
Net income			$ 36,050

Austin Sound
Statement of Owner's Equity
for the year ended December 31, 19X6

W. Nelson, capital, January 1, 19X6	$ 65,900
Add: Net income...	36,050 ←
	101,950
Less: Withdrawals...	34,100
W. Nelson, capital, December 31, 19X6	$ 67,850

Austin Sound
Balance Sheet
December 31, 19X6

Assets

Current		
Cash		$ 3,850
Accounts receivable		18,000
Note receivable..............		10,000
Interest receivable		400
Inventory....................		52,000
Prepaid insurance		200
Supplies		100
Total current assets		84,550
Plant		
Furniture and fixtures........	$6,800	
Less: Accumulated depreciation	3,000	3,800
Total assets		$88,350

Liabilities

Current	
Accounts payable	$ 7,000
Unearned sales revenue	700
Interest payable	200
Total current liabilities	7,900
Long-term	
Note payable....................	12,600
Total liabilities.................	20,500

Owner's Equity

W. Nelson, capital	67,850 ←
Total liabilities and owner's equity ..	$88,350

Adjusting and Closing Entries for a Merchandising Business

Exhibit 5-9A presents Austin Sound's adjusting entries, which are similar to those you have seen previously.

The closing entries in the exhibit include two new effects. The first closing entry debits Inventory for the ending balance of $52,000 and debits the temporary accounts that have credit balances. For Austin Sound, these accounts are Sales Revenue, Purchase Discounts, and Purchase Returns and Allowances. The offsetting credit of $196,500 transfers their sum to Income Summary. This amount comes directly from the credit column of the income statement on the work sheet (Exhibit 5-7).

EXHIBIT 5-9A *Journalizing and Posting the Adjusting and Closing Entries*

Journal
Adjusting Entries

a.	Dec.	31	Interest Receivable	400	
			Interest Revenue		400
b.		31	Supplies Expense ($650 − $100).......	550	
			Supplies.....................		550
c.		31	Insurance Expense	1,000	
			Prepaid Insurance		1,000
d.		31	Depreciation Expense..............	600	
			Accumulated Depreciation		600
e.		31	Unearned Sales Revenue............	1,300	
			Sales Revenue		1,300
f.		31	Interest Expense	200	
			Interest Payable		200

Closing Entries

	Dec.	31	Inventory (ending balance)..........	52,000	
			Sales Revenue	139,300	
			Interest Revenue	1,000	
			Purchase Discounts................	3,000	
			Purchase Returns and Allowances....	1,200	
			Income Summary		196,500
		31	Income Summary	160,450	
			Inventory (beginning balance) ..		50,500
			Sales Discounts		1,400
			Sales Returns and Allowances...		2,000
			Purchases		89,300
			Freight In		5,200
			Interest Expense		1,500
			Rent Expense		8,400
			Supplies Expense.............		550
			Insurance Expense		1,000
			Depreciation Expense..........		600
		31	Income Summary		
			($196,500 − $160,450)	36,050	
			W. Nelson, Capital.............		36,050
		31	W. Nelson, Capital	34,100	
			W. Nelson, Withdrawals........		34,100

EXHIBIT 5-9B Ledger Accounts of Austin Sound

Assets

Cash	
4,850	

Accounts Receivable	
17,000	

Note Receivable	
10,000	

Interest Receivable	
(A) 400	

Inventory	
50,500	(C) 50,500
(C) 52,000	

Supplies	
650	(A) 550
100	

Prepaid Insurance	
1,200	(A) 1,000
200	

Furniture and Fixtures	
6,800	

Accumulated Depreciation	
	2,400
	(A) 600
	3,000

Liabilities

Accounts Payable	
	7,000

Unearned Sales Revenue	
(A) 1,300	2,000
	700

Note Payable	
	12,600

Interest Payable	
	(A) 200

Owner's Equity

W. Nelson, Capital	
(C) 34,100	65,900
	(C) 36,050
	67,850

W. Nelson, Withdrawals	
34,100	(C) 34,100

Income Summary	
(C) 160,450	(C) 196,500
(C) 36,050	

Revenues

Sales Revenue	
	138,000
	(A) 1,300
(C) 139,300	139,300

Sales Discounts	
1,400	(C) 1,400

Sales Returns and Allowances	
2,000	(C) 2,000

Interest Revenue	
	600
	(A) 400
(C) 1,000	1,000

Expenses

Purchases					Purchase Discounts					Purchase Returns and Allowances		
89,300	(C)	89,300		(C)	3,000		3,000		(C)	1,200		1,200

Freight In					Rent Expense					Depreciation Expense		
5,200	(C)	5,200			8,400	(C)	8,400		(A)	600	(C)	600

Insurance Expense					Supplies Expense					Interest Expense		
(A) 1,000	(C)	1,000		(A)	550	(C)	550			1,300		
									(A)	200		
										1,500	(C)	1,500

A = Adjusting entry   C = Closing entry

The second closing entry includes a credit to Inventory for its beginning balance and credits to the temporary accounts with debit balances. These are Sales Discounts, Sales Returns and Allowances, Purchases, Freight In and the expense accounts. The offsetting $160,450 debit to Income Summary comes from the debit column of the income statement on the work sheet.

OBJECTIVE 5

Adjust and close the accounts of a merchandising business

The last two closing entries close net income from Income Summary, and also close owner Withdrawals, into the Capital account.

The entries to the Inventory account deserve additional explanation. As we have indicated, before the closing process, Inventory still has the period's beginning balance, as follows:

Inventory		
Beginning balance	50,500	

At the end of the period, this balance is one year old and must be replaced with the ending balance in order to prepare the financial statements at December 31. The closing entries give Inventory its correct ending balance of $52,000, as shown here:

Inventory		
Beginning balance (same as last period's ending balance) 50,500	Closing entry to eliminate beginning balance 50,500
Closing entry to set up ending balance 52,000	
Ending balance for this period's balance sheet 52,000	

The inventory amounts for these closing entries are taken directly from the income statement columns of the work sheet. The offsetting debits and credits to Income Summary in these closing entries also serve to place the dollar amount of cost of goods sold into the accounts. Income Summary contains the cost of goods sold amount after Purchases and its related contra accounts are closed.

Study Exhibits 5-7, 5-8 and 5-9 carefully. They illustrate the entire end-of-period process that leads to the financial statements. As you progress through this book, you may want to refer to these exhibits to refresh your understanding of the adjusting and closing process for a merchandising business.

Income Statement Format

We have seen that the balance sheet appears in two formats: the account format and report format. There are also two basic formats for the income statement: *single step* and *multiple step*.

<table>
<tr><td>

OBJECTIVE 6

Recognize different formats of the income statement

</td><td>

Multiple-Step Income Statement

The income statements presented thus far in this chapter have been multiple-step income statements. The **multiple-step format** contains subtotals to highlight significant relationships. In addition to net income, it also presents gross margin and income from operations. This format communicates a merchandiser's results of operations especially well, because gross margin and income from operations are two key measures of operating performance.

</td></tr>
</table>

Single-Step Income Statement

The **single-step format** contains only two sections, revenues and expenses, with a single net income amount at the bottom. The single-step format has the advantage of listing all revenues together and all expenses together, as shown in Exhibit 5-10. Thus it clearly distinguishes revenues from expenses. The income statements in Chapters 1 through 4 were single-step. This format works well for service entities because they have no gross margin to report. A recent survey of 600 companies indicated that 56 percent use the single-step format and 44 percent use the multiple-step format. Single-step income statements may become even more popular as Canada moves to a more service-oriented economy.

EXHIBIT 5-10   *Single-Step Income Statement*

Austin Sound
Income Statement
for the year ended December 31, 19X6

Revenues	
Net sales (net of sales discounts, $1,400,	
and returns and allowances, $2,000)	$135,900
Interest revenue	1,000
Total revenues	136,900
Expenses	
Cost of goods sold...............................	$ 88,800
Rent expense	8,400
Interest expense..................................	1,500
Insurance expense.................................	1,000
Depreciation expense	600
Supplies expense..................................	550
Total expenses	100,850
Net income.......................................	$ 36,050

Most published financial statements are highly condensed. Of course, condensed statements can be supplemented with desired details. For example, in Exhibit 5-10, the single-step income statement could be accompanied by a supporting schedule that gives the detailed computation of cost of goods sold.

Summary Problem for Your Review

The trial balance of Jan King Distributing Company follows on the next page.

Additional data at December 31, 19X3:

a. Supplies used during the year, $2,580.
b. Prepaid rent in force, $1,000.
c. Unearned sales revenue still not earned, $2,400. The company expects to earn this amount during the next few months.
d. Depreciation, $2,650.
e. Accrued salaries, $1,300.
f. Accrued interest expense, $600.
g. Inventory on hand, $195,800.

Jan King Distributing Company
Trial Balance
December 31, 19X3

| | Balance | |
Account Title	Debit	Credit
Cash.....................................	$ 5,670	
Accounts receivable	37,100	
Inventory	190,500	
Supplies..................................	3,930	
Prepaid rent	6,000	
Furniture and fixtures	26,500	
Accumulated depreciation...................		$ 21,200
Accounts payable		46,340
Salary payable		
Interest payable		
Unearned sales revenue....................		3,500
Note payable, long-term		35,000
Jan King, capital..........................		153,680
Jan King, withdrawals	48,000	
Income summary...........................		
Sales revenue		346,700
Sales discounts...........................	10,300	
Sales returns and allowances	8,200	
Purchases	175,900	
Purchases discounts		6,000
Purchase returns and allowances.............		7,430
Freight in	9,300	
Salary expense	82,750	
Rent expense	7,000	
Depreciation expense		
Utilities expense	5,800	
Supplies expense...........................		
Interest expense...........................	2,900	
Total....................................	$619,850	$619,850

Required

1. Make a single-summary journal entry to record King's
   a. Unadjusted sales for the year, assuming all sales were made on credit.
   b. Sales returns and allowances for the year.
   c. Sales discounts for the year, assuming the cash collected on account was $329,000 and the credit to Accounts Receivable was $339,300.

    d. Purchases of inventory for the year, assuming all purchases were made on credit.

    e. Purchase returns and allowances for the year.

    f. Purchase discounts for the year, $6,000. Cash paid on account was $188,400 and the debit to Accounts Payable was $194,400.

    g. Transportation costs for the year, assuming a cash payment in a separate entry.

2. Enter the trial balance on a work sheet and complete the work sheet.

3. Journalize the adjusting and closing entries at December 31. Post to the Income Summary account as an accuracy check on the entries affecting that account. The credit balance closed out of Income Summary should equal net income computed on the work sheet.

4. Prepare the company's multiple-step income statement, statement of owner's equity and balance sheet in account format.

SOLUTION TO REVIEW PROBLEM

Requirement 1

Sale, purchase and related return and discount entries

	19X3			
a.	Accounts Receivable	....	346,700	
	Sales Revenue	....		346,700
b.	Sales Returns and Allowances	....	8,200	
	Accounts Receivable	....		8,200
c.	Cash	....	329,000	
	Sales Discounts	....	10,300	
	Accounts Receivable	....		339,300
d.	Purchases	....	175,900	
	Accounts Payable	....		175,900
e.	Accounts Payable	....	7,430	
	Purchase Returns and Allowances	......		7,430
f.	Accounts Payable	....	194,400	
	Purchase Discounts	....		6,000
	Cash	....		188,400
g.	Freight In	....	9,300	
	Cash	....		9,300

Requirement 2

Jan King Distributing Company
Work Sheet
for the year ended December 31, 19X3

Account Title	Trial Balance Debit	Trial Balance Credit	Adjustments Debit	Adjustments Credit	Income Statement Debit	Income Statement Credit	Balance Sheet Debit	Balance Sheet Credit
Cash	5,670						5,670	
Accounts receivable	37,100						37,100	
Inventory	190,500				190,500	195,800	195,800	
Supplies	3,930			(a) 2,580			1,350	
Prepaid rent	6,000			(b) 5,000			1,000	
Furniture and fixtures	26,500						26,500	
Accumulated depreciation		21,200		(d) 2,650				23,850
Accounts payable		46,340						46,340
Salary payable				(e) 1,300				1,300
Interest payable				(f) 600				600
Unearned sales revenue		3,500	(c) 1,100					2,400
Note payable, long-term		35,000						35,000
Jan King, capital		153,680						153,680
Jan King, withdrawals	48,000						48,000	
Sales revenue		346,700		(c) 1,100		347,800		
Sales discounts	10,300				10,300			
Sales returns and allowances	8,200				8,200			
Purchases	175,900				175,900			
Purchase discounts		6,000				6,000		
Purchase returns and allowances		7,430				7,430		
Freight in	9,300				9,300			
Salary expense	82,750		(e) 1,300		84,050			
Rent expense	7,000		(b) 5,000		12,000			
Depreciation expense			(d) 2,650		2,650			
Utilities expense	5,800				5,800			
Supplies expense			(a) 2,580		2,580			
Interest expense	2,900		(f) 600		3,500			
	619,850	619,850	13,230	13,230	504,780	557,030	315,420	263,170
Net income					52,250			52,250
					557,030	557,030	315,420	315,420

Requirement 3
Adjusting entries:

19X3

Dec. 31	Supplies Expense		2,580	
	Supplies			2,580
31	Rent Expense............................		5,000	
	Prepaid Rent			5,000
31	Unearned Sales Revenue		1,100	
	Sales Revenue......................			1,100
31	Depreciation Expense		2,650	
	Accumulated Depreciation...........			2,650
31	Salary Expense		1,300	
	Salary Payable			1,300
31	Interest Expense		600	
	Interest Payable			600

Closing entries:

19X3

Dec. 31	Inventory (ending balance)		195,800	
	Sales Revenue		347,800	
	Purchase Discounts		6,000	
	Purchase Returns		7,430	
	Income Summary....................			557,030
31	Income Summary		504,780	
	Inventory (beginning balance)			190,500
	Sales Discounts.....................			10,300
	Sales Returns and Allowances			8,200
	Purchases...........................			175,900
	Freight In..........................			9,300
	Salary Expense			84,050
	Rent Expense			12,000
	Depreciation Expense			2,650
	Utilities Expense....................			5,800
	Supplies Expense			2,580
	Interest Expense....................			3,500
31	Income Summary ($557,030 − $504,780)		52,250	
	Jan King, capital			52,250
31	Jan King, capital		48,000	
	Jan King, withdrawals...............			48,000

Income Summary

Clo.	504,780	Clo.	557,030
Clo.	52,250	Bal.	52,250

Requirement 4

Jan King Distributing Company
Income Statement
for the year ended December 31, 19X3

Sales revenue			$347,800
Less: Sales discounts		$ 10,300	
Sales returns and allowances		8,200	18,500
Net sales revenue			$329,300
Cost of goods sold			
Beginning inventory			190,500
Purchases		175,900	
Less: Purchase discounts	$6,000		
Purchase returns and			
allowances	7,430	13,430	
Net purchases			162,470
Freight in			9,300
Cost of goods available for sale			362,270
Less: Ending inventory			195,800
Cost of goods sold			166,470
Gross margin			162,830
Operating expenses			
Salary expense			84,050
Rent expense			12,000
Utilities expense			5,800
Depreciation expense			2,650
Supplies expense			2,580
			107,080
Income from operations			55,750
Other expense			
Interest expense			3,500
Net income			$ 52,250

Jan King Distributing Company
Statement of Owner's Equity
for the year ended December 31, 19X3

Jan King, capital, December 31, 19X2	$153,680
Add: Net income	52,250
	205,930
Withdrawals	48,000
Jan King, capital, December 31, 19X3	$157,930

Jan King Distributing Company
Balance Sheet
December 31, 19X3

Assets			Liabilities		
Current			Current		
Cash............................		$ 5,670	Accounts payable................		$ 46,340
Accounts receivable		37,100	Salary payable		1,300
Inventory		195,800	Interest payable		600
Supplies.........................		1,350	Unearned sales revenue		2,400
Prepaid Rent		1,000	Total current liabilities		50,640
Total current assets		240,920	Long-term		
Plant			Note payable		35,000
Furniture and fixtures	$26,500		Total liabilities		85,640
Less: Accumulated			**Owner's Equity**		
depreciation	23,850	2,650	Jan King, capital..................		157,930
			Total liabilities and		
Total assets		$243,570	owner's equity		$243,570

Summary

The major revenue of a merchandising business is *sales revenue* or *sales*. The major expense is *cost of goods sold*. Sales minus cost of goods sold is called *gross margin, gross profit* or *gross income*. This amount measures the business's success or failure in selling its products at a higher price than it paid for them.

The merchandiser's major asset is *inventory*. In a merchandising entity resources flow from cash to inventory as the inventory is purchased for resale, and back to cash as the inventory is sold.

Cost of goods sold is unlike the other expenses in that it is not an account in the ledger. Instead, cost of goods sold is the remainder when beginning inventory and net purchases are added and ending inventory is subtracted from that sum.

The *invoice* is the business document generated by a purchase/sale transaction. Most merchandising entities offer *discounts* to their customers and allow them to *return* unsuitable merchandise. They also grant *allowances* for damaged goods that the buyer chooses to keep. Discounts and Returns and Allowances are *contra* accounts to Purchases and Sales.

The end-of-period adjusting and closing process of a merchandising business is similar to that of a service business. In addition, a merchandiser makes inventory entries at the end of the period. These closing entries replace the period's beginning balance with the cost of inventory on hand at the end. A by-product of these closing entries is the computation of cost of goods sold for the income statement.

The income statement may appear in the *single-step format* or the *multiple-step format*. A single-step income statement has only two sections — one for revenues and the other for expenses—and a single income amount for net income. A multiple-step income statement has numerous sections and subtotals, such as gross margin, operating expenses and other revenues and expenses. Both formats are widely used in practice.

Self-Study Questions

Test your understanding of the chapter by marking the correct answer for each of the following questions:

1. The major expense of a merchandising business is *(p. 176)*
   a. Cost of goods sold
   b. Depreciation
   c. Rent
   d. Interest

2. Sales total $440,000, cost of goods sold is $210,000, and operating expenses are $160,000. How much is gross margin? *(p. 176)*
   a. $440,000
   b. $230,000
   c. $210,000
   d. $70,000

3. A purchase discount results from *(p. 179)*
   a. Returning goods to the seller
   b. Receiving a purchase allowance from the seller
   c. Buying a large enough quantity of merchandise to get the discount
   d. Paying within the discount period

4. Which one of the following pairs includes items that are the most similar? *(pp. 183, 184)*
   a. Purchase discounts and purchase returns
   b. Cost of goods sold and inventory
   c. Net sales and sales discounts
   d. Sales returns and sales allowances

5. Which of the following is *not* an account? *(pp. 184, 185)*
   a. Sales revenue
   b. Net sales
   c. Inventory
   d. Supplies expense

6. Cost of goods sold is computed by adding beginning inventory and net purchases and subtracting X. What is X? *(p. 184)*
   a. Net sales
   b. Sales discounts
   c. Ending inventory
   d. Net purchases

7. Which account causes the main difference between a merchandiser's adjusting and closing process and that of a service business? *(p. 187)*
   a. Purchases
   b. Sales revenue
   c. Inventory
   d. Sales returns and allowances

8. The major item on a merchandiser's income statement that a service business does not have is *(p. 192)*
   a. Cost of goods sold
   b. Inventory
   c. Net purchases
   d. Net sales

9. The closing entry for Sales Discounts is *(p. 193)*
   a. Sales Discounts
        Income Summary
   b. Sales Discounts
        Sales Revenue
   c. Income Summary
        Sales Discounts
   d. Not used because Sales Discounts is a permanent account, which is not closed.

10. Which income statement format reports income from operations? *(p. 196)*
    a. Account format
    b. Report format
    c. Single-step format
    d. Multiple-step format

Answers to the self-study questions are at the end of the chapter.

Accounting Vocabulary

cost of goods sold *(p. 183)*
cost of sales *(p. 183)*
gross margin *(p. 176)*
gross profit *(p. 176)*
income from operations
 (p. 191)
invoice *(p. 177)*
multiple-step income
 statement *(p. 196)*

net purchases *(p. 181)*
net sales *(p. 183)*
operating expenses *(p. 191)*
operating income *(p. 191)*
other expense *(p. 191)*
other revenue *(p. 191)*
purchase discount *(p. 179)*
purchase returns and
 allowances *(p. 180)*

purchases *(p. 177)*
sales discount *(p. 182)*
sales returns and allowances
 (p. 182)
sales revenue *(p. 182)*
single-step income statement
 (p. 196)
trade discount *(p. 180)*

Assignment Material _____

Questions

1. Gross margin is often mentioned in the business press as an important measure of success. What does gross margin measure, and why is this important?
2. Describe the flow of resources for (a) the purchase and cash sale of inventory and (b) the purchase and sale of inventory on account.
3. Identify 10 items of information on an invoice.
4. What is the similarity and what is the difference between purchase discounts and trade discounts?
5. Indicate what accounts are debited and credited for (a) a credit purchase of inventory and the subsequent cash payment and (b) a credit sale of inventory and subsequent cash collection. Assume no discounts, returns, allowances or freight.
6. Inventory costing $1,000 is purchased and invoiced on July 28 under terms of 3/10 n/30. Compute the payment amount on August 6. How much would the payment be on August 8? What explains the difference? What is the latest acceptable payment date under the terms of sale?
7. Inventory listed at $35,000 is sold subject to a trade discount of $3,000 and under payment terms of 2/15 n/45. What is the net sales revenue on this sale, if the customer pays within 15 days?
8. Name four contra accounts introduced in this chapter.
9. Briefly discuss the similarity in computing supplies expense and computing cost of goods sold.
10. Why is the title of cost of goods sold especially descriptive? What type of account is cost of goods sold?
11. Beginning inventory is $5,000, net purchases total $30,000 and freight in is $1,000. If ending inventory is $8,000, what is cost of goods sold?
12. Identify two ways that cost of goods sold differs from operating expenses such as Salary Expense and Depreciation Expense.
13. Suppose you are evaluating two companies as possible investments. One entity sells its services and the other entity is a merchandiser. How can you identify the merchandiser by examining the two entities' balance sheets and their income statements?
14. You are beginning the adjusting and closing process at the end of your company's fiscal year. Does the trial balance carry the beginning or the ending amount of inventory? Will the balance sheet that you prepare report the beginning or the ending inventory?
15. Give the two closing entries for inventory, using no specific amount.
16. After the closing entries have been journalized and posted, what account contains the amount of cost of goods sold for the period?

17. What is the identifying characteristic of the "other" category of revenues and expenses? Give an example of each.
18. Name and describe the two income statement formats and identify the type of business to which each format best applies.
19. List eight different operating expenses.
20. Which financial statement reports sales discounts, sales returns and allowances, purchase discounts, and purchase returns and allowances? Show how they are reported, using any reasonable amounts in your illustration.

Exercises

Exercise 5-1   *Computing the elements of a merchandiser's income statement*

Supply the missing income statement amounts in each of the following situations:

Sales	Sales Discounts	Net Sales	Beginning Inventory	Net Purchases	Ending Inventory	Cost of Goods Sold	Gross Margin
$96,000	(a)	$92,800	$32,500	$66,700	$39,400	(b)	$33,000
82,400	$2,100	(c)	27,450	43,000	(d)	$44,100	36,200
91,500	1,800	89,700	(e)	54,900	22,600	59,400	(f)
(g)	3,000	(h)	40,700	(i)	48,230	62,500	36,600

Exercise 5-2   *Journalizing transactions from a purchase invoice*

As the proprietor of Davidson Tire Company, you receive the following invoice from a supplier:

ABC TIRE WHOLESALE DISTRIBUTORS, INC.
2600 Victoria Avenue
Regina, Saskatchewan S4P 1B3

Invoice date: May 14, 19X3   Payment terms: 2/10 n/30

Sold to: Davidson Tire Co.
          4219 Cumberland Avenue
          Saskatoon, SK S7M 1X3

Quantity Ordered	Description	Quantity Shipped	Price	Amount
6	P135-X4 Radials	6	$37.14	$222.84
8	L912 Belted-bias.	8	41.32	330.56
14	R39 Truck tires	10	50.02	500.20

Total $1,053.60

Due date: Amount:
  May 24, 19X3 $1,032.53
  May 25 through June 13, 19X3 $1,053.60

Paid:

Required

1. Record the May 15 purchase on account.
2. The R39 truck tires were ordered by mistake and therefore were returned to ABC. Journalize the return on May 19, assuming no refund of shipping charges.
3. Record the May 22 payment of the amount owed.

Exercise 5-3   *Journalizing purchase and sale transactions*

Journalize, without explanations, the following transactions of Mattox, Inc. during July:

July 3   Purchased $1,200 of inventory under terms of 2/10 n/eom (end of month) and fob shipping point.

   7   Returned $300 of defective merchandise purchased on July 3.

   9   Paid freight bill of $90 on July 3 purchase.

   10   Sold inventory for $2,200, collecting cash of $400. Payment terms on the remainder were 2/15 n/30.

   12   Paid amount owed on credit purchase of July 3, less the discount and the return.

   16   Granted a sales allowance of $800 on the July 10 sale.

   23   Received cash from July 10 customer in full settlement of her debt, less the return and the discount.

Exercise 5-4   *Journalizing purchase transactions*

On April 30, Reagan Jewelers purchased inventory of $3,800 on account from a wholesale jewelry supplier. Terms were 3/15 n/45. On receiving the goods May 3, Reagan checked the order and found $800 of items that were not ordered. Therefore, Reagan returned this amount of merchandise to the supplier on May 4.

To pay the remaining amount owed, Reagan had to borrow $2,910 from the bank because of a temporary cash shortage. On May 14, Reagan signed a short-term note payable to the bank and immediately paid the borrowed funds to the wholesale jewelry supplier. On May 31, Reagan paid the bank $2,940, which included $30 interest.

Required

Record the indicated transactions in the journal of Reagan Jewelers. Explanations are not required.

Exercise 5-5   *Journalizing sale transactions*

Refer to the business situation in Exercise 5-4. Journalize the transactions of the wholesale jewelry supplier. Explanations are not required.

Exercise 5-6   *Computing cost of goods sold for an actual company*

For the year ended December 31, 19X3, General Motors of Canada, Ltd., the auto maker, reported net sales of $16.3 billion and cost of goods sold of $13.2 billion. The company's balance sheet at December 31, 19X2 and 19X3 reported inventories of $1.2 billion and $1.4 billion respectively. What were General Motors' net purchases during 19X3? Hint: Set up the computation of cost of goods sold.

Exercise 5-7 *Preparing a merchandiser's multiple-step income statement*

Accounts receivable	$48,300	Purchase discounts	$ 3,000
Accumulated depreciation	18,700	Purchase returns............	2,000
Freight in	2,200	Capital, May 31	126,070
General expenses	23,800	Sales revenue	186,000
Interest revenue	1,500	Sales discounts	9,000
Inventory, May 31	39,450	Sales returns	4,600
Inventory, June 30	41,870	Selling expenses	37,840
Purchases...................	71,300		

Required

Prepare the business's multiple-step income statement for June of the current year.

Exercise 5-8 *Preparing a single-step income statement for a merchandising business*

Prepare Fortier Hardware Company's single-step income statement for June, using the data from the preceding exercise. In a separate schedule, show the computation of cost of goods sold.

Exercise 5-9 *Using work sheet data to prepare a merchandiser's income statement*

The trial balance and adjustments columns of the work sheet of Brownlee Supply Company include the following accounts and balances at March 31, 19X2:

	Trial Balance		Adjustments	
Account Title	**Debit**	**Credit**	**Debit**	**Credit**
Cash	2,000			
Accounts receivable	8,500		(a) 2,100	
Inventory	76,070			
Supplies	13,000			(b) 8,600
Store fixtures	22,500			
Accumulated depreciation		11,250		(c) 2,250
Accounts payable		9,300		
Salary payable				(d) 1,200
Note payable, long-term		27,500		
K. Brownlee, capital		53,920		
K. Brownlee, withdrawals..........	35,000			
Sales revenue....................		203,000		(a) 2,100
Sales discounts	2,000			
Purchases	94,200			
Purchase returns.................		2,600		
Selling expense	31,050		(b) 5,200	
			(d) 1,200	
General expense	20,500		(b) 3,400	
			(c) 2,250	
Interest expense	2,750			
Total	307,570	307,570	14,150	14,150

Ending inventory at March 31, 19X2 is $74,500.

Prepare the company's multiple-step income statement for the year ended March 31, 19X2.

Exercise 5-10   *Use work sheet data to prepare the closing entries of a merchandising business*

Use the data from Exercise 5-9 to journalize Brownlee Supply Company's closing entries at March 31, 19X2.

Problems   *(Group A)*

Problem 5-1A   *Journalizing purchase and sale transactions*

Jastrow Distributing Company engaged in the following transactions during May of the current year:

May 3 Purchased office supplies for cash, $300.

  7 Purchased inventory on credit terms of 3/10 net eom (end of month), $2,000.

  8. Returned half the inventory purchased on May 7. It was not the inventory ordered.

 10 Sold goods for cash, $450.

 13 Sold inventory on credit terms of 2/15 n/45, $3,900, less $600 trade discount offered to customers who purchased in large quantities.

 16 Paid the amount owed on account from the purchase of May 7, less the discount and the return.

 17 Received defective inventory returned from May 13 sale, $900.

 18 Purchased inventory of $4,000 on account. Payment terms were 2/10 n/30.

 26 Owing to cash shortage, borrowed $3,920 from the bank to take advantage of the discount offered on May 18 purchase. Signed a note payable to the bank for this amount.

 26 Paid supplier for goods purchased on May 18, less the discount.

 28 Received cash in full settlement of his account from the customer who purchased inventory on May 13 less the discount and the return.

 29 Purchased inventory for cash, $2,000, less a trade discount of $400, plus freight charges of $160.

Required

1. Journalize the above transactions.
2. Assume the note payable signed on May 26 requires the payment of $30 interest expense. Was the decision wise or unwise to borrow funds to take advantage of the cash discount? Support your answer by comparing the discount earned to the interest paid.

Problem 5-2A   *Preparing a merchandiser's financial statements*

The accounts of Banff Trading Company are listed in alphabetical order.

Accounts receivable	$43,700	Office equipment	$ 33,680
Accounts payable	16,950	Purchases	364,000
Accumulated depreciation—		Purchase discounts	1,990
office equipment	22,450	Purchase returns and	
Accumulated depreciation—		allowances	3,400
store equipment	16,000	Salary payable	2,840
Capital, April 30	74,620	Sales revenue	706,000
Cash	7,890	Sales discounts	10,400
General expenses	116,700	Sales returns and allowances	18,030
Interest expense	5,400	Selling expenses	132,900
Interest payable	1,100	Store equipment	48,000
Inventory: April 30	69,350	Supplies	5,100
May 31	71,520	Unearned sales revenue	13,800
Note payable, long-term	45,000	Withdrawals	49,000

Required

1. Prepare the business's multiple-step income statement for May of the current year.
2. Prepare the income statement in single-step format.
3. Prepare the balance sheet in report format at May 31 of the current year. Show your computation of the May 31 balance of Capital.

Problem 5-3A   *Using work sheet data to prepare financial statements*

The trial balance and adjustments columns of the work sheet of Schepps Auto Supply include the following accounts and balances at November 30, 19X4:

	Trial Balance		Adjustments	
Account Title	**Debit**	**Credit**	**Debit**	**Credit**
Cash	4,000			
Accounts receivable	14,500		(a) 6,000	
Inventory	67,340			
Supplies	2,800			(b) 1,900
Furniture	19,600			
Accumulated depreciation		4,900		(c) 2,450
Accounts payable		12,600		
Salary payable				(e) 1,000
Unearned sales revenue		13,570	(d) 6,700	
Note payable, long-term		15,000		
A. J. Schepps, capital		60,310		
A. J. Schepps, drawing	42,000			
Sales revenue		164,000		(a) 6,000
				(d) 6,700
Sales returns	6,300			
Purchases	73,200			
Purchase discounts		2,040		
Selling expense	28,080		(e) 1,000	
General expense	13,100		(b) 1,900	
			(c) 2,450	
Interest expense	1,500			
Total	272,420	272,420	18,050	18,050

Inventory on hand at November 30, 19X4 is $72,650.

Required

Without entering the preceding data on a formal work sheet, prepare the company's multiple-step income statement for the year ended November 30, 19X4 and its November 30, 19X4, balance sheet. Show your computation of the ending balance of A. J. Schepps, Capital. Drawing is another name for Withdrawals.

Problem 5-4A   *Preparing a merchandiser's work sheet*

Nicosia Shoe Store's trial balance at December 31 of the current year follows:

Nicosia Shoe Store
Trial Balance
December 31, 19XX

Account Title	Balance	
	Debit	Credit
Cash	$ 1,270	
Accounts receivable	4,430	
Inventory	73,900	
Prepaid rent	4,400	
Store fixtures	22,100	
Accumulated depreciation		$ 8,380
Accounts payable		6,290
Salary payable		
Interest payable		
Note payable, long term		18,000
Angelina Nicosia, capital		55,920
Angelina Nicosia, withdrawals	39,550	
Sales revenue		170,150
Purchases	67,870	
Salary expense	24,700	
Rent expense	7,700	
Advertising expense	4,510	
Utilities expense	3,880	
Depreciation expense		
Insurance expense	2,770	
Interest expense	1,660	
Total	$258,740	$258,740

Additional data at December 31, 19XX:

a. Rent expense for the year, $10,200
b. Depreciation for the year, $3,130
c. Accrued salaries at December 31, $900
d. Accrued interest expense at December 31, $360
e. Inventory on hand at December 31, $80,200

Required

Complete Nicosia's work sheet for the year ended December 31 of the current year.

Problem 5-5A   *Journalizing the adjusting and closing entries of a merchandising business*

Required

1. Journalize the adjusting and closing entries for the data in Problem 5-4A.
2. Determine the December 31 balance of Angelina Nicosia, Capital.

Problem 5-6A   *Preparing a merchandiser's work sheet, financial statements and adjusting and closing entries*

The year-end trial balance of McKee Sales Company at March 31 of the current year is as follows:

McKee Sales Company
Trial Balance
March 31, 19XX

	Balance	
Account Title	**Debit**	**Credit**
Cash......................................	$ 7,880	
Notes receivable, current	12,400	
Interest receivable		
Inventory	130,050	
Prepaid insurance	3,600	
Notes receivable, long-term..................	62,000	
Furniture.....................................	6,000	
Accumulated depreciation....................		$ 4,000
Accounts payable		12,220
Sales commission payable		
Salary payable		
Unearned sales revenue......................		9,610
J.R. McKee, capital..........................		167,380
J.R. McKee, withdrawals	66,040	
Income summary...........................		
Sales revenue		440,000
Interest revenue		8,600
Purchases	233,000	
Freight in	10,000	
Sales commission expense....................	78,300	
Salary expense..............................	24,700	
Rent expense	6,000	
Utilities expense	1,840	
Depreciation expense		
Insurance expense..........................		
Total......................................	$641,810	$641,810

Additional data at March 31, 19XX:

a. Accrued interest revenue, $1,030
b. Insurance expense for the year, $3,000
c. Depreciation for the year, $1,000
d. Unearned sales revenue still unearned, $8,200
e. Accrued salaries, $1,200

f. Accrued sales commissions, $1,700
g. Inventory on hand, $133,200

Required

1. Enter the trial balance on a work sheet, and complete the work sheet for the year ended March 31 of the current year.
2. Prepare the company's multiple-step income statement and statement of owner's equity for the year ended March 31 of the current year. Also prepare its balance sheet at that date. Long-term notes receivable should be reported on the balance sheet between current assets and plant assets in a separate section labeled Investments.
3. Journalize the adjusting and closing entries at March 31.
4. Post to the J.R. McKee, Capital account and to the Income Summary account as an accuracy check on the adjusting and closing process.

Problem 5-7A   *Completing a merchandiser's accounting cycle*

The end-of-month trial balance of Bucyk Trading Company at October 31 of the current year is

Bucyk Trading Company
Trial Balance
October 31, 19XX

Account Number	Account Title	Debit	Credit
11	Cash	$ 8,310	
12	Accounts receivable	14,390	
13	Inventory	82,300	
14	Supplies	4,100	
15	Building	140,000	
16	Accumulated depreciation—building		$ 23,000
17	Furniture	17,500	
18	Accumulated depreciation—furniture		7,500
21	Accounts payable		16,380
22	Salary payable		
23	Interest payable		
24	Unearned sales revenue		5,300
25	Note payable, long-term		79,000
31	Stu Bucyk, capital		105,860
32	Stu Bucyk, withdrawals	6,000	
33	Income summary		
41	Sales revenue		143,000
42	Sales discounts	4,290	
43	Sales returns and allowances	4,100	
51	Purchases	81,000	
52	Purchase discounts		3,750
53	Purchase returns and allowances		1,800
54	Selling expense	14,360	
55	General expense	9,240	
56	Interest expense		
	Total	$385,590	$385,590

Additional data at October 31, 19XX:

a. Supplies consumed during the month, $2,400. Two thirds is selling expense and one third is general expense.

b. Depreciation for the month: building, $7,000 and furniture, $1,700. Depreciation is evenly divided between selling expense and general expense.

c. Of the unadjusted balance of Unearned Sales Revenue, $2,000 was earned during October.

d. Accrued salaries, a selling expense, $1,400

e. Accrued interest expense, $900

f. Inventory on hand, $86,000

Required

1. Using T-accounts, open the accounts listed on the trial balance and insert their unadjusted balances. Date the balances of the following accounts October 1: Inventory; Supplies; Building; Accumulated Depreciation—Building; Furniture; Accumulated Depreciation—Furniture; Unearned Sales Revenue; and Stu Bucyk, Capital. Date all other unadjusted balances October 31.

2. Enter the trial balance on a work sheet, and complete the work sheet for the month ended October 31 of the current year. Bucyk Trading Company groups all operating expenses under two accounts, Selling Expense and General Expense. Leave three blank lines under Selling Expense and two blank lines under General Expense.

3. Prepare the company's multiple-step income statement and statement of owner's equity for the month ended October 31 of the current year. Also prepare the balance sheet at that date in report form.

4. Journalize the adjusting and closing entries, using page 6 of the journal.

5. Post the adjusting and closing entries, using dates and posting references.

(Group B)

Problem 5-1B   *Journalizing purchase and sale transactions*

Rogers Furniture Company engaged in the following transactions during July of the current year:

July 2   Purchased inventory for cash, $800, less a trade discount of $150.

5   Purchased store supplies on credit terms of net eom (end of month), $450.

8   Purchased inventory of $3,000 less a trade discount of 10 percent, plus freight charges of $230 on credit terms of 3/15 n/30.

9   Sold goods for cash, $1,200.

11   Returned $200 of the inventory purchased on July 8. It was damaged in shipment.

12   Purchased inventory on credit terms of 3/10 n/30, $3,330.

14   Sold inventory on credit terms of 2/10 n/30, $9,600, less a $600 trade discount.

16   Paid the electricity and water bills, $275.

20   Received returned inventory from July 14 sale, $400. Rogers shipped the wrong goods by mistake.

21   Owing to a cash shortage, borrowed the amount owed on the July 8 purchase. Signed a note payable to the bank for $2,655, which takes into account the return of inventory on July 11.

21   Paid supplier for goods purchased on July 8, less the discount and the return.

23   Received $6,860 cash in partial settlement of his account from the customer who purchased inventory on July 14. Granted the customer a 2 percent discount and credited his account receivable for $7,000.

30   Paid for the store supplies purchased on July 5.

Required

1.   Journalize the above transactions.
2.   Compute the amount of the receivable at July 31 from the customer to whom Rogers sold inventory on July 14. What amount of cash discount applies to this receivable at July 31?

Problem 5-2B   *Preparing a merchandiser's financial statements*

The accounts of Big Bend Trading Company are listed in alphabetical order.

Accounts receivable	$31,200	Office equipment	$ 49,000
Accounts payable	27,380	Purchases	273,100
Accumulated depreciation—		Purchase discounts	4,670
office equipment	9,500	Purchase returns and	
Accumulated depreciation—		allowances	10,190
store equipment	6,880	Salary payable	6,120
Capital, June 30	73,720	Sales revenue	501,580
Cash	12,320	Sales discounts	8,350
General expenses	75,830	Sales returns and allowances	17,900
Interest expense	7,200	Selling expenses	84,600
Interest payable	3,000	Store equipment	47,500
Inventory: June 30	60,060	Supplies	4,350
July 31	57,390	Unearned sales revenue	9,370
Note payable, long-term	30,000	Withdrawals	11,000

Required

1.   Prepare the entity's multiple-step income statement for July of the current year.
2.   Prepare the income statement in single-step format.
3.   Prepare the balance sheet in report format at July 31 of the current year. Show your computation of the July 31 balance of Capital.

Problem 5-3B   *Using work sheet data to prepare financial statements*

The trial balance and adjustments columns of the work sheet of Francis Toy Company include the following accounts and balances at September 30, 19X5:

Account Title	Trial Balance		Adjustments	
	Debit	Credit	Debit	Credit
Cash	7,300			
Accounts receivable	4,360		(a) 1,800	
Inventory	51,530			
Supplies	10,700			(b) 7,640
Equipment	79,450			
Accumulated depreciation		29,800		(c) 9,900
Accounts payable		13,800		
Salary payable				(e) 800
Unearned sales revenue		3,780	(d) 2,600	
Note payable, long-term		10,000		
M. Francis, capital................		78,360		
M. Francis, drawing	35,000			
Sales revenue.....................		182,000		(a) 1,800
				(d) 2,600
Sales returns	3,100			
Purchases	67,400			
Purchase discounts................		3,700		
Selling expense	40,600		(b) 7,640	
			(e) 800	
General expense	21,000		(c) 9,900	
Interest expense	1,000			
Total	321,440	321,440	22,740	22,740

Required

Inventory on hand at September 30, 19X5 is $52,580. Without entering the preceding data on a formal work sheet, prepare the company's multiple-step income statement for the year ended September 30, 19X5 and its September 30, 19X5 balance sheet. Show your computation of the ending balance of M. Francis, Capital. Drawing is another name for Withdrawals.

Problem 5-4B   Preparing a merchandiser's work sheet

Fairview Hardware's trial balance at December 31 of the current year is on the next page.

Additional data at December 31, 19XX:

a. Insurance expense for the year, $6,090
b. Depreciation for the year, $7,240
c. Accrued salaries at December 31, $1,260
d. Accrued interest expense at December 31, $870
e. Store supplies on hand at December 31, $760
f. Inventory on hand at December 31, $99,350

Fairview Hardware
Trial Balance
December 31, 19XX

	Balance	
Account Title	**Debit**	**Credit**
Cash	$ 2,910	
Accounts receivable	6,560	
Inventory	101,760	
Store supplies............................	1,990	
Prepaid insurance	3,200	
Store fixtures	63,920	
Accumulated depreciation..................		$ 37,640
Accounts payable		29,770
Salary payable		
Interest payable		
Note payable, long-term		37,220
Ed Sanger, capital		63,120
Ed Sanger, withdrawals....................	36,300	
Sales revenue		286,370
Purchases	161,090	
Salary expense	46,580	
Rent expense	14,630	
Utilities expense	6,780	
Depreciation expense		
Insurance expense.........................	5,300	
Store supplies expense		
Interest expense...........................	3,100	
Total.....................................	$454,120	$454,120

Required

Complete Fairview's work sheet for the year ended December 31 of the current year.

Problem 5-5B *Journalizing the adjusting and closing entries of a merchandising business*

Required

1. Journalize the adjusting and closing entries for the data in Problem 5-4B.
2. Determine the December 31 balance of Ed Sanger, Capital.

Problem 5-6B *Preparing a merchandiser's work sheet, financial statements and adjusting and closing entries*

The year-end trial balance of Thunder Bay Sales Company at July 31 of the current year is as follows:

Thunder Bay Sales Company
Trial Balance
July 31, 19XX

Account Title	Balance	
	Debit	Credit
Cash	$ 3,120	
Notes receivable, current	6,900	
Interest receivable		
Inventory	104,000	
Prepaid insurance	2,810	
Notes receivable, long-term	19,300	
Furniture	16,000	
Accumulated depreciation		$ 12,000
Accounts payable		14,360
Salary payable		
Sales commission payable		
Unearned sales revenue		4,090
G.M. Blake, capital		97,790
G.M. Blake, withdrawals	59,000	
Income summary		
Sales revenue		337,940
Interest revenue		1,910
Purchases	163,200	
Freight in	11,100	
Salary expense	39,030	
Sales commission expense	31,500	
Rent expense	10,000	
Utilities expense	2,130	
Insurance expense		
Depreciation expense		
Total	$468,090	$468,090

Additional data at July 31, 19XX:

a. Accrued interest revenue, $350
b. Prepaid insurance still in force, $310
c. Depreciation for the year, $2,000
d. Unearned sales revenue still unearned, $1,900
e. Accrued salaries, $1,640
f. Accrued sales commissions, $1,430
g. Inventory on hand, $102,600

Required

1. Enter the trial balance on a work sheet, and complete the work sheet for the year ended July 31 of the current year.
2. Prepare the company's multiple-step income statement and statement of owner's equity for the year ended July 31 of the current year. Also prepare its balance sheet at that date. Long-term notes receivable should be reported on the balance sheet between current assets and plant assets in a separate section labeled Investments.
3. Journalize the adjusting and closing entries at July 31.

4. Post to the G.M. Blake, capital account and to the Income Summary account as an accuracy check on the adjusting and closing process.

Problem 5-7B   *Completing a merchandiser's accounting cycle*

The end-of-month trial balance of Lansing Building Materials at January 31 of the current year is

Lansing Building Materials
Trial Balance
January 31, 19XX

Account Number	Account Title	Balance Debit	Balance Credit
11	Cash..	$ 6,430	
12	Accounts receivable	19,090	
13	Inventory	65,400	
14	Supplies.....................................	2,700	
15	Building......................................	195,000	
16	Accumulated depreciation—building		$ 36,000
17	Fixtures	45,600	
18	Accumulated depreciation—fixtures		5,800
21	Accounts payable		28,300
22	Salary payable		
23	Interest payable		
24	Unearned sales revenue.......................		6,560
25	Note payable, long-term		87,000
31	Ed Lansing, capital		144,980
32	Ed Lansing, withdrawals	9,200	
33	Income summary...............................		
41	Sales revenue		177,970
42	Sales discounts...............................	7,300	
43	Sales returns and allowances	8,140	
51	Purchases	103,000	
52	Purchase discounts		4,230
53	Purchase returns and allowances................		2,600
54	Selling expense	21,520	
55	General expense	10,060	
56	Interest expense..............................		
	Total..	$493,440	$493,440

Additional data at January 31, 19XX:

a. Supplies consumed during the month, $1,500. One half is selling expense and the other half is general expense.
b. Depreciation for the month: building, $4,000 and fixtures, $4,800. One fourth of depreciation is selling expense and three fourths is general expense.
c. Unearned sales revenue still unearned, $1,200
d. Accrued salaries, a general expense, $1,150
e. Accrued interest expense, $780
f. Inventory on hand, $60,720

Required

1. Using T-accounts, open the accounts listed on the trial balance and insert their unadjusted balances. Date the balances of the following accounts January 1: Inventory; Supplies; Building; Accumulated Depreciation — Building; Fixtures; Accumulated Depreciation — Fixtures; Unearned Sales Revenue; and Ed Lansing, Capital. Date the balance of Ed Lansing, Withdrawals, January 31.

2. Enter the trial balance on a work sheet, and complete the work sheet for the month ended January 31 of the current year. Lansing groups all operating expenses under two accounts, Selling Expense and General Expense. Leave two blank lines under Selling Expense and three blank lines under General Expense.

3. Prepare the company's multiple-step income statement and statement of owner's equity for the month ended January 31 of the current year. Also prepare the balance sheet at that date in report form.

4. Journalize the adjusting and closing entries at January 31, using page 3 of the journal.

5. Post the adjusting and closing entries, using dates and posting references.

Decision Problems

1. *Using the financial statements to decide on a business expansion*

Lynn Kraft owns Westlake Pharmacy, which has prospered during the first year of operation. In deciding whether to open another pharmacy in the area, Lynn has prepared the following current financial statements of the business:

Westlake Pharmacy
Income Statement
for the year ended December 31, 19X1

Sales revenue		$175,000
Interest revenue		24,600
Total revenue		199,600
Cost of goods sold		
Beginning inventory.	$ 27,800	
Net purchases	87,500	
Cost of goods available for sale	115,300	
Less: Ending inventory	30,100	
Cost of goods sold.		85,200
Gross margin		114,400
Operating expenses		
Salary expense	18,690	
Rent expense	12,000	
Interest expense.	6,000	
Depreciation expense	4,900	
Utilities expense	2,330	
Supplies expense	1,400	
Total operating expense.		45,320
Income from operations.		69,080
Other expense		
Sales discounts ($3,600) and returns ($7,100) .		10,700
Net income		$ 58,380

Westlake Pharmacy
Statement of Owner's Equity
for the year ended December 31, 19X1

L. Kraft, capital, January 1, 19X1..............	$20,000
Add: Increases in owner's equity	
Net income............................	58,380
L. Kraft, capital, December 31, 19X1	$78,380

Westlake Pharmacy
Balance Sheet
December 31, 19X1

Assets

Current	
Cash....................................	$ 5,320
Accounts receivable	9,710
Inventory	30,100
Supplies...............................	2,760
Store fixtures	63,000
Total current assets	110,890
Other	
Withdrawals...........................	45,000
Total assets	$155,890

Liabilities

Current	
Accumulated depreciation — store fixtures ..	$ 6,300
Accounts payable	10,310
Salary payable	900
Total current liabilities	17,510
Other	
Note payable due in 90 days..............	60,000
Total liabilities	77,510

Owner's Equity

L. Kraft, capital	78,380
Total liabilities and owner's equity	$155,890

Lynn recently read in an industry trade magazine that a successful pharmacy meets these criteria:

a. Gross margin is at least one half of net sales.
b. Current assets are at least two times current liabilities.
c. Owner's equity is at least as great as total liabilities.

Basing her opinion on the entity's financial statement data, Lynn believes the business meets all three criteria. She plans to go ahead with her expansion plan and asks your advice on preparing the pharmacy's financial statements in accordance with generally accepted accounting principles. She assures you that all amounts are correct.

Required

1. Prepare a correct multiple-step income statement, a statement of owner's equity and a balance sheet in report format.
2. Based on the corrected financial statements, compute correct measures of the three criteria listed in the trade journal.
3. Assuming the criteria are valid, make a recommendation about whether to undertake the expansion at this time.

2. *Understanding the operating cycle of a merchandiser*

A. Gayle Yip-Chuk has come to you for advice. Two years ago, she opened a record store in a plaza near the university she had attended. The store sells records, cassettes and compact discs for cash and on credit cards and, as a special feature, on credit to certain students. Many of the students at the university are co-op students who alternate school and work terms. Gayle allows co-op students to buy the products her store sells on credit while they are on a school term, with the understanding that the account will be paid shortly after the student starts his or her work-term.

　　Business has been very good. Gayle is sure it is because of the competitive prices her store offers and especially because of the unique credit facility she offers. Her problem is that she seems to be short of operating cash, and her loan with the bank has grown significantly. The bank manager has indicated that she wishes to reduce her line of credit because she is worried that Gayle will get into financial difficulties.

Required

1. Explain to Gayle why you think she is in the predicament she is in.
2. Gayle has asked you to come with her to meet the bank manager to explain her problem and to assist her in asking for more credit. What do you think you might say to the bank manager to assist Gayle?

B. The employees of Schneider Ltd. made an error when they performed the periodic inventory count at year end, October 31, 19X2: part of one warehouse was not counted and included in inventory.

Required

1. Indicate the effect of the inventory error on net income for the year ended October 31, 19X2.
2. Will the error affect net income in 19X3? If so, what will the effect be?

Financial Statement Problem

Closing entries for a merchandising operation
This problem uses both the income statement (statement of earnings) and the balance sheet of John Labatt Limited in Appendix E. It will aid in your understanding of the closing process of a merchandising business.

　　Assume that the inventory and closing procedures outlined in this chapter are appropriate for John Labatt. Further, do not use total inventories shown on the balance sheet, but rather the amounts shown in the financial statements for finished and in process inventories as well as materials and supplies inventories. Assume net purchases totaled $3,295.3 million.

Required

1. Show the computation of John Labatt's cost of goods sold for the year ended April 30, 1989 by this formula from the chapter:

$$
\begin{array}{l}
\textbf{Beginning inventory} \\
\underline{+ \textbf{Net purchases}} \\
= \textbf{Cost of goods available for sale} \\
\underline{- \textbf{Ending inventory}} \\
= \textbf{Cost of goods sold}
\end{array}
$$

2. Using Net Purchases and Net Sales (Gross Sales less sales and excise taxes) from the income statement, journalize John Labatt's closing entries for the year ended April 30, 1989. Selling and Administrative Expenses total $1,116.5 million. Close out Unusual Items (an expense), [total] Income Taxes (an expense) and Share of Net Earnings (losses) in Partly Owned Businesses (income) separately. Corporations like John Labatt close Income Summary into an account called Retained Earnings (instead of Capital). Also, corporations have no withdrawals account to close.

3. What amount was closed to Retained Earnings? How is this net income amount labeled on John Labatt's income statement?

Answers to Self-Study Questions

1.	a	6.	c
2.	b ($440,000 − $210,000 = $230,000)	7.	c
3.	d	8.	a
4.	d	9.	c
5.	b	10.	d

PART TWO

Introduction to Accounting Systems

6

Accounting Information Systems

LEARNING OBJECTIVES

After studying this chapter, you should be able to

1 Describe the features of an effective information system

2 Use the sales journal

3 Use control accounts and subsidiary ledgers

4 Use the cash receipts journal

5 Use the purchases journal

6 Use the cash disbursements journal

An **accounting information system**—often called, simply, an *information system*—is the combination of personnel, records and procedures that a business uses to meet its needs for financial data. Because each business has different information demands, each uses a different accounting information system. For example, a jewelry store earns revenue by selling inventory, so the store's management usually wants an up-to-the-minute, accurate record of the level of goods on hand for sale. A physician, however, earns revenue by providing service, and there is little or no inventory to control. The physician needs to keep track of the time spent on each patient. The jewelry store and the physician, then, need different information systems to answer the special sorts of questions that arise as they conduct their business. For maximum effectiveness, the information system is tailored to the business's specific needs.

A basic understanding of accounting systems is important for managing and evaluating a business. As a manager, you may be tempted to reply, "I can always hire an accountant to design the information system and do the accounting." Perhaps, but you will be better able to communicate with the members of your organization if you understand how the accounting system operates. The accounting system is the glue that holds the various parts of an organization together. It helps managers stay on top of their responsibilities. Indeed, a potential buyer of a business examines its accounting system to understand how the organization works.

Also, you do not want your employees to take advantage of you by manipulating your accounting system to cover theft. Business owners who are unfamiliar with accounting systems are victims of this practice to an alarming degree.

This chapter looks at accounting information system designs and how they are implemented. It also provides a basic model of information processing and discusses what makes an information system effective. The chapter then discusses computer data processing and illustrates special journals and ledgers that accountants use to streamline information systems.

Accounting System Design and Installation _____

System Design   An accounting information system begins with a design. The manager and the designer study the business's goals and organizational structure. They also identify management's information needs, then break down the required information-processing tasks. The designer must consider the personnel who will operate the system, the documents and reports to be produced, and the equipment to be used. Almost every information system uses a computer for at least some tasks. Some public accounting firms specialize in system design and install the accounting system for their clients.

System Installation   Installation includes selecting and training employees to operate the system, testing the system and modifying it as needed. For a large system, installation may take months or even years. Often installation is more difficult than planned. Even after careful consideration in the design phase, unforeseen difficulties may emerge. If the system is not debugged, the business will have a well-designed system that is not performing its intended tasks.

Basic Model of Information Processing _____

Processing accounting information means collecting data, organizing the data and communicating the information to statement users. The accounting data are also used by managers. For example, accounts receivable might be analysed to identify the biggest customers, who will receive special privileges. Exhibit 6-1 shows how the *basic model of information processing* ties us to an accounting system.

EXHIBIT 6-1   *Information-Processing Model and the Accounting System*

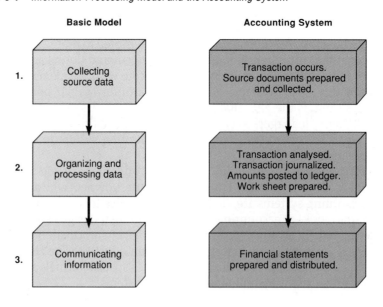

1. The *source data* for the accounting system are the *documents*, such as invoices and canceled cheques, that business transactions generate.
2. *Organizing and processing* data requires transaction analysis, journalizing, posting, and preparation of the work sheet.
3. The output is *information* — the *financial statements*.

Notice that the system converts data to reports, fulfilling accounting's role of providing information.

An Effective Information System

Each business's accounting information system follows the basic model of information processing shown in Exhibit 6-1. Besides following these steps, a well-designed information system offers control, compatibility, flexibility and an acceptable cost/benefit relationship.

Control

A good accounting information system gives management control over operations. **Internal controls** are the methods and procedures a business uses to protect its assets and to ensure the accuracy of its accounting records. For example, most companies exert tight controls over cash disbursement to avoid theft through unauthorized payments. Also, keeping accurate records of accounts receivable is the only way to ensure that customers are billed and collections are received on time. The accounting system controls assets to different degrees. Usually control over cash is tighter than control over supplies and prepaid expenses, because cash is more open to theft. Chapter 7 details internal control procedures.

> **OBJECTIVE 1**
> Describe the features of an effective information system

Compatibility

An information system meets the compatibility guideline when it works smoothly with the particular structure, personnel and special features of the business. For example, one company may be organized by geographical region and another company by product line. The accounting system for the first company would accumulate revenues and expenses by region. The second company's system would group revenues and expenses by product. Any combination of data accumulation by region and by product is possible, whatever best suits the business. The compatibility guideline means designing the information system with the human factor in mind.

Flexibility

Organizations evolve. They develop new products, sell off unprofitable operations and adjust employee pay scales. Changes in the business often call for changes in the accounting system. A well-designed system meets the flexibility guideline if it can accommodate such changes without needing a complete overhaul. In most organizations, systems are rarely replaced in their entirety. For example, a system for control of cash might be installed one year and a system for controlling inventories a year later.

Acceptable Cost/Benefit Relationship

Control, compatibility and flexibility can be achieved in an accounting system, but they cost money. At some point, the cost of the system outweighs its benefits. Identifying that point is the job of the accountant as systems analyst and the manager as user of the information.

Consider the growing number of businesses that have bought computers. For many companies, an elaborate computer system saves time and money and results in improved decisions. In these cases, the benefits far exceed the cost of the computer. In other cases, the savings are not sufficient to justify the cost of an increasingly complex system.

Computer Data Processing

Much data processing in business is done by computer. Computers offer significant advantages in accuracy and in the volume of accounting work that can be performed.

Components of a Computer System

The components of a computer data processing system are *hardware, software* and *personnel.*

Hardware   Computer **hardware** is the equipment that makes up the system. Exhibit 6-2 shows the hardware components of a mainframe system. A **main-**

EXHIBIT 6-2   *Mainframe Computer System*

Source: IBM 3090 Model 600E. Reproduced courtesy of IBM Corporation.

frame system is characterized by a single computer. It can be used locally or by employees at various locations. Employees enter data into the mainframe through remote terminals. In large systems, the employees may be scattered all over the world yet have access to the same computer. Smaller mainframe systems, called **minicomputers**, operate like large systems but on a smaller scale.

Exhibit 6-3 shows a microcomputer system, which is based on a different concept. In a **microcomputer** system, each work station has its own computer, often called a personal computer. Microcomputers can be connected so that employees can work on the same project together. A group of microcomputers connected for common use is called a network, which achieves many of the benefits of a mainframe system. Micro systems are popular because they are more flexible and less expensive than large mainframes.

Software Computer **software** is the set of programs or instructions that cause the computer to perform the work desired. In a computer system, transactions are not entered into the accounting records by writing entries in a journal. They are entered by typing data on a keyboard similar to that of a typewriter. The keyboard is wired to the computer, which converts the typed data into instructions the computer uses to process the data. In a few systems, the data are entered into the computer on punched cards.

Mainframe software includes programs written in computer languages such as FORTRAN, COBOL and PL/1. Microcomputers use software based on computer languages such as BASIC and PASCAL. Other micro software is designed to do specialized tasks. For example, LOTUS® 1-2-3 performs financial analysis, and dBASE III organizes, stores and retrieves vast quantities of data. ACCPAC®'s General Ledger and Financial Reporter program processes data and prints the balance sheet, income statement and subsidiary records of accounts receivable, accounts payable and payroll, among many other

EXHIBIT 6-3 *Microcomputer System*

Source: IBM Personal System/2 Model 60. Reproduced courtesy of IBM Corporation.

accounting tasks. Microcomputer software is popular because much of it is menu driven. This means by following instructions, the "menu", you can do complex tasks with little or no computer training.

Personnel   Computer personnel in a mainframe system include a systems analyst, a programmer and a machine operator. The *systems analyst* designs the system, based on managers' information needs and the available accounting data. It is the analyst's job to design systems that convert data into useful information — at the lowest cost. The *programmer* writes the programs (instructions) that direct the computer's actions. The computer *operator* runs the machine.

In microcomputer systems, the distinction between the programmer and the operator becomes blurry, because employees may handle both responsibilities. For example, a marketing manager may use a microcomputer to identify the territory needing an advertising campaign. The company treasurer may use a micro to analyse the effects of borrowing money at various interest rates. The controller may prepare the budget on a micro. These people may program the computer to meet their specific needs and also operate the machine.

Batch versus On-line Processing

Computers process data in two main ways: in batches and on-line. **Batch processing** handles similar transactions in a group or batch; batch processing is done on a periodic basis (e.g., once a day, once a week). Payroll accounting systems use batch processing. Suppose each employee fills out a weekly time sheet showing the number of hours he or she worked. Stored in the computer are the employee's hourly pay and payroll deductions. The machine operator enters the hours worked, and the computer multiplies hours by hourly pay to determine each employee's gross pay. The computer subtracts deductions to compute net pay and prints payroll cheques for the net amount. It also prints the weekly payroll report and updates the ledger accounts — all in one batch operation. Batch processing uses a limited portion of computer capacity.

On-line processing handles transaction data continuously, often from various locations, rather than in batches at a single location. In retail stores like The Bay and Eaton's, the cash register does more than make change. It also doubles as a computer terminal. When you charge merchandise at an Eaton's store, the transaction is recorded at Eaton's dataprocessing centre directly from the store cash register. For any one transaction the computer at the centre may perform the following steps:

1. Accounts Receivable
   a. Compares your account number to the list of approved accounts.
      Assume your account is approved.
   b. Adds the amount of this transaction to your previous balance and determines whether the new balance, including this transaction amount, exceeds your credit limit.
      Assume it does not exceed your credit limit.
   c. Debits the Accounts Receivable account and updates your personal account balance to include the effect of this transaction.
2. Sales Revenue: Credits the Sales Revenue account.
3. Inventory
   a. Updates inventory records for the decrease due to this transaction.
   b. Prepares an order for replacement merchandise if the updated quantity on hand is below the reorder point.

The interactive nature of on-line processing—accounting for accounts receivable, sales and inventory simultaneously—requires a large share of the computer's capacity. On-line processing, therefore, is used more in mainframe systems than in micro systems.

Overview of an Accounting Information System

The purpose of an accounting information system is to produce the financial statements and other reports used by managers, creditors and interested people to evaluate the business. To achieve this, companies often use computers, but in various ways determined by their specific needs. One company's accounting system may use a computer for accounts receivable and cash receipts and a manual system for the rest of its business. Another business may computerize payroll, accounts payable and cash disbursements, with the remainder accounted for manually. Many large companies have completely computerized accounting information systems, and many small businesses use mostly manual systems. Each entity designs its system to achieve the goals of control, compatibility, flexibility and an acceptable cost/benefit relationship. Exhibit 6-4 diagrams a typical accounting information system for a merchandising business.

Accounting procedures may be manual or computerized, mainframe or microcomputer, batch or on-line. The remainder of the chapter describes some of the more important aspects of the system described in Exhibit 6-4. Later chapters discuss the remaining system topics diagrammed in the exhibit.

EXHIBIT 6-4   *Overview of an Accounting Information System*

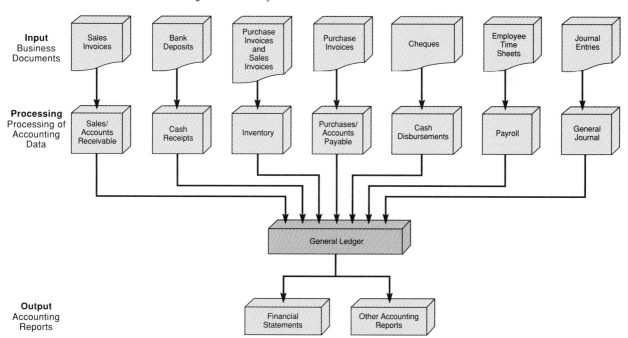

Special Accounting Journals

The journal entries illustrated so far in this book have been made in the **general journal**. In practice, however, it is inefficient to record all transactions there.

Think of using the general journal to debit Accounts Receivable and credit Sales Revenue for each credit sale made in a department store on a busy Saturday! Assuming you survived that, consider posting each journal entry to the ledger. Not only would the work be tedious, but it would be time-consuming and expensive.

In fact, most of a business's transactions fall into one of four categories, so accountants use special journals to record these transactions. This system reduces the time and cost otherwise spent journalizing, as we will see. The four categories of transactions, the related special journal and the posting abbreviations follow:

Transaction	Special Journal	Posting Abbreviation
1. Sales on account	Sales journal	S.
2. Cash receipt	Cash receipts journal	CR.
3. Purchase on account	Purchases journal	P.
4. Cash disbursement	Cash disbursements journal	CD.

Businesses use the *general journal* for transactions that do not fit one of the special journals. For example, adjusting and closing entries are entered in the general journal. Its posting abbreviation is J.

OBJECTIVE 2
Use the sales journal

Sales Journal

Most merchandisers sell at least some of their inventory on account. These *credit sales* are recorded in the **sales journal**, also called the *credit sales journal*. Credit sales of assets other than inventory (for example, buildings) occur infrequently and are recorded in the general journal.

Exhibit 6-5 illustrates a sales journal (Panel A) and the related posting to the ledgers (Panel B) of Austin Sound, the stereo shop we introduced in Chapter 5.

The sales journal in Exhibit 6-5 (Panel A) has only one amount column, on the far right. Each entry in this column is a debit (Dr.) to Accounts Receivable and a Credit (Cr.) to Sales Revenue, as the heading above this column indicates. For each transaction, the accountant enters the date, invoice number and customer account, along with the transaction amount. This streamlined way of recording sales on account saves a vast amount of time that would be spent writing account titles and dollar amounts in the general journal.

In recording credit sales in previous chapter, we did not keep a record of the names of credit sale customers. In practice the business must know the amount receivable from each customer. How else can the company keep track of who owes it money—and how much?

Consider the first transaction. On November 2, Austin Sound sold stereo equipment on account to Claudette Trudeau for $935. The invoice number is 422. All this information appears on a single line in the sales journal. Note that no explanation is necessary. The transaction's presence in the sales journal means that it is a credit sale: debited to Accounts Receivable—Claudette Trudeau and credited to Sales Revenue. To gain any additional information about the transaction, a person looks up the actual invoice.

Posting to the General Ledger   Note the term **general ledger**. The ledger accounts we have used so far are held in the general ledger, which holds the accounts reported in the financial statements. However, we will soon introduce other ledgers.

EXHIBIT 6-5   *Sales Journal and Posting to Ledgers*

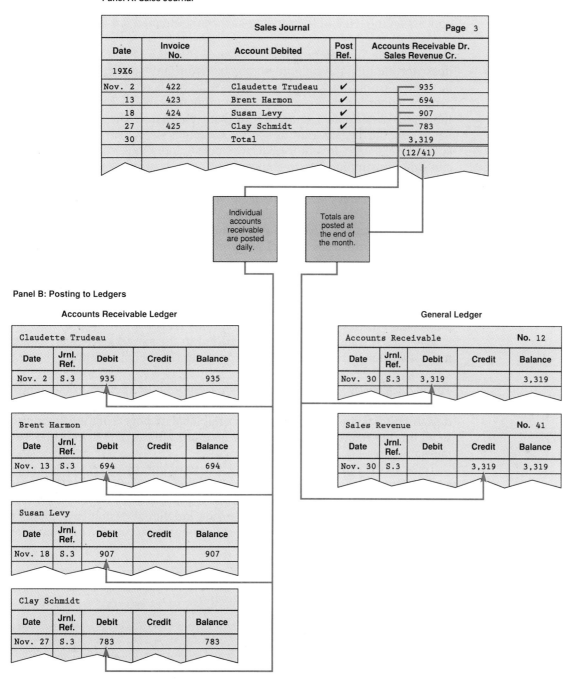

Panel A: Sales Journal

Panel B: Posting to Ledgers

Posting from the sales journal to the general ledger is done monthly. First, the amounts in the journal are added up. In Exhibit 6-5, the total credit sales for November are $3,319. Recall that this column has two headings, Accounts Receivable and Sales Revenue. When the $3,319 is posted to these accounts in the general ledger, the accountant enters their account numbers beneath the total in the sales journal. Note in Panel B of Exhibit 6-5 that the account number for Accounts Receivable is 12 and the account number for Sales Revenue is 41. These account numbers are written beneath the credit sales total in the sales journal to signify that the $3,319 has been posted to the two accounts. The $3,319 is a debit to Accounts Receivable and a credit to Sales Revenue, as the heading in the sales journal states. The number of the account debited (12) appears on the left and the number of the account credited (41) on the right.

Posting to the Subsidiary Ledger   The $3,319 sum of the November debits does not identify the amount receivable from any specific customer. Most businesses would find keeping a separate accounts receivable account in the general ledger for each customer to be unmanageable. A business may have thousands of customers. Imagine how many pages thick the general ledger for Eaton's would be. Locating a specific customer's account among the other accounts (like Cash, Inventory, Salary Expense, and so on) would be frustrating and time-consuming. To streamline operations, businesses instead place the accounts of their individual credit customers in a subsidiary ledger, called the Accounts Receivable ledger. A **subsidiary ledger** is a book of accounts that provides supporting details on individual balances, the total of which appears in the general ledger. The customer accounts are filed alphabetically.

OBJECTIVE 3

Use control accounts and
subsidiary ledgers

Amounts in the sales journal are posted to the subsidiary ledger daily to keep a current record of the amount receivable from each customer. Note that the amounts are debits. Daily posting allows the business to answer customer inquiries promptly. Suppose Claudette Trudeau telephones Austin Sound on November 11 to ask how much money she owes. Austin Sound has that information readily available in the subsidiary ledger.

When each transaction amount is posted to the subsidiary ledger, a check mark is written in the posting reference column of the sales journal.

Posting References in the Ledgers   When amounts are posted to the ledgers, the journal page number is written in the account to identify the source of the data. All transaction data in Exhibit 6-5 originated on page 3 of the sales journal so all posting references in the ledger accounts are S.3. The S. indicates sales journal.

Trace all the postings in Exhibit 6-5. The most effective way to learn about accounting systems and special journals is to study the flow of data. The arrows indicate the direction of the information.

The arrows show the links between the individual customer accounts in the subsidiary ledger and the Accounts Receivable account. These links are summarized as follows:

Accounts Receivable debit balance		$3,319
Balances of individual customer accounts in the subsidiary ledger		
Claudette Trudeau	$935	
Brent Harmon	694	
Susan Levy	907	
Clay Schmidt	783	
Total		$3,319

Accounts Receivable in the general ledger is a **control account**. In this simple illustration, its balance is the total amount of credit sales. The individual credit customer accounts are subsidiary accounts. They are "controlled" by the Accounts Receivable account in the general ledger.

Let us look at the advantages the sales journal offers. Each transaction is entered on a single line, and the account titles do not have to be written. The accountant, then, does not have to write as much in the sales journal as in the general journal. Also, the sales journal streamlines posting. Suppose that Austin

Sound had 400 credit sales for the month. How many postings to the general ledger would be made from the sales journal? There are only two: one to Accounts Receivable and one to Sales Revenue. How many postings would there be from the general journal? The total would be 800 — 400 debits to Accounts Receivable and 400 credits to Sales Revenue.

Additional data can be recorded in the sales journal. For example, a company may add a column to record sale terms, such as 2/10 n/30. The design of the journal depends on the business's needs for information.

Cash Receipts Journal

OBJECTIVE 4
Use the cash receipts journal

Cash transactions are common in most businesses because cash receipts from customers are the lifeblood of business. To streamline the recording of repetitive cash receipt transactions, accountants use the **cash receipts journal**.

Panel A in Exhibit 6-6 illustrates the cash receipts journal. The related posting to ledgers is shown in Panel B. The exhibit illustrates November transactions for Austin Sound.

Every transaction recorded in this journal is a cash receipt, so the first column is for debits to the Cash account. The next column is for debits to Sales Discounts on collections from customers. In a typical merchandising business, the main sources of cash are collections on account and cash sales. Thus the cash receipts journal has credit columns for Accounts Receivable and Sales Revenue. The journal also has a credit column for Other Accounts, which lists sources of cash other than cash sales and collections on account. This Other Accounts column is also used to record the names of customers from whom cash is received on account.

In Exhibit 6-6, cash sales occurred on November 6, 19 and 28. Observe the debits to Cash and the credits to Sales Revenue ($517, $853 and $1,802).

On November 11, Austin Sound borrowed $1,000 from Georgian Bay Bank. Cash is debited, and Note Payable to Georgian Bay Bank is credited in the Other Accounts column because no specific credit column is set up to account for borrowings. For this transaction, it is necessary to write the account title, Note Payable to Georgian Bay Bank, in the Other Accounts/Account Title column to record the source of cash.

On November 25, Austin Sound collected $762 of interest revenue. The account credited, Interest Revenue, must be written in the Other Accounts column. The November 11 and 25 transactions illustrate an important fact about business. Different entities have different types of transactions, and they design their special journals to meet their particular needs. In this case, the Other Accounts Credit column is the catch-all that is used to record all nonstandard cash receipt transactions.

On November 14, Austin Sound collected $900 from Claudette Trudeau. Referring back to Exhibit 6-5, we see that on November 2 Austin Sound sold inventory valued at $935 to Ms. Trudeau. Assume that the terms of sale allowed a $35 discount for prompt payment and that she paid within the discount period. Austin's cash receipts is recorded by debiting Cash for $900 and Sales Discounts for $35 and by crediting Accounts Receivable for $935. Note that the customer's name appears in the Other Accounts/Account Title column. This enables the business to keep exact track of each customer's account.

On November 22, the business collected $300 on account from Brent Harmon, who was paying for part of the November 13 purchase. Assume no discount applied to this collection.

Total debits should equal total credits in the cash receipts journal. This equality holds for each transaction and for the monthly totals. For example, the first transaction has a $517 credit and an equal debit. For the month, total

EXHIBIT 6-6   *Cash Receipts Journal and Posting to Ledgers*

Panel A: Cash Receipts Journal

Date	Cash (Debits)	Sales Discounts (Debits)	Accounts Receivable (Credits)	Sales Revenue (Credits)	Account Title (Other Accounts)	Post. Ref.	Amount
19X6							
Nov. 6	517			517			
11	1,000				Note Payable to First Bank	22	1,000
14	900	35	935		Claudette Trudeau	✔	
19	853			853			
22	300		300		Brent Harmon	✔	
25	762				Interest Revenue	46	762
28	1,802			1,802			
30	6,134	35	1,235	3,172	Totals		1,762
	(11)	(42)	(12)	(41)			(✔)

Totals are posted at the end of the month.

Individual accounts receivable are posted daily.

Individual amounts are posted at the end of the month.

Total is not posted.

Panel B: Posting to Ledgers

Accounts Receivable Ledger

Claudette Trudeau

Date	Jrnl. Ref.	Debit	Credit	Balance
Nov. 2	S.3	935		935
14	CR.5		935	-0-

Brent Harmon

Date	Jrnl. Ref.	Debit	Credit	Balance
Nov. 13	S.3	694		694
22	CR.5		300	394

Susan Levy

Date	Jrnl. Ref.	Debit	Credit	Balance
Nov. 18	S.3	907		907

Clay Schmidt

Date	Jrnl. Ref.	Debit	Credit	Balance
Nov. 27	S.3	783		783

General Ledger

Cash   No. 11

Date	Jrnl. Ref.	Debit	Credit	Balance
Nov. 30	CR.5	6,134		6,134

Accounts Receivable   No. 12

Date	Jrnl. Ref.	Debit	Credit	Balance
Nov. 30	S.3	3,319		3,319
30	CR.5		1,235	2,084

Note Payable to First Bank   No. 22

Date	Jrnl. Ref.	Debit	Credit	Balance
Nov. 11	CR.5		1,000	1,000

Sales Revenue   No. 41

Date	Jrnl. Ref.	Debit	Credit	Balance
Nov. 30	S.3		3,319	3,319
30	CR.5		3,172	6,491

Sales Discounts   No. 42

Date	Jrnl. Ref.	Debit	Credit	Balance
Nov. 30	CR.5	35		35

Interest Revenue   No. 46

Date	Jrnl. Ref.	Debit	Credit	Balance
Nov. 25	CR.5		762	762

debits ($6,134+$35=$6,169) equal total credits ($1,235+$3,172+$1,762= $6,169).

Posting to the General Ledger   The column totals are posted monthly. To indicate their posting, the account number is written below the column total in the cash receipts journal. Note the account number for Cash (11) below the column total $6,134, and trace the posting to Cash in the general ledger. Likewise, the Sales Discounts, Accounts Receivable and Sales Revenue column totals also are posted to the general ledger.

The column total for *Other Accounts* is not posted. Instead, these credits are posted individually. In Exhibit 6-6, the November 11 transaction reads "Note Payable to Georgian Bay Bank." This account's number (22) in the Post. Ref. column indicates that the transaction amount was posted individually. The check mark, instead of an account number, below the column total indicates that the column total was not posted. The November 25 collection of interest revenue is also posted individually. These amounts can be posted to the general ledger at the end of the month. However, they should be dated in the ledger accounts based on their actual date in the journal. This makes it easy to trace the amounts back to the journal.

Posting to the Subsidiary Ledger   Amounts from the cash receipts journal are posted to the subsidiary accounts receivable ledger daily to keep the individual balances up to date. The postings to the accounts receivable ledger are credits. Trace the $935 posting to Claudette Trudeau's account. It reduces the balance in her account to zero. The $300 receipt from Brent Harmon reduces his accounts receivable balance to $394.

After posting, the sum of the individual balances that remain in the accounts receivable ledger equals the general ledger balance in Accounts Receivable ($2,084). Austin Sound may prepare a November 30 list of account balances from the subsidiary ledger as a check of the accuracy of journalizing and posting.

Customer Accounts Receivable

Customer	Balance
Brent Harmon	$394
Susan Levy	907
Clay Schmidt	783
Total accounts receivable	$2,084

Keeping good accounts receivable records reduces errors and helps customer relations.

The cash receipts journal offers the same advantages as the sales journal: streamlined journalizing of transactions and fewer postings to the ledgers.

Summary Problem for Your Review

A company completed the following selected transactions during March:

Mar. 4   Received $500 from a cash sale to a customer.
     6   Received $60 on account from Brady Lee. The full invoice amount

was $65, but Lee paid within the discount period to gain the $5 discount.

9 Received $1,080 on a note receivable from Beverly Mann. This amount includes the $1,000 note receivable plus $80 of interest revenue.

15 Received $800 from a cash sale to a customer.

24 Borrowed $2,200 by signing a note payable to the Bank of the Rockies.

27 Received $1,200 on account from Lance Albert. Payment was received after the discount period lapsed.

The general ledger showed the following balances at February 28: Cash, debit balance of $1,117; Accounts Receivable, debit balance of $2,790; Note Receivable—Beverly Mann, debit balance of $1,000. The accounts receivable subsidiary ledger at February 28 contained debit balances as follows: Lance Albert, $1,840; Melinda Fultz, $885; Brady Lee, $65.

Required

1. Record the transactions in the cash receipts journal, page 7.
2. Compute column totals at March 31. Show that total debits equal total credits in the cash receipts journal.
3. Post to the general ledger and the accounts receivable subsidiary ledger. Use complete posting references, including the account numbers illustrated: Cash, 11; Accounts Receivable, 12; Note Receivable—Beverly Mann, 13; Note Payable—Bank of the Rockies, 22; Sales Revenue, 41; Sales Discounts, 42; Interest Revenue, 46. Insert a check mark (✔) in the posting reference column for each February 28 account balance.
4. Prove the accuracy of posting by showing that the total of the balances in the subsidiary ledger equals the general ledger balance in Accounts Receivable.

SOLUTION TO REVIEW PROBLEM

Requirements 1 and 2

Cash Receipts Journal   **Page 7**

| | Debits | | Credits | | | | |
| | | | | | Other Accounts | | |
Date	Cash	Sales Discounts	Accounts Receivable	Sales Revenue	Account Title	Post. Ref.	Amount
Mar. 4	500			500			
6	60	5	65		Brady Lee	✔	
9	1,080				Note Receivable —Beverly Mann	13	1,000
					Interest Revenue	46	80
15	800			800			
24	2,200				Note Payable— Bank of the Rockies	22	2,200
27	1,200		1,200		Lance Albert	✔	
31	5,840	5	1,265	1,300	Total		3,280
	(11)	(42)	(12)	(41)			(✔)

5,845   5,845

Requirement 3

Accounts Receivable Subsidiary Ledger

Lance Albert

Date	Post. Ref.	Debit	Credit	Balance
Feb. 28	✔			1,840
Mar. 27	CR. 7		1,200	640

Melinda Fultz

Date	Post. Ref.	Debit	Credit	Balance
Feb. 28	✔			885

Brandy Lee

Date	Post. Ref.	Debit	Credit	Balance
Feb. 28	✔			65
Mar. 6	CR. 7		65	

General Ledger

Cash   No. 11

Date	Post. Ref.	Debit	Credit	Balance
Feb. 28	✔			1,117
Mar. 31	CR. 7	5,840		6,957

Accounts Receivable   No. 12

Date	Post. Ref.	Debit	Credit	Balance
Feb. 28	✔			2,790
Mar. 31	CR. 7		1,265	1,525

Note Receivable — Beverly Mann   No. 13

Date	Post. Ref.	Debit	Credit	Balance
Feb. 28	✔			1,000
Mar. 9	CR. 7		1,000	

Note Payable — Bank of the Rockies   No. 22

Date	Post. Ref.	Debit	Credit	Balance
Mar. 24	CR. 7		2,200	2,200

Sales Revenue   No. 41

Date	Post. Ref.	Debit	Credit	Balance
Mar. 31	CR. 7		1,300	1,300

Sales Discount   No. 42

Date	Post. Ref.	Debit	Credit	Balance
Mar. 31	CR. 7	5		5

Interest Revenue   No. 46

Date	Post. Ref.	Debit	Credit	Balance
Mar. 9	CR. 7		80	80

Requirement 4

Lance Albert	$ 640
Melinda Fultz	885
Total	$1,525

This total agrees with the balance in Accounts Receivable.

OBJECTIVE 5
Use the purchases journal

Purchases Journal

A merchandising business purchases inventory and supplies frequently. Such purchases are usually made on account. The **purchases journal** is designed to account for all purchases of inventory, supplies and other assets *on account*. Cash purchases are recorded in the **cash disbursements journal**.

Exhibit 6-7 illustrates Austin Sound's purchases journal (Panel A) and posting to ledgers (Panel B).[1]

The purchases journal in Exhibit 6-7 has amount columns for credits to Accounts Payable and debits to Purchases, Supplies and Other Accounts. The Other Accounts columns accommodate purchases of assets other than inventory and supplies. These columns make the journal flexible enough to accommodate a wide variety of transactions. Each business designs its purchases journal to meet its own needs for information and efficiency. Accounts Payable is credited for all transactions recorded in the purchases journal. Inventory purchases are debited to Purchases. Purchases of supplies are debited to Supplies.

On November 2, Austin Sound purchased from JVC Corporation stereo inventory costing $700. The creditor's name (JVC Corporation) is entered in the Account Credited column. The purchase terms of 3/15 n/30 are also entered to help identify the due date and the discount available. Accounts Payable is credited and Purchases is debited for the transaction amount. On November 19, a credit purchase of supplies is entered as a debit to Supplies and a credit to Accounts Payable.

Note the November 9 purchase of fixtures from City Office Supply. Since the purchases journal contains no column for fixtures, the Other Accounts debit column is used. Because this was a credit purchase, the accountant enters the creditor name (City Office Supply) in the Account Credited column and writes "Fixtures" in the Other Accounts/Account Title column.

The total credits in the journal ($2,876) are compared to the total debits ($1,706 + $103 + $1,067 = $2,876) to prove the accuracy of the entries in the purchases journal.

To pay debts efficiently, a company must know how much it owes particular creditors. The Accounts Payable account in the general ledger shows only a single total, however, and therefore does not indicate the amount owed to each creditor. Companies keep an accounts payable subsidiary ledger. The accounts payable ledger lists the creditors in alphabetical order, along with the amounts owed to them. Exhibit 6-7 shows Austin Sound's accounts payable subsidiary ledger, which includes accounts for Audio Electronics, City Office

---

[1] This is the only special journal that we illustrate with the credit column placed to the left and the debit columns to the right. This arrangement of columns focuses on Accounts Payable, which is credited for each entry to this journal and on the individual supplier to be paid.

EXHIBIT 6-7   *Purchases Journal and Posting to Ledgers*

Panel A: Purchases Journal

Date	Account Credited	Terms	Post. Ref.	Credit — Accounts Payable	Debits — Purchases	Debits — Supplies	Other Accounts — Account Title	Other Accounts — Post. Ref.	Other Accounts — Amount
19X6									
Nov. 2	JVC Corp.	3/15 n/30	✔	700	700				
5	Pioneer Sound	n/30	✔	319	319				
9	City Office Supply	2/10 n/30	✔	440			Fixtures	19	440
12	Audio Electronics, Inc.	n/30	✔	236	236				
13	JVC Corp.	3/15 n/30	✔	451	451				
19	City Office Supply Co.	2/10 n/30	✔	103		103			
23	O'Leary Furniture Co.	n/60	✔	627			Furniture	18	627
30	Totals			2876	1706	103			1067
				(21)	(51)	(16)			(✔)

Purchases Journal   Page 8

- Individual accounts payable are posted daily.
- Totals are posted at the end of the month.
- Total is not posted
- Individual amounts are posted at the end of the month.

Panel B: Posting to Ledgers

Accounts Payable Subsidiary Ledger

Audio Electronics

Date	Jrnl. Ref.	Debit	Credit	Balance
Nov. 12	P.8		236	236

City Office Supply Co.

Date	Jrnl. Ref.	Debit	Credit	Balance
Nov. 9	P.8		440	440
19	P.8		103	543

JVC Corp.

Date	Jrnl. Ref.	Debit	Credit	Balance
Nov. 2	P.8		700	700
13	P.8		451	1,151

O'Leary Furniture Co.

Date	Jrnl. Ref.	Debit	Credit	Balance
Nov. 23	P.8		627	627

Pioneer Sound

Date	Jrnl. Ref.	Debit	Credit	Balance
Nov. 5	P.8		319	319

General Ledger

Supplies   No. 16

Date	Jrnl. Ref.	Debit	Credit	Balance
Nov. 30	P.8	103		103

Furniture   No. 18

Date	Jrnl. Ref.	Debit	Credit	Balance
Nov. 23	P.8	627		627

Fixtures   No. 19

Date	Jrnl. Ref.	Debit	Credit	Balance
Nov. 9	P.8	440		440

Accounts Payable   No. 21

Date	Jrnl. Ref.	Debit	Credit	Balance
Nov. 30	P.8		2,876	2,876

Purchases   No. 51

Date	Jrnl. Ref.	Debit	Credit	Balance
Nov. 30	P.8	1,706		1,706

Supply and others. After posting at the end of the period, the total of the individual balances in the subsidiary ledger equals the balance in the Accounts Payable control account in the general ledger. This system is much like the accounts receivable system discussed earlier in the chapter.

Posting from the Purchases Journal   Posting from the purchases journal is similar to posting from the sales journal and the cash receipts journal. Panel B in Exhibit 6-7 illustrates the posting process.

Individual accounts payable in the *accounts payable subsidiary ledger* are posted daily, and column totals and other amounts are posted to the *general ledger* at the end of the month. In the ledger accounts, P. 8 indicates the source of the posted amounts, that is, page 8 of the purchases journal.

Use of the special purchases journal offers advantages over the general journal. Each transaction is *journalized* on one line, and the general ledger accounts do not have to be written. A written explanation of each transaction is unnecessary because each transaction is a purchase on account. *Posting* to the general ledger is streamlined with the special journal because monthly totals can be posted to the general ledger. Contrast the number of postings from the purchases journal in Exhibit 6-7 with the number that would be required, if the general journal were used to record the same seven transactions. Use of the purchases journal requires only five general ledger postings— $2,876 to Accounts Payable, $1,706 to Purchases, $103 to Supplies, $440 to Fixtures and $627 to Furniture. Without the purchases journal, there would have been 14 postings, 2 for each of the 7 transactions.

| **OBJECTIVE 6** |
| Use the cash disbursements journal |

Cash Disbursements Journal

Most businesses make cash disbursements in two ways: by cheque or with currency and coin from a petty cash fund. *Petty* means "minor," and petty cash disbursements are small. We discuss accounting for petty cash in Chapter 7.

Businesses make most cash disbursements by cheque. All payments by cheque are recorded in the cash disbursements journal. Other titles of this special journal are the *cheque register* and *cash payments journal*. Like the other special journals, it has multiple columns for recording cash payments that occur frequently.

Panel A in Exhibit 6-8 illustrates the cash disbursements journal, and Panel B shows the postings to the ledgers of Austin Sound.

The cash disbursements journal in the exhibit has two debit columns (for Accounts Payable and Other Accounts) and two credit columns (for Cash and Purchase Discounts). It also has columns for the date and cheque number of each cash payment.

Suppose a business makes numerous cash purchases of inventory. What additional column would its cash disbursements journal need to be most useful? A column for Purchases, which would appear under the Debits heading, would streamline the accounting.

All entries in the cash disbursements journal include a credit to Cash. Payments on account are debits to Accounts Payable. On November 15, Austin Sound paid JVC on account, with credit terms of 3/15 n/30 (for details, see the first transaction in Exhibit 6-7). Therefore, Austin took the 3 percent discount and paid $679 ($700 less the $21 discount).

The Other Accounts column is used to record debits to accounts for which no special column exists. For example, on November 3, Austin Sound paid rent expense of $1,200, and on November 8, the business purchased supplies for $61.

EXHIBIT 6-8   *Cash Disbursements Journal and Posting to Ledgers*

Panel A: Cash Disbursements Journal

				Debits		Credits	
						Cash Disbursements Journal	Page **6**
Date	Ck. No.	Account Debited	Post. Ref.	Other Accounts	Accounts Payable	Purchase Discounts	Cash
19X6							
Nov. 3	101	Rent Expense	54	1,200			1,200
8	102	Supplies	16	61			61
15	103	JVC Corp.	✔		700	21	679
20	104	Pioneer Sound	✔		119		119
26	105	Purchases	51	1,900			1,900
30		Totals		3,161	819	21	3,959
				(✔)	(21)	(52)	(11)

> Total is not posted

> Totals are posted at the end of the month.

> Individual accounts payable are posted daily.

> Individual amounts are posted at the end of the month.

Panel B: Posting to Ledgers

Accounts Payable Subsidiary Ledger

Audio Electronics

Date	Jrnl. Ref.	Debit	Credit	Balance
Nov. 12	P.8		236	236

City Office Supply

Date	Jrnl. Ref.	Debit	Credit	Balance
Nov. 9	P.8		440	440
19	P.8		103	543

JVC Corp.

Date	Jrnl. Ref.	Debit	Credit	Balance
Nov. 2	P.8		700	700
13	P.8		451	1151
15	CD.6	700		451

O'Leary Furniture Co.

Date	Jrnl. Ref.	Debit	Credit	Balance
Nov. 23	P.8		627	627

Pioneer Sound

Date	Jrnl. Ref.	Debit	Credit	Balance
Nov. 5	P.8		319	319
20	CD.6	119		200

General Ledger

Cash   No. 11

Date	Jrnl. Ref.	Debit	Credit	Balance
Nov. 30	CR.5	6,134		6,134
30	CD.6		3,959	2,175

Supplies   No. 16

Date	Jrnl. Ref.	Debit	Credit	Balance
Nov. 30	P.8	103		103
8	CD.6	61		164

Accounts Payable   No. 21

Date	Jrnl. Ref.	Debit	Credit	Balance
Nov. 30	P.8		2,876	2,876
30	CD.6	819		2,057

Purchases   No. 51

Date	Jrnl. Ref.	Debit	Credit	Balance
Nov. 30	P.8	1,706		1,706
26	CD.6	1,900		3,606

Purchase Discounts   No. 52

Date	Jrnl. Ref.	Debit	Credit	Balance
Nov. 30	CD.6		21	21

Rent Expense   No. 54

Date	Jrnl. Ref.	Debit	Credit	Balance
Nov. 3	CD.6	1,200		1,200

As with all other journals, the total debits ($3,161 + $819 = $3,980) should equal the total credits ($21 + $3,959 = $3,980).

Posting from the Cash Disbursements Journal   Posting from the cash disbursements journal is similar to posting from the cash receipts journal. Individual creditor amounts are posted daily, and column totals and Other Accounts are posted at the end of the month. Panel B in Exhibit 6-8 illustrates the posting process.

Observe the effect of posting to the Accounts Payable account in the general ledger. The first posted amount in the Accounts Payable account (credit $2,876) originated in the purchases journal, page 8 (P.8). The second posted amount (debit $819) came from the cash disbursements journal, page 6 (CD.6). The resulting credit balance in Accounts Payable is $2,057. Also, see the Cash account. After posting, its debit balance is $2,175.

Amounts in the Other Accounts column are posted individually (for example, Rent Expense—debit $1,200). When each Other Accounts amount is posted to the general ledger, the account number is written in the Post. Ref. column of the journal.

As a proof of accuracy, companies total the individual creditor balances in the accounts payable subsidiary ledger for comparison with the Accounts Payable balance in the general ledger.

Creditor Accounts Payable

Creditor	Balance
Audio Electronics	$ 236
City Office Supply	543
JVC Corp.	451
O'Leary Furniture	627
Pioneer Sound	200
Total accounts payable	$2,057

This total, computed at the end of the period, agrees with the Accounts Payable balance in Exhibit 6-8. Agreement of the two amounts suggests that journalizing and posting have been performed correctly and that the resulting account balances are correct.

Use of the cash disbursements journal streamlines journalizing and posting in the same way as for the other special journals.

The Credit Memorandum: A Basic Business Document

Customers sometimes bring merchandise back to the seller, and sellers grant sales allowances to customers because of product defects and for other reasons. The effect of sales returns and sales allowances is the same: both decrease net sales in the same way a sales discount does. The document issued by the seller to indicate that the customer's Account Receivable is called a **credit memorandum** or **credit memo**. When a company issues a credit memo, it

EXHIBIT 6-9   *Credit Memorandum*

```
                    Credit Memorandum                No.  27

  Austin Sound                    Date   November 6, 19X6
  305 Robie Street
  Halifax, Nova Scotia B3H 4K7


  Customer Name      Maria Schultz

                     3007 Cobourg Road

                     Halifax, Nova Scotia B3H 2Y8


  Reason for Credit  Defective merchandise returned


            Description                          Amount
     2  Trailblazer JU170456 Speakers           $198
```

records the transaction by debiting Sales Returns and Allowances and crediting Accounts Receivable.

Suppose Austin Sound sold two stereo speakers for $198 on account to Maria Schultz. Later she discovered a defect and returned the speakers. Austin Sound would issue to Ms. Schultz a credit memo like the one in Exhibit 6-9.

To record the *sale return*, Austin Sound would make the following entry in the general journal:

	General Journal			Page 9
Date	**Accounts**	**Post. Ref.**	**Debit**	**Credit**
Nov. 6	Sales Returns and Allowances	43	198	
	Accounts Receivable — Maria Schultz	12/✔		198

The debit side of the entry is posted to Sales Return and Allowances. Its account number (43) is written in the posting reference column when $198 is posted. The credit side of the entry requires two $198 postings: one to Accounts Receivable, the control account in the general ledger (account number 12), and the other to Maria Schultz's account in the accounts receivable subsidiary ledger. These credit postings explain why the document is called a *credit memo*.

Observe that the posting references of the credit include two notations. The account number (12) denotes the posting to Accounts Receivable in the general ledger. The check mark (✔) denotes the posting to Ms. Schultz's account in the subsidiary ledger. Two postings are needed because this is the general journal. Without specially designed columns, it is necessary to write both posting references on the same line. Posting to the general ledger usually occurs monthly; and posting to the subsidiary ledger, daily.

Suppose Ms. Schultz had paid cash. Austin Sound would either give her a credit memo or refund her cash. Austin Sound would record the cash refund in the *cash disbursements journal* as follows:

				Debits		Credits	
Date	Ch. No.	Account Debited	Post. Ref.	Other Accounts	Accounts Payable	Purchase Discounts	Cash
Nov. 6	106	Sales Returns and Allowances	43	198			198

Cash Disbursements Journal   **Page 8**

A business with a high volume of sales returns, such as a department store chain, may find it efficient to use a specific journal for sales returns and allowances.

The Debit Memorandum: A Basic Business Document

Purchase Returns occur when a business returns goods to the seller. The procedures for handling purchase returns are similar to those dealing with sales returns. The purchaser gives the merchandise back to the seller and receives either a cash refund or replacement goods.

When a business returns merchandise to the seller, it may also send a business document known as a **debit memorandum** or **debit memo**. This document states that the buyer no longer owes the seller for the amount of the returned purchases. The buyer *debits* the Accounts Payable to the seller and credits Purchase Returns and Allowances. If the volume of purchase returns is high enough, the business may use a special journal for purchase returns.

Many businesses record their purchase returns in the general journal, not in a special journal. Austin Sound would record its return of defective speakers to JVC as follows:

General Journal   **Page 9**

Date	Accounts	Post Ref.	Debit	Credit
Nov. 6	Accounts Payable — JVC Corp...............	21/✔	137	
	Purchase Returns and Allowances..........	53		137
	Debits memo no. 16			

Sales Tax

Most provinces levy tax on sales (sales tax). Sellers must add the tax to the sale amount, then pay the tax to the provincial government. In most jurisdictions, sales tax is levied only on final consumers, so retail businesses usually do not pay sales tax on the goods they purchase for resale. For example, Gabor Stereo would not pay tax on a purchase of equipment from JVC, a wholesaler. However, when retailers like Gabor Stereo make sales, they must collect sales tax from the consumer. In effect, retailers serve as collecting agents for the taxing authorities. The amount of tax depends on the total sales.

Retailers set up procedures to collect the tax, account for it and pay it on time. Invoices may be preprinted with a place for entering the sales tax amount, and the general ledger has an account entitled Sales Tax Payable. The sales journal may include a special column for sales tax, such as the one illustrated in Exhibit 6-10. The sales tax rate is 5 percent.

EXHIBIT 6-10 *Sales Journal Designed to Account for Sales Tax*

				Sales Journal		Page 4
Date	Invoice No.	Account Debited	Post. Ref.	Accounts Receivable Dr.	Sales Tax Payable Cr.	Sales Revenue Cr.
19X6						
Nov. 2	422	Anne Fortin	✔	981.75	46.75	935.00
13	423	Brent Mooney	✔	728.70	34.70	694.00
18	424	Debby Levy	✔	952.35	45.35	907.00
27	425	Dan Girardi	✔	822.15	39.15	783.00
30		Totals		3,484.95	165.95	3,319.00

Note that the amount debited to Accounts Receivable ($3,484.95) is the sum of the credits to Sales Tax Payable ($165.95) and Sales Revenue ($3,319.00). This is so because the customers' payments, the Accounts Receivable figures, are partly for the purchase of merchandise (Sales Revenue) and partly for tax created by the sale. Each column total is posted at the end of the month, and individual customer accounts are posted daily to the accounts receivable subsidiary ledger. The check marks in the Posting Reference column show that individual amounts have been posted to the customer accounts. The absence of account numbers under the column totals shows that the total amounts have not yet been posted.

Another, but much less common, way to account for sales tax is to enter a single amount — which is the sum of sales revenue and sales tax — in the Sales Revenue account. This amount is what the customer pays the retailer. At the end of the period, the business computes the tax collected and transfers that amount from Sales Revenue to Sales Tax Payable through a general journal entry. This procedure eliminates the need for a special multicolumn journal.

Suppose a retailer's Sales Revenue account shows a $10,500 balance at the end of the period. This retailer chooses to enter the full amount of each sale — the actual sales revenue and the sales tax — as Sales Revenue. How does the retailer divide the total amount into its two parts?

To compute the actual sales revenue, the Sales Revenue balance is divided by 1 plus the tax rate. Assume that sales tax is 5 percent. Thus the retailer divides $10,500 by 1.05 (1+.05), which yields $10,000. Subtracting the actual sales revenue, the $10,000, from the $10,500 total yields $500, the sales tax. The retailer makes the following entry in the general journal:

	General Journal			**Page 9**

Date	Accounts	Post. Ref.	Debit	Credit
July 31	Sales Revenue	41	500	
	Sales Tax Payable	28		500
	To transfer sales tax to the liability account			

Sales tax is levied by many of the provinces as well as by the federal government; it is more fully discussed in Chapter 11.

Balancing the Ledgers

At the end of the period, after all postings, equality should exist between

1. Total debits and total credits in the general ledger. These amounts are used to prepare the trial balance that has been used throughout Chapters 3 to 5.
2. The balance of the Accounts Receivable control account in the general ledger and the sum of individual customer accounts in the accounts receivable subsidiary ledger.
3. The balance of the Accounts Payable control account in the general ledger and the sum of individual creditor accounts in the accounts payable subsidiary ledger.

This process is called **balancing the ledgers** or proving the ledgers. It is an important control procedure because it helps assure the accuracy of the accounting records. Equality between Accounts Receivable control and the accounts receivable subsidiary ledger was proved as shown in Exhibit 6-6 (p. 238). A simpler and less costly procedure is to total the individual customer balances on a calculator tape for comparison to Accounts Receivable control. Balancing the accounts payable ledger follows the same pattern as illustrated on p. 246.

Documents as Journals

Many small businesses streamline their accounting systems to save money by using the actual business documents as the journals. For example, Austin Sound could let its sales invoices serve as its sales journal and keep all invoices for credit sales in a looseleaf binder. At the end of the period, the accountant simply totals the sales on account and posts that amount to Accounts Receivable and Sales Revenue. Also, the accountant can post directly from invoices to customer accounts in the accounts receivable ledger. This "journal-less" system reduces accounting cost, because the accountant does not have to write in journals the information already in the business documents.

Summary Problem for Your Review

Identify the journal in which each of the following transactions would be recorded. Use journal abbreviations: sales journal = S; cash receipts journal = CR; purchases journal = P; cash disbursements journal = CD; general journal = J.

Cash sale_____

Sale on account_____

Loaned cash on note receivable_____

Received cash on account_____

Purchase of building on long-term
   note payable_____

Paid cash on account_____

Cash purchase of inventory_____

Owner investment of cash in
   the business_____

Closing entries_____

Purchase of supplies on account_____

Receipt of cash on account_____

Adjusting entry for accrued salaries_____

Cash purchase of land_____

Credit purchase of inventory_____

Collection of interest revenue_____

Paid interest expense_____

Cash sale of equipment_____

Owner withdrawal of cash_____

Owner investment of land in
   the business_____

SOLUTION TO REVIEW PROBLEM

Cash sale	CR
Sale on account	S
Loaned cash on note receivable	CD
Received cash on account	CR
Purchase of building on long-term note payable	J
Paid cash on account	CD
Cash purchase of inventory	CD
Owner investment of cash in the business	CR
Closing entries	J
Purchase of supplies on account	P

Receipt of cash on account	CR
Adjusting entry for accrued salaries	J
Cash purchase of land	CD
Credit purchase of inventory	P
Collection of interest revenue	CR
Paid interest expense	CD
Cash sale of equipment	CR
Owner withdrawal of cash	CD
Owner investment of land in the business	J

Summary

An efficient accounting system combines *personnel, records* and *procedures* to meet information needs of the business. Processing accounting information means collecting data from source documents, organizing and recording the data, and communicating the information; one source of communication is through the financial statements. Each business designs its accounting system to satisfy its particular information needs.

To be effective, the system must provide management with the information needed to *control* the organization. Also, the system must be *compatible* with the operations of the business. Further, businesses change, so the system must be *flexible* enough to handle new needs. Finally, the system must be *cost beneficial*. The best system in the world is not useful if the business cannot afford it.

Many businesses use computers to process the required information. Computer data processing systems include *hardware, software* and *personnel*. Hardware may consist of a mainframe computer or microcomputers. Computer operators use software to process data on-line or in batches. However, regardless of the nature of the system — computerized, manual, or a combination of the two — a system needs to account for sales, accounts receivable, inventory, cash, accounts payable, payroll and general journal transactions.

Many businesses use special journals to account for repetitive transactions such as credit sales, cash receipts, credit purchases, cash disbursements, and sales returns and allowances. Special journals cut down the amount of writing required and reduce the number of postings.

Some businesses find it efficient to use source documents as journals. Posting directly to the ledger from these documents eliminates having to journalize repetitive transactions.

Businesses use a subsidiary ledger to account for individual customer accounts receivable. The subsidiary ledger makes information on each customer's account readily available. The total of the subsidiary ledger's individual account balances must match the balance in the Accounts Receivable control account in the general ledger. Determining that these amounts agree is called balancing the ledger. Companies may also keep a subsidiary ledger for accounts payable.

Self-Study Questions

Test your understanding of the chapter by marking the correct answer for each of the following questions:

1. Why does a jewelry store need a different kind of accounting system than that a physician uses? *(p. 227)*
    a. They have different kinds of employees.
    b. They have different kinds of journals and ledgers.
    c. They have different kinds of business transactions.
    d. They work different hours.
2. Which feature of an effective information system is most concerned with safeguarding assets? *(p. 229)*
    a. Control   c. Flexibility
    b. Compatibility   d. Acceptable cost/benefit relationship
3. Which of the following components of a computerized accounting system is more likely to be developed in-house rather than by outsiders? Why? *(pp. 230-232)*
    a. Hardware, because of the desire for control
    b. Hardware, because of the desire for compatibility
    c. Software, because of the desire for control
    d. Software, because of the desire for compatibility
4. Special journals help most by *(pp. 233, 234)*
    a. Limiting the number of transactions that have to be recorded
    b. Reducing the cost of operating the accounting system
    c. Improving accuracy in posting to subsidiary ledgers
    d. Easing the preparation of the financial statements
5. Galvan Company recorded 523 credit sale transactions in the sales journal. How many postings would be required if these transactions were recorded in the general journal? *(p. 237)*
    a. 523   c. 1,569
    b. 1,046   d. 2,092
6. Which two dollar-amount columns in the cash receipts journal will be used the most by a department store that makes half of its sales for cash and half on credit? *(p. 238)*
    a. Cash Debit and Sales Discounts Debit
    b. Cash Debit and Accounts Receivable Credit
    c. Cash Debit and Other Accounts Credit
    d. Accounts Receivable Debit and Sales Revenue Credit
7. Entries in the purchases journal are posted to the *(p. 243)*
    a. General ledger only

b. General ledger and the Accounts payable ledger
c. General ledger and the Accounts receivable ledger
d. Accounts receivable ledger and the Accounts payable ledger

8. Every entry in the cash disbursements journal includes a *(p. 245)*
   a. Debit to Accounts Payable   c. Credit to Purchase Discounts
   b. Debit to an Other Account   d. Credit to Cash

9. Mazarotti Company has issued a debit memo. The related journal entry is *(p. 248)*

   a. Accounts Payable   XXX
       Purchase Returns and Allowances   XXX
   b. Purchase Returns and Allowances   XXX
       Accounts Payable........................   XXX
   c. Accounts Receivable   XXX
       Sales Returns and Allowances..............   XXX
   d. Sales Returns and Allowances   XXX
       Accounts Receivable   XXX

10. Balancing the ledgers at the end of the period is most closely related to *(p. 250)*
    a. Control   c. Flexibility
    b. Compatibility   d. Acceptable cost/benefit relationship

Answers to the self-study questions are at the end of the chapter.

Accounting Vocabulary

accounting information system *(p. 227)*
balancing the ledgers *(p. 250)*
batch processing *(p. 232)*
cash disbursements journal *(p. 242)*
cash receipts journal *(p. 237)*
control account *(p. 236)*

credit memo *(p. 246)*
debit memo *(p. 248)*
general journal *(p. 233)*
general ledger *(p. 234)*
hardware *(p. 230)*
internal controls *(p. 229)*
mainframe system *(p. 230)*

microcomputers *(p. 231)*
minicomputers *(p. 231)*
on-line processing *(p. 232)*
purchases journal *(p. 242)*
sales journal *(p. 234)*
software *(p. 231)*
subsidiary ledger *(p. 236)*

Assignment Material

Questions

1. Briefly describe the two phases of implementing an accounting system.
2. Describe the basic information processing model of an accounting system.
3. What are the attributes of an effective information system? Briefly describe each attribute.
4. How does a mainframe computer system differ from a microcomputer system?
5. Identify three computer languages used with mainframes. Identify four software programs used with microcomputers.
6. Distinguish batch computer processing from on-line processing.
7. Describe an on-line computer processing operation for accounts receivable, sales and inventory by a large retailer, such as Eaton's or The Bay.
8. Name four special journals used in accounting systems. For what type of transaction is each designed?
9. Describe the two advantages that special journals have over recording all transactions in the general journal.
10. What is a control account, and how is it related to a subsidiary ledger? Name two common control accounts.

11. Graff Company's sales journal has one amount column headed Accounts Receivable Dr. and Sales Revenue Cr. In this journal, 86 transactions are recorded. How many posting references appear in the journal? State what each posting reference represents.

12. Use S = Sales; CR = Cash Receipts; P = Purchases; CD = Cash Disbursements; and SRA = Sales Returns and Allowances to identify the special journal in which the following column headings appear. Some headings may appear in more than one journal.

Sales Revenue Cr._____   Invoice No._____

Accounts Payable Dr._____   Sales Discounts Dr._____

Cash Dr._____   Other Accounts Cr._____

Purchase Discounts Cr._____   Purchases Dr._____

Accounts Receivable Cr._____   Cash Cr._____

Cheque No._____   Credit Memo No._____

Other Accounts Dr._____   Accounts Payable Dr._____

Post. Ref._____   Accounts Receivable Dr._____

13. Identify two ways a check mark (✔) is used as a posting reference in the cash receipts journal.

14. The accountant for Bannister Company posted all amounts correctly from the cash receipts journal to the general ledger. However, she failed to post three credits to customer accounts in the accounts receivable subsidiary ledger. How would this error be detected?

15. In posting from the cash receipts journal of Enfield Homebuilders, the accountant failed to post the amount of the sales revenue credit column. Identify two ways this error can be detected.

16. At what two times is posting done from a special journal? What items are posted at each time?

17. For what purposes are a credit memo and a debit memo issued? Who issues each document, the seller or the purchaser?

18. The following entry appears in the general journal:

Nov. 25   Sales Returns and Allowances.................   539
                   Accounts Receivable — B. Goodwin.......   539

Prepare likely posting references.

19. Describe two ways to account for sales tax collected from customers.

20. What is the purpose of balancing the ledgers?

21. Posting from the journals of McKedrick Realty is complete. However, the total of the individual balances in the accounts payable subsidiary ledger does not equal the balance in the Accounts Payable control account in the general ledger. Does this necessarily indicate that the trial balance is out of balance? Give your reason.

22. Assume that posting is completed. The trial balance shows no errors, but the sum of the individual accounts payable does not equal the Accounts Payable control balance in the general ledger. What two errors could cause this problem?

23. Describe how some businesses use their documents as journals.

Exercises

Exercise 6-1 *Using the sales and cash receipts journals*

The sales and cash receipts journals of Advanced Design Company include the following entries:

Sales Journal

Date	Account Debited	Post. Ref.	Amount
Oct. 7	C. Carlson	✔	730
10	T. Muecke	✔	1,960
10	E. Lovell	✔	190
12	B. Goebel	✔	5,470
31	Total		8,350

Cash Receipts Journal

	Debits		Credits				
					Other Accounts		
Date	Cash	Sales Discounts	Accounts Receivable	Sales Revenue	Account Title	Post. Ref.	Amount
Oct. 16					C. Carlson	✔	
19					E. Lovell	✔	
24	100			100			
30					T. Muecke	✔	

Advanced Design makes all sales on credit terms of 2/10 n/30. Complete the cash receipts journal for those transactions indicated. Also, total the journal and show that total debits equal total credits. Assume that each cash receipt was for the full amount of the receivable.

Exercise 6-2   *Classifying postings from the cash receipts journal*

The cash receipts journal of Cranbrook, Inc. follows:

Cash Receipts Journal   Page 26

	Debits		Credits				
					Other Accounts		
Date	Cash	Sales Discounts	Accounts Receivable	Sales Revenue	Account Title	Post. Ref.	Amount
Dec. 2	794	16	810		Johnson-McBee	(a)	
9	1,291		1,291		B. R. Blake Co.	(b)	
14	3,904			3,904		(c)	
19	4,480				Note Payable	(d)	4,000
					Interest Revenue	(e)	480
30	314	7	321		L. M. Roose	(f)	
31	4,235			4,235		(g)	
31	15,018	23	2,422	8,139	Totals		4,480
	(h)	(i)	(j)	(k)			(l)

Required

Identify each posting reference (a) through (l) as (1) a posting to the general ledger as a column total, (2) a posting to the general ledger as an individual amount, (3) a posting to a subsidiary ledger account, or (4) an amount not posted.

Exercise 6-3   *Recording purchase transactions in the general journal and purchases journal*

During April, Monarch Tile Company completed the following credit purchase transactions:

April 4   Inventory, $912, from McGraw Ltd.
      7   Supplies, $107, from Paine Corp.
     19   Equipment, $1,903, from Liston-Fry Co. Ltd.
     27   Inventory, $2,210, from Milan, Inc.

Record these transactions first in the general journal, with explanations, and then in the purchases journal. Omit credit terms and posting references. Which procedure for recording transactions is quicker?

Exercise 6-4   *Identifying transactions from postings to the accounts receivable ledger*

An account in the accounts receivable ledger of McCray Company follows:

William H. Crocker

Date		P.R.	Dr.	Cr.	Balance Dr.	Balance Cr.
May 1	....				703	
10	....	S.5	1,180		1,883	
15	....	J.8		191	1,692	
21	....	CA.9		703	989	

Required

Describe the three posted transactions.

Exercise 6-5   *Posting from the purchases journal; balancing the ledgers*

The purchases journal of Marino Merchandise Company follows:

Purchases Journal   Page 7

Date	Account Credited	Terms	Post. Ref.	Account Payable Cr.	Purchases Dr.	Supplies Dr.	Other Accounts Dr. Acct. Title	Post. Ref.	Amt. Dr.
Sept. 2	Audio-Video	n/30		600	600				
5	Green Stationers	n/30		175		175			
13	Audio-Video	2/10 n/30		347	347				
26	Marks Equipment Co.	n/30		916			Equipment		916
30	Totals			2,038	947	175			916

Required

1. Open general ledger accounts for Supplies, Equipment, Accounts Payable and

Purchases. Post to these accounts from the purchase journal. Use dates and posting references in the ledger accounts.

2. Open accounts in the accounts payable subsidiary ledger for Audio-Video, Green Stationers and Marks Equipment Company. Post from the purchase journal. Use dates and posting references in the ledger accounts.

3. Balance the Accounts Payable control account in the general ledger with the total of the balances in the accounts payable subsidiary ledger.

Exercise 6-6 *Using business documents to record transactions*

The following documents describe two business transactions:

<table>
<tr><td colspan="3">**Invoice**</td></tr>
<tr><td>Date:</td><td colspan="2">August 14, 19X0</td></tr>
<tr><td>Sold to:</td><td colspan="2">Zephyr Bicycle Shop</td></tr>
<tr><td>Sold by:</td><td colspan="2">CCM Company</td></tr>
<tr><td>Terms:</td><td colspan="2">2/10 n/30</td></tr>
<tr><td colspan="3">Items Purchased   Bicycles</td></tr>
<tr><td>Quantity</td><td>Price</td><td>Total</td></tr>
<tr><td>3</td><td>$90</td><td>$270</td></tr>
<tr><td>2</td><td>70</td><td>140</td></tr>
<tr><td>5</td><td>60</td><td>300</td></tr>
<tr><td>Total . . . .</td><td></td><td>$710</td></tr>
</table>

<table>
<tr><td colspan="3">**Debit Memo**</td></tr>
<tr><td>Date:</td><td colspan="2">August 20, 19X0</td></tr>
<tr><td>Issued to:</td><td colspan="2">CCM Company</td></tr>
<tr><td>Issued by:</td><td colspan="2">Zephyr Bicycle Shop</td></tr>
<tr><td colspan="3">Items Returned   Bicycles</td></tr>
<tr><td>Quantity</td><td>Price</td><td>Total</td></tr>
<tr><td>1</td><td>$90</td><td>$ 90</td></tr>
<tr><td>1</td><td>70</td><td>70</td></tr>
<tr><td>Total . . . .</td><td></td><td>$160</td></tr>
<tr><td colspan="3">Reason: Wrong sizes</td></tr>
</table>

Use the general journal to record these transactions and Zephyr's cash payment on August 21. Record the transactions first on the books of Zephyr Bicycle Shop and, second, on the books of the CCM Company, which makes and sells bicycles. Explanations are not required. Set up your answer in the following format:

Date	Zephyr Journal Entries	CCM Journal Entries

Exercise 6-7 *Using the cash disbursements journal*

During July, Mancini Company had the following transactions:

July 3   Paid $392 on account to Miller, Inc., net of an $8 discount.
   6   Purchased inventory for cash, $599.
   11   Paid $375 for supplies.
   13   Purchased inventory on credit from Monroe Corporation, $774.
   16   Paid $8,062 on account to LaGrange Associates. There was no discount.
   21   Purchased furniture for cash, $960.
   26   Paid $3,910 on account to Graff Software. The discount was $90.
   31   Made a semiannual interest payment of $800 on a long-term note payable. The entire payment was for interest.

Required

1. Draw a cash disbursements journal similar to the one illustrated in this chapter. Omit the cheque number (Ch. No.) and posting reference (Post. Ref.) columns.

2. Record the transactions in the journal. Note that one transaction should *not* be recorded in the cash disbursement journal. Which is it? In what journal does it belong?
3. Total the amount columns of the journal. Determine that the total debits equal the total credits.

Exercise 6-8   *Journalizing return and allowance transactions*

Greenberg Company records returns and allowances in its general journal. During April, the company had the following transactions:

April 4	Issued credit memo to W. A. Wang for inventory that Wang returned to us..	$ 369
10	Received debit memo from B. R. Inman, who purchased merchandise from us on April 6. We shipped the wrong items, and Inman returned them to us.......................................	1,238
14	Issued debit memo for merchandise we purchased from Wyle Supply Company that was damaged in shipment. We returned the damaged inventory to Wyle...............................	4,600
22	Received credit memo from Dietrich Distributing Co., from whom we purchased inventory on April 15. Dietrich discovered that they overcharged us.......................................	900

Required

Journalize the transactions in the general journal. Explanations are not required.

Exercise 6-9   *Posting directly from sales invoices; balancing the ledgers*

Papadopoulos Ltd. uses its sales invoices as the sales journal and posts directly from them to the accounts receivable subsidiary ledger. During June the company made the following sales on account:

Date	Invoice No.	Customer Name	Amount
June 6	256	Anita Harris	$1,404
9	257	Forrest Ashworth	798
13	258	Paul Scott	550
16	259	Jan Childres	3,678
22	261	Anita Harris	1,915
30	262	Jan Childres	800
		Total..................	$9,145

Required

1. Open general ledger accounts for Accounts Receivable and Sales Revenue and post to those accounts. Use dates and use June Sales as the posting reference.
2. Open customer accounts in the accounts receivable subsidiary ledger and post to those accounts. Use dates and invoice numbers as posting references.
3. Balance the ledgers.

Exercise 6-10   *Detecting errors in the special journals*

Monarch Sales Company uses special journals for credit sales, cash receipts, credit purchases and cash disbursements and the subsidiary ledgers illustrated in this chapter.

During March the accountant made four errors. State the procedure that will detect each error described in the following:

a. Posted a $40 debit to J. B. Carnes's account in the accounts receivable subsidiary ledger as a $400 credit.

b. Added the Cash Credit column of the cash disbursements journal as $3,976 and posted this incorrect amount to the Cash account. The correct total was $3,796.

c. Recorded receipt of $500 on account from Electrosystems, Inc. incorrectly as a credit to Sales Revenue in the cash receipts journal.

d. Failed to post the total of the Accounts Receivable Dr./Sales Revenue Cr. column of the sales journal.

Problems   (Group A)

Problem 6-1A   *Using the sales, cash receipts and general journals*

The general ledger of Geoffrion Plaza, Inc. includes the following accounts, among others:

Cash	11	Sales Revenue	41
Accounts Receivable	12	Sales Discounts	42
Notes Receivable	15	Sales Returns and Allowances	43
Supplies	16	Interest Revenue	47
Land	18	Gain on Sale of Land	48

All credit sales are on the company's standard terms of 2/10 n/30. Transactions in May that affected sales and cash receipts were as follows:

May 2	Sold inventory on credit to Dockery Co., $550.
4	As an accommodation to a competitor, sold supplies at cost, $85, receiving cash.
7	Cash sales for the week totaled $1,890.
9	Sold merchandise on account to A. L. Beaubien, $7,320.
10	Sold land that cost $10,000 for cash of $10,000.
11	Sold goods on account to Sloan Electric, $5,104.
12	Received cash from Dockery Co. in full settlement of its account receivable, net of the discount, from May 2.
14	Cash sales for the week were $2,106.
15	Sold inventory on credit to the partnership of Citron & Mahen, $3,650.
18	Issued credit memo to A. L. Beaubien for $600 of merchandise returned to us by Beaubien. The goods shipped were unsatisfactory.
20	Sold merchandise on account to Sloan Electric, $629.
21	Cash sales for the week were $990.
22	Received $4,000 cash from A. L. Beaubien in partial settlement of his account receivable. There was no discount.
25	Received cash from Citron & Mahen for the discounted amount of their account receivable from May 15.
25	Sold goods on account to Olsen Co., $720.
27	Collected $5,125 on a note receivable, of which $125 was interest.
28	Cash sales for the week totaled $3,774.
29	Sold inventory on account to R. O. Marchand, $242.

30   Issued credit memo to Olsen Co. for $40 for inventory they returned to us because it was damaged in shipment.

31   Received $2,720 cash on account from A. L. Beaubien. There was no discount.

Required

1. Geoffrion Plaza records sales returns and allowances in the general journal. Use the appropriate journal to record the above transactions in a single-column sales journal (omit the Invoice No. column), a cash receipts journal and a general journal.

2. Total each column of the cash receipts journal. Show that the total debits equal the total credits.

3. Show how postings would be made from the journals by writing the account numbers and check marks in the appropriate places in the journals.

Problem 6-2A   *Using the purchases, cash disbursements and general journals*

The general ledger of Dreyfuss Company includes the following accounts:

Cash	11	Purchases	51
Prepaid Insurance	16	Purchase Discounts	52
Supplies	17	Purchase Returns and Allowances	53
Furniture	19	Rent Expense	56
Accounts Payable	21	Utilities Expense	58

Transactions in August that affected purchases and cash disbursements were as follows:

Aug. 1   Purchased inventory on credit from Wood Co., $3,900. Terms were 2/10 n/30.

1   Paid monthly rent, debiting Rent Expense for $2,000.

5   Purchased supplies on credit terms of 2/10 n/30 from Ross Supply, $450.

8   Paid electricity bill, $588. Debit Utilities Expense.

9   Purchased furniture on account from A-1 Office Supply, $4,100. Payment terms were net 30.

10   Returned the furniture to A-1 Office Supply. It was the wrong colour. Issued a debit memo for $4,100 and mailed a copy to A-1 Office Supply.

11   Paid Wood Co. the discounted amount owed on the purchase of August 1.

12   Purchased furniture on account from Wynne, Inc., $4,400. Terms were 3/10 n/30.

13   Purchased inventory for cash, $655.

14   Paid a semiannual insurance premium, debiting Prepaid Insurance, $1,200.

15   Paid our account payable to Ross Supply, less the discount, from August 5.

18   Paid gas and water bills, $196. Debit Utilities Expense.

21   Purchased inventory on credit terms of 1/10 n/45 from Software, Inc., $5,200.

21   Paid account payable to Wynne, Inc., less discount, from August 12.

22   Purchased supplies on account from Office Sales, Inc., $274. Terms were net 30.

25   Returned part of the inventory purchased on August 21 to Software, Inc., issuing a debit memo for $1,200.

31   Paid Software, Inc. the net amount owed from August 21, less the return, on August 25.

Required

1. Dreyfuss Company records purchase returns in the general journal. Record the above transactions in a purchase journal, a cash disbursements journal (omit the Cheque No. column) and a general journal.

2. Total each column of the special journals. Show that the total debits equal the total credits in each special journal.
3. Show how postings would be made from the journals by writing the account numbers and check marks in the appropriate places in the journals.

Problem 6-3A *Using the sales, cash receipt and general journals, posting and balancing the ledgers*

During April, North Bay Sales Company had these transactions:

Apr. 2 Issued invoice no. 436 for credit sale to Whistler Co., $5,200. All credit sales are made on the company's standard terms of 2/10 n/30.
  3 Collected cash of $3,038 from H.M. Burger in payment of his account receivable, $3,100, within the discount period.
  5 Cash sales for the week totaled $2,057.
  7 Collected note receivable, $2,000, plus interest of $210.
  10 Issued invoice no. 437 for sale on account to Van Allen Co., $1,850.
  11 Sold supplies to an employee for cash of $54, which was the cost.
  12 Received $5,096 cash from Whistler Co. in full settlement of their account receivable, net of the discount, from the sale of April 2.
  12 Cash sales for the week were $1,698.
  14 Sold inventory on account to Electro, Inc., issuing invoice no. 438 for $2,000.
  16 Issued credit memo to Electro, Inc., for $610 of merchandise returned to us by Electro. Part of the shipped goods were damaged.
  19 Cash sales for the week were $3,130.
  20 Received $1,813 from Van Allen Co. in full settlement of its account receivable, $1,850, from April 10.
  25 Received cash of $7,455 from Electro, Inc. on account. There was no discount.
  26 Cash sales for the week totaled $2,744.
  27 Issued invoice no. 439 to Clay Co. for credit sales of inventory, $3,640.
  28 Sold goods on credit to H.M. Burger, issuing invoice no. 440 for $2,689.
  30 Issued credit memo to H.M. Burger for $873 for inventory he returned to us because it was unsatisfactory.

The general ledger of North Bay Sales Company includes the following accounts and balances at April 1:

Account Number	Account Title	Balance	Account Number	Account Title	Balance
111	Cash	$ 3,579	411	Sales Revenue.......	
112	Accounts Receivable .	10,555	412	Sales Discounts......	
116	Supplies	1,756	413	Sales Returns and	
141	Notes Receivable	5,000		Allowances	
			418	Interest Revenue	

North Bay's accounts receivable subsidiary ledger includes the following accounts and balances at April 1: H.M. Burger, $3,100; Clay Company, -0-; Electro, Inc., $7,455; Whistler Company, -0-; and Van Allen Co., -0-.

Required

1. Open the general ledger and the accounts receivable subsidiary ledger accounts given, inserting their balances at April 1.

2. Record the transactions on page 4 of a single-column sales journal, page 13 of a cash receipts journal and page 7 of a general journal as appropriate. North Bay records sales returns and allowances in the general journal.

3. Post daily to the accounts receivable subsidiary ledger, and on April 30 post to the general ledger.

4. Determine that the total debits equal the total credits in each special journal.

5. Balance the total of the customer account balances in the accounts receivable subsidiary ledger against the Accounts Receivable balance in the general ledger.

Problem 6-4A   *Using the purchases, cash disbursements and general journals; posting and balancing the ledgers*

Windsor Company's November purchases and cash disbursement transaction are as follows:

Nov. 1   Issued cheque no. 346 for $2,058 to pay ENTEL Ltd. on account. Windsor received a $42 discount for prompt payment.

1   Issued cheque no. 347 to pay quarterly rent, debiting Prepaid Rent for $2,400.

2   Issued cheque no. 348 to pay net amount owed to Arbor Machine Co., $637. Windsor took a $13 discount.

5   Purchased supplies on credit terms of 1/10 n/30 from Chin Music Co., $264.

7   Paid delivery expense, issuing cheque no. 349 for $388. Debit Delivery Expense.

10   Purchased inventory on account from W. A. Mozart, Inc., $1,681. Payment terms were net 30.

11   Returned the inventory to W. A. Mozart, Inc. It was defective. We issued a debit memo for $1,681 and mailed a copy to Mozart.

15   Issued cheque no. 350 for a cash purchase of inventory, $2,889.

15   Paid semimonthly payroll with cheque no. 351, debiting Salary Expense for $1,595.

19   Issued cheque no. 352 to pay our account payable to Chin Music Co. from November 5. We did not earn the discount.

21   Purchased inventory on credit terms of 2/10 n/30 from Arbor Machine Co., $3,250.

24   Purchased machinery on credit terms of 2/10 n/30 from ENTEL Ltd., $1,558.

26   Purchased supplies on account from W. A. Mozart, Inc., $309. Terms were net 30.

29   Issued cheque no. 353 to Arbor Machine Co., paying the net amount owed from November 21.

30   Paid semimonthly payroll with cheque no. 354, debiting Salary Expense for $1,595.

The general ledger of Windsor Company includes the following accounts and balances at November 1:

Account Number	Account Title	Balance	Account Number	Account Title	Balance
111	Cash	$17,674	511	Purchases...........	
115	Prepaid Rent........	800	512	Purchase Discounts ..	
116	Supplies	884	513	Purchase Returns	
151	Machinery	33,600		and Allowances ...	
211	Accounts Payable	2,750	521	Salary Expense	
			551	Delivery Expense	

Windsor's accounts payable subsidiary ledger includes the following balances at

November 1: Arbor Machine Co., $650; Chin Music, Inc., -0-; ENTEL Ltd., $2,100; W. A. Mozart, Inc., -0-.

Required

1. Open the general ledger and the accounts payable subsidiary ledger accounts given, inserting their balances at November 1.
2. Record the above transactions on page 3 of a purchases journal, page 8 of a cash disbursements journal and page 12 of a general journal as appropriate. Windsor records purchase returns in the general journal.
3. Post daily to the accounts payable subsidiary ledger. Post to the general ledger on November 30.
4. Total each column of the special journals. Determine that the total debits equal the total credits in each special journal.
5. Balance the total of the creditor account balances in the accounts payable subsidiary ledger against the balance of the Accounts Payable control account in the general ledger.

Problem 6-5A   *Using all the journals, posting and balancing the ledgers*

Kent Sales Company had these transactions during January:

Jan. 2   Issued invoice no. 191 for sale on account to L. E. Wooten, $2,350.

3   Purchased inventory on credit terms of 3/10 n/60 from Delwood Plaza, $1,900.

4   Sold inventory for cash, $808.

5   Issued cheque no. 473 to purchase furniture for cash, $1,087.

8   Collected interest revenue of $440.

9   Issued invoice no. 192 for sale on account to Messier Co., $6,250.

10   Purchased inventory for cash, $776, issuing cheque no. 474.

12   Received $2,303 cash from L. E. Wooten in full settlement of her account receivable, net of the discount, from the sale of January 2.

13   Issued cheque no. 475 to pay Delwood Plaza net amount owed from January 3, $1,843. We received a $57 discount.

13   Purchased supplies on account from Havrilla Corp., $689. Terms were net end-of-month.

15   Sold inventory on account to J. R. Wakeland, issuing invoice no. 193 for $743.

17   Issued credit memo to J. R. Wakeland for $743 for defective merchandise returned to us by Wakeland.

18   Issued invoice no. 194 for credit sale to L. E. Wooten, $1,825.

19   Received $6,125 from Messier Co. in full settlement of its account receivable, $6,250, from January 9.

20   Purchased inventory on credit terms of net 30 from Howie Jasper Sales, $2,150.

22   Purchased furniture on credit terms of 3/10 n/60 from Delwood Plaza, $775.

22   Issued cheque no. 476 to pay for insurance coverage, debiting Prepaid Insurance for $1,345.

24   Sold supplies to an employee for cash of $86, which was their cost.

25   Issued cheque no. 477 to pay utilities. Debit Utilities Expense for $388.

28   Purchased inventory on credit terms of 2/10 n/30 from Havrilla Corp., $421.

29   Returned damaged inventory to Havrilla Corp., issuing a debit memo for $421.

29   Sold goods on account to Messier Co., issuing invoice no. 195 for $567.

30   Issued cheque no. 478 to pay Havrilla Corp. $689 on account from January 13.

31   Received $1,825 on account from L. E. Wooten on credit sale of January 18. There was no discount.

31   Issued cheque no. 479 to pay monthly salaries, debiting Salary Expense for $2,600.

Required

1. Open the following general ledger accounts using the account numbers given:

Cash	111	Sales Returns and Allowances..	413
Accounts Receivable	112	Interest Revenue	419
Supplies	116	Purchases....................	511
Prepaid Insurance	117	Purchase Discounts	512
Furniture	151	Purchase Returns	
Accounts Payable	211	and Allowances	513
Sales Revenue................	411	Salary Expense	531
Sales Discounts	412	Utilities Expense.............	541

2. Open these accounts in the subsidiary ledgers—Accounts receivable subsidiary ledger: Messier Co., J. R. Wakeland and L. E. Wooten. Accounts payable subsidiary ledger: Delwood Plaza, Havrilla Corp., and Howie Jasper Sales.
3. Enter the transactions in a sales journal (page 8), a cash receipts journal (page 3), a purchases journal (page 6), a cash disbursements journal (page 9) and a general journal (page 4).
4. Post daily to the accounts receivable subsidiary ledger and to the accounts payable subsidiary ledger. On January 31, post to the general ledger.
5. Total each column of the special journals. Determine that the total debits equal the total credits in each special journal.
6. Balance the total of the customer account balances in the accounts receivable subsidiary ledger against Accounts Receivable in the general ledger. Do the same for the accounts payable subsidiary ledger and Accounts Payable in the general ledger.

Problem 6-6A   *Correcting errors in the cash receipts journal*

The cash receipts journal below contains five entries. All five entries are for legitimate cash receipt transactions, but the journal contains some errors in recording the transactions. In fact, only one entry is correct, and each of the other four entries contains one error.

Cash Receipts Journal   **Page 13**

	Debits			Credits			
					Other Accounts		
Date	Cash	Sales Discounts	Accounts Receivable	Sales Revenue	Account Title	P.R.	Amount
5/6		500		500			
7	429	22			Ron Bynum	✔	451
12	3,170				Note		
					Receivable	13	3,000
					Interest		
					Revenue	45	170
18				330			
24	1,100		770				
	4,699	522	770	830	Totals		3,621
	(11)	(42)	(12)	(41)			(/)

Total Dr. = $5,221   Total Cr. = $5,221

Required

1. Identify the correct entry.
2. Identify the error in each of the other four entries.
3. Using the following format, prepare a corrected cash receipts journal.

Cash Receipts Journal   **Page 13**

	Debits		Credits				
					Other Accounts		
Date	Cash	Sales Discounts	Accounts Receivable	Sales Revenue	Account Title	P.R.	Amount
5/6 7 12					Ron Bynum Note Receivable Interest Revenue	✔ 13 45	
18 24							
	5,199	22	1,221	830	Totals		3,170
	(11)	(42)	(12)	(41)			(✔)

Total Dr. = $5,221   Total Cr. = $5,221

(Group B)

Problem 6-1B *Using the sales, cash receipts and general journals*

The general ledger of Carmel Trading Company includes the following accounts:

Cash	111	Sales Revenue	411
Accounts Receivable	112	Sales Discounts	412
Notes Receivable	115	Sales Returns and Allowances	413
Equipment	141	Interest Revenue	417
Land	142	Gain on Sale of Land	418

All credit sales are on the company's standard terms of 2/10 n/30. Transactions in February that affected sales and cash receipts were as follows:

Feb. 1 Sold inventory on credit to G. M. Titcher, $900.
5 As an accommodation to another company, sold new equipment for its cost of $770, receiving cash in this amount.
6 Cash sales for the week totaled $1,007.
8 Sold merchandise on account to McNair Co., $2,830.
9 Sold land that cost $22,000 for cash of $40,000, which includes a gain of $18,000.
11 Sold goods on account to Nickerson Builders, $6,099.

11   Received cash from G. M. Titcher in full settlement of her account receivable, net of the discount, from February 1.

13   Cash sales for the week were $1,995.

15   Sold inventory on credit to Montez and Montez, a partnership, $800.

18   Issued credit memo to McNair Co. for $120 of merchandise returned to us by McNair. The goods we shipped were unsatisfactory.

19   Sold merchandise on account to Nickerson Builders, $3,900.

20   Cash sales for the week were $2,330.

21   Received $1,200 cash from McNair Co. in partial settlement of their account receivable. There was no discount.

22   Received cash from Montez and Montez for the discounted amount of their account receivable from February 15.

22   Sold goods on account to Diamond Co., $2,022.

25   Collected $4,200 on a note receivable, of which $200 was interest.

27   Cash sales for the week totaled $2,970.

27   Sold inventory on account to Littleton Corporation, $2,290.

28   Issued credit memo to Diamond Co. for $680 for goods they returned to us because they were damaged in shipment.

28   Received $1,510 cash on account from McNair Co. There was no discount.

Required

1. Use the appropriate journal to record the above transactions in a single-column sales journal (omit the Invoice No. column), a cash receipts journal and a general journal. Carmel records sales returns and allowances in the general journal.
2. Total each column of the cash receipts journal. Determine that the total debits equal the total credits.
3. Show how postings would be made from the journals by writing the account numbers and check marks in the appropriate places in the journals.

Problem 6-2B   *Using the purchases, cash disbursements and general journals*

The general ledger of Enfield Corporation includes the following accounts:

Cash	111	Purchases	511
Prepaid Insurance	116	Purchase Discounts	512
Supplies	117	Purchase Returns and Allowances	513
Equipment	149	Rent Expense	562
Accounts Payable	211	Utilities Expense	565

Transactions in March that affected purchases and cash disbursements were as follows:

Mar. 1   Paid monthly rent, debiting Rent Expense for $1,600.

3   Purchased inventory on credit from Broussard Co., $4,600. Terms were 2/15 n/45.

6   Purchased supplies on credit terms of 2/10 n/30 from Harmon Sales, $800.

7   Paid gas and water bills, $406. Debit Utilities Expenses.

10   Purchased equipment on account from Lancer Co., $1,050. Payment terms were 2/10 n/30.

11   Returned the equipment to Lancer Co. It was defective. We issued a debit memo for $1,050 and mailed a copy to Lancer.

12   Paid Broussard Co. the discounted amount owed on the purchase of March 3.

12   Purchased inventory on account from Lancer Co., $1,100. Terms were 2/10 n/30.

14   Purchased inventory for cash, $1,585.

15   Paid an insurance premium, debiting Prepaid Insurance, $2,416.

16   Paid our account payable to Harmon Sales, less the discount, from March 6.

17   Paid electricity bill, $165. Debit Utilities Expenses.

20   Paid account payable to Lancer Co., less the discount, from March 12.

21   Purchased supplies on account from Master Supply, $754. Terms were net 30.

22   Purchased inventory on credit terms of 1/10 n/30 from Linz Brothers, $3,400.

26   Returned inventory purchased on March 22 to Linz Brothers, issuing a debit memo for $500.

31   Paid Linz Brothers the net amount owed from March 22, less the return on March 26.

Required

1. Use the appropriate journal to record the above transactions in a purchase journal, a cash disbursements journal (omit the Cheque No. column) and a general journal. Enfield Corporation records purchase returns in the general journal.

2. Total each column of the special journals. Determine that the total debits equal the total credits in each special journal.

3. Show how postings would be made from the journals by writing the account numbers and check marks in the appropriate places in the journals.

Problem 6-3B   *Using the sales, cash receipts and general journal; posting and balancing the ledgers*

During June, Harwood Systems engaged in the following transactions:

June 1   Issued invoice no. 113 for credit sale to Laurentian Co., $4,750. All credit sales are on the company's standard terms of 2/10 n/30.

    3   Collected cash of $882 from Leah Burnet in payment of her account receivable, $900, within the discount period.

    6   Cash sales for the week totaled $1,748.

    7   Collected note receivable, $3,400, plus interest of $367.

    9   Issued invoice no. 114 for sale on account to Wilder Co., $4,300.

  11   Received $4,655 cash from Laurentian Co. in full settlement of its account receivable, net of the discount, from the sale on June 1.

  13   Cash sales for the week were $2,964.

  14   Sold inventory on account to Goss Corp., issuing invoice no. 115 for $858.

  15   Issued credit memo to Goss Corp. for $154 of merchandise returned to us by Goss. Part of the goods we shipped were defective.

  19   Received $4,214 from Wilder Co. in full settlement of its account receivable, $4,300, from June 9.

  20   Cash sales for the week were $2,175.

  22   Received cash of $2,904 from Goss Corporation on account. There was no discount.

  24   Sold supplies to an employee for cash of $106, which was their cost.

  27   Cash Sales for the week totaled $1,650.

  28   Issued invoice no. 116 to Thompson Co. for credit sale of inventory, $5,194.

  29   Sold goods on credit to Leah Burnett, issuing invoice no. 117 for $3,819.

  29   Issued credit memo to Leah Burnett for $1,397 inventory she returned to us because it was unsatisfactory.

The general ledger of Harwood Systems includes the following accounts and balances at June 1:

Account Number	Account Title	Balance	Account Number	Account Title	Balance
111	Cash	$4,217	411	Sales Revenue	
112	Accounts Receivable .	3,804	412	Sales Discounts	
116	Supplies	1,290	413	Sales Returns and	
141	Notes Receivable	7,100		Allowances	
			418	Interest Revenue	

Harwood's accounts receivable subsidiary ledger includes the following accounts and balances at June 1: Laurentian Company, -0-; Leah Burnett, $900; Goss Corporation, $2,904; Thompson Company, -0-; Wilder Co., -0-.

Required

1. Open the general ledger and the accounts receivable subsidiary ledger accounts given, inserting their balances at June 1.
2. Record the above transactions on page 6 of a single-column sales journal, page 9 of a cash receipts journal and page 5 of a general journal. Harwood Systems records sales returns and allowances in the general journal.
3. Post daily to the accounts receivable subsidiary ledger. On June 30, post to the general ledger.
4. Total each column of the special journals. Determine that the total debits equal the total credits in each special journal.
5. Balance the total of the customer account balances in the accounts receivable subsidiary ledger against the Accounts Receivable balance in the general ledger.

Problem 6-4B *Using the purchases, cash disbursements and general journals; posting and balancing the ledgers*

Manitoba Company's September transactions affecting purchases and cash disbursements were as follows:

Sept. 1   Issued cheque no. 406 for $1,176 to pay Flin Flon Co. on account. Manitoba received a $24 discount for prompt payment.

1   Issued cheque no. 407 to pay a quarterly rent, debiting Prepaid Rent for $1,800.

2   Issued cheque no. 408 to pay net amount owed to Lynn Co., $1,455. Manitoba took a $45 discount.

5   Purchased supplies on credit terms of 2/10 n/30 from Westside Supply, $121.

7   Paid delivery expense, issuing cheque no. 409 for $739. Debit Delivery Expense.

10   Purchased inventory on account from Hayden, Inc., $2,008. Payment terms were net 30.

11   Returned the inventory to Hayden, Inc. because it was defective. We issued a debit memo for $2,008 and mailed a copy to Hayden.

15   Issued cheque no. 410 for a cash purchase of inventory, $2,332.

15   Paid semimonthly payroll with cheque no. 411, debiting Salary Expense for $1,224.

19   Issued cheque no. 412 to pay our account payable to Westside Supply from September 5. We did not earn the discount.

21   Purchased inventory on credit terms of 2/10 n/30 from Lynn Co., $4,150.

24   Purchased machinery on credit terms of 2/10 n/30 from Flin Flon Co., $3,195.

26 Purchased supplies on account from Hayden, Inc., $467. Terms were net 30.

29 Issued cheque no. 413 to Lynn Co., paying the net amount owed from September 21.

30 Paid semimonthly payroll with cheque no. 414, debiting Salary Expense for $1,224.

The general ledger of Manitoba Company includes the following accounts and balances at September 1:

Account Number	Account Title	Balance	Account Number	Account Title	Balance
111	Cash	$15,996	511	Purchases...........	
115	Prepaid Rent........	600	512	Purchase Discounts ..	
116	Supplies	703	513	Purchase Returns	
151	Machinery	21,800		and Allowances ...	
211	Accounts Payable	2,700	521	Salary Expense	
			551	Delivery Expense	

Manitoba's accounts payable subsidiary ledger includes the following balances at September 1: Flin Flon Co., $1,200; Hayden, Inc., -0-; Lynn Company, $1,500; Westside Supply, -0-.

Required

1. Open the general ledger and the accounts payable subsidiary ledger accounts, inserting their balances at September 1.

2. Record the above transactions on page 10 of a purchases journal, page 5 of a cash disbursements journal and page 8 of a general journal. Manitoba records purchase returns in the general journal.

3. Post daily to the accounts payable subsidiary ledger. On September 30, post to the general ledger.

4. Total each column of the special journals. Determine that the total debits equal the total credits in each special journal.

5. Balance the total of the creditor account balances in the accounts payable subsidiary ledger against the balance of the Accounts Payable control account in the general ledger.

Problem 6-5B *Using all the journals; posting and balancing the ledgers*

Lang Company completed the following transactions during July:

July 2 Issued invoice no. 913 for sale on account to N.J. Seiko, $4,100.

3 Purchased inventory on credit terms of 3/10 n/60 from Chicosky Co., $2,467.

5 Sold inventory for cash, $1,077.

5 Issued cheque no. 532 to purchase furniture for cash, $2,185.

8 Collected interest revenue of $1,775.

9 Issued invoice no. 914 for sale on account to Bell Co., $5,550.

10 Purchased inventory for cash, $1,143, issuing cheque no. 533.

12 Received $4,018 cash from N.J. Seiko in full settlement of her account receivable, net of the discount, from the sale on July 2.

13 Issued cheque no. 534 to pay Chicosky Co. the net amount owed from July 3, $2,393. We received a $74 discount.

13 Purchased supplies on account from Manley, Inc., $441. Terms were net end-of-month.

15 Sold inventory on account to M.O. Brown, issuing invoice no. 915 for $665.

17 Issued credit memo to M.O. Brown for $665 for defective merchandise returned to us by Brown.

18 Issued invoice no. 916 for credit sale to N.J. Seiko, $357.

19 Received $5,439 from Bell Co. in full settlement of its account receivable, $5,550, from July 9.

20 Purchased inventory on credit terms of net 30 from Sims Distributing, $2,047.

22 Purchased furniture on credit terms of 3/10 n/60 from Chicosky Co., $645.

22 Issued cheque no. 535 to pay for insurance coverage, debiting Prepaid Insurance for $1,000.

24 Sold supplies to an employee for cash of $54, which was their cost.

25 Issued cheque no. 536 to pay utilities, $453. Debit Utilities Expense.

28 Purchased inventory on credit terms of 2/10 n/30 from Manley, Inc., $675.

29 Returned damaged inventory to Manley, Inc., issuing a debit memo for $675.

29 Sold goods on account to Bell Co., issuing invoice no. 917 for $496.

30 Issued cheque no. 537 to pay Manley, Inc., $441 on account from July 13.

31 Received $357 on account from N.J. Seiko on credit sale of January 18. There was no discount.

31 Issued cheque no. 538 to pay monthly salaries, debiting Salary Expense for $2,347.

Required

1. Open the following general ledger accounts using the account numbers given:

Cash	111	Sales Returns and Allowances	413
Accounts Receivable	112	Interest Revenue	419
Supplies	116	Purchases	511
Prepaid Insurance	117	Purchase Discounts	512
Furniture	151	Purchase Returns	
Accounts Payable	211	and Allowances	513
Sales Revenue	411	Salary Expense	531
Sales Discounts	412	Utilities Expense	541

2. Open these accounts in the subsidiary ledgers —
Accounts receivable subsidiary ledger: Bell Co., M.O. Brown, and N.J. Seiko.
Accounts payable subsidiary ledger: Chicosky Co., Manley, Inc., and Sims Distributing.

3. Enter the transactions in a sales journal (page 7), a cash receipts journal (page 5), a purchases journal (page 10), a cash disbursements journal (page 8) and a general journal (page 6).

4. Post daily to the accounts receivable subsidiary ledger and the accounts payable subsidiary ledger. On July 31, post to the general ledger.

5. Total each column of the special journals. Determine that the total debits equal the total credits in each special journal.

6. Balance the total of the customer account balances in the accounts receivable subsidiary ledger against Accounts Receivable in the general ledger. Do the same for the accounts payable subsidiary ledger and Accounts Payable in the general ledger.

Problem 6-6B *Correcting errors in the cash receipts journal*

The cash receipts journal on the next page contains five entries. All five entries are for legitimate cash receipt transactions, but the journal contains some errors in recording the transactions. In fact, only one entry is correct, and each of the other four entries contains one error.

Cash Receipts Journal　　　　　　　　　　　**Page 5**

| | Debits | | Credits | | | | |
| | | | | | Other Accounts | | |
Date	Cash	Sales Discounts	Accounts Receivable	Sales Revenue	Account Title	P.R.	Amount
7/5	611	34	645		Meg Davis	✔	
9			229	229	Lou Metz	✔	
10	8000			8000	Land	19	
19	73						
31	1060			1133			
	9744	34	874	9362	Totals		
	(11)	(42)	(12)	(41)			(✔)

Total Dr. = $9,778　　　　　　Total Cr. = $10,236

Required

1. Identify the correct entry.
2. Identify the error in each of the other four entries.
3. Using the following format, prepare a corrected cash receipts journal.

Cash Receipts Journal　　　　　　　　　　　**Page 5**

| | Debits | | Credits | | | | |
| | | | | | Other Accounts | | |
Date	Cash	Sales Discounts	Accounts Receivable	Sales Revenue	Account Title	P.R.	Amount
7/5					Meg Davis	✔	
9					Lou Metz	✔	
10					Land	19	
19							
31							
	9973	34	874	1133	Totals		8000
	(11)	(42)	(12)	(41)			(✔)

Total Dr. = $10,007　　　　　　Total Cr. = $10,007

Decision Problems

1. Reconstructing transactions from posted amounts to the accounts receivable ledger

A fire destroyed some accounting records of Dimkoff Company. The owner, Greg Dimkoff, asks your help in reconstructing the records. He needs to know the beginning and ending balances of Accounts Receivable and the credit sales and cash receipts on account from customers during March. All Dimkoff Company's sales are on credit, with payment terms of 2/10 n/30. All cash receipts on account reached Dimkoff within the

10-day discount period, except as noted. The only accounting record preserved from the fire is the accounts receivable subsidiary ledger, which follows:

Grant Adams

Date	Item	Jrnl. Ref.	Debit	Credit	Balance
Mar. 8		S.6	2,178		2,178
16		S.6	903		3,081
18		CR.8		2,178	903
19		J.5		221	682
27		CR.8		682	-0-

Lou Gross

Date	Item	Jrnl. Ref.	Debit	Credit	Balance
Mar. 1	Balance				1,096
5		CR.8		1,096	-0-
11		S.6	396		396
21		CR.8		396	-0-
24		S.6	2,566		2,566

Norris Associates

Date	Item	Jrnl. Ref.	Debit	Credit	Balance
Mar. 1	Balance				883
15		S.6	2,635		3,518
29		CR.8		883*	2,635

---

* Cash receipt did not occur within the discount period.

Suzuki, Inc.

Date	Item	Jrnl. Ref.	Debit	Credit	Balance
Mar. 1	Balance				440
3		CR.8		440	-0-
25		S.6	3,655		3,655
29		S.6	1,123		4,778

Hint: Use the journal references to reconstruct the entries in the sales journal and the cash receipts journal. Then compute the amounts for total credit sales and total cash receipts on account. Round all sales discounts to the nearest dollar.

2. Understanding the accounting information system

The external auditor is concerned that the amounts shown on the balance sheet for accounts receivable represent amounts actually owing to the company (that is, each account receivable listed represents an actual sale on credit of goods or services by the company to the person or company indicated and the amount owing has not been paid). The concept is known as *validity*. The auditor is also concerned that the amounts shown on the balance sheet for accounts payable represents all amounts owing by the company (that is, there are no purchases of goods or services made by the company unpaid and not reflected in the total accounts payable). The concept is known as *completeness*.

Based on your knowledge of the accounting information system, suggest how an auditor might test an accounts receivable balance for validity and an accounts payable balance for completeness.

Hint: Do not worry about how much work the auditor would have to do but rather indicate what the auditor would have to do.

Answers to Self-Study Questions

1. c
2. a
3. d
4. b
5. c [523 × 3 (one debit, one credit and one to the accounts receivable ledger) = 1,569]
6. b
7. b
8. d
9. a
10. a

Practice Set

DeHaviland Company closes its books and prepares financial statements at the end of each month. The company completed the following transactions during August:

Aug. 1 Issued cheque no. 682 for August office rent of $2,000. (Debit Rent Expense.)

2 Issued cheque no. 683 to pay salaries of $1,240, which includes salary payable of $930 from July 31.

2 Issued invoice no. 503 for sale on account to R. T. Loeb, $600.

3 Purchased inventory on credit terms of 1/15 n/60 from Grant Publishers, $1,400.

4 Received net amount of cash on account from Fullam Company, $2,156, within the discount period.

4 Sold inventory for cash, $330.

5 Issued credit memo no. 267 to Park-Hee, Inc. for merchandise returned to us, $550.

5 Issued cheque no. 684 to purchase supplies for cash, $780.

6 Collected interest revenue of $1,100.

7 Issued invoice no. 504 for sale on account to K. D. Skipper, $2,400.

8 Purchased inventory on credit terms of 3/15 n/30 from Beaver Corporation, $4,300.

8 Issued cheque no. 685 to pay Federal Company $2,600 of the amount owed at July 31. This payment occurred after the end of the discount period.

9 Issued invoice no. 505 for sale on account to Iba & Frazier, $5,100.

11 Issued cheque no. 686 to pay Grant Publishers the net amount owed from August 3.

12 Received cash from R. T. Loeb in full settlement of her account receivable from August 2.

15 Sold inventory on account to Fullam Company, issuing invoice no. 506 for $466.

16 Issued cheque no. 687 to pay salary expense of $1,240.

18 Received $4,998 from Iba & Frazier in full settlement of their account receivable from August 9.

19 Purchased inventory for cash, $850, issuing cheque no. 688.

20 Purchased inventory on credit terms of net 30 from McMinn Sales, $2,150.

22 Purchased furniture on credit terms of 3/15 n/60 from Beaver Corporation, $510.

22 Issued cheque no. 689 to pay Beaver Corporation the net amount owed from August 8.

24 Received half the July 31 amount receivable from K. D. Skipper, after the end of the discount period.

25 Issued cheque no. 690 to pay utilities, $432.

26 Purchased supplies on credit terms of 2/10 n/30 from Federal Company, $180.

27 Returned damaged inventory to company from whom we made the cash purchase on August 19, receiving cash of $850.

28 Paid the amount payable to McMinn Sales at July 31, issuing cheque no. 691. There was no discount.

29 Sold goods on account to Iba & Frazier, issuing invoice no. 507 for $3,970.

30 Granted a sales allowance of $175 to K. D. Skipper, issuing credit memo no. 268.

31 Received $7,000 on account from Park-Hee, Inc. There was no discount.

31 Purchased inventory on credit terms of 1/10 n/30 from Suncrest Supply, $1,330.

31 Issued cheque no. 692 to J. M. DeHaviland, owner of the business, for personal withdrawal, $1,700.

Required

1. Open these accounts with their account numbers and July 31 balances in the various ledgers:

General Ledger

101	Cash....................................	$ 4,490
102	Accounts Receivable	22,560
104	Interest Receivable	
105	Inventory	41,800
109	Supplies..................................	1,340
117	Prepaid Insurance	2,200
140	Note Receivable, Long-term	11,000
160	Furniture.................................	37,270
161	Accumulated Depreciation	10,550
201	Accounts Payable	19,050
204	Salary Payable	930
207	Interest Payable	320
208	Unearned Sales Revenue	
220	Note Payable, Long-Term	42,000
301	J. M. DeHaviland, Capital	47,810
302	J. M. DeHaviland, Withdrawals	
400	Income Summary	
401	Sales Revenue	
402	Sales Discounts	
403	Sales Returns and Allowances	
410	Interest Revenue	
501	Purchases	
502	Purchase Discounts.......................	
503	Purchase Returns and Allowances............	
510	Salary Expense............................	
513	Rent Expense	
514	Depreciation Expense.......................	
516	Insurance Expense	
517	Utilities Expense	
519	Supplies Expense	
523	Interest Expense	

Accounts Receivable Subsidiary Ledger   Fullam Company, $2,200; Iba & Frazier; R. T. Loeb; Park-Hee, Inc., $11,590; K. D. Skipper, $8,770.

Accounts Payable Subsidiary Ledger   Beaver Corporation; Federal Company, $12,600; Grant Publishers; McMinn Sales, $6,450; Suncrest Supply.

2. Journalize the August transactions in a sales journal (page 4), a cash receipts journal (page 11), a purchases journal (page 8), a cash disbursements journal (page 5) and a general journal (page 9). Use the journals as illustrated in Chapter 6. DeHaviland makes all credit sales on terms of 2/10 n/30.

3. Post daily to the accounts receivable subsidiary ledger and the accounts payable subsidiary ledger. On August 31, post to the general ledger.

4. Prepare a trial balance in the Trial Balance columns of a work sheet and use the following information to complete the work sheet for the month ended August 31:

   a. Accrued interest revenue, $100
   b. Supplies on hand, $990
   c. Prepaid insurance expired, $550
   d. Depreciation expense, $230

   e. Accrued salary expense, $1,030
   f. Accrued interest expense, $320
   g. Unearned sales revenue, $450
   h. Inventory on hand, $47,700

5. Prepare DeHaviland's multiple-step income statement and statement of owner's equity for August. Prepare the balance sheet at August 31.

6. Journalize and post the adjusting and closing entries.

7. Prepare a post-closing trial balance at August 31. Also, balance the total of the customer accounts in the accounts receivable subsidiary ledger against the Accounts Receivable balance in the general ledger. Do the same for the accounts payable subsidiary ledger and Accounts Payable in the general ledger.

7

Internal Control and Cash Transactions

LEARNING OBJECTIVES

After studying this chapter, you should be able to

1 Define internal control

2 Identify the characteristics of an effective system of internal control

3 Prepare a bank reconciliation and related journal entries

4 Apply internal controls to cash receipts

5 Apply internal controls to cash disbursements

6 Account for petty cash transactions

7 Use the voucher system

You learned in Chapter 6 that a well-designed accounting system helps managers control the business. Chapter 7 looks in more detail at **internal control**, which is the organizational plan and all the related measures adopted by an entity to ensure the orderly and efficient conduct of its business. Management's objectives in setting up the system of internal control are

1. Discharge of statutory responsibilities such as maintaining accountability to owners.
2. Profitability and minimization of costs.
3. Prevention and detection of fraud and error.
4. Safeguarding of assets.
5. Reliability of accounting records.
6. Timely preparation of reliable financial information.[1]

OBJECTIVE 1
Define internal control

Notice that safeguarding of assets and reliability of accounting records relate to the assets and records of the entity, while the other objectives relate to managing the entity. This chapter focuses on internal controls that relate to the safeguarding of cash and the accuracy of records of cash transactions.

During the 1970s, illegal payments, embezzlements and other criminal business practices came to light. Some very large, otherwise well-run, companies in Canada and the United States discovered that parts of their systems of internal control were flawed, permitting these illegal activities. Concerned

[1] *CICA Handbook*, 1990, Section 5205.

citizens wanted to know why the companies' internal controls had failed to alert management that these illegalities had occurred. Formerly, internal control was viewed as an auditing consideration. Management generally has now become more concerned about internal control and usually mentions it specifically in the management letter included in the annual report (Exhibit 7-1). Since June 1977, instructions to auditors for evaluating internal control have been made more explicit in the Canadian Institute of Chartered Accountants' *Handbook*.

Wise management has always been interested in a system of strong internal control; many businesses have had such systems in place for years. However,

EXHIBIT 7-1 *Excerpts from Management Statements of TransCanada PipeLines Limited and Four Seasons Hotels Inc.*

Report of Management
TransCanada PipeLines Limited

The accompanying consolidated financial statements included in the Annual Report are the responsibility of management and have been approved by the Board of Directors of the Company....

The Board of Directors has appointed an Audit Committee consisting solely of directors who are not officers of the Company to review with management and the independent auditors the annual consolidated financial statements of the Company prior to submission to the Board of Directors for final approval. The Audit Committee also meets periodically during the year with management and the internal and external auditors either individually or as a group. Internal and external auditors have free access to the Audit Committee without obtaining prior management approval.

The independent auditors, Peat Marwick, have been appointed by the shareholders to express an opinion as to whether the consolidated financial statements present fairly the Company's financial position, operating results and changes in financial position in conformity with generally accepted accounting principles....

Management's Responsibility for Financial Reporting
Four Seasons Hotels Inc.

The management of Four Seasons Hotels Inc. is responsible for the preparation and integrity of the financial statements and related financial information of the Company. The consolidated financial statements, notes and other financial information included in the Annual Report were prepared in accordance with accounting principles generally accepted in Canada. The statements also include estimated amounts based on informed judgement of current and future events. These estimates are made with appropriate consideration of the materiality of the amounts involved. The financial information presented elsewhere in the Annual Report is consistent with that in the financial statements.

Management maintains a system of internal controls and budgeting procedures which are designed to provide reasonable assurance that assets are safeguarded and transactions are executed and recorded in accordance with management's authorization. To augment the internal control system, the Company maintains a comprehensive program of internal audits covering significant aspects of the Company's operations.

The Company's Audit Committee is appointed by the Board of Directors annually. The Committee meets with management and with the independent auditors (who have free access to the Audit Committee) to satisfy itself that each group is properly discharging its responsibilities and to review the financial statements and the independent auditors' report. The Audit Committee reports its findings to the Board of Directors for their consideration in approving the financial statements for issuance to the shareholders.

Peat Marwick, the independent auditors appointed by the shareholders of the Company, have examined the financial statements in accordance with generally accepted auditing standards and their report follows.

Isadore Sharp,
Chairman and President

H. Roger Garland,
Executive Vice-President
Development, Finance and
Administration

the concerns of the 1970s have increased management's interest. Often, the audit committee[2] of the board of directors has responsibility for accepting reports on the systems of internal control from both the internal and external auditors. Note the statements to that effect in the management report from TransCanada PipeLines in Exhibit 7-1 and the discussion of who bears the responsibility for the financial statements of John Labatt in Appendix E. If the auditors report problems with some or all of the systems of internal control to the audit committee, that body can suggest to the full board of directors that management be required to make necessary changes to the internal control systems in question.

Exhibit 7-1 presents excerpts from two fairly typical reports from management by TransCanada PipeLines Limited and Four Seasons Hotels Inc. Trans-Canada PipeLines' report, taken from the December 31, 1987 annual report, indicates that management is responsible for the financial statements. It points out that the audit committee is independent, that is, none of its members are officers or part of management. The audit committee meets "... periodically with management and the internal and external auditors either independently or in a group." Note that the internal and external auditors report directly to the audit committee and do not need management approval to do so. The responsibilities of the external auditors, Peat Marwick, are described.

The management report issued by Four Seasons Hotels Inc., included in the December 31, 1987 annual report, is signed by the chairman and president and by the executive vice-president. Note the statement in the second paragraph of management's responsibility for the system of internal control and of how management discharges that responsibility. The relationship between the audit committee and the auditors is explained as is the case with TransCanada PipeLines.

Effective Systems of Internal Control

Whether the business is Air Canada or a local department store, its system of internal control, if effective, has the following noteworthy characteristics.

Competent and Reliable Personnel

Employees should be *competent* and *reliable*. Paying top salaries to attract top-quality employees, training them to do their job well and supervising their work all help to build a competent staff. A business adds flexibility to its staffing by rotating employees through various jobs. If one employee is sick or on vacation, a second employee is already trained to step in and do the job.

Rotating employees through various jobs also promotes reliability. An employee is less likely to handle his/her job improperly if he/she knows that his/her misconduct may come to light when a second employee takes over the

> **OBJECTIVE 2**
> Identify the characteristics of an effective system of internal control

---

[2] An audit committee is a committee of the board of directors of a corporation. Incorporating acts such as the *Canada Business Corporations Act*, which require that a corporation has an audit committee, also require that a majority of the members of the audit committee be independent of the company, that is, that they not be officers or employees of the company. In many companies, both the internal and external auditors report to the audit committee (Exhibit 7-2).

job. This same reasoning leads businesses to require that employees take an annual vacation. A second employee, stepping in to handle the position, may uncover any wrongdoing.

Assignment of Responsibilities

In a business with an effective internal control system, no important duty is overlooked. A model of such *assignment of responsibilities* appears in the corporate organizational chart in Exhibit 7-2.

Notice that the corporation has a vice-president of finance and accounting. Two other officers, the treasurer and the controller, report to the vice-president.

EXHIBIT 7-2 *Organization Chart of a Corporation*

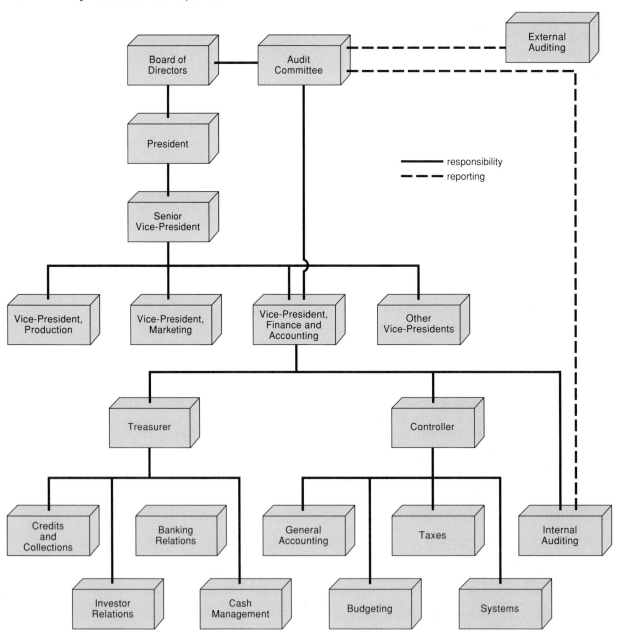

The treasurer is responsible for cash management. The controller performs accounting duties.

Within this organization, the controller may be responsible for approving invoices for payment and the treasurer may actually sign the cheques. Working under the controller, one accountant may be responsible for property taxes and another for income taxes. In sum, all duties are clearly defined and assigned to individuals who bear responsibility for carrying them out.

Obviously, the organization chart in Exhibit 7-2 is for a large corporation. Smaller entities have simpler structures with fewer officers and levels. For example, a car dealer may have a president, a treasurer/controller, a sales manager and a service manager.

Proper Authorization

An organization generally has a written set of rules that outlines approved procedures. Any deviation from standard policy requires *proper authorization*. For example, managers or assistant managers of retail stores must approve customer cheques for amounts above the store's usual limit. Likewise, deans or department chairpersons of colleges and universities must give the authorization for a first- or second-year student to enroll in courses otherwise restricted to upper-year students.

Separation of Duties

Smart management divides the responsibilities for transactions between two or more people or departments. Separation of duties limits chances for fraud and promotes the accuracy of accounting records. This crucial and often neglected component of the internal control system may be subdivided into four parts.

1. *Separation of operations from accounting*   The entire accounting function should be completely separate from operating departments so that objective records may be kept. For example, product inspectors, not machine operators, should count units produced by a manufacturing process; and accountants, not salespersons, should keep inventory records. Observe the separation of accounting from production and marketing in Exhibit 7-2.

2. *Separation of the custody of assets from accounting*   To reduce temptation and fraud, the accountant should not handle cash and the cashier should not have access to ledger accounts. If one employee had both cash-handling and accounting duties, this person would be able to steal cash and conceal the theft by making a bogus entry on the books. We see this component of internal control in the organization chart in Exhibit 7-2. Note that the treasurer has custody of cash and the controller accounts for cash. Neither person has both responsibilities.

Warehouse employees with no accounting duties should control inventory. If they were allowed to account for the inventory, they could steal it and write it off as obsolete. In a computerized accounting system, a person with custody of assets should not have access to the computer programs. Similarly, the programmer should not have access to tempting assets like cash.

3. *Separation of the authorization of transactions from the custody of related assets*
If possible, persons who authorize transactions should not control the related

asset. For example, the same individual should not authorize the payment of a supplier's invoice and also sign the cheque to pay the bill. With both duties, the person can authorize payments to himself and then sign the cheques. By separating these duties, only legitimate bills get paid.

For another example, an individual who handles cash receipts should not have the authority to write off accounts receivable. (Businesses that sell on credit declare certain of their accounts receivable as uncollectible, realizing that these receivables will never be collected. Chapter 8 looks at uncollectible accounts receivable in detail.) Suppose the company shown in Exhibit 7-2 employs V. Saucier. He works in credits and collections (under the treasurer) and handles cash receipts from customers.

Among the business's accounts receivable in the subsidiary ledger is Gina Kowalski's $500 balance. Saucier could label Kowalski's account as uncollectible, and the business might cease trying to collect from her. When Kowalski mails a $500 cheque to pay off her balance, Saucier forges the endorsement and pockets the money. Kowalski, of course, has no reason to notify anyone else at the business that she has mailed a cheque so that Saucier's crime goes undetected. This theft would have been avoided by denying Saucier either the access to cash receipts or the authority to declare accounts uncollectible.

4. *Separation of duties within the accounting function*   Independent performance of various phases of accounting helps minimize errors and the opportunities for fraud. For example, different accountants in a manual system keep the cash receipts and cash disbursements journals. In a large scale computerized system, the employees who enter data into the computer do not operate the machines as well; such separation is not practical in a microcomputer system.

Internal and External Audits

It is not economically feasible for auditors to examine all the transactions during a period. They must rely to some degree on the accounting system to produce accurate accounting records. To gauge the reliability of the company's accounting system, auditors evaluate its system of internal control. Auditors also spot weaknesses in the system and recommend corrections. Auditors offer *objectivity* in their reports, while managers, immersed in operations, may overlook the weaknesses.

Audits are internal or external. Exhibit 7-2 shows *internal auditors* as employees of the business, under the vice-president of finance and accounting. Some organizations have internal auditors report directly to the audit committee. Throughout the year, they audit various segments of the organization. *External auditors* are entirely independent of the business. These people, employed by an accounting firm, are hired by an entity as outsiders to audit the entity as a whole. The external auditors are and the internal auditors should be independent of the operations they examine, and their reviews of internal controls often are similar.

An auditor may find that an employee has both cash-handling and cash-accounting duties, or may learn that a cash shortage has resulted from lax efforts to collect accounts receivable. In such cases, the auditor suggests improvements. Auditors' recommendations assist the business in running smoothly and economically.

Documents and Records

Business *documents and records* vary considerably, from source documents like sales invoices and purchase orders to special journals and subsidiary ledgers.

Specially designed records, like the special journals discussed in the last chapter, speed the flow of paper work and enhance efficiency.

Documents should be prenumbered and access to them controlled. A gap in the numbered sequence calls attention to a missing document.

Prenumbering cash sale receipts discourages theft by the cashier because the copy retained by the cashier, which lists the amount of sale, can be checked against the actual amount of cash received. If receipts are not prenumbered, the cashier can destroy the copy and pocket the cash sale amount. However, if receipts are prenumbered, the missing copy can easily be identified.

Limitations of Internal Control

Most internal control measures can be overcome. Systems designed to thwart an individual employee's fraud may be beaten by two or more employees working as a team — colluding — to defraud the firm. Consider a movie theatre. The ticket seller takes in the cash, and the ticket taker tears the tickets in half so that they cannot be reused, retaining the torn ticket stubs. But suppose they put a scheme together in which the ticket seller pockets the cash for ten tickets and the ticket taker pockets ten stubs. Who would catch them? The manager could take the additional control measure of counting the people in the theatre and matching that figure against the number of ticket stubs retained. But that takes time away from other duties. As you see, the stricter the internal control system, the more expensive it becomes.

A system of internal control that is too complex may strangle people in red tape. Efficiency and control are hurt rather than helped. The more complicated the system, the more time and money it takes to maintain. Just how tight should an internal control system be? Managers must make sensible judgments. Investments in internal control must be judged in the light of costs and benefits.

The Bank Account as a Control Device

Keeping cash in a *bank account* is part of internal control because banks have established practices for safeguarding cash. Banks also provide depositors with detailed records of cash transactions. To take full advantage of these control features, the business should deposit all cash receipts in the bank account and make all cash payments through it (except petty cash disbursements, which we look at later). We now discuss banking records and documents.

For many businesses, cash is the most important asset. After all, cash is the most common means of exchange, and most transactions ultimately affect cash. Managers need an accurate record of this asset and all the transactions that affect it.

Cash is the most tempting asset for theft. Consequently, internal controls for cash are more elaborate than for most other assets. The rest of this chapter describes internal control over cash. We consider cash to be not just paper money and coins but also cheques, money orders and money kept in bank accounts. Cash does not include stamps because they are supplies, nor IOUs payable to the business because they are receivables.

Signature Card Banks require each person authorized to transact business through an account in that bank to sign a *signature card*. The bank compares the signatures on documents against the signature card to protect the bank and the depositor against forgery.

Deposit Ticket   Banks supply standard forms as *deposit tickets* or *deposit slips*. The customer fills in the dollar amount and date of deposit. The customer retains either a duplicate copy of the deposit ticket or a deposit receipt, depending on the bank's practice, as proof of transaction.

Cheque   To draw money from an account, the depositor writes a **cheque**, which is a document that instructs the bank to pay the designated person or business the specified amount of money. There are three parties to a cheque: the *maker*, who signs the cheque; the *payee*, to whose order the cheque is drawn; and the *bank* on which the cheque is drawn.

Most cheques are serially numbered and preprinted with the name and address of the depositor and the bank. The cheques have places for the date, the name of the payee, the signature of the maker, and the amount. The bank name and identification number and the depositor account number are usually imprinted in magnetic ink for machine processing.

Exhibit 7-3 shows a cheque drawn on the bank account of Business Research, Inc. The cheque has two parts: the cheque itself and the remittance advice. The *remittance advice*, an optional attachment, tells the payee the reason for payment. The maker (Business Research) retains a carbon copy of the cheque for its recording in the cheque register (cash disbursements journal). Note that internal controls at Business Research require two signatures on cheques.

Bank Statement   Most banks send monthly **bank statements** to their depositors. The statement shows the account's beginning and ending balance for the

EXHIBIT 7-3   *Cheque with Remittance Advice*

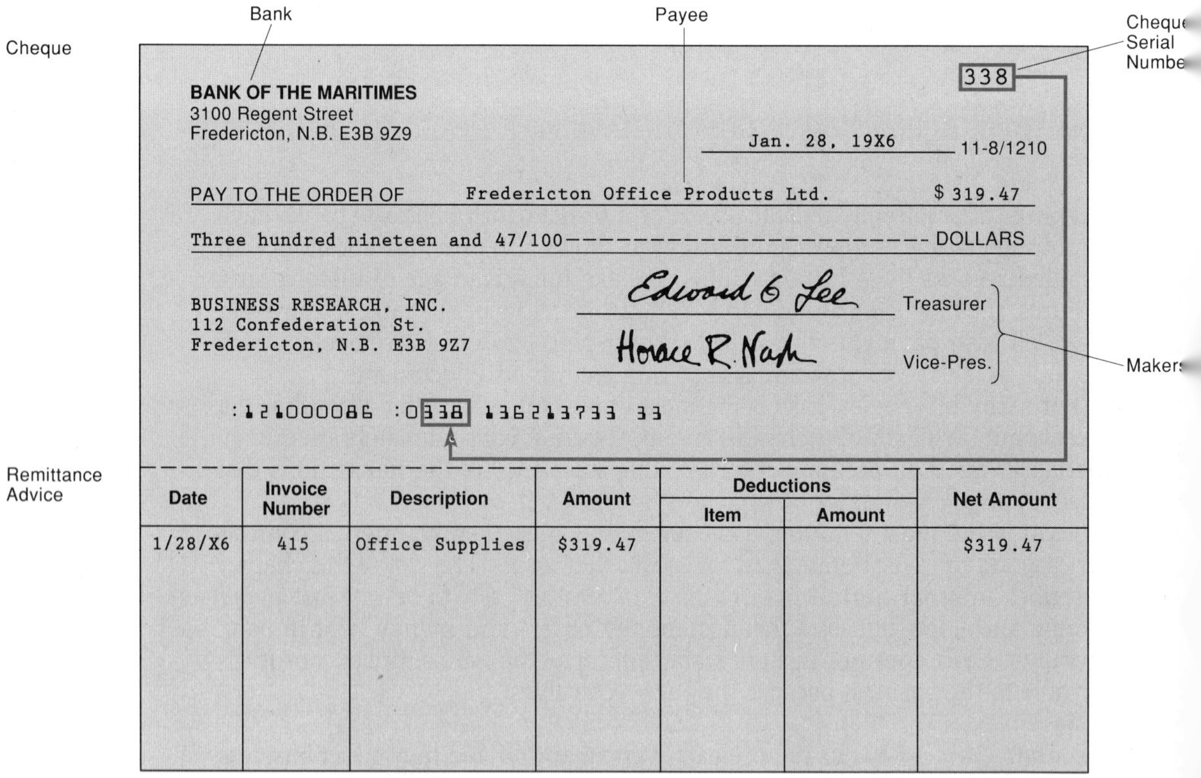

period and lists the month's transactions. Included with the statement are the maker's *canceled cheques* and those cheques that have been paid by the bank on behalf of the depositor. The bank statement also lists any other deposits and changes in the account. Deposits appear in chronological order, and cheques in cheque number order, along with the date each cheque cleared the bank.

Exhibit 7-4 is the bank statement of Business Research, Inc., for the month ended January 31, 19X6. At many banks, some depositors receive their statements on the first of the month, some on the second, and so on. This spacing eliminates the clerical burden of supplying all the statements at one time. Most businesses, like Business Research, receive their bank statement for the calendar month.

EXHIBIT 7-4 *Bank Statement*

BANK OF THE MARITIMES
3100 Regent Street
Fredericton, N.B. E3B 9Z9

ACCOUNT STATEMENT

Business Research, Inc.
112 Confederation St.
Fredericton, N.B. E3B 9Z7

CHEQUING ACCOUNT 136-213733

CHEQUING ACCOUNT SUMMARY AS OF 01-31-X6

BEGINNING BALANCE	TOTAL DEPOSITS	TOTAL WITHDRAWALS	SERVICE CHARGES	ENDING BALANCE
6556.12	3448.61	4602.00	14.25	5388.48

—————————————————CHEQUING ACCOUNT TRANSACTIONS—————————————————

DEPOSITS

DEPOSIT	01-04	1000.00
DEPOSIT	01-04	112.00
DEPOSIT	01-08	194.60
BANK COLLECTION	01-31	2114.00
INTEREST	01-31	28.01

CHARGES

SERVICE CHARGE	01-31	14.25

CHEQUES:

CHEQUES			CHEQUES			BALANCES	
NUMBER	DATE	AMOUNT	NUMBER	DATE	AMOUNT	DATE	BALANCE
332	01-12	3000.00	334	01-12	100.00	12-31	6556.12
656	01-06	100.00	335	01-06	100.00	01-04	7616.12
333	01-12	150.00	336	01-31	1100.00	01-06	7416.12
						01-08	7610.72
						01-12	4360.72
						01-26	6474.72
						01-31	5388.48

OTHER CHARGES		DATE	AMOUNT
NSF		01-04	52.00

MONTHLY SUMMARY

7 WITHDRAWALS	4360 MINIMUM BALANCE	5812 AVERAGE BALANCE

Bank Reconciliation There are two records of the business's cash: its Cash account in its own general ledger and the bank statement, which tells the actual amount of cash the business has in the bank. The balance in the business's Cash account rarely equals the balance shown on the bank statement.

The books and the bank statement may disagree, although both are correct. The difference arises because of a time-lag in recording certain transactions. When a firm writes a cheque, it immediately credits its Cash account. The bank, however, will not subtract the amount of the cheque until the cheque reaches it for payment. This may take days, even weeks, if the payee waits to cash the cheque. Likewise, the business debits Cash for all cash receipts, and it may take a day or so for the bank to add this amount to the business's bank balance.

Good internal control means knowing where a company's money is. How else can the accountant keep the accurate records that management needs to make informed decisions? The accountant must explain the reasons for the difference between the firm's records and bank statement figures and determine the actual amount of cash in the bank on a certain date. This process is called the **bank reconciliation**. Properly done, the bank reconciliation assures that all cash transactions have been accounted for and that bank and book records of cash are correct.

Common items that cause differences between the bank balance and the business are

1. Items recorded by the *company* but not yet recorded by the *bank*
   a. **Outstanding cheques** These cheques have been issued by the company and recorded on its books but have not yet been paid by its bank.
   b. **Deposits in transit** (outstanding deposits) The company has recorded these deposits, but the bank has not.

2. Items recorded by the *bank* but not yet recorded by the *company*
   a. **Service charge** This amount is the bank's fee for processing the depositor's transactions. Banks commonly base service charge on the balance in the account. The depositor learns the amount of service charge from the bank statement.
   b. **Bank collections** The bank sometimes collects money on behalf of depositors. Some businesses have their customers pay directly to the company bank account. This practice, called a lock-box system, reduces the possibility of theft and places the business's cash in circulation faster than if the cash had to be collected and deposited by company personnel. An example is a bank's collecting cash on a note receivable and interest revenue for the depositor. The bank may notify the depositor of these bank collections on the bank statement.
   c. *Interest revenue on chequing account* Many banks pay interest to depositors who keep a large enough balance of cash in the account. This is generally the case with business chequing accounts. The bank notifies the depositor of this interest on the bank statement.
   d. **NSF (nonsufficient funds) cheques** To understand how to handle NSF cheques, also called hot cheques, you first need to know the route a cheque takes. The maker writes the cheque, credits Cash to record the payment on the books and gives the cheque to the payee. On receiving the cheque, the payee debits Cash on his or her books and deposits the cheque in the bank. The payee's bank immediately adds the receipt amount to the payee's bank balance on the assumption that the cheque is good. The cheque is returned to the maker's bank, which then deducts the cheque amount from the maker's bank balance. If the maker's bank balance is insufficient to pay the cheque, the maker's bank refuses to

pay the cheque, reverses this deduction and sends an NSF notice back to the payee's bank. That bank subtracts the cheque amount from the payee's bank balance and notifies the payee of this action. This process may take from three to seven days. The company may learn of NSF cheques through the bank statement, which lists the NSF cheque as a charge (subtraction), as shown near the bottom of Exhibit 7-4.

    e. *Cheques collected, deposited and returned to the payee by the bank for reasons other than NSF*   Banks return cheques to the payee if (1) the maker's account has closed, (2) the date is stale, usually six months or more, before the cheque is deposited, (3) the signature is not authorized, (4) the cheque has been altered or (5) the cheque form is improper. Accounting for all returned cheques is the same as for NSF cheques.

    f. *Cost of printed cheques*   This charge against the company's bank account balance is handled like a service charge.

3. Errors by either the company or the bank. For example, a bank may improperly charge (decrease) the bank balance of Business Research, Inc. for a cheque drawn by another company, perhaps Business Research Associates. Or a company may miscompute its bank balance on its own books. Computational errors are becoming less frequent with the widespread use of computers. Nevertheless, all errors must be corrected, and the corrections will be a part of the bank reconciliation.

Internal Control and the Bank Reconciliation

Good internal control dictates that the person preparing the bank reconciliation should be separate from the handling of cash, the issuing of cheques and the recording of cash receipts and disbursements. Otherwise, an independent person should check the reconciliation after it is prepared.

Steps in Preparing the Bank Reconciliation

The steps in preparing the bank reconciliation are

1. Start with two figures, the balance shown on the bank statement (*balance per bank*) and the balance in the company's Cash account (*balance per books*). These two amounts will probably disagree because of the timing differences discussed earlier.

2. Add to, or subtract from, the *bank* balance those items that appear on the books but not on the bank statement.

    a. Add *deposits in transit* to the bank balance. Deposits in transit are identified by comparing the deposits listed on the bank statement to the company list of cash receipts. They show up as cash receipts on the books but not as deposits on the bank statement. As a control measure, the accountant should also ensure that deposits in transit from the preceding month appear on the current month's bank statement. If they do not, the deposits may be lost.

    b. Subtract *outstanding cheques* from the bank balance. Outstanding cheques are identified by comparing the canceled cheques returned with the bank statement to the company list of cheques in the cash disbursements journal. They show up as cash payments on the books but not as paid cheques on the bank statement. This comparison also verifies that all cheques paid by the bank were valid company cheques and correctly recorded by the bank and by the company. Outstanding cheques are usually the most numerous item on a bank reconciliation.

3. Add to, or subtract from, the *book* balance those items that appear on the bank statement but not on the company books.
   a. Add to the book balance (1) *bank collections* and (2) any *interest revenue* earned on the money in the bank. These items are identified by comparing the deposits listed on the bank statement to the company list of cash receipts.
   b. Subtract from the book balance (1) *service charges*, (2) *cost of printed cheques* and (3) *other bank charges* (for example, charges for NSF or stale date cheques). These items are identified by comparing the other charges listed on the bank statement to the cash disbursements recorded on the company books.
4. Compute the *adjusted bank balance* and *adjusted book balance*. The two should be equal.
5. Journalize each item in step 3, that is, each item listed on the book portion of the bank reconciliation. These items must be recorded on the company books because they affect cash.
6. Correct all book errors and notify the bank of any errors it has made.

Bank Reconciliation Illustrated

The bank statement in Exhibit 7-4 indicates that the January 31 bank balance of Business Research, Inc. is $5,388.48. However, the company's Cash account has a balance of $3,294.21. The bank statement arrives at the Business Research, Inc. office on February 2, and the accountant prepares the reconciliation immediately. In following the steps outlined above, the accountant finds these reconciling items:

OBJECTIVE 3

Prepare a bank reconciliation and related journal entries

1. The January 30 deposit of $1,591.63 does not appear on the bank statement.
2. The bank erroneously charged a $100 cheque written by Business Research Associates against the Business Research, Inc. account.
3. Five company cheques issued late in January and recorded in the cash disbursements journal have not been paid by the bank.

Cheque No.	Date	Amount
337	Jan. 27	$286.00
338	28	319.47
339	28	83.00
340	29	203.14
341	30	458.53

4. The bank collected on behalf of the company a note receivable, $2,114 (including interest revenue of $214). This cash receipt has not been recorded in the cash receipts journal.
5. The bank statement shows interest revenue of $28.01 that the bank has paid the company on its cash balance.
6. Cheque number 333 for $150 paid to Brown Company on account was recorded in the cash disbursements journal as a $510 amount, creating a $360 understatement of the cash balance per books.
7. The bank service charge for the month was $14.25.
8. The bank statement shows an NSF cheque for $52 that was received from customer L. Ross.

Exhibit 7-5 is the bank reconciliation based on the above data. Panel A lists the reconciling items, which are keyed by number to the actual reconciliation

EXHIBIT 7-5   *Bank Reconciliation*

Panel A: Reconciling Items

1. Deposit in transit, $1,591.63.
2. Bank error; add $100 to bank balance.
3. Outstanding cheques: no. 337, $286; no. 338, $319.47; no. 339, $83; no. 340, $203.14; no. 341, $458.53.

4. Bank collection, $2,114, including interest revenue of $214.
5. Interest earned on bank balance, $28.01.
6. Book error; add $360 to book balance.
7. Bank service charge, $14.25.
8. NSF cheque from L. Ross, $52.

Panel B: Bank Reconciliation

Business Research, Inc.
Bank Reconciliation
February 2, 19X6

Bank				Books			
Balance, January 31			$5,388.48	Balance, January 31			$3,294.21
Add:				Add:			
1. Deposit of January 30 in transit			1,591.63	4. Bank collection of note receivable, including interest revenue			
2. Correction of bank error—Business Research Associates cheque erroneously charged against company account			100.00	of $214			2,114.00
			$7,080.11	5. Interest revenue earned on bank balance			28.01
3. Less outstanding cheques:				6. Correction of book error—Overstated amount of cheque no. 333.			360.00
No. 337	$286.00						5,796.22
No. 338	319.47			Less:			
No. 339	83.00			7. Service charge	$14.25		
No. 340	203.14			8. NSF cheque	52.00		(66.25)
No. 341	458.53	(1,350.14)					
Adjusted bank balance			$5,729.97	Adjusted book balance			$5,729.97

in Panel B. Note that after the reconciliation, the adjusted bank balance equals the adjusted book balance. This equality is the accuracy check for the reconciliation.

Recording Entries from the Reconciliation

The bank reconciliation does not directly affect the journals or ledgers. Like the work sheet, the reconciliation is an accountant's tool, separate from the company's books.

The bank reconciliation acts as a control device by signaling the company to record transactions listed as reconciling items in the Books section because the company has not yet done so. For example, the bank collected the note receivable on behalf of the company, but the company has not yet recorded this cash receipt. In fact, the company learned of the cash receipt only when it received the bank statement.

Why does the company *not* need to record the reconciling items on the Bank side of the reconciliation? Those items have already been recorded on the company books.

Based on the reconciliation in Exhibit 7-5, Business Research, Inc. makes these entries. They are dated January 31 to bring the Cash account to the correct balance on that date.

Jan. 31	Cash....................................	2,114.00	
	Notes Receivable		1,900.00
	Interest Revenue		214.00
	Note receivable collected by bank.		
31	Cash....................................	28.01	
	Interest Revenue		28.01
	Interest earned on bank balance.		
31	Cash....................................	360.00	
	Accounts Payable—Brown Co.........		360.00
	Correction of Cheque Register, cheque no. 333.		
31	Miscellaneous Expense	4.25	
	Cash		4.25
	Bank service charge		
	Note: Miscellaneous Expense is debited for the bank service charge because the service charge pertains to no particular expense category.		
31	Accounts Receivable—L. Ross	62.00	
	Cash		62.00
	NSF cheque returned by bank.		

These entries bring the business's books up to date.

The entry for the NSF cheque needs explanation. Upon learning that L. Ross's $62 cheque was no good, Business Research credits Cash to bring the Cash account up to date. Since Business Research still has a receivable from Ross, it debits Accounts Receivable—L. Ross and pursues collection from him.

Summary Problem for Your Review

1. The cash account of Bain Company at February 28, 19X3 follows. (CR stands for cash receipts journal. CD stands for cash disbursements journal.)

Cash

Feb. 1	Balance	4,195	Feb. 3	CD 5	400
6	CR 14	800	12	CD 5	3,100
15	CR 15	1,800	19	CD 6	1,100
23	CR 15	900	25	CD 6	500
28	CR 15	2,400	27	CD 6	900
Feb. 28	Balance	4,095			

2. Bain Company receives this bank statement on February 28, 19X3. (Negative amounts appear in parentheses.)

Bank Statement for February, 19X3

Beginning balance		$4,195
Deposits		
Feb. 7	$ 800	
15	1,800	
24	900	3,500
Cheques (total per day)		
Feb. 8	$ 400	
16	3,100	
23	1,100	(4,600)
Other items		
Service charge		(10)
NSF cheque from M. E. Crown		(700)
Bank collection of note receivable for the company		1,000*
Interest on account balance		15
Ending balance		$3,400

---

* Includes interest of $119.

Additional data: Bain Company deposits all cash receipts in the bank and makes all cash disbursements by cheque.

Required

1. Prepare the bank reconciliation of Bain Company at February 28, 19X3.
2. Record the entries based on the bank reconciliation.

SOLUTION TO REVIEW PROBLEM

Requirement 1

Bain Company
Bank Reconciliation
February 28, 19X3

Bank

Balance, February 28, 19X3		$3,400
Add: Deposit of February 28 in transit		2,400
		5,800
Less: Outstanding cheques issued on Feb. 25 ($500) and		
Feb. 27 ($900)		(1,400)
Adjusted bank balance, February 28, 19X3		$4,400

Books

Balance, February 28, 19X3		$4,095
Add: Bank collection of note receivable, including interest		
of $119		1,000
Interest earned on bank balance		15
		5,110
Less: Service charge	$ 10	
NSF cheque	700	(710)
Adjusted book balance, February 28, 19X3		$4,400

Requirement 2

Feb. 28	Cash	1,000	
	Note Receivable ($1,100 – $119)		881
	Interest Revenue		119
	Note receivable collected by bank.		
28	Cash	15	
	Interest Revenue		15
	Interest earned on bank balance.		
28	Miscellaneous Expense	10	
	Cash		10
	Bank service charge.		
28	Accounts Receivable — M. E. Crown	700	
	Cash		700
	NSF cheque returned by bank.		

Reporting of Cash

Cash is the first current asset listed on the balance sheet of most companies. Even small businesses have several bank accounts and one or more petty cash funds that are kept on hand for making small disbursements. However, companies usually combine all cash amounts into a single total for reporting on the balance sheet. They also include liquid assets like time deposits and certificates of deposit. These are interest-bearing accounts that can be withdrawn with no penalty after a short period of time. Although they are slightly less liquid than cash, they are sufficiently similar to be reported along with cash. For example, the balance sheet of T.C.C. Beverages Ltd., bottler of Coca Cola products in British Columbia, Alberta, Ontario, Quebec and Nova Scotia, recently reported (in thousands of dollars):

Current Assets

Cash	$ 5,650
Trade accounts receivable	90,498
Inventories	49,736
Prepaid expenses and other assets	30,759
	$176,643

It is important to perform the bank reconciliation on the balance sheet date in order to be assured of reporting the correct amount of cash.

Internal Control over Cash Receipts

OBJECTIVE 4

Apply internal controls to cash receipts

Internal control over cash receipts ensures that all cash receipts are deposited in the bank and the company's accounting record is correct. Many businesses receive cash over the counter and through the mail. Each source of cash receipts calls for specific controls.

The cash register offers management control over cash received in a store. First, the machine should be positioned so that customers can see the amounts the cashier enters into the register. No person willingly pays more than the marked price for an item, so the customer helps prevent the sales clerk from overcharging and pocketing the excess over actual prices. Also, customers should be encouraged to request a receipt to make sure each sale is recorded in the register.

Second, the register's cash drawer opens only when the sales clerk enters an amount on the keys. A roll of tape locked inside the machine records each amount. At the end of the day, a manager proves the cash by comparing the total amount in the cash drawer against the tape's total. This step helps prevent outright theft by the clerk. For security reasons, the clerk should not have access to the tape.

Third, pricing merchandise at "uneven" amounts, say, $3.95 instead of $4.00, means that the clerk generally must make change, which in turn means having to get into the cash drawer. This requires entering the amount of the sale on the keys and so onto the register tape.

At the end of the day, the cashier or other employee with cash-handling duties deposits the cash in the bank. The tape goes to the accounting department as the basis for an entry in the cash receipts journal. These security measures, coupled with periodic on-site inspection by a manager, discourage fraud.

All incoming mail should be opened by a mail-room employee. This person should compare the actual enclosed amount of cash or cheque with the attached remittance advice. If no advice was sent, the mail-room employee should prepare one and enter the amount of each receipt on a control tape. At the end of the day, this control tape is given to a responsible official, such as the controller, for verification. Cash receipts should be given to the cashier, who combines them with any cash received over the counter and prepares the bank deposit.

Having a mail-room employee be the first to handle postal cash receipts is just another application of a good internal control procedure — in this case, separation of duties. If the accountants opened postal cash receipts, they could easily hide a theft.

The mail-room employee forwards the remittance advices to the accounting department. They provide the data for entries in the cash receipts journal and postings to customers' accounts in the accounts receivable ledger. As a final step, the controller compares the three records of the day's cash receipts: (1) the control tape total from the mail room, (2) the bank deposit amount from the cashier and (3) the debit to Cash from the accounting department.

An added measure used to control cash receipts is a *fidelity bond*, which is an insurance policy that the business buys to guard against theft. The fidelity bond helps in two ways. First, the insurance company that issues the policy investigates the backgrounds of the workers whose activities will be covered, such as the mail-room employees who handle incoming cash and the employees who handle inventory. Second, if the company suffers a loss due to the misconduct of a covered employee, the insurance company reimburses the business.

Cash Short and Over   A difference often exists between actual cash receipts and the day's record of cash received. Usually the difference is small and results from honest errors. Suppose the cash register tapes of a large department store indicate sales revenue of $25,000, but the cash received is $24,980. To record the day's sales, the store would make this entry:

Cash 24,980
Cash Short and Over 20
    Sales Revenue 25,000

As the entry shows, *Cash Short and Over* is debited when sales revenue exceeds cash receipts. This account is credited when cash receipts exceed sales. A debit balance appears on the income statement as Miscellaneous Expense, a credit balance as Other Income.

This account's balance should be small. The debits and credits for Cash Short and Over collected over an accounting period tend to cancel each other out. A large balance signals the accountant to investigate. For example, too large a debit balance may mean an employee is stealing. Cash Short and Over, then, acts as an internal control device.

Internal Control over Cash Disbursements _____

> **OBJECTIVE 5**
>
> Apply internal controls to cash disbursements

Payment by *cheque* is an important control over cash disbursements. First, the cheque acts as a source document. Second, to be valid the cheque must be signed by an authorized official, so that each payment by cheque draws the attention of management. Before signing the cheque, the manager should study the invoice, receiving report, purchase order and other supporting documents. (A discussion of these documents follows.) As further security and control over cash disbursements, many firms require two signatures on a cheque, as in Exhibit 7-3. To avoid document alteration, some firms also use machines that indelibly stamp the amount on the cheque.

In very small businesses, the proprietor or partners may control cash disbursements by reviewing the supporting documents themselves and personally writing all cheques. In larger businesses, however, this is impractical. Therefore the duties of approving invoices for payment and writing cheques are performed by authorized employees. Strong internal control is achieved through clear-cut assignment of responsibility, proper authorization and separation of duties.

Controlling the Cost of Inventory

Cost of goods sold is the major expense of most merchandising businesses. Therefore, it is important to control the cost of inventory purchases. Overall control is achieved by the same measures used to control all other cash disbursements—assignment of responsibility, authorization for payment, separation of duties, and so on.

A measure that is designed specifically to control the cost of inventory concerns the manner of recording purchases. There are two ways to record purchases: (1) at the *gross* cost, as illustrated thus far; and (2) at the *net* cost, which takes into account any discount on the purchase. For example, a $2,000 invoice subject to credit terms of 2/10 n/30 could be recorded at gross ($2,000) or net ($1,960). The discount terms of 2/10 n/30 (that is, a 2 percent discount for payment within 10 days, or the full $2,000 within 30 days) indicate a very high rate of interest when expressed as an annual rate. Paying after the discount period costs 2 percent for the extra 20 days of credit, an annual rate of 36 percent (.02×360 days/20 days=.36). For this reason, companies adopt the policy of taking all such discounts.

Recording the purchase at its net amount has a control advantage because it highlights the inefficiency of paying late. Recorded at net cost, the purchase entry is

Purchases ($2,000 – $40)	1,960	
Accounts Payable.........................		1,960
Purchase on account.		

The actual cost of the inventory is $1,960 because this is the cash cost of the goods if they are paid for immediately. The gross cost of $2,000 includes a $40 charge for payment beyond the discount period. Therefore, the net cost method is preferable. To see the control advantage of the net cost approach, suppose the invoice is *not* paid within the discount period. This inefficiency costs an extra $40, debited to Purchase Discounts Lost as follows:

Accounts Payable	1,960	
Purchase Discounts Lost	40	
Cash in Bank		2,000
Payment after discount period.		

Purchase Discounts Lost is an expense account reported as Other Expense on the income statement.

Grant Company
Income Statement
year ended December 31, 19X8

Sales revenue..	$700,000
Cost of goods sold	380,000
Gross margin	320,000
Operating expenses	230,000
Income from operations	90,000
Other revenue (expense)	
Purchase discounts lost............................	**(2,000)**
Net income	$ 88,000

Reporting Purchase Discounts Lost on the income statement draws attention to the inefficiency of losing the discounts. The net method thus captures the information needed to evaluate employee performance. Managers can then correct those persons whose oversight or carelessness led to payment of the full amount. Contrast this accounting treatment with recording the purchases at gross cost. There is no record of the discount because the purchase and related payment are both recorded at $2,000. Managers lose the notification provided by the Purchase Discounts Lost account.

Petty Cash Disbursements

It would be uneconomical for a business to write a separate cheque for an executive's taxi fare, a box of pencils needed right away, or the delivery of a special message across town. Therefore, companies keep a small amount of cash on hand to pay for such minor amounts. This fund is called **petty cash**.

Even though the individual amounts paid through the petty cash fund may be small, such expenses occur so often that the total amount over an accounting period may grow quite large. Thus the business needs to set up these controls over petty cash: (1) designate an employee to administer the fund as its custodian, (2) keep a specific amount of cash on hand, (3) support all fund disbursements with a petty cash ticket and (4) replenish the fund through normal cash disbursement procedures.

To open the petty cash fund, a payment is approved for a predetermined amount and a cheque for this amount is issued to Petty Cash. Assume that on February 28 the business decides to establish a petty cash fund of $200. The custodian cashes the cheque and places the currency and coin in the fund, which may be a cash box, safe, or other device. The petty cash custodian is assigned the responsibility for controlling the fund. Starting the fund is recorded as follows:

OBJECTIVE 6

Account for petty cash transactions

Feb. 28	Petty Cash....................................	200	
	Cash in Bank		200
	To open the petty cash fund.		

For each petty cash disbursement, the custodian prepares a *petty cash ticket* like the one illustrated in Exhibit 7-6.

EXHIBIT 7-6   *Petty Cash Ticket*

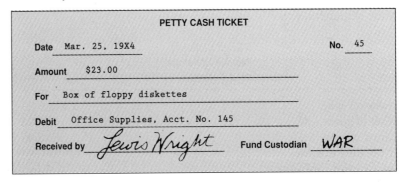

Observe the signatures (or initials, for the custodian) that identify the recipient of petty cash and the fund custodian. Requiring both signatures reduces unauthorized cash disbursements. The custodian keeps all the petty cash tickets in the fund. The sum of the cash plus the total of the ticket amounts should equal the opening balance at all times—in this case, $200. Also, the Petty Cash account keeps its prescribed $200 balance at all times. Maintaining the Petty Cash account at this balance, supported by the fund (cash plus tickets totaling the fund amount) is a characteristic of an **imprest system**. The control feature of an imprest system is that it clearly identifies the amount of money that the fund custodian is responsible for.

Disbursements reduce the amount of cash in the fund, so that periodically the fund must be replenished. Suppose that on March 31 the fund has $118 in cash and $82 in tickets. A cheque for $82 is issued, made payable to Petty Cash. The fund custodian cashes this cheque for currency and coins and puts the money in the fund to return its actual cash to $200. The petty cash tickets identify the accounts to be debited: Store Supplies for $23, Delivery Expense for $17 and Miscellaneous Selling Expense for $42. The entry to record replenishment of the fund is

Mar. 31	Store Supplies	23	
	Delivery Expense	17	
	Miscellaneous Selling Expense...................	42	
	Cash in Bank............................		82
	To replenish the petty cash fund.		

If this cash payment exceeds the sum of the tickets — that is, if the fund comes up short, Cash Short and Over is debited for the missing amount. If the sum of the tickets exceeds the payment, Cash Short and Over is credited. Note that replenishing the fund does *not* affect the Petty Cash account. Petty Cash keeps its $200 balance at all times.

Whenever petty cash runs low, the fund is replenished. It *must* be replenished on the balance sheet date. Otherwise, the reported balance for Petty Cash will be overstated by the amount of the tickets in the fund. The income statement will understate the expenses listed on these tickets.

Petty Cash is debited only when starting the fund (see the February 28 entry) or changing its amount. In our illustration, suppose the business decides to raise the fund amount from $200 to $250 because of increased demand for petty cash. This step would require a $50 debit to Petty Cash.

The Voucher System

As we saw in Chapter 6, some businesses use the purchases journal and the cash disbursements journal to record cash payments. Other businesses use a **voucher system**. The voucher system of recording cash payments offers the business greater internal control by formalizing the process of approving and recording invoices for payment. We will examine the voucher system as it is used by a merchandising business.

The voucher system uses (1) vouchers, (2) a voucher register, (3) an unpaid voucher file, (4) a cheque register and (5) a paid voucher file. The merchandising business we discuss has separate departments for purchasing goods, receiving goods, disbursing cash and accounting.

> **OBJECTIVE 7**
> Use the voucher system

Vouchers   A **voucher** is a document authorizing cash disbursement. The accounting department prepares vouchers. Exhibit 7-7 illustrates the voucher of Bliss Wholesale Company. In addition to places for writing in the *payee, due date, terms, description* and *invoice amount,* the voucher includes a section for designated officers to sign their *approval* for payment. The back of the voucher has places for recording the *account debited, date paid* and *cheque number.* You should locate these nine items in Exhibit 7-7.

To better understand the voucher system, let us take an in-depth look at the purchasing process. Exhibit 7-8 lists the various business documents used to

EXHIBIT 7-7 *Voucher*

Front of
Voucher

			Voucher No. 326
	BLISS WHOLESALE COMPANY		

Payee John Forsyth Co.
Address 31 Young St.
Kitchener, Ontario N2H 4Y7

Due Date March 7
Terms 2/10 n/30

Date	Invoice No.	Description	Amount
Mar. 1	6380	144 men's shirts stock no. X14	$1,800

Approved *Jane Trent*   **Approved** *Bob Kraft*
Controller   Treasurer

Back of
Voucher

Voucher No. 326
Payee   John Forsyth Co.

Invoice Amount   1,800

Discount   36

Net Amount $1,764

Due Date   Mar. 7

Date Paid   Mar. 6

Cheque No.   694

Account Distribution

Account Debited	Acct. No.	Amount
Purchases	501	1,800
Store Supplies	145	
Salary Expense	538	
Advertising Expense	542	
Utilities Expense	548	
Delivery Expense	544	
Total		$1,800

ensure that the company receives the goods it ordered and pays only for the goods it has actually received.

The purchasing process starts when the sales department identifies the need for merchandise and prepares a *purchase request* (or requisition). A separate purchasing department specializes in locating the best buys and mails a *purchase order* to the supplier, the outside company that sells the needed goods. When the supplier ships the goods to the requesting business, the supplier also mails the *invoice* (or bill), which is a notification of the need to pay. As the goods arrive, the receiving department checks them for any damage and lists the merchandise received on a document called the *receiving report*. The accounting department prepares a *voucher* and attaches all the foregoing documents, checks them for accuracy and agreement, and forwards this voucher packet to designated officers for approval and payment. Exhibit 7-9 shows how a voucher packet looks.

Before approving the voucher, the controller and the treasurer should examine a sample of vouchers to determine that the following control steps have been performed by the accounting department:

EXHIBIT 7-8   *Purchasing Process*

Business Document	Prepared by	Sent to
Purchase request	Sales department	Purchasing department
Purchase order	Purchasing department	Outside company that sells the needed merchandise (supplier or vendor)
Invoice	Outside company that sells the needed merchandise (supplier or vendor)	Accounting department
Receiving report	Receiving department	Accounting department
Voucher	Accounting department	Officer who signs the cheque

1. The invoice is compared to a copy of the purchase order and purchase request to ensure that the business pays cash only for the goods that it ordered. A purchasing agent prepares the purchase order and mails it to the supplier as the first step in the purchase transaction.
2. The invoice is compared to the receiving report to ensure that cash is paid only for the goods that are actually received. The receiving department prepares the receiving report when the goods arrive.
3. The mathematical accuracy of the invoice is proved.

The voucher packet includes the voucher, invoice, receiving report, purchase order and purchase request, as shown in Exhibit 7-9.

EXHIBIT 7-9   *Voucher Packet*

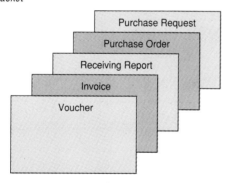

Voucher Register   After approval by the designated officers, the voucher goes to the accounting department where it is recorded in the **voucher register**. This journal is similar to the purchases journal (discussed in Chapter 6), but the voucher register is more comprehensive. In a voucher system, *all* expenditures are recorded first in the voucher register. This is a fundamental control feature of the voucher system because it centralizes the initial recording of all expenditures in this one journal. That is, all cash payments must be vouchered and approved prior to payment. For each transaction, the debit is to the account for which payment is being made, and the credit is to Vouchers Payable, the account that replaces Accounts Payable if a voucher system is used. Exhibit 7-10 illustrates the voucher register of Bliss Wholesale Company.

EXHIBIT 7-10 *Voucher Register*

Voucher Register — Page 16

Date	Voucher No.	Payee	Payment Date	Cheque No.	Credit Vouchers Payable	Debit Purchases	Store Supplies	Salary Expense	Advertising Expense	Utilities Expense	Delivery Expense	Other Accounts Title	No.	Amount
Mar. 1	326	John Forsyth Co.	3/6	694	1,800	1,800								
1	327	Howell Properties	3/2	693	1,500							Rent Expense	547	1,500
4	328	Bell Telephone	3/10	696	128					128				
5	329	Schick Supplies	3/11	697	85		85							
8	330	Daily Journal			369				369					
9	331	Ace Delivery Service	3/9	695	37						37			
26	348	Carr Products			1,638	1,638								
28	349	Petty Cash	3/31	717	82		23				17	Miscelaneous Selling Expense	563	42
29	350	Consumers Gas Co.			195					195				
30	351	Foothills Bank	3/31	718	360							Interest Expense	546	360
31	352	Ralph Grant	3/31	719	864			864						
31		Totals			12,580	6,209	137	1,781	753	602	185			2,913
					(201)	(501)	(145)	(538)	(542)	(548)	(544)			(✓)

Account numbers in parentheses indicate the accounts to which these amounts have been posted.

The voucher register has columns to record payment date and cheque number, which are entered when the voucher is paid. The absence of a payment date and cheque number means that the voucher is unpaid. In Exhibit 7-10, for example, Bliss Wholesale has a $2,202 liability at March 31 for vouchers 330 ($369 payable to the *Daily Journal*), 348 ($1,638 payable to Carr Products) and 350 ($195 payable to Consumers Gas Company). If these were the company's only unpaid vouchers at March 31, the balance sheet, which usually records unpaid vouchers as Accounts Payable rather than Vouchers Payable, would report:

Current liabilities
    Accounts payable $2,202

Unpaid Voucher File   After recording a voucher in the voucher register, the accountant places the voucher packet in the *unpaid voucher file*, where it stays until the voucher is paid. The unpaid voucher file acts as the accounts payable subsidiary ledger because each voucher serves as an individual account payable. Thus no need exists for a separate accounts payable ledger.

The unpaid voucher file has 31 slots, one for each day of the month. Each voucher is filed according to its due date. For example, voucher no. 326 in Exhibit 7-7 was due March 7, so that it was filed in the slot marked 7.

Cheque Register   The **cheque register** is the journal in which are recorded all cheques issued in a voucher system. It replaces the cash disbursements journal. All entries in the cheque register debit Vouchers Payable and credit Cash (and Purchase Discounts, as appropriate).

Exhibit 7-11 shows a cheque register. Notice that the cash account is entitled Cash in Bank.

EXHIBIT 7-11   *Cheque Register*

				Debit	Credit	
Date	Cheque No.	Payee	Voucher No.	Vouchers Payable	Purchase Discounts	Cash in Bank
Mar. 1	692	Trent Co.	322	600	18	582
2	693	Howell Properties	327	1,500		1,500
6	694	John Forsyth Co.	326	1,800	36	1,764
9	695	Ace Delivery Service	331	37		37
10	696	Bell Telephone	328	128		128
11	697	Schick Supplies	329	85		85
31	717	Petty Cash	349	82		82
31	718	Foothills Bank	351	360		360
31	719	Ralph Grant	352	864		864
31	720	Krasner Supply Co.	336	92		92
31		Totals		11,406	317	11,089
				(201)	(503)	(103)

Cheque Register   Page 9

Account numbers in parentheses indicate the accounts to which these amounts have been posted.

On or before the due date, the accountant removes the voucher packet from the unpaid voucher file and sends it to the officers for signing. After the cheques are signed, the cheque number and payment date are entered on the back of the voucher, in the register and in the voucher register.

Paid Voucher File   After payment, the voucher packet is canceled to avoid paying the bill twice. Typically, a hole is punched through the voucher packet. It is then filed alphabetically by payee name. Most businesses also file a copy in numerical sequence by voucher number as a cross reference. With this dual filing system, a voucher can be located using either classification scheme.

In summary, the voucher system works as follows:

1. The accounting department prepares a *voucher* for each invoice to be paid.
2. Supporting documents (invoice, receiving report, purchase order and purchase request) are compared in the accounting department for accuracy and attached to the voucher. These make up the *voucher packet*.
3. Designated officials examine the supporting documents and approve the voucher for payment.
4. The accounting department enters the voucher in the *voucher register*. The entry is a debit to the account of the item purchased (for example, Purchases) and a credit to Vouchers Payable. The voucher remains in the *unpaid voucher file* until payment.
5. Prior to the invoice due date, a cheque is issued to pay the voucher. The official reviews the supporting document and signs the *cheque*.
6. The accounting department enters the cheque in the *cheque register* and updates the voucher and voucher register to record payment. All cheques are debits to Vouchers Payable and credits to Cash.
7. Paid vouchers are canceled and filed by payee name and by voucher number.

To gain a complete understanding of the voucher system, trace voucher no. 326 from Exhibit 7-7 through the voucher register in Exhibit 7-10 to the cheque register in Exhibit 7-11. Also, trace the cheque register entries from Exhibit 7-11 back to Exhibit 7-10.

Computers and Internal Control

Computers have had both positive and negative effects on internal control. On the positive side, their speed of operation and high reliability increase efficiency. On the negative side, computer systems are less flexible than manual systems. Computers can take data in only one programmed format, whereas humans can process data if it is merely legible.

Effective internal control is as important to computer systems as it is to manual systems. For example, consider the separation of duties. Programmers should not be allowed to physically operate the computers. A computer consultant commented that he had opportunities to steal when he ran computer operations for a large bank. "I alone designed the dividend-payment operation, wrote the program for it, and ran the job on the machine. The operation was so big that it had a mistake tolerance of nearly $100,000. I could have paid at least half that much to myself, in small cheques, and the money wouldn't even have been missed." To avoid theft, no one person should have complete control over system design, programming and machine operation.

The computer has brought about an important development in cash payments. **Electronic funds transfer (EFT)** is a system that relies on electronic impulses—not paper documents—to handle cash transactions. To manage payroll, an employer enters the employee's name, wages and any other needed data on a magnetic tape, which is transferred to a bank. The bank runs the tape, which automatically decreases the business's cash account and increases the employee's cash account. Some retailers use EFT to handle sales. Customers pay with a card that activates a computer. The computer automatically decreases the customer's bank account balance and increases the store's account balance.

EFT systems reduce the cost of processing cash transactions. However, this savings is achieved by reducing the documentary evidence of transactions. Traditional approaches to internal control have relied on documents, so that EFT and other computer systems pose a significant challenge to managers and accountants who design and enforce internal control systems. Computer systems also create problems in protecting private information. For example, a group of students gained access to highly confidential hospital patient data by computer! Such situations point to the need for computer security measures.

Summary Problem for Your Review

Grudnitski Ltd. established a $300 petty cash fund. James C. Brown is the fund custodian. At the end of the first week, the petty cash fund contains the following:

1.   Cash: $171

2.   Petty cash tickets

No.	Amount	Issued to	Signed by	Account Debited
44	$14	B. Jarvis	B. Jarvis and JCB	Office Supplies
45	9	S. Bell	S. Bell	Miscellaneous Expense
47	43	R. Tate	R. Tate and JCB	—
48	33	G. Ghiz	G. Ghiz and JCB	Travel Expense

Required

1. Identify the four internal control weaknesses revealed in the above data.
2. Prepare the general journal entries to record
   a. Establishment of the petty cash fund.
   b. Replenishment of the fund. Assume petty cash ticket no. 47 was issued for the purchase of office supplies.
3. What is the balance in the Petty Cash account immediately before replenishment? Immediately after replenishment?

SOLUTION TO REVIEW PROBLEM

Requirement 1   The four internal control weaknesses are

a. Petty cash ticket no. 46 is missing. Coupled with weakness b, this omission raises questions about the administration of the petty cash fund and about how the petty cash funds were used.

b. The $171 cash balance means that $129 has been disbursed ($300 − $171 = $129). However, the total amount of the petty cash tickets is only $99 ($14 + $9 + $43 + $33). The fund, then, is $30 short of cash ($129 − $99 = $30). Was petty cash ticket no. 46 issued for $30? The data in the problem offer no hint that helps answer this question. In a real-world setting, management would investigate the problem.

c. The petty cash custodian (JCB) did not sign petty cash ticket no. 45. This omission may have been an oversight on his part. However, it raises the question of whether he authorized the disbursement. Both the fund custodian and recipient of cash should sign the ticket.

d. Petty cash ticket no. 47 does not indicate which account to debit. This omission raises two internal control questions. What did Tate do with the money, and what account should be debited? At worst, the funds have been stolen. At best, asking the custodian to reconstruct the transaction from memory is a haphazard way to identify the account to debit.

Requirement 2   Petty cash journal entries

a.   Entry to establish the petty cash fund

Petty Cash......................................	300	
Cash in Bank		300

b.   Entry to replenish the fund

Office Supplies ($14 + $43)	57	
Miscellaneous Expense ($9)........................	9	
Travel Expense	33	
Cash Short and Over	30	
Cash in Bank		129

Requirement 3   The balance in Petty Cash is *always* its specified balance, in this case $300, as shown by posting the above entries to the account.

Petty Cash

(a)	300	

Note that the entry to establish the fund (entry a) debits Petty Cash. The entry to replenish the fund (entry b) neither debits nor credits Petty Cash.

Summary

Internal controls should safeguard assets, ensure accurate accounting records, promote operational efficiency and encourage adherence to company policies. An effective internal control system includes these features: *reliable personnel, clear-cut assignment of responsibility, proper authorization* and *separation of duties*, which is the primary element of internal control. Many businesses use security devices, audits, and specially designed documents and records in their internal control systems.

The *bank account* helps control and safeguard cash. Businesses use the *bank statement* and *bank reconciliation* to account for banking transactions. An *imprest system* is used to control petty cash disbursements. Many companies record purchases at *net cost* in order to highlight the inefficiency of paying invoices late and thus losing purchase discounts.

Businesses often control cash disbursements by using a *voucher system*, which features the voucher, unpaid voucher file, voucher register and cheque register.

Businesses may handle their payroll by computer and through *electronic funds transfers*. Effective computerized internal control systems must meet the same basic standards that good manual systems do.

Self-Study Questions

Test your understanding of the chapter by marking the correct answer for each of the following questions:

1. Which of the following is an element of internal control? *(p. 279)*
   a. Safeguarding assets
   b. Ensuring accurate and reliable accounting records
   c. Promoting operational efficiency
   d. Encouraging adherence to company policies
   e. All the above are elements of internal control.
2. Which of the characteristics of an effective system of internal control is violated by allowing the employee who handles inventory to also account for inventory? *(p. 283)*
   a. Competent and reliable personnel   c. Proper authorization
   b. Assignment of responsibilities   d. Separation of duties
3. What control function is performed by auditors? *(p. 284)*
   a. Objective opinion of the effectiveness of the internal control system
   b. Assurance that all transactions are accounted for correctly
   c. Communication of the results of the audit to regulatory agencies
   d. Guarantee that a proper separation of duties exists within the business
4. The bank account serves as a control device over *(pp. 285, 294-297)*
   a. Cash receipts   c. Both of the above
   b. Cash disbursements   d. None of the above
5. Which of the following items appears on the bank side of a bank reconciliation? *(p. 291)*
   a. Book error   c. NSF cheque
   b. Outstanding cheque   d. Interest revenue earned on bank balance
6. Which of the following reconciling items requires a journal entry on the books of the company? *(pp. 291, 292)*
   a. Book error   d. Interest revenue earned on bank balance
   b. Outstanding cheque   e. All but b
   c. NSF cheque   f. None of the above
7. What is the major internal control measure over the cash receipts of a Zellers store? *(pp. 294, 295)*
   a. Reporting the day's cash receipts to the controller
   b. Preparing a petty cash ticket for all disbursements from the fund

    c. Pricing merchandise at uneven amounts, coupled with use of a cash register

    d. Channeling all cash receipts through the mail room, whose employees have no cash-accounting responsibilities

8. What is the control advantage of the net method of accounting for inventory purchases? *(p. 297)*

    a. It highlights the inefficiency of losing purchase discounts.

    b. It guarantees that all purchase discounts will be taken.

    c. It automatically increases the business's cash balance.

    d. It results in a higher quality of inventory on hand for customers.

9. The internal control feature that is specific to petty cash is *(p. 298)*

    a. Separation of duties   c. Proper authorization

    b. Assignment of responsibility   d. The imprest system

10. The most fundamental control feature provided by a voucher system is *(p. 301)*

    a. Assuring that only approved invoices are paid

    b. Centralizing the recording of all expenditures in one place—the voucher register

    c. Using the cheque register along with the voucher register

    d. Placing all incoming invoices in the unpaid voucher file

Answers to the self-study questions are at the end of the chapter.

Accounting Vocabulary

bank collections *(p. 288)*	electronic fund transfer (EFT)	petty cash *(p. 298)*
bank reconciliation *(p. 288)*	*(p. 305)*	service charge *(p. 288)*
bank statement *(p. 286)*	imprest system *(p. 298)*	voucher *(p. 299)*
cheque *(p. 286)*	nonsufficient fund (NSF)	voucher register *(p. 301)*
cheque register *(p. 303)*	cheque *(p. 288)*	voucher system *(p. 299)*
deposit in transit *(p. 288)*	outstanding cheque *(p. 288)*	

Assignment Material ———————————————

Questions

1. Which of the four features of effective internal control is the most fundamental? Why?

2. What is the role of the Audit Committee? Do the examples of the reports from management in the text support your answer? How?

3. Which company employees bear primary responsibility for a company's financial statements and for maintaining the company's system of internal control? How do these persons carry out this responsibility?

4. Identify six features of an effective system of internal control.

5. Separation of duties may be divided into four parts. What are they?

6. How can internal control systems be circumvented?

7. Are internal control systems designed to be foolproof and perfect? What is a fundamental constraint in planning and maintaining systems?

8. Briefly state how each of the following serves as an internal control measure over cash: bank account, signature card, deposit ticket and bank statement.

9. What is the remittance advice of a cheque? What use does it serve?
10. Each of the items in the following list must be accounted for in the bank reconciliation. Next to each item enter the appropriate letter from the following possible treatments: (a) bank side of reconciliation—add the item; (b) bank side of reconciliation—subtract the item; (c) book side of reconciliation—add the item; and (d) book side of reconciliation—subtract the item.

    _____ Outstanding cheque   _____ Bank collection
    _____ NSF cheque   _____ Customer's cheque returned
    _____ Bank service charge   owing to unauthorized
    _____ Cost of printed cheques   signature
    _____ Bank error that decreased   _____ Book error that increased
             bank balance   balance of Cash account
    _____ Deposit in transit

11. What purpose does a bank reconciliation serve?
12. Suppose a company has six bank accounts, two petty cash funds and three certificates of deposit that can be withdrawn on demand. How many cash amounts would this company likely report on its balance sheet?
13. What role does a cash register play in an internal control system?
14. Describe internal control procedures for cash received by mail.
15. Large businesses often have elaborate internal control systems that may be uneconomical for small businesses. Where does the internal control rest in small proprietorships, and how do they control cash disbursements?
16. What is the internal control advantage of recording purchases at net cost?
17. What balance does the Petty Cash account have at all times? Does this balance always equal the amount of cash in the fund? When are the two amounts equal? When are they unequal?
18. List the five elements of a voucher system and briefly describe the purpose of each.
19. Describe how a voucher system works.
20. What documents make up the voucher packet? Describe three procedures that use the voucher packet to ensure that each payment is appropriate.
21. Why should the same employee not write the computer programs for cash disbursements, sign cheques and mail the cheques to payees?

Exercises

Exercise 7-1   *Identifying internal control strengths and weaknesses*

The following situations suggest either a strength or weakness in internal control. Identify each as *strength* or *weakness* and give the reason for your answer.

a. Cash received over the counter is controlled by the sales clerk, who rings up the sale and places the cash in the register. The sales clerk has access to the control tape stored in the register.
b. Cash received by mail goes straight to the accountant, who debits Cash and credits Accounts Receivable from the customer.
c. The vice-president who signs cheques assumes the accounting department has matched the invoice with other supporting documents and therefore does not examine the voucher packet.
d. Purchase invoices are recorded at net amount to highlight Purchase Discounts Lost because of late payment.
e. The accounting department orders merchandise and approves vouchers for payment.
f. The operator of the computer has no other accounting or cash-handling duties.

Exercise 7-2 *Identifying internal controls*

Identify the missing internal control characteristic in the following situations:

a. Business is slow at Westwood Movie Theatre on Tuesday, Wednesday and Thursday nights. To reduce expenses the owner decides not to use a ticket taker on those nights. The ticket seller (cashier) is told to keep the tickets as a record of the number sold.

b. The manager of a discount store wants to speed the flow of customers through checkout. She decides to reduce the time spent by cashiers making change, so she prices merchandise at round dollar amounts, such as $8.00 and $15.00, instead of the customary amounts, $7.95 and $14.95.

c. Grocery stores such as Loblaws and Mr. Grocer purchase large quantities of their merchandise from a few suppliers. At another grocery store the manager decides to reduce paper work. He eliminates the requirement that a receiving department employee prepare a receiving report, which lists the quantities of items received from the supplier. Instead, the employee is simply to make a note of the items received.

d. When business is brisk, Mac's Milk and many other retail stores deposit cash in the bank several times during the day. The manager at another convenience store wants to reduce the time spent by employees delivering cash to the bank, so he starts a new policy. Cash will build up over Saturdays and Sundays, and the total two-day amount will be deposited on Sunday evening.

e. In the course of auditing the records of a company, you find that the same employee orders merchandise and approves invoices for payment.

Exercise 7-3 *Classifying bank reconciliation items*

The following seven items may appear on a bank reconciliation:

a. Outstanding cheques
b. Bank error: the bank charged our account for a cheque written by another customer.
c. Service charge
d. Deposits in transit
e. NSF cheque
f. Bank collections of a note receivable on our behalf
g. Book error: we debited Cash for $1,000. The correct debit was $100.

Classify each item as (1) an addition to the bank balance, (2) a subtraction from the bank balance, (3) an addition to the book balance, or (4) a subtraction from the book balance.

Exercise 7-4 *Bank reconciliation*

Rachel Lagimy's chequebook lists the following:

Date	Cheque No.	Item	Cheque	Deposit	Balance
9/1					$525
4	622	Apple Tree Gift Shop	$19		506
9		Dividends		$ 116	622
13	623	Bell Telephone Co.	43		579
14	624	Gulf Oil Co.	58		521
18	625	Cash	50		471
26	626	St. Alban's Anglican Church	25		446
28	627	Bent Tree Apartments	275		171
30		Paycheque		1,000	1,171

The September bank statement shows:

Balance			$525
Add: Deposits			116
Deduct cheques:	No.	Amount	
	622	$19	
	623	43	
	624	68*	
	625	50	(180)
Other charges			
Printed cheques		$8	
Service charge		6	(14)
			$447

* This is the correct amount of cheque number 624.

Required

Prepare Rachel's bank reconciliation at September 30.

Exercise 7-5   *Bank reconciliation*

Gary Walters operates four Petro Canada stations. He has just received the monthly bank statement at October 31 from the Prairie Bank, which shows an ending balance of $3,968. Listed on the statement are a service charge of $12, two NSF cheques totaling $46, and a $9 charge for printed cheques. In reviewing his cash records, Walters identifies outstanding cheques totaling $467 and an October 31 deposit of $788 which does not appear on the bank statement. During October he recorded a $190 cheque for the salary of a part-time employee by debiting Salary Expense and crediting Cash for $19. Walters's cash account shows an October 31 cash balance of $4,527. Prepare the bank reconciliation at October 31.

Exercise 7-6   *Journal entries from a bank reconciliation*

Using the data from Exercise 7-5, record the entries that Walters should make in the general journal on October 31. Include an explanation for each entry.

Exercise 7-7   *Income statements with purchases at gross and at net*

Motorex Ltd. began July with inventory of $470,000 and ended the month with inventory of $510,000. During July the company purchased $800,000 of inventory and took the 2 percent discount on $700,000 of the purchase. The remaining $100,000 in inventory cost was paid after the discount period. Sales during July were $1,600,000 and operating expenses (including income tax) were $490,000.

Required

1. Prepare the company's income statement for July assuming Motorex records inventory purchases at gross cost.
2. Prepare the company's income statement for July assuming the company records inventory purchases at net cost.
3. Which method provides the internal control advantage? Give your reason.

Exercise 7-8   *Accounting for petty cash*

United Way of Fredericton, New Brunswick created a $100 imprest petty cash fund. During the first month of use, the fund custodian authorized and signed petty cash tickets as follows:

Ticket No.	Item	Account Debited	Amount
1	Delivery of pledge cards to donors	Delivery Expense	$19.22
2	Mail package	Postage Expense	2.80
3	Newsletter	Supplies Expense	4.14
4	Key to closet	Miscellaneous Expense	.85
5	Waste basket	Miscellaneous Expense	3.78
6	Staples	Supplies Expense	5.37

Required

1. Make general journal entries for creation of the petty cash fund and its replenishment. Include explanations.
2. Immediately prior to replenishment, describe the items in the fund.
3. Immediately after replenishment, describe the items in the fund.

Exercise 7-9   *Purchases at gross and at net*

Singh Hardware Company uses a voucher system. Prepare its general journal entries for the following transactions under two assumptions (explanations are not required):

Assumption 1—Inventory purchases recorded at gross cost
Assumption 2—Inventory purchases recorded at net cost

May 3   Purchased inventory costing $3,600 on account, subject to terms of 2/10 n/30.
    11   Paid the liability created on May 3.
    14   Purchased inventory costing $2,200 on account, subject to terms of 2/10 n/30.
    27   Paid the liability created on May 14.

Which method provides the hardware store with a measure of discounts lost? Give your reason.

Exercise 7-10   *Petty cash; cash short and over*

Record the following selected transactions in general journal format (explanations are not required):

April 1   Issued voucher no. 637 to establish a petty cash fund with a $250 balance.
    1   Issued cheque no. 344 to pay voucher no. 637.
    2   Journalized the day's cash sales. Cash register tapes show a $2,859 total, but the cash in the register is only $2,853.
    10   The petty cash fund has $119 in cash and $131 in petty cash tickets issued to pay for Office Supplies ($61), Delivery Expense ($23) and Entertainment Expense ($47). Issued voucher no. 669 to replenish the fund.
    10   Issued cheque no. 402 to pay voucher no. 669.

Problems   (Group A)

Problem 7-1A   *Identifying internal control weaknesses*

Each of the following situations has an internal control weakness:

a. Myra Jones, a widow with no known sources of outside income, has been a trusted employee of Stone Products Company for 15 years. She performs all cash handling and accounting duties, including opening the mail, preparing the bank deposit, accounting for all aspects of cash and accounts receivable, and preparing the bank reconciliation. She has just purchased a new Cadillac and a new home in an expensive suburb. Lou Stone, the owner of the company, wonders how she can afford these luxuries on her salary.

b. Linda Cyert employs three professional interior designers in her design studio. She is located in an area with a lot of new construction, and her business is booming. Ordinarily, Linda does all the purchasing of furniture, draperies, carpets, fabrics, sewing services and other materials and labour needed to complete jobs. During the summer she takes a long vacation. In her absence she allows each designer to purchase materials and labour. At her return, Cyert reviews operations and notes that expenses are much higher and net income much lower than in the past.

c. Discount stores such as Bargain Harold's and Bi-Rite receive a large portion of their sales revenue in cash, with the remainder in credit card sales. To reduce expenses, a store manager ceases purchasing fidelity bonds on the cashiers.

d. The office supply company from which Dysan Stereo Centre purchases cash receipt forms recently notified Dysan that the last shipped receipts were not prenumbered. Stan Dysan, the owner, replied that he did not use the receipt numbers, so the omission is not important.

e. Lancer Computer Programs is a software company that specializes in computer programs with accounting applications. Their most popular program prepares the general journal, cash receipts journal, voucher register, cheque register, accounts receivable subsidiary ledger and general ledger. In the company's early days, the owner and eight employees wrote the computer programs, lined up manufacturers to produce the diskettes, sold the products to stores such as ComputerLand and MicroAge, and performed the general management and accounting of the company. As the company has grown, the number of employees has increased dramatically. Recently, the development of a new software program stopped while the programmers redesigned Lancer's accounting system. Lancer's own accountants could have performed this task.

Required

1. Identify the missing internal control characteristic in each situation.
2. Identify the business's possible problem.
3. Propose a solution to the problem.

Problem 7-2A   *Bank reconciliation and related journal entries*

The May 31 bank statement of Malcolm & Fisk, a partnership, has just arrived from Lake Huron Bank. To prepare the Malcolm & Fisk bank reconciliation, you gather the following data:

a. The May 31 bank balance is $4,119.82.
b. The bank statement includes two charges for returned cheques from customers. One is an NSF cheque in the amount of $67.50 received from Harley Doherty, a customer, recorded on the books by a debit to Cash and deposited on May 19. The other is a $195.03 cheque received from Maria Gucci and deposited on May 21. It was returned by Ms. Gucci's bank with the imprint "Unauthorized Signature."
c. The following Malcolm & Fisk cheques are outstanding at May 31:

Cheque No.	Amount
616	$403.00
802	74.25
806	36.60
809	161.38
810	229.05
811	48.91

d. The bank statement includes two special deposits: $688.14, which is the amount of dividend revenue the bank collected from Canadian General Electric on behalf of Malcolm & Fisk; and $16.86, the interest revenue Malcolm & Fisk earned on its bank balance during May.

e. The bank statement lists a $6.25 subtraction for the bank service charge.

f. On May 31 the Malcolm & Fisk treasurer deposited $381.14, but this deposit does not appear on the bank statement.

g. The bank statement includes a $410.00 deduction for a cheque drawn by Marimont Freight Company. Malcolm & Fisk promptly notified the bank of its error.

h. Malcolm & Fisk's Cash account shows a balance of $3,521.55 on May 31.

Required

1. Prepare the bank reconciliation for Malcolm & Fisk at May 31.

2. Record in general journal form the entries necessary to bring the book balance of Cash into agreement with the adjusted book balance on the reconciliation. Include an explanation for each entry.

Problem 7-3A   *Bank reconciliation and related journal entries*

Assume selected columns of the cash receipts journal and cheque register of Radio Shack store no. 147 appear as follows at March 31, 19X5:

Cash Receipts Journal (Posting reference: CR)		Cheque Register (Posting reference: CD)	
Date	Cash Debit	Cheque No.	Cash Credit
Mar. 4	$2,716	1413	$ 1,465
9	544	1414	1,004
11	1,655	1415	450
14	896	1416	8
17	367	1417	775
25	890	1418	88
31	2,038	1419	4,126
Total	$9,106	1420	760
		1421	200
		1422	2,267
		Total	$11,143

Assume the Cash account of the Radio Shack store shows the following information on March 31, 19X5:

Cash

Date	Item	P.R.	Debit	Credit	Balance
Mar. 1	Balance				14,188
31		CR 10	9,106		23,294
31		CD 16		11,143	12,151

Radio Shack store no. 147 received the following bank statement on March 31, 19X5:

Bank Statement for March 19X5

Beginning balance		$14,188
Deposits and other Credits		
Mar. 5	$2,716	
10	544	
11	1,655	
15	896	
18	367	
25	890	
31	1,000 BC	8,068
Cheques and other Debits		
Mar. 8	441 NSF	
9	1,465	
13	1,004	
14	450	
15	8	
22	775	
29	88	
31	4,216	
31	25 SC	(8,472)
Ending balance		$13,784

BC: Bank Collection   NSF: Nonsufficient Fund Cheque   SC: Service Charge

Additional data for the bank reconciliation include

a.   The NSF cheque was received late in February from L.M. Arnett.
b.   The $1,000 bank collection of a note receivable on March 31 included $122 interest revenue.
c.   The correct amount of cheque no. 1419, a payment on account, is $4,216. (The Radio Shack accountant mistakenly recorded the cheque for $4,126.)

Required

1.   Prepare the bank reconciliation of Radio Shack store no. 147 at March 31, 19X5.
2.   Record the entries based on the bank reconciliation. Include explanations.

Problem 7-4A   *Recording and reporting purchases at gross and at net*

Superior Products Company does not use a voucher system. On May 1 of the current year the company had inventory of $58,000. On May 31 the company had inventory of $53,700. Net sales for May were $212,800 and operating expenses were $65,100. During May, Superior completed the following transactions:

May 3   Purchased inventory costing $38,500 under terms of 2/10 n/30.
      7   Returned $2,000 of the inventory purchased on May 3.
     10   Purchased inventory costing $28,500 on credit terms of 2/10 n/45.
     12   Paid the amount owed from the May 3 invoice, net of the return on May 7 and also net of the discount.
     18   Purchased inventory costing $31,900 on credit terms of 2/10 n/30.
     19   Paid for the inventory purchased on May 10, less the discount.
     29   Paid the gross amount of the purchase on May 18, missing the discount because payment occurred after the discount period.

Required

1. Assuming Superior records inventory purchases at gross cost,
   a. Record the transactions in a general journal. Explanations are not required.
   b. Prepare the company's income statement for May of the current year.
2. Assuming Superior records inventory purchases at net cost,
   a. Record the transactions in a general journal. Explanations are not required.
   b. Prepare the company's income statement for May of the current year.
3. Which method of recording purchases offers the internal control advantage? Give your reason.

Problem 7-5A   *Accounting for petty cash transactions*

Suppose that on April 1 Ontario Hydro opens a regional office in Orillia and creates a petty cash fund with an imprest balance of $200. During April, Eleanor McGillicuddy, the fund custodian, signs the following petty cash tickets:

Ticket Number	Item	Amount
101	Pencils	$ 6.89
102	Cab fare for executive	14.50
103	Delivery of package across town	7.75
104	Dinner money for executives entertaining a customer	80.00
105	Postage for package received	10.00
106	Decorations for office party	18.22
107	Two boxes of floppy disks	14.37

On April 30, prior to replenishment, the fund contains these tickets plus $45.27. The accounts affected by petty cash disbursements are Office Supplies Expense, Travel Expense, Delivery Expense, Entertainment Expense and Postage Expense.

Required

1. Discuss the characteristics and internal control features of an imprest fund.
2. Make general journal entries to create the fund and to replenish it. Include explanations. Also, briefly describe what the custodian does on these dates.
3. Make the entry on May 1 to increase the fund balance to $300. Include an explanation and briefly describe what the custodian does.

Problem 7-6A   *Voucher system entries*

Assume Eaton's, the department-store chain, uses a voucher system and records purchases at *gross* cost. Assume further that an Eaton's store completed the following transactions during July:

July 2   Issued voucher no. 614 payable to Hathaway Shirt Company for the purchase of inventory costing $16,000, with payment terms of 2/10 n/30.

3   Issued voucher no. 615 payable to London Public Utilities Commission for electricity usage of $2,589.

5   Issued cheque no. 344 to pay voucher no. 614, less the discount.

6   Issued voucher no. 616 payable to Baylor Supply Company for store supplies costing $850, with payment terms of 2/10 n/45.

7   Issued cheque no. 345 to pay voucher no. 615.

13   Issued voucher no. 617 payable to replenish the petty cash fund. The payee is Petty Cash, the amount is $203, and the petty cash tickets list Store Supplies

($119), Delivery Expense ($48) and Miscellaneous Expense ($36). Also issued cheque no. 346 to pay the voucher.

14   Issued cheque no. 347 to pay voucher no. 616, less the discount.

18   Issued voucher no. 618 payable to the *London Free Press* for advertising, $2,800.

19   Issued voucher no. 619 payable to Levi Strauss & Company for inventory costing $65,800, with payment terms of 3/10 n/30.

28   Issued voucher no. 620 payable to city of London for property tax of $9,165.

30   Issued cheque no. 348 to pay voucher no. 619. Because of a filing error, we failed to earn the discount.

31   Issued voucher no. 621 payable to Middlesex Bank for interest expense of $7,000.

31   Issued voucher no. 622 to pay executive salary of $4,644 to Sharon Kratzman. Also issued cheque no. 349 to pay the voucher.

Required

1. Record Eaton's transactions in a voucher register and a cheque register like those illustrated in the chapter. Posting references are unnecessary.
2. Open the Vouchers Payable account with a zero beginning balance and post amounts to that account.
3. Prepare the list of unpaid vouchers at July 31 and check that the total matches the balance of Vouchers Payable.

Problem 7-7A   *Voucher system; purchases at net*

Assume that the Eaton's store in Problem 7-6A records its purchases of inventory and supplies at *net* cost.

Required

1. Record the transactions of Problem 7-6A in a voucher register and a cheque register. To account for purchase discounts lost, it is necessary to use a cheque register designed as follows:

Cheque Register

				Debit		Credit
Date	Cheque No.	Payee	Voucher No.	Vouchers Payable	Purchase Discounts Lost	Cash in Bank

2. Post to the Vouchers Payable account.
3. Prepare the list of unpaid vouchers at July 31 and check that the total matches the balance of Vouchers Payable.

(Group B)

Problem 7-1B   *Identifying internal control weaknesses*

Each of the following situations has an internal control weakness:

a. Most large companies have internal audit staffs that continuously evaluate the business's internal control. Part of the auditor's job is to evaluate how efficiently the company is running. For example, is the company purchasing inventory from the least expensive wholesaler? After a particularly bad year, Mason Tile company eliminates its internal audit department to reduce expenses.

b. Public accounting firms, law firms and other professional organizations use para-professional employees to do some of their routine tasks. For example, an accounting paraprofessional might examine documents to assist a public accountant in conducting an audit. In the public accounting firm of Grosso Howe, Lou Grosso, the senior partner, turns over a significant portion of his high-level audit work to his paraprofessional staff.

c. In evaluating the internal control over cash disbursements, an auditor learns that the purchasing agent is responsible for purchasing diamonds for use in the company's manufacturing process, approving the invoices for payment, and signing the cheques. No supervisor reviews the purchasing agent's work.

d. Grant Kowalzyak owns a firm that performs engineering services. His staff consists of twelve professional engineers, and he manages the office. Often his work requires him to travel to meet with clients. During the past six months he has observed that when he returns from a business trip, the engineering jobs in the office have not progressed satisfactorily. He learns that when he is away, several of his senior employees take over office management and neglect their engineering duties. One employee could manage the office.

e. Lew Jackson has been an employee of Brazleton Lumber Company for many years. Because the business is relatively small, Lew performs all accounting duties, including opening the mail, preparing the bank deposit and preparing the bank reconciliation.

Required

1. Identify the missing internal control characteristic in each situation.
2. Identify the business's possible problem.
3. Propose a solution to the problem.

Problem 7-2B   *Bank reconciliation and related journal entries*

The August 31 bank statement of Spinnaker Software has just arrived from United Bank. To prepare the Spinnaker bank reconciliation, you gather the following data:

a. Spinnaker's Cash account shows a balance of $5,503.77 on August 31.
b. The bank statement includes two charges for returned cheques from customers. One is a $395.00 cheque received from Shoreline Express, deposited on August 20 and returned by Shoreline's bank with the imprint "Unauthorized Signature." The other is an NSF cheque in the amount of $146.67 received from Lipsey, Inc. This cheque had been deposited on August 17.
c. The following Spinnaker cheques are outstanding at August 31:

Cheque No.	Amount
237	$ 46.10
288	141.00
291	578.05
293	11.87
294	609.51
295	8.88
296	101.63

d. The bank statement includes a deposit of $1,191.17, collected by the bank on behalf of Spinnaker. Of the total, $1,011.81 is collection of a note receivable, and the remainder is interest revenue.

e. The bank statement shows that Spinnaker earned $38.19 on its bank balance during August. This amount was added into Spinnaker's account by the bank.

f. The bank statement lists a $10.50 subtraction for bank service charge.

g. On August 31 the Spinnaker treasurer deposited $193.78, but this deposit does not appear on the bank statement.

h. The bank statement includes a $300.00 deposit that Spinnaker did not make. The bank had erroneously credited the Spinnaker account for another bank customer's deposit.

i. The August 31 bank balance is $7,784.22.

Required

1. Prepare the bank reconciliation for Spinnaker Software at August 31.
2. Record in general journal form the entries necessary to bring the book balance of Cash into agreement with the adjusted book balance on the reconciliation. Include an explanation for each entry.

Problem 7-3B   *Bank reconciliation and related bank entries*

Assume selected columns of the cash receipts journal and the cheque register of Microage store no. 15 appear as follows at April 30, 19X4:

Cash Receipts Journal (Posting reference: CR)		Cheque Register (Posting reference: CD)	
Date	Cash Debit	Cheque No.	Cash Credit
Apr. 2	$ 4,174	3113	$ 991
8	407	3114	147
10	559	3115	1,930
16	2,187	3116	664
22	1,854	3117	1,472
29	1,060	3118	1,000
30	337	3119	632
Total	$10,578	3120	1,675
		3121	100
		3122	2,413
		Total	$11,024

Assume the Cash account of the Microage store shows the following information at April 30, 19X4:

Cash

Date	Item	P.R.	Debit	Credit	Balance
Apr. 1	Balance				7,911
30		CR 6	10,578		18,489
30		CD 11		11,024	7,465

Microage store no. 15 received the following bank statement on April 30, 19X4:

Bank Statement for April 19X4

Beginning balance		$ 7,911
Deposits and other Credits		
Apr. 4	$4,174	
9	407	
12	559	
17	2,187	
22	1,185 BC	
23	1,854	10,366
Cheques and other Debits		
Apr. 7	$ 991	
13	1,390	
14	903 US	
15	147	
18	664	
26	1,472	
30	1,000	
30	20 SC	(6,587)
Ending balance		$11,690

BC: Bank Collection   US: Unauthorized Signature   SC: Service Charge

Additional data for the bank reconciliation include

a. The unauthorized signature cheque was received from S.M. Holt.
b. The $1,185 bank collection of a note receivable on April 22 included $185 interest revenue.
c. The correct amount of cheque number 3115, a payment on account, is $1,390. (The Microage accountant mistakenly recorded the cheque for $1,930.)

Required

1. Prepare the bank reconciliation of Microage store no. 15 at April 30, 19X4.
2. Record the entries based on the bank reconciliation. Include explanations.

Problem 7-4B   *Recording and reporting purchases at gross and at net*

Randolph Distributing company does not use a voucher system. On June 1 of the current year, the company had inventory of $71,300. On June 30 the company had inventory of $74,100. Net sales for June were $263,700, and operating expenses were $106,200. During June, Randolph completed the following transactions:

June 2   Purchased inventory costing $41,800 under terms of 2/10 n/30.
     8   Returned $5,800 of the inventory purchased on June 2.
    11   Purchased inventory costing $39,000 on credit terms of 2/10 n/45.
    11   Paid the amount owed from the June 2 invoice, net of the return on June 8 and also net of the discount.
    17   Purchased inventory costing $52,300 on credit terms of 2/10 n/30.
    20   Paid for the inventory purchased on June 11, less the discount.
    30   Paid the gross amount of the purchase on June 17, missing the discount because payment occurred after the discount period.

Required

1. Assuming Randolph records inventory purchases at gross cost,
   a. Record the transactions in a general journal. Explanations are not required.
   b. Prepare the company's income statement for June of the current year.
2. Assuming Randolph records inventory purchases at net cost,
   a. Record the transactions in a general journal. Explanations are not required.
   b. Prepare the company's income statement for June of the current year.
3. Which method of recording purchases offers the internal control advantage? Give your reason.

Problem 7-5B *Accounting for petty cash transactions*

Suppose that on June 1, Uniroyal Goodrich Canada Inc., the tire and rubber products company, opens a district office in Gander, Newfoundland and creates a petty cash fund with an imprest balance of $350. During June, Mordecai Klever, the fund custodian, signs the following petty cash tickets:

Ticket Number	Item	Amount
1	Postage for package received	$26.20
2	Decorations and refreshments for office party	13.19
3	Two boxes of floppy disks	16.82
4	Printer ribbons	27.13
5	Dinner money for sales manager entertaining a customer	50.00
6	Plane ticket for executive business trip to St. Johns	69.00
7	Delivery of package across town	6.30

On June 30, prior to replenishment, the fund contains these tickets plus $155.51. The accounts affected by petty cash disbursements are Office Supplies Expense, Travel Expense, Delivery Expense, Entertainment Expense and Postage Expense.

Required

1. Discuss the characteristics and internal control features of an imprest fund.
2. Make the general journal entries to create the fund and to replenish it. Include explanations. Also, briefly describe what the custodian does on these dates.
3. Make the entry on July 1 to increase the fund balance to $500. Include an explanation and briefly describe what the custodian does.

Problem 7-6B *Voucher system entries*

Assume a ComputerLand store in Chilliwack, B.C. uses a voucher system and records purchases at *gross* cost. Assume further that the store completed the following transactions during January:

Jan. 3 Issued voucher no. 135 payable to B.C. Telephone for telephone service of $1,007.

5 Issued voucher no. 136 payable to IBM for the purchase of inventory costing $21,500, with payment terms of 3/10 n/30.

6 Issued voucher no. 137 payable to City Supply Company for store supplies costing $250, with payment terms of 2/10 n/45.

7 Issued cheque no. 404 to pay voucher no. 136, less the discount.

10 Issued cheque no. 405 to pay voucher no. 135.

14 Issued cheque no. 406 to pay voucher no. 137, less the discount.

15   Issued voucher no. 138 payable to *The Chilliwack Progress* for advertising of $1,990.

17   Issued voucher no. 139 payable to replenish the petty cash fund. The payee is Petty Cash, the amount is $176, and the petty cash tickets list Store Supplies ($16), Delivery Expense ($96) and Miscellaneous Expense ($64). Also issued cheque no. 407 to pay the voucher.

18   Issued voucher no. 140 payable to Apple Computer Company for inventory costing $27,600, with payment terms of 2/10 n/30.

24   Issued voucher no. 141 payable to city of Chilliwack for property tax of $4,235. Debit Property Tax Expenses.

27   Issued voucher no. 142 payable to Western Bank for payment of a note payable ($10,000) and interest expense ($1,200).

30   Issued cheque no. 408 to pay voucher no. 140. Because of a filing error, we paid after the discount period and failed to earn the discount.

31   Issued voucher no. 143 to pay salesperson salary of $2,309 to Lester Gibbs. Also issued cheque no. 409 to pay the voucher.

Required

1. Record ComputerLand's transactions in a voucher register and a cheque register like those illustrated in the chapter. Posting references are unnecessary.
2. Open the Vouchers Payable account and post amounts to that account.
3. Prepare the list of unpaid vouchers at January 31 and check that the total matches the balances of Vouchers Payable.

Problem 7-7B   *Voucher system; purchases at net*

Assume that the ComputerLand store in Problem 7-6B records its purchases of inventory and supplies at *net* cost.

Required

1. Record the transactions of Problem 7-6B in a voucher register and a cheque register. To account for Purchase Discounts Lost, it is necessary to use a cheque register designed as follows:

				Cheque Register		Page 4
					Debit	**Credit**
Date	**Cheque No.**	**Payee**	**Voucher No.**	**Vouchers Payable**	**Purchase Discounts Lost**	**Cash in Bank**

2. Post to the Vouchers Payable account.
3. Prepare the list of unpaid vouchers at July 31, and check that the total matches the balance of Vouchers Payable.

Decision Problems

1.   *Using the bank reconciliation to detect a thief*

Schaeffer Art Supply has poor internal control over its cash transactions. Recently G.M. Schaeffer, the owner, has suspected the cashier of stealing. Details of the business's cash position at September 30 follow:

1. The Cash account shows a balance of $19,502. This amount includes a September 30 deposit of $3,794 that does not appear on the September 30 bank statement.
2. The September 30 bank statement shows a balance of $17,924. The bank statement lists a $200 credit for a bank collection, an $8 debit for the service charge and a $36 debit for an NSF cheque. The Schaeffer accountant has not recorded any of these items on the books.
3. At September 30 the following cheques are outstanding:

Cheque No.	Amount
154	$116
256	150
278	253
291	190
292	206
293	145

4. The cashier handles all incoming cash and makes bank deposits. He also reconciles the monthly bank statement. His September 30 reconciliation follows:

Balance per books, September 30			$19,502
Add:	Outstanding cheques			2,060
	Bank collection			200
				21,762
Less:	Deposits in transit	$3,794		
	Service charge	8		
	NSF cheque	36		3,838
Balance per bank, September 30			$17,924

Schaeffer has requested that you determine whether the cashier has stolen cash from the business and, if so, how much. Schaeffer also asks you to identify how the cashier has attempted to conceal the theft. To make this determination, you perform your own bank reconciliation using the format illustrated in the chapter. There are no bank or book errors. Schaeffer also asks you to evaluate the internal controls and recommend any changes needed to improve them.

2. *The role of internal control*

The questions below are unrelated except that they all pertain to internal control:

1. It has been said that the most important characteristic of a system of internal control is the quality of the people. What do you think this statement means? Do you agree with it?
2. Separation of duties is an important consideration if a system of internal control is to be effective. Why is this so?
3. Cash may be a relatively small item on the financial statements; yet internal control over cash is a very important consideration to a company. Why do you think such is the case?
4. Archer Ltd. requires all documents supporting a cheque be cancelled by the person signing the cheque. Why do you think this practice is required? What might happen if it were not required?
5. Many students think that safeguarding assets is the most important objective of internal control systems; yet both external and internal auditors emphasize reliable accounting data. Explain the auditors' focus. Why do you think auditors are less concerned about safeguarding assets?

Financial Statement Problem

Internal controls and cash

Study the audit opinion of John Labatt's financial statements, given in Appendix E. Answer the following questions about John Labatt's internal controls and cash position:

1. What is the name of John Labatt's outside auditing firm? What office of the firm signed the auditor's report? How long after John Labatt's fiscal year end did the auditors issue their opinion? Who recommends the appointment of the outside auditing firm?

2. Who assumes the responsibility for the preparation of the financial statements? Does it appear that John Labatt's internal controls are adequate? How can you tell?

3. What standard of auditing did the outside auditors use in examining the John Labatt financial statements? By what accounting standards were the John Labatt financial statements evaluated?

4. By how much did John Labatt's cash position increase during fiscal 1989? The consolidated statement of changes in financial position (discussed in detail in a later chapter) tells why this increase occurred. Which type of activity — operations, investment or financing — contributed most to this increase?

Answers to Self-Study Questions

1. e	3. a	5. b	7. c	9. d
2. d	4. c	6. e	8. a	10. b

PART THREE

Accounting for Noncash Assets and Liabilities

8

Accounts and Notes Receivable

From automobiles to houses to bicycles to dinners, people buy on credit every day. As high as annual credit sales for retailers are, credit sales are even higher for manufacturers and wholesalers. Clearly, credit sales lie at the heart of the Canadian economy, as they do in other developed countries.

Each credit transaction involves at least two parties: the **creditor**, who sells a service or merchandise, and the **debtor**, who makes the purchase. This chapter focuses on the creditor's accounting. The accounts that generally appear on a creditor's balance sheet are highlighted in Exhibit 8-1. We will discuss these accounts in our study of receivables.

Different Types of Receivables

A receivable arises when a business (or person) sells goods or services to a second business (or person) on credit. A receivable is the seller's claim against the buyer for the agreed-on amount of the transaction.

Receivables are monetary claims against businesses and individuals. They are acquired mainly by selling goods and services and by lending money.

The two basic types of receivables are accounts receivable and notes receivable. A business's *accounts receivable* are the amounts that its customers owe it. These accounts receivables are sometimes called *trade receivables*. They are *current assets*.

> **OBJECTIVE 1**
> Define different types of receivables

Accounts receivable should be distinguished from accruals, notes and other assets not arising from everyday sales because accounts receivable pertain to the main thrust of the business's operations. Moreover, amounts included as accounts receivable should be collectible according to the business's normal sale terms (such as net 30, or 2/10 n/30).

Notes receivable are more formal than accounts receivable. The debtor in a note receivable arrangement promises in writing to pay the creditor a definite sum at a definite future date. The terms of these notes usually extend for at

EXHIBIT 8-1 *Balance Sheet*

Example Company
Balance Sheet
Date

Assets			Liabilities		
Current			Current		
Cash		$X,XXX	Accounts payable		$X,XXX
Accounts Receivable	**X,XXX**		Notes payable, short-term		X,XXX
Less: Allowance for uncollectible			Accrued current liabilities		X,XXX
accounts	**(XXX)**	**X,XXX**	Total current liabilities		X,XXX
Notes receivable, short-term		**X,XXX**			
Inventories		X,XXX	Long-term		
Prepaid expenses		X,XXX	Notes payable, long-term		X,XXX
Total		X,XXX	Total liabilities		$X,XXX
Investments and long-term receivables			**Owner's Equity**		
Investments in other companies		X,XXX			
Notes receivable, long-term		**X,XXX**	Capital		X,XXX
Other receivables		**X,XXX**	Total liabilities and owner's		
Total		X,XXX	equity		$X,XXX
Plant assets					
Property, plant and equipment		X,XXX			
Total assets		$X,XXX			

least 60 days. A written document known as a *promissory note* serves as evidence of the receivable (see Exhibit 8-2, p. 339). A note may require the debtor to pledge *security* for the loan. This means that the borrower promises that the lender may claim certain assets if the borrower fails to pay the amount due at maturity.

Notes receivable due within one year or less are *current assets*. Those notes due beyond one year are *long-term receivables*. Some notes receivable are collected in periodic installments. The portion due within one year is a current asset, with the remaining amount a long-term asset. The Toronto-Dominion Bank may hold a $6,000 note receivable from you, but only the $1,500 you owe on it this year is a current asset to the Toronto-Dominion Bank.

Other receivables include loans to employees and branch companies. Usually these are long-term assets, but they are current if receivable within one year or less. Long-term notes receivable and other receivables are often reported on the balance sheet after current assets and before plant assets.

Each type of receivable is a separate account in the general ledger and may be supported by a subsidiary ledger if needed.

The Credit Department

A customer who buys goods using a credit card is buying on account. This transaction creates a receivable for the store. Most companies with a high proportion of sales on account have a separate credit department. This department evaluates customers who apply for credit cards by using standard formulas — which include the applicant's income and credit history, among other factors — for deciding which customers the store will sell to on account. After approving a customer, the credit department monitors customer payment records. Customers with a history of paying on time may receive higher and higher credit limits. Those who fail to pay on time have their limits reduced or eliminated. The credit department also assists the accounting department in measuring collection losses on customers who do not pay.

Uncollectible Accounts (Bad Debts) _____

Selling on credit creates both a benefit and a cost. Customers unwilling or unable to pay cash immediately may make a purchase on credit. Revenue and profit rise as sales increase. The cost to the seller of extending credit arises when credit customers do not pay off their debts. Accountants label this cost **uncollectible account expense, doubtful account expense,** or **bad debt expense**.

The extent of uncollectible account expense varies from company to company. It depends on the credit risks that managers are willing to accept. Many small retail businesses accept a higher level of risk than large stores like The Bay. Why? Small businesses often have personal ties to customers, which increases the likelihood that customers will pay their accounts.

Measuring Uncollectible Accounts

For a firm that sells on credit, uncollectible account expense is as much a part of doing business as salary expense and depreciation expense. Uncollectible Account Expense — an operating expense — must be measured, recorded and reported. To do so, accountants use the direct write-off method or the allowance method.

Direct Write-off Method Under the **direct write-off method** of accounting for bad debts, the company waits until the credit department decides that a customer's account receivable is uncollectible. Then the accountant debits Uncollectible Account Expense and credits the customer's account receivable to write off the account.

Assume it is 19X2 and most credit customers have paid for their 19X1 purchases. At this point, the credit department believes that two customers, Chi and Smith, will never pay. The department directs the accountant to write off Chi and Smith as bad debts.

The following entries show the business's accounting for 19X1 credit sales, and 19X2 collections and uncollectible accounts:

19X1	Accounts Receivable — Chi	800	
	Accounts Receivable — Smith	1,200	
	Accounts Receivable — Various Customers........	98,000	
	Sales Revenue		100,000
	To record credit sales of $100,000.		
19X2	Cash	97,000	
	Accounts Receivable — Various Customers ..		97,000
	To record cash collections of $97,000.		

19X2	Uncollectible Account Expense	2,000
	Accounts Receivable — Chi	800
	Accounts Receivable — Smith	1,200
	To write off uncollectible accounts and record bad debt expense of $2,000.	

Of course, this company would continue making credit sales as an important part of doing business. But what we want to know right now is how the direct write-off method affects financial statements. To see its impact most clearly, let us assume that the company stopped making credit sales altogether in 19X2. Consider the following partial financial statements for 19X1 and 19X2, based on the above journal entries:

Income Statement	**19X1**	**19X2**
Revenue		
Sales revenue	$100,000	$ -0-
Expense		
Uncollectible account expense	-0-	2,000

	December 31,	
Balance Sheet	**19X1**	**19X2**
Accounts receivable.	$100,000	$1,000

Let us ask two important questions about this approach to accounting for bad debts.

1. How accurately does the direct write-off method measure income? As we have seen, following generally accepted accounting principles means matching an accounting period's expenses against its revenues. This provides the most accurate picture of operating income, which measures how well a business's operations are running. But the direct write-off method does not match a period's bad debt expense against the same period's sales revenues. In our example, the full amount of sales revenues appears for 19X1, but the expenses incurred to generate this revenue — the bad debts — appear in 19X2. This gives misleading income figures for both years, as would failing to report any other expense, such as salary, depreciation, and so on, in the correct period. The $2,000 bad debt expense should be matched against the $100,000 sales revenues.

2. How accurately does the direct write-off method value accounts receivable? The 19X1 balance sheet shows accounts receivable at the full $100,000 figure. But any businessperson knows that bad debts are unavoidable when selling on credit. No intelligent manager expects to collect the entire amount. Is the $100,000 figure, then, the expected realizable value of the account? No, showing the full $100,000 in the balance sheet falsely implies that these accounts receivable are worth their face value.

The direct write-off method is simple to use, and it causes no great error if collection losses are insignificant in amount. However, you see that the resulting accounting records are not as accurate as they could be. The allowance method is the better way to account for uncollectible expense.

Allowance Method　　To present the most accurate financial statements possible, accountants in firms with large credit sales use the **allowance method** of measuring bad debts. This method records collection losses based on estimates prior to determining that specific customers will not pay their accounts.

Smart managers know that not every customer will pay in full. But they should not simply credit Accounts Receivable for the amount they believe will not be collected. That would cause the balance of Accounts Receivable to be less than the total of the individual accounts, and managers do not simply write off a customer's account on a hunch.

Rather than try to guess which accounts will go bad, managers, based on collection experience, estimate the total bad debt expense for the period. The business debits Uncollectible Account Expense (or Doubtful Account Expense) for the estimated amount and credits **Allowance for Uncollectible Accounts** (or **Allowance for Doubtful Accounts**), a contra account related to Accounts Receivable. This account holds the estimated amount of collection losses.

Assume the company's sales for 19X1 are $240,000 and that past collection experience suggests estimated bad debts of $3,100. The 19X1 journal entries are as follows, with accounts receivable from customers Rolf and Anderson shown separately for emphasis:

19X1	Accounts Receivable — Rolf	1,300	
	Accounts Receivable — Anderson	1,700	
	Accounts Receivable — Various Customers	237,000	
	Sales Revenue		240,000
	To record credit sales		
19X1	Uncollectible Account Expense	3,100	
	Allowance for Uncollectible Accounts		3,100
	To record estimated bad debt expense, based on past collection experience.		

> **OBJECTIVE 2**
> Use the allowance method of accounting for uncollectibles

To properly match expense against revenue, the uncollectible account expense is estimated, based on past collection experience, and recorded in 19X1 when the sales were made. This expense entry has two effects: (1) it decreases net income by debiting an expense account, and (2) it decreases *net* accounts receivable by crediting the allowance account. (Allowance for Uncollectible Accounts, the contra account, is subtracted from Accounts Receivable to measure *net* accounts receivable.) The account balances at December ⌐, 19X1 are as follows:

Accounts Receivable	Allowance for Uncollectible Accounts	Sales Revenue	Uncollectible Account Expense
240,000	3,100	240,000	3,100

Net accounts receivable
= $236,900

The 19X1 financial statements will report

Income Statement	19X1
Revenue	
Sales revenue	$240,000
Expense	
Uncollectible account expense	3,100

Balance Sheet	December 31, 19X1
Current assets	
Accounts receivable	$240,000
Less: Allowance for uncollectible accounts	3,100
Net accounts receivable	$236,900

Writing off Uncollectible Accounts

During 19X2, the company collects on most of the accounts receivable. However, the credit department determines that customers Rolf and Anderson cannot pay the amounts they owe. The accountant writes off their receivables and makes the following entries:

19X2	Cash	235,000	
	Accounts Receivable — Various Customers .		235,000
	To record collections on account		
19X2	Allowance for Uncollectible Accounts	3,000	
	Accounts Receivable — Rolf		1,300
	Accounts Receivable — Anderson		1,700
	To write off uncollectible accounts.		

The write-off entry has no effect on net income because it includes no debit to an expense account. The entry also has no effect on *net* accounts receivable because both the Allowance account debited and the Accounts Receivable account credited are part of *net* accounts receivable. The account balances at December 31, 19X2 are as follows:

Accounts Receivable		Allowance for Uncollectible Accounts	
240,000	235,000	3,000	3,100
	3,000		
			100
2,000			

The financial statements for 19X1 and 19X2 will report the following. In order to highlight the matching of expense and revenue, we are assuming no sales are made in 19X2.

Income Statement	19X1	19X2
Revenue		
Sales revenue	$240,000	$ 0
Expense		
Uncollectible account expense	3,100	0

	December 31,	
Balance Sheet	19X1	19X2
Current assets		
Accounts receivable................................	$240,000	$2,000
Less: Allowance for uncollectible accounts	3,100	100
Net accounts receivable	$236,900	$1,900

Compare these income statement and balance sheet effects with those for the direct write-off method on page 330. Which method better matches bad debt expense with sales revenue? The allowance method ties this expense of generating 19X1 sales to 19X1 revenue, and provides a more realistic picture of the business's operations. The allowance method also reports accounts receivable at their expected realizable value.

When a company sets up an allowance for doubtful accounts, it is estimating the dollar value of the accounts receivable that it will have to write off. It is unlikely that the company is able to predict exactly what the dollar value of the accounts to be written-off will be, and so the allowance will rarely, if ever, be equal to the accounts written off against it. Usually the difference between write-offs and the allowance is small, as shown in the preceding example. If the allowance is too large for one period, the estimate of bad debts for the next period can be cut back. If the allowance is too low, an additional entry debiting Uncollectible Account Expense and crediting Allowance for Uncollectible Accounts can be made at the end of the period. This credit brings the Allowance account to a realistic balance. Estimating uncollectibles will be discussed shortly.

Recoveries of Uncollectible Accounts

When an account receivable is written off as uncollectible, the receivable does not die. The customer still has an obligation to pay. However, the likelihood of receiving cash is so low that the company ceases its collection effort and writes off the account. Such accounts are filed for use in future credit decisions. Some companies turn them over to a lawyer for collection in the hope of recovering part of the receivable. To record a recovery, the accountant reverses the write-off and records the collection in the regular manner. The reversal of the write-off is needed to give the customer account receivable a debit balance.

Assume that the write-off of Rolf's account ($1,300) occurs in February 19X2. In August, Rolf pays the account in full. The journal entries for this situation follow:

Feb. 19X2	To write off Rolf's account as uncollectible (same as above)		
	Allowance for Uncollectible Accounts	1,300	
	Accounts Receivable — Rolf		1,300
Aug. 19X2	To reinstate Rolf's account		
	Accounts Receivable — Rolf.	1,300	
	Allowance for Uncollectible Accounts . . .		1,300
	To record collection from Rolf		
	Cash	1,300	
	Accounts Receivable — Rolf		1,300

Estimating Uncollectibles

We have seen that the allowance method results in more realistic financial statements. The more accurate the estimate, the more reliable the information in the statements. How are bad debt estimates made?

The most logical way to estimate bad debts is to look at the business's past records. Both the *percent of sales* method and the *aging of accounts receivable* method use the company's collection experience.

OBJECTIVE 3

Estimate uncollectibles by the percentage of sales and the aging approaches

Percentage of Sales A business may compute uncollectible account expense as a percentage of total credit sales (or total sales). Uncollectible account expense is recorded as an adjusting entry at the end of the period.

Basing its decision on figures from the last four periods, a business estimates that bad debt expense will be 2.5 percent of credit sales. If credit sales for 19X3 total $500,000, the adjusting entry to record bad debt expense for the year is

Adjusting Entries

Dec. 31	Uncollectible Account Expense ($500,000 × .025)	12,500	
	Allowance for Uncollectible Accounts		12,500

A business may change the percentage rate from year to year, depending on its collection experience. Suppose collections of accounts receivable in 19X4 are greater and write-offs are less than expected. The credit balance in Allowance for Doubtful Accounts would be too large in relation to the debit balance of Accounts Receivable. How would the business change its bad debt percentage rate in this case? *Decreasing* the percentage rate would reduce the credit entry to the allowance account, and the allowance account balance would not grow too large.

New businesses, with no credit history on which to base their rates, may obtain estimated bad debts percentages from industry trade journals, government publications and other sources of collection data.

Aging the Accounts The second popular method of estimating bad debts is called **aging the accounts**. In this approach, individual accounts receivable are analysed according to the length of time that they have been due. Performed manually, this is time-consuming. Computers greatly ease the burden. Schmidt Home Builders groups its accounts receivable into 30-day periods, as the following table shows:

Customer Name	Age of Account				
	1–30 Days	31–60 Days	61–90 Days	Over 90 Days	Total Balance
Oxwall Tools Co.	$20,000				$ 20,000
Calgary Pneumatic Parts Ltd.	10,000				10,000
Red Deer Pipe Corp.		$13,000	$10,000		23,000
Seal Coatings, Inc.			3,000	$1,000	4,000
Other accounts*	39,000	12,000	2,000	2,000	55,000
Totals	$69,000	$25,000	$15,000	$3,000	$112,000
Estimated percentage uncollectible	0.1%	1%	5%	90%	
Allowance for Uncollectible Accounts	$69	$250	$750	$2,700	$3,769

* Each of the "Other accounts" would appear individually.

Schmidt bases the percentage figures on the company's collection experience. In the past, the business has collected all but 0.1 percent of accounts aged from 1 to 30 days, all but 1 percent of accounts aged 31 to 60 days, and so on.

The total amount receivable in each age group is multiplied by the appropriate percentage figure. For example, the $69,000 in accounts aged 1 to 30 days is multiplied by 0.1 percent (.001), which comes to $69.00. The total balance needed in the Allowance for Uncollectible Accounts—$3,769—is the sum of the amounts computed for the various groups ($69+$250+$750+$2,700).

Suppose the Allowance account has a $2,100 *credit* balance from the previous period.

Allowance for Uncollectible Accounts	
	Unadjusted balance 2,100

Under the aging method, the adjusting entry is designed to adjust this account balance from $2,100 to $3,769, the needed amount. To bring the Allowance balance up to date, Schmidt makes this entry:

Adjusting Entries

Dec. 31	Uncollectible Account Expense	1,669	
	Allowance for Uncollectible Accounts		
	($3,769 – $2,100)		1,669

Now the Allowance account has the correct balance.

Allowance for Uncollectible Accounts	
	Unadjusted balance 2,100
	Adjustment amount 1,669
	Adjusted balance 3,769

It is possible that the allowance account might have a *debit* balance at year end prior to the adjusting entry. How can this occur? Bad debit write-offs during the year could have exceeded the allowance amount. Suppose the unadjusted Allowance for Uncollectible Accounts balance is a *debit* amount of $1,500.

Allowance for Uncollectible Accounts	
Unadjusted balance 1,500	

In this situation, the adjusting entry is

Adjusting Entries

Dec. 31	Uncollectible Account Expense ($3,769+$1,500)	5,269	
	Allowance for Uncollectible Accounts		5,269

After posting, the allowance account is up to date.

Allowance for Uncollectible Accounts	
Unadjusted balance 1,500	Adjustment amount 5,269
	Adjusted balance 3,769

On the balance sheet, the $3,769 is subtracted from the Accounts Receivable figure, which the table shows is $112,000, to report the expected realizable value of the accounts receivable, $108,231 ($112,000 – $3,769).

In addition to supplying the information needed for sound financial reporting, the aging method directs management's attention to the accounts that need to be pursued for payment.

Comparing the Two Methods   In practice, many companies use both the percentage of sales and the aging of accounts methods. For interim statements, monthly or quarterly, companies use the percent of sales method because it is easier to apply. At the end of the year, these companies use the aging method to ensure that they report Accounts Receivable at their expected realizable value. For this reason, auditors usually require an aging of the accounts on the year-end date. The two methods work well together, because the percent of sales approach focuses on measuring bad debt expense, whereas the aging approach is designed to measure net accounts receivable.

Credit Balances in Accounts Receivable

Occasionally, customers overpay their accounts or return merchandise for which they have already paid. The result is a credit balance in the customer's accounts receivable. Assume the company's subsidiary ledger contains 213 accounts, with balances as shown:

210 accounts with *debit* balances totaling	$185,000
3 accounts with *credit* balances totaling	2,800
Net total of debit balances	$182,200

The company should not report the asset Accounts Receivable at the net amount, $182,200. Why not? The credit balance — the $2,800 — is a liability. Like any other liability, customer credit balances are debts of the business. A balance sheet that did not indicate to management or to other financial statement users that the company had this liability amount would be misleading. Therefore, the company would report on its balance sheet:

Assets		**Liabilities**	
Current		Current	
Accounts receivable	$185,000	Credit balances in	
		customer accounts	$2,800

Credit Card Sales

Credit card sales are common in the retail industry. Cards that are issued by one company but accepted by many companies in a wide variety of businesses are American Express, Diners Club, En Route, VISA and MasterCard; they are popular nationally and internationally.

The customer presents the credit card as payment for a purchase. The seller prepares a sales invoice in triplicate. The customer and the seller keep copies as receipts. The third copy goes to the credit card company, which then pays the seller the amount charged and bills the customer.

Credit cards offer consumers the convenience of buying without having to pay the cash immediately. Also, consumers receive a monthly statement from the credit card company, detailing each credit card transaction. They can write a single cheque to cover the entire month's credit card purchases or pay less than the balance owing and pay interest on the unpaid balance.

Retailers also benefit from credit card sales. They do not have to check a customer's credit rating. The company that issues the card has already done so. Retailers do not have to keep an accounts receivable subsidiary ledger account for each customer, and they do not have to collect cash from customers. The copy of the sales invoice that retailers send to the credit card company signals the card issuer to pursue payment. Further, retailers receive cash more quickly from the credit card companies than they would from the customers themselves. Of course, these services to the seller do not come free.

The seller receives less than 100 percent of the face value of the invoice. The credit card company takes a 5 percent[1] discount on the sale to cover its services. The seller's entry to record a $100 En Route sale is

Accounts Receivable — En Route	100	
Sales Revenue		100

On collection of the discounted value, the seller records

Cash...	95	
Credit Card Discount Expense	5	
Accounts Receivable — En Route		100

Internal Control over Collections of Accounts Receivable

Businesses that sell on credit receive most of their cash receipts by mail. Internal control over collections on account is an important part of the overall internal control system. Chapter 7 detailed control procedures over cash receipts, but a critical element of internal control deserves emphasis here: the separation of cash-handling and cash-accounting duties. Consider the following case.

Butler Supply Co. is a small, family-owned business that takes pride in the loyalty of its workers. Most company employees have been with the Butlers for at least five years. The company makes 90 percent of its sales on account.

The office staff consists of a bookkeeper and a supervisor. The bookkeeper maintains the general ledger and the accounts receivable subsidiary ledger. He also makes the daily bank deposit. The supervisor prepares monthly financial statements and any special reports the Butlers require. She also takes sales orders from customers and serves as office manager.

Can you identify the internal control weakness? The bookkeeper has access to the general ledger, accounts receivable subsidiary ledger and cash. The bookkeeper could take a customer cheque and write off the customer's account as uncollectible.[2] Unless the supervisor or some other manager reviews the bookkeeper's work regularly, the theft may go undetected. In small businesses like Butler Supply Co., such a review may not be routinely performed.

How can this control weakness be corrected? The supervisor could open incoming mail and make the daily bank deposit. The bookkeeper should not be allowed to handle cash. Only the remittance slips would be forwarded to

> **OBJECTIVE 4**
> Identify internal control weaknesses in accounts receivable

---

[1] The rate varies among companies and over time.

[2] The bookkeeper would need to forge the endorsements of the cheques and deposit them in a bank account he controls. This is easier to do than you might imagine.

the bookkeeper to indicate which customer accounts to credit. Removing cash-handling duties from the bookkeeper — and keeping the accounts receivable subsidiary ledger away from the supervisor — separates duties and strengthens internal control. It reduces an employee's opportunity to steal cash and then cover it up with a false credit to a customer account. Also, the owner should prepare the bank reconciliation.

Summary Problem for Your Review

Pizza Inn Ltd. is a chain of family restaurants concentrated in the Maritimes. The company's year-end balance sheets for 19X3 and 19X2 reported

	19X3	19X2
Receivables	$7,455,648	$8,803,342
Less: Allowance for doubtful receivables	1,124,458	1,064,360
	$6,331,190	$7,738,982

Required

1. Suppose Pizza Inn estimated doubtful account (uncollectible account) expense for 19X4 to be $1,200,000. Prepare the journal entry using Pizza Inn's terminology (Doubtful Account Expense and Allowance for Doubtful Accounts).
2. Assume that during 19X4 Pizza Inn wrote off as uncollectible an account receivable of $35,000 from Fundy Company. Journalize this transaction using Pizza Inn's terminology.
3. Which entry records a decrease in net income? Which entry records a decrease in net accounts receivable?

SOLUTION TO REVIEW PROBLEM

a.	Doubtful Account Expense	1,200,000	
	Allowance for Doubtful Accounts..........		1,200,000
b.	Allowance for Doubtful Accounts	35,000	
	Account Receivable — Fundy Company		35,000

c. Entry *a* records both a decrease in net income and a decrease in net accounts receivable. The debit to Doubtful Account Expense indicates the decrease in net income. The credit to Allowance for Doubtful Accounts indicates the decrease in net accounts receivable. The Allowance account is a contra account to Accounts Receivable. Therefore, crediting the Allowance account increases its own balance and decreases net accounts receivable.

Entry *b* has no effect on net accounts receivable. The $35,000 debit to the Allowance account records an increase in net accounts receivable, and the $35,000 credit to Accounts Receivable records a decrease in net accounts receivable. The debit and credit counterbalance.

Notes Receivable _____

As we pointed out earlier in this chapter, notes receivable are more formal arrangements than accounts receivable. Often the debtor signs a promissory note, which serves as evidence of the debt. Let us take a moment to define the special terms used to discuss notes receivable.

OBJECTIVE 5
Use notes receivable terminology

1. **Promissory note**   A written promise to pay a specified sum of money at a particular future date.
2. **Maker** of a note   The person or business that signs the note and promises to pay the amount required by the note agreement. The maker is the debtor.
3. **Payee** of the note   The person or business to whom the maker promises future payment. The payee is the creditor.
4. **Principal amount** or **principal**   The amount loaned out by the payee and borrowed by the maker of the note.
5. **Interest**   The revenue to the payee for loaning out the principal and the expense to the maker for borrowing the principal.
6. **Interest period**   The period of time during which interest is to be computed. It extends from the original date of the note to the maturity date.
7. **Interest rate**   The percentage rate that is multiplied by the principal amount to compute the amount of interest on the note.
8. **Maturity date** or **due date**   The date on which final payment of the note is due. Notes with a maturity date are normally due three days after the maturity dates. These three days are called "days of grace."
9. **Maturity value**   The sum of principal and interest due at the maturity date.
10. *Note period* or *note term*   Synonyms for the interest period.

Exhibit 8-2 illustrates a promissory note. Study it carefully, and identify each of the above items for the note agreement.

EXHIBIT 8-2   *A Promissory Note*

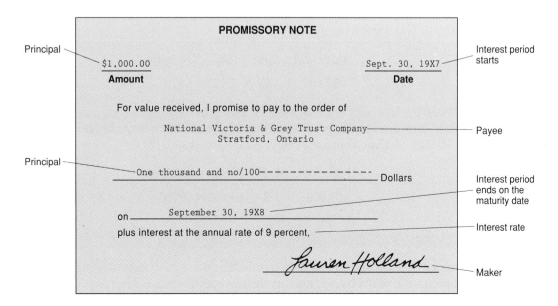

Identifying the Maturity Date of a Note

Some notes specify the maturity date of a note, as shown in Exhibit 8-2. Other notes state the period of the note, in days or months. When the period is given in months, the note's maturity date falls on the same day of the month as the date the note was issued. For example, a 6-month note dated February 16 matures on August 16.

When the period is given in days, the maturity date is determined by counting the days from date of issue. A 120-day note dated September 14, 19X2, matures on January 12, 19X3, as shown below:

Month	Number of Days	Cumulative Total
Sept. 19X2	16*	16
Oct. 19X2	31	47
Nov. 19X2	30	77
Dec. 19X2	31	108
Jan. 19X3	12	120

* $30 - 14 = 16$

Computing Interest on a Note

The formula for computing interest is

$$\text{Principal} \times \text{Rate} \times \text{Time} = \text{Amount of Interest}$$

Using the data in Exhibit 8-2, National Trust Company computes its interest revenue for 1 year on its note receivable as

Principal   Rate   Time   Interest
$1,000   × .09 × 1 (yr.) = $90

The *maturity value* of the note is $1,090 ($1,000 principal + $90 interest). Note that the time element is one (1) because interest is computed over a 1-year period.

When the interest period of a note is stated in months, we compute the interest based on the 12-month year. Interest on a $2,000 note at 15 percent for 3 months is computed as

Principal   Rate   Time   Interest
$2,000   × .15 × 3/12 = $75

When the interest period of a note is stated in days, we sometimes compute interest based on a 360-day year rather than a 365-day year. The interest on a $5,000 note at 12 percent for 60 days is computed as

Principal   Rate   Time   Interest
$5,000   × .12 × 60/360 = $100

Recording Notes Receivable

Consider the loan agreement shown in Exhibit 8-2. After Holland signs the note and presents it to the trust company, the trust company gives her $1,000 cash. At maturity date Holland pays the trust company $1,090 ($1,000 principal plus $90 interest). The trust company's entries are

Sept. 30, 19X7	Note Receivable — L. Holland	1,000	
	Cash		1,000
	To record the loan.		
Sept. 30, 19X8	Cash	1,090	
	Note Receivable — L. Holland		1,000
	Interest Revenue ($1,000 × .09 × 1)		90
	To record collection at maturity.		

> **OBJECTIVE 6**
>
> Account for notes receivable

Some companies sell merchandise in exchange for notes receivable (promissory notes) that are made payable to the seller. This arrangement occurs often when the payment term extends beyond the customary accounts receivable period, which generally ranges from 30 to 60 days.

Suppose that on October 20, 19X3, Canadian General Electric (CGE) sells equipment for $15,000 to Dorman Builders. Dorman signs a 90-day promissory note at 10 percent interest. CGE's entries to record the sale and collection from Dorman are

Oct. 20, 19X3	Note Receivable — Dorman Builders	15,000	
	Sales Revenue		15,000
	To record sale.		
Jan. 18, 19X4	Cash	15,375	
	Note Receivable — Dorman Builders . .		15,000
	Interest Revenue ($15,000 × .10 × 90/360)		375
	To record collection at maturity.		

A company may accept a note receivable from a trade customer who fails to pay an account receivable within the customary 30 to 60 days. The customer signs a promissory note, that is, becomes the maker of the note, and gives it to the creditor, who becomes the payee.

Suppose Maison Fortin Inc. sees that it will not be able to pay off its account payable to Hoffman Supply, which is due in 15 days. Hoffman may accept a note receivable from Maison Fortin. Hoffman's entry is

May 3	Note Receivable — Maison Fortin Inc.	2,400	
	Accounts Receivable — Maison Fortin Inc.		2,400
	To receive a note on account from a customer.		

Hoffman later records interest and collection as illustrated in the preceding examples.

Why does a company accept a note receivable instead of pressing its demand for payment of the account receivable? The company may pursue payment but learn that its customer does not have the money. A note receivable gives the company written evidence of the maker's debt, which may aid any legal action for collection. Also, the note receivable may carry a pledge by the maker that gives the payee certain assets if cash is not received by the due date. The company's reward for its patience in collecting is the interest revenue that it earns on the note receivable.

Discounting a Note Receivable

A note receivable is a *negotiable instrument,* which means it is readily transferable from one business or person to another and may be sold for cash. To get cash quickly, payees sometimes sell a note receivable to another party before the note matures. The payee endorses the note and hands it over to the note purchaser—often a bank—who collects the maturity value of the note at the maturity date.

Selling a note receivable before maturity is called **discounting a note receivable** because the purchaser pays less than the maturity value of the note. This lower price decreases the amount of interest revenue the original payee earns on the note. Giving up some of this interest is the price the payee pays for the convenience of receiving cash early.

Return to the preceding example with Canadian General Electric and Dorman. Recall that the maturity date of the Dorman note is January 18, 19X4. Let us assume CGE discounts the Dorman note at St. Lawrence Bank on December 9, 19X3. The discount period, which is the number of days from the date of discounting to the date of maturity (this is the period the bank will hold the note), is 40 days: 22 days in December and 18 days in January. Assume the bank applies a 12 percent interest rate in computing the discounted value of the note. The bank will want to use a discount rate that is higher than the interest rate on the note in order to increase its earnings. CGE may be willing to accept this higher rate in order to get cash quickly. The discounted value, called the *proceeds,* is the amount that CGE receives from the bank. The proceeds are computed as follows:

Principal amount	$15,000	
+ Interest ($15,000 × .10 × 90/360)	375	
= Maturity value	$15,375	$170 $170
− Discount ($15,375 × .12 × 40/360)	(205)	
= Proceeds	$15,170	

At maturity the bank collects $15,375 from the maker of the note, earning $205 of interest revenue.

Observe two points in the above computation: (1) the discount is computed on the *maturity value* of the note (principal plus interest) rather than on the original principal amount; and (2) the discount period extends *backward* from the maturity date (January 18, 19X4) to the date of discounting (December 9, 19X3). Follow this diagram:

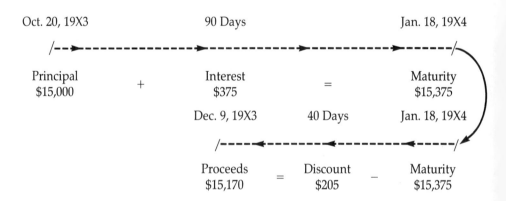

Canadian General Electric's entry to record discounting the note is

Dec. 9, 19X3 Cash 15,170
                        Note Receivable — Dorman Builders   15,000
                        Interest Revenue ($15,170 − $15,000)   170
                   To record discounting a note receivable.

When the proceeds from discounting a note receivable are less than the principal amount of the note, the payee records a debit to Interest Expense for the amount of the difference. The term *discount* has been used here to distinguish the interest earned by the payee of the note from the interest to be earned by the purchaser of the note. Fundamentally, the discount is interest.

Contingent Liabilities on Discounted Notes Receivable

Discounting a note receivable creates a **contingent** — that is, potential — **liability** for the endorser. The contingent liability is, if the maker of the note (Dorman, to continue our example) fails to pay the maturity value to the new payee (the bank), the original payee (Canadian General Electric, the note's endorser) legally must pay the bank the amount due.[3] Now we see why the liability is "potential." If Dorman pays the bank, CGE can forget the note. But if Dorman dishonours the note (fails to pay it), CGE has an actual liability.

This contingent liability exists from the time of endorsement to the maturity date of the note. In our example, the contingent liability exists from December 9, 19X3, when CGE endorsed the note, to the January 18, 19X4 maturity date.

Contingent liabilities are not reported with actual liabilities on the balance sheet. After all, they are not real debts. However, financial-statement users should be alerted that the business has incurred *potential* debts. Many businesses report contingent liabilities in a footnote to the financial statements. Canadian General Electric's end-of-period balance sheet might carry this note:

> As of December 31, 19X3, the Company is contingently liable on notes receivable discounted in the amount of $15,000.

Dishonoured Notes Receivable

If the maker of a note does not pay a note receivable at maturity, the maker is said to **dishonour** or **default on** the note. Because the term of the note has expired, the note agreement is no longer in force, nor is it negotiable. However, the payee still has a claim against the maker of the note for payment and usually transfers the claim from the note receivable account to Accounts Receivable. The payee records interest revenue earned on the note and debits Accounts Receivable for full maturity value of the note.

Suppose Rubinstein Jewelers has a six-month, 10 percent note receivable for

---

[3] The discounting agreement between the endorser and the purchaser may specify that the endorser has no liability if the note is dishonoured at maturity.

$1,200 from D. Hatachi. On the February 3 maturity date, Hatachi defaults. Rubinstein Jewelers would record the default as follows:

Feb. 3	Accounts Receivable — D. Hatachi	
	[$1,200 + ($1,200 × .10 × ⁶⁄₁₂)]	1,260
	Note Receivable — D. Hatachi		1,200
	Interest Revenue ($1,200 × .10 × ⁶⁄₁₂)		60
	To record dishonour of note receivable.	

Rubinstein would pursue collection from Hatachi as a promissory note default. The company may treat accounts receivable such as this as a special category to highlight them for added collection efforts. If the account receivable later proves uncollectible, the account is written off against Allowance for Uncollectible Accounts in the manner previously discussed.

The maker may dishonour a note after it has been discounted by the original payee. For example, suppose Dorman Builders dishonours its note (maturity value, $15,375) to Canadian General Electric after CGE has discounted the note to the bank. On dishonour, the bank adds a *protest fee* to cover the cost of a statement about the facts of the dishonour and requests payment from CGE, which then becomes the holder of the dishonoured note. Assume CGE pays the maturity value of the note, plus the $25 protest fee, to the bank. This creates an obligation for Dorman to CGE. CGE then presents the statement to Dorman and makes the following entry on the maturity date of the note:

Jan. 18, 19X4	Accounts Receivable — Dorman Builders	
	($15,375 + $25)	15,400
	Cash		15,400
	To record payment of dishonoured note receivable that has been discounted.	

CGE's collection of cash or write-off of the uncollected account receivable would be recorded in the normal manner, depending on the ultimate outcome. If CGE charges Dorman additional interest, CGE's collection entry debits Cash and credits Accounts Receivable and Interest Revenue.

Accruing Interest Revenue

Notes receivable may be outstanding at the end of the accounting period. The interest revenue that was accrued on the note up to that point should be recorded as part of that period's earnings. Recall that interest revenue is earned over time, not just when cash changes hands.

Suppose Yukon Bank receives a one-year, $1,000 note receivable, with 9 percent interest, on October 1, 19X7. The bank's accounting period ends December 31. How much of the total interest revenue does Yukon Bank earn in 19X7? How much in 19X8?

The bank will earn three months' interest in 19X7 for October, November and December. In 19X8, the bank will earn nine months' interest for January through September. Therefore, at December 31, 19X7, Yukon Bank will make the following adjusting entry to accrue interest revenue:

Dec. 31, 19X7	Interest Receivable ($1,000 × .09 × ³⁄₁₂)	22.50
	Interest Revenue		22.50
	To accrue interest revenue earned in 19X7 but not yet received.	

Then, on the maturity date Yukon Bank may record collection of principal and interest as follows:

Sept. 30, 19X8   Cash [$1,000 + ($1,000 × .09)] 1,090.00

                   Note Receivable 1,000.00

                   Interest Receivable

                   ($1,000 × .09 × $^{3}/_{12}$) 22.50

                   Interest Revenue

                   ($1,000 × .09 × $^{9}/_{12}$) 67.50

          To record collection of note receivable on

          which interest has been previously

          accrued.

The entries to accrue interest revenue earned in 19X7 and record collection in 19X8 assign the correct amount of interest to each year.

Reporting Receivables and Allowances: Actual Reports _____

Let us take a look at how some well-known companies report their receivables and allowances for uncollectibles on the balance sheet. The terminology and setup vary, but you can understand these actual presentations based on what you have learned in this chapter.

Bobbie Brooks, a manufacturer of women's clothing, reports under Current Assets (in thousands)

     Accounts receivable

       Less: Allowance for doubtful accounts of $602 . . . . $35,873

To figure the total accounts receivable amount, add the allowance to the net accounts receivable amount: $602 + $35,873 = $36,475.

Another form of disclosure is to indicate the allowance amount and show only the net accounts receivable amount.

> **OBJECTIVE 7**
>
> Report receivables on the balance sheet

     Accounts receivable

       Less: Allowance of $19.5 . . . . $309.9

While some companies such as Bobbie Brooks may show the total accounts receivable, allowance and net accounts receivable, other companies in Canada such as Canadian General Electric tend to show only net accounts receivable. They do not show the allowance. For example, Canadian General Electric Company reports a single amount for its current receivables in the body of the balance sheet and supplements it with a detailed note (amounts in thousands).

    Current receivables (note 8) $340,182

      Note 8: Current receivables

               Customer accounts $294,790

               Parent company   23,932

               Advance to related company   1,086

               Progress payments to suppliers   3,888

               Other receivables   16,486

                                                       $340,182

CGE also has long-term receivables of $10,598,000. The balance is located between Current Assets and Plant and Equipment on the balance sheet. MacLean Hunter, the publishing, broadcasting and cable television conglomerate, includes long-term receivables after fixed assets. The exact placement is less important than the fact that the long-term receivables are properly described and not included with current assets.

Bell Canada provides more detail in the body of the financial statements (amounts in millions).

> Accounts receivable
>   Principally from customers, including $5.3 ($6.4 — 1986) from
>   parent, affiliated and associated companies
>   Less $11.8 ($9.3 — 1986) for provision for uncollectibles. $954.5

Campeau Corporation, the real estate giant, disclosed in a note to the financial statements the following information about its amounts receivable shown on the balance sheet at $803,000,000 (in U.S. dollars):

> Note 4:   Accounts Receivable
>
> | | |
> |---|---:|
> | Revolving credit accounts . . . . | $601 |
> | Installment accounts . . . . | 47 |
> | | 648 |
> | Less: Allowance for doubtful accounts . . . . | 13 |
> | | 635 |
> | Others . . . . | 168 |
> | | $803 |

Anthes Industries, a company that manufactures machinery related to construction, reported in a note to the financial statements that the company was contingently liable under sales contracts financed by others in the amount of $1,500,000. The note to the financial statements suggests that Anthes sold equipment on a finance contract and then sold the contract to a financial institution. As the seller, Anthes is contingently liable if the purchaser does not pay the financial institution.

Using Computers to Account for Receivables

A computer greatly enhances accounting for receivables. Painstaking work like posting credit sales and collections, aging accounts receivable and computing interest can be performed with a computer in far less time than it takes to do them manually, and with fewer errors. Once the program is written and the data are entered, the machine can perform the calculations again and again. Commercial software is available to perform these tasks on a microcomputer. Even small businesses use them.

Suppose a homebuilder uses an Apple micro and commercial software to handle routine accounting work. Assume the business accepts notes receivable for its work and, rather than hold the notes for several years, sells them to a bank. The owner can use a program to compute a range of cash proceeds amounts that depend on different discount rates the bank is likely to propose. With this knowledge, the business person can probably strike a better deal with the bank. Instead of having to perform a half dozen such calculations by hand, the business owner or accountant can program the micro to do the arithmetic.

Suppose the homebuilder's accountant "roughs out" the calculations for discounting prior to writing the program in BASIC programming language. In computer programming, symbols are less cumbersome to work with than full terms, because each term may be lengthy and may have to be written several times. For each note receivable

Let: M = Maturity value
P = Principal value
R = Interest rate
T = Time period
D = Dollar amount of the discount
BR = Bank's interest rate used to discount the note (the discount rate)
BT = Time period the bank will hold the note (the discount period)
C = Cash proceeds from discounting the note

Then the cash proceeds (C) can be computed as follows:

$$M = P + (P \times R \times T)$$
$$D = M \times BR \times BT$$
$$C = M - D$$

Prior to discounting a note, the builder or his accountant can simply enter the value of each variable into the computer, and it will determine the cash proceeds. The program and all the data on notes receivable and discounting can be stored on a floppy disk for future use. The information can be retrieved when needed, for example, for preparation of the financial statements, including the note for contingent liabilities.

Summary Problem for Your Review

Suppose Petro-Canada engaged in the following transactions:

19X4

Apr. 4 Loaned $8,000 to Bland Co., a service station. Received a one-year, 10 percent note.

June 4 Discounted the Bland note at the bank at a discount rate of 12 percent.

Nov. 30 Loaned $6,000 to Houle, Inc., a regional distributor of Petro-Canada products, on a three-month, 11 percent note.

19X5

Feb. 28 Collected the Houle note at maturity.

Petro-Canada's accounting period ends on December 31.

Required

Explanations are not needed.

1. Record the 19X4 transactions on April 4, June 3 and November 30 on Petro-Canada's books.

2. Make any adjusting entries needed on December 31, 19X4.
3. Record the February 28, 19X5 collection of the Houle note.
4. Which transaction creates a contigent liability for Petro-Canada? When does the contingency begin? When does it end?
5. Write a footnote that Petro-Canada could use in its 19X4 financial statements to report the contingent liability.

SOLUTION TO REVIEW PROBLEM

19X4
1. Apr. 4 Note Receivable — Bland Co. 8,000

                Cash   8,000

June 4 Cash...................................... 7,920*

              Interest Expense 80

              Note Receivable — Bland Co............   8,000

Nov. 30 Note Receivable — Houle, Inc. 6,000

              Cash   6,000

* Computation of proceeds

Principal	$8,000
+ Interest ($8,000 × .10 × $\frac{12}{12}$)	800
= Maturity value...................	8,800
− Discount ($8,800 × .12 × $\frac{10}{12}$)	880
= Proceeds	$7,920

2.   Adjusting Entry

19X4
Dec. 31 Interest Receivable ($6,000 × .11 × $\frac{1}{12}$) 55

              Interest Revenue   55

Accrual of interest revenue on note receivable from Houle, Inc.

19X5
3. Feb. 28 Cash [$6,000 + ($6,000 × .11 × $\frac{3}{12}$)] 6,165

              Note Receivable — Houle, Inc...........   6,000

              Interest Receivable   55

              Interest Revenue ($6,000 × .11 × $\frac{2}{12}$)   110

4. Discounting the Bland note receivable creates a contingent liability for Petro-Canada. The contingency exists from the date of discounting the note receivable (June 4) to the maturity date of the note (April 4, 19X5).

5. Note XX — Contingent liabilities: At December 31, 19X4, the Company is contingently liable on notes receivable discounted in the amount of $8,000.

Summary

Credit sales create receivables. Accounts receivable are usually current assets, and notes receivable may be current or long-term.

Uncollectible receivables are accounted for by the direct write-off method or the allowance method. The *direct write-off method* is easy to apply, but it fails to match the uncollectible account expense to the corresponding sales revenue. Also, Accounts Receivable are reported at their full amount, which misleadingly suggests that the company expects to collect all its accounts receivable. The *allowance method* does match expenses to sales revenue and results in a more realistic measure of net accounts receivable. The *percent of sales method* and *aging of accounts receivable method* are two approaches to estimating bad debts under the allowance method.

In credit card sales, the seller receives cash from the credit card company, En Route, for example, which bills the customer. For the convenience of receiving cash immediately, the seller pays a fee, which is a percentage of sales.

Companies that sell on credit receive most customer payments in the mail. Good internal control over mailed-in cash receipts means separating cash-handling duties from cash-accounting duties.

Notes receivable are formal credit agreements. Interest earned by the creditor is computed by multiplying the note's principal amount by the interest rate times the length of the interest period.

Because notes receivable are negotiable, they may be sold. Selling a note receivable — called discounting a note — creates a contingent (possible) liability for the note's payee.

All accounts receivable, notes receivable and allowance accounts appear in the balance sheet. However, companies use various formats and terms to report these assets.

Self-Study Questions

Test your understanding of the chapter by marking the correct answer for each of the following questions:

1. The party that holds a receivable is called the *(p. 327)*
   a. Creditor
   b. Debtor
   c. Maker
   d. Security holder

2. The function of the credit department is to *(p. 329)*
   a. Collect accounts receivable from customers
   b. Report bad credit risks to other companies
   c. Evaluate customers who apply for credit
   d. Write off uncollectible accounts receivable

3. Longview, Inc. made the following entry related to uncollectibles:

Uncollectible Account Expense	1,900	
Allowance for Uncollectible Accounts		1,900

   The purpose of this entry is to *(p. 331)*
   a. Write off uncollectibles
   b. Close the expense account
   c. Age the accounts receivable
   d. Record bad debt expense

4. Longview, Inc. also made this entry:

Allowance for Uncollectible Accounts	2,110	
Accounts Receivable (detailed)		2,110

The purpose of this entry is to *(p. 332)*

a. Write off uncollectibles

b. Close the expense account

c. Age the accounts receivable

d. Record bad debt expense

5. The credit balance in Allowance for Uncollectibles is $14,300 prior to the adjusting entries at the end of the period. The aging of accounts indicates that an allowance of $78,900 is needed. The amount of expense to record is *(p. 335)*

a. $14,300

b. $64,600

c. $78,900

d. $93,200

6. The most important internal control over cash receipts is *(p. 337)*

a. Assigning an honest employee the responsibility for handling cash

b. Separating the cash-handling and cash-accounting duties

c. Ensuring that cash is deposited in the bank daily

d. Centralizing the opening of incoming mail in a single location

7. A six-month, $30,000 note specifies interest of 9 percent. The full amount of interest on this note will be *(p. 340)*

a. $450

b. $900

c. $1,350

d. $2,700

8. The note in the preceding question was issued on August 31, and the company's accounting year ends on December 31. The year-end balance sheet will report interest receivable of *(p. 345)*

a. $450

b. $900

c. $1,350

d. $2,700

9. Discounting a note receivable is a way to *(p. 342)*

a. Collect on a note

b. Increase interest revenue

c. Both of the above

d. None of the above

10. Discounting a note receivable creates a (an) *(p. 342)*

a. Cash disbursement

b. Interest expense

c. Protest fee

d. Contingent liability

Answers to the self-study questions are at the end of the chapter.

Accounting Vocabulary

aging of accounts receivable
(p. 334)

allowance for doubtful
accounts (p. 331)

allowance for uncollectible
accounts (p. 331)

allowance method (p. 330)

bad debt expense (p. 329)

contingent liability (p. 343)

creditor (p. 327)

debtor (p. 327)

default on a note (p. 343)

direct write-off method
(p. 329)

discounting a note receivable
(p. 342)

dishonour of a note (p. 343)

doubtful account expense
(p. 329)

interest (p. 339)

interest period (p. 339)

interest rate (p. 339)

maker of a note (p. 339)

maturity date (p. 339)

maturity value (p. 339)

other receivables (p. 328)

payee of a note (p. 339)

principal amount (p. 339)

promissory note (p. 339)

receivable (p. 327)

uncollectible accounts
expense (p. 329)

Assignment Material _____

Questions

1. Name the two parties to a receivable/payable transaction. Which party has the receivable? Which party has the payable? Which party has the asset? Which party has the liability?

2. List the three categories of receivables. State how each category is classified for reporting on the balance sheet.

3. Name the two methods of accounting for uncollectible receivables. Which method is easier to apply? Which method is consistent with generally accepted accounting principles?

4. Which of the two methods of accounting for uncollectible accounts is preferable? Why?

5. Identify the accounts debited and credited to account for uncollectibles under the direct write-off method and the allowance method.

6. What is another term for Allowance for Uncollectible Accounts? What are two other terms for Uncollectible Account Expense?

7. Which entry decreases net income under the allowance method of accounting for uncollectible accounts: the entry to record uncollectible account expense or the entry to write off an uncollectible account receivable?

8. May a customer pay his or her account receivable after it has been written off? If not, why not? If so, what entries are made to account for reinstating the customer's account and collecting cash from the customer?

9. Identify and briefly describe the two ways to estimate bad debt expense and uncollectible accounts.

10. Briefly describe how a company may use both the percentage of sales method and aging method to estimate uncollectibles.

11. How does a credit balance arise in a customer's account receivable? How does the company report this credit balance on its balance sheet?

12. Many businesses receive most of their cash on credit sales through the mail. Suppose you own a business so large that you must hire employees to handle cash receipts and perform the related accounting duties. What internal control feature should you use to ensure that cash received from customers is not taken by a dishonest employee?

13. Use the terms *maker, payee, principal amount, maturity date, promissory note* and *interest* in an appropriate sentence or two.

14. For each of the following notes receivable, compute the amount of interest revenue earned during 19X6:

		Principal	Interest Rate	Interest Period	Maturity Date
a.	Note 1	$ 10,000	9%	90 days	11/30/19X6
b.	Note 2	$ 50,000	10%	6 months	9/30/19X6
c.	Note 3	$100,000	8%	5 years	12/31/19X7
d.	Note 4	$ 15,000	13%	60 days	1/15/19X7

15. Name three situations in which a company might receive a note receivable. For each situation, show the account debited and the account credited to record receipt of the note.

16. Suppose you hold a 180-day, $5,000 note receivable that specifies 10 percent interest. After 60 days you discount the note at 12 percent. How much cash do you receive?

17. How does a contingent liability differ from an ordinary liability? How does discounting a note receivable create a contingent liability? When does the contingency cease to exist?

18. When the maker of a note dishonors it at maturity, what account does the payee debit and credit?

19. Why does the payee of a note receivable usually need to make adjusting entries for interest at the end of the accounting period?

20. Recall the real-world disclosurers of receivables the chapter presents. Show three ways to report Accounts Receivable of $100,000 and Allowance for Uncollectible Accounts of $2,800 on the balance sheet or in the related notes.

Exercises

Exercise 8-1   *Using the direct write-off method for bad debts*

On September 30, Maxwell Co. had a $32,000 debit balance in Accounts Receivable. During October the company had sales revenue of $135,000, which included $88,000 in credit sales. Other data for October include

Collections on accounts receivable, $91,000
Write-offs of uncollectible receivables, $1,520

Required

1. Record uncollectible account expense for October by the *direct write-off* method.
2. What amount of *net* accounts receivable would Maxwell report on its October 31 balance sheet under the direct write-off method? Does Maxwell expect to collect this much of the receivable? Give your reason.

Exercise 8-2   *Using the allowance method for bad debts*

Refer to the situation in Exercise 8-1 and add these facts:

September 30 credit balance in Allowance for Uncollectible Accounts, $2,100
Uncollectible account expense, estimated as 2 percent of credit sales

Required

1. Prepare journal entries to record sales, collections, uncollectible account expense by the allowance method, and write-offs of uncollectibles during October.
2. Show the ending balances in Accounts Receivable, Allowance for Uncollectible Accounts, and *net* accounts receivable at October 31. Does Maxwell expect to collect the net amount of the receivable?

Exercise 8-3   *Recording bad debts by the allowance method*

Prepare general journal entries to record the following transactions under the allowance method of accounting for uncollectibles:

Apr. 2   Sold merchandise for $4,650 on credit terms of 2/10 n/30 to McBee Sales Company.
May 28   Received legal notification that McBee Sales Company was bankrupt. Wrote off McBee's accounts receivable balance.
Aug. 11   Received $2,000 from McBee Sales Company, together with a letter indicating that the company intended to pay its account within the next month.
     30   Received the remaining amount due from McBee.

Exercise 8-4   *Recording bad debts by the allowance method*

At December 31, 19X5, Knudsen Company has an accounts receivable balance of $129,000. Sales revenue for 19X5 comes to $950,000, including credit sales of $600,000. For each of the following situations, prepare the year-end adjusting entry to record doubtful account expense. Show how the accounts receivable and the allowance for doubtful accounts are reported on the balance sheet.

a. Allowance for Doubtful Accounts has a credit balance before adjustment of $1,600. Knudsen Company estimates that doubtful account expense for the year is ¾ of 1 percent of credit sales.

b. Allowance for Doubtful Accounts has a debit balance before adjustment of $1,100. Knudsen Company estimates that $6,100 of the accounts receivable will prove uncollectible.

Exercise 8-5   *Using the aging approach to estimate bad debts*

At December 31, 19X7, the accounts receivable balance of Granite Shoals Co. is $266,000. The allowance for doubtful accounts has a $3,910 credit balance. Accountants for Granite Shoals Company prepare the following aging schedule for its accounts receivable:

Total Balance	Age of Accounts			
	1–30 Days	*31–60 Days*	*61–90 Days*	*Over 90 Days*
$266,000	$104,000	$78,000	$69,000	$15,000
Estimated percentage uncollectible	0.3%	1.2%	4.0%	50%

Journalize the adjusting entry for doubtful accounts based on the aging schedule. Show the T-account for the allowance.

Exercise 8-6   *Reporting receivables with credit balances*

The accounts receivable subsidiary ledger includes the following summarized data:

83 accounts with debit balances totaling $63,240
9 accounts with credit balances totaling   2,690
Net total of balances $60,550

Show how these data would be reported on the balance sheet.

Exercise 8-7   *Recording a note receivable and accruing interest revenue*

Record the following transactions in the general journal:

Nov. 1   Loaned $10,000 cash to E. Trembley on a 1-year 9 percent note.
Dec. 3   Sold goods to Lofland, Inc. receiving a 90-day 12 percent note for $3,750.
      16   Received a $2,000, 6-month, 12 percent note on account from J. Baker.
      31   Accrued interest revenue on all notes receivable.

Exercise 8-8   *Recording notes receivable, discounting a note and reporting the contingent liability in a note*

Prepare general journal entries to record the following transactions:

Aug. 14   Sold goods on account to Bert Lewis, $4,000.
Dec. 2   Received a $4,000, 90-day, 10 percent note from Bert Lewis in satisfaction of his past-due account receivable.
      30   Sold the Lewis note by discounting it to a bank at 15 percent. (Use a 360-day year, and round amounts to the nearest dollar.)

Write the note to disclose the contingent liability at December 31.

Exercise 8-9 *Accounting for a dishonoured note receivable*

Record the following transactions in the general journal, assuming the company uses the allowance method to account for uncollectibles:

May 18   Sold goods to Computer Specialties, receiving a 120-day, 10 percent note for $2,700.

Sept.15   The note is dishonoured. Added a $25 protest fee to the receivable from Computer Specialties.

Nov. 30   After pursuing collection from Computer Specialties, wrote off their account as uncollectible.

Exercise 8-10 *Recording a note receivable and accruing interest revenue*

Record the following transactions in the general journal:

Apr. 1, 19X2   Loaned $4,800 to Linda Rutishauser on a 1-year, 9 percent note.
Dec. 31, 19X2   Accrued interest on the Rutishauser note.
Dec. 31, 19X2   Closed the interest revenue account.
Apr. 1, 19X3   Received the maturity value of the note from Linda Rutishauser.

Problems   *(Group A)*

Problem 8-1A *Accounting for uncollectibles by the direct write-off and allowance methods*

On February 28 Gallery Lafleur had a $61,800 debit balance in Accounts Receivable. During March the company had sales revenue of $509,000, which includes $443,000 in credit sales. Other data for March include

Collections on account receivable, $451,600
Write-offs of uncollectible receivables, $4,990
February 28 unadjusted balance in Allowance for Uncollectible Accounts, $800 (debit)
Uncollectible account expense, estimated as 2 percent of credit sales

Required

1.   Record uncollectible account expense for March by the *direct write-off* method. Show all March activity in Accounts Receivable and Uncollectible Account Expense.
2.   Record uncollectible account expense and write-offs of customer accounts for March by the *allowance* method. Show all March activity in Accounts Receivable, Allowance for Uncollectible Accounts and Uncollectible Account Expense.
3.   What amount of uncollectible account expense would Gallery Lafleur report on its March income statement under the two methods? Which amount better matches expense with revenue? Give your reason.
4.   What amount of *net* accounts receivable would Gallery Lafleur report on its March 31 balance sheet under the two methods? Which amount is more realistic? Give your reason.

Problem 8-2A *Using the percent of sales and aging approaches for uncollectibles*

Masters Company completed the following transactions during 19X1 and 19X2:

19X1
Dec. 31   Estimated that uncollectible account expense for the year was ¾ of 1 percent on credit sales of $300,000, and recorded that amount as expense.

31   Made the appropriate closing entry.

19X2

Jan. 17   Sold inventory to Mary Lee, $652, on credit terms of 2/10 n/30.

June 29   Wrote off Mary Lee account as uncollectible after repeated efforts to collect from her.

Aug. 6   Received $250 from Mary Lee, along with a letter stating her intention to pay her debt in full within 30 days. Reinstated her account in full.

Sept. 4   Received the balance due from Mary Lee.

Dec. 31   Made a compound entry to write off the following accounts as uncollectible: Bernard Klaus, $737; Louis Mann, $348; and Millie Burnett, $622.

31   Estimated that uncollectible account expense for the year was ⅔ of 1 percent on credit sales of $420,000, and recorded that amount as expense.

31   Made the appropriate closing entry.

Required

1.   Open general ledger accounts for Allowance for Uncollectible Accounts and Uncollectible Account Expense. Keep running balances.

2.   Record the transactions in the general journal, and post to the two ledger accounts.

3.   The December 31, 19X2 balance of Accounts Receivable is $139,000. Show how Accounts Receivable would be reported at that date.

4.   Assume that Masters Company begins aging accounts receivable on December 31, 19X2. The balance in Accounts Receivable is $139,000; the credit balance in Allowance for Uncollectible Accounts is $543; and the company estimates that $2,600 of its accounts receivable will prove uncollectible.
     a. Make the adjusting entry for uncollectibles.
     b. Show how Accounts Receivable will be reported on the December 31, 19X2 balance sheet.

Problem 8-3A   *Using the percent of sales and aging approaches for uncollectibles*

The December 31, 19X6 balance sheet of Marlin Products Co. reports the following:

Accounts Receivable	$256,000
Allowance for Doubtful Accounts (credit balance)	7,100

At the end of each quarter, Marlin Products Company estimates doubtful account expense to be 2 percent of credit sales. At the end of the year, the company ages its accounts receivable, and adjusts the balance in Allowance for Doubtful Accounts to correspond to the aging schedule. During 19X7, Marlin completes the following selected transactions:

Jan. 31   Wrote off as uncollectible the $855 account receivable from Spinelli Company and the $3,287 account receivable from J. M. Bartlett.

Mar. 31   Recorded doubtful account expense based on credit sales of $120,000.

May 2   Received $1,000 from J. M. Bartlett after prolonged negotiations with Bartlett's lawyer. Marlin has no hope of collecting the remainder.

June 15   Wrote off as uncollectible the $1,120 account receivable from Lisa Brown.

June 30   Recorded doubtful account expense based on credit sales of $166,000.

July 14   Made a compound entry to write off the following uncollectible accounts: C. H. Harris, $766; Graphics Unlimited, $2,413; and Ben McQueen, $134.

Sept. 30   Recorded doubtful account expense based on credit sales of $141,400.

Nov. 22   Wrote off the following accounts receivable as uncollectible: Monet Corp., $1,345; Blocker, Inc., $2,109; and Main Street Plaza, $755.

Dec. 31   Recorded doubtful accounts expense based on the following summary of the aging of accounts receivable:

| Total Balance | Age of Accounts | | | |
	1–30 Days	31–60 Days	61–90 Days	Over 90 Days
$287,600	$154,500	$86,000	$32,000	$15,100
Estimated percentage uncollectible	0.2%	0.5%	3.0%	40.0%

Dec. 31   Made the closing entry for Doubtful Account Expense for the entire year.

Required

1. Record the transactions in the general journal.
2. Open the Allowance for Doubtful Accounts, and post entries affecting that account. Keep a running balance.
3. Most companies report two-year comparative financial statements. If Marlin's Accounts Receivable balance is $287,600 at December 31, 19X7, show how the company would report its accounts receivable in a comparative balance sheet for 19X7 and 19X6, as follows:

	19X7	19X6
Accounts receivable		
Less: Allowance for doubtful accounts		
Net accounts receivable		

✓ **Problem 8-4A**   *Accounting for notes receivable, including discounting notes and accruing interest revenue*

A company received the following notes during 19X3. Notes 1, 2 and 3 were discounted on the dates and at the rates indicated:

Note	Date	Face Amount	Interest Rate	Term	Date Discounted	Discount Rate
1	July 12	$10,000	10%	3 months	Aug. 12	15%
2	Aug. 4	6,000	11%	90 days	Aug. 30	13%
3	Oct. 21	8,000	15%	60 days	Nov. 3	18%
4	Nov. 30	12,000	12%	6 months	—	—
5	Dec. 7	9,000	10%	30 days	—	—
6	Dec. 23	15,000	9%	1 year	—	—

Required

As necessary in questions 1 through 5, identify each note by number, compute interest using a 360-day year for those notes with terms specified in days or years, round all interest amounts to the nearest dollar, and present entries in general journal form.

1. Determine the due date and maturity value of each note.
2. For each discounted note, determine the discount and proceeds from sale of the note.
3. Journalize the discounting of notes 1 and 2.

4. Journalize a single adjusting entry at December 31, 19X3 to record interest revenue earned but not received on notes 4, 5 and 6.

5. Journalize the collection of principal and interest on note 5.

Problem 8-5A   *Notes receivable, discounted notes, dishonoured notes and accrued interest revenue*

Record the following selected transactions in the general journal:

19X1

Dec. 19   Received a $2,000, 60-day, 12 percent note on account from Claude Bernard.

    31   Made an adjusting entry to accrue interest on the Bernard note.

    31   Made an adjusting entry to record doubtful account expense in the amount of 1 percent of credit sales of $474,500.

    31   Made a compound closing entry for interest revenue and doubtful account expense.

19X2

Feb. 17   Collected the maturity value of the Bernard note.

Mar. 22   Sold merchandise to Kamloops Power Co., receiving $1,400 cash and a 90-day, 10 percent note for $6,000.

May 3   Discounted the Kamloops Power Co. note to the Bank of the Rockies at 15 percent.

June 1   Loaned $10,000 cash to Linz Brothers, receiving a 6-month, 11 percent note.

Oct. 31   Received a $1,500, 60-day, 12 percent note from Ned Pierce on his past-due account receivable.

Dec. 1   Collected the maturity value of the Linz Brothers note.

    1   Sold goods to McNamara Company, receiving a $24,000, 3-month, 10 percent note.

    30   Ned Pierce dishonored his note at maturity; wrote off the note receivable as uncollectible, debiting Allowance for Doubtful Accounts.

    31   Wrote off as uncollectible the accounts receivable of Al Bynum, $435 and Ray Sharp, $276.

Dec. 31   Made an adjusting entry to accrue interest on the McNamara note.

    31   Made an adjusting entry to record doubtful account expense based on an aging of accounts receivable. The aging analysis indicates that $355,800 of accounts receivable will not be collected. Prior to this adjustment, the credit balance in Allowance for Uncollectible Accounts is $341,900.

19X3

Feb. 18   Received a 90-day, 10 percent, $5,000 note from Dilley, Inc. on account. (Assume February has 28 days.)

Mar. 1   Collected the maturity value of the McNamara Company note.

    8   Discounted the Dilley note to the Bank of the Rockies at 16 percent.

Apr. 21   Sold merchandise to Brown Group, receiving a 60-day, 9 percent note for $4,000.

June 20   Brown Group dishonored its note at maturity and converted the maturity value of the note to an account receivable.

July 12   Loaned $60,000 cash to Consolidated Investments, receiving a 90-day, 13 percent note.

    13   Sold merchandise to Scott Corp., receiving a 4-month, 12 percent, $2,500 note.

Aug. 2   Collected $4,060 on account from Brown Group.

Sept.13   Discounted the Scott Corp. note to the Bank of the Rockies at 18 percent.

Oct. 10   Collected the maturity value of the Consolidated Investments note.

Nov. 13   Scott Corp. dishonored its note at maturity; paid the Bank of the Rockies the maturity value of the note plus a protest fee of $35 and debited an account receivable from Scott Corp.

Dec. 31   Wrote off as uncollectible the account receivable from Scott Corp.

Required

Record the transactions in the general journal.

(Group B)

Problem 8-1B   *Accounting for uncollectibles by the direct write-off and allowance methods*

On May 31, Krakow Tool Company had a $104,300 debit balance in Accounts Receivable. During June the company had sales revenue of $788,000, which includes $640,000 in credit sales. Other data for June include

Collections on accounts receivable, $599,400
Write-offs of uncollectible receivables, $6,100
May 31 unadjusted balance in Allowance for Uncollectible Accounts, $2,200 (credit)
Uncollectible account expense, estimated as 2 percent of credit sales

Required

1. Record uncollectible account expense for June by the *direct write-off* method. Show all June activity in Account Receivable and Uncollectible Account Expense.
2. Record uncollectible account expense and write-offs of customer accounts for June by the *allowance* method. Show all June activity in Accounts Receivable, Allowance for Uncollectible Accounts and Uncollectible Account Expense.
3. What amount of uncollectible account expense would Krakow Tool Company report on its June income statement under the two methods? Which amount better matches expense with revenue? Give your reason.
4. What amount of net accounts receivable would Krakow Tool Company report on its June 30 balance sheet under the two methods? Which amount is more realistic? Give your reason.

Problem 8-2B   *Using the percent of sales and aging approaches for uncollectibles*

Reynaldo Company completed the following selected transactions during 19X1 and 19X2:

19X1
Dec. 31   Estimated that uncollectible account expense for the year was ⅔ of 1 percent on credit sales of $450,000 and recorded that amount as expense.
   31   Made the appropriate closing entry.

19X2
Feb. 4   Sold inventory to Gary Carter, $1,521, on credit terms of 2/10 n/30.
July 1   Wrote off Gary Carter's account as uncollectible after repeated efforts to collect from him.
Oct. 19   Received $521 from Gary Carter, along with a letter stating his intention to pay his debt in full within 30 days. Reinstated his account in full.
Nov. 15   Received the balance due from Gary Carter.
Dec. 31   Made a compound entry to write off the following accounts as uncollectible: Kris Moore, $899; Marie Mandue, $530; and Grant Frycer, $1,272.
   31   Estimated that uncollectible account expense for the year was ⅔ of 1 percent on credit sales of $540,000 and recorded the expense.
   31   Made the appropriate closing entry.

Required

1. Open general ledger accounts for Allowance for Uncollectible Accounts and Uncollectible Account Expense. Keep running balances.
2. Record the transactions in the general journal and post to the two ledger accounts.
3. The December 31, 19X2, balance of Accounts Receivable is $164,500. Show how Accounts Receivable would be reported at that date.
4. Assume that Richard Company begins aging its accounts receivable on December 31, 19X2. The balance in Accounts Receivable is $164,500; the credit balance in Allowance for Uncollectible Accounts is $299; and the company estimates that $3,545 of its accounts receivable will prove uncollectible.
   a. Make the adjusting entry for uncollectibles.
   b. Show how Accounts Receivable will be reported on the December 31, 19X2 balance sheet.

Problem 8-3B   *Using the percent of sales and aging approaches for uncollectibles*

The December 31, 19X4 balance sheet of Bonini Limited reports the following:

Accounts Receivable	$141,000
Allowance for Doubtful Accounts (credit balance)	3,200

At the end of each quarter, Bonini estimates doubtful account expense to be $1\frac{1}{2}$ percent of credit sales. At the end of the year, the company ages its accounts receivable and adjusts the balance in Allowance for Doubtful Accounts to correspond to the aging schedule. During 19X5 Bonini completes the following selected transactions:

Jan. 16   Wrote off as uncollectible the $403 account receivable from Platt Co. and the $1,719 account receivable from Wise Corp.

Mar. 31   Recorded doubtful account expense based on credit sales of $100,000.

Apr. 15   Received $300 from Wise Corp. after prolonged negotiations with Wise's lawyer. Bonini has no hope of collecting the remainder.

May 13   Wrote off as uncollectible the $2,980 account receivable from M. E. Cate.

June 30   Recorded doubtful account expense based on credit sales of $114,000.

Aug. 9   Made a compound entry to write off the following uncollectible accounts: Clifford Ltd. $235; Matz Co., $188; and Lew Norris, $1,006.

Sept. 30   Recorded doubtful account expense based on credit sales of $130,000.

Oct. 18   Wrote off as uncollectible the $767 account receivable from Bliss Co. and the $430 account receivable from Micro Data.

Dec. 31   Recorded doubtful account expense based on the following summary of the aging of accounts receivable:

Total Balance	Age of Accounts			
	1–30 Days	*31–60 Days*	*61–90 Days*	*Over 90 Days*
$167,400	$114,600	$31,100	$12,000	$9,700
Estimated percentage uncollectible	0.1%	0.4%	5.0%	30.0%

Dec. 31   Made the closing entry for Doubtful Account Expense for the entire year.

Required

1. Record the transactions in the general journal.
2. Open the Allowance for Doubtful Accounts and post entries affecting that account.

3. Most companies report two-year comparative financial statements. If Bonini's Accounts Receivable balance is $167,400 at December 31, 19X5, show how the company would report its accounts receivable on a comparative balance sheet for 19X5 and 19X4, as follows:

	19X5	19X4
Accounts receivable	_____	_____
Less: Allowance for doubtful accounts.......	_____	_____
Net accounts receivable	_____	_____

Problem 8-4B *Accounting for notes receivable, including discounting notes and accruing interest revenue*

A company received the following notes during 19X5. Notes 1, 2 and 3 were discounted on the dates and at the rates indicated.

Note	Date	Face Amount	Interest Rate	Term	Date Discounted	Discount Rate
1	July 15	$ 6,000	10%	6 months	Oct. 15	12%
2	Aug. 19	9,000	12%	90 days	Aug. 30	15%
3	Sept. 1	8,000	15%	120 days	Nov. 2	20%
4	Oct. 30	7,000	12%	3 months	—	—
5	Nov. 19	15,000	10%	60 days	—	—
6	Dec. 1	12,000	9%	1 year	—	—

Required

As necessary in questions 1 through 5, identify each note by number, compute interest using a 360-day year for those notes with terms specified in days or years, round all interest amounts to the nearest dollar, and present entries in general journal form.

1. Determine the due date and maturity value of each note.
2. For each discounted note, determine the discount and proceeds from sale of the note.
3. Journalize the discounting of notes 1 and 2.
4. Journalize a single adjusting entry at December 31, 19X5 to record interest revenue earned but not received on notes 4, 5 and 6.
5. Journalize the collection of principal and interest on note 4.

Problem 8-5B *Notes receivable, discounted notes, dishonoured notes and accrued interest revenue*

Record the following selected transactions in the general journal:

19X2
Dec. 21 Received a $3,600, 30-day, 10 percent note on account from Myron Blake.
  31 Made an adjusting entry to accrue interest on the Blake note.
  31 Made an adjusting entry to record doubtful account expense in the amount of ¾ of 1 percent on credit sales of $604,800.
  31 Made a compound closing entry for interest revenue and doubtful account expense.
19X3
Jan. 20 Collected the maturity value of the Blake note.
Apr. 19 Sold merchandise to the city of Lethbridge, receiving $500 cash and a 120-day, 12 percent note for $5,000.

May 1 Discounted the city of Lethbridge note to Prairie Bank at 15 percent.

Sept. 14 Loaned $6,000 cash to Banff Investors, receiving a 3-month, 13 percent note.

30 Received a $1,675, 60-day, 16 percent note from Matt Kurtz on his past-due account receivable.

Nov. 29 Matt Kurtz dishonoured his note at maturity; wrote off the note as uncollectible, debiting Allowance for Doubtful Accounts.

Dec. 14 Collected the maturity value of the Banff Investors note.

31 Wrote off as uncollectible the accounts receivable of Ty Larson, $1,005 and Terry Gee, $140.

Problem 8-6B *Uncollectibles, notes receivable, discounting notes, dishonoured notes and accrued interest revenue*

Assume Canada Packers manufacturer of meat products, completed the following selected transactions:

19X5
Nov. 1 Sold goods to Eckerd Grocery Co., receiving a $15,000, 3-month, 12 percent note.

Dec. 31 Made an adjusting entry to accrue interest on the Eckerd Grocery.

31 Made an adjusting entry to record doubtful account expense based on an aging of accounts receivable. The aging analysis indicates that $202,670 of accounts receivable will not be collected. Prior to this adjustment, the credit balance in Allowance for Uncollectible Accounts is $189,900.

19X6
Feb. 1 Collected the maturity value of the Eckerd Grocery note.

23 Received a 90-day, 15 percent, $4,000 note from Bliss Company on account. (Assume February has 28 days.)

Mar. 31 Discounted the Bliss Co. note to Bytown Bank at 20 percent.

Apr. 23 Sold merchandise to K Lynn Ltd., receiving a 60-day, 10 percent note for $9,000.

June 22 K Lynn Ltd. dishonoured its note at maturity; converted the maturity value of the note to an account receivable.

July 15 Loaned $8,500 cash to McNeil, Inc., receiving a 30-day, 12 percent note.

17 Sold merchandise to Grant Corp., receiving a 3-month, 10 percent, $8,000 note.

Aug. 5 Collected $9,150 on account from K Lynn Ltd.

14 Collected the maturity value of the McNeil, Inc. note.

17 Discounted the Grant Corp. note to Bytown Bank at 15 percent.

Oct. 17 Grant Corp. dishonoured its note at maturity; paid Bytown Bank the maturity value of the note plus a protest fee of $50 and debited an account receivable from Grant Corp.

Dec. 15 Wrote off as uncollectible the account receivable from Grant Corp.

Required

Record the transactions in the general journal.

Decision Problems

1. Uncollectible accounts and evaluating a business

Bentwood Appliances sells its products either for cash or on notes receivable that earn interest. The business uses the direct write-off method to account for bad debts. Mark

Moore, the owner, has prepared the financial statements of the store. The most recent comparative income statements, for 19X3 and 19X2, are as follows:

	19X3	19X2
Total revenue...........................	$210,000	$195,000
Total expenses...........................	157,000	153,000
Net income...............................	$ 53,000	$ 42,000

Based on the increase in net income, Moore seeks to expand his operations. He asks you to invest $50,000 in the business. You and Moore have several meetings, at which you learn that notes receivable from customers were $100,000 at the end of 19X1 and $300,000 at the end of 19X2. Also, total revenues for 19X2 and 19X3 include interest at 15 percent on the year's beginning notes receivable balance. Total expenses include bad debt expense of $5,000 each year, based on the direct write-off basis. Moore estimates that doubtful account expense would be 4 percent of sales revenue if the allowance method were used.

Required

1. Prepare for the Bentwood Appliances a comparative single-step income statement that identifies sales revenue, interest revenue, doubtful account expense and other expenses.
2. Is Bentwood's future as promising as Moore's income statement makes it appear? Give the reason for your answer.

2. Estimating the collectibility of accounts receivable

You work in the corporate credit department of Brunswick Bank. Maria Presti, owner of MP Manufacturing Inc., a manufacturer of wooden furniture, has come to you to arrange a loan for $350,000 to buy new manufacturing equipment to expand her operations. She proposes to use her accounts receivable as collateral for the loan and has provided you with the following information from her most recent audited financial statements (all figures to the nearest $1,000):

	19X9	19X8	19X7
Sales	$1,375	$1,589	$1,502
Cost of goods sold	876	947	905
Gross profit	499	642	597
Other expenses	518	487	453
Net profit or (loss) before taxes	(19)	155	144
Accounts receivable	458	387	374
Allowance for doubtful accounts	23	31	29

Required

1. Would you grant the loan based on the information Ms. Presti has provided? What analysis would you perform on the information? What would you base your decision on?
2. What additional information would you request from Ms. Presti?
3. Assume Ms. Presti provided you with the information requested in question 2. What would make you change the decision you made in question 1?

Financial Statement Problem

Use data from the John Labatt balance sheet in Appendix E to answer these questions. Show all amounts in millions, rounded to the nearest $100,000. For example, show $8,600,000 as $8.6 million.

1. How much did John Labatt customers owe the company at April 30, 1988? (Assume an allowance for doubtful accounts of $4.5 million.)
2. Journalize the following for the fiscal year ended April 30, 1989 using John Labatt's account titles. Explanations are not required.
    a. Revenues net of sales and excise taxes, $4,856.8 million, assuming all net revenues are earned on account.
    b. Cash collections of $4,846.1 million.
    c. Doubtful account expense estimated at 0.1 percent of net revenues.
    d. Write-offs of uncollectibles totaling $4.8 million.
3. Post the entries in question 2 to Accounts Receivable and Allowance for Doubtful Accounts, inserting the April 30, 1988 balances to these accounts.
4. Show Accounts Receivable as John Labatt would report this asset on the April 30, 1989 balance sheet. Did John Labatt have any other significant receivables at April 30, 1989?

Answers to Self-Study Questions

1. a	6. b
2. c	7. c ($30,000 × .09 × 6/12 = $1,350)
3. d	8. b ($30,000 × .09 × 4/12 = $ 900)
4. a	9. a
5. b ($78,900 − $14,300 = $64,600)	10. d

9

Merchandise Inventory

LEARNING OBJECTIVES

After studying this chapter, you should be able to

1 Apply four inventory costing methods

2 Describe the income effects of the inventory costing methods

3 Read and understand actual company inventory disclosures

4 Apply the lower-of-cost-or-market rule to inventory

5 Explain why inventory errors counterbalance

6 Estimate inventory by two methods

7 Account for inventory by the periodic and perpetual systems

Merchandise inventory is the largest *current asset* on the balance sheet of most businesses that manufacture or buy inventory for resale. John Labatt, in Appendix E, reported inventories of $345 million, compared to receivables of $307 million. Inventories are important to merchandisers of all sizes. Buying and selling inventory is the heart of wholesaling and retailing, whether the business is Eaton's, Loblaws, or the corner hardware store.

Inventory is the major current asset of most merchandisers. What is their major expense? It is *cost of sales* or *cost of goods sold*. Cost of goods sold is the total cost of inventory sold during the period. It includes all costs relating to the inventory sold: the cost of manufacturing or purchasing the inventory, and such acquisition costs as freight and insurance. Selling costs including shipping are normally excluded. For many other companies, cost of goods sold is greater than all other expenses combined. National Sea Products reported for 1987 its cost of sales at $410 million, compared to other operating expenses of $71 million.

Exhibit 9-1 traces the flow of inventory costs during the accounting period. The model presented in Exhibit 9-1 is fundamental to accounting for inventory.

The business starts each period with **beginning inventory**, the goods that are left over from the preceding period. During the period, the business purchases additional goods for resale. Together, beginning inventory and purchases make up **goods available for sale**. Over the course of the period, the business sells some of the available goods. The cost of the inventory sold to customers is called the cost of goods sold. This cost is an expense because the inventory is no longer of use to the company. The goods still on hand at the end of the

EXHIBIT 9-1   *Flow of Inventory Costs*

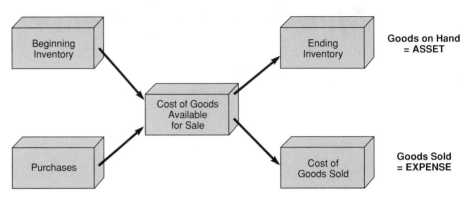

period is called **ending inventory**. Its cost is an asset because these goods are still available for sale.

Exhibit 9-2 uses data from the financial statements of Gillespie Hardware Ltd., a chain of hardware stores, to present the flow of inventory costs in a different format. Notice that ending inventory is subtracted from cost of goods available for sale to figure the cost of goods sold.

The rest of this chapter fills in the details of our inventory cost flow model.

Figuring the Cost of Inventory

A necessary step in accounting for inventory is determining the cost of *ending inventory*. At the end of each period the *quantity* of inventory is multiplied by the *unit cost* of inventory to compute the cost of ending inventory.

Determining the Quantity of Inventory   Most businesses physically count their inventory at least once each year, often on the last day of the fiscal year. Inventory, an asset, must be reported accurately on the balance sheet.

You may have worked at a grocery store or some other type of retail business. If so, you will recall the process of "taking the inventory." Some entities shut the business down to get a good count of inventory on hand. Others count the goods on a weekend. Still others inventory the merchandise while business is being conducted. How is it done in a large organization?

Assume Gillespie Hardware takes a complete physical inventory on its year-end date. Teams of counters in the company's approximately 17 stores record

EXHIBIT 9-2   *Inventory and Cost of Goods Sold for Gillespie Hardware Ltd.*

	(amounts in thousands)
Beginning inventory	$ 276
+ Purchases	1,348
= Cost of goods available for sale	1,624
− Ending inventory	317
= Cost of goods sold	$1,307

the quantities of each inventory item on hand. Each store forwards its total count to corporate headquarters, where home office employees determine the inventory grand total.

Complications may arise in determining the inventory quantity. Suppose the business has purchased some goods that are in transit when the inventory is counted. Even though these items are not physically present, they should be included in the inventory count if title to the goods has passed to the purchaser. When title passes from seller to purchaser, the purchaser becomes the legal owner of the goods.

The FOB (free on board) terms of the transaction govern when title passes from the seller to the purchaser. **FOB shipping point** indicates that title passes when the goods leave the seller's place of business. **FOB destination** means that title passes when the goods arrive at the purchaser's location. Therefore, goods in transit that are purchased FOB shipping point should be included in the purchaser's inventory. Goods in transit that are bought FOB destination should not be included.

Usually, the business has a purchase invoice, which lists the quantity of goods in transit and shows the FOB terms. Similarly, the business may have sold inventory that has not yet been shipped to the customer. If title has passed, these goods should be excluded from the seller's inventory, even though they may still be at the seller's place of business.

Another complication in counting inventory arises from consigned goods. In a **consignment** arrangement, the owner of the inventory (the consignor) transfers the goods to another business (the consignee). For a fee, the consignee sells the inventory on the owner's behalf. The consignee does *not* take title to the consigned goods and, therefore, should not include them in its own inventory. Consignments are common in retailing. Suppose Gillespie Hardware is the consignee for some Stanley tools in its stores. Should Gillespie include this consigned merchandise in its inventory count? No, because Gillespie does not own the goods. Instead, the Stanley wholesaler (the consignor) includes the consigned goods in his or her inventory. A rule of thumb is to include in inventory only what the business owns.

Determining the Unit Cost of Inventory   Inventories are normally accounted for at historical cost, as the *cost principle* requires. **Inventory cost** is the price the business pays to acquire the inventory, not the selling price of the goods. Suppose a business purchases inventory for $10 and offers it for sale at $15. The inventory cost is reported at $10, not $15. Inventory cost includes its invoice price, less any purchase discount, plus sales tax, tariffs, transportation charges, insurance while in transit, and all other costs incurred to make the goods ready for sale.

The inventory quantity multiplied by the unit cost equals the cost of inventory. Thirty tape recorders at a cost to the retailer of $100 each results in an inventory cost of $3,000.

Inventory Costing Methods _____

Determining the unit cost of inventory is easy when the unit cost remains constant during the period. However, the unit cost often changes. For example, during times of inflation, prices rise. The tape recorder model that cost the retailer $100 in January may cost $115 in June and $122 in October. Suppose the retailer sells 15 tape recorders in November. How many of them cost $100, $115 and $122? To compute the cost of goods sold and ending inventory

OBJECTIVE 1

Apply four inventory
costing methods

amounts, the accountant must have some means of assigning the business's cost to each item sold. The four costing methods that GAAP allows are

1. Specific unit cost
2. Average cost
3. First-in, first-out (FIFO) cost
4. Last-in, first-out (LIFO) cost

A company may use any of these methods.

Specific Unit Cost

Some businesses deal in inventory items that may be identified individually, like automobiles, jewels and real estate. These businesses usually cost their inventory at the **specific cost** of the particular unit. For instance, a Chevrolet dealer may have two vehicles in the showroom — a "stripped-down" model that cost $12,000 and a "loaded" model that cost $15,000. If the dealer sells the loaded model for $16,700, cost of goods sold is $15,000, the cost of the specific unit. The gross margin on this sale is $1,700 ($16,700 − $15,000). If the stripped-down auto is the only unit left in inventory at the end of the period, ending inventory is $12,000, the cost to the retailer of the specific unit on hand.

The specific unit cost method is also called the *specific identification* or *specific invoice cost* method. This method is not practical for inventory items that do not have unique characteristics, such as bushels of wheat, gallons of paint or boxes of laundry detergent.

Average Cost, FIFO Cost and LIFO Cost

The average cost, first-in, first-out (FIFO), and last-in, first-out (LIFO) methods are fundamentally different from the specific unit cost method. These methods do not assign to inventory the specific cost of particular units. Instead, they assume different flows of costs into and out of inventory.

Average Cost   The **average cost method** is based on the average cost of inventory during the period. Average cost is determined by dividing the cost of goods available for sale (beginning inventory plus purchases) by the number of units available. Ending inventory and cost of goods sold are computed by multiplying the number of units by average cost per unit. Assume that cost of goods available for sale is $90, and 60 units are available. Average cost is $1.50 ($90/60 = $1.50). Ending inventory of 20 units has an average cost of $30 (20 × $1.50 = $30). Cost of goods sold (40 units) is $60 (40 × $1.50). Panel A of Exhibit 9-3 gives the data in more detail. Panel B of the exhibit shows the average cost computations.

First-in, First-out (FIFO) Cost   Under the **first-in, first-out (FIFO) method**, the first units of inventory purchased are assumed to be the first units sold, and so their costs are the first to be included in the cost of goods sold, Therefore, costs used in computing the ending inventory may be different from the unit costs used in computing the cost of goods sold — hence the name first-in, first-out. Ending inventory is based on the costs of the most recent purchases. In our example, the FIFO cost of ending inventory is $36. Cost of goods sold is $54. Panel A of Exhibit 9-3 gives the data, and Panel B shows the FIFO computations.

EXHIBIT 9-3 *Inventory and Cost of Goods Sold under Average, FIFO and LIFO Inventory Costing Methods*

Panel A: Illustrative Data

Beginning inventory (10 units @ $1 per unit)		$ 10
Purchases		
No. 1 (25 units @ $1.40 per unit)	$ 35	
No. 2 (25 units @ $1.80 per unit)	45	
Total		80
Cost of goods available for sale		$ 90
Ending inventory (20 units @ $? per unit)		?
Cost of goods sold (40 units @ $? per unit)		$?

Panel B: Ending Inventory and Cost of Goods Sold

Average Cost Method

Cost of goods available for sale — see Panel A (60 units @ average cost of $1.50* per unit)		$ 90
Ending inventory (20 units @ $1.50 per unit)		$ 30
Cost of goods sold (40 units @ $1.50 per unit)		$ 60

* Cost of goods available for sale		$ 90
Number of units available for sale		÷ 60
Average cost per unit		$1.50

FIFO Cost Method

Cost of goods available for sale (60 units — see Panel A)		$ 90
Ending inventory (cost of the *last* 20 units available)		
20 units @ $1.80 per unit		36
Cost of goods sold (cost of the *first* 40 units available)		
10 units @ $1.00 per unit	$ 10	
25 units @ $1.40 per unit	35	
5 units @ $1.80 per unit	9	
Total		$ 54

LIFO Cost Method

Cost of goods available for sale (60 units — see Panel A)		$ 90
Ending inventory (cost of the *first* 20 units available)		
10 units @ $1.00 per unit	$ 10	
10 units @ $1.40 per unit	14	
Total		24
Cost of goods sold (cost of the *last* 40 units available)		
25 units @ $1.80 per unit	$ 45	
15 units @ $1.40 per unit	21	
Total		$ 66

Last-in, First-out (LIFO) Cost   The **last-in, first-out (LIFO) method** also depends on the costs of particular inventory purchases. LIFO is the opposite of FIFO. Under LIFO, the last costs into inventory are the first costs out to cost of goods sold. This leaves the oldest costs — those of beginning inventory and the earliest purchases of the period — in ending inventory. In our example, the LIFO cost of ending inventory is $24. Cost of goods sold is $66. Panel A of Exhibit 9-3 gives the data, and Panel B shows the LIFO computations.

<table>
<tr><td>**OBJECTIVE 2**

Describe the income effects of the inventory costing methods</td></tr>
</table>

Income Effects of FIFO, LIFO and Average Cost _____

In our discussion and examples, the cost of inventory rose over the accounting period. When prices change, different costing methods produce different cost of goods sold and ending inventory figures, as Exhibit 9-3 shows. When prices are increasing, FIFO ending inventory is *highest* because it is priced at the most recent costs, which are the highest. LIFO ending inventory is *lowest* because it is priced at the oldest costs, which are the lowest. *Average* cost avoids the extremes of FIFO and LIFO. When inventory costs are decreasing, FIFO ending inventory is lowest, and LIFO is highest.

Exhibit 9-4 summarizes the income effects of the three inventory methods using the data from Exhibit 9-3. Study the exhibit carefully, focusing on ending inventory, cost of goods sold and gross margin.

EXHIBIT 9-4   *Income Effects of FIFO, LIFO and Average Cost Inventory Methods*

	FIFO		**LIFO**		**Average**	
Sales revenue (assumed)		$100,000		$100,000		$100,000
Cost of goods sold						
Goods available for sale (assumed)...	$ 90,000		$ 90,000		$ 90,000	
Ending inventory.................	36,000		24,000		30,000	
Cost of goods sold		54,000		66,000		60,000
Gross margin		$ 46,000		$ 34,000		$ 40,000

Summary of Income Effects: When Inventory Costs Are Increasing

FIFO—Highest ending inventory
    Lowest cost of goods sold
    Highest gross margin
	LIFO—Lowest ending inventory
	    Highest cost of goods
	    sold
	    Lowest gross margin
		Average—Results fall between
		    the extremes of FIFO
		    and LIFO

Comparison of the Inventory Methods _____

We may ask two questions to judge the inventory costing methods. (1) How well does each method match inventory expense — the cost of goods sold — to sales revenue on the income statement? (2) Which method reports the most up-to-date inventory amount on the balance sheet? The average cost method produces amounts between the extremes of LIFO and FIFO. The specific unit cost method is used only for inventory made up of individually identifiable units. Therefore, we focus these questions on the differences between LIFO and FIFO.

LIFO better matches the current value of cost of goods sold with current revenue by assigning to this expense the most recent inventory costs. By contrast, FIFO matches the oldest inventory costs against the period's revenue — a poor matching of current expense with current revenue.

FIFO reports the most current inventory costs on the balance sheet. LIFO can result in absurd balance sheet valuations of inventories because the oldest prices are left in ending inventory.

FIFO is criticized because it overstates income by so-called inventory profit during periods of inflation. Briefly, inventory profit is the difference between gross margin figured on the FIFO basis and gross margin figured on the LIFO basis. Exhibit 9-4 illustrates inventory profit. The $12,000 difference between FIFO and LIFO gross margins ($46,000 − $34,000 = $12,000) results from the difference in cost of goods sold and in ending inventory. This $12,000 amount is called FIFO inventory profit, phantom profit or illusory profit. Why? Because to stay in business the company must replace the inventory it has sold. The replacement cost of the merchandise is essentially the same as the cost of goods sold under LIFO ($66,000), not the FIFO amount ($54,000).

LIFO is criticized because it allows managers to manipulate net income. Assume inventory prices are rising rapidly, and a company wants to show less income for the year. Managers can buy a large amount of inventory near the end of the year. Under LIFO these high inventory costs immediately become expense — as cost of goods sold. As a result, the income statement reports a lower net income. Conversely, if the business is having a bad year, management may wish to increase reported income. To do so, managers can delay a large purchase of high-cost inventory until the next period. This inventory is not expensed as cost of good sold in the current year. Thus management avoids decreasing the current year's reported income.

LIFO is very popular in the United States where its use is permitted for tax purposes. As you can see in Exhibit 9-4, in a period of rising prices (such as we have had since World War II), LIFO leads to the lowest income of the three methods and, in the United States, to the lowest taxes.

LIFO is not allowed for income tax purposes in Canada, but a company can use it for accounting purposes. Probably that is why in Canada, almost no companies use LIFO (4 percent); here most use FIFO (46 percent), while a few use average cost (35 percent).[1]

A company may want to report the highest income, and FIFO meets this need when prices are rising. When prices are falling, LIFO reports the highest income.

Which inventory method is best? There is no single answer to this question. Different companies have different motives for the inventory method they choose. National Sea Products and Chrysler Canada use FIFO. Imasco, the tobacco, restaurant and drug store conglomerate, uses average cost for tobacco products and FIFO for inventory in its restaurants and drug stores. Lake Ontario Cement uses average cost for all inventory. Arrowhead Metals Ltd., a division of AHL Group Limited, is one of the few companies that uses LIFO. The companies disclose the method used under the heading "Significant Accounting Policies" (National Sea Products) or "Summary of Accounting Policies" (Imasco) in the notes to the financial statements. National Sea Products' specific disclosure is:

INVENTORY VALUATION

Inventories are valued . . . with cost determined principally on a FIFO (first-in, first-out) basis.

Imasco's disclosure is:

INVENTORIES

. . . Cost is determined substantially as follows:
Tobacco: average cost
Drug Store: first-in, first-out
Restaurant: first-in, first-out

> **OBJECTIVE 3**
> Read and understand actual company inventory disclosures

---

[1] *Financial Reporting in Canada, 1989*, Toronto: *CICA*, 1990, p. 103.

Consistency Principle

The **consistency principle** states that businesses must use the same accounting methods and procedures from period to period. Consistency makes it possible to compare a company's financial statements from one period to the next.

Suppose you are analysing a company's net income pattern. The company has switched from LIFO to FIFO. Its net income has increased dramatically, but only as a result of the change in inventory method. If you did not know of the change, you might believe that the company's increased income arose from improved operations, which is not the case.

The consistency principle does not require that all companies within an industry use the same accounting method. Nor does it mean that a company may *never* change its own accounting method. However, a company making an accounting change must disclose the effect of the change on net income. Also, auditors mention their clients' accounting changes in the audit report on a company's financial statements.

Summary Problem for Your Review

Suppose a Northern Telecom division that handles telephone components has these inventory records for January 19X6:

Date	Item	Quantity	Unit Co.t	Sale Price
Jan. 1	Beginning inventory	100 units	$ 8	$—
6	Purchase	60 units	9	—
13	Sale	70 units	—	20
21	Purchase	150 units	9	—
24	Sale	210 units	—	22
27	Purchase	90 units	10	—
30	Sale	30 units	—	25

Company accounting records reveal that related operating expense for January was $1,900.

Required

1. Prepare the January income statement, using the following format. (Round figures to whole dollar amounts.)

Northern Telecom Ltd.
Partial Income Statement
for the month ended January 31, 19X6

	LIFO	FIFO	Average
Sales revenue............................	—	—	—
Cost of goods sold			
Beginning inventory	—	—	—
Purchases	—	—	—
Cost of goods available for sale	—	—	—
Ending inventory	—	—	—
Cost of goods sold	—	—	—
Gross margin	—	—	—
Operating expenses	—	—	—
Operating income.........................	—	—	—

2. Suppose you are the financial vice-president of Northern Telecom. Which inventory method would you use if your motive is to
   a. Minimize income taxes?
   b. Report the highest operating income?
   c. Report operating income between the extremes of FIFO and LIFO?
   d. Report inventory at the most current cost?
   e. Attain the best matching of current expense with current revenue?

   State the reason for each of your answers.

SOLUTION TO REVIEW PROBLEM

Requirement 1

Northern Telecom Ltd.
Partial Income Statement
for the month ended January 31, 19X6

	LIFO		FIFO		Average	
Sales revenue.................		$6,770		$6,770		$6,770
Cost of goods sold						
Beginning inventory	$ 800		$ 800		$ 800	
Purchases	2,790		2,790		2,790	
Cost of goods available						
for sale	3,590		3,590		3,590	
Ending inventory	720		900		808	
Cost of goods sold		2,870		2,690		2,782
Gross margin		3,900		4,080		3,988
Operating expenses		1,900		1,900		1,900
Operating income.............		$2,000		$2,180		$2,088

Computations

Sales revenue	$(70 \times \$20) + (210 \times \$22) + (30 \times \$25) = \$6,770$
Beginning inventory	$100 \times \$8 = \$800$
Purchases	$(60 \times \$9) + (150 \times \$9) + (90 \times \$10) = \$2,790$
Ending inventory: LIFO	$90^* \times \$8 = \$720$
FIFO	$90 \times \$10 = \$900$
Average	$90 \times \$8.75^{**} = \$808$ (rounded from $807.75)

* Number of units in ending inventory $= 100 + 60 - 70 + 150 - 210 + 90 - 30 = 90$
** $3,590/400$ units $= \$8.975$ per unit

Requirement 2

a. Use *average cost* to minimize income taxes. Operating income under LIFO is lowest when inventory unit costs are increasing, as they are in this case (from $8 to $10). Remember, LIFO cannot be used for income tax purposes. Average cost produces the next lowest income and, since it can be used for tax purposes, the lowest income taxes.

b. Use FIFO to report the highest operating income. Income under FIFO is highest when inventory unit costs are increasing, as in this situation.

c. Use average cost to report an operating income amount between the LIFO and FIFO extremes. This is true in this problem situation and in others whether inventory unit costs are increasing or decreasing.

d. Use FIFO to report inventory at the most current cost. The oldest inventory costs are expensed as cost of goods sold, leaving in ending inventory the most recent (most current) costs of the period.

e. Use LIFO to attain the best matching of current expense with current revenue. The most recent (most current) inventory costs are expensed as cost of goods sold.

Accounting Conservatism

Conservatism in accounting means presenting the gloomiest possible figures on the financial statements. What advantage does conservatism give a business? Management often looks on the brighter side of operations and may overstate a company's income and asset values. Many accountants regard conservatism as a counterbalance to management's optimistic tendencies. The goal is for financial statements to present realistic figures.

Conservatism appears in accounting guidelines like "anticipate no gains, but provide for all probable losses" and "if in doubt, record an asset at the lowest reasonable amount and a liability at the highest reasonable amount."

Accountants generally regard the historical cost of acquiring an asset as its maximum value. Even if the current market value of the asset increases above its cost, businesses do *not* write up (that is, increase) the asset's accounting value. Assume that a company purchased land for $100,000, and its value increased to $300,000. Accounting conservatism dictates that the historical cost $100,000 be maintained as the accounting value of the land.

Conservatism also directs accountants to decrease the accounting value of an asset if it appears unrealistically high—even if no transaction occurs. Assume that a company paid $35,000 for inventory that has become obsolete, and its current value is only $12,000. Conservatism dictates that the inventory be written down (that is, decreased) to $12,000. A write-down entry debits an expense account and credits the asset account for the amount of the decrease in value.

Lower-of-Cost-or-Market Rule

The **lower-of-cost-or-market rule** (abbreviated as LCM) shows accounting conservatism in action. LCM requires that an asset be reported at the lower of its historical cost or its market value. Applied to inventories, *market value* may mean *current replacement cost* (that is, how much the business would have to pay in the market on that day to purchase the same amount of inventory on hand), or it may mean *net realizable value* (that is, the gross amount the business could get if it sold the inventory less the costs of selling it). If the replacement cost or net realizable value of inventory falls below its historical cost, the business must write down the value of its goods. The business reports ending inventory at its LCM value on the balance sheet.

Suppose a business paid $3,000 for inventory on September 26. By December 31, its value has fallen. The inventory can now be replaced for $2,200. Market value, defined in this instance as current replacement cost, is below cost, and the December 31 balance sheet reports this inventory at its LCM value of $2,200. Usually, the market value of inventory is higher than historical cost, so that inventory's LCM value is cost for most companies. Exhibit 9-5 presents the effects of LCM on the income statement and the balance sheet. The point of the exhibit is to show that the lower of (1) cost or (2) market value (replacement cost) is the relevant amount for valuing inventory on the income statement and the balance sheet. Companies are not required to show both cost and market value amounts. However, they may report the higher amount in parentheses, as shown on the balance sheet in the exhibit.

EXHIBIT 9-5   *Lower-of-Cost-or-Market (LCM) Effects*

> **OBJECTIVE 4**
> Apply the lower-of-cost-or-market rule to inventory

Income Statement

Sales revenue		$20,000
Cost of goods sold		
Beginning inventory (LCM = Cost)	$ 2,800	
Purchases..	11,000	
Cost of goods available for sale	13,800	
Ending inventory		
Cost = $3,000		
Replacement cost (market value) = $2,200		
LCM = Market	2,200	
Cost of goods sold		11,600
Gross margin.....................................		$ 8,400

Balance Sheet

Current assets		
Cash	$ XXX	
Short-term investments	XXX	
Accounts reveivable............................	XXX	
Inventories, at LCM (Cost, $3,000)	2,200	
Prepaid investments	XXX	
Total current assets	$X,XXX	

LCM states that of the $3,000 cost of ending inventory in Exhibit 9-5, $800 is considered to have expired even though the inventory was not sold during the period. Its replacement cost is only $2,200, and that amount is carried forward to the next period as the cost of beginning inventory. Suppose during the next period the replacement cost of this inventory increases to $2,500. Accounting conservatism states that it would not be appropriate to write up the book value of inventory. The LCM value of inventory ($2,200 in this case) is used as its cost in future LCM determinations.

Examine the income statement effect of LCM in Exhibit 9-5. What expense absorbs the impact of the $800 inventory write down? *Cost of goods sold* is increased by $800 because ending inventory is $800 less at LCM ($2,200) than it would have been at cost ($3,000).

	Ending Inventory at		
	Cost	LCM	
Cost of goods available for sale	$13,800	$13,800	
Ending inventory			
Cost	3,000		$800 Lower at LCM
Replacement cost (market value)...		2,200	
Cost of goods sold	$10,800	$11,600	$800 Higher at LCM

Exhibit 9-5 also reports the application of LCM for inventories in the body of the balance sheet. Companies often *disclose* LCM in notes to their financial statements, as shown below for Spar Aerospace Limited:

FROM NOTE 1

(c) Inventories
Inventories of raw materials and finished goods are valued at the lower of cost ... and market value determined as the lesser of replacement cost or net realizable value.

Federal Pioneer Limited, a manufacturing company, states the following in the notes to the financial statements:

FROM NOTE 2—SIGNIFICANT ACCOUNTING POLICIES

Inventories
Raw material inventories are valued at lower of cost and replacement cost while work in process and finished goods are valued at the lower of cost and net realizable value ...

Effect of Inventory Errors

Businesses determine inventory amounts at the end of the period. In the process of counting the items, applying unit costs and computing amounts, errors may arise. As the period 1 segment of Exhibit 9-6 shows, an error in the ending inventory amount creates errors in the cost of goods sold and gross margin amounts.

Recall that one period's ending inventory is the next period's beginning inventory. Thus the error in ending inventory carries over into the next period. Note the highlighted amounts in Exhibit 9-6.

Because the same ending inventory figure that is subtracted from cost of goods available for sale in one period is added to cost of goods sold in the next period, the error's effect cancels out. The overstatement of cost of goods sold

EXHIBIT 9-6 *Effects of Inventory Errors*

	Period 1 Ending Inventory Overstated by $5,000		Period 2 Beginning Inventory Overstated by $5,000		Period 3 Correct	
Sales revenue		$100,000		$100,000		$100,000
Cost of goods sold						
Beginning inventory	$10,000		$15,000		$10,000	
Net purchases.	50,000		50,000		50,000	
Cost of goods available for sale	60,000		65,000		60,000	
Ending inventory.	15,000		10,000		10,000	
Cost of goods sold		45,000		55,000		50,000
Gross margin.		$ 55,000		$ 45,000		$ 50,000
			$100,000			

The authors thank Carl High for this example.

in period 2 counterbalances the understatement in cost of goods sold in period 1. Thus the total gross margin amount for the two periods is the correct $100,000 figure, whether or not an error entered into the computation.

However, inventory errors should not be dismissed lightly. Suppose you are analysing trends in the business's operations. The correct figures show a $5,000 increase in gross margin from period 2 to period 3, but the incorrect figures for period 2 indicate a misleadingly low gross margin. To provide accurate information for decision-making, all inventory errors should be corrected.

OBJECTIVE 5
Explain why inventory errors counterbalance

Methods of Estimating Inventory

OBJECTIVE 6
Estimate inventory by two methods

Often a business must *estimate* the value of its inventory. Because of cost and inconvenience, few companies physically count their inventories at the end of each month, Yet they may need monthly financial statements. A fire or a flood may destroy inventory, and to file an insurance claim, the business must estimate the value of its loss. In both cases, the business needs to know the value of ending inventory without being able to count it. Two methods for estimating ending inventory are the *gross margin method* (or *gross profit method*) and the *retail method*. These methods are widely used in practice.

Gross Margin (Gross Profit) Method

The **gross margin method** is a way of estimating inventory based on the familiar cost of goods sold model:

Beginning inventory
+ Net purchases (purchases minus purchase returns and purchase discounts)
= Cost of goods available for sale
− Ending inventory
= Cost of goods sold

Rearranging *ending inventory* and *cost of goods sold*, the model becomes useful for estimating ending inventory:

> **Beginning inventory**
> **+ Net purchases**
> ─────────────────────
> **= Cost of goods available for sale**
> **− Cost of goods sold**
> ─────────────────────
> **= Ending inventory**

Suppose a fire destroys your business's inventory. To collect insurance, you must estimate the cost of the ending inventory. If the fire did not also destroy your accounting records, beginning inventory and net purchases amounts may be taken directly from the accounting records. The Sales Revenue, Sales Returns and Sales Discounts accounts indicate net sales up to the date of the fire. Using the entity's normal *gross margin rate* (that is, gross margin divided by net sales revenue), you can estimate cost of goods sold. The last step is to subtract cost of goods sold from goods available to estimate ending inventory. Exhibit 9-7 illustrates the gross margin method.

EXHIBIT 9-7   *Gross Margin Method of Estimating Inventory (amounts assumed)*

Beginning inventory		$14,000
Net purchases		66,000
Cost of goods available for sale		80,000
Cost of goods sold		
Net sales revenue	$100,000	
Less estimated gross margin of 40%	40,000	
Estimated cost of goods sold		60,000
Estimated cost of *ending inventory*		$20,000

Accountants, managers and auditors use the gross margin method to test the overall reasonableness of an ending inventory amount that has been determined by a physical count for all types of businesses. This method helps detect large errors.

Retail Method

Retail establishments (department stores, drug stores, hardware stores, and so on) use the **retail method** to estimate their inventory cost. The retail method, like the gross margin method, is based on the cost of goods sold model. However, the retail method requires that the business record inventory purchases both at *cost*, as shown in the purchase records, and at *retail* (selling) price, as shown on the price tags. This is not a burden because price tags show the retail price of inventory, and most retailers set their retail prices by adding standard markups to their cost. For example, a department store may pay $6 for a man's belt, mark it up $4, and price the belt at $10 retail. In the retail method, the seller's inventory cost is determined by working backward from its retail value. Exhibit 9-8 illustrates the process.

In Exhibit 9-8 the accounting records show the goods available for sale at cost ($168,000) and at retail ($280,000). The cost ratio is .60 ($168,000/$280,000).

EXHIBIT 9-8 *Retail Method of Estimating Inventory (amounts assumed)*

	Cost	Retail
Beginning inventory	$ 24,000	$ 40,000
Net purchases	144,000	240,000
Goods available for sale..........................	$168,000	$280,000
Cost ratio: $168,000/$280,000 = .60		
Less: Net sales revenue (which is stated at retail)		(230,000)
Ending inventory, at retail		$ 50,000
Ending inventory, at cost ($50,000 × .60)	$ 30,000	

For simplicity, we round all such percentages to two decimal places in this chapter. Subtracting *net sales revenue* (a retail amount) from *goods available for sale at retail* yields *ending inventory at retail* ($50,000). The business multiplies *ending inventory at retail* by the cost ratio to figure *ending inventory at cost* ($30,000).

Suppose the retailer has four categories of inventory, each with a different cost ratio. How would the business use the retail method to estimate the overall cost of the ending inventory? Apply the retail method separately to each category of inventory, using its specific cost ratio; then add the costs of the four categories to determine the overall cost of inventory.

Even though the retail method is an estimation technique, some retailers use it to compute inventory value for their financial statements. They make physical counts of inventory at times other than the end of the year. For example, Silcorp Limited, whose operations include several convenience store chains, reports in the notes to the financial statements that "Cost is determined by the retail method . . . for convenience stores' inventories. . . . "

Periodic and Perpetual Inventory Systems _____

Different businesses have different inventory information needs. We now look at the two inventory systems: the *periodic system* and the *perpetual system.*

Periodic Inventory System   In the **periodic inventory system**, the business does not keep a continuous record of the inventory on hand. Instead, at the end of the period, the business makes a physical count of the on-hand inventory and applies the appropriate unit costs to determine the cost of ending inventory. The business makes the standard end-of-period inventory entries, as discussed in Chapter 5 and shown in the example that follows. This system is also called the *physical system* because it relies on the actual physical count of inventory. The periodic system is used to account for inventory items that have a low unit cost. Low-cost items may not be valuable enough to warrant the cost of keeping a running record of the inventory on hand.

Entries under the Periodic System   In the periodic system, the business records purchases of inventory in the Purchases account (an expense account). At the end of the period, the business removes the beginning balance from the

Inventory account and enters the ending balance, as determined by the physical count. Assume the following data for a K-Mart store's April transactions:

OBJECTIVE 7

Account for inventory by the periodic and perpetual systems

Beginning inventory	$ 80,000
Ending inventory	102,000
Credit purchases (net of discounts and returns)	600,000
Credit and cash sales (net of discounts and returns)	900,000

Summary entries for April

To record credit purchases

Purchases	600,000	
Accounts Payable		600,000

To record credit sales

Accounts Receivable/Cash	900,000	
Sales Revenue		900,000

Inventory entries at the end of the period

Income Summary	80,000	
Inventory (beginning balance)		80,000
Inventory (ending balance)	102,000	
Income Summary		102,000

Reporting on the financial statements

Balance sheet at April 30

Inventory	$102,000

Income statement for April

Sales revenue		$900,000
Cost of goods sold		
Begining inventory	$ 80,000	
Purchases	600,000	
Cost of goods available	680,000	
Ending inventory	102,000	
Cost of goods sold		$578,000
Gross margin		$322,000

Perpetual Inventory System   In the **perpetual inventory system,** the business keeps a continuous record for each inventory item. The records thus show the inventory on hand at all times. Perpetual records are useful in preparing monthly, quarterly or other interim financial statements. The business can determine the cost of ending inventory and the cost of goods sold directly from the accounts without having to physically count the merchandise.

The perpetual system offers a higher degree of control over inventory than the periodic system does because information is always up to date. Consequently businesses use the perpetual system for high-unit-cost inventories such as gemstones and automobiles. Nevertheless, companies physically count their inventory at least once each year to check the accuracy of their perpetual records.

Perpetual inventory records can be computer listings of inventory items or inventory cards like the Infotech World record shown in Exhibit 9-9. The accountant adds information to the computer list or the card on a daily basis. A running balance conveniently shows the latest inventory value. The perpetual record serves as a subsidiary record to the inventory account in the general ledger.

EXHIBIT 9-9   *Perpetual Inventory Card*

Item: Home Computer Model RK-42

Date	Received Qty.	Received Unit Cost	Received Total	Sold Qty.	Sold Unit Cost	Sold Total	Balance Qty.	Balance Unit Cost	Balance Total
Nov. 1							14	$300	$4,200
5				4	$300	$1,200	10	300	3,000
7				9	300	2,700	1	300	300
12	5	$320	$1,600				1	300	300
							5	320	1,600
26	7	$330	2,310				1	300	300
							5	320	1,600
							7	330	2,310
30				1	300	300	1	320	320
				4	320	1,280	7	330	2,310
Totals	12	—	$3,910	18	—	$5,480	8	—	$2,630

The perpetual inventory record indicates that the business uses the FIFO basis, as shown by the November 30 sale. The cost of the first unit sold is the oldest unit cost on hand. Perpetual records may also be kept on the LIFO basis or the average basis. Perpetual inventory records provide information such as the following:

1. When customers inquire about how soon they can get a home computer, the salesperson can answer the question after referring to the perpetual inventory record. On November 8 the salesperson would reply that the company's stock is low, and the customer may have to wait a few days. On November 27 the salesperson could offer immediate delivery.

2. The perpetual records alert the business to reorder when inventory becomes low. On November 8 the company would be wise to purchase inventory. Sales might be lost if the business could not promise immediate delivery.

3. At November 30 the company prepares monthly financial statements. The perpetual inventory records show the company's ending inventory of home computers at $2,630, and its cost of goods sold for this product at $5,480. No physical count is necessary at this time. However, a physical inventory is needed once a year to verify the accuracy of the records.

Entries under the Perpetual System   In the perpetual system, the business records purchases of inventory by debiting the Inventory account. When the business makes a sale, two entries are necessary. The company records the sale in the usual manner—debits Cash or Accounts Receivable and credits Sales Revenue. The company also debits Cost of Goods Sold and credits Inventory. The debit to Inventory (for purchases) and the credit to Inventory (for sales) serve to keep an up-to-date record of inventory on hand. Therefore, no end-of-period adjusting entries are needed. The Inventory account already carries the correct ending balance.

In the perpetual system, Cost of Goods Sold is an account in the general ledger. By contrast, in the periodic system, cost of goods sold is simply a total on the income statement.

To illustrate the entries under the perpetual system, let us use the same data we used in discussing the periodic system, which follow:

Ending inventory	$102,000
Credit purchases (net of discounts and returns)	600,000
Credit and cash sales (net of discounts and returns)	900,000
Cost of goods sold	578,000

Summary entries for April

To record credit purchases

Inventory	600,000	
Accounts Payable		600,000

To record credit sales

Accounts Receivable/Cash	900,000	
Sales revenue		900,000
Cost of Goods Sold	578,000	
Inventory		578,000

Reporting on the financial statements

Balance sheet at April 30

Inventory	$102,000

Income statement for April

Sales revenue	$900,000
Cost of goods sold	578,000
Gross margin	$322,000

You should compare the entries and financial statement presentations under the *periodic* and *perpetual* systems. Note that the entries to record purchases and sales differ under the two systems, but that the financial statement amounts are the same.

Internal Control over Inventory

Internal control over inventory is important because inventory is the lifeblood of a merchandiser. Successful companies take great care to protect their inventory. Elements of good internal control over inventory include

1. Physically counting inventory at least once each year no matter which system is used.
2. Maintaining efficient purchasing, receiving and shipping procedures.
3. Storing inventory to protect it against theft, damage and decay.
4. Limiting access to inventory to personnel who do *not* have access to the accounting records.
5. Keeping perpetual inventory records for high-unit-cost merchandise.
6. Purchasing inventory in economical quantities.
7. Keeping enough inventory on hand to prevent shortages which lead to lost sales.
8. Not keeping too large an inventory stockpiled, thus avoiding the expense of tying up money in unneeded items.

The annual physical count of inventory (Item 1) is necessary because the only way to be certain of the amount of inventory on hand is to count it. Errors arise in the best accounting systems, and the count is needed to establish the correct value of the inventory. When an error is detected, the records are brought into agreement with the physical count.

Keeping inventory handlers away from the accounting records (Item 4) is an essential separation of duties, discussed in Chapter 7. An employee with access to inventory and the accounting records can steal the goods and make an entry to conceal the theft. For example, he or she could increase the amount of an inventory write-down to make it appear that goods decreased in value when in fact they were stolen.

Computerized Inventory Records _____

Computer systems have revolutionized accounting for inventory. They can provide up-to-the-minute inventory data useful for managing the business. They help cut accounting cost by processing large numbers of transactions without computational error. Computer systems also enhance internal control. Computerized inventory systems also increase efficiency because managers always know the quantity and cost of inventory on hand. They can make better decisions about quantities to buy, prices to pay for the inventory, prices to charge customers and sale terms to offer. Knowing the quantity on hand helps safeguard the inventory.

Computer inventory systems vary considerably. At one extreme are complex systems used by huge retailers like Eaton's, Woodward's and Canadian Tire. Purchases of inventory are recorded in perpetual records stored in a central computer. The inventory tags are coded electronically for updating the perpetual records when a sale is recorded on the cash register. Have you noticed sales clerks passing the inventory ticket over a particular area of the checkout counter? A sensing device in the counter decodes the stock number, quantity, cost and sale price of the item sold. In other systems, the sales clerk passes an electronic device over the inventory tag. The computer records the sale and updates the inventory records. In effect, a journal entry is recorded for each sale, a procedure that is not economical without a computer.

Small companies also use minicomputers and microcomputers to keep perpetual inventory records. These systems may be similar to the systems used by large companies. In less sophisticated systems, a company may have sales clerks write inventory stock numbers on sales slips. The stock number identifies the particular item of inventory such as men's shirts or children's shoes. The business may accumulate all sales slips for the week. If the company has its own computer system, an employee may type the sales information into the computer and store the perpetual records on a magnetic disk. To learn the quantity, cost or other characteristic of a particular item of inventory, a manager can view the inventory record on the computer monitor. For broader-based decisions affecting the entire inventory, managers use printouts of all items in stock. Many small businesses hire outside computer service centers to do much of the accounting for inventory. Regardless of the arrangement, managers get periodic printouts showing inventory data needed for managing the business. Manual reporting of this information is more time-consuming and expensive.

Summary Problems for Your Review

Problem 1

Centronics Data Computer Ltd. reported a net loss for the year. In its financial statements, the company noted:

Balance Sheet

Current assets
  Inventories (notes 1C and 2)..................... $48,051,000

Note 1C: Inventories are stated at the lower of cost or market. Cost is determined on a first-in, first-out (FIFO) basis.

Note 2: Declining ... market conditions during [the] fiscal [year] adversely affected anticipated sales of the Company's older printer products; ... Accordingly, the statement of loss ... includes a [debit] of $9,600,000.

Required

1. At which amount did Centronics report its inventory, cost or market value? How can you tell?
2. If the reported inventory of $48,051,000 represents market value, what was the cost of the inventory?

Problem 2

Beaver Building Supply Limited reported using the FIFO inventory method. Its inventory amount was $176 million.

Required

1. Suppose that during the period covered by this report, the company made an error that understated its inventory by $15 million. What effect would this error have on *cost of goods sold* and *gross margin* of the period? On *cost of goods sold* and *gross margin* of the following period? On *total gross margin* of both periods combined?
2. When Beaver Building Supply reported the above amount for inventory, prices were rising. Would FIFO or LIFO have shown a higher gross margin? Why?

SOLUTIONS TO REVIEW PROBLEMS

Problem 1

1. Centronics reported its inventory at *market value*, as indicated by (a) their valuing inventories at LCM and (b) the declining market conditions that caused the company to "include a [debit] of $9,600,000" in "the statement of loss." The company debited the $9,600,000 to a loss account or to cost of goods sold. The credit side of the entry was to Inventory—for a write-down to market value.
2. The cost of inventory before the write-down was $57,651,000 ($48,051,000 + $9,600,000). The $48,051,000 market value is what is left of

the original cost. Thus the amount to be carried forward to future periods is $48,051,000.

Problem 2

1. Understating ending inventory by $15 million has the following effects on *cost of goods sold* and *gross margin*:

	Cost of Goods Sold	Gross Margin
Period during which error was made	OVERSTATED by $15 million	UNDERSTATED by $15 million
Following period	UNDERSTATED by $15 million	OVERSTATED by $15 million
Combined total	CORRECTLY STATED	CORRECTLY STATED

2. When prices are rising, FIFO results in higher gross margin than LIFO. FIFO matches against sales revenue the lower inventory costs of beginning inventory and purchases made during the early part of the period.

Summary

Accounting for inventory plays an important part in merchandisers' accounting systems because selling inventory is the heart of their business. Inventory is generally the largest current asset on their balance sheet, and inventory expense—called cost of goods sold—is usually the largest expense on the income statement.

Businesses multiply the quantity of inventory items by their unit cost to determine inventory cost. Inventory costing methods are *specific unit cost; average cost; first-in, first-out (FIFO) cost;* and *last-in, first-out (LIFO) cost.* Businesses that sell individually identifiable items like automobiles and jewels use the specific unit cost method. Most other companies use the other methods.

FIFO reports ending inventory at the most current cost. LIFO reports cost of goods sold at the most current cost. When inventory costs increase, LIFO produces the highest cost of goods sold and the lowest income. FIFO results in the highest income. The average cost method avoids the extremes of FIFO and LIFO.

The *consistency principle* demands that a business stick with the inventory method it chooses. If a change in inventory method is warranted, the company must report the effect of the change on income. The *lower-of-cost-or-market rule,* an example of accounting *conservatism,* requires that businesses report inventory on the balance sheet at the lower of its cost or market, which may be the current replacement value or net realizable value.

The *gross profit method* and *retail method* are two techniques for estimating the cost of inventory. These methods come in handy for preparing interim financial statements and for estimating the cost of inventory destroyed by fire and other casualties.

Merchandisers with high-price-tag items generally use the *perpetual inventory system,* which features a running inventory balance. Merchandisers handling low-price-tag items usually use the *periodic system.* A physical count of inventory is needed in both systems for control purposes.

Self-Study Questions

Test your understanding of the chapter by marking the correct answer to each of the following questions:

1. Which of the following items is the greatest in dollar amount? *(p. 366)*
   a. Beginning inventory
   b. Purchases
   c. Cost of goods available for sale
   d. Ending inventory
   e. Cost of goods sold

2. Sound Warehouse counts 15,000 stereo albums, including 1,000 albums held on consignment, in its Halifax store. The business has purchased an additional 2,000 units on FOB destination terms. These goods are still in transit. Each album cost $3.40. The cost of the inventory to report on the balance sheet is *(p. 367)*
   a. $47,600
   b. $51,000
   c. $54,400
   d. $57,800

3. The inventory costing method that best matches current expense with current revenues is *(p. 370)*
   a. Specific unit cost
   b. Average cost
   c. FIFO
   d. LIFO
   e. FIFO or LIFO, depending on whether inventory costs are increasing or decreasing

4. The consistency principle has the most direct impact on *(p. 372)*
   a. Whether to include or exclude an item in inventory
   b. Whether to change from one inventory method or another
   c. Whether to write inventory down to a market value below cost
   d. Whether to use the periodic or the perpetual inventory system

5. Application of the lower-of-cost-or-market rule often results in *(p. 375)*
   a. Higher ending inventory
   b. Lower ending inventory
   c. A counterbalancing error
   d. A change from one inventory method to another

6. An error understated ending inventory of 19X7. This error will *(pp. 376, 377)*
   a. Overstate 19X7 cost of sales
   b. Understate 19X8 cost of sales
   c. Not affect owner's equity at the end of 19X8
   d. All of the above

7. Beginning inventory was $35,000, purchases were $146,000 and sales totaled $240,000. With a normal gross margin rate of 35 percent, how much is ending inventory? *(pp. 377, 378)*
   a. $25,000
   b. $35,000
   c. $97,000
   d. $181,000

8. Beginning inventory was $20,000 at cost and $40,000 at retail. Purchases were $120,000 at cost and $210,000 at retail. Sales were $200,000. How much is ending inventory at cost? *(pp. 378, 379)*
   a. $22,000
   b. $26,000
   c. $28,000
   d. $50,000

9. The year-end entry to close beginning inventory in a perpetual inventory system is *(pp. 381, 382)*
   a. Income Summary XXX
       Inventory XXX
   b. Inventory XXX
       Income Summary XXX
   c. Either of the above, depending on whether inventory increased or decreased during the period
   d. Not needed

10. Which of the following statements is true? *(pp. 382, 383)*
    a. Separation of duties is not an important element of internal control for inventories.
    b. The perpetual system is used primarily for low-unit-cost inventory.

    c. An annual physical count of inventory is needed regardless of the type of inventory system used.

    d. All the above are true.

Answers to the self-study questions are at the end of the chapter.

Accounting Vocabulary

average cost method *(p. 368)*
beginning inventory *(p. 365)*
conservatism *(p. 374)*
consignment *(p. 367)*
consistency principle *(p. 372)*
ending inventory *(p. 366)*
first-in, first-out (FIFO) method
    (p. 368)
FOB destination *(p. 367)*

FOB shipping point *(p. 367)*
goods available for sale
    (p. 365)
gross margin (gross profit)
    method *(p. 377)*
inventory cost *(p. 367)*
last-in, first-out (LIFO) method
    (p. 369)

lower-of-cost-or-market (LCM)
    rule *(p. 375)*
periodic inventory system
    (p. 379)
perpetual inventory system
    (p. 380)
retail method *(p. 378)*
specific cost method *(p. 368)*

Assignment Material _____

Questions

1.   Why is merchandise inventory so important to a retailer or wholesaler?

2.   If beginning inventory is $10,000, purchases total $85,000 and ending inventory is $12,700, how much is cost of goods sold?

3.   If beginning inventory is $32,000, purchases total $119,000 and cost of goods sold is $127,000, how much is ending inventory?

4.   What role does the cost principle play in accounting for inventory?

5.   What two items determine the cost of ending inventory?

6.   Briefly describe the four generally accepted inventory cost methods. During a period of rising prices, which method produces the highest reported income? Which produces the lowest reported income?

7.   Which inventory costing method produces the ending inventory valued at the most current cost? Which method produces the cost-of-goods-sold amount valued at the most current cost?

8.   Why is LIFO the most popular method in the United States? Why is it so little used in Canada? Do these reasons accord with the notion that the inventory costing method should produce the most accurate data on the income statement?

9.   Which inventory costing method produces the most accurate data on the balance sheet? Why?

10. What is inventory profit? Which inventory costing method indicates it?

11. How does the consistency principle affect accounting for inventory?

12. Briefly describe the influence that the concept of conservatism has on accounting for inventory.

13. Manley Company's inventory has a cost of $48,000 at the end of the year, and the current replacement cost of the inventory is $51,000. At which amount should the company report the inventory on its balance sheet? Suppose the current replacement cost of the inventory is $45,000 instead of $51,000. At which amount should Manley report the inventory? What rule governs your answers to these questions?

14. Gabriel Company accidentally overstated its ending inventory by $10,000 at the end of period 1. Is gross margin of period 1 overstated or understated? Is gross margin of period 2 overstated, understated, or unaffected by the period 1 error?

Is total gross margin for the two periods overstated, understated or correct? Give the reason for your answer.

15. The market referred to in the lower-of-cost-or-market rule may have two meanings. Describe each of them.

16. Identify two methods of estimating inventory amounts. What familiar model underlies both estimation methods?

17. A fire destroyed the inventory of Olivera Company, but the accounting records were saved. The beginning inventory was $22,000, purchases for the period were $71,000, and sales were $141,000. Olivera's customary gross margin is 45 percent of sales. Use the gross margin method to estimate the cost of the inventory destroyed by the fire.

18. Suppose your company deals in expensive jewelry. Which inventory system should you use to achieve good internal control over the inventory? If your business is a hardware store that sells low-cost goods, what inventory system would you be likely to use? Why would you choose this system?

19. Identify the accounts debited and credited in the standard purchase and sale entries under (a) the periodic inventory system and (b) the perpetual inventory system.

20. What is the role of the physical count of inventory in (a) the periodic inventory system and (b) the perpetual inventory system?

21. A company that sells inventory of low unit cost needs no internal controls over the goods. Any inventory loss would probably be small. — True or false?

Exercises

Exercise 9-1 *Computing ending inventory by four methods*

The inventory records for stereo tuner/amplifiers indicate the following at October 31:

Oct.	1	Beginning inventory	10 units @ $130
	8	Purchase	4 units @ 140
	15	Purchase	11 units @ 150
	26	Purchase	5 units @ 156

The physical count of inventory at October 31 indicates that seven units are on hand, and the company owns them. Compute ending inventory and cost of goods sold using each of the following methods:

1. Specific unit cost, assuming five $150 units and two $130 units are on hand
2. Average cost
3. First in, first out
4. Last in, first out

Exercise 9-2 *Recording periodic inventory transactions*

Assume the data in Exercise 9-1 pertain to Ching Company. Prepare the general journal entries under the periodic inventory system to record:

1. Total October purchases in one summary entry. All purchases were on credit.
2. Total October sales in one summary entry. Assume the selling price was $300 per unit, and all sales were on credit.
3. October 31 entries for inventory. Ching uses FIFO.

Exercise 9-3 *Comparing the tax impact of FIFO and average cost*

Use the data in Exercise 9-1 to illustrate the income tax difference under FIFO and average cost, assuming sales revenue is $6,500, operating expenses are $1,100 and the income tax rate is 40 percent.

Exercise 9-4   *Converting LIFO financial statements to the FIFO basis*

Maxus Corporation reported:

Balance sheet	19X5	19X4
Inventories — Note 4	$ 65,800	$ 59,300

Income statement		
Purchases	404,100	372,700
Cost of sales	397,600	381,400

Note 4: The company determines inventory cost by the last-in, first-out method. If the first-in, first-out method were used, inventories would be $8,200 higher at year end 19X5 and $7,500 higher at year end 19X4.

Required

Show the cost of goods sold computations for 19X5 under LIFO and FIFO. Which method would result in higher reported income?

Exercise 9-5   *Note disclosure of a change in inventory method*

A company has used the first-in, first-out inventory method for many years. At the start of the current year the company switched to the last-in, first-out method. This change decreased net income by $263,000. Write the note to disclose this accounting change in the company's financial statements.

Exercise 9-6   *The effect of lower of cost or market on the income statement*

From the following inventory records of Barnet, Inc., for 19X7, prepare the company's income statement down to the gross margin amount. Apply the lower-of-cost-or-market rule.

Beginning inventory (average cost)	300 @ $41.33	= $ 12,399
(replacement cost) ..	300 @ 41.91	= 12,573
Purchases during the year	2,600 @ 45.50	= 118,300
Ending inventory (average cost).........	400 @ 45.07	= 18,028
(replacement cost)	400 @ 42.10	= 16,840
Sales during the year	2,500 @ 91.00*	= 227,500

* Selling price per unit.

Exercise 9-7   *Applying the lower-of-cost-or-market rule*

Danos Company's income statement and balance sheet for March reported the following data:

Income Statement

Sales revenue		$83,000
Cost of goods sold		
Beginning inventory	$17,200	
Purchases...............................	51,700	
Cost of goods available for sale	68,900	
Ending inventory........................	22,800	
Cost of goods sold		46,100
Gross margin...............................		$36,900

Prior to releasing the financial statements, it was discovered that the current replacement cost of ending inventory was $19,600. Correct the above data to include the lower-of-cost-or-market value of ending inventory.

Exercise 9-8 *Correcting an inventory error*

Lee Corporation reported the following comparative income statement for the years ended September 30, 19X5 and 19X4:

Lee Corporation
Income Statements
for the years ended September 30,

	19X5		19X4	
Sales revenue		$132,300		$121,700
Cost of goods sold				
Beginning inventory	$14,000		$12,800	
Purchases	72,000		66,000	
Cost of goods available	86,000		78,800	
Ending inventory	16,600		14,000	
Cost of goods sold		69,400		64,800
Gross margin		62,900		56,900
Operating expenses		30,300		26,100
Net income		$ 32,600		$ 30,800

During 19X5 accountants for the company discovered that ending 19X4 inventory was overstated by $1,500. Prepare the corrected comparative income statement for the two-year period. What was the effect of the error on net income for the two years combined? Explain your answer.

Exercise 9-9 *Estimating inventory by the gross margin method*

McIntosh Company began April with inventory of $41,000. The business made net purchases of $37,600 and had net sales of $51,000 before a fire destroyed the company's inventory. For the past several years, McIntosh's gross margin on sales has been 30 percent. Estimate the cost of the inventory destroyed by the fire.

Exercise 9-10 *Estimating inventory by the retail method*

Assume the inventory records of the menswear department of The Bay, a large chain of department stores, revealed the following:

	At Cost	At Retail
Beginning inventory........................	$ 26,000	$ 48,000
Net purchases	103,000	191,000
Net sales		201,000

Use the retail inventory method to estimate the ending inventory of the department.

Exercise 9-11 *Recording perpetual inventory transactions*

King Chevrolet Company keeps perpetual inventory records for its automobile inventory. During May the company made credit purchases of inventory costing $111,300. Cash sales came to $26,800, credit sales came to $130,400 and cost of goods sold reached $119,550. Record these summary transactions in the general journal.

Problems   (Group A)

Problem 9-1A   *Computing inventory by three methods*

Marchand Imports began the year with 230 units of inventory that cost $80 each. During the year Marchand made the following purchases:

Feb. 3	217 @ $81
Apr. 12	95 @ 82
Aug. 8	210 @ 84
Oct. 24	248 @ 88

The company uses the periodic inventory system, and the physical count at December 31 indicates that ending inventory consists of 319 units.

Required

Compute the ending inventory and cost of goods sold amounts under (a) average cost, (b) FIFO cost and (c) LIFO cost. Round average cost per unit to the nearest cent and all other amounts to the nearest dollar.

Problem 9-2A   *Computing inventory, cost of goods sold and FIFO inventory profits*

Campus Sportswear specializes in men's shirts. The store began operations on January 1, 19X1, with an inventory of 200 shirts that cost $13 each, a $2,600 total. During the year the store purchased inventory as follows:

Purchase no. 1	110 @ $14
Purchase no. 2	80 @ 15
Purchase no. 3	320 @ 15
Purchase no. 4	100 @ 18

The ending inventory consists of 250 shirts.

Required

1. Complete the following tabulation:

	Ending Inventory	Cost of Goods Sold
a. Average cost	_____	_____
b. FIFO cost	_____	_____
c. LIFO cost	_____	_____

2. Compute the amount of inventory profit under FIFO.
3. Which method produces the most current ending inventory cost? Which method produces the most current cost-of-goods-sold amount? Give the reason for your answers.

Problem 9-3A   *Preparing an income statement directly from the accounts*

The records of Janeway Retailers include the accounts on the next page for one of its products at December 31 of the current year:

Required

1. Compute the quantities of goods in (a) ending inventory and (b) cost of goods sold during the year.
2. Prepare the partial income statement on the next page under the average cost, FIFO cost and LIFO cost methods.

Inventory

Jan. 1	Balance	{ 300 units @ $3.00	1,210	
		100 units @ 3.10 }		

Purchases

Feb. 6	200 units @ $3.15	630	
May 19	600 units @ 3.35	2,010	
Aug. 22	1,000 units @ 3.50	3,500	
Nov. 4	800 units @ 3.75	3,000	
Dec. 31	Balance	9,140	

Sales Revenue

	Mar. 12	500 units @ $4.00	2,000
	June 9	1,100 units @ 4.20	4,620
	Aug. 21	300 units @ 4.50	1,350
	Oct. 2	400 units @ 4.50	1,800
	Dec. 18	100 units @ 4.75	475
	Dec. 31	Balance	10,245

Janeway Retailers
Income Statement
for the year ended December 31, 19XX

	Average Cost	FIFO Cost	LIFO Cost
Sales revenue	$ _____	$ _____	$ _____
Cost of goods sold			
Beginning inventory	$ _____	$ _____	$ _____
Purchases	_____	_____	_____
Cost of goods available	_____	_____	_____
Ending inventory	_____	_____	_____
Cost of goods sold	_____	_____	_____
Gross margin	_____	_____	_____

Problem 9-4A   *Recording periodic and perpetual inventory transactions*

Using the data in Problem 9-3A, make summary entries in the general journal to record:

1. Purchases, sales and end-of-period inventory entries, assuming Janeway Retailers uses the periodic inventory system and the average cost method. All purchases are on credit. Cash sales are $4,000, with the remaining sales on account.
2. Purchases, sales and cost of goods sold, assuming Janeway Retailers uses the perpetual inventory system and the average cost method. All purchases are on credit. Cash sales total $4,000, with the remainder on account.

Problem 9-5A   *Applying the lower-of-cost-or-market rule*

Assume that accountants prepare the financial statements of Dysan Company on the cost basis without considering whether the replacement value of ending inventory is less than cost. Following are selected data from those statements:

From the income statement

Sales revenue		$832,000
Cost of goods sold		
Beginning inventory	$104,000	
Purchases	587,000	
Cost of goods available for sale	691,000	
Ending inventory	143,000	
Cost of goods sold		548,000
Gross margin		$284,000

From the balance sheet

Current assets	
Inventory	$143,000

The replacement costs were $122,000 for beginning inventory and $138,000 for ending inventory.

Required

1. Revise the data to include the appropriate lower-of-cost-or-market value of inventory.
2. How is the lower-of-cost-or-market rule conservative?

Problem 9-6A   *Correcting inventory errors over a three-year period*

The Power & Masters Company books show these data (in millions):

	19X3		19X2		19X1	
Net sales revenue		$200		$160		$175
Cost of goods sold						
Beginning inventory	$ 15		$ 25		$ 40	
Net purchases	135		100		90	
Cost of goods available	150		125		130	
Less ending inventory	30		15		25	
Cost of goods sold		120		110		105
Gross margin		80		50		70
Operating expenses		74		38		46
Net income		$ 6		$ 12		$ 24

In early 19X4 a team of internal auditors discovered that the ending inventory of 19X1 had been overstated by $20 million. Also, the ending inventory for 19X3 had been understated by $5 million. The ending inventory at December 31, 19X2 was correct.

Required

1. Prepare corrected income statements for the three years.
2. State whether each year's net income and owners' equity amounts are understated or overstated. For each incorrect figure, indicate the amount of the understatement or overstatement.

Problem 9-7A *Estimating inventory by the gross margin method; preparing a multiple-step income statement*

Assume Swiss Chalet Chicken and Ribs Ltd. estimates its inventory by the gross margin method when preparing monthly financial statements. For the past two years, gross margin has averaged 35 percent of net sales. Assume further that the company's inventory records for stores in the Ontario Region reveal the following data:

Inventory, March 1......................	$ 398,000
Transactions during March	
Purchases	5,685,000
Purchase discounts...................	49,000
Purchase returns.....................	8,000
Sales	8,667,000
Sales returns	17,000

Required

1. Estimate the March 31 inventory using the gross martin method.
2. Prepare the March income statement through gross margin, for the Swiss Chalet Chicken and Ribs Ltd., stores in the Ontario Region. Use the multiple-step format.

Problem 9-8A *Estimating inventory by the retail method; recording periodic inventory transactions*

The fiscal year of Woodward's Ltd. (and many other retailers) ends in January. Assume the following inventory data for the women's sportswear department of a Woodward's store:

	Cost	Retail
Inventory, Jan. 26, 19X5	$ 84,500	$153,636
Transactions during the year ended		
January 26, 19X6		
Purchases	419,220	762,500
Purchase returns	9,690	17,450
Purchase discounts	8,400	15,722
Sales.................................		783,740
Sales returns.........................		9,676

Required

1. Use the retail method to estimate the cost of the store's ending inventory of women's sportswear at January 26, 19X6. Round off the ratio to two decimal places.
2. Assuming Woodward's uses the periodic inventory system, prepare general journal entries to record:
   a. Inventory purchases and sales during fiscal year 19X6. Assume all purchases and one half of company sales were on credit. All other sales were for cash.
   b. Inventory entries at January 26, 19X6. Closing entries for Purchases, Purchase Returns and Purchase Discounts are not required.

Problem 9-9A *Using the perpetual inventory system; applying the lower-of-cost-or-market rule*

Spar Aerospace Ltd. manufactures high-technology products used in the aviation and space industries. Perhaps its most famous product is the space arm used in NASA projects. Assume the following data for Spar's product AB477:

	Purchased	Sold	Balance
Dec. 31, 19X1			110 @ $5 = $550
Feb. 10, 19X2	80 @ $6 = $480		
Apr. 7		60	
May 29	110 @ 7 = 770		
July 13		120	
Oct. 4	100 @ 8 = 800		
Nov. 22		80	

Required

1. Prepare a perpetual inventory card for product AB477, using the FIFO method.
2. Assume Spar sold the 60 units on April 7 on account for $13 each. Record the sale and related cost of goods sold in the general journal under the FIFO method.
3. Suppose the current replacement cost of the ending inventory of product AB477 is $970 at December 31, 19X2. Use the answer to question 1 to compute the lower-of-cost-or-market (LCM) value of the ending inventory.

(Group B)

Problem 9-1B   *Computing inventory by three methods*

Microdot Software began the year with 73 units of inventory that cost $26 each. During the year Microdot made the following purchases:

Mar. 11	113 @ $27
May 2	81 @ 29
July 19	167 @ 32
Nov. 18	44 @ 36

The company uses the periodic inventory system, and the physical count at December 31 indicates that ending inventory consists of 131 units.

Required

Compute the ending inventory and cost of goods sold amounts under (a) average cost, (b) FIFO cost and (c) LIFO cost. Round average cost per unit to the nearest cent and all other amounts to the nearest dollar.

Problem 9-2B   *Computing inventory, cost of goods sold and FIFO inventory profit*

University Paperbacks specializes in softcover books. The store began operations on January 1, 19X1, with an inventory of 500 books that cost $2.01 each, a $1,005 total. During the first month of operations the store purchased inventory as follows:

Purchase no. 1	60 @ $2.10
Purchase no. 2	120 @ 2.35
Purchase no. 3	600 @ 2.50
Purchase no. 4	40 @ 2.75

The ending inventory consists of 600 books.

Required

1. Complete the following tabulation:

	Ending Inventory	Cost of Goods Sold
a. Average cost	_____	_____
b. FIFO cost	_____	_____
c. LIFO cost	_____	_____

2. Compute the amount of inventory profit under FIFO.
3. Which method produces the most current ending inventory cost? Which method produces the most current cost-of-goods-sold amount? Give the reason for your answers.

Problem 9-3B   *Preparing an income statement directly from the accounts*

The records of Blaine Wholesale Company include the following accounts for one of its products at December 31 of the current year:

Inventory

Jan. 1	Balance	700 units @ $7.00	4,900	

Purchases

Jan. 6	300 units @ $7.05	2,115	
Mar. 19	1,100 units @ 7.35	8,085	
June 22	8,400 units @ 7.50	63,000	
Oct. 4	500 units @ 8.80	4,400	
Dec. 31	Balance	77,600	

Sales Revenue

	Feb. 5	1,000 units @ $12.00	12,000
	Apr. 10	700 units @ 12.10	8,470
	July 31	1,800 units @ 13.25	23,850
	Sept. 4	2,200 units @ 13.50	29,700
	Nov. 27	3,100 units @ 15.00	46,500
	Dec. 31	Balance	120,520

Required

1. Compute the quantities of goods in (a) ending inventory and (b) cost of goods sold during the year.
2. Prepare the following partial income statement under the average cost, FIFO cost and LIFO cost methods:

Blaine Wholesale Company
Income Statement
for the year ended December 31, 19XX

	Average Cost		FIFO Cost		LIFO Cost	
Sales revenue		$ _____		$ _____		$ _____
Cost of goods sold						
Beginning inventory	$ _____		$ _____		$ _____	
Purchases	_____		_____		_____	
Cost of goods available	_____		_____		_____	
Ending inventory	_____		_____		_____	
Cost of goods sold		_____		_____		_____
Gross margin		_____		_____		_____

Problem 9-4B   *Recording periodic and perpetual inventory transactions*

Using the data in Problem 9-3B, make summary journal entries in the general journal to record:

1. Purchases, sales and end-of-period inventory entries, assuming Blaine Wholesale Company uses the periodic inventory system and the FIFO cost method. All purchases are on credit. Cash sales are $50,000, with the remaining sales on account.

2. Purchases, sales and cost of goods sold, assuming Blaine Wholesale Company uses the perpetual inventory system and the FIFO cost method. All purchases are on credit. Cash sales are $50,000, with the remaining sales on account.

Problem 9-5B   *Applying the lower-of-cost-or-market rule*

The financial statements of LaValle Company were prepared on the cost basis without considering whether the replacement value of ending inventory was less than cost. Following are selected data from those statements:

From the income statement

Sales revenue		$278,000
Cost of goods sold		
Beginning inventory...................	$ 54,000	
Purchases	119,000	
Cost of goods available for sale	173,000	
Ending inventory	53,000	
Cost of goods sold...................		120,000
Gross margin		$158,000

From the balance sheet

Current assets		
Inventory		$ 53,000

The replacement costs were $57,000 for beginning inventory and $49,000 for ending inventory.

Required

1. Revise the data to include the appropriate lower-of-cost-or-market value of inventory.
2. How is the lower-of-cost-or-market rule conservative? How is conservatism shown in LaValle's situation?

Problem 9-6B   *Correcting inventory errors over a three-year period*

The Cornerbrook Company books show these data (in millions):

	19X6		19X5		19X4	
Net sales revenue...............		$350		$280		$240
Cost of goods sold						
Beginning inventory	$ 65		$ 55		$ 70	
Net purchases.................	195		135		130	
Cost of goods available	260		190		200	
Less ending inventory	70		65		55	
Cost of goods sold		190		125		145
Gross margin....................		160		155		95
Operating expenses..............		113		109		76
Net income		$ 47		$ 46		$ 19

In early 19X7 a team of internal auditors discovered that the ending inventory of 19X4 had been understated by $12 million. Also, the ending inventory for 19X6 had been overstated by $8 million. The ending inventory at December 31, 19X5 was correct.

Required

1. Prepare corrected income statements for the three years.
2. State whether each year's net income and owner's equity amount are understated or overstated. For each incorrect figure, indicate the amount of the understatement or overstatement.

Problem 9-7B   *Estimating inventory by the gross margin method; preparing a multiple-step income statement*

Assume Harvey's Restaurants estimates its inventory by the gross margin method when preparing monthly financial statements. For the past two years, the gross margin has averaged 40 percent of net sales. Assume further that the company's inventory records for stores in the Southwest Ontario region reveal the following data:

Inventory, July 1.........................	$ 267,000
Transactions during July	
Purchases	3,589,000
Purchase discounts....................	26,000
Purchase returns.....................	12,000
Sales	5,773,000
Sales returns	22,000

Required

1. Estimate the July 31 inventory using the gross margin method.

2. Prepare the July income statement through gross margin for Harvey's Restaurants stores in the Southwest Ontario region. Use the multiple-step format.

Problem 9-8B *Estimating inventory by the retail method; recording periodic inventory transaction*

The fiscal year of K-Mart Canada ends on January 31. Assume the following inventory for the hardware department of a K-Mart Store:

	Cost	Retail
Inventory, Jan. 31, 19X3	$ 31,200	$ 63,000
Transactions during the year ended January 31, 19X4		
Purchases	154,732	301,190
Purchase returns	2,390	4,760
Purchase discounts	3,410	6,530
Sales		283,420
Sales returns		3,320

Required

1. Use the retail method to estimate the cost of the store's ending inventory of hardware at January 31, 19X4.
2. Assuming K-Mart uses the periodic inventory system, prepare general journal entries to record:
   a. Inventory purchases and sales during fiscal year 19X4. Assume all purchases and one half of company sales were on credit. All other sales were for cash.
   b. Inventory entries at January 31, 19X4. Closing entries for Purchases, Purchase Returns and Purchase Discounts are not required.

Problem 9-9B *Using the perpetual inventory system; applying the lower-of-cost-or-market rule*

Coachman Industries Ltd. manufacturers recreational vehicles and products. Assume the following data for Coachman's product EK-133:

	Purchased	Sold	Balance
Dec. 31, 19X3			120 @ $6 = $720
Mar. 15, 19X4	50 @ $7 = $350		
Apr. 10		80	
May 29	100 @ 8 = 800		
Aug. 3		110	
Nov. 16	90 @ 9 = 810		
Dec. 12		70	

Required

1. Prepare a perpetual inventory card for product EK-133, using the FIFO method.
2. Assume Coachman sold the 110 units on August 3 on account for $16 each. Record the sale and related cost of goods sold in the general journal under the FIFO method.
3. Suppose the current replacement cost of the ending inventory of product EK-133 is $750 at December 31, 19X4. Use the answer to question 1 to compute the lower-of-cost-or-market (LCM) value of the ending inventory.

Decision Problems

1. Assessing the impact of a year-end purchase of inventory

Yakima Paper Corporation is nearing the end of its first year of operations. The company made the following inventory purchases:

January	1,000	$10	$10,000
March	1,000	10	10,000
May	1,000	11	11,000
July	1,000	13	13,000
September	1,000	14	14,000
November	1,000	15	15,000
Totals	6,000		$73,000

Sales for the year will be 5,000 units for $120,000 revenue. Expenses other than cost of goods sold and income taxes will be $20,000. The president of the company is undecided about whether to adopt FIFO or LIFO.

The company has storage capacity for 5,000 additional units of inventory. Inventory prices are expected to stay at $15 per unit for the next few months. The president is considering purchasing 4,000 additional units of inventory at $15 each before the end of the year. He wishes to know how the purchase would affect net income before taxes under both FIFO and LIFO.

Required

1. To aid company decision making, prepare income statements under FIFO and under LIFO, both without and with the year-end purchase of 4,000 units of inventory at $15 per unit.
2. Compare net income under FIFO without and with the year-end purchase. Make the same comparison under LIFO. Under which method does the year-end purchase have the greater effect on net income before taxes.
3. Under which method can a year-end purchase be made in order to manipulate net income?

2. Assessing the impact of the inventory costing method on the financial statements

The inventory costing method chosen by a company can have an impact on the financial statements and thus on the decisions of the users of those statements.

Required

1. A leading accounting researcher stated that one inventory costing method results in the most recent costs being incorporated in the income statement, while another results in the most recent costs being incorporated in the balance sheet, and that this results in one or the other of the statements being "inaccurate" when prices are rising. What did the researcher mean?
2. Conservatism is an accepted accounting convention. Would you want management to be conservative in valuing inventory if you were (a) a shareholder and (b) a prospective shareholder?
3. Beechwood Ltd. follows the conservatism convention and writes the value of its inventory of bicycles down to market which has declined below cost. The following year, a cycling craze results in a demand for bicycles that far exceeds supply, and the market price increases way above the previous cost. What will the impact of conservatism have been on the income of Beechwood over the two years?

Financial Statement Problem

Inventories

The notes are an important part of a company's financial statements, giving valuable details that would clutter the tabular data presented in the statements. This problem will help you to learn to use a company's inventory notes. Refer to the John Labatt statements and the related notes in Appendix E. Answer the following questions:

1. How much were John Labatt's total inventories at April 30, 1989? What was the change in the total from April 30, 1988?
2. How many different types of inventory are shown? Name them and explain what you think each includes.
3. John Labatt's notes indicate two basic categories of inventory. How are these two categories described in the notes? How does John Labatt value each of the two categories of inventory?
4. The section of the John Labatt annual report in Appendix E entitled "Financial Review" is a summary financial information that users may find useful. Included in the section is a note relating to inventory. What does the note say? Why is it helpful in understanding the information in question 1 above?

Answers to Self-Study Questions

1. c
2. a $(15,000 - 1,000) \times \$3.40 = \$47,600$
3. d
4. b
5. b
6. d
7. a $\$35,000 + \$146,000 = \$181,000$
   $\$240,000 - (.35 \times \$240,000) = \$156,000$
   $\$181,000 - \$156,000 = \$25,000$
8. c

	Cost	Retail	
Beginning inventory	$ 20,000	$ 40,000	
Purchases	120,000	210,000	**Cost Ratio**
Goods available	140,000 ÷	250,000 =	.56
Sales		200,000	
Ending inventory—at retail....		$ 50,000	
at cost ($50,000 × .56)	$ 28,000		

9. d
10. c

Plant Assets, Wasting Assets, Intangible Assets and Related Expenses

LEARNING OBJECTIVES

After studying this chapter, you should be able to

1 Identify the elements of a plant asset's cost

2 Explain the concept of depreciation

3 Account for depreciation by three methods

4 Identify the best depreciation method for income tax purposes

5 Account for disposal of plant assets

6 Account for wasting assets and depletion

7 Account for intangible assets and amortization

8 Distinguish capital expenditures from revenue expenditures

Business assets are separated into current assets — those useful for one year or less, and long-lived assets — those useful for longer than a year. Long-lived assets share an additional similarity. They are used in business operations. Unlike inventory, they are not held for sale.

Long-lived assets include four types: land, plant and equipment, natural resources and intangibles. Land, plant and equipment make up the category known as plant assets. **Plant assets** are those long-lived assets that are tangible. Their physical form provides their usefulness, for instance, land, buildings and equipment. Of the plant assets, land is unique. Its cost is *not* depreciated (expensed over time) because its value does not decrease like that of other assets. Most companies report plant assets under the heading Property, Plant and Equipment.

Natural resources are also called **wasting assets**. They are consumed through the process of depletion or removal.

Intangible assets are useful not because of their physical characteristics, but because of the special rights they carry. Patents, copyrights and trademarks are intangible assets. An example of a famous patent is the Dolby noise-reduction process. Accounting for intangibles is similar to accounting for plant assets.

This area has its own terminology. Different names apply to the expense for the cost of the various assets, as shown in Exhibit 10-1.

The first half of the chapter discusses and illustrates how to identify the cost of a plant asset and to expense its cost. The second half considers disposing of plant assets and how to account for natural resources and intangible assets. Unless stated otherwise, we describe accounting in accordance with generally accepted accounting principles, as distinguished from reporting to Revenue Canada for income tax purposes.

EXHIBIT 10-1   *Terminology Used in Accounting for Plant Assets, Wasting Assets and Intangible Assets*

Asset Account on Balance Sheet	Related Expense Account on Income Statement
Land	None
Buildings, Machinery and Equipment, Furniture and Fixtures	Depreciation
Natural Resources	Depletion
Intangibles	Amortization

The Cost of a Plant Asset

The cost principle directs a business to carry an asset on the balance sheet at the amount paid for it. The **cost of a plant asset** is the purchase price, sales tax, purchase commissions, and all other amounts paid to acquire the asset and to ready it for its intended use. As the types of cost differ for various categories of plant assets, we discuss the major groups individually.

> **OBJECTIVE 1**
>
> Identify the elements of a plant asset's cost

Buildings

The cost of constructing a building includes architectural fees, building permits, contractors' charges, and payments for materials, labour and overhead. When an existing building (new or old) is purchased, its cost includes the purchase price, brokerage commission, sales and other taxes, and expenditures for repairing and renovating the building for its intended purpose.

Machinery and Equipment

The cost of machinery and equipment includes its purchase price (less any discounts), transportation charges, insurance while in transit, sales and other taxes, purchase commission, installation costs, and any expenditures to test the asset before placing it in service.

Land

The cost of land includes its purchase price (cash plus any note payable given), the broker's commission, survey fees, legal fees, and any back property taxes that the purchaser pays. Land cost also includes any expenditures for grading and clearing the land and for demolishing or removing any unwanted buildings.

The cost of land does *not* include the cost of fencing, paving, sprinkler systems and lighting. These are separate plant assets.

Suppose you are a real estate developer, and you sign a $300,000 note payable to purchase 100 hectares of land for subdivision into 5-hectare lots. You also pay $10,000 in brokerage commission, $8,000 in transfer taxes, $5,000 for removal of an old building, a $1,000 survey fee and $260,000 for the construction of roads, all in cash. What is the cost of this land?

Purchase price of land	$300,000
Add incidental costs, paid in cash	
Brokerage commission $10,000	
Transfer taxes 8,000	
Removal of building 5,000	
Survey fee 1,000	
Total incidental costs	24,000
Total cost of land	$324,000

The entry to record purchase of the land is

Land	324,000	
Note Payable		300,000
Cash		24,000

Land Improvements   In the above example, the cost of the roads ($260,000) is not part of the cost of the land. Instead, the $260,000 would be recorded in a separate account entitled Land Improvements. This account includes cost for such other items as fences, driveways, parking lots and sprinkler systems. Although these assets are located on the land, they are subject to decay. Therefore their cost should be depreciated, as we discuss later in this chapter. Also, the cost of a new building constructed on the land is a debit to the asset account Building.

Group (or Basket) Purchases of Assets

Businesses often purchase several assets (as a group or in a "basket") for a single amount. For example, a company may pay one price for land and an office building. The company must identify the cost of each asset. The total cost is divided between the assets according to their relative sales (or market) values. This allocation technique is called the **relative-sales-value method**.

Suppose Magna International Inc. purchases land and a building in Saint John for a Maritime plant. The building sits on two hectares of land and the combined purchase price of land and building is $2,800,000. An appraisal indicates that the land's market (sales) value is $300,000 and the building's market (sales) value is $2,700,000.

An accountant first figures the ratio of each asset's market price to the total market price. Total appraised value is $3,000,000. Thus land, valued at $300,000, is 10 percent of the total market value. Building's appraised value is 90 percent of the total.

Asset	Market (Sales) Value		Total Market Value		Percentage
Land	$ 300,000	÷	$3,000,000	=	10%
Building	2,700,000	÷	$3,000,000	=	90%
Total	$3,000,000				100%

The percentage for each asset is multiplied by the total purchase price to give its cost in the purchase.

Asset	Total Purchase Price		Percentage		Allocated Cost
Land	$2,800,000	×	.10	=	$ 280,000
Building	$2,800,000	×	.90	=	$2,520,000
					$2,800,000

Assuming Magna pays cash, the entry to record the purchase of the land and building is

Land	280,000	
Building	2,520,000	
Cash		2,800,000

Depreciation of Plant Assets

When a company buys a plant asset, it acquires the benefit of using the asset. As the business uses up the asset, less and less of its future benefit remains. The portion of the asset that has been consumed becomes an expense to the business. At the end of the asset's useful life, when ready for the salvage yard, it holds no future benefit to the business — its entire cost has become expense. The process of allocating a plant asset's cost to expense is called *depreciation*. It is designed to match the cost of an asset against the revenue earned by that asset over that asset's useful life. For example, if an automobile purchased for use as a taxi for $15,000 had an expected useful life of 300,000 kilometers, the cost per kilometer would be $.05. If the taxi earned $2,000 in fares from carrying passengers 10,000 kilometers, the depreciation cost incurred in earning that revenue would be $500 (10,000 × .05).

Suppose a company buys a computer. The business believes the computer offers four years of service after which obsolescence will make it worthless. Using straight-line depreciation (which we discuss later in this chapter), the business expenses one quarter of the asset's cost in each of its four years of use.

Let us contrast what depreciation accounting is with what it is *not*. (1) *Depreciation is not a process of valuation.* Businesses do not record depreciation based on appraisals of their plant assets made at the end of each period. Instead, businesses allocate the asset's cost to the periods of its useful life based on a specific depreciation method. (We discuss these methods in this chapter.) (2) *Depreciation does not mean that the business sets aside cash to replace assets as they become fully depreciated.* Establishing such a cash fund is a decision entirely separate from depreciation. *Accumulated depreciation* is that portion of the plant asset's cost that has already been debited to expense. Accumulated depreciation does not represent a growing amount of cash.

Determining the Useful Life of a Plant Asset

No asset (other than land) offers an unlimited useful life. For some plant assets physical *wear and tear* from operations and the elements may be the important cause of depreciation. For example, physical deterioration takes its toll on the usefulness of trucks and furniture.

Assets like computers, other electronic equipment and airplanes may become *obsolete* before they physically deteriorate. An asset is obsolete when another asset can do the job better or more efficiently. Thus an asset's useful life may be much shorter than its physical life. Accountants usually depreciate computers over a short period — perhaps four years — even though they know the computers will remain in working condition much longer. Whether wear and tear or obsolescence causes depreciation, the asset's cost is depreciated over its expected useful life.

Measuring Depreciation

To measure depreciation for a plant asset, we must know its *cost, estimated useful life* and *estimated residual value.*

Cost is the purchase price of the asset. We discussed cost under the heading The Cost of a Plant Asset at the beginning of this chapter.

Estimated useful life is the length of the service the business expects to get from the asset. Useful life may be expressed in years (as we have seen so far), units of output, miles or other measures. For example, the useful life of a building is stated in years. The useful life of a bookbinding machine may be stated as the number of books the machine is expected to bind, that is, its expected units of output. A reasonable measure of a delivery truck's useful life is the total number of kilometers the truck is expected to travel. Companies base such estimates on past experience and information from industry trade magazines and government publications.

Estimated residual value, also called *scrap value* and *salvage value*, is the expected cash value of the asset at the end of its useful life. It is an estimate by management based on their experience and knowledge of the asset. For example, a business may believe that a machine's useful life will be seven years. After that time, the company expects to sell the machine as scrap metal. The amount the business believes it can get for the machine is the estimated residual value. In computing depreciation, estimated residual value is *not* depreciated, because the business expects to receive this amount from disposing of the asset. The full cost of a plant asset is depreciated if the asset is expected to have no residual value. The plant asset's cost minus its estimated residual value is called the depreciable cost.

Of the factors entering the computation of depreciation, only one factor is known—cost. The other two factors—residual value and useful life—must be estimated. Depreciation, then, is an estimated amount.

The basic equation for computing depreciation is

$$\text{depreciation} = \frac{\text{cost} - \text{estimated residual value}}{\text{expected useful life}} = \frac{\text{depreciable cost}}{\text{expected useful life}}$$

The equation shows that depreciable cost is depreciated over the useful life of the asset.

Depreciation Methods

OBJECTIVE 3
Account for depreciation by three methods

Three methods for computing depreciation will be discussed in this text: straight-line, units-of-production and declining-balance. These three methods allocate different amounts of depreciation expense to different periods. However, they all result in the same total amount of depreciation over the life of the asset—the asset's depreciable cost. Exhibit 10-2 presents the data used to illustrate depreciation computations by the three methods.

Straight-Line (SL) Method

In the **straight-line (SL)** method, an equal amount of depreciation expense is assigned to each year (or period) of asset use. Depreciable cost is divided by

EXHIBIT 10-2   *Data for Depreciation Computations*

Data Item	Amount
Cost of limousine	$41,000
Estimated residual value	1,000
Depreciable cost	$40,000
Estimated useful life	
Years.	5 years
Units of production	400,000 units

useful life in years to determine the annual depreciation expense. The equation for SL depreciation, applied to the limo data from Exhibit 10-2, is

$$\text{straight-line depreciation per year} = \frac{\text{cost} - \text{residual value}}{\text{useful life in years}}$$

$$= \frac{\$41{,}000 - \$1{,}000}{5}$$

$$= \$8{,}000$$

Assume that the limo was purchased on January 1, 19X1, and the business's fiscal year ends on December 31. A *straight-line depreciation schedule* is presented in Exhibit 10-3.

EXHIBIT 10-3   *Straight-Line Depreciation Schedule*

Date	Asset Cost	Depreciation Rate		Depreciable Cost		Depreciation Amount	Accumulated Depreciation	Asset Book Value
				Depreciation for the Year				
1-1-X1	$41,000							$41,000
12-31-X1		1/5	×	$40,000	=	$8,000	$ 8,000	33,000
12-31-X2		1/5	×	40,000	=	8,000	16,000	25,000
12-31-X3		1/5	×	40,000	=	8,000	24,000	17,000
12-31-X4		1/5	×	40,000	=	8,000	32,000	9,000
12-31-X5		1/5	×	40,000	=	8,000	40,000	1,000

The final column of Exhibit 10-3 shows the asset's *book value*, which is its cost less accumulated depreciation. Book value is also called carrying value.

As an asset is used, accumulated depreciation increases and the book value decreases. (Note the Accumulated Depreciation and Book Value columns.) An asset's final book value is its *residual value* ($1,000 in Exhibit 10-3). At the end of its useful life, the asset is said to be fully depreciated.

Units-of-Production (UOP) Method

In the **units-of-production (UOP)** method, a fixed amount of depreciation is assigned to each unit of output produced by the plant asset. Depreciable cost is divided by useful life in units to determine this amount. This per-unit depreciation expense is multiplied by the number of units produced each

EXHIBIT 10-4 *Units-of-Production Depreciation Schedule*

Date	Asset Cost	Depreciation for the Year			Accumulated Depreciation	Asset Book Value
		Depreciation Per Unit	Number of Units	Depreciation Amount		
1-1-19X1	$41,000					$41,000
12-31-19X1		$.10	× 90,000 =	$ 9,000	$ 9,000	32,000
12-31-19X2		.10	× 120,000 =	12,000	21,000	20,000
12-31-19X3		.10	× 100,000 =	10,000	31,000	10,000
12-31-19X4		.10	× 60,000 =	6,000	37,000	4,000
12-31-19X5		.10	× 30,000 =	3,000	40,000	1,000

period to compute depreciation for the period. The UOP depreciation equation for the limo data in Exhibit 10-2 is

$$\frac{\text{units-of-production depreciation}}{\text{per unit of output}} = \frac{\text{cost} - \text{residual value}}{\text{useful life in units}}$$

$$= \frac{\$41,000 - \$1,000}{400,000 \text{ units}}$$

$$= \$.10$$

Assume the limo was driven 90,000 kilometres (*kilometres* are the *units* in our example) during the first year, 120,000 during the second, 100,000 during the third, 60,000 during the fourth and 30,000 during the fifth. The UOP depreciation schedule for this asset is shown in Exhibit 10-4.

The amount of UOP depreciation per period varies with the number of units the asset produces. Note that the total number of units produced is 400,000 — the measure of this asset's useful life. Therefore, UOP depreciation does not depend directly on time as the other methods do.

Declining-Balance (DB) Method

The declining-balance method (DB) is one of the accelerated-depreciation methods; and the other is sum-of-years-digits, which is not widely used in Canada and so will not be discussed in this text. An **accelerated-depreciation** method writes off a relatively larger amount of the asset's cost nearer the start of its useful life than does straight-line. There are two methods in common use in Canada for computing **DB depreciation**; each is discussed in turn below.

Depreciation Based on Revenue Canada Rates   Revenue Canada publishes the maximum depreciation rates for various fixed assets that it will allow taxpayers to deduct from income for income tax purposes. Depreciation allowed for income tax purposes is called **capital cost allowance**; and the rates allowed are called *capital cost allowance rates*.

Some typical Revenue Canada rates are

Automobiles. 30%
Brick, concrete or stone buildings 5%
Computer software 100%
Office furniture and fixtures. 20%
Video games, coin-operated 40%

EXHIBIT 10-5 *Revenue Canada Rate Depreciation Schedule*

		Depreciation for the Year				
Date	Asset Cost	Revenue Canada Rate	Asset Book Value	Depreciation Amount	Accumulated Depreciation	Asset Book Value
1-1-19X1	$41,000					$41,000
12-31-19X1		.30	× $41,000 =	$12,300	$12,300	28,700
12-31-19X2		.30	× 28,700 =	8,610	20,910	20,090
12-31-19X3		.30	× 20,090 =	6,027	26,937	14,063
12-31-19X4		.30	× 14,063 =	4,219	31,156	9,844
12-31-19X5				8,844*	40,000	1,000

* Last-year depreciation is the amount needed to reduce asset book value to the residual value ($9,844 − $1,000 = $8,844).

Thus, since the capital cost allowance rate allowed for automobiles is 30 percent, a company choosing to use the Revenue Canada rates would use a depreciation rate of 30 percent. Many companies, who use accelerated depreciation for accounting purposes, use the rates allowed by Revenue Canada for convenience. We now discuss the issue of depreciation and income taxes.

When a company uses the Revenue Canada rates, the annual depreciation is computed as follows:

First, the rate, which is obtained from Revenue Canada's *Income Tax Regulations*, is multiplied by the period's beginning asset book value (cost less accumulated depreciation). The residual value of the asset is ignored in computing depreciation by the DB method except during the last year.

Second, the final year's depreciation amount is used to reduce the asset's book value to its residual value. In Exhibit 10-5, the fifth and final year's depreciation is $8,844.

Double-Declining Balance (DDB)   This method involves computing annual depreciation by multiplying the asset's book value by a constant percentage, which is two times the straight-line depreciation rate. DDB rates are computed as follows:

First, the straight-line depreciation rate per year is computed. For example, a 5-year limousine has a straight-line depreciation rate of 1/5 or 20 percent. A 10-year asset has a straight-line rate of 1/10 or 10 percent, and so on.

Second, the straight-line rate is multiplied by 2 to compute the DDB rate. The DDB rate for a 5-year asset is 40 percent ($20\% \times 2 = 40\%$). For a 10-year asset the DDB rate is 20 percent ($10\% \times 2 = 20\%$).

Third, the DDB rate is multiplied by the period's beginning asset book value (cost less accumulated depreciation). Residual value of the asset is ignored in computing depreciation by the DDB method, except during the last year.

The DDB rate for the limousine in Exhibit 10-2 is

$$\text{DDB rate per year} = \left(\frac{1}{\text{useful life in years}} \times 2\right) = \left(\frac{1}{5 \text{ years}} \times 2\right) = 20\% \times 2 = 40\%$$

The DDB depreciation schedule for the asset is illustrated in Exhibit 10-6.

Fourth, the final year's depreciation amount is the amount needed to reduce the asset's book value to its residual value. In the following schedule, the fifth

EXHIBIT 10-6   *Double-Declining Balance Depreciation Schedule*

| Date | Asset Cost | Depreciation for the Year | | | Accumulated Depreciation | Asset Book Value |
		DDB Rate	Asset Book Value	Depreciation Amount		
1-1-19X1	$41,000					$41,000
12-31-19X1		.40	× $41,000 =	$16,400	$16,400	24,600
12-31-19X2		.40	× 24,600 =	9,840	26,240	14,760
12-31-19X3		.40	× 14,760 =	5,904	32,144	8,856
12-31-19X4		.40	× 8,856 =	3,542	35,686	5,314
12-31-19X5				4,314*	40,000	1,000

* Last-year depreciation is the amount needed to reduce asset book value to the residual value
($5,314 − $1,000 = $4,314).

and final year's depreciation is $4,314—the $5,314 book value less the $1,000 residual value.

The DB method differs from the other methods in two ways: (1) the asset's residual value is ignored initially and (2) the final year's calculation is changed in order to bring the asset's book value to the residual value.

Comparison of the Depreciation Methods

Compare the three methods in terms of the yearly amount of depreciation:

Amount of Depreciation Per Year

| | | | Accelerated Methods | |
Year	Straight-Line	Units-of-Production	Double-Declining-Balance	Revenue Canada Rates
1	$ 8,000	$ 9,000	$16,400	$12,300
2	8,000	12,000	9,840	8,610
3	8,000	10,000	5,904	6,027
4	8,000	6,000	3,542	4,219
5	8,000	3,000	4,314	8,844
Total	$40,000	$40,000	$40,000	$40,000

The yearly amount of depreciation varies by method, but the total $40,000 depreciable cost systematically becomes expense under all three methods.

Generally accepted accounting principles (GAAP) direct a business to match the expense of an asset to the revenue that the asset produces. For a plant asset that generates revenue fairly evenly over time, the straight-line method best meets the matching principle. As the clock ticks, the asset marches toward the scrap heap—through wear and tear, obsolescence, or both. An example of an asset for which straight-line depreciation is appropriate is a brick building, since the value provided by the building is fairly constant over its useful life.

EXHIBIT 10-7   *Depreciation Patterns*

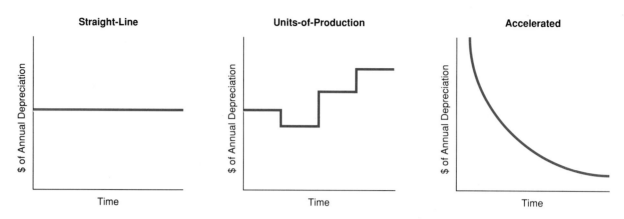

The units-of-production method best fits those assets that wear out because of physical use, not obsolescence. For example, the more (or less) a drill-press is used, the faster (or slower) it wears out and must be replaced. Depreciation in this method is recorded only when the asset is used. The more units the asset generates in a given year, the greater the depreciation expense.

The accelerated method applies best to those assets that generate greater revenue earlier in their useful lives, such as taxis. The greater expense recorded under the accelerated method in the early periods matches best against those periods' greater revenue.

Exhibit 10-7 graphs the relationship between annual depreciation amounts for straight-line, units-of-production and the accelerated depreciation methods.

The graph of straight-line depreciation is flat because annual depreciation is the same amount in each period. Units-of-production depreciation follows no particular pattern because annual depreciation depends on the use of the asset. The greater the use, the greater is the amount of depreciation. Accelerated depreciation is greatest in the asset's first year and less in the later years.

A recent survey indicated that over 57 percent of companies use the straight-line method, approximately 22 percent use an accelerated method, approximately 18 percent use the units of production method, and the remainder use other methods. For example, John Labatt uses straight-line while George Weston uses straight-line and units-of-production. Maclean Hunter uses straight-line for most fixed assets and declining balance for some buildings, some equipment and all vehicles.

Summary Problem for Your Review

Hubbard Company purchased office furniture on January 1, 19X5 for $44,000. The expected life of the equipment is 10 years and its residual value is $4,000. Under two depreciation methods, the annual depreciation expense and the balance of accumulated depreciation at the end of 19X5 and 19X6 are

	Method A		Method B	
Year	*Annual Depreciation Expense*	*Accumulated Depreciation*	*Annual Depreciation Expense*	*Accumulated Depreciation*
19X5	$4,000	$4,000	$8,800	$ 8,800
19X6	4,000	8,000	7,040	15,840

Required

1. Identify the depreciation method used in each instance, and show the equation and computation for each. (Round off to the nearest dollar.)
2. Assume continued use of the same method through year 19X7. Determine the annual depreciation expense, accumulated depreciation and book value of the equipment for 19X5 through 19X7 under each method.

SOLUTION TO REVIEW PROBLEM

Requirement 1

Method A: Straight-line

Depreciable cost = $40,000 ($44,000 − $4,000)

each year: $40,000/10 years = $4,000

Method B: Declining-balance (Revenue Canada rate)

Rate = 20%

19X5: .20 × $44,000 = $8,800

19X6: .20 × ($44,000 − $8,800) = $7,040

Requirement 2

	Method A Straight-Line			Method B Declining-Balance (Revenue Canada)		
Year	*Annual Depreciation Expense*	*Accumulated Depreciation*	*Book Value*	*Annual Depreciation Expense*	*Accumulated Depreciation*	*Book Value*
Start			$44,000			$44,000
19X5	$4,000	$4,000	40,000	$8,800	$ 8,800	35,200
19X6	4,000	8,000	36,000	7,040	15,840	28,160
19X7	4,000	12,000	32,000	5,632	21,472	22,528

Computations for 19X7

Straight-line: **$40,000/10 years = $4,000**

Declining-balance (Revenue Canada):   **.20 × $28,160 = $5,632**

Depreciation and Income Taxes

The majority of companies use the straight-line method for reporting to their shareholders and creditors on their financial statements. They keep a separate set of records of the capital cost allowance they claim on their tax return. The capital cost allowance rates published by Revenue Canada are maximums. A company may claim from zero to the maximum capital cost allowance allowed in a year. Most companies claim the maximum capital cost allowance using the declining-balance method.

Suppose you are a business manager. Revenue Canada will allow you to use any one of the three methods we have discussed as long as the amount you are claiming does not exceed their maximum. Which method would you choose? You will probably choose Revenue Canada's capital cost allowance rate because it is the maximum allowed. It provides the largest deduction from income as quickly as possible, thus decreasing your immediate tax payments. The cash you save may be applied to best fit your business needs. This is the strategy most businesses follow. For example, George Weston Limited reports in its summary of accounting policies that the company uses the straight-line method and the units-of-production method to depreciate assets for financial statement purposes. Still, the company could use the declining-balance method for tax purposes, even though a review of George Weston's financial statements does not disclose the method it uses for taxes.

To understand the relationships among cash flow (cash provided by operations), depreciation and capital cost allowance and income tax, consider the following example. Straight-line depreciation is $8,000 while the maximum capital cost allowance allowed is $16,400. Assume the business has $400,000 in cash sales and $300,000 in operating expenses during the asset's first year, and the income tax rate is 40 percent. The cash flow analysis appears in Exhibit 10-8.

> **OBJECTIVE 4**
>
> Identify the best depreciation method for income tax purposes

EXHIBIT 10-8 *Cash Flow Advantage of Declining-Balance (DB) Depreciation over Straight-Line (SL) Depreciation for Income Tax Purposes*

	Income Tax Rate 40 Percent	
	SL	DB
Revenues	$400,000	$400,000
Cash operating expense	300,000	300,000
Cash provided by operations before income tax	100,000	100,000
Capital cost allowance		
(Depreciation — a noncash expense)	8,000	16,400
Income before income tax	92,000	83,600
Income tax expense (40%)	36,800	33,440
Net income	$ 55,200	$ 50,160
Supplementary cash flow analysis		
Cash provided by operations before income tax	$100,000	$100,000
Income tax expense	36,800	33,440
Cash provided by operations	$ 63,200	$ 66,560
Extra cash available for investment if DB is used		
($66,560 – $63,200)		$ 3,360
Assumed earnings rate on investment of extra cash		× .10
Cash advantage of using DB over SL		$ 336

Exhibit 10-8 highlights several important business relationships. Compare the amount of cash provided by operations before income tax. Both columns show $100,000. If there were no income taxes, the total cash provided by operations would be the same regardless of the depreciation method used. Depreciation is a noncash expense and so does not affect cash from operations.

However, capital cost allowance is a tax-deductible expense. The higher the capital cost allowance, the lower the income before tax and thus the lower the income tax payment. Therefore, using the maximum capital cost allowance available helps conserve cash for use in the business. Exhibit 10-8 indicates that the business will have $3,360 more cash at the end of the first year if it uses DB depreciation instead of SL ($66,560 against $63,200). Suppose the company invests this money to earn a return of 10 percent during the second year. Then the company will be better off by $336 ($3,360 × 10% = $336). The cash advantage of using the DB method is the $336 of additional revenue.

Special Issues in Depreciation Accounting

Two special issues in depreciation accounting are (1) depreciation for partial periods and (2) change in the useful life of a depreciable asset.

Depreciation for Partial Years

Companies purchase plant assets as needed. They do not wait until the beginning of a year or a month. Therefore, companies must develop policies to compute *depreciation for partial years*. Suppose a company purchases a building on April 1 for $500,000. The building's estimated life is 20 years and its estimated residual value is $20,000. The company's fiscal year ends on December 31. Consider how the company computes depreciation for the year ended December 31.

Many companies compute partial-year depreciation by first computing a full year's depreciation. They then multiply this amount by the fraction of the year they held the asset. Assuming the straight-line method, the year's depreciation is $18,000, computed as follows:

$$\frac{(\$500,000 - \$20,000)}{20} = \$24,000 \text{ per year} \times \frac{9}{12} = \$18,000$$

What if the company bought the asset on April 18? A widely used policy suggests businesses record no depreciation on assets purchased after the fifteenth of the month and record a full month's depreciation on an asset bought on or before the fifteenth. Thus the company would record no depreciation for April on an April 18 purchase. In this case, the year's depreciation would be $16,000 ($24,000 × 8/12).

How is partial-year depreciation computed under the other depreciation methods? Suppose this building is acquired on October 4 and the company uses the declining-balance method. For a 20-year asset, the DB rate is 10 percent ($\frac{1}{20} = 5\% \times 2 = 10\%$). First-year depreciation is $50,000 ($500,000 × .10), and the DB amount for October, November and December is $12,500 ($50,000 × 3/12).

No special computation is needed for partial-year depreciation under the units-of-production method. Simply use the number of units produced, regardless of the time period the asset is held.

Change in the Useful Life of a Depreciable Asset

As previously discussed, a business must estimate the useful life of a plant asset to compute depreciation. This prediction is the most difficult part of accounting for depreciation. After the asset is put into use, the business is able to refine its estimate based on experience and new information. Such a change is called a *change in accounting estimate*. In an actual example, Harding Carpets Limited included the following note in its October 31, 1984 financial statements:

> **4. CHANGES IN ACCOUNTING ESTIMATES**
>
> . . . management reassessed the remaining useful lives of all the corporation's machinery and equipment and product sample costs. . . . these changes have resulted in a reduction in depreciation written on fixed assets and a decrease in product sample costs expensed resulting in an increase in net income for the year of $1,094,000.

Such accounting changes resulting from a change in estimated useful life are common because no business has perfect foresight. Generally accepted accounting principles require the business to report the nature, reason and effect of the change on net income, as the Harding Carpets example shows. To *record* a change in accounting estimate, the remaining book value of the asset is spread over its adjusted remaining useful life. The adjusted useful life may be longer or shorter than the original useful life.

Assume that a Harding Carpets machine cost $40,000 and the company originally believed the asset had an 8-year useful life with no residual value. Using the straight-line method, the company would record $5,000 depreciation each year ($40,000/8 years = $5,000). Suppose Harding Carpets used the asset for 2 years. Accumulated depreciation reached $10,000, leaving a book value of $30,000 ($40,000 − $10,000). From its experience with the asset during the first 2 years, management believes the asset will remain useful for an additional 10 years. The company would compute a revised annual depreciation amount and record it as follows:

Asset's Remaining Book Value	÷	(New) Estimated Useful Life Remaining	=	(New) Annual Depreciation Amount
$30,000		10 years		$3,000

Yearly depreciation entry based on new estimated useful life is

Depreciation Expense — Machine......................	3,000	
Accumulated Depreciation — Machine		3,000

Using Fully Depreciated Assets

A fully depreciated asset is one that has reached the end of its estimated useful life. No more depreciation is recorded for the asset. If the asset is no longer suitable for its purpose, the asset is disposed of, as discussed in the next section. However, the company may be in a cash bind and unable to replace the asset. Or the asset's useful life may have been underestimated at the outset. In any event, companies sometimes continue using fully depreciated assets. The asset account and its related accumulated depreciation account remain in the ledger, even though no additional depreciation is recorded for the asset.

Disposal of Plant Assets _____

Eventually, a plant asset ceases to serve a company's needs. The asset may have become worn out, obsolete or, for some other reason, no longer useful to the business. Generally, a company disposes of a plant asset by selling or exchanging it. If the asset cannot be sold or exchanged, then disposal takes the form of junking the asset. Whatever the method of disposal, the business should bring depreciation up to date to measure the asset's final book value properly.

To account for disposal, credit the asset account and debit its related accumulated depreciation account. Suppose the final year's depreciation expense has just been recorded for a machine that cost $6,000 and was estimated to have zero residual value. The machine's accumulated depreciation thus totals $6,000. Assuming this asset cannot be sold or exchanged, the entry to record its disposal is

Accumulated Depreciation—Machine	6,000	
Machine		6,000
To dispose of fully depreciated machine.		

> **OBJECTIVE 5**
> Account for disposal of plant assets

If assets are junked prior to being fully depreciated, the company records a loss equal to the asset's book value. Suppose store fixtures that cost $4,000 are disposed of in this manner. Accumulated depreciation is $3,000 and book value is therefore $1,000. Disposal of these store fixtures is recorded as follows:

Accumulated Depreciation—Store Fixtures...............	3,000	
Loss on Disposal of Store Fixtures	1,000	
Store Fixtures		4,000
To dispose of store fixtures.		

Loss accounts such as Loss on Disposal of Store Fixtures have the same effect as expenses. They decrease net income. Losses are reported on the income statement and are closed to Income Summary along with expenses.

Selling a Plant Asset

Suppose the business sells furniture on September 30, 19X4 for $5,000 cash. The furniture cost $10,000 when purchased on January 1, 19X1 and has been depreciated on a straight-line basis. The business estimated a 10-year useful life and no residual value. Prior to recording the sale of the furniture, the business must update depreciation. Since the business uses the calendar year as its accounting period, partial depreciation must be recorded for the asset's expense from January 1, 19X4 to the sale date. The straight-line depreciation entry at September 30, 19X4 is

19X4			
Sept. 30	Depreciation Expense ($10,000/10 years × $\frac{9}{12}$)	750	
	Accumulated Depreciation—Furniture		750
	To update depreciation.		

After this entry is posted, the Furniture and the Accumulated Depreciation—Furniture accounts appear as follows. The furniture book value is $6,250 ($10,000 − $3,750).

Furniture		Accumulated Depreciation — Furniture	
Jan. 1, 19X1 10,000			Dec. 31, 19X1 1,000
			Dec. 31, 19X2 1,000
			Dec. 31, 19X3 1,000
			Sept. 30, 19X4 750
			Sept. 30, 19X4 3,750

The entry to record sale of the furniture for $5,000 cash is

19X4
Sept. 30   Cash 5,000
                Loss on Sale of Furniture 1,250
                Accumulated Depreciation — Furniture 3,750
                      Furniture 10,000
                To sell furniture.

When recording the sale of a plant asset, the business must remove the balances in the asset account (Furniture, in this case) and its related accumulated depreciation account, and also record a gain or a loss if the amount of cash received differs from the asset's book value. In our example, cash of $5,000 is less than the book value of the furniture, $6,250. The result is a loss of $1,250.

Suppose the sale price had been $7,000. The business would have had a gain of $750 (Cash, $7,000 – asset book value, $6,250). The entry to record this transaction would be

Cash 7,000
Accumulated Depreciation — Furniture 3,750
      Furniture 10,000
      Gain on Sale of Furniture 750
To sell furniture.

A gain is recorded when an asset is sold for a price greater than the asset's book value. A loss is recorded when the sale price is less than book value. Gains increase net income, as revenues do. They are reported on the income statement and closed to Income Summary along with the revenues.

Exchanging a Plant Asset

Businesses often exchange (trade in) their old plant assets for similar assets that are newer and more efficient. For example, a pizzeria may decide to trade in its 5-year-old delivery car for a newer model. To record the exchange, the business must remove from the books the balances for the asset being exchanged and its related accumulated depreciation account.

Assume that the pizzeria's old delivery car cost $7,000 and has accumulated depreciation totaling $6,000. The book value, then, is $1,000. The new delivery car, say a Ford Escort, costs $10,200, and the auto dealer offers a $1,000 trade-in allowance. The pizzeria pays cash for the remaining $9,200. The trade-in is recorded with this entry:

Delivery Auto (new) 10,200
Accumulated Depreciation (old) 6,000
      Delivery Auto (old) 7,000
      Cash 9,200

In this example, the book value and the trade-in allowance are both $1,000, and so no gain or loss occurs on the exchange. Usually, however, an exchange results in a gain or a loss. If the trade-in allowance received is greater than the book value of the asset being given, the business has a gain. If the trade-in allowance received is less than the book value of the asset given, the business has a loss. Generally accepted accounting principles allow losses and gains to be recognized on the exchange of similar assets. We now turn to the entries for gains and losses on exchanges, continuing our delivery-car example and its data.[1]

Situation 1   Loss recognized on asset exchange

Assume that the new Escort has a cash price of $10,200, and the dealer gives a trade-in allowance of $600 on the old vehicle. The pizzeria pays the balance, $9,600 in cash. The loss on the exchange is $400 (book value of old asset given, $1,000, minus trade-in allowance received, $600). The account Loss on Exchange of Delivery Auto is debited for $400. The entry to record this exchange is

Delivery Auto (new)	10,200	
Accumulated Depreciation—Delivery Auto (old).	6,000	
Loss on Exchange of Delivery Auto	400	
Delivery Auto (old)		7,000
Cash		9,600

Situation 2   Gain recognized on asset exchange

Assume that the new Escort's cash price is $10,200, and the dealer gives a $1,300 trade-in allowance. The pizzeria pays the balance in cash. The gain is $300 (trade-in allowance received, $1,300, minus book value of old asset given, $1,000). The account Gain on Exchange of Delivery Auto is credited for $300. The entry to record this exchange is

Delivery Auto (new)	10,200	
Accumulated Depreciation—Delivery Auto	6,000	
Delivery Auto (old)		7,000
Cash		8,900
Gain on Exchange of Delivery Auto		300

Control of Plant Assets

Control of plant assets includes safeguarding them and having an adequate accounting system. To see the need for controlling plant assets, consider the following actual situation. The home office and top managers of the company are in Calgary. The company manufactures gas pumps in Michigan, which are sold in Europe. Top managers and owners of the company rarely see the manufacturing plant and therefore cannot control plant assets by on-the-spot management. What features does their internal control system need?

---

[1] GAAP rules for exchanges may differ from income tax rules. In this discussion, we are concerned with the accounting rules.

Safeguarding plant assets includes:

1. Assigning responsibility for custody of the assets.
2. Separating custody of assets from accounting for the assets. (This is a cornerstone of internal control in almost every area.)
3. Setting up security measures, for instance, guards and restricted access to plant assets, to prevent theft.
4. Protecting them from the elements (rain, snow, and so on).
5. Having adequate insurance against fire, storm and other casualty losses.
6. Training operating personnel in the proper use of the asset.
7. Keeping a regular maintenance schedule.

Plant assets are controlled in much the same way that high-priced inventory is controlled—with subsidiary records. For plant assets, companies use a plant asset ledger. Each plant asset is represented by a card describing the asset and listing its location and the employee responsible for it. These details aid in safeguarding the asset. The ledger card also shows the asset's cost, useful life and other accounting data. Exhibit 10-9 is an example.

The ledger card provides the data for computing depreciation on the asset. It serves as a subsidiary record of accumulated depreciation. The asset balance ($190,000) and accumulated depreciation amount ($45,000) agree with the balances in the respective general ledger accounts (Store Fixtures and Accumulated Depreciation—Store Fixtures).

EXHIBIT 10-9 *Plant Asset Ledger Card*

Asset Clothing racks **Location** Ladies better dresses
Employee responsible for the asset Department manager

Cost $190,000 **Purchased From** Boone Supply Co.
Depreciation Method SL
Useful Life 10 years **Residual Value** $10,000
General Ledger Account Store fixtures

| Date | Explanation | Asset | | | Accumulated Depreciation | | |
		Dr	Cr	Bal	Dr	Cr	Bal
Jul. 3, 19X4	Purchase	190,000		190,000			
Dec. 31, 19X4	Deprec.					9,000	9,000
Dec. 31, 19X5	Deprec.					18,000	27,000
Dec. 31, 19X6	Deprec.					18,000	45,000

Accounting for Wasting Assets and Depletion

OBJECTIVE 6

Account for wasting assets and depletion

Natural resources or *wasting assets* such as iron ore, coal, oil, gas and timber are plant assets of a special type. An investment in natural resources could be described as an investment in inventories in the ground (coal) or on top of the ground (timber). As plant assets (such as machines) are expensed through depreciation, natural resource assets are expensed through depletion. **Depletion** expense is that portion of the cost of natural resources that is used up in a particular period. Depletion expense is computed in the same way as *units-of-production* depreciation.

An oil well may cost $100,000 and contain an estimated 10,000 barrels of oil. The depletion rate would be $10 per barrel ($100,000/10,000 barrels). If 3,000 barrels are extracted during the first year, depletion expense is $30,000 (3,000 barrels $\times$ $10 per barrel). If 4,500 barrels are removed the second year, that period's depletion is $45,000 (4,500 barrels $\times$ $10 per barrel). The depletion entry for the first year is

Depletion Expense (3,000 barrels $\times$ $10)	30,000	
Accumulated Depreciation — Oil		30,000

Accumulated Depletion is a contra account similar to Accumulated Depreciation.

Natural resource assets can be reported as follows:

Property, Plant and Equipment		
Land.		$120,000
Buildings.	$800,000	
Equipment	160,000	
	960,000	
Less: Accumulated Depletion.	410,000	550,000
Coal	$340,000	
Less: Accumulated Depletion	90,000	250,000
Total Property, Plant and Equipment		$920,000

Accounting for Intangible Assets and Amortization _____

Intangible assets are a class of long-lived assets that are not physical in nature. Instead, these assets consist of special rights to current and expected future benefits from patents, copyrights, trademarks, franchises, leaseholds and goodwill.

The acquisition cost of an intangible asset is debited to an asset account. The intangible is expensed through **amortization**, which applies to intangible assets in the same way depreciation applies to plant assets and depletion applies to natural resources. All three methods of expensing assets are conceptually the same; that is, they are different names for the same concept.

Amortization is generally computed on a straight-line basis over the asset's estimated useful life — up to a maximum of 40 years, according to convention, and thus GAAP. However, obsolescence often cuts an intangible asset's useful life shorter than its legal life. Amortization expense is written off directly against the asset account rather than held in an accumulated amortization account. The residual value of most intangible assets is zero, because once the rights represented by the intangible asset expire, the asset has no value.

Assume that a business purchases a patent on a special manufacturing process. Legally, the patent may run for 17 years. However, the business realizes that new technologies will limit the patented process's life to 4 years. If the patent cost $80,000, each year's amortization expense is $20,000 ($80,000/4). The balance sheet reports the patent at its acquisition cost less amortization expense to date. After 1 year, the patent has a $60,000 balance ($80,000 – $20,000), after 2 years a $40,000 balance, and so on.

Patents are federal government grants giving a holder the exclusive right for 17 years to produce and sell an invention. Patented products include Bombardier Skidoos and the Spar Aerospace "Arm" that has been used on the space shuttle flights. Like any other asset, a patent may be purchased. Suppose a company pays $170,000 to acquire a patent and the business believes the expected useful life of the patent is only 5 years. Amortization expense is $34,000 per year ($170,000/5 years). The company's acquisition and amortization entries for this patent are

OBJECTIVE 7

Account for intangible assets and amortization

19X4				
Jan. 1	Patent		170,000	
	Cash			170,000
	To acquire a patent.			
Dec. 31	Amortization Expense—Patents ($170,000/5) ..		34,000	
	Patents			34,000
	To amortize the cost of a patent.			

Copyrights are exclusive rights to reproduce and sell a book, musical composition, film or other work of art. Issued by the federal government, copyrights extend 50 years beyond the author's (composer's, artist's) life. The cost of obtaining a copyright from the government is low, but a company may pay a large sum to purchase an existing copyright from the owner. For example, a publisher may pay the author of a popular novel $1 million or more for the book's copyright. The useful life of a copyright is usually no longer than two or three years, so that each period's amortization amount is a considerable portion of the copyright's cost.

Trademarks and **trade names** are distinctive identifications of products or services. For example, The Sports Network has its distinct logo of the yellow letters TSN on a black television screen-shaped background. Apple Computer has the multi-coloured apple with the bite out of it. The Toronto Maple Leafs and the Montreal Canadiens have insignia that identify their respective hockey teams. Molson Export, Swiss Chalet chicken, Petro-Canada and Roots are everyday trade names. Advertising slogans such as "At Speedy you're a somebody," Japan Camera Centre's "Where memories develop... right before your eyes" or Burger King's "Fast Food for Fast Times" are also legally protected.

The cost of a trademark or trade name is amortized over its useful life, not to exceed 40 years. The cost of advertising and promotions that use the trademark or trade name is not a part of the asset's cost but a debit to the advertising expense account.

Franchises and **licences** are privileges granted by a private business or a government to sell a product or service in accordance with specified conditions. The Calgary Flames hockey organization is a franchise granted to its owners by the National Hockey League. IGA Food Markets and Re/Max Ltd. are well-known franchises. Union Gas holds a franchise to provide gas to residents and businesses in certain parts of the country. The acquisition costs of franchises and licences are amortized over their useful lives rather than over legal lives, subject to the 40-year maximum.

A **leasehold** is a prepayment that a lessee (renter) makes to secure the use of an asset from a lessor (landlord). Often leases require the lessee to make this prepayment in addition to monthly rental payments. The lessee debits the monthly lease payments to the Rent Expense account. The prepayment, however, is a debit to an intangible asset account entitled Leaseholds. This amount is amortized over the life of the lease by debiting Rent Expense and crediting Leaseholds. Some leases stipulate that the last year's rent must be paid in advance when the lease is signed. This prepayment is debited to Leaseholds and transferred to Rent Expense during the last year of the lease.

Sometimes lessees modify or improve the leased asset. For example, a lessee may construct a fence on leased land. The lessee debits the cost of the fence to a separate intangible asset account, Leasehold Improvements, and amortizes its cost over the term of the lease.

Goodwill in accounting is a more limited term than in everyday use, as in "goodwill among men." In accounting, *goodwill* is defined as the excess of the cost of an acquired company over the sum of the market values of its net assets (assets minus liabilities). Suppose Company A acquires Company B at a cost of $10 million. The market value of Company B's assets is $9 million, and its liabilities total $1 million. In this case, Company A paid $2 million for goodwill, computed as follows:

Purchase price paid for Company B...............		$10 million
Market value of Company B's assets	$9 million	
Less: Company B's liabilities......................	1 million	
Market value of Company B's net assets............		8 million
Excess is called *goodwill*.........................		$ 2 million

Company A's entry to record the acquisition of Company B, including its goodwill, would be

Assets (Cash, Receivables, Inventories,		
Plant Assets, all at market value)	9,000,000	
Goodwill	2,000,000	
Liabilities..................................		1,000,000
Cash......................................		10,000,000

Goodwill has the following special features:

1. Goodwill is recorded, at its cost, only when it is purchased in the acquisition of another company. Even though a favourable location, a superior product or an outstanding reputation may create goodwill for a company, it is never recorded by that entity. Instead, goodwill is recorded only by another company that purchases the entity with goodwill. A purchase transaction provides objective evidence of the value of the goodwill.

2. According to generally accepted accounting principles, goodwill is amortized on a straight-line basis over a period not to exceed 40 years. In reality, the goodwill of many entities increases in value.

Capital Expenditures versus
Revenue Expenditures (Expenses)

When a company makes a plant asset expenditure, it must decide whether to debit an asset account or an expense account. In this context, *expenditure* refers to either a cash or credit purchase of goods or services related to the asset. Examples of these expenditures range from replacing the windshield wipers on an automobile to adding a wing to a building.

Expenditures that increase the capacity or efficiency of the asset or extend its useful life are called **capital expenditures**. For example, the cost of a major overhaul that extends a taxi's useful life is a capital expenditure. Repair work that generates a capital expenditure is called an **extraordinary repair**. The amount of the capital expenditure, said to be capitalized, is a debit to an asset

OBJECTIVE 8
Distinguish capital expenditures from revenue expenditures

EXHIBIT 10-10   *Delivery Truck Expenditures*

Debit an Asset Account for Capital Expenditures	Debit Repair and Maintenance Expense for Revenue Expenditures
Extraordinary repairs	*Ordinary repairs*
Major engine overhaul	Repair of transmission or other
Modification of body for new use	mechanism
of truck	Oil change, lubrication, and so on
Addition to storage capacity of	Replacement tires, windshield, and
truck	the like
	Paint job

account. For the extraordinary repair on the taxi, we would debit the asset account Automobile.

Other expenditures do not extend the asset's capacity or efficiency. Expenditures that merely maintain the asset in its existing condition or restore the asset to good working order are called **revenue expenditures** because these costs are matched against revenue. Examples include the costs of repainting a taxi, repairing a dented fender and replacing tires. The work that creates the revenue expenditure, said to be expensed, is a debit to an expense account. For the **ordinary repairs** on the taxi, we would debit Repair Expense.

The distinction between capital and revenue expenditures is often a matter of opinion. Does the work extend the life of the asset, or does it only maintain the asset in good order? When doubt exists as to whether to debit an asset or an expense, companies tend to debit an expense for two reasons. First, many expenditures are minor in amount, and most companies have a policy of debiting expense for all expenditures below a specified minimum, such as $1,000. Second, the income tax motive favours debiting all borderline expenditures to expense in order to create an immediate tax deduction. Capital expenditures are not immediate tax deductions.

Exhibit 10-10 illustrates the distinction between capital expenditures and revenue expenditures (expense) for several delivery truck expenditures. Note also the difference between extraordinary and ordinary repairs.

Treating a capital expenditure as a revenue expenditure, or vice versa, creates errors in the financial statements. Suppose a company makes an extraordinary repair to equipment and erroneously expenses this cost. It is a capital expenditure that should have been debited to an asset account. This accounting error overstates expenses and understates net income on the income statement. On the balance sheet, the equipment account is understated, and so is owner's equity. Capitalizing the cost of an ordinary repair creates the opposite error. Expenses are understated and net income is overstated on the income statement. The balance sheet reports overstated amounts for assets and owners' equity.

Summary Problems for Your Review

Problem 1   The figures that follow appear in requirement 2, the Solution to Review Problem, on p. 413.

| | Method A | | | Method B | | |
| | Straight-Line | | | Declining-Balance (Revenue Canada) | | |
Year	Annual Depreciation Expense	Accumulated Depreciation	Book Value	Annual Depreciation Expense	Accumulated Depreciation	Book Value
Start			$44,000			$44,000
19X5	$4,000	$4,000	40,000	$8,800	$ 8,800	35,200
19X6	4,000	8,000	36,000	7,040	15,840	28,160
19X7	4,000	12,000	32,000	5,632	21,472	22,528

Required

Which depreciation method would you select for income tax purposes? Why?

Problem 2   A corporation purchased a building at a cost of $500,000 on January 1, 19X3. Management has depreciated the building by using the straight-line method, a 35-year life, and a residual value of $150,000. On July 1, 19X7, the company sold the building for $575,000 cash. The fiscal year of the corporation ends on December 31.

Required

Record depreciation for 19X7 and record the sale of the building on July 1, 19X7.

SOLUTIONS TO REVIEW PROBLEMS

1. For tax purposes, most companies select the maximum amount allowed by Revenue Canada, which results in accelerated depreciation of the equipment. Accelerated depreciation minimizes taxable income and income tax payments in the early years of the asset's life, thereby maximizing the business's cash at the earliest possible time.

2.

19X7			
July 1	Depreciation Expense—Building		
	[($500,000 – $150,000)/35 years × ½ year]	5,000	
	Accumulated Depreciation—Building		5,000
To record depreciation to date of sale.			
July 1	Cash......................................	575,000	
	Accumulated Depreciation—Building		
	[($500,000 – $150,000)/35 years × 4½ years].....	45,000	
	Building		500,000
	Gain on Sale of Building................		120,000
To record sale of building.			

Summary _____

Plant assets are long-lived assets that the business uses in its operation. These assets are not held for sale as inventory. The cost of all plant assets but land is expensed through *depreciation*. The cost of natural resources, a special category of long-lived assets, is expensed through *depletion*. A third category of long-lived assets, *intangibles*, are rights that have no physical form. The cost of intangibles is expensed through *amortization*. Depreciation, depletion and amortization are identical in concept.

Businesses usually compute the depreciation of plant assets by one of three methods: *straight-line, units-of-production*, and the *accelerated* method — *double-declining-balance* or Revenue Canada rates. Most companies use the straight-line method for financial reporting purposes, and almost all companies use an accelerated method for income tax purposes. Accelerated depreciation results in greater tax deductions early in the asset's life. These deductions decrease income tax payments and conserve cash that the company can use in its business.

Before disposing of a plant asset, the business updates the asset's depreciation. Disposal is recorded by removing the book balances from both the asset account and its related accumulated depreciation account. Disposal often results in recognition of a gain or a loss.

Depletion of natural resources is computed on a units-of-production basis. *Amortization* of intangibles is computed on a straight-line basis over a maximum of 40 years. However, the useful lives of most intangibles are shorter than their legal lives.

Capital expenditures increase the capacity or the efficiency of an asset, or extend its useful life. Accordingly, they are debited to an asset account. *Revenue expenditures*, on the other hand, merely maintain the asset's usefulness and are debited to an expense account.

Self-Study Questions

Test your understanding of the chapter by marking the correct answer for each of the following questions:

1. Which of the following payments is *not* included in the cost of land? *(p. 404)*
    a. Broker's commission   c. Back property taxes paid at acquisition
    b. Legal fees   d. Cost of fencing and lighting

2. A business paid $120,000 for two machines valued at $90,000 and $60,000. The business will record these machines at *(p. 404)*
    a. $90,000 and $60,000   c. $72,000 and $48,000
    b. $60,000 each   d. $70,000 and $50,000

3. Which of the following definitions fits depreciation? *(pp. 405, 406)*
    a. Allocation of the asset's market value to expense over its useful life
    b. Allocation of the asset's cost to expense over its useful life
    c. Decreases in the asset's market value over its useful life
    d. Increases in the fund set aside to replace the asset when it is worn out

4. Which depreciation method's amounts are not computed based on time? *(pp. 408, 409)*
    a. Straight-line   c. Declining balance
    b. Units-of-production

5. Which depreciation method gives the largest amount of expense in the early years of using the asset and therefore is best for income tax purposes? *(pp. 414, 415)*
    a. Straight-line   c. Accelerated
    b. Units of-production   d. All are equal

6. A company paid $450,000 for a building and was depreciating it by the straight-line method over a 40-year life with estimated residual value of $50,000. After 10 years, it became evident that the building's useful life would be 50 years. Depreciation for the eleventh year is *(p. 416)*
    a. $7,500   c. $10,000
    b. $8,750   d. $12,500

7. Labrador, Inc. scrapped an automobile that cost $14,000 and had book value of $1,100. The entry to record this disposal is *(p. 417)*

    a. Loss on Disposal of Automobile   1,100
           Automobile   1,100

b. Accumulated Depreciation 14,000

       Automobile.................................   14,000

c. Accumulated Depreciation 12,900

       Automobile.................................   12,900

d. Accumulated Depreciation 12,900

   Loss of Disposal of Automobile.................... 1,100

       Automobile.................................   14,000

8. Depletion is computed in the same manner as which depreciation method? *(p. 421)*
   a. Straight-line   c. Declining balance
   b. Units-of-production

9. Lacy Corporation paid $550,000 to acquire Gentsch, Inc. Gentsch's assets had a market value of $900,000 and its liabilities were $400,000. In recording the acquisition, Lacy will record goodwill of *(p. 423)*
   a. $50,000   c. $550,000
   b. $100,000   d. $0

10. Which of the following items is a revenue expenditure? *(p. 424)*
    a. Property tax paid on land one year after it is acquired
    b. Survey fee paid during the acquisition of land
    c. Legal fee paid to acquire land
    d. Building permit paid to construct a warehouse on the land

Answers to the self-study questions are at the end of the chapter.

Accounting Vocabulary

accelerated depreciation
  (p. 409)
amortization *(p. 421)*
capital cost allowance
  (p. 409)
capital expenditure *(p. 423)*
copyright *(p. 422)*
cost of plant asset
  (p. 404)
depletion *(p. 421)*
declining-balance (DB) method
  (p. 409)
estimated residual value
  (p. 407)

estimated useful life
  (p. 407)
extraordinary repair
  (p. 423)
franchises and licences
  (p. 422)
goodwill *(p. 423)*
intangible assets
  (p. 403)
leaseholds *(p. 422)*
ordinary repairs *(p. 424)*
patents *(p. 422)*
relative-sales-value method
  (p. 405)

Revenue Canada rates
  (p. 409)
revenue expenditure
  (p. 424)
straight-line (SL) method
  (p. 407)
trademarks and trade names
  (p. 422)
units-of-production (UOP)
  method *(p. 408)*
wasting assets *(p. 403)*

Assignment Material _____

Questions

1. To what types of long-lived assets do the following expenses apply: depreciation, depletion and amortization?
2. Describe how the cost of a plant asset is measured. Would the cost of repairing the asset after it is placed in service be included in the asset's cost?
3. Suppose land is purchased for $100,000. How do you account for the $8,000 cost of removing an unwanted building?
4. When assets are purchased as a group for a single price and no individual asset cost is given, how is each asset's cost determined?
5. Define depreciation. Present the common misconceptions about depreciation.

6. Which depreciation method does each of the following graphs characterize: straight-line, units-of-production or accelerated?

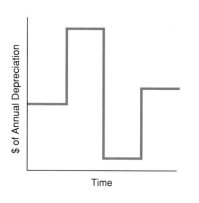 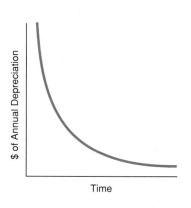 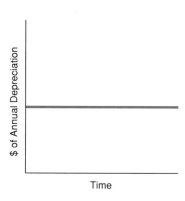

7. Which of the three depreciation methods results in the most depreciation in the first year of the asset's life?

8. Explain the concept of accelerated depreciation. Which depreciation methods are used in the definition of accelerated depreciation?

9. The level of business activity fluctuates widely for Harwood Delivery Service, reaching its peak around Christmas each year. At other times, business is slow. What depreciation method is most appropriate for the company's fleet of Chevy Luv trucks?

10. Oswalt Computer Service Center uses the most advanced computers available to keep a competitive edge over other service centres. To maintain this advantage, Oswalt usually replaces its computers before they are worn out. Describe the major factors affecting the useful life of a plant asset and indicate which seems more relevant to Oswalt's computers.

11. Estimated residual value is not considered in computing depreciation during the early years of the asset's life by one of the methods. Which method is it?

12. Which depreciation method is best from the standpoint of income tax? Why?

13. How does depreciation affect income taxes? How does depreciation affect cash provided by operations?

14. Describe how an accountant computes depreciation for less than a full year and how an accountant accounts for depreciation for less than a full month.

15. Ragland Company paid $10,000 for office furniture. The company expected it to remain in service for 6 years and to have a $1,000 residual value. After 2 years' use, company accountants believe the furniture will last an additional 6 years. How much depreciation will Ragland record for each of these 6 years, assuming straight-line depreciation and no change in the estimated residual value?

16. What three pieces of information should a company disclose about a change in accounting estimate, such as extending the useful life of a depreciable asset?

17. When a company sells a plant asset before the year's end, what must it record before accounting for the sale?

18. Describe how an accountant determines whether a company experiences a gain or a loss when an old plant asset is exchanged for a new one.

19. Identify seven elements of internal control designed to safeguard plant assets.

20. What expense applies to natural resources? By which depreciation method is this expense computed?

21. How do intangible assets differ from most other assets? Why are they assets at all? What expense applies to intangible assets?

22. Why is the cost of patents and other intangible assets often expensed over a shorter period than the legal life of the asset?

23. Your company has just purchased another company for $400,000. The market

value of the other company's net assets is $325,000. What is the $75,000 excess called? What type of asset is it? What is the maximum period over which its cost is amortized under generally accepted accounting principles?

24. Northern Telecom is recognized as a world leader in the manufacture and sale of telephone equipment. The company's success has created vast amounts of business goodwill. Would you expect to see *this* goodwill reported on Northern Telecom's financial statements? Why, or why not?

25. Distinguish a capital expenditure from a revenue expenditure. The title Revenue Expenditure is curious in that a revenue expenditure is a debit to an expense account. Explain why revenue expenditures are so named.

26. Are ordinary repairs capital expenditures or revenue expenditures? Which type of expenditures are extraordinary repairs?

Exercises

Exercise 10-1 *Identifying the elements of a plant asset's cost*

A company purchased land, paying $30,000 cash as a down payment and signing a $120,000 note payable for the balance. In addition, the company paid a purchase commission of $6,000, a legal fee of $500 and a $3,100 charge for leveling the land and removing an unwanted building. The company constructed an office building on the land at a cost of $640,000. It also paid $12,000 for a fence around the boundary of the property, $2,400 for the company sign near the entrance to the property and $6,000 for special lighting of the grounds. Determine the cost of the company's land, land improvements and building.

Exercise 10-2 *Allocating cost to assets acquired in a basket purchase*

Dartmouth Research Centre bought three used machines in a $21,000 purchase. An independent appraisal of the machines produced the following figures:

Machine No.	Appraised Value
1	$ 4,000
2	12,000
3	8,000

Assuming Dartmouth paid cash for the machines, record the purchase in the general journal, identifying each machine's individual cost in a separate Machine account.

Exercise 10-3 *Computing depreciation*

A company delivery truck was acquired on January 2, 19X1 for $12,000. The truck was expected to remain in service for 4 years and last 88,000 kilometres. At the end of its useful life, company officials estimated that the truck's residual value would be $1,000. The truck travelled 24,000 kilometres in the first year, 28,000 in the second year, 21,000 in the third year, and 15,000 in the fourth year. Prepare a schedule of *depreciation expense* per year for the truck under the following depreciation methods. The Revenue Canada rate is 30 percent. Show your computations.

Depreciation Expense Per Year

Year	Straight-line	Units-of-Production	Double-Declining-Balance	Revenue Canada Rate
19X1				
19X2				
19X3				
19X4				

Exercise 10-4   *Identifying depreciation methods for income tax and financial reporting purposes*

Using the data in Exercise 10-3, identify the depreciation method that is most advantageous from an income tax perspective. Which depreciation method do most companies use for reporting to their shareholders and creditors on their financial statements?

Exercise 10-5   *Recording depreciation computed by two methods*

Situation 1   Hunt Corporation purchased office furniture on March 3, 19X4 for $2,600 cash. Donna Hunt expects it to remain useful for 8 years and to have a residual value of $200. Hunt uses the straight-line depreciation method. Record Hunt's depreciation on the furniture for the year ended December 31, 19X4.

Situation 2   Chen Company purchased equipment on May 19, 19X2 for $19,500, signing a note payable for that amount. Chen estimated that this equipment will be useful for 3 years and have a residual value of $1,500. Assuming Chen uses double-declining-balance depreciation, record Chen's depreciation on the machine for the year ended December 31, 19X2.

Exercise 10-6   *Journalizing a change in a plant asset's useful life*

A company purchased a building for $680,000 and depreciated it on a straight-line basis over a 30-year period. The estimated residual value was $80,000. After using the building for 10 years, the company realized that wear and tear on the building would force the company to replace it before 30 years. Starting with the 11th year, the company began depreciating the building over a revised total life of 20 years, retaining the $80,000 estimate of residual value. Record depreciation expense on the building for years 10 and 11.

Exercise 10-7   *Recording the sale of a plant asset*

On January 2, 19X1, Oakwood Sales Company purchased store fixtures for $7,700 cash, expecting the fixtures to remain in service for 10 years. Oakwood has depreciated the fixtures by the Revenue Canada rate of 20 percent, assuming no estimated residual value. On June 30, 19X8, Oakwood sold the fixtures for $1,600 in cash. Record depreciation expense on the fixtures for the 6 months ended June 30, 19X8, and also record the sale of the fixtures.

Exercise 10-8   *Exchanging plant assets*

A machine cost $10,000. At the end of 4 years, its accumulated depreciation was $4,500. For each of the following situations, record the trade-in of this old machine for a new, similar machine.

Situation 1   The new machine had a cash price of $12,400; the dealer allowed a trade-in allowance of $5,200 on the old machine; and you paid the $7,200 balance in cash.

Situation 2   The new machine had a cash price of $13,000; the dealer allowed a trade-in allowance of $6,300 on the old machine; and you signed a note payable for the $6,700 balance.

Exercise 10-9   *Preparing a plant ledger card*

McBee Delivery Service uses a plant ledger card to account for its delivery vehicles, which are located at the company's service garage. The fleet of vehicles cost $96,000 when purchased from Ericksen Ford Ltd. on September 1, 19X2. This cost is the debit balance in the Delivery Vehicles account in the general ledger. McBee uses the straight-line depreciation method and estimates a 4-year useful life and a $6,000 residual value for the trucks. The garage supervisor is responsible for the vehicles. The company's fiscal year ends on December 31. Complete a plant ledger card for these vehicles through December 31, 19X4, using a format similar to Exhibit 10-9.

Exercise 10-10 *Recording wasting assets and depletion*

Sasquatch Mining Company Ltd. paid $178,500 for the right to extract ore from a 200,000-tonne mineral deposit. In addition to the purchase price, Sasquatch also paid a $500 filing fee and a $1,000 license fee to the Province of British Columbia. Because Sasquatch purchased the rights to the minerals only, the company expected the asset to have zero residual value when fully depleted. During the first year of production, Sasquatch removed 35,000 tonnes of ore. Make general journal entries to record (1) purchase of the mineral rights (debit Mineral Asset), (2) payment of fees and (3) depletion for first-year production.

Exercise 10-11 *Recording intangibles, amortization and a change in the asset's useful life*

Part 1   Lutz Corporation manufactures high-speed printers and has recently purchased for $4 million a patent for the design for a new laser printer. Although it gives legal protection for 17 years, the patent is expected to provide a competitive advantage for Lutz for only 8 years. Assuming the straight-line method of amortization, use general journal entries to record (1) the purchase of the patent and (2) amortization for 1 year.

Part 2   After using the patent for 3 years, Lutz learns at an industry trade show that another company is designing a more efficient printer. Based on this new information, Lutz decides, starting with year 4, to amortize the remaining cost of the patent over 2 additional years, giving the patent a total useful life of 5 years. Record amortization for year 4.

Exercise 10-12 *Computing and recording goodwill*

Company P purchased Company S, paying $1 million cash. The market value of Company S assets was $1.7 million, and Company S had liabilities of $.9 million.

a. Compute the cost of the goodwill purchased by Company P.
b. Record the purchase by Company P.
c. Record amortization of goodwill for 1 year, assuming the straight-line method and a useful life of 20 years.

Exercise 10-13 *Distinguishing capital expenditures from revenue expenditures*

Classify each of the following expenditures as a capital expenditure or a revenue expenditure (expense) related to machinery: (a) purchase price, (b) sales tax paid on the purchase price, (c) transportation and insurance while machinery is in transport from seller to buyer, (d) installation, (e) training of personnel for initial operation of the machinery, (f) special reinforcement to the machinery platform, (g) income tax paid on income earned from the sale of products manufactured by the machinery, (h) major overhaul to extend useful life by three years, (i) ordinary recurring repairs to keep the machinery in good working order, (j) lubrication of the machinery before it is placed in service, (k) periodic lubrication after the machinery is placed in service.

Problems   *(Group A)*

Problem 10-1A *Identifying the elements of a plant asset's cost*

Mazzoti Ltd. incurred the following costs in acquiring land and a garage, making land improvements, and constructing and furnishing a home office building:

a. Purchase price of 3½ acres of land, including an old building that will be used as a garage for company vehicles (land market value is $600,000; building market value is $60,000) $605,000

b. Delinquent real estate taxes on the land to be paid by Mazzoti 14,600

c. Landscaping (additional dirt and earth moving) 3,550

d. Legal fees on the land acquisition 1,000

e. Fence around the boundary of the land 12,500

f. Building permit for the home office building 200

g. Architect fee for the design of the home office building........... 25,000

h. Company signs near front and rear approaches to the company property 23,550

i. Renovation of the garage 23,800

j. Concrete, wood, steel girders and other materials used in the construction of the home office building 385,000

k. Masonry, carpentry, roofing and other labour to construct home office building 734,000

l. Repair of vandalism damage to home office building during construction 4,100

m. Parking lots and concrete walks on the property................. 17,450

n. Lights for the parking lot, walkways and company signs 8,900

o. Supervisory salary of construction supervisor (90 percent to home office building, 6 percent to fencing, parking lot and concrete walks, and 4 percent to garage renovation)............................ 55,000

p. Office furniture for the home office building 267,500

q. Transportation of furniture from seller to the home office building.. 700

r. Landscaping (trees and shrubs)................................ 9,100

Mazzoti depreciates buildings over 40 years, land improvements over 20 years and furniture over 8 years, all on a straight-line basis with zero residual value.

Required

1. Using the following format, account for each cost by listing it as a debit to Land, Land Improvements, Home Office Building, Garage or Furniture:

Item	Land	Land Improvements	Home Office Building	Garage	Furniture
a	$	$	$	$	$
⋮					
r	———	———	———	———	———
Totals $		$	$	$	$

2. Assuming that all construction was complete and the assets were placed in service on March 19, record depreciation for the year ended December 31. (Round figures to the nearest dollar.)

Problem 10-2A   *Computing depreciation and the cash flow advantage of accelerated depreciation for tax purposes*

On January 2, 19X1, Morse, Inc. purchased three used delivery trucks at a total cost of $41,000. Before placing the trucks in service, the company spent $1,200 painting them, $1,800 replacing their tires and $4,000 overhauling their engines and reconditioning their bodies. Morse management estimates that the trucks will remain in service for 6 years and have a residual value of $6,000. The trucks' combined annual usage is expected to be 16,000 kilometers in each of the first 4 years and 18,000 kilometers in each of the next 2 years. In trying to decide which depreciation method to use, Ted Morse requests a depreciation schedule for each of the following generally accepted depreciation methods: straight-line, units-of-production and declining-balance using the Revenue Canada rate of 30 percent.

Required

1. Assuming Morse depreciates its delivery trucks as a unit, prepare a depreciation schedule for each of the above generally accepted depreciation methods, showing asset cost, depreciation expense, accumulated depreciation and asset book value. Use the formats of Exhibits 10-3 through 10-5.
2. Morse reports to shareholders and creditors in the financial statements, using the depreciation method that maximizes reported income in the early years of asset use. For income tax purposes, however, the company uses the depreciation method that minimizes income tax payments in those early years. Consider the first year that Morse uses the delivery trucks. Identify the depreciation methods that meet Morse's objectives.
3. Assume cash provided by operations before income tax is $80,000 for the delivery truck's first year. The income tax rate is 40 percent. For the two depreciation methods identified in question 2, compare the net income and cash provided by operations (cash flow). Use the following outline for your answer:

	Depreciation Method that in the Early Years	
	A **Maximizes** **Reported** **Income**	**B** **Minimizes** **Income Tax** **Payments**
Comparison of Net Income for First Year		
Cash provided by operations before income tax ..	$	$
Depreciation expense		
Income before income tax		
Income tax expense (40%)......................		
Net income	$	$
Advantage of Method A over Method B	$	
Cash Flow Analysis for First Year		
Cash provided by operations before income tax ..	$	$
Income tax expense		
Cash provided by operations (called cash flow) ...	$	$
Advantage of Method B over Method A	$	

Problem 10-3A *Journalizing and posting plant asset transactions; capital expenditures versus revenue expenditures*

Saskatchewan Power Corporation provides electrical power to Saskatchewan. Assume that the company completed the following transactions:

19X4

Jan. 3   Paid $16,000 cash for a used service truck.

Jan. 5   Paid $1,200 to have the truck engine overhauled.

Jan. 7   Paid $300 to have the truck modified for business use.

Oct. 3   Paid $855 for transmission repair and oil change.

Dec. 31 Used the double-declining-balance method to record depreciation on the truck. (Assume a 4-year life.)

31 Closed the appropriate accounts.

19X5

Mar. 13 Replaced the truck's broken windshield for $275 cash.

June 26 Traded in the service truck for a new truck costing $22,000. The dealer granted a $6,000 allowance on the old truck, and Saskatchewan Power paid the balance in cash. Recorded 19X5 depreciation for the year to date and then recorded the exchange of trucks.

Dec. 31 Used the double-declining-balance method to record depreciation on the new truck. (Assume a 4-year life.)

31 Closed the appropriate accounts.

Required

1. Open the following accounts in the general ledger: Service Trucks, Accumulated Depreciation—Service Trucks, Truck Repair Expense, Depreciation Expense—Service Trucks and Loss on Exchange of Service Trucks.

2. Record the transactions in the general journal and post to the ledger accounts opened.

Problem 10-4A   *Recording plant asset transactions; exchanges; changes in useful life*

A. C. Nielsen Co. surveys Canadian viewing trends. Nielsen's balance sheet reports the following assets under Property and Equipment: land and improvements, buildings, furniture and equipment, and leasehold improvements. The company has a separate accumulated depreciation account for each of these assets except land and leasehold improvements. Depreciation on leasehold improvements is credited directly to the Leasehold Improvements account rather than to Accumulated Depreciation—Leasehold Improvements.

Assume that Nielsen completed the following transactions:

Jan. 4 Traded in communication equipment with book value of $22,000 (cost of $51,000) for similar new equipment with a cash cost of $78,000. The seller gave Nielsen a trade-in allowance of $15,000 on the old equipment, and Nielsen paid the remainder in cash.

19 Purchased office furniture for $45,000 plus 6 percent sales tax and $300 shipping charge. The company gave a 90-day, 10 percent note in payment.

Apr. 19 Paid the furniture note and related interest.

Aug. 29 Sold a building that had cost $475,000 and had accumulated depreciation of $353,500 through December 31 of the preceding years. Depreciation is computed on a straight-line basis. The building has a 30-year useful life and a residual value of $47,500. Nielsen received $250,000 cash and a $750,000 note receivable.

Sept. 6 Paid cash to improve leased assets at a cost of $39,000.

Nov. 10 Purchased used communication and televideo equipment from the Decima Research polling organization. Total cost was $90,000 paid in cash. An independent appraisal valued the communication equipment at $65,000 and the televideo equipment at $35,000.

Dec. 31 Recorded depreciation as follows:
Equipment is depreciated by the double-declining-balance method over a 6-year life with zero residual value. Record depreciation on the equipment purchased on January 4 and on November 10 separately.
Office furniture has an expected useful life of 8 years with an estimated residual value of $5,000. Depreciation is computed using the Revenue Canada rate (20 percent).
Depreciation on leasehold improvements is computed on a straight-line basis over the life of the lease, which is 6 years, with zero residual value.

Depreciation on buildings is computed by the straight-line method. The company had assigned buildings an estimated useful life of 30 years and a residual value that is 10 percent of cost. After using the buildings for 20 years, the company has come to believe that their useful life will extend to 35 years. Residual value remains unchanged. The buildings cost $16,000,000.

Required

Record the transactions in the general journal.

Problem 10-5A   *Distinguishing capital expenditures from revenue expenditures; preparing a plant ledger card*

Suppose Nova Scotia Boat Repair Co. Ltd. uses plant ledger cards to control its service trucks, purchased from Wallen Motor Company. The supervisor is responsible for the trucks, which are located at the company's service garage. The following transactions were completed during 19X6 and 19X7:

19X6

Jan. 10	Paid $14,000 cash for a used service truck (truck no. 21).
Jan. 11	Paid $1,500 to have the truck engine overhauled.
Jan. 12	Paid $250 to have the truck modified for business use.
Aug. 3	Paid $603 for transmission repair and oil change.
Dec. 31	Recorded depreciation on the truck by the double-declining-balance method, based on a 4-year life and a $1,500 residual value.

19X7

Mar. 13	Replaced a damaged bumper on truck no. 21 at a cash cost of $295.
Aug. 12	Traded in service truck no. 21 for a new one (truck no. 26) with a cash cost of $20,000. The dealer granted a $7,000 allowance on the old truck, and Nova Scotia Boat Repair Co. paid the balance in cash. Recorded 19X7 depreciation for year to date and then recorded exchange of the trucks.
Dec. 31	Recorded depreciation on truck no. 26 by the double-declining-balance method, based on a 4-year life and a $2,000 residual value.

Required

1. Identify the capital expenditures and the revenue expenditures in the transactions. Which expenditures are debited to an asset account? Which expenditures are debited to an expense account?
2. Prepare a separate plant ledger card for each of the trucks.

Problem 10-6A   *Recording intangibles, wasting assets and the related expenses*

Part 1   Newfoundland Telephone provides telephone service to most of Newfoundland and Labrador. Suppose that the company's balance sheet reports the asset Cost of Acquisitions in Excess of the Fair Market Value of the Net Assets of Subsidiaries. Assume that Newfoundland Telephone purchased this asset as part of the acquisition of another company, which carried these figures:

Book value of assets	$215,000
Market value of assets	300,000
Liabilities	135,000

Required

1. What is another title for the asset Cost of Acquisitions in Excess of the Fair Market Value of the Net Assets of Subsidiaries?

2. Make the general journal entry to record Newfoundland Telephone's purchase of the other company for $220,000 cash.

3. Assuming Newfoundland Telephone amortizes Cost of Acquisitions in Excess of the Fair Market Value of the Net Assets of Subsidiaries over 20 years, record the straight-line amortization for 1 year.

Part 2   Suppose Northern Telecom purchased a patent for $455,000. Before using the patent, Northern Telecom incurred an additional cost of $25,000 for a lawsuit to defend the company's right to purchase it. Even though the patent gives Northern Telecom legal protection for 17 years, company management has decided to amortize its cost over an 8-year period because of the industry's fast-changing technologies.

Required

Make general journal entries to record the patent transactions, including straight-line amortization for 1 year.

Part 3   TransCanada PipeLines Ltd. owns gas transmission facilities and other energy related assets. The company's balance sheet includes the asset Oil Properties.

Suppose TransCanada paid $2,800,000 cash for an oil lease that contained an estimated reserve of 300,000 barrels of oil. Assume that the company paid $350,000 for additional geological tests of the property and $50,000 to prepare the surface for drilling. Prior to production, the company signed a $40,000 note payable to have a building constructed on the property. Because the building provides on-site headquarters for the drilling effort and will be abandoned when the oil is depleted, its cost is debited to the Oil properties account and included in depletion charges. During the first year of production, TransCanada removed 26,000 barrels of oil, which it sold on credit for $19 per barrel.

Required

Make general journal entries to record all transactions related to the oil and gas property, including depletion and sale of the first-year production.

(Group B)

Problem 10-1B   *Identifying the elements of a plant asset's cost*

Anotelli Company incurred the following costs in acquiring land, making land improvements, and constructing and furnishing an office building:

a.	Purchase price of four hectares of land, including an old building that will be used for storage (land market value is $380,000; building market value is $20,000)	$350,000
b.	Landscaping (additional dirt and earth moving)	8,100
c.	Fence around the boundary of the land	23,650
d.	Legal fee for title search on the land	600
e.	Delinquent real estate taxes on the land to be paid by Anotelli	5,900
f.	Company signs at front of the company property	7,600
g.	Building permit for the office building	350
h.	Architect fee for the design of the office building	19,800
i.	Masonry, carpentry, roofing and other labor to construct office building	509,000
j.	Concrete, wood, steel girders and other materials used in the construction of the office building	453,000
k.	Renovation of the storage building	41,800

l.	Repair of storm damage to storage building during construction....	2,200
m.	Landscaping (trees and shrubs)	6,400
n.	Parking lot and concrete walks on the property	19,750
o.	Lights for the parking lot, walkways and company signs	7,300
p.	Supervisory salary of construction supervisor (85 percent to office building, 9 percent to fencing, parking lot and concrete walks, and 6 percent to storage building renovation)	40,000
q.	Office furniture for the office building	174,400
r.	Transportation and installation of furniture	1,100

Anotelli depreciates buildings over 40 years, land improvements over 20 years and furniture over 8 years, all on a straight-line basis with zero residual value.

Required

1. Using the following format, account for each cost by listing it as a debit to Land, Land Improvements, Office Building, Storage Building, or Furniture:

Item	Land	Land Improvements	Office Building	Storage Building	Furniture
a	$	$	$	$	$
⋮					
r	____	____	____	____	____
Totals	$____	$____	$____	$____	$____

2. Assuming that all construction was complete and the assets were placed in service on May 4, record depreciation for the year ended December 31. (Round off figures to the nearest dollar.)

Problem 10-2B   *Computing depreciation and the cash flow advantage of accelerated depreciation for tax purposes*

On January 9, 19X1, Lynch, Inc. paid $82,000 for equipment that manufactures stereo cassette tapes. In addition to the basic purchase price, the company paid $700 transportation charges, $100 insurance for the goods in transit, $4,100 sales tax and $3,100 for a special platform on which to place the equipment in the plant. Lynch management estimates that the equipment will remain in service for 5 years and have a residual value of $11,250. The equipment will produce 45,000 units in the first year, with annual production decreasing by 5,000 units during each of the next 4 years (that is, 40,000 units in year 2; 35,000 units in year 3; and so on). In trying to decide which depreciation method to use, Charlene Lynch has requested a depreciation schedule for each of the following generally accepted depreciation methods: straight-line, units-of-production and declining-balance, using the Revenue Canada rate of 20 percent.

Required

1. For each of the above generally accepted depreciation methods, prepare a depreciation schedule showing asset cost, depreciation expense, accumulated depreciation and asset book value. Use the format of Exhibits 10-3 through 10-5.
2. Lynch reports to shareholders and creditors in the financial statements using the depreciation method that maximizes reported income in the early years of asset use. For income tax purposes, however, the company uses the depreciation method that minimizes income tax payments in those early years. Consider the first year Lynch uses the equipment. Identify the depreciation methods that meet Lynch's objectives.

3. Assume cash provided by operations before income tax is $110,000 for the equipment's first year. The income tax rate is 40 percent. For the two depreciation methods identified in question 2, compare the net income and cash provided by operations (cash flow). Use the following outline for your answer:

	Depreciation Method that in the Early Years	
Comparison of Net Income for First Year	**A Maximizes Reported Income**	**B Minimizes Income Tax Payments**
Cash provided by operations before income tax ..	$	$
Depreciation expense		
Income before income tax		
Income tax expense (40%)......................		
Net income	$	$
Advantage of Method A over Method B	$	
Cash Flow Analysis for First Year		
Cash provided by operations before income tax ..	$	$
Income tax expense		
Cash provided by operations (called cash flow) ...	$	$
Advantage of Method B over Method A	$	

Problem 10-3B   *Journalizing and posting plant asset transactions; capital expenditures versus revenue expenditures*

Assume that a Shoppers Drug Mart drugstore completed the following transactions:

19X2

Jan. 6   Paid $6,000 cash for a used delivery truck.
Jan. 7   Paid $800 to have the truck engine overhauled.
Jan. 8   Paid $200 to have the truck modified for business use.
Aug. 21   Paid $127 for a minor tuneup.
Dec. 31   Recorded depreciation on the truck by the double-declining-balance method. (Assume a 4-year life and a $1,500 residual value).
     31   Closed the appropriate accounts.

19X3

May 8   Traded in the delivery truck for a new truck costing $10,000. The dealer granted a $4,000 allowance on the old truck, and the store paid the balance in cash. Recorded 19X3 depreciation for the year to date and then recorded exchange of trucks.
July 8   Repaired the new truck's damaged fender for $625 cash.
Dec. 31   Recorded depreciation on the new truck by the double-declining-balance method. (Assume a 4-year life and a residual value of $2,000).
     31   Closed the appropriate accounts.

Required

1. Open the following accounts in the general ledger: Delivery Trucks, Accumulated Depreciation—Delivery Trucks, Truck Repair Expense, Depreciation Expense—Delivery Trucks and Loss on Exchange of Delivery Trucks.
2. Record the transactions in the general journal and post to the ledger accounts opened.

Problem 10-4B   *Recording plant asset transactions; exchanges; changes in useful life*

Laidlaw Transportation Ltd. provides freight service, waste management and school bus service. The company's balance sheet includes the following assets under Property, Plant and Equipment: land, buildings, motor carrier equipment and leasehold improvements. Assume the company has a separate accumulated depreciation account for each of these assets except land and leasehold improvements. Depreciation on leasehold improvements is credited directly to the Leasehold Improvements account rather than to Accumulated Depreciation—Leasehold Improvements.

Assume that Laidlaw completed the following transactions:

Sept. 5   Traded in motor-carrier equipment with book value of $34,000 (cost of $90,000) for similar new equipment with a cash cost of $128,000. The seller gave Laidlaw a trade-in allowance of $40,000 on the old equipment, and Laidlaw paid the remainder in cash.

Oct. 22   Purchased motor-carrier equipment for $136,000 plus 5 percent and $200 legal fee. The company gave a 60-day, 12 percent note in payment.

Dec. 23   Paid the equipment note and related interest.

Mar. 9   Sold a building that had cost $550,000 and had accumulated depreciation of $247,500 through August 31 of the preceding year. Depreciation is computed on a straight-line basis. The building has a 30-year useful life and a residual value of $55,000. Laidlaw received $100,000 cash and a $600,000 note receivable.

Apr. 16   Paid cash to improve leased assets at a cost of $21,600.

June 26   Purchased land and a building for a single price of $300,000. An independent appraisal valued the land at $115,000 and the building at $230,000.

Aug. 31   Recorded depreciation as follows:

Motor-carrier equipment has an expected useful life of 6 years and an estimated residual value of 5 percent of cost. Depreciation is computed by the Revenue Canada rate of 20 percent. Make separate depreciation entries for equipment acquired on September 5 and October 22.

Depreciation on leasehold improvements is computed on a straight-line basis over the life of the lease, which is 5 years, with zero residual value.

Depreciation on buildings is computed by the straight-line method. The company had assigned to its older buildings, which cost $100,000,000, an estimated useful life of 30 years with a residual value equal to 10 percent of the asset cost. However, management has come to believe that the buildings will remain useful for a total of 40 years. Residual value remains unchanged. The company has used all its buildings, except for the one purchased on June 26, for 10 years. The new building carries a 40-year useful life and a residual value equal to 10 percent of its cost. Make separate entries for depreciation on the building acquired on June 26 and the other buildings purchased in earlier years.

Required

Record the transactions in the general journal.

Problem 10-5B   *Distinguishing capital expenditures from revenue expenditures; preparing a plant ledger card*

Suppose Pacific Tire Supply Company Ltd. uses plant ledger cards to control its service trucks, purchased from Paproski Motor Co. The supervisor is responsible for the trucks, which are located at the company's service garage. The following transactions were completed during 19X3 and 19X4:

19X3
Jan. 6   Paid $13,800 cash for a used service truck (truck no. 5).
Jan. 7   Paid $2,500 to have the truck engine overhauled.

Jan. 8   Paid $180 to have the truck modified for business use.

Nov. 5   Paid $107 for replacement of one tire.

Dec. 31   Recorded depreciation on the truck by the double-declining-balance method, based on a 4-year useful life and a $2,000 residual value.

19X4

Apr. 19   Repaired a damaged fender on truck no. 5 at a cash cost of $877.

Nov. 6   Traded in service truck no. 5 for a new one (truck no. 6) with a cash cost of $18,000. The dealer granted a $6,000 allowance on the old truck, and Pacific Tire paid the balance in cash. Recorded 19X4 depreciation for year to date and then recorded exchange of the trucks.

Dec. 31   Recorded depreciation on truck no. 6 by the double-declining-balance method, on a 4-year life and a $2,500 residual value.

Required

1. Identify the capital expenditures and the revenue expenditures in the transactions. Which expenditures are debited to an asset account? Which expenditures are debited to an expense account?
2. Prepare a separate plant ledger card for each of the trucks.

Problem 10-6B   *Recording intangibles, wasting assets and the related expenses*

Part 1   Scott's Hospitality Inc., among its other businesses, operates Kentucky Fried Chicken franchised restaurants. The company's balance sheet reports the asset Cost in Excess of Net Assets of Purchased Businesses. Assume that Scott purchased this asset as part of the acquisition of another company, which carried these figures:

Book value of assets	$275,000
Market value of assets	420,000
Liabilities	167,500

Required

1. What is another title for the asset Cost in Excess of Net Assets of Purchased Businesses?
2. Make the general journal entry to record Scott's Hospitality's purchase of the other company for $292,500 cash.
3. Assuming Collins amortizes Cost in Excess of Net Assets of Purchased Businesses over ten years, record the straight-line amortization for one year.

Part 2   Suppose Scott's Hospitality purchased a Kentucky Fried Chicken franchise license for $162,000. In addition to the basic purchase price, Scott's Hospitality also paid a lawyer $8,000 for assistance with the negotiations. Management believes the appropriate amortization period for its cost of the franchise license is eight years.

Required

Make general journal entries to record the franchise transactions, including straight-line amortization for one year.

Part 3   Canadian Pacific Ltd. is one of Canada's largest holding companies owning companies in the forest products, coal, iron ore, and oil and gas industries. The company's balance sheet includes the assets Natural Gas, Oil and Coal.

Suppose Canadian Pacific paid $800,000 cash for a lease giving the firm the right to work a mine that contained an estimated 80,000 tonnes of coal. Assume that the company paid $5,000 to remove unwanted buildings from the land and $15,000 to prepare the surface for mining. Further assume that Canadian Pacific signed a $20,000 note payable for a landscaping company to return the land surface to its original condition after the lease ends. During the first year, Canadian Pacific removed 15,000 tonnes of coal, which it sold on account for $17 per tonne.

Required

Make general journal entries to record all transactions related to the coal, including depletion and sale of the first-year production.

Decision Problems

1. Measuring profitability based on different inventory and depreciation methods

Suppose you are considering investing in two businesses, Frycer Company and Bergdahl Company. The two companies are virtually identical, and both began operations at the beginning of the current year. During the year, each company purchased inventory as follows:

Jan. 4	12,000 units at $4 =	$ 48,000
Apr. 6	5,000 units at 5 =	25,000
Aug. 9	7,000 units at 6 =	42,000
Nov. 27	10,000 units at 7 =	70,000
Totals	34,000	$185,000

Over the first year, both companies sold 25,000 units of inventory.

In early January, both companies purchased equipment costing $100,000 that had a 10-year estimated useful life and a $10,000 residual value. Frycer Company uses the first-in, first-out (FIFO) method for its inventory and straight-line depreciation for its equipment. Bergdahl Company uses last-in, first-out (LIFO) and double-declining-balance depreciation. Both companies' trial balances at December 31 included the following:

Sales revenue	$250,000
Purchases.................................	185,000
Operating expenses	80,000

Required

1. Prepare both companies' income statements.
2. Prepare a schedule that shows why one company appears to be more profitable than the other. Explain the schedule and amounts in your own words. What accounts for the different amounts?
3. Is one company more profitable than the other? Give your reason.

2. Plant assets and intangible assets

The following questions are unrelated except that they apply to fixed assets and intangible assets:

1. The manager of Meadowlake Ltd. regularly buys plant assets and charges the cost to Repairs and Maintenance Expense. Why would he do that, since he knows such action is in violation of GAAP?
2. The manager of Spruce Lake Inc. regularly charges the cost of repairs and maintenance of plant assets to Plant and Equipment, a fixed asset account. Why would she do that, since she knows such action is in violation of GAAP?
3. It has been suggested that, since many intangible assets have no value except to the company that owns them, they should be valued at $1.00 or zero on the balance

sheet. Many accountants disagree with that view. Which view do you support? Why?

4. GAAP specifies a maximum time-period for writing off intangible assets. However, some companies use a shorter period than the maximum allowed. Why would a company do that? Are there any reasons for using the maximum period? What effect does using a shorter period have on net income over the life of the asset?

Financial Statement Problem

Plant assets and intangible assets

Refer to the John Labatt financial statements in Appendix E and answer the following questions:

1. Which depreciation method does John Labatt use for the purposes of reporting to shareholders and other users of the financial statements?

2. What was the amount of depreciation and amortization expense for the year ended April 30, 1989? How much of the depreciation and amortization related to the brewing part of John Labatt's business (Hint: see note 16)? How much of the depreciation and amortization related to the Canadian operations of John Labatt (Hint: see note 16)?

3. The statement of changes in financial position also reports the purchase and disposal of plant assets during the year. What was the net (that is, cost of additions less proceeds on disposal) cost of plant assets acquired in fiscal 1989? Were these capital expenditures or revenue expenditures?

4. What is the amount reported for intangible assets at April 30, 1989? What is the basis of amortization of the intangible assets? Is John Labatt complying with GAAP with respect to amortization of intangibles? How do you know?

Answers to Self-Study Questions

1. d
2. c [$90,000/($90,000 + $60,000) × $120,000 = $72,000;
   $60,000/($90,000 + $60,000) × $120,000 = $48,000]
3. b
4. b
5. c
6. a Depreciable cost = $450,000 − $50,000 = $400,000
   $400,000/40 years = $10,000 per year
   $400,000 − ($10,000 × 10 years) = $300,000/40 years = $7,500 per year
7. d
8. b
9. a $550,000 − ($900,000 − $400,000) = $50,000
10. a

11

Current Liabilities and Payroll Accounting

LEARNING OBJECTIVES

After studying this chapter, you should be able to

1 Classify liabilities as current or long-term

2 Account for current liabilities

3 Account for contingent liabilities

4 Make basic payroll entries

5 Use a payroll-accounting system

6 Report current liabilities

A *liability* is an obligation to transfer assets or to provide services in the future. The obligation may arise from a transaction with an outside party. For example, a business incurs a liability when it issues a note payable to buy equipment or to borrow money. Also, the obligation may arise in the absence of individual transactions. For example, interest expense accrues with the passage of time. Until this interest is paid it is a liability. Income tax, another liability, accrues as income is earned. Proper accounting for liabilities is as important as proper accounting for assets. The failure to record an accrued liability causes the balance sheet to understate the related expense and thus overstate owner's equity. A misleadingly positive view of the business is the result.

All liabilities may be classified as current—those that are due within the year or the company's operating cycle if longer than a year, or long term—those liabilities not classified as current. We discuss long-term liabilities in Chapter 16. We now turn to accounting for current liabilities, including those arising from payroll expenses.

> **OBJECTIVE 1**
> Classify liabilities as current or long-term

Current Liabilities of Known Amount _____

Current liabilities fall into one of two categories: those of a known amount and those whose amount must be estimated. We look first at current liabilities of known amount.

Trade Accounts Payable

Amounts owed to suppliers for products or services that are purchased on open account are accounts payable. We have seen many accounts payable examples in previous chapters. For example, a business may purchase inventories and office supplies on an account payable.

Short-Term Notes Payable

Short-term notes payable, a common form of financing, are notes payable that are due within one year. Companies often issue short-term notes payable to borrow cash or to purchase inventory or plant assets. In addition to recording the note payable and its eventual payment, the business must also accrue interest expense and interest payable at the end of the period. The following entries are typical of this liability:

<table>
<tr><td colspan="4">19X1</td></tr>
<tr><td>Sept. 30</td><td>Purchases ....</td><td>8,000</td><td></td></tr>
<tr><td></td><td>   Note Payable, Short-Term...............</td><td></td><td>8,000</td></tr>
<tr><td></td><td>Purchase of inventory by issuing a one-year
10 percent note payable.</td><td></td><td></td></tr>
<tr><td>Dec. 31</td><td>Interest Expense ($8,000 × .10 × 3/12) ....</td><td>200</td><td></td></tr>
<tr><td></td><td>   Interest Payable ....</td><td></td><td>200</td></tr>
<tr><td></td><td>Adjusting entry to accrue interest expense at
year end.</td><td></td><td></td></tr>
</table>

OBJECTIVE 2
Account for current liabilities

The balance sheet at December 21, 19X1, will report the Note Payable of $8,000 and the related Interest Payable of $200 as current liabilities. The 19X1 income statement will report interest expense of $200.

The following entry records the note's payment:

<table>
<tr><td colspan="4">19X2</td></tr>
<tr><td>Sept. 30</td><td>Note Payable, Short-Term ....</td><td>8,000</td><td></td></tr>
<tr><td></td><td>Interest Payable ....</td><td>200</td><td></td></tr>
<tr><td></td><td>Interest Expense ($8,000 × .10 × 9/12)</td><td>600</td><td></td></tr>
<tr><td></td><td>   Cash [$8,000 + ($8,000 × .10)] ....</td><td></td><td>8,800</td></tr>
<tr><td></td><td>Payment of a note payable and interest at
maturity.</td><td></td><td></td></tr>
</table>

The cash payment entry must split the total interest on the note between the portion accrued at the end of the previous period ($200) and the period's expense ($600).

Short-Term Notes Payable Issued at a Discount

In another common borrowing arrangement, a company may **discount a note payable** at the bank. Discounting means that the bank subtracts the interest amount from the note's face value. The borrower receives the net amount. In effect, the borrower prepays the interest, which is computed on the principal of the note.

Suppose Inco discounts a $100,000, 60-day note payable to their bank at 12 percent. The company will receive $98,000—that is, the $100,000 face value less interest of $2,000 ($100,000 × .12 × 60/360). Assume this transaction occurs on November 25, 19X1. Inco's entries to record discounting the note would be

<table>
<tr><td colspan="4">19X1</td></tr>
<tr><td>Nov. 25</td><td>Cash ($100,000 − $2,000) ....</td><td>98,000</td><td></td></tr>
<tr><td></td><td>Discount on Note Payable
    ($100,000 × .12 × 60/360) ....</td><td>2,000</td><td></td></tr>
<tr><td></td><td>   Note Payable, Short-Term ....</td><td></td><td>100,000</td></tr>
<tr><td></td><td>Discounted a $100,000, 60-day, 12-percent note
payable to borrow cash.</td><td></td><td></td></tr>
</table>

Discount on Note Payable is a contra account to the liability Note Payable, Short-Term. A balance sheet prepared immediately after this transaction would report the note payable at its net amount of $98,000, as follows:

Current liabilities
Note payable, short-term $100,000
 Less: Discount on note payable .... (2,000)
Note payable, short-term, net .... $ 98,000

The accrued interest at year end must still be recorded, as it would for any note payable. The adjusting entry at December 31 records interest for 36 days as follows:

19X1
Dec. 31   Interest Expense ($100,000 × .12 × $36/360$) 1,200
               Discount on Note Payable 1,200
          Adjusting entry to accrue interest expense at
          year end.

This entry credits the Discount account instead of Interest Payable. Why? It is because the Discount balance is like prepaid interest, and the accrual of interest uses up part of the prepayment. Furthermore, crediting the Discount reduces this contra account's balance and increases the net amount of the Note Payable. After the adjusting entry, only $800 of the Discount remains, and the carrying value of the Note Payable increases to $99,200, as follows:

Current liabilities
Note payable, short-term $100,000
 Less: Discount on note payable ($2,000 − $1,200) .... (800)
Note payable, short-term, net .... $ 99,200

Finally, the business records the note's payment:

19X2
Jan. 24   Interest Expense ($100,000 × .12 × $24/360$) 800
               Discount on Note Payable 800
          To record interest expense.

          Note Payable, Short-Term 100,000
               Cash 100,000
          To pay note payable at maturity.

After these entries, the balances in the note payable account and the discount account are zero. Each period's income statement reports the appropriate amount of interest expense.

Goods and Services Tax and Sales Tax Payable

There are (or will be) two basic consumption taxes levied on purchases in Canada that will be visible to the consumer: the goods and services tax proposed by the federal government and provincial sales taxes levied by all the provinces except Alberta. The federal government presently collects a federal sales tax at rates ranging from 9 to 19 percent on goods produced or manufactured in or imported into Canada; it is proposed to eliminate this tax and replace it with the goods and services tax. The federal sales tax is hidden in that it is collected by the manufacturer, producer or importer and remitted by them to the government; the consumer does not know the amount of tax he or she is paying because it is buried in the price. There are also excise or luxury taxes, sometimes called "sin taxes," which are a form of sales tax levied by the federal and provincial governments on products such as cigarettes, jewellery and alcoholic beverages; these taxes are also hidden in that they are collected by the manufacturer. The focus of discussion in this section will be on the consumption or visible taxes.

At the present time, the federal government is planning to implement a goods and services tax (GST) that will be collected from the ultimate consumer of most goods and services; basic groceries and some prepared foods are not subject to the tax. The proposed GST rate is 7 percent.

The tax will be collected by the individual or entity supplying the good or service to the consumer and remitted to the Receiver General. Suppliers of goods and services will have to pay tax on their purchases, but will be able to recover it from the government. For example, Mary Janicek purchases a power lawn-mower with a view to earning money by cutting grass during the summer. The lawn-mower cost $250; the GST would be $17.50. Because Mary is planning to use the mower exclusively to cut grass for a fee, she could recover the $17.50. However, she would have to charge all her customers the 7 percent GST and remit it to the government.

As was mentioned above, all the provinces, except Alberta, the Yukon and Northwest Territories, levy a sales tax on retail sales. Retailers charge their customers the sales tax in addition to the price of the item sold. Because the retailers owe the province the sales tax collected, the account Sales Tax Payable is a current liability. For example, John Labatt reports excise and sales taxes in the amount of $420 million on sales of $3,581 million; some portion of that $420 million is included in the current liability, Taxes Payable, of $25 million at year end.

Sales taxes are levied by those provinces on sales to the final consumers of products; they are not levied on sales to wholesalers or retailers. For example, Super Stereo Products does not pay sales tax on its purchase of your CD player from RCA but you pay sales tax to Super Stereo when you buy the CD player. Super Stereo pays the sales tax to the provincial government. RCA would not have a sales tax liability at its year end but Super Stereo probably would have.

Suppose one Saturday's sales at a Super Stereo Store in Ontario totaled $2,000. The business would have collected an additional 8 percent in sales tax, which would equal $160 ($2,000 × .08). The business would record that day's sales as follows:

Cash ($2,000 × 1.08)......................................	2,160	
Sales Revenue....................................		2,000
Sales Tax Payable ($2,000 × .08)		160
To record cash sales of $2,000 subject to 8 percent		
sales tax.		

Companies forward the collected sales tax to the taxing authority at regular intervals, at which time they debit Sales Tax Payable and credit Cash. Observe that Sales Tax Payable does *not* correspond to any sales tax expense that the business is incurring. Nor does this liability arise from the purchase of any asset. Rather, it is the cash that the business is collecting for the government.

Many companies consider it inefficient to credit Sales Tax Payable when recording sales. They record the sale in an amount that includes the tax. Then prior to paying tax to the province, they make a single entry for the entire period's transactions to bring Sales Revenue and Sales Tax Payable to their correct balances.

Suppose a company made July sales of $100,000, subject to a tax of 6 percent. Its summary entry to record the month's sales could be

July 31	Cash ($100 × 1.06)	106,000	
	Sales Revenue		106,000
	To record sales for the month.		

The entry to adjust Sales Revenue and Sales Tax Payable to their correct balances is

July 31	Sales Revenue [$106,000 − ($106,000 ÷ 1.06)]	6,000	
	Sales Tax Payable		6,000
	To record sales tax.		

Companies that follow this procedure need to make an adjusting entry at the end of the period in order to report the correct amounts of revenue and liability on their financial statements.

Current Portion of Long-Term Debt

Some long-term notes payable and long-term bonds payable must be paid in installments. The **current portion of long-term debt**, or *current maturity*, is the amount of the principal that is due within one year. This amount does not include the interest due. Of course, any liability for accrued interest payable must also be reported but a separate account, Interest Payable, is used for that purpose.

Fisheries Products International owed almost $20½ million on long-term debt at December 31, the end of its fiscal year. Slightly more than $3 million was a current liability because it was due within one year. The remaining $17½ million was a long-term liability. Suppose the interest rate on the debt was 9 percent and that interest was last paid the preceding September 30. Fishery Products International's December 31 balance sheet would report:

Current Liabilities (in part)	millions
Portion of long-term debt due within one year	$ 3.0
Interest payable ($20.5 × .09 × 3/12)	.46
Long-Term Debt and Other Liabilities (in part)	
Long-term debt	$17.5

Accrued Expenses

As shown in the Fishery Products presentation, *accrued expenses*, such as interest expense, create current liabilities because the interest is due within the year. Therefore, the interest payable (accrued interest) is reported as a current liability. Other important liabilities for accrued expenses are payroll and the related payroll withholdings which we discuss in the second part of this chapter.

Unearned Revenues

Unearned revenues are also called *deferred revenues, revenues collected in advance* and *customer prepayments*. Each account title indicates that the business has received cash from its customers before earning the revenue. The company has an obligation to provide goods or services to the customer.

The Dun & Bradstreet (D&B) Corporation provides credit evaluation services on a subscription basis. When companies pay in advance to have D&B investigate the credit histories of potential customers, D&B incurs a liability to provide future service. The liability account is called Unearned Subscription Revenue (which could also be titled Unearned Subscription Income).

Assume that Dun & Bradstreet charges $150 for a finance company's three-year subscription. Dun & Bradstreet's entries would be

19X1

Jan. 1	Cash......................................	150	
	Unearned Subscription Revenue..........		150
	To record receipt of cash at start of the three-year subscription agreement.		

19X1, 19X2, 19X3

Dec. 31	Unearned Subscription Revenue	50	
	Subscription Revenue ($150/3) ..		50
	To record subscription revenue earned at the end of each of three years.		

Dun & Bradstreet's financial statements would report this sequence:

Balance Sheet	Year 1	Year 2	Year 3
Current liabilities			
Unearned subscription revenue	$100	$50	$-0-
(Computations			
Year 1: $150 − $50 = $100			
Year 2: $150 − $50 − $50 = $50			
Year 3: $150 − $50 − $50 − $50 = $0.)			

Income Statement	Year 1	Year 2	Year 3
Revenues			
Subscription revenue	$ 50	$50	$50

Customer Deposits Payable

Some companies require cash deposits from customers as security on borrowed assets. These amounts are called Customer Deposits Payable because the company must refund the cash to the customer under certain conditions.

For example, telephone companies may demand a cash deposit from a customer before installing a telephone. Utility companies and businesses that lend tools and appliances commonly demand a deposit as protection against damage and theft. When the customer ends the service or returns the borrowed asset, the company refunds the cash deposit—if the customer has paid all the bills and has not damaged the company's property. Because the company generally must return the deposit, that cash is a liability. The uncertainty of when the deposits will be refunded and their relatively small amounts cause many companies to classify Customer Deposits Payable as current liabilities. This is consistent with the concept of conservatism.

Certain manufacturers of products sold in the home, such as Avon, demand deposits from merchandisers who sell their products; the deposit is usually equal to the cost of the sample kit given to the merchandiser. Companies, whose products are sold in returnable containers, collect deposits on those containers. The most common example is the deposit on soda pop bottles. In both cases the deposits are shown as current liabilities by the manufacturers. The amounts are relatively small and so are included with accounts payable and accrued charges.

Current Liabilities That Must Be Estimated _____

A business may know that a liability exists but not know the amount. The liability may not simply be ignored. The unknown amount of a liability must be estimated for reporting on the balance sheet.

Estimated current liabilities vary among companies. As an example, let us look at Warranties Payable, a liability account common among merchandisers.

Warranties Payable

Many merchandising companies guarantee their products against defects under *warranty* agreements. The warranty period may extend for any length of time. Ninety-day warranties and one-year warranties are common.

Whatever the warranty's lifetime, the matching principle demands that the company record the *warranty expense* in the same period that the business recognizes sales revenue. After all, offering the warranty—and incurring any possible expense through the warranty agreement—is a part of generating revenue through sales. At the time of the sale, however, the company does not know which products are defective. The exact amount of warranty expense cannot be known with certainty, so the business must estimate its warranty expense and open the related liability account, Estimated Warranties Payable, also called Accrued Warranty Costs and Product Warranty Liability.

Companies may make a reliable estimate of their warranty expense based on their experience. Assume a company made sales of $200,000, subject to product warranties. Company management, noting that in past years between 2 percent and 4 percent of products proved defective, estimates that 3 percent of the products will require repair or replacement during the one-year warranty period. The company records warranty expense of $6,000 ($200,000 × .03) for the period:

Warranty Expense	6,000	
Estimated Warranty Payable		6,000
To accrue warranty expense.		

Assume that defective merchandise totals $5,800. The company may either repair or replace it. Corresponding entries follow.

Estimated Warranty Payable	5,800	
Cash		5,800
To repair defective products sold under warranty.		

Estimated Warranty Payable 5,800
      Inventory   5,800
To replace defective products sold under warranty.

Note that the expense is $6,000 on the income statement no matter what the cash payment or the cost of the replacement inventory. In future periods, the company may come to debit the liability Estimated Warranty Payable for the remaining $200. However, *when* the company repairs or replaces defective merchandise has no bearing on when the company records warranty expense. The reason for recognizing the expense is the *sale* in order to match expense against revenue. The business records warranty expense in the same period as the sale.

Contingent Liabilities

A *contingent liability* is not an actual liability. Instead, it is a potential liability that depends on a *future* event arising out of a past transaction. For example, a town government may sue the company that installed new street lights, claiming that the electrical wiring is faulty. The past transaction is the street-light installation. The future event is the court case that will decide the suit. The lighting company thus faces a contingent liability, which may or may not become an actual obligation. The amount of the liability will not be known until the court case is settled.

Sometimes the amount that will have to be paid, if the contingent liability becomes an actual liability, is known at the balance sheet date. From Chapter 8 recall that the payee of a discounted note has a contingent liability. If the maker of the note pays at maturity, the contingent liability ceases to exist. However, if the maker defaults, the payee, who sold the note, must pay its maturity value to the purchaser. In this case, the payee knows the note's maturity value, which is the amount of the contingent liability the payee faces.

Another contingent liability of known amount arises from guaranteeing that another company will pay a note payable that it owes a third party. This practice, called cosigning a note, obligates the guarantor to pay the note and interest if, and only if, the primary debtor fails to pay. Thus the guarantor has a contingent liability until the note becomes due. If the primary debtor pays off, the contingent liability ceases to exist. If the primary debtor fails to pay, the guarantor's liability becomes actual.

Sometimes the amount that will have to be paid, if the contingent liability becomes an actual liability, is not known at the balance sheet date. For example, companies face lawsuits, which may cause possible future obligations of amounts to be determined by the courts. Revenue Canada may have indicated to the entity that a reassessment of its income and taxes has been made or is forthcoming but the company may not know the amount of its liability at the time the financial statements are prepared.

OBJECTIVE 3
Account for contingent liabilities

Contingent liabilities are normally disclosed in the notes to the financial statements unless both the confirming future event is likely *and* the amount of the loss can be reasonably estimated in which case the amount of the loss should be accrued in the financial statements. When the loss is both likely and estimable, then it is less a contingent loss than a real loss; that is why the loss is accrued or put through the books as of the statement date. For example, suppose Revenue Canada had reassessed a company prior to its year-end at December 31, 19X7 disallowing expenses claimed by the company on its 19X5 tax return. If the company decided to accept the reassessment (in which case the confirming future event is likely and the amount known), it should accrue the additional tax payable. If, on the other hand, the company had decided to appeal the reassessment (that is neither condition is met), the reassessment should be treated as a contingency and shown in the notes.

Some companies draw attention to the footnote describing the contingent liability by making reference to it on the balance sheet. The most common locations for the reference are between liabilities and owners' equity and after owners' equity.

General Electric Canada Inc. reports the following in the notes to the financial statements under the heading "Commitments and contingencies":

> The company is contingently liable under guarantees for notes payable by a related finance company, Genelcan Limited, which at December 31, 1987 amounted to $454.8 million. This guarantee, in turn, is guaranteed by General Electric Holdings Limited. Operating lease commitments, liabilities under purchase commitments and performance bonds, and pending litigation and claims are not considered by management to be material in relation to the Company's financial position.

Summary Problem for Your Review

This problem consists of three independent parts:

1. Suppose a Harvey's hamburger restaurant made cash sales of $4,000 subject to a 10 percent sales tax. Record the sales and the related sales tax. Also record payment of the tax to the provincial government.

2. Suppose at April 30, 19X2, Fisheries Products International reported a 9 percent long-term debt as follows:

Current Liabilities (in part)	millions
Portion of long-term debt due within one year	$ 3.0
Interest payable $(20.5 \times .09 \times \frac{3}{12})$	.46

Long-Term Debt and Other Liabilities (in part)	
Long-term debt	$17.5

The company pays interest on its long-term debt on January 31.

Show how Fisheries Products would report its liabilities on the year-end balance sheet at April 30, 19X3. Assume the current maturity of its long-term debt is $4 million and the long-term portion is $18 million.

3. What distinguishes a contingent liability from an actual liability?

SOLUTION TO REVIEW PROBLEM

1. Cash ($4,000×1.10) 4,400
        Sales Revenue 4,000
        Sales Tax Payable ($4,000×.10)...................... 400
  To record cash sales and related sales tax.

        Sales Tax Payable..................................... 400
        Cash.. 400
  To pay sales tax to the provincial government.

2. Fisheries Products International balance sheet at April 30, 19X3 would be as follows:

Current Liabilities (in part)	millions
Portion of long-term debt due within one year	$ 4.0
Interest payable (22×.09×³⁄₁₂)	.50

Long-Term Debt and Other Liabilities (in part)	
Long-term debt	$18.0

3. A contingent liability is a *potential liability*, which may or may not become an actual liability.

Accounting for Payroll

Payroll, also called *employee compensation*, is a major expense of many businesses. For service organizations, such as public accounting firms, real estate brokers and travel agents, payroll is *the* major expense of conducting business. Service organizations sell their employees' service, so employment compensation is their primary cost of doing business, just as cost of goods sold is the largest expense in merchandising.

Employment compensation takes different forms. Some employees collect a **salary**, which is income stated at a yearly, monthly or weekly rate. Other employees work for **wages**, which is employee pay stated at an hourly figure. Sales employees often receive a **commission**, which is a percentage of the sales the employee has made. Some companies reward excellent performance with a **bonus**, an amount over and above regular compensation.

Businesses often pay employees at a base rate for a set number of hours called straight time. For working any additional hours, called overtime, the employee receives a higher rate.

Assume that Lucy Childres is an accountant for an electronics company. Lucy earns $600 per week straight time. The company work week runs 40 hours, so Lucy's hourly wage is $15 ($600/40). Her company pays her **time and a half** for overtime. The rate is 150 percent (1.5 times) the straight-time rate. Thus Lucy earns $22.50 for each hour of overtime she works ($15.00×1.5=$22.50). For working 42 hours during a week, she earns $645, computed as follows:

Straight-time pay for 40 hours.........................	$600
Overtime pay for 2 overtime hours—	
2 × $22.50	45
Total pay	$645

Gross Pay and Net Pay

Many years ago, employees brought home all that they had earned. For example, Lucy Childres would have taken home the full $645 total that she made. Payroll accounting was straightforward. Those days are long past.

The federal government, and most provincial governments demand that employers act as collection agents for employee taxes, which are deducted from employee cheques. Insurance companies, labour unions and other organizations may also take pieces of employees' pay. Amounts withheld from an employee's cheque are called deductions.

Gross pay is the total amount of salary, wages, commissions, or any other employee compensation before taxes and other deductions are taken out. **Net pay** is the amount that the employee actually takes home.

In addition to employee taxes that employers must withhold from paycheques, employers themselves must pay some payroll taxes. Many companies also pay employee **fringe benefits**, such as health and life insurance and retirement pay. Payroll accounting has become quite complex. Let us turn now to a discussion of payroll deductions.

Payroll Deductions

Payroll deductions that are *withheld* from employees' *pay* fall into two categories: (1) *required deductions*, which include employee income tax, unemployment insurance, and Canada Pension or Quebec Pension Plan deductions; and (2) *optional deductions*, which include union dues, insurance premiums, charitable contributions, and other amounts that are withheld at the employee's request. After they are withheld, payroll deductions become the liability of the employer who assumes responsibility for paying the outside party. For example, the employer pays the government the employee income tax withheld and pays the union the employee union dues withheld.

Required Payroll Deductions

Employee Withheld Income Tax Payable   The law requires most employers to withhold income tax from their employees' salaries and wages. The amount of income tax deducted from gross pay is called **withheld income tax**. For many employees, this deduction is the largest. The amount withheld depends on the employee's gross pay and on the number of withholding allowances the employee claims.

Each employee files a Form TD1 with the employer. Exhibit 11-1 is an example of Form TD1; it has been completed by Roberta C. Dean who has a spouse Pierre, who is an author with an estimated income of $3,000, and two children under the age of 18, for which the Dean family gets monthly Family Allowance payments. Roberta claims $6,169 for herself, $2,655 for Pierre and

EXHIBIT 11-1 *1990 Personal Tax Credit Return (Form TDI)*

1990 PERSONAL TAX CREDIT RETURN (Form TD1)

Revenue Canada Taxation	Revenu Canada Impôt

page 1.

TD1 (E)
Rev. 1990

1990 PERSONAL TAX CREDIT RETURN

FAMILY NAME (Please Print): DEAN
USUAL FIRST NAME AND INITIALS: Roberta C.
EMPLOYEE NUMBER: 3637
ADDRESS: 3817 29th Avenue
For NON-RESIDENTS ONLY Country of Permanent Residence:
SOCIAL INSURANCE NUMBER: 767 676 767
Owen Sound, Ontario Postal Code N4K 2x9
DATE OF BIRTH: Day 7 Month 2 Year 39

Instructions

• Please fill out this form so your employer or payer will know how much tax to deduct regularly from your pay. Regular deductions will help you avoid having to pay when you file your income tax return.

• **You must complete this form if you receive** • salary, wages, commissions or any other remuneration;
  • superannuation or pension benefits including an annuity payment made under a superannuation or pension fund or plan;
  • Unemployment Insurance benefits including training allowances.

• You may also complete this form if you receive annuity payments under registered retirement income funds and registered retirement savings plans.

• Give the completed form to your employer or payer. Otherwise, you will be allowed **only** the basic personal amount of $6,169.

• All amounts on this form should be rounded to the nearest dollar.

• **Need Help?** If you need help to complete this form, you may ask your employer or payer, or call the Source Deductions Section of your local Revenue Canada district taxation office. Before you do this, please refer to the additional information on page 2 under "Notes to Employees and Payees."

1. **Are you a non-resident of Canada?** (see note 1 on page 2). If so, and **less than** 90 per cent of your 1990 total world income will be included when calculating taxable income earned in Canada, enter 0 in the box on line 17 and sign the form. If you are a resident of Canada, go to item 2.

2. **Basic personal amount.** (everyone may claim $6,169) ▶ $6,169 **2.**

3. (a) **Are you married and supporting your spouse?** (see notes 4 and 5 on page 2)
   or
   (b) **Are you single, divorced, separated or widowed and supporting a relative who lives with you who is either your parent or grandparent, OR who is under 19 at the end of 1990, OR 19 or older and infirm?** (see notes 2, 3 and 4 on page 2)
   Note: A spouse or dependant claimed here cannot be claimed again on lines 4 or 5.
   If you answered yes to either (a) or (b) and your spouse's or dependant's 1990 net income will be
   • under $514, CLAIM $5,141
   • between $514 and $5,655, CLAIM (e) →
   • over $5,655, CLAIM $0

Minus: spouse or dependant s net income	$5,655 (c)
	3,000 (d)
Claim (c minus d)	2,655 (e)

   ▶ 2,655 **3.**

4. **Do you have any dependants who will be under 19 at the end of 1990?** (see notes 2 and 4 on page 2). If so, and your 1990 net income will be **higher** than your spouse's, calculate the amount to claim for **each** dependant. If you are not married, please refer to notes 2, 3 and 4 on page 2.
   Note: If you have three or more dependants who will be under 19 years old at the end of the year, you do not have to claim them in the order they were born. You may claim them in the **most beneficial** order. For example, a dependant who is 16 years old with a net income of $3,500 could be claimed as the first dependant (claim 0) while the other two, with no income, could be claimed as second and third dependants.

   First and second dependant:
   If your dependant's 1990 net income will be
   • under $2,570, CLAIM $399
   • between $2,570 and $2,969, CLAIM (e) →
   • over $2,969, CLAIM $0

Minus: dependant s net income	$2,969 (c)
	200 (d)
Claim (c minus d)	2,769 (e)

   dependants
   1st 399
   2nd 399

   Third and each additional dependant:
   If your dependant's 1990 net income will be
   • under $2,570, CLAIM $798
   • between $2,570 and $3,368, CLAIM (e) →
   • over $3,368, CLAIM $0

Minus: dependant s net income	$3,368 (c)
	(d)
Claim (c minus d)	(e)

   3rd
   4th
   5th
   Total ▶ 798 **4.**

5. **Do you have any infirm dependants who will be 19 or older at the end of 1990?** (see notes 2 and 4 on page 2). If so, and your dependant's net income will be
   • under $2,570, CLAIM $1,512
   • between $2,570 and $4,082, CLAIM (e)
   • over $4,082, CLAIM $0

Minus: dependant s net income	$4,082 (c)
	(d)
Claim (c minus d)	(e)

   dependants
   1st
   2nd
   3rd
   Total ▶ Nil **5.**

6. **Do you receive eligible pension income?** (see note 6 on page 2). If so, claim your pension income amount or $1,000, whichever is less. ▶ Nil **6.**

7. **Will you be 65 or older at the end of 1990?** If so, claim $3,327. ▶ Nil **7.**

8. **Are you disabled?** (see note 7 on page 2). If so, claim $3,327. ▶ Nil **8.**

9. **Are you a student?** If so, claim
   • **tuition fees** paid for courses you take in 1990 to attend either a university, college or a certified educational institution. If you receive any scholarships, fellowships or bursaries in 1990, subtract the amount over $500 from your tuition fees before you claim them.
   • **$60** for each month in 1990 that you will be in **full-time attendance** in a qualifying program, at either a university, college or a school offering job re-training courses.
   Total ▶ Nil **9.**

10. Total (add lines 2 to 9 - please enter this amount on line 11 on page 2) 9,622 **10.**
(See reverse)

$399 for each of the children for a total claim of $9,623. From this total, the Family Allowance payments of $786 are deducted to arrive at a net claim of $8,837. The net claim translates into a net claim code of 3. Roberta's employer will use the net claim code number to compute the amount of income tax that should be withheld from Roberta's monthly salary.

Revenue Canada provides tax tables each year that the employer uses with the TD1's to calculate the amount of income tax to be withheld each pay period.

The employer sends its employees' withheld income tax to the government. The amount of the income tax withheld determines how often the employer submits tax payments. Most employers must remit the taxes to the government at least monthly; larger employers must remit two or four times a month, depending on the amounts withheld. Every business must account for payroll taxes on a calendar-year basis regardless of its fiscal year.

The employer accumulates taxes in the Employees' Withheld Income Tax Payable account. The word *payable* indicates that the account is a liability to the employer, even though the employees are the people taxed.

Employee Withheld Canada (or Quebec) Pension Plan Contributions Payable
The Canada (or Quebec) Pension Plan provides retirement, disability and death benefits to employees who are covered by it. Employers are required to deduct premiums from each employee required to make a contribution (basically all employees between 18 and 70 years of age). The premium is 2.2 percent of wages in excess of $2,800, up to a maximum contribution in a year of $574.20.

Revenue Canada provides tables that the employer uses to calculate how much to deduct from each employee's pay each pay period; the tables take into account the basic exemption of $2,800 of income. Once the employee reaches the maximum contribution of $574.20, the employer stops deducting for that year. Some employees may have had more than one employer in a year; for example, you may have had a job for the summer and now have a part-time job while you are back at school. Canada requires each employer to deduct Canada Pension Plan contributions; however, you recover the overpayment when you file your income tax return for the year.

The employer must remit the Canada Pension Plan contributions withheld and the employer's share, discussed below, every month to Revenue Canada. Larger employers must remit two or four times a month, depending on the amounts withheld.

Employee Withheld Unemployment Insurance Premiums Payable
The **Unemployment Insurance** Act requires employers to deduct unemployment insurance premiums from each employee each time that employee is paid. The purpose of the Unemployment Insurance Fund is to provide assistance to contributors to the fund who cannot work for a variety of reasons. The most common reason is that the employee has been laid off; another reason is maternity leave.

Revenue Canada provides tables for calculating deductions for a range of pay periods. The employee premium is 2.25 percent of earnings exceeding $6,656 per year to a maximum contribution of $748.80 (2.25 percent of maximum insurable earnings of $33,279.96). As with the Canada Pension Plan, Revenue Canada requires every employer to deduct Unemployment Insurance premiums from every eligible employee. Overpayments may be recovered when the employee files his or her income tax return.

The employer must remit the Unemployment Insurance premiums withheld and the employer's share, discussed below, every month to Revenue Canada. Larger employers must remit two or four times a month depending on the amounts withheld.

Optional Payroll Deductions

As a convenience to its employees, many companies make payroll deductions and disburse cash according to employee instructions. Union dues, insurance payments, payroll savings plans and gifts to charities such as the United Way are examples. The account Employees' Union Dues Payable holds employee deductions for union membership.

Employer Payroll Costs

Employers bear expenses for at least three payroll costs: (1) Canada Pension Plan contributions, (2) Unemployment Insurance Plan premiums and (3) Workers' Compensation Plan premiums. As mentioned above, most employers must remit both employee and employer shares monthly. Larger employers must remit twice monthly. Workers' Compensation payments are remitted quarterly.

Employer Canada (or Quebec) Pension Plan Contributions   In addition to being responsible for deducting and remitting the employee contribution to the Canada Pension plan, the employer must also pay into the program. The employer must match the employee's contribution of 2.2 percent of gross pay in excess of $2,800 to a maximum payment of $574.20. Every employer must do so whether or not the employee also contributes elsewhere. Unlike the employee, the employer may not obtain a refund for overpayment.

Employer Unemployment Insurance Premiums   The employer calculates the employee's premium and remits it together with the employer's share, which is generally 1.4 times the employee's premium, to Revenue Canada. The dollar amount of the employer's contribution would be 1.4 times the maximum employee's contribution of $748.80 or $1,048. Almost all employers and employees are covered by this program.

Workers' Compensation Premiums   Unlike the previous two programs, which are administered by the federal government, the **Workers' Compensation** plan is provincially administered. The purpose of the program is to provide financial support for workers injured on the job. The cost of the coverage is borne by the employer; the employee does not pay a premium to the fund.

In Manitoba, almost all employees are covered by the program. There are over 70 different categories that the Workers' Compensation Board uses to ascertain the cost of coverage. The category a group of workers is assigned to is based on the risk of injury to workers in that group based on that group's and like group's experience. The employer pays a premium equal to the rate assessed times the employer's gross payroll. Thus, in February 19X2, the employer estimates gross payroll for 19X2 and sends that information plus any premium owing from 19X1 to the provincial government. Premiums, based on that estimated payroll, are remitted quarterly in most cases. In February 19X3, the employer estimates gross payroll for 19X3, calculates any premium owing for 19X2 based on the excess of actual wages over estimated wages for 19X2, and sends the estimate and premium owing to the provincial government.

Payroll Withholding Tables

We have discussed the tables that employers use in calculating the withholdings that must be made from employees' wages for income taxes, Canada (or Quebec) Pension contributions and Unemployment Insurance premiums. Exhibit 11-2 provides illustrations of all three tables for a resident of Ontario.

EXHIBIT 11-2   Payroll Withholding Tables

Panel A
Table 3
Ontario
Semi-Monthly Tax Deductions
Basis: 24 Pay Periods Per Year

Semi-Monthly Pay Use appropriate bracket	If the employee's "Net Claim Code" on Form TD1 is										
	0	**1**	**2**	**3**	**4**	**5**	**6**	**7**	**8**	**9**	**10**
From Less than	Deduct from each pay										
1912—1938	608.45	539.40	530.95	514.00	497.10	480.20	463.50	446.35	429.45	412.55	395.60
1938—1964	619.10	550.10	541.60	524.70	507.80	490.85	474.20	457.05	440.10	423.20	406.30
1964—1990	629.80	560.75	552.30	535.40	518.45	501.55	484.85	467.70	450.80	433.90	416.95
1990—2016	640.50	571.45	563.00	**546.05**	529.15	512.25	495.55	478.40	461.50	444.60	427.65
2016—2042	651.15	582.10	573.65	556.75	539.85	522.90	506.20	489.10	472.15	455.25	438.35

Panel B
Canada Pension Plan Contributions

Semi-Monthly Pay Period

Remuneration From To	C.P.P.	Remuneration From To	C.P.P.	Remuneration From To	C.P.P.	Remuneration From To	C.P.P.
1171.89 — 1172.34	23.22	1204.62 — 1214.61	24.05	1924.62 — 1934.61	39.89	2644.62 — 2654.61	55.73
1172.35 — 1172.79	23.23	1214.62 — 1224.61	24.27	1934.62 — 1944.61	40.11	2654.62 — 2664.61	55.95
1172.80 — 1173.25	23.24	1224.62 — 1234.61	24.49	1944.62 — 1954.61	40.33	2664.62 — 2674.61	56.17
1173.26 — 1173.70	23.25	1234.62 — 1244.61	24.71	1954.62 — 1964.61	40.55	2674.62 — 2684.61	56.39
1173.71 — 1174.15	23.26	1244.62 — 1254.61	24.93	1964.62 — 1974.61	40.77	2684.62 — 2694.61	56.61
1174.16 — 1174.61	23.27	1254.62 — 1264.61	25.15	1974.62 — 1984.61	40.99	2694.62 — 2704.61	56.83
1174.62 — 1175.06	23.28	1264.62 — 1274.61	25.37	1984.62 — 1994.61	41.21	2704.62 — 2714.61	57.05
1175.07 — 1175.52	23.29	1274.62 — 1284.61	25.59	1994.62 — 2004.61	**41.43**	2714.62 — 2724.61	57.27
1175.53 — 1175.97	23.30	1284.62 — 1294.61	25.81	2004.62 — 2014.61	41.65	2724.62 — 2734.61	57.49

Panel C
Unemployment Insurance Premiums

For minimum and maximum insurable earnings amounts for various pay periods see Schedule II.
For the maximum premium deduction for various pay periods see bottom of this page.

Remuneration From To	U.I. Premium	Remuneration From To	U.I. Premium	Remuneration From To	U.I. Premium	Remuneration From To	U.I. Premium
1932.23 — 1932.66	43.48	1964.23 — 1964.66	44.20	1996.23 — 1996.66	44.92	2028.23 — 2028.66	45.64
1932.67 — 1933.11	43.49	1964.67 — 1965.11	44.21	1996.67 — 1997.11	44.93	2028.67 — 2029.11	45.65
1933.12 — 1933.55	43.50	1965.12 — 1965.55	44.22	1997.12 — 1997.55	44.94	2029.12 — 2029.55	45.66
1933.56 — 1933.99	43.51	1965.56 — 1965.99	44.23	1997.56 — 1997.99	44.95	2029.56 — 2029.99	45.67
1934.00 — 1934.44	43.52	1966.00 — 1966.44	44.24	1998.00 — 1998.44	44.96	2030.00 — 2030.44	45.68
1934.45 — 1934.88	43.53	1966.45 — 1966.88	44.25	1998.45 — 1998.88	44.97	2030.45 — 2030.88	45.69
1934.89 — 1935.33	43.54	1966.89 — 1967.33	44.26	1998.89 — 1999.33	44.98	2030.89 — 2031.33	45.70
1935.34 — 1935.77	43.55	1967.34 — 1967.77	44.27	1999.34 — 1999.77	44.99	2031.34 — 2031.77	45.71
1935.78 — 1936.22	43.56	1967.78 — 1968.22	44.28	1999.78 — 2000.22	**45.00**	2031.78 — 2032.22	45.72

Maximum Premium Deduction for a Pay Period of the stated frequency.	Weekly: 14.40	10 pp per year: 74.88
	Bi-Weekly: 28.80	13 pp per year: 57.60
	Semi-Monthly: 31.20	22 pp per year: 34.04
	Monthly: 62.40	

Roberta Dean is paid a salary of $2,000 twice a month (semi-monthly). From Panel A, you can see that, based on her net claim code of 3, she would have income tax of $546.05 withheld. Her Canada Pension deduction, Panel B, would be $41.43 and her Unemployment Insurance premium, Panel C, would be $31.20. The Unemployment Insurance table reads $45.00 but remember the maximum premium is $748.80; the box at the bottom of the table confirms the amount of $31.20. The employer's share would be $41.43 for Canada Pension (matches employee's share), while the employer's share for Unemployment Insurance would be $43.68 (1.4 times employee share).

Payroll Entries

Exhibit 11-3 summarizes an employer's entries to record a monthly payroll of $10,000 (all amounts are assumed for illustration only).

Entry 1 in Exhibit 11-3 records the employer's *salary expense*, which is the *gross salary* of all employees ($10,000) for a month. From this amount the employer collects for the federal government income tax, Canada Pension (except in Quebec where it is Quebec Pension) and Unemployment Insurance. Union dues are also collected from this amount by the employer on behalf of the union that represents the employees. The remaining amount is the employees' net (take-home) pay of $7,964. In this payroll transaction the employer acts as a collection agent for Revenue Canada (income tax and Canada Pension), the Unemployment Insurance Commission and the union, withholding the employees' contributions from their gross pay.

Entry 2 represents the employer's *share of Canada Pension* and *Unemployment Insurance*. Remember, the employer's share is 1.0 times and 1.4 times the employee's share respectively for these two deductions.

OBJECTIVE 4
Make basic payroll entries

EXHIBIT 11-3   *Payroll Accounting by the Employer*

1.	Salary Expense (or Wage or Commission Expense)	10,000	
	Employee Withheld Income Tax Payable		1,200
	Canada Pension Plan Payable		387
	Unemployment Insurance Payable		294
	Employee Union Dues Payable		155
	Salaries Payable to Employees (net pay).........		7,964
	To record *salary expense* and *employee withholdings*.		
2.	Canada Pension and Unemployment Insurance Expense)	799	
	Canada Pension Plan Payable (1.0 × $387)		387
	Unemployment Insurance Payable (1.4 × $294) ...		412
	To record *employer's share of Canada Pension* and *Unemployment Insurance*.		
3.	Provincial Health Insurance Premiums Expense	618	
	Employee Life Insurance Expense	182	
	Employee Benefits Payable		800
	To record employee *fringe benefits* payable by employer.		

Entry 3 records employee *fringe benefits* paid by the employer. Some employers pay employee provincial health insurance premiums as a benefit to the employee and other employers do not. Since provincial health insurance premiums must be paid by law, if the employer did not pay them, they would be deducted from the employees' pay in Entry A. This company also has a life insurance plan for its employees for which it pays the premiums.

In the exhibit, the total payroll expense for the month is made up of base salary ($10,000) plus the employer's share of Canada Pension and Unemployment Insurance ($799) plus fringe benefits ($618 + $182) for a total of $11,599. There would also be Workers' Compensation, which, you will recall, is paid completely by the employer.

A company's payments to people who are not employees — outsiders called independent contractors — are *not* company payroll expenses. Consider two CAs, Fermi and Scott. Fermi is the corporation's chief financial officer. Scott is the corporation's outside auditor. Fermi is an employee, and his compensation is a debit to Salary Expense. Scott, on the other hand, performs auditing service for many clients, and her payments are debits to Auditing Expense. Any payment for services performed by a person outside the company is a debit to an expense account other than payroll. The account to debit depends on the type of work the independent contractor performs for the business.

The Payroll System

Good business means paying employees all that they have earned — and paying them on time. Also, companies face the legal responsibility of remitting amounts withheld from employees, as we have seen. These demands require companies to process a great deal of payroll data. Efficient accounting is important. To make payroll accounting accurate and effective, accountants have developed the payroll system.

The components of the payroll system are a *payroll register*, a *special payroll bank account, payroll cheques* and an *earnings record* for each employee.

Payroll Register

Each pay period, the company organizes the payroll data in a special journal called the *payroll register* or *payroll journal*. This register lists each employee and the figures the business needs to record payroll amounts. The payroll register, which resembles the cash disbursement register, or cheque register, also serves as a cheque register by providing a column for recording each payroll cheque number.

The payroll register in Exhibit 11-4 includes sections for recording Gross Pay, Deductions, Net Pay, and Account Debited. *Gross Pay* has columns for straight-time pay, overtime pay, and total gross pay for each employee. Columns under the *Deductions* heading vary from company to company. Of course the employer must deduct federal income tax, Canada Pension contributions and Unemployment Insurance premiums. Additional column headings depend on which optional deductions the business handles. In the exhibit, the employer deducts employee withholdings and gifts to United Way and then sends the amounts to the proper parties. The business may add deduction columns as needed. The *Net Pay* section lists each employee's net (take-home) pay and the number of the cheque issued to him or her. The last two columns indicate the *Account Debited* for the employees's gross pay. (The company has office workers and sales people.)

EXHIBIT 11-4   *Payroll Register*

Week ended December 27, 19X3

		a	*b*	*c*	*d*	*e*	*f*	*g*	*h*	*i*	*j*	*k*	*l*
		Gross Pay			**Deductions**					**Net Pay**		**Account Debited**	
Employee Name	Hours	Straight-time	Overtime	Total	Federal Income Tax	Canada Pension Plan	Unemploy-ment Insurance	United Way Charities	Total	(c-h) Amount	Cheque No.	Office Salary Expense	Sales Salary Expense
Chen, W. L.	40	500.00		500.00	85.85	9.82	11.25	2.00	108.92	391.08	1621	500.00	
Drago, C. L.	46	400.00	90.00	490.00	73.90	9.60	11.03	2.00	96.53	393.47	1622		490.00
Ellis, M.	41	560.00	21.00	581.00	119.90	11.60	13.07		144.57	436.43	1623	581.00	
Trimble, E. A.	40	1,360.00		1,360.00	432.85	28.76	14.40	15.00	491.01	868.99	1641		1,360.00
Total		12,940.00	714.00	13,654.00	3,167.76	300.39	327.10	155.00	3,950.25	9,703.75		4,464.00	9,190.00

In the exhibit, W.L. Chen earned gross pay of $500. His net pay was $391.08, paid with cheque number 1621. Chen is an office worker, so his salary is debited to Office Salaries Expense.

The payroll register in Exhibit 11-4 gives the employer the information needed to record salary expense for the pay period. Using the total amounts for columns 4 through 12, the employer records total salary expense as follows:

Dec. 27	Office Salaries Expense.....................	4,464.00	
	Sales Salaries Expense......................	9,190.00	
	Employee Withheld Income Tax Payable..........................		3,167.76
	Employee Withheld Canada Pension Plan Payable		300.39
	Employee Withheld Unemployment Insurance Payable..................		327.10
	Employee Gifts to United Way Payable..........................		155.00
	Salaries Payable to Employees		9,703.75

Payroll Bank Account

Once the payroll has been recorded, the company books include a credit balance in Salaries Payable to Employees for net pay of $9,703.75. (See column *i* in Exhibit 11-4). How the business pays this liability depends on its payroll system. Many companies disburse paycheques to employees from a special payroll bank account. The employer draws a cheque for net pay ($9,703.75 in our illustration) on its regular bank account and deposits this in the special payroll bank account. Then the company writes paycheques to employees out of the payroll account. When all the paycheques clear the bank, the payroll account has a zero balance, ready for the activity of the next pay period. Disbursing paycheques from a separate bank account isolates net pay for analysis and control, as discussed later in the chapter.

Other payroll disbursements, for withholdings, union dues, and so on, are neither as numerous nor as frequent as weekly or monthly paycheques. The employer pays taxes, union dues and charities from its regular bank account.

Payroll Cheques

Most companies pay employees by cheque. A *payroll cheque* is like any other cheque except that its perforated attachment lists the employee's gross pay, payroll deductions, and net pay. These amounts are taken from the payroll register. Exhibit 11-5 shows payroll cheque number 1622, issued to C.L. Drago for net pay of $393.47 earned during the week ended December 27, 19X3. To check your ability to use payroll data, trace all amounts on the cheque attachment to the payroll register in Exhibit 11-4.

Recording Cash Disbursements for Payroll _____

Most employers must make at least three entries to record payroll cash disbursements: payments of earnings to employees, payments of payroll withholdings to the government and payments to third parties for employee fringe benefits.

EXHIBIT 11-5   *Payroll Cheque*

Blumenthal's	1622
Payroll Account	
Winnipeg, Manitoba	

12-27   19 X3

Pay to the
Order of _____ C.L. Drago _____ $ | 393.47

Three hundred and ninety-three & 47/100------------------- Dollars

Toronto-Dominion Bank
Winnipeg,
Manitoba R2W 3Y1

Anna Figaro
Treasurer

⊙ ⑈⑈⑈⑈⑈⑈⑈⑈⑈ 0787⑈ 50000454⑈

Pay			Deductions					Net	Cheque
Straight-time	Over-time	Gross	Income Tax	C.P.P.	Unemploy-ment Ins.	United Way	Total	Pay	No.
400.00	90.00	490.00	73.90	9.60	11.03	2.00	96.53	393.47	1622

Cash Payments to Employees   When the employer issues payroll cheques to employees, the company debits Salaries Payable to Employees and credits Cash.

Using the data in Exhibit 11-4, the company would make the following entry to record the cash payment (column i) for the December 27 weekly payroll:

Dec. 27   Salaries Payable to Employees 9,703.75
Cash 9,703.75

Sending Payroll Withholdings to the Government and Other Organizations
The employer must send income taxes withheld from employees pay and the employee deductions and employer's share of Canada (or Quebec) Pension Plan contributions and Unemployment Insurance premiums to Revenue Canada. In addition, the employer has to remit any withholdings for union dues, charitable gifts, etc. Based on Exhibit 11-4, columns d through j, the business would record payments to Revenue Canada for $4,553.58 and United Way Charities for $155.00 as follows:

Dec. 27   Employee Withheld Income Tax Payable 3,167.76
Employee Withheld Canada Pension Plan
Payable 300.39
Employee Withheld Unemployment
Insurance Payable 327.10
Employee Gifts to United Way Payable 155.00
Canada Pension Plan Expense 300.39
Unemployment Insurance Expense 457.94
Cash 4,708.58

Payments to Third Parties for Fringe Benefits   The employer sometimes pays for employees' provincial health insurance coverage and for a company pension plan. Assuming the total cash payment for these benefits is $1,927.14, this entry would be

| Dec. 27 | Employee Benefits Payable . . . . | 1,927.14 | |
| | Cash . . . . | | 1,927.14 |

Earnings Record

The employer must file Summary of Remuneration Paid returns with Revenue Canada and must provide the employee with a statement of Remuneration Paid, Form T4, at the end of the year. Therefore, employers maintain an earnings record for each employee. Exhibit 11-6 is a five-week excerpt from the earnings record of employee C.L. Drago.

The employee earnings record is not a journal or a ledger, and it is not required by law. It is an accounting tool, like the worksheet, that the employer uses to prepare payroll tax reports. Year-to-date earnings also indicate when an employee has earned $26,100, the point at which employer can stop deducting Canada Pension.

Exhibit 11-7 is the Statement of Remuneration paid, Form T4 Supplementary, for employee C. L. Drago. The employer prepares this form for each employee and a form called a T4 Summary, which summarizes the information on the T4 Supplementaries issued by the employer for that year. The employer sends the T4 Summary and one copy of each T4 Supplementary to Revenue Canada by February 28 each year. Revenue Canada uses the documents to ensure that the employer has correctly paid to the government all amounts withheld on its behalf from employees together with the employer's share. The employee gets two copies of the T4 Supplementary; one copy must be filed with the employee's income tax return while the second copy is for the employee's records. Revenue Canada matches the income on the T4 supplementary filed by the employer against the income reported on the employee's income tax return, filed by the employee, to ensure that the employee properly reported his or her income from employment.

Internal Control over Payrolls _____

The internal controls over cash disbursements discussed in Chapter 7, such as making all disbursements by cheque, apply to payroll. In addition, companies adopt special controls in payroll accounting. The large number of transactions and the many different parties involved increase the risk of a control failure. Accounting systems feature two types of special controls over payroll: controls for efficiency and controls for safeguarding cash.

Controls for Efficiency

For companies with many employees, reconciling the bank account can be time consuming owing to the large number of outstanding payroll cheques. For example, a March 30 payroll cheque would probably not have time to clear the

EXHIBIT 11-6 Employee Earnings Record for 19X3

Employee Name and Address:

Drago, C.I.
1400 Wellington Crescent
Winnipeg, Manitoba R3P 1E5

Social Insurance No.: 987-010-789
Marital Status: Married
Net Claims Code: 4
Pay Rate: $400 per week
Job Title: Salesperson

Week Ended	Gross Pay					Deductions					Net Pay	
	Hours	Straight-time	Overtime	Total	To Date	Federal Income Tax	Canada Pension Plan	Unemploy-ment Insurance	United Way Charities	Total	Amount	Cheque No.
Nov. 29	40	400.00		400.00	21,340.00	51.85	7.62	9.00	2.00	70.47	329.53	1525
Dec. 6	40	400.00		400.00	21,740.00	51.85	7.62	9.00	2.00	70.47	329.53	1548
Dec. 13	44	400.00	60.00	460.00	22,200.00	67.75	8.94	10.35	2.00	89.04	370.96	1574
Dec. 20	48	400.00	120.00	520.00	22,720.00	82.15	10.26	11.70	2.00	106.11	413.89	1598
Dec. 27	46	400.00	90.00	490.00	23,210.00	73.90	9.60	11.03	2.00	96.53	393.47	1622
Total		20,800.00	2,410.00	23,210.00		3,249.40	449.02	522.23	104.00	4,324.65	18,885.35	

EXHIBIT 11-7 *Employee Statement of Remuneration Paid (Form T4)*

Revenue Canada Taxation | Revenu Canada Impôt

T4-1989 Supplementary / *Supplémentaire*

STATEMENT OF REMUNERATION PAID
ÉTAT DE LA RÉMUNÉRATION PAYÉE

00-000-000

(C) EMPLOYMENT INCOME BEFORE DEDUCTIONS / *REVENUS D'EMPLOI AVANT RETENUES*	(D) EMPLOYEE'S PENSION CONTRIBUTION CANADA PLAN / *DU CANADA*	QUEBEC PLAN / *DU QUÉBEC* (*COTISATION DE PENSION (EMPLOYÉ)*)	(E) U.I. PREMIUM / *PRIME D'A-C*	(F) REGISTERED PENSION PLAN CONTRIBUTION / *COTISATIONS RÉGIME ENREGISTRÉ DE PENSIONS*	(G) INCOME TAX DEDUCTED / *IMPÔT SUR LE REVENU RETENU*	(H) U.I. INSURABLE EARNINGS / *GAINS ASSURABLES A-C*	(I) C.P.P. PENSIONABLE EARNINGS / *GAINS OUVRANT DROIT À PENSIONS - R.P.C.*	(J) EXEMPT C.P.P./Q.P.P. (RPC/RRQ) · U.I. (A-C) / *EXONÉRATION*
→ 23,210 : 00	449 : 02	:	522 : 23	:	3,249 : 40	23,210 : 00	20,410 : 32	

BOX (C) AMOUNT ALREADY INCLUDES ANY AMOUNTS IN BOXES (K), (L), (M), (N), (O), and (P) / *LE MONTANT DE LA CASE (C) COMPREND DÉJÀ TOUS LES MONTANTS DES CASES (K), (L), (M), (N), (O), ET (P)*	TAXABLE ALLOWANCES AND BENEFITS ▶ / *AVANTAGES IMPOSABLES*	(K) HOUSING BOARD AND LODGING / *LOGEMENT, PENSION ET LOGEMENT*	(L) TRAVEL IN A PRESCRIBED AREA / *VOYAGE DANS UNE RÉGION VISÉE PAR RÈGLEMENT*	(M) PERSONAL USE OF EMPLOYER'S AUTO / *USAGE PERSONNEL DE L'AUTO DE L'EMPLOYEUR*	(N) INTEREST FREE AND LOW INTEREST LOANS / *PRÊTS SANS INTÉRÊT OU À FAIBLE INTÉRÊT*	(O) OTHER TAXABLE ALLOW. AND BENEFITS / *AUTRES AVANTAGES IMPOSABLES*	(P) EMPLOYMENT COMMISSIONS / *COMMISSIONS D'EMPLOI*
		:	:	:	:	:	

(Q) UNION DUES / *COTISATIONS SYNDICALES*	(R) CHARITABLE DONATIONS / *DONS DE CHARITÉ*	(S) PAYMENTS TO DPSP / *PAIEMENTS À UN RPDB*	(T) PENSION PLAN OR DEFERRED PROFIT SHARING PLAN REGISTRATION NUMBER / *N° ENREGISTREMENT DE RÉGIME DE PENSION OU DE PARTICIPATION DIFFÉRÉE AUX BÉNÉFICES*	(A) PROVINCE OF EMPLOYMENT / *PROVINCE D'EMPLOI*	(B) SOCIAL INSURANCE NUMBER* / *N° D'ASSURANCE SOCIALE**
:	104 : 00	:		Manitoba	978 : 010 : 789

* IF YOUR SOCIAL INSURANCE NUMBER IS NOT SHOWN IN THIS BOX, SEE INFORMATION ON REVERSE.
* *SI VOTRE NUMÉRO D'ASSURANCE SOCIALE N'EST PAS IMPRIMÉ DANS CETTE CASE, VOIR LES RENSEIGNEMENTS AU VERSO.*

EMPLOYEE: SURNAME FIRST (in capital letters), USUAL FIRST NAME AND INITIALS AND FULL ADDRESS
EMPLOYÉ: NOM DE FAMILLE D'ABORD (en capitales), PRÉNOM USUEL ET ADRESSE COMPLÈTE
SURNAME *NOM DE FAMILLE* — USUAL FIRST NAME AND INITIALS - *PRÉNOM USUEL*

FOOTNOTES:
NOTES:

→ Drago, C.L.
1400 Wellington Crescent
Winnipeg, Manitoba
R3P 1E5

EMPLOYER NAME / *NOM DE L'EMPLOYEUR*: Blumenthal's
ACCOUNT NUMBER / *NUMÉRO DE COMPTE*: 387-035
EMPLOYEE NO. / *N° DE L'EMPLOYÉ*:

TO BE RETURNED WITH T4-T4A SUMMARY
À RETOURNER AVEC LA T4-T4A SOMMAIRE 1

Source: Revenue Canada Taxation. Reproduced with permission of the Minister of Supply and Services Canada.

bank before a bank statement on March 31. This cheque and others in a March 30 payroll would be outstanding. Identifying a large number of outstanding cheques for the bank reconciliation increases accounting expense. To limit the number of outstanding cheques, many companies use two payroll bank accounts. They make payroll disbursements from one payroll account one month and from the other payroll account the next month. By reconciling each account every other month, a March 30 paycheque has until April 30 to clear the bank before the account is reconciled. This essentially eliminates outstanding cheques, cuts down the time it takes to prepare the bank reconciliation, and decreases accounting expense. Also, many companies' cheques become void if not cashed within a certain period of time. This too limits the number of outstanding cheques.

Other payroll controls for efficiency include following established policies for hiring and firing employees and complying with government regulations. Hiring and firing policies provide guidelines for keeping a qualified, diligent work force dedicated to achieving the business's goals. Complying with government regulations avoids paying fines and penalties.

Controls for Safeguarding of Cash

Owners and managers of small businesses can monitor their payroll disbursements by personal contact with their employees. Large corporations cannot do so. These businesses must establish controls to assure that payroll disbursements are made only to legitimate employees and for the correct amounts. A particular danger is that payroll cheques may be written to a fictitious employee and cashed by a dishonest employee. To guard against this crime and other possible breakdowns in internal control, large businesses adopt strict internal control policies.

The duties of hiring and firing employees should be separated from the duties of distributing paycheques. Otherwise, a dishonest supervisor, for example, could add a fictitious employee to the payroll. When paycheques are issued, the supervisor could simply pocket the nonexistent person's paycheque for his or her own use.

Requiring an identification badge bearing an employee's photograph helps internal control: issuing paycheques only to employees with the appropriate badge ensures only actual employees receive pay. This safeguard ensures that only actual employees receive pay.

On occasion management should instruct an employee from the home office, perhaps an internal auditor, to distribute cheques in the branch office personally rather than have the payroll department mail the cheques. No one will claim a paycheque that has been issued to a fictitious employee. Any cheque left over after the distribution signals that payroll fraud has been attempted. Management would pursue an investigation.

A time-keeping system helps ensure that employees have actually worked the number of hours claimed. Having employees punch time cards at the start and end of the work day proves their attendance—as long as management makes sure that no employee punches in and out for other too. Some companies have their workers fill in weekly or monthly time sheets.

Again we see that the key to good internal control is separation of duties. The responsibilities of the personnel department, payroll department, accounting department, time-card management, and paycheque distribution should be kept separate.

Reporting Payroll Expense and Liabilities _____

At the end of its fiscal year, the company reports the amount of *payroll liability* owed to all parties: employees, Revenue Canada, provincial governments, unions, and so forth. Payroll liability is *not* the payroll expense for the year. The liability at year end is the amount of the expense that is still unpaid. Payroll expense appears on the income statement, payroll liability on the balance sheet.

Burroughs Corporation reported accrued payrolls and commissions of approximately $164 million as a current liability on its year-end balance sheet (Exhibit 11-8). However, Burroughs's payroll expense for the year far exceeded $164 million. Exhibit 11-8 also presents the other current liabilities that we have discussed in this chapter.

Exhibit 11-9 summarizes all the current liabilities that we have discussed in this chapter.

EXHIBIT 11-8 *Partial Burroughs Corporation Balance Sheet*

OBJECTIVE 6
Report current liabilities

Current Liabilities	millions
Notes payable within one year	$ 397
Current maturities of long-term debt	31
Accounts payable	397
Accrued payrolls and commissions	164
Customers' deposits and prepayments...........	155
Dividends payable to shareholders	28
Estimated income taxes	111
Total current liabilities	$1,283

EXHIBIT 11-9 *Categories of Current Liabilities*

Amount of liability known when recorded	Amount of liability that must be estimated when recorded
Trade accounts payable	Warranties payable
Short-term notes payable	Income tax payable
Sales tax payable	
Current portion of long-term debt	
Accrued expenses payable:	
Interest payable	
Payroll liabilities (salaries payable, wages payable and commissions payable)	
Payroll withholdings payable (employee and employer)	
Unearned revenues (revenues collected in advance of being earned)	
Customer deposits payable	
Customer prepayments	

Computer Accounting Systems for Current Liabilities

Current liabilities arising from a high volume of similar transactions are well suited for computerized accounting. One of the most common transactions of a merchandiser is the credit purchase of inventory. It is efficient to integrate the accounts payable and inventory systems. When merchandise dips below a predetermined level, the system automatically prepares a purchase request. After the order is placed and the goods are received, inventory and accounts payable data are entered on magnetic tape. The computer reads the tape, then debits Inventory and credits Accounts Payable to account for the purchase. For payments, the computer debits Accounts Payable and credits Cash. The program may also update account balances and print journals, ledger accounts, and the financial statements.

The face amount of notes payable and their interest rates and payment dates can be stored for electronic data processing. Computer programs calculate interest, print the interest cheques, journalize the transactions and update account balances.

Payroll transactions are also ideally suited for computer processing. Employee pay rates and withholding data are stored on magnetic tape. Each payroll period, computer operators enter the number of hours worked by each employee. The machine performs the calculations, prints the payroll register and paycheques, and updates the employee earnings records. The program also computes and prepares semi-monthly, monthly, quarterly or annual reports as required by government agencies such as Revenue Canada. Expense and liability accounts are automatically updated for the payroll transactions.

The estimated amounts of current liabilities for warranties and income taxes may require personal attention. However, once accountants estimate these liabilities, their amounts can be entered into accounts that are maintained in computerized form.

Summary Problem for Your Review

Beth Denius Ltd., a clothing store employs one salesperson, Alan Kingsley. His straight-time pay is $300 per week. He earns time and a half for hours worked in excess of 40 per week. For Kingsley's wage rate and deductions, the income tax withholding rate is approximately 15 percent. Canada Pension is 2.2 percent on income in excess of $53.84 per week while Unemployment Insurance premiums are 2.25 percent. In addition, Denius pays Kingsley's Blue Cross supplemental health insurance premiums of $31.42 a month and dental insurance premiums of $18.50 a month.

During the week ended February 28, 19X3, Kingsley worked 48 hours.

Required

1. Compute Kingsley's gross pay and net pay for the week.
2. Record the following payroll entries that Denius would make:
   a. Expense for Kingsley's wages including overtime pay
   b. Cost of employer's share of Kingsley's withholdings

c. Expense for fringe benefits
d. Payment of cash to Kingsley
e. Payment Denius must make to Revenue Canada
f. Payment of fringe benefits

3. How much total payroll expense did Denius incur for the week? How much cash did the business spend on its payroll?

Requirement 1

Gross pay

Straight time for 40 hours		$300.00
Overtime pay		
Rate per hour ($300/40×1.5)	$11.25	
Hours (48–40)	× 8	90.00
Total gross pay		$390.00

Net pay

Gross pay		$390.00
Less: Withheld income tax ($390×.15)	$ 58.50	
Withheld Canada Pension (($390−53.84)×.022)	7.40	
Withheld Unemployment Insurance ($390×.0225)	8.78	74.68
Net pay		315.32

Requirement 2

a.
Sales Wages Expense	390.00	
Employee Withheld Income Tax Payable		58.50
Employee Canada Pension Payable		7.40
Employee Unemployment Insurance Payable		8.78
Wages payable to employee		315.32

b.
Canada Pension Plan Expense ($7.40×1)	7.40	
Unemployment Insurance Expense ($8.78×1.4)	12.29	
Employer Canada Pension Plan Payable		7.40
Employer Unemployment Insurance Payable		12.29

c.
Medical and Dental Expense ($31.42 + $18.50)	49.92	
Employee Benefits Payable		49.92

d.
Wages Payable to Employee	315.32	
Cash		315.32

e.
Employee Withheld Income Tax Payable	58.50	
Employee Canada Pension Payable	7.40	
Employee Unemployment Insurance Payable	8.78	
Employer Canada Pension Plan Payable	7.40	
Employer Unemployment Insurance Payable	12.29	
Cash		94.37

f.
Employee Benefits Payable	49.92	
Cash		49.92

Requirement 3

Denius incurred *total payroll expense* of $459.61 (gross salary of $390.00+ employer's cost re Canada Pension of $7.40+ employer's cost re Unemployment Insurance of $12.29+ fringe benefits of $49.92). See entries a to c.

Denius *paid cash* of $459.61 on payroll (Kingsley's net pay of $315.32+ payment to Revenue Canada of $94.37+ fringe benefits of $49.92). See entries d to f.

Summary _____

Current liabilities may be divided into those of *known amount* and those that must be *estimated*. Trade accounts payable, short-term notes payable, and the related liability for accrued expenses are among current liabilities of known amount. Current liabilities that must be estimated are warranties payable and some businesses' income tax payable.

Contingent liabilities are not actual liabilities but potential liabilities that may arise in the future. Contingent liabilities, like current liabilities, may be of known amount or an indefinite amount. A business that faces a lawsuit not yet decided in court has a contingent liability of indefinite amount.

Payroll accounting handles the expenses and liabilities arising from compensating employees. Employers must withhold income taxes, Canada (or Quebec) Pension Plan contributions and Unemployment Insurance premiums from employees' pay and send these withholdings together with the employer's share of the latter two to the government. In addition, many employers allow their employees to pay for insurance and union dues and to make gifts to charities through payroll deductions. An employee's net pay is the gross pay less all withholdings and optional deductions.

An *employer's* payroll expenses include the employer's share of Canada (or Quebec) Pension contributions and Unemployment Insurance premiums and Workers' Compensation, which are separate from the withholdings borne by the employees. Also, most employers provide their employees with fringe benefits, like payment of the employee's provincial health insurance, life insurance coverage and retirement pensions.

A *payroll system* consists of a payroll register, a payroll bank account, payroll cheques and an earnings record for each employee. Good *internal controls* over payroll disbursements help the business to conduct payroll accounting efficiently and to safeguard the company's cash. The cornerstone of internal controls is the separation of duties.

Current liabilities arising from a high volume of repetitive transactions are well suited for computer processing. Trade accounts payable, notes payable and the related interest, and payrolls are three examples.

Self-Study Questions

Test your understanding of the chapter by marking the correct answer for each of the following questions.

1. A $10,000, 9 percent, one-year note payable was issued on July 31. The balance sheet at December 31 will report interest payable of *(p. 444)*
   a. $0 because the interest is not due yet   c. $375
   b. $300   d. $900

2. If the note payable in the preceding question had been discounted, the cash proceeds from issuance would have been *(p. 444)*
   a. $9,100   c. $9,700
   b. $9,625   d. $10,000

3. Which of the following liabilities creates *no* expense for the company? *(p. 446)*
   a. Interest   c. Unemployment Insurance
   b. Sales tax   d. Warranty

4. Suppose Canadian Tire estimates that warranty costs will equal 1 percent of tire sales. Assume that November sales totaled $900,000, and the company's outlay in tires and cash to satisfy warranty claims was $7,400. How much warranty expense should the November income statement report? *(p. 449)*
   a. $1,600   c. $9,000
   b. $7,400   d. $16,400

5. XYZ Company is a defendant in a lawsuit that claims damages of $55,000. On the balance sheet date, it appears unlikely that the court will render a judgment against the company. How should XYZ report this event in its financial statements? *(pp. 450, 451)*
   a. Omit mention because no judgment has been rendered
   b. Disclose the contingent liability in a note

c. Report the loss on the income statement and the liability on the balance sheet

d. Both b and c

6. Emilie Frontenac's weekly pay for 40 hours is $320, plus time and half for overtime. The tax rate, based on her income level and deductions, is 16 percent, the Quebec Pension Plan rate is 2.2 percent on her weekly earnings in excess of $53.84, and the Unemployment Insurance rate 2.25 percent. What is Emilie's take-home pay for a week in which she works 50 hours? *(pp. 453, 458)*

    a. $351.20   c. $345.80

    b. $319.38   d. $331.59

7. Which of the following represents a cost to the employer? *(p. 456)*

    a. Withheld income tax   c. Unemployment Insurance

    b. Canada Pension   d. Both b and c

8. The main reason for using a separate payroll bank account is to *(p. 461)*

    a. Safeguard cash by avoiding writing payroll cheques to fictitious employees

    b. Safeguard cash by limiting paycheques to amounts based on time cards

    c. Increase efficiency by isolating payroll disbursements for analysis and control

    d. All of the above

9. The key to good internal controls in the payroll area is *(p. 466)*

    a. Using a payroll bank account   c. Using a payroll register

    b. Separating payroll duties   d. Using time cards

10. Which of the following items is reported as current liability on the balance sheet? *(p. 468)*

    a. Short-term notes payable   c. Accrued payroll withholdings

    b. Estimated warranties   d. All of the above

Answers to the self-study questions are at the end of the chapter.

Accounting Vocabulary

bonus *(p. 452)*	fringe benefits *(p. 453)*	time and a half *(p. 452)*
Canada (or Quebec) Pension Plan *(p. 455)*	gross pay *(p. 453)*	Unemployment Insurance *(p. 455)*
commission *(p. 452)*	net pay *(p. 453)*	wages *(p. 452)*
current portion of long-term debt *(p. 447)*	payroll *(p. 452)*	withheld income tax *(p. 453)*
discounting a note payable *(p. 444)*	salary *(p. 452)*	Workers' Compensation *(p. 456)*
	short-term note payable *(p. 444)*	

Assignment Material _____

Questions

1. Give a more descriptive account title for each of the following current liabilities: Accrued Interest, Accrued Salaries, Accrued Income Tax.

2. What distinguishes a current liability from a long-term liability? What distinguishes a contingent liability from an actual liability?

3. A company purchases a machine by signing a $21,000, 10 percent, one-year note payable on July 31. Interest is to be paid at maturity. What two current liabilities related to this purchase does the company report on its December 31 balance sheet? What is the amount of each liability?

4. A company borrowed cash by discounting a $15,000, 8 percent, six-month note payable to the bank, receiving cash of $14,400. (a) Show how the amount of cash was computed. Also, identify (b) the total amount of interest expense to be recognized on this note and (c) the amount of the borrower's cash payment at maturity.

5. Explain how sales tax that is paid by consumers is a liability of the store that sold the merchandise.

6. What is meant by the term *current portion of long-term debt*, and how is this item reported in the financial statements?

7. At the beginning of the school term, what type of account is the tuition that your college or university collects from students? What type of account is the tuition at the end of the school term?

8. Why is a customer deposit a liability? Give an example.

9. Patton Company warrants its products against defects for three years from date of sale. During the current year, the company made sales of $300,000. Store management estimates warranty costs on those sales will total $18,000 over the three-year warranty period. The company paid $22,000 cash on warranties. What is the company's warranty expense for the year? What accounting principle governs this answer?

10. Identify two contingent liabilities of a definite amount and two contingent liabilities of an indefinite amount.

11. Describe how contingent liabilities are reported.

12. Why is payroll expense relatively more important to a service business, a CA firm, than it is to a merchandising company?

13. Two persons are studying Allen Company's manufacturing process. One person is Allen's factory supervisor, and the other person is an outside consultant who is an expert in the industry. Which person's salary is the payroll expense of Allen Company? Identify the expense account that Allen would debit to record the pay of each person.

14. What are two elements of an employee's payroll expense in addition to salaries, wages, commissions, and overtime pay?

15. What determines the amount of income tax that is withheld from employee paycheques?

16. What is the Canada Pension Plan? Who pays it? What are the funds used for?

17. Identify three required deductions and four optional deductions from employee paycheques.

18. Identify three employer payroll costs that are not optional.

19. Who pays Unemployment Insurance premiums? What are these funds used for?

20. Briefly describe a payroll accounting system's components and their functions.

21. How much Unemployment Insurance has been withheld from the pay of an employee who has earned $42,000 during the current year? How much must the employer pay for this employee?

22. Briefly describe the two principal categories of internal controls over payroll.

23. Why do some companies use two special payroll bank accounts?

24. Identify three internal controls designed to safeguard payroll cash.

Exercises

Exercise 11-1 *Recording note payable transactions*

Record the following note payable transactions of McBee Company in the company's general journal:

19X2

May 1 Purchased equipment costing $4,500 by issuing a one-year, 10 percent note payable.

Dec. 31 Accrued interest on the note payable.

19X3

May 1 Paid the note payable at maturity.

Exercise 11-2 *Discounting a note payable*

On November 1, 19X4, Maxwell Company discounted a six-month, $8,000 note payable to the bank at 12 percent.

Required

1. Prepare general journal entries to record (a) issuance of the note, (b) accrual of interest at December 31 and (c) payment of the note at maturity in 19X5.
2. Show how Maxwell would report the note on the December 31, 19X4, balance sheet.

Exercise 11-3 *Recording sales tax two ways*

Make general journal entries to record the following transactions of Ransom Distributors, Inc. for a two-month period:

Mar. 31   Recorded cash sales of $68,100 for the month, plus sales taxes of 11 percent collected on behalf of the Province of New Brunswick. Record sales tax in a separate account.

Apr. 6   Sent March sales tax to the province.

Journalize these transactions a second time. Record the sales tax initially in the Sales Revenue account.

Exercise 11-4 *Reporting current and long-term liabilities*

Suppose Woodward's borrowed $400,000 on December 31, 19X0, by issuing 9 percent long-term debt that must be paid in annual installments of $100,000 plus interest each January 2. By inserting appropriate amounts in the following excerpts from the company's partial balance sheet, show how Woodward's would report its long-term debt.

	December 31,			
	19X1	**19X2**	**19X3**	**19X4**
Current liabilities				
Current portion of long-term debt	$ ____	$ ____	$ ____	$ ____
Interest payable	____	____	____	____
Long-term liabilities				
Long-term debt	____	____	____	____

Exercise 11-5 *Accounting for warranty expense and the related liability*

The accounting records of Shotwell, Inc. included the following balances at the end of the period:

Estimated Warranty Payable	Sales Revenue	Warranty Expense
Beg. bal 3,800	141,000	

In the past, Shotwell's warranty expense has been 8 percent of sales. During the current period, Shotwell paid $11,790 to satisfy the warranty claims of customers.

Required

1. Record Shotwell's warranty expense for the period and the company's cash payments during the period to satisfy warranty claims.

2. What ending balance of Estimated Warranty Payable will Shotwell report on its balance sheet?

Exercise 11-6 *Reporting a contingent liability*

Falcon Lamp Corp. is a defendant in lawsuits brought against the marketing and distribution of its products. Damages of $2 million are claimed against Falcon, but the company denies the charges and is vigorously defending itself. In a recent talk-show interview, the president of the company stated that he could not predict the outcome of the lawsuits. Nevertheless, he said, management does not believe that any actual liabilities resulting from the lawsuits will significantly affect the company's financial position.

Required

Prepare a partial balance sheet to show how Falcon Lamp Corp. would draw attention to the contingent liability. Total liabilities are $3 million. Also, write the disclosure note to describe the contingency.

Exercise 11-7 *Accruing a contingency*

Refer to the Falcon Lamp Corp. situation in the preceding exercise. Suppose that Falcon Lamp's lawyers believe it is probable that a judgment of $350,000 will be rendered against the company.

Required

Describe how to report this situation in the Falcon Lamp Corp. financial statements. Journalize any entry required under GAAP.

Exercise 11-8 *Computing net pay*

Chil Pilsbury is a salesclerk in the men's department of The Bay in Calgary. He earns a base monthly salary of $550 plus an 8 percent commission on his sales. Through payroll deductions, Chil donates $5 per month to a charitable organization and pays dental insurance premiums of $38.25. Compute Chil's gross pay and net pay for December, assuming his sales for the month are $61,300. The income tax rate on his earnings is 20 percent, the Canada Pension Plan contribution is 2.2 percent (subject to the basic deduction of $2,800 and the maximum contribution of $574.20), and the Unemployment Insurance Plan premium rate is 2.25 percent (subject to the maximum premium of $748.80). During the first 11 months of the year, Chil earned $37,140.

Exercise 11-9 *Computing and recording gross pay and net pay*

Rosemarie Libbus works for a Quik Trip convenience store for straight-time earnings of $8 per hour, with time-and-a-half for hours in excess of 40 per week. Rosemarie's payroll deductions include income tax of 7 percent, Canada Pension is 2.2 percent on earnings in excess of $54 per week, and Unemployment Insurance is 2.25 percent on earnings. In addition, Rosemarie contributes $5 per week to the United Way. Assuming Rosemarie worked 43 hours during the week, (1) compute her gross pay and net pay for the week, and (2) make a general journal entry to record the store's wage expense for Rosemarie's work, including her payroll deductions. Round all amounts to the nearest cent.

Exercise 11-10 *Recording a payroll*

Emilio's Department Store incurred salary expense of $42,000 for December. The store's payroll expense includes Canada Pension of 2.2 percent (ignore the basic exemption for this question) and Unemployment Insurance of 1.4 times the employee rate of 2.25

percent. Also the store provides the following fringe benefits for employees: dental insurance (cost to the store $1,134.68); life insurance (cost to the store $351.07); and pension benefits through a private plan (cost to the store $707.60). Record Emilio's payroll expenses for Canada Pension and Unemployment Insurance and employee fringe benefits.

Problems   (Group A)

Problem 11-1A   *Reporting current liabilities*

Following are six pertinent facts about events during the current year at Woodhaven Sales.

a. On September 30 signed a six-month, 9 percent note payable to purchase inventory costing $22,000. The note requires payment of principal and interest at maturity.

b. On October 31 discounted a $50,000 note payable to the Bank of Newfoundland and received cash of $44,000. The interest rate on the one-year note is 12 percent.

c. On November 30 received rent of $4,200 in advance for a lease on a building. This rent will be earned evenly over three months.

d. December sales totaled $38,000 and Woodhaven Sales collected provincial sales tax of 12 percent. This amount will be sent to the province early in January.

e. Woodhaven owes $100,000 on a long-term note payable. At December 31, $20,000 of this principal plus accrued interest of $2,100 are payable within one year.

f. Sales of $430,000 were covered by Woodhaven's product warranty. At December 31 estimated warranty payable is $8,100.

Required

For each item, indicate the account and the related amount to be reported as a current liability on Woodhaven's December 31 balance sheet.

Problem 11-2A   *Journalizing liability-related transactions*

The following transactions of Ortega, Inc., occurred during 19X4 and 19X5. Record the transactions in the company's general journal.

19X4

Jan.   9   Purchased inventory for $3,100, signing a six-month, 8 percent note payable.

29   Recorded the month's sales of $80,240, three fourths on credit and one fourth for cash. All sales amounts are subject to a 5 percent provincial sales tax.

Feb.   5   Sent last month's sales tax to the province.

28   Borrowed $300,000 on a 10 percent, long-term note payble that calls for annual installment payments of $50,000 principal plus interest.

Apr.   8   Received $778 in deposits from distributors of company products. Ortega refunds the deposits after six months.

July   9   Paid the six-month, 8 percent note at maturity.

Oct.   8   Refunded security deposits of $778 to distributors.

22   Discounted a $5,000, 10 percent, 90-day note payable to the bank, receiving cash for the net amount after interest was deducted from the note's maturity value.

Nov. 30   Purchased a machine at a cost of $3,000, signing a 12 percent, six-month note payable for that amount.

Dec. 31   Accrued warranty expense, which is estimated at 2½ percent of sales of $650,000.

31   Accured interest on all outstanding notes payable. Make a separate interest accrual entry for each note payable.

19X5

Jan. 20   Paid off the 10 percent discounted note payable. Made a separate entry for the interest.

Feb. 28   Paid the first installment and interest for one year on the long-term note payble.

May 31   Paid off the 12 percent machine note plus interest at maturity.

Problem 11-3A   *Journalizing, posting and reporting liabilities*

The general ledger of Mayes Company at June 30, 19X3, end of the company's fiscal year, includes the following account balances before adjusting entries. Parentheses indicate a debit balance.

Notes Payable, Short-Term . .	$ 21,000	Employer Payroll	
Discount on Notes Payable . .	(900)	Expense Payable	$ —
Accounts Payable	105,520	Employee Benefits Payable . . .	—
Current Portion of Long-		Sales Tax Payable	738
Term Debt Payable	—	Customer Deposits Payable . .	6,950
Interest Payable	—	Estimated Warranty Payable .	—
Salaries Payable	—	Unearned Rent Revenue	4,800
Employee Payroll		Long-Term Debt Payable	120,000
Withholdings Payable	—	Contingent Liabilities	—

The additional data needed to develop the adjusting entries at June 30 are as follows:

a.   The $21,000 balance in Notes Payable, Short-Term consists of two notes. The first note, with a principal amount of $15,000, was issued on January 31. It matures six months from date of issuance and was discounted at 12 percent. Interest was last paid on July 31 of the preceding year. The second note, with a principal amount of $6,000, was issued on April 22 for a term of 90 days. It bears interest at 10 percent. It was not discounted.

b.   The long-term debt is payable in annual installments of $20,000 with the next installment due on July 31. On that date, Mayes will also pay one year's interest at 9 percent. Interest was last paid on July 31 of the preceding year. To shift the current installment of the long-term debt to a current liability, debit Long-Term Debt Payable and credit Current Portion of Long-Term Debt Payable.

c.   Gross salaries for the last payroll of the fiscal year were $5,044. Of this amount, employee payroll withholdings payable were $1,088, and salaries payable were $3,956.

d.   Employer payroll expense payable was $876, and Mayes's liability for employee health insurance was $1,253.

e.   Mayes estimates that warranty expense is 2 percent of sales, which were $494,000. The company has not yet recorded warranty expense for the year.

f.   On February 1, the company collected one year's rent of $4,800 in advance.

g.   At June 30, Mayes is the defendant in a $200,000 lawsuit, which the company expects to win. However, the outcome is uncertain. Mayes reports contingent liabilities only with an explanatory note.

Required

1.   Open the listed accounts, inserting their unadjusted June 30 balances.

2. Journalize and post the June 30 adjusting entries to the accounts opened. Key adjusting entries by letter.
3. Prepare the liability section of the balance sheet at June 30.

Problem 11-4A   *Computing and recording payroll amounts*

The partial monthly records of Wilcox Company show the following figures:

Employee Earnings

a. Straight-time employee earnings	$16,246
b. Overtime pay	?
c. Total employee earnings ...	?

Deductions and Net Pay

d. Withheld income tax	4,360
e. Canada Pension	?

f. Unemployment Insurance .	$ 466
g. Medical insurance	668
h. Total deductions	5,890
i. Net pay	13,930

Accounts Debited

j. Salary Expense	?
k. Wage Expense	4,573
l. Sales Commission Expense	5,077

Required

1. Determine the missing amounts on lines b, c, e and j.
2. Prepare the general journal entry to record Wilcox's payroll for the month. Credit Payrolls Payable for net pay.

Problem 11-5A   *Computing and recording payroll amounts*

Assume that Joyce Stankov is Vice-President for Leasing Operations for the Bank of Prince Edward Island (BPEI) in Charlottetown. During 19X6 she worked for the company at a $3,625 monthly salary. She also earned a year-end bonus equal to 10% of her salary.

The income tax withheld each month during 19X6 from Stankov's pay was $974.40. Also, she had tax of $652.50 withheld from her bonus when it was paid in December 19X6. She paid $74.58 per month into the Canada Pension Plan until she had paid the maximum. In addition, Stankov paid $62.40 per month to the Unemployment Insurance Commission through her employer. She had authorized the BPEI to make the following payroll deductions: life insurance of $19 per month; United Way of Charlottetown of $35 per month.

The Bank of Prince Edward Island incurred Canada Pension expense equal to the amount deducted from Stankov's pay and Unemployment Insurance expense equal to 1.4 times the amount Stankov paid. In addition, the bank paid dental and drug insurance of $32.00 per month and pension benefits of 8% of her salary.

Required

1. Compute Stankov's gross pay, payroll deductions, and net pay for the full year 19X6. Round all amounts to the nearest dollar.
2. Compute Bank of Prince Edward Island's total 19X6 payroll cost for Stankov.
3. Prepare BPEI's summary general journal entries to record its expense for
   a. Stankov's total earnings for the year, her payroll deductions, and her net pay. Debit Salary Expense and Executive Bonus Compensation as appropriate. Credit liability accounts for the payroll deductions and Cash for net pay.
   b. Employer payroll expenses on Stankov. Credit liability accounts.
   c. Fringe benefits provided to Stankov. Credit a liability account.

Problem 11-6A *Selecting the correct data to record a payroll*

Assume that the following payroll information appeared in the records of the St. Marys *Journal-Argus* newspaper:

	Payroll for Week Ended Friday, March 31, 19X9	Payroll for Month of March 19X9
Salaries		
Editorial salaries	$6,455	$27,178
Warehousing salaries.	3,118	13,128
Deductions		
Employee withheld income tax	2,297	9,673
Employee Canada Pension Plan		
contributions.	192	806
Employee Unemployment Insurance	225	947
Employee contributions to United Way. .	367	1,545
Employee Canada Savings Bonds	288	1,213
Net pay	6,204	26,122
Employer Payroll Expense		
Canada Pension Plan.	192	806
Unemployment Insurance	315	1,325
Worker's Compensation	77	320
Employer Cost of Fringe Benefits for Employees		
Dental insurance	663	2,791
Life insurance	324	1,368
Pensions.	451	1,899

Note: One challenge of this problem is to use only the relevant data. Not all the information given is necessary for making the required journal entries.

Required

1. Prepare the general journal entries to record the payroll for the week ended March 31, including all payroll withholdings and expenses.

2. Prepare the general journal entry to record the payment of the week's salaries to employees on March 31.

3. Assume that the *Journal-Argus* pays its liabilities to the federal government once a month while payments to the Worker's Compensation Board are made quarterly. Prepare the general journal entry to record the April 19X9 payment to Revenue Canada. (Liabilities to Revenue Canada include income tax withheld and the employee's share and employer's share of Canada Pension and Unemployment Insurance.)

4. Assume the *Journal-Argus* pays all other payroll liabilities (except Worker's Compensation) shortly after the end of the month. Prepare a single general journal entry to record the payment on April 4, 19X9 for these March liabilities.

Problem 11-7A *Using payroll register; recording a payroll*

Assume that the payroll records of a district sales office of Regina Freight Corporation provided the following information for the weekly pay period ended December 21, 19X5:

Employee	Hours Worked	Hourly Earnings Rate	Income Tax	Canada Pension	Unemployment Insurance	Earnings through Previous Week
Maria Kokoros	42	$18	182.80	0	14.40	$42,474
James English	47	8	52.90	7.70	9.09	23,154
Louise French	40	11	77.75	8.50	9.90	4,880
Robert LaFlair	41	16	136.80	0	14.40	39,600

James English and Louise French work in the office, and Maria Kokoros and Robert LaFlair work in sales. All employees are paid time and a half for hours worked in excess of 40 per week. For convenience, round all amounts to the nearest dollar. Show computations.

Required

1. Enter the appropriate information in a payroll register similar to Exhibit 11-4.
2. Record the payroll information in the general journal.
3. Assume that the first payroll cheque is number 319, paid to Maria Kokoros. Record the cheque numbers in the payroll register. Also, prepare the general journal entry to record payment of net pay to the employees.
4. The employer's payroll costs include matching the employee's Canada Pension Plan contribution and paying 1.4 times the employee's Unemployment Insurance premium. Record the employer's payroll costs in the general journal.
5. Why was no Canada Pension deducted for Kokoros and LaFlair?

(Group B)

Problem 11-1B   *Reporting current liabilities*

Following are six pertinent facts about events during the current year at Chevalier Products.
a. On August 31 signed a six-month, 12 percent note payable to purchase a machine costing $14,000. The note requires payment of principal and interest at maturity.
b. On September 30 discounted a $10,000 note payable to St. Lawrence Bank and received cash of $9,000. The interest rate on the one-year note is 10 percent.
c. On October 31 received rent of $2,000 in advance for a lease on a building. This rent will be earned evenly over four months.
d. December sales totaled $63,000 and Chevalier collected sales tax of 9 percent. This amount will be sent to the Province of Quebec early in January.
e. Chevalier owes $75,000 on a long-term note payable. At December 31, $25,000 of this principal plus accrued interest of $900 are payable within one year.
f. Sales of $509,000 were covered by Chevalier's product warranty. At December 31, estimated warranty payable is $11,300.

Required

For each item, indicate the account and the related amount to be reported as a current liability on Chevalier's December 31 balance sheet.

Problem 11-2B   *Journalizing liability-related transactions*

The following transactions of Lancaster Company occurred during 19X2 and 19X3. Record the transactions in the company's general journal.

19X2

Feb. 3   Purchased a machine for $2,200, signing a six-month, 11 percent note payable.

28   Recorded the month's sales of $90,000, one third for cash, and two thirds on credit. All sales amounts are subject to a 7 percent provincial sales tax.

Mar. 7   Sent the last month's sales tax to the Province of British Columbia.

Apr. 30   Borrowed $500,000 on a 9 percent, long-term note payble that calls for annual installment payments of $100,000 principal plus interest.

May 10   Received $1,125 in security deposits from customers. Lancaster refunds most deposits within three months.

Aug. 3   Paid the six-month, 11 percent note at maturity.

10   Refunded security deposits of $1,125 to customers.

Sept.14   Discounted a $6,000, 12 percent, 60-day note payable to the bank, receiving cash for the net amount after interest was deducted from the note's maturity value.

Nov. 13   Recognized interest on the 12 percent discounted note and paid off the note at maturiry.

30   Purchased inventory at a cost of $7,200, signing a 10 percent, three-month note payable for that amount.

Dec. 31   Accrued warranty expense, which is estimated at 3 percent of sales of $145,000.

31   Accured interest on all outstanding notes payable. Make a separate interest accrual entry for each note payable.

19X3

Feb. 28   Paid off the 10 percent inventory note, plus interest, at maturity.

Apr. 30   Paid the first installment and interest for one year on the long-term note payable.

Problem 11-3B   *Journalizing, posting and reporting liabilities*

The Loflin Company general ledger at September 30, 19X7, the end of the company's fiscal year, includes the following account balances before adjusting entries. Parentheses indicate a debit balance.

Notes Payable, Short-Term ..	$ 32,000	Employer Payroll Costs	
Discount on Notes Payable ..	(2,100)	Payable..................	$ —
Accounts Payable	88,240	Employee Benefits Payable...	—
Current Portion of Long-		Sales Tax Payable	372
Term Debt Payable	—	Property Tax Payable	1,433
Interest Payable............	—	Estimated Warranty Payable .	—
Salaries Payable............	—	Unearned Rent Revenue	3,900
Employee Withholdings		Long-Term Debt Payable	165,000
Payable	—	Contingent Liabilities	—

The additional data needed to develop the adjusting entries at September 30 are as follows:

a. The $32,000 balance in Notes Payable, Short-Term consists of two notes. The first note, with a principal amount of $21,000, was issued on August 31, matures six months from date of issuance, and was discounted at 10 percent. The second note, with a principal amount of $11,000, was issued on September 2 for a term of 90 days and bears interest at 9 percent. It was not discounted.

b. The long-term debt is payable in annual installments of $55,000, with the next installment due on January 31, 19X8. On that date, Loflin will also pay one year's interest at 10.5 percent. Interest was last paid on January 31. To shift the current installment of the long-term debt to a current liability, debit Long-Term Debt Payable and credit Current Portion of Long-Term Debt Payable.

c.   Gross salaries for the last payroll of the fiscal year were $4,319. Of this amount, employee withholdings were $958, and salaries payable were $3,361.

d.   Employer payroll costs were $755, and Loflin's liability for employee life insurance was $1,004.

e.   Loflin estimates that warranty expense is 3 percent of sales, which were $387,000. The company has not yet recorded warranty expense for the year.

f.   On August 1, the company collected six months' rent of $3,900 in advance.

g.   At June 30, Loflin is the defendant in a $50,000 lawsuit, which the company expects to win. However, the outcome is uncertain.

Required

1.   Open the listed accounts, inserting their unadjusted September 30 balances.
2.   Journalize and post the September 30 adjusting entries to the accounts opened. Key adjusting entries by letter.
3.   Prepare the liability section of Loflin's balance sheet at September 30.

Problem 11-4B   *Computing and reporting payroll amounts*

The partial monthly records of Friedrich Company show the following figures:

Employee Earnings

a. Straight-time earnings	?	g. Medical insurance	$ 1,373
b. Overtime pay	$ 5,109	h. Total deductions	?
c. Total employee earnings...	?	i. Net pay	53,754

Deductions and Net Pay

Accounts Debited

d. Withheld income tax	16,466	j. Salary Expense	31,278
e. Canada Pension	1,497	k. Wage Expense............	?
f. Unemployment Insurance .	1,759	l. Sales Commission Expense	27,931

Required

1.   Determine the missing amounts on lines a, c, h and k.
2.   Prepare the general journal entry to record Friedrich's payroll for the month. Credit Payrolls Payable for net pay.

Problem 11-5B   *Computing and recording payroll amounts*

Assume that Greta Gunderson is a commercial lender in Northwest Bank's mortgage department in Dawson Creek. During 19X2, she worked for the bank all year at a monthly salary of $4,195. She also earned a year-end bonus equal to 12 percent of her salary.

Gunderson's monthly income tax withholding for 19X2 was $1,109.90. Also, she paid a one-time withholding of $2,316.00 on her bonus cheque. She paid $87.12 per month towards the Canada Pension Plan until the maximum had been withheld. In addition, Gunderson's employer deducted $62.40 per month for unemployment insurance. Gunderson authorized the following deductions: 1 percent per month of her monthly pay to the Northwest Bank's charitable donation fund and $28.00 per month for life insurance.

Northwest Bank incurred Canada Pension expense equal to the amount deducted from Gunderson's pay. Unemployment Insurance cost the bank 1.4 times the amount deducted from Gunderson's pay. In addition, the bank provided Gunderson with the following fringe benefits: dental and drug insurance at a cost of $48 per month, and pension benefits to be paid to Gunderson upon retirement. The pension contribution is based on her income and was $3,564.00 in 19X2.

Required

1. Compute Gunderson's gross pay, payroll deductions and net pay for the full year 19X2. Round all amounts to the nearest dollar.
2. Compute Northwest Bank's total 19X2 payroll cost for Gunderson.
3. Prepare Northwest Bank's summary general journal entries to record its expense for
   a. Gunderson's total earnings for the year, her payroll deductions and her net pay. Debit Salary Expense and Executive Bonus Compensation as appropriate. Credit liability accounts for the payroll deductions and Cash for net pay.
   b. Employer payroll expenses for Gunderson. Credit liability accounts.
   c. Fringe benefits provided to Gunderson. Credit a liability account.

Problem 11-6B   *Selecting the correct data to record a payroll*

Assume the following payroll information appeared in the records of a small plant operated by Ford Motor Co. of Canada:

	Payroll for Week Ended Friday, July 31, 19X4	Payroll for Month of July 19X4
Salaries		
Supervisor salaries	$39,668	$162,639
Office salaries	9,088	37,261
Deductions		
Employee withheld income tax	12,677	51,974
Employee withheld Canada Pension		
Plan contributions	975	3,998
Employee Unemployment Insurance....	1,146	4,698
Employee union dues	708	2,903
Employee Canada savings bonds	665	2,727
Net Pay	32,585	136,660
Employer Payroll Costs		
Canada Pension Plan.................	975	3,998
Unemployment Insurance	1,604	6,577
Worker's Compensation	390	1,599
Employer Cost of Fringe Benefits for		
Employees		
Dental insurance	2,034	8,339
Life insurance	1,857	7,614
Pension	1,667	6,835

Note: One challenge of this problem is to use only the relevant data. Not all the information given is necessary for making the required journal entries.

Required

1. Prepare the general journal entries to record the payroll for the week ended July 31, including all payroll withholdings and expenses.

2. Prepare the general journal entry to record the payment of the week's salaries to employees on July 31.

3. Assume that Ford pays its liabilities to the federal government once a month while payments to the Worker's Compensation Board are made quarterly. Prepare the general journal entry to record the August 19X9 payment to Revenue Canada. (Liabilities to Revenue Canada include income tax withheld and the employee's share and employer's share of Canada Pension and Unemployment Insurance.)

4. Assume Ford pays all other payroll liabilities (except Worker's Compensation) shortly after the end of the month. Prepare a single general journal entry to record the payment on August 4, 19X9 for these July liabilities.

Problem 11-7B   *Using a payroll register; recording a payroll*

Assume that payroll records of a district sales office of Purolator Courier provided the following information for the weekly pay period ended December 18, 19X3:

Employee	Hours Worked	Weekly Earnings Rate	Income Tax	Canada Pension	Unemployment Insurance	Earnings through Previous Week
Tina Fortin	43	$400	78.75	8.61	10.01	$17,060
Leroy Dixon	46	480	107.55	11.82	13.23	22,365
Karol Stastny	41	800	198.00	0	14.40	39,247
David Trent	40	240	30.30	4.10	5.40	3,413

Tina Fortin and David Trent work in the office, and Leroy Dixon and Karol Stastny work in sales. All employees are paid time and a half for hours worked in excess of 40 per week. For convenience, round all amounts to the nearest dollar. Show computations.

Required

1. Enter the appropriate information in a payroll register similar to Exhibit 11-4.
2. Record the payroll information in the general journal.
3. Assume that the first payroll cheque is number 178, paid to Tina Fortin. Record the cheque numbers in the payroll register. Also, prepare the general journal entry to record payment of net pay to the employees.
4. The employer's payroll costs derive from matching the employee's Canada Pension Plan contribution and paying 1.4 times the employee's Unemployment Insurance premium. Record the employer's payroll costs in the general journal.
5. Why is no Canada Pension deducted for Stastny?

Decision Problems

1. *Identifying internal control weaknesses and their solution*

Hall Custom Homes is a large home-building business in Edmonton, Alberta. The owner and manager is Lawrence Hall, who oversees all company operations. He employs 15 work crews, each made up of 6 to 10 members. Construction supervisors, who report directly to Hall, lead the crews. Most supervisors are long-time employees, so Hall trusts them greatly. Hall's office staff consists of an accountant and an office manager.

Because employee turnover is rapid in the construction industry, supervisors hire and terminate their own crew members. Supervisors notify the office of all personnel changes. Also, supervisors forward to the office the employee TD1 forms, which the crew members fill out to claim tax-withholding exemptions. Each Thursday the supervisors submit weekly time sheets for their crews, and the accountant prepares the payroll. At noon on Friday the supervisors come to the office to get paycheques for distribution to the workers at 5 P.M.

Hall's accountant prepares the payroll, including the payroll cheques, which are written on a single payroll bank account. Hall signs all payroll cheques after matching the employee name to the time sheets submitted by the supervisor. Often the construction workers wait several days to cash their paycheques. To verify that each construction worker is a bona fide employee, the accountant matches the employee's endorsement signature on the back of the canceled payroll cheque with the signature on that employee's TD1 form.

Required

1. List one *efficiency* weakness in Hall's payroll accounting system. How can Hall correct this weakness?
2. Identify one way that a supervisor can defraud Hall under the present system.
3. Discuss a control feature Hall can use to *safeguard* against the fraud you identified in question 2.

2. Questions about liabilities

The following questions are not related.

a. A friend comments that he thought that liabilities represented amounts owed by a company and asks why unearned revenues are shown as a current liability. How would you respond?

b. A warranty is like a contingent liability in that the amount that will have to be paid out is not known at year end. Why are warranties payable shown as a current liability while contingent liabilities are included in the notes to the financial statements?

c. Give an example of a long-term warranty. Where would it be shown on the financial statements?

d. Auditors have a set of procedures that they use in determining whether or not they have discovered all of a company's contingent liabilities. These procedures, differ from the procedures used for determining that accounts payable are correctly stated. What is it about contingent liabilities that necessitates this difference?

Financial Statement Problem

Current and contingent liabilities

Details about a company's current and contingent liabilities appear in a number of places in the annual report. Use the John Labatt financial statements in Appendix E to answer these questions.

1. What is the balance of John Labatt's accounts payable at April 30, 1989? What do you think the major components of the accounts payable are?

2. How much were the current maturities of John Labatt's long-term debt at April 30, 1989? Are any debt issues due to mature in the fiscal year ended April 30, 1990? If there are, describe the issue (Hint: see notes 10 and 11).

3. Does John Labatt have any contingent liabilities at April 30, 1989?

4. John Labatt has a number of operating leases outstanding at April 30, 1989. The payments on those leases are not a liability at April 30, 1989, but a specified amount is due in the fiscal year ended April 30, 1990. What is that amount? Why do you think it is reported in the financial statements?

Answers to Self-Study Questions

1. c $\$10,000 \times .09 \times 5/12 = \$375$
2. a $\$10,000 - (\$10,000 \times .09) = \$9,100$
3. b
4. c $\$900,000 \times .01 = \$9,000$
5. b
6. a   Overtime pay: $\$320/40 = \$8 \times 1.5 = \$12$ per hour $\times 10$ hours $= \$120$
      Gross pay $= \$320 + \$120 = \$440$
      Deductions $= (\$440 \times .16) + (\$440 - \$53.84) \times .022 + (\$440 \times .0225) = \$70.40 + 8.50 + 9.90 = \$88.80$
      Take-home pay $= \$440.00 - 88.80 = \$351.20$
7. d
8. c
9. b
10. d

PART FOUR

Generally Accepted Accounting Principles

12

The Foundation
for Generally Accepted
Accounting Principles

LEARNING OBJECTIVES

After studying this chapter, you should be able to

1 Identify the basic objective of financial reporting

2 Identify and apply the underlying concepts of accounting

3 Identify and apply the principles of accounting

4 Allocate revenue to the appropriate period by four methods

5 Report information that satisfies the disclosure principle

6 Apply two constraints to accounting

7 Name and define the elements of financial statements

Throughout the first eleven chapters, we have introduced key concepts and principles as they have applied to the topics under discussion. For example, Chapter 1 introduced the entity concept so that we could account for the transactions of a particular business. In Chapter 2, we discussed the revenue and matching principles as the guidelines for measuring income. Now that you have an overview of the accounting process, we consider the full range of accounting concepts and principles. Collectively, they form the foundation for accounting practice — GAAP.

The Development of Standards

Every technical field seems to have professional associations and regulatory bodies that govern its practice. Accounting is no exception. In Canada, the Canadian Institute of Chartered Accountants (CICA) has had the responsibility for issuing accounting standards that form the basis of generally accepted accounting principles or GAAP. Initially, from 1946, when the first accounting standard was issued by the CICA's Accounting and Auditing Research Committee, until 1972, the CICA assumed for itself the responsibility for issuing accounting standards.[1]

---

[1] This material is from Murphy, George J., "A Chronology of the Development of Corporate Financial Reporting in Canada: 1850 to 1983." *The Accounting Historians Journal*, Spring, 1986, pp. 31–62.

Then in 1972, the Canadian Securities Administrators, a body composed of officials appointed by the provincial governments with securities exchanges to set securities law, issued National Policy Statement 27 (NP 27) designating the *CICA Handbook* as generally accepted accounting principles (GAAP). In 1975, the Canada Business Corporations Act did likewise. The Ontario Securities Act in 1978 also designated the *CICA Handbook* as GAAP (Exhibit 12-1). In these ways, the CICA became the official promulgator of generally accepted accounting principles. Exhibit 12-1 illustrates how the authority for setting GAAP is delegated to the CICA by the federal and provincial governments and the Securities Administrators.

EXHIBIT 12-1   *Flow of Authority for Developing GAAP*

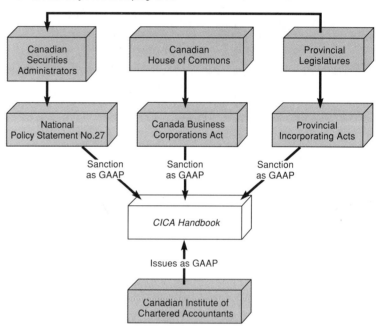

From the date of the first accounting standard in 1946 until 1968, some 26 "bulletins" were issued by the Accounting and Auditing Research Committee. In 1968, the CICA changed the format of pronouncements; from that date they became *Recommendations* and were the italicized portions of a looseleaf binder entitled the *CICA Handbook*. Sections 1500 to 4999 (Volume I) of the *Handbook* are concerned with accounting, while Sections 5000 to 9200 (Volume II) are concerned with auditing. The Recommendations are standards or regulations that must be followed, except in those rare cases where a particular Recommendation or Recommendations would not lead to fair presentation. In those cases, the accountant should, using professional judgment, select the appropriate accounting principle. An accountant, who determines that the *Handbook* is not appropriate and selects some other basis of accounting, must be prepared to defend that decision. The *Handbook* also includes Accounting Guidelines and Auditing Guidelines. They do not have the force of Recommendations and are issued simply to suggest methods for dealing with issues that are not covered by Recommendations. Frequently, they become replaced eventually by Recommendations on the issues.

In 1972, the Accounting and Auditing Research Committee was split into two committees—the Accounting Research Committee (ARC), renamed in 1982, the Accounting Standards Committee (AcSC) and the Auditing Standards Committee (AuSC). The former has the responsibility for establishing accounting standards, while the latter has the responsibility for establishing auditing standards. The CICA established another standards committee in 1981, the Public Sector Accounting and Auditing Standards Committee (PSAAC), and a new handbook to contain the standards promulgated by that body. The PSAAC issues standards dealing with accounting by and auditing of public sector entities, such as Transport Canada, provincial liquor commissions, municipalities, hospitals and school boards. The Recommendations issued by PSAAC have the same force as standards issued by AcSC ad AuSC, except that they apply only to public sector entities.

Each new accounting Recommendation issued by the Accounting Standards Committee becomes part of GAAP, the "accounting law of the land." In the same way that our laws draw authority from their acceptance by the people, GAAP depends on the general acceptance by the business community. Throughout this book, we refer to GAAP as the proper way to do accounting.

Setting accounting standards is a complex process. The Accounting Standards Committee does research on a particular issue, for example, the proper accounting for a lease. A document called an exposure draft is issued; it is a draft of the proposed new *Handbook* material. It is distributed by the AcSC to all interested parties who are asked to make comments by a specified date. The AcSC considers the responses to the exposure draft and issues a new Recommendation, which becomes part of the *Handbook*. Occasionally, the proposed *Handbook* section is redrafted and re-exposed as a re-exposure draft to get additional comments before it is incorporated into the *Handbook*.

Individuals and companies often exert pressure on the AcSC in their efforts to shape accounting decisions to their advantage. Occasionally governmental bodies have exerted pressure when they perceived that a proposed standard was not in harmony with government policy. Accountants also try to influence accounting decisions.

We have seen that GAAP guides companies in their financial statement preparation. Independent auditing firms of public accountants hold the responsibility for making sure companies do indeed follow GAAP.

Sources of Generally Accepted Accounting Principles

While the primary source of GAAP is the *CICA Handbook*, the *Handbook* cannot possibly cover all the situations that accountants encounter. When situations not covered by the *Handbook* arise, Section 1000 of the *Handbook* suggests that the accountant must exercise professional judgment utilizing one or more of the following sources:

1. *General practice*   These are accounting principles that have general acceptance even though they are not codified.
2. *Industry practice*   Some industries, such as the Canadian Institute of Real Estate Companies (CIPREC), have developed and enunciated principles for their industry.
3. *Accounting Guidelines*   The Accounting Standards Steering Committee issues Guidelines which are that body's interpretations of Recommendations or opinions on issues that are not yet codified as Recommendations.

4. *Emerging Issues Committee*   This committee was established in 1988 by the CICA to deal with emerging accounting issues on a more timely basis than was possible under the process of standard setting by the AcSC described above. The CICA's Emerging Issues Committee issues consensus views entitled "Abstracts" that have the full support of the CICA.

5. *International Accounting Standards*   The Canadian Institute of Chartered Accountants, along with the Certified General Accountants Association of Canada and the Society of Management Accountants of Canada, are charter members of the International Accounting Standards Committee (IASC). This body, which includes as members professional accounting organizations in more than 50 countries, is attempting to harmonize GAAP in those countries by issuing international accounting standards. Other members include the U.K., the U.S., the member countries of the European Economic Community, Japan and Australia. Section 1501 of the *Handbook* lists the more than 25 international accounting standards (IASs) that have been issued to date.

    IASs do not override Canadian GAAP as set forth in the *Handbook*, which has precedence as local regulation. The AcSC is attempting, where possible, to harmonize the Recommendations in the *CICA Handbook* with the IASs.

6. *Authoritative pronouncements from other countries*   The Financial Accounting Standards Board (FASB), the body responsible for setting accounting standards in the United States, has issued a number of accounting standards in areas where there may not be a pronouncement from the CICA.

7. *CICA research studies*   The CICA has issued a number of research studies such as *Financial Statements for Pension Plan Participants* that provide guidance to accountants. In addition, the Certified General Accountants Association of Canada and the Society of Management Accountants of Canada publish research studies dealing with accounting issues.

8. *Accounting texts and professional journals* such as *CAmagazine* and the *Journal of Accountancy*.

If confronted with an accounting issue that is not dealt with by the *CICA Handbook*, you should consider these sources and select the most appropriate treatment, the one that provides the most informative disclosure.

Overview of Generally Accepted Accounting Principles

In December 1988, the Accounting Standards Committee issued *CICA Handbook* Section 1000, "Financial Statement Concepts." The new section's purpose is to " ... describe the concepts underlying the development and use of accounting principles in the general purpose financial statements ... of profit oriented enterprises." The AcSC expects the section to be used by accountants in guiding their professional judgment in the preparation and audit of financial statements.

Accounting principles differ from natural laws like the law of gravity. Accounting principles draw their authority from their acceptance in the business community rather than from their ability to explain physical phenomena. Thus they really are *generally accepted* by those people and organizations who need guidelines in accounting for their financial undertakings. Exhibit 12-2 diagrams how we move from the objectives of financial reporting to the financial statements.

We now look at the objective of financial reporting. This objective tells what financial accounting is intended to accomplish. Thus it provides the goal for

EXHIBIT 12-2 *Overview of Generally Accepted Accounting Principles*

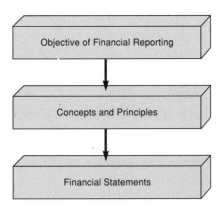

accounting information. Next, we examine particular accounting concepts and principles used to implement the objective. What is the difference between a concept and a principle? The concepts are broader in their application, and the principles are more specific. Last, we discuss the financial statements, the end product of financial accounting, and their elements — assets, liabilities, owner's equity, revenues, expenses, and so on.

Objective of Financial Reporting

The basic objective of financial reporting is to provide useful information to users of financial statements in making investment and lending decisions and in evaluating management's stewardship. To be useful in decision-making, the AcSC, in Section 1000, believes that information in financial statements should be *understandable, relevant, reliable* and *comparable*.

The information must be *understandable* to users if they are to be able to use it. *Relevant* information is useful for making predictions and for evaluating past performance. *Reliable* information is free from error and the bias of a particular viewpoint. *Comparable* information can be compared from period to period to help investors and creditors track the business's progress through time. These characteristics combine to shape the concepts and principles that make up GAAP.

> **OBJECTIVE 1**
> Identify the basic objective of financial reporting

Underlying Concepts

Entity Concept

The *entity concept* is the most basic concept in accounting because, as Chapter 1 points out, it draws a boundary around the organization being accounted for. That is, the transactions of each entity are accounted for separately from transactions of all other organizations and persons, including the owners of the entity. This separation allows us to measure the performance and the financial position of each entity independent of all other entities.

> **OBJECTIVE 2**
> Identify and apply the underlying concepts of accounting

A business entity may be a sole proprietorship, a partnership or a large corporation like Petro-Canada. The entity concept applies with equal force to all types and sizes of organizations. The proprietor of a travel agency, for example, accounts for his or her personal transactions separately from those of the business. At the other end of the spectrum, Petro-Canada is a giant company with oil exploration, oil-refining, and retail gasoline sales operations. Petro-Canada accounts for each division separately in order to know which part of the business is earning a profit, which needs to borrow money, and so on.

The entity concept also applies to nonprofit organizations such as churches, synagogues and government agencies. A hospital, for example, may have an emergency room, a pediatrics unit and a surgery unit. The accounting system of the hospital should account for each separately to allow the managers to evaluate the progress of each unit.

The entity concept also provides the basis for consolidating subentities into a single set of financial statements. For example, the directors want to know the overall result of operating the entire hospital. Accountants, therefore, summarize the results of the various subentities into a consolidated set of financial statements. This is also done for profit-oriented businesses like Petro-Canada, which has a single set of consolidated financial statements.

Going-Concern Concept

In following the **going-concern concept**, accountants assume the business will continue operating for the foreseeable future. The logic behind the going-concern concept is best illustrated by considering the alternative assumption: going out of business.

When a business stops, it sells its assets, converting them to cash. This process is called *liquidation*. With the cash, the business pays off its liabilities, and the owners keep any remaining cash. In liquidation, the amount of cash for which the assets are sold measures their current value. Likewise, the liabilities are paid off at their current value. If the business were to prepare a balance sheet between making the decision to liquidate and the actual liquidation, the assets and liabilities would be written down from historical cost (the values at which they were originally recorded) to current or liquidation values.

On the other hand, when a business plans to continue in operation, that is, remain a going concern, it reports the historical cost of its assets and liabilities. In a normal buyer-seller transaction, cost is an objective measure of an asset's worth. Under the going-concern concept, it is assumed the entity will continue long enough for it to recover its costs. Considering what an asset may be worth on the current market requires making an estimate. This estimate may or may not be objective.

The going-concern concept allows for the reporting of assets and liabilities as current (due within one year) or long-term, a distinction that investors and creditors find useful in evaluating a company. For example, a creditor wants to know the portion of a company's liabilities that are scheduled to come due within the next year and the portion payable beyond the year. The assumption is that the entity will continue in business and honour its commitment.

Time-Period Concept

The **time-period concept** ensures that accounting information is reported at regular intervals. This timely presentation of accounting data aids the comparison of business operations over time—from year to year, quarter to quarter, and so on. Managers, owners, lenders and other people and businesses need regular reports to assess the business's success — or failure. These persons make decisions constantly. Although the ultimate success of a company cannot be known for sure until the business liquidates, decision-makers cannot wait until liquidation to learn whether operations yielded a profit.

Nearly all companies use the year as their basic time period. *Annual* reports are common in business. Companies also prepare quarterly and monthly reports, called interim reports, to meet managers', investors' and creditors' need for helpful, up-to-the-minute information.

The time-period concept underlies the use of accruals. Suppose the business's accounting year ends at December 31 and the business has accrued — but will not pay until the next accounting period — $900 in salary expense. To tie this expense to the appropriate period, the accountant enters this adjusting entry, as we have seen:

Salary Expense	900	
Salary Payable		900

Accrual entries assign revenue and expense amounts to the correct accounting period and thus help produce the most meaningful financial statements.

Approximately 63 percent of all companies report their financial statements on a calendar-year basis, January through December. The remaining 37 percent use a fiscal year that ends at the business's annual low point in operations. For example, Hudson's Bay Co. and most large retailers use a fiscal year ending January 31. Their operations reach their most active point during December and then taper off at the end of January when the after-Christmas sales have finished.

Stable Monetary Unit Concept

Accounting information is expressed primarily in monetary terms. The monetary unit is the prime means of measuring assets. This measure is not surprising given that money is the common denominator in business transactions. In Canada, the monetary unit is the dollar; in Great Britain, the pound sterling; and in Japan, the yen. The stable monetary unit concept provides an orderly basis for handling account balances to produce the financial statements.

Unlike a litre, a metre and many other measurements, the value of the monetary unit may change over time. Most of us are familiar with inflation. Groceries that cost $50 three years ago may cost $60 today. The value of the dollar changes. In view of the fact that the dollar does not maintain a constant value, how does a business measure the worth of assets and liabilities acquired over a long span of time? The business records all assets and liabilities at cost. Each asset and each liability on the balance sheet is the sum of all the individual dollar amounts added over time. For example, if a company bought 100 acres of land in 1975 for $60,000 and another 100 acres of land in 1985 for $300,000, the asset Land on the balance sheet carries a $360,000 balance, and the change in the purchasing power of the dollar is ignored. The **stable-monetary-unit concept** is the accountant's basis for ignoring the effect of inflation and making no adjustments for the changing value of the dollar. Let us look at the shortcomings of this concept.

The December 31, 1989, balance sheet of Crown Development Corporation reported Land at $38.5 million. Assume that Crown Development purchased land in 1971 for $4 million and land in 1989 for $34.5 million. The period from 1971 to 1989 witnessed high inflation. We know, therefore, that the dollar had significantly higher value in 1971. Crown Development may have bought more land in 1971 for $4 million than it did in 1989 for so much more money. Now suppose that a second company spent a full $38.5 million on land in 1989. The area of land it purchased would be much smaller than the area purchased with mixed 1971 and 1989 dollars. How do we compare the two companies' balance sheets? The comparison based on the stable monetary unit concept may not be valid, because mixing dollar values at different times is like mixing apples and oranges.

Many businesspeople believe that accounting information must be adjusted for changes in the dollar's purchasing power. The CICA encourages large companies to present supplementary inflation-adjusted information in their financial reports, a topic we examine in Chapter 17. Generally, however, accounting is based on historical costs.

Accounting Principles

Reliability (Objectivity) Principle

OBJECTIVE 3

Identify and apply the principles of accounting

The **reliability principle**, as Chapter 1 discusses, requires that accounting information be dependable. Reliable information is free from error and bias. Users of this accounting information may rely on its truthfulness. To be reliable, information must be verifiable by people outside the business. Financial statement users may consider information reliable if independent experts agree that the information is based on objective and honest measurement. Information that contains errors or bias would not be considered reliable.

Consider the error from a company's failure to accrue interest revenue at the end of an accounting period. This error results in understated interest revenue and understated net income. Clearly, this company's accounting information is unreliable.

Biased information, data prepared from a particular viewpoint and not based on objective facts, is also unreliable. Suppose a company purchased inventory for $25,000. At the end of the accounting period, the inventory has declined in value and can be replaced for $20,000. Under the lower-of-cost-or-market rule, the company must record a $5,000 loss for the decrease in the inventory's value. Company management may believe that the appropriate value for the inventory is $22,000, but that amount is only an opinion. If management reports the $22,000 figure, total assets and owner's equity will be overstated on the balance sheet. Income will be overstated on the income statement.

To establish a reliable figure for the inventory's value, management could get a current price list from the inventory supplier or call in an outside professional appraiser to revalue the inventory. Evidence obtained from outside the company leads to reliable, verifiable information. The reliability principle applies to all financial accounting information—from assets to owner's equity on the balance sheet and from revenue to net income on the income statement.

Comparability Principle

The **comparability principle** has two requirements. First, accounting information must be comparable from business to business. Second, a single business's financial statements from one period must be comparable to those from the next period. The CICA encourages comparability in order to make possible a useful analysis of one business against another business, and one period against another period.

Standard formats for financial statements (balance sheets, income statements, and so on) promote comparability among companies. Using the same terms to describe the statement elements (assets, liabilities, revenues, and so on) also aids the comparison process.

Complete comparability even among companies that adhere to standard formats and standard terms, may not always be possible. Comparisons of companies that use different inventory methods (LIFO and FIFO, for example) are difficult. Likewise, comparisons of companies that use different depreciation methods (straight-line and accelerated, for example) are also quite complex. When GAAP allows a choice among acceptable accounting methods, in inventory, depreciation and other areas, comparability may be harder to achieve.

Recall that the comparability principle directs each individual company to produce accounting information that is comparable over time. To achieve this quality, which accountants call *consistency*, companies must follow the same accounting practices from period to period. The business that uses FIFO for inventory and straight-line for depreciation in one period ought to use those same methods in the next period. Otherwise, a financial statement user could not tell whether changes in income and asset values result from operations or from the way the business accounts for operations.

Companies may change accounting methods, however, in response to a change in business operations. A company may open up a new product line that calls for a different inventory method. GAAP allows the company to make a change in accounting method, but the business must disclose the change, the reason for making the change and the effect of the change on net income. This disclosure is made in a note to the financial statements.

Cost Principle

As presented in Chapter 1, the **cost principle** states that assets and services are recorded at their purchase cost and that the accounting record of the asset continues to be based on cost rather than current market value. This principle also governs the recording of liabilities and owner's equity. Suppose that a land developer purchased 20 hectares of land for $50,000 plus a real estate commission of $2,000. Additional costs included fees paid to the municipality ($1,500), utility hookups ($8,000) and landscaping ($20,000), for a total cost of $81,500. The Land account carries this balance because it is the cost of bringing the land to its intended use. Assume that the developer holds the land for one year, then offers it for sale at a price of $200,000. The cost principle requires the accounting value of the land to remain at $81,500.

The developer may wish to lure buyers by showing them a balance sheet that reports the land at $200,000. However, this would be inappropriate under GAAP because $200,000 is merely the developer's opinion of what the land is worth.

The underlying basis for the cost principle is the reliability principle. Cost is a reliable value for assets and services, because cost is supported by completed transactions between parties with opposing interests. Buyers try to pay the lowest price possible and sellers try to sell for the highest price. The actual cost of an asset or service is objective evidence of its value.

Revenue Principle

The revenue principle provides guidance on the *timing* of the recording of revenue and the *amount* of revenue to record. The general rule is that revenue should be recorded when it is earned and not before.

Some revenues, such as interest and rent, accrue with the passage of time.

Their timing and amount are easy to figure. The accountant records the amount of revenue earned over each accounting period.

Other revenues are earned by selling goods or rendering services. Identifying *when* these revenues are earned depends on more factors than the passage of time. Under the revenue principle, three conditions must be met before revenue is recorded: (1) the seller has done everything necessary to expect to collect from the buyer; (2) the amount of revenue can be objectively measured; and (3) collectibility is reasonably assured. In most cases, these conditions are met at the point of sale or when services are performed.

The amount of revenue to record is the value of the assets received — usually cash or a receivable. However, situations may arise in which the amount of revenue or the timing of earning the revenue is not easily determined. We turn now to four methods that guide the accountant in applying the revenue principle in different circumstances.

OBJECTIVE 4

Allocate revenue to the appropriate period by four methods

Sales Method   Under the **sales method**, revenue is recorded at the point of sale. Consider a retail sale in a hardware store. At the point of sale, the customer pays the store and takes the merchandise. The store records the sale by debiting Cash and crediting Sales Revenue. In other situations, the point of sale occurs when the seller ships the goods to the buyer. Suppose a mining company sells iron ore to Dofasco. By shipping the ore to Dofasco, the mining company has completed its duty and may expect to collect revenue. If the amount of revenue can be objectively measured and collection is reasonably certain, the mining company can then record revenue. The sale entry is a debit to Accounts Receivable and a credit to Sales Revenue. The sales method is used for most sales of goods and services.

Collection Method   The **collection method** is used only if the receipt of cash is uncertain. Under this method, the seller waits until cash is received to record the sale. This method is a form of cash-basis accounting and, as such, its use is discouraged by Revenue Canada. Companies that use the collection method do so because they often find it difficult to collect their receivables. They may not reasonably assume that they can collect the revenue, so they wait until the cash is actually received before recording it. The collection method is conservative because revenue is not recorded in advance of its receipt.

Installment Method   The **installment method** is a type of collection method that is used for installment sales. In a typical installment sale, the buyer makes a down payment when the contract is signed and pays the remainder in installments. Department stores (such as Sears and Simpsons), auto dealers and real estate companies sell on the installment plan. This method is also used for income tax purposes. Under the installment method, gross profit (sales revenue minus cost of goods sold) is recorded as cash is collected.

Suppose a real estate developer sells land for a down payment of $80,000 plus three annual installments of $120,000, $140,000 and $160,000 (a total of $500,000). The developer's cost of the land is $300,000, so the gross profit is $200,000, computed as follows:

Installment sale	$500,000
Cost of the land sold	300,000
Gross profit	$200,000

To determine the gross profit associated with each collection under the installment method, we must compute the gross profit percentage as follows:

$$\text{Gross profit percentage} = \frac{\text{Gross profit}}{\text{Installment sale}} = \frac{\$200,000}{\$500,000} = 40\%$$

We next apply the gross profit percentage to each collection. The result is the amount of gross profit recorded as revenue at the time of cash receipt.

Year	Collections	×	Gross Profit Percentage	=	Gross Profit
1	$ 80,000	×	40%	=	$ 32,000
2	120,000	×	40%	=	48,000
3	140,000	×	40%	=	56,000
4	160,000	×	40%	=	64,000
Total	$500,000	×	40%	=	$200,000

Accountants would record gross profit of $32,000 in year 1, $48,000 in year 2, and so on. The total gross profit ($200,000) is the same as under the sales method. However, under the sales method, the full $200,000 of gross profit would be recorded at the beginning of the contract.

Of course, companies make installment sales year after year. If the company's sales mix changed from year to year, each year's sales may have a different gross profit percentage. In the preceding example, year 1 installment sales earned gross profit of 40 percent. Suppose year 2 sales earn gross profit of 45 percent, year 3 sales earn 42 percent, and year 4 sales earn 35 percent. The total gross profit for a year is the sum of all the gross profit amounts recorded on cash collections made that year.

Using assumed cash receipts on installment sales made in years 2, 3 and 4, the gross profit computations for years 1 through 4 follow. All year 1 amounts are taken from our computations above.

	Year 1 Sales	Year 2 Sales	Year 3 Sales	Year 4 Sales
Gross profit percentage	40%	45%	42%	35%

Gross profit by year

	Year 1	Year 2	Year 3	Year 4
Year 1 sales	$80,000 × .40 = $32,000	$120,000 × .40 = $48,000	$140,000 × .40 = $56,000	$160,000 × .40 = $64,000
Year 2 sales		90,000 × .45 = 40,500	100,000 × .45 = 45,000	20,000 × .45 = 9,000
Year 3 sales			75,000 × .42 = 31,500	65,000 × .42 = 27,300
Year 4 sales				30,000 × .35 = 10,500
Total gross profit	$32,000	$88,500	$132,500	$110,800

The installment method is attractive for income tax purposes, because it postpones the recording of revenue and thus the payment of taxes. Under generally accepted accounting principles, this method is permissible only when no reasonable basis exists for estimating collections. It is seldom used in financial statements.

Percentage-of-Completion Method   Construction of office buildings, bridges, dams and other large assets often extends over several years. The accounting issue for the construction company is when to record the revenue. The most conservative approach is to record all the revenue earned on the project in the period when the project is completed. This procedure, called the **completed-contract method**, is acceptable under GAAP.

Under the alternative acceptable method, called the **percentage-of-completion method**, the construction company recognizes revenue as work is performed. Each year the company estimates the percentage of project completion as construction progresses. One way to make this estimate is to compare the cost incurred for the year to the total estimated project cost. This percentage is then multiplied by the total project revenue to compute the construction revenue for the year. Construction income for the year is revenue minus cost.

Assume Mannix Construction Company receives a contract to build a power plant for a price of $42 million. Mannix estimates total costs of $36 million over the three-year construction period: $6 million in year 1, $18 million in year 2, and $12 million in year 3. Construction revenue and income during the three years are as follows (amounts in millions):

Year	Cost for year	Total Project Cost	Percentage of Project Completion for Year	Total Project Revenue	Construction Revenue for Year	Construction Income for Year
1	$ 6	$36	$ 6/$36 = 1/6	$42	$42 × 1/6 = $ 7	$ 7 − $ 6 = $1
2	18	36	18/ 36 = 1/2	42	42 × 1/2 = 21	21 − 18 = 3
3	12	36	12/ 36 = 1/3	42	42 × 1/3 = 14	14 − 12 = 2
	$36	$36		$42	$42	$42 $36 $6

The percentage-of-completion method is appropriate when the company can estimate the degree of completion during the construction period, which most construction companies can do. When estimates are not possible, the completed-contract method is required. However, the completed-contract method does not relate the revenues and expenses of each period in a systematic manner. If Mannix Construction had used the completed-contract method, its income statement for year 3 would report total project revenue of $42 million, total project expenses of $36 million, and income of $6 million. The income statements of years 1 and 2 would report nothing concerning this project. Most accountants believe the results under the percentage-of-completion method are more realistic.

Matching Principle

The *matching principle* governs the recording and reporting of expenses. This principle goes hand in hand with the revenue principle to govern income recognition in accounting. Recall that income is revenue minus expense. During any period, the company first measures its revenues by the revenue principle. The company then identifies and measures all the expenses it incurred during the period to earn the revenues. To *match* the expenses against the revenues means to subtract the expenses from the revenues. The result is the income for the period.

Some expenses are easy to match against particular revenues. For example, cost of goods sold relates directly to sales revenue because without the sales, there would be no cost of goods sold. Commissions and fees paid for selling the goods, delivery expense and sales supplies expense relate to sales revenue for the same reason.

Other expenses are not so easily linked to particular sales because they occur whether or not any revenues arise. Depreciation, salaries and all types of home-office expense are in this category. Accountants usually match these expenses against revenue on a time basis. For example, the company's home-office building may be used for general management, manufacturing and marketing. Straight-line depreciation of a 40-year-old building assigns one fortieth of the building's cost to expense each year, whatever the level of revenue. The annual salary expense for an employee is the person's total salary for the year, regardless of revenue.

Losses, like expenses, are matched against revenue on a time basis. For example, if an asset like inventory loses value, the loss is recorded when it occurs, without regard for the revenues earned during the period.

Disclosure Principle

The **disclosure principle** holds that a company's financial statements should report enough information for outsiders to make knowledgeable decisions about the company. In short, the company should report sufficient *understandable, relevant, reliable* and *comparable* information about its economic affairs. This section of the chapter discusses and illustrates nine types of disclosures.

Summary of Significant Accounting Policies　To evaluate a company, investors and creditors need to know how its financial statements were prepared. This consideration is especially important when the company can choose from several acceptable methods. Companies summarize their accounting policies in the first note to their financial statements. The note may include both monetary amounts and written descriptions. Companies commonly disclose how they have applied accounting principles. For example, the depreciation method, consolidation basis and inventory valuation are three procedures commonly disclosed. John Labatt reported the following in its notes to its April 30, 1986 financial statements:

> **OBJECTIVE 5**
> Report information that satisfies the disclosure principle

NOTE 1. ACCOUNTING POLICIES [in part]

The financial statements have been prepared in accordance with accounting principles generally accepted in Canada and also conform in all material respects with International Accounting Standards. Significant accounting policies observed in their preparation are summarized below:

Principles of consolidation
The consolidated financial statements include the accounts of all subsidiary companies. The results of operations of subsidiaries acquired or sold during the year are included from or to their respective dates of acquisition or sale.

Inventories
Inventories, other than containers, are valued at the lower of cost and net realizable value, cost being determined on a first-in, first-out basis. Containers are valued at redemption price or at amortized cost, which does not exceed replacement cost. Inventory values are as follows:

(in thousands)	1986	1985
Finished and in process	$209,475	$194,571
Materials and supplies	89,896	86,930
Containers	39,434	46,598
	$338,805	$328,099

Investments

Partly owned businesses are companies and partnerships in which the Company has significant influence and are accounted for using the equity method of accounting.

Investments in other companies are carried at the lower of cost and net realizable value, and income is recognized when dividends are received.

Fixed assets

Fixed assets are recorded at cost. Depreciation is provided on a straight-line basis over the estimated useful lives of the assets, generally at rates of 2½% for buildings, 10% for machinery and equipment, and 20% for vehicles.

Contingent Liabilities   Companies are usually eager to disclose good news. The disclosure principle requires them to report bad news as well. For example, a company may be a defendant in a lawsuit with an uncertain outcome. Will the contingency — the possibility of a negative outcome — result in an actual loss to the company? Will it endanger the company's ability to continue as a going concern? Investors, lenders and other interested parties need the full financial picture. A bank may decide not to loan additional money because of the contingency. A labor union may note the contingency and lower its demand for an increase in employee wages. The disclosure principle requires the company to report whether the lawsuit is likely to result in a liability and, if so, the expected amount.

As discussed in Chapter 11, most companies disclose their contingent liabilities in notes to the financial statements. An example is the following note excerpted from the December 30, 1987 financial statements of George Weston Limited. George Weston reported that its contingent liabilities arose from endorsements and guarantees, from assigned leases and from a lawsuit against the company:

10. COMMITMENTS AND CONTINGENT LIABILITIES [amounts in millions]

Endorsements and guarantees arising in the normal course of business amount to $178.4 [millions]. In addition, there are assigned leases of $84.3 [millions] which relate to the sale of a U.S. subsidiary of Loblaw Companies. In addition to various claims arising in the normal course of business, there is a class action lawsuit, involving a substantial amount, filed by a former employee of a U.S. division of Loblaw Companies sold in 1982. Although the outcome of this action cannot be predicted with certainty, management believes that it will not have a material effect on the Company's financial position.

Probable Losses   The disclosure principle directs a business to record and report a probable loss *before* it occurs if the loss is likely and its amount can be estimated. Phillips Petroleum Company reported such a loss in its 1985 financial statements. Observe that the disposal of assets has not occurred yet, but the company does *expect* the disposal to result in a loss.

NOTE 1. DISCONTINUED OPERATION [in part]

During 1985, the company announced plans to discontinue its minerals operation. Assets associated with these operations were sold, abandoned, or written down ... in anticipation of their future sale or abandonment, resulting in an estimated net loss on disposal in 1985 of $171 million, net of income tax. ...

The $171 million loss on disposal appeared on Phillips's 1985 income statement as follows:

	millions
Income from Continuing Operations	$ 596
Discontinued operations (net of income taxes)	
Loss from operations	(7)
Loss on disposal	(171)
Net Income	$ 418

Accounting Changes   Consistent use of accounting methods and procedures is important, as we saw in discussing comparability. When a company does change from one accounting method or procedure to another, it must disclose the change, the reason for making the change and the effect of the change on net income. Two common accounting changes are *changes in accounting principles* and *changes in accounting estimates*.

A **change-in-accounting principle** is a change in accounting method. A switch from the FIFO method to the LIFO method for inventories and a switch from the accelerated depreciation method to the straight-line method are examples of accounting changes. Special rules that apply to changes in accounting principles are discussed in later accounting courses. Whatever the change in principle, the notes to the financial statements must inform the reader that the change has occurred.

Saskatchewan Economic Development Corporation disclosed the following accounting change in its December 31, 1984 financial statements, after the company had changed its method of depreciation:

2. CHANGE IN ACCOUNTING POLICY

Retained earnings at December 31, 1983 and December 31, 1982 have been increased by $383,000 and $240,000 respectively to reflect a retroactive change in the Corporation's method of depreciation for its buildings from the straight-line method to the sinking fund method. This change in accounting policy has been retroactively applied to the 1983 comparative figures and has reduced depreciation expense from $685,000 as previously reported to $542,000. The remainder of the change is applicable to years prior to 1983.

A **change-in-accounting estimate** occurs in the course of business as the company alters earlier expectations. A company may record uncollectible accounts expense based on the estimate that bad debts will equal 2 percent of sales. If actual collections exceed this estimate, the company may lower its estimated expense to 1½ percent of sales in the future.

A company may originally estimate that a new Ford Econoline delivery van will provide four years' service. After two years of using the truck, the company sees that the truck's full useful life will stretch to six years. The company must recompute depreciation based on this new information at the start of the truck's third year of service. Assume that this truck cost $16,000, has an estimated residual value of $2,000 and is depreciated by the straight-line method.

Annual depreciation for each of the first two years of the asset's life is $3,500, computed as follows:

$$\textbf{Depreciation per year} = \frac{\$16,000 - \$2,000}{4 \text{ years}} = \$3,500$$

Changes in estimate are accounted for by spreading the asset's remaining book value over its remaining life. Annual depreciation after the accounting change is $1,750, computed in the following manner:

$$\text{Depreciation per year} = \frac{\text{Asset book value}}{\text{Remaining life}}$$

$$= \frac{\$16,000 - \$2,000 - (3,500 \times 2)}{6 \text{ total years} - 2 \text{ years used}}$$

$$= \frac{\$7,000}{4 \text{ years}}$$

$$= \$1,750$$

This revised amount of depreciation is recorded in the usual manner.

Harding Carpets Limited disclosed a similar change in accounting estimate in its financial statements for the year ended October 31, 1984. Observe that Harding reported the nature of the change, the reason for making the change, and its effect on income:

4. CHANGES IN ACCOUNTING ESTIMATES

During 1984 management reassessed the remaining useful lives of all the corporation's machinery and equipment and product sample costs. They have determined that such remaining lives are in the range of 7 to 17 years for machinery and equipment and are 24 months for product samples. Accordingly, 1984 depreciation on machinery and equipment has been taken on a straight-line basis using these revised estimated remaining lives. Product sample costs have been expensed over 24 months. For the year ended October 31, 1984 these changes in estimates have resulted in a reduction in depreciation written on fixed assets and a decrease in product sample costs expensed resulting in an increase in net income for the year of $1,094,000.

Subsequent Events   A company usually takes several weeks after the end of the year to close its books and to publish its financial statements. Occasionally, events occur during this period that affect the interpretation of the information in those financial statements. Such an occurrence is called a **subsequent event** and should be disclosed in the prior period's statements. The most common examples of subsequent events are borrowing money, paying debts, making investments, selling assets and becoming a defendant in a lawsuit.

Bell Canada reported the following subsequent event in its financial statements for the year ended December 31, 1987:

20. SUBSEQUENT EVENT

On January 27, 1988, Bell Canada entered into an agreement for a public issue in Canada of $125 million of 10.55% Debentures, Series DW, Due 2015. This issue is expected to be completed on February 15, 1988.

Business Segments   Most large companies operate in more than one area. Each area is called a *business segment*. Lord Kenneth Thomson not only controls Thomson newspapers through a holding company but also The Bay, Simpsons, Zellers, an oil company and other differing businesses. Olympia and York owns real estate companies, paper companies, oil and gas refiners and other energy companies. Canadian Pacific owns hotels, mining companies, steamships, trucking companies, oil companies, paper companies as well as real estate interests. Diversification like this is not limited to large international companies. A realtor may also own a restaurant. A farmer may sell farm implements. An automobile dealer may also own a furniture store.

Suppose you are considering investing in a company that is active in the footwear industry but also owns a meat packer and several leisure resorts.

Assume the Canadian footwear industry is in retreat because of intense foreign competition. With income and asset data broken down by business segments, you can determine how much of the company's assets are committed to each segment and which lines of business are most (and least) profitable. Companies disclose segment data in notes to their financial statements.

The following John Labatt note in its April 30, 1986 financial statements meets the GAAP requirement for adequate disclosure of segmented information:

NOTE 9. SEGMENTED FINANCIAL INFORMATION

Information by class of business

The classes of business of the Company are as follows:

Brewing comprises the Company's brewing activities in Canada and the sale of Canadian-made beer and ale in the United States and overseas.

Agri Products includes operations that process agricultural products into basic foods in Canada and the United States.

Packaged Food includes operations that manufacture and distribute grocery food products, fruit juices and wines in Canada and the United States. The following is a summary of key financial information by business segment for the year ended April 30, 1986:

(in thousands)	1986 Gross sales	Inter-segment sales
Brewing	$1,274,382	$ 1,447
Agri products	1,605,020	41,130
Packaged food	702,039	712
	$3,581,441	$ 43,289

	Capital expenditures	Depreciation & amortization
Brewing	$ 54,705	$ 25,425
Agri products	35,356	27,554
Packaged food	25,515	17,937
	$ 115,576	$ 70,916

	Contribution	Assets employed
Brewing	$ 93,305	$ 343,421
Agri products	92,063	403,689
Packaged food	50,604	372,175
	235,972	1,119,285
Interest	(49,700)	
Unallocated expense	(509)	
Earnings before income taxes	$ 185,763	
Short-term investments		206,498
Investments in partly owned businesses		70,568
Current liabilities other than bank advances and short-term notes		388,901
Total assets per consolidated balance sheet		$1,785,252

Information by geographic segment

The Company operates principally in the geographic areas of Canada and the United States. Geographic segmentation is determined on the basis of the business location where the sale originates. Financial information by geographic segment for the year ended April 30, 1986 follows:

(in thousands)	1986	
	Gross sales	Inter-segment sales
Canada	$2,675,523	$ 36,802
United States	905,918	898
	$3,581,441	$ 37,700

	Capital expenditures	Depreciation & amortization
Canada	$ 91,324	$ 52,021
United States	24,252	18,895
	$ 115,576	$ 70,916

	Contribution	Assets employed
Canada	$ 189,051	$ 768,691
United States	46,921	350,594
	235,972	1,119,285
Interest	(49,700)	
Unallocated expense	(509)	
Earnings before income taxes	$ 185,763	
Short-term investments		206,498
Investments in partly owned businesses		70,568
Current liabilities other than bank advances and short-term notes		388,901
Total assets per consolidated balance sheet		$1,785,252

To satisfy the disclosure principle, John Labatt breaks down sales, income before taxes and assets two ways: by business segments and by geographic area. GAAP also requires companies to disclose capital expenditures and depreciation by business segment.

Long-term Commitments Many companies make long-term commitments that involve making payments that may be unequal in amount over a series of years. Users of the company's financial statements will have an incomplete picture of the company's future cash flows unless information about the future committed payments is disclosed in the notes. An example of such a future commitment of payments is a capital lease, such as the lease Air Canada enters into when it acquires a plane for its fleet. Capital leases are studied in later financial accounting courses; all you need to know at this point is that the company, Air Canada, acquires an asset, a plane, and a liability, a series of payments over a number of years. So a reader of Air Canada's financial statements is aware of these future payments and when they are to be made, GAAP requires the year-by-year payments to be disclosed.

Maclean Hunter Limited, the media giant with interests in publishing (newspapers and periodicals), printing, radio, cable television and communication services, discloses information about future capital and operating lease payments in the following note:

17. LEASES

Future minimum lease payments under capital leases (note 8) and operating leases at December 31, 1987 are as follows:

	Capital leases	Operating leases
	(millions)	
1988	$ 1.9	$ 17.9
1989	1.7	14.5
1990	1.8	13.9
1991	1.5	12.7
1992	1.6	11.5
1993 and thereafter	10.2	74.7
Total lease payments	18.7	$145.2
Less interest included in capital leases	(6.0)	
Present value of minimum capital lease payments (including current installments of $0.6 million)	$12.7	

Related Party Transactions   A basic assumption underlying the financial statements is that the transactions underlying the numbers in the financial statements were made at arm's length. The usual definition of an arm's length transaction is a transaction between a buyer and a seller who are independent of each other or unrelated; as such, each can and will work to obtain the most favourable terms for the transaction. Most, and perhaps even all, of a company's transactions will be with unrelated parties. However, some transactions may be between the company and a party related to it. For example, Loblaws stores, owned through Loblaw Companies by George Weston Limited, buy baked goods from Weston Bakeries, owned through Weston Foods by George Weston Limited. Because the two companies have the same parent, they are considered to be related parties.

While most related party or non-arm's length transactions are conducted at fair prices (—the same prices that arm's length transactions would be), there is a possibility that the buyer or seller obtained a financial advantage that would not have otherwise been possible. For that reason, GAAP requires that related party transactions be disclosed. In its December 31, 1987 financial statements TransCanada Pipelines Limited disclosed information about transactions with two subsidiaries, Great Lakes Transmission Company and Trans Quebec and Maritimes Pipeline Inc. (TQM), in the following note:

NOTE 14. RELATED PARTY TRANSACTIONS [in part]

Sales revenue from and payments by the Company for gas transportation services to each of Great Lakes and TQM, affiliates of the Company, were as follows:

Year Ended December 31 (millions of dollars)	1987	1986	1985
Gas Sales			
Great Lakes	168.0	214.1	245.2
TQM	59.7	69.0	62.6
Charges for Gas Transportation Services			
Great Lakes	155.3	195.5	144.4
TQM	80.3	81.8	86.9

The recovery in the Company's regulated cost of service of charges by Great Lakes and TQM for gas transportation services is subject to the [National Energy Board's] toll-making process.

Economic Dependence   Some companies become dependent on other companies as either suppliers or customers. For example, a small manufacturer of furniture may sell all or most of its output to one customer, a department store chain. A small brewer may buy all its bottles from one large glassmaking company. The small manufacturer and the small brewer are said to be economically dependent.

If the department store chain stops buying from the manufacturer, the manufacturer may go out of business before it can develop a new customer base. If the glassmaker stops selling bottles to the brewer, the brewer may get into financial difficulty unless a new supplier can be found quickly. It is important that users of financial statements be aware of **economic dependence** and so GAAP requires that companies that are economically dependent disclose that fact.

TransCanada Pipelines provides the following information on its principal customers in the notes to its December 31, 1987 financial statements. Total natural gas sales for the period were $3,057,100,000.

(C) PRINCIPAL CUSTOMERS

The following table sets forth the Company's revenues generated by the Pipeline segment from natural gas sales under long-term contracts and transportation services to its five principal customers:

Year Ended December 31 (millions of dollars)	1987	1986	1985
The Consumers' Gas Company Ltd.	943.0	1,195.0	1,206.2
Union Gas Limited	598.9	885.7	958.8
Gaz Metropolitain, inc.	373.8	482.1	506.7
ICG (Ontario) Ltd.	302.3	391.3	438.9
Great Lakes Gas Transmission Company	168.0	214.1	245.2

Constraints on Accounting

Do financial statements report every detail, no matter how small, to meet the need for understandable, relevant, reliable and comparable information? If they did, the result would be an avalanche of data. To avoid such a deluge of data, accountants use the *materiality concept*. They also exercise another constraint in the compilation of the accounting information. To balance the optimism of the top managers of a company, who are responsible for the financial statements, which could bias the statements and present too favourable a picture of company operations, accountants follow the *conservatism concept*. This section discusses these constraints on accounting information.

Materiality Concept

The **materiality concept** states that a company must perform strictly proper accounting only for items and transactions that are significant to the business's financial statements. Information is significant — what accountants call material — when its inclusion and correct presentation in the financial statement would cause a statement user to change a decision because of that information. Immaterial (insignificant) items justify less than perfect accounting. The inclusion and proper presentation of immaterial items would not affect a statement user's decision. The materiality concept frees accountants from having to compute and report every last item in strict accordance with GAAP. Thus the materiality concept reduces the cost of recording accounting information.

OBJECTIVE 6
Apply two constraints to accounting

How does a business decide where to draw the line between what is material and what is immaterial? This decision rests to a great degree on how large the business is. Canadian Tire, for example, holds close to $1.5 billion in assets. Management would likely treat as immaterial a $100 purchase of wastebaskets. These wastebaskets may well remain useful for ten years. Strictly speaking, Canadian Tire should capitalize their cost and depreciate the wastebaskets. However, this treatment is not practical. The accounting cost of computing, recording and properly reporting this asset outweighs the information provided. No statement user, a potential investor or lender, for example, would change a decision based on so insignificant (immaterial) an amount. The cost of accounting in this case outweighs the benefit of the resulting information.

Large companies may draw the materiality line at as high a figure as $10,000. An asset having an expected life longer than one year and costing more than $10,000 would be capitalized as fixed asset and depreciated over their life, while assets having the same expected life but costing less than $10,000 would be charged to expense in the year acquired. Smaller firms may choose to expense only those items less than $50. Materiality varies from company to company. An amount that is material to the local service station may not be material to General Motors.

The materiality concept does not free a business from having to account for every item. Canadian Tire, for example, must still account for the wastebaskets. They would credit Cash (or Accounts Payable) to record their purchase, of course, but what account would they debit? Because the amount is immaterial, management may decide to debit Supplies, an asset account, or Supplies Expense. No matter what account receives the debit, no statement user's decision would be changed by the information.

Conservatism Concept

Business managers are often optimists. Asked how well the company is doing, its president will likely answer, "Great, we're having our best year ever." Without constraints this optimism could find its way into the company's reported assets and profits. Managers may try to present too favorable a view of the company. For example, they may pressure accountants to capitalize costs associated with fixed assets that should be expensed. This would result in less immediate expense and higher current income on the income statement. The balance sheet would report unduly high fixed asset values and owner's equity. The overall result would be that the managers' performance would appear to be better than it actually was. Traditionally, accountants have been conservative, to counter management's optimism.

Conservatism has been interpreted as "Anticipate no profits, but anticipate all losses." A clear-cut example is the lower-of-cost-or-market (LCM) method for inventories. Under LCM, inventory is reported at the *lower* of its cost or market value, which results in higher cost of goods sold and lower net income. Thus profits and assets are reported at their lowest reasonable amount. Other conservative accounting practices include the LIFO method for inventories when inventory costs are increasing, accelerated depreciation and the completed-contract method for construction revenues. These methods result in earlier recording of expenses or later recording of revenues. Both effects postpone the reporting of net income and therefore are conservative.

In recent years, conservatism's effect on accounting has decreased. Conservatism should not mean deliberate understatement of assets, profits and owner's equity. However, if two different values can be used for an asset or a liability, the concept suggests using the less optimistic value. Conservatism is a secondary consideration in accounting. Relevant, reliable and comparable information is the goal, and conservatism is a factor only after these primary goals are met.

Financial Statements and Their Elements

We have examined the concepts and principles that guide businesses in shaping accounting practice. The CICA aims for financial statements that best meet user needs for business information.

This accounting information appears in four statements: the balance sheet, the income statement, the statement of owner's equity and the statement of changes in financial position (which we cover in Chapter 18). The CICA provides definitions for the elements that make up these statements. Financial information presentation, to be most useful to the greatest number of statements users, must be presented in a standard format with well-defined terms, as we learned in our discussion of the comparability concept.

The Canadian Institute of Chartered Accountants in "Financial Statement Concepts," Section 1000 of the *Handbook* provides authoritative definitions of the elements of financial statements.

OBJECTIVE 7

Name and define the elements of financial statements

Balance Sheet Elements

Assets are economic resources controlled by an entity as a result of past transactions or events from which future economic benefits may be obtained.

Liabilities are obligations of an entity arising from past transactions or events, the settlement of which may result in the transfer or use of assets, provision of services or other yielding of economic benefits in the future.

Equity (Owner's Equity) is the ownership interest in the assets of an entity after deducting its liabilities.

Income Statement Elements

Revenues are increases in economic resources, either by way of inflows or enhancements of assets or reductions of liabilities, resulting from the ordinary activities of an entity, normally from the sale of goods, the rendering of services or the use by others of entity resources yielding rent, interest, royalties or dividends.

Expenses are decreases in economic resources, either by way of outflows or reductions of assets or incurrences of liabilities, resulting from the ordinary revenue-earning activities of an entity.

Gains are increases in equity from peripheral or incidental transactions and events affecting an entity and from all other transactions, events and circumstances affecting the entity except those that result from revenues or equity contributions.

Losses are decreases in equity from peripheral or incidental transactions and events affecting an entity and from all other transactions, events and circumstances affecting the entity except those that result from expenses or distributions of equity.

Note that *revenues* and *expenses* arise from the business's ongoing central operations, but *gains* and *losses* do not. For example, sales and interest are revenues because most companies make sales and earn interest as part of their central operations. For example, selling cars and trucks lies at the heart of an automobile dealership. To this business, a gain on the sale of a truck is revenue and a loss on the sale is expense. However, a gain on the sale of a truck is not revenue for a trucking company because that entity buys trucks for use rather than for sale. Selling a truck is not a part of central operations. Exhibit 12-3 shows how to report revenues, expenses, gains and losses on a multiple-step and a single-step income statement.

EXHIBIT 12-3   *Reporting Revenues, Expenses, Gains and Losses*

Multiple-Step Income Statement			Single-Step Income Statement		
Sales revenue		$XXX	Revenues and gains		
Cost of goods sold		XXX	Sales revenue		$XXX
Gross profit		XXX	Gain on sale of land		XXX
Operating expenses		XXX	Total revenues and gains		XXX
Income from operations		XXX	Expenses and losses		
Other items			Cost of goods sold	$XXX	
Gain on sale of land	$XXX		Operating expenses	XXX	
Loss due to fire	XXX	XXX	Loss due to fire	XXX	
			Total expenses and losses . . .		XXX
Net income		$XXX	Net income		$XXX

Statement of Owner's Equity Elements

Investments by owners are increases in owner's equity that result from the owner's transferring to the entity something of value. The most common investment is cash, but owners sometimes invest land, buildings, legal services or other assets. In some cases, an owner's investment in the business may consist of paying off its liabilities.

Distributions to owners are decreases in owner's equity that result from the owner's transferring assets or services from the business to himself or herself, or from the business taking on the owner's liabilities. When the business is a corporation, owner withdrawals are called dividends. The most commonly distributed asset is cash, but businesses sometimes distribute other assets, such as stock investments they hold in other companies, to their owners.

Summary Problem for Your Review

This chapter has discussed the following principles and concepts:

Entity concept	Cost principle
Going-concern concept	Revenue principle
Time-period concept	Matching principle
Reliability principle	Disclosure principle
Comparability principle	Materiality concept

Indicate which of these concepts is being violated in each of the following situations:

1. A construction company signs a two-year contract to build a bridge for the province of Nova Scotia. The president of the company immediately records the full contract price as revenue.

2. Competition has taken away much of the business of a small airline. The airline is unwilling to report its plans to sell half its fleet of planes.

3. After starting the business in February 19X2, a coal-mining company keeps no accounting records for 19X2, 19X3 and 19X4. The owner is waiting until the mine is exhausted to determine the success or failure of the business.

4. Assets recorded at cost by a drug store chain are written up to their fair market value at the end of each year.

5. The accountant for a manufacturing company keeps detailed depreciation records on every asset no matter how small its value.

6. A physician mixes her personal accounting records with those of the medical practice.

7. Expenses are reported whenever the bookkeeper records them rather than when related revenues are earned.

8.   The damaged inventory of a discount store is being written down. The store manager bases the write-down entry on his own subjective opinion in order to minimize income taxes.

9.   A quick-copy centre changes accounting methods every year in order to report the maximum amount of net income possible under generally accepted accounting principles.

10. The owners of a private nursing home base its accounting records on the assumption that the nursing home might have to close at any time. The nursing home has a long record of service to the community.

SOLUTION TO REVIEW PROBLEM

1. Revenue principle
2. Disclosure principle
3. Time-period concept
4. Cost principle
5. Materiality concept

6. Entity concept
7. Matching principle
8. Reliability principle
9. Comparability principle
10. Going-concern concept

Summary

The Canadian Institute of Chartered Accountants (CICA) formulates generally accepted accounting principles (GAAP) to provide understandable, relevant, reliable and comparable accounting information. Information must be *understandable* by users if it is to be used. *Relevant* information allows users to make business predictions and to evaluate past decisions. *Reliable* data are free from error and bias. Accounting information is also intended to be *comparable* from company to company and from period to period.

Four concepts underlie accounting. The most basic, the *entity concept*, draws clear boundaries around the accounting unit or entity. The entity, according to the *going-concern concept*, is assumed to remain in business for the foreseeable future. The *time-period concept* holds that accounting information is reported for particular time periods such as months, quarters and years. Under the *stable-monetary-unit concept*, no adjustment is made for the changing value of the dollar.

Accounting principles provide detailed guidelines for recording transactions and preparing the financial statements. The reliability and comparability principles require that accounting information be based on objective data and be useful for comparing companies across different time periods. The *cost principle* governs accounting for assets and liabilities, and the *revenue principle* governs accounting for revenues. *Matching* is the basis for recording expenses. The *disclosure principle* requires companies to report their accounting policies, contingent liabilities, probable future losses, accounting changes, subsequent events, business-segment data, long-term commitments, related party transactions and economic dependence.

Two constraints on accounting are materiality and conservatism. The *materiality concept* allows companies to avoid the cost of accounting for immaterial items. *Conservatism* constrains the optimism of managers by insisting on realistic accounting practices.

Financial statements and their elements include

1.   *Balance sheet: assets, liabilities* and *equity (owner's equity)*
2.   *Income statement: revenues, expenses, gains* and *losses*
3.   *Statement of owner's equity: investments by owners* and *distributions to owners.*

Self-Study Questions

Test your understanding of the chapter by marking the correct answer for each of the following questions:

1. The organization that issues accounting pronouncements that make up GAAP is the *(p. 491)*
   a. Government of Canada
   b. National Securities Administrators
   c. Accounting Standards Committee
   d. Ontario Securities Commission

2. Which of the following characteristics of accounting information does the objective of financial reporting omit? *(p. 493)*
   a. Timeliness
   b. Understandability
   c. Relevance
   d. Reliability
   e. Comparability

3. A new business is starting. The president wishes to wait until significant contracts have been fulfilled before reporting the results of the business's operations. Which underlying concept serves as the basis for preparing financial statements at regular intervals? *(p. 494)*
   a. Entity
   b. Going concern
   c. Time period
   d. Stable monetary unit

4. Which of these revenue methods is the most conservative? *(pp. 498, 510)*
   a. Sales method
   b. Collection method
   c. Percentage-of-completion method
   d. All the above are equally conservative

5. Suppose a Woodwards store sells $10,000 worth of kitchen appliances on the installment plan and collects a down payment of $1,500. Woodwards's cost of the appliances is $7,000. How much gross profit will the company report under the installment revenue method *(pp. 498, 499)*
   a. $450
   b. $1,500
   c. $3,000
   d. $10,000

6. A construction company spent $180,000 during the current year on a building with a contract price of $900,000. The company estimated total construction cost at $720,000. How much construction *income* will the company report under the percentage-of-completion method? *(p. 500)*
   a. $45,000
   b. $144,000
   c. $180,000
   d. $225,000

7. Which of the following items should be disclosed to satisfy the adequate disclosure principle? *(pp. 501–503)*
   a. Contingent liabilities
   b. Probable losses
   c. Accounting changes
   d. All of the above

8. Important subsequent events should be disclosed because they *(p. 504)*
   a. Occur immediately after the current period
   b. Describe changes in accounting methods
   c. Reveal losses that have a high probability of occurring in the future
   d. May affect the interpretation of the current-period financial statements

9. Which of the following statements is most in keeping with the materiality concept? *(p. 509)*
   a. Accountants record material losses but are reluctant to record material gains.
   b. Different companies have different materiality limits, depending on their size.
   c. Business-segment data are disclosed to fulfill the materiality concept.
   d. Companies report all the information needed to communicate a material view of the entity.

10. Gains and losses are most similar to *(p. 511)*
    a. Assets and liabilities
    b. Revenues and expenses
    c. Investments by owners and distributions to owners

Answers to the self-study questions are at the end of the chapter.

Accounting Vocabulary

change-in-accounting estimate
   (p. 503)
change in accounting principle
   (p. 503)
collection method (p. 498)
comparability principle
   (p. 496)
completed-contract method
   (p. 500)
cost principle (p. 497)

disclosure principle
   (p. 501)
economic dependence
   (p. 508)
gains (p. 511)
going-concern concept
   (p. 494)
installment method (p. 498)
losses (p. 511)
materiality concept (p. 509)

percentage of completion
   method (p. 500)
reliability principle (p. 496)
sales method (p. 498)
stable monetary unit concept
   (p. 495)
subsequent event (p. 504)
time-period concept
   (p. 494)

Assignment Material

Questions

1. How do accounting principles differ from natural laws?
2. State the basic objective of financial reporting.
3. What four characteristics make accounting information useful for decision making? Briefly discuss each characteristic.
4. What is the entity concept?
5. How does the going-concern concept affect accounting? What is liquidation?
6. Identify two practical results of the time-period concept.
7. What is the shortcoming of the stable monetary-unit concept?
8. What are the two requirements of the comparability principle?
9. Why is consistency important in accounting?
10. Discuss the relationship between the cost principle and the reliability principle.
11. What three conditions must be met before revenue is recorded? What determines the amount of the revenue?
12. Which revenue recognition method is more conservative, the sales method or the collection method? Give your reason.
13. Suppose Eaton's sold a lawn mower on an installment basis, receiving a down payment of $50 to be followed by 12 monthly installments of $12.50 each. If the cost of the mower to Eaton's was $120, how much gross profit would Eaton's record under the installment method (a) when the down payment is received and (b) when each installment is received?
14. Briefly discuss two methods of recognizing revenue on long-term construction contracts.
15. Give two examples of expenses that are easy to relate to sales revenue and two examples of expenses that are not so easy to relate to particular sales. On what basis are the latter expenses matched against revenue?
16. ABC Company agreed on November 22, 19X7 to sell an unprofitable manufacturing plant. ABC estimates on December 31, its fiscal year end, that the company is likely to incur a $4 million loss on the sale when it is finalized in 19X8. In which year should ABC report the loss? What accounting principle governs this situation?
17. Identify three items commonly disclosed in a company's summary of significant accounting policies.
18. What is a subsequent event? Why should companies disclose important subsequent events in their financial statements?

19. How does information on business segments help an investor?
20. Classify each of the following as a change in accounting principle or a change in accounting estimate:
    a. Change from straight-line to accelerated depreciation.
    b. Change in the uncollectibility of accounts receivable.
    c. Change to FIFO from LIFO for inventory.
    d. Change from the percentage-of-completion method to the completed-contract method for revenue on long-term construction contracts.
    e. Change from an 8-year life to a 10-year life for a machine.
    f. Change in estimated warranty expense rate stated as a percent of sales.
21. Sloan Sales Company expenses the cost of plant assets below $500 at the time of purchase. What accounting concept allows this departure from strictly proper accounting? Why would Sloan Sales follow such a policy?
22. Give three examples of conservative accounting methods, stating why the methods are conservative.
23. Briefly define each of the following terms and explain why information about each is important to users of financial statements:
    a. Related party transactions
    b. Economic dependence
24. The four income statement elements may be divided into two pairs of similar elements. What elements make up these two pairs?

Exercises

Exercise 12-1   *Reporting assets under GAAP*

Identify the amount at which each of the following assets should be reported in the financial statements of Gravel Company. Cite the principle or concept that is most applicable to each answer.

a. Gravel purchased land for $100,000 and paid $2,500 to have the land surveyed, $15,400 to have old buildings removed, and $40,300 for landscaping. Gravel is offering the land for sale at $225,000 and has received a $200,000 offer.
b. Inventory has a cost of $45,000, but its current market value is $39,600.
c. Gravel purchased a machine for $25,000, less a $2,100 cash discount. To ship the machine to the office, Gravel paid transportation charges of $500 and insurance of $200 while in transit. After using the machine for one month, Gravel purchases lubricating oil costing $150 for use in operating the machine.

Exercise 12-2   *Reporting assets as a going concern and as a liquidating entity*

Robarts Company has the following assets:

Cash, $15,000

Accounts Receivable, $25,600; allowance for uncollectible accounts, $4,300

Office supplies, cost $280; scrap value $70

Office machinery, cost $72,000; accumulated depreciation $54,000; current sales value, $8,400

Land, cost $85,000; current sales value $135,000

Required

1. Assume Robarts continues as a going concern. Compute the amount of its assets for reporting on the balance sheet.

2. Assume Robarts is going out of business by liquidating its assets. Compute the amount of its assets at liquidation value.

Use the following format for your answers:

	Assets of a Going Concern	Assets at Liquidation Value
Cash	$	$
Accounts receivable	$	
Less: Allowance for uncollectible accounts		
Office supplies....................		
Office machinery	$	
Less: Accumulated depreciation ...		
Land		
Total	$	$

Exercise 12-3 *Reporting revenues under GAAP*

For each of the following situations, indicate the amount of revenue to report for the current year ended December 31 and for the following year:

a. On July 1, collected one year's rent of $12,000 in advance on a building leased to another company.

b. Sold gift certificates, collecting $4,000 in advance. At December 31, $2,200 of the gifts have been claimed. The remainder were claimed during the next year.

c. Sold merchandise for $5,900, receiving a down payment of $1,100 and the customer's receivable for the balance. The company accounts for these sales by the sales method.

d. On April 1, loaned $25,000 at 12 percent on a three-year note.

e. Performed $900 of services for a high-risk customer on August 18, accounting for the revenue by the collection method. At December 31, the company had received $200 of the total; $330 was received the following year.

Exercise 12-4 *Reporting income under GAAP*

Lotus Management Company failed to record the following items at December 31, 19X4, the end of its fiscal year:

Accrued salary expense, $2,800
Accrued interest expense, $600
Prepaid insurance, $400
Depreciation expense, $500

Instead of recording the accrued expenses at December 31, 19X4, Lotus recorded the expenses when it paid them in 19X5. The company recorded the insurance as expense when it was prepaid for one year, early in 19X4. Depreciation expense for 19X5 was correctly recorded.

Lotus incorrectly reported net income of $9,000 in 19X4 and $5,300 in 19X5 because of the above errors.

Required

Compute Lotus's correct net income for 19X4 and 19X5.

Exercise 12-5   *Computing gross profit under the sales method and the installment method*

Allied Appliance Store sells on the installment plan. The store's installment sales figures for 19X7 follow:

Sales	$420,000
Down payments received on the sales	80,000
Collections on installments	170,000
Inventory at beginning of 19X7	60,000
Inventory at end of 19X7	45,000
Purchases	216,000

Required

Compute the store's gross profit if it uses (1) the sales method of revenue recognition and (2) the installment method.

Exercise 12-6   *Computing construction revenue under the completed-contract method and the percentage-of-completion method*

McMinn Construction Company builds bridges for the province of Alberta. The construction period typically extends for several years. During 19X5, McMinn completed a small bridge with a contract price of $400,000. McMinn's $320,000 cost of the bridge was incurred as follows: $20,000 in 19X3; $180,000 in 19X4; and $120,000 in 19X5. Compute McMinn's revenue for each year 19X3 through 19X5 if the company uses (a) the completed-contract method and (b) the percentage-of-completion method.

Exercise 12-7   *Changing the useful life of a depreciable asset*

McMinn Construction Company uses a crane on its construction projects. The company purchased the crane early in January 19X3 for $500,000. For 19X3 and 19X4 depreciation was taken by the straight-line method based on a six-year life and an estimated residual value of $80,000. In early 19X5, it became evident that the crane would be useful beyond the original life of six years. Therefore, beginning in 19X5, McMinn changed the depreciable life of the crane to a total life of nine years. The company retained the straight-line method and did not alter the residual value.

Required

Prepare McMinn's depreciation entries for 19X4 and 19X5.

Exercise 12-8   *Identifying subsequent events for the financial statements*

Champlain Inc. experienced the following events after May 31, 19X8, the end of the company's fiscal year, but before publication of its financial statements on July 12:

a. Champlain collected $126,000 of the $480,000 accounts receivable reported on the May 31 balance sheet. Champlain expects to collect the remainder in the course of business during the next fiscal year.

b. A major customer, who owed Champlain $220,000 at May 31, declared bankruptcy on June 21.

c. Champlain sales personnel received a contract to supply Bronson Company with laser equipment.

d. Increased demand for Champlain products suggests that the next fiscal year will be the best in the company's history.

e. On July 6, Champlain is sued for $3 million. Loss of the lawsuit could lead to Champlain's bankruptcy.

Required

Identify the subsequent events that Champlain should disclose in its May 31, 19X8 financial statements.

Exercise 12-9 *Using accounting concepts and principles*

Identify the accounting concept or principle, if any, that is violated in each of the following situations. You may choose from among *disclosure, conservatism, cost, entity* and *matching*.

a. The owner of a travel agency used the business bank account to pay her family's household expenses, making no note that the expenses were personal.
b. A manufacturing company changed from the FIFO inventory method to the LIFO method and failed to disclose the accounting change in the financial statements.
c. A paper company that purchased 5,000 hectares of timberland at $150 per hectare in 1953 reports the land at its current market value of $3,000 per hectare.
d. A railroad records depreciation during years when net income is high but fails to record depreciation when net income is low. Revenues are relatively constant.
e. The inventory of a clothing store has a current market value of $80,000. The store reports the inventory at its cost of $124,000.

Exercise 12-10 *Using accounting concepts and principles*

Indicate the accounting concept or principle that applies to the following situations. Choose from among *comparability, materiality, reliability, revenue* and *time period*.

a. New Wave Distributors expenses the cost of plant assets that cost less than $300.
b. Although Bracken Company could increase its reported income by changing depreciation methods, Bracken management has decided not to make the change.
c. Lim Ting Restaurant was recently sued for $200,000, but the plaintiff has indicated a willingness to settle for less than that amount. Lim Ting hopes to settle for $50,000, but their lawyers believe the settlement will be between $90,000 and $100,000. Lim Ting's auditor reports it as a real liability on the balance sheet. The only remaining issue is whether to report the liability at $50,000 or at $95,000.
d. Northern Lights Company is considering publishing quarterly financial statements to provide more timely information about its affairs.
e. POA, Inc. is negotiating the sale of $500,000 of inventory. POA has been in financial difficulty and desperately needs to report this revenue on its income statement of the current year. At December 31, the end of the company's accounting year, the sale has not been closed.

Problems   (Group A)

Problem 12-1A *Identifying the basis for good accounting practices*

The following accounting practices are in accord with generally accepted accounting principles. Identify all the accounting concepts and principles that form the basis for each accounting practice. More than one concept or principle may apply.

a. The personal residence of the owner of a freight company is not disclosed in the financial statements of the business.
b. A manufacturing company's plant assets are carried on the books at cost under the assumption that the company will remain in operation for the foreseeable future.
c. A clothing store discloses in notes to its financial statements that it uses the FIFO inventory method.

d. A real estate developer paid $450,000 for land and held it for three years before selling it for $800,000. There was significant inflation during this period, but the developer reports the $350,000 gain on sale with no adjustment for the change in the value of the dollar.

e. Liabilities are reported in two categories, current and long-term.

f. A travel agent's payments for fire insurance are so small that the company expenses them and makes no year-end adjustment for prepaid insurance.

g. The inventory of a personal computer store declined substantially in value because of changing technology, and the store wrote its computer inventory down to the lower of cost or market.

h. A construction company changed from the completed-contract method to the percentage-of-completion method of recording revenue on its long-term construction contracts. The company disclosed this accounting change in the notes to its financial statements.

i. A mining company recorded an intangible asset at the cost of the mineral lease and all other costs necessary to bring the mine to the point of production. After the mine was in operation, the company amortized the asset's cost as expense in proportion to the revenues from sale of the minerals.

j. Owing to a downturn in the economy, a jeweler increased his business's allowance for doubtful accounts.

Problem 12-2A   *Identifying the concepts and principles violated by bad accounting practices*

The following accounting practices are *not* in accord with generally accepted accounting principles. Identify the single accounting concept or principle that is most clearly violated by each accounting practice.

a. Royal Iron Works regularly changes accounting methods in order to report a target amount of net income each year.

b. Texas Land Company reports land at its market value of $820,000, which is greater than the cost of $400,000.

c. A flood on July 2 caused $150,000 in damage to Yukon Construction property. The company did not report the flood as a subsequent event in the June 30 financial statements.

d. Austin, Inc. overstates depreciation expense in order to report low amounts of net income.

e. The balance sheet of Rhonda Green's dental practice includes receivables that she will probably never collect. Nevertheless, Green's accountant refuses to use the collection method to account for revenue.

f. The current market value of Miska Electronics's inventory is $65,000, but the company reports its inventory at cost of $91,000. The decline in value is permanent.

g. The liabilities of Waco Jet Company exceed the company's assets. In order to get a loan from the bank, Waco Jet's owner, Slade McQueen, includes his personal investments as assets on the balance sheet of the business.

h. Singh Corporation increases the carrying value of its land based on recent sales of adjacent property.

i. Mission Ford Sales records expenses on an irregular basis without regard to the pattern of the company's revenues.

j. Waterloo Software Company omits the significant accounting policies note from its financial statements, because the company uses the same accounting methods that its competitors use.

Problem 12-3A   *Recording and reporting transactions according to GAAP*

The accounting records of P.E.I. Wholesale Distributors reveal the following information prior to closing the books at September 30, the end of the current fiscal year:

a. Accounts receivable include $42,000 from Glenwood Drug Company, which has declared bankruptcy. P.E.I., which uses the allowance method to account for bad debts, expects to receive one third of the amount receivable from Glenwood.

b. No interest has been accrued on a $50,000, 12 percent, six-month note receivable that was received on May 31.

c. The merchandise inventory, with a cost of $69,000, has a current market value of only $31,000. P.E.I. uses a periodic inventory system and has not made the September 30 entry to record ending inventory.

d. Accrued salaries of $21,800 have been earned by P.E.I. employees but have not been recorded at September 30, because the company plans to record the salaries when it pays them in October.

e. The company's office building has been valued recently by independent appraisers at $400,000. This valuation is $180,000 more than P.E.I. paid for the building and is $270,000 more than its cost less accumulated depreciation.

f. P.E.I. paid $120,000 for its delivery trucks on October 1 one year ago. During the current year, the company has depreciated the trucks by the straight-line method over an expected useful life of four years, using a residual value of $20,000. After using the trucks for the first year, P.E.I. decides the trucks will remain in service for a total of five years. The company will continue to use the straight-line method and the $20,000 residual value for accounting purposes.

g. On October 19, before P.E.I. issued its financial statements for the year ended September 30, a competitor sued the company for damages of $500,000. Lawyers for P.E.I. believe P.E.I. will win the case. However, a $500,000 loss would make it difficult for the company to continue in business.

Required

Make all journal entries needed at September 30 to record this information. Explanations are not required. Identify those items *not* requiring a journal entry, giving the reason why an entry is not needed. If a note to the financial statements is needed, write the note.

Problem 12-4A   *Using the installment revenue method*

Nickel City Appliances sells on the installment plan. Collections of installment receivables have deteriorated. The store's accountants are considering the different methods of recording revenues. Revenue, expense and collection data for the current year are as follows:

	19X3
Installment sales	$90,000
Cost of goods sold	54,000
Collections of installment receivables from sales of 19X5	20,000
19X6	24,000

The gross profit percentage on 19X5 installment sales was 42 percent.

Required

1. Which method should be used to account for revenues if collections are reasonably assured? If collections are extremely doubtful? Which method is more advantageous for income tax purposes? Why?

2. Compute gross profit for 19X6 under the sales method, the collection method and the installment method.

Problem 12-5A   *Using the installment-revenue method*

Pine Valley Appliance Store makes all sales on the installment basis but uses the sales method to record revenue. The company's income statements for the most recent three years follow:

	Year 1	Year 2	Year 3
Sales	$240,000	$210,000	$290,000
Cost of goods sold	144,000	121,800	179,800
Gross profit.......................	96,000	88,200	110,200
Operating expenses	51,400	49,300	61,300
Net income	$ 44,600	$ 38,900	$ 48,900
Collections from sales of year 1	$ 80,000	$105,000	$ 40,000
Collections from sales of year 2		68,000	120,000
Collections from sales of year 3			145,000

Required

Compute the amount of net income Pine Valley would have reported if the company had used the installment method for revenue. Ignore the effect of uncollectible accounts and present your answer in the following format:

Installment-Method Net Income	Year 1	Year 2	Year 3
Gross profit.......................	$	$	$
Operating expenses	51,400	49,300	61,300
Net income	$	$	$

Problem 12-6A   *Accounting for construction income*

B.C. Shipbuilding Company participates in the construction of small ships under long-term contracts. During 19X7 B.C. began three projects that progressed according to the following schedule during 19X7, 19X8 and 19X9:

Project	Contract Price	Total Project Cost	19X7 Cost for Year	19X7 Percent Completed	19X8 Cost for Year	19X8 Percent Completed	19X9 Cost for Year	19X9 Percent Completed
1	$3,500,000	$2,800,000	$ 924,000	33%	$1,876,000	67%	—	—
2	1,200,000	880,000	880,000	100	—	—	—	—
3	7,400,000	6,300,000	1,260,000	20	2,205,000	35	$2,835,000	45%

Required

1. Assume B.C. Shipbuilding uses the completed-contract method for construction revenue. Compute the company's construction revenue and income to be reported in 19X7, 19X8, and 19X9.
2. Compute B.C.'s construction revenue and income to be reported in the three years if the company uses the percentage-of-completion method.

Problem 12-7A   *Accounting for revenues and expenses according to GAAP*

Nathan Nielsen established Nielsen Furniture Importers in January 19X4 to import furniture from Denmark. During 19X4 and 19X5 Nielsen kept the company's books and prepared the financial statements, although he had no training or experience in accounting. As a result, the accounts contain numerous errors. Nielsen recorded revenue from sales on the collection method, which is not appropriate for the company. Nielsen should have been using the sales method for revenues. He also recorded inventory purchases as the cost of goods sold.

When the value of the company warehouse increased by $35,000 in 19X6, Nielsen recorded an increase in the Warehouse Building account and credited Revenue. On January 2, 19X4, he borrowed $100,000 on a 9 percent, three-year note. He intended to wait until 19X7, when the note was due, to record the full amount of interest expense for three years. The company's records reveal the following amounts:

	19X4	19X5	19X6
Reported net income (net loss)	$ (24,200)	$ 41,600	$ 44,100
Sales	256,700	303,500	366,800
Cash collections from customers	210,400	309,000	317,800
Purchases of inventory	141,000	187,400	202,300
Ending inventory	35,800	59,900	73,400
Accrued expenses not recorded at year end; these expenses were recorded during the next year, when paid	13,500	22,600	30,100
Interest expense recorded	-0-	-0-	-0-
Revenue recorded for increase in the value of the warehouse building			35,000

Required

In early 19X7 Nielsen employed you as an accountant. Apply the concepts and principles of GAAP to compute the correct net income of Nielsen Furniture Importers for 19X4, 19X5 and 19X6.

(Group B)

Problem 12-1B   *Identifying the basis for good accounting practices*

The following accounting practices are in accord with generally accepted accounting principles. Identify all the accounting concepts and principles that form the basis for each accounting practice. More than one concept or principle may apply.

a. The cost of office equipment such as staplers and wastebaskets is not capitalized and depreciated because of their relative insignificance.

b. A fire destroyed the company warehouse after December 31, 19X7 and before the financial statements were published in early February 19X8. Although the fire loss is insured, reconstruction of the warehouse will disrupt the company's operations. This subsequent event will be reported in the 19X7 financial statements.

c. A chemical company accounts for its operations by dividing the business into four separate units. This division enables the company to evaluate each unit apart from the others.

d. A building-materials company accrues employee salaries at year end even though the salaries will be paid during the first few days of the new year.

e. Assets are reported at liquidation value on the financial statements of a company that is going out of business.

f. The cost of machinery is being depreciated over a five-year life, because independent engineers believe the machinery will become obsolete after that time. (The company had hoped to depreciate the machinery over ten years. In this way, lower depreciation and higher net income would have been reported in the early years of the asset's life.)

g. A manufacturing firm built some specialized equipment for its own use. The equipment would have cost $75,000 if purchased from an outside company, but the cost of constructing the equipment was only $48,000. The firm recorded the equipment at cost of $48,000.

h. Depreciation of the home-office building is difficult to relate to particular sales. Therefore, the company records depreciation expense on a time basis.

i. A company wishes to change its method of accounting for revenue. However, the company does not switch because it wants to use the same accounting method that other companies in the industry use.

j. Because it is often difficult to collect installment receivables, a retailer uses the installment method of revenue recognition rather than the sales method.

Problem 12-2B *Identifying the concepts and principles violated by bad accounting practices*

The following accounting practices are *not* in accord with generally accepted accounting principles. A few of the practices violate more than one concept or principle. Identify all the accounting concepts and principles not followed in each situation.

a. Butler Manufacturing does not report a lawsuit in which it is the defendant. Alvin Butler, the president, argues that the outcome of the case is uncertain and that to report the lawsuit would introduce subjective data into the financial statements.

b. Todd Department Store records cost of goods sold in a predetermined amount each month regardless of the level of sales.

c. Tim Ihnacek is having difficulty evaluating the success of his advertising firm because he fails to separate business assets from personal assets.

d. Tapes Unlimited is continuing in business, but its owner accounts for assets as though the store were liquidating.

e. Major Construction Company recognizes all revenue on long-term construction projects at the start of construction.

f. All amounts on the balance sheet and income statement of Business Products Company have been adjusted for changes in the value of the dollar during the period.

g. Rizzuto Grain Company records one half of the depreciation of its grain silos when it purchases them and the other half over their estimated useful lives.

h. Day's Boutique sells high-fashion clothing to customers on credit. Thus far, collection losses on receivables have been very small. Nevertheless, Bonnie Day, the owner, uses the collection method to recognize revenue. The entity's revenue is understated because credit sales are not accounted for properly.

i. Alvarez Importers changed from the FIFO method to the LIFO method for inventory but did not report the accounting change in the financial statements.

j. Martin Supply Company applied the lower-of-cost-or-market method to account for its inventory. Martin used an estimate of the inventory value developed by its management. This estimate differed widely from estimates supplied by two independent appraisers. The estimates of the two appraisers were close together.

Problem 12-3B *Recording and reporting transactions according to GAAP*

The accounting records of Mortensen Publishing Company reveal the following information prior to closing the books at April 30, the end of the current fiscal year:

a. Accounts receivable include $29,800 from Miller Bookstore, which has declared bankruptcy. Mortensen, which uses the allowance method to account for bad debts, expects to receive only one fourth of the amount receivable from Miller.

b. No interest has been accrued on a $60,000, 11 percent, 90-day note payable issued on March 31.

c. The merchandise inventory, with a cost of $54,000, has a current market value of only $40,700. Mortensen uses a periodic inventory system and has not made the April 30 entry to record ending inventory.

d. Property tax is due each April 30, and Mortensen has received the city property tax bill of $3,650. However, the company has not recorded property tax at April 30 because Mortensen plans to record the tax when it is paid in May.

e. The company's office building was recently valued by independent appraisers at $640,000. This valuation is $290,000 more than Mortensen paid for the building and is $410,000 more than its cost less accumulated depreciation.

f. Mortensen paid $440,000 for its printing equipment on May 1, 2 years ago. The company has depreciated the equipment by the straight-line method over an expected useful life of ten years using a residual value of $40,000. Having used the equipment for two years, Mortensen determines that it will remain in service for a total of only eight years. The company will continue to use the straight-line method and $40,000 residual value for accounting purposes.

g. On May 13, before Mortensen issued its financial statements for the year ended April 30, the company's principal customer, Mears Co., declared its intention to cease doing business with Mortensen. This event is significant because for the past ten years Mears has accounted for approximately 65 percent of Mortensen's sales. Consequently, Mortensen's ability to sustain its recent level of sales in future years is seriously in doubt.

Required

Make all journal entries needed at April 30 to record this information. Explanations are not required. Identify those items *not* requiring a journal entry, giving the reason why an entry is not needed. If a note to the financial statements is needed, write the note.

Problem 12-4B   *Using the installment-revenue method*

Bayview Resorts sells land on the installment plan. Collections of installment receivables have deteriorated. The company's accountants are considering the different methods of recording revenues. Revenue, expense and collection data for the current year are as follows:

	19X6
Installment sales.......................................	$1,200,000
Cost of land sold	660,000
Collections of installment receivables from sales of 19X2	240,000
19X3	210,000

The gross profit percentage of 19X2 installment sales was 46 percent.

Required

1. Which method should be used to account for revenues if collections are extremely doubtful? If collections are reasonably assured? Which method is more advantageous for income tax purposes? Why?

2. Compute gross profit for 19X3 under the sales method, the collection method and the installment method.

Problem 12-5B   *Using the installment-revenue method*

Meridian Electrical makes all sales on the installment basis but uses the sales method to record revenue. The company's income statements for the most recent three years are as follows:

	Year 1	Year 2	Year 3
Sales..............................	$380,000	$404,000	$370,000
Cost of goods sold.................	190,000	181,800	199,800
Gross profit.......................	190,000	222,200	170,200
Operating expenses	110,600	130,700	125,100
Net income	$ 79,400	$ 91,500	$ 45,100
Collections from sales of year 1	$108,000	$181,000	$ 82,000
Collections from sales of year 2		143,000	209,000
Collections from sales of year 3			163,000

Required

Compute the amount of net income Meridian would have reported if the company had used the installment method for revenue. Ignore the effect of uncollectible accounts and present your answer in the following format:

Installment-Method Net Income	Year 1	Year 2	Year 3
Gross profit.......................	$	$	$
Operating expenses	110,600	130,700	125,100
Net income	$	$	$

Problem 12-6B   *Accounting for construction income*

Diamond Bridge Company constructs bridges under long-term contracts. During 19X5, Diamond began three projects that progressed according to the following schedule during 19X5, 19X6 and 19X7:

Project	Contract Price	Total Project Cost	19X5 Cost for Year	19X5 Percent Completed	19X6 Cost for Year	19X6 Percent Completed	19X7 Cost for Year	19X7 Percent Completed
1	$2,100,000	$1,600,000	$1,600,000	100%	—	—	—	—
2	3,100,000	2,200,000	484,000	22	1,716,000	78%	—	—
3	1,800,000	1,400,000	140,000	10	840,000	60	420,000	30%

Required

1. Assume Diamond uses the completed-contract method for construction revenue. Compute the company's construction revenue and income to be reported in 19X5, 19X6 and 19X7.

2. Compute Diamond's construction revenue and income to be reported in the three years if the company uses the percentage-of-completion method.

Problem 12-7B   *Accounting for revenues and expenses according to GAAP*

Roberta Katz established Katz Home Furnishings in January 19X7. During 19X7, 19X8 and most of 19X9, Katz kept the company's books and prepared its financial statements, although she had no training or experience in accounting. As a result, the accounting and statements contain numerous errors. For example, Katz recorded only cash receipts from customers as revenue. The sales method is appropriate for the business. She recorded inventory purchases as the cost of goods sold. When the value of her company's inventory increased by $15,600 in 19X7 and by $3,900 in 19X9, Katz debited the Inventory account and credited Revenue. She recorded no depreciation during 19X7, 19X8 and 19X9.

Late in 19X9 Katz employed an accountant, who determined that depreciable assets of the firm cost $170,000 on June 30, 19X7, had an expected residual value of $10,000,

and a total useful life of eight years. The accountant believes the straight-line depreciation method is appropriate for Katz's plant assets. The company's fiscal year ends
December 31. At the end of 19X9 the company's records reveal the following amounts:

	19X7	19X8	19X9
Reported net income (net loss)	$ 9,300	$ (11,200)	$ 52,900
Sales	131,800	164,700	226,100
Cash collections from customers	106,500	151,300	239,600
Purchases of inventory	100,600	136,000	191,700
Ending inventory	20,800	47,400	83,700
Accrued expenses not recorded at year end; these expenses were recorded during the next year, when paid	3,800	2,700	6,800
Depreciation expense recorded	-0-	-0-	-0-
Revenue recorded for increase in the value of inventory	15,600		3,900

Required

Apply the concepts and principles of GAAP to compute the correct net income of Katz
Home Furnishings for 19X7, 19X8 and 19X9.

Decision Problems

1. Measuring income according to GAAP

O'Hara Furniture Company was founded in January 19X5 by Bernard and Virginia
O'Hara, who share the management of the business. Virginia does the purchasing and
manages the sales staff. Bernard keeps the books and handles financial matters. The
O'Haras believe the store has prospered, but they are uncertain about precisely how
well it has done. It is now December 31, 19X5, and they are trying to decide whether
to borrow a substantial sum in order to expand the business.

They have asked your help because of your accounting knowledge. You learn that
the O'Haras opened the store with an initial investment of $45,000 cash and a building
valued at $100,000. The cash receipts totaled $180,000, which included collections,
$15,000 invested by the O'Haras, $50,000 borrowed from the bank in the name of the
furniture store, and $7,500 of earnings from a family inheritance. The store made credit
sales of $95,000 that have not been collected at December 31. The O'Haras purchased
furniture inventory on credit for $160,000, and inventory at December 31, 19X5, was
$75,000. The store paid $90,000 on account.

The 19X5 cash expenses were $92,000. Additional miscellaneous expenses totaled
$2,700 at year's end. These expenses included the O'Haras' household costs of $10,000
and interest on the business debt. The $5,000 of depreciation on the store building was
omitted.

Bernard and Virginia have decided to proceed with the expansion plan only if net
income for the first year was $40,000 or more. Bernard's analysis of the cash account
leads him to believe that net income was $43,000, so he is ready to expand. You are less
certain than Bernard of the wisdom of this decision primarily because the O'Haras have
mixed personal and business assets.

Required

1. Use a Cash T-account to show how Bernard arrived at the $43,000 amount.
2. Prepare the income statement of the furniture store of 19X5.
3. Should the O'Haras borrow to expand their business?
4. Which accounting concept or principle is most fundamental to this problem
    situation?

2. *Examining the disclosure principle*

1. It has been suggested that the disclosure principle is perhaps one of the most important concepts and principles and concepts underlying financial reporting. Why do you think it is considered so important?

2. "Disclosure of Accounting Policies," Section 1505 of the *CICA Handbook*, was added to the *Handbook* in October, 1974. Discuss the probable impact the addition of Section 1505 had on users of financial statements. Consider users before and after its introduction.

3. Accounting researchers are studying the understandability of financial statements. Why are they doing this? What contribution might their research make?

4. The text suggests that *subsequent events* and *long-term commitments* should be disclosed in the notes to the financial statements. What is it about these two that makes their disclosure so important to users?

5. *Financial Reporting in Canada*[2] reported that about one in five of the companies surveyed for its 1989 edition reported the revenue principle or revenue recognition method used in preparing their financial statements. Why do you think these companies reported that information? What might we assume about the other 234 companies (over 200) in the survey with respect to revenue recognition?

Financial Statement Problem

Disclosure in action

The notes to the financial statements are an integral part of the financial statements. Examine John Labatt's financial statements in Appendix E, and answer these questions:

1. Note 1, "Accounting Policies," is perhaps the most important of the notes; it describes the accounting policies followed in preparing the financial statements. John Labatt, as a brewer, has a large inventory of returnable bottles and kegs; how are these accounted for in the financial statements? How does the company account for research and development costs? What is the basis for valuing short-term investments?

2. Do the notes indicate any important subsequent events? If so, describe them.

3. What proportion of the company's gross sales comes from the brewing part of their operations? What is the value of assets employed in Canada? In the United States?

4. John Labatt has diversified interests. What percentage does it own of the Toronto Blue Jays? During the year, John Labatt purchased a share interest in International Talent Group (ITG); how do the notes describe the business ITG is in?

5. Explain how the concept of materiality is evident in the financial statements.

Answers to Self-Study Questions

1. c		7. d
2. a		8. d
3. c		9. b
4. b		10. b

5. a $(\$10,000 - \$7,000)/\$10,000 = .30 \times \$1,500 = \$450$

6. a $\$180,000/\$720,000 = .25 \times \$900,000 = \$225,000$;
   $\$225,000 - \$180,000 = \$45,000$

---

[2] *Financial Reporting in Canada, Seventeenth Edition 1987*, Toronto: Canadian Institute of Chartered Accountants, 1987, p. 14.

PART FIVE

Accounting for Partnerships and Corporations

13

Accounting for Partnerships

LEARNING OBJECTIVES

After studying this chapter, you should be able to

1 Identify the characteristics, including advantages and disadvantages, of a partnership

2 Account for partners' initial investments in a partnership

3 Use different methods to allocate profits and losses to the partners

4 Account for the admission of a new partner to the business

5 Account for the withdrawal of a partner from the business

6 Account for the liquidation of a partnership

Forming a partnership is easy. It requires no permission from government authorities and involves no legal procedures. When two persons decide to go into business together, a partnership is automatically formed.

A **partnership** is an association of two or more persons who co-own a business for profit. This definition is common to the various provincial partnership acts which tend to prescribe similar rules with respect to the organization and operation of partnerships in their jurisdiction.

A partnership brings together the capital, talents and experience of the partners. Business opportunities closed to an individual may open up to a partnership. Suppose neither Pedigo nor Yu has enough capital individually to buy a $300,000 parcel of land. They may be able to afford it together in a partnership. Or VanAllen, a tax accountant, and Kahn, an investment counselor, may pool their talents and know-how. Their partnership may offer a fuller range of money management services than either person could offer alone. Combining their experience may increase income for each of them.

Partnerships come in all sizes. Many partnerships have fewer than ten partners. Some physician and law firms may have twenty or more partners. The largest CA firms have several hundred partners.

Characteristics of a Partnership _____

Several features are unique to the partnership form of business. The following characteristics distinguish partnerships from sole proprietorships, the form of business organization that we have covered so far, and from corporations, which we examine in later chapters.

531

Starting a partnership is voluntary. A person cannot be forced to join a partnership, and partners cannot be forced to accept another person as a partner. Although the partnership agreement may be oral, a written agreement between the partners reduces the chance of a misunderstanding.

The Written Partnership Agreement

OBJECTIVE 1

Identify the characteristics, including advantages and disadvantages, of a partnership

A business partnership is like a marriage. To be successful, the partners must cooperate. However, business partners do not vow to remain together for life. Business partnerships come and go. To make certain that each partner fully understands how a particular partnership operates and to cut down on the chances that any partner might misunderstand how the business is run, partners may draw up a **partnership agreement**, also called the **articles of partnership**. This agreement is a contract between the partners, so transactions involving the agreement are governed by contract law. The articles of partnership should make the following points clear:

1. Name, location and nature of the business
2. Name, capital investment and duties of each partner
3. Method of sharing profits and losses by the partners
4. Withdrawals allowed to the partners
5. Procedures for settling disputes between the partners
6. Procedures for admitting new partners
7. Procedures for settling up with a partner who withdraws from the business
8. Procedures for liquidating the partnership: selling the assets, paying the liabilities and disbursing any remaining cash to the partners

As partners enter and leave the business, the old partnership is dissolved and a new partnership is formed. Drawing up a new agreement for each new partnership may be expensive and time consuming.

Limited Life

A partnership has a life limited by the length of time that all partners continue to own the business. When a partner withdraws from the business, that partnership ceases to exist. A new partnership may emerge to continue the same business, but the old partnership has been *dissolved*. **Dissolution** is the ending of a partnership. Likewise, the addition of a new partner dissolves the old partnership and creates a new partnership. Partnerships are sometimes formed for a particular business venture, like a mining operation or a real estate investment. When the mine is depleted or the real estate is sold, the partnership may be dissolved.

Mutual Agency

Mutual agency in a partnership means that every partner can bind the business to a contract within the scope of the partnership's regular business operations. If an individual partner in a CA firm enters into a contract with a person or another business to provide accounting service, then the firm—not the individual who signs the contract—is bound to provide that service. However, if that same CA signs a contract to purchase home lawn services for the summer months, the partnership would not be bound to pay. Contracting for lawn services does not fall within the partnership's regular business operations.

Unlimited Liability

Each partner has an **unlimited personal liability** for the debts of the partnership. When a partnership cannot pay its debts with business assets, the partners must use their personal assets to meet the debt.

Avilla and Davis are the two partners in AD Company. The business has had an unsuccessful year, and the partnership's liabilities exceed its assets by $120,000. Davis and Avilla must pay this amount with their personal assets.

Recall that each partner has *unlimited* liability. If a partner is unable to pay his or her part of the debt, the other partner (or partners) must make payment. If Davis can pay only $50,000 of the liability, Avilla must pay $70,000 ($120,000 − $50,000). Avilla would then seek $10,000 ($70,000 − $60,000) from Davis in a separate business action.

Unlimited liability and mutual agency are closely related. A dishonest partner or a partner with poor judgment may commit the partnership to a contract under which the business loses money. In turn, creditors may force *all* the partners to pay the debt from their personal assets. Hence, a business partner should be chosen with great care.

Co-ownership of Property

Any asset (cash, inventory, machinery, and so on) that a partner invests into the partnership becomes the joint property of all the partners. Also, each partner has a claim to the business's profits.

No Partnership Income Taxes

A partnership pays no income tax on its business income. Instead, the net income of the partnership is divided and becomes the taxable income of the partners. Suppose AD Company earned net income of $80,000, shared equally by partners Avilla and Davis. AD Company would pay no income tax *as a business entity*. However, Avilla and Davis would pay income tax as individuals on their $40,000 shares of partnership income.

Accounting for a partnership is much like accounting for a proprietorship. We record buying and selling, collecting and paying in a partnership just as we do for a business with only one owner. However, because a partnership has more than one owner, the partnership must have more than one owner's equity account. Every partner in the business, whether the firm has two or two hundred partners, has an individual owner's equity account. Often these accounts carry the name of the particular partner and the word *capital*. For example, the owner's equity account for Larry Insdorf would read "Insdorf, Capital." Similarly, each partner has a withdrawal account. If the number of partners is large, the general ledger may contain the single account Partners' Capital or Owners' Equity. A subsidiary ledger can be used for individual partner accounts.

Let us see how to account for the multiple owners' equity accounts—and learn how they appear on the balance sheet—by taking a look at how to account for starting up a partnership.

Initial Investments by Partners _____

Partners in a new partnership may invest assets and liabilities in the business. These contributions are entered in the books in the same way that a proprietor's assets and liabilities are recorded. Subtracting each person's liabilities from his or her assets yields the amount to be credited to the owner's equity account for that person. Often the partners hire an independent firm to appraise their assets and liabilities at current market value at the time a partnership is formed. This outside evaluation assures an objective valuation for what each partner brings into the business.

Assume Benz and Hanna form a partnership to manufacture and sell computer software. Benz brings to the partnership cash of $10,000, accounts receivable of $30,000, inventory of $70,000, computer equipment with a book value of $400,000, and accounts payable of $85,000. Hanna contributes cash of $5,000 and a software program. The development of this program cost Hanna $18,000, but its current market value is much greater. Suppose the partners agree on the following values based on an independent appraisal:

Benz's contributions
Cash, $10,000; inventory, $70,000; and accounts payable, $85,000 (the appraiser believes Benz's book values for these items equal their current market value)
Accounts receivable, $30,000, less allowance for doubtful accounts of $5,000
Computer equipment, $450,000

Hanna's contributions
Cash, $5,000
Computer software, $100,000

Note that current market value differs only slightly from book value for Benz's computer equipment. However, the appraiser valued Hanna's $18,000 computer software at the much higher $100,000 figure. The partners record their initial investments at the current market values. The title of each owner's equity account includes the owner's name and *Capital*.

Benz's investment

June 1	Cash.....................................	10,000	
	Accounts Receivable........................	30,000	
	Inventory	70,000	
	Computer Equipment	450,000	
	Allowance for Doubtful Accounts.........		5,000
	Accounts Payable		85,000
	Benz, Capital		470,000
	To record Benz's investment in the partnership.		

> **OBJECTIVE 2**
> Account for partners' initial investments in a partnership

Hanna's investment

June 1	Cash.....................................	5,000	
	Computer Software	100,000	
	Hanna, Capital		105,000
	To record Hanna's investment in the partnership.		

The initial partnership balance sheet reports these amounts as follows:

Benz and Hanna
Balance Sheet
June 1, 19X5

Assets			Liabilities	
Cash.............		$ 15,000	Accounts payable ...	$ 85,000
Accounts receivable	$30,000			
Less: Allowance for			**Capital**	
doubtful accounts	(5,000)	25,000		
Inventory		70,000	Benz, capital	470,000
Computer equipment		450,000	Hanna, capital......	105,000
Computer software .		100,000	Total liabilities and	
Total assets		$660,000	capital..........	$660,000

Each owner's equity account appears under the heading Capital. Having more than one capital account distinguishes a partnership balance sheet from a proprietorship balance sheet.

Sharing Partnership Profits and Losses

How to distribute profits and losses among partners is one of the most challenging aspects of managing a partnership. If the partners have not drawn up an agreement, or if the agreement does not state how the partners will divide profits and losses, then, according to law, the partners must share profits and losses equally. If the agreement specifies a method for sharing profits but not losses, then losses are shared in the same proportion as profits. For example, a partner receiving 75 percent of the profits would likewise absorb 75 percent of any losses.

In some cases, an equal division is not fair. One partner may perform more work for the business than the other partner, or one partner may make a larger capital contribution. In the preceding example, Hanna might agree to work longer hours for the partnership than Benz in order to earn a greater share of profits. Benz could argue that he should receive more of the profits because he contributed more net assets ($470,000) than Hanna did ($105,000). Hanna might contend that her computer software program is the partnership's most important asset and that her share of the profits should be greater than Benz's share. Arriving at fair sharing of profits and losses in a partnership may be difficult. We now discuss the options available in determining partners' shares.

Sharing Based on a Stated Fraction

Partners may agree to any profit and loss-sharing method they desire. Suppose the partnership agreement of Cagle and Elias allocates two thirds of the business profits and losses to Cagle and one third to Elias. If net income for the

OBJECTIVE 3
Use different methods to allocate profits and losses to the partners

year is $90,000 and all revenue and expense accounts have been closed, the Income Summary account has a credit balance of $90,000 as follows:

Income Summary
Bal. 90,000

The entry to close this account and allocate the profit to the partners' capital account is

Dec. 31	Income Summary	90,000	
	Cagle, Capital ($90,000 × ⅔)		60,000
	Elias, Capital ($90,000 × ⅓)		30,000
	To allocate net income to partners.		

Consider the effect of this entry. Does Cagle get cash of $60,000 and Elias cash of $30,000? No. The increase in the capital accounts of the partners cannot be linked to any particular asset, including cash. Instead, the entry indicates that Cagle's ownership in *all* the assets of the business increased by $60,000 and Elias's by $30,000.

If the year's operations resulted in a net loss of $66,000, the Income Summary account would have a debit balance of $66,000. In that case, the closing entry to allocate the loss to the partners' capital accounts would be

Dec. 31	Cagle, Capital ($66,000 × ⅔)	44,000	
	Elias, Capital ($66,000 × ⅓)	22,000	
	Income Summary		66,000
	To allocate net loss to partners.		

Sharing Based on Partners' Capital Contributions

Profits and losses are often allocated in proportion to the partners' capital contributions in the business. Suppose Antoine, Barber and Cabañas are partners in ABC Company. Their capital accounts have the following balances at the end of the year, before the closing entries:

Antoine, Capital...........................	$ 40,000
Barber, Capital	60,000
Cabañas, Capital	50,000
Total capital balances	$150,000

Assume that the partnership earned a profit of $120,000 for the year. To allocate this amount based on capital contributions, each partner's percentage share of the partnership's total capital balance must be computed. We simply divide each partner's contribution by the total capital amount. These figures, multiplied by the $120,000 profit amount, yield each partner's share of the year's profits:

Antoine:	$40,000/$150,000 × $120,000	=	$ 32,000
Barber:	$60,000/$150,000 × $120,000	=	48,000
Cabañas:	$50,000/$150,000 × $120,000	=	40,000
	Net income allocated to partners	=	**$120,000**

The closing entry to allocate the profit to the partners' capital accounts is

Dec. 31	Income Summary	120,000	
	Antoine, Capital		32,000
	Barber, Capital.......................		48,000
	Cabañas, Capital		40,000
	To allocate net income to partners.		

After this closing entry, the partners' capital balances are

Antoine, Capital ($40,000 + $32,000)	$ 72,000
Barber, Capital ($60,000 + $48,000)	108,000
Cabañas, Capital ($50,000 + $40,000)	90,000
Total capital balances after allocation of net income ..	$270,000

Sharing Based on Capital Contributions and Service to the Partnership

One partner, regardless of his or her capital contribution, may put more work into the business than the other partners. Even among partners who log equal service time, one person's superior experience and knowledge may command a greater share of income. To reward the harder-working or more valuable person, the profit-and-loss-sharing method may be based on a combination of contributed capital *and* service to the business.

Assume Randolph and Scott formed a partnership in which Randolph invested $60,000 and Scott invested $40,000, a total of $100,000. Scott devotes more time to the partnership and earns the larger salary. Accordingly, the two partners have agreed to share profits as follows:

1. The first $50,000 of partnership profits is to be allocated based on partners' capital contributions to the business.
2. The next $60,000 of profits is to be allocated based on service, with Randolph receiving $24,000 and Scott receiving $36,000.
3. Any remaining amount is allocated equally.

If net income for the first year is $125,000, the partners' shares of this profit are computed as follows:

	Randolph	Scott	Total
Total net income			$125,000
Sharing of first $50,000 of profit, based on capital contributions			
Randolph ($60,000/$100,000 × $50,000)	$30,000		
Scott ($40,000/$100,000 × $50,000)		$20,000	
Total			50,000
Net Income left for allocation			75,000
Sharing of next $60,000, based on service			
Randolph	24,000		
Scott		36,000	
Total			60,000
Net income left for allocation			15,000
Remainder shared equally			
Randolph ($15,000 × ½)	7,500		
Scott ($15,000 × ½)		7,500	
Total			15,000
Net income left for allocation			$ -0-
Net income allocated to the partners	$61,500	$63,500	$125,000

Based on this allocation, the closing entry is

Dec. 31	Income Summary	125,000	
	Randolph, Capital.....................		61,500
	Scott, Capital		63,500
	To allocate net income to partners.		

Sharing Based on Salaries and Interest

Partners may be rewarded for their service and their capital contributions to the business in other ways. In one sharing plan, the partners are allocated salaries plus interest on their capital balances. Assume Massey and Vanier form an oil-exploration partnership. At the beginning of the year, their capital balances are $80,000 and $100,000 respectively. The partnership agreement allocates annual salary of $43,000 to Massey and $35,000 to Vanier. After salaries are allocated, each partner earns 8 percent interest on his beginning capital balance. Any remaining net income is divided equally. Partnership profit of $96,000 would be allocated as follows:

	Massey	Vanier	Total
Total net income			$96,000
First, salaries			
Massey.....................................	$43,000		
Vanier		$35,000	
Total..			78,000
Net income left for allocation			18,000
Second, interest on beginning capital balances			
Massey ($80,000 × $.08)........................	6,400		
Vanier ($100,000 × $.08).......................		8,000	
Total..			14,400
Net income left for allocation			3,600
Third, remainder shared equally			
Massey ($3,600 × ½)...........................	1,800		
Vanier ($3,600 × ½)...........................		1,800	
Total..			3,600
Net income left for allocation			$ -0-
Net income allocated to the partners	$51,200	$44,800	$96,000

Based on this allocation, the closing entry is

Dec. 31	Income Summary	96,000	
	Massey, Capital		51,200
	Vanier, Capital........................		44,800
	To allocate net income to partners.		

These salaries and interest amounts are *not* business expenses in the usual sense. Partners do not work for their own business to earn a salary, as an employee does. They do not loan money to their own business to earn interest. Their goal is for the partnership to earn a profit. Therefore, salaries and interest in partnership agreements are simply ways of expressing the allocation of profits and losses to the partners. For example, the salary component of partner income rewards service to the partnership. The interest component rewards a partner's investment of cash or other assets in the business.

In the preceding illustration, net income exceeded the sum of salary and interest. If the partnership profit is less than the allocated sum of salary and interest, a negative remainder will occur at some stage in the allocation process. Even so, the partners use the same method for allocation purposes. For example, assume that Massey and Vanier Partnership earned only $82,000.

	Massey	**Vanier**	**Total**
Total net income			$82,000
First, salaries			
Massey...	$43,000		
Vanier		$35,000	
Total.......................................			78,000
Net income left for allocation			4,000
Second, interest on beginning capital balances			
Massey ($80,000 × $.08)	6,400		
Vanier ($100,000 × $.08)		8,000	
Total.......................................			14,400
Net income left for allocation			(10,400)
Third, remainder shared equally			
Massey ($10,400 × ½)	(5,200)		
Vanier ($10,400 × ½)		(5,200)	
Total.......................................			(10,400)
Net income left for allocation			$ -0-
Net income allocated to the partners	$44,200	$37,800	$82,000

A net loss would be allocated to Massey and Vanier in the same manner outlined for net income. The sharing procedure would begin with the net loss and then allocate salary, interest and any other specified amounts to the partners.

We see that partners may allocate profits and losses based on a stated fraction, contributed capital, service, interest on capital, or any combination of these factors. Each partnership shapes its profit-and-loss-sharing ratio to fit its own needs.

Partner Drawings _____

Partners, like anyone else, need cash for personal living expenses. Partnership agreements usually allow partners to withdraw cash or other assets from the business. Drawings from a partnership are recorded exactly as illustrated in previous chapters for drawings from a proprietorship. Assume Massey and Vanier are each allowed a monthly withdrawal of $3,500. The partnership records the March withdrawal with this entry:

Mar. 31	Massey, Drawing............................	3,500	
	Vanier, Drawing	3,500	
	Cash		7,000
	Monthly partner withdrawals.		

During the year, each partner's drawing account accumulates 12 such amounts, a total of $42,000 ($3,500 × 12). At the end of the period, the general ledger shows the following account balances immediately after net income has been closed to the partners' capital accounts. Assume these beginning balances for Massey and Vanier at the start of the year and that $82,000 of profit has been allocated based on the preceding illustration.

Massey, Capital		
	Jan. 1 Bal.	80,000
	Dec. 31 Net inc.	44,200

Vanier, Capital		
	Jan. 1 Bal.	100,000
	Dec. 31 Net inc.	37,800

Massey, Drawing		
Dec. 31 Bal.	42,000	

Vanier, Drawing		
Dec. 31 Bal.	42,000	

The withdrawal accounts must be closed at the end of the period. The final closing entries transfer their balances to the partner's capital account as follows:

Dec. 31	Massey, Capital	42,000	
	Massey, Drawing		42,000
	Vanier, Capital	42,000	
	Vanier, Drawing		42,000
	To close partner drawing accounts.		

After closing, the accounts appear as follows:

Massey, Capital			
Dec. 31 Clo.	42,000	Jan. 1 Bal.	80,000
		Dec. 31 Net inc.	44,200
		Dec. 31 Bal.	82,200

Vanier, Capital			
Dec. 31 Clo.	42,000	Jan. 1 Bal.	100,000
		Dec. 31 Net inc.	37,800
		Dec. 31 Bal.	95,800

Massey, Drawing			
Dec. 31 Bal.	42,000	Dec. 31 Clo.	42,000

Vanier, Drawing			
Dec. 31 Bal.	42,000	Dec. 31 Clo.	42,000

In this case, Massey withdrew less than his share of the partnership net income. Consequently, his capital account grew during the period. Vanier, however, withdrew more than his share of net income. His capital account decreased.

Partnerships, as we have mentioned, do not last forever. We turn now to a discussion of how partnerships dissolve—and how new partnerships arise.

Dissolution of a Partnership

A partnership lasts only as long as its partners remain in the business. The addition of a new member or the withdrawal of an existing member dissolves the partnership.

Often a new partnership is formed to carry on the former partnership's business. In fact, the new partnership may choose to retain the dissolved partnership's name. Price Waterhouse, for example, is an accounting firm that retires and hires partners during the year. Thus the former partnership dissolves and a new partnership begins many times. The business, however, retains the name and continues operations. Other partnerships may dissolve and then reform under a new name. Let us look now at the ways that a new member may gain admission into an existing partnership.

Admission by Purchasing a Partner's Interest

A person may become a member of a partnership by gaining the approval of the other partner (or partners) for entrance into the firm *and* by purchasing a present partner's interest in the business. Let us assume that Fisher and Levesque have a partnership that carries these figures:

Cash	$ 40,000	Total liabilities	$120,000
Other assets	360,000	Fisher, capital	110,000
		Levesque, capital	170,000
Total assets	$400,000	Total liabilities and capital ...	$400,000

Business is going so well that Fisher receives an offer from Dynak, an outside party, to buy her $110,000 interest in the business for $150,000. Fisher agrees to sell out to Dynak, and Levesque approves Dynak as a new partner. The firm records the transfer of capital interest in the business with this entry:

Apr. 16	Fisher, Capital	110,000	
	Dynak, Capital.......................		110,000
	To transfer Fisher's equity in the business to Dynak.		

OBJECTIVE 4

Account for the admission of a new partner to the business

The debit side of the entry closes Fisher's capital account because she is no longer a partner in the firm. The credit side opens Dynak's capital account because Fisher's equity has been transferred to Dynak. Notice that the entry amount is Fisher's capital balance ($110,000) and not the $150,000 price that Dynak paid Fisher to buy into the business. The full $150,000 goes to Fisher. In this example, the partnership receives no cash because the transaction was between Dynak and Fisher, not between Dynak and the partnership. Suppose Dynak pays Fisher less than Fisher's capital balance. That does not affect the entry on the partnership books. Fisher's equity is transferred to Dynak at book value ($110,000).

The old partnership has dissolved. Levesque and Dynak draw up a new partnership agreement, with a new profit-and-loss-sharing ratio, and continue business operations.

Admission by Investing in the Partnership

A person may also be admitted as a partner by investing directly in the partnership rather than by purchasing an existing partner's interest. The new partner contributes assets (for example, cash, inventory, or equipment) to the business. Assume that the partnership of Ingel and Jay has the following assets, liabilities and capital:

Cash	$ 20,000	Total liabilities	$100,000
Other assets	240,000	Ingel, capital	70,000
		Jay, capital	90,000
Total assets	$260,000	Total liabilities and capital ...	$260,000

Kahn offers to invest equipment and land (Other assets) with a market value of $80,000 to persuade the existing partners to take her into the business. Ingel and Jay agree to dissolve the existing partnership and to start up a new business, giving Kahn one-third interest in exchange for the contributed assets. The entry to record Kahn's investment is

July 18	Other Assets	80,000	
	Kahn, Capital		80,000
	To admit L. Kahn as a partner with a one-third interest in the business.		

After this entry, the partnership books show:

Cash	$ 20,000	Total liabilities..............	$100,000
Other assets		Ingel, capital	70,000
($240,000 + $80,000)	320,000	Jay, capital	90,000
		Kahn, capital	80,000
	$340,000	Total liabilities and capital ...	$340,000

Kahn's one-third interest in the partnership [$80,000/($70,000 + $90,000 + $80,000) = 1/3] does not necessarily entitle her to one third of the profits. The sharing of profits and losses is a separate consideration in the partnership agreement.

In the previous example, Dynak paid an individual member (Fisher), not the partnership. Note that Kahn's payment (the other assets) goes into the partnership.

Admission by Investing in the Partnership — Bonus to the Old Partners   The more successful a partnership, the higher the payment the partners may demand from a person entering the business. Partners in a business that is doing quite well might require an incoming person to pay them a bonus. The bonus increases the current partners' capital accounts.

Suppose that Nagasawa and Osburn's partnership has earned above-average profits for ten years. The two partners share profits and losses equally. The balance sheet carries these figures:

Cash	$ 40,000	Total liabilities..............	$100,000
Other assets	210,000	Nagasawa, capital..........	70,000
		Osburn, capital	80,000
Total assets	$250,000	Total liabilities and capital ...	$250,000

The partners agree to admit Parker to a one-fourth interest with his cash investment of $90,000. Parker's capital balance on the partnership books is $60,000, computed as follows:

Partnership capital before Parker is admitted ($70,000 + $80,000)	$150,000
Parker's investment in the partnership	90,000
Partnership capital after Parker is admitted	$240,000
Parker's capital in the partnership ($240,000 × ¼)	$ 60,000

The entry on the partnership books to record Parker's investment is

```
Mar. 11   Cash .......................................   90,000
              Parker, Capital.........................              60,000
              Nagasawa, Capital ($30,000 × ½) .........            15,000
              Osburn, Capital ($30,000 × ½) ...........            15,000
          To admit G. Parker as a partner with a one-
          fourth interest in the business.
```

Parker's capital account is credited for his one-fourth interest in the partnership. The other partners share the $30,000 difference between Parker's investment ($90,000) and her equity in the business ($60,000). This difference is accounted for as income to the old partners and is, therefore, allocated to them based on their profit-and-loss ratio.

The new partnership's balance sheet reports these amounts:

Cash ($40,000 + $90,000)	$130,000	Total liabilities	$100,000
Other assets	210,000	Nagasawa, capital ($70,000 + $15,000)	85,000
		Osburn, capital ($80,000 + $15,000)	95,000
		Parker, capital	60,000
Total assets	$340,000	Total liabilities and capital ...	$340,000

Admission by Investing in the Partnership — Bonus to the New Partner   A potential new partner may be so important that the existing partners offer him or her a partnership share that includes a bonus. A law firm may strongly desire a former premier, cabinet minister or other official as a partner because of the person's reputation. A restaurant owner may want to go into partnership with a famous sports personality like Mario Lemieux or Carolyn Waldo.

Suppose Page and Osuka is a law partnership. The firm's balance sheet appears as follows:

Cash	$140,000	Total liabilities	$120,000
Other assets	360,000	Page, capital	230,000
		Osuka, capital	150,000
Total assets	$500,000	Total liabilities and capital ...	$500,000

The partners admit Schiller, a former attorney general, as a partner with a one-third interest in exchange for his cash investment of $100,000. At the time of Schiller's admission, the firm's capital is $380,000 — Page, $230,000 and Osuka, $150,000. Page and Osuka share profits and losses in the ratio of two thirds to Page and one third to Osuka. The computation of Schiller's equity in the partnership is

Partnership capital before Schiller is admitted ($230,000 + $150,000) .	$380,000
Schiller's investment in the partnership...........................	100,000
Partnership capital after Schiller is admitted.....................	$480,000
Schiller's capital in the partnership ($480,000 × ⅓).................	$160,000

The capital accounts of Page and Osuka are debited for the $60,000 difference between the new partner's equity ($160,000) and his investment ($100,000). The existing partners share this decrease in capital, which is accounted for as though it were a loss, based on their profit-and-loss ratio.

The entry to record Schiller's investment is

Aug. 24	Cash.....................................	100,000	
	Page, Capital ($60,000 × ⅔)	40,000	
	Osuka, Capital ($60,000 × ⅓)	20,000	
	Schiller, Capital.......................		160,000
	To admit M. Schiller as a partner with a one-third interest in the business.		

The new partnership's balance sheet reports these amounts:

Cash		Total liabilities..............	$120,000	
($140,000 + $100,000)	$240,000	Page, capital		
Other assets...............	360,000	($230,000 − $40,000)	190,000	
		Osuka, capital		
		($150,000 − $20,000)	130,000	
		Schiller, capital	160,000	
Total assets	$600,000	Total liabilities and capital ...	$600,000	

Summary Problem for Your Review

The partnership of Taylor and Uvalde is considering admitting Vaughn as a partner on January 1, 19X8. The partnership general ledger includes the following balances on that date:

Cash	$ 9,000	Total liabilities..............	$ 50,000
Other assets...............	110,000	Taylor, capital	45,000
		Uvalde, capital	24,000
Total assets	$119,000	Total liabilities and capital ...	$119,000

Taylor's share of profits and losses is 60 percent and Uvalde's share is 40 percent.

Required

1. Suppose Vaughn pays Uvalde $31,000 to acquire Uvalde's interest in the business. Taylor approves Vaughn as a partner.
   a. Record the transfer of owner's equity on the partnership books.
   b. Prepare the partnership balance sheet immediately after Vaughn is admitted as a partner.
2. Suppose Vaughn becomes a partner by investing $31,000 cash to acquire a one-fourth interest in the business.
   a. Compute Vaughn's capital balance.
   b. Prepare the partnership balance sheet immediately after Vaughn is admitted as a partner. Include the heading.
3. Which way of admitting Vaughn to the partnership increases its total assets? Give your reason.

SOLUTION TO REVIEW PROBLEM

Requirement 1

a. Jan. 1   Uvalde, Capital 24,000

  Vaughn, Capital 24,000

  To transfer Uvalde's equity in the partnership to
  Vaughn.

b. The balance sheet for the partnership of Taylor and Vaughn is identical to
the balance sheet given for Taylor and Uvalde in the problem, except for
Vaughn's name replaces Uvalde's name in the title and in the listing of
capital accounts.

Requirement 2

a. Computation of Vaughn's capital balance

Partnership capital before Vaughn is admitted ($45,000 + $24,000)	$ 69,000
Vaughn's investment in the partnership......................	31,000
Partnership capital after Vaughn is admitted..................	$100,000
Vaughn's capital in the partnership ($100,000 × ¼)	$ 25,000

Jan. 1   Cash 31,000

  Vaughn, Capital 25,000
  Taylor, Capital
   [($31,000 − $25,000) × .60] 3,600
  Uvalde, Capital
   [($31,000 − $25,000) × .40] 2,400
  To admit Vaughn as a partner with a one-fourth
  interest in the business.

b.

Taylor, Uvalde and Vaughn
Balance Sheet
January 1, 19X8

Cash		Total liabilities	$ 50,000
($9,000 + $31,000)	$ 40,000	Taylor, capital	
Other assets	110,000	($45,000 + $3,600)	48,600
		Uvalde, capital	
		($24,000 + $2,400)	26,400
		Vaughn, capital	25,000
Total assets	$150,000	Total liabilities and capital	$150,000

Requirement 3

Vaughn's investment in the partnership increases its total assets by the amount
of his contribution. Total assets of the business are $150,000 after his investment,
compared to $119,000 before. By contrast, Vaughn's purchase of Uvalde's inter-
est in the business is a personal transaction between the two individuals. It
does not affect the assets of the partnership regardless of the amount Vaughn
pays Uvalde.

Withdrawal of a Partner _____

OBJECTIVE 5

Account for the withdrawal of a partner from the business

A partner may withdraw from the business for many reasons, including retirement or a dispute with the other partners. The partnership agreement should contain a provision to govern how to settle with a withdrawing partner. In the simplest case, as illustrated on p. 541, a partner may withdraw and sell his or her interest to another partner in a personal transaction. The only entry needed to record this transfer of equity debits the withdrawing partner's capital account and credits the purchaser's capital account. The dollar amount of the entry is the capital balance of the withdrawing partner, regardless of the price paid by the purchaser. The accounting when one current partner buys a second partner's interest is the same as when an outside party buys a current partner's interest.

If the partner withdraws in the middle of the accounting period, it is necessary to update the partnership books to determine the withdrawing partner's capital balance. The business must measure net income or net loss for the fraction of the year up to the withdrawal date and allocate profit or loss according to the existing ratio. After closing the books, the business then accounts for the change in partnership capital.

The withdrawing partner may receive his or her share of the business in partnership assets other than cash. The question then arises of what value to assign the partnership assets: book value or current market value. The settlement procedure may specify that an independent appraisal of the assets take place to determine their current market value. If market values have changed, the appraisal will result in a revaluing of the partnership assets. In this way the withdrawing partner shares with the remaining partners in any market value changes that their efforts caused.

Suppose Isaac is retiring in midyear from the partnership of Green, Maslowski and Isaac. After the books have been adjusted for partial-period income but before the asset appraisal, revaluation and closing entries, the balance sheet reports:

Cash		$ 39,000	Total liabilities		$ 80,000
Inventory		44,000	Green, capital		54,000
Land		55,000	Maslowski, capital		43,000
Building	$95,000		Isaac, capital		21,000
Less: Accumulated depreciation	35,000	60,000			
			Total liabilities		
Total assets		$198,000	and capital		$198,000

Assume an independent appraiser revalues the inventory at $38,000 (down from $44,000) and the land at $101,000 (up from $55,000). The partners share the differences between these assets' market values and their prior book values based on their profit and loss ratio. The partnership agreement has allocated one fourth of the profits to Green, one half to Maslowski and one fourth to Isaac. (This ratio may be written 1:2:1 for one part to Green, two parts to Maslowski and one part to Isaac.) For each share that Green or Isaac has, Maslowski has two. The entries to record the revaluation of the inventory and land are

July 31	Green, Capital ($6,000 × ¼)	1,500	
	Maslowski, Capital ($6,000 × ½)	3,000	
	Isaac, Capital ($6,000 × ¼)	1,500	
	Inventory ($44,000 − $38,000)		6,000
	To revalue the inventory and allocate the loss in value to the partners.		
July 31	Land ($101,000 − $55,000)	46,000	
	Green, Capital ($46,000 × ¼)		11,500
	Maslowski, Capital ($46,000 × ½)		23,000
	Isaac, Capital ($46,000 × ¼)		11,500
	To revalue the land and allocate the gain in value to the partners.		

After the revaluations, the partnership balance sheet reports:

Cash	$ 39,000	Total liabilities		$ 80,000
Inventory	38,000	Green, capital		
Land	101,000	($54,000 − $1,500 +		
Building	$95,000	$11,500)		64,000
Less: Accumulated		Maslowski, capital		
depreciation	35,000	($43,000 − $3,000 +		
	60,000	$23,000)		63,000
		Isaac, capital		
		($21,000 − $1,500 +		
		$11,500)		31,000
Total assets		Total liabilities		
	$238,000	and capital		$238,000

The books now carry the assets at current market value, which becomes the new book value; the capital accounts have been adjusted accordingly. Isaac has a claim to $31,000 in partnership assets. How is his withdrawal from the business accounted for?

Withdrawal at Book Value

If Isaac withdraws by taking cash equal to the book value of his owner's equity, the entry would be

July 31	Isaac, Capital	31,000	
	Cash		31,000
	To record withdrawal of K. Isaac from the partnership.		

This entry records the payment of partnership cash to Isaac and the closing of his capital account upon withdrawal from the business.

Withdrawal at Less Than Book Value

The withdrawing partner may be so eager to leave the business that he is willing to take less than his equity. This situation has occurred in real estate and oil-drilling partnerships. Assume Isaac withdraws from the business and agrees to take partnership cash of $10,000 and the new partnership's note for $15,000. This $25,000 settlement is $6,000 less than Isaac's $31,000 equity in the business. The remaining partners share this $6,000 difference, which is a gain to them, according to their profit-and-loss ratio. However, since Isaac has withdrawn from the partnership, a new agreement — and a new profit-and-loss ratio — must be drawn up. Maslowski and Green, in forming a new partnership, may decide on any ratio that they see fit. Let us assume they agree that Maslowski will earn two thirds of partnership profits and losses and Green one third. The entry to record Isaac's withdrawal at less than book value is

July 31	Isaac, Capital	31,000	
	Cash		10,000
	Note Payable to K. Isaac		15,000
	Green, Capital ($6,000 × ⅓)		2,000
	Maslowski, Capital ($6,000 × ⅔)		4,000
	To record withdrawal of K. Isaac from the partnership.		

Isaac's account is closed, and Maslowski and Green may or may not continue the business.

Withdrawal at More Than Book Value

The settlement with a withdrawing partner may allow him to take assets of greater value than the book value of his capital. Also, the remaining partners may be so eager for the withdrawing partner to leave the firm that they pay him a bonus to withdraw from the business. In either case, the partner's withdrawal causes a decrease in the book equity of the remaining partners. This decrease is allocated to the partners based on their profit-and-loss ratio.

Assume Chang, Daley and Evans share profits in a ratio of 3:2:1. Their partnership accounts include the following balances:

Cash	$ 50,000	Total liabilities..............	$110,000
Other assets	220,000	Chang, capital	80,000
		Daley, capital...............	50,000
		Evans, capital	30,000
Total assets	$270,000	Total liabilities and capital ...	$270,000

Assume Evans withdraws, taking $15,000 in cash and the new partnership's note for $25,000. This $40,000 settlement exceeds Evans's capital balance by $10,000. Chang and Daley share this loss in equity according to their profit-and-loss ratio (3:2). The withdrawal entry is

Nov. 30	Evans, Capital	30,000	
	Chang, Capital ($10,000 × ⅗)	6,000	
	Daley, Capital ($10,000 × ⅖)	4,000	
	Cash		15,000
	Note Payable to R. Evans		25,000
	To record withdrawal of R. Evans from the partnership.		

The withdrawal entry closes Evans's capital account and updates those of Chang and Daley.

Death of a Partner

The death of a partner, like any other form of partnership withdrawal, dissolves a partnership. The partnership accounts are adjusted to measure net income or loss for the fraction of the year up to the date of death, then closed to determine the partners' capital balances on that date. Settlement with the deceased partner's estate is based on the partnership agreement, with the estate commonly receiving partnership assets equal to the partner's capital balance. The partnership closes the deceased partner's capital account with a debit crediting a payable to the estate.

Alternatively, a remaining partner may purchase the deceased partner's equity. The deceased partner's equity is debited and the purchaser's equity is credited. The amount of this entry is the ending credit balance in the deceased partner's capital account.

Liquidation of a Partnership

Admission of a new partner or withdrawal or death of an existing partner dissolves the partnership. However, the business may continue operating with no apparent change to outsiders such as customers and creditors. Business **liquidation**, however, is the process of going out of business by selling the entity's assets and paying its liabilities. The final step in liquidation of a business is the *distribution of the remaining cash to the owners*. Before liquidating the business, the books should be adjusted and closed. After closing, only asset, liability and partners' capital accounts remain open.

Liquidation of a partnership includes three basic steps:

1. Sell the assets. Allocate the gain or loss to the partners' capital accounts based on the profit-and-loss ratio.
2. Pay the partnership liabilities.
3. Disburse the remaining cash to the partners based on their capital balances.

In actual practice, the liquidation of a business can stretch over weeks or months. Selling every asset and paying every liability of the entity may take a long time. To avoid excessive detail in our illustrations, we include only two asset categories, Cash and Noncash Assets, and a single liability category, Liabilities. Our examples also assume that the business sells the noncash assets in a single transaction and pays the liabilities in a single transaction.

Assume that Aviron, Bloch and Crane have shared profits and losses in the ratio of 3:1:1. (This ratio is equal to $\frac{3}{5}$, $\frac{1}{5}$, $\frac{1}{5}$, or a 60-percent, 20-percent, 20-percent sharing ratio.) They decide to liquidate their partnership. After the books are adjusted and closed, the general ledger contains the following balances:

Cash	$ 10,000	Liabilities	$ 30,000
Noncash assets	90,000	Aviron, capital	40,000
		Bloch, capital	20,000
		Crane, capital	10,000
Total assets	$100,000	Total liabilities and capital	$100,000

We will use the Aviron, Bloch and Crane partnership data to illustrate accounting for liquidation in three different situations.

Sale of Noncash Assets at a Gain

Assume the partnership sells its noncash assets (shown on the balance sheet at $90,000) for cash of $150,000. The partnership realizes a gain of $60,000, which is allocated to the partners based on their profit-and-loss-sharing ratio. The entry to record this sale and allocation of the gain is

<table>
<tr><td>Oct. 31</td><td>Cash ....</td><td>150,000</td><td></td></tr>
<tr><td></td><td>   Noncash Assets ....</td><td></td><td>90,000</td></tr>
<tr><td></td><td>   Aviron, Capital ($60,000 × .60)...........</td><td></td><td>36,000</td></tr>
<tr><td></td><td>   Bloch, Capital ($60,000 × .20) ....</td><td></td><td>12,000</td></tr>
<tr><td></td><td>   Crane, Capital ($60,000 × .20) ....</td><td></td><td>12,000</td></tr>
<tr><td></td><td>To sell noncash assets in liquidation and allocate gain to partners.</td><td></td><td></td></tr>
</table>

OBJECTIVE 6

Account for the liquidation of a partnership

The partnership must next pay off its liabilities:

<table>
<tr><td>Oct. 31</td><td>Liabilities ....</td><td>30,000</td><td></td></tr>
<tr><td></td><td>   Cash..................................</td><td></td><td>30,000</td></tr>
<tr><td></td><td>To pay liabilities in liquidation.</td><td></td><td></td></tr>
</table>

In the final liquidation transaction, the remaining cash is disbursed to the partners. The partners share in the cash according to their capital balances. (By contrast, *gains* and *losses* on the sale of assets are shared by the partners based on their profit-and-loss-sharing ratio.) The amount of cash left in the partnership is $130,000 – the $10,000 beginning balance plus the $150,000 cash sale of assets minus the $30,000 cash payment of liabilities. The partners divide the remaining cash according to their capital balances.

<table>
<tr><td>Oct. 31</td><td>Aviron, Capital ($40,000 + $36,000) ....</td><td>76,000</td><td></td></tr>
<tr><td></td><td>Bloch, Capital ($20,000 + $12,000) ....</td><td>32,000</td><td></td></tr>
<tr><td></td><td>Crane, Capital ($10,000 + $12,000) ....</td><td>22,000</td><td></td></tr>
<tr><td></td><td>   Cash..................................</td><td></td><td>130,000</td></tr>
<tr><td></td><td>To disburse cash to partners in liquidation.</td><td></td><td></td></tr>
</table>

A convenient way to summarize the transactions in a partnership liquidation is given in Exhibit 13-1.

EXHIBIT 13-1   *Partnership Liquidation: Sale of Assets at a Gain*

				Capital		
	Cash	+ Noncash Assets =	Liabilities +	Aviron (60%) +	Bloch (20%) +	Crane (20%)
Balances before sale of assets....	$ 10,000	$90,000	$30,000	$40,000	$20,000	$10,000
Sale of assets and sharing of gain	150,000	(90,000)		36,000	12,000	12,000
Balances......................	160,000	-0-	30,000	76,000	32,000	22,000
Payment of liabilities...........	(30,000)		(30,000)			
Balances......................	130,000	-0-	-0-	76,000	32,000	22,000
Disbursement of cash to partners	(130,000)			(76,000)	(32,000)	(22,000)
Balances......................	$ -0-	$ -0-	$ -0-	$ -0-	$ -0-	$ -0-

After the disbursement of cash to the partners, the business has no assets, liabilities or owners' equity. The balances are all zero. At all times, partnership assets must equal partnership liabilities plus partnership capital, according to the accounting equation:

	Total assets	=	Total liabilities	+	Total capital
Before liquidation	$100,000	=	$30,000	+	$ 70,000
After sale of assets	160,000	=	30,000	+	130,000
After payment of liabilities	130,000	=	0	+	130,000
After final disbursement to the partners	0	=	0	+	0

Sale of Noncash Assets at a Loss

Assume that Aviron, Bloch and Crane sell the noncash assets for $75,000, realizing a loss of $15,000.

The summary of transactions appears in Exhibit 13-2. The journal entries to record the liquidation transactions are

Oct. 31	Cash	75,000	
	Aviron, Capital ($15,000 × .60)	9,000	
	Bloch, Capital ($15,000 × .20)	3,000	
	Crane, Capital ($15,000 × .20)	3,000	
	Noncash Assets		90,000
	To sell noncash assets in liquidation and allocate loss to partners.		
31	Liabilities	30,000	
	Cash..................................		30,000
	To pay liabilities in liquidation.		
31	Aviron, Capital ($40,000 − $9,000)	31,000	
	Bloch, Capital ($20,000 − $3,000)	17,000	
	Crane, Capital ($10,000 − $3,000)	7,000	
	Cash..................................		55,000
	To disburse cash to partners in liquidation.		

EXHIBIT 13-2 *Partnership Liquidation: Sale of Assets at a Loss*

				Capital		
	Cash	+ Noncash Assets =	Liabilities +	Aviron (60%) +	Bloch (20%) +	Crane (20%)
Balances before sale of assets	$ 10,000	$90,000	$30,000	$40,000	$20,000	$10,000
Sale of assets and sharing of loss................	75,000	(90,000)		(9,000)	(3,000)	(3,000)
Balances	85,000	-0-	30,000	31,000	17,000	7,000
Payment of liabilities	(30,000)		(30,000)			
Balances	55,000	-0-	-0-	31,000	17,000	7,000
Disbursement of cash to partners	(55,000)			(31,000)	(17,000)	(7,000)
Balances	$ -0-	$ -0-	$ -0-	$ -0-	$ -0-	$ -0-

Sale of Noncash Assets at a Loss — Deficiency in a Partner's Capital Account The sale of noncash assets at a loss may result in a debit balance in a partner's capital account. This situation is called a **capital deficiency** because the partner's capital balance is insufficient to cover his or her share of the partnership's loss. The unlimited liability of partners forces the other partners to absorb this deficiency through debits to their own capital accounts if the deficient partner does not erase the deficiency. The deficiency is a loss to the other partners, and they share it based on their profit-and-loss ratio.

Deficient Partner Unable to Erase Deficiency   Assume that Aviron, Bloch and Crane's partnership has had losses for several years. The market value of the noncash assets of the business is far less than book value ($90,000). In liquidation, the partnership sells these assets for $30,000, realizing a loss of $60,000. Crane's 20 percent share of this loss is $12,000. Because the loss exceeds his $10,000 capital balance, Crane's account has a $2,000 deficit. Crane is obligated to contribute personal funds to the business in order to meet this debt. Assume that Crane cannot erase the deficiency by contributing personal assets. Because of mutual agency, the other partners must absorb the deficiency before the final distribution of cash.

Because Aviron and Bloch share losses in the ratio of 3:1, Aviron absorbs three fourths of the deficiency and Bloch absorbs one fourth. Aviron's share of Crane's $2,000 deficiency is $1,500 ($2,000 × ¾), and Bloch's share is $500 ($2,000 × ¼).

The journal entries to record the foregoing liquidation transactions are

Oct. 31	Cash	30,000	
	Aviron, Capital ($60,000 × .60)	36,000	
	Bloch, Capital ($60,000 × .20)	12,000	
	Crane, Capital ($60,000 × .20)	12,000	
	Noncash Assets		90,000
	To sell noncash assets in liquidation and allocate loss to partners.		
31	Liabilities	30,000	
	Cash		30,000
	To pay liabilities in liquidation.		
31	Aviron, Capital ($2,000 × ¾)	1,500	
	Bloch, Capital ($2,000 × ¼)	500	
	Crane, Capital		2,000
	To allocate Crane's capital deficiency to the other partners.		
31	Aviron, Capital ($40,000 − $36,000 − $1,500)	2,500	
	Bloch, Capital ($20,000 − $12,000 − $500)	7,500	
	Cash		10,000
	To disburse cash to partners in liquidation.		

The summary of transactions in Exhibit 13-3 includes a separate transaction (highlighted) to allocate Crane's deficiency to Aviron and Bloch.

Deficient Partner Erases Deficiency   A partner may erase his or her deficiency by contributing cash or other assets to the partnership. Such contributions are credited to the deficient partner's account and then distributed to the other

EXHIBIT 13-3   *Deficient Partner Unable to Erase a Capital Deficiency*

				Capital		
	Cash	+ Noncash Assets =	Liabilities +	Aviron (60%) +	Bloch (20%) +	Crane (20%)
Balances before sale of assets	$ 10,000	$90,000	$30,000	$40,000	$20,000	$10,000
Sale of assets and sharing of loss..............	30,000	(90,000)		(36,000)	(12,000)	(12,000)
Balances......................	40,000	-0-	30,000	4,000	8,000	(2,000)
Payment of liabilities...........	(30,000)		(30,000)			
Sharing of Crane's deficiency by Aviron and Bloch.........				(1,500)	(500)	2,000
Balances......................	10,000	-0-	-0-	2,500	7,500	-0-
Disbursement of cash to partners	(10,000)			(2,500)	(7,500)	-0-
Balances......................	$ -0-	$ -0-	$ -0-	$ -0-	$ -0-	$ -0-

partners. Suppose Crane erases his deficiency by investing $2,000 cash in the partnership.

The journal entries to record Crane's contribution and the disbursement of cash to the partners are

Oct. 31   Cash   2,000
                Crane, Capital   2,000
           Crane's contribution to erase his capital
           deficiency in liquidation.

    31   Aviron, Capital   4,000
         Bloch, Capital   8,000
                Cash..................................   12,000
         To disburse cash to partners in liquidation.

In this case, the summary of transactions, beginning with the balances after payment of the liabilities, appears in Exhibit 13-4.

EXHIBIT 13-4   *Partnership Liquidation: Partner Erases Capital Deficiency*

				Capital		
	Cash	+ Noncash Assets =	Liabilities +	Aviron (60%) +	Bloch (20%) +	Crane (20%)
Balances after payment of liabilities	$ 10,000	$ -0-	$ -0-	$ 4,000	$ 8,000	$(2,000)
Crane's contribution to erase his deficiency	2,000					2,000
Balances	12,000	-0-	-0-	4,000	8,000	-0-
Disbursement of cash to partners ...	(12,000)			(4,000)	(8,000)	-0-
Balances	$ -0-	$ -0-	$ -0-	$ -0-	$ -0-	$ -0-

Partnership Financial Statements _____

Partnership financial statements are much like those of a proprietorship. However, a partnership income statement includes a section showing the division of net income to the partners. For example, the partnership of Gray and Hayward might report its income statement for the year ended June 30, 19X6 as follows:

Gray and Hayward Income Statement for the year ended June 30, 19X6	
Sales revenue	$381,000
Net income	$ 79,000
Allocation of net income	
M. Gray	$ 36,600
L. Hayward	42,400
Total	$ 79,000

Large partnerships may not find it feasible to report the net income of every partner. Instead, the firm may report the allocation of net income to active and retired partners and average earnings per partner. For example, the CA firm of Arthur Andersen & Company reported the following:

The Arthur Andersen Worldwide Organization Combined Statement of Earnings for the year ended August 31, 19X0	
dollar amounts in thousands	
Fees for Professional Services	$805,492
Earnings for the year	$181,880
Allocation of earnings	
To partners active during the year —	
Resigned, retired and deceased partners	$ 9,901
Partners active at year end	160,270
To retired and deceased partners —	
Retirement and death benefits	4,310
Not allocated to partners —	
Retained for specific partnership purposes	7,399
	$181,880
Average earnings per partner active at year end	
(1,170 partners)	$137

Exhibit 13-5 summarizes the financial statements of a proprietorship and a partnership.

EXHIBIT 13-5   *Financial Statements of a Proprietorship and a Partnership*

Income Statements
for the year ended December 31, 19X1

Proprietorship		Partnership		
Revenues	$460	Revenues		$460
Expenses	(270)	Expenses		(270)
Net income	$190	Net income		$190
		Allocation of net income		
		To Smith	$114	
		To Jones..............	76	$190

Statements of Owner's Equity
for the year ended December 31, 19X1

Proprietorship		Partnership		
			Smith	*Jones*
Capital,		Capital,		
December 31, 19X0	$ 90	December 31, 19X0	$ 50	$ 40
Additional investments	10	Additional investments...	10	—
Net income	190	Net income	114	76
Subtotal	290	Subtotal	174	116
Drawings	(120)	Drawings	(72)	(48)
Capital,		Capital,		
December 31, 19X1	$170	December 31, 19X1.....	$102	$ 68

Balance Sheets
December 31, 19X1

Proprietorship		Partnership	
		Assets	
Cash and other assets	$170	Cash and other assets	$170
		Equities	
		Smith, capital..................	$102
		Jones, capital	68
Smith, capital	$170	Total capital	$170

Summary Problem for Your Review

The partnership of Prolux, Roberts and Satulsky is liquidating. Its accounts
have the following balances after closing:

Cash	$ 22,000	Liabilities	$ 77,000
Noncash assets	104,000	Prolux, capital	23,000
		Roberts, capital	10,000
		Satulsky, capital	16,000
Total assets	$126,000	Total liabilities and capital ...	$126,000

The partnership agreement allocates profits to Prolux, Roberts and Satulsky in the ratio of 3:4:3. In liquidation, the noncash assets were sold in a single transaction for $64,000 on May 31, 19X7. The partnership paid the liabilities the same day.

Required

1. Journalize the liquidation transactions. The partnership books remain open until June 7 to allow Roberts to make an additional $4,000 contribution to the business in view of her capital deficiency. This cash is immediately disbursed to the other partners. Use T-accounts if necessary.

2. Prepare a summary of the liquidation transactions, as illustrated in the chapter. Roberts invests cash of $4,000 in the partnership in partial settlement of her capital deficiency. The other partners absorb the remainder of Roberts's capital deficiency.

SOLUTION TO REVIEW PROBLEM

Requirement 1

May 31	Cash	64,000	
	Prolux, Capital		
	[($104,000 − $64,000) × .30]	12,000	
	Roberts, Capital		
	[($104,000 − $64,000) × .40]	16,000	
	Satulsky, Capital		
	[($104,000 − $64,000) × .30]	12,000	
	Noncash Assets		104,000
	To sell noncash assets in liquidation and distribute loss to partners.		
31	Liabilities	77,000	
	Cash		77,000
	To pay liabilities in liquidation.		
June 7	Cash	4,000	
	Roberts, Capital		4,000
	Roberts's contribution to erase part of her capital deficiency in liquidation.		

After posting the entries, Roberts's capital account still has a $2,000 deficiency, indicated by its debit balance:

Roberts, Capital			
Loss on sale	16,000	Bal.	10,000
		Investment	4,000
Bal.	2,000		

Prolux and Satulsky must make up Roberts's remaining $2,000 deficiency.

Since Prolux and Satulsky had equal shares in the partnership profit-and-loss ratio (30 percent each), they divide Roberts's deficiency equally.

June 7	Prolux, Capital ($2,000 × ½)	1,000
	Satulsky, Capital ($2,000 × ½)	1,000
	Roberts, Capital.	2,000
	To allocate Roberts's capital deficiency to the other partners.	

At this point, the capital accounts of Prolux and Satulsky appear as follows:

Prolux, Capital

Loss on sale 12,000		Bal.	23,000
Loss on Roberts 1,000			
		Bal.	10,000

Satulsky, Capital

Loss on sale 12,000		Bal.	16,000
Loss on Roberts 1,000			
		Bal.	3,000

The final disbursement entry is

June 7	Prolux, Capital	10,000
	Satulsky, Capital	3,000
	Cash	13,000
	To disburse cash to partners in liquidation.	

Activity in the Cash account appears as follows:

Cash

Bal.	22,000	Payment of liabilities	77,000
Sale of assets	64,000		
Roberts's contribution	4,000		
Bal.	13,000	Final distribution	13,000

Requirement 2

					Capital		
	Cash	+ Noncash Assets	= Liabilities +	**Prolux** *(30%)*	+	**Roberts** *(40%)*	+ **Satulsky** *(30%)*
Balances before sale of assets	$ 22,000	$ 104,000	$ 77,000	$ 23,000		$ 10,000	$ 16,000
Sale of assets and sharing of loss . . .	64,000	(104,000)		(12,000)		(16,000)	(12,000)
Balances	86,000	-0-	77,000	11,000		(6,000)	4,000
Payment of liabilities	(77,000)		(77,000)				
Balances	9,000	-0-	-0-	11,000		(6,000)	4,000
Roberts's investment of cash to erase part of her deficiency	4,000					4,000	
Balances	13,000	-0-	-0-	11,000		(2,000)	4,000
Sharing of Roberts's deficiency by Prolux and Satulsky				(1,000)		2,000	(1,000)
Balances	13,000	-0-	-0-	10,000		-0-	3,000
Disbursement of cash to partners . .	(13,000)			(10,000)			(3,000)
Balances	$ -0-	$ -0-	$ -0-	$ -0-		$ -0-	$ -0-

Summary

A *partnership* is a business co-owned by two or more persons for profit. The characteristics of this form of business organization are its *ease of formation, limited life, mutual agency, unlimited liability* and *no partnership income taxes.*

A written *partnership agreement* or *articles of partnership* establishes procedure for admission of a new partner, withdrawals of a partner, and the sharing of profits and losses among the partners.

When a new partner is admitted to the firm or an existing partner withdraws, the old partnership is *dissolved* or ceases to exist. A new partnership may or may not emerge to continue the business.

Accounting for a partnership is similar to accounting for a proprietorship. However, a partnership has more than one owner. Each partner has an individual capital account and a withdrawal account.

Partners share net income or loss in any manner they choose. Common sharing agreements base the *profit-and-loss ratio* on a stated fraction, partners' capital contributions, and/or their service to the partnership. Some partnerships call the cash withdrawals of partners *salaries* and *interest*, but these amounts are not expenses of the business. Instead, they are merely ways of allocating partnership net income to the partners.

An outside person may become a partner by purchasing a current partner's interest or by investing in the partnership. In some cases the new partner must pay the current partners a bonus to join. In other situations the new partner may receive a bonus to join.

When a partner withdraws, partnership assets may be reappraised. Partners share any gain or loss on the asset revaluation based on their profit-and-loss ratio. The withdrawing partner may receive payment equal to, greater than or less than his or her capital book value, depending on the agreement with the other partners.

In *liquidation*, a partnership goes out of business by selling the assets, paying the liabilities and disbursing any remaining cash to the partners. Any partner's capital deficiency, which may result from sale of assets at a loss, must be absorbed before remaining cash is distributed.

Partnership *financial statements* are similar to those of a proprietorship. However, the partnership income statement commonly reports the allocation of net income to the partners.

Self-Study Questions

Test your understanding of the chapter by marking the correct answer for each of the following questions:

1. Which of these characteristics does *not* apply to a partnership? *(p. 532)*
   a. Unlimited life
   b. Mutual agency
   c. Unlimited liability
   d. No business income tax
2. A partnership records a partner's investment of assets in the business at *(p. 534)*
   a. The partner's book value of the assets invested
   b. The market value of the assets invested
   c. A special value set by the partners
   d. Any of the above, depending upon the partnership agreement
3. The partnership of Lane, Murdock and Nu divides profits in the ratio of 4:5:3. During 19X6, the business earned $40,000. Nu's share of this income is *(p. 535)*
   a. $10,000
   b. $13,333
   c. $16,000
   d. $16,667
4. Suppose the partnership of Lane, Murdock and Nu in the preceding question lost $40,000 during 19X6. Murdock's share of this loss is *(p. 535)*
   a. Not determinable because the ratio applies only to profits
   b. $13,333
   c. $16,000
   d. $16,667

5. Placido, Quinn and Rolfe share profits and losses ⅕, ⅙ and ¹⁹⁄₃₀. During 19X3, the first year of their partnership, the business earned $120,000 and each partner withdrew $50,000 for personal use. What is the balance in Rolfe's capital account after all closing entries? *(p. 540)*
   a. Not determinable because Rolfe's beginning capital balance is not given
   b. Minus $10,000
   c. $26,000
   d. $70,000
6. Fuller buys into the partnership of Graff and Harrell by purchasing a one-third interest for $55,000. Prior to Fuller's entry, Graff's capital balance was $46,000, and Harrell's balance was $52,000. The entry to record Fuller's buying into the business is *(p. 543)*

   a. Cash.............. 55,000
          Fuller, Capital ...   55,000

   b. Graff, Capital 27,500
      Harrell, Capital 27,500
          Fuller, Capital ...   55,000

   c. Cash.............. 55,000
          Fuller, Capital ...   51,000
          Graff, Capital   2,000
          Harrell, Capital ..   2,000

   d. Cash.............. 51,000
      Graff, Capital 2,000
      Harrell, Capital 2,000
          Fuller, Capital ...   55,000
7. Thomas, Valik and Wollenberg share profits and losses equally. Their capital balances are $40,000, $50,000 and $60,000 respectively, when Wollenberg sells her interest in the partnership to Valik for $90,000. Thomas and Valik continue the business. Immediately after Wollenberg's retirement, the total assets of the partnership are *(p. 546)*
   a. Increased by $30,000
   b. Increased by $90,000
   c. Decreased by $60,000
   d. The same as before Wollenberg sold her interest to Valik
8. Prior to Hogg's withdrawal from the partnership of Hogg, Hamm and Bacon, the partners' capital balances were $140,000, $110,000 and $250,000 respectively. The partners share profits and losses ⅓, ¼ and ⁵⁄₁₂. The appraisal indicates that assets should be written down by $36,000. Hamm's share of the write-down is *(p. 546)*
   a. $7,920   c. $12,000
   b. 9,000   d. $18,000
9. Closing the business, selling the assets, paying the liabilities and disbursing remaining cash to the owners is called *(p. 549)*
   a. Dissolution   c. Withdrawal
   b. Forming a new partnership d. Liquidation
10. A and B have shared profits and losses equally. Immediately prior to the final cash disbursement in a liquidation of their partnership, the books show:

Cash	=	Liabilities	+	A, Capital	+	B, Capital
$100,000		$-0-		$60,000		$40,000

How much cash should A receive? *(p. 550)*
   a. $40,000   c. $60,000
   b. $50,000   d. None of the above

Answers to the self-study questions are at the end of the chapter.

Accounting Vocabulary

articles of partnership (p. 532)
capital deficiency (p. 552)
dissolution (p. 532)
liquidation (p. 549)
mutual agency (p. 532)
partnership agreement (p. 532)
unlimited personal liability (p. 533)

Assignment Material _____

Questions

1. What is another name for a partnership agreement? List eight items that the agreement should specify.

2. Montgomery, who is a partner in M&N Associates, commits the firm to a contract for a job within the scope of its regular business operations. What term describes Montgomery's ability to obligate the partnership?

3. If a partnership cannot pay a debt, who must make payment? What term describes this obligation of the partners?

4. How is partnership income taxed?

5. Identify the advantages and disadvantages of the partnership form of business organization.

6. Randall and Smith's partnership agreement states that Randall gets 60 percent of profits and Smith gets 40 percent. If the agreement does not discuss the treatment of losses, how are losses shared? How do the partners share profits and losses if the agreement specifies no profit-and-loss-sharing ratio?

7. Are salary and interest allocated to partners' expenses of the business? Why or why not?

8. What determines the amount of the credit to a partner's capital account when the partner contributes assets other than cash to the business?

9. Do partner withdrawals of cash for personal use affect the sharing of profits and losses by the partner? If so, explain how. If not, explain why not.

10. Name two events that can cause the dissolution of a partnership?

11. Briefly describe how to account for the purchase of an existing partner's interest in the business.

12. Malcolm purchases Brown's interest in the Brown & Kareem partnership. What right does Malcolm obtain from the purchase? What is required for Malcolm to become Kareem's partner?

13. Assissi and Carter each have capital of $75,000 in their business and share profits in the ratio of 55:45. Denman acquires a one-fifth share in the partnership by investing cash of $50,000. What are the capital balances of the three partners immediately after Denman is admitted?

14. When a partner resigns from the partnership and receives assets greater than her capital balance, how is the excess shared by the other partners?

15. Why are the assets of a partnership often revalued when a partner is about to withdraw from the firm?

16. Distinguish between dissolution and liquidation of a partnership.

17. Name the three steps in liquidating a partnership.

18. Why does the cash of a partnership equal the sum of its partner capital balances after the business sells its noncash assets and pays its liabilities?

19. The partnership of Ralls and Sauls is in the process of liquidation. How do the partners share (a) gains and losses on the sale of noncash assets and (b) the final cash disbursement?

20. Fernandez, Chretien and Ghiz are partners, sharing profits and losses in the ratio of 3:2:1. In liquidation, Ghiz's capital balance is less than his share of losses on the sale of assets. What becomes of Ghiz's capital deficiency if Ghiz cannot make it up?

21. Compare and contrast the financial statements of a proprietorship and a partnership.

22. Summarize the situations in which partnership allocations are based on (a) the profit-and-loss ratio and (b) the partners' capital balances.

Exercises

Exercise 13-1   *Recording a partner's investment*

Ann Clinton has operated an apartment-locater service as a proprietorship. She and Amanda Doss have decided to reorganize the business as a partnership. Ann's investment in the partnership consists of cash, $8,100; accounts receivable, $13,600 less allowance for uncollectibles, $800; office furniture, $2,700 less accumulated depreciation, $1,100; a small building, $55,000 less accumulated depreciation, $27,500; accounts payable, $3,300; and a note payable to the bank, $10,000.

To determine Ann's equity in the partnership, she and Amanda hire an independent appraiser. This outside party provides the following market values of the assets and liabilities that Ann is contributing to the business: cash, accounts receivable, office furniture and a related accumulated depreciation, accounts payable, and note payable — the same as Ann's book value; allowance for uncollectible accounts, $2,900; building, $70,000 less accumulated depreciation, $35,000; and accrued expenses payable (including interest on the note payable), $1,200.

Required

Make the entry on the partnership books to record Ann's investment.

Exercise 13-2   *Preparing a partnership balance sheet*

On October 31, 19X9, Alpha and Beta agree to combine their proprietorships as a partnership. Their balance sheets on October 31 are as follows:

	Alpha's Business		**Beta's Business**	
	Book Value	**Current Market Value**	**Book Value**	**Current Market Value**
Assets				
Cash	$ 8,000	$ 8,000	$ 3,700	$ 3,700
Accounts receivable (net)	13,000	11,800	22,000	20,200
Inventory	34,000	35,100	51,000	46,000
Plant assets (net)	53,500	57,400	121,800	123,500
Total assets.................	$108,500	$112,300	$198,500	$193,400
Liabilities				
Accounts payable	$ 9,100	$ 9,100	$ 23,600	$ 23,600
Accrued expenses payable	$ 800	$ 800	$ 2,200	$ 2,200
Notes payable	—	—	75,000	75,000
Alpha, capital................	98,600	102,400		
Beta, capital			97,700	92,600
Total liabilities and capital	$108,500	$112,300	$198,500	$193,400

Required

Prepare the partnership balance sheet at October 31, 19X9.

Exercise 13-3   *Computing partners' shares of net income*

Roy Dean and Joe Edwards form a partnership, investing $30,000 and $60,000 respectively. Determine their shares of net income or net loss for each of the following situations:

a. Net loss is $69,000, and the partners have no written partnership agreement.

b.   Net income is $84,000, and the partnership agreement states that the partners share profits and losses based on their capital contributions.

c.   Net loss is $63,000, and the partnership agreement states that the partners share profits based on their capital contributions.

d.   Net income is $105,000. The first $40,000 is shared based on the partner capital contributions. The next $30,000 is based on partner service, with Dean receiving 30 percent and Edwards receiving 70 percent. The remainder is shared equally.

Exercise 13-4   *Computing partners' capital balances*

Roy Dean withdrew cash of $52,000 for personal use and Joe Edwards withdrew cash of $60,000 during the year. Using the data from situation d in Exercise 13-3, journalize the entries to close the (a) income summary account and (b) the partners' drawing accounts. Explanations are not required.

Indicate the amount of increase or decrease in each partner's capital balance. What was the overall effect on partnership capital?

Exercise 13-5   *Admitting a new partner*

Jack Phillips is admitted to a partnership. Prior to the admission of Phillips, the partnership books show Susan Recker's capital balance at $80,000 and Lewis Schmitz's capital balance at $40,000. Compute the amount of each partner's equity on the books of the new partnership under each of the following plans:

a.   Phillips pays $30,000 for Schmitz's equity. Phillips's payment is not an investment in the partnership but instead goes directly to Schmitz.

b.   Phillips invests $30,000 to acquire a one-fifth interest in the partnership.

c.   Phillips invests $60,000 to acquire a one-fourth interest in the partnership.

Exercise 13-6   *Recording the admission of a new partner*

Make the partnership journal entry to record the admission of Phillips under plans a, b and c in Exercise 13-5. Explanations are not required.

Exercise 13-7   *Withdrawal of a partner*

After closing the books, T&W's partnership balance sheet reports owner's equity of $50,000 for T. and $70,000 for W. T. is withdrawing from the firm. The partners agree to write down partnership assets by $30,000. They have shared profits and losses in the ratio of one third to T. and two thirds to W. If the partnership agreement states that a withdrawing partner will receive assets equal to the book value of his owner's equity, how much will T. receive?

W. will continue to operate the business as a proprietorship. What is W.'s beginning owner's equity on the proprietorship books?

Exercise 13-8   *Withdrawal of a partner*

Lana Brown is retiring from the partnership of Brown, Green and White on May 31. After the books are closed on that date, the partner capital balances are Brown, $36,000; Green, $51,000; and White, $22,000. The partners agree to have the partnership assets revalued to current market values. The independent appraiser reports that the book value of the inventory should be decreased by $8,000, and the book value of the building should be increased by $32,000. The partners agree to these revaluations. The profit-and-loss ratio has been 5:3:2 for Brown, Green and White respectively. Brown receives $25,000 cash and a $25,000 note from the partnership. Journalize (a) the asset revaluations and (b) Brown's withdrawal from the firm.

Exercise 13-9   *Liquidation of a partnership*

Marsh, Ng and Orsulak are liquidating their partnership. Before selling the noncash assets and paying the liabilities, the capital balances are Marsh, $23,000; Ng, $14,000; and Orsulak, $11,000. The partnership agreement divides profits and losses equally.

a.   After selling the noncash assets and paying the liabilities, the partnership has cash of $48,000. How much cash will each partner receive in final liquidation?

b.   After selling the noncash assets and paying the liabilities, the partnership has cash of $45,000. How much cash will each partner receive in final liquidation?

Exercise 13-10   *Liquidation of a partnership*

Prior to liquidation, the accounting records of Pratt, Qualls and Ramirez included the following balances and profit-and-loss-sharing percentages:

				Capital		
	Cash +	Noncash Assets	= Liabilities +	*Pratt* *(40%)*	*Qualls* *(30%)*	*Ramirez* *(30%)*
Balances before sale of assets	$8,000	$57,000	$19,000	$20,000	$15,000	$11,000

The partnership sold the noncash assets for $73,000, paid the liabilities and disbursed the remaining cash to the partners. Complete the summary of transactions in the liquidation of the partnership. Use the format illustrated in the chapter.

Problems   *(Group A)*

Problem 13-1A   *Investments by partners*

Papineau and Hutton formed a partnership on March 15. The partners agreed to invest equal amounts of capital. Hutton invested her proprietorship's assets and liabilities (credit balances in parentheses):

	Hutton's Book Value	Current Market Value
Accounts receivable	$ 12,000	$ 12,000
Allowance for doubtful accounts . . .	(740)	(1,360)
Inventory	43,850	51,220
Prepaid expenses	2,400	2,400
Store equipment	36,700	31,000
Accumulated depreciation	(9,200)	(7,800)
Accounts payable	(22,300)	(22,300)

On March 15, Papineau invested cash in an amount equal to the current market value of Hutton's partnership capital, which was $65,160. The partners decided that Hutton would earn 70 percent of partnership profits because she would manage the business. Papineau agreed to accept 30 percent of profits. During the period ended December 31, the partnership earned $55,000. Papineau's drawings were $12,000 and Hutton's drawings were $36,000.

Required

1.   Journalize the partners' initial investments.
2.   Prepare the partnership balance sheet immediately after its formation on March 15.
3.   Journalize the December 31 entries to close the income summary account and the partner drawing accounts.

Problem 13-2A   *Computing partners' shares of net income and net loss*

J. Warner, S. Deitmer and R. Mullaney have formed a partnership. Warner invested $20,000, Deitmer $40,000 and Mullaney $60,000. Warner will manage the store, Deitmer will work in the store three quarters of the time, and Mullaney will not work in the business.

Required

1. Compute the partners' shares of profits and losses under each of the following plans. Use this format for your answer:

	Warner	Deitmer	Mullaney	Total
Total net income (net loss)				
Allocation to the partners				
Warner				
Deitmer				
Mullaney.				
Total.				
Net income (loss) left for allocation . . .				
Add a line for "Net income allocated to partners" as necessary.				

a. Net income is $27,000, and the articles of partnership do not specify how profits and losses are shared.

b. Net loss is $47,000, and the partnership agreement allocates 45 percent of profits to Warner, 35 percent to Deitmer and 20 percent to Mullaney. The agreement does not discuss the sharing of losses.

c. Net income is $104,000. The first $50,000 is allocated based on salaries of $34,000 for Warner and $16,000 for Deitmer. The remainder is allocated based on partner capital contributions.

d. Net income for the year ended September 30, 19X4 is $81,000. The first $42,000 is allocated based on partner capital contributions. The next $30,000 is based on service, with $20,000 going to Warner and $10,000 going to Deitmer. Any remainder is shared equally.

2. Revenues for the year ended September 30, 19X4 were $621,000 and expenses were $540,000. Under plan d, prepare the partnership income statement for the year.

Problem 13-3A   *Recording changes in partnership capital*

Red River Resort is a partnership, and its owners are considering admitting Greg Lake as a new partner. On July 31 of the current year, the capital accounts of the three existing partners and their shares of profits and losses are as follows:

	Capital	Profit-and-Loss Ratio
Ellen Urlang	$48,000	1/6
Amy Sharp	64,000	1/3
Bob Hayes.	88,000	1/2

Required

Journalize the admission of Lake as a partner on July 31 for each of the following independent situations:

1. Urlang gives her partnership share to Lake, who is her nephew.

2. Lake pays Hayes $50,000 cash to purchase one half of Hayes's interest.
3. Lake invests $50,000 in the partnership, acquiring a one-fifth interest in the business.
4. Lake invests $40,000 in the partnership, acquiring a one-eighth interest in the business.
5. Lake invests $30,000 in the partnership, acquiring a 15 percent interest in the business.

Problem 13-4A   *Recording changes in partnership capital*

Boat Town is a partnership owned by three individuals. The partners share profits and losses in the ratio of 30 percent to Golden, 30 percent to Ramos and 40 percent to Miller. At December 31, 19X6, the firm has the following balance sheet:

Cash		$ 25,000	Total liabilities	$103,000
Accounts receivable	$ 16,000			
Less: Allowance for uncollectibles ..	1,000	15,000		
Inventory.............		51,000	Golden, capital	23,000
Equipment............	130,000		Miller, capital.........	41,000
Less: Accumulated depreciation	30,000	100,000	Ramos, capital .... Total liabilities and	24,000
Total assets		$191,000	capital	$191,000

Golden withdraws from the partnership on this date.

Required

Record Golden's withdrawal from the partnership under the following plans:

1. Golden gives his interest in the business to Kamanga, his son-in-law.
2. In personal transactions, Golden sells his equity in the partnership to Meyers and Shankar, who each pay Golden $15,000 for one half of his interest. Miller and Ramos agree to accept Meyers and Shankar as partners.
3. The partnership pays Golden cash of $5,000 and gives him a note payable for the remainder of his book equity in settlement of his partnership interest.
4. Golden receives cash of $10,000 and a note for $20,000 from the partnership.
5. The partners agree that the equipment is worth $150,000 and that accumulated depreciation should remain at $30,000. After the revaluation, the partnership settles with Golden by giving him cash of $10,000 and inventory for the remainder of his book equity.

Problem 13-5A   *Liquidation of a partnership*

The partnership of Yagoda, Kelly and Dobbs has experienced operating losses for three consecutive years. The partners, who have shared profits and losses in the ratio of Yagoda 15 percent, Kelly 60 percent and Dobbs 25 percent, are considering the liquidation of the business. They ask you to analyse the effects of liquidation under various assumptions about the sale of the noncash assets. They present the following condensed partnership balance sheet at December 31, end of the current year:

Cash	$ 18,000	Liabilities	$ 74,000
Noncash assets	163,000	Yagoda, capital	19,000
		Kelly, capital	66,000
		Dobbs, capital	22,000
Total assets	$181,000	Total liabilities and capital ...	$181,000

Required

1. Prepare a summary of liquidation transactions (as illustrated in the chapter) for each of the following situations:
   a. The noncash assets are sold for $175,000.
   b. The noncash assets are sold for $133,000.
   c. The noncash assets are sold for $63,000, and the partner with a capital deficiency is personally bankrupt.
   d. The noncash assets are sold for $60,000, and the partner with a capital deficiency pays cash of $1,500 to the partnership to erase part of the deficiency.
2. Make the journal entries to record the liquidation transactions in question 1d.

Problem 13-6A   *Liquidation of a partnership*

Triad Company is a partnership owned by Ryan, St. Laurent and Goldberg, who share profits and losses in the ratio of 1:3:4. The adjusted trial balance of the partnership (in condensed form) at June 30, end of the current fiscal year, follows:

Triad Company		
Adjusted Trial Balance		
June 30, 19XX		
Cash	$ 14,000	
Noncash assets	116,000	
Liabilities		$100,000
Ryan, capital		22,000
St. Laurent, capital		41,000
Goldberg, capital..............		62,000
Ryan, drawing................	24,000	
St. Laurent, drawing	35,000	
Goldberg, drawing	54,000	
Revenues		108,000
Expenses.....................	90,000	
Totals	$333,000	$333,000

Required

1. Prepare the June 30 entries to close the revenue, expense, income summary and drawing accounts.
2. Insert the opening capital balances in the partner capital accounts, post the closing entries to the capital accounts and determine each partner's ending capital balance.
3. The partnership liquidates on June 30 by selling the noncash assets for $100,000. Using the ending balances of the partner capital accounts, prepare a summary of liquidation transactions (as illustrated in the chapter). Any partner with a capital deficiency is unable to contribute assets to erase the deficiency.

(Group B)

Problem 13-1B   *Investments by partners*

On June 30, McMinn and Pellerin formed a partnership. The partners agreed to invest equal amounts of capital. McMinn invested her proprietorship's assets and liabilities (credit balances in parentheses):

	McMinn's Book Value	Current Market Value
Accounts receivable	$ 8,100	$ 8,100
Allowance for doubtful accounts ...	(-0-)	(1,050)
Inventory	22,340	29,000
Prepaid expenses.................	1,700	1,700
Office equipment.................	45,900	41,400
Accumulated depreciation.........	(15,300)	(13,800)
Accounts payable	(19,100)	(19,100)

On June 30, Pellerin invested cash in an amount equal to the current market value of McMinn's partnership capital, which was $46,250. The partners decided that McMinn would earn two thirds of partnership profits because she would manage the business. Pellerin agreed to accept one third of profits. During the remainder of the year, the partnership earned $48,000. McMinn's drawings were $35,200, and Pellerin's drawings were $14,000.

Required

1. Journalize the partners' initial investments.
2. Prepare the partnership balance sheet immediately after its formation on June 30.
3. Journalize the December 31 entries to close the income summary account and the partner drawing accounts.

Problem 13-2B   *Computing partners' shares of net income and net loss*

D. Hogan, E. Stanford and S. Reichlin have formed a partnership. Hogan invested $6,000, Stanford $18,000 and Reichlin $36,000. Hogan will manage the store, Stanford will work in the store half time, and Reichlin will not work in the business.

Required

1. Compute the partners' shares of profits and losses under each of the following plans. Use this format for your answer:

	Hogan	Stanford	Reichlin	Total
Total net income (net loss)				
Allocation to the partners:				
Hogan				
Stanford				
Reichlin				
Total........................				
Net income (loss) left for allocation ...				
Add a line for "Net income allocated to partners" as necessary.				

a. Net loss is $51,600, and the articles of partnership do not specify how profits and losses are shared.
b. Net loss is $70,000, and the partnership agreement allocates 40 percent of profits to Hogan, 25 percent to Stanford and 35 percent to Reichlin. The agreement does not discuss the sharing of losses.

c. Net income is $88,000. The first $40,000 is allocated based on salaries, with Hogan receiving $28,000 and Stanford receiving $12,000. The remainder is allocated based on partner capital contributions.

d. Net income for the year ended January 31, 19X8 is $132,000. The first $75,000 is allocated based on partner capital contributions and the next $36,000 is based on service, with Hogan receiving $28,000 and Stanford receiving $8,000. Any remainder is shared equally.

2. Revenues for the year ended January 31, 19X8 were $872,000 and expenses were $740,000. Under plan d, prepare the partnership income statement for the year.

Problem 13-3B   *Recording changes in partnership capital*

Englewood Consulting Associates is a partnership and its owners are considering admitting Hilda Newton as a new partner. On March 31 of the current year, the capital accounts of the three existing partners and their shares of profits and losses are as follows:

	Capital	Profit-and-Loss Percent
Jim Zook.............	$ 40,000	15%
Richard Land.........	100,000	30
Jennifer Lim..........	160,000	55

Required

Journalize the admission of Newton as a partner on July 31 for each of the following independent situations:

1. Land gives his partnership share to H. Newton, who is his daughter.
2. Newton pays Lim $145,000 cash to purchase Lim's interest in the partnership.
3. Newton invests $60,000 in the partnership, acquiring a one-sixth interest in the business.
4. Newton invests $60,000 in the partnership, acquiring a one-fifth interest in the business.
5. Newton invests $40,000 in the partnership, acquiring a 10 percent interest in the business.

Problem 13-4B   *Recording changes in partnership capital*

Pediatric Associates is a partnership owned by three individuals. The partners share profits and losses in the ratio of 31 percent to Turman, 38 percent to Herron and 31 percent to Tyler. At December 31, 19X7, the firm has the following balance sheet:

Cash		$ 31,000	Total liabilities		$ 94,000
Accounts receivable	$ 22,000				
Less: Allowance					
for uncollectibles ..	4,000	18,000	Turman, capital.......		61,000
Office equipment	$310,000		Herron, capital		72,000
Less: Accumulated			Tyler, capital		62,000
depreciation	70,000	240,000	Total liabilities		
Total assets		$289,000	and capital		$289,000

Herron withdraws from the partnership on December 31, 19X7 to establish her own medical practice.

Required

Record Herron's withdrawal from the partnership under the following plans:

1. Herron gives her interest in the business to Zagat, her niece.
2. In personal transactions, Herron sells her equity in the partnership to Grimes and Hirsh, who each pay Herron $50,000 for one half of her interest. Turman and Tyler agree to accept Grimes and Hirsh as partners.
3. The partnership pays Herron cash of $15,000 and gives her a note payable for the remainder of her book equity in settlement of her partnership interest.
4. Herron receives cash of $10,000 and a note for $70,000 from the partnership.
5. The partners agree that the office equipment is worth only $280,000 and that its accumulated depreciation should remain at $70,000. After the revaluation, the partnership settles with Herron by giving her cash of $10,600 and a note payable for the remainder of her book equity.

Problem 13-5B   *Liquidation of a partnership*

The partnership of Monet, Dixon and Palma has experienced operating losses for three consecutive years. The partners, who have shared profits and losses in the ratio of Monet 20 percent, Dixon 30 percent and Palma 50 percent, are considering the liquidation of the business. They ask you to analyse the effects of liquidation under various assumptions about the sale of the noncash assets. They present the following condensed partnership balance sheet at December 31, end of the current year:

Cash	$ 27,000	Liabilities	$131,000
Noncash assets	202,000	Monet, capital	13,000
		Dixon, capital	39,000
		Palma, capital	46,000
Total assets	$229,000	Total liabilities and capital ...	$229,000

Required

1. Prepare a summary of liquidation transactions (as illustrated in the chapter) for each of the following situations:
    a. The noncash assets are sold for $212,000.
    b. The noncash assets are sold for $194,000.
    c. The noncash assets are sold for $122,000, and the partner with a capital deficiency pays cash to the partnership to erase the deficiency.
    d. The noncash assets are sold for $124,000, and the partner with a capital deficiency is personally bankrupt.
2. Make the journal entries to record the liquidation transactions in question 1d.

Problem 13-6B   *Liquidation of a partnership*

BP&O is a partnership owned by Bell, Pastena and O'Donnell, who share profits and losses in the ratio of 5:3:2. The adjusted trial balance of the partnership (in condensed form) at September 30, end of the current fiscal year, follows:

BP&O
Adjusted Trial Balance
September 30, 19XX

Cash	$ 7,000	
Noncash assets	177,000	
Liabilities		$135,000
Bell, capital..................		57,000
Pastena, capital		44,000
O'Donnell, capital............		18,000
Bell, drawing	45,000	
Pastena, drawing	37,000	
O'Donnell, drawing	18,000	
Revenues		211,000
Expenses.....................	181,000	
Totals	$465,000	$465,000

Required

1. Prepare the September 30 entries to close the revenue, expense, income summary and drawing accounts.
2. Insert the opening capital balances in the partner capital accounts, post the closing entries to the capital accounts, and determine each partner's ending capital balance.
3. The partnership liquidates on September 30 by selling the noncash assets for $132,000. Using the ending balances of the partner capital accounts, prepare a summary of liquidation transactions (as illustrated in the chapter). Any partner with a capital deficiency is unable to contribute assets to erase the deficiency.

Decision Problems

1. Disagreements among partners

Clay Grant invested $20,000 and Elaine Marsh invested $10,000 in a public relations firm that has operated for ten years. Neither partner has made an additional investment. They have shared profits and losses in the ratio of 2:1, which is the ratio of their investments in the business. Grant manages the office, supervises the 16 employees and does the accounting. Marsh, the moderator of a television talk show, is responsible for marketing. Her high profile generates important revenue for the business. During the year ended December 19X4, the partnership earned net income of $87,000, shared in the 2:1 ratio. On December 31, 19X4, Grant's capital balance was $120,000 and Marsh's capital balance was $80,000.

Required

Respond to each of the following situations:

1. What explains the difference between the ratio of partner capital balances at December 31, 19X4 and the 2:1 ratio of partner investments and profit sharing?
2. Marsh believes the profit-and-loss-sharing ratio is unfair. She proposes a change, but Grant insists on keeping the 2:1 ratio. What two factors may underlie Marsh's unhappiness?
3. During January 19X5, Grant learned that revenues of $18,000 were omitted from the reported 19X4 income. He brings this to Marsh's attention, pointing out that his

share of this added income is two thirds, or $12,000, and Marsh's share is one third, or $6,000. Marsh believes they should share this added income based on their capital balances. 60 percent, or $10,800, to Grant and 40 percent, or $7,200, to Marsh. Which partner is correct? Why?

4. Assume the 19X4 $18,000 omission was an account payable for an operating expense. How would the partners share this amount?

2. *Questions about partnerships*

1. The text suggests that a written partnership agreement may be drawn up between the partners in a partnership. One benefit of such an agreement is that it provides a mechanism for resolving disputes between the partners. List five areas of dispute that might be resolved by a partnership agreement.

2. The statement has been made that "If you must take on a partner, make sure the partner is richer than you are." What does the statement mean? Is it valid?

3. Jardine, Kitchen and Wong is a partnership of CGAs who practice public accounting. Wong enters into a contract with Lime Computers Ltd. on behalf of the partnership to sell Lime computers and related software. What liabilities does the partnership have under the contract?

4. Zalinski, Waller and Gunz is a partnership of CMAs. Gunz is planning to move to Australia. What are the options open to her to convert her share of the partnership assets to cash so that she may take her share with her?

Answers to Self-Study Questions

1. a
2. b
3. a ($40,000 \times {}^{3}\!/_{12} = $10,000)
4. d ($40,000 \times {}^{5}\!/_{12} = $16,667)
5. a
6. c ($46,000 + $52,000 + $55,000) \times {}^{1}\!/_{3} = $51,000$; $55,000 - $51,000 = $4,000;
   $4,000 \div 2 = $2,000 each to Graff and Harrell]
7. d
8. b ($36,000 \times {}^{1}\!/_{4} = $9,000)
9. d
10. c

14

Corporations: Organization, Capital Stock and the Balance Sheet

LEARNING OBJECTIVES

After studying this chapter, you should be able to

1 Identify the characteristics of a corporation

2 Record the issuance of stock

3 Prepare the shareholders' equity section of a corporation balance sheet

4 Account for the incorporation of a going business

5 Allocate dividends to preferred and common stock

6 Distinguish among various stock "values"

The corporation is the dominant form of business organization in Canada. Although proprietorships and partnerships are more numerous, corporations transact more business and are larger in terms of total assets, sales revenue, and number of employees. Most well-known companies, such as Canadian Pacific Ltd., Noranda Inc. and Moore Corp., are corporations. Their full names include *Limited, Incorporated* or *Corporation* (abbreviated *Ltd., Inc.* and *Corp.*) to indicate they are corporations. This chapter and the next three discuss corporations and how to account for them.

Characteristics of a Corporation

Why is the corporation form of business so attractive? We now look at the features that distinguish corporations from proprietorships and partnerships.

Separate Legal Entity

A **corporation** is a business entity formed under federal or provincial law. The federal or provincial government grants **articles of incorporation**, which consist of a document that gives the governing body's permission to form a corporation.

A corporation is a distinct entity from a legal perspective. We may consider the corporation as an artificial person that exists apart from its owners, who

> **OBJECTIVE 1**
>
> Identify the characteristics of a corporation

573

are called **shareholders** or stockholders. The corporation has many of the rights that a person has. For example, a corporation may buy, own and sell property. Assets and liabilities in the business belong to the corporation. The corporation may enter into contracts, sue and be sued.

The owners' equity of a corporation is divided into shares of **stock**. A person becomes a shareholder by purchasing the stock of the corporation. The articles of incorporation specify how much stock the corporation can issue (sell) and lists the other details of its relationships with the federal or provincial government.

Continuous Life and Transferability of Ownership

Most corporations have continuous lives regardless of changes in the ownership of their stock. Shareholders may transfer stock as they wish. They may sell or trade the stock to another person, give it away, bequeath it in a will or dispose of it in any other way they desire. The transfer of the stock does not affect the continuity of the corporation. Proprietorships and partnerships, on the other hand, terminate when their ownership changes.

No Mutual Agency

Mutual agency of the owners is *not* present in a corporation. The shareholder of a corporation cannot commit the corporation to a contract (unless he or she is also an officer in the business). For this reason, a shareholder need not exercise the care that partners must in selecting co-owners of the business.

Limited Liability of Shareholders

A shareholder has **limited liability** for corporation debts. He or she has no personal obligation for corporation liabilities. The most that a shareholder can lose on an investment in a corporation's stock is the cost of the investment. Recall that proprietors and partners are personally liable for the debts of their businesses.

The combination of limited liability and no mutual agency means that persons can invest limited amounts in a corporation, without fear of losing all their personal wealth because of a business failure. This feature enables a corporation to raise more capital from a wider group of investors than proprietorships and partnerships.

Separation of Ownership and Management

Shareholders own the business, but a board of directors, elected by the shareholders, appoints corporate officers to manage the business. Thus shareholders may invest $1,000 or $1 million in the corporation without having to manage the business or disrupt their personal affairs.

However, this separation between owners, shareholders and management may create problems. Corporate officers may decide to run the business for their own benefit and not to the shareholders' advantage. Shareholders may find it difficult to lodge an effective protest against management policy because of the distance between them and management.

Corporate Taxation

Corporations are separate taxable entities. They pay a variety of taxes not borne by proprietorships or partnerships such as federal and provincial income taxes. Corporate earnings are subject to **double taxation**. First, corporations pay their own income taxes on corporate income. Then, the shareholders pay personal income tax on the cash dividends that they receive from corporations. This is different from proprietorships and partnerships, which pay no business income tax. Instead, the tax falls solely on the owners.

Government Regulation

Strong government regulation is an important disadvantage to the corporation. Because shareholders have only limited liability for corporation debts, outsiders doing business with the corporation can look no further than the corporation itself for any claims that may arise against the business. To protect persons who loan money to a corporation or who invest in its stock, the federal and provincial governments monitor the affairs of corporations. This government regulation consists mainly of ensuring that corporations disclose the business information that investors and creditors need to make informed decisions. For many corporations, adhering to this government regulation is expensive.

Organization of a Corporation

Creation of a corporation begins when its organizers, called the **incorporators**, obtain articles of incorporation from the federal or provincial government. The articles of incorporation include the authorization for the corporation to issue a certain number of shares of stock, which are shares of ownership in the corporation. The incorporators pay fees and file the required documents with the incorporating jurisdiction. Then the corporation comes into existence. The incorporators agree to a set of **bylaws**, which act as the constitution for governing the corporation.

The ultimate control of the corporation rests with the shareholders, who receive one vote for each share of voting stock they own. The shareholders elect the members of the **board of directors**, which sets policy for the corporation and appoints the officers. The board elects a **chairperson**, who usually is the most powerful person in the corporation. The board also designates the **president**, who is the chief operating officer in charge of managing day-to-day operations. Most corporations also have vice-presidents in charge of sales, manufacturing, accounting and finance and other key areas. Often the president and one or more vice-presidents are also elected to the board of directors. Exhibit 14-1 shows the authority structure in a corporation.

All corporations have an annual meeting at which the shareholders elect directors and make other shareholder decisions. Shareholders unable to attend this annual meeting may vote on corporation matters by use of a **proxy**, which is a legal document that expresses the shareholder's preference and appoints another person to cast the vote.

The structure of proprietorships, partnerships and corporations is similar in that all three types of business have owners, managers and employees. In proprietorships and partnerships, policy decisions are usually made by the owners—the proprietor or the partners. In a corporation, however, the

EXHIBIT 14-1   Authority Structure in a Corporation

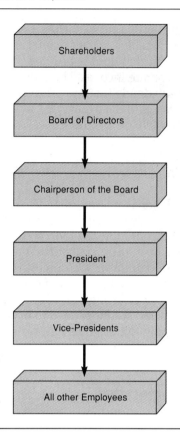

managers who set policy — the board of directors — may or may not be owners (shareholders).

A corporation keeps a subsidiary record of its shareholders. The business must notify the shareholders of the annual shareholder meeting and mail them dividend payments (which we discuss later in this chapter). Large companies use a registrar to maintain the shareholder list and a transfer agent to issue stock certificates. Banks or trust companies provide these registration and transfer services. The transfer agent handles the change in stock ownership from one shareholder to another.

Capital Stock

A corporation issues stock certificates to its owners in exchange for their investments in the business. The basic unit of capital stock is called a *share*. A corporation may issue a share certificate for any number of shares it wishes — one share, one hundred shares, or any other number. Exhibit 14-2 depicts an actual stock certificate for fifty shares of National Trust stock. The certificate shows the company name, shareholder name and number of shares.

Stock in the hands of a shareholder is said to be **outstanding**. The total number of shares of stock outstanding at any time represents 100 percent ownership of the corporation. Because stock represents the corporation's capital, it is often called capital stock.

EXHIBIT 14-2   *Share Certificate*

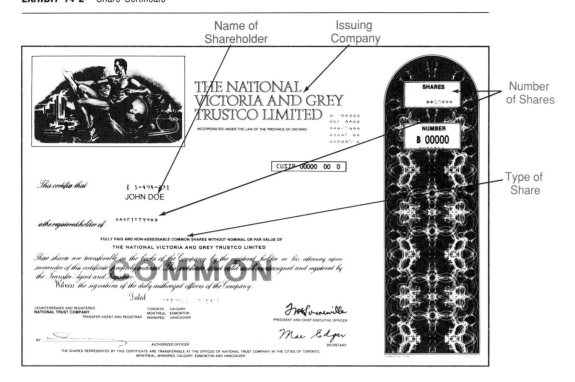

Shareholders' Equity

The balance sheet of a corporation reports assets and liabilities in the same way as a proprietorship or a partnership. However, owners' equity of a corporation called **shareholders' equity**, is reported differently. Incorporating acts require corporations to report the sources of their capital. The two most basic sources of capital are investments by the shareholders, called **capital stock** or **share capital**, and the capital earned through the profitable operations of the business, called **retained earnings**. While the *Canada Business Corporations Act* and several of the provincial incorporating acts use the term **stated capital** to describe capital stock, this text will use the more common term, capital stock. Exhibit 14-3 outlines a simplified corporation balance sheet to show how to report these categories of shareholders' equity.

EXHIBIT 14-3   *Simplified Corporation Balance Sheet*

Assets..................	$600,000	Liabilities	$240,000
		Shareholders' Equity	
		Capital stock	200,000
		Retained earnings	160,000
		Total shareholders' equity	360,000
		Total liabilities and	
Total assets	$600,000	shareholders' equity	$600,000

An investment of cash or any other asset in a corporation increases its assets and shareholders' equity. The corporation's entry for receipt of a $20,000 shareholder investment in the business is

Oct. 20	Cash	20,000	
	Capital Stock		20,000
	Investment by shareholders.		

Capital stock is regarded as the permanent capital of the business because it is *not* subject to withdrawal by the shareholders.

Profitable operations produce income, which increases shareholders' equity through an account called Retained Earnings. At the end of the year, the balance of the Income Summary account is closed to Retained Earnings. For example, if net income is $95,000, Income Summary will have a $95,000 credit balance. The closing entry will debit Income Summary to transfer net income to Retained Earnings as follows:

Dec. 31	Income Summary	95,000	
	Retained Earnings		95,000
	To close Income Summary by transferring		
	net income to Retained Earnings.		

If operations produce a net *loss* rather than net income, the Income Summary account will have a debit balance. Income Summary must be credited to close it. With a $60,000 loss, the closing entry is

Dec. 31	Retained Earnings..........................	60,000	
	Income Summary		60,000
	To close Income Summary by transferring		
	net loss to Retained Earnings.		

A large loss may cause a debit balance in the Retained Earnings account. This condition, called a Retained Earnings **deficit**, or accumulated deficit, is reported on the balance sheet as a negative amount in shareholders' equity. Assume a $50,000 deficit:

Shareholders' Equity

Capital stock	$200,000
Deficit...	(50,000)
Total shareholders' equity	$150,000

If the corporation has been profitable and has sufficient cash, a distribution of cash may be made to the shareholders. Such distributions, called **dividends**, decrease both the assets and the retained earnings of the business. The balance of the Retained Earnings account at any time is the sum of earnings accumulated since incorporation, minus any losses, and minus all dividends distributed to shareholders. Retained Earnings is entirely separate from the capital stock invested in the business by the shareholders.

Some people think of Retained Earnings as a fund of cash. It is not, because Retained Earnings is an element of shareholders' equity, representing a claim against all assets resulting from earnings that have not been distributed to the owners.

Shareholder Rights _____

The owner of a share of stock has certain rights that are set out in the corporation's articles of incorporation; these vary from company to company and even from class of stock to class of stock within a company. In addition, the shareholder may have other rights granted by the legislation under which the corporation receives its articles. While those rights outlined in the articles of incorporation are specific to an individual company, those set forth by legislation are shared by shareholders of all companies incorporated under that legislation. The articles of incorporation, for example, may specify that the shareholder of a Class A common share is entitled to one vote at shareholders' meetings, while the shareholder of a Class B common share is not entitled to vote. An example of a shared right is that under the *Canada Business Corporations Act*, shareholders may require the directors of the company to call a meeting of the shareholders.

Some of the rights that *normally* are attached to common shares are:

1. The right to sell the shares.
2. The right to vote at shareholders' meetings.
3. The right to a proportionate share of any dividends declared by the directors for that class of shares.
4. The right to receive a proportionate share of any assets, on the winding-up of the company, after the creditors and any classes of shares that rank above that class have been paid.

Classes of Stock _____

Corporations issue different types of stock to appeal to a wide variety of investors. The stock of a corporation may be either common or preferred.

Common and Preferred Stock

Every corporation issues **common stock**, the most basic form of capital stock. Unless designated otherwise, the word *stock* is understood to mean "common stock." Companies may issue different classes of common stock. For example, some companies issue Class A common stock, which usually carries the right to vote, and Class B common stock, which may be nonvoting. (Classes of common stock may also be designated Series A, Series B, and so on.) The general ledger has a separate account for each class of common stock. In describing a corporation, we would say the common shareholders are the owners of the business.

Some corporations issue **preferred stock**. Often the right to vote is withheld from preferred shareholders. Preferred stock usually gives its owners certain advantages over common shareholders. These benefits frequently include the priority to receive dividends before the common shareholders and the priority to receive assets before the common shareholders if the corporation liquidates. Because of the priorities that preferred shareholders often have, we see that common stock represents the residual ownership in the corporation's assets after subtracting the liabilities and the claims of preferred shareholders. Preferred shares usually indicate the annual dividend. Lefarge Corporation, the cement and building materials company, has $1.88 convertible preferred shares and $2.44 convertible preferred shares; $1.88 and $2.44 are the annual dividend rates. Companies may issue different classes of preferred stock. (Class A and Class B or Series A and Series B, for example). Each class is recorded in a separate account.

Par Value and No-Par Stock

Par value is an arbitrary amount assigned to a share of stock in the articles of incorporation by the company issuing it. For example, National Trust, through a predecessor company, used to issue common shares with a $2.00 par value. When a common share was sold, $2.00 would be allocated to Common Stock and any consideration received in excess of $2.00 would be recorded as a premium on (that) common stock. Par value shares, however, today exist only in a few jurisdictions in Canada.

No-par shares are shares of stock that do not have a value assigned to them by the articles of incorporation. The board of directors assigns a value to the shares when they are issued; this value is known as the *stated value*. For example, suppose Dajol Inc. has authorization to issue 100,000 shares of common stock having *no-par value* assigned to them by the articles of incorporation. Dajol needs $50,000 at incorporation and might issue 10,000 shares for $5.00 per share, 2,000 shares at $25.00 per share or 1,000 shares at $50.00 per share, and so on. The point is that Dajol can assign whatever value to the shares the board of directors wishes. Normally, the stated value would be credited to Common Stock when the stock is issued.

The value of a corporation's capital stock or stated capital is the sum of the shares issued times the stated values of those shares at the time of issue. For example, if YDR Ltd. issued 1,000 common shares at a stated value of $8.00 per share, 2,000 shares at $12.00 per share and 500 shares at $15.00 per share, its capital stock or stated capital would be $39,500 [(1,000 × $8) + (2,000 × $12) + (500 × $15)].

The *Canada Business Corporations Act* and most provincial incorporating acts now require common and preferred shares to be issued without nominal or par value. The full value of the proceeds from the sale of stock by a company must be allocated to the capital account for that stock. For example, if National Trust were to issue 100 shares of common stock for $2,500 (that is, at a stated value of $25.00 per share), $2,500 would be credited to Common Stock.

Issuing Stock

The articles of incorporation that the incorporators receive from the federal government or province includes an **authorization** for the business to issue (that is, to sell) a certain number of shares of stock. Corporations may sell the stock directly to the shareholders or they may use the service of an *underwriter*, such as the brokerage firms Dominion Securities and Richardson Greenshields. An underwriter agrees to buy all the stock it cannot sell to its clients.

The corporation need not issue all the stock that the articles allows. Management may hold some stock back and issue it later if the need for additional capital arises. The stock that the corporation does issue to shareholders is called *issued stock*. Only by issuing stock (not by receiving authorization) does the corporation increase the asset and equity amounts on its balance sheet.

The price that the shareholder pays to acquire stock from the corporation is called the *issue price*. A combination of market factors, including the company's comparative earnings record, financial position, prospects for success and general business conditions, determines issue price. Investors will not pay more than market value for the stock. The following sections show how to account for the issuance of stock.

Issuing Common Stock

Issuing Common Stock at a Stated Value   Suppose Medina Corporation issues 500 shares of its common stock for cash with a stated value of $10 per share. The stock issuance entry is

OBJECTIVE 2	
Record the issuance of stock	

Jan. 8	Cash (500 × $10)	5,000	
	Common Stock..........................		5,000
	To issue common stock at $10 per share.		

The amount invested in the corporation, $5,000 in this case, is called capital stock. The credit to Common Stock records an increase in the capital stock of the corporation.

The following example illustrates the shareholders' equity section of Medina Corporation after it had issued the 500 shares. Assume that the articles of Medina authorize it to issue 5,000 common shares, that 1,500 shares had been issued for a stated value of $6.00 per share prior to January, and that the company had $3,000 in retained earnings. The corporation would report shareholders' equity as follows:

Shareholders' Equity

Capital stock	
Common stock, 5,000 shares authorized,	
2,000 shares issued.................................	$14,000
Retained earnings	3,000
Total shareholders' equity	$17,000

Issuing Par Value Common Stock at a Premium   A corporation, in a province that permits par value stock, usually issues its common stock for a price above par value. The excess amount above par is called a **premium**. Assume Olde Corp. issues $10 par common stock for a price of $25. The $15 difference is a premium. This sale of stock increases the corporation's capital stock by $25, the total issue price of the stock. Both the par value of the stock and the premium are part of capital stock. A premium on the sale of stock is not gain, income, or profit to the corporation, because the entity is dealing with its own shareholders. This illustrates one of the fundamentals of accounting: a company cannot earn a profit, nor can it incur a loss, when it sells its stock to, or buys its stock from, its own shareholders.

Suppose Olde Corp. issues 4,000 shares of its $10 par common stock for $25 per share — a total of $100,000 (4,000 × $25). The premium per share is $15 ($25 − $10), and the entry to record the issuance of the stock is

Jan. 23	Cash (4,000 × $25)	100,000	
	Common Stock (4,000 × $10)		40,000
	Premium on Common Stock (4,000 × $15) .		60,000
	To issue common stock at a premium.		

Since both par value and premium amounts increase the corporation's capital, they appear in the shareholders' equity section of the balance sheet.

At the end of the first year, Olde Corp. would report shareholders' equity on its balance sheet as follows, assuming the corporate articles authorizes 20,000 shares of common stock and retained earnings is $85,000:

Shareholders' Equity

Capital stock	
Common stock, $10 par, 20,000 shares authorized, 4,500 shares issued..............................	$ 45,000
Premium on common stock...........................	60,000
Total capital stock	105,000
Retained earnings	85,000
Total shareholders' equity	$190,000

We determine the dollar amount reported for common stock by multiplying the total number of shares *issued* (500 issued previously + 4,000) by the par value per share. The *authorization* reports the maximum number of shares the company may issue under its articles.

Issuing Common Stock for Assets Other Than Cash   When a corporation issues stock in exchange for assets other than cash, it debits the assets received for their current market value and credits the capital accounts accordingly. The assets' prior book value does not matter because the shareholder will demand stock equal to the market value of the asset given. Assume Kahn Corporation issues 15,000 shares of its common stock for equipment worth $15,000 and a building worth $120,000. The entry is

Nov. 12	Equipment	15,000	
	Building	120,000	
	Common Stock (15,000 × $9)............		135,000
	To issue 15,000 shares of common stock in exchange for equipment and a building.		

Capital stock increases by the amount of the assets' current market value, $135,000 in this case; the stated value would be $9.00 per share.

Issuing Common Stock through Subscriptions   Established companies usually issue stock and receive the full price in a single transaction. New corporations, to gauge their ability to raise capital, often take subscriptions for their stock. A **stock subscription** is a contract that obligates an investor to purchase the corporation's stock at a later date. Because a contract exists between the two parties, the corporation acquires an asset, Subscription Receivable, when it receives the subscription. The investor gains an equity in the corporation by promising to pay the subscription amount. Depending on the subscription agreement, the subscriber may pay the subscription in a lump sum or in installments.

The *Canada Business Corporations Act* and several of the provincial incorporating acts do not permit a corporation to issue shares until the full subscription price has been paid. The purchaser does not have any shareholder rights until the shares have been fully paid and issued.

Assume Medina Corporation receives a subscription on May 31 for 1,000 shares of common stock. The subscription price is $22 per share. The subscriber makes a down payment of $6,000 and agrees to pay the $16,000 balance in two monthly installments of $8,000 each. Medina Corporation will issue the shares when the subscriber pays in full. The entry to record receipt of the subscription is

May 31	Cash	6,000	
	Subscription Receivable — Common		
	($22,000 − $6,000)	16,000	
	Common Stock Subscribed		
	(1,000 × $22)		22,000
	To receive common stock subscription at		
	$22 per share.		

Subscription Receivable — Common is a current asset if collection is expected within one year. Otherwise it is long-term and is reported in the Other Assets category on the balance sheet. Common Stock Subscribed is an element of shareholders' equity, reported immediately beneath Common Stock on the balance sheet. The "subscribed" label will be eliminated when the subscription is paid off and the stock is issued. The entries to record receipt of the two installments and issuance of the stock are

June 30	Cash ($16,000 × ½)	8,000	
	Subscription Receivable — Common		8,000
	To collect first installment on common stock		
	subscription.		
July 31	Cash ($16,000 × ½)	8,000	
	Subscription Receivable — Common		8,000
	To collect second installment on common		
	stock subscription.		
31	Common Stock Subscribed	22,000	
	Common Stock		22,000
	To issue common stock under subscription		
	agreement.		

The last entry is needed to transfer the value of the stock from the Subscribed account to Common Stock.

Because the subscription is a legally binding contract, subscribers are obliged to pay their subscriptions in full. If a subscriber does not, the company may cancel the subscription and claim the amount already paid, cancel the subscription and refund the amount already paid, or issue shares with a value of the amount already paid.

Issuing Preferred Stock

Not all corporations issue preferred stock. The Canadian Institute of Chartered Accountants, in the 1989 edition of *Financial Reporting in Canada*, reports that in 1988 just slightly more than two thirds of the companies reporting mentioned preferred shares in the shareholders' equity section of the balance sheet. Accounting for preferred shares follows the pattern illustrated for common stock. Assume the Medina Corporation incorporating articles authorizes issuance of 5,000 preferred shares with an annual dividend of $11.00 per share. On July 31, the company issues 400 shares at a stated price of $110.00 per share.

The issuance entry is

July 31	Cash (400×$110)	44,000	
	Preferred Stock........................		44,000
	To issue preferred stock.		

Let us review the first half of this chapter by showing the shareholders' equity section of Medina Corporation's balance sheet. (Assume that all figures, which are arbitrary, are correct.) Note the two sections of shareholders' equity: capital stock and retained earnings. Also observe the order of the equity accounts: preferred stock, common stock and common stock subscribed. If Medina had a Preferred Stock Subscribed account, it would appear after Preferred Stock (corresponding to the order illustrated for the common stock accounts).

Shareholders' Equity

Capital stock	
Preferred stock, $11.00, 5,000 shares authorized,	
400 shares issued	$44,000
Common stock, 5,000 shares authorized,	
2,000 shares issued...............................	14,000
Common stock subscribed, 1,000 shares	22,000
Total capital stock	80,000
Retained earnings	3,000
Total shareholders' equity	$83,000

OBJECTIVE 3

Prepare the shareholders' equity section of a corporation balance sheet

Summary Problems for Your Review

1. Test your understanding of the first half of this chapter by answering whether each of the following statements is true or false:

   a. A shareholder may bind the corporation to a contract.

   b. The policy-making body in a corporation is called the board of directors.

   c. The owner of 100 shares of preferred stock has greater voting rights than the owner of 100 shares of common stock.

   d. A company incorporated under the *Canada Business Corporations Act* must assign the proceeds of a stock issue to the capital account for that stock.

   e. Par value stock is worth more than no-par stock.

   f. Issuance of 1,000 shares of stock at $12 increases stated capital by $12,000.

g. The stated value of a stock is the value assigned to the stock by the company issuing it at the date issued or subscribed.

h. A corporation issues its preferred stock in exchange for land and a building with a combined market value of $200,000. This transaction increases the corporation's owner equity by $200,000 regardless of the assets' prior book value.

i. Receipt of a subscription contract does not increase the shareholders' equity of the corporation unless the subscriber makes a down payment.

j. Common Stock Subscribed is a part of shareholders' equity.

2. Tundra Co. Ltd., incorporated under the *Canada Business Corporations Act*, had three transactions during the year involving its common shares. On January 15, 10,000 shares were issued with a stated value of $7.80 per share. On February 28, subscriptions were received for 4,000 shares with a stated value of $8.50 per share; $4.50 was received on each share subscribed. On August 8, 6,000 shares were issued in exchange for land with a market value of $52,000. Tundra's articles of incorporation state that 50,000 common shares are authorized.

Required

1. Prepare the journal entry to record the transaction of January 15.
2. Prepare the journal entry to record the transaction of February 28.
3. Prepare the journal entry to record the transaction of August 8.
4. Set up the shareholders' equity section for Tundra Co. Ltd. after the three transactions have taken place.
5. What is the total capital stock of the company?

SOLUTIONS TO SUMMARY PROBLEMS

1. Answers to true-false statements:
   a. False   b. True   c. False   d. True   e. False
   f. True   g. True   h. True   i. False j. True

2. a. Jan. 15   Cash 78,000
                    Common Stock   78,000
                To issue common stock at $7.80
                per share.

   b. Feb. 28   Cash 18,000
                Subscriptions Receivable 16,000
                    Common Stock Subscribed   34,000
                To receive common stock
                subscription at $8.50 per share.

   c. Aug. 8   Land 52,000
                    Common Stock   52,000
                To issue 6,000 shares of common
                stock in exchange for land.

d.   Shareholders' Equity
      Capital stock
          Common stock, 50,000 shares
              authorized, 16,000 shares issued $130,000
          Common stock subscribed
              but not issued .... <u>34,000</u>
                                         <u>$164,000</u>

e.   Capital stock is $164,000.

Donated Capital

Corporations occasionally receive gifts or donations. For example, city council members may offer a company free land to encourage it to locate in their city. The free land is called a donation. Also, a shareholder may make a donation to the corporation in the form of cash, land, or other assets or stock that the corporation can resell.

A donation is a gift that increases the assets of the corporation. However, the donor (giver) receives no ownership interest in the company in return. A transaction to receive a donation does not increase the corporation's revenue, and thus it does not affect income. Instead, the donation creates a special category of shareholders' equity called **donated capital**. The corporation records a donation by debiting the asset received at its current market value and by crediting Donated Capital, a shareholders' equity account.

Suppose Burlington Ltd. receives 100 hectares of land as a donation from the city of Lethbridge, Alberta. The current market value of the land is $250,000. Burlington records receipt of the donation as follows:

Apr. 18   Land   250,000
            Donated Capital   250,000
        To receive land as a donation from the city.

Donated capital is reported on the balance sheet after the stock accounts in the capital stock section of shareholders' equity.

Incorporation of a Going Business

You may dream of having your own business someday, or you may currently be a business proprietor or partner. Businesses that begin as a proprietorship or a partnership often incorporate at a later date. By incorporating a going business, the proprietor or partners avoid the unlimited liability for business debts. And as we discussed earlier, incorporating also makes it easier to raise capital.

To account for the incorporation of a going business, we close the owner equity accounts of the prior entity and set up the shareholder equity accounts of the corporation. Suppose B. C. Coast Travel Associates is a partnership owned by Joe Suzuki and Monica Lee. The partnership balance sheet, after all adjustments and closing entries, reports Joe Suzuki, Capital, of $50,000 and

Monica Lee, Capital, of $70,000. They incorporate the travel agency as B. C. Coast Travel Company, Inc. with an authorization to issue 200,000 shares of common stock. Joe and Monica agree to receive common stock equal in stated value to their partnership owner equity balances. The entry to record the incorporation of the business is

Feb.1	Joe Suzuki, Capital............................	50,000	
	Monica Lee, Capital...........................	70,000	
	Common Stock..........................		120,000
	To incorporate the business, close the capital accounts of the partnership and issue common stock to the incorporators.		

> **OBJECTIVE 4**
>
> Account for the incorporation of a going business

Organization Cost _____

The costs of organizing a corporation include legal fees for preparing documents and advising on procedures, fees and taxes paid to the incorporating jurisdiction and charges by promoters for selling the company's stock. These costs are grouped in an account titled Organization Cost, which is an asset because these costs contribute to a business's start-up. Suppose Mary's Good Wings and Ribs Ltd. pays legal fees and incorporation fees of $15,000 to organize the corporation under a federal charter in Newfoundland. In addition, a promoter charges a fee of $24,000 for selling the stock and receives 2,000 common shares as payment. Mary's Good Wings and Ribs Ltd.'s journal entries to record these organization costs are

Mar. 31	Organization Cost..........................	15,500	
	Cash..................................		15,500
	Legal fees and incorporation fees to organize the corporation.		
Apr. 3	Organization Cost..........................	24,000	
	Common Stock		24,000
	Promoter fee for selling stock in organization.		

Organization Cost is an *intangible asset*, reported on the balance sheet along with patents, trademarks, goodwill and any other intangibles. We know that an intangible asset should be amortized over its useful life, and organization costs will benefit the corporation for as long as the corporation operates. But how long will that be? We cannot know in advance. Revenue Canada allows corporations to write organization expenses off against taxable income. While the *CICA Handbook* does not require organization costs to be amortized, most companies write organization costs off quickly because of their relatively small size. As is true with other intangibles, amortization expense for the year should be disclosed.

Dividends on Preferred and Common Stock _____

A corporation must declare a dividend before paying it. The board of directors alone has the authority to declare a dividend. The corporation has no obligation to pay a dividend until the board declares one; but once declared, the dividend becomes a legal liability of the corporation. Declaration of a cash dividend is recorded by debiting Retained Earnings and crediting Dividends Payable as follows:

June 19	Retained Earnings	XXX	
	Dividends Payable		XXX
	To declare a cash dividend.		

Payment of the dividend, which usually follows declaration by a few weeks, is recorded by debiting Dividends Payable and crediting Cash.

July 2	Dividends Payable	XXX	
	Cash		XXX
	To pay a cash dividend.		

Dividends Payable is a current liability. When a company has issued both preferred and common stock, the preferred shareholders receive their dividends first. The common shareholders receive dividends only if the total declared dividend is large enough to pay the preferred shareholders first.

Pine Industries, Inc., in addition to its common stock, has 9,000 shares of preferred stock outstanding. Preferred dividends are paid at the annual rate of $1.75 per share. Assume Pine declares an annual dividend of $150,000. The allocation to preferred and common shareholders is

<table>
<tr><td></td><td style="text-align:right">Total Dividend
of $150,000</td></tr>
<tr><td>Preferred dividend (9,000 shares × $1.75 per share) ......</td><td style="text-align:right">$ 15,750</td></tr>
<tr><td>Common dividend (remainder: $150,000 − $15,750) .....</td><td style="text-align:right">134,250</td></tr>
<tr><td>Total dividend ....</td><td style="text-align:right">$150,000</td></tr>
</table>

> **OBJECTIVE 5**
>
> Allocate dividends to preferred and common stock

If Pine declares only a $20,000 dividend, preferred shareholders receive $15,750 and the common shareholders receive $4,250 ($20,000 − $15,750).

This example illustrates an important relationship between preferred stock and common stock. To an investor, the preferred stock is safer because it receives dividends first. For example, if Pine Industries earns only enough net income to pay the preferred shareholders' dividends, the owners of common stock receive no dividends at all. However, the earnings potential from an investment in common stock is much greater than from an investment in preferred stock. Preferred dividends are usually limited to the specified amount, but there is no upper limit on the amount of common dividends.

We have noted that preferred shareholders enjoy the advantage of priority over common shareholders in receiving dividends. The dividend preference is normally stated as a dollar amount. (If the preferred shares have a par value, the dividend preference may be stated as a percentage of the par value rate.) For example, the preferred stock may be "$3 preferred," meaning that the shareholders receive an annual dividend of $3 per share.

Cumulative and Noncumulative Preferred Stock

The allocation of dividends may be complex if the preferred stock is *cumulative*. Corporations sometimes fail to pay a dividend to their preferred shareholders. The passed dividends are said to be **in arrears**. The owners of **cumulative**

preferred stock must receive all dividends in arrears before the corporation pays dividends to the common shareholders.

The preferred stock of Pine Industries is cumulative. Suppose the company passed the 19X4 preferred dividend of $15,750. Before paying dividends to its common shareholders in 19X5, the company must first pay preferred dividends of $15,750 for both 19X4 and 19X5, a total of $31,500.

Assume that Pine Industries passes its 19X4 preferred dividend. In 19X5 the company declares a $50,000 dividend. The entry to record the declaration is

Sept. 6	Retained Earnings	50,000	
	Dividends Payable, Preferred	
	($15,750 × 2)		31,500
	Dividends Payable, Common	
	($50,000 − $31,500)		18,500
	To declare a cash dividend.	

If the preferred stock is *noncumulative*, the corporation is not obligated to pay dividends in arrears in the notes to the financial statements. Suppose that the Pine Industries preferred stock was noncumulative, and the company passed the 19X4 preferred dividend of $15,750. The preferred shareholders would lose the 19X4 dividend forever. Of course, the common shareholders would not receive a 19X4 dividend either. Before paying any common dividends in 19X5, the company would have to pay the 19X5 preferred dividend of $15,750.

Having dividends in arrears on cumulative preferred stock is *not* a liability to the corporation. (A liability for dividends arises only after the board of directors declares the dividend.) Nevertheless, a corporation should report cumulative preferred dividends in arrears. This information alerts common shareholders to how much in cumulative preferred dividends must be paid before any dividends will be paid on the common stock. This gives the common shareholders an idea about the likelihood of receiving dividends and satisfies the disclosure principle.

Dividends in arrears are often disclosed in notes, as follows (all dates and amounts assumed.) Observe the two references to Note 3 in this section of the balance sheet. The "$3.00" after "Preferred stock" is the dividend rate.

Preferred stock, $3.00, 2,000 shares issued (note 3)	$100,000
Retained earnings (note 3)	414,000

Note 3: Cumulative preferred dividends in arrears. At December 31, 19X2, dividends on the company's $3.00 preferred stock were in arrears for 19X1 and 19X2, in the amount of $12,000 ($3.00 × 2,000 × 2 years).

Participating and Nonparticipating Preferred Stock

The owners of **participating preferred stock** may receive (that is, *participate in*) dividends beyond the stated amount or stated percentage. Assume that the corporation declares a dividend. First, the preferred shareholders receive their dividends. If the corporation has declared a large enough dividend, then the common shareholders receive their dividends. If an additional dividend amount remains to be distributed, common shareholders and participating preferred shareholders share it. For example, the owners of a $4 preferred stock must receive the specified annual dividend of $4 per share before the common shareholders receive any dividends. Then a $4 dividend is paid on each common share. The participation feature takes effect only after the preferred and common shareholders have received the specified $4 rate. Payment of an extra *common* dividend of, say, $1.50 is accompanied by a $1.50 dividend on each participating preferred share.

Participating preferred stock is rare. In fact, preferred stock is nonparticipating unless it is specifically described as participating in the articles of incorporation. Therefore, if the preferred stock in our example is nonparticipating (the usual case), the largest annual dividend that a preferred shareholder will receive in our illustration is $4.

Convertible Preferred Stock

Convertible preferred stock may be exchanged by the preferred shareholders, if they choose, for another class of stock in the corporation. For example, the Pine Industries preferred stock may be converted into the company's common stock. A note to Pine's balance sheet describes the conversion terms as follows:

> The ... preferred stock is convertible at the rate of 6.51 shares of common stock for each share of preferred stock outstanding.

If you owned 100 shares of Pine's convertible preferred stock, you could convert it into 651 (100 × 6.51) shares of Pine common stock. Under what condition would you exercise the conversion privilege? You would do so if the market value of the common stock that you could receive from conversion exceeded the market value of the preferred stock that you presently held. This way you, as an investor, could increase your personal wealth.

Pine Industries convertible preferred stock was issued at $100 per share, and the common stock at $1. The company would record the conversion at the value of the 100 preferred shares on the Pine Industries books, or $10,000 (100 × $100). The conversion of the 100 shares of preferred stock into 651 shares of common stock would be recorded as follows:

Mar. 7	Preferred Stock (100 × $100)	10,000	
	Common Stock (651 shares)		10,000
	Conversion of preferred stock into common.		

Preferred stock, as we see, offers alternative features not available to common stock. Preferred stock may be cumulative or noncumulative, participating or nonparticipating, and convertible or not convertible. In addition, preferred stock is usually preferred when dividends are distributed and when the assets are distributed to shareholders upon liquidation of the company.

Different Values of Stock

OBJECTIVE 6

Distinguish among various stock "values"

The business community refers to several different *stock values* in addition to par value. These values include market value, redemption value, liquidation value and book value.

Market Value

A stock's **market value** is the price for which a person could buy or sell a share of the stock. The issuing corporation's net income, financial position, its future prospects and the general economic conditions determine market value (also called *market price*). Daily newspapers report the market price of many stocks. In almost all cases, shareholders are more concerned about the market value of a stock than any of the other values discussed below. A stock *listed at* (an alternative term is *quoted at*) 29¼ sells for, or may be bought for, $29.25 per share. The purchase of 100 shares of this stock would cost $2,925 ($29.25 × 100), plus a commission. If you were selling 100 shares of this stock, you would receive cash of $2,925 less a commission. The commission is the fee an investor pays to a stockbroker for buying or selling the stock.

Redemption Value

Preferred stock's fixed dividend rate makes it somewhat like debt. However, companies do not get a tax deduction for preferred dividend payments. Thus they may wish to buy back (or redeem) their preferred stock to avoid paying the dividends. Preferred stock that provides for redemption at a set price is called redeemable preferred stock. In some cases, the company has the *option* of redeeming its preferred stock at a set price. In other cases, the company is *obligated* to redeem the preferred stock. The price the corporation agrees to pay for the stock, which is set when the stock is issued, is called **redemption value**.

The redeemable preferred stock of Pine Industries, Inc. is "redeemable at the option of the Company at $25 per share." Beginning in 1992, Pine is "required to redeem annually 6,765 shares of the preferred stock ($169,125 annually)." Pine's annual redemption payment to the preferred shareholders will include this redemption value plus any dividends in arrears.

Book Value

The **book value** of a stock is the amount of owners' equity on the company's books for each share of its stock. Corporations often report this amount in their annual reports. If the company has only common stock outstanding, its book value is computed by dividing total shareholders' equity by the number of shares outstanding. A company with shareholders' equity of $180,000 and 5,000 shares of common stock outstanding has book value of $36 per share ($180,000/ 5,000 shares).

If the company has both preferred and common stock outstanding, the preferred shareholders usually have the first claim to owners' equity. Ordinarily, preferred stock has a specified liquidation or redemption value. The book value of preferred is its redemption value plus any cumulative dividends in arrears on the stock. After the corporation figures the preferred shares' book value, it computes the common stock book value per share. The corporation divides the common equity (total shareholders' equity minus preferred equity) by the number of common shares outstanding.

Assume that the company balance sheet reports the following amounts:

Shareholders' Equity

Capital stock	
Preferred stock, $6.00, 5,000 shares authorized,	
400 shares issued	$ 44,000
Common stock, 20,000 shares authorized,	
4,500 shares issued................................	117,000
Common stock subscribed, 1,000 shares	10,000
Total capital stock	171,000
Retained earnings	85,000
Total shareholders' equity	$256,000

Suppose that four years (including the current year) of cumulative preferred dividends are in arrears and preferred stock has a redemption value of $130 per share. Note that book value computations do not treat subscribed stock as though it were issued stock.

The book value per share computations for this corporation follow:

Preferred:	
Redemption value (400 shares × $130)	$ 52,000
Cumulative dividends (400 × $6.00 × 4)	9,600
Shareholders' equity allocated to preferred	$ 61,600
Book value per share ($61,600/400 shares)	$ 154.00
Common:	
Total shareholders' equity	$256,000
Less: Shareholders' equity allocated to preferred.......	61,600
	$194,400
Less: Common stock subscribed	10,000
Shareholders' equity available	
for common shareholders	$184,400
Book value per share [$184,400/(4,500 shares)]	$40.98

How is book value per share used in decision making? Companies may agree to buy a corporation based on the book value of its stock. Corporations may settle with a shareholder, agreeing to pay the book value of the person's stock in the company. In general, however, book value is not directly related to the market value of stock.

Liquidation Value

The **liquidation value** of a share of company stock is equal to the net realizable value of the assets less the cash required to pay the liabilities divided by the number of shares outstanding. Liquidation value is rarely equal to either market value or book value.

For example, Douglas Ltd. has 10,000 common shares outstanding. The shares have a book value of $25.75 per share and are trading on the stock market at $29.50; that is, they have a market value of $29.50 per share. The company's assets have a net realizable value of $336,000, while liabilities amount to $62,000; the liquidation value per share is $27.40 ($336,000 − $62,000) divided by 10,000 shares).

Occasionally, you will read in a business newspaper like *The Financial Post* that a company's *break-up value* (liquidation value) per share is greater than its market value per share. That means that the total market value of the company's individual assets, minus its liabilities, exceeds the total market value of the company's shares.

Summary Problems for Your Review

1. Use the following accounts and related balances to prepare the classified balance sheet of Whitehall, Inc. at September 30, 19X4. Use the account format of the balance sheet.

Common stock,		Inventory	$ 85,000
50,000 shares authorized,		Property, plant and	
20,000 shares issued	$135,000	equipment, net.........	225,000
Dividends payable	4,000	Donated capital	18,000
Cash	9,000	Accounts receivable, net...	23,000
Accounts payable........	28,000	Preferred stock, $3.75	
Stock subscription		10,000 shares authorized,	
receivable		2,000 shares issued	24,000
— common	2,000	Common stock subscribed	
Retained earnings	38,000	3,000 shares............	21,000
Organization cost, net	1,000	Accrued liabilities	3,000
Long-term note payable....	74,000		

2. The balance sheet of Trendline Corporation reported the following at March 31, 19X6, end of its fiscal year.

Shareholders' Equity

Preferred stock, $4.00, cumulative 1,000 shares authorized and issued	$110,000
Common stock, 100,000 shares authorized, 50,000 shares issued...................................	464,000
Common stock subscribed (1,700 shares)	17,500
Donated capital	55,000
Retained earnings	330,000
Total shareholders' equity	$976,500

Required

a. Is the preferred stock cumulative or noncumulative? Is it participating or nonparticipating? How can you tell?

b. What is the total amount of the annual preferred dividend?

c. Assume the common shares were all issued at the same time. What was the selling price per share?

d. What is the subscription price per share of the common stock?

e. What was the market value of the assets donated to the corporation?

f. Compute the book value per share of the preferred stock and the common stock. The preferred stock has no specified redemption value. No prior year preferred dividends are in arrears, but Trendline has not declared the current-year dividend.

SOLUTIONS TO REVIEW PROBLEMS

1.

Whitehall, Inc.
Balance Sheet
September 30, 19X4

Assets		Liabilities	
Current		**Current**	
Cash	$ 9,000	Accounts payable	$ 28,000
Accounts receivable, net	23,000	Dividends payable	4,000
Stock subscription receivable—		Accrued liabilities	3,000
common	2,000	Total current liabilities	35,000
Inventory	85,000	Long-term note payable	74,000
Total current assets	119,000	Total liabilities	109,000
Property, plant and equipment, net..	225,000		
Intangible assets		**Shareholders' Equity**	
Organization cost, net	1,000		
		Capital stock	
		Preferred stock, $3.75,	
		10,000 shares authorized,	
		2,000 shares issued	$ 24,000
		Common stock, 50,000	
		shares authorized,	
		20,000 shares issued	135,000
		Common stock subscribed,	
		3,000 shares	21,000
		Donated capital	18,000
		Total capital stock	198,000
		Retained earnings	38,000
		Total shareholders' equity	236,000
		Total liabilities and	
Total assets	$345,000	shareholders' equity	$345,000

2. Answers to Trendline Corporation questions:

a. The preferred stock is *noncumulative* and *nonparticipating* because it is not specifically labeled otherwise; it is *cumulative* as is noted in its description.

b. Total annual preferred dividend: $4,000 (1,000 × $4.00)

c. Price per share: $9.28 ($464,000/50,000 shares issued)

d. Subscription price: $10.29 ($17,500/1,700)

e. Market value of donated assets: $55,000

f. Book values per share of preferred and common stock:

      Preferred:

Book value	$110,000
Cumulative dividend for current year (1,000 × $4.00)....	4,000
Shareholders' equity allocated to preferred	$114,000
Book value per share ($114,000/1,000 shares)	$114.00

      Common:

Total shareholders' equity	$976,500
Less: Shareholders' equity allocated to preferred	114,000
	$862,500
Less: Common stock subscribed	17,500
Shareholders' equity available	
for common shareholders	$845,000
Book value per share	
($845,000/50,000 shares)	$16.90

Summary

A corporation is a separate legal and business entity. *Continuous life*, the ease of raising large amounts of capital and transferring ownership, and *limited liability* are among the advantages of the corporate form of organization. An important disadvantage is *double taxation*. Corporations pay *income taxes*, and shareholders pay tax on dividends. Shareholders are the owners of corporations. They elect a *board of directors*, which elects a chairperson and appoints the officers to manage the business.

Corporations may issue different classes of stock: *common* and *preferred*. Corporations may also issue stock under a *subscription* agreement. The balance sheet carries the capital raised through stock issuance under the heading Capital Stock or Share Capital in the shareholders' equity section.

Corporations may receive *donations* from outsiders or from shareholders. Donated Capital is a shareholders' equity account.

Only when the board of directors declares a *dividend* does the corporation incur the liability to pay dividends. Preferred stock usually has priority over common stock in the distribution of dividends, which are normally stated as a dollar amount per share. In addition, preferred stock has a claim to dividends in arrears if it is *cumulative* and a claim to further dividends if it is *participating*. *Convertible* preferred stock may be exchanged for the corporation's common stock.

A stock's *market value* is the price for which a share may be bought or sold. *Redemption value, book value* — the amount of owners' equity per share of company stock — and *liquidation value* are other values that may apply to stock.

Self-Study Questions

Test your understanding of the chapter by marking the best answer for each of the following questions:

1. Which of the following is a *disadvantage* of the corporate form of business organization? *(p. 575)*

      a. Limited liability of shareholders   c. No mutual agency
      b. Government regulation   d. Transferability of ownership

2. The person with the most power in a corporation is the *(p. 575)*
   a. Incorporator   c. President
   b. Chairperson of the board   d. Vice-president

3. The dollar amount of the shareholder investments in a corporation is called *(p. 577)*
   a. Outstanding stock   c. Capital stock
   b. Total shareholders' equity   d. Retained earnings

4. The unique rights that attach to a share of stock are defined by *(p. 580)*
   a. The federal government   c. The provincial government
   b. Generally accepted accounting   d. The articles of incorporation
      principles

5. Stock issued by a corporation incorporated under the *Canada Business Corporations Act* normally has *(p. 580)*
   a. No par value   c. A par value set by the government
   b. A par value set by management   d. A par value of $10.00

6. Mangum Corporation receives a subscription for 1,000 shares of preferred stock at $104 per share. This transaction increases Mangum's capital stock by *(pp. 583, 584)*
   a. $0 because the corporation   c. $100,000
      received no cash   d. $104,000
   b. $4,000

7. Organization cost is classified as a (an) *(p. 587)*
   a. Operating expense   c. Contra item in shareholders' equity
   b. Current asset   d. None of the above

8. Trade Days, Inc. has 10,000 shares of $3.50 cumulative preferred stock, and 100,000 of common stock outstanding. Two years' preferred dividends are in arrears. Trade Days declares a cash dividend large enough to pay the preferred dividends in arrears, the preferred dividend for the current period, and a $1.50 dividend to common. What is the total amount of the dividend? *(p. 588)*
   a. $255,000   b. $220,000   c. $150,000   d. $105,000

9. The preferred stock of Trade Days, Inc. in the preceding question was issued at $55 per share. Each preferred share can be converted into 10 common shares. The entry to record the conversion of this preferred stock into common is *(p. 590)*

a. Cash	550,000	
Preferred Stock		500,000
Common Stock		50,000
b. Preferred Stock	500,000	
Capital Stock in Excess of Par		
— Preferred Stock	50,000	
Common Stock		550,000
c. Preferred Stock	550,000	
Common Stock		550,000
d. Preferred Stock	550,000	
Common Stock		400,000
Capital Stock in Excess of Par		
— Common Stock		150,000

10. When an investor is buying stock as an investment, the value of most direct concern is *(p. 591)*
   a. Par value   b. Market value   c. Liquidation value   d. Book value

Answers to the self-study questions are at the end of the chapter.

Accounting Vocabulary

articles of incorporation
   (p. 573)
authorization of stock *(p. 580)*
board of directors *(p. 575)*
book value of stock *(p. 591)*
bylaws *(p. 575)*
capital stock *(p. 577)*
chairperson of the board
   (p. 575)
common stock *(p. 579)*
convertible preferred stock
   (p. 590)
cumulative preferred stock
   (p. 588)

deficit *(p. 578)*
dividends *(p. 578)*
dividends in arrears *(p. 588)*
donated capital *(p. 586)*
double taxation *(p. 575)*
incorporator *(p. 575)*
limited liability *(p. 574)*
liquidation value of stock
   (p. 592)
market value of stock *(p. 591)*
organization cost *(p. 587)*
outstanding stock *(p. 576)*
par value *(p. 580)*

participating preferred stock
   (p. 589)
preferred stock *(p. 579)*
president *(p. 575)*
proxy *(p. 575)*
redemption value of stock
   (p. 591)
retained earnings *(p. 577)*
share capital *(p. 577)*
shareholders' equity
   (p. 577)
stated capital *(p. 577)*
stock *(p. 574)*
stock subscription *(p. 582)*

Assignment Material _____

Questions

1. Why is a corporation called a creature of the government?
2. Identify the characteristics of a corporation.
3. Explain why corporations face a tax disadvantage.
4. Briefly outline the steps in the organization of a corporation.
5. How are the structures of a partnership and a corporation similar and different?
6. List four rights common shares normally have.
7. Dividends on preferred stock may be stated as a percentage rate or a dollar amount. What is the annual dividend on these preferred stocks: 4 percent, $100 par; $3.50?
8. Which event increases the assets of the corporation: authorization of stock or issuance of stock? Explain.
9. Suppose Watgold Ltd. issued 1,000 shares of its $3.65 preferred stock for $120. How much would this transaction increase the company's capital stock? How much would it increase retained earnings? How much would it increase annual cash dividend payments?
10. Woodstock Ltd. issued 100 shares of no par common stock for $15.00 per share. What would the journal entry to record the sale be? Paris Ltd. issued 100 shares of $10 par common stock for $15.00 per share. What would the journal entry to record the sale be?
11. Yukon Corp.'s financial statements show that 100,000 common shares are authorized. Where does the "authority" to issue shares come from?
12. How does issuance of 1,000 shares of common stock for land and a building, together worth $150,000, affect capital stock?
13. Why does receipt of a stock subscription increase the corporation's assets and owners' equity?
14. Give an example of a transaction that creates donated capital for a corporation.
15. Journalize the incorporation of the Barnes & Connally partnership. (Omit amounts.)
16. Rank the following accounts in the order they would appear on the balance sheet: Common Stock, Organization Cost, Donated Capital, Preferred Stock, Common Stock Subscribed, Stock Subscription Receivable (due within six months), Retained Earnings, Dividends Payable. Also, give each account's balance sheet classification.

17. What type of account is Organization Cost? Briefly describe how to account for organization cost.

18. Mancini Inc. has 3,000 shares of its $2.50 preferred stock outstanding. Dividends for 19X1 and 19X2 are in arrears, and the company has declared no dividends on preferred stock for the current year, 19X3. Assume that Mancini declares total dividends of $35,000 at the end of 19X3. Show how to allocate the dividends to preferred and common (a) if preferred is cumulative and (b) if preferred is noncumulative.

19. As a preferred shareholder, would you rather own cumulative or noncumulative preferred? If all other factors are the same, would the corporation rather the preferred stock be cumulative or noncumulative? Give your reason.

20. How are cumulative preferred dividends in arrears reported in the financial statements? When do dividends become a liability of the corporation?

21. Distinguish between the market value of stock and the book value of stock.

22. How is book value per share of common stock computed when the company has both preferred stock and common stock outstanding?

Exercises

Exercise 14-1   *Issuing stock*

Journalize the following stock issuance transactions of Dartmouth Corporation. Explanations are not required.

Feb. 19   Issued 4,000 shares of common stock for cash of $12.50 per share.
Mar. 3   Sold 300 shares of $2.25 Class A preferred stock for $6,000 cash.
Mar. 11   Received inventory valued at $25,000 and equipment with market value of $16,000 for 3,300 shares of the common stock.
Mar. 15   Issued 1,000 shares of $2.50, Class B preferred stock. The issue price was cash of $55 per share.

Exercise 14-2   *Shareholders' equity section of a balance sheet*

The articles of incorporation for Dartmouth Corporation authorizes the issuance of 5,000 shares of Class A preferred stock, 1,000 shares of Class B preferred stock, and 10,000 shares of common stock. Prepare the shareholders' equity section of the Dartmouth balance sheet for the transactions given in the preceding exercise. Retained Earnings has a balance of $63,000.

Exercise 14-3   *Stock subscriptions*

Durham Ltd. has just been organized and is selling its stock through stock subscriptions. Record the following selected transactions that occurred during June 19X6.

June 3   Received a subscription to 200 shares of common stock at the subscription price of $20 per share. The subscriber paid one fourth of the subscription amount as a down payment. The corporation will issue the stock when it is fully paid.
June 18   Collected one half of the amount receivable from the subscriber.
July 3   Collected the remainder from the subscriber and issued the stock.

Exercise 14-4   *Capital stock for a corporation*

Errico Inc. has recently organized. The company issued common stock to a lawyer who gave Errico legal services of $2,400 to help her in organizing the corporation. It issued common stock to another person in exchange for his patent with a market value of $40,000. In addition, Errico received cash both for 2,000 shares of its preferred stock at

$110 per share and for 32,000 shares of its common stock at $15 per share. The city of North Bay donated 50 hectares of land to the company as a plant site. The market value of the land was $180,000. Without making journal entries, determine the total capital stock created by these transactions.

Exercise 14-5   *Recording issuance of stock*

The following partial shareholders' equity section is taken from the balance sheet of Northern Woodlands Ltd. Note that Northern has two separate classes of preferred stock, labeled as Series A and Series B.

Shareholders' Equity

Preferred stock, authorized 4,000,000 shares (note 7)	
Series A, issued and outstanding 58,451 shares	$ 175,353
Series B, issued and outstanding 375,765 shares	7,515,300
Common stock, authorized 20,000,000 shares, issued and	
outstanding 9,125,390 shares	69,198,304

Required

Make the summary journal entries to record issuance of all the Northern Woodlands stock. Explanations are not required.

Exercise 14-6   *Incorporating a partnership*

The Kingston Jaybirds are a semiprofessional baseball team that has been operated as a partnership by D. Robertson and G. Childres. In addition to their management responsibilities, Robertson also plays second base and Childres sells hot dogs. Journalize the following transactions in the first month of operation as a corporation:

May 14   The incorporators paid legal fees of $1,440 and fees of $600 to obtain articles of incorporation.

May 14   Issued 2,500 shares of common stock to Robertson and 1,000 shares to Childres. Robertson's capital balance on the partnership books was $30,000, and Childres's capital balance was $12,000.

May 18   The city of Kingston donated 20 hectares of land to the corporation for a stadium site. The land value was $20,000.

Exercise 14-7   *Recording issuance of no-par stock*

Fanous, Inc. is an importer of European furniture and Oriental rugs. The corporation issues 10,000 shares of non-par common stock for $75 per share. Record issuance of the stock (a) if the stock is true no-par stock and (b) if the stock has stated value of $5 per share.

Exercise 14-8   *Computing dividends on preferred and common stock*

The following elements of shareholders' equity are excerpted from the balance sheet of Northern Woodlands Ltd:

Shareholders' Equity

Preferred stock, cumulative and nonparticipating,	
authorized 4,000,000 shares (note 7)	
Series A, issued and outstanding 58,451 shares	$ 175,353
Series B, issued and outstanding 375,765 shares	7,515,300
Common stock, authorized 20,000,000 shares, issued and	
outstanding 9,125,390 shares	69,198,304

Note 7. Preferred stock

**Designated Annual
Cash Dividend**

Series A .... $ .20
Series B 1.30
The series A preferred has preference over series B pre-
ferred with respect to liquidation and dividends.

Assume the company has paid all dividends through 19X4.

Required

Compute the dividends to both series of preferred and common for 19X5 and 19X6 if total dividends are $0 in 19X5 and $1,500,000 in 19X6. (Round to the nearest dollar.)

Exercise 14-9   *Shareholders' equity section of a balance sheet*

China Palace Corporation has the following selected account balances at June 30, 19X7. Prepare the shareholders' equity section of the company's balance sheet. (Not all accounts listed are part of shareholders' equity).

Common stock, no-par, 500,000 shares authorized, 120,000 shares issued	$660,000	Inventory	$112,000
		Machinery and equipment ...	109,000
Donated capital	34,000	Preferred stock subscription receivable	8,000
Accumulated depreciation— machinery and equipment .	62,000	Preferred stock, $1.00, 20,000 shares authorized,	
Retained earnings	119,000	10,000 shares issued	200,000
Preferred stock subscribed 1,000 shares	20,000	Organization cost, net	3,000

Exercise 14-10   *Book value per share of preferred and common stock*

The balance sheet of International Graphics Corporation reported the following:

Redeemable preferred stock; redemption value $5,103,000	$ 4,860,000
Common shareholders' equity 8,120,375 shares issued and outstanding	216,788,000
Total shareholders' equity..........................	$221,648,000

Assume the International has paid preferred dividends for the current year and all prior years (no dividends in arrears), and the company has 100,000 shares of preferred stock outstanding. Compute the book value per share of the preferred stock and the common stock.

Exercise 14-11   *Book value per share of preferred and common stock; preferred dividends in arrears*

Refer to Exercise 14-10. Compute the book value per share of the preferred stock and the common stock, assuming that three years' preferred dividends (including dividends for the current year) are in arrears. Assume the preferred stock is cumulative and its dividend rate is $3.00.

Problems

(Group A)

Problem 14-1A *Journalizing corporation transactions and preparing the shareholders' equity section of the balance sheet*

Greenlawn Inc. was organized under the laws of the province of Nova Scotia. The articles of incorporation authorize Greenlawn to issue 100,000 shares of $3, no-par preferred stock and 500,000 shares of no par common stock. During its start-up phase, the company completed the following transactions:

July 5 Paid fees of $1,500 to the Province of Nova Scotia to obtain the articles of incorporation and file the required documents for incorporation.

6. Issued 500 shares of common stock to the promoters who organized the corporation. Their fee was $15,000.

7 Accepted subscriptions for 1,000 shares of common stock at $30 per share and received a down payment of one third of the subscription amount.

12 Issued 300 shares of preferred stock for cash of $18,000.

14 Issued 800 shares of common stock in exchange for land valued at $24,000.

31 Collected one half of the stock subscription receivable.

31 Earned a small profit for July and closed the $4,000 credit balance of Income Summary into the Retained Earnings account.

Required

1. Record the transactions in the general journal.
2. Prepare the shareholders' equity section of the Greenlawn balance sheet at July 31.

Problem 14-2A *Shareholders' equity section of the balance sheet*

The following summaries for Beliveau Inc. and Monroe Corporation provide the information needed to prepare the shareholders' equity section of the company balance sheet. The two companies are independent.

Beliveau, Inc.   Beliveau, Inc. is authorized to issue 25,000 shares of no par common stock. All the stock was issued at $6 per share. The company incurred net losses of $30,000 in 19X1 and $14,000 in 19X2. It earned net incomes of $8,000 in 19X3 and $41,000 in 19X4. The company declared no dividends during the four-year period.

Monroe Corporation   Monroe's articles of incorporation authorizes the company to issue 5,000 shares of $5.00 preferred stock and 500,000 shares of no-par common stock. Monroe issued 1,000 shares of the preferred stock at $105 per share. It issued 200,000 shares of the common stock for $300,000. The company's retained earnings balance at the beginning of 19X4 was $120,000. Net income for 19X4 was $65,000, and the company correctly subtracted the $5.00 preferred dividend for 19X4 from retained earnings. No preferred dividends are in arrears.

Required

For each company, prepare the shareholders' equity section of its balance sheet at December 31, 19X4. Show the computation of all amounts. Entries are not required.

Problem 14-3A *Journalizing corporation transactions and preparing the shareholders' equity section of the balance sheet*

The partnership of Starr & Wagner needed additional capital to expand into new markets, so the business incorporated as Micro Devices, Inc. The articles of incorporation from the Government of Canada authorizes Micro Devices to issue 50,000 shares of $1.00, no-par preferred stock and 100,000 shares of no-par common stock. In its first month, Micro Devices completed the following transactions:

Dec. 1   Paid incorporation fees of $2,100 to the Government of Canada and paid legal fees of $1,000 to organize as a corporation.

2   Issued 500 shares of common stock to the promoter for assistance with issuance of the common stock. The promotional fee was $3,000.

2   Issued 9,000 shares of common stock to Starr and 12,000 shares to Wagner in return for the net assets of the partnership. Starr's capital balance on the partnership books was $54,000, and Wagner's capital balance was $72,000.

4   Accepted subscriptions for 4,000 shares of common stock at $6 per share and received a down payment of 20 percent of the subscription amount.

8   Received a small parcel of land valued at $35,000 as a donation from the city of Brandon.

10   Issued 400 shares of preferred stock to acquire a patent with a market value of $10,000.

16   Issued 600 shares of common stock for cash of $3,600.

30   Collected one third of the stock subscription receivable.

Required

1. Record the transactions in the general journal.
2. Prepare the shareholders' equity section of the Micro Devices balance sheet at December 31. Retained Earnings' balance is $19,970.

Problem 14-4A   *Analysing the shareholders' equity of a corporation*

The purpose of this problem is to familiarize you with the financial statement information of a real company. The Toronto-Dominion Bank is one of Canada's major banks. Toronto-Dominion included the following in its shareholders' equity section on its balance sheet:

		(thousands of dollars)
Shareholders' equity	Capital stock: (note 12)	
	Preferred	346,651
	Common	875,336
	Retained earnings	2,534,251
		3,756,238

Note 12. The share capital of the Bank consists of

Authorized

25,000,000 Class A First Preferred shares and 25,000,000 Class B First Preferred shares.

An unlimited number of common shares whose aggregate consideration shall not exceed $3 billion.

Issued and fully paid

1,866,025 $1.835 Cumulative Redeemable Class A First Preferred Shares...........................	$ 46,651
6,000,000 Variable Rate* Cumulative Redeemable Class A First Preferred Shares, Series D......................................	150,000
1,500,000 Price Adjusted Floating Rate* Cumulative Redeemable Class B First Preferred Shares, Series 1	150,000
	346,651
150,499,187 Common Shares..............................	875,336

* The dividend rate for these shares is based on the Bank's prime lending rate and determined annually.

Required

1. Identify the different issues of stock Toronto-Dominion has outstanding.
2. Is the preferred stock participating or nonparticipating? How can you tell?
3. Can you tell at what price the Class A First Preferred Series D shares are redeemable at? Why do you think the Toronto-Dominion Bank issued redeemable preferred shares?
4. How does the capital stock section of the Toronto-Dominion Bank differ from that illustrated on page p. 592?
5. All three preferred share issues are cumulative? What effect does that feature have on the common shares?
6. The dividend rates for this year are

Class A First Preferred, Series D	$2.15
Class B First Preferred, Series 1	8.75

What is the total dividend that must be paid this year before the common shareholders receive any dividend? Assume that there are no arrears on the preferred shares from prior years.

7. Pierre Richard wishes to earn 10 percent on his money and is thinking of buying 100 common shares of Toronto-Dominion stock. The market price is presently $40.00 per share. What dividend would have to be paid on the common shares so that Pierre could earn his 10 percent? What would the total dividend paid by Toronto-Dominion have to be so that Pierre could earn his 10 percent (Hint: use the information from question 6 above)?

Problem 14-5A *Computing dividends on preferred and common stock*

Ayr Ltd. has 5,000 shares of $.40 preferred stock and 100,000 shares of common stock outstanding. During a three-year period Ayr declared and paid cash dividends as follows: 19X1, $0; 19X2, $5,000; and 19X3, $34,000.

Required

1. Compute the total dividends to preferred stock and common stock for each of the three years if
   a. Preferred is noncumulative and nonparticipating.
   b. Preferred is cumulative and nonparticipating.
2. For case 1b, record the declaration of the 19X3 dividends on December 22, 19X3 and the payment of the dividends on January 14, 19X4.

Problem 14-6A *Analysing the shareholders' equity of an actual corporation*

The balance sheet of Oak Manufacturing, Inc. reported the following:

Shareholders' Investment (same as shareholders' equity)	($ thousands)
Cumulative convertible preferred stock	$ 45
Common stock, authorized 40,000,000 shares; issued 16,000,000 shares	192,000
Retained earnings	(77,165)
Total shareholders' investment	$114,880

Notes to the financial statements indicate that 9,000 shares of $1.60 preferred stock were issued and outstanding. The preferred stock has a redemption value of $25 per share, and preferred dividends are in arrears for two years, including the current year. On the balance sheet date, the market value of the Oak Manufacturing common stock was $7.50 per share.

Required

1. Is the preferred stock cumulative or noncumulative, participating or nonparticipating? How can you tell?
2. What is the amount of the annual preferred dividend?
3. What is the total capital stock of the company?
4. What was the total market value of the common stock?
5. Compute the book value per share of the preferred stock and the common stock.

Problem 14-7A   *Preparing a corporation balance sheet*

The following accounts and related balances of Maritimes Ltd. are arranged in no particular order. Use them to prepare the company's classified balance sheet in the account format at November 30, 19X7.

Accounts payable	$ 47,000	Preferred stock,	
Stock subscription receivable,		25,000 shares authorized,	
preferred	1,000	3,000 shares issued	$ 30,000
Retained earnings	101,000	Cash	41,000
Common stock,		Inventory	176,000
100,000 shares authorized,		Property, plant, and	
42,000 shares issued	283,000	equipment, net	328,000
Dividends payable	3,000	Organization cost, net	6,000
Donated capital	109,000	Prepaid expenses	13,000
Accrued liabilities	17,000	Preferred stock subscribed	
Long-term note payable	86,000	700 shares	7,000
Accounts receivable, net	87,000	Patent, net	31,000

(Group B)

Problem 14-1B   *Journalizing corporation transactions and preparing the shareholders' equity section of the balance sheet*

Multipurpose Corporation received articles of incorporation from the Government of Canada. The company is authorized to issue 50,000 shares of $2.00 preferred stock and 300,000 shares of common stock. During its start-up phase, the company completed the following transactions:

Oct. 2   Paid incorporation and legal fees of $2,800 to obtain the articles of incorporation.

4   Issued 900 shares of common stock to the promoters who organized the corporation. Their fee was $45,000.

5   Accepted subscriptions for 1,000 shares of common stock at $50 per share and received a down payment of one fourth of the subscription amount.

9   Issued 1,000 shares of common stock in exchange for equipment valued at $50,000.

14   Issued 600 shares of preferred stock for cash of $44 per share.

30   Collected one third of the stock subscription receivable.

31   Earned a small profit for October and closed the $6,100 credit balance of Income Summary into Retained Earnings.

Required

1. Record the transactions in the general journal.
2. Prepare the shareholders' equity section of the Multipurpose balance sheet at October 31.

Problem 14-2B *Shareholders' equity section of the balance sheet*

Shareholders' equity information is given for Baker Corporation and Wang, Inc. The two companies are independent.

Baker Corporation   Baker Corporation is authorized to issue 10,000 shares of common stock. All the stock was issued at $8 per share. The company incurred a net loss of $12,000 in 19X1. It earned net incomes of $5,000 in 19X2 and $21,000 in 19X3. The company declared no dividends during the three-year period.

Wang, Inc.   Wang's articles of incorporation authorizes the company to issue 7,500 shares of $2.50 preferred stock and 120,000 shares of common stock. Wang issued 800 shares of the preferred stock at $60 per share. It issued 20,000 shares of the common stock for a total of $240,000. The company's retained earnings balance at the beginning of 19X3 was $72,000 and net income for the year was $49,000. During 19X3, the company correctly subtracted the specified dividend on preferred and a $.50 per share dividend on common from retained earnings. No preferred dividends are in arrears.

Required

For each company, prepare the shareholders' equity section of its balance sheet at December 31, 19X3. Show the computation of all amounts. Entries are not required.

Problem 14-3B *Journalizing corporation transactions and preparing the shareholders' equity section of the balance sheet*

The partners who owned Wolfson & Stauffer wished to avoid the unlimited personal liability of the partnership form of business, so they incorporated the partnership as Financial Consultants, Inc. The articles of incorporation from the federal government authorizes the corporation to issue 10,000 shares of $6.00 preferred stock and 250,000 shares of common stock. In its first month, Financial Consultants completed the following transactions:

Dec. 1   Paid incorporation fees of $2,000 and paid legal fees of $1,900 to organize as a corporation.

3   Issued 750 shares of common stock to the promoter for assistance with issuance of the common stock. The promotion fee was $7,500.

3   Issued 4,100 shares of common stock to Wolfson and 3,800 shares to Stauffer in return for the net assets of the partnership. Wolfson's capital balance on the partnership books was $41,000, and Stauffer's capital balance was $38,000.

5   Accepted subscriptions for 5,000 shares of common stock at $10 per share and received a down payment of 25 percent of the subscription amount.

7   Received a small parcel of land valued at $42,000 as a donation from the city of Moose Jaw.

12   Issued 1,000 shares of preferred stock to acquire a patent with a market value of $110,000.

22   Issued 1,500 shares of common stock for $10 cash per share.

28   Collected 20 percent of the stock subscription receivable.

Required

1. Record the transactions in the general journal.
2. Prepare the shareholders' equity section of the Financial Consultants balance sheet at December 31. Retained Earnings balance is $20,820.

Problem 14-4B *Analysing the shareholders' equity of an actual corporation*

The purpose of this problem is to familiarize you with the financial statement information of a real company, U and I, Inc. U and I included the following shareholders' equity on its year-end balance sheet at February 28:

Shareholders' Equity	($ thousands)
Voting Preferred Stock, $1.265 cumulative; authorized 100,000 shares in each class:	
Class A—issued 75,473 shares	$ 1,736
Class B—issued 92,172 shares	2,120
Common stock, authorized 5,000,000 shares;	19,903
issued 2,870,950 shares	
Retained earnings	8,336
	$32,095

Required

1. Identify the different issues of stock U and I has outstanding.
2. Is the preferred stock participating or nonparticipating? How can you tell?
3. Give the summary entries to record issuance of all the U and I stock. Assume that all the stock was issued for cash. Explanations are not required.
4. How does the capital stock section of U and I differ from that illustrated on p. 592?
5. Suppose U and I passed its preferred dividends for one year. Would the company have to pay these dividends in arrears before paying dividends to the common shareholders? Give your reason.
6. What amount of preferred dividends must U and I declare and pay each year to avoid having preferred dividends in arrears?
7. Assume preferred dividends are in arrears for 19X8.
    a. Write Note 5 of the February 28, 19X8 financial statements to disclose the dividends in arrears.
    b. Record the declaration of a $500,000 dividend in the year ended February 28, 19X9. An explanation is not required.

Problem 14-5B *Computing dividends on preferred and common stock*

Continental Corporation has 10,000 shares of $4.25, preferred stock and 40,000 shares of common stock outstanding. Continental declared and paid the following dividends during a three-year period: 19X1, $10,000; 19X2, $80,000; and 19X3, $265,000.

Required

1. Compute the total dividends to preferred stock and common stock for each of the three years if
    a. Preferred is noncumulative and nonparticipating.
    b. Preferred is cumulative and nonparticipating.
2. For case 1b, record the declaration of the 19X3 dividends on December 28, 19X3 and the payment of the dividends on January 17, 19X4.

Problem 14-6B   *Analysing the shareholders' equity of an actual corporation*

The balance sheet of Fort Murray Drilling Company Limited reported the following:

**Shareholders' Investment
(same as Shareholders' Equity)**

Redeemable non-voting preferred stock, no-par (Redemption value $358,000)	$320,000
Common stock, authorized 60,000 shares; issued 28,000 shares	259,000
Retained earnings	7,000
Total shareholders' investment	$586,000

Notes to the financial statements indicate that 8,000 shares of $3.90 preferred stock were issued and outstanding. Preferred dividends are in arrears for three years, including the current year. On the balance sheet date, the market value of the Fort Murray common stock was $4.50 per share.

Required

1. Which class of shareholders controls the company? Give your reason.
2. Is the preferred stock cumulative or noncumulative, participating or nonparticipating? How can you tell?
3. What is the amount of the annual preferred dividend?
4. What is the total capital stock of the company?
5. What was the total market value of the common stock?
6. Compute the book value per share of the preferred stock and the common stock.

Problem 14-7B   *Preparing a corporation balance sheet*

The following accounts and related balances of Superior Coal and Iron, Inc. are arranged in no particular order. Use them to prepare the company's classified balance sheet in the account format at June 30, 19X2.

Trademark, net	$ 9,000	Dividends payable	$ 9,000
Organization cost, net	14,000	Retained earnings	48,000
Preferred stock, $.65 no-par, 10,000 shares authorized, 2,700 shares issued	27,000	Accounts payable	53,000
		Property, plant, and equipment, net	167,000
Stock subscription receivable —common	3,000	Common stock, no par, 500,000 shares authorized, 214,000 shares issued	126,000
Cash	19,000	Prepaid expenses	10,000
Accounts receivable, net	34,000	Common stock subscribed 22,000 shares	11,000
Accrued liabilities	26,000		
Long-term note payable	72,000		
Inventory	122,000	Donated capital	6,000

Decision Problems

1.   *Evaluating alternative ways of raising capital*
J. McDade and M. Fineberg have written a computer program for a video game that they believe will rival Nintendo. They need additional capital to market the product,

and they plan to incorporate their partnership. They are considering alternative capital structures for the corporation. Their primary goal is to raise as much capital as possible without giving up control of the business. The partners plan to receive 120,000 shares of the corporation's common stock in return for the net assets of the partnership. After the partnership books are closed and the assets adjusted to current market value, McDade's capital balance is $65,000 and Fineberg's balance is $55,000.

The corporation's plans for the articles of incorporation include an authorization to issue 5,000 shares of preferred stock and 500,000 shares of common stock. McDade and Fineberg are uncertain about the most desirable features for the preferred stock. Prior to incorporating, the partners have discussed their plans with two investment groups. The corporation can obtain capital from outside investors under either of the following plans:

Plan 1 Group 1 will invest $75,000 to acquire 600 shares of $5, no-par preferred stock and $100,000 to acquire 100,000 shares of common stock. Each preferred share receives 50 votes on matters that come before the shareholders. The investors in Group 1 would attempt to control the corporation if they have the majority of the corporate votes.

Plan 2 Group 2 will invest $150,000 to acquire 1,000 shares of $6.00, nonvoting, noncumulative, participating preferred stock.

Required

Assume the corporation receives its articles of incorporation.
1. Journalize the issuance of common stock to McDade and Fineberg.
2. Journalize the issuance of stock to the outsiders under both plans.
3. Assume net income for the first year is $130,000 and total dividends of $19,800 are properly subtracted from retained earnings. Prepare the shareholders' equity section of the corporation balance sheet under both plans.
4. Recommend one of the plans to McDade and Fineberg. Give your reasons.

2. Questions about corporations
1. Why do you think capital stock and retained earnings are shown separately in the shareholders' equity section?
2. Mary Reznick, major shareholder of M-R Inc., proposes to sell some land she owns to the company for common shares in M-R. What problem does she face in recording the transaction?
3. Preferred shares generally are preferred with respect to dividends and on liquidation. If that is the case, why would investors buy common shares when preferred shares are available?
4. What does it mean if the liquidation value of a company's stock is greater than the market value?
5. If you owned 100 shares of stock in Magna Corporation and someone offered to buy the stock for its book value, would you accept their offer? Why or why not?

Financial Statement Problem

Shareholders' equity
The John Labatt balance sheet appears in Appendix E. Answer these questions about the company's capital stock.

1. Describe the different classes of stock that John Labatt can issue. How many shares of each class are authorized at April 30, 1989? How many shares of each class are issued?

2. What is the average stated value per common share? What was the average stated value of shares issued during the year ended April 30, 1989?

3. What is the total shareholders' equity at April 30, 1989? Exclude convertible debentures from your calculation.

4. Journalize the issuance of 10,000 common shares with a stated value of $22.00 per share. Use John Labatt terminology. No explanation is required.

5. Ignoring the foreign currency translation adjustment, what is the book value per common share?

Answers to Self-Study Questions

1. b
2. b
3. c
4. d
5. a
6. d (1,000 shares $\times$ $104 = $104,000)
7. d Intangible asset
8. a [(10,000 $\times$ $3.50 $\times$ 3 = $105,000) + (100,000 $\times$ $1.50 = $150,000) = $255,000]
9. c
10. b

15

Corporations: Retained Earnings, Dividends, Treasury Stock and the Income Statement

---

LEARNING OBJECTIVES

After studying this chapter, you should be able to

1 Account for stock dividends

2 Distinguish stock splits from stock dividends

3 Account for treasury stock

4 Report restrictions of retained earnings

5 Identify the elements of a corporation income statement

6 Account for prior period adjustments

Chapter 14 introduced the corporate form of business. Chapter 15 continues our discussion of corporation retained earnings and cash dividends and also considers stock dividends, treasury stock and the corporate income statement.

Retained Earnings and Dividends

We have seen that the equity section on the corporation balance sheet is called shareholders' equity. The capital stock accounts and retained earnings make up the shareholders' equity section.

Retained Earnings is the corporation account that carries the balance of the business's net income from operations accumulated over the corporation's lifetime less its net loses and any declared dividends. *Retained* means "held on to." Retained Earnings is accumulated income to cover dividends and any future losses. Because Retained Earnings is an owners' equity account, it normally has a credit balance. Corporations may use other labels for Retained Earnings, among them Earnings Reinvested in the Business and Retained Income.

A debit balance in Retained Earnings, which arises when a corporation's accumulated net losses and any declared dividends exceed its accumulated net income, is called a *deficit*. This amount is subtracted from the sum of the credit balances in the other equity accounts on the balance sheet to determine total shareholders' equity. In a recent survey, 31 of 300 companies (10 percent) had a retained earnings deficit.

At the end of each accounting period, the Income Summary account, which carries the balance of net income for the period, is closed to the Retained Earnings account. Assume the following amounts are drawn from a corporation's temporary accounts:

Income Summary

Dec. 31, 19X1	Expenses	750,000	Dec. 31, 19X1	Revenues	850,000
			Dec. 31, 19X1	Bal.	100,000

This final closing entry transfers net income from Income Summary to Retained Earnings:

19X1			
Dec. 31	Income Summary	100,000	
	Retained Earnings		100,000
	To close net income to Retained Earnings.		

If 19X1 was the corporation's first year of operations, the Retained Earnings account now has an ending balance of $100,000:

Retained Earnings

	Jan. 1, 19X1	Bal.	-0-
	Dec. 31, 19X1	Net income	100,000
	Dec. 31, 19X1	Bal.	100,000

A $60,000 net loss for the year would produce this debit balance in Income Summary:

Income Summary

Dec. 31, 19X1	Expenses	470,000	Dec. 31, 19X3	Revenues	410,000
Dec. 31, 19X3	Bal.	60,000			

To close a $60,000 loss, we would credit Income Summary and debit Retained Earnings, as follows:

19X3			
Dec. 31	Retained Earnings	60,000	
	Income Summary		60,000
	To close net loss to Retained Earnings.		

After posting, Income Summary's balance is zero, and the Retained Earnings balance is decreased by $60,000.

Remember that the account title includes the word *earnings*. Credits to the Retained Earnings account arise only from net income. When we examine a corporation income statement and want to learn how much net income has the corporation earned and retained in the business, we turn to Retained Earnings.

After the corporation has earned net income, its board of directors may declare and pay a cash dividend to the shareholders. The entry on January 15, 19X2 to record the declaration of a $35,000 dividend is

19X2			
Jan. 15	Retained Earnings	35,000	
	Dividends Payable		35,000
	To declare a cash dividend.		

After the dividend declaration is posted, the Retained Earnings account has a $65,000 credit balance:

Retained Earnings

Jan. 15, 19X2	Dividend	35,000	Jan. 1, 19X2	Bal.	100,000
			Jan. 15, 19X2	Bal.	65,000

The Retained Earnings account is not a reservoir of cash waiting for the board of directors to pay dividends to the shareholders. Instead, Retained Earnings is an owners' equity account representing a claim on all assets in general and not on any asset in particular. Its balance is the cumulative, lifetime earnings of the company less its cumulative losses and dividends. In fact, the corporation may have a large balance in Retained Earnings but not have the cash to pay a dividend because the company purchased a building or the company may have abundant cash from borrowing but very little retained earnings. To *declare* a dividend, the company must have an adequate balance in Retained Earnings. To *pay* the dividend, it must have the cash. Cash and Retained Earnings are two entirely separate accounts sharing no necessary relationship.

Dividend Dates

Three relevant dates for dividends are

1. **Declaration date** On the declaration date, the board of directors announces the intention to pay the dividend. The declaration creates a liability for the corporation. Declaration is recorded by debiting Retained Earnings and crediting Dividends Payable.
2. **Date of record** The people who own the stock on the date of record receive the dividend. The corporation announces the record date, which follows the declaration date by a few weeks, as part of the declaration. The corporation makes no journal entry on the date of record because no transaction occurs. Nevertheless, much work takes place behind the scenes to properly identify the shareholders of record on this date because the stock is being traded continuously.
3. **Payment date** Payment of the dividend usually follows the record date by two to four weeks. Payment is recorded by debiting Dividends Payable and crediting Cash.

Stock Dividends

A **stock dividend** is a proportional distribution by a corporation of its own stock to its shareholders. Stock dividends are fundamentally different from cash dividends because stock dividends do not transfer the assets of the corporation to the shareholders. Cash dividends are distributions of the asset cash, but stock dividends cause changes *only* in the shareholders' equity of the corporation. The effect of a stock dividend is an increase in the stock account and a decrease in Retained Earnings. Because both of these accounts are elements of shareholders' equity, total shareholders' equity is unchanged. There is merely a transfer from one shareholders' equity account to another, and no asset or liability is affected by a stock dividend.

The corporation distributes stock dividends to shareholders in proportion to the number of shares they already own. For example, suppose a shareholder owned 300 shares of Canadian Pacific Ltd. common stock. If Canadian Pacific distributed a 10 percent common stock dividend, he/she would receive 30 (300×.10) additional shares. He/she would now own 330 shares of the stock. All other Canadian Pacific shareholders would receive additional shares equal to 10 percent of their prior holdings. He/she would all be in the same relative position after the dividend as before.

In distributing a stock dividend, the corporation gives up no assets. Why, then, do companies issue stock dividends?

Reasons for Stock Dividends

A corporation may choose to distribute stock dividends for the following reasons:

1. To continue dividends but conserve cash. A company may want to keep cash in the business in order to expand, buy inventory, pay off debts, and so on. Yet the company may wish to continue dividends in some form. To do so, the corporation may distribute a stock dividend. The debit to Retained Earnings also conserves cash by decreasing the Retained Earnings available for the declaration of future cash dividends.

2. To reduce the market price per share of its stock. Many companies pay low cash dividends and grow by reinvesting their earnings in operations. As they grow, the company's stock price increases. If the price gets high enough, eventually some potential investors may be prevented from purchasing the stock. Distribution of a stock dividend may cause the market price of a share of the company's stock to decrease because of the increased supply of the stock.

Suppose the market price of a share of stock is $50. If the corporation doubles the number of shares of its stock outstanding by issuing a stock dividend, the market price of the stock would drop by approximately one half, to $25 per share. The objective is to make the stock less expensive and thus attractive to a wider range of investors because less cash is required for the investor to buy a block of shares.

Entries for Stock Dividends

The board of directors announces stock dividends on the declaration date. The date of record and the distribution date follow. (This is the same sequence of dates used for a cash dividend.) The declaration of a stock dividend does *not* create a liability because the corporation is not obligated to pay assets. (Recall that a liability is a claim on *assets*.) Instead, the corporation has declared its intention to distribute its stock. Assume General Lumber Corporation has the following shareholders' equity prior to the dividend:

Shareholders' Equity

Capital stock	
Common stock, 50,000 shares authorized, 20,000 shares issued	$270,000
Total capital stock	270,000
Retained earnings	85,000
Total shareholders' equity	$355,000

Of concern about stock dividends is how to determine the amount to transfer from retained earnings to the capital stock account. The *Canada Business Corporations Act* suggests that the market value of the shares issued is the appropriate amount to transfer, while other incorporating acts allow the directors to set a value on the shares. If market value were to be used, it would be the market value on the date the dividend is declared. If any other value were to be used, it would be determined by the directors at the time of declaration. This issue is not dealt with in the *CICA Handbook*. The market value of the shares issued would seem to be an appropriate valuation in any event and will be used in this text.

Assume General Lumber Corporation declares a 10 percent common stock dividend on November 17. The company will distribute 2,000 ($20,000 \times .10$) shares in the dividend. On November 17 the market value of its common stock is $16 per share. Using the market value approach, Retained Earnings is debited for the market value of the 2,000 dividend shares and Common Stock Dividend Distributable is credited. General Lumber makes the following entry on the declaration date.

Nov. 17	Retained earnings ($20,000 \times .10 \times \$16$)	32,000	
	Common Stock Dividend Distributable		32,000
	To declare a 10 percent common stock dividend.		

OBJECTIVE 1

Account for stock dividends

On the distribution (payment) date, the company records issuance of the dividend shares as follows:

Dec. 12	Common Stock Dividend Distributable	32,000	
	Common Stock		32,000
	To issue common stock in a stock dividend.		

Common Stock Dividend Distributable is an owner's equity account. (It is *not* a liability because the corporation has no obligation to pay assets.) If the company prepares financial statements after the declaration of the stock dividend but before issuing it, Common Stock Dividend Distributable is reported in the shareholders' equity section of the balance sheet immediately after Common Stock and Common Stock Subscribed. However, this account holds the value of the dividend shares only from the declaration date to the date of distribution.

The following tabulation shows the changes in shareholders' equity caused by the stock dividend:

Shareholders' Equity	Before the Dividend	After the Dividend	Change
Capital stock			
Common stock, 50,000 shares			
authorized, 20,000 shares issued	$270,000		
22,000 shares issued		$302,000	**up by $32,000**
Total capital stock.................	270,000	302,000	**up by $32,000**
Retained earnings	85,000	53,000	down by $32,000
Total shareholders' equity	$355,000	$355,000	Unchanged

Compare shareholders' equity before and after the stock dividend. Observe the increase in the balance of Common Stock and the decrease in Retained Earnings. Also observe that total shareholders' equity is unchanged from $355,000.

Amount of Retained Earnings Transferred in a Stock Dividend   Stock dividends are said to be *capitalized retained earnings* because they transfer an amount from retained earnings to capital stock. The capital stock accounts are more permanent than retained earnings because they are not subject to owner withdrawals through dividends. As we saw in the preceding illustration, the amount transferred from Retained Earnings in a stock dividend is the market value of the dividend shares. Therefore, many shareholders view stock dividends as distributions of earnings.

Stock Splits

A large stock dividend may decrease the market price of the stock. The stock then becomes attractive to more people. A stock split also decreases the market price of stock — with the intention of making the stock more attractive. A **stock split** is an increase in the number of outstanding shares of stock coupled with a proportionate reduction in the book value per share of the stock. For example, if the company splits its stock 2 for 1, the number of outstanding shares is doubled and each share's book value is halved. Many large companies in Canada, Dofasco, Toronto-Dominion Bank, St. Lawrence Cement, National Trust, and others, have split their stock.

Assume that the market price of a share of Star Ltd. common stock is $120 and that the company wishes to decrease the market price to approximately $30. Star Ltd. decides to split the common stock 4 for 1 in the expectation that the stock's market price would fall from $120 to $30. A 4-for-1 stock split means that the company would have four times as many shares of stock outstanding after the split as it had before and that each share's book value would be quartered. Assume Star had 150 thousand shares of common stock issued and outstanding before the split.

Shareholders' Equity	($ thousands)
Capital stock	
Common stock, 900 thousand shares authorized,	
150 thousand shares issued	$ 5,950
Total capital stock	5,950
Retained earnings	20,000
Total sharesholders' equity	$25,950

After the 4-for-1 split, Star would have 600 thousand shares (150 thousand shares × 4) of common stock outstanding. Total shareholders' equity would be exactly as before the stock split. Indeed, the balance in the Common Stock account does not even change. Only the number of shares issued and the book value per share change. Compare the highlighted figures in the two shareholders' equity presentations.

Shareholders' Equity	($ thousands)
Capital stock	
Common stock, 900 thousand shares authorized,	
600 thousand shares issued	$ 5,950
Total capital stock	5,950
Retained earnings	20,000
Total shareholders' equity	$25,950

The book value per share was $173 ($25,950/150) before the stock split and $43.25 ($25,950/600) after the split.

Because the stock split affects no account balances, no formal journal entry is necessary. Instead, the split is recorded in a memorandum entry such as the following:

Aug. 19   Distributed three additional shares of common stock for each old share previously outstanding.

Stock Dividends and Stock Splits

A stock dividend and a stock split both increase the number of shares of stock owned per shareholder. Also, neither a stock dividend nor a stock split changes the investor's total cost of the stock owned. For example, assume you paid $3,000 to acquire 150 shares of National Sea Products common stock. If National Sea distributes a 100 percent stock dividend, your 150 shares increase to 300, but your total cost is still $3,000. Likewise, if National Sea distributes a 2-for-1 stock split, your shares increase in number to 300, but your total cost is unchanged. Neither type of stock action is taxable income to the investor.

> **OBJECTIVE 2**
> Distinguish stock splits from stock dividends

Both a stock dividend and a stock split increase the corporation's number of shares outstanding. For example, a 100 percent stock dividend and a 2-for-1 stock split both double the outstanding shares and cut the stock's market price per share in half. They differ in that a stock *dividend* shifts an amount from retained earnings to capital stock, leaving book value per share unchanged. A stock *split* affects no account balances whatsoever but instead changes the book value of the stock.

Exhibit 15-1 summarizes the effects of dividends and stock splits on total shareholders' equity.

EXHIBIT 15-1   *Effects on Total Shareholders' Equity*

	Declaration	Payment of Cash or Distribution of Stock
Cash dividend	Decrease	None
Stock dividend	None	None
Stock split	None	None

Source: Adapted from Beverly Terry.

Treasury Stock

Corporations may purchase their own stock from their shareholders for several reasons: (1) the company may have issued all its authorized stock and need the stock for distributions to officers and employees under bonus plans or stock purchase plans; (2) the purchase may help support the stock's current market price by decreasing the supply of stock available to the public; and (3) management may gather in the stock to avoid a takeover by an outside party. Stock that is purchased in this way is called **treasury stock**, because it is in the issuing corporation's treasury; in that state, it may be cancelled or reissued.

The *Canada Business Corporations Act* requires a corporation that purchases its own stock to cancel the shares bought. It may do so by treating the purchased shares as authorized but unissued, and issue them in the normal way at a later date or it may cancel them outright. Several of the provincial incorporating acts require that the shares be treated this way, too, while others permit the corporation to hold the shares as treasury stock and resell them.

The *Canada Business Corporations Act* and most provincial incorporating acts do not permit a corporation to reacquire its own shares if such reacquisition would result in the corporation being unable to pay its liabilities as they become due.

For practical purposes, treasury stock is like unissued stock: neither category of stock is outstanding in the hands of shareholders. The company does not receive cash dividends on its treasury stock, and treasury stock does not entitle the company to vote or to receive assets in liquidation. The difference between unissued stock and treasury stock is that treasury stock has been issued and bought back.

The purchase of treasury stock decreases the company's assets and its shareholders' equity. The size of the company literally decreases, as shown on the balance sheet. For companies incorporated under the *Canada Business Corporations Act*, the Common Stock account is debited. In those jurisdictions where treasury stock is permitted, the Treasury Stock account has a debit balance, which is the opposite of the other owners' equity accounts. Therefore, Treasury Stock is a contra shareholders' equity account.

Purchase of Treasury Stock

The *CICA Handbook* requires a company that purchases its own shares at a price equal to or greater than the issue price to debit Common Stock (or Preferred Stock as the case may be) for the issue price; any excess should be debited to Retained Earnings. When the shares are purchased at a price less than the issue price, the excess of the issue price over the purchase price should be credited to Contributed Surplus. In situations where the shares are issued at different prices, the average issue price should be used. (In jurisdictions where par value stock is permitted, the excess of the price paid over par would be debited to Contributed Surplus.)

Suppose Farwest Drilling Inc. had the following shareholders' equity before purchasing 1,000 of its own shares; its 8,000 shares were issued at the same price, as follows:

Shareholders' Equity

Capital stock
    Common stock, 10,000 shares authorized, 8,000 shares issued $20,000
       Total capital stock   20,000
Retained earnings   14,600
       Total shareholders' equity $34,600

On November 22, Farwest purchases 1,000 shares of its common stock paying cash of $7.50 per share; the shares had been issued at $2.50 (20,000/8,000). Farwest records the purchase as follows:

Nov. 22	Common Stock	2,500	
	Retained Earnings	5,000	
	Cash		7,500
	Purchased 1,000 shares of stock at $7.50 per share.		

> **OBJECTIVE 3**
> Account for treasury stock

The shareholders' equity section of Farwest's balance sheet would appear as follows after the transaction:

Shareholders' Equity

Capital stock
    Common stock, 10,000 shares authorized, 7,000 shares issued $17,500
       Total capital stock   17,500
Retained earnings   9,600
       Total shareholders' equity $27,100

Observe that the purchase of the stock did not affect the number of shares authorized but did decrease the number of shares issued and outstanding. Only outstanding shares have a vote, receive cash dividends, and share in assets if the corporation liquidates. Notice that the dollar amount shown for Capital Stock and Retained Earnings decreased by $2,500 and $5,000 respectively.

The articles of incorporation, issued under the *Canada Business Corporations Act*, for Eastern Exploration Ltd., authorized it to issue 100,000 shares of common stock. By February 28 of this year, Eastern had issued 40,000 shares at an average price of $20.00 per share. Common Stock on the balance sheet amounted to $800,000. Retained Earnings was $187,396.

On March 20, Eastern purchases 2,000 shares at $15.00 per share and records the transaction as follows:

March 20	Common Stock (2,000 × $20)	40,000	
	Contributed Surplus [2,000 × ($20 − 15)] . . .		10,000
	Cash (2,000 × $15)		30,000
	Purchased 2,000 shares of stock at $15 per share.		

The shareholders' equity section of Eastern Exploration's balance sheet would appear as follows after the transaction:

Shareholders' Equity

Capital stock
   Common stock, 100,000 shares authorized, 38,000 shares issued $760,000
   Contributed Surplus (note 6)   10,000
     Total capital stock $770,000
Retained earnings   187,396
     Total shareholders' equity $957,396

Note 6: During the year, the company acquired 2,000 shares of common stock at a price of $15.00 per share; the shares had been issued at $20.00 per share.

How a company accounts for the purchase of its own stock is different in those jurisdictions that do not require such shares to be cancelled as the *Canada Business Corporations Act* does.

Sale of Treasury Stock

A company incorporated under the *Canada Business Corporations Act* may re-issue the shares that it previously had repurchased. The sale would be treated like a normal sale of authorized but unissued stock. As with accounting for the purchase of its own stock, accounting for the re-sale of the stock is different for companies in those jurisdictions that do not require such shares to be cancelled as the *Canada Business Corporations Act* does.

No Gain or Loss from Treasury Stock Transactions

The purchase and sale of treasury stock do not affect net income. Sale of treasury stock above cost is an increase in capital stock, not income. Likewise, sale of treasury stock below cost is a decrease in capital stock, not a loss. Treasury stock transactions take place between the business and its owner's, the shareholders. If the company is able to issue the shares at a price in excess of the price paid for them, the company would earn a "profit" on the transaction. However the profit is not a real profit; it does not appear on the income statement. Instead, it would be reflected in the Common Stock account, since the proceeds of the sale of shares is credited in total to the Common Stock account. Similarly, if the company issued the shares at a price that was less than the price paid for them, the "loss" would be reflected in the Common Stock account.

Suppose Farwest Drilling sold 500 shares of common stock at $10.00 per share shortly after the purchase of 1,000 shares described above. Farwest records the sale as follows:

Dec. 5	Cash	5,000	
	Common Stock		5,000
	To sell 500 shares of stock at $10.00 per share.		

If Farwest had sold the 500 shares for $2.00 per share, the sale would be recorded as follows:

Dec. 5	Cash	1,000	
	Common Stock		1,000
	To sell 500 shares of stock at $2.00 per share.		

Does this mean that a company cannot increase its net assets by buying treasury stock low and selling it high? Not at all. Management may buy treasury stock because it believes the market price of its stock is too low. For example, a company may buy 500 shares of its stock at $10 per share. Suppose it holds the stock as the market price rises and resells the stock at $14 per share. The net assets of the company increase by $2,000 [500 shares × ($14 − $10 = $4 difference per share)]. This increase is reported as capital stock and not as income.

Summary Problem for Your Review

Pierre Caron, Inc. reported the following shareholders' equity:

Shareholders' Equity

Preferred stock $1.00	
Authorized: 10,000 shares	
Issued: None	$ —
Common stock	
Authorized, 30,000 shares	
Issued 13,733 shares	49,266
Earnings retained in business	89,320
	$138,586

Required

1. What was the average issue price per share of the common stock?
2. Journalize the issuance of 1,200 shares of common stock at $4 per share. Use Caron's account titles.
3. How many shares of Caron's common stock are outstanding?
4. How many shares of common stock would be outstanding after Caron splits its common stock 3 for 1?
5. Using Caron account titles, journalize the declaration of a stock dividend when the market price of Caron common stock is $3 per share. Consider each of the following stock dividends independently:
    a. Caron declares a 10 percent common stock dividend on the shares outstanding, computed in question 3.
    b. Caron declares a 50 percent common stock dividend on the shares outstanding, computed in question 3.
6. Journalize the following treasury stock transactions, assuming they occur in the order given:
    a. Caron purchases 500 shares at $8 per share.
    b. Caron purchases 500 shares at $3 per share.
    c. Caron sells 100 shares for $9 per share.
7. How many shares of Caron's common stock would be outstanding after the transactions in question 6 take place. Ignore the transactions in questions 4 and 5.

SOLUTION TO SUMMARY PROBLEM

1. Average issue price of the common stock was $3.59 per share ($49,266/13,733 shares = $3.59).

2. Cash (1,200 × $4) 4,800
   Common Stock 4,800
   To issue common stock.

3. Shares outstanding = 13,733.

4. Shares outstanding after a 3-for-1 stock split = 41,199, (13,733 shares outstanding × 3).

5. a. Earnings Retained in Business
      (13,733 × .10 × $3) 4,120
         Common Stock Dividend Distributable 4,120
      To declare a 10 percent common stock dividend.

   b. Earnings Retained in Business
      (13,733 × .50 × $3) 20,600
         Common Stock Dividend Distributable 20,600
      To declare a 50 percent common stock dividend.

6. a. Common Stock (500 × $3.59) 1,795
      Retained Earnings [500 × ($8.00 − $3.59)] 2,205
         Cash 4,000
      To purchase 500 shares at $8.00 per share.

   b. Common Stock (500 × $3.59) 1,795
         Contributed Surplus [500 × ($3.59 − $3.00)] 295
         Cash 1,500
      To purchase 500 shares at $3.00 per share.

   c. Cash (100 × $9.00) 900
         Common Stock 900
      To sell 100 shares at $9.00 per share.

7. Shares outstanding = 12,833 (13,733 − 500 − 500 + 100)

Retirement of Stock

Under the heading "Treasury Stock," you learned that corporations incorporated under the *Canada Business Corporations Act* may reacquire their own shares and that the shares must be either cancelled outright or treated as authorized but unissued. You further learned that corporations incorporated in other jurisdictions could treat such purchased shares as treasury shares and later resell them.

Shares that are cancelled may not be re-issued. The effect of purchasing an outstanding share is to reduce the number of shares issued; the effect of cancelling a share is to reduce the number of shares authorized.

As with treasury stock, a corporation may purchase its own shares when the price is more than or less than the issue price. When a corporation incorporated under the *Canada Business Corporations Act* purchases its own shares at a price greater than the issue price and the shares are to be cancelled or retired, it would make the entry shown below. Assume that the company is acquiring 500 shares of its own shares and that the shares, issued at $10.00, are being acquired at $14.00:

May 15	Common Stock (500 × $10).....................	5,000	
	Retained Earnings [50 × ($14 − $10)]............	2,000	
	Cash (500 × $14)........................		7,000
	To purchase 500 shares of stock at $14 per share.		

The excess of the purchase price over the (average) issue price is debited to Retained Earnings as is the case with treasury stock, as illustrated on p. 619.

When a corporation is able to purchase its own shares (the common case) at a price that is less than the issue price and the shares are to be cancelled or retired, it would make the following entry. Assume the company is acquiring 1,000 of its own shares and that the shares, issued at $10.00, are being acquired at $8.00.

June 15	Common Stock (1,000 × $10)	10,000	
	Contributed Surplus [1,000 × ($10 − $8)] ...		2,000
	Cash................................		8,000
	To purchase 1,000 shares of stock at $8 per share.		

Again as is the case with treasury stock on p. 619, the excess of the issue price over the purchase price is credited to Contributed Surplus.

Retiring stock, like purchasing stock, is a transaction that does not affect net income. No gain or loss arises from stock retirement because the company is doing business with its owners. The entries we presented in illustrating stock retirement affect *balance sheet accounts*, not income statement accounts.

Restrictions on Retained Earnings

Dividends, purchases of treasury stock, and retirements of stock require payments by the corporation to its shareholders. In fact, treasury stock purchases and stock retirements are returns of capital stock to the shareholders. These outlays decrease the corporation's assets, so fewer assets are available to pay liabilities. Therefore, its creditors may seek to restrict a corporation's dividend payments and treasury stock purchases. For example, a bank may agree to loan $500,000 only if the borrowing corporation limits dividend payments and purchases of its stock.

To ensure that corporations maintain a minimum level of shareholders' equity for the protection of creditors, incorporating acts restrict the amount of its own stock that a corporation may purchase. The maximum amount a corporation can pay its shareholders without decreasing capital stock is its balance of retained earnings. Therefore, restrictions on dividends and stock purchases focus on the balance of retained earnings.

Companies usually report their retained earnings restrictions in notes to the financial statements. The following actual disclosure in the 1987 financial statements by Westcoast Transmission Company Limited is typical:

NOTE 9. DIVIDEND RESTRICTION

The First Mortgage and the indentures relating to the company's long term debt and preferred shares contain restrictions as to the declaration or payment of dividends, other than stock dividends, on common shares. Under the most restrictive provision, the amount available for dividends at December 31, 1987 was $146,000,000 (December 31, 1986—$132,000,000; December 31, 1985—$143,00,000).

In another actual example, Reynolds Aluminum Co. of Canada Ltd. indicates restrictions on the payment of dividends on common stock in note 4 to the financial statements in its 1986 annual report:

NOTE 4. RESTRICTION ON DIVIDENDS

The First Mortgage Bond agreements restrict cash dividends on common stock. The restriction covenant states that, so long as any of the debentures remain outstanding, the Company will not declare or pay any dividends (other than stock dividends) on its common shares unless, at a date not more than ninety days prior to the date of declaration of such dividend, the amount of Net Current Assets of the Company shall not be less than 50% of the aggregate principal amount of all Debentures outstanding under the Trust Deed.

Under the terms of the Credit agreement the Company shall not, directly or indirectly, redeem its shares or declare, distribute or pay any dividends of any nature or kind whatsoever on its common shares.

At December 31, 1986, the Company is not in violation of these agreements.

Appropriations of Retained Earnings

Appropriations are restrictions of Retained Earnings that are recorded by formal journal entries. A corporation may appropriate (segregate in a separate account) a portion of Retained Earnings for a specific use. For example, the board of directors may appropriate part of Retained Earnings for building a new manufacturing plant, for meeting possible future liabilities or other reasons. A debit to Retained Earnings and a credit to a separate account, Retained Earnings Restricted for Plant Expansion, records the appropriation.

An appropriation does *not* decrease total retained earnings. Any appropriated amount is simply a portion of retained earnings that is earmarked for a particular purpose. When the need for the appropriation no longer exists, an entry debits the Retained Earnings Appropriated account and credits Retained Earnings. This entry closes the Appropriation account and returns its amount back to the regular Retained Earnings account.

Retained earnings appropriations are rare. Corporations generally disclose any retained earnings restrictions in the notes to the financial statements. The notes give the corporation more room to describe the nature and amounts of any restrictions. Thus corporations satisfy the requirement for adequate disclosure.

Disclosing any restriction on retained earnings is important to shareholders and possible investors because the restricted amounts may not be used for dividends. A corporation with a $100,000 balance in Retained Earnings and a $60,000 restriction may declare a maximum dividend of $40,000—if the cash is available and the board of directors so decides.

Variations in Reporting Shareholders' Equity ⎯⎯⎯⎯⎯

One of the most important skills you will learn in this course is the ability to understand the financial statements of real companies. Therefore it is important that you realize that the format of shareholders' equity sections of actual companies will often differ from that illustrated in the text. One difference is that many corporations provide only cursory information on the balance sheet and more detailed information in the notes to the financial statements. Another difference is that sub-totals with labels are not much used in the real world. An example of an actual shareholders' equity section and the related notes is shown in the extracts from the December 31, 1987 Bell Canada financial statements as in Exhibit 15-2.

EXHIBIT 15-2   *Real-World Format for Shareholders' Equity*

Shareholders' equity		
Share capital authorized (note 9)		
Preferred shares (note 10)		
Non-convertible (redeemable)	481.9	360.5
Convertible (redeemable)	254.1	257.9
	736.0	618.4
Common shareholders' equity		
Stated capital of common shares (note 11)	2,321.2	2,017.4
Premium on share capital (note 11)	1,033.5	1,033.5
Retained earnings	1,920.4	1,766.0
	5,275.1	4,816.9

Notes to the Financial Statements

9. Share capital authorized

The articles of incorporation of Bell Canada provide that its authorized share capital shall be divided into an unlimited number of common shares and an unlimited number of Class A preferred shares issuable in series, all without nominal or par value. The articles authorize the directors of Bell Canada to fix the number of preferred shares of each series to be issued, and the respective attaching conditions prior to their issue.

10. Preferred shares

Class A Preferred Shares series 1 to 5 are owned by BCE.

During the three-year period ended December 31, 1987, Bell Canada issued for cash: 250 Class A preferred shares, series 6 on December 10, 1985, 6,000,000 Class A preferred shares, series 8 on November 13, 1986, and 5,000,000 Class A preferred shares, series 9 on June 16, 1987. On May 20, 1987, 1,250,000 Cumulative Redeemable Price Adjusted Floating Rate Class A preferred shares, series 7 were issued upon conversion of all outstanding Cumulative Redeemable Class A preferred shares, series 6 pursuant to the terms attaching thereto.

| | (dollars in millions) | | | |
| | December 31, 1987 | | December 31, 1986 | |
Outstanding	Number of shares	Stated capital	Number of shares	Stated capital
Class A preferred shares (a)				
Non-convertible preferred shares				
$2.25 shares, series 1	986,000	$ 29.6	1,037,000	$ 31.1
$1.80 shares, series 2	2,616,300	52.3	2,721,300	54.4
Series 7 (Series 6–1986) (b)	1,250,000	125.0	250	125.0
$1.94 shares, series 8 (retractable) (c)	6,000,000	150.0	6,000,000	150.0
7.50% shares, series 9 (retractable) (d)	5,000,000	125.0	—	—
		481.9		360.5
Convertible preferred shares				
$1.96 shares, series 3	204,431	5.1	233,526	5.8
$2.05 shares, series 4	639,022	12.8	793,075	15.9
$2.70 shares, series 5	11,810,400	236.2	11,810,400	236.2
		254.1		257.9
Aggregate stated capital of outstanding preferred shares		$736.0		$618.4

a. All Class A preferred shares are non-voting and the holders of Class A preferred shares series 1 to 5 and series 8 and 9 are entitled to cumulative dividends at the respective rates per share set out in the designation of each series. The holders of preferred shares series 7 are entitled to cumulative monthly dividends. Dividend rates are determined monthly and are generally based on 65 per cent of the average of the prime commercial lending rates of interest announced during the month by two specified Canadian chartered banks, subject to a further adjustment based on trading values of these shares during the month. The monthly dividend rate in effect for December 1987 was $0.585 per share. All Class A preferred shares are redeemable at Bell Canada's option.

b. The series 7 preferred shares are redeemable from time to time at $101 per share.

c. The $1.94 series 8 preferred shares are redeemable on December 1, 1996, at $26 per share to December 1, 1997, and at reducing amounts thereafter to $25 after December 1, 2000. The series 8 preferred shares are retractable at the option of the holder on December 1, 2001, at a price of $25 per share.

d. The 7.50% series 9 preferred shares are redeemable on June 15, 1995, at $26 per share to June 15, 1996, and at reducing amounts thereafter to $25 after June 15, 1999. The series 9 preferred shares are retractable at the option of the holder on June 15, 1999, at a price of $25 per share.

Except for series 7, 8 and 9, all preferred share issues are subject to purchase fund requirements and, taking into account purchases to December 31, 1987, the maximum aggregate stated capital of shares that Bell Canada may be required to purchase, if available pursuant to the terms of the purchase funds, in the years 1988 to 1992 are $21.0, $6.4, $3.6, $3.6 and $12.5 million, respectively.

The convertible preferred shares are in aggregate convertible into 12,697,396 common shares as at December 31, 1987. The decreases in the convertible preferred shares in 1987 resulted from the conversion of preferred shares to common shares. The cumulative number of preferred shares converted as at December 31, 1987 for each of Series 3, 4 and 5 are 6,795,569; 9,360,978 and 2,100 respectively. The decreases in the non-convertible preferred shares during the same period were due to purchases for cancellation to meet purchase fund requirements.

11. Common shares

All outstanding common shares of Bell Canada are owned by BCE.

	(dollars in millions)			
	December 31, 1987		December 31, 1986	
	Number of shares	Stated capital	Number of shares	Stated capital
Outstanding	217,725,289	$2,321.2	204,967,839	$2,017.4

The number of common shares issued during the last three years are as follows:

	1987	1986	1985
For cash	12,568,104	6,610,841	—
Upon conversion of preferred shares	189,346	296,176	966,780
	12,757,450	6,907,017	966,780

Premium on share capital represents the consideration received in excess of the then par value of common shares issued before Bell Canada was continued under the Canada Business Corporations Act on April 21, 1982.

Corporation Income Statement

A corporation's net income receives more attention than any other item in the financial statements. Net income measures the business's ability to earn a profit and answers the question of how successfully the company has managed its operations. To shareholders, the larger the corporation's profit, the greater the likelihood of dividends will be. To creditors, the larger the corporation's profit, the better able it is to pay its debts. Net income builds up a company's assets and owners' equity. It also helps to attract capital from new investors who hope to receive dividends from future successful operations.

Suppose you are considering investing in the stock of two manufacturing companies. In reading their annual reports and examining their past records, you learn that the companies showed the same net income figure for last year and that each company has increased its net income by 15 percent annually over the last five years. You observe, however, that the two companies have generated income in different ways.

Company A's income has resulted from the successful management of its central operations (manufacturing). Company B's manufacturing operations have been flat for two years. Its growth in net income has resulted from selling off segments of its business at a profit. Which company would you invest in?

Company A holds the promise of better future earnings. This corporation earns profits from continuing operations. We may reasonably expect the business to match its past earnings in the future. Company B shows no growth from operations. Its net income results from one-time transactions, the selling off of its operating assets. Sooner or later, Company B will have sold off the last of its assets used in operations. When that occurs, the business will have no means of generating income. Based on this reasoning, your decision is to invest in the stock of Company A.

This example points to two important investment considerations: the *trend* of a company's earnings and the *makeup* of its net income. The probability of making intelligent investment decisions is improved if the income statement separates the results of central, continuing operations from special, one-time gains and losses. We now discuss the components of the corporation income statement. We will see how the income statement reports the results of operations in a manner that allows statement users to get a good look at the business's operations. Exhibit 15-3 will be used throughout these discussions; it presents the detailed income statement of Electronics Corporation for the year ended December 31, 19X5. The income statement is in multiple-step format. The items of primary interest are highlighted for emphasis.

Continuing Operations

We have seen that income from a business's continuing operations helps financial statement users make predictions about the business's future earnings. In the income statement of Exhibit 15-3, the upper-most section reports income from continuing operations. This part of the business is expected to continue from period to period. We may use this information to predict that Electronics Corporation will earn income of approximately $54,000 next year.

Note that income tax expense has been deducted in arriving at income from continuing operations. The tax that corporations pay on their income is a significant expense. The combined federal and provincial income tax rates for corporations varies from time to time, and the current maximum rate is 46 percent. For computational ease, let us use an income tax rate of 40 percent in our illustrations. This is a reasonable estimate of combined federal and provincial income taxes. The $36,000 income tax expense in Exhibit 15-3 equals the pretax income from continuing operations multiplied by the tax rate ($90,000 \times .40 = \$36,000$).

Discontinued Operations

Most large corporations engage in several lines of business. For example, Canadian Pacific is best known for transportation, but it also has subsidiaries in mining, forestry products, real estate, hotels, securities and insurance; it recently sold off CP Air. Olympia and York, best known for its real estate holdings in Canada, the United States and England, is also into oil and gas, distilling and transportation. We call each significant part of a company a **segment of the business**.

A company may sell a segment of its business. Such a sale is not a regular source of income because a company cannot keep on selling its segments indefinitely. The sale of a business segment is viewed as a one-time transaction. The income statement carries information on the segment that has been disposed of under the heading Discontinued Operations. This section of the income statement is divided into two components: (1) operating income or (loss) on the segment that is disposed of and (2) and gain (or loss) on the disposal. Income and gain are taxed at the 40 percent rate and reported as follows:

Discontinued operations
    Operating income, $30,000, less income tax, $12,000.... $18,000
    Gain on disposal, $5,000, less income tax, $2,000 ....   <u>3,000</u>
                                                   $21,000

Trace this presentation to Exhibit 15-3.

EXHIBIT 15-3 *Corporation Income Statement*

> **OBJECTIVE 5**
>
> Identify the elements of a corporation income statement

Electronics Corporation
Income Statement
for the year ended December 31, 19X5

Sales revenue..		$500,000
Cost of goods sold		240,000
Gross margin		260,000
Operating expenses (detailed)		181,000
Operating income....................................		79,000
Other gains (losses)		
Gain on sale of machinery		11,000
Income from continuing operations before income tax ...		90,000
Income tax expense		36,000
Income before discontinued operations and extraordinary		
items		54,000
Discontinued operations		
Operating income, $30,000, less income tax		
of $12,000	$18,000	
Gain on disposal, $5,000, less income tax of		
$2,000	3,000	21,000
Income before extraordinary items		75,000
Extraordinary tornado loss	(10,000)	
Less income tax saving	4,000	(6,000)
Net income		$ 69,000
Earnings per share of common stock (30,000 shares outstanding)		
Income before discontinued operations and extraordinary items		$1.80
Income from discontinued operations		.70
Income before extraordinary items................................		2.50
Extraordinary loss		(.20)
Net income		$2.30

It is necessary to separate discontinued operations into these two components because the company may operate the discontinued segment for part of the year. This is the operating income (or loss) component; it should include the results of operations of the segment from the beginning of the period to the disposal date. There is usually also a gain (or loss) on disposal. The transaction may not have been completed at the company's year end and so the gain (or loss) may have to be estimated. Following the conservatism concept, the estimated loss should be recorded in the accounts at year end while an estimated gain would not be recognized until it was realized.

It is important that the assets, liabilities and operations of the segment can be clearly identified as separate from those of other operations of the company. The notes to the financial statements should disclose fully the nature of the discontinued operations and other relevant information about the discontinued operations, such as revenue to the date of discontinuance.

Discontinued operations are common in business. Recent examples include the sale, mentioned above, by Canadian Pacific of CP Air to Pacific Western Airways and the sale of its interest in Algoma Steel to Dofasco. Other recent examples are the sale by Rogers Cable of its U.S. cable systems to a U.S. company and the sale by Canada Development Corp. of De Havilland Aircraft to Boeing.

Extraordinary Gains and Losses

Extraordinary gains and losses, also called **extraordinary items**, must meet three criteria to be classed as extraordinary. They must have *all* of these characteristics (*CICA Handbook*, Section 3480):

1. An item is extraordinary only if it is not expected to occur frequently. For example, a company that had property on a flood plain that was covered with water every four or five years could not treat losses from flood waters as extraordinary.
2. An item is extraordinary only if it is not typical of the normal business activities of the company. For example, inventory losses or gains, or losses from the sale of property would not be considered extraordinary, since a company that owned either one might normally expect to suffer a loss as a result of that ownership.
3. A gain or loss is extraordinary only if it does not depend on decisions or determinations made by management. For example, the gain on the sale of property held for expansion would not be an extraordinary gain whereas the gain on the expropriation of land by a municipality would normally be considered extraordinary.

In short, to be classed as extraordinary, a transaction must be infrequent, unusual and its result determined externally.

Extraordinary items are reported along with their income tax effect. Assume Electronics Corporation lost $10,000 of inventory in a tornado. This loss, which reduces income, also reduces the company's income tax. The tax effect of the loss is computed by multiplying the amount of the loss by the tax rate. The tax effect decreases the net amount of the loss in the same way that the tax effect of income reduces the amount of net income. An extraordinary loss is reported along with its tax effect as follows:

Extraordinary tornado loss	$(10,000)	
Less income tax saving	4,000	$(6,000)

Trace this item to the income statement in Exhibit 15-3. An extraordinary gain is reported the same way, net of the income tax on the gain.

Gains and losses from unusual or infrequent transactions, such as gains or losses from fixed asset disposals or losses resulting from employee strikes, would be separately disclosed on the income statement as part of income before discontinued operations and extraordinary items. An example is the gain on the sale of machinery in Exhibit 15-3.

Earnings Per Share (EPS)

The final segment of a corporation income statement presents the company's earnings per share, abbreviated as EPS. In fact, GAAP requires that corporations disclose EPS figures on the income statement or in a note to the financial statements.

Earnings per share is the amount of a company's net income per share of its outstanding common stock. EPS is a key measure of a business's success. Consider a corporation with net income of $200,000 and 100,000 shares of common stock outstanding. Its EPS is $2 ($200,000/100,000). A second corporation may also have net income of $200,000 but only 50,000 shares of common stock outstanding. Its EPS is $4 ($200,000/50,000).

Just as the corporation lists separately its different sources of income from continuing operations, discontinued operations, and so on, it must list separately the EPS figure for income before discontinued operations and extraordinary items and net income for the period. The *CICA Handbook*, in Section 3500.12, suggests that "it may also be desirable to show the per share figure for discontinued operations and extraordinary items to emphasize their significance to the overall results."

Consider the income statement of Electronics Corporation shown in Exhibit 15-3; in 19X5, it had 30,000 common shares outstanding. Income before discontinued operations and extraordinary items was $54,000, income from discontinued operations net of tax was $21,000, and there was an extraordinary loss, net of tax saving, of $6,000. Adhering to the *CICA Handbook* it also presents the following disclosures:

```
Disclosure required
    Income per share before discontinued operations and
        extraordinary items ($54,000/30,000) ........................    $1.80
    Net income per share [($54,000 + $21,000 − $6,000)/30,000] ..........    $2.30
Disclosure not required, but suggested for clarity
    Income per share from discontinued operations ($21,000/30,000) ...     $.70
    Loss per share from extraordinary items ($6,000/30,000) ...........    ($.20)
```

Remember that the disclosure required by the *CICA Handbook* is a minimum. It is often in the users' interest to exceed that minimum as was done in Exhibit 15-3. The income statement user can better understand the sources of the business's EPS amounts when presented in this detail.

Weighted Average Number of Shares of Common Stock Outstanding   Computing EPS is straightforward if the number of common shares outstanding does not change over the entire accounting period. For many corporations, however, this figure varies over the course of the year. Consider a corporation that had 100,000 shares outstanding from January through November, then purchased 60,000 of its own shares for cancellation. This company's EPS would be misleadingly high if computed using 40,000 (100,000 − 60,000) shares. To make EPS as meaningful as possible, corporations use the weighted average number of common shares outstanding during the period.

Let us assume the following figures for Diskette Demo Corporation. From January through May, the company had 240,000 shares of common stock outstanding; from June through August, 200,000 shares; and from September through December, 210,000 shares. We compute the weighted average by considering the outstanding shares per month as a fraction of the year:

Number of Common Shares Outstanding		Fraction of Year		Weighted Average Number of Common Shares Outstanding
240,000	×	$\frac{5}{12}$	(January through May)	= 100,000
200,000	×	$\frac{3}{12}$	(June through August)	= 50,000
210,000	×	$\frac{4}{12}$	(September through December)	= 70,000
			Weighted average number of common shares outstanding during the year	220,000

The 220,000 weighted average would be divided into net income to compute the corporation's EPS.

Preferred Dividends   Throughout the EPS discussion we have used only the number of shares of common stock outstanding. Holders of preferred stock have no claim to the business's income beyond the stated preferred dividend (unless the preferred stock is participating preferred, but such stock is rare and will be ignored for purposes of this discussion). Even though preferred stock has no claims, preferred dividends do affect the EPS figure. Recall, the EPS is earnings per share of *common* stock. Also recall that dividends on preferred stock are paid first. Therefore, preferred dividends must be subtracted from income subtotals (income before discontinued operations and extraordinary items and net income) in the computation of EPS.

If Electronics Corporation had 10,000 shares of preferred stock outstanding, each with a $1.50 dividend, the annual preferred dividend would be $15,000 (10,000 × $1.50). The $15,000 would be subtracted from the two income subtotals resulting in the following EPS computations:

Income before discontinued operations and extraordinary items
    [($54,000 − $15,000)/30,000] $1.30
Net income [($69,000 − $15,000)/30,000] $1.80

Dilution   Some corporations make their bonds or preferred stock more attractive to investors by offering conversion privileges which permit the holder to convert the bond or preferred stock into some specified number of shares of common stock. Holders of convertible bonds or convertible preferred stock may exchange their securities for common shares. If in fact the bonds or preferred shares are converted into common stock, then the EPS will be *diluted* (reduced) because more common shares are divided into net income. Because convertible bonds or convertible preferred shares can be traded in for common stock, the common shareholders want to know the amount of the decrease in EPS that would occur if conversion took place. To provide this information, corporations, with convertible bonds or preferred shares outstanding, present two sets of EPS amounts: EPS based on outstanding common shares (*basic EPS*), and EPS based on outstanding common shares plus the number of additional common shares that would arise from conversion of the convertible bonds and convertible preferred shares into common (*fully diluted EPS*).

Use of EPS   EPS is the most widely used accounting figure. Many income statement users place top priority on EPS. Also, a stock's market price is related to a company's EPS. By dividing the market price of a company's stock by its EPS, we compute a statistic called the price-to-earnings or price-earnings ratio. *The Financial Post* reports the price-earnings ratios (listed as P/E) daily for hundreds of companies listed on the Toronto and Montreal and the New York Stock Exchanges.

Statement of Retained Earnings _____

Retained earnings may be a significant portion of a corporation's owner's equity. The year's income increases the retained earnings balance, and dividends decrease it. Retained earnings are so important that corporations draw up a financial statement outlining the major changes in this equity account, much as the statement of owner's equity presents information on changes in the equity of a proprietorship. The statement of retained earnings for Electronics Corporation appears in Exhibit 15-4.

Some companies report income and retained earnings on a single statement. Exhibit 15-5 illustrates how Electronics would combine its income statement and its statement of retained earnings.

EXHIBIT 15-4   *Statement of Retained Earnings*

Electronics Corporation Statement of Retained Earnings for the year ended December 31, 19X5	
Retained earnings balance, December 31, 19X4	$130,000
Net income for 19X5	69,000
	199,000
Dividends for 19X5	(21,000)
Retained earnings balance, December 31, 19X5	$178,000

EXHIBIT 15-5 *Statement of Income and Retained Earnings*

Electronics Corporation **Statement of Income and Retained Earnings** **for the year ended December 31, 19X5**	
Sales revenue	$500,000
Cost of goods sold	240,000

Net income for 19X5	69,000
Retained earnings, December 31, 19X4	130,000
	199,000
Dividends for 19X5	(21,000)
Retained earnings, December 31, 19X5	$178,000
Earnings per share of common stock (30,000 shares outstanding)	
Income before discontinued operations and extraordinary items	$1.80
Income from discontinued operations	.70
Income before extraordinary items	2.50
Extraordinary loss	(.20)
Net income	$2.30

OBJECTIVE 6

Account for prior period adjustments

Prior Period Adjustments

What happens when a company makes an error in recording revenues or expenses? Detecting the error in the period in which it occurs allows the company to make a correction before preparing that period's financial statements. But failure to detect the error until a later period means that the business will have reported an incorrect amount of income on its income statement. After closing the revenue and expense accounts, the Retained Earnings account will absorb the effect of the error, and its balance will be wrong until the error is corrected.

Corrections to the beginning balance of Retained Earnings for errors of an earlier period are called **prior period adjustments**. The correcting entry includes a debit or credit to Retained Earnings for the error amount and a debit or credit to the asset or liability account that was misstated. The prior period adjustment appears on the corporation's statement of retained earnings to indicate to readers the amount and the nature of the change in the Retained Earnings balance.

Assume that Paquette Corporation recorded income tax expense for 19X4 as $30,000. The correct amount was $40,000. This error resulted in understanding 19X4 expenses by $10,000 and overstating net income by $10,000. A bill from the government in 19X5 for the additional $10,000 in taxes alerts the Paquette management to the mistake. The entry to record this prior period adjustment in 19X5 is

19X5			
June 19	Retained Earnings	10,000	
	Income Tax Payable		10,000
	Prior period adjustment to correct error in recording income tax expense of 19X4.		

The debit to Retained Earnings excludes the error correction from the income statement of 19X5. Recall the matching principle. If Income Tax Expense is debited when the prior period adjustment is recorded in 19X5, then this $10,000 in taxes would appear on the 19X5 income statement. This would not be proper since the expense arose from 19X4 operations.

This prior period adjustment would appear on the statement of retained earnings, as follows:

Paquette Corporation
Statement of Retained Earnings
for the year ended December 31, 19X5

Retained earnings balance, December 31, 19X4, **as originally reported**	$390,000
Prior period adjustment — debit to correct error in recording income tax expense of 19X4	(10,000)
Retained earnings balance, December 31, 19X4, **as adjusted**	380,000
Net income for 19X5	114,000
	494,000
Dividends for 19X5	(41,000)
Retained earnings balance, December 31, 19X5	$453,000

Our example shows a prior period adjustment for additional expense. To make a prior period adjustment for additional income, retained earnings is credited and the misstated asset or liability is debited.

Summary Problem for Your Review

The following information was taken from the ledger of Ansong Corporation:

Loss on sale of discontinued operations	$ 20,000	Selling expenses	$ 78,000
Prior period adjustment — credit to Retained Earnings	5,000	Common stock, 40,000 shares issued	155,000
		Sales revenue	620,000
		Interest expense	30,000
Gain on sale of plant assets	21,000	Extraordinary gain	26,000
Cost of goods sold	380,000	Operating income, discontinued operations	30,000
Income tax expense (saving)			
Continuing operations	32,000	Loss due to lawsuit	11,000
Discontinued operations		General expenses	62,000
Operating income	12,000	Preferred stock, $8.00, 500 shares issued	57,000
Loss on sale	(8,000)		
Extraordinary gain	10,000	Retained earnings, beginning, as originally reported	103,000
Dividends	16,000		

Required

Prepare a single-step income statement and a statement of retained earnings for Ansong Corporation for the current year ended December 31. Include the earnings per share presentation and show computations. Assume no changes in the stock accounts during the year.

SOLUTION TO SUMMARY PROBLEM

Ansong Corporation
Income Statement
for the year ended December 31, 19XX

Revenue and gains			
Sales revenue			$620,000
Gain on sale of plant assets			21,000
Total revenues and gains....................			641,000
Expenses and losses			
Cost of goods sold...........................		$380,000	
Selling expenses		78,000	
General expenses		62,000	
Interest expense.............................		30,000	
Loss due to lawsuit		11,000	
Income tax expense..........................		32,000	
Total expenses and losses			593,000
Income before discontinued operations and extraordinary items..........................			48,000
Discontinued operations			
Operating income	$30,000		
Less income tax	12,000	18,000	
Loss on sale of discontinued operations	20,000		
Less income tax saving.....................	8,000	(12,000)	6,000
Income before extraordinary items			54,000
Extraordinary gain		26,000	
Less income tax		10,000	16,000
Net income			$ 70,000

Earnings per share
  Income before discontinued operations and
    extraordinary item [($48,000 − $4,000)/40,000 shares] $1.10*
  Income from discontinued operations ($6,000/40,000 shares) .... .15
  Income before extraordinary items [($54,000 − $4,000)/40,000 shares] 1.25
  Extraordinary gain ($16,000/40,000 shares)............................ .40
  Net income [($70,000 − $4,000)/40,000 shares] $1.65*

Computations

$$\text{EPS} = \frac{\text{Income} - \text{Preferred dividends}}{\text{Common shares outstanding}}$$

Preferred dividends: $500 \times \$8.00 = \$4,000$

---

* These calculations are required; the other EPS calculations are included to make the statements more informative for users.

Ansong Corporation
Statement of Retained Earnings
for the year ended December 31, 19XX

Retained earnings balance, beginning, as originally reported	$103,000
Prior period adjustment—credit	5,000
Retained earnings balance, beginning, as adjusted	108,000
Net income for current year	70,000
	178,000
Dividends for current year	(16,000)
Retained earnings balance, ending	$162,000

Summary

Retained Earnings carries the balance of the business's net income accumulated over its lifetime, less its declared dividends and any net losses. *Cash dividends* are distributions of corporate assets made possible by earnings. *Stock dividends* are distributions of the corporation's own stock to its shareholders. Stock dividends and *stock splits* increase the number of shares outstanding and generally lower the market price per share of stock.

Treasury stock is the corporation's own stock that has been issued and reacquired. The corporation may issue reacquired stock in the normal way but more often cancels the reacquired shares.

Retained earnings may be *restricted* by law or contract or by the corporation itself. An *appropriation* is a restriction of retained earnings that is recorded by formal journal entries.

The corporate *income statement* lists separately the various sources of income—*income before discontinued operations and extraordinary items*, which includes other gains and losses, *discontinued operations*, and *extraordinary gains and losses*. The bottom line of the income statement reports *net income* or *net loss* for the period. *Income tax expense* and *earnings-per-share* figures also appear on the income statement, likewise divided into different categories based on the nature of income. The *statement of retained earnings* reports the causes for changes in the Retained Earnings account. This statement may be combined with the income statement.

Self-Study Questions

Test your understanding of the chapter by marking the best answer for each of the following questions:

1. A corporation has total shareholders' equity of $100,000, including retained earnings of $19,000. The cash balance is $35,000. The maximum cash dividend the company can declare and pay is *(p. 613)*
   a. $19,000   c. 65,000
   b. 35,000   d. $100,000

2. An entry debiting Dividends Payable and crediting Cash is recorded on the *(p. 613)*
   a. Declaration date   c. Payment date
   b. Date of record   d. None of the above

3. Meyer's Thrifty Acres Ltd. has 10,000 shares of common stock outstanding; the stated value of the stock was $20.00 per share at the time of issue. The stock's

market value is $37 per share. Meyer's board of directors declares and distributes a common stock dividend of one share for every ten held. Which of the following entries shows the full effect of declaring and distributing the dividend? *(p. 615)*

a. Retained Earnings	37,000	
Common Stock Dividend Distributable		20,000
Paid-in Capital in Excess of Par—Common		17,000
b. Retained Earnings	20,000	
Common Stock		20,000
c. Retained Earnings	17,000	
Paid-in Capital in Excess of Par—Common		17,000
d. Retained Earnings	37,000	
Common Stock		37,000

4. Lang Real Estate Investment Corporation declared and distributed a 50 percent stock dividend. Which of the following stock splits would have the same effect on the number of Lang shares outstanding? *(pp. 616, 617)*
   a. 2 for 1   c. 4 for 3
   b. 3 for 2   d. 5 for 4

5. A company purchased 10,000 shares of its common stock that had been issued at $1.50 a share paying $6 per share. This transaction *(pp. 619, 620)*
   a. Has no effect on company assets   c. Decreases owners' equity by $15,000
   b. Has no effect on owners' equity   d. Decreases owners' equity by $60,000

6. A restriction of retained earnings *(pp. 623, 624)*
   a. Has no effect on total retained earnings
   b. Reduces retained earnings available for the declaration of dividends
   c. Is usually reported by a note
   d. All of the above

7. Which of the following items is *not* reported on the income statement? *(p. 629)*
   a. Issue price of stock   c. Income tax expense
   b. Extraordinary gains and losses d. Earnings per share

8. The income statement item that is likely to be most useful for predicting income from year to year is *(p. 628)*
   a. Extraordinary items   c. Income from continuing operations
   b. Discontinued operations   d. Net income

9. In computing earnings per share (EPS), dividends on preferred stock are *(p. 632)*
   a. Added because they represent earnings to the preferred shareholders
   b. Subtracted because they represent earnings to the preferred shareholders
   c. Ignored because they do not pertain to the common stock
   d. Reported separately on the income statement

10. A corporation accidentally overlooked an accrual of property tax expense at December 31, 19X4. Accountants for the company detect the error early in 19X5 before the expense is paid. The entry to record this prior period adjustment is *(p. 634)*

a. Retained Earnings	XXX		c. Retained Earnings	XXX	
Property Tax Expense		XXX	Property Tax Payable		XXX
b. Property Tax Expense .	XXX		d. Property Tax Payable . .	XXX	
Property Tax Payable		XXX	Property Tax Expense		XXX

Answers to the self-study questions are at the end of the chapter.

Accounting Vocabulary

appropriation of retained earnings *(p. 624)*	declaration date *(p. 613)*	extraordinary item *(p. 630)*
date of record *(p. 613)*	earnings per share (EPS) *(p. 631)*	prior period adjustment *(p. 634)*

segment of a business
(p. 628)

stock dividend
(p. 613)

stock split *(p. 616)*
treasury stock *(p. 618)*

Assignment Material

Questions

1. Identify the two main parts of shareholders' equity.
2. Identify the account debited and the account credited from the last closing entry a corporation makes each year. What is the purpose of this entry?
3. Ametek, Inc. reported a cash balance of $73 million and a retained earnings balance of $162.5 million. Explain how Ametek can have so much more retained earnings than cash. In your answer, identify the nature of retained earnings and state how it ties to cash.
4. Briefly discuss the three important dates for a dividend.
5. A friend of yours receives a stock dividend on an investment. He believes stock dividends are the same as cash dividends. Explain why this is not true.
6. Give two reasons for a corporation to distribute a stock dividend.
7. A corporation declares a stock dividend on December 21 and reports Stock Dividend Payable as a liability on the December 31 balance sheet. Is this correct? Give your reason.
8. What value is normally assigned to shares issued as a stock dividend?
9. To an investor, a stock split and a stock dividend have essentially the same effect. Explain the similarity and difference to the corporation between a 100 percent stock dividend and a 2-for-1 stock split.
10. Give three reasons a corporation would purchase its own shares.
11. What effect does the purchase of its own shares have on the (a) assets, (b) issued stock, and (c) authorized stock of the corporation?
12. What does the *Canada Business Corporations Act* (CBCA) require a company to do when it purchases its own stock?
13. Are there any exceptions to the requirement of the CBCA mentioned in 12? If so, what are they?
14. Incorporating legislation frequently has a prohibition on a corporation purchasing its own stock in certain circumstances. What are those circumstances? Why does the prohibition exist?
15. Why do creditors wish to restrict a corporation's payment of cash dividends and purchases of treasury stock?
16. What are two ways to report a retained earnings restriction? Which way is more common?
17. Identify three items on the income statement for which income tax expense (saving) is shown. What is an income tax saving, and how does it arise?
18. Why is it important for a corporation to report income before discontinued operations and extraordinary items separately from discontinued operations and extraordinary items?
19. Give two examples of extraordinary gains and losses and four examples of gains and loses that are *not* extraordinary.
20. What is the most widely used of all accounting statistics? What is the price-earnings ratio? Compute the price-earnings ratio for a company with an EPS of $2 and a market price of $12 per share of common stock.
21. What is the earnings per share of a company with net income of $5,500 and issued common stock of 12,000 shares?
22. What account do all prior period adjustments affect? On what financial statement are prior period adjustments reported?

Exercises

Exercise 15-1   *Journalizing dividends and reporting shareholders' equity*

Eatmore Hamburger System, Inc. is authorized to issue 300,000 shares of common stock. The company issued 100,000 shares at $6 per share, and all 100,000 shares are outstanding. When the retained earnings balance was $300,000, Eatmore declared and distributed a 50 percent stock dividend, assigning a value of $1.00 per share. Later, Eatmore declared and paid a $.20 per share cash dividend.

Required

1. Journalize the declaration and distribution of the stock dividend.
2. Journalize the declaration and payment of the cash dividend.
3. Prepare the shareholders' equity section of the balance sheet after both dividends.

Exercise 15-2   *Journalizing a stock dividend and reporting shareholders' equity*

The shareholders' equity for Tick Tock Jewelry Ltd. on September 30, 19X4, end of the company's fiscal year, follows:

Shareholders' Equity

Common stock, 100,000 shares authorized, 50,000 shares issued	$550,000
Retained earnings	280,000
Total shareholders' equity	$830,000

On November 16, the market price of Tick Tock's common stock was $15 per share and the company declared a 10 percent stock dividend. Tick Tock issued the dividend shares on November 30.

Required

1. Journalize the declaration and distribution of the stock dividend.
2. Prepare the shareholders' equity section of the balance sheet after the stock dividend.

Exercise 15-3   *Journalizing treasury stock transactions*

Journalize the following transactions of Shoe Renewry, Inc., a national chain of shoe repair shops:

May 19   Issued 3,000 shares of common stock at $12 per share.
Aug. 22   Purchased 600 shares of stock at $14 per share.
Nov. 11   Sold 200 shares of stock at $15 per share.
Dec. 28   Sold 100 shares of stock at $11 per share.

Exercise 15-4   *Journalizing treasury stock transactions and reporting shareholders' equity*

Northwest Distributing Ltd. had the following shareholders' equity on November 30:

Shareholders' Equity

Common stock, 500,000 shares authorized, 50,000 shares issued	$400,000
Retained earnings	220,000
Total shareholders' equity	$620,000

On December 19, the company purchased 1,000 shares of treasury stock at $6 per share. Journalize the purchase of the treasury stock and prepare the shareholders' equity section of the balance sheet at December 31.

Exercise 15-5 *Reporting shareholders' equity after a stock split*

Assume Northwest Distributing Ltd. (the business in the preceding exercise) split its common stock 4 for 1 on December 10. Make the memorandum entry to record the stock split, and prepare the shareholders' equity section of the balance sheet immediately after the split. Assume the number of authorized shares increases to 2,000,000.

Exercise 15-6 *Reporting a retained earnings restriction*

The agreement under which Brookview Sales, Inc. issued its long-term debt requires the restriction of $351,000 of the company's retained earnings balance. Total retained earnings is $609,000, and total capital stock is $822,000.

Required

Show how to report shareholders' equity (including retained earnings) on Brookview's balance sheet, assuming:

1. Brookview discloses the restriction in a note. Write the note.
2. Brookview appropriates retained earnings in the amount of the restriction and includes no note in its statements.

Exercise 15-7 *Preparing a multiple-step income statement*

The ledger of a corporation contains the following information for 19X7 operations:

Cost of goods sold	$45,000	Income tax saving — loss on	
Loss on discontinued		discontinued operations .	$ 20,000
operations	50,000	Extraordinary gain	12,000
Income tax expense —		Sales revenue.............	130,000
extraordinary gain	4,800	Operating expenses	
		(including income tax)...	60,000

Required

Prepare a multiple-step income statement for 19X7. Omit earnings per share.

Exercise 15-8 *Computing earnings per share*

Benavides Inc. earned net income of $5ɔ,000 for the second quarter of 19X6. The ledger reveals the following figures:

Preferred stock, $2.50, 1,400 shares issued and outstanding	$ 50,000
Common stock, 32,000 shares issued	320,000

Required

Compute EPS for the quarter, assuming no changes in the stock accounts during the quarter.

Exercise 15-9 *Preparing a statement of retained earnings with a prior period adjustment*

Posen Inc., a soft-drink company, reported a prior period adjustment in 19X9. An accounting error caused net income of prior years to be overstated by $3.8 million. Retained earnings at January 1, 19X9, as previously reported, stood at $395.3 million. Net income for 19X9 was $78.1 million, and dividends were $39.8 million. Prepare the company's statement of retained earnings for the year ended December 31, 19X9.

Exercise 15-10   *Preparing a combined statement of income and retained earnings*

Kroger Ltd. had retained earnings of $792.6 million at the beginning of 19X3. The company showed these figures at December 31, 19X3:

	($ millions)
Increases in retained earnings	
Net income	$127.1
Decreases in retained earnings	
Cash dividends, preferred	2.3
common	85.2
Debit to retained earnings due to purchase of preferred stock . .	11.3

Required

Beginning with net income, prepare a combined statement of income and retained earnings for the Kroger Company for 19X3. The debit to Retained Earnings was caused by Kroger's paying $11.3 more to retire its preferred stock than the original issue price of the stock.

Exercise 15-11   *Computing earnings per share*

Greenlawn Supply Ltd. had 40,000 shares of common stock and 10,000 shares of preferred stock outstanding that paid a dividend of $.50 on December 31, 19X8. On April 30, 19X9, the company issued 9,000 additional common shares and ended 19X9 with 49,000 shares of common stock outstanding. Income from continuing operations of 19X9 was $106,200, and loss on discontinued operations (net of tax) was $8,280. The company had an extraordinary gain (net of tax) of $50,600.

Required

Compute Greenlawn's EPS amounts for 19X9, starting with income before discontinued operations and extraordinary items.

Problems   *(Group A)*

Problem 15-1A   *Journalizing owner's equity transactions*

Yukon Corporation completed the following selected transactions during the current year:

Jan. 9   Discovered that income tax expense of the preceding year was overstated by $8,000. Recorded a prior period adjustment to correct the error.

Feb. 10   Split common stock 2 for 1 on the 20,000 shares of common stock outstanding by issuing 20,000 more shares to the shareholders.

Mar. 18   Declared a cash dividend on the $5.00 preferred stock (1,000 shares outstanding). Declared at $.20 per share dividend on the 40,000 shares of common stock outstanding. The date of record was April 2, and the payment date was April 23

Apr. 23   Paid the cash dividends.

July 30   Declared a 10 percent stock dividend on the common stock to holders of record August 21, with distribution set for September 11. The market value of the common stock was $21 per share.

Sept. 11   Issued the stock dividend shares.

Sept. 26   Purchased 3,000 shares of the company's own common stock at $18 per share.

Nov. 8   Sold 1,000 shares of common stock for $20 per share.
Dec. 13   Sold 500 shares of common stock for $17 per share.

Required

Record the transactions in the general journal.

Problem 15-2A   *Journalizing prior period adjustments and dividend and treasury stock transactions; reporting retained earnings and shareholders' equity*

The balance sheet of Flin Flon Inc. at December 31, 19X1 reported the following shareholders' equity:

Capital stock	
Common stock, 100,000 shares	
authorized, 20,000 shares issued	$500,000
Total capital stock	500,000
Retained earnings......................	240,000
Total shareholders' equity............	$740,000

During 19X2, Flin Flon completed the following selected transactions:

Jan. 11   Discovered that income tax expense of 19X1 was understated by $14,000. Recorded a prior period adjustment to correct the error.

Apr. 30   Declared a 10 percent stock dividend on the common stock. The market value of Flin Flon common stock was $24 per share. The record date was May 21, with distribution set for June 5.

June 5   Issued the stock dividend shares.

July 29   Purchased 2,000 shares of the company's own common stock at $19 per share.

Nov. 13   Sold 1,000 shares of common stock for $24 per share.

Nov. 27   Declared a $.30 per share dividend on the 21,000 shares of common stock outstanding. The date of record was Dec. 17, and the payment date was January 7, 19X3.

Dec. 31   Closed the $103,000 credit balance of Income Summary to Retained Earnings.

Required

1. Record the transactions in the general journal.
2. Prepare a retained earnings statement at December 31, 19X2.
3. Prepare the shareholders' equity section of the balance sheet at December 31, 19X2.

Problem 15-3A   *Journalizing dividend and treasury stock transactions and reporting shareholders' equity*

The balance sheet of Summerside Sales Ltd. at December 31, 19X5 reported 100,000 shares of common stock authorized, with 30,000 shares issued and a Common Stock balance of $180,000. Summerside sales also had 5,000 shares of $.50 preferred stock authorized and outstanding. The preferred stock was issued in 19X1 at $10.00 per share. Retained Earnings had a credit balance of $65,000. During the two-year period ended December 31, 19X7, the company completed the following selected transactions:

19X6
Mar. 15   Purchased 2,000 shares of the company's own common stock at $5 per share.

July 2   Declared the annual $.50 cash dividend on the preferred stock and a $.75-per-share cash dividend on the common stock. The date of record was July 16, and the payment date was July 31.

July 31   Paid the cash dividends.

Nov. 30   Declared a 20 percent stock dividend on the *outstanding* common stock to holders of record December 21, with distribution set for January 11, 19X7. The market value of Summerside Sales common stock was $10 per share.

Dec. 31   Earned net income of $60,000 for the year.

19X7

Jan. 11   Issued the stock dividend shares.

June 30   Declared the annual $.50 cash dividend on the preferred stock. The date of record was July 14, and the payment date was July 29.

July 29   Paid the cash dividends.

Aug. 2   Purchased and retired all the preferred stock at $14 per share.

Oct. 8   Sold 800 shares of common stock for $12 per share.

Dec. 19   Split the common stock 2 for 1 by issuing two new shares for each old share previously issued.

31   Earned net income of $81,000 during the year.

Required

1. Record the transactions in the general journal. Explanations are not required.
2. Prepare the shareholders' equity section of the balance sheet at two dates: December 31, 19X6 and December 31, 19X7.

Problem 15-4A   *Preparing a single-step income statement and a statement of retained earnings: reporting shareholders' equity on the balance sheet*

The following information was taken from the ledger and other records of Rivera Corporation at September 30, 19X6:

Loss on sale of plant assets	$ 8,000	Interest revenue	$ 4,000
Sales returns	9,000	Extraordinary loss	30,000
Income tax expense (saving)		Operating loss, discontinued segment	15,000
Continuing operations	72,000	Loss on insurance settlement	12,000
Discontinued segment		General expenses	113,000
Operating loss	(6,000)	Preferred stock, $3, 10,000 shares	
Gain on sale	8,000	authorized, 5,000 shares issued	200,000
Extraordinary loss	(12,000)	Retained earnings, beginning,	
Sales revenue	903,000	as originally reported	88,000
Dividends	35,000	Selling expenses	136,000
Gain on sale of discontinued segment	20,000	Common stock, 24,000 shares	
Prior period adjustment—		authorized and issued	266,000
credit to Retained Earnings	6,000	Sales discounts	18,000
Cost of goods sold	420,000	Interest expense	11,000

Required

Prepare a single-step income statement and a statement of retained earnings for Rivera Corporation for the fiscal year ended September 30, 19X6. Also prepare the shareholders' equity section of the balance sheet at that date. Include the earnings-per-share presentation, and show computations.

Problem 15-5A   *Preparing a corrected combined statement of income and retained earnings*

Monica Hearn, accountant for International Food Incorporated, was injured in a skiing accident. Another employee prepared the income statement for the fiscal year ended December 31, 19X3.

The individual amounts listed on the income statement are correct. However, some accounts are reported incorrectly, and others do not belong on the income statement at all. Also, income tax (40 percent) has not been applied to all appropriate figures. International issued 52,000 shares of common stock in 19X1 and repurchased 2000 shares in 19X2. The retained earnings balance, as originally reported at December 31, 19X2, was $92,000.

Required

Prepare a corrected combined statement of income and retained earnings for 19X3. Prepare the income statement in single-step format.

International Foods Incorporated
Income Statement
19X3

Revenue and gains		
Sales		$349,000
Prior period adjustment—credit		14,000
Gain on retirement of preferred stock		
(issued for $100,000; purchased for $93,000)		7,000
Total revenues and gains		370,000
Expenses and losses		
Cost of goods sold	$145,000	
Selling expenses	76,000	
General expenses	61,000	
Sales returns	11,000	
Dividends	7,000	
Sales discounts	6,000	
Income tax expense	20,000	
Total expenses and losses		326,000
Income from operations		44,000
Other gains and losses		
Gain on sale of discontinued operations	10,000	
Flood loss	(20,000)	
Operating loss on discontinued segment	(15,000)	
Total other losses		(25,000)
Net income		$ 19,000
Earnings per share		$.38

Problem 15-6A *Using actual-company data to record transactions and report earnings per share*

The following items have been adapted from the financial statements of actual companies that showed amounts in millions and rounded to the nearest $100,000:

A. The General Tire & Rubber Company declared and paid cash dividends of $35.2 million to its common shareholders, and also declared and issued a 2 percent stock dividend on its 23.6 million common shares outstanding. The market value of General's common stock at the time of the stock dividend was $60 per share.

Required

1. Journalize the declaration and payment of the cash dividend.
2. Journalize declaration and issuance of the stock dividend.

B. During the year, IU International Corporation paid $2.2 million to purchase its common shares, which had been issued for $1.3 million. The company also paid $19.6 million to purchase and retire preferred shares that had been issued for $18.8 million two years previously.

Required

1. Journalize the purchase and retirement of its common shares by IU International.
2. Journalize the purchase and retirement of its preferred shares.

C. Chesapeake Corporation reported that it had been able to pay off long-term debt of $16.5 million by paying $4.5 million in cash and issuing 200,000 common shares. The corporation proposed to recognize an extraordinary gain of $4.0 million on the transaction, because its common shares were trading at $40 a share at the time of the transaction.

Required

1. Journalize the transaction.
2. Can Chesapeake show an extraordinary gain on the transaction?

Problem 15-7A   *Computing earnings per share and reporting a retained earnings restriction*

The capital structure of Montpelier Gardens Inc. at December 31, 19X6, included 20,000 shares of $1.25 preferred stock and 44,000 shares of common stock. Common shares outstanding during 19X7 were 44,000 January through May; 50,000 June through August; and 60,500 September through December. Income from continuing operations during 19X7 was $47,440. The company discontinued a segment of the business at a loss of $6,630, and an extraordinary item generated a gain of $33,660. Montpelier's board of directors restricts $60,000 of retained earnings for contingencies.

Required

1. Compute Montpelier's earnings per share. Start with income from continuing operations. Assume figures shown are net of tax.
2. Show two ways of reporting Montpelier's retained earnings restriction. Assume total retained earnings is $190,000 and total capital stock is $230,000.

(Group B)

Problem 15-1B   *Journalizing owner's equity transactions*

Trail Corporation completed the following selected transactions during 19X6:

Jan. 13   Discovered that income tax expense of 19X5 was understated by $11,000. Record a prior period adjustment to correct the error.

Jan. 21   Split common stock 3 for 1 by calling in the 10,000 shares of old common and issuing 30,000 shares of new common.

Feb. 6   Declared a cash dividend on the 4,000 shares of $2.25, preferred stock. Declared a $.50 per share dividend on the 30,000 shares of common stock outstanding. The date of record was February 27, and the payment date was March 20.

Mar. 20   Paid the cash dividends.

Apr. 18	Declared a 50 percent stock dividend on the common stock to holders of record April 30, with distribution set for May 30. The market value of the common stock was $11 per share.
May 30	Issued the stock dividend shares.
June 18	Purchased 2,000 shares of the company's own common stock at $12 per share.
Nov. 14	Sold 800 shares of common stock for $10 per share.
Dec. 22	Sold 1,000 shares of common stock for $16 per share.

Required

Record the transactions in the general journal.

Problem 15-2B   *Journalizing prior period adjustments and dividend and treasury stock transactions; reporting retained earnings and shareholders' equity*

The balance sheet of Camrose Corporation at December 31, 19X3 presented the following shareholder's equity:

Capital stock	
Common stock, 250,000 shares authorized,	
50,000 shares issued	$400,000
Total capital stock	400,000
Retained earnings.............................	110,000
Total shareholders' equity....................	$510,000

During 19X4, Camrose completed the following selected transactions:

Jan. 7	Discovered that income tax expense of 19X3 was overstated by $7,000. Recorded a prior period adjustment to correct the error.
Mar. 29	Declared a 10 percent stock dividend on the common stock. The market value of Camrose common stock was $9 per share. The record date was April 19, with distribution set for May 19.
May 19	Issued the stock dividend shares.
July 13	Purchased 5,000 shares of the company's own common stock at $6 per share.
Oct. 4	Sold 3,000 shares of common stock for $9 per share.
Dec. 27	Declared a $.20 per share dividend on the 53,000 shares of common stock outstanding. The date of record was January 17, 19X5, and the payment date was January 31.
31	Closed the $62,000 credit balance of Income Summary to Retained Earnings.

Required

1. Record the transactions in the general journal.
2. Prepare the retained earnings statement at December 31, 19X4.
3. Prepare the shareholders' equity section of the balance sheet at December 31, 19X4.

Problem 15-3B   *Journalizing dividend and treasury stock transactions and reporting shareholders' equity*

The balance sheet of Carmel Service Inc. at December 31, 19X7 reported 10,000 shares of $.50 cumulative preferred stock authorized and outstanding. The preferred was issued in 19X1 at $8 per share. Carmel also had 500,000 shares of common stock authorized with 100,000 shares issued for $400,000. Retained Earnings had a balance of $18,000, and the preferred dividend for 19X7 was in arrears. During the two-year period ended December 31, 19X9, the company completed the following selected transactions:

19X8

Feb. 15 Purchased 5,000 shares of the company's own common stock at $3 per share.

Apr. 2 Declared the cash dividend on the preferred stock in arrears for 19X7 and the current cash dividend on preferred. The date of record was April 16, and the payment date was May 1.

May 1 Paid the cash dividends.

May 2 Purchased and retired all the preferred stock at $7.50 per share.

Dec. 31 Earned net income of $45,000 for the year.

19X9

Mar. 8 Sold 2,000 shares of common stock for $4 per share.

Sept. 28 Declared a 5 percent stock dividend on the *outstanding* common stock to holders of record October 15, with distribution set for October 31. The market value of Carmel common stock was $5 per share.

Oct. 31 Issued the stock dividend shares.

Nov. 5 Split the common stock 2 for 1 by issuing 2 new common shares for each old share previously issued.

Dec. 31 Earned net income of $62,000 during the year.

Required

1. Record the transactions in the general journal. Explanations are not required.
2. Prepare the shareholders' equity section of the balance sheet at two dates: December 31, 19X8 and December 31, 19X9.

Problem 15-4B *Preparing a single-step income statement and a statement of retained earnings and reporting shareholders' equity on the balance sheet*

The following information was taken from the ledger and other records of Mancini Corporation at June 30, 19X5:

General expenses	$ 71,000	Sales revenue	$559,000
Loss on sale of discontinued segment	8,000	Retained earnings, beginning, as originally reported	79,000
Prior period adjustment—debit to Retained Earnings	4,000	Selling expenses	87,000
Cost of goods sold	319,000	Common stock, 20,000 shares authorized and issued	322,000
Interest expense	23,000		
Gain on settlement of lawsuit	8,000	Sales discounts	7,000
Sales returns	15,000	Interest revenue	5,000
Income tax expense (saving)		Extraordinary gain	27,000
Continuing operations	16,000	Operating loss, discontinued segment	9,000
Discontinued segment		Loss on sale of plant assets	10,000
Operating loss	(3,600)	Dividends on preferred stock	?
Loss on sale	(3,200)	Preferred stock, $1.50, 20,000 shares authorized, 4,000 shares issued	100,000
Extraordinary gain	10,800		
Dividends on common stock	12,000		

Required

Prepare a single-step income statement and a statement of retained earnings for Mancini Corporation for the fiscal year ended June 30, 19X5. Also prepare the shareholders' equity section of the balance sheet at that date. Include the earnings-per-share presentation and show computations.

Problem 15-5B *Preparing a corrected combined statement of income and retained earnings*

Leslie Gose, accountant for Stinnett Catering Company Ltd., was injured in a sailing accident. Another employee prepared the following income statement for the fiscal year ended June 30, 19X4:

Stinnett Catering Company Ltd.
Income Statement
June 30, 19X4

Revenue and gains		
Sales		$622,000
Gain on retirement of preferred stock		
(issued for $50,000; purchased for $48,000)		2,000
Total revenues and gains		624,000
Expenses and losses		
Cost of goods sold	$233,000	
Selling expenses	103,000	
General expenses	74,000	
Sales returns	22,000	
Prior period adjustment — debit	4,000	
Dividends	15,000	
Sales discounts	10,000	
Income tax expense	32,000	
Total expenses and losses.......................		493,000
Income from operations		131,000
Other gains and losses		
Extraordinary gain..............................	30,000	
Operating income on discontinued segment	25,000	
Loss on sale of discontinued operations	(40,000)	
Total other gains		15,000
Net income		$146,000
Earnings per share................................		$7.30

The individual amounts listed on the income statement are correct. However, some accounts are reported incorrectly, and others do not belong on the income statement at all. Also, income tax (40 percent) has not been applied to all appropriate figures. Stinnett issued 24,000 shares of common stock in 19X1 and repurchased 4,000 shares during the fiscal year 19X4. The retained earnings balance, as originally reported at June 30, 19X3, was $56,000.

Required

Prepare a corrected combined statement of income and retained earnings for fiscal year 19X4. Prepare the income statement in single-step format.

Problem 15-6B   *Using actual-company data to record transactions and report earnings per share*

The following items have been adapted from actual financial statements that reported amounts in millions, rounded to the nearest $100,000:

A. Hampton Industries, Inc. declared and paid cash dividends of $.1 million to preferred shareholders and also declared and issued a 10 percent stock dividend on its 2.0 million common shares outstanding. The issue price of Hampton's common stock was $1.00 per share, and the market value of the stock at the time of the stock dividend was $6.50 per share.

Required

1. Journalize the declaration and payment of the cash dividend.
2. Journalize the declaration and issuance of the stock dividend.

B. During the year, the Louisiana Land and Exploration Company paid $212.8 million for common shares that had been issued for $105 million.

Required

Journalize the purchase of the shares.

C. Crown Cork & Seal Company, Inc., purchased and retired 800,000 shares of its common stock at a cost of $40 per share. Assume that the common stock was issued for $9 per share.

Required

Journalize the purchase and retirement of the common stock.

D. G.C. Murphy Corp. reported that it had been able to pay off long-term debt of $4.5 million by issuing 100,000 common shares. The corporation proposed to recognize an extraordinary gain of $1.3 million on the transaction because its common shares were trading at $32 a share at the time of the transaction.

Required

1. Journalize the transaction.
2. Can Murphy Corp. show an extraordinary gain on the transaction?

Problem 15-7B   *Computing earnings per share and reporting a retained earnings restriction*

Tradewinds Travel Ltd.'s capital structure at December 31, 19X2, included 5,000 shares of $2.50 preferred stock and 130,000 shares of common stock. Common shares outstanding during 19X3 were 130,000 January through February; 119,000 during March; 121,000 April through October; and 128,000 during November and December. Income from continuing operations during 19X7 was $349,655. The company discontinued a segment of the business at a gain of $69,160, and an extraordinary item generated a loss of $49,510. The board of directors of Tradewinds has restricted $240,000 of retained earnings for expansion of the company's office facilities.

Required

1. Compute Tradewind's earnings per share. Start with income from continuing operations. Assume figures shown are net of tax.
2. Show two ways of reporting Tradewinds's retained earnings restriction. Assume total retained earnings is $739,800 and total capital stock is $947,610.

Decision Problems

1. *Analysing cash dividends and stock dividends*
Pacific Coast Ltd. had the following shareholders' equity on June 30 of the current year:

Common stock, 100,000 shares issued	$ 750,000
Retained earnings	830,000
Total shareholders' equity	$1,580,000

In the past, Pacific Coast has paid an annual cash dividend of $1.50 per share. Despite the large retained earnings balance, the board of directors wished to conserve cash for expansion. The board delayed the payment of cash dividends by one month and in the meantime distributed a 20 percent stock dividend. During the following year, the company's cash position improved. The board declared and paid a cash dividend of $1.25 per share.

Suppose you own 1,000 shares of Pacific Coast common stock, acquired three years ago. The market price of the stock was $24 per share before any of the above dividends.

Required

1. How does the stock dividend affect your proportionate ownership in the company? Explain.
2. What amount of cash dividends did you receive last year? What amount of cash dividends will you receive after the above dividend action?
3. Immediately after the stock dividend was distributed, the market value of Pacific Coast stock decreased from $24 per share to $20 per share. Does this represent a loss to you? Explain.
4. Suppose Pacific Coast announces at the time of the stock dividend that the company will continue to pay the annual $1.50 cash dividend per share, even after the stock dividend. Would you expect the market price of the stock to decrease to $20 per share as in question 3? Explain.

2. Earnings and dividends

1. A researcher noted that the market price of stocks seemed to decline after the date of record. Why do you think that would be the case?
2. The treasurer of Miske Brewing Corp. wanted to disclose a large loss that the company had incurred, because it had produced too much product just prior to a very cool summer, as an extraordinary item. Why do you think the treasurer wanted to use that particular disclosure? Would such disclosure be acceptable?
3. Certain public companies have purchased their stock on the market recently. When asked why they had done so, management responded that they felt the stock was under-valued. What do you think management meant? What advantage would the company gain by buying its own shares for cancellation?
4. The text states that EPS must be shown for income before discontinued operations and extraordinary items but more extensive EPS disclosure may be appropriate. Why do you think the additional disclosure is encouraged?
5. Carter Ltd. earned a significant profit in the year ended November 30, 19X2 because land it held was expropriated for a new highway. The company proposes to treat the sale of land to the government as other revenue. Why do you think Carter is proposing such treatment? Is such disclosure appropriate?

Financial Statement Problem

Retained earnings and the corporation income statement

Use the John Labatt financial statements in Appendix E to answer these questions.

1. How many shares of common stock did John Labatt have outstanding at April 30, 1989?
2. Did John Labatt purchase any shares of its own stock during the year ended April 30, 1989? Did the company issue any shares during the year?
3. Does John Labatt have any bonds or preferred shares outstanding that are convertible into common shares? How can you tell from the Income Statement? What is another source of information in the financial statements you can use to answer the question?

4. What was the retained earnings balance at April 30, 1989? Were there any restrictions on retained earnings?

5. Were any events such as discontinuance of operations of a significant segment of John Labatt's business or an extraordinary item reported on the Income Statement? Did John Labatt consider all events reported on the income statement to be in the normal course of business?

6. What was the total of income taxes charged against income for the year ended April 30, 1989 by John Labatt?

Answers to Self-Study Questions

1. a	3. d	5. d	7. a	9. b
2. c	4. b	6. d	8. c	10. c

16

Corporations: Long-Term Liabilities and Bond Investments

LEARNING OBJECTIVES

After studying this chapter, you should be able to

1 Amortize bond discount and premium by the straight-line method

2 Amortize bond discount and premium by the effective interest method

3 Account for retirement of bonds payable

4 Account for conversion of bonds payable

5 Account for operating leases and capital leases

6 Explain the advantages and disadvantages of borrowing

7 Account for investments in bonds

Corporations may finance—that is, raise money for—their operations in different ways. As we have seen, they may issue stock to their owners, and they may reinvest assets earned by profitable operations. This chapter discusses the third way of financing operations, long-term liabilities.

Two common long-term liabilities are notes payable and bonds payable. A note payable, which we studied in Chapter 11, is a promissory note issued by the company to borrow money from a single lender, like a bank or an insurance company. **Bonds payable** are groups of notes payable issued to multiple lenders, called bondholders. This chapter focuses on bonds and bond investments and also discusses accounting for lease liabilities.

The Nature of Bonds

A company needing millions of dollars may be unable to borrow so large an amount from a single lender. To gain access to more investors, the company may issue bonds. Each bond is, in effect, a long-term note payable that bears interest. Bonds are debts to the company for the amounts borrowed from the investors.

Purchasers of bonds receive a bond certificate, which carries the issuing company's name. The certificate also states the *principal*, which is the amount that the company has borrowed from the bondholder. This figure, typically stated in units of $1,000, is also called the bond's face value, maturity value or par value. The bond obligates the issuing company to pay the holder the principal amount at a specific future date, called the maturity date, which also appears on the certificate.

Bondholders loan their money to companies for a price: interest on the principal. The bond certificate states the interest rate that the issuer will pay

653

EXHIBIT 16-1   *Bond (Note) Certificate*

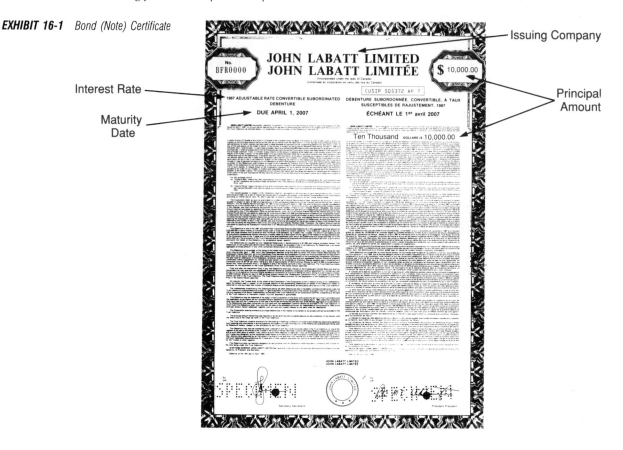

the holder and the dates that the interest payments are due (generally twice a year). Some bond certificates name the bondholder (the investor). When the company pays back the principal, the holder returns the certificate, which the company retires (or cancels). Exhibit 16-1 shows an actual bond certificate, with the various features highlighted.

The board of directors may authorize a bond issue. In some companies the shareholders—as owners—may also have to vote their approval.

Issuing bonds usually requires the services of a securities firm, like Wood Gundy, to act as the *underwriter* of the bond issue. The **underwriter** purchases the bonds from the issuing company and resells them to its clients, or it may sell the bonds for a commission from the issuer, agreeing to buy all unsold bonds.

Types of Bonds

Bonds may be *registered* bonds or *coupon* bonds. The owner of a **registered bond** receives interest cheques from the issuing company, which keeps a listing of the names and addresses of the bondholders. Owners of **coupon bonds** receive interest by detaching a perforated coupon—which states the interest due and the date of payment—from the bond and depositing it in a bank for collection. A company with coupon bonds needs no registry of bondholders. The responsibility for cashing coupons rests with the bondholders. All registered bonds and most coupon bonds are registered in the name of the owner for safe keeping.

All the bonds in a particular issue may mature at the same time (**term bonds**), or they may mature in installments over a period (**serial bonds**). By issuing serial bonds, the company spreads its principal payments over time and avoids paying the entire principal at one time. Serial bonds are like installment notes payable.

The contract between the corporation issuing a series of bonds and the holders of the bonds is called a **bond indenture**. All the details of the contract such as the security pledged as collateral for the bonds (for example, the corporation's land and buildings), any restrictions on the payment of dividends while the bond issue is outstanding, and any commitments in connection with the bond issue made by the corporation (for example, maintaining a certain working capital ratio) are among the terms specified in the indenture. The trustee for the bond issue, often a trust company such as National Trust, acts on behalf of the bondholders to ensure that all the terms of the indenture are fulfilled.

Secured or *mortgage* bonds give the bondholder the right to take specified assets of the issuer if the company *defaults*, that is, fails to pay interest or principal. Unsecured bonds, called **debentures**, are backed only by the good faith of the borrower.

A secured bond is not necessarily more attractive to an investor than is a debenture. The primary motive of a person investing in bonds is to receive the interest amounts and the bonds' maturity value on time. Thus a debenture from a business with an excellent record in meeting obligations may be more attractive to an investor than is a secured bond from a business that has just been started or that has a bad credit record.

Bond Prices

Investors may transfer ownership through bond markets. The bond market in Canada is called the *over the counter (OTC)* market. It is a network of investment dealers who trade bonds issued by the Government of Canada and Crown corporations, the provinces, municipalities and regions, and corporations.

Bond prices are quoted at a percentage of their maturity value using $100 as a base. For example, a $1,000 maturity value bond trading at $1,000 would be listed at $100 while a $1,000 bond trading at $1,050 would be listed at $105. A $100 maturity value bond trading at $102 would be listed at $102.

Exhibit 16-2 contains actual price information for bonds of Ontario Hydro, taken from *The Financial Post*.

EXHIBIT 16-2 *Bond Price Information*

Bonds	Int. Rate %	Maturity Date	Bid $	Yield %
Ontario Hydro	10.250	Jul 12 98	102.95	9.75

On this particular day, Ontario Hydro's 10¼ percent $1,000 par value bonds maturing July 12, 1998 (indicated by 98) had a bid price of $1,029.50 which provided a yield of 9.75 percent (the yield rate is the same as the market interest rate discussed below). *The Financial Post*, six days later, showed a bid price for the same bonds of 103.13; the yield was 9.72 percent.

The factors that affect the market price of a bond include the length of time left until the bond matures. The sooner the maturity date, the more attractive the bond, and the more an investor is willing to pay for it. Also, the bonds issued by a company with a proven ability to meet all payments commands a higher price than an issue from a company with a poor record. Bond price hinges, too, on the rates of other available investment plans. Is a 12 percent bond the best way to invest $1,000, or does another investment strategy pay a higher rate? Of course, the higher the percentage rate, the higher the market price will be. Buying a 13 percent bond will cost you more than buying an 8 percent bond, given that both issues have the same maturity date and have been issued by equally sound businesses.

A bond issued at a price above its maturity (par) value is said to be issued at a **premium**, and a bond issued at a price below maturity (par) value has a **discount**. Both of these practices are discussed below. As a bond nears maturity, its market price moves toward par value. On the maturity date the market value of a bond exactly equals its par value because the company that issued the bond pays that amount to retire the bond.

Present Value

A dollar received today is worth more than a dollar received in the future. You may invest today's dollar and earn income from it. Likewise, deferring any payment gives your money a period to grow. Money earns income over time, a fact called the *time value of money*. Let us examine how the time value of money affects the pricing of bonds.

Assume a bond with a face value of $1,000 reaches maturity three years from today and carries no interest. Would you pay $1,000 to purchase the bond? No, because the payment of $1,000 today to receive the same amount in the future provides you with no income on the investment. You would not be taking advantage of the time value of money. Just how much would you pay today in order to receive $1,000 at the end of three years? The answer is some amount *less* than $1,000. Let us suppose that you feel $750 is a good price. By investing $750 now to receive $1,000 later, you earn $250 interest revenue over the three years. The issuing company sees the transaction this way: It pays you $250 interest expense for the use of your $750 for three years.

The amount that a person would invest *at the present time* to receive a greater amount at a future date is called the **present value** of a future amount. In our example, $750 is the present value of the $1,000 amount to be received three years later.

Our $750 bond price is a reasonable estimate. The exact present value of any future amount depends on (1) the amount of the future payment (or receipt) (2) the length of time from the investment to the date when the future amount is to be received (or paid), and (3) the interest rate during the period. Present value is always less than the future amount. We discuss the method of computing present value in the appendix that follows this chapter. We need to be aware of the present-value concept, however, in the discussion of bond prices that follows.

Bond Interest Rates

Bonds are sold at market price, which is the amount that investors are willing to pay. Market price is the bond's present value, which equals the present value of the principal payment plus the present value of the cash interest payments (which are made quarterly, semiannually or annually over the term of the bond).

Two interest rates work to set the price of a bond. The **contract interest rate** or **stated rate** is the interest rate that determines the amount of cash interest the borrower pays—and the investor receives—each year. For example, the Toronto-Dominion Bank's 8 percent bonds have a contract interest rate of 8 percent. Thus Toronto-Dominion pays $8,000 of interest annually on each $100,000 bond. Each semiannual interest payment is $4,000 ($100,000 × .08 × ½).

The **market interest rate** or **effective rate** is the rate that investors demand in order to loan their money. The market rate varies, sometimes daily. A company may issue bonds with a contract interest rate that differs from the prevailing market interest rate. Toronto-Dominion may issue its 8 percent bonds when the market rate has risen to 9 percent. Will the Toronto-Dominion bonds attract investors in this market? No, because investors can earn 9 percent on other bonds. Therefore, investors will purchase Toronto-Dominion bonds only at a price less than par value. The difference between the lower price and face value is a *discount*. Conversely, if the market interest rate is 7 percent, Toronto-Dominion's 8 percent bonds will be so attractive that investors will pay more than face value for them. The difference between the higher price and face value is a *premium*.

Issuing Bonds Payable

Suppose the Toronto-Dominion Bank has $50 million in 8 percent bonds that mature in 10 years. Assume that Toronto-Dominion issues these bonds at par on January 1, 1991. The issuance entry is

```
1991
Jan. 1   Cash ...............................   50,000,000
               Bonds Payable ..................                50,000,000
         To issue 8%, 10-year bonds at par.
```

The corporation that is borrowing money makes a one-time entry similar to this to record the receipt of cash and the issuance of bonds. Afterward, investors buy and sell the bonds through the bond markets. The buy-and-sell transactions between investors do not involve the corporation that issued the bonds. It keeps no records of these transactions, except for the names and addresses of the bondholders. This information is needed for mailing the interest and principal payments.

Interest payments for these bonds occur each January 1 and July 1. Toronto-Dominion's entry to record the first semiannual interest payment is

```
1991
July 1   Interest Expense ($50,000,000 × .08 × 6/12) ....   2,000,000
               Cash ............................                2,000,000
         To pay semiannual interest on bonds
         payable.
```

At maturity, Toronto-Dominion will record payment of the bonds as follows:

```
2001
Jan. 1   Bonds Payable ......................   50,000,000
               Cash...........................                50,000,000
         To pay bonds payable at maturity.
```

Issuing Bonds Payable between Interest Dates

The foregoing entries to record Toronto-Dominion's bond transactions are straightforward because the company issued the bonds on an interest payment date (January 1). However, corporations often issue bonds between interest dates.

Suppose Nova Scotia Power issues $75 million of 12 percent debentures due June 15, 2001. These bonds are dated June 15, 1991, and carry the price "100 plus accrued interest from date of original issue." An investor purchasing the bonds after the bond date must pay market value *plus accrued interest*. The issuing company will pay the full semiannual interest amount to the bond-holder at the next interest payment date. Companies do not split semiannual interest payments.

Assume that Nova Scotia Power sells $100,000 of its bonds on July 15, 1991, one month after the date of original issue on June 15. Also assume that the market price of the bonds on July 15 is the face value. The company receives one month's accrued interest in addition to the bond's face value. Nova Scotia Power's entry to record issuance of the bonds payable is

1991			
July 15	Cash	101,000	
	Bonds Payable		100,000
	Interest Payable ($100,000 × .12 × $\frac{1}{12}$)		1,000
	To issue 12%, 10-year bonds at par, one month after the original issue date.		

Nova Scotia Power's entry to record the first semiannual interest payment is

1991			
Dec. 15	Interest Expense ($100,000 × .12 × $\frac{5}{12}$)	5,000	
	Interest Payable	1,000	
	Cash ($100,000 × .12 × $\frac{6}{12}$)		6,000
	To pay semiannual interest on bonds payable.		

The debit to Interest Payable eliminates the credit balance in that account (from July 15). Nova Scotia Power has now paid off that liability.

Note that Nova Scotia Power pays a full six months' interest on December 15. After subtracting the one month's accrued interest received at the time of issuing the bond, Nova Scotia Power has recorded interest expense for five months ($5,000). This interest expense is the correct amount for the five months that the bonds have been outstanding.

Selling bonds between interest dates at market value plus accrued interest simplifies the borrower's bookkeeping. The business pays the same amount of interest on each bond regardless of the length of time the person has held the bond. The business need not compute each bondholder's interest payment on an individual basis. Imagine the paperwork necessary to keep track of the interest due hundreds of bondholders who each bought bonds on a different date.

When an investor sells bonds to another investor, the price is always "plus accrued interest." Suppose you hold bonds as an investment for two months of a semiannual interest period and sell the bonds to another investor before receiving your interest. The person who buys the bonds will receive your two months of interest on the next specified interest date. Business practice dictates that you must collect your share of the interest when you sell the bonds. For this reason, all bond transactions are "plus accrued interest."

Issuing Bonds Payable at a Discount

We know that market conditions may force the issuing corporation to accept a discount price for its bonds. Suppose Bell Canada issues $100,000 of its 8 percent, 10-year bonds when the market interest rate is slightly above 8 percent. The market price of the bonds drops to 98, which means 98 percent of par value. Bell receives $98,000 ($100,000 × .98) at issuance. The entry is

```
1991
Jan. 1   Cash ($100,000 × .98)..........................   98,000
         Discount on Bonds Payable ....................    2,000
              Bonds Payable .........................               100,000
         To issue 8%, 10-year bonds at a discount.
```

After posting, the bond accounts have the following balances:

Bonds Payable	Discount on Bonds Payable
100,000	2,000

Bell Canada's balance sheet immediately after issuance of the bonds reports

```
Long-term liabilities
    Bonds payable, 8%, due 2001...........   $100,000
    Less: Discount on bonds payable .......      2,000   $98,000
```

Discount on Bonds Payable is a contra account to Bonds Payable. Subtracting its balance from Bonds Payable yields the book value, or carrying value, of the bonds. The relationship between Bonds Payable and the Discount account is similar to the relationships between Equipment and Accumulated Depreciation and between Accounts Receivable and Allowance for Uncollectible Accounts. Thus Bell's liability is $98,000, which is the amount the company borrowed. If Bell were to pay off the bonds immediately (an unlikely occurrence), Bell's required outlay would be $98,000 because the market price of the bonds is $98,000.

Interest Expense on Bonds Issued at a Discount   We earlier discussed the difference between the contract interest rate and the market interest rate. Suppose the market rate is 8¼ percent when Bell issues its 8 percent bonds. The ¼ percent interest rate difference creates the $2,000 discount on the bonds. Bell borrows $98,000 cash but must pay $100,000 cash when the bonds mature, 10 years later. What happens to the $2,000 balance of the discount account over the life of the bond issue?

The $2,000 is in reality an additional interest expense to the issuing company. That amount is a cost (beyond the stated interest rate) that the business pays for borrowing the investors' money.

The discount amount is an interest expense not paid until the bond matures. However, the borrower (the bond issuer) benefits from the use of the investors' money each accounting period over the full term of the bond issue. The matching principle directs the business to match expense against its revenues

> **OBJECTIVE 1**
> Amortize bond discount and premium by the straight-line method

on a period-by-period basis. The discount is allocated to interest expense through amortization each accounting period over the life of the bonds.

Straight-Line Amortization of Discount We may amortize bond discount by dividing it into equal amounts for each interest period. This method is called straight-line amortization. In our example, the beginning discount is $2,000, and there are 20 semiannual interest periods during the bonds' 10-year life. Therefore, $\frac{1}{20}$ of the $2,000 ($100) of bond discount is amortized each interest period. Bell's semiannual interest entry on July 1, 1991 is

1991				
July 1	Interest Expense	4,100	
	Cash ($100,000 × .08 × $\frac{6}{12}$)		4,000
	Discount on Bonds Payable ($2,000/20)		100
	To pay semiannual interest and amortize discount on bonds payable.		

Interest expense of $4,100 is the sum of the contract interest ($4,000, which is paid in cash) plus the amount of discount amortized ($100). Discount on Bonds Payable is credited to amortize (reduce) the account's debit balance. Because Discount on Bonds Payable is a contra account, each reduction in its balance increases the book value of Bonds Payable. Twenty amortization entries will decrease the discount balance to zero, which means that Bonds Payable will have increased by $2,000 up to its face value of $100,000. The entry to pay off the bonds at maturity is

2001				
Jan. 1	Bonds Payable	100,000	
	Cash................................		100,000
	To pay bonds payable at maturity.		

Issuing Bonds Payable at a Premium

To illustrate issuing bonds at a premium, let us change the Bell Canada example. Assume that the market interest rate is $7\frac{1}{2}$ percent when the company issues its 8 percent, 10-year bonds. Because 8 percent bonds are attractive in this market, investors pay a premium price to acquire them. If the bonds are priced at $103\frac{1}{2}$ (103.5 percent of par value) Bell receives $103,500 cash upon issuance. The entry is

1991				
Jan. 1	Cash ($100,000 × 1.035)	103,500	
	Bonds Payable		100,000
	Premium on Bonds Payable		3,500
	To issue 8%, 10-year bonds at a premium.		

After posting, the bond accounts have the following balances:

Bonds Payable	Premium on Bonds Payable
100,000	3,500

Bell Canada's balance sheet immediately after issuance of the bonds reports:

Long-term liabilities:
Bonds payable, 8%, due 2001 .... $100,000
Premium on bonds payable........... __3,500__ $103,500

Premium on Bonds Payable is added to Bonds Payable to show the book value, or carrying value, of the bonds. Bell's liability is $103,500, which is the amount that the company borrowed. Immediate payment of the bonds would require an outlay of $103,500 because the market price of the bonds at issuance is $103,500. The investors would be unwilling to give up bonds for less than their market value.

Interest Expense on Bonds Issued at a Premium   The ½ percent difference between the 8 percent contract rate on the bonds and the 7½ percent market interest rate creates the $3,500 premium. Bell borrows $103,500 cash but must pay only $100,000 cash at maturity. We treat the premium as a savings of interest expense to Bell. The premium cuts Bell's cost of borrowing the money. We account for the premium much as we handled the discount. We amortize the bond premium as a decrease in interest expense over the life of the bonds.

Straight-Line Amortization of Premium   In our example, the beginning premium is $3,500, and there are 20 semiannual interest periods during the bonds' 10-year life. Therefore, $\frac{1}{20}$ of the $3,500 ($175) of bond premium is amortized each interest period. Bell's semiannual interest entry on July 1, 1991 is

1991
July 1   Interest Expense 3,825
       Premium on Bonds Payable ($3,500/20) 175
          Cash ($100,000 × .08 × $\frac{6}{12}$) 4,000
       To pay semiannual interest and amortize premium
       on bonds payable.

Interest expense of $3,825 is the remainder of the contract cash interest ($4,000) less the amount of premium amortized ($175). The debit to Premium on Bonds Payable reduces its credit balance. Twenty amortization entries will decrease the premium balance to zero. The payment at maturity will debit Bonds Payable and credit Cash for $100,000.

Adjusting Entries for Interest Expense _____

Companies issue bonds when they need cash. The interest payments seldom occur on December 31 (or the end of the fiscal year). Nevertheless, interest expense must be accrued at the end of the period to properly measure income. The accrual entry may often be complicated by the need to amortize a discount or a premium for only a partial interest period.

Suppose Nova Corp. issues $100,000 of its 8 percent, 10-year bonds at a $2,000 discount on October 1, 1991. Assume that interest payments occur on March 31 and September 30 each year. On December 31, Nova records interest for the three-month period (October, November and December) as follows:

1991

Dec. 31   Interest Expense............................   2,050

    Interest Payable ($100,000 × .08 × 3/12)........   2,000

    Discount on Bonds Payable ($2,000/10 × 3/12) .   50

  To accrue three months' interest and amortize
  discount on bonds payable for three months.

Interest Payable is credited for the three months of cash interest that have accrued since September 30. Discount on Bonds Payable is credited for three months of amortization.

The balance sheet at December 31, 1991 reports Interest Payable of $2,000 as a current liability. Bonds Payable appears as a long-term liability, presented as follows:

Long-term liabilities
 Bonds payable, 8%, due 2001...................... $100,000
 Less: Discount on bonds payable ($2,000 − $50).......   1,950 $98,050

Observe that the balance of Discount on Bonds Payable decreases by $50. The bonds' carrying value increases by the same amount. The bonds' carrying value continues to increase over its 10-year life, reaching $100,000 at maturity when the discount will be fully amortized.

The next semiannual interest payment occurs on March 31, 1992 as follows:

1992

Mar. 31   Interest Expense............................   2,050

  Interest Payable   2,000

    Cash ($100,000 × .08 × 6/12).................   4,000

    Discount on Bonds Payable ($2,000/10 × 3/12) .   50

  To pay semiannual interest, part of which was
  accrued, and amortize three months' discount
  on bonds payable.

Amortization of a premium over a partial interest period is similar except that Premium on Bonds Payable is debited.

Summary Problem for Your Review

Assume that Hydro-Québec has outstanding an issue of 9 percent bonds that mature on May 1, 2010. Further, assume that the bonds are dated May 1, 1990 and Hydro-Québec pays interest each April 30 and October 31.

Required

1. Will the bonds be issued at par, at a premium, or at a discount if the market interest rate is 8 percent at date of issuance? if the market interest rate is 10 percent?

2. Assume Hydro-Québec issued $1,000,000 of the bonds at 104 on May 1, 1990.
   a. Record issuance of the bonds.
   b. Record the interest payment and amortization of premium or discount on October 31, 1990.
   c. Accrue interest and amortize premium or discount on December 31, 1990.
   d. Show how the company would report the bonds on the balance sheet at December 31, 1990.
   e. Record the interest payment on April 30, 1991.

SOLUTION TO REVIEW PROBLEM

Requirement 1   If the market interest rate is 8 percent, 9 percent bonds will be issued at a *premium*. If the market rate is 10 percent, the 9 percent bonds will be issued at a *discount*.

Requirement 2

1990				
a. May 1	Cash ($1,000,000 × 1.04)	1,040,000		
	Bonds Payable		1,000,000	
	Premium on Bonds Payable		40,000	
	To issue 9%, 20-year bonds at a premium.			
b. Oct. 31	Interest Expense	44,000		
	Premium on Bonds Payable ($40,000/40) . .	1,000		
	Cash ($1,000,000 × .09 × 6/12)		45,000	
	To pay semiannual interest and amortize premium on bonds payable.			
c. Dec. 31	Interest Expense	14,667		
	Premium on Bonds Payable ($40,000/40 × 2/6)	333		
	Interest Payable ($1,000,000 × .09 × 2/12)		15,000	
	To accrue interest and amortize bond premium for two months.			
d. Long-term liabilities				
	Bonds payable, 9%, due 2010	$1,000,000		
	Premium on bonds payable ($40,000 − $1,000 − $333)	38,667	$1,038,667	
1991				
e. Apr. 30	Interest Expense	29,333		
	Interest Payable	15,000		
	Premium on Bonds Payable ($40,000/40 × 4/6)	667		
	Cash ($1,000,000 × .09 × 6/12)		45,000	
	To pay semiannual interest, part of which was accrued, and amortize four months' premium on bonds payable.			

SUPPLEMENT TO SUMMARY PROBLEM SOLUTION

Bond problems include many details. You may find it helpful to check your work. We verify the answers to the Summary Problem in this supplement.

On April 30, 1991, the bonds have been outstanding for one year. After the entries have been recorded, the account balances should show the results of one year's cash interest payments and one year's bond premium amortization.

Fact 1	Cash interest payments should be $90,000 ($1,000,000 × .09).
Accuracy check	Two credits to Cash of $45,000 each = $90,000. Cash payments are correct.
Fact 2	Premium amortization should be $2,000 ($40,000/40 semiannual periods × 2 semiannual periods in 1 year).
Accuracy check	Three debits to Premium on Bonds Payable ($1,000 + $333 + $667) = $2,000. Premium amortization is correct.
Fact 3	Also we can check the accuracy of interest expense recorded during the year ended December 31, 1990.

The bonds in this problem will be outstanding for a total of 20 years, or 240 (that is, 20×12) months. During 1990 the bonds are outstanding for 8 months (May through December).

Interest expense for 8 months *equals* payment of cash interest for 8 months *minus* premium amortization for 8 months.

Interest expense should therefore be ($1,000,000 × .09 × $\frac{8}{12}$ = $60,000) minus [($40,000/240) × 8 = $1,333] or ($60,000 − $1,333 = $58,667).

Accuracy check	Two debits to Interest Expense ($44,000 + $14,667) = $58,667. Interest expense for 1990 is correct.

Effective Interest Method of Amortization _____

The straight-line amortization method has a theoretical weakness. Each period's amortization amount for a premium or discount is the same dollar amount over the life of the bonds. However, over that time the bonds' carrying value continues to increase (with a discount) or decrease (with a premium). Thus the fixed dollar amount of amortization changes as a percentage of the bonds' carrying value, making it appear that the bond issuer's interest rate changes over time. This appearance is misleading because in fact the issuer locked in a fixed interest rate when the bonds were issued. The interest rate on the bonds does not change.

We will see how the effective interest method keeps each interest expense amount at the same percentage of the bonds' carrying value for every interest payment over the bonds' life. The total amount amortized over the life of the bonds is the same under both methods. GAAP does not specify which method should be used. U.S. GAAP favors the effective interest method because it does a better job of matching. However, the straight-line method is popular because of its simplicity.

Effective Interest Method of Amortizing Discount

Assume that Dofasco Inc. issues $100,000 of its 9 percent bonds at a time when the market rate of interest is 10 percent. Also assume that these bonds mature in five years and pay interest semiannually, so there are 10 semiannual interest payments. The issue price of the bonds is $96,149.[1] The discount on these bonds is $3,851 ($100,000 − $96,149).

Exhibit 16-3 illustrates amortization of the discount by the effective interest method.

EXHIBIT 16-3   *Effective Interest Method of Amortizing Bond Discount*

Panel A: Bond Data

Maturity value, $100,000
Contract interest rate, 9%
Interest paid, 4½% semiannually, $4,500 ($100,000 × .045)
Market interest rate at time of issue, 10% annually, 5% semiannually
Issue price, $96,149

Panel B: Amortization Table

Semiannual Interest Period	A Interest Payment (4½% of Maturity Value)	B Interest Expense (5% of Preceding Bond Carrying Value)	C Discount Amortization (B − A)	D Discount Account Balance (D − C)	E Bond Carrying Value ($100,000 − D)
Issue Date				$3,851	$ 96,149
1	$4,500	$4,807	$307	3,544	96,456
2	4,500	4,823	323	3,221	96,779
3	4,500	4,839	339	2,882	97,118
4	4,500	4,856	356	2,526	97,474
5	4,500	4,874	374	2,152	97,848
6	4,500	4,892	392	1,760	98,240
7	4,500	4,912	412	1,348	98,652
8	4,500	4,933	433	915	99,085
9	4,500	4,954	454	461	99,539
10	4,500	4,961*	461	-0-	100,000

* Adjusted for effect of rounding.

The exhibit reveals the following important facts about effective interest method amortization of bond discount:

Column A   The semiannual interest payments are constant because they are governed by the contact interest rate and the bonds' maturity value.

Column B   The interest expense each period is computed by multiplying the

---

[1] We compute this present value using the tables that appear in the appendix to this chapter.

preceding bond carrying value by the market interest rate (5 percent semiannually). This rate is the *effective interest rate* because its effect determines the interest expense each period. The amount of interest each period increases as the effective interest rate, a constant, is applied to the increasing bond carrying value (column E).

Column C   The excess of each interest expense amount (column B) over each interest payment amount (column A) is the discount amortization for the period.

Column D   The discount balance decreases by the amount of amortization for the period (column C). The discount decreases from $3,851 at the bonds' issue date to zero at their maturity. The balance of the discount plus the bonds' carrying value equal the bonds' maturity value.

Column E   The bonds' carrying value increases from $96,149 at issuance to $100,000 at maturity.

Recall that we want to present interest expense amounts over the full life of the bonds at a fixed percentage of the bonds' carrying value. The 5 percent rate—the effective interest rate—*is* that percentage. We have figured the cost of the money borrowed by the bond issuer—the interest expense—as a constant percentage of the carrying value of the bonds. The dollar *amount* of interest expense varies from period to period but not the interest percentage *rate*.

The accounts debited and credited under the effective interest amortization method and the straight-line method are the same. Only the amounts differ. We may take the amortization amounts directly from the table in the exhibit. We assume that the first interest payment occurs on July 1 and use the appropriate amounts from Exhibit 16-3, reading across the line for the first interest payment date:

July 1	Interest Expense (column B)	4,807	
	Discount on Bonds Payable (column C).		307
	Cash (column A)		4,500
	To pay semiannual interest and amortize discount on bonds payable.		

OBJECTIVE 2

Amortize bond discount and premium by the effective interest method

Effective Interest Method of Amortizing Premium

Let us modify the Dofasco example to illustrate the interest method of amortizing bond premium. Assume that Dofasco issues $100,000 of five-year, 9 percent bonds that pay interest semiannually. If the bonds are issued when the market interest rate is 8 percent, their issue price is $104,100.[2] The premium on these bonds is $4,100, and Exhibit 16-4 illustrates amortization of the premium by the interest method.

Exhibit 16-4 reveals the following important facts about the effective interest method of amortizing bond premium:

Column A   The semiannual interest payments are a constant amount fixed by the contract interest rate and the bonds' maturity value.

---

[2] Again, we compute the present value of the bonds using the tables in this chapter's appendix.

EXHIBIT 16-4   *Interest Method of Amortizing Bond Premium*

Panel A: Bond Data

Maturity value, $100,000
Contract interest rate, 9%
Interest paid, 4½% semiannually, $4,500 ($100,000 × .045)
Market interest rate at time of issue, 8% annually, 4% semiannually
Issue price, $104,100

Panel B: Amortization Table

	A	B	C	D	E
Semiannual Interest Period	Interest Payment (4½% of Maturity Value)	Interest Expense (4% of Preceding Bond Carrying Value)	Premium Amortization (A − B)	Premium Account Balance (D − C)	Bond Carrying Value ($100,000 + D)
Issue Date				$4,100	$104,100
1	$4,500	$4,164	$336	3,764	103,764
2	4,500	4,151	349	3,415	103,415
3	4,500	4,137	363	3,052	103,052
4	4,500	4,122	378	2,674	102,674
5	4,500	4,107	393	2,281	102,281
6	4,500	4,091	409	1,872	101,872
7	4,500	4,075	425	1,447	101,447
8	4,500	4,058	442	1,005	101,005
9	4,500	4,040	460	545	100,545
10	4,500	3,955*	545	-0-	100,000

* Adjusted for effect of rounding.

Column B   The interest expense each period is computed by multiplying the preceding bond carrying value by the effective interest rate (4 percent semiannually). Observe that the amount of interest decreases each period as the bond carrying value decreases.

Column C   The excess of each interest payment (column A) over the period's interest expense (column B) is the premium amortization for the period.

Column D   The premium balance decreases by the amount of amortization for the period (column C) from $4,100 at issuance to zero at maturity. The bonds' carrying value plus the premium balance equal the bonds' maturity value.

Column E   The bonds' carrying value decreases from $104,100 at issuance to $100,000 at maturity.

Assuming that the first interest payment occurs on October 31, we read across the line for the first interest payment date and pick up the appropriate amounts.

Oct. 31	Interest Expense (column B)	4,164	
	Premium on Bonds Payable (column C)	336	
	Cash (column A)		4,500

To pay semiannual interest and amortize discount
on bonds payable.

At year end it is necessary to make an adjusting entry for accrued interest and amortization of the bond premium for a partial period. In our example, the last interest payment occurred on October 31. The adjustment for November and December must cover two months, or one third of a semiannual period. The entry, with amounts drawn from line 2 in Exhibit 16-4 is

Dec. 31	Interest Expense ($4,151 × ⅓)	1,384	
	Premium on Bonds Payable ($349 × ⅓)	116	
	Interest Payable ($4,500 × ⅓)		1,500

To accrue two months' interest and amortize
premium on bonds payable for two months.

The second interest payment occurs on April 30 of the following year. The payment of $4,500 includes interest expense for four months (January through April), the interest payable at December 31, and premium amortization for four months. The payment entry is

Apr. 30	Interest Expense ($4,151 × ⅔)	2,767	
	Interest Payable	1,500	
	Premium on Bonds Payable ($349 × ⅔)	233	
	Cash		4,500

To pay semiannual interest, some of which was
accrued, and amortize premium on bonds
payable for four months.

If these bonds had been issued at a discount, procedures for these interest entries would be the same, except that Discount on Bonds Payable would be credited.

Bond Sinking Fund

Bond indentures, the contracts under which bonds are issued, often require the borrower to make regular periodic payments to a *bond sinking fund*. A fund is a group of assets that are segregated for a particular purpose. A **bond sinking fund** is used to retire bonds payable at maturity. A trustee manages this fund for the issuer, investing the company's payments in income-earning assets. The company's payments into the fund and the interest revenue, which the trustee reinvests in the fund, accumulate. The target amount of the sinking fund is the face value of the bond issue at maturity. When the bonds come due, the trustee sells the sinking-fund assets and uses the cash proceeds to pay off the bonds. The bond sinking fund provides security of payment to investors in unsecured bonds.

Most companies report sinking funds under the heading Investments, a separate asset category between current assets and plant assets on the balance sheet. A bond sinking fund is not a current asset because it may not be used to pay current liabilities. Accounting for the interest, dividends, and other earnings on the bond sinking fund requires use of the accounts Sinking Fund and Sinking Fund Revenue.

Sobey's Stores Limited has outstanding $9.25 million of 13 percent sinking fund debentures. The company must make annual sinking-fund payments. The entry to deposit $500,000 with the trustee is

Jan. 5	Sinking Fund	500,000	
	Cash................................		500,000
	To make annual sinking fund deposit.		

If the trustee invests the cash and reports annual sinking fund revenue of $50,000, the fund grows by this amount, and Sobey's makes the following entry at year end:

Dec. 31	Sinking Fund	50,000	
	Sinking Fund Revenue		50,000
	To record sinking fund earnings.		

Assume that Sobey's has made the required sinking fund payments over a period of years and that these payments plus the fund earnings have accumulated a cash balance of $9.45 million at maturity. The trustee pays off the bonds and returns the excess cash to Sobey's, which makes the following entry:

Jan. 4	Cash..................................	200,000	
	Bonds Payable	9,250,000	
	Sinking Fund.......................		9,450,000
	To record payment of bonds payable and receipt of excess sinking fund cash at maturity.		

If the fund balance is less than the bonds' maturity value, the entry is similar to the foregoing entry. However, the company pays the extra amount and credits Cash.

Retirement of Bonds Payable

Normally companies wait until maturity to pay off, or retire, their bonds payable. All bond discount or premium has been amortized, and the retirement entry debits Bonds Payable and credits Cash for the bonds' maturity value.

Companies sometimes retire their bonds payable prior to maturity. The main reason for retiring bonds early is to relieve the pressure of making interest payments. Interest rates fluctuate. The company may be able to borrow at a lower interest rate and use the proceeds from new bonds to pay off the old bonds, which bear a higher rate.

Some bonds are **callable**, which means that the issuer may *call* or pay off the bonds at a specified price whenever the issuer wants. The call price is usually a few percent above par, perhaps 104 or 105. Callable bonds give the issuer the benefit of being able to take advantage of low interest rates by paying off the bonds at the most favorable time. As an alternative to calling the bonds the issuer may purchase them in the open market at their current market price.

OBJECTIVE 3
Account for retirement of bonds payable

Say Air Products Canada Ltd. has $7,000,000 of debentures outstanding with unamortized discount of $35,000. Lower interest rates in the market may convince management to pay off these bonds now. Assume that the bonds are callable at 103. If the market price of the bonds is 99¼, will Air Products call the bonds or purchase them in the open market? The market price is lower than the call price, so market price is the better choice, as shown in the following tabulation:

Par value of bonds being retired..................	$7,000,000
Unamortized discount	35,000
Book value	6,965,000
Market price ($7,000,000 × .9925).................	6,947,500
Gain on retirement	$ 17,500

The entry to record retirement of the bonds, immediately after an interest date, is

June 30 Bonds Payable.......................	7,000,000	
Discount on Bonds Payable		35,000
Cash ($7,000,000 × .9925)		6,947,500
Gain on Retirement of Bonds		
Payable.....................		17,500
To retire bonds payable before maturity.		

The entry removes the bonds payable and the related discount from the accounts and records a gain on retirement. Of course, any existing premium would be removed with a debit. If Air Products Canada had retired only half of these bonds, the accountant would remove half of the discount or premium. Likewise, if the price paid to retire the bonds exceeds their carrying value, the retirement entry would record a loss with a debit to the account Loss on Retirement of Bonds. GAAP requires that gains and losses on early retirement of debt, that are both abnormal in size and unusual, be classified as *unusual* and be reported separately as a line item on the income statement before discontinued operations and extraordinary items.

Convertible Bonds and Notes _____

OBJECTIVE 4
Account for conversion of bonds payable

Many corporate bonds and notes payable may be converted into the common stock of the issuing company at the option of the investor. These bonds and notes, called **convertible bonds** (or **notes**), combine the safety of assured receipts of principal and interest on the bonds with the opportunity for large gains on the stock. The conversion feature is so attractive that investors usually accept a lower interest rate than they would on nonconvertible bonds. The lower interest rate benefits the issuer. Convertible bonds are recorded like any other debt at issuance.

The bond indenture will specify how many shares (usually common shares) the bond will be convertible into at specified dates after the bond is first sold. If a $100 bond is convertible into five shares, the purchaser of the bond is buying a $100 bond or five shares of stock. If the market price of the stock increases from the date of issue of the bonds to say $45 a share at the conversion date, the bondholder could convert the $100 bond into five shares, sell the shares for $225 and realize a profit of $125 ($225 – $100, the price paid for the shares).

In other words, if the market price of the issuing company's stock gets high enough, the bondholders will convert the bonds into stock. The corporation records conversion by debiting the bond accounts and crediting the shareholders' equity accounts. The carrying value of the bonds becomes the book value of the newly issued stock. No gain or loss is recorded.

Maclean Hunter Limited has 8¼ percent convertible *debentures* outstanding with a carrying value of $52.3 million; the debentures are due May 1, 2004. They are convertible into Class X voting shares up to May 1, 1994, at $10.125 per Class X voting share. Assume that $2 million of debentures were converted into 197,531 ($2,000,000/$10.125) Class X shares on May 1, 1991. Maclean Hunter's entry to record conversion is

```
1991
May 1   Debentures Outstanding . . . . . . . . . . . . . . . . .   2,000,000
            Common Stock — Class X . . . . . . . . . . .              2,000,000
        To record conversion of $2,000,000
        debentures outstanding into 197,531
        Class X shares.
```

Observe that the carrying value of the debentures becomes the amount of increase in shareholders' equity.

Current Portion of Long-Term Debt ———————————————

Serial bonds and serial notes are payable in serials, or installments. The portion payable within one year is a current liability, and the remaining debt is long-term. At December 31, 1991, Mapco, Inc. had $70 million of 8.7 percent notes payable. The notes are due in $8 million annual installments through 1999 with a final installment of $6 million due in 2000. Therefore, $8 million is a current liability at December 31, 1991, and $62 million is a long-term liability. Mapco reported this installment note payable among its liabilities as follows:

	$ millions
Current liabilities	
Current portion of long-term debt	$ 8
Long-term debt, excluding amounts payable within one year	62

Mortgage Notes Payable ———————————————

Many notes payable are mortgage notes, which actually contain two agreements. The *note* is the borrower's promise to pay the lender the amount of the debt. The **mortgage** is the borrower's promise to transfer the legal title to certain assets to the lender if the debt is not paid on schedule. The borrower is said to pledge these assets as security for the note. Often the asset that is pledged was acquired with the borrowed money. For example, most homeowners sign mortgage notes to purchase their residences, pledging that property as security for the loan. Businesses sign mortgage notes to acquire buildings, equipment, and other long-term assets. Mortgage notes are usually serial notes that require monthly or quarterly payments.

Lease Liabilities

A **lease** is a rental agreement in which the tenant (**lessee**) agrees to make rent payments to the property owner (**lessor**) in exchange for the use of the asset. Leasing allows the lessee to acquire the use of a needed asset without having to make the large initial cash down payment that purchase agreements require. Accountants divide leases into two types: operating and capital. Capital leases are further divided into two kinds: *sales-type leases*, where the lessor is usually a manufacturer or dealer, and *direct financing leases*, where the lessor is usually not a manufacturer or dealer but provides financing. This text will consider the broader term, capital lease, and not the kinds of capital lease.

Distinguishing a Capital Lease from an Operating Lease   The *CICA Handbook* suggests that a lease is a **capital lease** if one or more of the following conditions are present at the beginning of the lease:

1. There is reasonable assurance that the lessee will obtain ownership of the leased asset at the end of the lease term.
2. The lease term is of such a length that the lessee will obtain almost all of the benefits from the use of the leased asset.
3. The lessor would both recover the original investment and earn a return on that investment from the lease.

A lease which does not meet any of the above conditions is probably an operating lease and should be accounted for as such.

Operating Leases

OBJECTIVE 5
Account for operating leases and capital leases

Operating leases are usually short-term or cancelable. Many apartment leases and most car-rental agreements extend a year or less. These operating leases give the lessee the right to use the asset but provide the lessee with no continuing rights to the asset. The lessor retains the usual risks and rewards of owning the leased asset. To account for an operating lease, the lessee debits Rent Expense (or Lease Expense) and credits Cash for the amount of the lease payment. The lessee's books do not report the leased asset or any lease liability (except perhaps a prepaid rent amount or a rent accrual at the end of the period).

Capital Leases

More and more businesses nationwide are turning to capital leasing to finance the acquisition of assets. A *capital lease* is long-term and noncancelable. Accounting for a capital lease is much like accounting for a purchase. The lessor removes the asset from her books. The lessee enters the asset into his accounts and records a lease liability at the beginning of the lease term.

Many companies lease some of their plant assets rather than buy them. A recent survey of 300 companies indicates that while almost 90 percent (260) have long-term debt, one third (101) have capital leases.

Becker Milk Co. Ltd. owns Becker's convenience stores. Suppose the company leases a building, agreeing to pay $10,000 annually for a 20-year period, with the first payment due immediately. This arrangement is similar to purchasing the building on an installment plan. In an installment purchase, Becker would debit Building and credit Cash and Installment Note Payable. The company would then pay interest and principal on the note payable and record depreciation on the building. Accounting for a capital lease follows this pattern.

Becker records the building at cost, which is the sum of the $10,000 initial payment plus the present value of the 19 future lease payments of $10,000 each. The company credits Cash for the initial payment and credits Lease Liability for the present value of the future lease payments. Assume the interest rate on Becker's lease is 10 percent and the present value (PV) of the future lease payments is $83,650.[3] At the beginning of the lease term, Becker makes the following entry:

May 1	Building ($10,000 + $83,650)	93,650	
	Cash.		10,000
	Lease Liability (PV of future lease		
	payments).		83,650
	To acquire a building and make the first annual		
	lease payment on a capital lease.		

Because Becker has capitalized the building, the company records depreciation. Assume the building has an expected life of 25 years. It is depreciated over the lease term of 20 years because the lessee has the use of the building only for that period. No residual value enters into the depreciation computation because the lessee will have no residual asset when the building is returned to the lessor at the expiration of the lease. Therefore, the annual depreciation entry is

19X2			
Apr. 30	Depreciation Expense ($93,650/20)	4,683	
	Accumulated Depreciation — Building		4,683
	To record depreciation on leased building.		

At year end Becker must also accrue interest on the lease liability. Interest expense is computed by multiplying the lease liability by the interest rate on the lease. The following entry credits Lease Liability (not Interest Payable) for this interest accrual:

19X2			
Apr. 30	Interest Expense ($83,650 × .10)	8,365	
	Lease Liability.		8,365
	To accrue interest on the lease liability.		

---

[3] This computation appears in the chapter appendix.

The balance sheet at December 31, 19X1 reports:

Assets

Plant assets
Building...	$93,650	
Less Accumulated depreciation	4,683	$88,967

Liabilities

Current liabilities
Lease liability (next payment due on May 1, 19X2).................	$10,000

Long-term liabilities
Lease liability [beginning balance ($83,650 + interest accrual ($8,365) —current portion ($10,000)]	82,015

In addition, the lessee must report the minimum capital lease payments for the next five years in the notes to the financial statements.

The lease liability is split into current and long-term portions because the next payment ($10,000) is a current liability and the remainder is long-term. The May 1, 19X2 lease payment is recorded as follows:

May 1	Lease Liability...............................	10,000	
	Cash..................................		10,000
	To make second annual lease payment on building.		

Off-Balance-Sheet Financing

An important part of business is obtaining the funds needed to acquire assets. To finance operations a company may issue stock, borrow money, or retain earnings in the business. Notice that all three of these financing plans affect the right-hand side of the balance sheet. Issuing stock affects preferred or common stock. Borrowing creates notes or bonds payable. Internal funds come from retained earnings.

Off-balance-sheet financing is the acquisition of assets or services whose resulting debt is not reported on the balance sheet. A prime example is an operating lease. The lessee has the use of the leased asset, but neither the asset nor any lease liability is reported on the balance sheet. In the past, most leases were accounted for by the operating method. However, *CICA Handbook* Section 3065 has required businesses to account for an increasing number of leases by the capital lease method. Also, *CICA Handbook* Section 3065 has brought about detailed reporting of operating lease payments in the notes to the financial statements; minimum operating lease payments for the next five years must be reported. The inclusion of more lease information, be they capital or operating leases, makes the accounting information for decision-making more complete.

Pension Liabilities

Most companies have a pension plan for their employees. A **pension** is employee compensation that is received during retirement. Employees earn the pensions by their service, so the company records pension expense while employees work for the company. While employees may also contribute to a company pension plan, the following discussion relates to employer contributions to a pension plan for employees.

CICA Handbook, Section 3460, gives the rules for measuring pension expense. To record the company's payment into a pension plan, the company debits Pension Expense and credits Cash. Trustees such as trust companies and pension trusts manage pension plans. They receive the employer payments and any employee contributions, then invest these amounts for the future benefit of the employees. The goal is to have the funds available to meet any obligations to retirees, much as a bond sinking fund is designed to retire bonds payable at maturity.

While employees are perhaps those most interested in the status of their employer's pension plan, others such as creditors are also interested because pension plan assets and obligations can be large in proportion to a company's financial position. A company with a large underfunded pension liability could find itself in financial difficulties that would affect all creditors. For example, the financial statements of Maclean Hunter recently reported that while the company's total assets were $873 million, the assets in the company's pension plans were $180 million.

Section 3460 defines two types of pension plan: a **defined benefit plan**, where the benefits to be paid to the employee upon retirement are specified and the company must ensure that adequate funds will be available to make the specified payments, and a **defined contribution plan**, where the contribution is defined and the benefits depend on what is available when the employee retires. Each will be discussed in turn.

A defined benefit plan must have an actuarial evaluation at least every three years to ensure that there will be sufficient funds available to make the required payments to each member of the plan on his or her retirement. In conducting the valuation, the plan actuaries will determine the actuarial present value of the plan benefits, compare that to the plan assets and determine whether the plan has a surplus or deficit. Section 3460 requires that the actuarial present value of plan benefits, for employee services to the reporting date, and the value of pension plan assets be disclosed in the financial statements. A recent annual report issued by St. Lawrence Cement Inc. includes the following note to the financial statements:

8. PENSION PLANS

The Company's pension plans were valued as of January 1, 1987 by actuaries based on projection of employees' compensation levels to the time of retirement and the assets and obligations were projected to December 31, 1987. As a result, the contributions for the current year to the pension plans have exceeded the pension expense by $160,000. This amount has been included in other assets in the balance sheet.

As at December 31, 1987 the present value of accrued pension benefits and the net assets, at market value, available to provide for these benefits are as follows:

Accrued pension benefits, $52,263,000
Pension plan assets, $54,506,000

The accounting for defined benefits pension plans is complex and is demonstrated in subsequent accounting courses.

A defined contribution plan is an accumulation of the employer and employee contributions. The required disclosure is the present value of required future contributions by the company for employee services to the reporting date. For example, the disclosure for Elora Ltd. could be as follows:

NOTES TO THE FINANCIAL STATEMENTS

8. The company has a defined contribution pension plan which covers all the company's employees. The present value of required future contributions in respect of past service by employees of the company was $759,256 at the year end.

Section 3460 of the *CICA Handbook* required companies to report pension assets and liabilities for defined benefit plans and unfunded obligations for defined contribution plans, starting in 1987. Before that date, pensions were another example of off-balance-sheet financing. Companies received the benefit of their employees' service but could avoid reporting pension liabilities on the balance sheet.

Advantage of Financing Operations with Debt versus Stock

OBJECTIVE 6

Explain the advantages and disadvantages of borrowing

Businesses use different ways to acquire assets. Management may decide to purchase or to lease equipment.

The buy or lease decision is complex and is demonstrated in subsequent accounting courses. The money to finance the asset may come from the business's retained earnings, a note payable, a stock issue or a bond issue. Each financing strategy has its advantages and disadvantages. The principal advantage of financing an asset purchase out of retained earnings is that there is no interest charge to pay to an outside party; the disadvantage is that a company following this course uses up cash resources in acquiring the asset. If the company does not have surplus cash to use in this way, it will be forced to select one of the other options. Notes payable tend to be fairly short-term and to have a higher interest rate than bonds. Notes are more flexible than bonds, however, in that the business itself can issue them. As you have already learned in this chapter, a bond issue requires the services of an investment dealer and may be expensive. Another option is to issue stock.

Now let us examine how issuing stock compares to issuing bonds. Bonds differ from stocks in important ways. Stock shares give the holder part ownership of the corporation and a voice in management. Bonds merely give the holder a creditor's claim to the debtor's assets. Bond certificates carry dates for maturity and interest payments, unlike stock, which does not come due at any specific time. Companies are not obligated to declare dividends on stock.

Issuing stock raises capital without incurring the liabilities and interest expense that accompany bonds. However, by issuing stock the business spreads the ownership, control and income of the corporation among more shares. Management may wish to avoid this dilution of its ownership. Borrowing money through bonds raises liabilities and interest expense, which the corporation must pay whether or not it earns a profit. But borrowing does not affect shareholder control: bondholders are creditors with no voice in management. Borrowing also provides a tax advantage in that interest expense is tax deductible. Dividends paid to shareholders are not tax deductible because they are not an expense.

Exhibit 16-5 illustrates the earnings-per-share (EPS) advantage of borrowing. Suppose a corporation with 100,000 shares of common stock outstanding needs $500,000 for expansion. Management is considering two financing plans. Plan 1 is to issue $500,000 of 10 percent bonds payable, and Plan 2 is to issue 50,000

EXHIBIT 16-5 *Earnings-per-Share Advantage of Borrowing*

	Plan 1 Borrow $500,000 at 10%	Plan 2 Issue $500,000 of Common Stock
Income before interest and income tax.....	$200,000	$200,000
Less interest expense ($500,000 × .10)	50,000	-0-
Income before income tax	150,000	200,000
Less income tax expense (40%)	60,000	80,000
Net income............................	$ 90,000	$120,000
Earnings per share on new project		
Plan 1 ($90,000/100,000 shares)..........	$ .90	
Plan 2 ($120,000/150,000 shares).........		$ .80

shares of common stock for $500,000. Management believes the new cash can be invested in operations to earn income of $200,000 before interest and taxes.

The earnings-per-share amount is higher if the company borrows. The business earns more on the investment ($90,000) than the interest it pays on the bonds ($50,000). Earning more income than the borrowed amount increases the earnings for common shareholders and is called **trading on the equity**. It is widely used in business to increase earnings per share of common stock.

Dividend payments to the new shareholders under Plan 2 would also make borrowing more attractive than issuing stock. Assume that net income is entirely an increase in cash. If under Plan 2 the company were to pay dividends of $50,000 (the same as the interest expense under Plan 1) its net cash inflow would be $70,000 ($120,000 – $50,000), compared to $90,000 under Plan 1.

Borrowing, however, has its disadvantages. If the interest rate is high enough, the advantage of borrowing disappears as the interest expense reduces net income. In addition, borrowing creates liabilities that accrue during bad years as well as during good years. In contrast, a company that issues stock can omit its dividends during a bad year.

Investments in Bonds and Notes

For every issuer of bonds payable, at least one investor owns the bonds. The relationship between the issuer and the investor may be diagrammed as follows:

Issuing Corporation		**Investor (Bondholder)**
Bonds payable	⟷	Investment in bonds
Interest expense	⟷	Interest revenue

The dollar amount of a bond transaction is the same for issuer and investor, but the accounts debited and credited differ. However, the accounts are parallel. For example, the issuer's interest expense is the investor's interest revenue.

An investment in bonds is classified either as short-term (a current asset) or as long-term. An investment is a current asset if (1) the investment is liquid (can readily be sold for cash, such as a Government of Canada bond) and (2) the owner intends to convert it to cash within one year or to use it to pay

OBJECTIVE 7
Account for investments in bonds

a current liability. An investment that is intended to be held longer than a year is classified as long-term. **Long-term investments** is a separate asset category reported on the balance sheet between current assets and plant assets.

Bond investments are recorded at cost, which includes the purchase price and any brokerage fees. Amortization of bond premium or discount is *not* recorded on short-term investments because the investor plans to hold the bonds for so short a period that any amortization would be immaterial. On the other hand, investors hold long-term investments for a significant period and therefore amortize any premium or discount on the bonds.

Let us look at accounting for a *short-term* bond investment. Suppose that an investor purchases $10,000 of bonds on August 1, 19X2, paying 93 plus accrued interest and a brokerage commission of $250. The annual contract interest rate is 12 percent, paid semiannually on April 1 and October 1. The cost of the bonds is $9,550 [($10,000 × .93) + $250]. In addition, the investor pays accrued interest for the four months (April through July) since the last interest payment. The investor records the purchase on August 1 as follows:

Aug. 1	Short-Term Investment in Bonds		
	[($10,000 × .93) + $250]	9,550	
	Interest Receivable ($10,000 × .12 × 4/12)	400	
	Cash		9,950
	To purchase short-term bond investment.		

Accrued interest is *not* included in the cost of the investment but is debited to Interest Receivable.

The investor's entry for receipt of the first semiannual interest amount on October 1 is

Oct. 1	Cash ($10,000 × .12 × 6/12)	600	
	Interest Receivable		400
	Interest Revenue ($10,000 × .12 × 2/12)		200
	To receive semiannual interest, part of which was accrued.		

At October 1, the investor has held the bonds for two months. The entry correctly credits Interest Revenue for two months' interest. This entry does not include discount amortization on the bonds because the investment is short-term.

At December 31, the investor accrues interest revenue for three months (October, November and December), debiting Interest Receivable and crediting Interest Revenue for $300 ($10,000 × .12 × 3/12). The investor's December 31 balance sheet reports the following information (we assume that the market price of the bonds is 96):

Current assets
    Short-term investment in bonds (note 4) $9,550
    Interest receivable 300

Note 4: Short-term investments. At December 31, the current market value of short-term investments in bonds was $9,600.

Observe that the investment is reported at cost, with the current market value disclosed in a note. The market value may also be reported parenthetically.

Current assets
    Short-term investment in bonds (Current market value, $9,600) $9,550
    Interest receivable   300

The investor measures any gain or loss on sale as the difference between the sale price and the cost of the investment. For example, sale of the bonds for $9,700 will result in a gain of $150. This gain is reported as Other Revenue on a multiple-step income statement or beneath Sales Revenue among the revenues and gains on a single-step statement. A loss would be reported as Other Expense on a multiple-step statement or among the expenses on a single-step statement.

Accounting for *long-term* investments in bonds follows the general pattern illustrated for short-term investments. For long-term investments, however, discount or premium is amortized to account more precisely for interest revenue. This additional step is needed because the bond investment will be held for longer than a year and, therefore, the amortization amount is likely to be material. The amortization of discount or premium on a bond investment affects Interest Revenue in the same way that the amortization affects Interest Expense for the company that issued the bonds.

The accountant records amortization on the cash interest dates and at year end, along with the accrual of interest receivable. Accountants rarely use separate discount and premium accounts for investments. Amortization of a discount is recorded by directly debiting the Long-Term Investment in Bonds account and crediting Interest Revenue. Amortization of a premium is credited directly to the Long-Term Investment account. This entry debits Interest Revenue. These entries bring the investment balance to the bonds' face value on the maturity date and record the correct amount of interest revenue each period.

Suppose the $10,000 of 12 percent bonds in the preceding illustration were purchased on August 1, 19X2, as a long-term investment. Interest dates are April 1 and October 1. These bonds mature on October 1, 19X6, so they will be outstanding for 50 months. Assume amortization of the discount by the straight-line method. The following entries for a long-term investment highlight the differences between accounting for a short-term bond investment and for a long-term bond investment:

Aug. 1	**Long-Term** Investment in Bonds		
	[($10,000 × .93) + $250]	9,550	
	Interest Receivable ($10,000 × .12 × $\frac{4}{12}$)	400	
	Cash		9,950
	To purchase long-term bond investment.		
Oct. 1	Cash ($10,000 × .12 × $\frac{6}{12}$)	600	
	Interest Receivable		400
	Interest Revenue ($10,000 × .12 × $\frac{2}{12}$)		200
	To receive semiannual interest, part of which was accrued.		
Oct. 1	**Long-Term Investment in Bonds**		
	[($10,000 − $9,550)/50 × 2]	**18**	
	Interest Revenue		**18**
	To amortize discount on bond investment for two months.		

Dec. 31   Interest Receivable ($10,000 × .12 × ³⁄₁₂)   300
                    Interest Revenue   300
            To accrue interest revenue for three months.

Dec. 31   Long-term Investment Bonds [($10,000 − $9,550)/50 × 3]..   27
                    Interest Revenue **27**
            **To amortize discount on bond investment for three
            months.**

The financial statements at December 31, 19X2 report the following effects of this long-term investment in bonds (assume the bonds' market price is 102):

Balance sheet at December 31, 19X2
Current assets
    Interest receivable.. $ 300
    Total current assets......................................   X,XXX
Long-term investments in bonds ($9,550 + $18 + $27) — note 6   9,595
Property, plant and equipment ....   X,XXX

Note 6: Long-term investments. At December 31, 19X1, the current market value of long-term investments in bonds was $10,200.

Income statement (multiple-step) for the year ended December 31, 19X2
  Other revenues
    Interest revenue ($200 + $18 + $300 + $27) .... $ 545

The amortization entry for a premium debits Interest Revenue and credits Long-Term Investment in Bonds. Where discount or premium is amortized by the effective interest method, accounting for long-term investments follows the pattern illustrated here. Effective interest amortization amounts are computed as shown for bonds payable in Exhibits 16-3 and 16-4.

Summary Problem for Your Review

Say Quebecor Inc. has outstanding an issue of 8 percent convertible bonds that mature in 2008. Suppose the bonds were dated October 1, 1988, and pay interest each April 1 and October 1.

Required

1.   Complete the following effective amortization table through October 1, 1990.

Bond data:

Maturity value, $100,000
Contract interest rate, 8%
Interest paid, 4% semiannually, $4,000 ($100,000 × .04)
Market interest rate at time of issue, 9% annually, 4½% semiannually
Issue price, 90¾

Amortization table:

Semiannual Interest Date	A Interest Payment (4% of Maturity Value)	B Interest Expense (4½% of Preceding Bond Carrying Value)	C Discount Amortization (B − A)	D Discount Account Balance (D − C)	E Bond Carrying Value ($100,000 − D)
10-1-88					
4-1-89					
10-1-89					
4-1-90					
10-1-90					

2. Using the amortization table, record the following transactions:
   a. Issuance of the bonds on October 1, 1988.
   b. Accrual of interest and amortization of discount on December 31, 1988.
   c. Payment of interest and amortization of discount on April 1, 1989.
   d. Conversion of one third of the bonds payable into common stock on October 2, 1990.
   e. Retirement of two thirds of the bonds payable on October 2, 1990. Purchase price of the bonds was 102.

SOLUTION TO REVIEW PROBLEM

Requirement 1

Semiannual Interest Date	A Interest Payment (4% of Maturity Value)	B Interest Expense (4½% of Preceding Bond Carrying Value)	C Discount Amortization (B − A)	D Discount Account Balance (D − C)	E Bond Carrying Value ($100,000 − D)
10-1-88				$9,250	$90,750
4-1-89	$4,000	$4,084	$84	9,166	90,834
10-1-89	4,000	4,088	88	9,078	90,922
4-1-90	4,000	4,091	91	8,987	91,013
10-1-90	4,000	4,096	96	8,891	91,109

Requirement 2

       1988
a. Oct. 1   Cash ($100,000 × .9075)   90,750
            Discount on Bonds Payable   9,250
                  Bonds Payable   100,000
            To issue 8%, 20-year bonds at a discount.

b. Dec. 31 Interest Expense ($4,084 × ³⁄₆)   2,042
                  Discount on Bonds Payable ($84 × ³⁄₆)   42
                  Interest Payable ($4,000 × ³⁄₆)   2,000
            To accrue interest and amortize bond discount for three months.

1989

c. Apr. 1   Interest Expense   2,042

Interest Payable.............................   2,000

    Discount on Bonds Payable ($84 × ⅜)   42

    Cash   4,000

To pay semiannual interest, part of which was
accrued, and amortize three months' discount on
bonds payble.

1990

d. Oct. 2   Bonds Payable ($100,000 × ⅓)   33,333

    Discount on Bonds Payable ($8,891 × ⅓)   2,964

    Common Stock ($91,109 × ⅓)   30,369

To record conversion of bonds payable.

e. Oct. 2   Bonds Payable ($100,000 × ⅔)   66,667

Loss on Retirement of Bonds   7,260

    Discount on Bonds Payable ($8,891 × ⅔)   5,927

    Cash ($100,000 × ⅔ × 1.02)   68,000

To retire bonds payable before maturity.

Summary

A corporation may borrow money by issuing bonds and long-term notes payable. A bond contract, called an *indenture*, specifies the maturity value of the bonds, the contact interest rate, and the dates for paying interest and principal. The owner of *registered* bonds receives an interest cheque from the company. The owner of *coupon* bonds deposits an interest coupon in the bank. Bonds may be secured (*mortgage* bonds) or unsecured (*debenture* bonds).

Bonds are traded through organized markets, like the Over-the-Counter market. Bonds are typically divided into $1,000 units. Their prices are quoted at a percentage of face value.

Market interest rates fluctuate and may differ from the contract rate on a bond. If a bond's contract rate exceeds the market rate, the bond sells at a *premium*. A bond with a contract rate below the market rate sells at a *discount*.

Money earns income over time, a fact that gives rise to the present value concept. An investor will pay a price for a bond equal to the present value of the bond principal plus the present value of the bond interest.

Straight-line amortization allocates an equal amount of premium or discount to each interest period. In the *effective interest method* of amortization, the market rate at the time of issuance is multiplied by the bonds' carrying value to determine the interest expense each period and to compute the amount of discount or premium amortization.

A *bond sinking fund* accumulates the money to pay the bonds' face value at maturity. Companies may retire their bonds payable before maturity through *callable* bonds which give the borrower the right to pay off the bonds at a specified call price, or by purchasing the bonds in the open market. Any gain or loss on an early extinguishment of debt is classified as an *unusual* item.

Convertible bonds and notes give the investor the privilege of trading the bonds for stock of the issuing corporation. The carrying value of the bonds becomes the book value of the newly issued stock.

A lease is a rental agreement between the *lessee* and the *lessor*. In an *operating lease* the lessor retains the usual risks and rights of owning the asset. The lessee debits Rent Expense and credits Cash when making lease payments. A *capital lease* is long-term, noncancelable, and similar to an installment purchase of the leased asset. In a capital lease, the lessee capitalizes the leased asset and reports a lease liability. Companies report *accrued pension benefits* and *pension assets* in the financial statements in the case of *defined benefit pension plans*.

Bonds and notes are assets to the investor. These assets are short-term or long-term depending on how long the investor plans to hold them and whether they can be readily sold for cash.

Self-Study Questions

Test your understanding of the chapter by marking the best answer for each of the following questions.

1. An unsecured bond is called a *(p. 655)*
   a. Serial bond
   b. Registered bond
   c. Debenture bond
   d. Mortgage bond

2. How much will an investor pay for a $100,000 bond priced at 101⅞, plus a brokerage commission of $1,100? *(p. 655)*
   a. $100,000
   b. $101,000
   c. $101,875
   d. $102,975

3. A bond with a stated interest rate of 9½ percent is issued when the market interest rate is 9¾ percent. This bond will sell at *(p. 657)*
   a. Par value
   b. A discount
   c. A premium
   d. A price minus accrued interest

4. Ten-year, 11 percent bonds payable of $500,000 were issued for $532,000. Assume the straight-line amortization method is appropriate. The total annual interest expense on these bonds is *(pp. 660, 661, 663)*
   a. $51,800
   b. $55,000
   c. $58,200
   d. A different amount each year because the bonds' book value decreases as the premium is amortized

5. Use the facts in the preceding question but assume the effective interest method of amortization is used. Total annual interest expense on the bonds is *(pp. 667, 668)*
   a. $51,800
   b. $55,000
   c. $58,200
   d. A decreasing amount each year because the bonds' book value decreases as the premium is amortized

6. Bonds payable with face value of $300,000 and carrying value of $288,000 are retired before their scheduled maturity with a cash outlay of $292,000. Which of the following entries correctly records this bond retirement? *(pp. 669, 670)*

a.
Bonds Payable	300,000	
Discount on Bonds Payable	12,000	
Cash		292,000
Gain on Retirement of Bonds Payable		20,000

b.
Bonds Payable	300,000	
Loss on Retirement of Bonds Payable	4,000	
Discount on Bonds Payable		12,000
Cash		292,000

c.
Bonds Payable	300,000	
Discount on Bonds Payable		6,000
Cash		292,000
Gain on Retirement of Bonds Payable		2,000

d. Bonds Payable	288,000	
Discount on Bonds Payable	12,000	
Gain on Retirement of Bonds Payable		8,000
Cash......................................		292,000

7. In a capital lease, the lessee records *(pp. 671–674)*
   a. A leased asset and a lease liability   c. Interest on the lease liability
   b. Depreciation on the leased asset   d. All of the above

8. Which of the following is an example of off-balance-sheet financing? *(p. 674)*
   a. Operating lease   c. Debenture bonds
   b. Current portion of long-term debt   d. Convertible bonds

9. An advantage of financing operations with debt versus stock is *(pp. 676, 677)*
   a. The tax deductibility of interest expense on debt
   b. The legal requirement to pay interest and principal
   c. Lower interest payments compared to dividend payments
   d. All of the above

10. The main difference between accounting for long-term investments in bonds and accounting for short-term investments in bonds in *(p. 679)*
    a. Lower cost of short-term investments
    b. Higher cost of short-term investments
    c. No amortization of premium or discount on short-term investments in bonds
    d. No amortization of premium or discount on long-term investments in bonds

Answers to the self-study questions are at the end of the chapter.

Accounting Vocabulary

bond discount *(p. 656)*	defined benefit pension plan	off-balance-sheet financing
bond indenture *(p. 655)*	*(p. 675)*	*(p. 674)*
bond premium *(p. 656)*	defined contribution pension	operating lease *(p. 672)*
bond sinking fund *(p. 668)*	plan *(p. 675)*	pension *(p. 674)*
bonds payable *(p. 653)*	effective interest rate *(p. 657)*	present value *(p. 656)*
callable bonds *(p. 669)*	lease *(p. 672)*	registered bonds *(p. 654)*
capital lease *(p. 672)*	lessee *(p. 672)*	serial bonds *(p. 654)*
contract interest rate *(p. 657)*	lessor *(p. 672)*	stated interest rate *(p. 657)*
convertible bonds *(p. 670)*	long-term investment *(p. 678)*	term bonds *(p. 654)*
coupon bonds *(p. 654)*	market interest rate *(p. 657)*	trading on the equity *(p. 677)*
debentures *(p. 655)*	mortgage *(p. 671)*	underwriter *(p. 654)*

Assignment Material _____

Questions

1. Identify three ways to finance the operations of a corporation.
2. How do bonds payable differ from a note payable?
3. How does an underwriter assist with the issuance of bonds?
4. Why would an investor require the borrower to set up a sinking fund?
5. Compute the price to the nearest dollar for the following bonds with a face value of $10,000:
   a. 93   b. 88¾   c. 101⅜   d. 122½   e. 100
6. In which of the following situations will bonds sell at par, at a premium and at a discount?
   a. 9% bonds sold when the market rate is 9%.
   b. 9% bonds sold when the market rate is 10%.
   c. 9% bonds sold when the market rate is 8%.

7. Identify the accounts to debit and credit for transactions (a) to issue bonds at *par*, (b) to pay interest, (c) to accrue interest at year end, and (d) to pay off bonds at maturity.

8. Identify the account to debit and credit for transactions (a) to issue bonds at a *discount*, (b) to pay interest, (c) to accrue interest at year end, and (d) to pay off bonds at maturity.

9. Identify the accounts to debit and credit for transactions (a) to issue bonds at a *premium*, (b) to pay interest, (c) to accrue interest at year end, and (d) to pay off bonds at maturity.

10. Why are bonds sold for a price "plus accrued interest"? What happens to accrued interest when bonds are sold by an individual?

11. How does the straight-line method of amortizing bond discount (or premium) differ from the effective interest method?

12. A company retires ten-year bonds payable of $100,000 after five years. The business issued the bonds at 104 and called them at 103. Compute the amount of gain or loss on retirement. How is this gain or loss reported on the income statement?

13. Bonds payable with a maturity value of $100,000 are callable at 102½. Their market price is 101¼. If you are the issuer of these bonds, how much will you pay to retire them before maturity?

14. Why are convertible bonds attractive to investors? Why are they popular with borrowers?

15. Describe how to report serial bonds payable on the balance sheet.

16. Identify the accounts a lessee debits and credits when making operating lease payments.

17. What characteristics distinguish a capital lease from an operating lease?

18. A business signs a capital lease for the use of a building. What accounts are debited and credited (a) to begin the lease term and make the first lease payment, (b) to record depreciation, (c) to accrue interest on the lease liability, and (d) to make the second lease payment?

19. Show how a lessee reports on the balance sheet any leased equipment and the related lease liability under a capital lease.

20. What is off-balance-sheet financing? Give two examples.

21. Distinguish a defined benefit plan from a defined contribution pension plan. What must be reported for each in the financial statements?

22. Contrast the effects on a company of issuing bonds versus issuing stock.

23. What is the same in accounting for bonds payable and accounting for a long-term investment in bonds? What is different?

24. What distinguishes a short-term investment (current asset) from a long-term investment? Describe premium and discount amortization for a short-term bond investment.

Exercises

Exercise 16-1   *Issuing bonds payable and paying interest*

Electronix, Inc. issues $500,000 of 10 percent, 20-year bonds payable that are dated April 30. Record (a) issuance of bonds at par on May 31 and (b) the next semiannual interest payment on October 31.

Exercise 16-2   *Issuing bonds payable, paying and accruing interest, and amortizing discount by the straight-line method*

On February 1, MiniCalc Ltd. issues 20-year, 10 percent bonds payable with a face value of $1,000,000. The bonds sell at 96½ and pay interest on January 31 and July 31. MiniCalc amortizes bond discount by the straight-line method. Record (a) issuance of the bonds on February 1, (b) the semiannual interest payment on July 31, and (c) the interest accrual on December 31.

Exercise 16-3 *Issuing bonds payable, paying and accruing interest, and amortizing premium by the straight-line method*

XIT Transportation Inc. issues 30-year, 8 percent bonds payable with a face value of $5,000,000 on March 31. The bonds sell at 103 and pay interest on March 31 and September 30. Assume XIT amortizes bond premium by the straight-line method. Record (a) issuance of the bonds on March 31, (b) payment of interest on September 30, and (c) accrual of interest on December 31.

Exercise 16-4 *Preparing an effective interest amortization table; recording interest payments and the related discount amortization*

Optic Devices Incorporated is authorized to issue $1,000,000 of 11 percent, 10-year bonds payable. On January 2, when the market interest rate is 12 percent, the company issues $500,000 of the bonds and receives cash of $471,325. Optic Devices amortizes bond discount by the effective interest method.

Required

1. Prepare an amortization table for the first four semiannual interest periods. Follow the format of Panel B in Exhibit 16-3.
2. Record the first semiannual interest payment on June 30 and the second payment on December 31.

Exercise 16-5 *Preparing an effective interest amortization table; recording interest accrual and payment and the related premium amortization*

On August 31, 1990, the market interest rate is 11 percent. Lancer Limited issues $300,000 of 12 percent, 20-year sinking-fund bonds payable at 108. The bonds pay interest on February 28 and August 31. Lancer amortizes bond premium by the effective interest method.

Required

1. Prepare an amortization table for the first four semiannual interest periods. Follow the format of Panel B in Exhibit 16-4.
2. Record issuance of the bonds on August 31, 1990, the accrual of interest at December 31, 1990 and the semiannual interest payment on February 28, 1991.

Exercise 16-6 *Journalizing sinking fund transactions*

Lancer established a sinking fund for the bond issue in Exercise 16-5. Record payment of $6,000 into the sinking fund on February 28, 1991. Also record sinking-fund revenue of $900 on December 31, 1991, and the payment of the bonds at maturity on August 31, 2010. At maturity date the sinking-fund balance was $291,500.

Exercise 16-7 *Recording early retirement and conversion of bonds payable*

High Value Hardware Corp. reported the following at September 30:

Long-term liabilities
Convertible bonds payable, 9%, 8 years to maturity $200,000
Discount on bonds payable 6,000 $194,000

Required

1. Record retirement of one fourth of the bonds on October 1 at the call price of 101.
2. Record conversion of one half of the bonds into 8,000 shares of High Value's common stock on October 1.

Exercise 16-8   *Reporting long-term debt and pension liability on the balance sheet*

a. A note to the financial statements of Mapco, Inc. reports:

> Note 5: Long-Term Debt
> Total $537,888
> Less: Current portion.......................... 22,085
> Unamortized discount .... <u>1,391</u>
> Long-term debt $514,412

Assume that none of the unamortized discount relates to the current portion of long-term debt. Show how Mapco's balance sheet would report these liabilities.

b. El Campo Incorporated's defined benefit pension plan has assets with a market value of $720,000. The plan's accumulated benefit obligation is $840,000. What will El Campo report on its balance sheet?

Exercise 16-9   *Journalizing capital lease and operating lease transactions*

A capital lease agreement for equipment requires 10 annual payments of $8,000, with the first payment due on January 2, 19X5. The present value of the 9 future lease payments at 10 percent is $46,072.

a. Journalize the following lessee transactions:

19X5

Jan.   2   Beginning of lease term and first annual payment.

Dec. 31   Depreciation of equipment.

     31   Interest expense on lease liability.

19X6

Jan.   2   Second annual lease payment.

b. Journalize the January 2, 19X5 lease payment if this is an operating lease.

Exercise 16-10   *Analysing alternative plans for raising money*

MJ-R Corporation is considering two plans for raising $1,000,000 to expand operations. Plan A is to borrow at 9 percent, and Plan B is to issue 200,000 shares of common stock. Before any new financing, MJ-R has 300,000 shares of common stock outstanding. Management believes the company can use the new funds to earn income of $420,000 before interest and taxes. The income tax rate is 40 percent.

Required

Prepare an analysis like Exhibit 16-5 to determine which plan will result in higher earnings per share.

Exercise 16-11   *Recording short-term bond investment transactions*

On June 30, Cartwright Corporation paid 92¼ for 8 percent bonds of Klein, Inc. as a short-term investment. The maturity value of the bonds is $50,000, and they pay interest on March 31 and September 30. Record Cartwright's purchase of the bond investment, the receipt of semiannual interest on September 30, and the accrual of interest revenue on December 31.

Exercise 16-12   *Recording long-term bond investment transactions*

Assume the Cartwright Corporation bonds in the preceding exercise are purchased as a long-term investment on June 30, 19X3. The bonds mature on September 30, 19X7.

Required

1. Using the straight-line method of amortizing the discount, journalize all transactions on the bonds for 19X3.
2. How much more interest revenue would the investor record in 19X3 for a long-term investment than for a short-term investment in these bonds? What accounts for this difference?

Problems   *(Group A)*

Problem 16-1A   *Journalizing bond transactions (at par) and reporting bonds payable on the balance sheet*

The board of directors of Duck Lake Ltd. authorizes the issue of $3 million of 9 percent, 10-year bonds payable. The semiannual interest dates are May 31 and November 30. The bonds are issued through an underwriter on July 31, 19X5, at par plus accrued interest.

Required

1. Journalize the following transactions:
   a. Issuance of the bonds on July 31, 19X5.
   b. Payment of interest on November 30, 19X5.
   c. Accrual of interest on December 31, 19X5.
   d. Payment of interest on May 31, 19X6.
2. Check your recorded interest expense for 19X5, using as a model the supplement to the summary problem on p. 663.
3. Report interest payable and bonds payable as they would appear on the Duck Lake Ltd. balance sheet at December 31, 19X5.

Problem 16-2A   *Issuing bonds at a discount, amortizing by the straight-line method and reporting bonds payable on the balance sheet*

On March 1, 19X4, Daigle, Inc. issues 10½ percent, 20-year bonds payable with a face value of $500,000. The bonds pay interest on February 28 and August 31. Daigle amortizes premium and discount by the straight-line method.

Required

1. If the market interest rate is 9 percent when Daigle issues its bonds, will the bonds be priced at par, at a premium or at a discount? Explain.
2. If the market interest rate is 11¼ percent when Daigle issues its bonds, will the bonds be priced at par, at a premium, or at a discount? Explain.
3. Assume the issue price of the bonds is 92. Journalize the following bond transactions:
   a. Issuance of the bonds on March 1, 19X4.
   b. Payment of interest and amortization of discount on August 31, 19X4.
   c. Accrual of interest and amortization of discount on December 31, 19X4.
   d. Payment of interest and amortization of discount on February 28, 19X5.
4. Check your recorded interest expense for the year ended February 28, 19X5, using as a model the supplement to the summary problem on p. 663.
5. Report interest payable and bonds payable as they would appear on the Daigle balance sheet at December 31, 19X4.

Problem 16-3A   *Issuing convertible bonds at a premium, amortizing by the effective interest method, retiring bonds early, converting bonds and reporting the bonds payable on the balance sheet*

On December 31, 19X1, Gander Distributing Corp. issues 12 percent, 10-year convertible bonds with a maturity value of $500,000. The semiannual interest dates are June 30 and

December 31. The market interest rate is 11 percent, and the issue price of the bonds is 106. Gander amortizes bond premium and discount by the effective interest method.

Required

1. Prepare an effective interest method amortization table like Exhibit 16-4 for the first four semiannual interest periods.
2. Journalize the following transactions:
   a. Issuance of the bonds on December 31, 19X1. Credit Convertible Bonds Payable.
   b. Payment of interest on June 30, 19X2.
   c. Payment of interest on December 31, 19X2.
   d. Retirement of bonds with face value of $100,000 on July 1, 19X3. Gander pays the call price of 102.
   e. Conversion by the bondholders on July 1, 19X3, of bonds with face value of $300,000 into 10,000 shares of Gander's common stock.
3. Prepare the balance sheet presentation of the bonds payable that are outstanding at December 31, 19X3.

Problem 16-4A *Analysing a company's long-term debt, journalizing its transactions, and reporting the long-term debt on the balance sheet*

The notes to Baker Incorporated's financial statements recently reported the following data on September 30, Year 1 (the end of the fiscal year):

NOTE 4: INDEBTEDNESS

Long-term debt at September 30, Year 1 included the following:

6.00% debentures due Year 20 with an effective interest rate of 14.66%, net of unamortized discount of $123,152	$101,848
Other indebtedness with an interest rate of 10.30%, due $12,108 in Year 6 and $19,257 in Year 7	31,365

Assume Baker amortizes discount by the effective interest method.

Required

1. Answer the following questions about Baker's long-term liabilities:
   a. What is the maturity value of the 6.00% debenture bonds?
   b. What are Baker's annual cash interest payments on the 6.00% debenture bonds?
   c. What is the carrying value of the 6.00% debenture bonds at September 30, Year 1?
2. Prepare an amortization table through September 30, Year 5 for the 6.00% debenture bonds. Assume Baker pays interest annually on September 30. Use the following format for the amortization table:

End of Annual Interest Period	A Interest Payment (6% of Maturity Value)	B Interest Expense (14.66% of Preceding Bond Carrying Value)	C Discount Amortization (B − A)	D Discount Balance (D − C)	E Bond Carrying Value ($225,000 − D)
Sept. 30, Yr. 1					
Sept. 30, Yr. 2					
Sept. 30, Yr. 3					
Sept. 30, Yr. 4					
Sept. 30, Yr. 5					

3. Record the September 30, Year 2 and Year 3 interest payments on the 6.00% debenture bonds.

4. There is no problem or discount on the other indebtedness. Assuming annual interest is paid on September 30 each year, record Baker's September 30, Year 2 interest payment on the other indebtedness.

5. Show how Baker would report the debenture bonds payable and other indebtedness of September 30, Year 5.

Problem 16-5A   *Journalizing bonds payable, bond investment and capital lease transactions*

Journalize the following transactions of Gundersen Corporation:

19X1

Jan. 1   Issued $1,000,000 of 8 percent, 10-year bonds payable at 93.

1   Signed a 5-year capital lease on equipment. The agreement requires annual lease payments of $20,000, with the first payment due immediately. At 12 percent, the present value of the four future lease payments is $60,750.

Mar. 31   Purchased a short-term investment in the 9 percent bonds of another company, paying 95½ plus interest accrued since January 31. Maturity value of the bonds is $50,000.

July 1   Paid semiannual interest and amortized discount by the straight-line method on our 8 percent bonds payable.

1   Made the $50,000 sinking-fund payment required by the indenture on our 8 percent bonds payable.

July 31   Received semiannual interest on the bond investment purchased March 31.

Dec. 31   Accrued semiannual interest expense, and amortized discount by the straight-line method on our 8 percent bonds payable.

31   Recorded depreciation on leased equipment.

31   Accrued interest expense on the lease liability.

31   Accrued interest revenue on the bond investment.

31   Recorded bond sinking-fund earnings of $2,000.

19X11

Jan. 1   Paid the 8 percent bonds at maturity from the sinking fund and received excess cash of $22,400.

Problem 16-6A   *Reporting bond investments and liabilities on the balance sheet*

The accounting records of Musberger, Inc. include the following items:

Bond sinking fund	$130,000	Mortgage note payable,	
Accumulated pension benefit		long-term	$ 67,000
obligation	260,000	Building acquired under	
Bonds payable, long-term	300,000	capital lease	190,000
Short-term investment		Interest expense	47,000
in bonds	49,000	Pension plan assets	
Premium on bonds payable . .	22,000	(market value)	205,000
Interest payable	9,200	Bonds payable,	
Interest revenue	5,300	current portion	60,000
Capital lease liability,		Accumulated depreciation,	
long-term	111,000	building	108,000
Interest receivable	1,100		

Required

Show how these items would be reported on the Musberger balance sheet, including headings for current assets, current liabilities, and so on. The company has a defined benefit pension plan. Note disclosures are not required. Not all the items are reported on the balance sheet.

Problem 16-7A   *Accounting for a long-term bond investment purchased at a discount*

Financial institutions such as insurance companies and pension plans hold large quantities of bond investments. Suppose The Manufacturers Life Insurance Co. purchases $500,000 of 9 percent bonds of Henry Birks & Sons Ltd. for 97 on March 31, 19X0. These bonds pay interest on January 31 and July 31 each year. They mature on July 31, 19X8.

Required

1. Journalize Manufacturers' purchase of the bonds as long-term investment on March 31, 19X0 receipt of cash interest and amortization of discount on July 31, 19X0, and accrual of interest revenue and amortization of discount at December 31, 19X0. The straight-line method is used for amortizing discount.
2. Show all financial statement effects of this long-term bond investment at December 31, 19X0. Assume a multiple-step income statement.
3. Repeat question 2 under the assumption that Manufacturers purchased these bonds as a short-term investment.

(Group B)

Problem 16-1B   *Journalizing bond transactions (at par) and reporting bonds payable on the balance sheet*

The board of directors of Alberta Stampede Ltd. authorizes the issue of $2 million of 8 percent, 20-year bonds payable. The semiannual dates are February 28 and August 31. The bonds are issued through an underwriter on June 30, 19X7 at par plus accrued interest.

Required

1. Journalize the following transactions:
    a. Issuance of the bonds on June 30, 19X7.
    b. Payment of interest on August 31, 19X7.
    c. Accrual of interest on December 31, 19X7.
    d. Payment of interest on February 28, 19X8.
2. Check your recorded interest expense for 19X7, using as a model the supplement to the summary problem on p. 663.
3. Report interest payable and bonds payable as they would appear on the Alberta Stampede Ltd. balance sheet at December 31, 19X7.

Problem 16-2B   *Issuing notes at a premium, amortizing by the straight-line method and reporting notes payable on the balance sheet*

On March 1, 19X6, Crown Centre Corporation issues $9\frac{1}{4}$ percent, 10-year notes payable with a face value of $300,000. The notes pay interest on February 28 and August 31, and Crown Centre amortizes premium and discount by the straight-line method.

Required

1. If the market interest rate is 10 percent when Crown Centre issues its notes, will the notes be priced at par, at a premium or at a discount? Explain.
2. If the market interest rate is 8½ percent when Crown Centre issues its notes, will the notes be priced at par, at a premium, or at a discount? Explain.
3. Assume the issue price of the notes is 106. Journalize the following note payable transactions:
   a. Issuance of the notes on March 1, 19X6.
   b. Payment of interest and amortization of premium on August 31, 19X6.
   c. Accrual of interest and amortization of premium on December 31, 19X6.
   d. Payment of interest and amortization of premium on February 28, 19X7.
4. Check your recorded interest expense for the year ended February 28, 19X7, using as a model the supplement to the summary problem on p. 663.
5. Report interest payable and notes payable as they would appear on the Crown Centre balance sheet at December 31, 19X6.

Problem 16-3B   *Issuing convertible bonds at a discount, amortizing by the effective interest method, retiring bonds early, converting bonds and reporting the bonds payable on the balance sheet*

On December 31, 19X1, Youth Development Institute Inc. issues 11 percent, 10-year convertible bonds with a maturity value of $400,000. The semiannual interest dates are June 30 and December 31. The market interest rate is 13 percent, and the issue of the bonds is 89. The Institute amortizes bond premium and discount by the effective interest method.

Required

1. Prepare an effective interest method amortization table like Exhibit 16-3 for the first four semiannual interest periods.
2. Journalize the following transactions:
   a. Issuance of the bonds on December 31, 19X1. Credit Convertible Bonds Payable.
   b. Payment of interest on June 30, 19X2.
   c. Payment of interest on December 31, 19X2.
   d. Retirement of bonds with face value of $100,000 on July 1, 19X3. The Institute purchases the bonds at 94 in the open market.
   e. Conversion by the bondholders on July 1, 19X3 of bonds with face value of $250,000 into 50,000 shares of Youth Development common stock.
3. Prepare the balance sheet presentation of the bonds payable that are outstanding at December 31, 19X3.

Problem 16-4B   *Analysing a company's long-term debt, journalizing its transactions and reporting the long-term debt on the balance sheet*

The notes to Park Lane Towers Ltd.'s financial statements reported the following data on July 31, Year 1 (the end of the fiscal year):

NOTE E: LONG-TERM DEBT

7% debentures due Year 20, net of unamortized discount of $71,645 (effective interest rate of 11%)	$159,855
Notes payable, interest of 8.67%, due in annual amounts of $22,840 in Years 6 through 17	274,080

Assume Park Lane amortizes discount by the effective interest method.

Required

1. Answer the following questions about Park Lane's long-term liabilities:
   a. What is the maturity value of the 7% debenture bonds?
   b. What are Park Lane's annual cash interest payments on the 7% debenture bonds?
   c. What is the carrying value of the 7% debenture bonds at July 31, Year 1?

2. Prepare an amortization table through July 31, Year 5 for the 7% debenture bonds. Assume Park Lane pays interest annually on July 31. Use the following format for the amortization table:

End of Annual Interest Period	A Interest Payment (7% of Maturity Value)	B Interest Expense (11% of Preceding Bond Carrying Value)	C Discount Amortization (B – A)	D Discount Balance (D – C)	E Bond Carrying Value ($231,500 – D)
July 31, Yr. 1					
July 31, Yr. 2					
July 31, Yr. 3					
July 31, Yr. 4					
July 31, Yr. 5					

3. Record the July 31, Year 2 and Year 3 interest payments on the 7% debenture bonds.

4. There is no premium or discount on the notes payable. Assuming annual interest is paid on July 31 each year, record Park Lane's July 31, Year 2 interest payment on the notes payable. Round interest to the nearest dollar.

5. Show how Park Lane would report the debenture bonds payable and notes payable at July 31, Year 5.

Problem 16-5B *Journalizing bonds payable, bond investment and capital lease transactions*

Journalize the following transactions of Oriental Rug Corporation:

19X1

Jan. 1 Issued $2,000,000 of 9 percent, 10-year bonds payable at 97.

   1 Signed a 10-year capital lease on machinery. The agreement requires annual lease payments of $16,000, with the first payment due immediately. At 12 percent, the present value of the nine future lease payments is $85,250.

Mar. 31 Purchased a short-term investment in the 7 percent bonds of another company, paying 88¼ plus interest accrued since January 31. Maturity value of the bonds is $60,000.

July 1 Paid semiannual interest and amortized discount by the straight-line method on our 9 percent bonds payable.

   1 Made the $100,000 sinking-fund payment required by the indenture on our 9 percent bonds payable.

July 31 Received semiannual interest on the bond investment purchased March 31.

Dec. 31 Accrued semiannual interest expense and amortized discount by the straight-line method on our 9 percent bonds payable.

   31 Recorded depreciation on leased equipment.

   31 Accrued interest expense on the lease liability.

   31 Accrued interest revenue on the bond investment.

   31 Recorded bond sinking-fund earnings of $5,500.

19X11

Jan. 1   Paid the 9 percent bonds at maturity from the sinking fund ($1,981,000) and the remainder from the company cash.

Problem 16-6B   *Reporting bond investments and liabilities on the balance sheet*

The Silverstein Corporation accounting records include the following items:

Pension plan assets (market value)............	$ 93,000	Mortgage note payable, long-term...............	$ 82,000
Interest payable	13,000	Accumulated depreciation, equipment...............	97,000
Interest expense	57,000	Bond sinking fund..........	119,000
Bonds payable, current portion.................	75,000	Capital lease liability, current.................	18,000
Capital lease liability, long-term...............	81,000	Mortgage note payable, current.................	19,000
Discount on bonds payable.................	7,000	Accumulated pension benefit obligation...............	89,000
Interest receivable..........	2,000	Bonds payable, long-term....	400,000
Interest revenue............	5,000	Equipment acquired under capital lease..............	208,000
Short-term investment in bonds................	38,000		

Required

Show how these items would be reported on the Silverstein balance sheet, including headings for current assets, current liabilities, and so on. The company has a defined benefit pension plan. Note disclosures are not required. Not all the items are reported on the balance sheet.

Problem 16-7B   *Accounting for a long-term bond investment purchased at a premium*

Financial institutions such as insurance companies and pension plans hold large quantities of bond investments. Suppose Variable Life Insurance Company (VALIC) purchases $600,000 of 8 percent bonds of Acadia Corporation for 102 on July 1, 19X1. These bonds pay interest on March 1 and September 1 each year. They mature on March 1, 19X8.

Required

1. Journalize VALIC's purchase of the bonds as a long-term investment on July 1, 19X1, receipt of cash interest and amortization of premium on September 1, 19X1, and accrual of interest revenue and amortization of premium at December 31, 19X1. The straight-line method is used for amortizing premium.
2. Show all financial statement effects of this long-term bond investment at December 31, 19X1. Assume a multiple-step income statement.
3. Repeat question 2 under the assumption that VALIC purchased these bonds as a short-term investment.

Decision Problems

1. Analysing alternative ways of raising $5 million

Business is going well for BPI Systems, Inc. The board of directors of this family-owned company believes that BPI could earn an additional $1,500,000 in income before interest and taxes by expanding into new markets. However, the $5,000,000 that the business needs for growth cannot be raised within the family. The directors, who strongly wish to retain family control of BPI, must consider issuing securities to outsiders. They are considering three financing plans.

Plan A is to borrow at 9 percent. Plan B is to issue 200,000 shares of common stock. Plan C is to issue 100,000 shares of nonvoting, $3.75 preferred stock. BPI presently has 500,000 shares of common stock outstanding. The income tax rate is 40 percent.

Required

1. Prepare an analysis similar to Exhibit 16-5 to determine which plan will result in the highest earnings per share of common stock.
2. Recommend one plan to the board of directors. Give your reasons.

2. Questions about long-term debt

The following questions are not related.

a. The text suggests a principal reason why a company might issue convertible bonds. What reason(s) are given by John Labatt in its financial statements in note 11 of Appendix E for issuing convertible bonds? Do both sources agree or disagree?

b. Why do you think corporations like off-balance sheet financing? How do you think a shareholder would view off-balance sheet financing?

c. Companies like to borrow for longer terms when interest rates are low and for shorter terms when interest rates are high? Why is this statement true?

d. If you were to win $2,000,000 from Lotto 6-49, you would receive the $2,000,000, whereas if you win $2,000,000 in one of the big U.S. lotteries, you would receive 20 annual payments of $100,000. Are the prizes equivalent? If not, why not?

Financial Statement Problem

Long-term debt

John Labatt's balance sheet and related notes 10 and 11, all given in Appendix E, provide details about the company's long-term debt. Use those data to answer the following questions:

1. Examine note 10. How much long-term debt, excluding convertible debentures, did John Labatt pay off during fiscal 1989? How much new long-term debt, excluding convertible debentures, did the company create during fiscal 1989? Hint: Use a T-Account for Long-Term Debt, as follows (amounts in millions):

Long-Term Debt
(including Portion Due Within One Year)

Fiscal 1989 Payments	?	April 30, 1988	Bal. 492.2
		Fiscal 1989 New Debt	?
		April 30, 1989	Bal. 547.8

Journalize the entry for payment and the entry for the issuance of new debt.

2. How much of the April 30, 1989 balance in the T-account did John Labatt expect to pay during fiscal 1990? Journalize the payment during fiscal 1990.
3. Note 10 indicates that John Labatt borrows beyond Canada's borders. Where else does John Labatt borrow?
4. What long-term debt is secured? How much is outstanding at April 30, 1989?
5. John Labatt has convertible debentures outstanding at April 30, 1989. What is the total amount outstanding at April 30, 1989? Where do they appear on the balance sheet? Why does John Labatt say they are classified the way they are?

Appendix: Present Value

After studying this appendix, you should be able to

1. Compute the market value of a note or a bond.
2. Determine the cost of an asset acquired through a capital lease.

Present value (PV) has many applications in accounting. Take the example of a company that issues 10 percent bonds payable when the market interest rate is 11 percent. The company needs to know how much cash it will receive from issuing the bonds. The investors must determine how much to pay for the bonds. Both parties must compute the present value of the bonds. Another example is the acquisition of an asset through a capital lease. The lessee in this case (tenant) must know the cost of the asset. The concept of time value of money requires us to evaluate bonds, leases, and investments in terms of present value.

Suppose an investment promises to pay you $5,000 at the *end* of one year. How much would you pay *now* to acquire this investment? You would be willing to pay the present value of the $5,000, which is a future amount.

Present value depends on three factors: (1) the amount of payment (or receipt), (2) the length of time between investment and future receipt (or payment), and (3) the interest rate. The process of computing a present value is called **discounting** because the present value is *less* than the future value.

In our investment example, the future receipt is $5,000. The investment period is one year. Assume that you demand an annual interest rate of 10 percent on your investment. With all three factors specified, you can compute the present value of $5,000 at 10 percent for one year. The computation is

$$\frac{\text{Future value}}{(1 + \text{Interest rate})} = \frac{\$5,000}{1.10} = \$4,545$$

(Throughout this discussion we round off to the nearest dollar.) By turning the problem around, we verify the present value computation:

Amount invested (present value)	$4,545
Expected earnings ($4,545 × .10)	455
Amount to be received one year from now (future value)	$5,000

The $455 income amount is interest revenue, also called the return on the investment.

If the $5,000 is to be received two years from now, you would pay only $4,132 for the investment, computed as follows:

Present value			Future amount
0	**1**		**2**
?			$5,000
$4,132	$4,545		$5,000

$$\frac{\$4,545}{1.10} = \$4,132 \qquad\qquad \frac{\$5,000}{1.10} = \$4,545$$

By turning the problem around, we verify that $4,132 accumulates to $5,000 at 10 percent for two years.

Amount invested (present value)	$4,132
Expected earnings for first year ($4,132 × .10)	413
Amount invested after one year	4,545
Expected earnings for second year ($4,545 × .10)	455
Amount to be received two years from now (future value)	$5,000

You would pay $4,132 (the present value of $5,000) to receive the $5,000 future amount at the end of two years at 10 percent per year. The $868 difference between the amount invested ($4,132) and the amount to be received ($5,000) is the return on the investment, the sum of the two interest receipts: $413 + $455 = $868.

Present-Value Tables

We can compute present value by using the formula, as we have shown,

$$\frac{\textbf{Future value}}{\textbf{(1 + interest rate)}}$$

However, figuring present value "by hand" for investments spanning many years becomes drawn out. The "number crunching" presents too many opportunities for arithmetical errors. Present-value tables ease our work. Let us re-examine our examples of present value by using Table 16-1.

For the 10 percent investment for one year, we find the junction under 10% and across from 1 in the period column. The table figure of 0.909 is computed as follows: $\frac{1}{1.10} = 0.909$. This work has been done for us, and only the present values are given in the table. Note that the table heading states $1. To figure present value for $5,000, we multiply 0.909 by $5,000. The result is $4,545, which matches the result we obtained by hand.

For the two-year investment, we read down from 10 percent and across from period 2. We multiply 0.826 (which is computed as follows: $\frac{.909}{1.10} = 0.826$) by $5,000 and get $4,130, which confirms our earlier computation of $4,132 (the difference is due to rounding in the present-value table). We can compute the present value of any single future amount using the table.

Table 16-1 *Present Value of $1*

Periods	4%	5%	6%	7%	8%	10%	12%	14%	16%
1	0.962	0.952	0.943	0.935	0.926	0.909	0.893	0.877	0.862
2	0.925	0.907	0.890	0.873	0.857	0.826	0.797	0.769	0.743
3	0.889	0.864	0.840	0.816	0.794	0.751	0.712	0.675	0.641
4	0.855	0.823	0.792	0.763	0.735	0.683	0.636	0.592	0.552
5	0.822	0.784	0.747	0.713	0.681	0.621	0.567	0.519	0.476
6	0.790	0.746	0.705	0.666	0.630	0.564	0.507	0.456	0.410
7	0.760	0.711	0.665	0.623	0.583	0.513	0.452	0.400	0.354
8	0.731	0.677	0.627	0.582	0.540	0.467	0.404	0.351	0.305
9	0.703	0.645	0.592	0.544	0.500	0.424	0.361	0.308	0.263
10	0.676	0.614	0.558	0.508	0.463	0.386	0.322	0.270	0.227
11	0.650	0.585	0.527	0.475	0.429	0.350	0.287	0.237	0.195
12	0.625	0.557	0.497	0.444	0.397	0.319	0.257	0.208	0.168
13	0.601	0.530	0.469	0.415	0.368	0.290	0.229	0.182	0.145
14	0.577	0.505	0.442	0.388	0.340	0.263	0.205	0.160	0.125
15	0.555	0.481	0.417	0.362	0.315	0.239	0.183	0.140	0.108
16	0.534	0.458	0.394	0.339	0.292	0.218	0.163	0.123	0.093
17	0.513	0.436	0.371	0.317	0.270	0.198	0.146	0.108	0.080
18	0.494	0.416	0.350	0.296	0.250	0.180	0.130	0.095	0.069
19	0.475	0.396	0.331	0.277	0.232	0.164	0.116	0.083	0.060
20	0.456	0.377	0.312	0.258	0.215	0.149	0.104	0.073	0.051

Present Value of an Annuity

The investment in the preceding example provided the investor with only a single future receipt ($5,000 at the end of two years). Some investments, called annuities, provide multiple receipts of an equal amount at fixed intervals over the investment's duration.

Consider an investment that promises *annual* cash receipts of $10,000 to be received at the end of each of three years. Assume that you demand a 12 percent return on your investment. What is the investment's present value? What would you pay today to acquire the investment? The investment spans three periods, and you would pay the sum of three present values. The computation is

Year	Annual Cash Receipt	Present Value of $1 at 12% (Table 1)	Present Value of Annual Cash Receipt
1	$10,000	0.893	$ 8,930
2	10,000	0.797	7,970
3	10,000	0.712	7,120
Total present value of investment			$24,020

The present value of this annuity is $24,020. By paying this amount today, you would receive $10,000 at the end of each of three years while earning 12 percent on your investment.

The example illustrates repetitive computations of the three future amounts, a time-consuming process. One way to ease the computational burden is to add the three present values of $1 (0.893 + 0.797 + 0.712) and multiply their sum (2.402) by the

Table 16-2 *Present Value of Annuity of $1*

Periods	4%	5%	6%	7%	8%	10%	12%	14%	16%
1	0.962	0.952	0.943	0.935	0.926	0.909	0.893	0.877	0.862
2	1.886	1.859	1.833	1.808	1.783	1.736	1.690	1.647	1.605
3	2.775	2.723	2.673	2.624	2.577	2.487	2.402	2.322	2.246
4	3.630	3.546	3.465	3.387	3.312	3.170	3.037	2.914	2.798
5	4.452	4.329	4.212	4.100	3.993	3.791	3.605	3.433	3.274
6	5.242	5.076	4.917	4.767	4.623	4.355	4.111	3.889	3.685
7	6.002	5.786	5.582	5.389	5.206	4.868	4.564	4.288	4.039
8	6.733	6.463	6.210	5.971	5.747	5.335	4.968	4.639	4.344
9	7.435	7.108	6.802	6.515	6.247	5.759	5.328	4.946	4.607
10	8.111	7.722	7.360	7.024	6.710	6.145	5.650	5.216	4.833
11	8.760	8.306	7.887	7.499	7.139	6.495	5.938	5.453	5.029
12	9.385	8.863	8.384	7.943	7.536	6.814	6.194	5.660	5.197
13	9.986	9.394	8.853	8.358	7.904	7.103	6.424	5.842	5.342
14	10.563	9.899	9.295	8.745	8.244	7.367	6.628	6.002	5.468
15	11.118	10.380	9.712	9.108	8.559	7.606	6.811	6.142	5.575
16	11.652	10.838	10.106	9.447	8.851	7.824	6.974	6.265	5.669
17	12.166	11.274	10.477	9.763	9.122	8.022	7.120	6.373	5.749
18	12.659	11.690	10.828	10.059	9.372	8.201	7.250	6.467	5.818
19	13.134	12.085	11.158	10.336	9.604	8.365	7.366	6.550	5.877
20	13.590	12.462	11.470	10.594	9.818	8.514	7.469	6.623	5.929

annual cash receipt ($10,000) to obtain the present value of the annuity ($10,000 × 2.402 = $24,020).

An easier approach is to use a present value of an annuity table. Table 16-2 shows the present value of $1 to be received periodically for a given number of periods. The present value of a three-period annuity at 12 percent is 2.402. Thus $10,000 received annually at the end of each of three years, discounted at 12 percent, is $24,020 ($10,000 × 2.402), which is the present value.

Present Value of Bonds Payable

The present value of a bond (its market price) is the present value of the future principal amount at maturity plus the present value of the future contract interest payments. The principal is a single amount to be paid at maturity. The interest is an annuity because it occurs periodically.

Let us compute the present value of the 9 percent, five-year bonds of John Labatt. The face value of the bonds is $100,000, and they pay 4½ percent contract (cash) interest semiannually. At issuance the market interest rate is 10 percent, and so the effective interest rate for each of the 10 semiannual periods is 5 percent. We use 5 percent in computing the present value of the maturity and of the interest. The market price of these bonds is $96,149, as follows:

	Effective annual interest rate ÷ 2		Number of semiannual interest payments	
PV of principal				
$100,000 × PV of single amount at 5%		for	10 periods	
($100,000 × .614 — Table 1)				$61,400
PV of interest				
($100,000 × .045) × PV of annuity at 5%		for	10 periods	
($4,500 × 7.722 — Table 2)				34,749
PV (market price) of bonds				$96,149

The market price of the John Labatt bonds shows a discount because the contract interest rate on the bonds (9 percent) is less than the market interest rate (10 percent). We discuss these bonds in more detail on pp. 664–666.

Let us consider a premium price for the John Labatt bonds. Assume that the market interest rate is 8 percent at issuance. The effective interest rate is 4 percent for each of the 10 semiannual periods.

	Effective annual interest rate ÷ 2		Number of semiannual interest payments	
PV of principal				
$100,000 × PV of single amount at 4%		for	10 periods	
($100,000 × .676 — Table 1)				$67,600
PV of interest				
($100,000 × .045) × PV of annuity at 4%		for	10 periods	
($4,500 × 8.111 — Table 2)				36,500
PV (market price) of bonds				$104,100

We discuss accounting for these bonds on pp. 666–668.

Capital Leases

How does a lessee compute the cost of an asset acquired through a capital lease? Consider that the lessee gets the use of the asset but does *not* pay for the leased asset in full at the beginning of the lease. Therefore, the lessee must record the leased asset at the present value of the lease liability. The time value of money must be weighed.

The cost of the asset to the lessee is the sum of any payment made at the beginning of the lease period plus the present value of the future lease payments. The lease payments are equal amounts occurring at regular intervals, that is, they are annuity payments.

Consider a 20-year building lease of the Oshawa Group Limited, which owns Towers Department Stores. The lease requires 20 annual payments of $10,000 each, with the first payment due immediately. The interest rate in the lease is 10 percent, and the present value of the 19 future payments is $83,650 ($10,000 × PV of annuity at 10 percent for 19 periods, or 8.365 from Table 16-2). Oshawa Group's cost of the building is $93,650 (the sum of the initial payment, $10,000, plus the present value of the future payments, $83,650). The entries for a capital lease are illustrated on pp. 673–674.

Problems

Problem PV-1   *Computing the present values of notes and bonds*

Determine the present value of the following notes and bonds:

a. $20,000, five-year note payable with contract interest rate of 11 percent, paid annually. The market interest rate at issuance is 12 percent.
b. Ten-year bonds payable with maturity value of $100,000 and contract interest rate of 12 percent, paid semiannually. The market rate of interest is 12 percent at issuance.
c. Same bonds payable as in question b, but the market interest rate is 10 percent.
d. Same bonds payable as in question b, but the market interest rate is 14 percent.

Problem PV-2   *Computing a bond's present value; recording its issuance at a discount and interest payments*

On December 31, 19X1, when the market interest rate is 8 percent, Unitrode Corporation issues $500,000 of 10-year, 7.25 percent bonds payable. The bonds pay interest semiannually.

Required

1. Determine the present value of the bonds at issuance.
2. Assume that the bonds are issued at the price computed in question 1. Prepare an effective interest method amortization table for the first two semiannual interest periods.
3. Using the amortization table prepared in question 2, journalize issuance of the bonds and the first two interest payments.

Problem PV-3   *Computing a bond's present value; recording its issuance at a premium and interest payments*

On December 31, 19X1, when the market interest rate is 10 percent, RTE Ltd. issues $4,000,000 of 10-year, 12.5 percent bonds payable. The bonds pay interest semiannually.

Required

1. Determine the present value of the bonds at issuance.
2. Assuming the bonds were issued at the price computed in question 1, prepare an effective interest method amortization table for the first two semiannual interest periods.
3. Using the amortization table in question 2, journalize issuance of the bonds on December 31, 19X1, and the first two interest payments on June 30 and December 31, 19X2.

Problem PV-4   *Computing the cost of equipment acquired under a capital lease and recording the lease transactions*

Montgomery Limited acquired equipment under a capital lease that requires six annual lease payments of $5,000. The first payment is due when the lease begins, on January 1, 19X6. Future payments are due on January 1 of each year of the lease term. The interest rate in the lease is 16 percent.

Required

1. Compute Montgomery's cost of the equipment.
2. Journalize the (a) acquisition of the equipment, (b) depreciation for 19X6, (c) accrued interest at December 31, 19X6, and (d) second lease payment on January 1, 19X7.

Problem PV-5   *Computing the cost of a bond investment and journalizing its transactions*

An investor purchases $400,000 of the RTE bonds (Problem PV-3) at issuance. Determine the cost (present value) of the bond investment. Assume that the investment is short-term. Journalize the purchase on December 31, 19X1, the first semiannual interest receipt on June 30, 19X2, and the year-end interest receipt on December 31, 19X2.

Answers to Self-Study Questions

1. c
2. d [($100,000 × 1.01875) + $1,100 = $102,975]
3. b
4. a [($500,000 × .11) − ($32,000/10) = $51,800]
5. d

6. b
7. d
8. a
9. a
10. c

17

Corporations: Investments in Stock and Accounting for the Effects of Changing Prices

In the preceding chapter, we discussed accounting for bond investments. In this chapter, we discuss how to account for investments in stock. We also consider the challenging area of accounting for the effects of changing prices.

Accounting for Investments in Stock

Stock Prices

Investors buy more stocks in transactions among themselves than in purchases directly from the issuing company. Each share of stock is issued only once, but it may be traded among investors many times thereafter. People and businesses buy and sell stocks from each other in markets, such as the Toronto, Montreal, Vancouver and Alberta Stock Exchanges. Recall that stock ownership is transferable. Investors trade millions of stock shares each day. Brokers like RBC Dominion Securities and Richardson Greenshields handle stock transactions for a commission.

A broker may "quote you a stock price," which means state the current market price per share. The financial community quotes stock prices in dollars and one-eighth fractions. A stock selling at 32⅛ costs $32.125 per share. A stock listed at 55¾ sells at $55.75. Financial publications and many newspapers carry daily information on the stock issues of thousands of corporations. These one-line summaries carry information as of the close of trading the previous day.

Exhibit 17-1 presents information for the common stock of John Labatt, a brewer and food and beverage company, just as it appears in the daily *Financial Post*.

EXHIBIT 17-1   *Stock Price Information*

52 Weeks		Stock	Div Rate	High	Low	Cls or Latest	Net Chge	Vol 100s	Yield %	P/E Ratio
High	Low									
25⅜	20½	Labatt, John	0.70	25⅜	24⅞	25⅜	+½	702	2.8	14.1

During the previous 52 weeks, Labatt common stock reached a high of $25.375 and a low of $20.50. The annual cash dividend is $.70 per share. *The Financial Post* comes out in the morning so the information relates to the previous day; the high and low prices were $25.375 and $24.875 while the closing price was $25.375 (if there had been no trading on the previous day, the latest, or most recent price, would be given). The closing price on the previous day was up $.50 from the closing price of one trading day earlier. During the previous day, 702,00 (702 × 100) shares of John Labatt stock were traded. The yield (dividend per share divided by price per share) is 2.8% while the P/E ratio (ratio of earnings per share to the share price) is 14.1/1.

What causes a change in a stock's price? The company's net income trend, the development of new products, court rulings, new legislation, business success and upward market trends drive a stock's price up, and business failures and bad economic news pull it down. The market sets the price at which a stock changes hands.

Stock Investments

As we begin the discussion of investments in stock, let's define two key terms. The person or company that owns stock in a corporation is the *investor*. The corporation that issued the stock is the *investee*. If you own shares of Labatt common stock, you are an investor and Labatt is the investee.

A business may purchase another corporation's stock simply to put extra cash to work in the hope of earning dividends and gains on the sale of the stock. Alternatively, the business may make the investment to gain a degree of control over the investee's operation. After all, stock is ownership. An investor holding 25 percent of the outstanding stock of the investee owns one fourth of the business. This one-quarter voice in electing the directors of the corporation is likely to give the investor a lot of say in how the investee conducts its business. An investor holding more than 50 percent of the outstanding shares controls the investee.

Let us consider why one corporation might want to gain a say in another corporation's business. The investor may want to exert some control over the level of dividends paid by the investee. Or perhaps the investee has a line of products closely linked to the investor's own sales items. By influencing the investee's business, the investor may be able to exert some control on product distribution, product-line improvements, pricing strategies and other important business considerations. A swimming-pool manufacturer might want to purchase stock in a diving-board company, a swimsuit maker or some other corporation with related business.

Why doesn't the investor simply diversify its own operations, expanding into diving boards, swimsuits and other related products? The cost may be too great. Also, the investor may not have experience with these other products. Why challenge a successful business in the marketplace when the investor can "buy into" a successful corporation's existing operations? The reasons for investing in a corporation in order to affect its operations to some degree make corporate investments attractive to many businesses.

Investments are not without risk. To offset the ill effects of a sudden downturn in the operations of any one investee, smart investors hold a portfolio of stocks. The portfolio holds investments in different companies. By diversifying its holdings, the investor gains protection from losing too much if any one investee runs into problems and its stock price plummets.

Classifying Stock Investments

Investments in stock are assets to the investor. The investments may be short-term or long-term. Short-term investments are current assets. Because short-term investments may be sold any time the investor wishes, they are also called **marketable securities**. To be listed on the balance sheet as short-term, investments must be liquid (readily convertible to cash). Also, the investor's *intent* is important; the investor must intend either to convert the investments to cash within one year or to use them to pay a current liability. Investments not meeting these two requirements are classified on the balance sheet as long-term.

Short-term investments include treasury bills, certificates of deposit, and stocks and bonds of other companies. *Long-term investments* include bond sinking funds, and stocks, bonds and other assets that the investor expects to hold longer than one year or that are not readily marketable, for instance, real estate not used in the operations of the business. Exhibit 17-2 shows the positions of short-term and long-term investments on the balance sheet.

Observe that we report assets in the order of their liquidity. Cash is the most liquid asset, followed by Short-Term Investments, Accounts Receivable, and so on. Long-Term Investments are less liquid than Current Assets but more liquid than Property, Plant and Equipment.

EXHIBIT 17-2 *Reporting Investments on the Balance Sheet*

Current Assets		
Cash	$X	
Short-term investments	X	
Accounts receivable	X	
Inventories	X	
Prepaid expenses	X	
Total current assets		$X
Long-term investments (or simply **Investments**)		X
Property, plant and equipment		X
Intangible assets		X
Other assets		X

Accounting for Stock Investments _____

Accounting for stock investments varies with the nature and extent of the investment. The specific accounting method that GAAP directs us to follow depends first on whether the investment is short-term or long-term and second on the percentage of the investee's voting stock that the investor holds.

Short-term Investments: The Cost Method (with LCM)

The **cost method** (with lower of cost or market) is used to account for short-term investments in stock. *Cost* is used as the initial amount for recording investments and as the basis for measuring gains and losses on their sale. These investments are reported on the balance sheet at the *lower of their cost or market value*. Therefore, we refer to the overall method as cost (with lower of cost or market).

All investments, including short-term investments, are recorded initially at cost. Cost is the price paid for the stock plus the brokerage commission. Suppose that Dade, Inc. purchases 1,000 shares of Noranda Inc. common stock at the market price of 36¼ and pays a $500 commission. Dade intends to sell this investment within one year or less and, therefore, classifies it as short-term. Dade's entry to record the investment is

Aug. 22   Short-term Investment in Noranda Common
                  Stock [(1,000 × $36.25) + $500]   36,750
                        Cash   36,750
                  Purchased 1,000 shares of Noranda common
                  stock at $36.25 plus commission of $500.

OBJECTIVE 1	
Account for investments by the cost (LCM) method	

Assume Dade receives a $.22 per share cash dividend on the Noranda stock. Dade's entry to record receipt of the dividends is

Oct. 14   Cash (1,000 × $.22)   220
                  Dividend Revenue   220
                  Received $.22 per share cash dividend on Noranda
                  common stock.

Dividends do not accrue with the passage of time (as interest does). The investee has no liability for dividends until the dividends are declared. An investor makes no accrual entry for dividend revenue at year end in anticipation of a dividend declaration.

However, if a dividend declaration *does* occur before year end (say, on December 28) the investor may debit Dividend Receivable and credit Dividend Revenue on that date. The investor would then report this receivable and the revenue in the December 31 financial statements. Receipt of the cash dividend in January would be recorded by a debit to Cash and a credit to Dividend Receivable. The more common practice, however, is to record the dividend as income when it is received.

Receipt of a *stock* dividend is *not* income to the investor, and no formal journal entry is needed. As we have seen, a stock dividend increases the number of shares held by the investor but does not affect the total cost of the investment. The cost per share of the stock investment therefore decreases. The investor usually makes a memorandum entry of the number of dividend shares received and the new cost per share. Assume that Dade, Inc. receives a

10 percent stock dividend on its 1,000-share investment in Noranda, which cost $36,750. Dade would make a memorandum entry along this line:

Nov. 22   Received 100 shares of Noranda common stock in
　　　　　 10 percent stock dividend. New cost per share is $33.41
　　　　　 ($36,750/1,100 shares).

Any gain or loss on the sale of the investment is the difference between the sale proceeds and the cost of the investment. Assume that Dade sells 400 shares of Noranda stock for $35 per share, less a $280 commission. The entry to record the sale is

Dec. 18   Cash [(400×$35)−$280].....................   13,720
　　　　　　 Short-Term Investment in Noranda
　　　　　　 Common Stock (400×$33.41)   13,364
　　　　　　 Gain on Sale of Investment..............   356
　　　　　 Sold 400 shares of investment in Noranda
　　　　　 common stock.

Observe that the cost per share of the investment ($33.41) is based on the total number of shares held, including those received as a dividend.

Reporting Short-Term Investments at Lower of Cost or Market (LCM)

Because of accounting conservatism, short term investments are reported at the lower of their cost or market (LCM or LOCAM) value. Canadian practice, in the absence of standards in the *CICA Handbook*, is to calculate market value on an investment-by-investment basis or on the portfolio as a whole. In either event, the basis of valuation for cost and market values should be disclosed. Assume a company owns three short term investments with the following costs and market values:

Short-term Investment Portfolio

Stock	Cost	Current Market Value
Dofasco Inc.........................	$155,625	$126, 275
Toronto-Dominion Bank..............	67,000	86,200
George Weston Limited	186,000	174,500
Total	$408,625	$386,975

The investor owning the portfolio has two choices when determining the value of the portfolio for balance sheet purposes. The first considers the portfolio on a security-by-security basis. The investor would write the book value of the two stocks (Dofasco and Weston) whose market price has dropped below the price paid for them, down to their market values of $126,275 and $174,500 respectively. The market price of Toronto-Dominion is greater than cost, so no adjustment would be made to its book value. The journal entry to record the write down would be as follows:

Loss of Marketable Securities..........................   40,850
　　 Marketable Securities   40,850
To write down investment in Dofasco
($155,625−$126,275=$29,350) and George Weston
($186,000−$174,500=$11,500) to market.

The investor's balance sheet would report short-term investments as follows:

Current Assets

Cash	$ XXX
Short-term investments, at lower of cost or market value (note 4) ...	367,775
Accounts receivable, net of allowance of $XXX	XXX

NOTE 4. SHORT-TERM INVESTMENTS

Short-term investments are reported at the lower of their cost or market value. At December 31, 19XX, market value was $386,975.

Under this option, the investor would write down the book value of individual stocks to their market values, where cost was greater than market, irrespective of whether or not the total market value of the portfolio was greater than or less than cost.

The investor's other option would be to apply the LCM rule to the entire portfolio and write it down to market. The journal entry to record the write down would be

Loss on Marketable Securities	21,650	
Marketable Securities		21,650
To write down investment portfolio to market.		

The investor's balance sheet would report short-term investments as follows:

Current Assets

Cash	$ XXX
Short-term investments, at market value (note 4).................	386,975
Accounts receivable, net of allowance of $XXX	XXX

NOTE 4. SHORT-TERM INVESTMENTS

Short-term investments are reported at the lower of their cost or market value. At December 31, 19XX, cost was $408,625.

Under the second option, if the portfolio cost is lower than market value, the investor reports short-term investments at cost and discloses market value in the note.

Conservatism requires that an investor write the book value of stocks or portfolios down to market when cost exceeds market, but does not permit the investor to write up the book value of those same stocks or portfolios when their market value subsequently rises above the written down book values.

Long-Term Investments

An investor may own numerous investments, some short-term and others long-term. For accounting purposes, the two investment portfolios are *not* mixed. They are reported separately on the balance sheet, as shown in Exhibit 17-2. *Long-term* is not often used in the account title. An investment is understood to be long-term unless specifically labeled as short-term.

Long-term investments may be of several different types depending on the purpose of the investment and thus the percentage of voting interest acquired. Each of the three types will be discussed in turn below.

An investor may make a portfolio investment where the purpose is similar to that of short-term investing; the investor will hold the investment to earn dividends or interest but has no long term interest in the investee. In such a situation, the investor will generally hold less than 20 percent of the voting interest of the investee. Such an investor would normally account for the investment using the cost method.

An investor may also make an investment in the investee of such magnitude that the investor exerts a *significant influence* on the investee. An investor holding more than 20 percent of the voting interest of the investee generally, but not always, is considered to exert significant influence. Such an investor would normally account for the investment using the **equity method**.

The investor may make an investment in the investee that exceeds 50 percent of the voting interest. Such investees are called *subsidiaries*; subsidiaries financial statements are normally *consolidated* with those of the parent.

Long-Term Investments Accounted for by the Cost Method

Accounting for portfolio investments follows the procedures outlined for short-term investments. The beginning accounting value is cost, which is debited to an Investments account at the date of purchase. Dividends are treated as income. Gains and losses are recorded on sales. Long-term investments are normally reported on the balance sheet at cost. If the market price of one of the stocks in the portfolio drops below cost, and the decline is thought to be other than temporary, the stock's book value would be written down to market and carried at that value in the future. The determination of whether or not the decline is temporary is management's.

Long-Term Investments Accounted for by the Equity Method

The *cost* method of accounting for long-term investments applies when an investor holds less than 20 percent of the investee's voting stock. Such an investor usually plays no important role in the investee's operations. However, an investee with a larger stock holding (between 20 percent and 50 percent of the investee's voting stock) may *significantly influence* how the investee operates the business. Such an investor can likely affect the investee's decisions on dividend policy, product lines, sources of supply and other important matters. Since the investor has a voice in shaping business policy and operations, accountants believe that some measure of the business's success and failure should be included in accounting for the investment. We use the equity method to account for investments in which the investor can significantly influence the decision of the investee.

Investments accounted for by the equity method are recorded initially at cost. Suppose Nova Corp. pays $400,000 for 30 percent of the common stock of White Rock Corporation. Nova's entry to record the purchase of this investment is

Jan. 6	Investment in White Rock Common Stock	400,000	
	Cash		400,000
	To purchase 30% investment in White Rock common stock.		

Under the equity method, Nova, as the investor, applies its percentage of ownership, 30 percent in our example, in recording its share of the investee's net income and dividends. If White Rock reports net income of $250,000 for the year, Nova records 30 percent of this amount as an increase in the investment account and as equity-method investment revenue, as follows:

OBJECTIVE 2

Use the equity method for investments

Dec. 31	Investment in White Rock Common Stock		
	($250,000 × .30)	75,000	
	Equity-Method Investment Revenue		75,000
	To record 30% of White Rock net income.		

The Investment Revenue account carries the Equity-Method label to identify its source. This labeling is similar to distinguishing Sales Revenue from Service Revenue.

The investor increases the Investment account and records Investment Revenue when the investee reports income because of the close relationship between the two companies. As the investee's owner equity increases, so does the Investment account on the books of the investor.

Nova records its proportionate part of cash dividends received from White Rock. Assuming White Rock declares and pays a cash dividend of $100,000, Nova receives 30 percent of this dividend, recording it as follows:

Jan. 17	Cash ($100,000 × .30)	30,000	
	Investment in White Rock Common Stock .		30,000
	To record receipt of 30% of White Rock cash dividend.		

Observe that the Investment account is credited for the receipt of a dividend on an equity-method investment. Why? It is because the dividend decreases the investee's owner equity and so it also reduces the investor's investment. In effect, the investor received cash for this portion of the investment.

After the above entries are posted, Nova's investment account reflects its equity in the net assets of White Rock:

Investment in White Rock Common Stock

19X1			19X2		
Jan. 6	Purchase	400,000	Jan. 17	Dividends	30,000
Dec. 31	Net income	75,000			
19X2					
Jan. 17	Balance	445,000			

Gain or loss on the sale of an equity-method investment is measured as the difference between the sale proceeds and the carrying value of the investment. For example, sale of one tenth of the White Rock common stock for $41,000 would be recorded as follows:

Feb. 13	Cash	41,000	
	Loss on Sale of Investment....................	3,500	
	Investment in White Rock Common Stock		
	($445,000 × 1/10)		44,500
	Sold one-tenth of investment in White Rock common stock.		

Companies with investments accounted for by the equity method often refer to the investee as an *affiliated company*. The account title Investments in Affiliated Companies refers to investments that are accounted for by the equity method.

Consolidation Method

Most large corporations own controlling interests in other corporations. A **controlling** (or **majority**) **interest** is the ownership of more than 50 percent of the investee's voting stock. Such an investment enables the investor to elect a majority of the investee's board of directors and so control the investee. The investor is called the **parent company**, and the investee company, as mentioned earlier, is called the **subsidiary**. For example, Zellers Inc., the department store chain, is 100% owned by Hudson's Bay Co. Lord Thomson of Fleet and the other shareholders of Hudson's Bay Co. control that company and, because Hudson's Bay owns Zellers, they also control Zellers.

Consolidation accounting is a method of combining the financial statements of two or more companies that are controlled by the same owners. This method implements the entity concept by reporting a single set of financial statements for the consolidated entity, which carries the name of the parent company. The assets, liabilities, revenues and expenses of each subsidiary are added to the parent's accounts. The consolidated financial statements (balance sheet, income statement, and so on) present the combined account balances. For example, the balance in the Cash account of Zellers is added to the balance in the Hudson's Bay Co. Cash account, and the sum of the two amounts is presented as a single amount in the consolidated balance sheet of Hudson's Bay Co. Each account balance of a subsidiary loses its identity in the consolidated statements. Hudson's Bay Co. financial statements are entitled "Hudson's Bay Co. and Consolidated Subsidiaries." Zellers and the names of all other Hudson's Bay Co. subsidiaries do not appear in the statement titles. But the names of the subsidiary companies are listed in the parent company's annual report.

No separate set of books exists for the consolidated entity. The parent company and the subsidiary company prepare their own financial statements separately. Accountants for the parent company then combine the two companies' statements into a single set of consolidated statements.

Combining balances in consolidation accounting requires special eliminating journal entries on a work sheet, which we examine later in the chapter. For example, the parent's books contain an Investment in Subsidiary account.[1] The subsidiary's books include its own owners' equity accounts. At least a part of its owners' equity balance is represented in the parent's investment account. That is, the same amount appears in the Investment in Subsidiary account of the parent and in the Common Stock account of the subsidiary. If these two accounts are combined in the consolidated statements, the *same resources* would be counted twice, which is clearly improper. In fact, intercompany accounts (those that appear in both the parent's books and the subsidiary's books) should *not* be included in consolidated statements at all.

Consider also an account receivable that the parent has from the subsidiary, or vice versa. The receivable and the payable represent the *same resources*.

---

[1] The parent company may use either the cost method or the equity method for journal entries to the Investment account. Regardless of the method used, the consolidated statements are the same. Advanced accounting courses deal with this topic.

Because the receivable and the payable are entirely within the consolidated entity, they must be eliminated from the consolidated financial statements. Another way to state this is that the consolidated entity can have neither a receivable from, nor a payable to, itself. All intercompany accounts must be eliminated in the consolidated statements. Accountants accomplish this by making special eliminating journal entries, which we look at later in the chapter.

Consolidated Balance Sheet: Parent Owns All of Subsidiary's Stock   Companies usually prepare a consolidated balance sheet immediately after the parent acquires a controlling interest in the subsidiary. This balance sheet provides the basis for evaluating the future progress of the consolidated entity.

Exhibit 17-3 shows the work sheet used to prepare a consolidated balance sheet immediately after Parent Limited purchases Subsidiary Corporation. The amounts in the Parent and Subsidiary columns are taken directly from those companies' separate financial statements. The column labeled Eliminations summarizes the journal entries needed to eliminate amounts arising from intercompany transactions. The Consolidated Amounts column lists the balances that appear on the consolidated balance sheet.

We assume in this illustration that Parent Limited has purchased all the outstanding common stock of Subsidiary Corporation at its book value of $150,000. Also, Subsidiary owes an $80,000 note payable to Parent. Let us look now at the elimination entries.

OBJECTIVE 3

Consolidate parent and subsidiary balance sheets

Explanation of Elimination Entries   *Entry (a).* Parent Limited loaned $80,000 to Subsidiary Corporation, and Subsidiary signed a note payable to Parent. Therefore, Parent's balance sheet includes an $80,000 note receivable and Subsidiary's balance sheet reports a note payable for this amount. This

EXHIBIT 17-3   *Work Sheet for Consolidated Balance Sheet: Parent Owns All of Subsidiary's Stock*

Assets	Parent Limited	Subsidiary Corporation	Eliminations Debit	Eliminations Credit	Consolidated Amounts
Cash	12,000	18,000			30,000
Notes receivable from Subsidiary	80,000	—		(a) 80,000	—
Inventory	104,000	91,000			195,000
Investment in Subsidiary	150,000	—		(b) 150,000	—
Other assets	218,000	138,000			356,000
Total	564,000	247,000			581,000

Liabilities and Shareholders' Equity					
Accounts payable	43,000	17,000			60,000
Notes payable	190,000	80,000	(a) 80,000		190,000
Common stock	176,000	100,000	(b) 100,000		176,000
Retained earnings	155,000	50,000	(b) 50,000		155,000
Total	564,000	247,000	230,000	230,000	581,000

loan was entirely within the consolidated entity and so must be eliminated. Entry (*a*) accomplishes this. The $80,000 credit in the elimination column of the work sheet offsets Parent's debit balance in Notes Receivable from Subsidiary. After this work sheet entry, the consolidated amount for notes receivable is zero. The $80,000 debit in the elimination column offsets the credit balance of Subsidiary's notes payable, and the resulting consolidated amount for notes payable is the amount owed to businesses and people outside the consolidated entity.

Entity (b). In Exhibit 17-3, the Parent balance sheet reports Investment in Subsidiary with a $150,000 debit balance. The balance sheet of Subsidiary Corporation includes Common Stock and Retained Earnings with combined balances totaling $150,000. Parent's investment is Subsidiary's owner equity. It would not be correct to include the same resources twice in the consolidated balance sheet. Therefore, the stock, and retained earnings balances of the subsidiary should be eliminated from the consolidated statement because they are entirely intercompany accounts. Entry (*b*) credits the Investment account to eliminate its debit balance. It also eliminates the Subsidiary owners' equity by debiting its Common Stock for $100,000 and Retained Earnings for $50,000. The resulting consolidated balance sheet reports no Investment in Subsidiary account, and the Common Stock and Retained Earnings balances are those of Parent Limited only. The consolidated balance sheet can be taken directly from the final column of the consolidation work sheet.

Parent Company Buys Subsidiary's Stock at a Price above Book Value   A company may acquire a controlling interest in a subsidiary by paying a price above the book value of the subsidiary's owner equity. The excess of the price paid by the parent over the fair value of the subsidiary's net assets is *goodwill.* What drives a company's market value up? The company may create goodwill through its superior products, service, or location. Goodwill was discussed in Chapter 10.

The subsidiary does not record goodwill. Doing so would violate the reliability principle. Goodwill is recorded only when a company purchases it as part of the acquisition of another company, that is, when a parent company purchases a subsidiary. The goodwill is recorded in the process of consolidating the parent and subsidiary financial statements.

Suppose Parent Limited paid $450,000 to acquire 100 percent of the common stock of Subsidiary Corporation, which had Common Stock of $200,000 and Retained Earnings of $180,000. Parent's payment included $70,000 for goodwill ($450,000 − $200,000 − $180,000 = $70,000). The entry to eliminate Parent's Investment account against Subsidiary's equity accounts is

Dec. 31	Common Stock, Subsidiary	200,000	
	Retained Earnings, Subsidiary	180,000	
	Goodwill	70,000	
	Investment in Subsidiary		450,000
	To eliminate cost of investment in subsidiary against Subsidiary's equity balances and to recognize Subsidiary's unrecorded goodwill.		

In actual practice, this entry would be made only on the consolidation work sheet. Here we show it in general journal form for instructional purposes.

The asset goodwill is reported on the consolidated balance sheet among the intangible assets, after plant assets. Goodwill is amortized to expense over its useful life.

Consolidated Balance Sheet: Parent Owns Less Than 100 Percent of Subsidiary's Stock When a parent company owns more than 50 percent (a majority) of the subsidiary's stock but less than 100 percent of it, a new category of owners' equity, called *minority interest*, must appear on the consolidated balance sheet. Suppose Parent buys 75 percent of Subsidiary's common stock. The minority interest is the remaining 25 percent of Subsidiary's equity. Thus **minority interest** is the subsidiary's equity that is held by shareholders other than the parent company. While the *CICA Handbook* is silent on where minority interest should be disclosed on the balance sheet, accepted practice is to disclose it between liabilities and owner's equity.

Assume P Corp. buys 75 percent of S Ltd.'s common stock. Also, P owes S $50,000 on a note payable. Exhibit 17-4 is the consolidation work sheet. Again, focus on the Eliminations columns and the Consolidation Amounts.

Entry (a) in Exhibit 17-4 eliminates S Ltd.'s $50,000 note receivable against P's note payable of the same amount. The consolidated amount of notes payable ($42,000) is the amount that S Company owes to outsiders.

Entry (b) eliminates P Corp.'s Investment balance of $120,000 against the $160,000 owner's equity of S Ltd. Observe that all of S's equity is eliminated even though P holds only 75 percent of S's stock. The remaining 25 percent interest in S's equity is credited to Minority Interest ($160,000 × .25 = $40,000). Thus Entry (b) reclassifies 25 percent of S Company's equity as minority interest.

EXHIBIT 17-4 *Work Sheet for Consolidated Balance Sheet: Parent Owns Less Than 100 Percent of Subsidiary's Stock*

Assets	P Corp.	S Ltd.	Eliminations Debit	Eliminations Credit	Consolidated Amounts
Cash	33,000	18,000			51,000
Notes receivable from P	—	50,000		(a) 50,000	—
Accounts receivable, net	54,000	39,000			93,000
Inventory	92,000	66,000			158,000
Investment in S	120,000	—		(b) 120,000	—
Plant and equipment, net	230,000	123,000			353,000
Total	529,000	296,000			655,000

Liabilities and Shareholders' Equity	P Corp.	S Ltd.	Eliminations Debit	Eliminations Credit	Consolidated Amounts
Accounts payable	141,000	94,000			235,000
Notes payable	50,000	42,000	(a) 50,000		42,000
Common stock	170,000	100,000	(b) 100,000		170,000
Retained earnings	168,000	60,000	(b) 60,000		168,000
Minority interest	—	—		(b) 40,000	40,000
Total	529,000	296,000	210,000	210,000	655,000

The consolidated balance sheet of P Corp., based on the work sheet of Exhibit 17-4, is

P Corp. and Consolidated Subsidiary
Consolidated Balance Sheet
December 31, 19XX

Assets

Cash..	$ 51,000
Accounts receivable, net	93,000
Inventory	158,000
Plant and equipment, net	353,000
Total assets.................................	$655,000

Liabilities and Shareholders' Equity

Accounts payable	$235,000
Notes payable	42,000
Minority interest............................	40,000
Common stock	170,000
Retained earnings...........................	168,000
Total liabilities and shareholders' equity	$655,000

The consolidated balance sheet reveals that ownership of P Corp. and its consolidated subsidiary is divided between P's shareholders (common stock and retained earnings totaling $338,000) and the minority shareholders of S Ltd. ($40,000).

Income of a Consolidated Entity   The income of a consolidated entity is the net income of the parent plus the parent's proportion of the subsidiaries' net income. Suppose Parent Inc. owns all the stock of Subsidiary S-1 and 60 percent of the stock of Subsidiary S-2. During the year just ended, Parent earned net income of $330,000, S-1 earned $150,000 and S-2 had a net loss of $100,000. Parent would report net income of $420,000, computed as follows:

	Net Income (Net Loss)	Parent Shareholders' Ownership	Parent Net Income (Net Loss)
Parent Inc.	$330,000	100%	$330,000
Subsidiary S-1	150,000	100	150,000
Subsidiary S-2	(100,000)	60	(60,000)
Consolidated net income .			$420,000

The parent's net income is the same amount that would be recorded under the equity method. However, the equity method stops short of reporting the investee's assets and liabilities on the parent balance sheet because with an investment in the range of 20–50 percent, the investor owns less than a controlling interest in the investee company.

The procedures for preparation of a consolidated income statement parallel those outlined above for the balance sheet. The consolidated income statement is discussed in an advanced course. Exhibit 17-5 summarizes the accounting methods for investments.

EXHIBIT 17-5   *Accounting Methods for Investments*

Type of Investments	Accounting Method
Short-term investment	Cost (lower of cost or market)
Long-term investment	
Investor owns less than 20 percent of investee stock	Cost (lower of cost or market if decline in market is not temporary)
Investor owns between 20 and 50 percent of investee stock	Equity
Investor owns greater than 50 percent of investee stock	Consolidation

Summary Problem for Your Review

This problem consists of four independent items.

1. Identify the appropriate accounting method for each of the following situations:
   a. Investment in 25 percent of investee's stock
   b. Investor intends to sell three months after year end
   c. Investment in more than 50 percent of investee's stock

2. At what amount should the following long-term investment portfolio be reported? All the investments are less than 5 percent of the investee's stock.

Stock	Investment Cost	Current Market Value
Loblaw Companies	$ 5,000	$12,500
National Sea Products	61,200	53,000
National Trust	3,680	6,230

3. Investor paid $67,900 to acquire a 40 percent equity-method investment in the common stock of Investee. At the end of the first year, Investee's net income was $80,000, and Investee declared and paid cash dividends of $55,000. Journalize Investor's (a) purchase of the investment, (b) share of Investee's net income, (c) receipt of dividends from Investee, and (d) sale of Investee stock for $80,100.

4. Parent Corp. paid $100,000 for all the common stock of Subsidiary Ltd., and Parent owes Subsidiary $20,000 on a note payable. Assume the fair

value of Subsidiary's net assets is equal to book value. Complete the following consolidation work sheet:

Assets	Parent Corp.	Subsidiary Ltd.	Eliminations Debit	Eliminations Credit	Consolidated Amounts
Cash	7,000	4,000			
Note receivable from Parent...................	—	20,000			
Investment in Subsidiary	100,000	—			
Goodwill	—	—			
Other assets...............................	108,000	99,000			
Total	215,000	123,000			

Liabilities and Shareholders' Equity					
Accounts payable	15,000	8,000			
Notes payable	20,000	30,000			
Common stock	135,000	60,000			
Retained earnings	45,000	25,000			
Total	215,000	123,000			

SOLUTION TO SUMMARY PROBLEM

1. a. Equity   b. Cost (LCM)   c. Consolidation

2. There are two possible solutions to this problem:

a. Report the investments at cost, $69,880, because total cost is less than total market.

Stock	Investment Cost	Current Market Value
Loblaw Companies	$ 5,000	$12,500
National Sea Products........................	61,200	53,000
National Trust...............................	3,680	6,230
Totals	$69,880	$71,730

b. Report the investments at the lower of cost or market on an investment-by-investment basis because the market value for one or more of the investments (National Sea Products) is less than cost.

Stock (Note)	Lower of Investment Cost and Current Market Value
Loblaw Companies................................	$ 5,000
National Sea Products	53,000
National Trust	3,680
Total	$61,680

Note: Market value is $71,730.

3.   a. Investment in Investee Common Stock   67,900
          Cash   67,900
       To purchase 40% investment in Investee common
       stock.

   b. Investment in Investee Common Stock
       ($80,000 × .40)   32,000
          Equity-Method Investment Revenue   32,000
       To record 40% of Investee net income.

   c. Cash ($55,000 × .40)   22,000
          Investment in Investee Common Stock   22,000
       To record receipt of 40% of Investee cash dividend.

   d. Cash.   80,100
       Investment in Investee Common Stock
          ($67,900 + $32,000 − $22,000)   77,900
       Gain on Sale of Investment   2,200
       Sold investment in Investee common stock.

4.   Consolidation work sheet:

Assets	Parent Corp.	Subsidiary Ltd.	Eliminations Debit	Eliminations Credit	Consolidated Amounts
Cash	7,000	4,000			11,000
Note receivable from Parent	—	20,000		(a) 20,000	—
Investment in Subsidiary	100,000	—		(b) 100,000	—
Goodwill	—	—	(b) 15,000		15,000
Other assets	108,000	99,000			207,000
Total	215,000	123,000			233,000

Liabilities and Shareholders' Equity					
Accounts payable	15,000	8,000			23,000
Notes payable	20,000	30,000	(a) 20,000		30,000
Common stock	135,000	60,000	(b) 60,000		135,000
Retained earnings	45,000	25,000	(b) 25,000		45,000
Total	215,000	123,000	120,000	120,000	233,000

Accounting for the Effects of Changing Prices

We use accounting information for making economic decisions. Of course, these decisions can only be as good as the information we weigh in making them. Critics charge that accounting fails to provide the most accurate information possible because it fails to measure the effects of changing prices. How intelligent, then, can our economic decisions be?

We know that GAAP directs companies to assume the stable-monetary-unit concept when preparing financial statements. For accounting purposes, companies use the historical cost of the building throughout the building's lifetime. However, critics maintain that historical-cost accounting does not provide the necessary information to allow statement users to make intelligent decisions. Is it valid to assume a stable monetary unit when prices — and the dollar's value itself — change over time?

There are two forces simultaneously at work on the price of an asset over time. They are changes in the general price level and changes in specific prices of particular assets and liabilities. These are now discussed in turn.

Changes in the general price level, which is a weighted average of all the prices of goods and services in the economy, lead to changes in the purchasing power of the dollar. When the general price level increases and the purchasing power of the dollar decreases, we call it **inflation**; when the general price level decreases and the purchasing power of the dollar increases, we call it *deflation*. Since World War II, the world has seen almost steady inflation, that is, an almost continuous fall in the purchasing power of the dollar.

Changes in the general price level can be measured by a general price index that assigns a value of 100 to a base year. The price index tracks the movement of prices in the economy over time. A 6 percent price increase during year 1 would cause the price index to rise to a value of 106 (100×1.06) at the end of the year. A 50 percent increase in prices over a six-year period would result in a price index of 150 (100×1.50) at the end of six years.

The most widely used price index in Canada is the **Consumer Price Index** (CPI) published monthly by Statistics Canada. The CPI is based on a representative sample of food, clothing, shelter, transportation and other items purchased by an average consumer. The present base period for the CPI is 1981. Each month the average of these items' prices is compared to their prices the preceding month, and a new price index is computed. The CPI, based on 1981 as 100, was 33.1 in 1964, indicating that prices tripled from 1964 to 1981. The CPI was 154.3 at the end of 1989, an increase of 54.3 percent over 1981.

As the CPI increases, the purchasing power of a dollar decreases, and it becomes more and more difficult to compare assets acquired in different years. For example, it is difficult to compare the cost of an asset bought in 19X1, when the CPI was at, say 120, with an asset that was purchased five years later in 19X6 when the CPI was at, say 140.

In order to make financial data comparable between years when inflation occurs, we restate amounts into **constant dollars**. We call dollars stated in terms of current purchasing power **nominal dollars**. We calculate constant dollars by using one year, for example, 19X1, as the base and deflating the dollars of the other year, for example, 19X6, by multiplying them by the CPI for 19X6 divided by the CPI for 19X1. Suppose Cathy Hanna bought 1 hectare of land for $2,000 in 19X1 (when the index was 120) and is considering buying a second hectare adjoining it in 19X6 (when the index is 140). The second hectare is for sale for $2,600. Cathy would compare the two prices by calculating the price of the second hectare in terms of constant or 19X1 dollars [$2,229 ($2,600 × (120/140))] and then comparing them; the first hecatre cost her $2,000 in 19X1 dollars.

Another way to describe inflation is in terms of decreases in the purchasing power of the dollar. A dollar today will buy less meat, less gasoline, less laundering for shirts and less of most other goods and services than a dollar would buy in 1981.

Changes in specific prices are caused by a variety of factors in addition to changes in the purchasing power of the dollar. The development of new technology can lead to falling prices for particular products. For example, computers and compact disc players have fallen in price over the past several years, in part, because of new technology. Market conditions can effect specific prices. A drought can lead to higher prices for grain because a shortage results, while a bumper crop can lead to a fall in prices.

> ### OBJECTIVE 5
> Discuss the effects of changes in the purchasing power of the dollar and of changes in specific prices of assets and liabilities

The specific price of an asset may also be described as its **current value**. Specific prices can be measured in a variety of ways; two different ways that were suggested in Chapter 9 are *current replacement cost* and *net realizable value*. Current replacement cost is also called an **entry** or buying price while net realizable value is an **exit** or selling price. An entry price is the amount of cash required to buy an asset that is similar to the asset being valued. An exit price is amount of cash that would be received from selling the asset, that is, the selling price less the cost of selling the asset.

Assume that Brehme Inc. bought land 20 years ago in June, 1970 for $500,000; the land was to be used for a planned expansion of the company's manufacturing facilities. Assume that inflation and an increase in demand for land have pushed the price of the land to $2,500,000. The specific price of the land increased by $2,000,000 ($2,500,000 – $500,000). The Consumer Price Index (based on 1981 as 100) was 41.0 in 1970 and is 157.8 in June, 1990.

The increase in the price of the land has two components: a *fictitious* component caused by inflation and a *real* component. The fictitious component is called fictitious because it is caused only by a decline in the purchasing power of the dollar; it represents no real change in the value of the asset. Thus you need $1.58 in 1990 dollars to buy what you could have bought for $.41 in 1970. The real increase is the difference between the increase in the specific price and the fictitious increase.

The fictitious gain is calculated by subtracting the historic cost from the inflation-adjusted cost:

$$[(\$500,000 \times (157.8/41.0)) - \$500,000] = \$1,424,390$$

The real gain is calculated by subtracting this amount from the increase in the specific price:

Specific price change............................	$2,000,000
Fictitious gain caused by inflation	1,424,390
Real Gain......................................	$ 575,610

By investing in the land in 1970, Brehme Inc. is $575,610, 1990 dollars better off in terms of general purchasing power than it was in 1970. Note that most of the specific price gain is illusory; it was caused by a decline in the purchasing power of the dollar.

Certain financial statement items, such as inventory, cost of goods sold, fixed assets and depreciation, are affected by changing prices more than others; providing information about the effects of changing prices on them is helpful to users of the financial statements. However, not all assets, liabilities, revenues and expenses are affected by inflation to the same extent. For example, sales are made at a price that accurately reflects current value at the time of sale; the receivable arising from the sale reflects that same current value. Similarly, wages and salaries reflect the current value of the services performed at the time they are performed. For these financial statement accounts, current cost is historical cost.

In the remainder of this chapter, we discuss, first, issues related to the reporting of changing prices and then summarize pronouncements by the Canadian Institute of Chartered Accountants on the effects of changing prices. Next we illustrate the purchasing-power losses that accrue from holding net financial assets (and vice versa the gains from liabilities) when the purchasing power of the dollar is decreasing. The discussion concludes with a consideration of the components of the profit that arise from the sale of inventory when specific prices are increasing.

Reporting the Effects of Changing Prices ————————————

There are three issues that must be resolved when determining how to report the effects of changing prices. Section 4510A of the *CICA Handbook* describes the three issues as follows:

1. Which attribute of the financial statement elements should be measured and reported?
2. Which capital maintenance concept should be followed?
3. What unit of measurement should be used?

The three issues are discussed below.

> **OBJECTIVE 6**
> Discuss the issues that must be resolved in determining how to report the effects of changing prices

Attribute of Financial Statement Elements   You learned in Chapter 12 that the elements of financial statements include assets, liabilities, revenue and expenses. The attribute to be measured could be, among others, the historical cost of the element or its current value. Remember that among the possible definitions of the current value of an asset are its buying price or its selling price. As you learned in Chapter 1 and again in Chapter 12, accountants usually use historical cost in preparing financial statements according to GAAP.

Capital Maintenance   A company must maintain its capital (that is, owner's equity) if it is to continue in operation. In other words, it should not pay out to its owners more than it earns as income. This is especially true in a period of rapidly rising prices. As is illustrated below, the concept of **capital maintenance** suggests that income can be earned only after capital is maintained. In the three examples that follow we will consider measuring income under the three different capital maintenance concepts most commonly favoured by accountants:

1. *Maintenance of financial capital in nominal dollars.* Financial capital is maintained in nominal dollars if the historical cost owner's equity is the same at the end of the period as it was at the beginning. Financial statements prepared under the historical cost principle are concerned with the maintenance of financial capital in nominal dollars. If they show owner's equity (ignoring dividends and capital transactions) at the end of the period is equal to owner's equity at the beginning of the period, financial capital has been maintained; if owner's equity is greater than owner's equity at the beginning of the period, income has been earned and is taken to be equal in amount to the increase.

   Suppose a company begins operations on January 1, 19X1 with cash of $10 and owner's equity of $10. The company buys one unit of product for $10 cash and sells the unit for $15 cash; income earned is $5. Following the historical cost principle, the company's balance sheet would be as follows after the transaction:

Assets		Owner's Equity	
Cash	$15	Owner's Equity	$15

   Opening owner's equity was $10 so income would be $5 ($15 − $10). A dividend of $5 could be paid and owner's equity would be maintained at

$10. The company's income statement for the period would be as follows:

Sales	$15
Cost of goods sold	10
Income	$ 5

2. *Maintenance of financial capital in constant dollars.* The second capital maintenance concept is like the first except that the capital to be maintained is opening owner's equity adjusted for inflation during the period. If owner's equity (ignoring dividends and capital transactions) at the end of the period is equal to owner's equity at the beginning of the period adjusted for inflation during the period, financial capital has been maintained. If owner's equity at the end of the period is greater than owner's equity at the beginning of the period adjusted for inflation during the period, income has been earned and is equal in amount to the increase.

    Suppose the Consumer Price Index (CPI) increased by 10 percent during 19X2. The price adjusted opening owner's equity would be $11 ($10 × 1.10). In order to maintain the purchasing power of its capital the company would have to retain $1 ($11 − $10) of the $5 excess of selling price over cost; the company's income would therefore be $4 ($5 − $1). The company's income statement for the period would be as follows:

Sales	$15
Cost of goods sold	10
Excess of sales over cost of goods sold	5
Amount required to maintain price-level-adjusted capital [($10 × 1.10) − $10]	1
Income	$ 4

3. *Maintenance of operating capability or capital.* This capital maintenance concept requires the entity to maintain its **operating capability** or capacity (that is, the same level of operations as the previous year) before income can be earned. Suppose the purchase price of the product increased to $12 per unit during 19X2. To maintain its ability to operate, the company must be able to replace the unit of product sold during 19X2 at a price of $12. In order to maintain the operating capacity of its capital, the company would have to retain $2 ($12 − $10) of the $5 excess of selling price over cost; the company's income would then be $3 ($5 − $2). The company's income statement for the period would be as follows:

Sales	$15
Cost of goods sold	10
Excess of sales over cost of goods sold	5
Additional amount required to maintain operating capability at one unit of inventory ($12 − $10)	2
Income	$ 3

Income is earned only after operating capacity (in this case $12, the new cost of a unit of product) has been maintained. Note that the maximum amount the company will be able to pay out as a dividend and still maintain operating capacity is $3. The assumption underlying this discussion is that the company wishes to maintain the same level of operations.

The above illustrations are simple; the situation becomes more complex when the company's assets include other kinds of assets and when activities are financed by both debt and owner's equity.

Unit of Measurement   The information reported could be in nominal dollars or constant (price-adjusted) dollars. Recall that:

1. The attribute to be measured in historical cost financial statements is the historical cost of the asset, liability, revenue and expense.
2. The capital maintenance concept followed in historical cost financial statements is the maintenance of financial capital in nominal dollars.

Thus historical cost financial statements, which have been the kind traditionally compiled, use nominal dollars as the unit of measurement. Economists report national income accounts, for example, in both nominal and real or constant dollars.

After decisions have been made about the attribute to be measured, the capital maintenance concept to be adopted and the unit of measurement to be used, a decision must be made on what information should be reported and whether complete financial statements or elements from the financial statements should be reported taking into account changes in prices. For example, as will be discussed below, Section 4510 from the *CICA Handbook* requires disclosure of information about the effects of changing prices on elements of both the income statement and balance sheet but not the complete statements themselves.

CICA Pronouncements on the Effects of Changing Prices ___

Until January 1983, with the exception of a few Canadian companies, annual reports contained only historical cost financial information, financial statements were prepared using the historical cost model. On that date, Section 4510 "Reporting the Effects of Changing Prices" was added to the *CICA Handbook*. The new section suggested that companies, whose shares were publicly traded and who met a size test (had inventories and fixed assets before depreciation of $50 million and total assets of $350 million) *should* issue information supplementary to the audited financial statements reporting the effects of changing prices. The information could be but did not have to be audited.

Companies meeting the size test could but were not required to provide the supplementary information about the effects of changing prices. Most companies elected not to provide it while those that did initially later discontinued the disclosure. The reasons that the Section 4510 experiment was not successful are not clear; two reasons put forward are the decline in the rate of inflation and the cost of the additional disclosures. The seventeenth and eighteenth editions of the CICA publication, *Financial Reporting in Canada*, which is a survey of the financial statement reporting practices of 300 Canadian companies, cover the years 1983 to 1988. During that period, the percentage of companies that were covered by Section 4510 and did report information about changing prices in some form decreased from 57 percent in 1983, 8 percent in 1986, to 1 percent in 1988.[1]

---

[1] *Financial Reporting in Canada*, 17th Edition, Toronto: Canadian Institute of Chartered Accountants, 1987, p. 79, and 18th Edition, Toronto: Canadian Institute of Chartered Accountants, 1990, pp. 92, 93.

A detailed discussion of the requirements of Section 4510 is beyond the scope of this text; the interested student is referred to Section 4510 in the *CICA Handbook*. The discussion that follows is a brief summary of some of the information for which disclosure is suggested. Section 4510 suggests that the information about the effects of changing prices be presented as supplementary information in the annual report that includes the historical cost financial statements. The information to be provided includes:

1. The current cost amount of cost of goods sold and of depreciation, depletion or amortization.
2. The current cost of inventory, of property, plant and equipment and of net assets.
3. The changes in the current cost of inventory and of property, plant and equipment from the previous year end.
4. An indication of how much of the change in the current value of the assets was brought about by changes in the CPI (fictitious gain) and by changes in the prices of the specific assets owned (real gain).
5. The effect on changes in the current cost of assets of the ratio of the company's debt to owner's equity.

In addition, the section suggests that information about purchasing power gains (or losses) arising from holding net monetary liabilities (or assets) be included.

Purchasing-Power Gain or Loss

A company may have a purchasing-power gain from holding net monetary liabilities (that is, monetary liabilities exceed monetary assets) in a period of rising prices; if the company held net monetary assets during the same period, it would suffer a purchasing-power loss. The gain occurs during inflation because the company is able to pay its liabilities with dollars that are cheaper than the dollars borrowed.

What does the purchasing-power gain mean? Suppose you borrow $5,000 to purchase a sailboat. You repay the loan after two years, during which time prices have risen 20 percent. If you are obligated to pay only $5,000 (ignoring interest for the moment), you experience a **purchasing-power gain** of $1,000 ($5,000 multiplied by the inflation rate of 20 percent). The creditor who loaned you the money incurs the corresponding **purchasing-power loss** of $1,000 because the dollars the creditor receives when you repay the loan are worth less than the dollars lent in terms of their command over goods and services. Interest rates are intended to compensate for this purchasing-power gain or loss, but interest is accounted for separately.

The purchasing-power gain or loss depends on the company's monetary assets and monetary liabilities. **Monetary assets** are assets whose values are stated in a fixed number of dollars. This amount does *not* change, regardless of inflation. Examples include cash and receivables. Cash of $1,000 remains cash of $1,000 whether inflation occurs or not. If you hold $1,000 cash during a period of inflation, your $1,000 will buy fewer goods and services at the end of the period. The result is a purchasing-power loss. Likewise, if you sell $1,500 of merchandise on account and you receive the cash after a period of inflation, you receive only $1,500. Holding the receivable results in a purchasing-power loss.

Nonmonetary assets are those assets whose prices do change during inflation. Examples include inventory, land, buildings and equipment. Holding nonmonetary assets does not result in a purchasing-power gain or loss.

Monetary liabilities are liabilities that are stated in a fixed number of dollars. Most liabilities are monetary. As discussed above in the sailboat example, you have a purchasing-power gain if you have a monetary liability during inflation.

The computation of the purchasing-power gain or loss is based on the company's *net monetary position* (monetary assets minus monetary liabilities). If the company has more monetary assets than monetary liabilities, it has **net monetary assets**. If its monetary liabilities exceed its monetary assets, it has **net monetary liabilities**. Most industrial corporations have net-monetary-liability positions and experience purchasing-power gains. Most financial institutions, such as banks, trust companies and insurance companies, have net-monetary-asset positions. They usually incur purchasing-power losses during inflation. A company's monetary assets and liabilities can be determined from its historical-cost balance sheet.

Exhibit 17-6 illustrates one way to calculate a purchasing-power gain or loss. Dajol Ltd. had monetary assets of $450,000 in 19X8 and $520,000 in 19X9 at December 31, its year end. Monetary liabilities were $640,000 at December 31, 19X8 and $812,000 at December 31, 19X9. The CPI was 146.1 at December 31, 19X8 and 153.5 at December 31, 19X9.

The computation of the purchasing power gain in Exhibit 17-6 follows the approach suggested in the appendix to Section 4510 of the *CICA Handbook.* At

EXHIBIT 17-6 *Purchasing-Power Gain*

> **OBJECTIVE 7**
>
> Compute a purchasing-power gain or loss

Dajol Ltd.
Gain from Purchasing Power of Net Amounts Owed
(Purchasing-Power Gain)
for the year ended December 31, 19X9
(thousands of dollars)

	Historical Cost	Conversion Factor	Average 19X9 Dollars
December 31, 19X8			
Monetary liabilities	$640		
Monetary assets	450		
Net monetary liabilities................	190	149.8	$194.8
		146.1	
Increase during year	102	149.8	102.0
		149.8	
			296.8
December 31, 19X9			
Monetary liabilities	$812		
Monetary assets	520		
Net monetary liability	292	149.8	285.0
		153.5	
Gain in general purchasing power from having net monetary liabilities during the year.			$ 11.8

Note: The change in dollar amount of net monetary liabilities during 19X9 is assumed to have occurred evenly over the year.

December 31, 19X8 (the beginning of 19X9), Dajol had a net-monetary-liability position of $190,000. During 19X9 the company increased its net monetary liabilities by $102 and ended 19X9 with a net-monetary-liability position of $292,000. These amounts are in the Historical Cost column. The net-monetary-liability positions are not comparable because they are stated in dollars of different purchasing power. The beginning position is stated in December 19X8 dollars, which are not comparable to the ending position which is stated in December 19X9 dollars. The reason is that the general price level and the CPI in Canada increased during 19X9, that is, inflation occurred. To compute Dajol's overall purchasing-power gain or loss, it is necessary to compare the beginning and ending positions in dollars of equal purchasing power.

The inflation adjustments of Dajol's net monetary liabilities are in Exhibit 17-6 under the columns Conversion Factor and Average 19X9 Dollars. The conversion factors are used to restate the beginning and ending net-monetary-liability positions to dollars of constant purchasing power. The Consumer Price Index (CPI) is used for the conversion. At the beginning of 19X9, when Dajol had net monetary liabilities of $190,000, the CPI was 146.1. For 19X9, the average was 149.8.

The beginning historical-cost balance is restated into average constant dollars of 19X9 by multiplying the ratio of the current-year average index (149.8) by the beginning price index (146.1). The numerator of the price-index ratio is the current-year average index, and the denominator is the price index that was in effect on the date of the balance. The adjustment of the beginning balance is (amounts rounded to the nearest thousand dollars)

$$\begin{array}{ccc} \text{Beginning} \\ \text{Net Monetary} \times \dfrac{\text{Current-Year Average Consumer Price Index}}{\text{Beginning-of-Year Consumer Price Index}} = \text{Beginning Net Monetary Liabilities Stated in Average Constant Dollars of the Current Year} \\ \text{Liabilities} \end{array}$$

$$\$190 \quad \times \quad \frac{149.8}{146.1} \quad = \quad \$194.8$$

The change in net monetary liabilities during 19X9 ($102,000) is *not* adjusted because it occurred as the company transacted business all during the year. The average price index (149.8) is both the numerator and the denominator of the index ratio, resulting in a ratio of 1.

The subtotal in Exhibit 17-6 ($296.8) is the sum of the adjusted beginning net monetary liabilities plus the increase (or minus the decrease) in net monetary liabilities that arose from the transactions of the year. During 19X9, Dajol *increased* its net monetary liabilities by $102,000. The subtotal of $295,000 is the amount of net monetary liabilities that Dajol would owe if the company's assets and liabilities had just kept pace with inflation during the year.

The ending historical-cost balance ($296.8) is restated into average constant dollars of 19X9 by multiplying it by the ratio of the current-year average index (148.9) to the ending price index (153.5). The adjustment of the ending balance is (amounts rounded to the nearest thousand dollars)

$$\begin{array}{ccc} \text{Ending} \\ \text{Net Monetary} \times \dfrac{\text{Current-Year Average Consumer Price Index}}{\text{End-of-Year Consumer Price Index}} = \text{Ending Net Monetary Liabilities Stated in Average Constant Dollars of the Current Year} \\ \text{Liabilities} \end{array}$$

$$\$292 \quad \times \quad \frac{149.8}{153.5} \quad = \quad \$285.0$$

The purchasing-power gain can now be computed. Its amount is determined by subtracting the ending adjusted net-monetary-liability balance ($285,000) from the subtotal ($296,800). If Dajol had just kept pace with general inflation during 19X9, its net-monetary-liability position would have been $296,800. But at year end, the company's net monetary liabilities are only $285,000. The result is a purchasing-power gain of $11,800. Dajol's gain resulted primarily from (1) inflation during 19X9 and (2) the company's net-monetary-liability position during the year. If the company had had more monetary assets than liabilities during the year and there had been inflation, the company would have experienced a purchasing-power loss.

The purchasing-power gain computation is useful for determining how well the entity is managing its monetary position during inflation. Purchasing-power gain (or loss) can be applied to individual persons as well as businesses of all sizes.

Trading Gains and Holding Gains

In order to simplify the discussion in this section, we assume that there is no change in the purchasing power of the dollar in the illustrations provided below. In this way, we can focus on the trading gain and the holding gain.

A company that sells a unit of product for more than it paid for it in a period of rising prices earns a profit which has two components. Part of the profit arises from selling the product; it is called a **trading gain**. The balance of the profit arises from holding the product in inventory; it is called a **holding gain**. Todd's Cycle and Sports Ltd. buys one bicycle for $100, holds it for six months, and sells it for $180. During the six months, the cost to Todd of replacing the bicycle in inventory (or entry price) increases to $120; $120 is the amount Todd must pay to replace the bicycle that was sold. The total profit on the transaction was $80 ($180 − $100). The profit can be broken down as follows:

> **OBJECTIVE 8**
> Understand the two components of profit on sales when specific prices are changing

Selling price	$180 ⎫	Trading gain	$60
Replacement cost	120 ⎬		
Original cost	100 ⎭	Holding gain	20

The trading profit arose from the sale of the bicycle while the holding profit arose from holding the bicycle while its replacement cost price rose from $100 to $120. The total profit ($80) is the amount we normally would recognize on the income statement; it is not broken down into components as we have done in the example.

The notion of earning a profit from simply holding an item in inventory may be difficult to grasp. Imagine two companies that sell Big Boom portable stereos. Company A buys one stereo on January 1, 19X1, from the manufacturer for $300, while Company B buys the same model from the same manufacturer for $350 on June 30, 19X1 (the cost price has increased to $350 because of an increase in the cost of components of the stereo). Both companies sell their stereos to customers on July 1, 19X1 for $500. Company A earns a total profit of $200; $50 ($350 − $300) is a holding profit, while the trading profit is $150 ($500 − $350). Company B earns a total profit of $150 ($500 − $350); there is no holding profit because Company B did not hold (own) the stereo while its cost price increased. You have probably noticed that we have assumed that the selling price increased as the cost price increased so that both companies sold the stereos for $500.

Companies that expect an increase in the replacement cost of inventory may try to earn a holding gain by purchasing more than is immediately needed. Of course, there are costs to buying the extra inventory, extra insurance coverage, extra storage costs and, perhaps, borrowing costs. If the holding gain exceeds these costs, then the decision to buy the extra inventory is sound. The situation may be complicated by the fact that there may be a change in general prices (inflation) during the holding period that may erode the potential holding gain.

Summary

Investments are classified as short term or long term. *Short-term investments* are liquid, and the investor intends to convert them to cash within one year or less or to use them to pay a current liability. All other investments are *long term*.

Different methods are used to account for stock investments, depending on the investor's degree of influence over the investee. All investments are recorded initially at *cost*. Short-term investments are accounted for by the cost method (with lower-of-cost-or-market). These investments are reported on the balance sheet at the lower of their cost or current market (LCM) value.

Long-term investments of less than 20 percent of the investee's stock are also accounted for using the cost method. The *equity* method is used to account for investments of between 20 and 50 percent of the investee company's stock. Such an investment enables the investor to significantly influence the investee's activities. Investee income is recorded by the investor by debiting the Investment account and crediting an account entitled Equity-Method Investment Revenue. The investor records receipt of dividends from the investee by crediting the Investment account.

Ownership of more than 50 percent of the voting stock creates a parent-subsidiary relationship, and the *consolidation* method must be used. Because the parent has control over the subsidiary, the subsidiary's financial statements are included in the consolidated statements of the parent company. Two features of consolidation accounting are (1) addition of the parent and subsidiary accounts to prepare the parent's consolidated statements and (2) elimination of intercompany items. When a parent owns less than 100 percent of the subsidiary's stock, the portion owned by outside investors is called *minority interest*. Purchase of a controlling interest at a cost greater than the fair value of the subsidiary's net assets creates an intangible asset called *goodwill*. A consolidation work sheet is used to prepare the consolidated financial statements.

Accounting for changing prices can include recognizing either or both of the effects of changes in the general price level, as indicated by a price index such as the *Consumer Price Index* (CPI), and changes in the prices of specific assets.

Consideration of which *attribute* to be measured, which *capital maintenance concept* to be followed and which *unit of measurement* to be used must be resolved in determining how to measure income and financial position under conditions of changing prices. Reporting of the effects of changing prices is not mandatory in Canada and, at this time, few companies do it.

Companies that have net monetary liabilities during a period of inflation will earn a *purchasing-power gain*, while companies that have net monetary assets will suffer a *purchasing-power loss*. Profit on sales during a period of rising prices consists of a *trading gain* and a *holding gain*; the latter, which is based on changes in buying prices, can be partly real and partly fictitious.

Self-Study Questions

Test your understanding of the chapter by marking the best answer for each of the following questions:

1. Short-term investments are reported on the balance sheet *(p. 705)*
    a. Immediately after cash
    b. Immediately after accounts receivable
    c. Immediately after inventory
    d. Immediately after current assets

2. Byforth, Inc. distributes a 10 percent stock dividend. An investor who owns Byforth stock should *(p. 706)*
   a. Debit Investment and credit Dividend Revenue for the book value of the stock received in the dividend distribution
   b. Debit Investment and credit Dividend Revenue for the market value of the stock received in the dividend distribution
   c. Debit Cash and credit Investment for the market value of the stock received in the dividend distribution
   d. Make a memorandum entry to record the new cost per share of Byforth stock held

3. Short-term investments are reported at the *(p. 707)*
   a. Total cost of the portfolio
   b. Total market value of the portfolio
   c. Lower of total cost or total market value of the portfolio or lower of cost or market value on an investment-by-investment basis
   d. Total equity value of the portfolio

4. Putsch Corporation owns 30 percent of the voting stock of Mazelli, Inc. Mazelli reports net income of $100,000 and declares and pays cash dividends of $40,000. Which method should Putsch use to account for this investment? *(pp. 709, 710)*
   a. Cost   c. Equity
   b. Market value   d. Consolidation

5. Refer to the facts of the preceding question. What effect do Mazelli's income and dividends have on Putsch's net income? *(pp. 709, 710)*
   a. Increase of $12,000   c. Increase of $30,000
   b. Increase of $18,000   d. Increase of $42,000

6. In applying the consolidation method, elimination entries are *(pp. 712, 713)*
   a. Necessary
   b. Required only when the parent has a receivable from or a payable to the subsidiary
   c. Required only when there is a minority interest
   d. Required only for the preparation of the consolidated balance sheet

7. Parent Corp. has separate net income of $155,000. Subsidiary A, which Parent owns 90 percent of, reports net income of $60,000, and Subsidiary B, which Parent owns 60 percent of, reports net income of $80,000. What is Parent Corp.'s consolidated net income? *(pp. 715, 716)*
   a. $155,000   c. $263,000
   b. $257,000   d. $295,000

8. The Consumer Price Index is useful for calculating the year-to-year change in *(p. 719)*
   a. The current-cost of an asset
   b. The general price level
   c. The carrying-value of an asset
   d. The gain or loss in the current cost of a non-monetary asset

9. Holding a net-monetary-asset position during a period of inflation results in a *(p. 725)*
   a. Purchasing-power gain
   b. Purchasing-power loss
   c. Neither a purchasing-power gain nor a loss
   d. Lower income from continuing operations

10. The issues to be resolved in determining how to report the effects of changing prices are *(p. 721)*
    a. The capital maintenance concept to be followed
    b. The attribute to be measured and reported
    c. The unit of measurement to be used
    d. All of the above

Answers to the self-study questions are at the end of the chapter.

Accounting Vocabulary

capital maintenance (p. 721)	equity method for investments (p. 709)	net monetary liabilities (p. 725)
consolidation method for investments (p. 711)	exit price (p. 720)	nominal dollars (p. 719)
constant dollars (p. 719)	holding gain (p. 727)	nonmonetary asset (p. 725)
consumer price index (p. 719)	inflation (p. 719)	operating capability (capital) (p. 722)
controlling (majority) interest (p. 711)	marketable security (p. 705)	parent company (p. 711)
cost method for investments (p. 706)	minority interest (p. 714)	purchasing-power gain (or loss) (p. 724)
current value (p. 720)	monetary asset (p. 724)	subsidiary company (p. 711)
entry price (p. 720)	monetary liability (p. 725) net monetary assets (p. 725)	trading gain (p. 727)

Assignment Material

Questions

1. How are stock prices quoted in the securities market? What is the investor's cost of 1,000 shares of BC Telephone $4.50 preferred stock at 55¾, with a brokerage commission of $1,350?
2. What distinguishes a short-term investment from a long-term investment?
3. Show the positions of short-term investments and long-term investments on the balance sheet.
4. Outline the accounting methods for the different types of investment.
5. How does an investor record the receipt of a cash dividend on an investment accounted for by the cost method? How does this investor record receipt of a stock dividend?
6. An investor paid $11,000 for 1,000 shares of stock and later received a 10 percent stock dividend. Compute the gain or loss on sale of 300 shares of the stock for $2,600.
7. At what amount are short-term investments reported on the balance sheet? Are the short-term and long-term investment portfolios mixed, or are they kept separate?
8. When is an investment accounted for by the equity method? Outline how to apply the equity method. Include in your answer how to record the purchase of the investment, the investor's proportion of the investee's net income, and receipt of a cash dividend from the investee. Describe how to measure gain or loss on sale of this investment.
9. Identify three transactions that cause debits or credits to an equity-method investment account.
10. What are two special features of the consolidation method for investments?
11. Why are intercompany items eliminated from consolidated financial statements? Name two intercompany items that are eliminated.
12. Name the account that expresses the excess of cost of an investment over the book value of the subsidiary's net assets. What type of account is this, and where in the financial statements is it reported?
13. When a parent company buys less than 100 percent of a subsidiary's stock, a certain type of equity is created. What is it called?
14. How would you measure the net income of a parent company with three subsidiaries? Assume that two subsidiaries are wholly (100 percent) owned and that the parent owns 60 percent of the third subsidiary.

15.   Identify one problem with the historical-cost balance sheet and one problem with the historical-cost income statement that arise because of inflation.

16.   What two assets and what two expenses are most likely to have current values that are different from their historical-cost values?

17.   How do monetary assets differ from non-monetary assets? Give examples of each.

18.   If a company holds net monetary *assets* during inflation, does it experience a purchasing-power gain or a loss? If the company holds net monetary *liabilities*, does it experience a purchasing-power gain or loss?

19.   St. Lawrence Cement Inc. had net monetary liabilities of $113 million at the beginning of 1988, when the CPI was 138.2. The average price index for the year was 141.5. What is the beginning net monetary liability stated in average constant dollars of the current year?

20.   What does the concept of capital maintenance mean? Explain maintenance of operating capability.

21.   If a company charged current-cost cost of goods sold against sales in a period of rising prices, would the company have a higher or lower gross margin than when historical-cost cost of goods sold was charged against income? Would your answer be different if prices were falling?

Exercises

Exercises 17-1   *Journalizing transactions under the cost method*

Journalize the following investment transactions of Chateau Rose, Inc.:

a.   Purchased 300 shares (2 percent) of Madison Corporation common stock at $44 per share, with brokerage commission of $300.

b.   Received cash dividend of $1 per share on the Madison investment.

c.   Received 150 shares of Madison common stock in a 50 percent stock dividend.

d.   Sold 200 shares of Madison stock for $29 per share, less brokerage commission of $270.

Exercise 17-2   *Reporting investments at the lower of cost or market*

Boiestown Ltd. recently reported the following information (not including the question mark) on its balance sheet:

Current Assets	(dollars in thousands)
Cash..	$7
Marketable securities [short-term investments], at the lower of cost or market (note 3)...............	?

NOTES TO THE FINANCIAL STATEMENTS
Note 3. Marketable Securities

	Cost	Market
St. Lawrence Cement common	$16,250	$20,625
Trail Ltd. 7.0% bonds	20,000	14,200
	$36,250	$34,825

Required

Apply the lower-of-cost-or-market method to Boiestown Ltd. short-term investments by inserting the appropriate amount in place of the question mark. Boiestown evaluates its short-term securities on a security-by-security basis.

Exercise 17-3 *Journalizing transactions under the equity method*

Canadian National Railway System (CN) owns equity-method investments in several companies. Suppose CN paid $180,000 to acquire a 25 percent investment in XYZ Corp. Further, assume XYZ reported net income of $120,000 for the first year and declared and paid cash dividends of $70,000. Record the following in CN's general journal: (1) purchase of the investment, (2) CN's proportion of XYZ's net income, and (3) receipt of the cash dividends.

Exercise 17-4 *Recording equity-method transactions directly in the accounts*

Without making journal entries, record the transactions of Exercise 17-3 directly in the Investment in XYZ Common Stock account. Assume that after all the above transactions took place, CN sold its entire investment in XYZ common stock for cash of $240,000. Journalize the sale of the investment.

Exercise 17-5 *Comparing the cost and equity methods for a long-term investment*

Sonar Devices Corporation paid $100,000 for a 25 percent investment in the common stock of El Marko, Inc. For the first year, El Marko reported net income of $84,000 and at year end declared and paid cash dividends of $16,000. On the balance sheet date the market value of Sonar's investment in El Marko stock was $91,000; the decline in market value is assumed to be temporary.

Required

1. On Sonar Device's books, journalize the purchase of the investment, recognition of Sonar's portion of El Marko's net income, and receipt of dividends from El Marko under the equity method, which is appropriate for these circumstances.
2. Repeat question 1 but follow the cost method for comparison purposes only.
3. Show the amount that Sonar Devices would report for the investment on Sonar's year-end balance sheet under the two methods.

Arrange the answer as follows:

Transaction	Equity Method	Cost Method
Investment		
El Marko net income..............................		
Receipt of El Marko dividend		
Investment amount to report on the balance sheet (show work)		

Exercise 17-6 *Elimination entries under the consolidation method*

Assume on December 31 that Walker Financial Consultants Ltd., a 100 percent-owned-subsidiary of Northern Express Corp., had the following owners' equity:

Common Stock........................	$200,000
Retained Earnings	160,000

Assume further that Northern Express's cost of its investment in Walker was $360,000 and that Walker owed Northern Express $45,000 on a note.

Required

Give the work-sheet entry to eliminate (1) the investment of Northern Express and the shareholders' equity of Walker and (2) the note receivable of Northern Express and note payable of Walker.

Exercise 17-7 *Completing a consolidation work sheet with minority interest*

Maxim Ltd., owns an 85 percent interest in Ultra Corporation. Complete the following consolidation work sheet:

Assets	Maxim Ltd.	Ultra Corporation
Cash	19,000	14,000
Accounts receivable, net	82,000	53,000
Note receivable from Maxim	—	12,000
Inventory.........................	114,000	77,000
Investment in Ultra	85,000	—
Plant assets, net	186,000	129,000
Other assets	22,000	8,000
Total	508,000	293,000

Liabilities and Equities		
Accounts payable...................	39,000	26,000
Notes payable.....................	47,000	36,000
Other liabilities....................	52,000	131,000
Common stock	200,000	80,000
Retained earnings	170,000	20,000
Minority interest	—	—
Total	508,000	293,000

Exercise 17-8 *Issues in inflation accounting*

The two problems that follow are not related:

a. Hanna Corp. sells bicycles. A CCM mountain bike was purchased for $240 and resold for $480 some months later when the cost price had increased to $320.

Required

Calculate the trading gain and the holding gain realized by Hanna on the sale of the bicycle.

b. Carter Ltd.'s accountant advised the president that the current-cost of a printing press owned by the company had increased in price by 17 percent to $117,000 during the year. The accountant further advised that the consumer price index had increased by 4.4 percent during the same period.

Required

Calculate how much of the increase was fictitious and how much was real.

Exercise 17-9 *Computing a purchasing-power gain or loss*

Loblaw Companies Limited, Canada's largest food distributor, had monetary assets of $192.1 million at December 31, 1988. Monetary liabilities were $1,259.0 million. Monetary assets were $281.6 million at December 31, 1987, while monetary liabilities totalled $1,221.5 million. The consumer price index was 146.1 at December 31, 1988 and 138.2 at December 31, 1987. The average CPI for the year was 142.2.

Required

Did Loblaw Companies have a purchasing-power gain or a purchasing-power loss during 1988? Compute Loblaw Companies purchasing-power gain (or loss).

Exercise 17-10 *Calculating income under the three capital maintenance concepts*

Boritz Cycle Corp. imports and sells mountain bikes. At December 31, 19X2, Boritz had 1,000 bicycles on hand that had cost $280 each; owner's equity was $42,800. The consumer price index was 132.4.

During 19X3, Boritz Cycle sold the 1,000 bicycles for $430 each and purchased 1,000 new bicycles for $320 each. The total of all other expenses of Boritz Cycle for the year was $90,000. The consumer price index was 138.2 at December 31, 19X3.

Required

Calculate Boritz Cycle's income under each of the three capital maintenance concepts discussed in the chapter. Use the format suggested in the chapter.

Problems   (Group A)

Problem 17-1A *Journalizing transactions under the cost and equity methods*

Imasco Limited, the conglomerate, owns numerous investments in the stock of other companies. Assume Imasco completed the following investment transactions:

19X4

Mar. 19 Purchased 500 shares of ROX Corporation common stock as a short-term investment, paying 22½ per share plus brokerage commission of $700.

Apr. 1 Purchased 8,000 shares, which exceeds 20 percent, of the common stock of MIC Ltd. at total cost of $720,000.

July 1 Purchased 1,600 additional shares of MIC Ltd. common stock at cost of $140,000.

Aug. 14 Received semiannual cash dividend of $.75 per share on the ROX investment.

Sept. 15 Received semiannual cash dividend of $1.40 per share (total of $13,440) on the MIC investment.

Oct. 12 Received 50 shares of ROX common stock in a 10 percent stock dividend. Round the new cost per share to the nearest cent.

Nov. 9 Sold 200 shares of ROX stock for 28¼ per share, less brokerage commission of $175.

Dec. 31 Received annual report from MIC Ltd. Net income for the year was $350,000. Of this amount, Imasco's proportion is 21.25 percent.

19X5

Feb. 6 Sold 1,920 shares of MIC stock for net cash of $189,700.

Required

Record the transactions in the general journal of Imasco Limited.

Problem 17-2A *Applying the cost method and the equity method*

The beginning balance sheet of NOVA Corp. of Alberta recently included:

> Investments $768,308,000

Investments refers to long-term investments accounted for by the equity method. NOVA included its short-term investments among the current assets. Assume the company completed the following investment transactions during the year:

Jan. 3   Purchased 5,000 shares of common stock as a short-term investment, pay-ing 9¼ per share plus brokerage commission of $1,350. Debit Short-Term Investments.

4   Purchased new long-term investment in affiliate at cost of $408,000. Debit Investments.

May 14   Received semiannual cash dividend of $.40 per share on the short-term investment purchased January 3.

June 15   Received cash dividend of $21,000 from affiliated company.

Aug. 28   Sold 1,000 shares of the short-term investment (purchased on January 3) for 11¼ per share, less brokerage commission of $750.

Oct. 24   Sold other short-term investments for $226,000, less brokerage commission of $11,400. Cost of these investments was $231,800.

Dec. 15   Received cash dividend of $23,000 from affiliated company.

31   Received annual reports from affiliated companies. Their total net income for the year was $740,000. Of this amount, NOVA's proportion is 30 percent.

Required

1.   Record the transactions in the general journal of NOVA Corp.
2.   Post entries to the Investments T-account, and determine its balance at December 31.
3.   Assume the beginning balance of Short-Term Investments was cost of $356,400. Post entries to the Short-Term Investments T-account and determine its balance at December 31.
4.   Assuming the market value of the short-term investment portfolio is $149,000 at December 31, show how NOVA Corp. would report short-term investments and investments in affiliates on the ending balance sheet. NOVA compares total portfolio cost to total portfolio market value in determining the lower of cost or market. Use the following format:

Cash .... $XXX
Short-term investments, at lower of cost or market (cost, $___) ....
Accounts receivable XXX
$\begin{cases}\end{cases}$ $\begin{cases}\end{cases}$
Total current assets XXX
Investments .... ___

Problem 17-3A *Preparing a consolidated balance sheet; no minority interest*

Prent Co. Ltd. paid $179,000 to acquire all the common stock of Stratford Corporation, and Stratford owes Prent $55,000 on a note payable. Immediately after the purchase on May 31, 19X7, the two companies' balance sheets were as follows:

Assets	Prent Co. Ltd.	Stratford Corporation
Cash..............................	$ 18,000	$ 14,000
Accounts receivable, net	64,000	43,000
Note receivable from Stratford	55,000	—
Inventory	171,000	103,000
Investment in Stratford	179,000	—
Plant assets, net.....................	205,000	138,000
Total	$692,000	$298,000

Liabilities and Shareholders' Equity		
Accounts payable	$ 76,000	$ 37,000
Notes payable	196,000	55,000
Other liabilities	44,000	27,000
Common stock	282,000	90,000
Retained earnings....................	94,000	89,000
Total	$692,000	$298,000

Required

1. Prepare a consolidation work sheet.
2. Prepare the consolidated balance sheet on May 31, 19X7. Show total assets, total liabilities, and total shareholders' equity. It is not necessary to classify assets and liabilities as current and long-term.

Problem 17-4A   *Preparing a consolidated balance sheet with goodwill*

On August 17, 19X8, Marble Corporation paid $229,000 to purchase all the common stock of Granite Inc., and Granite owes Marble $42,000 on a note payable. Immediately after the purchase, the two companies' balance sheets were as follows:

Assets	Marble Corporation	Granite Inc.
Cash..............................	$ 23,000	$ 37,000
Accounts receivable, net	104,000	54,000
Note receivable from Granite	42,000	—
Inventory	213,000	141,000
Investment in Granite	229,000	—
Plant assets, net.....................	197,000	175,000
Goodwill...........................	—	—
Total	$808,000	$407,000

Liabilities and Shareholders' Equity		
Accounts payable	$119,000	$ 77,000
Notes payable	223,000	42,000
Other liabilities	33,000	88,000
Common stock	219,000	113,000
Retained earnings....................	214,000	87,000
Total	$808,000	$407,000

Required

1. Prepare a consolidation work sheet.
2. Prepare the consolidated balance sheet on August 17, 19X8. Show total assets, total liabilities and total shareholders' equity. It is not necessary to classify assets and liabilities as current and long-term.

Problem 17-5A   *Calculating purchasing-power gain or loss*

Specific information from the balance sheets for the years ended December 31, 19X5 and 19X6 for Shen Ltd. is presented below. The information is in no particular order; the amounts shown are in thousands of dollars.

	19X6	19X5
Accounts payable	$37,988	$27,964
Accounts receivable	7,853	6,889
Allowance for doubtful accounts	129	105
Bank indebtedness	—	19,060
Capital stock	10,000	10,000
Cash and short-term investments	3,562	—
Convertible debentures	59,914	60,000
Deferred revenue	1,987	2,345
Goodwill	1,066	1,138
Inventory	47,996	49,089
Prepaid expenses	105	102

The consumer price index was 127.2 at December 31, 19X5 and 132.4 at December 31, 19X6.

Required

Calculate Shen Ltd.'s purchasing power gain or loss for 19X6.

Problem 17-6A   *Calculating income under three capital maintenance concepts*

YDR Inc. imports, sells and installs complex computer systems. The work is highly specialized, and each contract takes almost a year to complete. Because of the nature of the company's business, it owns no fixed assets; instead, all equipment and office space are rented. The company's year end is December 31. At December 31, 19X6, YDR's balance sheet is as follows:

YDR Inc.
Balance Sheet
December 31, 19X6

Assets		Liabilities and Owner's Equity	
Current		Current Liabilities	
Cash	$ 1,000	Accounts payable	$ 7,580
Accounts receivable	18,000	Taxes payable	25,000
Inventory	185,000		32,580
Total assets	$204,000	Long-term debt	70,000
		Owner's equity	101,420
		Liabilities and owner's equity	$204,000

During 19X7, YDR installed the computer system from inventory at Joba Corp. for $619,000; a new computer was purchased for inventory at $225,000. Expenses during 19X7 totalled $260,000; taxes on income were $68,000. The consumer price index was 132.4 at December 31, 19X6 and 138.2 at December 31, 19X7; the increase in the CPI was even over the year.

Required

Calculate YDR's income under each of the capital maintenance concepts discussed in the chapter.

(Group B)

Problem 17-1B   *Journalizing transactions under the cost and equity methods*

ConAgra, Inc. owns numerous investments in the stock of other companies. Assume ConAgra completed the following investment transactions:

19X6

Jan. 2   Purchased 24,000 shares, which exceeds 20 percent, of the common stock of Agribusiness, Inc. at total cost of $640,000.

Mar. 16   Purchased 800 shares of Apex Corp. common stock as a short-term investment, paying 41½ per share plus brokerage commission of $800.

July 1   Purchased 8,000 additional shares of Agribusiness common stock at cost of $200,000.

Aug. 9   Received annual cash dividend of $.90 per share (total of $28,800) on the Agribusiness investment.

30   Received semiannual cash dividend of $.60 per share on the Apex investment.

Sept. 14   Received 200 shares of Apex common stock in a 25 percent stock dividend.

Oct. 22   Sold 400 shares of Apex stock for 30¼ per share less brokerage commission of $450.

Dec. 31   Received annual report from Agribusiness, Inc. Net income for the year was $440,000. Of this amount, ConAgra's proportion is 35 percent.

19X7

Jan. 14   Sold 4,000 shares of Agribusiness stock for net cash of $141,000.

Required

Record the transactions in the general journal of ConAgra, Inc.

Problem 17-2B   *Applying the cost method and the equity method*

The beginning balance sheet of Ranco Limited recently included:

Investments in Affiliates $10,984,000

Investments in Affiliates refers to investments accounted for by the equity method. Ranco included its short-term investments among the current assets. Assume the company completed the following investment transactions during the year:

Jan. 2   Purchased 4,000 shares of common stock as a short-term investment, paying 12¼ per share plus brokerage commission of $1,000. Debit Short-Term Investments.

5   Purchased new long-term investment in affiliate at cost of $820,000. Debit Investments in Affiliates.

Apr. 21   Received semiannual cash dividend of $.35 per share on the short-term investment purchased January 2.

May 17 Received cash dividend of $47,000 from affiliated company.

July 16 Sold 1,600 shares of the short-term investment (purchased on January 2) for 10⅛ per share less brokerage commission of $720.

Sept. 8 Sold other short-term investments for $136,000 less brokerage commission of $5,100. Cost of these investments was $120,600.

Nov. 17 Received cash dividend of $49,000 from affiliated company.

Dec. 31 Received annual reports from affiliated companies. Their total net income for the year was $550,000. Of this amount, Ranco's proportion is 22 percent.

Required

1. Record the transactions in the general journal of Ranco Limited.
2. Post entries to the Investments in Affiliates T-account and determine its balance at December 31.
3. Assume the beginning balance of Short-Term Investments was cost of $293,600. Post entries to the Short-Term Investments T-account and determine its balance at December 31.
4. Assuming the market value of the short-term investment portfolio is $215,000 at December 31, show how Ranco would report short-term investments and investments in affiliates on the ending balance sheet. Ranco compares total portfolio cost to total portfolio market value in determining the lower of cost or market. Use the following format:

```
Cash .....................................................    $XXX
Short-term investments, at lower of cost or market (market, $___) ...........
Accounts receivable  ......................................    XXX
        ≷                                                       ≷

Total current assets ......................................    XXX
Investments in affiliates .................................    ____
```

Problem 17-3B *Preparing a consolidated balance sheet; no minority interest*

Lethbridge Ltd. paid $166,000 to acquire all the common stock of Calgary Corporation, and Calgary owes Lethbridge $81,000 on a note payable. Immediately after the purchase on June 30, 19X3, the two companies' balance sheets were as follows:

Assets	Lethbridge Ltd.	Calgary Corporation
Cash	$ 21,000	$ 20,000
Accounts receivable, net	91,000	42,000
Note receivable from Calgary	81,000	—
Inventory	145,000	114,000
Investment in Calgary	166,000	—
Plant assets, net	178,000	151,000
Total.............................	$682,000	$327,000

Liabilities and Shareholders' Equity		
Accounts payable	$ 54,000	$ 49,000
Notes payable	177,000	81,000
Other liabilities	29,000	31,000
Common stock.....................	274,000	118,000
Retained earnings	148,000	48,000
Total.............................	$682,000	$327,000

Required

1. Prepare a consolidation work sheet.
2. Prepare the consolidated balance sheet on June 30, 19X3. Show total assets, total liabilities and total shareholders' equity. It is not necessary to classify assets and liabilities as current and long-term.

Problem 17-4B   *Preparing a consolidated balance sheet with minority interest*

On March 22, 19X4, Abbott Corporation paid $180,000 to purchase 80 percent of the common stock of Zeta Inc., and Zeta owes Abbott $67,000 on a note payable. Immediately after the purchase, the two companies' balance sheets were as follows:

Assets	Abbott Corporation	Zeta Inc.
Cash...............................	$ 41,000	$ 43,000
Accounts receivable, net	86,000	75,000
Note receivable from Zeta.............	67,000	—
Inventory	128,000	107,000
Investment in Zeta	180,000	—
Plant assets, net.....................	277,000	168,000
Goodwill...........................	—	—
Total	$779,000	$393,000

Liabilities and Shareholders' Equity		
Accounts payable	$ 72,000	$ 65,000
Notes payable	301,000	67,000
Other liabilities	11,000	36,000
Common stock	141,000	160,000
Retained earnings....................	254,000	65,000
Minority interest	—	—
Total	$779,000	$393,000

Required

1. Prepare a consolidation work sheet.
2. Prepare the consolidated balance sheet on March 22, 19X4. Show total assets, total liabilities and total shareholders' equity. It is not necessary to classify assets and liabilities as current and long-term.

Problem 17-5B   *Calculating purchasing-power gain or loss*

Information taken from the balance sheets of Boyle Inc. for the years ended June 30, 19X9 and 19X8 is presented below. The information is in no particular order; the amounts shown are in millions of dollars.

	19X9	19X8
Accounts payable	$12.4	$11.6
Accounts receivable	35.8	32.4
Capital stock	1.7	1.5
Cash and short-term investments........	2.1	2.2
Convertible debentures	15.0	—
Goodwill	1.6	1.7
Inventory............................	14.7	12.8
Prepaid expenses	.1	.1

The consumer price index was 142.1 at June 30, 19X8, and 149.9 at June 30, 19X9.

Required

Calculate Boyle Inc.'s purchasing power gain or loss for the year ended June 30, 19X9.

Problem 17-6B   *Calculating income under three capital maintenance concepts*

Mitchell Ltd. buys plumbing supplies such as bathtubs and jacuzzis from manufacturers and sells them to builders and do-it-yourself stores. The lines that Mitchell carries are considered to be of the highest quality; Mitchell rarely has obsolete stock. The business is operated out of a rented warehouse and office. In addition, all equipment and fixtures and trucks are leased.

The company's year end is June 30. At June 30, 19X2, Mitchell Ltd.'s balance sheet is as follows:

Mitchell Ltd.
Balance Sheet
June 30, 19X2

Assets		Liabilities and Owner's Equity	
Current		Current Liabilities	
Cash	$ 18,000	Accounts payable	$ 46,900
Accounts receivable	67,450	Taxes payable	40,000
Inventory	128,000		86,900
Total assets	$213,450	Long-term debt...........	60,000
		Owner's equity	66,550
		Liabilities and	
		owner's equity	$213,450

During 19X3, Mitchell had sales of $498,000. The cost of replacing the entire opening inventory, which was sold, was $138,000. Expenses of operating the business (excluding cost of goods sold) were $237,000 during 19X3, taxes on income were $63,000. The consumer price index was 105.4 at June 30, 19X2 and 114.0 at June 30, 19X3. Assume the increase in the CPI was even over the year.

Required

Calculate Mitchell's income under each of the capital maintenance concepts discussed in the chapter.

Decision Problems

1. Understanding the cost and equity methods of accounting for investments

Bruce Joyce is the accountant for Dunrobin Inc. whose year end is December 31. The company made two investments during the first week of January, 19X7. Both investments are to be held for at least the next five years as investments. Information about each of the investments is as follows:

a. Forty percent of the common stock of Lonesome Dove Ltd. was purchased for its book value of $200,000. During the year ended December 31, 19X7, Lonesome Dove earned $85,000 and paid a total dividend of $30,000.

b. Ten percent of the common stock of M-J Western Music Inc. was purchased for its book value of $50,000. During the year ended December 31, 19X7, M-J paid Dunrobin a dividend of $3,000. The company had earned a profit of $85,000 for that period.

Bruce has come to you as his auditor to ask you how to account for the investments; the company has never had such investments before. You attempt to explain the proper accounting to him by indicating that the investment in M-J Western Music will be accounted for on the cost basis while that for Lonesome Dove will be accounted for on the equity basis. You realize that he does not understand what you are talking about.

Required

Help Bruce understand by:

1. Defining the two methods of accounting for the investments.
2. Explaining why different methods are appropriate in each of the two situations.
3. Drafting the journal entries to record the purchases and any other entries that are required for 19X7.

2.   *Understanding the consolidation method for investments and inflation accounting*

Indira Agarwal inherited some investments, and she has received the annual reports of the companies in which the funds are invested. The financial statements of the companies are puzzling to Indira, and she asks you the following questions:

a. The companies label their financial statements as *consolidated* balance sheet, *consolidated* income statement, and so on. What are consolidated financial statements?
b. Notes to the statements indicate that "certain intercompany transactions, loans, and other accounts have been eliminated in preparing the consolidated financial statements." Why does a company eliminate transactions, loans, and accounts? Indira states that she thought a transaction was a transaction and that a loan obligated a company to pay real money. She wonders if the company is juggling the books to defraud Revenue Canada.
c. The balance sheet lists the asset Goodwill. What is Goodwill? Does this mean that the company's stock has increased in value?
d. One of the sections of the annual report, not part of the financial statements, reports the "Net increase in current cost over effect of general inflation." What is the meaning of the number reported under this heading?
e. One company reports a "purchasing power gain of $62 million." What does the $62 million represent?

Required

Respond to each of Indira's questions.

Financial Statement Problem

The John Labatt financial statements and related notes in Appendix E describe some of the company's investment activity. The balance sheet and notes 8 and 9 reveal that John Labatt has a number of affiliated companies which are labelled "partly-owned businesses." Can you tell from the financial statements and notes the method used to account for these companies? Note that the equity interest owned ranges from 19.9 percent to 60 percent. (Hint: The income statement shows the method used; since the investor takes up a share of the investees' profit or loss, the method must be the equity method.) The statement of changes in financial position reports that John Labatt increased its investment in affiliated companies.

Required

1. Journalize the following transactions of fiscal 1989. Use the John Labatt account titles, and show amounts in millions rounded to the nearest $100,000.

a. Increase in investment in partly-owned businesses; the total was $30.2 million.

b. John Labatt's share of income from partly-owned businesses. Label this account Equity in Earnings of Affiliated Companies.

c. Receipt of cash dividends of $5.0 million from partly-owned businesses.

Insert the April 30, 1988 balance in Investment in Partly-owned Businesses, and post the foregoing entries to this account. Compare its balance to the amount shown in the financial statements at April 30, 1989.

2. What was John Labatt's balance of short-term investments at April 30, 1989? What is the basis of valuation? Where did you find both pieces of information?

3. What is the only word that appears in the title of all of John Labatt's financial statements? What does this word indicate? Name one company that John Labatt purchased 50 percent of the voting stock of in the year ended April 30, 1989. Name a company or business that John Labatt sold its interest in during the same year. What company does John Labatt own 45 percent of the voting interest?

Answers to Self-Study Questions

1. a
2. d
3. c
4. c
5. c ($100,000 × .30 = $30,000; dividends have *no* effect on investor net income under the equity method)
6. a
7. b [$155,000 + ($60,000 × .90) + ($80,000 × .60) = $257,000]
8. b
9. b
10. d

PART SIX

Using External
Accounting Information

18

Statement
of Changes in
Financial Position

Income statements and balance sheets are anchored to the accrual basis of accounting for measuring performance and financial position. Another major statement, the statement of changes in financial position (SCFP), is required to provide a more extensive picture of performance and position.

Consider some common questions asked by managers, investors and creditors. What were the company's sources of cash during the period? Did operations — buying and selling the company's major products — generate the bulk of its cash receipts, or did the business have to sell off plant assets to keep the cash balance at an acceptable level? Did the company have to borrow heavily during the period? How did the entity spend its cash? Was it busy paying off debts, or were cash disbursements devoted to expanding the business? This chapter discusses the statement of changes in financial position. As its title implies, the SCFP helps explain a company's performance in generating cash.

Cash flows are cash receipts and cash payments (disbursements). The **Statement of Changes in Financial Position** reports changes in cash or cash equivalents classified according to the entity's major activities: operating, financing and investing. The statement reports a net cash inflow or net cash outflow for each activity and for the business overall. The change of the requirements for the SCFP to their present form occurred in 1985 when the CICA issued a significantly revised Section 1540, "Statement of Changes in Financial Position."

While the most common title of the statement is "Statement of Changes in Financial Position," some Canadian companies use the title "Statement of Cash Flow" or "Statement of Cash Flows." Section 1540 does not specify a particular title.

Purposes of the Statement of Changes in Financial Position

The statement of changes in financial position is designed to fulfill the following purposes:

1. *To predict future cash flows.* Cash, not reported accounting income, pays the bills. In many cases, a business's sources and uses of cash do not change dramatically from year to year. Therefore, past cash receipts and disbursements are a reasonably good predictor of future cash receipts and disbursements.

2. *To evaluate management decisions.* If managers make wise investment decisions, their businesses prosper. If they make unwise decisions, the businesses suffer. The statement of changes in financial position reports the company's investment in plant and equipment and thus gives investors and creditors cash-flow information for evaluating managers' decisions.

3. *To determine the ability to pay dividends to shareholders and interest and principal to creditors.* Shareholders are interested in receiving dividends on their investments in the company's stock. Creditors want to receive their interest and principal amounts on time. The statement of changes in financial position helps investors and creditors predict whether the business can make these payments.

4. *To show the relationship of net income to changes in the business's cash.* Usually, cash and net income move together. High levels of income tend to lead to increases in cash, and vice versa. However, a company's cash balance can decrease when net income is high, and cash can increase when income is low. The failures of companies which were earning net income but had insufficient cash have pointed to the need for cash flow information.

Basic Concept of the Statement of Changes in Financial Position

The balance sheet reports the cash balance at the end of the period. By examining two consecutive balance sheets, you can tell whether cash increased or decreased during the period. However, the balance sheet does not indicate *why* the cash balance changed. The income statement reports revenues, expenses and net income — clues about the sources and uses of cash — but still does not tell *why* cash increased or decreased.

The SCFP reports the entity's cash receipts and cash payments during the period (where cash came from and how it was spent). It explains the *causes* for the change in the cash balance. This information cannot be learned solely from the other financial statements.

The balance sheet is the only financial statement that is dated as of the end of the period. The income statement and the statement of retained earnings cover the period from beginning to end. The SCFP also covers the entire period and therefore is dated "For the Year Ended XXX" or "For the Month Ended XXX." Its timing and its position among the statements is shown in this diagram:

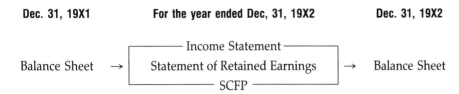

Operating, Financing and Investing Activities _____

Fundamentally, businesses undertake three distinctly different types of activities. First, they must *finance* their operations. That is, they must acquire the money necessary to launch and sustain the business. Think back to Chapter 1. What was the first transaction that we accounted for? It was receipt of cash from the owner to start the business. Those investors who finance the business expect a return on their money, so financing activities also include paying dividends to the shareholders.

What was the business's second transaction in Chapter 1? It was an *investment*. Companies invest in land, buildings, office furniture, equipment and other long-lived assets for use in the business. They pay close attention to their investing activities because the long-term assets they buy determine the future course of the business. Headlines such as "Stelco Investing in New Steel Making Technology" and "Japanese Company Opening New Plant in Cambridge, Ontario" are seen regularly in *The Financial Post* and other business periodicals.

Why do businesses exist? The main purpose is to generate revenues in order to earn a profit. The way a company earns revenues is called its *operations*. For a grocery store, operations include buying and selling food and other grocery products. For a law firm, operations consist of providing legal services for clients. The operations of a company define the type of business it is. For example, Moore Corp. operates in the business forms industry, Harveys in the fast-food business, and Magna manufactures automobile parts.

A good way to evaluate a business is based on these three types of business activities. After the business is up and running, operations are the most important activity, followed by financing activities and investing activities. The statement of cash flows therefore divides cash receipts and disbursements into operating activities, financing activities and investing activities.

Operating activities create revenues and expenses in the entity's major line of business. Therefore, operating activities affect the income statement, which reports the accrual-basis effects of operating activities. The statement of cash flows reports their impact on cash.

Financing activities obtain the funds from investors and creditors needed to launch and sustain the business. Financing activities include issuing stock, borrowing money by issuing notes and bonds payable, and making payments to the shareholders—dividends and purchases of treasury stock. Payments to the creditors include principal payments only. The payment of interest is an operating activity.

Investing activities increase and decrease the assets that the business has to work with. A purchase or sale of a plant asset like land, a building or equipment is an investing activity, as is the purchase or sale of an investment in stock or bonds of another company. On the SCFP, investing activities include more than the buying and selling of assets that are classified as investments on

> **OBJECTIVE 2**
> Distinguish among operating, financing and investing activities

the balance sheet. Making a loan (an investing activity because the loan creates a receivable for the lender) and collecting on the loan are also reported as investing activities on the statement of changes in financial position.

Each of these categories of activities includes both cash receipts and cash disbursements.

Extraordinary Items

Just as extraordinary items are to be shown separately on the income statement, so are they to be shown separately on the statement of changes in financial position. The cash inflow or outflow resulting from an extraordinary item should be shown as part of operating, financing or investing activities. For example, recent financial statements of Intermetco Ltd. show an extraordinary item among operating activities while those of Provigo Inc. and Selkirk Communications Ltd. include extraordinary items with investing activities.

Cash and Cash Equivalents

On a SCFP, *Cash* has a broader meaning than just cash on hand and cash in the bank. It includes **cash equivalents**, which are highly liquid short-term investments that can be converted into cash with little delay. Examples include money market investments and investments in Government of Canada Treasury bills. Businesses invest their extra cash in these types of liquid assets rather than let it remain idle. Throughout this chapter, the term *cash* refers to cash and cash equivalents. Companies usually use cash on the SCFP to describe cash and cash equivalents.

Format of the Statement of Changes in Financial Position

Exhibit 18-1 displays the 19X2 statement of changes in financial position for Anchor Ltd.

As the exhibit illustrates, each set of activities (operating, financing and investing) includes both cash inflows (receipts) and cash outflows (payments). Outflows are shown in parentheses to indicate that payments must be subtracted. Each section of the statement reports a net cash inflow or a net cash outflow.

The largest cash inflow from operations is the collection of cash from customers. Less important inflows are receipts of interest on loans and dividends on stock investments. The operating cash outflows include payments to suppliers and to employees and payments for interest and taxes. Anchor's net cash inflow from operating activities is $68,000.

Financing activities brought in net cash of $167,000. The acquisition of plant assets dominates the company's investing activities, which produce a net cash outflow of $255,000. Overall, cash decreased by $20,000 during 19X2. The company began the year with cash of $42,000 and ended with $22,000.

You may be puzzled by the listing of receipts of interest and dividends as operating activities. After all, these cash receipts result from investing activities. Interest comes from investments in loans, and dividends come from investments in stock. Equally puzzling is listing the payment of interest as part of operations. Interest expense results from borrowing money — a financing activity. These items are included as part of operations because they affect the computation of net income. Interest revenue and dividend revenue increase net income, and interest expense decreases income. Therefore, cash receipts of interest and dividends and cash payments of interest are reported as operating activities on the cash flow statement.

In contrast, notice that dividend payments are not listed among the operating activities of Exhibit 18-1. Why? It is because they do not enter the computation of income. Dividend payments are reported in the financing activities section of the cash flow statement because they go to the entity's owners, who finance the business by holding its stock.

Section 1540 of the *CICA Handbook* does not specify any particular format for the statement of changes in financial position except to require that activities generating or requiring cash or cash equivalents be classified as operating, financing or investing. This text orders the activities, operating, financing and investing, in the order suggested in Section 1540. However, many Canadian companies follow the order suggested by U.S. standards of operating, investing and financing. While either order is acceptable, it is appropriate to begin the statement with operating activities.

Preparing the Statement of Changes in Financial Position: The Direct Method _____

There are two basic ways to present the SCFP. Both methods arrive at the same subtotals for operating activities, financing activities, investing activities and the net change in cash for the period. They differ only in the manner of showing the cash flows from operating activities. The **direct method**, lists the major categories of operating cash receipts and cash disbursements as shown in Exhibit 18-1. We discuss the indirect method later in the chapter.

Illustrative Problem

Let us see how to prepare the SCFP by the direct method in Exhibit 18-1. Suppose Anchor Ltd. accountants have assembled the following summary of 19X2 transactions. Those transactions with cash effects are denoted by an asterisk.

Summary of 19X2 Transactions

Operating Activities

  1. Sales on credit, $284,000.

*2. Collections from customers, $271,000.

EXHIBIT 18-1   Statement of Changes in Financial Position

<table>
<tr><td colspan="3" align="center">Anchor Ltd.
Statement of Changes in Financial Position
for the year ended December 31, 19X2
(amounts in thousands)</td></tr>
</table>

Cash flows from operating activities		
Receipts		
Collections from customers...........................	$ 271	
Interest received on notes receivable	10	
Dividends received on investments in stock..............	9	
Total cash receipts		290
Payments		
To suppliers.....................................	$(133)	
To employees	(58)	
For interest.....................................	(16)	
For income tax..................................	(15)	
Total cash payments		(222)
Net cash inflow from operating activities		68
Cash flows from financing activities		
Proceeds from issuance of common stock	$ 101	
Proceeds from issuance of long-term debt..................	94	
Payment of long-term debt.............................	(11)	
Payment of dividends	(17)	
Net cash inflow from financing activities................		167
Cash flows from investing activities		
Acquisition of plant assets................................	$(306)	
Loan to another company...............................	(11)	
Proceeds from sale of plant assets	62	
Net cash outflow from investing activities..............		(255)
Net decrease in cash		$ (20)
Cash balance, December 31, 19X1		42
Cash balance, December 31, 19X2		$ 22

> **OBJECTIVE 3**
>
> Prepare a statement of changes in financial position using the direct method

3. Interest revenue on notes receivable, $12,000.

*4. Collection of interest receivable, $10,000.

*5. Cash receipt of dividend revenue on investments in stock, $9,000.

6. Cost of goods sold, $150,000.

7. Purchases of inventory on credit, $147,000.

*8. Payments to suppliers, $133,000.

9. Salary and wage expense, $56,000.

*10. Payments of salaries and wages, $58,000.

11. Depreciation expense, $18,000.

12. Other operating expense, $17,000.

*13. Interest expense and payments, $16,000.

*14. Income tax expense and payments, $15,000.

Financing Activities

*15. Proceeds from issuance of common stock, $101,000.
*16. Proceeds from issuance of long-term debt, $94,000.
*17. Payment of long-term debt, $11,000.
*18. Declaration and payment of cash dividends, $17,000.

Investing Activities

*19. Cash payments to acquire plant assets, $306,000.
*20. Loan to another company, $11,000.
*21. Proceeds from sale of plant assets, $62,000, including $8,000 gain.

These summary transactions give the data for both the income statement and the SCFP. Some transactions affect one statement, some the other. Sales, for example, are reported on the income statement, but cash collections appear on the SCFP. Other transactions, such as the cash receipt of dividend revenue, affect both statements. The statement of changes in financial position reports only those transactions with cash effects.

Preparation of the SCFP follows these steps: (1) identify the activities that increased cash and decreased cash (those items with asterisks in the Summary of 19X2 Transactions from p. 752); (2) classify each cash increase and each cash decrease as an operating activity, a financing activity or an investing activity; and (3) identify the cash effect of each transaction. Preparing the statement is discussed in the next section.

Cash Flows from Operating Activities   Operating cash flows are listed first because they are the largest and most important source of cash for most businesses. The failure of a company's operations to generate the bulk of its cash inflows for an extended period may signal trouble. This is not true of Anchor Ltd. in Exhibit 18-1. Its operating activities were the largest source of cash receipts, $290,000.

Cash Collections from Customers   Cash sales bring in cash immediately. Credit sales, however, increase Accounts Receivable but not Cash. Receipts of cash on account are a separate transaction, and only cash receipts are reported on the SCFP. "Collections from customers" on the statement includes both cash sales and collections of accounts receivable from credit sales. Collections from customers are Anchor's major operating source of cash, $271,000 in Exhibit 18-1.

Cash Receipts of Interest   Interest revenue is earned on notes receivable. The income statement reports interest revenue. As the clock ticks, interest accrues, but cash interest is received only on specified dates. Only the cash receipts of interest appear on the statement of changes in financial position, $10,000 in Exhibit 18-1.

Cash Receipts of Dividends   Dividends are earned on investments in stock. Unlike interest, dividends do not accrue with the passage of time. Therefore, dividend revenue is recorded when cash is received. This cash receipt is reported on the SCFP, $9,000 in Exhibit 18-1. (Note that dividends *received* are part of operating activities, but dividends *paid* are a financing activity.)

Payments to Suppliers   Payments to suppliers include all cash disbursements for inventory and operating expenses except employee compensation, interest and income taxes. Suppliers are those entities that provide the business with its inventory and essential services. For example, a clothing store's payments to John Forsythe, Dylex and Far West Mountain Wear are listed as payments to suppliers. A grocery store chain makes payments to suppliers like BC Sugar, Canada Packers and National Sea Products. Suppliers also provide advertising, utility, and other services that are classified as operating expenses. This category *excludes* payments to employees, payments for interest, and payments for income taxes because there are separate categories of operating cash payments. In Exhibit 18-1, Anchor Ltd. reports payments to suppliers of $133,000.

Payments to Employees   This category includes disbursements for salaries, wages, commissions, and other forms of employee compensation. Accrued amounts are excluded because they have not yet been paid. The income statement reports the expense, including accrued amounts. The statement of changes in financial position reports only the payments ($58,000) in Exhibit 18-1.

Payments for Interest Expense and Income Tax Expense   These cash payments are reported separately from the other expenses. Interest payments show the cash cost of borrowing money. Because excessive borrowing can lead to financial trouble, a large amount of interest payments may signal managers to examine this aspect of operations. Income tax payments also deserve emphasis because of their significant amount. In the Anchor Ltd. illustration, these expenses equal the cash payments. Therefore, the same amount appears on the income statement and the statement of changes in financial position. In actual practice, this is rarely the case. Year-end accruals and other transactions usually cause the expense and cash payment amounts to differ. The cash flow statement reports the cash payments for interest ($16,000) and income tax ($15,000).

Depreciation, Depletion and Amortization Expenses   These expenses are *not* listed on the statement of changes in financial position in Exhibit 18-1 because they do not affect cash. For example, depreciation is recorded by debiting the expense and crediting Accumulated Depreciation. No debit or credit to the Cash account occurs.

Cash Flows from Financing Activities   These cash flows include the following:

Proceeds from Issuance of Stock and Debt   Readers of the financial statements want to know how the entity obtains its financing. Issuing stock (preferred and common) and debt (short-term and long-term) are two common ways to finance operations. In Exhibit 18-1, Anchor Ltd. issued common stock of $101,000 and long-term debt of $94,000.

Payment of Debt and Purchases of the Company's Own Stock   The payment of debt (long-term and short-term) decreases Cash, which is the opposite of borrowing money. Anchor Ltd. reports debt payments of $11,000. Other transactions in this category are purchases of the company's own stock.

Payment of Cash Dividends   The payment of cash dividends decreases Cash and is therefore reported as a cash payment, as illustrated by Anchor's $17,000 payment in Exhibit 18-1. A dividend in another form (a stock dividend, for example) has no effect on Cash and is *not* reported on the statement of changes in financial position.

Cash Flows from Investing Activities   Many analysts regard investing as a critical activity because a company's investments determine its future course. Large purchases of plant assets signal expansion, which is usually a good sign about the company. Low levels of investing activities over a lengthy period mean the business is not replenishing its capital assets. Knowing these cash flows helps investors and creditors evaluate the direction that managers are charting for the business.

Cash Payments to Acquire Plant Assets and Investments, and Loans to Other Companies   These cash payments are similar because they acquire a noncash asset. The first transaction purchases plant assets, such as land, buildings and equipment ($306,000) in Exhibit 18-1. In the second transaction, Anchor Ltd. makes an $11,000 loan and obtains a note receivable. These are investing activities because the company is investing in assets for use in the business rather than for resale. These transactions have no effect on revenues or expenses and thus are not reported on the income statement. Another transaction in this category (not shown in Exhibit 18-1) is a purchase of an investment in stocks or bonds.

Proceeds from the Sale of Plant Assets and Investments, and Collections of Loans   These transactions are the opposites of acquisitions of plant assets and investments, and making loans. They are cash receipts from investment transactions.

The sale of the plant assets needs explanation. The statement of changes in financial position reports that Anchor Ltd. received $62,000 cash on the sale of plant assets. The income statement shows an $8,000 gain on this transaction. What is the appropriate amount to show on the statement of changes in financial position? It is $62,000, the cash proceeds from the sale. Assuming Anchor sold equipment that cost $64,000 and had accumulated depreciation of $10,000, the journal entry to record this sale is

Cash...	62,000	
Accumulated Depreciation	10,000	
Equipment......................................		64,000
Gain on Sale of Plant Assets (from income statement) .		8,000

The analysis indicates that the book value of the equipment was $54,000 ($64,000 − $10,000). However, the book value of the asset sold is not reported on the statement of changes in financial position. Only the cash proceeds of $62,000 are reported on the statement. For the income statement, only the gain is reported. Since a gain occurred, you may wonder why this cash receipt is not reported as part of operations. Operations consist of buying and selling merchandise or rendering services to earn revenue. Investing activities are the acquisition and disposition of assets used in operations. Therefore, the sale of plant assets and the sale of investments should be viewed as cash inflows from investing activities.

Investors and creditors are often critical of a company that sells large amounts of its plant assets. Such sales may signal an emergency. In other situations, selling off fixed assets may be good news about the company if it is getting rid of an unprofitable division. Whether sales of plant assets are good news or bad news should be evaluated in light of a company's operating and financing characteristics.

Exhibit 18-2 summarizes the more common cash receipts and cash disbursements that appear on the SCFP.

EXHIBIT 18-2   Cash Receipts and Disbursements Reported on the Statement of Changes in Financial Position

Operating Activities

Cash Receipts	Cash Disbursements
Collections from customers	Payments to suppliers
Receipts of interest and dividends on investments	Payments to employees
	Payments of interest and income tax
Other operating receipts	Other operating disbursements

Financing Activities

Cash Receipts	Cash Disbursements
Issuing stock	Purchase of own shares
Borrowing money	Payment of dividends
	Paying principal amounts of debts

Investing Activities

Cash Receipts	Cash Disbursements
Sale of plant assets	Acquisition of plant assets
Sale of investments that are not cash equivalents	Acquisition of investments that are not cash equivalents
Cash receipts on loans receivable	Making loans

Focus of the Statement of Changes in Financial Position

The statement of changes in financial position focuses on the increase or decrease in cash during the period (highlighted in Exhibit 18-1 for emphasis). This check figure is taken from the comparative balance sheet that shows the beginning and ending balances. The SCFP, which adds up to the change in cash, shows the reasons why cash changed.

Exhibit 18-1 illustrates how the cash-balance information may be shown at the bottom of an SCFP, a common format. Another common practice places the beginning cash balance at the top of the statement and the ending balance at the bottom. However, the CICA in Section 1540 does not require that the beginning and ending cash balances appear on the statement. Because the balance sheet reports these amounts, it is sufficient to show on the SCFP only the change that occurred during the period.

In our example, cash decreased by $20,000. Readers of the annual report might wonder why cash decreased during a good year. After all, Exhibit 18-3, Anchor's income statement, reports net income of $41,000. When a business is expanding, its cash often declines. Why? It is because cash is invested in plant assets such as land, buildings and equipment, as reported in the statement of changes in financial position. Conversely, cash may increase in a year when income is low, if the company borrows heavily. The SCFP gives its readers a direct picture of where cash came from (cash inflows) and how cash was spent (cash outflows).

EXHIBIT 18-3   *Income Statement*

Anchor Ltd.
Income Statement
for the year ended December 31, 19X2
(amounts in thousands)

Revenues and gains
  Sales revenue $284
  Interest revenue 12
  Dividend revenue 9
  Gain on sale of plant assets 8
    Total revenues and gains 313
Expenses
  Cost of goods sold $150
  Salary and wage expense 56
  Depreciation expense 18
  Other operating expense 17
  Interest expense 16
  Income tax expense 15
    Total expenses 272
Net income .... $ 41

Summary Problem for Your Review

Acadia Corporation accounting records include the following information for
the year ended June 30, 19X8:
 1. Salary expense, $104,000.
 2. Interest revenue, $8,000.
 3. Proceeds from issuance of common stock, $31,000.
 4. Declaration and payment of cash dividends, $22,000.
 5. Collection of interest receivable, $7,000.
 6. Payments of salaries, $110,000.
 7. Credit sales, $358,000.
 8. Loan to another company, $42,000.
 9. Proceeds from sale of plant assets, $18,000, including $1,000 loss.
10. Collections from customers, $369,000.
11. Cash receipt of dividend revenue on stock investments, $3,000.
12. Payments to suppliers, $319,000.
13. Cash sales, $92,000.
14. Depreciation expense, $32,000.
15. Proceeds from issuance of short-term debt, $38,000.
16. Payments of long-term debt, $57,000.
17. Interest expense and payments, $11,000.
18. Loan collections, $51,000.
19. Proceeds from sale of investments, $22,000, including $13,000 gain.

20. Amortization expense, $5,000.
21. Purchases of inventory on credit, $297,000.
22. Income tax expense and payments, $16,000.
23. Cash payments to acquire plant assets, $83,000.
24. Cost of goods sold, $284,000.
25. Cash balance: June 30, 19X7 — $83,000
    June 30, 19X8 — $54,000

Required

Prepare Acadia Corporation's statement of changes in financial position and income statement for the year ended June 30, 19X8. Follow the formats of Exhibits 18-1 and 18-3.

SOLUTION TO REVIEW PROBLEM

Acadia Corporation
Statement of Changes in Financial Position
for the year ended June 30, 19X8
(amounts in thousands)

Item No. (Reference Only)			
	Cash flows from operating activities		
	Receipts		
10, 13	Collections from customers ($369 + $92)	$ 461	
5	Interest received on notes receivable	7	
11	Dividends received on investments in stock	3	
	Total cash receipts		471
	Payments		
12	To suppliers	$(319)	
6	To employees.	(110)	
17	For interest	(11)	
22	For income tax.	(16)	
	Total cash payments.		(456)
	Net cash inflow from operating activities		15
	Cash flows from financing activities		
15	Proceeds from issuance of short-term debt	$ 38	
3	Proceeds from issuance of common stock	31	
16	Payments of long-term debt	(57)	
4	Dividends declared and paid	(22)	
	Net cash outlfow from financing activities		(10)
	Cash flows from investing activities		
23	Acquisition of plant assets.	$ (83)	
8	Loan to another company.	(42)	
19	Proceeds from sale of investments	22	
9	Proceeds from sale of plant assets	18	
18	Collection of loans	51	
	Net cash outflow from investing activities.		(34)
	Net decrease in cash.		$ (29)
25	Cash balance, June 30, 19X7		83
25	Cash balance, June 30, 19X8		$ 54

Acadia Corporation
Income Statement
for the year ended June 30, 19X8
(amounts in thousands)

Revenue and gains		
Sales revenue ($358 + $92)	$450	
Gain on sale of investments	13	
Interest revenue	8	
Dividend revenue	3	
Total revenues and gains		474
Expenses and losses		
Cost of goods sold	$284	
Salary expense...	104	
Depreciation expense	32	
Income tax expense	16	
Interest expense	11	
Amortization expense	5	
Loss on sale of plant assets	1	
Total expenses..		453
Net income		$ 21

Computing Individual Amounts for the Statement of Changes in Financial Position

OBJECTIVE 4
Use the financial statements to compute the cash effects of a wide variety of business transactions

How do accountants compute the amounts for the SCFP? Many accountants prepare the SCFP using the income statement amounts and *changes* in the related balance sheet accounts. Learning to analyse accounts in this manner is one of the most useful skills you will acquire from accounting. It will enable you to identify the cash effects of a wide variety of transactions. The following discussions use Anchor Ltd.'s comparative balance sheet in Exhibit 18-4 and income statement in Exhibit 18-3. For continuity, trace the cash amounts on the balance sheet in Exhibit 18-4 to the bottom part of the cash flow statement in Exhibit 18-1.

Computing the Cash Amounts of Operating Activities

Computing Cash Collections from Customers   Collections can be computed by converting sales revenue (an accrual-basis amount) to the cash basis. A decrease in the balance of Accounts Receivable during the period indicates that cash collections exceeded sales revenue. Therefore, we add the decrease to sales revenue to compute collections. An increase in Accounts Receivable means that sales exceeded cash receipts. This amount is subtracted to compute collec-

EXHIBIT 18-4 *Comparative Balance Sheet*

Anchor Ltd.
Comparative Balance Sheet
December 31, 19X2 and 19X1
(amounts in thousands)

Assets	19X2	19X1	Increase (Decrease)
Current			
Cash..	$ 22	$ 42	$ (20)
Accounts receivable	93	80	13
Interest receivable.............................	3	1	2
Inventory	135	138	(3)
Prepaid expenses	8	7	1
Long-term receivable from another company........	11	—	11
Plant assets, net...............................	453	219	234
Total	$725	$487	$238
Liabilities			
Current			
Accounts payable	$ 91	$ 57	$ 34
Salary and wage payable........................	4	6	(2)
Accrued liabilities	1	3	(2)
Long-term debt	160	77	83
Shareholders' Equity			
Common stock	359	258	101
Retained earnings..............................	110	86	24
Total	$725	$487	$238

tions. These relationships suggest the following computation for collections from customers:

$$\begin{matrix} \text{Collections} \\ \text{from} \\ \text{customers} \end{matrix} = \text{Sales Revenue} \begin{cases} +\text{Decrease in Accounts Receivable} \\ \text{or} \\ -\text{Increase in Accounts Receivable} \end{cases}$$

Anchor Ltd.'s income statement (Exhibit 18-3) reports sales of $284,000. Exhibit 18-4 shows that Accounts Receivable increased from $80,000 at the beginning of the year to $93,000 at year end, a $13,000 increase. Based on these amounts, collections equal $271,000: Sales Revenue, $284,000 minus the $13,000 increase in Accounts Receivable. Posting these amounts directly to Accounts Receivable highlights the collections amount, $271,000.

Accounts Receivable			
Beginning balance	80,000		
Sales	284,000	**Collections**	271,000
Ending balance	93,000		

We see that this computation required the income statement account Sales Revenue and the *change* in the related balance sheet account, Accounts Receivable. The amount of cash collections from customers is derived from these accounts. Cash collections — and the other amounts reported on the cash flow statement — are *not* the balances of separate ledger accounts. Instead, the cash flow amounts must be computed by analysis of related income statement and balance sheet accounts, as illustrated in this section.

All collections of receivables can be computed in the same way. For example, the illustrative problem indicates that Anchor Ltd. received cash interest. To compute this operating cash receipt, note that the income statement reports interest revenue of $12,000. Interest Receivable's balance in Exhibit 18-4 increased by $2,000. Cash receipts of interest must be $10,000 ($12,000 − $2,000).

Computing Payments to Suppliers   This computation includes two parts, payments for inventory and payments for expenses other than interest and income tax.

Payments for inventory are computed by converting cost of goods sold to the cash basis. We accomplish this by analysing Cost of Goods Sold and Accounts Payable. The computation of cash payments for inventory is

$$
\begin{array}{l}
\text{Payments} \\
\text{for} \\
\text{inventory}
\end{array}
=
\begin{array}{l}
\text{Cost of} \\
\text{goods sold}
\end{array}
\left\{
\begin{array}{c}
+ \text{ Increase in} \\
\text{Inventory} \\
\text{or} \\
- \text{ Decrease in} \\
\text{Inventory}
\end{array}
\right.
\text{and}
\left\{
\begin{array}{c}
+ \text{ Decrease in} \\
\text{Accounts Payable} \\
\text{or} \\
- \text{ Increase in} \\
\text{Accounts Payable}
\end{array}
\right.
$$

The logic behind this computation is that an increase in inventory leads to an increase in accounts payable that finds its way into a cash payment. A decrease in accounts payable can occur only if cash was paid. By contrast, an increase in accounts payable indicates that cash was *not* paid. A detailed analysis will show the validity of this computation.

Anchor Ltd. reports cost of goods sold of $150,000. The balance sheet shows that Inventory decreased by $3,000. Accounts Payable increased by $34,000. These amounts combine to compute payments for inventory of $113,000: Cost of Goods Sold, $150,000, minus the decrease in Inventory, $3,000, minus the increase in Accounts Payable, $34,000 — a total of $113,000.

The T-account analysis also indicates payments of $113,000 (with Purchases inserted for completeness):

Cost of Goods Sold

Beginning inventory	138,000	Ending inventory	135,000
Purchases	147,000		
Cost of goods sold	150,000		

Accounts Payable

		Beginning balance	57,000
Payments for inventory	113,000	Purchases	147,000
		Ending balance	91,000

Payments to suppliers ($133,000) equal the sum of payments for inventory ($113,000) plus payments for operating expenses ($20,000), as explained next.

Computing Payments for Operating Expenses   Payments for operating expenses other than interest and income tax can be computed by analysing Prepaid Expenses and Other Accrued Liabilities, as follows:

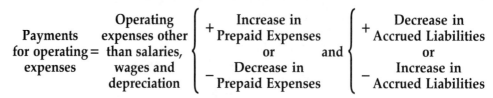

Increases in prepaid expenses require cash payments, and decreases indicate that payments were less than expenses. Decreases in accrued liabilities can occur only from cash payments, and increases mean that cash was *not* paid.

Anchor's income statement reports operating expenses (other than salaries, wages and depreciation) of $17,000. The balance sheet shows that prepaid expenses increased by $1,000, and accrued liabilities decreased by $2,000. Based on these data, payments for operating expenses total $20,000 ($17,000 + $1,000 + $2,000).

This result is confirmed by the T-account analysis, as follows:

Prepaid Expenses

Beginning balance	7,000	Expiration of prepaid expense ...	7,000
Payments	8,000		
Ending balance	8,000		

Accrued Liabilities

Payment of beginning balance	3,000	Beginning balance	3,000
		Accrual of expense at year end.................	1,000
		Ending balance	1,000

Operating Expenses (other than Salaries, Wages and Depreciation)

Expiration of prepaid expense	7,000		
Accrual of expense at year end.................	1,000		
Payments	9,000		
Ending balance	17,000		

Total payments = $20,000 ($8,000 + $3,000 + $9,000)

Computing Payments to Employees   The company may have separate accounts for salaries, wages and other forms of cash compensation to employees. To compute payments to employees, it is convenient to combine them into one account. Anchor's calculation begins with Salary and Wage Expense (an income statement account) and adjusts for the change in Salary and Wage

Payable (a balance sheet account). The computation follows:

$$
\begin{array}{c}
\text{Payments} \\
\text{to} \\
\text{employees}
\end{array}
=
\begin{array}{c}
\text{Salary} \\
\text{and Wage} \\
\text{Expense}
\end{array}
\left\{
\begin{array}{c}
\text{+Decrease in Salary and Wage Payable} \\
\text{or} \\
\text{-Increase in Salary and Wage Payable}
\end{array}
\right.
$$

A decrease in the liability is added because it requires a cash payment. An increase in the liability indicates that the expense exceeds cash payments, so the increase is subtracted. Anchor's salary and wage expense is $56,000. The balance sheet in Exhibit 18-4 reports a $2,000 decrease in the liability. Thus cash payments to employees are $58,000 ($56,000 + $2,000). This is confirmed by analysis of the Salary and Wage Payable account.

Salary and Wage Payable

		Beginning balance	6,000
Payments	58,000	Salary and wage expense	56,000
		Ending balance	4,000

Computing Payments of Interest and Income Taxes   In our illustrative problem, the expense and payment amount is the same for each of these expenses. Therefore, no analysis is required to determine the payment amount. If the expense and the payment differ, the payment can be computed by analysing the related liability account. The payment computation follows the pattern illustrated for payments to employees.

Computing the Cash Amounts of Financing Activities

Financing activities affect liability and shareholders' equity accounts, such as Notes Payable, Bonds Payable, Long-Term Debt, Common Stock and Retained Earnings. The cash amounts of financing activities can be computed by analysing these accounts.

Computing Issuances and Payments of Long-Term Debt   The beginning and ending balances of Long-Term Debt, Notes Payable or Bonds Payable are taken from the balance sheet. If either the amount of new issuances or the amount of the payments is known, the other amount can be computed. New debt issuances total $94,000. The computation of debt payments follows, using balances from Exhibit 18-4:

$$
\begin{array}{c}
\text{Beginning} \\
\text{Long-Term Debt} \\
\text{balance}
\end{array}
+
\begin{array}{c}
\text{Issuance of} \\
\text{new debt}
\end{array}
- \text{Payments} =
\begin{array}{c}
\text{Ending} \\
\text{Long-Term Debt} \\
\text{balance}
\end{array}
$$

$$\$77,000 \quad + \quad \$94,000 \quad - \text{Payments} = \quad \$160,000$$

Rearranging this equation results in the following:

$$-\text{Payments} = \$160,000 - \$77,000 - \$94,000$$

$$\text{Payments} = \$11,000$$

Computing Issuances and Retirements of Stock   The cash effects of these financing activities can be determined by analyzing the various stock accounts. It is convenient to work with a single summary account for stock as we do for plant assets. Using Exhibit 18-4 data, we have:

$$\begin{array}{c} \text{Beginning} \\ \text{stock} \\ \text{balance} \end{array} + \begin{array}{c} \text{Issuance of} \\ \text{new stock} \end{array} - \text{Retirements} = \begin{array}{c} \text{Ending} \\ \text{stock} \\ \text{balance} \end{array}$$

$$\$258{,}000 \ + \text{New Stock} - \quad \$0 \quad = \$359{,}000$$

Isolating new stock gives the final equation:

$$\textbf{Issuance of new stock} = \$359{,}000 - \$258{,}000$$

$$\textbf{Issuance of new stock} = \$101{,}000$$

Computing Dividend Payments   If the amount of the dividends is not given elsewhere (for example, in a statement of retained earnings), it can be computed by analysing the Retained Earnings account. Beginning and ending amounts come from the balance sheet, and the income statement reports net income. Dividend declarations can be computed as shown here, using net income from Exhibit 18-3 and Retained Earnings balances from Exhibit 18-4. We assume Anchor Ltd. had no stock dividends or other transactions that affected Retained Earnings during the year. If, for example, a stock dividend and a cash dividend occurred during the year, total dividends must be separated into stock dividends and cash dividends.

$$\begin{array}{c} \text{Beginning} \\ \text{Retained Earnings} \\ \text{balance} \end{array} + \text{Net income} - \begin{array}{c} \text{Dividend} \\ \text{declarations} \end{array} = \begin{array}{c} \text{Ending} \\ \text{Retained Earnings} \\ \text{balance} \end{array}$$

$$\$86{,}000 \quad + \quad \$41{,}000 \quad - \text{Dividends} = \quad \$110{,}000$$

Keeping dividends on the left-hand side produces the following equation:

$$- \text{Dividends} = \$110{,}000 - \$86{,}000 - \$41{,}000$$
$$\text{Dividends} = -\$110{,}000 + \$86{,}000 + \$41{,}000$$
$$\text{Dividends} = \$17{,}000$$

A change in the Dividends Payable account means that dividend payments differ from the amount declared. In this case, dividend payments are determined by first computing dividends declared as shown here. Then add the amount of any decrease in Dividends Payable or subtract the amount of any increase in that account. The result is the dividend payments figure.

Computing the Cash Amounts of Investing Activities

Investing activities affect asset accounts, such as Plant Assets, Investments and Notes Receivable. The cash amounts of investing activities can be identified by analysing these accounts.

Computing Acquisitions and Sales of Plant Assets   Most companies have separate accounts for Land, Buildings, Equipment, and other plant assets. It is helpful to combine these accounts into a single summary for computing the cash flows from acquisitions and sales of these assets. Also, we subtract accumulated depreciation from the assets' cost and work with a net figure for plant assets. This allows us to work with a single plant asset account as opposed to a large number of plant asset and related accumulated depreciation accounts.

To illustrate, observe that Anchor Ltd.'s balance sheet (Exhibit 18-4) reports beginning plant assets, net of depreciation, of $219,000 and an ending net amount of $453,000. The income statement shows depreciation of $18,000 and a $8,000 gain on sale of plant assets. Further, the acquisitions total $306,000. How much are the proceeds from the sale of plant assets? First, we must determine their book value, computed as follows:

Beginning				Book value	Ending
Plant Asset	+ Acquisitions	− Depreciation	−	of plant	= Plant Asset
balance (net)				assets sold	balance (net)
				Book	
$219,000	+ $306,000	− $18,000	−	value	= $453,000
				sold	

Isolating book value sold on the left-hand side rearranges the equation as follows:

$$-\text{Book value sold} = \$453,000 - \$219,000 - \$306,000 + \$18,000$$
$$\text{Book value sold} = \$54,000$$

Now we can compute the sale proceeds as follows:

$$\text{Sale proceeds} = \text{Book value sold, } \$54,000 + \text{Gain, } \$8,000 - \text{Loss, } \$0$$
$$= \$62,000$$

Trace the sale proceeds of $62,000 to the statement of cash flows in Exhibit 18-1. If the sale resulted in a loss of $3,000, the sale proceeds would be $51,000 ($54,000 − $3,000), and the statement would report $51,000 as a cash receipt from this investing activity.

The book value of plant assets sold can also be computed by analysis of the Plant Assets T-account:

Plant Assets (net)			
Beginning balance	219,000	Depreciation	18,000
Acquisitions	306,000	Book value of assets sold	54,000
Ending balance	453,000		

Computing Acquisitions and Sales of Assets Classified as Investments, and Loans and Their Collections   Accountants use a separate category of assets for investments in stocks, bonds and other types of assets. The cash amounts of transactions involving these assets can be computed in the manner illustrated for plant assets. Investments are easier to analyse, however, because there is no depreciation to account for.

Loan transactions follow the pattern illustrated on pp. 759 and 760 for collections from customers. New loans cause an outflow of cash, and collections increase cash.

Noncash Financing and Investing Activities _____

Companies make investments that do not require cash. They also obtain financing other than cash. Our illustrative problem included none of these transactions.

Suppose Anchor Ltd. issued common stock with a stated value of $320,000 to acquire a warehouse. Anchor would journalize this transaction as follows:

Warehouse	320,000	
Common Stock		320,000

<table>
<tr><td>

OBJECTIVE 5

Name some typical noncash financing and investing activities

</td></tr>
</table>

Despite the fact that this transaction has no net effect on the statement of changes in financial position, Section 1540 requires that it be disclosed on the statement and that both aspects of the transaction be disclosed separately. In this case, the proceeds from the issue of the common stock will be included with investing activities, while the purchase of the building will be included with financing activities. The SCFP should indicate that the two transactions are related. The appropriate disclosure is illustrated in the solution to the review problem on p. 771.

The transaction must be shown in its entirety; it is not appropriate to show only the net effects of the transaction. For example, if the purchase had been for common stock of $300,000 and for cash of $20,000, it would not be appropriate to show only the net effect on cash of $20,000.

Examples of other noncash transactions that should be reported include the acquisition of an asset in exchange for another asset (for example, the trading of property for marketable securities) or for debt and the exchange of shares in the company for debt.

Preparing the Statement of Changes in Financial Position: The Indirect Method _____

An alternative way to compute cash flows from *operating* activities is the **indirect method**. This method, also called the **reconciliation method**, starts with net income and shows the reconciliation from net income to operating cash flows. It shows the link between net income and cash flow from operations better than the direct method. The main drawback of the indirect method is that it does not report the detailed operating cash flows: collections from customers and other cash receipts, payments to suppliers, payments to employees, and payments for interest and taxes.

The indirect method and the direct method are both used in Canada. These methods of preparing the statement of changes in financial position affect only the operating activities section of the statement. No difference exists in the reporting of financing activities and investing activities.

Exhibit 18-5 is Anchor Ltd.'s statement prepared by the indirect method. You will see that only the operating section of the statement differs from the direct method format in Exhibit 18-1.

EXHIBIT 18-5   *Statement of Changes in Financial Position*

Anchor Ltd.		
Statement of Changes in Financial Position: Indirect Method for Operating Activities for the year ended December 31, 19X2 (amounts in thousands)		

<table>
<tr><td>Cash flows from operating activities</td><td></td><td></td></tr>
<tr><td>Net income ....</td><td></td><td>$ 41</td></tr>
<tr><td>Add (subtract) items that affect
net income and cash flow differently—</td><td></td><td></td></tr>
<tr><td>Depreciation ....</td><td>$ 18</td><td></td></tr>
<tr><td>Gain on sale of plant assets............................</td><td>(8)</td><td></td></tr>
<tr><td>Increase in accounts receivable ....</td><td>(13)</td><td></td></tr>
<tr><td>Increase in interest receivable ....</td><td>(2)</td><td></td></tr>
<tr><td>Decrease in inventory ....</td><td>3</td><td></td></tr>
<tr><td>Increase in prepaid expenses ....</td><td>(1)</td><td></td></tr>
<tr><td>Increase in accounts payable ....</td><td>34</td><td></td></tr>
<tr><td>Decrease in salary and wage payable ....</td><td>(2)</td><td></td></tr>
<tr><td>Decrease in accrued liabilities ....</td><td>(2)</td><td>27</td></tr>
<tr><td>Net cash inflow from operating activities ....</td><td></td><td>68</td></tr>
<tr><td>Cash flows from financing activities</td><td></td><td></td></tr>
<tr><td>Proceeds from issuance of common stock ....</td><td>$ 101</td><td></td></tr>
<tr><td>Proceeds from issuance of long-term debt..................</td><td>94</td><td></td></tr>
<tr><td>Payment of long-term debt...............................</td><td>(11)</td><td></td></tr>
<tr><td>Payment of dividends ....</td><td>(17)</td><td></td></tr>
<tr><td>Net cash inflow from financing activities...............</td><td></td><td>167</td></tr>
<tr><td>Cash flows from investing activities</td><td></td><td></td></tr>
<tr><td>Acquisition of plant assets...............................</td><td>$(306)</td><td></td></tr>
<tr><td>Loan to another company................................</td><td>(11)</td><td></td></tr>
<tr><td>Proceeds from sale of plant assets ....</td><td>62</td><td></td></tr>
<tr><td>Net cash outflow from investing activities...............</td><td></td><td>(255)</td></tr>
<tr><td>Net decrease in cash ....</td><td></td><td>$ (20)</td></tr>
<tr><td>Cash balance, December 31, 19X1 ....</td><td></td><td>42</td></tr>
<tr><td>Cash balance, December 31, 19X2 ....</td><td></td><td>$ 22</td></tr>
</table>

OBJECTIVE 6

Prepare a statement of changes in financial position using the indirect method

Logic behind the Indirect Method

The operating section of the statement begins with net income, taken directly from the income statement. A series of additions and subtractions follows. These are labeled "Add (subtract) items that affect net income and cash flow differently." In this section, we discuss those items.

Depreciation, Depletion and Amortization Expenses   It is necessary to add these noncash expenses back to net income when determining cash flow from operations. Let us see why. Depreciation is recorded as follows:

Depreciation Expense	18,000	
Accumulated Depreciation		18,000

This entry contains no debit or credit to Cash, so depreciation expense has no cash effect. However, depreciation is deducted from revenues in the computation of income. Therefore, in going from net income to cash flow from operations, we add depreciation back to net income. The addback simply cancels the earlier deduction. The following example should help. Suppose a company had two transactions during the period, a $1,000 cash sale and depreciation expense of $300. Net income is $700 ($1,000 – $300). Cash flow from operations is $1,000. To go from net income ($700) to cash flow ($1,000), we must add the depreciation amount of $300.

All expenses with no cash effects are added back to net income on the cash flow statement. Depletion and amortization are two other examples.

Gains and Losses on the Sale of Assets   Sales of plant assets are investing activities on the cash flow statement. A gain or loss on the sale is an adjustment to income. Exhibit 18-5 includes an adjustment for a gain. Recall that equipment with a book value of $54,000 was sold for $62,000, producing a gain of $8,000. The way to learn how to treat an item on the statement of changes in financial position is to examine the journal entry that recorded it, as discussed on p. 755.

The $8,000 gain is reported on the income statement and, therefore, is included in net income. However, the cash receipt from the sale is $62,000, which includes the gain. To avoid counting the gain twice, we need to remove its effect from income and report the cash receipt of $62,000 in the investing-activities section of the statement. Starting with net income, we subtract the gain. This deduction removes the gain's earlier effect on income. The sale of plant assets is reported as a $62,000 cash receipt from an investing activity, as shown in Exhibits 18-1 and 18-5.

A loss on the sale of plant assets is also an adjustment to net income on the SCFP. However, a loss is added back to income to compute cash flow from operations. The sale proceeds are reported under investing activities.

Changes in the Current Asset and Current Liability Accounts   Most current assets and current liabilities result from operating activities. Accounts receivable result from sales, inventory generates revenues, and prepaid expenses are used up in operations. On the liability side, accounts payable are incurred to buy inventory, and accrued liabilities relate to salaries, utilities and other expenses. Changes in these current accounts are reported as adjustments to net income on the statement of changes in financial position. The following rules apply:

1. An *increase* in a current asset other than cash is subtracted from net income to compute cash flow from operations. Suppose a company makes a sale. Income is increased by the sale amount. However, collection of less than the full amount leaves Accounts Receivable with an increase. To compute the impact of revenue on the cash flow amount, it is necessary to subtract the $13,000 increase in Accounts Receivable from net income in Exhibit 18-5. The same logic applies to the other current assets. If they increase during the period, subtract the increase from net income.

2. A *decrease* in a current asset other than cash is added to net income. For example, suppose Accounts Receivable's balance decreased by $4,000 during the period. Cash receipts cause the Accounts Receivable balance to decrease, so decreases in Accounts Receivable and the other current assets are added to net income.

3. A *decrease* in a current liability is subtracted from net income. The payment of a current liability causes it to decrease, so decreases in current liabilities are subtracted from net income. For example, in Exhibit 18-5, the $2,000 decrease

in Accrued Liabilities is subtracted from net income to compute net cash inflow from operating activities.

4. An *increase* in a current liability is added to net income. Suppose Accrued Liabilities increased during the year. This can occur only if cash is not spent to pay this liability, which means that cash payments are less than the related expense. Thus increases in current liabilities are added to net income.

The computation of net cash inflow or net cash outflow from *operating* activities by the indirect method takes a path that is very different from the computation by the direct method. However, the two methods arrive at the same amount of net cash flow. This is shown in Exhibits 18-1 and 18-6, which report a net cash inflow of $68,000.

EXHIBIT 18-6 *Statement of Changes in Financial Position*

The Oshawa Group Limited Consolidated Statement of Changes in Financial Position for the year ended January 29, 1989 (in thousands of dollars)	
	1989 **(53 weeks)**
Cash provided from—	
Operating activities	
Net earnings	$ 56,870
Charges to earnings not affecting cash	
Depreciation and amortization	29,022
Deferred income taxes	522
	86,414
Changes in working capital components other than cash	(54,132)
	32,282
Financing activities	
Issue of Class A shares	2,609
Issue of long term debt	885
Reduction of long term debt	(837)
	2,657
Investing activities	
Purchase of fixed assets	(91,680)
Disposal of fixed assets	1,464
Loans and mortgages receivable	298
Other	(1,926)
	(91,844)
Dividends	(11,208)
Change in cash position	(68,113)
Cash, beginning of year	12,561
Cash, end of year	$(55,552)
Represented by—	
Cash and short term investments	$ 3,058
Bank indebtedness	(58,610)
	$(55,552)

An Actual Statement of Changes in Financial Position

Exhibit 18-6 is an example of a statement of changes in financial position for an actual company, The Oshawa Group Limited. The Oshawa Group's activities include IGA Stores, Towers Department Stores, drug stores and wholesale food operations.

Exhibit 18-6, similar to Exhibit 18-5, illustrates the indirect method. Many companies use it because it allows users to more easily reconcile the SCFP to the income statement. There are, however, several differences between Exhibits 18-5 and 18-6. First, deferred income taxes in Exhibit 18-6 have been added back to net earnings in the operating section. Deferred taxes, which are the subject of more advanced accounting texts, arise from timing differences between the claiming of certain income or expenses for income statement purposes and for tax purposes. They do not require current cash payments and are, therefore, similar to depreciation. Second, the changes in working capital accounts such as accounts receivable, inventory and accounts payable are combined into a single number, $54,132, instead of being listed as they are in Exhibit 18-5. Third, dividends are shown as a separate item below investing activities and are not included with financing activities as they are in both Exhibits 18-5 and 18-1. Fourth, cash and cash equivalents are shown to be represented by cash and short term investments and by bank indebtedness.

Oshawa Wholesale's revenues come primarily from the wholesale and retail sale of food. Like many other companies in the retail food business, Oshawa Wholesale ends its fiscal year on a Saturday rather than on a specific date like December 31; in Oshawa Wholesale's case, the fiscal year end is the fourth Saturday in January. As a result of this practice, every few years Oshawa Wholesale will have 53 and not 52 weeks in their fiscal year.

Summary Problem for Your Review

Prepare the 19X3 statement of changes in financial position for Robins Corporation, using the indirect method to report cash flows from operating activities.

	December 31,	
	19X3	19X2
Current assets		
Cash and cash equivalents	$19,000	$ 3,000
Accounts receivable	22,000	23,000
Inventories	34,000	31,000
Prepaid expenses	1,000	3,000
Current liabilities		
Notes payable	$11,000	$ 7,000
Accounts payable	24,000	19,000
Accrued liabilities	7,000	9,000
Income tax payable	10,000	10,000

Transaction data for 19X3

Purchase of equipment.......	$98,000	Issuance of long-term note	
Payment of cash dividends ...	18,000	payable to borrow cash.....	$ 7,000
Net income	26,000	Issuance of common stock	
Issuance of common stock		for cash	19,000
to retire bonds payable	13,000	Sale of building	74,000
Purchase of long-term		Amortization expense	3,000
investment................	8,000	Purchase of stock shares	
Issuance of long-term note		for cancellation............	5,000
payable to purchase patent .	37,000	Loss on sale of building	2,000
Depreciation expense	7,000		

SOLUTION TO REVIEW PROBLEM

Robins Corporation
Statement of Changes in Financial Position
for the year ended December 31, 19X3

Cash flows from operating activities		
Net income		$26,000
Add (subtract) items that affect net income and cash flow differently		
Depreciation	$ 7,000	
Amortization.......................................	3,000	
Loss on sale of building	2,000	
Decrease in accounts receivable	1,000	
Increase in inventories	(3,000)	
Decrease in prepaid expenses	2,000	
Increase in notes payable, short-term	4,000	
Increase in accounts payable	5,000	
Decrease in accrued liabilities	(2,000)	19,000
Net cash inflow from operating activities		45,000
Cash flows from financing activities		
Issuance of long-term notes payable*	$ 44,000	
Issuance of common stock**	32,000	
Payment of cash dividends	(18,000)	
Retirement of bonds payable**	(13,000)	
Purchase of shares for cancellation......................	(5,000)	
Net cash inflow from financing activities		40,000
Cash flows from investing activities		
Purchase of equipment...............................	$(98,000)	
Sale of building	74,000	
Purchase of patent*	(37,000)	
Purchase of long-term investment	(8,000)	
Net cash outflow from investing activities		(69,000)
Net increase in cash.....................................		$ 16,000

---

* During the year, the company issued a long-term note payable in the amount of $37,000 and used the proceeds to purchase a patent.
** During the year, the company issued common stock in the amount of $13,000 and used the proceeds to retire bonds payable in the same amount.

Summary

The *statement of changes in financial position* reports a business's cash receipts, cash disbursements and net change in cash for the accounting period. It shows *why* cash increased or decreased during the period. A required financial statement, it gives a different view of the business from the accrual-basis statements. The statement of changes in financial position helps financial statement users predict the future cash flows of the entity. Cash includes cash on hand, cash in bank and *cash equivalents* such as liquid, short-term investments.

The statement is divided into *operating activities, financing activities* and *investing activities.* Operating activities create revenues and expenses; financing activities obtain the funds needed to launch and sustain the business; and investing activities affect long-term assets. Each section of the statement includes cash receipts and cash payments and concludes with a net cash increase or decrease. In addition, *non-cash investing activities and financing activities* are also included in the SCFP.

Two formats are used to report operating activities. The *direct method* lists the major sources of cash receipts and disbursements, for example, cash collections from customers and cash payments to suppliers and to employees. The *indirect method* shows the reconciliation from net income to cash flow from operations.

Self-Study Questions

Test your understanding of the chapter by marking the best answer for each of the following questions:

1. The income statement and the balance sheet *(p. 747)*
   a. Report the cash effects of transactions
   b. Fail to report why cash changed during the period
   c. Report the sources and uses of cash during the period
   d. Are divided into operating financing and investing activities
2. A new business's first activity is to *(p. 749)*
   a. Obtain financing   c. Earn revenues
   b. Make an investment   d. Incur expenses
3. A successful company's major source of cash should be *(pp. 749, 753)*
   a. Operating activities   c. Financing activities
   b. Investing activities   d. A combination of the above
4. Dividends paid to shareholders are usually reported on the statement of changes in financial position as a (an) *(pp. 752, 754)*
   a. Operating activity   c. Financing activity
   b. Investing activity   d. Combination of the above
5. Which of the following items appears on a statement of changes in financial position prepared by the direct method? *(p. 752)*
   a. Depreciation expense   c. Loss on sale of plant assets
   b. Decrease in accounts receivable   d. Cash payments to suppliers
6. Interest Receivable's beginning balance is $18,000, and its ending amount is $14,000. Interest revenue earned during the year is $43,000. How much cash interest was received? *(pp. 759-761)*
   a. $39,000   c. $45,000
   b. $43,000   d. $47,000
7. McGrath Ltd. sold an investment at a gain of $22,000. The Investment account reports a beginning balance of $104,000 and an ending balance of $91,000. During the year, McGrath purchased new investments costing $31,000. What were the proceeds from the sale of investments? *(pp. 764, 765)*
   a. $22,000   c. $66,000
   b. $44,000   d. $186,000
8. Noncash investing and financing activities *(p. 766)*
   a. Are reported in the main body of the SCFP
   b. Are reported in a separate schedule that accompanies the SCFP

c. Are reported on the income statement

d. Are not reported in the financial statements

9. The indirect method does a better job than the direct method at *(p. 766)*

   a. Reporting the cash effects of financing activities

   b. Reporting why the cash balance changed

   c. Showing the link between net income and cash flow from operations

   d. Reporting the separate components of operating cash flows such as collections from customers and payments to suppliers and employees

10. Net income is $17,000, depreciation is $9,000, and amortization is $3,000. In addition, the sale of a plant asset generated a $4,000 gain. Current assets other than cash increased by $6,000, and current liabilities increased by $8,000. What was the amount of cash flow from operations? *(p. 769)*

    a. $23,000   c. $31,000

    b. $27,000   d. $35,000

Answers to the self-study questions are at the end of the chapter.

Accounting Vocabulary

cash equivalents *(p. 750)*	indirect method *(p. 766)*	reconciliation method *(p. 766)*
cash flows *(p. 747)*	investing activities *(p. 749)*	statement of changes in
direct method *(p. 751)*	operating activities *(p. 749)*	financial position *(p. 747)*
financing activities *(p. 749)*		

Assignment Material _____

Questions

1. What information does the SCFP report that is not shown on the balance sheet, the income statement, or the statement of retained earnings?

2. Identify four purposes of the SCFP.

3. Identify and briefly describe the three types of activities reported on the SCFP.

4. How is the SCFP dated and why?

5. What is the check figure for the SCFP, where is it obtained, and how is it used?

6. What is the most important source of cash for most successful companies?

7. How can cash decrease during a year when income is high? How can cash increase during a year when income is low? How can investors and creditors learn these facts about the company?

8. DeBerg, Inc. prepares its SCFP using the *direct* method for operating activities. Identify the section of DeBerg's SCFP where each of the following transactions will appear. If the transaction does not appear on the SCFP, give the reason.

a.	Cash	14,000	
	Note Payable, Long-Term		14,000
b.	Salary Expense	7,300	
	Cash		7,300
c.	Cash	28,400	
	Sales Revenue.............................		28,400
d.	Amortization Expense	6,500	
	Goodwill		6,500
e.	Accounts Payable	1,400	
	Cash		1,400

9. Why are depreciation, depletion and amortization expenses *not* reported on an SCFP that reports operating activities by the direct method? Why and how are

these expenses reported on a statement prepared by the indirect method?

10. Mainline Distributing Inc. collected cash of $92,000 from customers and $6,000 interest on notes receivable. Cash payments included $24,000 to employees, $13,000 to suppliers, $6,000 as dividends to shareholders and $5,000 as a loan to another company. How much was Mainline's net cash inflow from operating activities?

11. Summarize the major cash receipts and cash disbursements in the three categories of activities that appear on the SCFP.

12. Kirchner, Inc. recorded salary expense of $51,000 during a year when the balance of Salary Payable decreased from $10,000 to $2,000. How much cash did Kirchner pay to employees that year? Where on the SCFP should Kirchner report this item?

13. Marshall Corporation's beginning plant asset balance, net of accumulated depreciation, was $193,000, and the ending amount was $176,000. Marshall recorded depreciation of $37,000 and sold plant assets with a book value of $9,000. How much cash did Marshall pay to purchase plant assets during the period? Where on the SCFP should Marshall report this item?

14. How should issuance of a note payable to purchase land be reported in the financial statements? Identify three other transactions that fall in this same category.

15. Which format of the SCFP gives a clearer description of the individual cash flows from operating activities? Which format better shows the relationship between net income and operating cash flow?

16. An investment that cost $65,000 was sold for $80,000, resulting in a $15,000 gain. Show how to report this transaction on a SCFP prepared by the indirect method.

17. Identify the cash effects of increases and decreases in current assets other than cash. What are the cash effects of increases and decreases in current liabilities?

18. Milano Corporation earned net income of $38,000 and had depreciation expense of $22,000. Also, noncash current assets decreased $13,000, and current liabilities decreased $9,000. What was Milano's net cash flow from operating activities?

19. What is the difference between the direct method and the indirect method of reporting financing activities and investing activities?

20. Milgrom Company reports operating activities by the direct method. Does this method show the relationship between net income and cash flow from operations? If so, state how. If not, how can Milgrom satisfy this purpose of the SCFP?

Exercises

Exercise 18-1   *Identifying activities for the statement of changes in financial position*

Identify each of the following transactions as an operating activity (O), a financing activity (F), an investing activity (I), a noncash financing and investing (NFI) activity, or a transaction that is not reported on the statement of changes in financial position (N). Assume the direct method is used to report cash flows from operating activities.

_____ a.	Cash sale of land	_____ k.	Collection of account receivable
_____ b.	Payment of stock dividend	_____ l.	Issuance of long-term note payable to borrow cash
_____ c.	Acquisition of equipment by issuance of note payable	_____ m.	Depreciation of equipment
_____ d.	Payment of long-term debt	_____ n.	Purchase of treasury stock
_____ e.	Acquisition of building by issuance of common stock	_____ o.	Issuance of common stock for cash
_____ f.	Accrual of salary expense	_____ p.	Payment of account payable
_____ g.	Purchase of long-term investment	_____ q.	Issuance of preferred stock for cash
_____ h.	Payment of wages to employees	_____ r.	Payment of cash dividend
_____ i.	Collection of cash interest	_____ s.	Sale of long-term investment
_____ j.	Amortization of bond discount		

Exercise 18-2   *Classifying transactions for the statement of changes in financial position*

Indicate where, if at all, each of the following transactions would be reported on a SCFP prepared by the *direct* method.

a. Equipment	18,000	
Cash		18,000
b. Cash	7,200	
Long-Term Investment		7,200
c. Bonds Payable	45,000	
Cash		45,000
d. Building	164,000	
Note Payable, Long-Term		164,000
e. Cash	1,400	
Accounts Receivable		1,400
f. Dividends Payable	16,500	
Cash		16,500
g. Furniture and Fixtures	22,100	
Note Payable, Short-Term		22,100
h. Accounts Payable	8,300	
Cash		8,300
i. Cash	81,000	
Common Stock		81,000
j. Common Stock	13,000	
Cash		13,000
k. Retained Earning	36,000	
Common Stock		36,000
l. Cash	2,000	
Interest Revenue		2,000
m. Land	87,700	
Cash		87,700
n. Salary Expense	4,300	
Cash		4,300

Exercise 18-3   *Computing cash flows from operating activities: direct method*

Analysis of the accounting records of Gibson Transfer Company Ltd. reveals the following:

Acquisition of land	$37,000	Payment of dividends	$ 7,000
Payment of accounts		Collection of accounts	
payable	45,000	receivable	89,000
Net income	24,000	Payment of salaries and	
Payment of income tax	13,000	wages	34,000
Collection of dividend		Depreciation	8,000
revenue	7,000	Decrease in current	
Payment of interest	16,000	liabilities	20,000
Cash sales	9,000	Increase in current assets other	
Loss on sale of land	2,000	than cash	17,000

Compute cash flows from operating activities by the direct method. Use the format of the operating activities section of Exhibit 18-1. Not all items are used.

Exercise 18-4   *Computing cash flows from operating activities: indirect method*

Use the data of Exercise 18-3 to compute cash flows from operating activities by the indirect method. Use the format of the operating activities section of Exhibit 18-5. Not all items are used.

Exercise 18-5   *Identifying items for the statement of changes in financial position: direct method*

Selected accounts of Bismark, Inc. show the following activity:

Interest Receivable

Beginning balance	11,000	Cash receipts of interest	40,000
Interest revenue	37,000		
Ending balance	8,000		

Investments in Stock

Beginning balance	0	Cost of investments sold	4,000
Acquisitions	27,000		
Ending balance	23,000		

Long-Term Debt

Payments	69,000	Beginning balance	134,000
		Issuance of debt for cash	17,000
		Ending balance	82,000

For each account, identify the item or items that should appear on a SCFP prepared by the direct method. State where to report the item.

Exercise 18-6   *Computing amounts for the statement of changes in financial position*

Compute the following items for the SCFP:

a. Beginning and ending Accounts Receivable are $14,000 and $19,000 respectively. Credit sales for the period total $81,000. How much are cash collections?
b. Cost of goods sold is $62,000. Beginning Inventory balance is $25,000 and ending Inventory balance is $21,000. Beginning and ending Accounts Payable are $11,000 and $8,000 respectively. How much are cash payments for inventory?

Exercise 18-7   *Computing amounts for the statement of changes in financial position*

Compute the following items for the SCFP:

a. Beginning and ending Plant Assets, net, are $79,000 and $83,000 respectively. Depreciation for the period is $16,000 and acquisitions of new plant assets are $27,000. Plant assets were sold at a $4,000 loss. What were the cash proceeds of the sale?
b. Beginning and ending Retained Earnings are $45,000 and $73,000 respectively. Net income for the period is $62,000 and stock dividends are $19,000. How much are cash dividend payments?

Exercise 18-8 *Classifying transactions for the statement of changes in financial position*

Two transactions of Ferrari's Restaurant are recorded as follows:

a. Cash	17,000	
Accumulated Depreciation	51,000	
Loss on Sale of Equipment	67,000	
Equipment		135,000
b. Land	110,000	
Cash		10,000
Note Payable		100,000

Required

1. Indicate where, how and in what amount to report these transactions on the SCFP. Ferrari reports cash flows from operating activities by the *direct* method.
2. Repeat question 1, assuming Ferrari reports cash flows from operating activities by the *indirect* method.

Exercise 18-9 *Preparing the statement of changes in financial position: direct method*

The income statement and additional data of Hillcrest Electric Company Ltd. follow:

Hillcrest Electric Company Ltd.
Income Statement
for the year ended September 30, 19X2

Revenues		
Sales revenue	$336,000	
Dividend revenue	22,000	$358,000
Expenses		
Cost of goods sold	163,000	
Salary expense	85,000	
Depreciation expense	21,000	
Advertising expense	19,000	
Interest expense	11,000	
Amortization expense — patent	8,000	307,000
Net income		$ 51,000

Additional data:

a. Collections from customers are $3,000 more than sales.
b. Payments to suppliers are $9,000 less than the sum of cost of goods sold plus advertising expense.
c. Payments to employees are $1,000 more than salary expense.
d. Dividend revenue and interest expense equal their cash amounts.
e. Acquisition of plant assets are $141,000. Of this amount, $91,000 is paid in cash, and $50,000 by signing a note payable.
f. Proceeds from sale of land, $19,000.
g. Proceeds from issuance of common stock, $30,000.
h. Payment of long-term note payable, $15,000.
i. Payment of dividends, $11,000.
j. Increase in cash balance, $23,000.

Prepare Hillcrest Electric Company Ltd.'s SCFP. Report operating activities by the *direct* method.

Exercise 18-10   *Reporting cash flows from operating activities: indirect method*

Use the information of Exercise 18-9 and the following changes in the current accounts to report Hillcrest Electric Company Ltd.'s cash flows from operating activities by the *indirect* method. All changes in the current accounts affected operations.

| | September 30, | |
	19X2	19X1
Current Assets		
Accounts receivable	$51,000	$58,000
Inventory	83,000	77,000
Prepaid expenses....................	9,000	8,000
Current Liabilities		
Notes payable	$20,000	$20,000
Accounts payable	35,000	22,000
Accrued liabilities	19,000	21,000

Problems   (Group A)

Problem 18-1A   *Preparing the statement of changes in financial position: direct method*

Athabasca Corporation accountants have developed the following data from the company's accounting records for the year ended July 31, 19X9:

a. Collection of interest revenue, $11,700.
b. Acquisition of equipment by issuing short-term note payable, $35,500.
c. Payments of salaries, $104,000.
d. Credit sales, $608,100.
e. Loan to another company, $35,000.
f. Income tax expense and payments, $56,400.
g. Depreciation expense, $27,700.
h. Collections on accounts receivable, $673,100.
i. Loan collections, $74,400.
j. Proceeds from sale of investments, $34,700, including $3,800 loss.
k. Payment of long-term debt by issuing preferred stock, $107,300.
l. Amortization expense, $23,900.
m. Cash sales, $222,000.
n. Proceeds from issuance of short-term debt, $44,100.
o. Payments of long-term debt, $78,800.
p. Proceeds from sale of plant assets, $49,700, including $10,600 gain.
q. Interest revenue, $12,100.
r. Cash receipt of dividend revenue on stock investments, $5,700.
s. Payments to suppliers, $683,300.
t. Interest expense and payments, $37,800.
u. Salary expense, $105,300.
v. Cash payments to purchase plant assets, $181,000.

w. Cost of goods sold, $481,100.

x. Proceeds from issuance of common stock, $116,900.

y. Payment of cash dividends, $50,500.

z. Cash balance: July 31, 19X8—$53,800
    July 31, 19X9—$59,300

Required

Prepare Athabasca Corporation's SCFP for the year ended July 31, 19X9. Follow the format of Exhibit 18-1, but do *not* show amounts in thousands. Warning: Some listed items are *not* used.

Problem 18-2A *Preparing the statement of changes in financial position: indirect method*

Accounts for LaDue Fashions Inc. have assembled the following data for the year ended December 31, 19X4:

Collection of loan	$10,300	Issuance of long-term debt	
Depreciation expense	19,200	to borrow cash	$21,000
Acquisition of equipment	69,000	Net income	83,600
Payment of long-term debt by		Issuance of preferred stock	
issuing common stock	89,400	for cash	36,200
Acquisition of long-term		Sale of long-term investment	12,200
investment	44,800	Amortization expense	1,100
Acquisition of building by		Payment of long-term debt	47,800
issuing long-term		Gain on sale of investment	3,500
note payable	94,000	Payment of cash dividends	48,300
Stock dividends	12,600		

	December 31,	
	19X4	**19X3**
Current accounts (all result from operations)		
Current assets		
Cash and cash equivalents	$21,700	$34,800
Accounts receivable	70,100	73,700
Inventories	90,600	96,500
Prepaid expenses	3,200	2,100
Current liabilities		
Notes payable	$36,300	$36,800
Accounts payable	72,100	67,500
Income tax payable	5,900	6,800
Accrued liabilities	28,300	23,200

Required

Prepare LaDue Fashion's SCFP, using the *indirect* method to report operating activities.

Problem 18-3A *Computing amounts for the statement of changes in financial position: direct method*

The 19X3 income statement and comparative balance sheet of Custom Trailers, Inc. follow:

Income Statement

Revenues		
Sales revenue		$436,800
Interest revenue....................		11,700
Total revenues		448,500
Expenses		
Cost of goods sold	$205,200	
Salary expense	76,400	
Depreciation expense	15,300	
Other operating expense	49,700	
Interest expense....................	24,600	
Income tax expense.................	16,900	
Total expenses		388,100
Net income		$ 60,400

Comparative Balance Sheet

	19X3	19X2	Increase (Decrease)
Current assets			
Cash and cash equivalents............	$ 12,500	$ 15,600	$ (3,100)
Accounts receivable.................	41,500	43,100	(1,600)
Interest receivable	600	900	(300)
Inventories	94,300	89,900	4,400
Prepaid expenses...................	1,700	2,200	(500)
Plant assets			
Land..............................	35,100	10,000	25,100
Equipment, net	100,900	93,700	7,200
Total assets	$286,600	$255,400	$ 31,200
Current liabilities			
Accounts payable...................	$ 16,400	$ 17,900	$ (1,500)
Interest payable	6,300	6,700	(400)
Salary payable	2,100	1,400	700
Other accrued liabilities	18,100	18,700	(600)
Income tax payable	6,300	3,800	2,500
Long-term liabilities			
Notes payable......................	55,000	65,000	(10,000)
Shareholders' equity			
Common stock	131,100	122,300	8,800
Retained earnings	51,300	19,600	31,700
Total liabilities and shareholders' equity .	$286,600	$255,400	$ 31,200

Custom Trailers had no noncash investing and financing transactions during 19X3.

Required

Compute the following items for the 19X3 SCFP:

Cash flows from operating activities
  Cash receipts
    Collections from customers .... $
    Receipts of interest...

Cash payments
   To suppliers—
      Inventory . . . .
      Operating expenses . . . .
   To employees . . . .
   For interest . . . .
   For income tax . . . .
      Net cash inflow from operating activities . . . . $ _____
Cash flows from financing activities
   Payment of dividends . . . . $
   Payment of note payable (there were no issuances of notes payable) . . . . . .
   Issuance of common stock (there were no retirements of stock) . . . .
      Net cash outflow from financing activities . . . . $ _____
Cash flow from investing activities
   Acquisition of land (there were no sales of land) . . . . $
   Acquisition of equipment (there were no sales of equipment) . . . .
      Net cash outflow from investing activities . . . . $ _____
Net decrease in cash $3,100

Problem 18-4A   *Preparing the statement of changes in financial position: indirect method*

The comparative balance sheet of Highland Recreation, Inc. at December 31, 19X5 reported the following:

	December 31,	
	19X5	**19X4**
Current Assets		
Cash and cash equivalents	$ 6,000	$ 2,500
Accounts receivable	28,600	29,300
Inventories	51,600	53,000
Prepaid expenses	4,200	3,700
Current liabilities		
Notes payable	$ 9,200	$ -0-
Accounts payable	21,900	28,000
Accrued liabilities	14,300	16,800
Income tax payable	11,000	14,300

Highland's transactions during 19X5 included the following:

Retirement of bonds payable		Sale of long-term	
by issuing common stock . . .	$40,000	investment	$ 6,000
Amortization expense	5,000	Depreciation expense	15,000
Payment of cash dividends . . .	17,000	Cash acquisition of building . .	84,000
Cash acquisition of		Net income	42,000
equipment	55,000	Issuance of common stock	
Issuance of long-term note		for cash	60,600
payable to borrow cash	32,000	Stock dividend	13,000

Required

Prepare Highland Recreation's SCFP for the year ended December 31, 19X5. Use the *indirect* method to report cash flows from operating activities. All current account balances result from operating transactions.

Problem 18-5A   *Preparing the statement of changes in financial position: direct and indirect methods*

To prepare the SCFP, accountants for Cartier Corporation have summarized 19X8 activity in two accounts as follows:

Cash

Beginning balance	37,100	Payments of operating	
Issuance of common stock	60,800	expenses.................	46,100
Receipts of dividends	1,900	Payment of long-term debt ...	78,900
Collection of loan	18,500	Purchase of own stock	
Sale of investments	9,900	for cancellation	10,400
Receipts of interest..........	7,700	Payment of income tax	8,000
Collections from customers ...	268,100	Payments on accounts payable	101,600
		Payments of dividends	1,800
		Payments of salaries	
		and wages	67,500
		Payments of interest	21,800
		Purchase of equipment	29,900
Ending balance	38,000		

Common Stock

Purchase for cancellation	10,400	Beginning balance	103,500
		Issuance for cash	60,800
		Issuance to acquire land	62,100
		Issuance to retire long-term	
		debt	21,100
		Ending balance	237,100

Required

1. Prepare Cartier Corporation's SCFP for the year ended December 31, 19X8, using the *direct* method to report operating activities.

Cartier's 19X8 income statement and selected balance sheet data follow:

Cartier Corporation
Income Statement
for the year ended December 31, 19X8

Revenues and gains		
Sales revenue		$251,800
Interest revenue....................		7,700
Dividend revenue		1,900
Gain on sale of investments		700
Total revenues and gains		262,100
Expenses		
Cost of goods sold	$103,600	
Salary and wage expense.............	66,800	
Depreciation expense	10,900	
Other operating expense	44,700	
Interest expense.....................	24,100	
Income tax expense..................	2,600	
Total expenses		252,700
Net income		$ 9,400

Cartier Corporation
Balance Sheet Data

	Increase (Decrease)
Current assets	
Cash and cash equivalents	$ 900
Accounts receivable	(16,300)
Inventories	5,700
Prepaid expenses	(1,900)
Current liabilities	
Accounts payable	$ 7,700
Interest payable	2,300
Salary payable................................	(700)
Other accrued liabilities	(3,300)
Income tax payable	(5,400)

2. Use these data to prepare a supplementary schedule showing cash flows from operating activities by the *indirect* method. All activity in the current accounts results from operations.

Problem 18-6A   *Preparing the statement of changes in financial position: direct and indirect methods*

Henke-Ward Corporations' comparative balance sheet at September 30, 19X4 included the following balances:

Henke-Ward Corporation
Partial Balance Sheet
September 30, 19X4 and 19X3

	19X4	19X3	Increase (Decrease)
Current assets			
Cash	$ 27,700	$ 17,600	$ 10,100
Accounts receivable..................	41,900	44,000	(2,100)
Interest receivable	4,100	2,800	1,300
Inventories	121,700	116,900	4,800
Prepaid expenses....................	8,600	9,300	(700)
Current liabilities			
Notes payable, short-term	$ 22,000	$ -0-	$ 22,000
Accounts payable....................	61,800	70,300	(8,500)
Income tax payable	21,800	24,600	(2,800)
Accrued liabilities	17,900	29,100	(11,200)
Interest payable	4,500	3,200	1,300
Salary payable	1,500	1,100	400

Transaction data for the year ended September 30, 19X4:

a. Net income, $72,900.
b. Depreciation expense on equipment, $8,500.

c. Acquired long-term investments, $37,300.

d. Sold land for $38,100, including $10,900 gain.

e. Acquired equipment by issuing long-term note payable, $26,300.

f. Paid long-term note payable, $24,700.

g. Received cash of $51,900 for issuance of common stock.

h. Paid cash dividends, $64,300.

i. Acquired equipment by issuing short-term note payable, $22,000.

Required

1. Prepare Henke-Ward's SCFP for the year ended September 30, 19X4, using the *indirect* method to report operating activities. All current accounts except short-term notes payable result from operating transactions.

2. Prepare a supplementary schedule showing cash flows from operations by the *direct* method. The income statement reports the following: sales, $349,600; gain on sale of land, $10,900; interest revenue $7,300; cost of goods sold, $161,500; salary expense, $63,400; other operating expenses, $29,600; income tax expense, $18,400; interest expense, $13,500; depreciation expense, $8,500.

(Group B)

Problem 18-1B *Preparing the statement of changes in financial position: direct method*

Chilliwack Corporation accountants have developed the following data from the company's accounting records for the year ended April 30, 19X5:

a. Cash receipt of dividend revenue on stock investments, $4,100.

b. Payments to suppliers, $478,500.

c. Cash sales, $171,900.

d. Depreciation expense, $59,900.

e. Proceeds from issuance of short-term debt, $19,600.

f. Payments of long-term debt, $50,000.

g. Interest expense and payments, $13,300.

h. Salary expense, $95,300.

i. Loan collections, $12,800.

j. Proceeds from sale of investments, $6,800, including $300 gain.

k. Payment of short-term note payable by issuing common stock, $14,000.

l. Amortization expense, $2,900.

m. Income tax expense and payments, $37,900.

n. Cash payments to acquire plant assets, $59,400.

o. Cost of goods sold, $382,600.

p. Proceeds from issuance of common stock, $8,000.

q. Payment of cash dividends, $48,400.

r. Collection of interest, $4,400.

s. Acquisition of equipment by issuing short-term note payable, $16,400.

t. Payments of salaries, $93,600.

u. Credit sales, $553,900.

v. Loan to another company, $12,500.

w. Proceeds from sale of plant assets, $22,400, including $6,800 loss.

x. Collections on accounts receivable, $521,100.

y. Interest revenue, $3,800.

z. Cash balance: April 30, 19X4 — $39,300

April 30, 19X5 — $16,800

Required

Prepare Chilliwack Corporation's SCFP for the year ended April 30, 19X5. Follow the format of Exhibit 18-1, but do *not* show amounts in thousands. Warning: Some listed items are *not* used.

Problem 18-2B *Preparing the statement of changes in financial position: indirect method*

McAlister Overhead Door Systems, Inc. accounts have assembled the following data for the year ended December 31, 19X7:

Collection of loan	$ 8,700	Issuance of long-term note payable to borrow cash	$ 34,400
Depreciation expense	26,800		
Acquisition of building	125,300	Net income	55,100
Retirement of bonds payable by issuing common stock . .	65,000	Issuance of common stock for cash	41,200
Acquisition of long-term investment	31,600	Sale of equipment	19,500
		Amortization expense	5,300
Acquisition of land by issuing long-term note payable	83,000	Payment of own shares for cancellation	14,300
		Loss on sale of equipment . . .	11,700
Stock dividends	31,800	Payment of cash dividends . .	18,300

	December 31,	
	19X7	**19X6**
Current accounts (all result from operations)		
Current assets		
Cash and cash equivalents	$35,200	$22,700
Accounts receivable	59,700	64,200
Inventories	88,600	83,000
Prepaid expenses.	5,300	4,100
Current liabilities		
Notes payable	$22,600	$18,300
Accounts payable	52,900	55,800
Income tax payable	18,600	16,700
Accrued liabilities	25,500	27,200

Required

Prepare McAlister's SCFP, using the *indirect* method to report operating activities.

Problem 18-3B *Computing amounts for the statement of changes in financial position: direct method*

The 19X5 income statement and comparative balance sheet of Casa Loma, Inc. follow:

Income Statement

Revenues		
Sales revenue		$194,000
Interest revenue		8,600
Total revenues		202,600
Expenses		
Cost of goods sold	$92,400	
Salary expense	27,800	
Depreciation expense	4,000	
Other operating expense	10,500	
Interest expense.	11,600	
Income tax expense.	9,100	
Total expenses		155,400
Net income		$ 47,200

Comparative Balance Sheet

	19X5	19X4	Increase (Decrease)
Current assets			
Cash and cash equivalents............	$ 6,400	$ 5,300	$ 1,100
Accounts receivable.................	28,600	26,900	1,700
Interest receivable	1,900	700	1,200
Inventories	83,600	87,200	(3,600)
Prepaid expenses...................	2,500	1,900	600
Plant assets			
Land...........................	69,000	60,000	9,000
Equipment, net	53,500	49,400	4,100
Total assets	$245,500	$231,400	$ 14,100
Current liabilities			
Accounts payable...................	$ 31,400	$ 28,800	$ 2,600
Interest payable	4,400	4,900	(500)
Salary payable	3,100	6,600	(3,500)
Other accrued liabilities	13,700	16,000	(2,300)
Income tax payable	8,900	7,700	1,200
Long-term liabilities			
Notes payable......................	75,000	100,000	(25,000)
Shareholders' equity			
Common stock	88,300	64,700	23,600
Retained earnings	20,700	2,700	18,000
Total liabilities and shareholders' equity .	$245,500	$231,400	$ 14,100

Casa Loma had no noncash investing and financing transactions during 19X5.

Required

Compute the following items for the 19X5 SCFP:

Cash flows from operating activities
  Cash receipts
    Collections from customers .... $
    Receipts of interest...
Cash payments
  To suppliers—
    Inventory..
    Operating expenses...
  To employees ....
  For interest ....
  For income tax ....
    Net cash inflow from operating activities .... $_____
Cash flows from financing activities
  Payment of dividends .... $
  Payment of note payable (there were no issuances of notes payable)......
  Issuance of common stock (there were no retirements of stock) ....
    Net cash outflow from financing activities .... $_____
Cash flow from investing activities
  Acquisition of land (there were no sales of land)...................... $
  Acquisition of equipment (there were no sales of equipment) ....
    Net cash outflow from investing activities .... $_____
Net increase in cash... $1,100

Problem 18-4B   *Preparing the statement of changes in financial position: indirect method*

The comparative balance sheet of Westwood Sales Inc. at March 31, 19X7 reported the following:

	March 31,	
	19X7	**19X6**
Current Assets		
Cash and cash equivalents	$ 2,800	$ 4,000
Accounts receivable	19,400	21,700
Inventories	63,200	60,600
Prepaid expenses....................	1,900	1,700
Current liabilities		
Notes payable	$ 4,000	$ 4,000
Accounts payable	30,300	27,600
Accrued liabilities	10,700	11,100
Income tax payable	8,000	4,700

Westwood's transactions during the year ended March 31, 19X7, included the following:

Acquisition of land by issuing note payable	$36,000	Sale of long-term investment..	$13,700
		Depreciation expense	9,000
Amortization expense	2,000	Cash acquisition of building ..	47,000
Payment of cash dividend	30,000	Net income	63,000
Cash acquisition of equipment	78,000	Issuance of common stock	
Issuance of long-term note payable to borrow cash.....	50,000	for cash	11,000
		Stock dividend	18,000

Required

Prepare Westwood Sales's SCFP for the year ended March 31, 19X7, using the *indirect* method to report cash flows from operating activities. All current account balances resulted from operating transactions.

Problem 18-5B   *Preparing the statement of changes in financial position: direct and indirect methods*

To prepare the SCFP, accountants for Fanshawe Corporation have summarized 19X3 activity in two accounts as follows:

Cash

Beginning balance	53,600	Payments of operating expenses	34,300
Issuance of common stock	27,500	Payment of long-term debt ...	41,300
Receipts of dividends	4,500	Purchase of own stock	
Collection of loan	13,000	for cancellation	26,400
Receipts of interest..........	12,600	Payment of income tax	18,900
Collections from customers ...	676,700	Payments on accounts payable	399,100
		Payments of dividends	27,200
		Payments of salaries and wages	143,800
		Payments of interest	26,900
		Purchase of equipment	31,400
Ending balance	38,600		

Common Stock

Purchase for cancellation	26,400	Beginning balance	84,400
		Issuance for cash	27,500
		Issuance to acquire land	41,100
		Issuance to retire long-term debt	19,000
		Ending balance	145,600

Required

1. Prepare Fanshawe Corporations's SCFP for the year ended December 31, 19X3, using the *direct* method to report operating activities.

   Fanshawe's 19X3 income statement and selected balance sheet data follow:

Fanshawe Corporation
Income Statement
for the year ended December 31, 19X3

Revenues		
Sales revenue		$704,300
Interest revenue....................		12,600
Dividend revenue		4,500
Total revenues		721,400
Expenses and losses		
Cost of goods sold	$402,600	
Salary and wage expense.............	150,800	
Depreciation expense	24,300	
Other operating expense	44,100	
Interest expense....................	28,800	
Income tax expense..................	16,200	
Loss on sale of investments	1,100	
Total expenses		667,900
Net income		$ 53,500

Fanshawe Corporation
Balance Sheet Data

	Increase (Decrease)
Current assets	
Cash and cash equivalents	$(15,000)
Accounts receivable	27,600
Inventories	(11,800)
Prepaid expenses	600
Current liabilities	
Accounts payable	$ (8,300)
Interest payable	1,900
Salary payable..............................	7,000
Other accrued liabilities	10,400
Income tax payable	(2,700)

2. Use these data to prepare a supplementary schedule showing cash flows from operating activities by the *indirect* method. All activity in the current accounts results from operations.

Problem 18-6B   *Preparing the statement of changes in financial position: direct and indirect methods*

Key-Steib Corporation's comparative balance sheet at June 30, 19X7, included the following balances:

	19X7	19X6	Increase (Decrease)
Key-Steib Corporation			
Partial Balance Sheet			
June 30, 19X7 and 19X6			
Current assets			
Cash	$17,600	$ 8,600	$ 9,000
Accounts receivable	45,900	48,300	(2,400)
Interest receivable	2,900	3,600	(700)
Inventories	68,600	60,200	8,400
Prepaid expenses....................	3,700	2,800	900
Current liabilities			
Notes payable, short-term	$13,400	$18,100	$(4,700)
Accounts payable	42,400	40,300	2,100
Income tax payble	13,800	14,500	(700)
Accrued liabilities	8,200	9,700	(1,500)
Interest payable	3,700	2,900	800
Salary payable	900	2,600	(1,700)

Transaction data for the year ended June 30, 19X7:

a. Net income, $52,500.
b. Depreciation expense on equipment, $10,200.
c. Purchased long-term investment, $4,900.
d. Sold land for $46,900, including $6,700 loss.
e. Acquired equipment by issuing long-term note payable, $14,300.
f. Paid long-term note payable, $61,000.
g. Received cash for issuance of common stock, $3,900.
h. Paid cash dividends, $38,100.
i. Paid short-term note payable by issuing common stock, $42,000.

Required

1. Prepare Key-Steib's SCFP for the year ended June 30, 19X7, using the *indirect* method to report operating activities. All current accounts except short-term notes payable result from operating transactions.
2. Prepare a supplementary schedule showing cash flows from operations by the *direct* method. The income statement reports the following: sales, $233,600; interest revenue, $10,600; cost of goods sold, $82,800; salary expense, $38,800; other operating expenses, $37,200; depreciation expense, $10,200; income tax expense, $9,900; loss on sale of land, $6,700; interest expense, $6,100.

Decision Problems

1.   Preparing and using the statement of changes in financial position to evaluate operations

The 19X6 comparative income statement and the 19X6 comparative balance sheet of Gruber Inc. have just been distributed at a meeting of the company's board of directors.

Gruber, Inc.
Comparative Income Statement
for the years ended December 31, 19X6 and 19X5
(amounts in thousands)

	19X6	19X5
Revenues and gains		
Sales revenue	$474	$310
Gain on sale of equipment (sale price, $33)	—	18
Totals	$474	$328
Expenses and losses		
Cost of goods sold	$221	$162
Salary expense	48	28
Depreciation expense	46	22
Interest expense	13	20
Amortization expense on patent	11	11
Loss on sale of land (sale price, $61)	—	35
Totals	339	278
Net income	$135	$ 50

Gruber, Inc.
Comparative Balance Sheet
December 31, 19X6 and 19X5
(amounts in thousands)

Assets	19X6	19X5
Cash	$ 13	$ 63
Accounts receivable, net	72	61
Inventories	194	181
Long-term investment	31	-0-
Property, plant and equipment	401	259
Accumulated depreciation	(244)	(198)
Patents	177	188
Totals	$ 644	$ 554

Liabilities and Owners' Equity		
Notes payable, short-term	$ 32	$ 101
Accounts payable	63	56
Accrued liabilities	12	17
Notes payable, long-term	147	163
Common stock	139	61
Retained earnings	251	156
Totals	$ 644	$ 554

In discussing the company's results of operations and year-end financial position, the members of the board of directors raise a fundamental question: Why is the cash balance so low? This question is especially troublesome to the board members because 19X6 showed record profits. As the controller of the company, you must answer the question.

Required

1. Prepare a SCFP for 19X6 in the format that best shows the relationship between net income and operating cash flow. The company sold no plant assets or long-term investments and issued no notes payable during 19X6. The changes in all current accounts except short-term notes payable arose from operations. There were *no* noncash investing and financing transactions during the year. Show all amounts in thousands.
2. Answer the board members' question: Why *is* the cash balance so low? In explaining the business's cash flows, identify two significant cash receipts that occurred during 19X5 but not in 19X6 (see the comparative income statement). Also point out the two largest cash disbursements during 19X6.
3. Considering net income and the company's cash flows during 19X6, was it a good year or a bad year? Give your reasons.

2.   Using the statement of changes in financial position to evaluate a company's operations

The statement of changes in financial position, in the not-too-distant past, included information in only two categories: sources of cash and uses of cash. The present-day statement provides information about cash flows from operating activities, financing activities and investing activities. The earlier statement permitted the information to be about changes in working capital (current assets minus current liabilities) or in cash, while today's SCFP deals specifically with information about flows in cash and cash equivalents.

Required

1. Explain why you think the present day SCFP, with its disclosure of the three different kinds of activities, is or is not an improvement over the earlier model. (Hint: Discuss the advantages to the user of the financial statements of having the information in the SCFP categorized into the three activities.)
2. Is information about cash flows more informative to users than information about working capital flows? Hint: Consider the information about changes in current asset and liability accounts included in the SCFP prepared under the indirect method; that information would not be included in a statement of changes in working capital.
3. Briefly explain why comparative balance sheets and a SCFP are more informative than just comparative balance sheets.

Financial Statement Problem

Using the statement of cash flows

See John Labatt's (consolidated) statement of changes in financial position in Appendix E. Use this statement along with the company's other financial statements to answer the following questions:

1. By which method does John Labatt report net cash flows from *operating* activities? How can you tell?

2. Calculate the fixed asset disposals and the related accumulated depreciation. Show all amounts to the nearest $1 million, rounded to the nearest $100,000.
   a. Set up T-accounts entitled "Fixed Assets" and "Accumulated Depreciation." The opening balances and closing balances come from the comparative balance sheet.
   b. The financial statements provide you with information about debits to Fixed Assets and credits to Accumulated Depreciation. Make the appropriate entries to your T-accounts.
   c. Calculate the cost of fixed asset disposals and the related accumulated depreciation. You may assume there were no transactions effecting the two accounts other than the purchases and sales of fixed assets and depreciation expense.
3. John Labatt's cash position changed rather dramatically between April 30, 1988 and April 30, 1989. What is the new cash position? What were the principal (that is, over $10 million) ways in which cash was provided or used during the year ended April 30, 1989?

Answers to Self-Study Questions

1. b
2. a
3. a
4. c
5. d
6. d ($43,000 + $4,000 decrease in Interest Receivable = $47,000)
7. c ($104,000 + $31,000 − cost of investment sold = $91,000; Cost = $44,000; Proceeds = Cost, $44,000 + Gain, $22,000 = $66,000)
8. a
9. c
10. b ($17,000 + $9,000 + $3,000 − $4,000 − $6,000 + $8,000 = $27,000)

19

Using Accounting
Information to Make
Business Decisions

Investors, creditors and other business people rely on accounting information to make intelligent, informed decisions. Should the bank officer lend money to the Joneses? Should the investor buy more stock in Noranda Inc. or sell those shares presently owned? People need information to make these decisions. The balance sheet, the income statement, and the statement of changes in financial position provide a large part of the information that is used for making decisions such as these. In Chapters 1 through 18, we have described the process of accounting and the preparation of the financial statements. We have tried to relate each topic to the real world of business by showing the relevance of the accounting data. In this chapter, we discuss in more detail how to use the information that appears in these statements. (Appendix E features the financial statements of John Labatt. You may apply the analytical skills you learn in this chapter to those real-world data.)

Financial Statement Analysis

We divide the tools and techniques that the business community uses in evaluating financial statement information into three broad categories: horizontal analysis, vertical analysis and ratio analysis. These three categories make up the broad area of financial statement analysis.

Horizontal Analysis

Many business decisions hinge on whether the numbers — in sales, income, expenses, and so on — are increasing or decreasing over time. Has the sales figure risen from last year? From two years ago? By how many dollars? We may find that the net sales figure has risen by $20,000. This may be interesting, but considered alone it is not very useful for decision making. An analysis of the *percentage change* in the net sales figure over time improves our ability to use the dollar amounts. It is more useful to know that sales have increased by 20 percent than to know that the increase in sales is $20,000.

The study of percentage changes in comparative statements is called **horizontal analysis**. Computing a percentage change in comparative statements requires two steps: (1) Compute the dollar amount of the change from the earlier (base) period to the later period, and (2) divide the dollar amount of change by the base period amount. Horizontal analysis is illustrated as follows:

| | | | | Increase (Decrease) | | | |
| | | | | During Year 3 | | During Year 2 | |
	Year 3	Year 2	Year 1	Amount	%	Amount	%
Sales.......	$120,000	$100,000	$80,000	$20,000	20%	$20,000	25%
Net income .	12,000	8,000	10,000	4,000	50%	(2,000)	(20%)

The increase in sales is $20,000 in both year 3 and year 2. However, the percentage increase in sales differs from year to year because of the change in the base amount. To compute the percentage change for year 2, we divide the amount of increase ($20,000) by the base period amount ($80,000), an increase of 25 percent. For year 3, the dollar amount increases again by $20,000. However, the base period amount for figuring this percentage change is $100,000. Dividing $20,000 by $100,000 computes a percentage increase of only 20 percent during year 3. Observe that net income *decreases* by 20 percent during year 2 and *increases* by 50 percent during year 3.

Detailed horizontal analyses of a comparative income statement and a comparative balance sheet are shown in the two right-hand columns of Exhibits 19-1 and 19-2.

OBJECTIVE 1

Perform a horizontal analysis of comparative financial statements

EXHIBIT 19-1   *Comparative Income Statement: Horizontal Analysis*

McColpin, Inc.
Comparative Income Statement
years ended December 31, 19X7 and 19X6

| | | | Increase (Decrease) | |
	19X7	19X6	Amount	Percent
Net sales	$858,000	$803,000	$55,000	6.8%
Cost of goods sold.............	513,000	509,000	4,000	0.8
Gross profit...................	345,000	294,000	51,000	17.3
Operating expenses				
Selling expenses.............	126,000	114,000	12,000	10.5
General expenses............	118,000	123,000	(5,000)	(4.1)
Total operating expenses	244,000	237,000	7,000	3.0
Income from operations........	101,000	57,000	44,000	77.2
Interest revenue...............	4,000	—	4,000	—
Interest expense...............	24,000	14,000	10,000	71.4
Income before income taxes	81,000	43,000	38,000	88.4
Income tax expense............	33,000	17,000	16,000	94.1
Net income	$ 48,000	$ 26,000	$22,000	84.6

EXHIBIT 19-2 *Comparative Balance Sheet: Horizontal Analysis*

McColpin, Inc.
Comparative Balance Sheet
December 31, 19X7 and 19X6

			Increase (Decrease)	
	19X7	19X6	Amount	Percent
Assets				
Currents assets				
Cash	$ 29,000	$ 32,000	$ (3,000)	(9.4%)
Accounts receivable, net	114,000	85,000	29,000	34.1
Inventories	113,000	111,000	2,000	1.8
Prepaid expenses	6,000	8,000	(2,000)	(25.0)
Total current assets	262,000	236,000	26,000	11.0
Long-term investments	18,000	9,000	9,000	100.0
Property, plant and equipment,				
net	507,000	399,000	108,000	27.1
Total assets	$787,000	$644,000	$143,000	22.2
Liabilities				
Current liabilities				
Notes payable	$ 42,000	$ 27,000	$ 15,000	55.6
Accounts payable	73,000	68,000	5,000	7.4
Accrued liabilities	27,000	31,000	(4,000)	(12.9)
Total current liabilities	142,000	126,000	16,000	12.7
Long-term debt	289,000	198,000	91,000	46.0
Total liabilities	431,000	324,000	107,000	33.0
Shareholders' Equity				
Common stock	186,000	186,000	—	0.0
Retained earnings	170,000	134,000	36,000	26.9
Total shareholders' equity . .	356,000	320,000	36,000	11.3
Total liabilities and				
shareholders' equity	$787,000	$644,000	$143,000	22.2

The comparative income statement in Exhibit 19-1 reveals that net sales increased by 6.8 percent during 19X7 and that the cost of goods sold grew by much less. As a result, gross profit rose by 17.3 percent. Note that general expenses actually decreased, and so the company significantly increased income from operations and net income during 19X7. Our analysis shows that 19X7 was a much better year than 19X6. We see that the growth in income resulted more from slowing the increase in expenses than from boosting sales revenue.

No percentage increase is computed for interest revenue because dividing the $4,000 increase by a zero amount would produce a meaningless percentage. Also, we compute no percentage change when a base-year amount is negative. For example, when a company goes from a net loss one year to a profit the next year, we would be dividing a positive number by a negative amount.

Throughout this chapter, we discuss only some of the elements of the various statements that we present. For example, we mention McColpin's cost of goods sold but not its selling expenses. Understand, however, that the manager of the sales staff (and likely top management also) would examine the selling expenses in conducting a full analysis of the company's operations.

The comparative balance sheet in Exhibit 19-2 shows that 19X7 was a year of expansion for the company. Property, plant, and equipment, net of depreciation, increased by 27.1 percent. To help finance this expansion, McColpin borrowed heavily, increasing short-term notes payable by 55.6 percent and long-term debt by 46 percent. The increase in assets was also financed in part by profitable operations, as shown by the 26.9 percent increase in retained earnings.

The sharpest percentage increase on the balance sheet is in long-term investments (100 percent). However, the dollar amounts are small compared to the other balance sheet figures. Note this key point of financial analysis: percentage changes must be evaluated in terms of the item's relative importance to the company as a whole. In this instance, the large percentage increase in long-term investments means little because the company holds such a small amount. The 27.1 percent increase in property, plant and equipment is more important because their cost represents the largest asset and their use is intended to generate profits for years to come.

Trend Percentages

Trend percentages are a form of horizontal analysis. Trends are important indicators of the direction a business is taking. How have sales changed over a five-year period? What trend does gross profit show? These questions can be answered by an analysis of trend percentages over a representative period, such as the most recent five years or the most recent 10 years. To gain a realistic view of the company, it is often necessary to examine more than just a two- or three-year period.

Trend percentages are computed by selecting a base year, with each amount during that year set equal to 100 percent. The amounts of each following year are expressed as a percent of the base amount. To compute trend percentages, divide each item for years after the base year by the corresponding amount during the base year. Suppose McColpin, Inc. showed sales, cost of goods sold and gross profit for the past six years as follows:

	(amounts in thousands)					
	19X7	19X6	19X5	19X4	19X3	19X2
Net sales	$858	$803	$781	$744	$719	$737
Cost of goods sold	513	509	490	464	450	471
Gross profit	$345	$294	$291	$280	$269	$266

Assume we want trend percentages for a five-year period starting with 19X3. We use 19X2 as the base year. Trend percentages for net sales are computed by dividing each net sales amount by the 19X2 amount of $737,000. Likewise, dividing each year's cost-of-goods-sold amount by the base-year amount ($471,000) yields the trend percentages for cost of goods sold. Gross-profit trend percentages are computed similarly. The resulting trend percentages follow (19X2, the base year = 100%):

	19X7	19X6	19X5	19X4	19X3	19X2
Net sales	116%	109%	106%	101%	98%	100%
Cost of goods sold	109	108	104	99	96	100
Gross profit	130	111	109	105	101	100

   McColpin's sales and cost of goods sold have trended upward since a downturn in 19X3. Gross profit has increased steadily, with the most dramatic growth coming during 19X7. What signal about the company does this information provide? It suggests that operations are becoming increasingly more successful. A similar analysis can be performed for any related set of items in the financial statements. For example, an increase in inventory and accounts receivable, coupled with a decrease in sales, may reveal difficulty in making sales and collecting receivables.

Vertical Analysis

Horizontal analysis highlights changes in an item over time. However, no single technique provides a complete picture of a business. Another way to analyse a company is called vertical analysis.

   Vertical analysis of a financial statement reveals the relationship of each statement item to the total, which is the 100 percent figure. For example, suppose under normal conditions a company's gross profit is 50 percent of net sales. A drop in gross profit to 40 percent may cause the company to report a net loss on the income statement. Management, investors and creditors view a large decline in gross profit with alarm.

   The percentages in Exhibits 19-3 and 19-4 show vertical analyses of McColpin, Inc.'s income statement and balance sheet. Percentages on the income statement are computed by dividing all amounts by net sales. The vertical analysis, therefore, presents each amount as a percentage of net sales. The vertical analysis of the balance sheet shows all amounts as a percentage of total assets or the sum of liabilities and shareholders' equity (recall that total assets equal total liabilities and shareholders' equity).

EXHIBIT 19-3 *Comparative Income Statement: Vertical Analysis*

> **OBJECTIVE 2**
> Perform a vertical analysis of financial statements

McColpin, Inc. Comparative Income Statement years ended December 31, 19X7 and 19X6				
	19X7		**19X6**	
	Amount	**Percent**	**Amount**	**Percent**
Net sales	$858,000	100.0%	$803,000	100.0%
Cost of goods sold	513,000	59.8	509,000	63.4
Gross profit	345,000	40.2	294,000	36.6
Selling expenses.............	126,000	14.7	114,000	14.2
General expenses............	118,000	13.7	123,000	15.3
Total operating expenses	244,000	28.4	237,000	29.5
Income from operations	101,000	11.8	57,000	7.1
Interest revenue...............	4,000	0.4	—	—
Interest expense...............	24,000	2.8	14,000	1.8
Income before income tax	81,000	9.4	43,000	5.3
Income tax expense............	33,000	3.8	17,000	2.1
Net income	$ 48,000	5.6%	$ 26,000	3.2%

EXHIBIT 19-4 *Comparative Balance Sheet: Vertical Analysis*

	19X7		19X6	
McColpin, Inc. Comparative Balance Sheet December 31, 19X7 and 19X6	Amount	Percent	Amount	Percent
Assets				
Current assets				
Cash	$ 29,000	3.7%	$ 32,000	5.0%
Accounts receivable, net	114,000	14.5	85,000	13.2
Inventories	113,000	14.3	111,000	17.2
Prepaid expenses	6,000	.8	8,000	1.2
Total current assets	262,000	33.3	236,000	36.6
Long-term investments	18,000	2.3	9,000	1.4
Property, plant and equipment, net	507,000	64.4	399,000	62.0
Total assets	$787,000	100.0%	$644,000	100.0%
Liabilities				
Current liabilities				
Notes payable	$ 42,000	5.3%	$ 27,000	4.2%
Accounts payable	73,000	9.3	68,000	10.6
Accrued liabilities	27,000	3.4	31,000	4.8
Total current liabilities	142,000	18.0	126,000	19.6
Long-term debt	289,000	36.7	198,000	30.7
Total liabilities	431,000	54.7	324,000	50.3
Shareholders' Equity				
Common stock	186,000	23.7	186,000	28.9
Retained earnings	170,000	21.6	134,000	20.8
Total shareholders' equity ..	356,000	45.3	320,000	49.7
Total liabilities and shareholders' equity	$787,000	100.0%	$644,000	100.0%

The 19X7 comparative income statement (Exhibit 19-3) reports that cost of goods sold dropped to 59.8 percent of net sales from 63.4 percent in 19X6. This explains why the gross profit percentage arose in 19X7. The gross profit percentage is one of the most important pieces of information in financial analysis because it shows the relationship between net sales and cost of goods sold. A company that can steadily increase its gross profit percentage over a long period is more likely to succeed than a business whose gross profit percentage is steadily declining. The net income percentage almost doubled in 19X7, mostly because of the decrease in the cost-of-goods-sold percentage.

Vertical analysis gives a view of the income statement that is different from the view provided by horizontal analysis. Decision-makers use these two forms of analysis together. For example, Exhibit 19-1 reports that gross profit increased by 17.3 percent, and net income increased by 84.6 percent from 19X6 to 19X7.

Exhibit 19-3 indicates that gross profit grew from 36.6 percent of sales in 19X6 to 40.2 percent of sales in 19X7 and that net income has increased from 3.2 percent of sales to 5.6 percent of sales. Together, vertical analysis and horizontal analysis show a favourable improvement in McColpin's operations.

We can apply trend analysis to the balance sheet of McColpin, Inc., as Exhibit 19-4 shows. For example, among the changes that occurred in the one-year period from 19X6 to 19X7, we note that current assets have become a smaller percentage of total assets. A decrease in current assets may make it difficult for the company to pay its bills. However, this does not present a problem for McColpin, Inc. because current liabilities also decreased as a percentage of total assets during 19X7. This kind of comparison is used in vertical analysis.

Common-Size Statements

The percentages in Exhibits 19-3 and 19-4 can be presented as a separate statement that reports only percentages (no dollar amounts). Such a statement, called a **common-size statement**, is a type of vertical analysis.

On a common-size income statement, each item is expressed as a percentage of the net sales amount. Net sales is the "common size" to which we relate the statement's other amounts. In the balance sheet, the "common size" is the total on each side of the accounting equation (total assets *or* the sum of total liabilities and shareholders' equity). A common-size statement eases the comparison of different companies because their amounts are stated in percentages.

Common-size statements may identify the need for corrective action. Exhibit 19-5 is the common-size analysis of current assets taken from Exhibit 19-4.

Exhibit 19-5 shows cash as a smaller percentage of total assets at December 31, 19X7 than at the previous year end. Accounts receivable, on the other hand, is a larger percentage of total assets. What could cause a decrease in cash and an increase in accounts receivable as percentages of total assets? McColpin may have been lax in collecting accounts receivable, which may explain a cash

EXHIBIT 19-5   *Common-Size Analysis of Current Assets*

McColpin, Inc. Common-Size Analysis of Current Assets December 31, 19X7 and 19X6		
	Percent of Total Assets	
	19X7	19X6
Current assets		
Cash	3.7%	5.0%
Accounts receivable, net	14.5	13.2
Inventories	14.3	17.2
Prepaid expenses	.8	1.2
Total current assets	33.3%	36.6%

shortage and reveal that the company needs to pursue collection more vigorously. Or the company may have sold to less creditworthy customers. In any event, the company should monitor its cash position and collection of accounts receivable to avoid a cash shortage. Common-size statements provide information useful for this purpose.

Industry Comparisons

We study the records of a company in order to understand past results and predict future performance. Still, the knowledge that we can develop from a single company's records is limited to that one company. We may learn that gross profit has decreased and net income has increased steadily for the last ten years. While this information is helpful, it does not consider how businesses in the same industry have fared over this time. Have other companies in the same line of business increased their sales? Is there an industrywide decline in gross profit? Has cost of goods sold risen steeply for other businesses that sell the same products? Managers, investors, creditors and other interested parties need to know how one company compares to other companies in the same line of business.

Exhibit 19-6 gives the common-size income statement of McColpin, Inc. compared to the average for its industry. This analysis compares McColpin to all other companies in its line of business. Analysts specialize in a particular industry and make such comparisons in deciding which companies' stocks to buy or sell. For example, financial-service companies like Richardson Greenshields have paper and forest products industry specialists, merchandising

OBJECTIVE 3

Prepare common-size financial statements

EXHIBIT 19-6   *Common-Size Income Statement Compared to the Industry Average*

McColpin, Inc. Common-Size Income Statement for Comparison with Industry Average year ended December 31, 19X7		
	McColpin, Inc.	**Industry Average**
Net sales	100.0%	100.0%
Cost of goods sold	59.8	61.8
Gross profit	40.2	38.2
Operating expenses		
Selling expenses	14.7	15.7
General expenses	13.7	12.9
Total operating expenses	28.4	28.6
Income from operations	11.8	9.6
Other revenue (expense)	(2.4)	(3.5)
Income before income tax	9.4	6.1
Income tax expense	3.8	2.4
Net income	5.6%	3.7%

industry specialists, and so on. Boards of directors evaluate top managers based on how well the company compares with other companies in the industry. Exhibit 19-6 shows that McColpin compares favourably with competing firms in its line of business. Its gross profit percentage, percentage of income from operations, and net income percentage are higher than the industry average.

Another use of common-size statements is to aid the comparison of different-sized companies. Suppose you are considering an investment in the stock of an automobile manufacturer, and you are choosing between General Motors (GM) and Chrysler. GM is so much larger than Chrysler that a direct comparison of their financial statements in dollar amounts is not meaningful. However, you can convert the two companies' income statements to common size and compare the percentages. You may find that one company has a higher percentage of its assets in inventory and the other company has a higher percentage of its liabilities in long-term debt.

Information Sources

Financial analysts draw their information from various sources. Annual and quarterly reports offer readers a good look at an individual business's operations. Publicly held companies must, in addition, submit more detailed annual reports to the provincial securities commission in each province where they are listed on a stock exchange (for example, the Alberta Securities Commission for the Alberta Stock Exchange). Business publications such as the daily and weekend *Financial Post* and the daily *Globe and Mail Report on Business* carry information about individual companies and Canadian industries. *InfoGlobe* and *The Financial Post Information Service* provide data to subscribers on public companies and industries in Canada, too. Credit agencies like Dun and Bradstreet Canada Limited, for example, and investment companies like Moodys, for example, offer industry averages as part of their financial service. *The Financial Post Survey of Industrials* and *Survey of Mines and Energy Resources* supply information on an annual basis about individual companies and the industries they are in.

The Statement of Changes in Financial Position in Decision-Making

The chapter so far has centered on the income statement and balance sheet. We may also perform horizontal and vertical analysis on the statement of changes in financial position. In the preceding chapter, we discussed how to prepare the statement. To discuss its role in decision-making, let us use Exhibit 19-7.

Some analysts use cash flow analysis to identify danger signals about a company's financial situation. For example, the statement in Exhibit 19-7 reveals what may be a weakness in DeMaris Corporation.

> **OBJECTIVE 4**
>
> Use the statement of changes in financial position in decision-making

EXHIBIT 19-7   *Statement of Changes in Financial Position*

DeMaris Corporation		
Statement of Changes in Financial Position		
for the Current Year		
Operating activities		
Income from operations		$ 35,000
Add (subtract) noncash items		
Depreciation	$ 14,000	
Net increase in current assets other than cash . . .	(5,000)	
Net increase in current liabilities	8,000	17,000
Net cash inflow from operating activities		52,000
Financing activities		
Issuance of bond payable	$ 72,000	
Payment of long term debt	(170,000)	
Payment of interest expense	(9,000)	
Payment of dividends	(33,000)	
Net cash outflow from financing activities		(140,000)
Investing activities		
Sale of property, plant and equipment	$ 91,000	
Net cash inflow from investing activities		91,000
Increase in cash		$ 3,000

First, operations provided a net cash inflow of $52,000, which is much less than the $91,000 generated by the sale of fixed assets. An important question arises: Can the company remain in business by generating the majority of its cash by selling its property, plant and equipment? No, because these assets will be needed to manufacture the company's products in the future. Note also that borrowing by issuing bonds payable brought in $72,000. No company can long survive living on borrowed funds. DeMaris must eventually pay off the bonds. Indeed, the company paid $170,000 on older debt. Also, interest expense must be incurred as the price of borrowing. Successful companies like John Labatt, St. Lawrence Cement, and Bell Canada generate the greatest percentage of their cash from operations, not from selling their fixed assets or from borrowing money. These conditions may be only temporary for DeMaris Corporation, but they are worth investigating.

The most important information that the statement of changes in financial position provides is a summary of the company's use of cash. How a company spends its cash today determines its sources of cash in the future. The company may wisely use its cash to purchase assets that will generate income in the years ahead. However, if a company invests unwisely, cash will eventually run short. DeMaris's statement of changes in financial position reveals problems. The exhibit information indicates that DeMaris invested in no fixed assets to replace those that it sold. The company may in fact be going out of business. Furthermore, DeMaris paid dividends of $33,000, an amount that is very close to its net income. Is the company retaining enough of its income to finance future operations without excessive borrowing? Analysts seek answers to questions such as this. They analyse the information from the statement of changes in financial position along with the information from the balance sheet and the income statement to form a well-rounded complete picture of the business.

Summary Problem for Your Review

Perform a horizontal analysis and a vertical analysis of the comparative income statement of TRE Corporation. State whether 19X3 was a good year or a bad year and give your reasons.

TRE Corporation
Comparative Income Statement
years ended December 31, 19X3 and 19X2

	19X3	19X2
Total revenues	$275,000	$225,000
Expenses		
Cost of products sold	$194,000	$165,000
Engineering, selling and administrative expenses	54,000	48,000
Interest expense	5,000	5,000
Income tax expense	9,000	3,000
Other expense (income)	1,000	(1,000)
Total expenses	263,000	220,000
Net earnings	$ 12,000	$ 5,000

SOLUTION TO REVIEW PROBLEM

TRE Corporation
Horizontal Analysis of Comparative Income Statement
years ended December 31, 19X3 and 19X2

	19X3	19X2	Increase (Decrease) Amount	Increase (Decrease) Percent
Total revenues	$275,000	$225,000	$50,000	22.2%
Expenses				
Cost of products sold	$194,000	$165,000	$29,000	17.6
Engineering, selling and administrative expenses	54,000	48,000	6,000	12.5
Interest expense	5,000	5,000	—	—
Income tax expense	9,000	3,000	6,000	200.0
Other expense (income)	1,000	(1,000)	2,000	—
Total expenses	263,000	220,000	43,000	19.5
Net earnings	$ 12,000	$ 5,000	$ 7,000	140.0

TRE Corporation
Vertical Analysis of Comparative Income Statement
years ended December 31, 19X3 and 19X2

	19X3		19X2	
	Amount	Percent	Amount	Percent
Total revenue	$275,000	100.0%	$225,000	100.0%
Expenses				
Cost of products sold	$194,000	70.5	$165,000	73.3
Engineering, selling and				
administrative expenses	54,000	19.6	48,000	21.3
Interest expense	5,000	1.8	5,000	2.2
Income tax expense	9,000	3.3	3,000	1.4
Other expense (income)	1,000	0.4	(1,000)	(0.4)
Total expenses	263,000	95.6	220,000	97.8
Net earnings	$ 12,000	4.4	$ 5,000	2.2

The horizontal analysis shows that total revenues increased 22.2 percent. This percentage increase was greater than the 19.5 percent increase in total expenses, resulting in a 140 percent increase in net earnings.

The vertical analysis shows decreases in the percentages of net sales consumed by the cost of products sold (from 73.3 percent to 70.5 percent) and the engineering, selling, and administrative expenses (from 21.3 percent to 19.6 percent). These two items are TRE's largest dollar expenses, so their percentage decreases are quite important. The relative reduction in expenses raised 19X3 net earnings to 4.4 percent of sales, compared to 2.2 percent the preceding year. The overall analysis indicates that 19X3 was significantly better than 19X2.

Using Ratios to Make Business Decisions

The preceding analyses were based on each financial statement considered alone. Another set of decision tools develops relationships among items taken from throughout the statements.

Ratios are important tools for financial analysis. A ratio expresses the relationship of one number to another number. For example, if the balance sheet shows current assets of $100,000 and current liabilities of $25,000, the ratio of current assets to current liabilities is $100,000 to $25,000. We simplify this numerical expression to the ratio of 4 to 1, which may also be written 4:1 and ⁴⁄₁. Other acceptable ways of expressing this ratio include (1) "current assets are 400 percent of current liabilities" and (2) "the business has four dollars in current assets for every one dollar in current liabilities."

We often reduce the ratio fraction by writing the ratio as one figure over the other, for example, ⁴⁄₁, and then dividing the numerator by the denominator. In this way, the ratio ⁴⁄₁ may be expressed simply as 4. The 1 that represents the denominator of the fraction is understood, not written. Consider the ratio $175,000:$165,000. After dividing the first figure by the second, we come to

1.06:1, which we state as 1.06. The second part of the ratio, the 1, again is understood. Ratios provide a convenient and useful way of expressing a relationship between numbers. For example, the ratio of current assets to current liabilities gives information about a company's ability to pay its current debts with existing current assets.

A manager, lender or financial analyst may use any ratio that is relevant to a particular decision. We discuss the more important ratios used in credit and investment analysis and in managing a business. Many companies include these ratios in a special section of their annual financial reports. Investment services, such as Moody's, Standard & Poor's, Robert Morris Associates, and others, report these ratios for companies and industries. They are widely used in all aspects of business, such as finance, management and marketing as well as accounting.

Measuring the Ability to Pay Current Liabilities _____

Working capital is defined as current assets minus current liabilities. Working capital is widely used to measure a business's ability to meet its short-term obligations with its current assets. The larger the working capital, the better able the business is to pay its debts. Recall that capital (or owners' equity) is total assets minus total liabilities. Working capital is like a "current" version of total capital. The working capital amount considered alone does not give a complete picture of the entity's working capital position, however. Consider two companies with equal working capital.

	Company A	Company B
Current assets	$100,000	$200,000
Current liabilities...................	50,000	150,000
Working capital	$ 50,000	$ 50,000

Both companies have working capital of $50,000, but Company A's working capital is as large as its current liabilities. Company B's working capital, on the other hand, is only one third as large as its current liabilities. Which business has a better working capital position? Company A, because its working capital is a higher percentage of current assets and current liabilities. To use working capital data in decision making, it is helpful to develop ratios. Two decision tools based on working capital data are the *current ratio* and the *acid-test ratio*.

Current Ratio

The most common ratio using current asset and current liability data is the **current ratio**, which is current assets divided by current liabilities. Recall the makeup of current assets and current liabilities. Inventory is converted to receivables through sales, the receivables are collected in cash, and the cash is used to buy inventory and pay current liabilities. A company's current assets and current liabilities represent the core of its day-to-day operations.

The current ratios of McColpin, Inc. at December 31, 19X7 and 19X6, follow (data from Exhibit 19-2):

OBJECTIVE 5
Compute the standard financial ratios used for decision-making

Current Ratio of McColpin, Inc.

Formula	19X7	19X6
$\text{Current ratio} = \dfrac{\text{Current assets}}{\text{Current liabilities}}$	$\dfrac{\$262,000}{\$142,000} = 1.85$	$\dfrac{\$236,000}{\$126,000} = 1.87$

The current ratio decreased slightly during 19X7. Lenders, shareholders and managers closely monitor changes in a company's current ratio. In general, a higher current ratio indicates a stronger financial position. A high current ratio suggests that the business has sufficient liquid assets to maintain normal business operations. Compare McColpin's current ratio of 1.85 to the current ratios of some actual companies.

Company	Current Ratio
Maclean Hunter Limited (Communications)	1.63
The Oshawa Group Limited (Merchandising)	1.54
St. Lawrence Cement Inc. (Building materials)	2.16
TransCanada PipeLines Limited (Energy)	1.26
George Weston Limited (Food processing and distribution and resources)	1.22

What is an acceptable current ratio? The answer to this question depends on the nature of the business. The companies listed above are typical of their industries.

Acid-Test Ratio

The **acid-test** (or **quick**) **ratio** tells us whether the entity could pay all its current liabilities if they came due immediately. That is, could the company pass this *acid test*? The company would convert its most liquid assets to cash. To compute the acid-test ratio, we add cash, short-term investments and net current receivables (accounts and notes receivable, net of allowances) and divide by current liabilities. Inventory and prepaid expenses are the two current assets not included in the acid-test computations. These accounts are omitted because they are the least liquid of the current assets. A business may not be able to convert them to cash immediately to pay current liabilities. The acid-test ratio measures liquidity using a narrower asset base than the current ratio does.

McColpin's acid-test ratios for 19X7 and 19X6 follow (data from Exhibit 19-2):

Acid-Test Ratio of McColpin, Inc.

Formula	19X7	19X6
$\text{Acid-test ratio} = \dfrac{\text{Cash} + \text{short-term investments} + \text{net current receivables}}{\text{Current liabilities}}$	$\dfrac{\$29,000 + \$0 + \$114,000}{\$142,000} = 1.01$	$\dfrac{\$32,000 + \$0 + \$85,000}{\$126,000} = .93$

The company's acid-test ratio improved considerably during 19X7. Its ratio of 1.01 is between those of Maclean Hunter (1.21), St. Lawrence Cement (1.37) and TransCanada PipeLines (1.13) and those of The Oshawa Group (0.60) and George Weston (0.41).

Measuring the Ability to Sell Inventory and Collect Receivables

The ability to sell inventory and collect receivables is fundamental to business success. Recall the operating cycle of a merchandiser: cash to inventory to receivables and back to cash. This section discusses three ratios that measure the ability to sell inventory and collect receivables.

Inventory Turnover

Companies generally seek to achieve the quickest possible return on their investments. A return on an investment in inventory — usually a substantial amount — is no exception. The faster inventory sells, the sooner the business creates accounts receivable, and the sooner it collects cash.

Inventory turnover is a measure of the number of times a company sells its average level of inventory during a year. A high rate of turnover indicates relative ease in selling inventory, whereas a low turnover indicates difficulty in selling. Generally, companies prefer a high inventory turnover. A value of 6 means that the company's average level of inventory has been sold 6 times during the year. In most cases this is better than a turnover of 3 or 4. However, a high value can mean that the business is not keeping enough inventory on hand, and this can result in lost sales if the company cannot fill a customer's order. Therefore, a business strives for the most profitable rate of inventory turnover, not necessarily the highest.

To compute the inventory turnover ratio we divide cost of goods sold by the average inventory for the period. We use the cost of goods sold — not sales — in the computation because both cost of goods sold and inventory are stated *at cost*. Sales is stated at the sales value of inventory and therefore is not comparable to inventory cost.

McColpin's inventory turnover for 19X7 is

Formula	Inventory Turnover of McColpin, Inc.
$\text{Inventory turnover} = \dfrac{\text{Cost of goods sold}}{\text{Average inventory}}$	$\dfrac{\$513,000}{\$112,000} = 4.58$

Cost of goods sold appears in the income statement (Exhibit 19-1). Average inventory is figured by averaging the beginning inventory ($111,000) and ending inventory ($113,000). (See the balance sheet, Exhibit 19-2). If inventory levels vary greatly from month to month, compute the average by adding the 12 monthly balances and dividing this sum by 12.

Inventory turnover varies widely with the nature of the business. For example, most manufacturers of farm machinery have an inventory turnover close to 3 times a year. By contrast, companies that remove natural gas from the ground hold their inventory for a very short period of time and have an average turnover of 30. McColpin's turnover of 4.58 times a year is similar to retailers of building materials (4.9) and to department stores (5.5).

To evaluate fully a company's inventory turnover, compare the ratio over time. A sudden sharp decline or a steady decline over a long period suggests the need for corrective action. Analysts also compare a company's inventory turnover to other companies in the same industry and to the industry average.

Accounts Receivable Turnover

Accounts receivable turnover measures a company's ability to collect cash from credit customers. Generally, the higher the ratio, the more successfully the business collects cash, and the better off its operations are. However, too high a receivable turnover may indicate that credit is too tight, causing the loss of sales to good customers. To compute the accounts receivable turnover we divide net credit sales by average net accounts receivable. The resulting ratio indicates how many times during the year the average level of receivables was turned into cash.

McColpin's accounts receivable turnover ratio for 19X7 is computed as follows, assuming that all sales were on credit:

Formula	Accounts Receivable Turnover of McColpin, Inc.
$\text{Accounts receivable turnover} = \dfrac{\text{Net credit sales}}{\text{Average net accounts receivable}}$	$\dfrac{\$858,000}{\$99,500} = 8.62$

The sales figure comes from the income statement (Exhibit 19-1). McColpin makes all sales on credit. If the company makes both cash and credit sales, this ratio is best computed using only net credit sales. Average net accounts receivable is figured using the beginning accounts receivable balance ($85,000) and the ending balance ($114,000). (See the balance sheet in Exhibit 19-2.) If accounts receivable balances exhibit a seasonal pattern, compute the average using the 12 monthly balances.

Receivable turnover ratios vary little from company to company. Most companies' ratios range between 7.0 and 10.0. McColpin's receivable turnover of 8.62 falls within this range.

Days' Sales in Receivables

Businesses must convert accounts receivable to cash. The lower the Accounts Receivable balance, the more successful the business has been in converting receivables into cash, and the better off the business.

The **days'-sales-in-receivables** ratio tells us how many days' sales remain in Accounts Receivable. We express the money amount in terms of an average day's sales. This relation becomes clearer as we compute the ratio, a two-step process. First, divide net sales by 365 days to figure the average sales amount for one day. Second, divide this average day's sales amount into the average net accounts receivable.

The data to compute this ratio for McColpin, Inc. for 19X7 are taken from the income statement and the balance sheet.

Formula	Days' Sales in Accounts Receivable of McColpin, Inc.
Days' Sales in AVERAGE Accounts Receivable:	
1. One day's sales $= \dfrac{\text{Net sales}}{365\ \text{days}}$	$\dfrac{\$858,000}{365\ \text{days}} = \$2,351$
2. Days' sales in average accounts receivable $= \dfrac{\text{Average net accounts receivable}}{\text{One day's sales}}$	$\dfrac{\$99,500}{\$2,351} = 42\ \text{days}$

The computation in two steps is designed to increase your understanding of the meaning of the ratio. We may compute days' sales in average receivables in one step: $99,500/($858,000/365 \text{ days}) = 42$ days.

McColpin's ratio tell us that 42 average days' sales remain in accounts receivable and need to be collected. The company will increase its cash inflow if it can decrease this ratio. To detect any changes over time in McColpin's ability to collect its receivables, let us compute the days' sales in receivables ratio at the beginning and the end of 19X7.

Days' Sales in ENDING 19X6 Accounts Receivable:

$$\text{One day's sales} = \frac{\$803,000}{365 \text{ days}} = \$2,200$$

$$\begin{array}{c}\text{Days' sales in} \\ \text{ending 19X6 accounts} = \\ \text{receivable}\end{array} \frac{\$85,000}{\$2,200} = 39 \text{ days at beginning of 19X7}$$

Days' Sales in ENDING 19X7 Accounts Receivable:

$$\text{One day's sales} = \frac{\$858,000}{365 \text{ days}} = \$2,351$$

$$\begin{array}{c}\text{Days' sales in} \\ \text{ending 19X7 accounts} = \\ \text{receivable}\end{array} \frac{\$114,000}{\$2,351} = 48 \text{ days at end of 19X7}$$

This analysis shows a drop in McColpin's collection of receivables: days' sales in accounts receivable has increased from 39 at the beginning of the year to 48 at year end. The credit and collection department should strengthen its collection efforts. Otherwise, the company may experience a cash shortage in 19X8 and beyond.

Measuring the Ability to Pay Long-Term Debt _____

The ratios discussed so far give us insight into current assets and current liabilities. They help us measure a business's ability to sell inventory, collect receivables and to pay current liabilities. Most businesses also have long-term debts. Bondholders and banks that loan money on long-term notes payable and bonds payable take special interest in a business's ability to meet long-term obligations. Two key indicators of a business's ability to pay long-term liabilities are the *debt ratio* and *times-interest-earned ratio*.

Debt Ratio

Suppose you are a loan officer at a bank and you are evaluating loan applications from two companies with equal sales revenue and total assets. Sales and total assets are the two most common measures of firm size. Both companies have asked to borrow $500,000, and each has agreed to repay the loan over a ten-year period. The first customer already owes $600,000 to another bank. The second owes only $250,000. Other things equal, which company is likely to get the loan at the lower interest rate? Why?

Company B is more likely to get the loan. The bank faces less risk by loaning to Company B because that company owes less to creditors than Company A owes.

This relationship between total liabilities and total assets, called the **debt ratio**, tells us the proportion of the company's assets that it has financed with debt. If the debt ratio is 1, then debt has been used to finance all the assets. A debt ratio of .50 means that the company has used debt to finance half its assets. The owners of the business have financed the other half. The higher the debt ratio, the higher the strain of paying interest each year and the principal amount at maturity. The lower the ratio, the less the business's future obligations. Creditors view a high debt ratio with caution. If a business seeking financing already has many liabilities, then additional debt payments may be too much for the business to handle. Creditors, to help protect themselves, generally charge higher interest rates on new borrowing to companies with an already high debt ratio.

McColpin's debt ratio at the end of 19X7 and 19X6 follow (data from Exhibit 19-2):

		Debt Ratio of McColpin, Inc.	
Formula		**19X7**	**19X6**
$\text{Debt ratio} = \dfrac{\text{Total liabilities}}{\text{Total assets}}$		$\dfrac{\$431{,}000}{\$787{,}000} = .55$	$\dfrac{\$324{,}000}{\$644{,}000} = .50$

Recall from our vertical and horizontal analyses that McColpin, Inc. expanded operations by financing the purchase of property, plant and equipment through borrowing, which is common.

Even after the increase in 19X7, McColpin's debt is not very high. The average debt ratio for most companies ranges around .57 to .67, with relatively little variation from company to company. McColpin's .55 debt ratio indicates a fairly low-risk debt position.

Times-Interest-Earned Ratio

The debt ratio measures the effect of debt on the company's *financial position* (balance sheet) but says nothing about its ability to pay interest expense. Analysts use a second ratio, the **times-interest-earned ratio**, to relate income to interest expense. To compute this ratio, we divide income from operations by interest expense. This ratio measures the number of times that operating income can *cover* interest expense. For this reason, the ratio is also called the **interest-coverage ratio**. A high ratio indicates ease in paying interest expense; a low value suggests difficulty.

McColpin's times-interest-earned ratios follow (data from Exhibit 19-1):

		Times-Interest-Earned Ratio of McColpin, Inc.	
Formula		**19X7**	**19X6**
$\begin{array}{l}\text{Times-} \\ \text{interest-earned} = \dfrac{\text{Income from operations}}{\text{Interest expense}} \\ \text{ratio}\end{array}$		$\dfrac{\$101{,}000}{\$24{,}000} = 4.21$	$\dfrac{\$57{,}000}{\$14{,}000} = 4.07$

McColpin's interest-coverage ratio increased in 19X7. This is a favourable sign about the company, especially since the company's short-term notes payable and long-term debt rose substantially during the year. (See the horizontal analysis of Exhibit 19-2). McColpin's new plant assets, we conclude, have earned more in operating income than they have cost the business in interest expense. The company's coverage ratio of around 4 is somewhat better than the norm for business, which is in the range of 2.0 to 3.0 for most companies.

Based on its debt ratio and times-interest-earned ratio, McColpin appears to have little difficulty paying its liabilities, also called *servicing its debt*.

Measuring Profitability

The fundamental goal of business is to earn a profit. Ratios that measure profitability play a large role in decision making. These ratios are reported in the business press, by investment services, and in the annual financial reports of companies.

Rate of Return on Net Sales

In business, the term *return* is used broadly and loosely as an evaluation of profitability. For example, consider a percentage called the **rate of return on net sales** or, simply **return on sales**. (The word *net* is usually omitted for convenience, even though the net sales figure is used to compute the ratio.) McColpin's rate of return on sales ratios follow:

		Rate of Return on Sales of McColpin, Inc.	
	Formula	**19X7**	**19X6**
Rate of return on sales	$= \dfrac{\text{Net income}}{\text{Net sales}}$	$\dfrac{\$48,000}{\$858,000} = .056$	$\dfrac{\$26,000}{\$803,000} = .032$

You will recognize this ratio from the vertical analysis of the income statement in Exhibit 19-3. The increase in McColpin's return on sales is significant. Companies strive for a high rate of return. The higher the rate of return, the more net sales dollars are providing income to the business and the fewer net sales dollars are absorbed by expenses. The 5.6 percent rate is less than Inco (1988: 21.2 percent), Echo Bay Mines (gold mining, 1988: 18.9 percent), Laidlaw Transportation (1988: 12.5 percent), and more than George Weston (1988: 1.3 percent) and Hudson's Bay Co. (1989: 1.1 percent). As these rates of return on sales indicate, this ratio varies widely from industry to industry.

One strategy for increasing the rate of return on sales is to develop a product that commands a premium price such as Bombardier's Ski-doo, Laura Secord chocolates and certain brands of clothing, such as Far West, Kettle Creek and Roots. Another strategy is to control costs. If successful, either strategy converts a higher proportion of sales into net income and increases the rate of return on net sales.

A return measure can be computed on any revenue and sales amount. Return on net sales, as we have seen, is net income divided by net sales. Return on total revenues is net income divided by total revenues. A company can compute a return on other specific portions of revenue as its information needs dictate.

Rate of Return on Total Assets

The **rate of return on total assets** or, simply, **return on assets** measures the success a company has in using its assets to earn a profit. Creditors have loaned money to the company, and the interest they receive is the return on their investment. Shareholders have invested in the company's stock, and net income is their return. The sum of interest expense and net income is the return to the two groups that have financed the company's operations, and this amount is the numerator of the return on assets ratio. Average total assets is the denominator.

McColpin's return on assets ratio follows:

Formula	Rate of Return on Total Assets of McColpin, Inc. 19X7
Rate of return on assets $= \dfrac{\text{Net income} + \text{interest expense}}{\text{Average total assets}}$	$\dfrac{\$48{,}000 + \$24{,}000}{\$715{,}500} = .101$

Net income and interest expense are taken from the income statement. To compute average total assets, we use beginning and ending total assets from the comparative balance sheet. McColpin's 10.1 percent return on assets is higher than the 5 to 6 percent average return on assets in many industries and compares favourably with Oshawa Wholesale (1989: 8.6 percent) and Union Enterprises (1989: 6.8 percent). St. Lawrence Cement (1987: 16.1 percent) and Dofasco (1987: 11.6 percent) earned somewhat higher returns.

Rate of Return on Common Shareholders' Equity

One of the most important measures of profitability is **rate of return on common shareholders' equity**. This ratio shows the relationship between net income and common shareholders' investment in the company. To compute this ratio, we first subtract preferred dividends from net income. This leaves only net income available to the common shareholders, which is needed to compute the ratio. We then divide net income available to common shareholders by the average shareholders' equity during the year. Common shareholders' equity is total shareholders' equity minus preferred equity. McColpin's rate of return on common shareholders' equity follows, (data from Exhibits 19-1 and 19-2):

**Rate of Return on Common
Shareholders' Equity of
McColpin, Inc.**

Formula		19X7
Rate of return on common shareholders' equity	$= \dfrac{\text{Net income} - \text{preferred dividends}}{\text{Average common shareholders' equity}}$	$\dfrac{\$48,000 - \$0}{\$338,000} = .142$

We compute average equity using the beginning and ending balances [($356,000 + $320,000)/2 = $338,000]. Observe that common shareholders' equity includes Retained Earnings.

McColpin's 14.2 percent return on common equity compares favourably with returns of companies in most industries, which average between 10 and 15 percent. However, some leading companies show higher ratios: Alcan Aluminum (1988: 23 percent), Thompson Newspapers (1988: 22.7 percent) and Noranda (1988: 17 percent).

Observe that return on equity (14.2 percent) is higher than return on assets (10.1 percent). This 4.1 percent difference results from borrowing at one rate, say 10 percent, and investing the funds to earn a higher rate, such as McColpin's 10.1 percent return on shareholders' asset. This practice is called **trading on the equity**, or the use of **leverage**. It is directly related to the debt ratio. The higher the debt ratio, the higher the leverage. Companies that finance operations with debt are said to *lever* their positions. Leverage increases the risk to common shareholders. For McColpin, Inc. and many other companies, leverage increases profitability. That is not always the case, however. Leverage can also have a negative impact on profitability. If revenues drop, debt and interest expense still must be paid. Therefore, leverage is a double-edged sword, increasing profits during good times but compounding losses during bad times.

Earnings per Share of Common Stock

Earnings per share of common stock or, simply, **earnings per share (EPS)** is perhaps the most widely quoted of all financial statistics. EPS is the only ratio that must appear on the face of the income statement. EPS is the amount of net income per share of the company's *common* stock. Earnings per share is computed by dividing net income available to common shareholders by the number of common shares outstanding during the year. Preferred dividends are subtracted from net income because the preferred shareholders have a prior claim to their dividends. McColpin has no preferred stock outstanding and so has no preferred dividends. McColpin's EPS for 19X7 and 19X6 follow. (Data are from Exhibits 19-1 and 19-2, and the company had 10,000 shares of common stock outstanding throughout 19X6 and 19X7).

**Earnings Per Share
of McColpin, Inc.**

Formula		19X7	19X6
Earnings per share of common stock (EPS)	$= \dfrac{\text{Net Income} - \text{preferred dividends}}{\text{Number of shares of common stock outstanding}}$	$\dfrac{\$48,000 - \$0}{10,000} = \$4.80$	$\dfrac{\$26,000 - \$0}{10,000} = \$2.60$

McColpin's EPS rose from $2.60 to $4.80, an increase of 85 percent. McColpin's shareholders should not expect such a significant boost in EPS every year. However, most companies strive to increase EPS by 10 to 15 percent annually, and the more successful companies do so. However, even the most dramatic upward trends include an occasional bad year.

Analysing Stock as an Investment

Investors purchase stock to earn a return on their investment. This return consists of two parts: (1) gains (or losses) from selling the stock at a price that is different from the investors' purchase price, and (2) dividends, the periodic distributions to shareholders. The ratios we examine in this section help analysts evaluate stock in terms of market price or dividend payments.

Price/Earnings Ratio

The **price/earnings ratio** is the ratio of the market price of a share of common stock to the company's earnings per share. This ratio, abbreviated P/E, appears in *The Financial Post* stock listings. P/E plays an important part in evaluating decisions to buy, hold, and sell stocks.

The price/earnings ratios of McColpin, Inc. follow. The market price of its common stock was $50 at the end of 19X7 and $35 at the end of 19X6. These prices can be obtained from a financial publication, a stockbroker or some other source outside the accounting records.

	Formula	Price/Earnings Ratio of McColpin, Inc. 19X7	Price/Earnings Ratio of McColpin, Inc. 19X6
Price/ earnings = ratio	Market price per share of common stock / Earnings per share	$\frac{\$50.00}{\$4.80} = 10.4$	$\frac{\$35.00}{\$2.60} = 13.5$

Given McColpin's 19X7 price/earnings ratio of 10.4, we would say that the company's stock is selling at 10.4 times earnings. The decline from the 19X6 P/E ratio of 13.5 is not a cause for alarm because the numerator (market price of the stock) is not under McColpin's control. The denominator (net income) is more controllable, and it increased during 19X7. Like most other ratios, P/E ratios vary from industry to industry, ranging in 1988 from 5 to 8 for companies that mine base metals (like Alcan Aluminum and Noranda) to 30 to 35 for companies that mine precious metals such as gold (like Echo Bay and Hemlo Gold). Some more glamourous companies (like BCE Mobile Communications) averaged more than 100 in 1988.

Dividend Yield

Dividend yield is the ratio of dividends per share of stock to the stock's market price per share. This ratio measures the percentage of a stock's market value that is returned annually as dividends, an important concern of shareholders. *Preferred* shareholders, who invest primarily to receive dividends, pay special attention to this ratio.

McColpin paid annual cash dividends of $1.20 per share in 19X7 and $1.00 in 19X6 and market prices of the company's common stock were $50 in 19X7 and $35.00 in 19X6. McColpin's dividend yields follow:

	Formula	Dividend Yield on Common Stock of McColpin, Inc.	
		19X7	**19X6**
Dividend yield on common stock	$= \dfrac{\text{Dividend per share of common stock}}{\text{Market price per share of common stock}}$	$\dfrac{\$1.20}{\$50.00} = .024$	$\dfrac{\$1.00}{\$35.00} = .029$

Investors who buy their McColpin common stock for $50 can expect to receive almost 2½ percent of investment annually in the form of cash dividends. Dividend yields vary widely, from 5 to 8 percent for older established firms (like Stelco and Bank of Montreal) down to a range of 0 to 3 percent for growth-oriented companies (like Rogers Communications and Magna). McColpin's dividend yield places the company in the second group.

Book Value per Share of Common Stock

Book value per share of common stock is simply common shareholders' equity divided by the number of shares of common stock outstanding. Common shareholders' equity equals total shareholders' equity less preferred equity. McColpin has no preferred stock outstanding. Its book value per share of common stock ratios follow. Recall that 10,000 shares of common stock were outstanding at the ends of years 19X7 and 19X6.

	Formula	Book Value per Share of the Common Stock of McColpin, Inc.	
		19X7	**19X6**
Book value per share of common stock	$= \dfrac{\text{Total shareholders' equity} - \text{preferred equity}}{\text{Number of shares of common stock outstanding}}$	$\dfrac{\$356,000 - \$0}{10,000} = \$35.60$	$\dfrac{\$320,000 - \$0}{10,000} = \$32.00$

The market price of a company's stock usually exceeds its book value. Some investors buy a stock when its market value approaches book value. Suppose you decided to buy McColpin stock at the end of 19X6, when its market price of $35 was close to book value of $32. That investment would have proved wise. The stock's price increased to $50 in 19X7. Of course, when you bought the stock in 19X6, there was no guarantee the stock price would increase.

The Complexity of Business Decisions

OBJECTIVE 6

Explain how to use ratios in decision-making

Business decisions are made in a world of uncertainty. Legislation, international affairs, competition, scandals and many other factors can turn profits into losses, and vice versa. To be most useful, ratios should be analysed over a period of years to take into account a representative group of these factors. Any one year, or even any two years, may not be representative of the company's performance over the long term.

For example, a business's acid-test ratio may show a substantial increase over a ten-year period. However, a two-year period during the early part of that decade might show a slight downturn. An evaluation based on the two-year analysis might lead to an unwise decision. To make the best use of ratios, we must consider them within a broad time frame.

As useful as ratios may be, they do have limitations. We may liken their use in decision making to a physician's use of a thermometer. A reading of 39 degrees Celsius indicates that something is wrong with the patient, but the temperature alone does not indicate what the problem is or how to cure it.

In financial analysis, a sudden drop in a company's current ratio signals that *something* is wrong, but this change does not identify the problem or show how to correct it. The business manager must analyse the figures that go into the ratio to determine whether current assets have decreased, current liabilities have increased, or both. If current assets have dropped, is the problem a cash shortage? Are accounts receivable down? Are inventories too low? Only by analysing the individual items that make up the ratio can the manager determine how to solve the problem. The manager must evaluate data on all ratios in the light of other information about the company and about its particular line of business, such as increased competition or a slowdown in the economy.

Uncertainty clouds business decisions. A decision-maker can never be sure how a course of action will turn out. For example, a careful analysis of ratios and other accounting information may suggest to management that the business should invest its excess cash in the stock of a microcomputer company. This industry may hold the prospect for the fastest return on an investment. A competing microcomputer company may come out with a new computer that sweeps the market, leaving the first company's stock worthless and the investing company with a loss. Ratio analysis cannot predict the future, but knowledge gained by a study of ratios and related information can help the analyst to make informed decisions.

Summary Problem for Your Review

This problem is based on the following financial data adapted from the financial statements of Big Bear Ltd., which operates approximately 400 convenience stores across Canada.

Big Bear Ltd.
Balance Sheets
19X3 and 19X2

	19X3	19X2
	(thousands of dollars)	

Assets

Current assets

Cash...	$ 4,123	$ 6,453
Marketable securities (same as short-term investments)	4,236	—
Receivables, net..	6,331	7,739
Inventories...	5,840	4,069
Prepaid expenses and others	3,830	2,708
Total current assets	24,360	20,969
Net property, plant and equipment	35,330	28,821
Net property under capital leases	23,346	20,886
Intangibles and other assets	10,493	11,349
	$93,529	$82,025

Liabilities and Shareholders' Equity

Current liabilities

Notes payable	$ 1,244	$ 785
Current installments of long-term debt and capital lease obligations	5,220	6,654
Accounts payable — trade	8,631	8,791
Accrued liabilities	5,822	5,983
Total current liabilities	20,917	22,213
Long-term debt, less current installments	22,195	15,549
Capital lease obligations, less current portion	24,296	22,350
Deferred income and deferred income taxes.................	2,211	1,522
Total common shareholders' equity (shares outstanding 3,017,381 at year end 19X3 and 2,729,274 at year end 19X2)	23,910	20,391
	$93,529	$82,025

Big Bear Ltd.
Statements of Earnings
19X3 and 19X2

	19X3	19X2
	(thousands of dollars)	

Total revenue..	$148,889	$140,539
Costs and expenses		
Cost of products sold	$114,335	$111,188
Selling, administrative and general expenses	23,475	20,816
	137,810	132,004
Earnings from operations	11,079	8,535
Interest expense	5,771	5,902
Earnings before income taxes.............................	5,308	2,633
Income taxes	1,713	932
Net earnings	$ 3,595	$ 1,701

Required

Compute the following ratios for Big Bear for 19X3:

1. Current ratio
2. Acid-test ratio
3. Inventory turnover
4. Days' sales (total revenue) in average receivables
5. Debt ratio
6. Times-interest-earned ratio
7. Rate of return on sales (total revenue)
8. Rate of return on total assets
9. Rate of return on common shareholders' equity
10. Price/earnings ratio, assuming the market price of common stock is $15.50 and earnings per share is $1.16.
11. Book value per share of common stock

SOLUTION TO REVIEW PROBLEM

1. $\text{Current Ratio} = \dfrac{\text{Current Assets}}{\text{Current Liabilities}} = \dfrac{\$24,360}{\$20,917} = 1.16$

2. $\text{Acid-Test Ratio} = \dfrac{\begin{array}{c}\text{Cash} + \text{Short-Term Investments} \\ + \text{Net Current Receivables}\end{array}}{\text{Current Liabilities}} = \dfrac{\$4,123 + \$4,236 + \$6,331}{\$20,917} = .70$

3. $\text{Inventory Turnover} = \dfrac{\text{Cost of Goods Sold}}{\text{Average Inventory}} = \dfrac{\$114,335}{(\$5,840 + \$4,069)/2} = 23.08$

4. Days' Sales (Total Revenue) in Average Receivables:

   a. $\text{One day's sales} = \dfrac{\text{Net Sales}}{365 \text{ Days}} = \dfrac{\$148,889}{365} = \$407.92$

   b. $\begin{array}{l}\text{Days' sales in} \\ \text{average accounts} \\ \text{receivable}\end{array} = \dfrac{\begin{array}{c}\text{Average} \\ \text{Accounts Receivables}\end{array}}{\text{One Day's Sales}} = \dfrac{(\$6,331 + \$7,739)/2}{\$407.92} = 17 \text{ days}$

5. $\text{Debt Ratio} = \dfrac{\text{Total Liabilities}}{\text{Total Assets}} = \dfrac{\$20,917 + \$22,195 + \$24,296 + \$2,211}{\$93,529} = .74$

6. $\begin{array}{l}\text{Times-} \\ \text{Interest-Earned} \\ \text{Ratio}\end{array} = \dfrac{\text{Income from Operations}}{\text{Interest Expense}} = \dfrac{\$11,079}{\$5,771} = 1.92$

7. $\dfrac{\text{Rate of Return on}}{\text{Sales (Total Revenue)}} = \dfrac{\text{Net Income}}{\text{Total Revenue}} = \dfrac{\$3,595}{\$148,889} = .024$

8. $\begin{array}{l}\text{Rate of} \\ \text{Return on} \\ \text{Total Assets}\end{array} = \dfrac{\text{Net Income} + \text{Interest Expense}}{\text{Average Total Assets}} = \dfrac{\$3,595 + \$5,771}{(\$93,529 + \$82,025)/2} = .107$

9. $\begin{array}{l}\text{Rate of Return} \\ \text{on Common} \\ \text{Shareholders' Equity}\end{array} = \dfrac{\begin{array}{c}\text{Net Income} \\ - \text{Preferred Dividends}\end{array}}{\begin{array}{c}\text{Average Common} \\ \text{Shareholders' Equity}\end{array}} = \dfrac{\$3,595 - \$0}{(\$23,910 + \$20,391)/2} = .162$

10. $\dfrac{\text{Price/}}{\text{Earnings}} = \dfrac{\text{Market Price per Share of Common Stock}}{\text{Earnings per Share}} = \dfrac{\$15.50^*}{\$1.16^*} = 13.4$

11. $\dfrac{\text{Book Value}}{\text{per Share of}} = \dfrac{\text{Total Shareholders' Equity} - \text{Preferred Equity}}{\text{Number of Shares of Common Stock Outstanding}} = \dfrac{\$23,910,000^* - \$0^*}{3,017,381^*} = \$7.92$

---

* All dollar amounts are expressed in thousands except those denoted by *.

Summary

Accounting provides information for decision making. Banks loan money, investors buy stocks, and managers run businesses based on the analysis of accounting information.

Horizontal analysis shows the dollar amount and the percentage change in each financial statement item from one period to the next. *Vertical analysis* shows the relationship of each item in a financial statement to its total: total assets on the balance sheet and net sales on the income statement.

Common-size statements (a form of vertical analysis) show the component percentages of the items in a statement. Investment advisory services report common-size statements for various industries, and analysts use them to compare a company to its competitors and to the industry averages.

The *statement of changes in financial position* shows the net cash inflow or outflow caused by a company's operating, investing and financing activities. By analysing the inflows and outflows of cash listed on this statement, an analyst can see where a business's cash comes from and how it is being spent.

Ratios play an important part in business decision making because they show relationships between financial statement items. Analysis of ratios over a period of time is an important way to track a company's progress. The accompanying list presents the ratios discussed in this chapter:

Know this column.

Ratio	Computation	Information Provided
Measuring the ability to pay current liabilities		
1. Current ratio	$\dfrac{\text{Current assets}}{\text{Current liabilities}}$	Measures ability to pay current liabilities from current assets.
2. Acid-test (quick) ratio	$\dfrac{\text{Cash} + \text{short-term investments} + \text{net current receivables}}{\text{Current liabilities}}$	Shows ability to pay current liabilities from the most liquid assets.
Measuring the ability to sell inventory and collect receivables		
3. Inventory turnover	$\dfrac{\text{Cost of goods sold}}{\text{Average inventory}}$	Indicates number of times inventory is turned or sold during the year.
4. Accounts receivable turnover	$\dfrac{\text{Net credit sales}}{\text{Average net accounts receivable}}$	Indicates company's ability to collect receivables.
5. Days' sales in receivables	$\dfrac{\text{Average net accounts receivable}}{\text{One day's sales}}$	Shows how many days it takes to collect average receivables.

Measuring the ability to pay long-term debts

6.	Debt ratio	$$\dfrac{\text{Total liabilities}}{\text{Total assets}}$$	Indicates percentage of assets financed through borrowing.
7.	Times-interest-earned ratio	$$\dfrac{\text{Income from operations}}{\text{Interest expense}}$$	Measures coverage of interest expense by operating income.

Measuring profitability

8.	Rate of return on net sales	$$\dfrac{\text{Net income}}{\text{Net sales}}$$	Shows the percentage of each sales dollar earned as net income.
9.	Rate of return on total assets	$$\dfrac{\text{Net income}+\text{interest expense}}{\text{Average total assets}}$$	Gauges how profitably assets are used.
10.	Rate of return on common shareholders' equity	$$\dfrac{\substack{\text{Net income}\\ -\text{preferred dividends}}}{\substack{\text{Average common}\\ \text{shareholders' equity}}}$$	Gauges how profitably the assets financed by the common shareholders are used.
11.	Earnings per share of common stock	$$\dfrac{\substack{\text{Net income}\\ -\text{preferred dividends}}}{\substack{\text{Number of share of}\\ \text{common stock outstanding}}}$$	Gives the amount of earnings per one share of common stock.

Analysing stock as an investment

12.	Price/earnings ratio	$$\dfrac{\substack{\text{Market price per}\\ \text{share of common stock}}}{\text{Earnings per share}}$$	Indicates the market price of one dollar of earnings.
13.	Dividend yield	$$\dfrac{\substack{\text{Dividend per share}\\ \text{of common stock}}}{\substack{\text{Market price per}\\ \text{share of common stock}}}$$	Shows the proportion of the market price of each share of stock returned as dividends to shareholders each period.
14.	Book value per share of common stock	$$\dfrac{\substack{\text{Total shareholders' equity}\\ -\text{preferred equity}}}{\substack{\text{Number of shares of}\\ \text{common stock outstanding}}}$$	Indicates the recorded accounting value of each share of common stock outstanding.

Self-Study Questions

Test your understanding of the chapter by marking the best answer for each of the following questions:

1. Net income was $240,000 in 19X4, $210,000 in 19X5, and $252,000 in 19X6. The change from 19X5 to 19X6 is a (an) *(p. 794)*
   a. Increase of 5 percent   c. Decrease of 10 percent
   b. Increase of 20 percent   d. Decrease of 12.5 percent
2. Vertical analysis of a financial statement shows *(p. 797)*
   a. Trend percentages
   b. The percentage change in an item from period to period
   c. The relationship of an item to its total on the statement
   d. Net income expressed as a percentage of shareholders' equity

3. Common-size statements are useful for comparing *(pp. 799, 800)*
   a. Changes in the makeup of assets from period to period
   b. Different companies
   c. A company to its industry
   d. All of the above
4. The statement of changes in financial position is used for decision making by *(pp. 801, 802)*
   a. Reporting where cash came from and how it was spent
   b. Indicating how net income was earned
   c. Giving the ratio relationships between selected items
   d. Showing a horizontal analysis of cash flows
5. Cash is $10,000, net accounts receivable amount to $22,000, inventory is $55,000, prepaid expenses total $3,000, and current liabilities are $40,000. What is the acid-test ratio? *(p. 806)*
   a. .25   c. 2.18
   b. .80   d. 2.25
6. Inventory turnover is computed by dividing *(p. 807)*
   a. Sales revenue by average inventory
   b. Cost of goods sold by average inventory
   c. Credit sales by average inventory
   d. Average inventory by cost of goods sold
7. Capp Corporation is experiencing a severe cash shortage due to inability to collect accounts receivable. The decision tool most likely to help identify the appropriate corrective action is the *(pp. 808, 809)*
   a. Acid-test ratio   c. Times-interest-earned ratio
   b. Inventory turnover   d. Day's sales in receivables
8. Analysis of Mendoza Ltd. financial statements over five years reveals that sales are growing steadily, the debt ratio is higher than the industry average and is increasing, interest coverage is decreasing, return on total assets is declining, and earnings per share of common stock is decreasing. Considered together, these ratios suggest that *(pp. 809–812)*
   a. Mendoza should pursue collections of receivables more vigorously
   b. Competition is taking sales away from Mendoza
   c. Mendoza is in a declining industry
   d. The company's debt burden is hurting profitability
9. Which of the following is most likely to be true? *(pp. 812, 813)*
   a. Return on common equity exceeds return on total assets.
   b. Return on total assets exceeds return on common equity.
   c. Return on total assets equals return on common equity.
   d. None of the above.
10. How are financial ratios used in decision-making? *(p. 816)*
    a. They remove the uncertainty of the business environment.
    b. They give clear signals about the appropriate action to take.
    c. They can help identify the reasons for success and failure in business, but decision-making requires information beyond the ratios.
    d. They aren't useful because decision-making is too complex.

Answers to the self-study questions are at the end of the chapter.

Accounting Vocabulary

accounts receivable turnover (p. 808)
acid-test ratio (p. 806)
book value per share of common stock (p. 815)

common-size statements (p. 799)
current ratio (p. 805)
days' sales in receivables (p. 808)

debt ratio (p. 810)
dividend yield (p. 815)
horizontal analysis (p. 794)
interest-coverage ratio (p. 810)

inventory turnover *(p. 807)*	rate of return on total assets *(p. 812)*	vertical analysis *(p. 797)*
leverage *(p. 813)*		working capital *(p. 805)*
price/earnings ratio *(p. 814)*	return on assets *(p. 812)*	
quick ratio *(p. 806)*	return on common	
rate of return on common	shareholders' equity	
shareholders' equity	*(p. 812)*	
(p. 812)	return on sales *(p. 811)*	
rate of return on net sales	times-interest-earned ratio	
(p. 811)	*(p. 810)*	

Assignment Material _____

Questions

1. Identify two groups of users of accounting information and the decisions they base on accounting data.
2. What are three analytical tools that are based on accounting information?
3. Briefly describe horizontal analysis. How do decision makers use this tool of analysis?
4. What is vertical analysis, and what is its purpose?
5. What use is made of common-size statements?
6. State how an investor might analyse the statement of changes in financial position. How might the investor analyse investing activities data?
7. Why are ratios an important tool of financial analysis? Give an example.
8. Identify two ratios used to measure a company's ability to pay current liabilities. Show how they are computed.
9. Why is the acid-test ratio called by this name?
10. What does the inventory-turnover ratio measure?
11. Suppose the days' sales in receivables ratio of Gomez, Inc. increased from 36 at January 1 to 43 at December 31. Is this a good sign or a bad sign about the company? What would Gomez management do in response to this change?
12. Company A's debt ratio has increased from .50 to .70. Identify a decision-maker to whom this increase is important, and state how the increase affects this party's decisions about the company.
13. Which ratio measures the *effect of debt* on (a) financial position (the balance sheet) and (b) the company's ability to pay interest expense (the income statement)?
14. Company A is a chain of grocery stores, and Company B is a computer manufacturer. Which company is likely to have the higher (a) current ratio, (b) inventory turnover, and (c) rate of return on sales? Give your reasons.
15. Identify four ratios used to measure a company's profitability. Show how to compute these ratios and state what information each ratio provides.
16. The average price/earnings ratio of Cominco was 7.4 in 1988, and the price/earnings ratio of Trizec was 45.7. Which company did the stock market favor? Explain.
17. Irwin Toy paid cash dividends of $.20 per share when the market price of the company's stock was $6⅜. What was the dividend yield on Irwin's stock. What does dividend yield measure?
18. Hold all other factors constant and indicate whether each of the following situations generally signals good or bad news about a company:
   a. Increase in current ratio   e. Increase in return on sales
   b. Decrease in inventory turnover   f. Decrease in earnings per share
   c. Increase in debt ratio   g. Increase in price/earnings ratio
   d. Decrease in interest-coverage ratio h. Increase in book value per share
19. Explain how an investor might use book value per share of stock in making an investment decision.
20. Describe how decision makers use ratio data. What are the limitations of ratios?

Exercises

Exercise 19-1   *Computing year-to-year changes in current assets and total assets*

Using the following financial statement data of Chin Corporation, compute the dollar amount of change and the percentage change in total current assets and total assets during years 5 and 4:

| | | | | Increase (Decrease) | | | |
| | | | | During Year 5 | | During Year 4 | |
	Year 5	Year 4	Year 3	Amount	%	Amount	%
Total current assets	$312,000	$260,000	$280,000				
Total assets	850,000	867,000	840,000				

Exercise 19-2   *Horizontal analysis of an income statement*

Prepare a horizontal analysis of the following comparative income statement of LaPaz Incorporated. Round percentage changes to the nearest one-tenth percent (three decimal places):

LaPaz Incorporated
Comparative Income Statement
years ended December 31, 19X9 and 19X8

	19X9	19X8
Total Revenue	$431,000	$373,000
Expenses		
Cost of goods sold	$202,000	$188,000
Selling and general expenses	118,000	93,000
Interest expense	7,000	4,000
Income tax expense	42,000	37,000
Total expenses	369,000	322,000
Net Income	$ 62,000	$ 51,000

Why did net income increase by a higher percentage than total revenues increased during 19X9?

Exercise 19-3   *Computing trend percentages*

Compute trend percentages for net sales and net income for the following five-year period, using year 1 as the base year:

	Year 5	Year 4	Year 3	Year 2	Year 1
		(amounts in thousands)			
Net sales	$1,448	$1,287	$1,106	$944	$1,043
Net income ..	127	114	93	71	85

Which grew more during the period, net sales or net income?

Exercise 19-4   *Vertical analysis of a balance sheet*

Quattlebaum Ltd. has requested that you perform a vertical analysis of its balance sheet to determine the component percentages of its assets, liabilities and shareholders' equity.

Quattlebaum Ltd.
Balance Sheet
December 31, 19X3

Assets

Total current assets..............................	$ 74,000
Long-term investments	23,000
Property, plant and equipment, net	227,000
Total assets....................................	$324,000

Liabilities

Total current liabilities	$ 48,000
Long-term debt	118,000
Total liabilities	166,000

Shareholders' Equity

Total shareholders' equity........................	158,000
Total liabilities and shareholders' equity	$324,000

Exercise 19-5 *Preparing a common-size income statement*

Prepare a comparative common-size income statement for LaPaz Incorporated, using the 19X9 and 19X8 data of Exercise 19-2 and rounding percentages to one-tenth percent (three decimal places).

Exercise 19-6 *Analysing the statement of changes in financial position*

Identify any weaknesses revealed by the statement of changes in financial position of Tanglewood Home Centres, Inc.

Tanglewood Home Centers, Inc.
Statement of Changes in Financial Position
for the Current Year

Operating activities		
Income from operations		$ 8,000
Add (subtract) noncash items		
Depreciation	$ 23,000	
Net increase in current assets other than cash ...	(15,000)	
Net increase in current liabilities exclusive of		
short-term debt	11,000	19,000
Net cash inflow from operating activities		27,000
Financing activities		
Issuance of bonds payable	$ 81,000	
Payment of short-term debt	(101,000)	
Payment of long-term debt	(79,000)	
Payment of dividends	(8,000)	
Net cash outflow from financing activities.......		(107,000)
Investing activities		
Sale of property, plant and equipment............		76,000
Decrease in cash		$ (4,000)

Exercise 19-7   *Computing five ratios*

The financial statements of Snyder Corp. include the following items:

	Current Year	Preceding Year
Balance sheet		
Cash......................	$ 17,000	$ 22,000
Short-term investments	21,000	26,000
Net receivables	64,000	73,000
Inventory	87,000	71,000
Prepaid expenses	6,000	8,000
Total current assets..........	195,000	200,000
Total current liabilities	107,000	91,000
Income statement		
Net credit sales	$444,000	
Cost of goods sold...........	237,000	

Required

Compute the following ratios for the current year: (1) current ratio, (2) acid-test ratio, (3) inventory turnover, (4) accounts receivable turnover and (5) day's sales in average receivables.

Exercise 19-8   *Analysing the ability to pay current liabilities*

Holmes, Inc., has requested that you determine whether the company's ability to pay its current liabilities and long-term debts has improved or deteriorated during 19X5. To answer this question, compute the following ratios for 19X5 and 19X4: (a) current ratio, (b) acid-test ratio, (c) debt ratio and (d) times-interest-earned ratio. Summarize the results of your analysis.

	19X5	19X4
Cash	$ 31,000	$ 37,000
Short-term investments	28,000	—
Net receivables........................	132,000	116,000
Inventory	226,000	263,000
Prepaid expenses.....................	11,000	9,000
Total assets	553,000	519,000
Total current liabilities	205,000	241,000
Total liabilities	261,000	273,000
Income from operations	165,000	158,000
Interest expense......................	26,000	31,000

Exercise 19-9   *Analysing profitability*

Compute four ratios that measure ability to earn profits for Gaspé, Inc. whose comparative income statement appears on the next page. Additional data follow:

a. Average total assets.....................................	$204,000	$191,000
b. Average common shareholders' equity	$ 96,000	$ 89,000
c. Preferred dividends	$ 3,000	$ 3,000
d. Shares of common stock outstanding....................	18,000	18,000

Did the company's operating performance improve or deteriorate during 19X1?

Gaspé, Inc.
Comparative Income Statement
years ended December 31, 19X1 and 19X0

	19X1	19X0
Net sales	$166,000	$158,000
Cost of goods sold	93,000	86,000
Gross profit	73,000	72,000
Selling and general expenses	48,000	41,000
Income from operations	25,000	31,000
Interest expense	9,000	10,000
Income before income tax	16,000	21,000
Income tax expense	6,000	8,000
Net income	$ 10,000	$ 13,000

Exercise 19-10 *Evaluating a stock as an investment*

Evaluate the common stock of Grand Banks, Inc. as an investment. Specifically, use the three stock ratios to determine whether the stock has increased or decreased in attractiveness during the past year.

	Current Year	Preceding Year
Net income	$ 58,000	$ 55,000
Dividends (half on preferred stock)	28,000	28,000
Common shareholders' equity at year end		
(100,000 shares)	530,000	500,000
Preferred shareholders' equity at year end	200,000	200,000
Market price per share of common stock at year end	$6.63	$5.75

Problems

Problem 19-1A *Trend percentages, return on common equity and comparison to the industry*

Net sales, net income, and common shareholders' equity for Nasdac Computing, Inc. for a six-year period follow:

	19X9	19X8	19X7	19X6	19X5	19X4
	(amounts in thousands)					
Net sales	$762	$714	$621	$532	$596	$634
Net income	49	45	42	38	37	40
Ending common shareholders' equity ...	386	354	330	296	272	252

Required

1. Compute trend percentages for 19X5 through 19X9, using 19X4 as the base year.
2. Compute the rate of return on average common shareholders' equity for 19X5 through 19X9, rounding to three decimal places. In this industry, rates of 13 percent

are average, rates above 16 percent are considered good, and rates above 20 percent are viewed as outstanding.

3. How does Nasdac's return on common shareholders' equity compare to the industry?

Problem 19-2A   *Common-size statements, analysis of profitability and comparison to the industry*

Middlebrook Sporting Goods Ltd. has asked your help in comparing the company's profit performance and financial position with the average for the sporting goods retail industry. The proprietor has given you the company's income statement and balance sheet and also the industry average data for retailers of sporting goods.

Middlebrook Sporting Goods Ltd. Income Statement Compared to Industry Average year ended December 31, 19X6		
	Middlebrook	**Industry Average**
Net sales.................	$781,000	100.0%
Cost of goods sold	476,000	65.8
Gross profit	305,000	34.2
Operating expenses	243,000	29.7
Operating income	62,000	4.5
Other expenses	5,000	.4
Net income	$ 57,000	4.1%

Middlebrook Sporting Goods Ltd. Balance Sheet Compared to Industry Average December 31, 19X6		
	Middlebrook	**Industry Average**
Current assets	$350,000	80.9%
Fixed assets, net	74,000	13.6
Intangible assets, net	4,000	.8
Other assets	22,000	4.7
Total	$450,000	100.0%
Current liabilities	$230,000	48.1%
Long-term liabilities	72,000	16.6
Shareholders' equity	148,000	35.3
Total	$450,000	100.0%

Required

1. Prepare a two-column common-size income statement and a two-column common-size balance sheet for Middlebrook. The first column of each statement should present Middlebrook's common-size statement, and the second column should show the industry averages.

2. For the profitability analysis, compute Middlebrook's (a) ratio of gross profit to net sales, (b) ratio of operating income to net sales, and (c) ratio of net income to net sales. Compare these figures to the industry averages. Is Middlebrook's profit performance better or worse than the industry average?

3. For the analysis of financial position, compute Middlebrook's (a) ratio of current assets to total assets and (b) ratio of shareholders' equity to total assets. Compare these ratios to the industry averages. Is Middlebrook's financial position better or worse than the industry averages?

Problem 19-3A   *Using the statement of changes in financial position for decision-making*

You have been asked to evaluate two companies as possible investments. The two companies, similar in size, buy computers, airplanes and other high-cost assets to lease to other businesses. Assume that all other available information has been analysed, and the decision on which company's stock to purchase depends on the information given in their statements of changes in financial position shown on the next page.

LeaseAlberta, Inc.
Statements of Changes in Financial Position
years ended September 30, 19X5 and 19X4

	19X5	19X4
Operating activities		
Income from operations	$ 37,000	$ 74,000
Add (subtract) noncash items:		
Total	14,000	(4,000)
Net cash inflow from operating activities	51,000	70,000
Financing activities		
Issuance of short-term notes payable	$ 73,000	$ 19,000
Issuance of long-term notes payable	31,000	42,000
Payment of short-term notes payable	(181,000)	(148,000)
Payment of long-term notes payable	(55,000)	(32,000)
Net cash outflow from financing activities	(132,000)	(119,000)
Investing activities		
Purchase of property, plant and equipment	$ (13,000)	$ (3,000)
Sale of property, plant and equipment	86,000	79,000
Sale of long-term investments	13,000	—
Net cash inflow from investing activities	86,000	76,000
Increase in cash	$ 5,000	$ 27,000
Cash summary from balance sheet		
Cash balance at beginning of year	$ 31,000	$ 4,000
Increase in cash during the year	5,000	27,000
Cash balance at end of year	$ 36,000	$ 31,000

Prairie Leasing Corporation
Statements of Changes in Financial Position
years ended September 30, 19X5 and 19X4

	19X5	19X4
Operating activities		
Income from operations	$ 79,000	$ 71,000
Add (subtract) noncash items:		
Total	19,000	—
Net cash inflow from operating activities	98,000	71,000
Financing activities		
Issuance of long-term notes payable	$ 46,000	$ 43,000
Payment of long-term notes payable	(15,000)	(40,000)
Payment of cash dividends	(12,000)	(9,000)
Net cash inflow (outflow) from financing activities	19,000	(6,000)
Investing activities		
Purchase of property, plant and equipment	$(121,000)	$(91,000)
Sale of long-term investments	13,000	18,000
Net cash inflow from investing activities	(108,000)	(73,000)
Increase (decrease) in cash	$ 9,000	$ (8,000)
Cash summary from balance sheet		
Cash balance at beginning of year	$ 72,000	$ 80,000
Increase (decrease) in cash during the year	9,000	(8,000)
Cash balance at end of year	$ 81,000	$ 72,000

Required

Discuss the relative strengths and weaknesses of each company. Conclude your discussion by recommending one company's stock as an investment.

Problem 19-4A   *Effects of business transactions on selected ratios*

Financial statement data of Bylinski Corp. include the following items:

Cash...	$ 22,000
Short-term investments	19,000
Accounts receivable, net	83,000
Inventories	141,000
Prepaid expenses	8,000
Total assets	657,000
Short-term notes payable	49,000
Accounts payable	103,000
Accrued liabilities	38,000
Long-term notes payable..........................	160,000
Other long-term liabilities	31,000
Net income......................................	71,000
Number of common shares outstanding	40,000

Required

1. Compute Bylinski's current ratio, debt ratio and earnings per share.
2. Compute each of the three ratios after evaluating the effect of each transaction that follows. Consider each transaction *separately*.
   a. Purchased merchandise of $26,000 on account, debiting inventory.
   b. Paid off long-term liabilities, $31,000.
   c. Declared, but did not pay, a $22,000 cash dividend on the common stock.
   d. Borrowed $85,000 on a long-term note payable.
   e. Sold short-term investments for $18,000 (cost, $11,000); assume no income tax on the gain.
   f. Issued 5,000 shares of common stock, receiving cash of $120,000.
   g. Received cash on account $19,000.
   h. Paid short-term notes payable, $32,000.

Use the following format for your answer:

Requirement 1		**Current Ratio**	**Debt Ratio**	**Earnings per Share**
Requirement 2	**Transaction (letter)**	**Current Ratio**	**Debt Ratio**	**Earnings per Share**

Problem 19-5A   *Using ratios to evaluate a stock investment*

Comparative financial statement data of Oaktree Realty Ltd. appear on the next page.

Other information:

a. Market price of Oaktree common stock: $31 at December 31, 19X7 and $25.50 at December 31, 19X6.
b. Common shares outstanding: 10,000 during 19X7 and 9,000 during 19X6.
c. Preferred shares outstanding: 1,000.
d. All sales on credit.

Required

1. Compute the following ratios for 19X7 and 19X6:
   a. Current ratio
   b. Inventory turnover
   c. Accounts receivable turnover
   d. Times-interest-earned ratio
   e. Return on assets
   f. Return on common shareholders' equity
   g. Earnings per share of common stock
   h. Price/earnings ratio
   i. Book value per share of common stock

2. Decide (a) whether Oaktree's financial position improved or deteriorated during 19X7 and (b) whether the investment attractiveness of its common stock appears to have increased or decreased.

Oaktree Realty Ltd.
Comparative Income Statement
years ended December 31, 19X7 and 19X6

	19X7	19X6
Net sales	$462,000	$427,000
Cost of goods sold	229,000	218,000
Gross profit	233,000	209,000
Operating expenses	136,000	134,000
Income from operations	97,000	75,000
Interest expense	21,000	12,000
Income before income tax	76,000	63,000
Income tax expense	30,000	27,000
Net income	$ 46,000	$ 36,000

Oaktree Realty Ltd.
Comparative Balance Sheet
December 31, 19X7 and 19X6
(selected 19X5 amounts given for computation of ratios)

	19X7	19X6	19X5
Current assets			
Cash	$ 71,000	$ 77,000	
Current receivables, net	137,000	146,000	$153,000
Inventories	202,000	182,000	237,000
Prepaid expenses	16,000	7,000	
Total current assets	426,000	412,000	
Property, plant and equipment, net	159,000	148,000	
Total assets	$585,000	$560,000	598,000
Total current liabilities	$206,000	$223,000	
Long-term liabilities	119,000	117,000	
Total liabilities	325,000	340,000	
Preferred shareholders' equity, $6.00	100,000	100,000	
Common shareholders' equity	160,000	120,000	90,000
Total liabilities and shareholders' equity	$585,000	$560,000	

Problem 19-6A   *Using ratios to decide between two stock investments*

Assume you are purchasing an investment and have decided to invest in a company in the air-conditioning and heating business. Suppose you have narrowed the choice to Linz Corp. and Hutton, Inc. You have assembled the following selected data:

Selected income statement data for current year

	Linz Corp.	Hutton, Inc.
Net sales (all on credit)	$371,000	$497,000
Cost of goods sold	209,000	258,000
Income from operations	79,000	138,000
Interest expense		19,000
Net income	48,000	72,000

Selected balance sheet and market price data at end of current year

	Linz Corp.	Hutton, Inc.
Current assets		
Cash	$ 22,000	$ 19,000
Short-term investments		18,000
Current receivables, net	42,000	46,000
Inventories	87,000	100,000
Prepaid expenses	2,000	3,000
Total current assets	153,000	186,000
Total assets	265,000	328,000
Total current liabilities	108,000	98,000
Total liabilities	108,000	131,000
Preferred stock: $5.00 (200 shares)		20,000
Common stock (10,000 shares)	10,000	
(5,000 shares)		12,500
Total shareholders' equity	157,000	197,000
Market price per share of common stock	$48	$108

Selected balance sheet data at beginning of current year

	Linz Corp.	Hutton, Inc.
Current receivables, net	$ 40,000	$ 48,000
Inventories	93,000	88,000
Total assets	259,000	270,000
Preferred shareholders' equity, $5.00 (200 shares)		20,000
Common stock (10,000 shares)	10,000	
(5,000 shares)		12,500
Total shareholders' equity	118,000	126,000

Your investment strategy is to purchase the stocks of companies that have low price/earnings ratios but appear to be in good shape financially. Assume you have analysed all other factors, and your decision depends on the results of the ratio analysis to be performed.

Required

Compute the following ratios for both companies for the current year and decide which company's stock better fits your investment strategy:

1. Current ratio
2. Acid-test ratio
3. Inventory turnover
4. Day's sales in average receivables
5. Debt ratio
6. Times-interest-earned ratio
7. Return on net sales

8. Return on total assets
9. Return on common shareholders' equity
10. Earnings per share of common stock
11. Book value per share of common stock
12. Price/earnings ratio

(Group B)

Problem 19-1B *Trend percentages, return on common equity and comparison to the industry*

Net sales, net income and total assets for LeClerc Manufacturing, Inc. for a six-year period follow:

	19X6	19X5	19X4	19X3	19X2	19X1
	(amounts in thousands)					
Net sales	$337	$303	$266	$271	$253	$241
Net income	24	21	12	17	14	13
Total assets	286	244	209	197	181	166

Required

1. Compute trend percentages for 19X2 through 19X6, using 19X1 as the base year.
2. Compute the rate of return on net sales for 19X2 through 19X6, rounding to three decimal places. In this industry, rates above 5 percent are considered good, and rates above 7 percent are viewed as outstanding.
3. How does LeClerc's return on net sales compare to the industry?

Problem 19-2B *Common-size statements, analysis of profitability and comparison to the industry*

The owners of Blanton & Bornhauser Ltd., a department store, have asked your help in comparing the company's profit performance and financial position with the average for the department-store industry. The accountant has given you the company's income statement and balance sheet and also the following actual data for the department-store industry.

Blanton & Bornhauser Ltd. Income Statement Compared to Industry Average year ended December 31, 19X3			Blanton & Bornhauser Ltd. Balance Sheet Compared to Industry Average December 31, 19X3		
	Blanton & Bornhauser	Industry Average		Blanton & Bornhauser	Industry Average
Net sales	$957,000	100.0%	Current assets..............	$440,000	74.4%
Cost of goods sold	653,000	65.9	Fixed assets, net	135,000	20.0
Gross profit	304,000	34.1	Intangible assets, net	42,000	.6
Operating expenses.........	306,000	31.1	Other assets	13,000	5.0
Operating income (loss)	(2,000)	3.0	Total	$630,000	100.0%
Other expenses	2,000	.4	Current liabilities	$246,000	35.6%
Net income (loss)	$ (4,000)	2.6%	Long-term liabilities	124,000	19.0
			Shareholders' equity	260,000	45.4
			Total	$630,000	100.0%

Required

1. Prepare a two-column common-size income statement and a two-column common-size balance sheet for Blanton & Bornhauser. The first column of each statement should present Blanton & Bornhauser's common-size statement, and the second column should show the industry averages.

2. For the profitability analysis, compute Blanton & Bornhauser's (a) ratio of gross profit to net sales, (b) ratio of operating income (loss) to net sales, and (c) ratio of net income (loss) to net sales. Compare these figures to the industry averages. Is Blanton & Bornhauser's profit performance better or worse than average for department stores?

3. For the analysis of financial position, compare Blanton & Bornhauser's (a) ratio of current assets to total assets and (b) ratio of shareholders' equity to total assets. Compare these ratios to the industry averages. Is Blanton & Bornhauser's financial position better or worse than the average for the industry?

Problem 19-3B   *Using the statement of changes in financial position for decision-making*

You are evaluating two companies as possible investments. The two companies, similar in size, are in the commuter airline business. They fly passengers from Toronto to smaller cities in Ontario. Assume that all other available information has been analysed, and that the decision on which company's stock to purchase depends on the information given in their statements of changes in financial position shown on the next page.

Required

Discuss the relative strengths and weaknesses of UC Air and Western Ontario Flight. Conclude our discussion by recommending one of the company's stocks as an investment.

UC Air, Inc.
Statements of Changes in Financial Position
years ended November 30, 19X9 and 19X8

	19X9	19X8
Operating activities		
Income from operations	$ 184,000	$ 131,000
Add (subtract) noncash items:		
Total	64,000	62,000
Net cash inflow from operating activities	248,000	193,000
Financing activities		
Issuance of long-term notes payable	$ 131,000	$ 83,000
Issuance of short-term notes payable	43,000	35,000
Payment of short-term notes payable	(66,000)	(18,000)
Net cash inflow from financing activities	108,000	100,000
Investing activities		
Purchase of property, plant and equipment	$(303,000)	$(453,000)
Sale of property, plant and equipment	46,000	39,000
Sale of long-term investments	—	33,000
Net cash outflow from investing activities	(257,000)	(381,000)
Increase (decrease) in cash	$ 99,000	$ (88,000)
Cash summary from balance sheet		
Cash balance at beginning of year	$ 116,000	$ 204,000
Increase (decrease) in cash during the year	99,000	(88,000)
Cash balance at end of year	$ 215,000	$ 116,000

Western Ontario Flight Corporation
Statements of Changes in Financial Position
years ended November 30, 19X9 and 19X8

	19X9	19X8
Operating activities		
Income (loss) from operations	$ (67,000)	$154,000
Add (subtract) noncash items:		
Total	84,000	(23,000)
Net cash inflow from operating activities	17,000	131,000
Financing activities		
Issuance of short-term notes payable	$ 122,000	$ 143,000
Payment of short-term notes payable	(179,000)	(134,000)
Payment of cash dividends	(45,000)	(64,000)
Net cash outflow from financing activities	(102,000)	(55,000)
Investing activities		
Purchase of property, plant and equipment	$(120,000)	$ (91,000)
Sale of property, plant and equipment	118,000	39,000
Sale of long-term investments	52,000	4,000
Net cash inflow (outflow) from investing activities	50,000	(48,000)
Increase (decrease) in cash	$ (35,000)	$ 28,000
Cash summary from balance sheet		
Cash balance at beginning of year	$ 131,000	$ 103,000
Increase (decrease) in cash during the year	(35,000)	28,000
Cash balance at end of year	$ 96,000	$ 131,000

Problem 19-4B   *Effects of business transactions on selected ratios*

Financial statement data of Goliad Corporation include the following items:

Cash..	$ 47,000
Short-term investments	21,000
Accounts receivable, net	102,000
Inventories.....................................	274,000
Prepaid expenses	15,000
Total assets....................................	933,000
Short-term notes payable	72,000
Accounts payable	96,000
Accrued liabilities	50,000
Long-term notes payable.........................	146,000
Other long-term liabilities........................	78,000
Net income....................................	119,000
Number of common shares outstanding	32,000

Required

1. Compute Goliad's current ratio, debt ratio, and earnings per share.
2. Compute each of the three ratios after evaluating the effect of each transaction that follows. Consider each transaction *separately*.
    a. Purchased merchandise of $48,000 on account, debiting Inventory.
    b. Paid off long-term liabilities, $78,000.
    c. Declared, but did not pay, a $31,000 cash dividend on the common stock.
    d. Borrowed $56,000 on a long-term note payable.
    e. Sold short-term investments for $34,000 (cost $46,000); assume no tax effect of the loss.
    f. Issued 14,000 shares of common stock, receiving cash of $168,000.
    g. Received cash on account, $6,000.
    h. Paid short-term notes payable, $51,000.

Use the following format for your answer to Problem 19-4B:

Requirement 1		**Current Ratio**	**Debt Ratio**	**Earnings per Share**

Requirement 2	**Transaction (letter)**	**Current Ratio**	**Debt Ratio**	**Earnings per Share**

Problem 19-5B   *Using ratios to evaluate a stock investment*

Comparative financial statement data of Manatee Furniture Inc. follow on p. 836.

Other information:

a. Market price of Manatee common stock: $42 at December 31, 19X4 and $51.00 at December 31, 19X3.
b. Common shares outstanding: 20,000 during 19X4 and 19,000 during 19X3. Preferred shares outstanding: 2,500 during 19X3 and 19X4.
c. Preferred shares outstanding: 2,500.
d. All sales on credit.

Required

1. Compute the following ratios for 19X4 and 19X3:
    a. Current ratio
    b. Inventory turnover
    c. Accounts receivable turnover
    d. Times-interest-earned ratio

Manatee Furniture Inc.
Comparative Income Statement
years ended December 31, 19X4 and 19X3

	19X4	19X3
Net sales...	$667,000	$599,000
Cost of goods sold	378,000	283,000
Gross profit	289,000	316,000
Operating expenses.................................	129,000	147,000
Income from operations	160,000	169,000
Interest expense	47,000	41,000
Income before income tax...........................	113,000	128,000
Income tax expense	44,000	53,000
Net income	$ 69,000	$ 75,000

Manatee Furniture Inc.
Comparative Balance Sheet
December 31, 19X4 and 19X3
(selected 19X2 amounts given for computation of ratios)

	19X4	19X3	19X2
Current assets			
Cash.................................	$ 37,000	$ 30,000	
Current receivables, net.................	188,000	151,000	$138,000
Inventories...........................	372,000	306,000	184,000
Prepaid expenses	5,000	10,000	
Total current assets...................	602,000	497,000	
Property, plant and equipment, net	287,000	276,000	
Total assets.............................	$889,000	$773,000	707,000
Total current liabilities	$286,000	$267,000	
Long-term liabilities	245,000	235,000	
Total liabilities	531,000	502,000	
Preferred shareholders' equity, $.80	50,000	50,000	
Common shareholders' equity	308,000	221,000	148,000
Total liabilities and shareholders' equity	$889,000	$773,000	

e. Return on assets
f. Return on common shareholders' equity
g. Earnings per share of common stock
h. Price/earnings ratio
i. Book value per share of common stock

2. Decide (a) whether Manatee's financial position improved or deteriorated during 19X4 and (b) whether the investment attractiveness of its common stock appears to have increased or decreased.

Problem 19-6B   *Using ratios to decide between two stock investments*

Assume you are purchasing stock in a company in the grain business. Suppose you have narrowed the choice to AgriCorp and MultiGrains, Inc., and have assembled the following data:

Selected income statement data for current year

	AgriCorp	MultiGrains, Inc.
Net sales (all on credit)	$603,000	$519,000
Cost of goods sold	454,000	387,000
Income from operations	93,000	72,000
Interest expense		8,000
Net income	56,000	38,000

Selected balance sheet and market price data at end of current year

	AgriCorp	Multigrains, Inc.
Current assets		
Cash	$ 35,000	$ 39,000
Short-term investments	16,000	13,000
Current receivables, net	189,000	164,000
Inventories	191,000	183,000
Prepaid expenses	5,000	15,000
Total current assets	436,000	414,000
Total assets	974,000	938,000
Total current liabilities	366,000	338,000
Total liabilities	667,000	691,000
Preferred stock, $4.00 (250 shares)		25,000
Common stock, (150,000 shares)	150,000	
(20,000 shares)		100,000
Total shareholders' equity	307,000	247,000
Market price per share of common stock	$6	$47.50

Selected balance sheet data at beginning of current year

	AgriCorp	MultiGrains, Inc.
Current receivables, net	$142,000	$193,000
Inventories	209,000	197,000
Total assets	842,000	909,000
Preferred shareholders' equity, $4.00 (250 shares) .		25,000
Common stock, (150,000 shares)	150,000	
(20,000 shares)		100,000
Total shareholders' equity	152,000	145,000

Your investment strategy is to purchase the stocks of companies that have low price/earnings ratios but appear to be in good shape financially. Assume you have analysed all other factors, and your decision depends on the results of the ratio analysis to be performed.

Required

Compute the following ratios for both companies for the current year and decide which company's stock better fits your investment strategy:

1. Current ratio
2. Acid-test ratio
3. Inventory turnover
4. Days' sales in average receivables
5. Debt ratio
6. Times-interest-earned ratio
7. Return on net sales
8. Return on total assets
9. Return on common shareholders' equity
10. Earnings per share of common stock
11. Book value per share of common stock
12. Price/earnings ratio

Decision Problems

1.   *Identifying action to cut losses and establish profitability*

Suppose you manage BiSports Ltd., a sporting goods and bicycle shop, which lost money during the past year. Before you can set the business on a successful course, you must first analyze the company and industry data for the current year in an effort to learn what is wrong. The data appear below.

BiSports Ltd. Balance Sheet Data

	BiSports	Industry Average
Cash and short-term investments.........	2.5%	6.8%
Trade receivables, net	14.3	8.0
Inventory.............................	64.6	63.5
Prepaid expenses	2.0	0.0
Total current assets	83.4	78.3
Fixed assets, net	12.6	15.2
Other assets	4.0	6.5
Total assets	100.0%	100.0%
Notes payable, short-term, 12%	19.6%	14.0%
Accounts payable.......................	18.6	25.1
Accrued liabilities......................	7.8	7.9
Total current liabilities	46.0	47.0
Long-term debt, 11%....................	19.7	16.4
Total liabilities	65.7	63.4
Common shareholders' equity	34.3	36.6
Total liabilities and shareholders' equity...	100.0%	100.0%

BiSports Ltd. Income Statement Data

	BiSports	Industry Average
Net sales	100.0%	100.0%
Cost of sales	(69.7)	(64.8)
Gross profit	30.3	35.2
Operating expense	(35.6)	(32.3)
Operating income (loss)	(5.3)	2.9
Interest expense	(6.8)	(1.3)
Other revenue	1.1	.3
Income (loss) before income tax	(11.0)	1.9
Income tax (expense) saving	4.4	(.8)
Net income (loss)	(6.6)%	1.1%

Required

Based on your analysis of these figures, suggest four courses of action BiSports should take to reduce its losses and establish profitable operations. Give your reasons for each suggestion.

2.   Understanding the components of accounting ratios

1. Harvey Drago is the controller of Hunan Industries Limited whose year end is December 31. He prepares cheques for suppliers in December and posts them to the appropriate books of account in that month. However, he holds on to the cheques and actually mails them to the suppliers in January. What is Drago's purpose in undertaking this activity? What financial ratio(s) are most affected by the action?

2. Janet Wong has asked you about the stock of a particular company. She finds it attractive because it has a high dividend yield relative to another stock she is also considering. Explain to her the meaning of the ratio and the danger of making a decision based on it alone.

3. Rick Bergman, a stock analyst, believes that net income after taxes but before extraordinary items should be used to measure profitability. Susan Blair, another stock analyst, believes that net income after extraordinary items is more appropriate. Explain why Rick and Susan have the beliefs they do. Which approach do you favour? Why?

4. A friend has asked you about a particular stock whose market price he believes is low. Suggest two ratios your friend might use to assess the market price. Suggest how your friend might assess the stock using the two ratios. To what might he compare the ratios?

5. Limeridge Ltd.'s owner is concerned because the number of days' sales in receivables has increased over the previous two years. Explain why the ratio might have increased.

Financial Statement Problem

Measuring profitability and analysing stock as an investment

Use the financial information in the John Labatt financial statements in Appendix E and the following financial information taken from earlier John Labatt financial statements to chart the company's progress through the fiscal years 1986 to 1989. Compute the ratios that measure profitability and ratios that are used to measure stock as an investment.

	Year ended April 30,	
	1987	1986
	(amounts in millions except as indicated)	
Net sales...	$3,802	$3,161
Net income	125	101
Shareholders' equity	771	671
Common share dividends (dollars per share)..........	$ .54¾	$ .50¼
Number of common shares outstanding (millions of shares)...............................	72.7	71.9

Profitability measures

a. Return on net revenues

b. Return on common shareholders' equity (Exclude convertible debentures. Ignore preferred stock because it was not issued until 1989; no dividends were paid on the preferred in the period under review.) Shareholders' equity at April 30, 1985 was $514 million.

Stock analysis measures

c. Price earnings ratio (Representative market prices for John Labatt Limited stock during fiscal years 1989, 1988, 1987 and 1986 were $22.53, $24.94, $23.75 and $17.44 respectively.)

d. Dividend yield

Is the trend in profitability measures consistent with the trend in the stock analysis measures?

Answers to Self-Study Questions

1. b $252,000 − $210,000 = $42,000; $42,000/$210,000 = .20
2. c
3. d
4. a
5. b ($10,000 + $22,000)/$40,000 = .80
6. b
7. d
8. d
9. a
10. c

Appendices

Taxation in Canada

Canadians are subject to a myriad of laws designed and written primarily to promote and encourage the smooth functioning of our democratic society. Of all these, tax law, in all its forms, probably impacts on each of us more directly and generates more discussion and controversy than the others. National tax policy impacts on business decisions, voting patterns, the rate of inflation, pollution control and many other aspects of daily life. Taxation legislation might be relatively simple if its only purpose was to generate revenue for the government. In fact tax policy and law have been used to encourage economic growth and investment, promote socially desirable goals such as donations to charities, and redress social inequities by allowing deductions and credits for medical expenses and child care expenses. Deductions for moving expenses, child support and union dues each have a special goal. What purpose does allowing an income tax credit for a political donation serve? The question perhaps hardly needs answering. It encourages support for the democratic process. The fact is that the income tax act in all its complexity serves many purposes in our society beyond the simple raising of funds for government operations.

The **income tax** is a general-purpose tax levied on the income of the taxpayer. Entirely separate from all other taxes, it is the federal government's largest source of revenue. Besides income tax, there are many kinds of taxes. For example, consider property taxes or, as they are more commonly known, municipal taxes. The primary source of revenue for our municipal governments, they use the value of land as their base. These revenues pay for municipal services and public education. At the provincial level the retail sales tax[1] has been a popular method of raising revenue for governments, and in 1991 the federal government will have entered this field by replacing the hidden or indirect manufacturers sales tax with a wide ranging goods and services tax (GST),[1] which is applied at the retail level. Not all taxes are visible, that is, itemized on the bill of sale. Some of the favourite targets for hidden taxes continue to be alcohol products, cigarettes and gasoline. These types of products are chosen at least in part because the demand for them remains more or less constant even with rising prices.

History of Taxation in Canada

Federal income taxes were first imposed in 1917 to finance World War I. This temporary measure, known as the Income War Tax Act, was required to supplement the sources of revenue existing then, primarily customs and excise taxes.

---

[1] Introduced in Chapter 11, pp. 445–447.

EXHIBIT A-1   *Revenues and Costs of Collections*

Net revenues from tax collections
$ billions

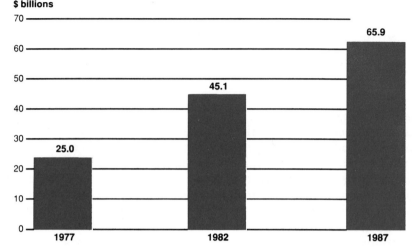

Total costs of tax collections
$ millions

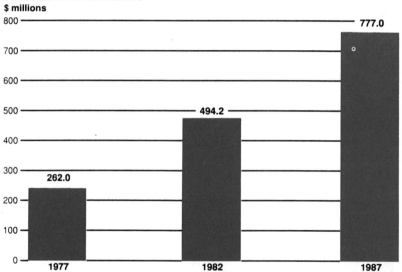

Net cost to collect $100 of tax

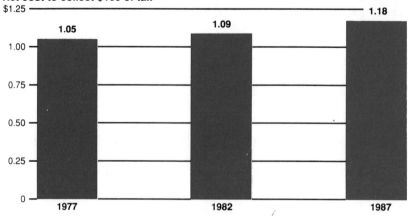

The so-called temporary arrangement remained in force until 1948, when the Income Tax Act was passed, confirming the permanency of this type of tax in Canadian lives. Since then income tax reform has been a frequent topic of public debate. Probably the most ambitious study undertaken was headed by the late Kenneth Carter, whose 1967 commission prepared a seven-volume work containing wide-ranging recommendations for reform to the income tax system. He will most likely be best remembered as the proponent of the philosophy "a buck is a buck," as he called for the equal taxation of all types of income and in particular capital gains, which up to this point had escaped the tax collectors' grasp. Edgar Benson, then Minister of Finance, introduced Bill C-259 to reform the Income Tax Act. Ultimately receiving Parliamentary approval, it came into law on January 1, 1972. Not surprisingly, it included the taxation of capital gains for the first time in Canadian history, albeit at a preferred rate.

More recently, Michael Wilson introduced a reform package in Parliament which has had a significant impact on the preparation of both the personal and corporate returns. Key among the features of this reform for individuals was a widening of the tax base and a conversion of many deductions into tax credits.

The ordinary taxpayers probably expected tax reform to result in a simpler system — one which they could better understand, and which would result in easier form completion. Equally important was the expectation for at least *their* taxes to be reduced. While the highest marginal rates have dropped slightly from previous years, any wholesale reduction during the taxpayer's lifetime is unrealistic. The current national debt would preclude any action of this nature. Expectations of a simpler tax law are equally unrealistic as long as the Income Tax Act is used for so many purposes beyond that of revenue generation. Overall, Canadians file more than 16 million personal income tax returns each year, with personal income taxes accounting for about 46 percent of taxation revenue. Exhibit A-1 gives an indication of the magnitude of these revenues and the cost of their collection.

The authority to collect taxes originally stemmed from the 1867 British North America Act, subsequently named the Constitution Act, 1967. In these acts, the Federal government was granted the right to use any system of taxation deemed necessary (direct or indirect) while the provinces were limited to forms of direct taxation. This has resulted in an overlapping of taxation powers between the governments and thus the need for federal-provincial taxation agreements. Currently all provinces and territories, except Quebec, have agreed to allow the federal government to collect its share of income taxes, thus avoiding to a large extent the duplication of ministries within their respective civil services.

The System of Income Taxation

The Canadian system of taxation is based on the principle of self-assessment, and is comparable in this respect to the taxation system in the United States and Australia. All Canadian residents are responsible for ensuring that their taxes have been paid according to the law through the completion and filing of a tax return, and that in turn they are able to check and confirm they have made use of all available opportunities to reduce their tax liability.

The development and administration of tax law in Canada involves two ministries in the federal government. The Department of Finance is responsible for the government's fiscal and tax policy and the resulting budgets. This department also formulates the legislation to raise the appropriate amount of revenue through various sources of taxation. Parliament approves these laws which, after receiving Royal Assent, become the responsibility of Revenue Canada, Taxation for their administration. This department's mandate is, first and foremost, the collection of taxes through voluntary compliance and disclosure, and the deterring of tax evasion and tax avoidance. Also of great importance is maintaining public confidence in the integrity of the tax system by administering tax and related legislation.

Taxpayers have rights, according to a declaration published by Revenue Canada in 1985 (Exhibit A-2).

The system by which personal income taxes are levied in Canada is described as **progressive**, meaning an individual pays an increasing percentage of his or her income in taxes as his or her income rises through specific brackets. We see this progression from a federal point of view in Exhibit A-3.

The Federal Marginal Rate is applied to **taxable income**, described in Exhibit A-7 to calculate Basic Federal Tax.

EXHIBIT A-2   *Declaration of Taxpayer Rights*

DECLARATION OF TAXPAYER RIGHTS

Revenue Canada   Revenu Canada
Taxation   Impôt

THE CONSTITUTION AND LAWS OF CANADA ENTITLE YOU TO MANY RIGHTS THAT PROTECT YOU IN MATTERS OF INCOME TAX. YOU ARE ENTITLED TO KNOW YOUR RIGHTS. YOU ARE ENTITLED TO INSIST ON THEM. YOU ARE ENTITLED TO BE HEARD, AND TO BE DEALT WITH FAIRLY.

HELPING YOU EXERCISE YOUR RIGHTS REMAINS AN IMPORTANT ROLE OF THE STAFF OF NATIONAL REVENUE TAXATION AT ITS DISTRICT OFFICES AND OTHER LOCATIONS. FAIR TREATMENT OF A COMPLAINT IS ONE OF YOUR GREATEST RIGHTS.

Canada

FAIR TREATMENT IN ALL DEALINGS WITH NATIONAL REVENUE TAXATION MEANS IMPORTANT RIGHTS TO:

Information
You are entitled to expect that the Government will make every reasonable effort to provide you with access to full, accurate and timely information about the Income Tax Act, and your rights under it.

Impartiality
You are entitled to an impartial determination of law and facts by departmental staff who seek to collect only the correct amount of tax, no more and no less.

Courtesy and Consideration
You are entitled to courtesy and considerate treatment from National Revenue Taxation at all times, including when it requests information or arranges interviews and audits.

Presumption of Honesty
You are entitled to be presumed honest unless there is evidence to the contrary.

FAIR TREATMENT UNDER THE CONSTITUTION AND LAWS OF CANADA INCLUDES IMPORTANT RIGHTS TO:

Privacy and Confidentiality
In addition to other constitutional and legal rights, you have a special right that personal and financial information you provide to National Revenue Taxation will be used only for purposes allowed by law.

Independent Review
You are entitled to object to an assessment or reassessment if you think the law has been applied incorrectly. To protect this right, you must file your objection within 90 days of the assessment or reassessment. Filing an objection will start an independent review by departmental appeals officers. If they don't resolve the matter to your satisfaction, they will explain how you can appeal to the courts.

An Impartial Hearing Before Payment
Until you have had an impartial review by the Department or a court, you may withhold amounts disputed in formal objections filed after January 1, 1985. If you appeal to a higher court, you will be able to provide equivalent security instead of paying those disputed amounts.
Certain exceptions, set out in legislation to guarantee these rights, are applicable to frivolous appeals to the courts, or where collection is clearly in jeopardy.

Bilingual Services
The Official Languages Act gives you the right to communicate with and receive services from National Revenue Taxation in either official language.

YOU ARE ENTITLED TO EVERY BENEFIT ALLOWED BY THE LAW

You have a right to arrange your affairs in order to pay the minimum tax required by law. You can also expect your government to administer tax law consistently, and to apply it firmly to those who try to avoid paying their lawful share.

EXHIBIT A-3 *Federal Tax Brackets and Rates for 1990*

Taxable Income	Federal Marginal Rate
$ 0 – $28,275	17%
27,276 – 56,549	26%
56,550 and up	29%

These rates do not take into account the provincial taxes, which the provinces levy and are collected on their behalf by the federal government, that is, with the exception of Quebec. Residents of Quebec file both a provincial and federal tax return. Excluded from these rates are surtaxes, which both the federal government and a number of provinces levy at various levels of income. Surtaxes are a flat tax calculated as a percentage applied to all **taxable income** or, in some cases, to taxable income above a certain level. Currently the federal government has placed a 5 percent surtax on the first $15,000 basic federal tax.

Each province sets its own tax rate, as indicated in Exhibit A-4. These rates are to be applied to the Basic Federal Tax.

EXHIBIT A-4 *1990 Rates of Provincial and Territorial Income Tax*

Newfoundland	62%	Manitoba	52%
Prince Edward Island	57%	Saskatchewan	50%
Nova Scotia	56.5%	Alberta	46.5%
New Brunswick	60%	British Columbia	51.5%
Quebec	Not applicable	Northwest Territories	43%
Ontario	53%	Yukon Territory	45%

The basic formula for the calculation of federal and provincial tax then becomes

Basic Federal Tax + (Basic Federal Tax × Provincial Tax Rate)

For Ontario the combined marginal rates for each bracket are shown in Exhibit A-5.

EXHIBIT A-5 *Combined Marginal Rates for Ontario*

Taxable Income	Combined Marginal Rate
$ 0 – $28,275	$.17 + (.17 \times .53) = .26$
28,276 – $56,549	$.26 + (.26 \times .53) = .40$
56,550 and up	$.29 + (.29 \times .53) = .44$

The combined marginal rates are useful, not for computing an individual's tax liability, but rather for measuring the impact of a change on an individual's marginal income. For example, if a taxpayer is eligible and makes a $1,000 contribution to his or her registered retirement savings plan, and his or her marginal taxable income falls in the highest bracket, then the tax savings of this particular action is estimated to be $440 ($1,000 × .44).

EXHIBIT A-6   *Maximum Personal Marginal Income Tax Rates, 1989 and 1990*

	B.C. %	Alta. %	Sask. %	Man. %	Ont. %	Que. %	N.S. %	N.B. %	P.E.I. %	Nfld. %
Ordinary Income										
1989	45.5	45.7	49.1	49.7	47.2	49.8	47.0	48.0	48.8	43.7
1990	46.3	46.8	49.9	50.4	48.2	50.5	47.7	48.7	49.5	49.3

If the system by which we tax individuals' income is described as progressive, then sales taxes are described as **regressive**. They are not levied on the basis of ability to pay, and result in the higher income earner paying less taxes when calculated as a percentage of his or her income.

Exhibit A-6 shows the highest combined marginal tax rates for all provinces, including the adjustment for surtaxes. **Marginal income** in the last paragraph, in its economic sense, means the last dollar earned by an individual, while the **marginal income tax rate** is the rate the marginal income is taxed.

Filing a Tax Return

Tax law identifies taxpayers as individuals, corporations and trusts. In this appendix we focus on the taxation of individuals and corporations.

Each taxpayer reports income and shows the computation of income tax on a document called a **tax return** (T1). Submitting the completed document to Revenue Canada is called *filing a tax return*. An individual must file his or her tax return by April 30 following the end of the taxation year, which is the calendar year for employees or any twelve-month period for a self-employed person operating through a proprietorship or partnership. It should be noted that proprietorships and partnerships pay no taxes, but rather the net income of the business is attributed to the proprietor or partner. In the case of a partnership, the partner reports the portion of the partnership income allocated to him or her according to the agreement, and includes any other income earned on the same return. From a general perspective, Canadian residents are taxable on their world income under Canadian law. Conversely, if an individual can establish that he or she was not a resident of Canada, he or she will generally—but not always—not be subject to tax in Canada.

Preparation of the T1 General, the individual income tax return, can be broken down into steps as illustrated in Exhibit A-7. Identification of income to be included in the calculation of total income is aided greatly by the issuance of information slips to the recipient of the income. For example, T3 (trust and estate income), T4 (employment income), T4A (pension and other income) and T5 (investment income) are some of the most common. There are slips for Unemployment Benefits (T4U), Family Allowance Payments (TFA1) and others as well.

Income from employment is by far the largest source of taxable income and is reported on a T4 issued by the individual's employer.[2] Box C of this document

---

[2] See also pp. 463–464 and Exhibit 11-7 (p. 465).

EXHIBIT A-7 *Personal Income Tax Computation*

1.	Calculation of Total Income	Employment, Pensions, Interest, Dividends, Self Employment, etc.
2.	Calculation of Net Income	Deduct: Pension Contributions, Childcare, Moving Expense, Carrying Charges, Employment Expense
3.	Calculation of Taxable Income	Deduct: Capital Gains Deduction, Other Losses
4.	Calculation of Non-refundable Tax Credits	Deduct: Personal Amounts CPP — UI Premiums, Disability, Tuition, Education Donations, Medical
5.	Summary of Tax and Credits	Calculation of Tax, Child Tax Credits, Federal Sales Tax Credit, Federal Political Credits

is the key figure and includes not only wages, salary and commissions but any benefit received by the individual as a result of the employment relationship. A good example of this would be the benefit a sales representative receives when supplied with an automobile and allowed to use it for personal use as well as business. The value attributed to the personal use of this auto, based on operating costs as well as the leasing or capital costs must be added to his or her employment income. A bank employee who is allowed to borrow money at interest rates below that which is normally paid is receiving a benefit and must have the amount included in his or her income. Using the information provided by these source documents one is then able to accumulate totals for many of the classifications of income required by the T1 tax return. A selection of these incomes are summarized in the following:

Pension Income from Old Age Security, the Canada Pension Plan, company registered pensions plans and individuals registered retirement savings plans are normally well documented on information slips and present no difficulty to preparers.

Family Allowance payments are normally sent to the mother of the child but for income tax purposes are reported by the spouse with the higher income.

Dividends from taxable Canadian corporations represent the after tax distributions of income to shareholders. Since this income has already been taxed at the corporate level, its inclusion in income by individuals at the personal level makes it subject to **double taxation**. This problem has been adjusted for, to some extent, if one examines the T5 shown in Exhibit A-8. Box A identifies the actual amount of dividends received, in this case $100. Box B identifies the taxable amount of dividends received and is the result of what is called the gross up calculation where the actual amount is multiplied by 125 per cent

EXHIBIT A-8 *T5 Information Slip*

Revenue Canada Taxation | Revenu Canada Impôt

T 5
Supplementary – *Supplémentaire*
Rev. 89

STATEMENT OF INVESTMENT INCOME
ÉTAT DES REVENUS DE PLACEMENTS

Dividends from Taxable Canadian Corporations
Dividendes de corporations canadiennes imposables

Year / *Année*	(A) Actual Amount of Dividends / *Montant réel des dividendes*	(B) Taxable Amount of Dividends / *Montant imposable des dividendes*	(C) Federal Dividend Tax Credit / *Crédit d'impôt fédéral pour dividendes*	(D) Interest from Canadian Sources / *Intérêts de source canadienne*	(E) Other Income from Canadian Sources / *Autres revenus de source canadienne*
	100.00	125.00	16.67		

(F) Gross Foreign Income / *Revenus étrangers bruts*	(G) Foreign Tax Paid / *Impôt étranger payé*	(H) Royalties from Canadian Sources / *Redevances de source canadienne*	(I) Capital Gains Dividends / *Dividendes sur gains en capital*	(J) Pension Income / *Revenu de pensions*	(K) Amount Eligible for Resource Allowance Deduction / *Montant donnant droit à la déduction en matière de ressources*

The Income Tax Act requires that you provide your Social Insurance Number upon request to any person who prepares an information slip on your behalf. If you do not have a Social Insurance Number, please contact your nearest Canada Employment Centre.
La Loi de l'impôt sur le revenu exige que vous fournissiez votre numéro d'assurance sociale sur demande à toute personne qui établit un feuillet de renseignements en votre nom. Si vous n'avez pas de numéro d'assurance sociale, veuillez communiquer avec votre Centre d'emploi du Canada.

RECIPIENT: SURNAME FIRST, AND FULL ADDRESS
BÉNÉFICIAIRE: NOM DE FAMILLE D'ABORD, ET ADRESSE COMPLÈTE

Social Insurance Number
Numéro d'assurance sociale

NAME AND ADDRESS OF PAYER (Must appear on each slip)
NOM ET ADRESSE DU PAYEUR (À inscrire sur chaque feuillet)

• **For Taxation Office**
• ***Pour le bureau d'impôt***

1

Source: Revenue Canada Taxation. Reproduced with permission of the Minister of Supply and Services Canada.

(\$100 × 1.25 = \$125). The grossed-up dividends are meant to reflect, in part, income before taxes at the corporate level. Finally, Box C identifies the dividend tax credit which is computed by multiplying the taxable amount of dividends by 13⅓ percent (\$125 × 0.1333 = \$16.67). The credit is taken as a reduction in basic federal tax at the point where federal taxes are calculated. It is worth noting that this credit reduces basic federal tax and results in the reduction of provincial taxes, since provincial taxes are a function of basic federal tax. Therefore, the full value of the tax credit to an Ontario taxpayer can be calculated as \$16.67 + (.52 × \$16.67) = \$25.34. The impact of the dividend tax credit can be graphically illustrated by the following example. A single person receiving only dividend income, about \$22,000 cash, would pay no income tax as a result of the credit. A taxpayer whose taxable income falls in the highest tax bracket would pay 32 percent on dividend income, as opposed to 47 percent on other income when analysed from a marginal point of view.

Interest Canadians purchase a wide ranging variety of interest bearing contracts, the most common being Canada Savings Bonds. Where interest is paid on a regular basis, at least yearly, there is no problem as T5 information slips are issued. For contracts where interest is compounded for a period greater than a year, taxpayers, as of 1990, must now use the annual accrual method, which requires the reporting of interest earned, though not actually received. Deferral of taxes will no longer be possible through the use of compound investments.

Rental Income has been a common source of investment, with gross rental income less operating expenses equalling net rental income. The primary restriction on this computation is that rental losses may not be created by the claiming of capital cost allowance (depreciation).

Taxable Capital Gains, first reported for tax purposes in 1972, are a result of the sale of a capital property. The most common is the sale of shares or common stock of a corporation which have increased in value since their purchase. Initially only one half of any capital gain was reported for tax purposes, effectively taxing this type of income at one half of the normal tax rate. As of 1990, three quarters of all capital gains income must now be reported for tax purposes. The calculation of a taxable capital gain is as follows (Exhibit A-9):

EXHIBIT A-9   *Calculation of Capital Gains*

Proceeds of disposition	$100.00
Adjusted cost base	50.00
Selling cost	2.00
Capital Gain	48.00
	.75
Taxable Capital Gain	$ 36.00

An individual who owns a condominium, house or similar dwelling and has lived there sometime during each of the years in question may claim this house as his or her principal residence and exempt any capital gain from tax. Opportunities for tax free income are rare and should be taken advantage of when there is one. Capital losses may only be offset against capital gains. Unclaimed capital losses, that is, capital losses that cannot be deducted in a particular year, may be carried forward or back to other tax years.

Scholarships, bursaries and grants are subject to tax with the first $500 being exempt.

Self-employment Income, gross and net, must be reported along with the appropriate financial statements, giving the sources of revenue and listing of all major expenses. These self-employed taxpayers are all working as proprietors or partners in such occupations as farmers, fishermen, doctors, lawyers and electricians.

Not many sources of income are exempt from tax, but it is worth noting that lottery winnings, most welfare and social assistance payments, veteran's disability and war allowances, and workers' compensation benefits fall in this category.

Deductions to Net Income and Taxable Income

Tax reform of 1988 resulted in a significant reduction in the number of deductions allowed in arriving at taxable income. As will be shown later, these deductions in all cases were converted into **tax credits**.

Registered Pension Plan (RPP) Contributions are deductible and usually matched with a contribution to the plan of a similar amount by the employer. While the sheltering of this income from tax is good, the amount the employee may contribute is controlled by the terms of the pension plan agreement;

employees are not able to make extra contributions even if they wished. In addition, many employees of small businesses and self-employed individuals do not have the opportunity to contribute to an RPP.

The term registered pension plan refers to specific pension plans that have been established by employers for their employees' benefit that meet and are designed according to federal government regulations. Funds held in trust will ultimately be used to buy an annuity at the time of the employee's retirement.

Registered Retirement Savings Plans (RRSP) is the vehicle provided by tax law for individuals who are not members of an RPP or whose RPP plans are insufficient to establish an adequate pension. Again, there are restrictions as to the amount of income a taxpayer may shelter in this type of plan; but as of 1991, an individual with sufficient *earned income* and not making any contributions to an RPP could contribute and deduct $11,500 (Exhibit A-10). In subsequent years that ceiling will rise to $15,500, but eligibility for this amount will be based on the formula of 18 percent of earned income and no contribution to an RPP in that year. To make a contribution of this size, one would require earned income of $86,111. Employment income and self-employment earnings are the major sources of earned income. Major exclusions are investment income and capital gains. Contributions to an RRSP by individuals who are already contributors to an RPP are restricted; and with the introduction of pension reform, the plan is to have the government actually compute the amount of eligibility and communicate this information to the taxpayer.

EXHIBIT A-10   *Maximum Contributions to a RRSP*

Year	Dollar Amount
1991	$11,500
1992	12,500
1993	13,500
1994	14,500
1995	15,500

The power of the RRSP to generate retirement funds through the sheltering of income from tax is demonstrated as follows. One thousand dollars contributed at the beginning of each year to an RRSP at 10 percent over a 35-year period will result in savings of approximately $300,000. On the other hand, if tax was paid on the $1,000 at the marginal rate of 45 percent, $550 would remain for investment and result in a savings of approximately $60,000 over 35 years.

Child Care Expenses may be deductible if they are paid to an individual or child care facility in order to permit parents or a single parent to earn employment or self-employment income. The deduction is gender neutral, going to the parent with the lowest net income. For children six years and younger or disabled, up to $4,000 may be deducted per child, while for older children up to the age of fourteen, the deduction is $2,000.

Moving Expenses related to a move that results in a taxpayer living 40 kilometres closer to his or her new work location can create a significant deduction. Normal family moving and travel expenses are included as well as the sales commission and legal fees on the sale of a house.

Alimony or Separation Allowances paid are deductible without limit provided they are periodic and paid under a decree order, judgement or written agreement.

Carrying Charges and interest expenses related to investments made to earn money are normally deductible. Charges for a safety deposit box, safe keeping fees and investment counsel fees are other examples. Interest expense can be significant where the investment is highly leveraged, but there should be a clear path tying the money borrowed to the investment.

Employment Expenses are most often permitted when the individual is a commission sales representative, but this is not an absolute requirement. Automobile, travel and entertainment are the most common, but the last item is limited to the commission salesperson. Any expenditure on food is limited to 80 percent of the bill; and even if a more expensive automobile is used, depreciation may not be taken on the value in excess of $24,000.

All of the above amounts may be attractive deductions to the taxpayer if he or she is eligible; and with a progressive tax system, the tax savings are the greatest when the individual is in the highest bracket, 47–48 percent.

Capital Gains Deduction   In a budget presented in 1985, Finance Minister Michael Wilson introduced a lifetime exemption which would have allowed $500,000 tax free capital gains, and which he described as an "economic engine", spurring capital investment. Others argued that this was an overly generous deduction primarily benefiting high income earners. Eventually the deduction was capped at $100,000 of capital gains or $75,000 in taxable capital gains. It is necessary to keep track of the amount of deductions taken from year to year as you have a lifetime to use it.

While not all deductions have been discussed, the most commonly used ones have been highlighted. The importance of reading all available materials cannot be overstressed.

Non-Refundable Tax Credits

The introduction of this extensive system of tax credits was probably the most significant change as far as individuals were concerned when dealing with the tax reform package of 1988. As mentioned before all of these items were formerly deductions.

The basic formula for the calculation of the **non-refundable tax credit** is simply to add up all the amounts to which you are entitled and multiply by 17 percent. The exception is donations. Medical expenses must be reduced by 3 percent of net income (to a maximum of $1,542).

The chief reason for this conversion of deductions to credits was fairness. Reference to and understanding of marginal rates is necessary because, as discussed previously, the value of a deduction in terms of tax savings depends on the taxpayer's marginal income bracket (Exhibit 27-5). The greatest tax savings accrue to those with income in the highest tax bracket. Tax credits, on the other hand, have a fixed value no matter what your marginal income bracket may be.

Personal Amounts (1990) _____

Basic personal amount (everyone may claim)	$6,169
Age amount (65 years of age or older)	3,327
Married amount (dependent spouse, net income under $514)	5,141
Dependent children under 19, net income under $2,570..............	399
19 or older, infirm, net income under $2,570......	1,512
Other dependents under 19, net income under $2,570	399
19 and over, infirm, net income under $2,570	1,512
Married equivalent, dependent, net income under $514	5,141

NOTES

Infirm   Not a defined term, but Revenue Canada has described this condition as an inability to be gainfully employed for a considerable period of time.

Married equivalent may be claimed by a person, who is single, divorced, separated or widowed and supporting a relative who lives with him or her and is either his or her parent or grand-parent, or who is under 19 at the end of 1990, or over 19 and infirm.

Common-law does not satisfy married requirements even though there are parts of the act where it is recognized, particularly when assessing family income.

Other dependents   Basically other relatives.
The deduction for dependent children increases if more than two children.

All of these amounts are subject to an indexing formula to which adjustments are made yearly by the amount the cost of living exceeds 3 percent. Assuming that incomes increase by at least the cost of living, there will be a gradual increase in taxable income and taxes collected all else being equal. The personal amount to which everyone is entitled provides an absolute base to taxable income. No person with income of less than $6,169 will pay any taxes. This is of course small comfort when your income is this low, but it does keep many students and some retired persons off the tax rolls.

Other Amounts

Canada or Quebec Pension Plan contributions, employment	$ 574
Unemployment Insurance premiums, maximum	749
Eligible Pension amount	1,000
Disability amount, for self or transferred	3,327
Tuition fees and Education amount, maximum	3,529
Transfer from spouse	no fixed amount
Medical expenses, deduct 3% of net income to a maximum of	$1,542
Charitable donations	no fixed amount

NOTES

Eligible Pension amount   Excludes Old Age Security and Canada Pension.

Disability amount Severely impaired mentally or physically with impairment markedly restricting daily living activities.

Tuition fees Over $100 at a post secondary institution; transferrable by the student if not needed to reduce his or her own taxes.

Education amount $60 a month for every month the individual is a full time student at a post secondary institution; transferrable by the student if not needed to reduce his or her own taxes.

Transfer from spouse May transfer unused age, disability, pension amount, tuition and education amounts if not needed to reduce his or her own taxes.

Medical expenses Must be out of pocket, falling within any twelve-month period ending in the taxation year.

Donations Maximum 20 percent of net income and receipted. Charity must be registered with Revenue Canada. The first $250 credit is calculated at 17 percent and above $250, at 29 percent.

Except for donations over $250, all credits are calculated at the rate of 17 percent. This makes their value the same for all taxpayers.

A final comment on the taxes Canadians pay comes from the Fraser Institute, an independent Canadian research institute that calculates "Tax Freedom Day" each year. This day for 1989, July 3, was designated as the day when the average Canadian family had done enough work to pay the total tax bill imposed on it by all levels of government. This calculation brings home to us the significant role that taxes play in our financial lives and that we spend about half the year just working to pay our taxes.

Summary Problem for Your Review

Bruce is a CA in public practice with employment income of $55,000 and several other sources of income (interest from the Bank of Commerce $1,300, cash dividends of $700, taxable capital gains from the sale of shares of $400). He contributed $1,800 to an RPP and $1,500 to an RRSP, paid professional dues of $420 as a chartered accountant, and had carrying charges and interest expense of $5,500. His wife Sheila has employment income of $4,000 and has paid $300 in tuition for credit courses at York University. They have three children. John, 15, is blind; Mary is 17; and Andrew, 23, a full-time student at York University, pays a tuition of $1,800. Also Bruce made charitable donations in the amount of $500 and the maximum Canada Pension and Unemployment Insurance contributions, tax withheld at source amounted to $13,222.

SOLUTION TO REVIEW PROBLEM

Total Income

Employment income		$55,000
Taxable family allowance		798
Interest, Bank of Commerce		1,300
Taxable amount of dividends ($700 × 1.25)		875
Taxable capital gains (sale of shares—$400 × .75)		300
Total income		$58,273

Less: Registered pension plan contributions	$ 1,800	
Contribution to RRSP	1,500	
Professional dues, Chartered Accountant	420	
Carrying charges and interest	550	4,270
Net Income		$54,003

Less: Capital Gains Deduction		300
Taxable Income		$53,703

Non-Refundable Tax Credits

Base Personal amount	$ 6,169	
Married amount ($5,655 − 4,000)	1,655	
Dependent children (2 × $399)	798	
Canada Pension contribution	574	
Unemployment Insurance premiums	749	
Disability amount from dependent	3,327	
Tuition and Education, transferred from son ($1,800 + 8 × $60)	2,280	
Tuition transferred from wife	300	
	$15,852	
Therefore ($15,852 × .17)		$ 2,695
Donations	$ 500	
($250 × .17)		43
($250 × .29)		73
Total Non-Refundable Tax Credits		$ 2,811

Computation of Tax, Federal

Taxable Income	$53,703		
Tax on first	28,275 × .17		$ 4,807
Tax on remainder	25,428 × .26		6,611
Federal Tax			$11,418
Less: Dividend tax credit ($875 × .133)		$ 116	
Non-Refundable Tax Credit		2,811	2,927
Basic Federal Tax			$ 8,491
Add: Federal Surtax ($8,491 × .05)			425
Total Federal Tax Payable			$ 8,916
Provincial Tax Payable ($8,491 × .53)			4,500
Total Federal and Provincial Taxes Payable			$13,416
Less: Tax withheld at source			13,222
Balance owing			$ 194

Income Taxation of Corporations _____

A corporation is a taxable entity entirely separate from its owners, the share-holders. Corporations must file a Federal T2, Corporate Income Tax Return, whether or not they have taxable income for the year, and these returns must be submitted within six months of the corporation's year end. A separate provincial return must be filed by corporations located in Quebec, Ontario and Alberta, since these provinces collect their own corporate income tax. While there are separate personal income tax returns for each province and territory, there is only one version of the corporate return for all of Canada. Corporate taxes account for approximately 12 percent of the revenues from taxation in comparison to the previously mentioned 46 percent from personal income taxes. The basic corporate tax rate is 38 percent, with a 10 percent abatement for provincial taxes giving a rate of 28 percent. This rate may in turn drop to 12 percent, where the corporation is eligible for the small business deduction.

Taxable Income of a Corporation

Corporations, in preparing their financial statements follow generally accepted accounting principles, discussed in Chapter 12. Taxation law, to a large extent, also adheres to GAAP. Revenue Canada and GAAP permit taxpayers to add amounts to or deduct amounts from income for **income tax** purposes that differ from amounts added to or deducted from income for *book* (that is, financial statement) *purposes*. This point was made in Chapter 10 with respect to de-preciation of plant assets. Recall that the statement was made that companies used straight-line depreciation for financial statement purposes and accelerated depreciation for income tax purposes and that such action allowed the companies to report higher incomes and pay less tax in the early years of a plant asset's life.

The use of different amounts for tax purposes and book purposes results in a reconciling balance called **deferred income taxes**. John Labatt shows deferred income taxes of $143.0 million at April 30, 1989 on the balance sheet in Appendix E. The topic of deferred taxes is covered more fully in advanced accounting courses.

The following discussion illustrates how differences arise between income for tax purposes and income for book purposes:

1. Corporations receiving dividends from other taxable Canadian corpora-tions are included in the calculation of net income of a business but are fully deductible in arriving at taxable income. Since dividends are distributions of after tax income, this deduction is necessary to avoid double taxation. As dividends are distributed to shareholders in after-tax dollars, the dividend tax credit (as previously explained) reduces the rate paid on this income by individuals, thereby avoiding to some extent double taxation at the personal level.

2. The treatment of capital gains within a corporation is similar to that of an individual with capital losses only being deductible against capital gains. Additional unclaimed capital losses may be carried back and forward simi-lar to individuals. On the other hand, corporations are not eligible for the $100,000 capital gains deduction. Income for book purposes would include the full amount of capital losses in any given year.

3. Differing methods for the computation of depreciation probably causes the major differences in book income and taxable income. As was mentioned above, many taxpayers use maximum capital cost allowance (accelerated depreciation using the Revenue Canada Rates, introduced in Chapter 10) for tax purposes and the straight-line method for financial reporting purposes. Since the former is always greater, income for tax purposes is less than income for book or reporting purposes.

The Small Business Deduction

The small business deduction is a tax credit that reduces taxes that would otherwise be payable on income "from an active business carried on in Canada and is designed to assist Canadian-controlled private corporations" to expand through retention of capital. A private corporation is primarily distinguished by the fact that none of its shares are listed on a prescribed Canadian stock exchange.

The application of this credit is limited to $200,000 of active business income in a year effectively reducing the federal tax rate to 12 percent and producing a combined federal and provincial rate of about 22 percent. Recalling the combined marginal rates for individuals of 26 percent, 40 percent and 44 percent, this is an attractive rate. However, the income must stay within the corporation and is not available for personal use.

Tax Factors in Business Decisions

Forms of Business Organizations

While proprietorships and partnerships are the simplest form of business organization, they do not automatically result in the lowest tax being paid. Since income from these sources flows to the individuals, income is taxed at the personal rates which may be substantially higher than the corporate rates, especially where the small business deduction is concerned. Also, it should be remembered that in very small businesses where the individual continues to have employment income, any losses from the operation of a proprietorship or partnership can be used to reduce employment income and the resulting taxes.

On the other hand, losses of a corporation can be carried back to the previous year or forward to future years to reduce corporate taxable income, but these can never be applied against personal income. One should choose the type of business organization that best meets his or her needs. An owner of a corporation will want to pay himself or herself a blend of salary and dividends. The salary, to him or her is a source of earned income, creating eligibility to contribute to the Canada Pension Plan and to an RRSP. By paying dividends, he or she may take advantage of the dividend tax credit.

Tax planning is critical to making wise business decisions. Tax planning is the legitimate reduction of and delay in paying taxes within the legal system.

Also called **tax avoidance,** it is the structuring of business transactions in order to pay the least amount of income tax at the latest possible time permitted by the law. Tax avoidance should not be confused with **tax evasion.**Tax evasion is the result of deliberate suppression of income or the deduction of expenses which are fraudulent in nature. An example of tax planning (tax avoidance) is delaying revenue until a year later, when tax rates are scheduled to decrease. Failing to report the income on the tax return or reporting less than the full amount of income is tax evasion. Revenue Canada also looks closely at tax avoidance schemes which legally circumvent the law and do not properly reveal the true facts.

Corporations and individuals pay so much taxes that financial strategies must always consider the tax effects of the transactions. The complexity of the law has resulted in public accountants who specialize in tax and earn the majority of their business income as tax consultants.

Accounting Vocabulary

deferred income taxes
  (p. 1121)
income tax *(p. 1107)*
marginal income *(p. 1112)*
marginal income tax rate
  (p. 1112)

non-refundable tax credit
  (p. 1117)
progressive tax *(p. 1110)*
regressive tax *(p. 1112)*
tax avoidance *(p. 1123)*
tax credit *(p. 1115)*

tax evasion *(p. 1123)*
tax return *(p. 1112)*
taxable income *(p. 1110)*

Accounting with Computers

Accounting has benefited more from computer technology than any other area of business. The application of computers to accounting is natural because the computer is ideally suited for repetitive calculations.

This chapter expands the Chapter 6 discussion of computer systems. It outlines a personal-computer (PC) system of accounting for general ledger, accounts receivable, accounts payable and payroll transactions.

The first computerized accounting systems were developed in the 1950s. Only the largest organizations could afford the expensive computer equipment available at that time. Since then, however, the price of computer equipment has dropped dramatically. Today even the smallest business can afford a computer capable of keeping its accounting records.

Advantages of Computer Systems

Computerized systems offer many advantages over manual systems, such as the following:

Speed   A computerized system can provide information more quickly than a manual system because the computer can perform tasks instantaneously that are time-consuming when done manually.

Volume of Output   A much larger volume of transactions can be handled using a computerized system because of its speed of processing.

Error Protection   Using a computer greatly reduces the number of errors because the computer does calculations more accurately than a human. Also, computerized accounting systems have many error-protection features. For example, most systems do not accept an entry that does not balance.

Automatic Posting   Posting is automatically performed in a computerized system — an enormous savings in time. Not only is the repetitive task of posting time-consuming, but it can also create many errors in a manual accounting system. Using a computer ensures that each entry is posted accurately. This prevents such errors as double posting, posting to the wrong account, posting a debit as a credit (and vice versa), and posting the wrong amount.

Automatic Report Preparation   Reports can be generated automatically in a computerized accounting system: journals, ledgers, financial statements and special reports to aid management in decision-making.

Automatic Document Printing   A computerized system can provide many of the documents used in a business: invoices, monthly statements for accounts receivable customers, payroll cheques and employee earnings statements, among others.

Computers can make errors if the information supplied to them or the programs run on them are incorrect. Therefore care must be taken both in designing programs and inputting data.

Accounting procedures are basically the same whether performed manually or on a computer. Exhibit B-1 reviews the accounting cycle from Chapter 4 and lists the corresponding steps which can be programmed into a computerized system. Observe how many steps the computer can perform automatically.

EXHIBIT B-1   *Comparison of the Accounting Cycle in a Manual System and in a Computerized System*

Accounting Cycle in a Manual System	Accounting Cycle in a Computerized System
1. Start with the account balances in the ledger at the beginning of the period.	1. Same.
2. Analyse and journalize transactions as they occur.	2. Analyse transactions and enter them in the computer, which automatically prepares a journal that can be printed at any time.
3. Post journal entries to the ledger accounts.	3. The computer automatically posts from the journal to the ledger.
4. Compute the unadjusted balance in each account at the end of the period.	4. The computer automatically computes the balance in each account.
5. Enter the trial balance on the work sheet and complete the work sheet.	5. The computer automatically prepares a trial balance. Enter adjusting entries in the computer. No work sheet is needed.
6. Using the work sheet as a guide, a. prepare the financial statements; b. journalize and post adjusting entries; c. journalize and post closing entries.	6. The computer automatically prepares the financial statements and posts the adjusting and closing entries.
7. Prepare the post-closing trial balance.	7. The computer automatically prepares the post-closing trial balance.

Computer Basics

A computer **program** is a set of instructions that tells the computer what to do. Without a program it cannot perform even the simplest tasks. This does not mean that you must become a programmer to use a computer for accounting. Since accounting is one of the computer's most important applications, many programs have been written to handle accounting data. To use the computer for accounting, a business can simply purchase a program that suits its needs and is compatible with its computer.

Hardware

Computers are classified according to their speed and the amount of data they can store. There are three basic classes of computers: mainframes, minicomputers and microcomputers. In the 1950s the only type of computer available for accounting applications was the mainframe. A *mainframe* computer can handle a large volume of transactions very quickly, but its cost is prohibitive for most small businesses. In the late 1960s the *minicomputer* was developed. It was less powerful and less expensive than the mainframe.

As technology progressed, a new type of computer was developed, the microcomputer, which is small enough for each employee to have one. At first microcomputers were not very powerful and were used mostly for playing computer games. However, new ones were soon developed with more memory and speed. Some microcomputers today are more powerful than the mainframes of the 1950s, and they are very affordable. A complete microcomputer system can be purchased for less than $2,000. Because of their low cost, programmers have a large market for their software programs. Hundreds of software packages have been produced for the microcomputer, making it a valuable business tool. Some medium and large-size businesses still require mainframes and minicomputers, but microcomputer packages now provide virtually all of the features offered by larger computers and can easily meet the needs of small businesses.

Although we concentrate on accounting procedures for microcomputers, the basic procedures are the same no matter what type of computer is used. Exhibit B-2 shows the hardware for a typical microcomputer system consisting of three main types of components:

1. Input devices (disk drive and keyboard)
2. Central processing unit (the "brain" of the computer)
3. Output devices (monitor, printer and disk drive)

EXHIBIT B-2   *Microcomputer Hardware*

Source: IBM Personal System/2 Model 25. Reproduced courtesy of IBM Corporation.

EXHIBIT B-3   *Floppy Diskette*

Source: A 3.5 diskette. Reproduced courtesy of IBM Corporation.

Input Devices   Input devices are used to feed instructions and data into the computer. An input device usually found on a computer system is a **disk drive**, which reads data and instructions from magnetic disks. The most common form of disk is the floppy **diskette**, also called a floppy disk. This thin, 5¼-inch diameter round diskette, enclosed in a square plastic envelope, can store approximately 360,000 characters of data and costs under $3. Exhibit B-3 is a picture of a floppy diskette.

To use the computer program or data stored on a diskette, place the diskette in the disk drive, and the computer can read the information from it. Some computers use a hard disk. This type of disk is metal and can hold much more information than a floppy diskette. However, it is also more expensive.

The other input device usually found in a microcomputer system is the *keyboard*. Much like a typewriter keyboard, this device is used to enter data and instructions.

Central Processing Unit   The **central processing unit (CPU)** is the "brain" of the microcomputer. The CPU does the "thinking" for the computer. It performs mathematical and logical operations and controls all the other components of the system.

Output Devices   *Output devices* give us the information we want to receive from the computer — in several ways. The **monitor** looks like a television screen and allows the user to view data being processed and to receive messages from the program being run.

The **printer** can provide printed copies of the information after it has been processed. Examples of the printed copies, also called *hard copies*, in an accounting system include printouts of the balance sheet and income statement, payroll cheques, and invoices for mailing to customers.

A third common output device is the disk drive (which we also listed as an input device). We can save the records that have been updated during processing by placing them on a diskette. When the computer is turned off at the end of a work session, the internal memory in the CPU "forgets" the data put into it. However, the diskette provides extra storage for later use.

Accounting Software Programs

Some firms prefer to have their accounting programs written specifically for their business, while others purchase off-the-shelf accounting programs. In the latter case, one program may handle all accounting transactions, or a total accounting system may be purchased in parts called *modules*. Each module handles a particular area of the total accounting function: general ledger, accounts receivable, accounts payable, inventory or payroll. Still other modules are available for billing, budgeting, asset management, order entry and job costing, to mention only a few. As new modules are purchased, they must be interfaced with the existing accounting system.

The payroll is often the first accounting function to be computerized. This area is ideally suited to computerization because of the repetitive nature of payroll activities and the large number of mathematical calculations. A computerized payroll function can therefore save the accountant a considerable amount of time while leaving other accounting functions on a manual basis.

There are many computerized accounting packages available in Canada. The Bedford integrated accounting program is perhaps the most inexpensive, simplest and easiest to use by both accountants and non-accountants alike. It is particularly suited to small businesses. Integrated accounting packages like the Bedford program are described as **integrated software** programs; the packages coordinate the functions and output of the different modules included such as general ledger, accounts receivable, accounts payable, inventory, payroll and job costing. Since all modules are integrated, it means that you only have to enter a particular business transaction in the appropriate module, all other modules are updated automatically. For example, if a sale is recorded through accounts receivable, the inventory will be adjusted automatically to reflect the sale, and both accounts in the general ledger will be updated to reflect the sale as well. Even though the Bedford accounting package is integrated, each of the modules can also be used independently if so desired. Because it is so inexpensive and has an excellent payroll module, the Bedford program is often used by small and medium-sized businesses solely for computerizing the payroll function.

A comprehensive integrated accounting program, Abacus, developed by Comsoft Inc., an Edmonton company, has been available since 1984. Various versions are available for small to large businesses with comprehensive accounting requirements. Abacus I contains all of the standard accounting modules present in the Bedford program in addition to purchase orders, order entry billing, summary billing and multiple branch accounting. Both Abacus I and Abacus II, the multi-user version, are suitable for construction job estimating and costing, manufacturing, order entry, time billing, service organizations and multiple branch accounting. A stand-alone payroll program is also available to handle all payroll needs for Canadian business without requiring customization. It can be integrated at any time with the full function Abacus accounting system.

Another comprehensive accounting package is ACCPAC — the Plus version is also a multi-user program. The ACCPAC program is purchased in modules. A basic accounting system requires the three major modules — general ledger, accounts payable and accounts receivable — and the report writer. The system can be extended further by adding the payroll module, inventory module and order entry among others. Many of the major modules allow additional packages for better information management. For example, by adding the sales analysis package to accounts receivable, a sales manager can obtain a report of all customers in his region.

Although ACCPAC may have some limitations for large corporations, it is a comprehensive package suitable for most business firms and provides a considerable amount of management information. A major difference between the Bedford and Abacus programs and ACCPAC is that the former are integrated packages, while ACCPAC is a *batch processing package*. This means transactions are not recorded the instant they occur. Instead, all accounting data are entered in groups into a *batch file*. For example, instead of recording each sale or purchase immediately when it is made, each day's sales would be recorded at one time, followed by the day's purchases. Only when the batch file is finally processed are the various accounts in the modules updated. An advantage of batch processing is that the data entered can be changed prior to processing if an error is found. On the other hand, the information produced by the accounting system is not always current if batches have not yet been processed.

NewViews, introduced in Canada in 1985, is an accounting program different from either Bedford or ACCPAC. Unlike many comprehensive accounting packages such as ACCPAC where individual modules have to be added and interfaced with each other, NewViews is one program that handles the accounting functions of general ledger, accounts receivable, accounts payable, financial statements and payroll. Other applications, such as time and billing, job costing, inventory and consolidations, are also available. The program is transaction based with each transaction linked to a particular file that is updated when the transaction is entered.

NewViews in effect resembles a series of nested spreadsheets, with each spreadsheet representing a file accessible through one of the four hierarchical accounting levels. These four accounting levels are called Home, Report, Account and Distribution. The Home level contains all the reports that can be produced for the business from the transaction data, such as the balance sheet, income statement, accounts receivable ledger and accounts payable ledger. When you place the cursor on the name of a report and give the appropriate command, you can expand it and view the report layout and accounts in it. This is the report level where the financial statements are formatted. You simply enter the account names and descriptions and place them where you want them to appear in the report. Each line in the report represents an account. The transactions making up the account balance can be viewed through the Account level by again placing the cursor on the account and giving the expand command. If a transaction affects more than one account, this breakdown can be viewed again through the Distribution level. Whenever a transaction is entered at the account or distribution level the balances of all accounts affected are automatically updated. Reports can be produced immediately with the accounts in these reports reflecting the updated balances. This means that the information available from the accounting system is always up-to-date.

NewViews has not gained the acceptance of the accounting profession, because the program allegedly does not produce an audit trail which allows a person to go back to the source of the transaction. Others claim that it has an excellent audit trail system but it has to be set up by the accountant first. On the other hand, NewViews is a real time-accounting program. This means that all accounts are instantly updated when a transaction is entered, providing managers with the most current information to make decisions.

Most computerized accounting programs have common features. Virtually all accounting programs are **menu-driven**. **Menus** simplify the task of learning to use an accounting program. When you start up the program, a list of options is displayed from which you can choose, like a menu in a restaurant. The first menu is called the master menu. It will guide you to the section of the program sought. When you choose an option, the computer will either perform the

EXHIBIT B-4   *Master Menu*

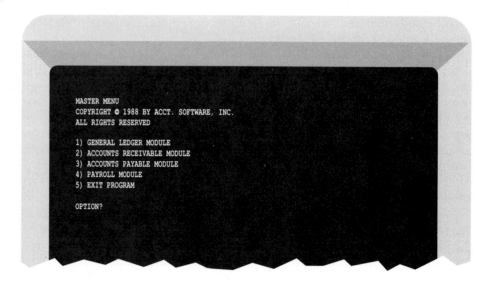

```
MASTER MENU
COPYRIGHT © 1988 BY ACCT. SOFTWARE, INC.
ALL RIGHTS RESERVED

1) GENERAL LEDGER MODULE
2) ACCOUNTS RECEIVABLE MODULE
3) ACCOUNTS PAYABLE MODULE
4) PAYROLL MODULE
5) EXIT PROGRAM

OPTION?
```

function or display a new set of menu choices. A typical master menu is shown in Exhibit B-4. To work with a particular module of this program, you would simply select from the menu. For example, to use the general ledger section of this program, you would type a "1".

General Ledger Module

The *general ledger module* is the centre of an integrated system. In this module, all of the general ledger accounts are maintained. Exhibit B-5 is a typical menu for using a general ledger module.

One option included in this module is the chart of accounts feature. The accountant sets up the chart of accounts by telling the computer each account's name, number, normal balance and type (current asset, plant asset, and so on). Since the program will remember this information, it need be entered only

EXHIBIT B-5   *Menu for General Ledger Module*

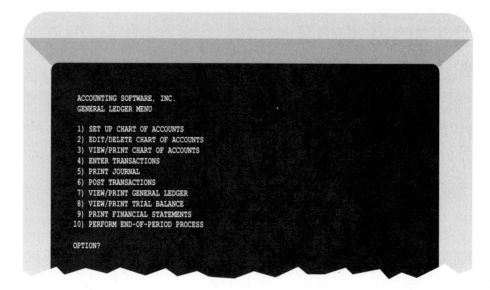

```
ACCOUNTING SOFTWARE, INC.
GENERAL LEDGER MENU

1) SET UP CHART OF ACCOUNTS
2) EDIT/DELETE CHART OF ACCOUNTS
3) VIEW/PRINT CHART OF ACCOUNTS
4) ENTER TRANSACTIONS
5) PRINT JOURNAL
6) POST TRANSACTIONS
7) VIEW/PRINT GENERAL LEDGER
8) VIEW/PRINT TRIAL BALANCE
9) PRINT FINANCIAL STATEMENTS
10) PERFORM END-OF-PERIOD PROCESS

OPTION?
```

once. This chart can be modified as necessary. Once the chart has been set up, the accountant can refer to an account simply by listing its account number. With this information, the program can supply the account name and other information by referring back to the chart of accounts.

Journal entries can also be entered through this module. Just as in the manual system of Chapters 1-5, some businesses choose to use the general journal as their only book of original entry. In Chapter 6 we saw the advantages of special journals. The same option exists in a computerized system. The general ledger module can be used on a stand-alone basis, with the general journal as the only book of original entry. Other modules with their special journals can also be used in an integrated system.

To make a journal entry, we list the number of each account affected (the computer will supply the account name), the amount of the transaction, and the choice of either debit or credit for that account. Once the transaction has been listed, the program will ask if the entry is correct before recording it. The computer will then check to see if the journal entry balances (debits equal credits).

After the entries have been recorded, the general journal can be printed. This printout, commonly called a *hard copy*, provides a permanent record of the journal entries. Most companies with computerized systems keep hard copies of all work to document the accounting records. Exhibit B-6 shows a sample page of *general journal entries*.

EXHIBIT B-6   *General Journal Entries*

J&L OFFICE SUPPLY
GENERAL JOURNAL
PAGE 08

TRANS	DATE	ACCT NO.	ACCT. NAME	DR.	CR.
32	4/20	1360	STORE EQUIP	1130.00	
		2200	ACCOUNTS PAYABLE		1130.00
33	4/20	5400	SALARY EXP	1900.00	
		2710	EMPLOYEE INCOME TAX PAY		399.00
		2711	FICA TAX PAY		135.85
		2712	EMPLOYEE HEALTH INS. PAY		16.00
		2713	EMPLOYEE UNION DUES PAY		35.00
		2720	SALARIES PAY		1314.15
34	4/20	5410	PAYROLL TAX EXP	212.65	
		2711	FICA TAX PAY		135.85
		2718	STATE UNEMPL TAX PAY		67.20
		2719	FED UNEMPL TAX PAY		9.60
35	4/20	4130	SALES RET & ALL	86.40	
		2370	SALES TAX PAY	6.05	
		1200	ACCOUNTS REC		92.45
36	4/20	2200	ACCOUNTS PAYABLE	651.00	
		5130	PURCH RET & ALL		651.00
39	4/21	1360	STORE EQUIP	400.00	
		2200	ACCOUNTS PAY		400.00
			PAGE TOTALS	5056.10	5056.10

Posting in a computer system is easy. In the system menu of Exhibit B-5, choose menu option 6, "Post Transactions." The program will post and also enter posting references automatically. This represents a considerable time-saving over the manual method of posting. It is also more accurate, because the computer is unlikely to make a posting error.

Accountants may wish to see (on the screen or printed out) the whole general ledger, in order to check each account, for example. A printout of a few general ledger accounts is shown in Exhibit B-7. Note that the posting references refer to other journals besides the general journal. These postings come from the other modules, as explained later.

At the end of the period, the program produces the trial balance as a basis for making the adjusting entries. Adjusting entries, like all other general journal entries, are recorded using the "Enter Transactions" option in Exhibit B-5. These entries are posted using the posting option on the menu. Once this is done, the account balances are updated and ready to be reported on the financial statements.

An important feature of a computerized system is that a work sheet is unnecessary. The reason for a work sheet in a manual system is to organize data to prepare the financial statements and the adjusting and closing entries. On the work sheet, ending balances are computed for the statements and

EXHIBIT B-7   *General Ledger Accounts*

```
J & L Office Supply
1908 Victoria Ave., E.
Brandon, Manitoba
R7B 6Y7


CASH                                                  ACCOUNT NO. 1100

DATE     EXPLANATION      REF      DR.          CR.          BALANCE

19XX
0401     BEG. BAL.        ---                                35540.00 DR
0430     TOTAL            CR12     23671.00                  59211.00 DR
0430     TOTAL            CD7                   31437.23     27773.77 DR



PETTY  CASH                                           ACCOUNT NO. 1120

DATE     EXPLANATION      REF      DR.          CR.          BALANCE

0401     BEG. BAL.        ---                                100.00 DR



ACCOUNTS RECEIVABLE                                   ACCOUNT NO. 1200

DATE     EXPLANATION      REF      DR.          CR.          BALANCE

0401     BEG. BAL.        ---                                8743.00 DR
0420                      J8                    92.45        8650.55 DR
0420                      J8                    107.00       8543.55 DR
0430     TOTAL            S16      19872.00                  28415.55 DR
0430     TOTAL            CR12                  25112.00     3303.55 DR
```

closing entries. Having the machine perform these steps automatically eliminates this time-consuming task. To print the financial statements, simply select this option from the menu, and the statements are created automatically.

Most accounting packages include an option allowing you to request that the temporary accounts be automatically closed at the end of the period. In Exhibit B-5, this menu option, "Perform End-of-Period Process," closes the accounts and prepares a post-closing trial balance. The post-closing trial balance can be printed by choosing the "View/Print Trial Balance" option in the general ledger menu. Just as in a manual system, this completes the accounting cycle, with balances updated and ready for use in the next accounting period.

Accounts Receivable Module

The *accounts receivable module* is used to keep track of the accounts receivable subsidiary ledger and to provide special journals for recording transactions that affect this asset account. In Chapter 6 we discussed the need for the sales journal and the cash receipts journal. A typical menu for the accounts receivable module is shown in Exhibit B-8.

The sales for each day are recorded at one time using this module. In some programs the sales are entered in the same format as in a manual sales journal:

Apr. 19	Accounts Receivable — Customer Name	1,300
	Sales Revenue	1,300

Other programs allow the accountant to enter each sale in the form of a sales invoice. The program creates an entry for the sales journal and also prints out the actual sale invoice to be sent to the customer, eliminating the manual

EXHIBIT B-8   *Menu for Accounts Receivable Module*

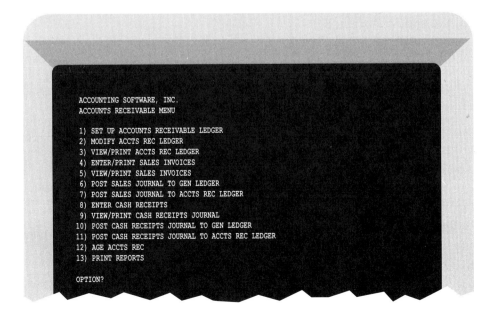

```
ACCOUNTING SOFTWARE, INC.
ACCOUNTS RECEIVABLE MENU

 1) SET UP ACCOUNTS RECEIVABLE LEDGER
 2) MODIFY ACCTS REC LEDGER
 3) VIEW/PRINT ACCTS REC LEDGER
 4) ENTER/PRINT SALES INVOICES
 5) VIEW/PRINT SALES INVOICES
 6) POST SALES JOURNAL TO GEN LEDGER
 7) POST SALES JOURNAL TO ACCTS REC LEDGER
 8) ENTER CASH RECEIPTS
 9) VIEW/PRINT CASH RECEIPTS JOURNAL
10) POST CASH RECEIPTS JOURNAL TO GEN LEDGER
11) POST CASH RECEIPTS JOURNAL TO ACCTS REC LEDGER
12) AGE ACCTS REC
13) PRINT REPORTS

OPTION?
```

EXHIBIT B-9   *Computer-Generated Sales Invoice*


```
J & L Office Supply              INVOICE        INVOICE NO.    2081
1908 Victoria Ave., E.                          INVOICE DATE   4-23-XX
Brandon, Manitoba                               ACCOUNT NO.    H01000
R7B 6Y7
                                                         PAGE  1


SOLD TO  Shaw Engineering Consultants    SHIP TO  Same
         1050 Wesbrook Mall
         Vancouver, B.C.
         V6S 1W8
```

PURCHASE ORDER NO.	SALESPERSON	SHIP VIA	FREIGHT	DATE SHIPPED	TERMS
628		Your Truck		April 23	2/10,N/30

QUANTITY	STOCK ITEM	UNIT	DESCRIPTION	UNIT PRICE	DISC %	AMOUNT
10	24X914		Staplers	7.00		70.00
50	87A827		Mechanical Pencils	1.25		62.50
20	24X820		Staples	1.50		30.00
100	428191		Memo Pads	.25		25.00

SALE AMOUNT	187.50
MISC CHARGES / SALES TAX / FREIGHT	13.13
TOTAL	200.63

ORIGINAL INVOICE

preparation of these invoices. An example of a computer-generated sale invoice is shown in Exhibit B-9.

After the day's sales have been entered, a sales journal can be printed. The hard copy is checked for correctness and saved as a permanent record. This journal can now be posted. Just as in a manual system, the sales journal should be posted to two ledgers, the accounts receivable ledger in the accounts receivable module and the general ledger in the general ledger module. See items 6 and 7 in Exhibit B-8.

The other journal in the accounts receivable module is the cash receipts journal, where all receipts of cash are recorded. A batch of cash receipt transactions is entered into the computer as it is in manual recording. As with the other journals, a hard copy is printed and checked for correctness. This journal is also posted to both the general ledger and accounts receivable ledger.

Some programs will keep a running balance of the customer accounts in the accounts receivable subsidiary ledger and can also print monthly statements to be sent to customers. An example of a monthly statement is shown in Exhibit B-10.

The accounts receivable module can perform an aging of the customer accounts to estimate uncollectible account expense. Using the computer for such tasks saves much time and money.

Exhibit B-11 shows how information flows through the accounts receivable module and interacts with the general ledger module.

Accounts Payable Module

A business can use the accounts payable program to maintain its accounts payable ledger, issue cheques to pay accounts payable, and generate both the

EXHIBIT B-10   *Customer Monthly Statement*

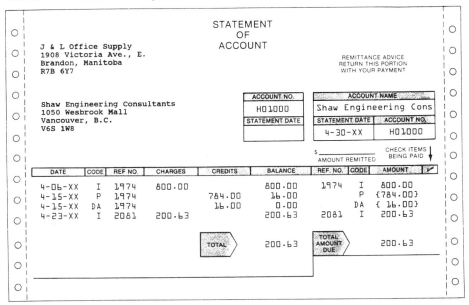

EXHIBIT B-11   *Information Flow in the Accounts Receivable Module*

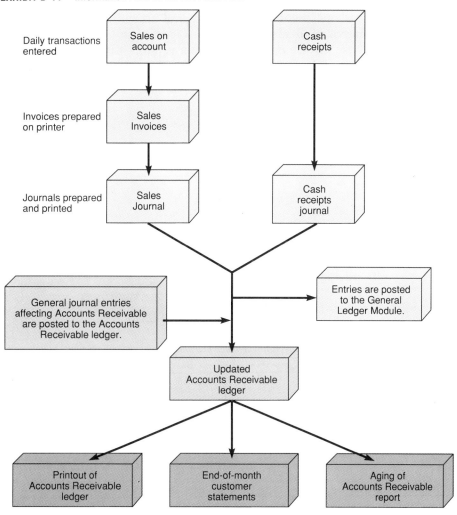

EXHIBIT B-12   *Menu for Accounts Payable Module*

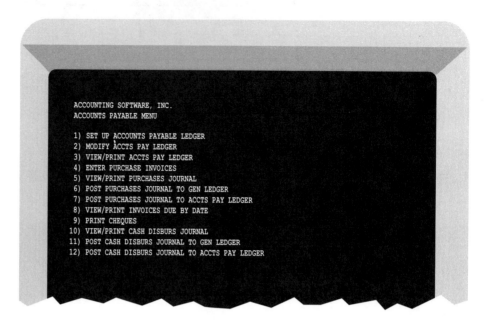

```
ACCOUNTING SOFTWARE, INC.
ACCOUNTS PAYABLE MENU

 1) SET UP ACCOUNTS PAYABLE LEDGER
 2) MODIFY ACCTS PAY LEDGER
 3) VIEW/PRINT ACCTS PAY LEDGER
 4) ENTER PURCHASE INVOICES
 5) VIEW/PRINT PURCHASES JOURNAL
 6) POST PURCHASES JOURNAL TO GEN LEDGER
 7) POST PURCHASES JOURNAL TO ACCTS PAY LEDGER
 8) VIEW/PRINT INVOICES DUE BY DATE
 9) PRINT CHEQUES
10) VIEW/PRINT CASH DISBURS JOURNAL
11) POST CASH DISBURS JOURNAL TO GEN LEDGER
12) POST CASH DISBURS JOURNAL TO ACCTS PAY LEDGER
```

purchases and cash payment journals. A typical accounts payable module menu is shown in Exhibit B-12.

When a purchase invoice is received from a vendor, it is entered into the accounts payable module. For each batch of purchase invoices the program will create a purchases journal. Its entries can be posted to both the accounts payable ledger and general ledger.

EXHIBIT B-13   *Cheque for Cash Payment*

					GUARANTY NATIONAL BANK	
	J & L Office Supply				CHECK 005074	
	1908 Victoria Ave., E.					
	Brandon, Manitoba		DATE	CONTROL NO	AMOUNT	
	R7B 6Y7		4-23-XX	4813	4471.60	

FOUR THOUSAND FOUR HUNDRED SEVENTY ONE AND 60/100-------------------

PAY TO THE ORDER OF   Franklin Paper Co.
3500 17th Avenue S.W.
Calgary, Alberta
T2P 1W7

J&L Office Supply

_____
AUTHORIZED SIGNATURE

J & L Office Supply, 1908 Victoria Ave., E., Brandon, Manitoba   R7B 6Y7

OUR REF. NO.	YOUR INVOICE NO.	INVOICE DATE	INVOICE AMOUNT	AMOUNT PAID	DISCOUNT TAKEN	NET CHECK AMOUNT
P1028	5673	4-10-XX	3080.00	3080.00		3080.00
P1264	5823	4-17-XX	1420.00	1420.00	28.40	1391.60
					TOTAL 4471.60	

Before invoices come due for payment, the system can provide a list of each invoice due on a particular date (item 8 of the Accounts Payable menu). The accountant can list the invoice to be paid and amount of the payment. Using preprinted forms, the computer can print the cheques (menu item 9). Exhibit B-13 is an example of a computer-generated cheque along with its stub showing information about the invoice paid.

The program records each cheque in the cash disbursements journal. This journal can be posted to both the accounts payable and general ledgers. Paid invoices can be shown along with the date of payment. A business may wish to print a list of all paid invoices for the records and delete them from the computer files. This step can prevent paying an invoice twice, paying the wrong amount, or mistakenly paying too late to receive the discount. Also, if an inventory module is added to this system, each purchase of merchandise can automatically be added into the inventory list. Exhibit B-14 shows how information flows in a system using an accounts payable module.

EXHIBIT B-14   *Information Flow in the Accounts Payable Module*

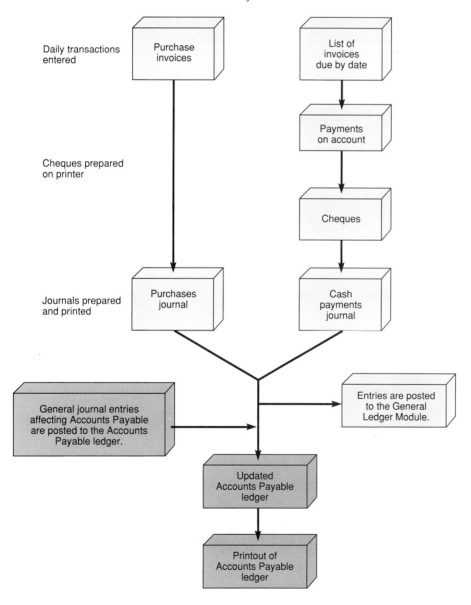

Payroll Module

As stated earlier, payroll accounting is ideally suited for a computerized system. A typical payroll module menu is shown in Exhibit B-15.

To use the payroll program, the business sets up a file on each employee. These files will contain such information as name, address, pay rate, marital status, and required and optional deductions. This information can be modified at any time, for example, when an employee moves or receives a raise, or when a new employee is hired.

For each pay period we will use the "Enter Current Payroll Data" option in the menu to calculate the period's payroll. The program will list each employee and show the current-period information: number of regular and overtime hours worked, bonuses or commissions to be received, and any optional deductions from this paycheque. For most employees this information does not change from pay period to pay period and will not have to be modified. After the information for the current payroll is entered, the computer will automatically calculate each paycheque. The program will calculate regular pay, overtime pay, gross pay, each deduction and net pay. Current tax, Canada or Quebec Pension Plan, and unemployment insurance tables should be built into the program so that the required deductions can be computed. Also, the computer keeps a record of year-to-date earnings and deductions for each employee.

The program can print the payroll register. After the information is verified, the payroll cheques are printed. Using preprinted cheques, the program can print cheques and the accompanying stubs, as illustrated in Exhibit B-16.

After the payroll cheques have been printed, the payroll register information is posted to the general ledger and the employee's individual earnings records are updated. Both tasks are performed by choosing the appropriate menu option.

At the end of the calendar year, the business prepares a T4 form for each employee (see Exhibit 11-7, p. 465).

Exhibit B-17 shows how information flows in a system using a payroll module.

EXHIBIT B-15   *Menu for a Payroll Module*

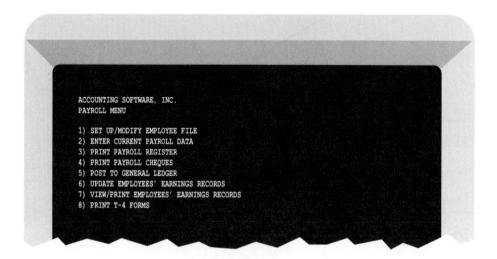

```
ACCOUNTING SOFTWARE, INC.
PAYROLL MENU

1) SET UP/MODIFY EMPLOYEE FILE
2) ENTER CURRENT PAYROLL DATA
3) PRINT PAYROLL REGISTER
4) PRINT PAYROLL CHEQUES
5) POST TO GENERAL LEDGER
6) UPDATE EMPLOYEES' EARNINGS RECORDS
7) VIEW/PRINT EMPLOYEES' EARNINGS RECORDS
8) PRINT T-4 FORMS
```

EXHIBIT B-16   *Paycheque*

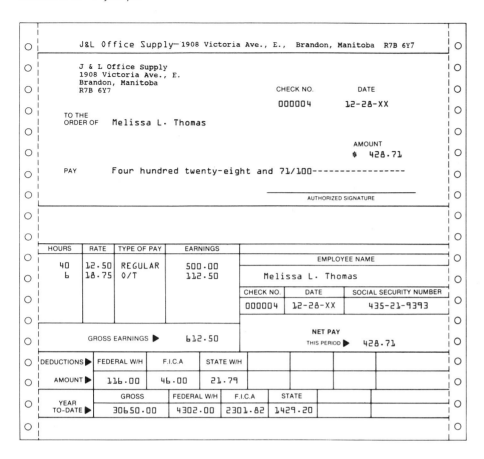

EXHIBIT B-17   *Information Flow in the Payroll Module*

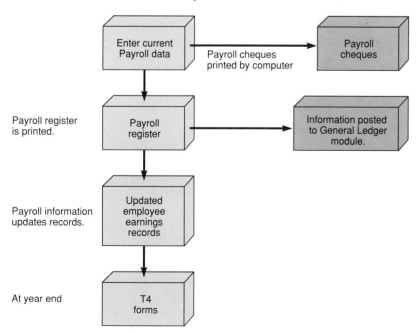

Spreadsheets

Spreadsheets are integrated software programs that can be used to solve many different problems. Spreadsheet programs replace the manual solution of problems. Typical accounting applications performed with a spreadsheet include budgets, depreciation schedules, debt amortization schedules, cost-volume-profit analysis and capital budgeting.

The most popular of the spreadsheet programs is Lotus 1-2-3™, which includes an electronic spreadsheet with graphics and data-management capabilities. Lotus 1-2-3 runs on a variety of personal computers and IBM-compatible computers. Other spreadsheet programs on the market that are structured similarly to Lotus 1-2-3 include VP Planner, Quattro and Super Calc.

Accounting Vocabulary

central processing unit (CPU) *(p. 1127)*
disk drive *(p. 1127)*
diskette *(p. 1127)*

integrated software *(p. 1128)*
menu *(p. 1129)*
menu-driven *(p. 1129)*

monitor *(p. 1127)*
printer *(p. 1127)*
program *(p. 1125)*

Mathematical Presentations

This appendix reviews some of the mathematical presentations in the book. You may find it helpful to refer to this appendix as you use the text.

Fractions, Decimals, Percentages and Ratios _____

There are four ways to describe mathematically a specific portion of something: as a fraction, a decimal, a percentage and a ratio. These expressions are interchangeable, as the following discussion shows.

Delwood Plaza, a shopping centre, consists of 40 stores. Thirty of the stores are occupied, ten are vacant. We can describe the portions of the shopping centre that are occupied and vacant in four ways:

	Portion of the Shopping Centre	
	Occupied	**Vacant**
Fraction	$^{30}\!/_{40} = \frac{3}{4}$	$^{10}\!/_{40} = \frac{1}{4}$
Decimal	$\frac{3}{4} = 3 \div 4 = .75$	$\frac{1}{4} = 1 \div 4 = .25$
Percentage	$.75 = 75\%$	$.25 = 25\%$
Ratio	$3 : 4$	$1 : 4$

Fractions, decimals, percentages and ratios are based on the relationship between two numbers. In this example, we are expressing the relationship between (1) the portion of the shopping centre that is occupied (or vacant) and (2) the total shopping centre.

As another example, suppose your daily drive to school is six kilometres. After driving two kilometres, you could describe your progress as $\frac{2}{6} = \frac{1}{3}$, or .333, or $33\frac{1}{3}\%$, or $1 : 3$. They all carry the same meaning. In this example, we are expressing the relationship between (1) the portion of the drive completed and (2) the total distance to be driven.

In all cases, there is a key question to ask before computing fractions, decimals, percentages and ratios: What is the base amount? That is, what is the denominator in the computation? For example, if a percentage is to be computed, the base amount is the number that represents 100 percent (40 stores in the shopping centre and 6 kilometres in the daily drive to school).

Percentage Changes _____

In business, percentage changes are widely used to measure achievement. For example, a company's total assets may increase from $200,000 to $240,000. This is a 20 percent increase, computed as follows:

Total assets now	$240,000	120%
Total assets previously	200,000	100
Increase in total assets	$ 40,000	20%
Percentage increase in total assets:		
Increase divided by previous amount		
($40,000 ÷ $200,000)	20%	

Suppose that during the next period total assets decrease to $180,000. The decrease is 25 percent, computed in exactly the same manner:

Total assets now	$180,000	75%
Total assets previously	240,000	100
Decrease in total assets..............	$ 60,000	25%
Percentage decrease in total assets:		
Decrease divided by previous amount		
($60,000 ÷ $240,000)	25%	

Dollar Signs and Double Underlines _____

In this book we show monetary figures by placing a dollar sign ($) with the first amount in each column and with each total that is underlined twice. This is the method used in companies' published annual reports. The preceding section, Percentage Changes, gives two examples.

Dollar signs are *not* used for amounts debited and credited in journals and ledgers. It is understood that these are monetary figures. However, we often use dollar signs in parenthetical explanations to aid your understanding of a particular entry. For example, two cash purchases of supplies for $50 and $40 could be combined into one entry:

	Amount	
	Debit	Credit
Supplies ($50 + $40)	90	
Cash......................		90

The ledger also omits dollar signs:

Supplies		Cash	
90			90

Double underlines indicate a final total, as presented in the Percentage Changes section.

Positive and Negative Amounts _____

In most mathematical presentations, the plus sign (+) denotes a positive amount, and the minus (−) denotes a negative amount: for example, $7 + 5 − 3 = 9$. In a columnar presentation it would be cumbersome to use a + or a − sign for each number. Accountants use a short-cut method that omits the plus sign for positive amounts and uses parentheses to denote negatives, as follows:

$$
\begin{array}{r}
7 \\
5 \\
\underline{(3)} \\
\underline{\underline{9}}
\end{array}
$$

Not all negative amounts are presented with parentheses, however. Parentheses are often omitted where the description clearly indicates that a subtraction occurs, as follows:

Males	7
Plus: Females	5
Less: Children	$\underline{3}$
Total adults	$\underline{\underline{9}}$

Reversing Entries

This appendix shows how accountants use a special technique called *reversing entries* to ease the burden of bookkeeping.

Accrued Expenses and the Related Liabilities

Some expenses accrue day by day (or even hour by hour), but they are paid at regular, longer intervals, often weekly or monthly. Many times the payment does not occur on the financial statement date. Therefore, at the end of the period the business must make an adjusting entry to record the expenses that have built up to that time but that will not be paid until later. Without an adjustment, the business's financial statements will overstate net income and owner's equity (because expenses and liabilities will be understated). These built-up expenses are called accrued expenses (or accrued liabilities because their recording includes a credit to a liability account). Examples include property taxes, interest on notes payable and employee salaries and wages.

Assume that at December 27, 19X1, (near the end of the accounting period) Salary Expense has a debit balance of $185,000 from salaries paid during the year. At year end the business owes employees $3,000 for their service during the last three work days of the year. This amount will be paid on January 3, the next payday, along with $2,000 in salaries for the first two work days of the new year. The next weekly payroll amount will be $5,000. However, to present the complete financial picture, the $3,000 in salaries incurred in 19X1 must be included in the 19X1 statements. Accordingly, the business makes the following adjusting entry on December 31:

Adjusting Entries

19X1

Dec. 31   Salary Expense   3,000

                 Salary Payable   3,000

After posting, the Salary Payable and Salary Expense accounts appear as follows:

Salary Payable

	19X1		
	Dec. 31	Adj.*	3,000
	Dec. 31	Bal.	3,000

Salary Expense

19X1			
Year's total through			
Dec. 27		185,000	
Dec. 31	Adj.	3,000	
Dec. 31	Bal.	188,000	

After the adjusting entry, the 19X1 *income statement* reports salary expense of $188,000, and the *balance sheet* at December 31, 19X1, reports Salary Payable, a liability, of $3,000. The $188,000 debit balance of Salary Expense will be eliminated by a closing entry at December 31, 19X1, as follows:

Closing Entries

19X1

Dec. 31   Income Summary   188,000

                 Salary Expense   188,000

After posting, Salary Expense appears as follows:

Salary Expense

Year's total through					
Dec. 27		185,000			
Dec. 31	Adj.	3,000			
Dec. 31	Bal.	188,000	Dec. 31	Clo.	188,000

---

* Entry explanations used throughout this appendix are
Adj. = Adjusting entry
Bal. = Balance
Clo. = Closing entry
CP   = Cash payment entry
CR   = Cash receipt entry
Rev. = Reversing entry, explained later in the appendix

Reversing Entries

Reversing entries are special types of entries that ease the burden of accounting after adjusting entries have been made in a preceding period. Let us see how reversing entries work. Suppose you are the accountant who records cash payments for salaries. In the normal course of recording salary payments during the year, you make the following payroll entry:

Salary Expense	5,000	
Cash		5,000

However, suppose that payday does not land on the day the accounting period ends and that you have made an adjusting entry to accrue salary payable of $3,000, as we have just seen. On January 3, 19X2, you record the weekly payroll of $5,000. You credit Cash for $5,000, but what account or accounts do you debit? The cash payment entry is

19X2			
Jan. 3	Salary Payable	3,000	
	Salary Expense................................	2,000	
	Cash		5,000

This method of recording the cash payment is *inefficient* because you must refer back to the adjusting entries of December 31, 19X1. Otherwise, you do not know the amount of the required debit (in this example, $3,000) to Salary Payable. Searching the preceding year's adjusting entries takes time, and in business, time is money. To avoid having to analyse the payment entry and having to separate the debit into two accounts, accountants have devised a technique called reversing entries.

Making a Reversing Entry   A **reversing entry** switches the debit and the credit of a previous adjusting entry. The reversing entry is dated the first day of the period following the adjusting entry.

Let us continue with our example of the end-of-period cash payment of $5,000 in salaries. On December 31, 19X1, the accountant made the following entry to accrue Salary Payable:

Adjusting Entries

19X1			
Dec. 31	Salary Expense	3,000	
	Salary Payable		3,000

The reversing entry simply flip-flops the position of the debit and the credit:

Reversing Entries

OBJECTIVE 1

Make a reversing entry for an accrued expense

19X2			
Jan. 1	Salary Payable	3,000	
	Salary Expense.........................		3,000

Notice that the reversing entry is dated the first day of the new period. It is the exact opposite of the December 31 adjusting entry. Ordinarily, the accountant who makes the adjusting entry also prepares the reversing entry at the same time. She postdates the reversing entry to January 1 of the next period, however, so that it affects the new period. Note how the accounts appear after the accountant posts the reversing entry:

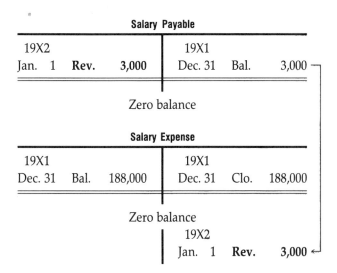

The arrow shows the transfer of the $3,000 credit balance from Salary Payable to Salary Expense. This credit balance in Salary Expense does not mean that the entity has negative salary expense, as might be suggested by a credit balance in an expense account. Instead, the odd credit balance is merely a temporary result of the reversing entry. The credit balance is eliminated on January 3, 19X2, when the $5,000 cash payment for salaries is debited to Salary Expense in the customary manner:

```
19X2
Jan. 3   Salary Expense...............................   5,000
             Cash ...................................           5,000
```

Then this cash payment entry is posted:

Salary Expense					
19X2			19X2		
Jan. 3	CP	5,000	Jan. 1	Rev.	3,000
Jan. 3	Bal.	2,000			

Now Salary Expense has its correct debit balance of $2,000, which is the amount of salary expense incurred thus far in 19X2. The $5,000 cash disbursement also pays the liability for Salary Payable. Thus the Salary Payable account has a zero balance which is correct, as shown at the top of this page.

The adjusting and reversing process is repeated year after year. Cash payments for salaries are debited to Salary Expense, and these amounts accumulate in that account. At the end of the year, the accountant makes an adjusting entry to accrue salary expense incurred but not yet paid. At the same time, the accountant also makes a reversing entry, which allows her to record all payroll entries in the customary manner—by routinely debiting Salary Expense. Even in computerized systems, making reversing entries is more efficient than writing a program to locate the amount accrued from the preceding period and making the more complicated journal entry.

Reversing entries deserve emphasis. Accountants often must deal with hundreds or even thousands of repetitive transactions. With reversing entries, accountants do not have to worry that a cash payment might apply in part to an accrued liability recognized at the end of the preceding period. Reversing entries allow them to debit an expense for the full cash expense payment. Reversing entries may be made for all types of accrued expenses. However, they are optional, and some companies do not use them.

Accrued Revenues and the Related Assets _____

Certain revenues, such as interest earned on notes receivable, accrue with the passage of time, just as expenses do. However, a business usually does not record *accrued revenues* daily, weekly or even monthly. Instead, it records them when it receives cash. Thus at the end of the accounting period, the business may have earned revenue that it has not yet recorded.

Assume the business has a note receivable on which it receives cash interest on February 1 and August 1. Interest accumulates at $200 per month. During 19X3 the business receives $1,200 of interest on August 1, and that amount is the balance in Interest Revenue at December 31, 19X3, before any adjustments. Suppose that between August 1 and December 31 the business has earned additional interest revenue of $1,000, which it will receive February 1, 19X4, along with $200 of interest revenue for January 19X4. The year-end adjusting entry on December 31, 19X3 is

Adjusting Entries

19X3			
Dec. 31	Interest Receivable...........................	1,000	
	Interest Revenue		1,000

After posting, the accounts appear as follows:

Interest Receivable

19X3			
Dec. 31	Adj.	1,000	
Dec. 31	Bal.	1,000	

Interest Revenue

			19X3		
			Aug. 1	CR	1,200
			Dec. 31	Adj.	1,000
			Dec. 31	Bal.	2,200

The 19X3 income statement reports interest revenue of $2,200, and the balance sheet reports interest receivable of $1,000.

Receipt of $1,200 cash interest on February 1, 19X4 eliminates the $1,000 receivable. This receipt also includes $200 interest revenue earned during January 19X4. A reversing entry, dated January 1, 19X4, avoids having to account for these dual effects. The reversing entry is

Reversing Entries

19X4		
Jan. 1 Interest Revenue..............................	1,000	
Interest Receivable........................		1,000

> **OBJECTIVE 2**
> Make a reversing entry for an accrued revenue

After posting the reversing entry, Interest Receivable and Interest Revenue appear as follows:

Interest Receivable

19X3			19X4			
Dec. 31	Bal.	1,000	Jan. 1	**Rev.**	**1,000**

Zero balance

Interest Revenue

19X3			19X3			
Dec. 31	Clo.	2,200	Dec. 31	Bal.	2,200

Zero balance

19X4		
Jan. 1	**Rev.**	**1,000**

The arrow shows the transfer of the debit balance from Interest Receivable to Interest Revenue. This debit will be eliminated on February 1, 19X4, when the business receives cash interest of $1,200. The cash receipt entry is then routinely recorded:

19X4		
Feb. 1 Cash	1,200	
Interest Revenue		1,200

After posting, the Interest Revenue account has the correct credit balance of $200, which is the amount of interest revenue earned in 19X4:

Interest Revenue

19X4			19X4			
Jan. 1	Rev.	1,000	Feb. 1	CR	1,200
			Feb. 1	Bal.	200

Accountants use reversing entries for all types of accrued revenues, but they are optional.

Summary Problem for Your Review

The fiscal year accounting period of Jeans 4 U Ltd., maker of Excellent jeans, ends on September 30. After going through the accounting process, including the adjusting entries, Jeans 4 U reported its *accrued liabilities* on a recent balance sheet as follows. These accrued liabilities resulted directly from the adjusting entries.

Liabilities

Notes payable: Banks and other	$135,419
Current maturities of long-term debt	3,664
Accounts payable, principally trade	120,697
Dividends payable	5,756
Accrued liabilities	
Compensation [salaries and wages]	**23,620**
Pension and profit sharing	**4,981**
Income taxes	**21,624**
Withholdings	**8,028**
Interest	**3,534**
Other	**7,983**
Total	$335,306

The company's accrued liability for compensation is its unpaid compensation expense for the year ended September 30.

Required

1. Journalize adjusting entries like those that Jeans 4 U made at September 30 to record accrued compensation expense and accrued interest expense.

2. Journalize the related reversing entries. Date them appropriately.

3a. Set up ledger accounts for Compensation Payable and Compensation Expense, on September 30, prior to the adjusting entries in question 1. Compensation Payable had a zero balance and Compensation Expense had a debit balance of $380,000.

  b. Journalize the closing entry for Compensation Expense at September 30.

  c. Assume Jeans 4 U paid compensation of $25 thousand on October 3. Journalize this cash payment, assuming a reversing entry was made.

  d. Post the adjusting, closing, reversing and cash payment entries to Compensation Payable and Compensation Expense. Use the appropriate dates and label adjusting entries as Adj., closing entries as Clo., reversing entries as Rev. and cash payments as CP.

  e. After all postings, what is the balance in Compensation Payable? What does this mean? What is the balance in Compensation Expense? What does this balance mean?

SOLUTION TO REVIEW PROBLEM

a.   Adjusting entries at September 30:

Adjusting Entries

Sept. 30	Compensation Expense	23,620	
	Compensation Payable		23,620
30	Interest Expense	3,534	
	Interest Payable....................		3,534

b.   Reversing entries at October 1:

Reversing Entries

Oct. 1	Compensation Payable	23,620	
	Compensation Expense................		23,620
1	Interest Payable...........................	3,534	
	Interest Expense		3,534

c.   (1) Ledger accounts and balances prior to September 30 adjusting entries:

Compensation Payable

Compensation Expense

CP		
CP		
Sept. 30 Bal. 380,000		

(2) Closing entry at September 30:

Closing Entries

Sept. 30	Income Summary ($380,000 + $23,620) .	403,620	
	Compensation Expense.........		403,620

(3) Cash payment for compensation at October 3:

Oct. 3	Compensation Expense	25,000	
	Cash		25,000

(4) Ledger accounts posted:

Compensation Payable

Oct. 1 Rev. 23,620		Sept. 30 Adj. 23,620	

Zero balance

Compensation Expense

CP		$\gtrless$				
CP		$\gtrless$				
		380,000				
Sept. 30	Adj.	23,620				
Sept. 30	Bal.	403,620	Sept. 30	Clo.	403,620	
Oct. 3	CP	25,000	Oct. 1	Rev.	23,620	
Oct. 3	Bal.	1,380				

(5) The balance in Compensation Payable is zero. This means Jeans 4 U has no compensation liability. The debit balance in Compensation Expense is $1,380. This amount is the portion of the October 3 payment that is compensation expense of the new year.

Prepaid Expenses

Prepaid expenses are advance payments of expenses. Prepaid Insurance, Prepaid Rent, Prepaid Advertising and Prepaid Legal Cost are prepaid expenses. Supplies that will be used up in the current period or within one year are also accounted for as prepaid expenses.

When a business prepays an expense for example, rent, it can debit an *asset* account (Prepaid Rent) as follows:

Prepaid Rent...	XXX	
Cash......................................		XXX

Alternatively, the accountant can debit an *expense* account in the entry to record this cash payment, as follows:

Rent Expense	XXX	
Cash...		XXX

Regardless of the account debited, the business must adjust the accounts at the end of the period. Making the adjustment allows the business to report the correct amount of expense for the period and the correct amount of asset at the period's end.

Prepaid Expense Recorded Initially as an Asset

Prepayments of expenses provide a future benefit to the business, so it is logical to record the prepayment by debiting an *asset* account. Suppose on August 1, 19X6, the business prepays one year's rent of $6,000 ($500 per month). The cash payment is recorded:

19X6			
Aug. 1	Prepaid Rent..................................	6,000	
	Cash....................................		6,000

On December 31, the end of the accounting period, five months' prepayment has expired and must be accounted for as *expense*. The adjusting entry is

Adjusting Entries

19X6
Dec. 31   Rent Expense ($6,000 × 5/12)   2,500
                    Prepaid Rent   2,500

The adjusting entry transfers $2,500 of the original $6,000 prepayment from Prepaid Rent to Rent Expense. This leaves a $3,500 debit balance in Prepaid Rent, which is seven months' rent still prepaid. After posting, the accounts appear as follows:

Prepaid Rent

19X6			19X6		
Aug. 1	CP	6,000	Dec. 31	Adj.	2,500
Dec. 31	Bal.	3,500			

Rent Expense

19X6				
Dec. 31	Adj.	2,500		
Dec. 31	Bal.	2,500		

The $2,500 balance of Rent Expense is closed to Income Summary, along with all other expenses and revenues, at the end of the accounting period.

No reversing entry is used under this approach. The asset account Prepaid Rent has a debit balance to start the new period. This is consistent with recording prepaid expenses initially as assets.

The balance sheet at December 31, 19X6, reports Prepaid Rent of $3,500 as an asset. The 19X6 income statement reports Rent Expense of $2,500 as an expense, which is the expired portion of the initial $6,000 rent prepayment. Keep this reporting result in mind as you study the next section.

Prepaid Expense Recorded Initially as an Expense

Prepaying an expense creates an asset. However, the asset may be so short-lived that it will expire in the current accounting period (within one year or less). Thus the accountant may decide to debit the prepayment to an expense account at the time of payment. Continuing with the rent example, the $6,000 cash payment on August 1 may be debited to Rent Expense:

19X6
Aug. 1   Rent Expense   6,000
                    Cash   6,000

At December 31 only five months' prepayment has expired, leaving seven months' rent still prepaid. In this case, the accountant must transfer 7/12 of the original prepayment of $6,000 or $3,500 to Prepaid Rent. The adjusting entry decreases the balance of Rent Expense to 5/12 of the original $6,000, or $2,500. The December 31 adjusting entry is

Adjusting Entries

19X6

Dec. 31   Prepaid Rent ($6,000 × 7/12)   3,500

              Rent Expense   3,500

After posting, the two accounts appear as follows:

Prepaid Rent

19X6			
Dec. 31	Adj.	3,500	
Dec. 31	Bal.	3,500	

Rent Expense

19X6			19X6			
Aug. 1	CP	6,000	Dec. 31	Adj.	3,500	
Dec. 31	Bal.	2,500				

The balance sheet for 19X6 reports Prepaid Rent of $3,500, and the income statement for 19X6 reports Rent Expense of $2,500. Whether the business initially debits the prepayment to an asset account or to an expense account, the financial statements report the same amounts for prepaid rent and rent expense. The Rent Expense's balance is closed at the end of the period.

During the next accounting period, the $3,500 balance in Prepaid Rent will expire and become expense. It is efficient on the beginning date of the new year to make a *reversing entry* that transfers the ending balance of Prepaid Rent back to Rent Expense:

Reversing Entries

OBJECTIVE 4

Reverse the adjustment for a prepaid expense recorded initially as an expense

19X7

Jan. 1   Rent Expense   3,500

          Prepaid Rent   3,500

This reversing entry avoids later worry about what prepayments become expenses. The arrow shows the transfer of the debit balance from Prepaid Rent to Rent Expense after posting:

Prepaid Rent

19X6			19X7			
Dec. 31	Bal.	3,500	Jan. 1	**Rev.**	**3,500**	

Zero balance

Rent Expense

19X6			19X6			
Aug. 1	CP	6,000	Dec. 31	Adj.	3,500	
Dec. 31	Bal.	2,500	Dec. 31	Clo.	2,500	

Zero balance

19X7		
Jan. 1	**Rev.**	**3,500**

After the reversing entry, the $3,500 amount is lodged in the expense account. This is consistent with recording prepaid expenses initially as expenses. Because this $3,500 amount will become expense during 19X7, no additional adjustment is needed. Subsequent expense prepayments are debited to Rent Expense and then adjusted at the end of the period as outlined here. Reversing entries ease the work of the accounting process for all types of prepaid expenses that are recorded initially as expenses. Reversing entries are *not* used for prepaid expenses that are recorded initially as assets.

Comparing the Two Approaches to Recording Prepaid Expenses

In summary, the two approaches to recording prepaid expenses are similar in that the asset amount reported on the balance sheet and the expense amount reported on the income statement are the same. They differ, however, in the prepayment entries and the adjusting entries. When a prepaid expense is recorded initially as an asset, (1) the adjusting entry transfers the *used* portion of the asset to the expense account and (2) no reversing entry is used. When a prepaid expense is recorded initially as an expense, (1) the adjusting entry transfers the *unused* portion of the expense to the asset account and (2) a reversing entry transfers the amount of the asset account back to the expense account to start the new accounting period.

Unearned (Deferred) Revenues _____

Unearned (deferred) revenues arise when a business collects cash in advance of earning the revenue. The recognition of revenue is *deferred* until later when it is earned. Unearned revenues are liabilities because the business that receives cash owes the other party goods or services to be delivered later.

Recall the prepaid expense examples listed on p. 1152: insurance, rent, advertising, and so on. Prepaid expenses create assets for the business that pays the cash. The business that receives the cash in advance, however, faces a liability. For example, the landlord who receives a tenant's rent in advance must provide future service to the tenant. This is a liability, and the cash the landlord receives is unearned rent revenue. Similarly, unearned revenue arises as magazine publishers sell subscriptions, colleges collect tuition, airlines sell tickets and lawyers accept advance fees.

When a business receives cash before earning the related revenue, the business debits Cash. It can credit either a *liability* account or a *revenue* account. In either case, the business must make adjusting entries at the end of the period to report the correct amounts of liability and revenue on the financial statements.

Unearned (Deferred) Revenue Recorded Initially as a Liability

Receipt of cash in advance of earning revenue creates a liability, so it is logical to debit Cash and credit a *liability* account. Assume a lawyer receives a $7,200 fee in advance from a client on October 1, 19X2. The lawyer will earn this amount at the rate of $800 per month during the nine-month period ending June 30, 19X3. The lawyer's cash receipt entry is

OBJECTIVE 5

Record unearned revenues in two ways

```
19X2
Oct. 1   Cash ..........................................   7,200
              Unearned Legal Revenue...................            7,200
```

On December 31, 19X2, the end of the law firm's accounting period, three months of the fee agreement have elapsed. The lawyer has earned $\frac{3}{9}$ of the $7,200, or $2,400. The adjusting entry to transfer $2,400 to the revenue account is

Adjusting Entries

```
19X2
Dec. 31   Unearned Legal Revenue ($7,200 × 3/9) ............   2,400
               Legal Revenue ...........................            2,400
```

After posting, the liability and revenue accounts are

Unearned Legal Revenue

19X2			19X2		
Dec. 31	Adj.	2,400	Oct. 1	CR	7,200
			Dec. 31	Bal.	4,800

Legal Revenue

			19X2		
			Dec. 31	Adj.	2,400
			Dec. 31	Bal.	2,400

The law firm's 19X2 income statement reports legal revenue of $2,400, while its balance sheet reports unearned legal revenue of $4,800 as a liability. During 19X3 the lawyer will earn the remaining $4,800 and will then make an adjusting entry to transfer $4,800 to the Legal Revenue account. No reversing entry is used. The balance in the liability account is consistent with recording the unearned revenue initially as a liability.

Unearned (Deferred) Revenue Recorded Initially as a Revenue

Receipt of cash in advance of earning the revenue can be credited initially to a *revenue* account. If the business has earned all the revenue within the period during which it received the cash, no adjusting entry is necessary. However, if the business earns only a part of the revenue at the end of the period, it must make adjusting entries.

Suppose on October 1, 19X2, the law firm records the nine-month advance fee of $7,200 as revenue. The cash receipt entry is

```
19X2
Oct. 1   Cash ..........................................   7,200
              Legal Revenue ...........................            7,200
```

After December 31 the lawyer has earned only ⅓ of the $7,200, or $2,400. Accordingly, the firm makes an adjusting entry to transfer the unearned portion (⅔ of $7,200, or $4,800) from the revenue account to a liability account.

Adjusting Entries

19X2
Dec. 31   Legal Revenue ($7,200 × ⅔) 4,800
                 Unearned Legal Revenue   4,800

The adjusting entry leaves the earned portion (⅓ or $2,400) of the original amount in the revenue account. After posting, the total amount ($7,200) is properly divided between the liability account ($4,800) and the revenue account ($2,400), as follows:

Unearned Legal Revenue

	19X2		
	Dec. 31	Adj.	4,800
	Dec. 31	Bal.	4,800

Legal Revenue

19X2			19X2		
Dec. 31	Adj.	4,800	Oct. 1	CR	7,200
			Dec. 31	Bal.	2,400

The lawyer's 19X2 income statement reports legal revenue of $2,400, and the balance sheet at December 31, 19X2, reports as a liability the unearned legal revenue of $4,800. Whether the business initially credits a liability account or a revenue account, the financial statements report the same amounts for unearned legal revenue and legal revenue.

The law firm will earn the $4,800 during 19X3. On January 1, 19X3, it is efficient to make a reversing entry in order to transfer the liability balance back to the revenue account. By making the reversing entry, the accountant avoids having to reconsider the situation one year later, when the 19X3 adjusting entries will be made. The reversing entry is

Reversing Entries

19X3
Jan. 1   Unearned Legal Revenue 4,800
                 Legal Revenue   4,800

OBJECTIVE 6
Reverse the adjustment for an earned revenue recorded initially as a revenue

After posting, the liability account has a zero balance. The $4,800 credit is now lodged in the revenue account because it will be earned during 19X3. The arrow in the following example shows the transfer from the liability account to the revenue account.

Unearned Legal Revenue

				19X2		
				Dec. 31	Adj.	4,800
19X3				19X2		
Jan. 1	**Rev.**	**4,800**		Dec. 31	Bal.	4,800

Zero balance

Legal Revenue

19X2				19X2		
Dec. 31	Adj.	4,800		Oct. 1	CR	7,200
Dec. 31	Clo.	2,400		Dec. 31	Bal.	2,400

Zero balance

19X3		
Jan. 1	**Rev.**	**4,800**

Subsequent advance receipts of revenue are credited to the Legal Revenue account. The year-end adjusting process is the same for every period.

Comparing the Two Approaches to Recording Unearned (Deferred) Revenues

The two approaches to recording unearned revenue are similar in that the liability amount reported on the balance sheet and the revenue amount reported on the income statement are the same. The approaches differ, though, in how adjustments are handled. When unearned revenues are recorded initially as liabilities, (1) the adjusting entry transfers to the revenue account the amount of the advance collection that has been *earned* during the period, and (2) *no* reversing entry is used. When unearned revenues are recorded initially as revenue, (1) the adjustment transfers to the liability account the amount of the advance collection that is still *unearned*, and (2) a reversing entry transfers the balance of the liability account to the revenue account to begin the next accounting period.

Summary Problem for Your Review

Pizza Time Theatre, Inc. reported prepaid expenses of $429,380 on a recent balance sheet. Assume that during the year the company paid cash in the amount of $1 million for prepaid insurance, rent, and so on.

Required

Record the company's prepaid expense transactions and related adjusting, closing, and reversing entries, assuming the company records prepaid expenses initially as (1) an asset and (2) an expense. Record entries in a single Prepaid Expense account and a single Expense account.

SOLUTION TO REVIEW PROBLEM

a. Prepaid expense recorded initially as an *asset*
    Cash payment of $1,000,000:

Prepaid Expense	1,000,000	
Cash		1,000,000

Year-end adjusting entry:

Expense ($1,000,000 – $429,380)	570,620	
Prepaid Expense		570,620

Year-end closing entry:

Income Summary	570,620	
Expense		570,620

Reversing entry: None

b. Prepaid expense recorded initially as an *expense*
    Cash payment of $1,000,000:

Expense......................................	1,000,000	
Cash		1,000,000

Year-end adjusting entry:

Prepaid Expense	429,380	
Expense		429,380

Year-end closing entry:

Income Summary	570,620	
Expense		570,620

Reversing entry dated January 1 of new year:

Expense......................................	429,380	
Prepaid Expense		429,380

Summary _____

Accrual entries may be accompanied by *reversing entries*, which eliminate the need to refer back to the adjusting entries of the preceding period when recording the cash payments and receipts of a new period. They are the exact opposite of the related adjusting entry. An efficiency device, they eliminate the need to refer back to a preceding period's adjusting entries when making cash entries in the next period. However, they are optional.

Prepared expenses may be recorded initially in an *asset* account or an *expense* account. When prepaid expenses are recorded initially as an asset, no need exists for a reversing entry because the asset account balance will be adjusted at the end of the next period. However, when prepaid expenses are recorded initially as an expense, a reversing entry eases accounting for the expense of the new period. Regardless of the approach taken, the financial statements should report the same amount of asset and expense.

Unearned (deferred) revenues may be recorded initially as a *liability* or a *revenue*. Recording unearned revenues initially as liabilities causes no need for a reversing entry. However, when recording them initially as revenues, a reversing entry eases accounting. Either recording approach is acceptable as long as the *financial statements* report the *correct* amounts.

Self-Study Questions

Test your understanding of this appendix by marking the best answer for each of the following questions:

1. The reversing entry for a $900 accrual of salary expense is *(p. 1146)*

   a. Salary Expense 900
      Salary Payable 900
   b. Salary Expense 900
      Cash 900
   c. Salary Payable 900
      Cash 900
   d. Salary Payable 900
      Salary Expense 900

2. Reversing entries are dated *(p. 1146)*
   a. The date on which the entry is made
   b. The beginning of the next period
   c. The end of the period
   d. Any of the above

3. The benefit of reversing entries is that they *(p. 1148)*
   a. Eliminate the need for adjusting entries
   b. Close out the balances in all the revenues and expenses
   c. Streamline the accounting for transactions in a period following an adjusting entry
   d. Increase the amounts of assets and decrease the amounts of liabilities reported on the balance sheet

4. Which of the following entries would it be helpful to reverse? *(pp. 1148–1149, 1154)*

   a. Interest Receivable XXX
      Interest Revenue XXX
   b. Rent Expense XXX
      Prepaid Rent XXX
   c. Cash XXX
      Interest Receivable XXX
   d. Supplies XXX
      Supplies Expense XXX
   e. Both a and b
   f. Both a and d
   g. None of the above

5. Recording a prepaid expense initially as an asset *(pp. 1152, 1155)*

a. Has no effect on the amount of asset and expense reported in the financial statements so long as the correct adjusting entry is made at the end of the period.

b. Leads to reporting the correct amount of asset and expense in the financial statements.

c. Leads to reporting an incorrect amount of asset and expense in the financial statements.

d. Is illogical. It is more logical to record the prepaid expense initially as an expense.

Answers to the self-study questions are at the end of the appendix.

Accounting Vocabulary

reversing entry *(p. 1146)*

ASSIGNMENT MATERIAL _____

Questions

1. What are the identifying characteristics of a reversing entry? What is the practical value of reversing entries?

2. The title Accrued Expenses does not include the word *liability* or *payable*. Why are accrued expenses liabilities?

3. What are the two ways to initially record a prepaid expense? How are they similar? How are they different?

4. Explain why recording a prepaid expense initially as an expense calls for a reversing entry.

5. Unearned revenues are also called deferred revenues. Why?

6. Suppose your company receives cash from customers in advance of earning the revenue. Which approach to recording the unearned revenue would you take and why?

7. Which approach to recording unearned (deferred) revenues calls for a reversing entry?

8. Each of the following adjusting entries is incomplete. Indicate the account debited or credited in the other half of the entry.

Accounts Receivable	XXX	
_____a_____		XXX
_____b_____	XXX	
Wage Payable.....................................		XXX
Supplies Expense	XXX	
_____c_____		XXX
Unearned Revenue	XXX	
_____d_____		XXX

9. Indicate whether each of the following accounts is (a) an asset, (b) a liability, (c) a revenue or (d) an expense: Unearned Legal Revenue, Interest Receivable, Prepaid Rent, Sales Revenue, Insurance Expense, Supplies, Salary Expense, Income Tax Expense, Property Tax Payable, Deferred Subscription Revenue, Service Fees Earned.

10. Where is the ultimate emphasis in financial accounting? How do adjusting entries tie into this emphasis?

Exercises

Exercise D-1 *Journalizing and posting wage payment and accrual transactions*

During 19X2 London Sales Company Ltd. pays wages of $40,800 to its employees. At December 31, 19X2, the company owes accrued wages of $900 that will be included in the $1,200 weekly payroll payment on January 4, 19X3.

Required

1. Open T-accounts for Wage Expense and Wage Payable.

2. Journalize all wage transactions for 19X2 and 19X3, including adjusting, closing and reversing entries. Record the $40,800 amount by a single debit to Wage Expense.

3. Post amounts to the two T-accounts, showing their balances at January 4, 19X3. Denote cash payment entries by CP, adjusting entries by Adj., closing entries by Clo., reversing entries by Rev. and balances by Bal.

Exercise D-2 *Recording supplies transactions two ways*

At the beginning of the year supplies of $1,490 were on hand. During the year the business paid $3,300 cash for supplies. At the end of the year the count of supplies indicates the ending balance is $1,260.

Required

1. Assume the business records supplies by initially debiting an *asset* account. Therefore, place the beginning balance in the Supplies T-account and record the above entries directly in the accounts without using a journal.

2. Assume the business records supplies by initially debiting an *expense* account. Therefore, place the beginning balance in the Supplies Expense T-account and record the above entries directly in the accounts without using a journal.

3. Compare the ending account balances under the two approaches. Are they the same or different? Why?

Exercise D-3 *Recording unearned revenues two ways*

At the beginning of the year the company owed customers $6,450 for unearned sales collected in advance. During the year the business received advance cash receipts of $10,000. At year end the unearned revenue liability is $3,900.

Required

1. Assume the company records unearned revenues by initially crediting a *liability* account. Open T-accounts for Unearned Sales Revenue and Sales Revenue and place the beginning balance in Unearned Sales Revenue. Journalize the cash collection and adjusting entries and post their dollar amounts. As references in the T-accounts, denote a balance by Bal., a cash receipt by CR and an adjustment by Adj.

2. Assume the company records unearned revenues by initially crediting a *revenue* account. Open T-accounts for Unearned Sales Revenue and Sales Revenue and place the beginning balance in Sales Revenue. Journalize the cash collection and adjusting entries and post their dollar amounts. As references in the T-accounts, denote a balance by Bal., a cash receipt by CR and an adjustment by Adj.

3. Compare the ending balances in the two accounts. Explain why they are the same or different.

Exercise D-4   *Using reversing entries to account for unearned revenues*

One approach to recording unearned revenue in Exercise D-3 calls for a reversing entry. Identify that approach. Journalize and post the entries in Exercise D-3 and also the closing and reversing entries. The end of the current period is December 31, 19X1. Use dates for all entries and postings except the cash collection, which is a summary of the year's transactions. As references in the ledger accounts, denote a balance by Bal., cash receipts by CR, adjusting entries by Adj., closing entries by Clo. and reversing entries by Rev.

Exercise D-5   *Recording accrued revenues with and without reversing entries*

Columbus Corporation receives a note receivable on November 1, 19X5. During the remainder of the year, Columbus earns accrued interest revenue of $3,000. This amount will be collected on May 1, 19X6, along with $6,000 of interest revenue for 19X6.

Required

1. Open T-accounts for Interest Receivable and Interest Revenue. Journalize and post the interest accrual and cash collection transactions and the closing entry, assuming reversing entries are not used. As references in the ledger accounts, denote a balance by Bal., cash receipts by CR, adjusting entries by Adj., closing entries by Clo. and reversing entries by Rev.
2. Repeat question 1, assuming reversing entries are used.
3. Compare the account balances achieved in questions 1 and 2.

Exercise D-6   *Identifying transactions from a ledger account*

McGraw Company Ltd. makes its annual insurance payment on June 30. Identify each of the entries (a) through (e) to the Insurance Expense account as a cash payment, an adjusting entry, a closing entry or a reversing entry. Also give the other account debited or credited in each entry.

Insurance Expense

Date	Item	Debit	Credit	Balance Debit	Balance Credit
19X4					
Jan. 1	(a)	800		800	
June 30	(b)	1,240		2,040	
Dec. 31	(c)		410	1,630	
Dec. 31	(d)		1,630	—	
19X5					
Jan. 1	(e)	410			410

Problems   **(Group A)**

Problem D-1A   *Recording prepaid rent and revenue collected in advance two ways*

DeGroot Sales and Service Inc. completes the following transactions during 19X4:

Aug. 31   Pays $9,000 store rent covering the six-month period ending February 28, 19X5.

Dec. 1   Collects $2,200 cash in advance from customers. The service revenue will be earned $550 monthly over the period ending March 30, 19X5.

Required

1. Journalize these entries by debiting an asset account for Prepaid Rent and by crediting a liability account for Unearned Service Revenue. Explanations are unnecessary.
2. Journalize the related adjustments at December 31, 19X4.
3. Post the entries to the ledger accounts and show their balances at December 31, 19X4. Posting references are unnecessary.
4. Repeat questions 1 through 3. This time debit Rent Expense for the rent payment and credit Service Revenue for the collection of revenue in advance.
5. Compare the account balances in questions 3 and 4. They should be equal.

Problem D-2A *Journalizing adjusting and reversing entries*

Vidmar Corp.'s accounting records reveal the following information before adjustments at December 31, 19X3, the end of the accounting period:

a. Wages owed to hourly employees total $3,400. Total salaries owed to salaried employees are $2,790. These amounts will be paid on the next scheduled payday in January 19X4.

b. On October 31 Vidmar loaned $40,000 to another business. The loan agreement requires the borrower to pay Vidmar interest of $2,400 on April 30, 19X4. One third of this interest is earned in 19X3.

c. Vidmar routinely debits Sales Supplies when it purchases supplies. At the beginning of 19X3 supplies of $800 were on hand, and during the year the company purchased supplies of $6,700. At year end the count of sales supplies on hand indicates the ending amount is $950.

d. Vidmar collects revenue in advance from customers and credits such amounts to Sales Revenue because the revenue is usually earned within a short time. At December 31, 19X3, however, the company has a liability of $6,840 to customers for goods they paid for in advance.

e. Rentals cost the company $1,000 per month. The company prepays rent of $6,000 each May 1 and November 1 and debits Rent Expense for such payments.

f. On December 23 Vidmar Corp. received a property tax bill from the city. The total amount, due on February 1, 19X4, is $4,600. Half of this amount is property tax expense for 19X3.

g. The company prepaid $3,500 for television advertising that will run daily for two weeks, December 27, 19X3 through January 9, 19X4. Vidmar debited Prepaid Advertising for the full amount on December 1.

Required

1. Journalize the adjusting entry needed for each situation at December 31, 19X3, identifying each entry by its corresponding letter.
2. Journalize reversing entries as needed. Use the corresponding letters for references. Date the entries appropriately.
3. Use the first situation that calls for a reversing entry to explain the practical value of the reversal.

Problem D-3A   *Preparing an adjusted trial balance; journalizing reversing entries*

The year-end trial balance of Hibbert Company at July 31 of the current year appears as follows:

Hibbert Company
Trial Balance
July 31, 19XX

Account Title	Balance Debit	Credit
Cash	$ 3,960	
Accounts receivable	14,700	
Note receivable	78,330	
Prepaid rent	6,000	
Prepaid insurance		
Furniture	9,600	
Accumulated depreciation		$ 4,200
Accounts payable		16,090
Wage payable		
Salary payable		
Interest payable		
Unearned service revenue		
Notes payable		30,000
C. Hibbert, capital		48,490
C. Hibbert, withdrawals	46,000	
Service revenue		129,000
Advertising expense	3,000	
Wage expense	31,750	
Salary expense	26,300	
Rent expense		
Utilities expense	3,640	
Depreciation expense		
Insurance expense	2,400	
Interest expense	2,100	
Total	$227,780	$227,780

The accounting records reveal the following additional data at July 31, 19XX:

a. Accrued wages of $1,400 and accrued salaries of $640 at July 31.
b. Hibbert records advance collections from customers by crediting Sales Revenue. At July 31, $2,400 of the balance of Sales Revenue has still not been earned. This amount of inventory will be shipped early in August.
c. Prepaid rent expired during the year, $5,300. When Hibbert pays rent, he debits Prepaid Rent.
d. Insurance expense for the year, $2,100. When Hibbert pays insurance, he debits Insurance Expense.
e. Depreciation on furniture for the year, $1,200.
f. Accrued interest expense at July 31, $430.

Required

1. Write the trial balance on a sheet of paper, enter the adjustments in adjacent columns, and prepare the adjusted trial balance at July 31 of the current year.
2. Journalize the reversing entries, as appropriate, at August 1.

Problem D-4A *Identifying adjustments and the related reversing entries*

The unadjusted and adjusted balances are shown below for selected accounts. Journalize the adjusting entries that were made and posted at May 31, 19X5, the end of the accounting period. Where appropriate, also journalize the reversing entries at June 1, 19X5.

	Unadjusted Balance	Adjusted Balance
Interest receivable	$ —	$ 1,465
Prepaid rent.........................	4,500	1,500
Supplies	—	940
Accumulated depreciation	12,900	15,300
Salary payable.......................	—	3,090
Property tax payable	—	1,300
Unearned sales revenue	—	790
Sales revenue	98,870	98,080
Interest revenue	3,590	5,055
Salary expense	49,550	52,640
Rent expense........................	—	3,000
Supplies expense	5,560	4,620
Property tax expense.................	2,110	3,410
Depreciation expense	—	2,400

Problem D-5A *Recording supplies and unearned revenue transactions two ways*

The accounting records of Stone Company reveal the following information about sales supplies and unearned sales revenue for 19X5:

Sales Supplies

19X5

Jan. 1	Beginning amount on hand	$ 420
Mar. 16	Cash purchase of supplies	3,740
Dec. 31	Ending amount on hand	290

Unearned Sales Revenue

19X5

Jan. 1	Beginning amount of advance collections................	6,590
July 22	Advance cash collection from customer..................	16,480
Nov. 4	Advance cash collection from customer..................	38,400
Dec. 31	Advance collections earned during the year..............	52,160

Required

1. Assume Stone Company records (a) supplies by initially debiting an asset account and (b) advance collections from customers by initially crediting a liability account
   a. Open T-accounts for Sales Supplies, Sales Supplies Expense, Unearned Sales Revenue and Sales Revenue. Insert the beginning balances in the appropriate accounts.
   b. Record the cash transactions during 19X5 directly in the accounts.
   c. Record the adjusting and closing entries at December 31, 19X5 directly in the accounts.
   d. If appropriate, record the reversing entries at January 1, 19X6 directly in the accounts.
2. Assume Stone Company records (a) supplies by initially debiting an expense account and (b) advance collections by initially crediting a revenue account. Perform Steps *a* through *d* as in question 1.
3. Using the following format, compare the amounts that would be reported for the above accounts in the 19X5 balance sheet and income statement under the two recording approaches of questions 1 and 2. Explain any similarity or difference.

	Question 1	Question 2
Balance sheet at December 31, 19X5 reports:		
Sales supplies	$_____	$_____
Unearned sales revenue	_____	_____
Income statement for year ended December 31, 19X5, reports:		
Sales revenue	_____	_____
Sales supplies expense.	_____	_____

(Group B)

Problem D-1B   *Recording prepaid rent and revenue collected in advance two ways*

Ngai Service Corp. completes the following transactions during 19X7:

Oct. 31   Pays $4,200 store rent covering the six-month period ending April 30, 19X8.

Nov. 1   Collects $1,800 cash in advance from customers. The service revenue will be earned $600 monthly over the period ending January 31, 19X8.

Required

1. Journalize these entries by debiting an asset account for Prepaid Rent and by crediting a liability account for Unearned Service Revenue. Explanations are unnecessary.
2. Journalize the related adjustments at December 31, 19X7.
3. Post the entries to the ledger accounts and show their balances at December 31, 19X7. Posting references are unnecessary.

4. Repeat questions 1 through 3. This time debit Rent Expense for the rent payment and credit Service Revenue for the collection of revenue in advance.
5. Compare the account balances in questions 3 and 4. They should be equal.

Problem D-2B   *Journalizing adjusting and reversing entries*

The accounting records of Conner Company reveal the following information before adjustments at December 31, 19X6, the end of the accounting period:

a. On December 29, the company prepaid $2,200 for newspaper advertising that will run for 10 days beginning December 29, 19X6. Conner debited Prepaid Advertising for the full amount.
b. On July 31, Conner deposited $25,000 in a savings account. The bank will pay Conner interest of $1,200 on January 31, 19X7. Of this amount, five sixths is earned in 19X6.
c. On November 29, Conner Company received a property tax bill from the city. The total amount, due on January 15, 19X7, is $3,900. Three fourths of this amount is property tax expense of 19X6.
d. Commissions owed to sales employees at December 31 are $2,565, and salaries owed to home office employees are $1,870.
e. Conner collected revenue of $12,400 in advance from customers during the year. The company expected to earn the revenue during the year, so it credited Sales Revenue for the full amount. However, at December 31, the company has not yet shipped $3,169 of these goods.
f. On December 1, the company paid $4,500 rent for December, January and February. It is company practice to debit Rent Expense for such prepayments.
g. Conner routinely debits Sales Supplies when it purchases supplies. At the beginning of 19X6 supplies of $380 were on hand, and during the year the company paid $4,000 for supplies. At year end, supplies of $510 are on hand.

Required

1. Journalize the adjusting entry needed for each situation at December 31, 19X6, identifying each entry by its corresponding letter.
2. Journalize reversing entries as needed. Use the corresponding letters for references. Date the entries.
3. Use the first situation that calls for a reversing entry to explain the practical value of the reversal.

Problem D-3B   *Preparing an adjusted trial balance; journalizing reversing entries*

The year-end trial balance of Saxman Company at June 30 of the current year appears as shown on the next page.
   The accounting records reveal the following additional data at June 30, 19XX:

a. Accrued wages of $970 and accrued salaries of $880 at June 30.
b. Saxman records advance collections from customers by crediting Sales Revenue. At June 30, $1,780 of the balance of Sales Revenue has still not been earned.
c. Prepaid rent expired during the year, $1,400. When Saxman pays rent, she debits Prepaid Rent.
d. Insurance expense for the year, $3,640. When Saxman pays insurance, she debits Insurance Expense.

e. Depreciation on furniture for the year, $2,600.

f. Accrued interest expense at June 30, $560.

Required

1. Write the trial balance on a sheet of paper, enter the adjustments in adjacent columns, and prepare the adjusted trial balance at June 30 of the current year.

2. Journalize the reversing entries, as appropriate, at July 1.

Saxman Company
Trial Balance
June 30, 19XX

Account Title	Balance Debit	Balance Credit
Cash	$ 4,120	
Accounts receivable.	23,800	
Note receivable	91,030	
Prepaid insurance		
Prepaid rent	1,500	
Furniture	14,700	
Accumulated depreciation		$ 6,280
Accounts payable.		24,630
Wage payable.		
Salary payable		
Interest payable		
Unearned service revenue		
Notes payable.		42,000
Betty Saxman, capital		55,170
Betty Saxman, withdrawals	41,000	
Service revenue		136,000
Advertising expense	3,750	
Wage expense	40,900	
Salary expense	31,200	
Rent expense		
Utilities expense.	4,200	
Depreciation expense		
Insurance expense.	3,880	
Interest expense.	4,000	
Total.	$264,080	$264,080

Problem D-4B   *Identifying adjustments and the related reversing entries*

The unadjusted and adjusted balances are shown on the next page for selected accounts. Journalize the adjusting entries that were made and posted at January 31, 19X2, the end of the accounting period. Where appropriate, also journalize the reversing entries at February 1, 19X2.

	Unadjusted Balance	Adjusted Balance
Interest receivable	$ —	$ 780
Prepaid insurance	3,400	860
Supplies	—	1,195
Accumulated depreciation	32,600	39,100
Wage payable	—	2,285
Income tax payable	—	2,860
Unearned sales revenue	—	2,390
Sales revenue	134,670	132,280
Interest revenue	3,300	4,080
Wage expense	24,660	26,945
Insurance expense	—	2,540
Depreciation expense	—	6,500
Supplies expense	7,990	6,795
Income tax expense	11,800	14,660

Problem D-5B *Recording prepaid expense and unearned revenue transactions two ways*

The accounting records of Waco Publications Ltd. reveal the following information about prepaid insurance and unearned subscription revenue for 19X7:

Prepaid Insurance

19X7		
Jan. 1	Beginning prepaid amount	$ 2,000
Aug. 31	Cash payment of insurance premiums	4,050
Dec. 31	Ending prepaid amount	2,700

Unearned Subscription Revenue

19X7		
Jan. 1	Beginning liability for unearned subscriptions............	9,640
June 30	Advance cash collections from customers	48,500
Dec. 31	Advance cash collections from customers	51,980
Dec. 31	Subscription revenue earned during the year	97,410

Required

1. Assume Waco records (a) prepaid insurance by initially debiting an asset account and (b) advance collections of subscriptions from customers by initially crediting a liability account.
   a. Open accounts for Prepaid Insurance, Insurance Expense, Unearned Subscription Revenue and Subscription Revenue. Insert the beginning balances in the appropriate accounts.
   b. Record the cash transactions during 19X7 directly in the accounts.
   c. Record the adjusting and closing entries at December 31, 19X7 directly in the accounts.
   d. If appropriate, record the reversing entries at January 1, 19X8 directly in the accounts.
2. Assume Waco records (a) prepaid insurance by initially debiting an expense account and (b) advance collections on subscriptions by initially crediting a revenue account. Perform Steps *a* through *d* as in question 1.

3. Using the following format, compare the amounts that would be reported for the above accounts in the 19X7 balance sheet and income statement under the two recording approaches of questions 1 and 2. Explain any similarity or difference.

	Question 1	Question 2
Balance sheet at December 31, 19X7, reports:		
Prepaid insurance	$_____	$_____
Unearned subscription revenue	_____	_____
Income statement for year ended December 31, 19X7, reports:		
Subscription revenue...........................	_____	_____
Insurance expense	_____	_____

Answers to Self-Study Questions

1. d   2. b   3. c   4. e   5. a

Published
Financial Statements

Highlights

(in millions except per share and other data)	1989	1988	% Change
Operating Results			
Gross sales	$5,424.2	$5,107.0	6.2%
Net earnings	135.1	140.6	(3.9)%
Funds provided from operations	279.7	288.8	(3.2)%
Common share dividends	50.6	45.5	11.2%
Acquisitions, capital expenditures and other investments	280.3	341.8	(18.0)%
Proceeds on divestitures	328.7	—	—
Financial Position			
Working capital	$ 543.9	$ 228.0	138.4%
Total assets	2,756.5	2,538.0	8.6%
Non-convertible long-term debt	532.3	481.6	10.5%
Convertible debentures and shareholders' equity	1,398.2	1,158.4	20.7%
Per Common Share Data			
Fully diluted net earnings	$ 1.60	$ 1.68	(4.8)%
Dividends	$ 0.685	$ 0.62	10.5%
Convertible debentures and common shareholders' equity	$ 13.90	$ 13.01	6.8%
Other Data			
Return on average common shareholders' equity	14.6%	17.2%	
Return on average common shareholders' equity and convertible debentures	11.9%	13.5%	
Number of common shareholders	13,999	14,838	
Number of employees	16,000	17,900	
Number of common shares outstanding — end of year (in millions)	74.6	73.8	

♤ JOHN LABATT

**John Labatt is a major North American food and
beverage company carrying on business in two principal
groups, Brewing and Food.**

1

Financial Review

Sales and Earnings

- Sales of $5.4 billion in fiscal 1989 increased by 6% over last year. Sales growth slowed compared to previous years, as good results in Labatt Brewing Company were somewhat offset by lower growth in the Labatt Food Company, which experienced intensely competitive market environments.

- Despite substantial productivity gains through facility improvements, operating costs rose more rapidly than revenues, largely as a result of significant increases in raw material costs in the Food Company, which could not be recovered through pricing due to very competitive market environments. In addition, after several years of rapid growth through acquisitions, the Company incurred substantial consolidation costs rationalizing operations and commissioning new facilities.

- During the year John Labatt conducted detailed reviews of business operations and the carrying values of operating assets and as a result made provisions for the estimated costs associated with the restructuring of certain business operations and the write-down of operating assets to net realizable value. This provision was applied against the net gains on dispositions, principally the sale of Catelli. Accordingly, a net pre-tax charge of $9.0 million as an unusual item was deducted in computing earnings for the year.

- The Company's apparent income tax rate declined, mainly as a result of a lower effective tax rate on the capital gain arising from the sale of Catelli.

- Net earnings of $135 million were 4% lower than last year's record level and fully diluted net earnings per share were $1.60, a decline of 5%.

- Return on average common shareholders' equity was 15%, 12% on a fully diluted basis, compared to 17% and 14% respectively for the prior year.

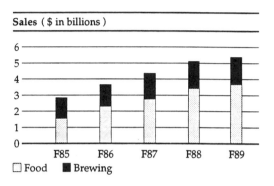

Sales ($ in billions)

☐ Food   ■ Brewing

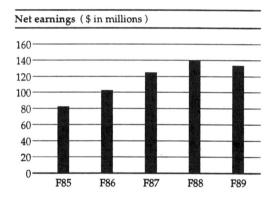

Net earnings ($ in millions)

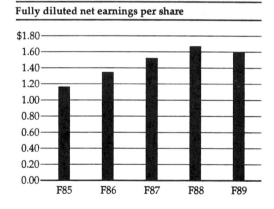

Fully diluted net earnings per share

23

Changes in Financial Position

- Cash from operating activities remained strong, generating $242 million.

- Dividends of 68.5 cents per common share were paid during the year, representing a 10% increase. The Company distributed total dividends of $50.6 million, compared with $45.5 million last year.

- Fixed asset additions of $238 million increased 24% over the $192 million invested in fiscal 1988. Brewing capital expenditures of $79 million accounted for 33% of total spending, supporting cost efficiencies, packaging flexibilities and capacity additions. Labatt Food Company spent $160 million, principally to upgrade existing facilities, expand capacities and improve efficiencies.

- Divestment activities provided net cash proceeds of $329 million, reflecting primarily the divestiture of Catelli and the Wine operations.

- In March 1989 the Company increased its equity base through the issue of $150 million of perpetual redeemable preferred shares with a dividend rate of 7.85% per annum until March 31, 1994 and at market rates thereafter.

- In addition, the Company arranged a US$50 million floating rate borrowing facility which provides access to the Euro-Short-term Paper Market for a period of eight years.

- As a result of these changes, the Company's net cash position improved $449 million during the year resulting in a $360 million cash surplus at April 30, 1989.

Financial Position

- The working capital ratio at 1.80 is substantially improved from a ratio of 1.31 last year, as a result of cash generated during the year.

- Average number of days sales in accounts receivable at 23 were comparable to last year. Average number of days sales in inventory at 40 declined from last year due to a shift in the business mix.

- The Company's financial position was significantly strengthened during the year. With the cash increase, the Company's overall borrowings declined by $393 million. Total convertible debentures and shareholders' equity increased by 21% to $1.4 billion, substantially improving the Company's debt/ equity and interest coverage ratios.

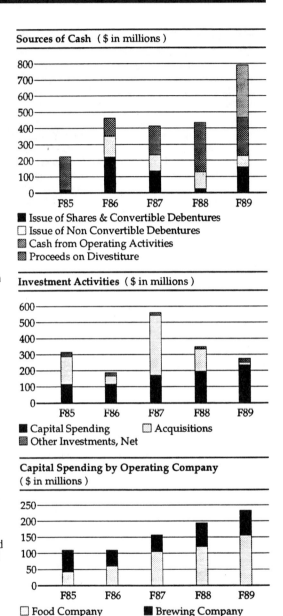

Sources of Cash ($ in millions)

■ Issue of Shares & Convertible Debentures
□ Issue of Non Convertible Debentures
▨ Cash from Operating Activities
▨ Proceeds on Divestiture

Investment Activities ($ in millions)

■ Capital Spending   □ Acquisitions
▨ Other Investments, Net

Capital Spending by Operating Company ($ in millions)

□ Food Company   ■ Brewing Company

24

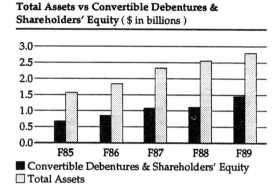

**Total Assets vs Convertible Debentures &
Shareholders' Equity ($ in billions)**

■ Convertible Debentures & Shareholders' Equity
▢ Total Assets

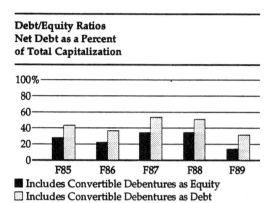

**Debt/Equity Ratios
Net Debt as a Percent
of Total Capitalization**

■ Includes Convertible Debentures as Equity
▢ Includes Convertible Debentures as Debt

Summary of Quarterly Financial Information

(in millions except per share amounts)

Year ended April 30, 1989	First	Second	Third	Fourth	Total
			Quarter		
Sales	$1,424.8	$1,386.1	$1,312.7	$1,300.6	**$5,424.2**
Net earnings	39.5	32.9	25.2	37.5	**135.1**
Net earnings per common share:					
Basic	0.53	0.45	0.34	0.48	**1.80**
Fully diluted	0.47	0.40	0.31	0.42	**1.60**
Dividends per common share	0.16	0.175	0.175	0.175	**0.685**

Year ended April 30, 1988	First	Second	Third	Fourth	Total
			Quarter		
Sales	$1,303.9	$1,313.1	$1,247.1	$1,242.9	**$5,107.0**
Net earnings	37.5	38.7	29.0	35.4	**140.6**
Net earnings per common share:					
Basic	0.52	0.52	0.39	0.49	**1.92**
Fully diluted	0.45	0.46	0.35	0.42	**1.68**
Dividends per common share	0.14	0.16	0.16	0.16	**0.62**

25

Responsibility for Financial Statements

Management

The accompanying consolidated financial statements of John Labatt were prepared by the management of the Company in conformity with generally accepted accounting principles.

The Company is responsible for the integrity and objectivity of the information contained in the financial statements. The preparation of financial statements necessarily involves the use of estimates requiring careful judgment in those cases where transactions affecting a current accounting period are dependent upon future events.

The Company's accounting procedures and related internal control systems are designed to provide assurance that accounting records are reliable and to safeguard the Company's assets. The accompanying consolidated financial statements have been prepared by qualified personnel in accordance with policies and procedures established by management. In management's opinion, these statements fairly reflect the financial position of the Company, the results of its operations and the changes in its financial position with reasonable limits of materiality and within the framework of the accounting policies outlined in Note 1 to the Consolidated Financial Statements.

External Auditors

Clarkson Gordon, Chartered Accountants, as the Company's external auditors appointed by the shareholders, have examined the consolidated financial statements for the year ended April 30, 1989, and their report is presented on page 30.

Their opinion is based upon an examination conducted in accordance with generally accepted auditing standards and a review of the Company's accounting systems and procedures and internal controls. Based upon the evaluation of these systems, the external auditors conduct appropriate tests of the Company's accounting records and obtain sufficient audit evidence to provide reasonable assurance that the financial statements are presented fairly in accordance with generally accepted accounting principles.

Audit Committee

The Audit Committee, none of the members of which are officers of the Company, meets quarterly to review the Company's financial statements before recommending the statements to the Board of Directors for approval. It also reviews, on a continuing basis, reports prepared by both the internal and external auditors of the Company on the Company's accounting policies and procedures and internal control systems. The Committee meets regularly with both the internal and external auditors, without management present, to review their activities and to consider the results of their audits. The Committee also recommends the appointment of the Company's external auditors, who are appointed annually by the Company's shareholders.

Consolidated Statement of Earnings

(in millions except per share amounts)

For the year ended April 30, 1989 (with comparative amounts for the year ended April 30, 1988)	1989	1988
Revenue		
Gross sales	**$5,424.2**	$5,107.0
Less excise and sales taxes	**567.4**	496.0
	4,856.8	4,611.0
Operating costs		
Cost of sales, selling and administration	**4,466.5**	4,202.0
Depreciation and amortization	**127.0**	114.3
Interest (note 2)	**69.4**	66.9
	4,662.9	4,383.2
Operating earnings	**193.9**	227.8
Unusual items (note 3)	**(9.0)**	—
Earnings before income taxes	**184.9**	227.8
Income taxes (note 4)		
— current	**53.6**	63.9
— deferred	**3.0**	22.0
	56.6	85.9
Earnings before share of net earnings (losses) in partly-owned businesses	**128.3**	141.9
Share of net earnings (losses) in partly-owned businesses	**6.8**	(1.3)
Net earnings	**$ 135.1**	$ 140.6
Net earnings per common share (note 5)		
Basic	**$ 1.80**	$ 1.92
Fully diluted	**$ 1.60**	$ 1.68

See accompanying notes

Consolidated Statement of Changes in Financial Position

(in millions)

For the year ended April 30, 1989 (with comparative amounts for the year ended April 30, 1988)	1989	1988
Operations		
Net earnings	$ 135.1	$ 140.6
Net charges to earnings which do not reduce funds	144.6	148.2
Funds provided from operations	279.7	288.8
Changes in non-cash working capital (note 6)	(37.2)	35.0
Cash provided from operating activities	242.5	323.8
Dividends paid to shareholders	(50.6)	(45.5)
Investment activities		
Additions to fixed assets, net	(238.4)	(192.5)
Acquisitions (note 15)	(16.0)	(135.4)
Proceeds on divestitures (note 15)	328.7	—
Other investments, net	(25.9)	(13.9)
Cash provided from (used for) investments	48.4	(341.8)
Financing activities		
Issue of common shares (note 12)	14.7	13.8
Issue of preferred shares (note 12)	150.0	—
Issue of non-convertible debt (note 10)	59.5	99.2
Net decrease in non-convertible and convertible debentures	(15.9)	(4.2)
Cash provided from financing	208.3	108.8
Increase in net cash	448.6	45.3
Net cash deficit beginning of year	(88.4)	(133.7)
Net cash surplus (deficit) end of year	$ 360.2	$ (88.4)
Net cash consists of:		
Cash receivable on divestitures	$ 315.2	$ —
Short-term investments	200.0	200.0
Bank advances and short-term notes	(155.0)	(288.4)
Net cash surplus (deficit) end of year	$ 360.2	$ (88.4)

See accompanying notes

28

Consolidated Balance Sheet

(in millions)

April 30, 1989 (with comparative amounts as at April 30, 1988)	1989	1988
Assets		
Current		
Cash receivable on divestitures	$ 315.2	$ —
Short-term investments	200.0	200.0
Accounts receivable	307.3	301.5
Inventories (note 7)	344.7	407.9
Prepaid expenses	59.7	54.6
	1,226.9	964.0
Fixed, at cost		
Land	46.6	49.9
Buildings and equipment	1,507.9	1,473.2
	1,554.5	1,523.1
Less accumulated depreciation	552.7	531.0
	1,001.8	992.1
Other assets (note 8)	527.8	581.9
	$2,756.5	$2,538.0
Liabilities		
Current		
Bank advances and short-term notes	$ 155.0	$ 288.4
Accounts payable	468.1	427.1
Taxes payable	44.4	9.9
Long-term debt due within one year	15.5	10.6
	683.0	736.0
Non-convertible long-term debt (note 10)	532.3	481.6
Deferred income taxes	143.0	162.0
Convertible debentures and shareholders' equity		
Convertible debentures (note 11)	289.4	290.7
Shareholders' equity		
Share capital (note 12)		
Preferred shares	150.0	—
Common shares	272.7	258.0
Retained earnings	706.5	622.0
Accumulated foreign currency translation adjustment	(20.4)	(12.3)
	1,108.8	867.7
	1,398.2	1,158.4
	$2,756.5	$2,538.0

See accompanying notes

On behalf of the Board

P.N.T. Widdrington, Director   *J.T. Eyton, Director*

29

Consolidated Statement of Retained Earnings

(in millions except per share amounts)

For the year ended April 30, 1989 (with comparative amounts for the year ended April 30, 1988)	1989	1988
Balance beginning of year	**$622.0**	$526.9
Net earnings	**135.1**	140.6
	757.1	667.5
Common dividends		
($0.685 per share fiscal year 1989)		
($0.62 per share fiscal year 1988)	**50.6**	45.5
Balance end of year	**$706.5**	$622.0

See accompanying notes

Auditors' Report

To the Shareholders of John Labatt Limited

We have examined the consolidated balance sheet of John Labatt Limited as at April 30, 1989 and the consolidated statements of earnings, retained earnings and changes in financial position for the year then ended. Our examination was made in accordance with generally accepted auditing standards and accordingly included such tests and other procedures as we considered necessary in the circumstances.

In our opinion, these consolidated financial statements present fairly the financial position of the company as at April 30, 1989 and the results of its operations and the changes in its financial position for the year then ended in accordance with generally accepted accounting principles applied on a basis consistent with that of the preceding year.

London, Canada   *Clarkson Gordon*
June 14, 1989   *Chartered Accountants*

Notes to the Consolidated Financial Statements

April 30, 1989

1. Accounting Policies

The financial statements have been prepared in accordance with accounting principles generally accepted in Canada and also conform in all material respects with International Accounting Standards. Significant accounting policies observed in the preparation of the financial statements are summarized below:

Principles of consolidation

The consolidated financial statements include the accounts of all subsidiary companies. The results of operations of subsidiaries acquired or sold during the year are included from or to their respective dates of acquisition or sale.

Foreign currency translation

The accounts of foreign subsidiaries are translated into Canadian dollars on the following basis:

Income and expenses — at average exchange rates prevailing during the year

Assets and liabilities — at the exchange rate in effect at the balance sheet date

The adjustments arising on translation of foreign subsidiaries' balance sheets are deferred and reported as a separate component of shareholders' equity.

Net earnings per common share

Net earnings per common share have been calculated using the weighted monthly average number of shares outstanding during the year.

Fully diluted net earnings per common share have been calculated assuming that the convertible debentures and common share options outstanding at the end of the year had been converted to common shares or exercised at the later of the beginning of the year or at the date of issuance.

Short-term investments

Short-term investments are carried at cost which approximates market value.

Inventories

Inventories, other than returnable containers, are valued at the lower of cost and net realizable value, cost being determined on a first-in, first-out basis. Returnable containers are valued at redemption price or at amortized cost which does not exceed replacement cost.

Fixed assets

Fixed assets are recorded at cost. Depreciation is provided on a straight-line basis over the estimated useful lives of the assets, generally at rates of 2½% for buildings, 10% for machinery and equipment and 20% for vehicles.

Income taxes

The Company follows the deferral method of tax allocation accounting. Investment tax credits arising from the acquisition of fixed assets are applied to reduce the cost of the fixed assets.

Research and development costs

Research and development costs amounting to $9.1 million in 1989 ($9.5 million in 1988) are charged to earnings as incurred.

2. Interest Expense

(in millions)	1989	1988
Long-term debt	$50.3	$39.0
Convertible debentures	16.4	16.3
Short-term debt	2.7	11.6
	$69.4	$66.9

Short-term interest is net of income from short-term investments as follows:

(in millions)	1989	1988
Interest expense on bank advances and short-term notes	$22.5	$28.9
Income from short-term investments	(19.8)	(17.3)
	$ 2.7	$11.6

31

3. Unusual Items

The consolidated statement of earnings includes the following unusual items:

(in millions)	
Unusual expenses	
Labatt Brewing Company	$ 45.0
Labatt Food Company	104.5
	149.5
Net gain on dispositions	(140.5)
	$ 9.0

During the year, the Company disposed of several businesses which no longer held strategic relevance, including most notably, Catelli and the Canadian Wine operations. These transactions resulted in an unusual pre-tax gain of $140.5 million. During its strategic review, management concluded that as a result of the changes in the environment in which several of its food businesses compete, the net carrying value of certain components of Labatt Food Company businesses had been impaired. Accordingly, the Company, in recognition of these changed circumstances, recorded an unusual pre-tax charge to earnings of $104.5 million. Similarly, a review of Labatt Brewing Company resulted in a pre-tax charge of $45.0 million for the impairment in the carrying value of certain assets.

4. Income Taxes

The effective income tax rate is comprised of the following:

	1989	1988
Combined basic federal, provincial and state income tax rates	45.4%	47.6%
Less:		
Manufacturing and processing deduction	3.0	4.4
Reduction in income tax rates for income taxed as capital gains	10.4	—
Non-taxable income, net of non-allowable expenses	1.4	5.5
	30.6%	37.7%

5. Net Earnings Per Common Share

The number of shares used in calculating net earnings per common share is as follows:

(in millions)	1989	1988
Basic	74.0	73.4
Fully diluted	90.6	89.8

6. Changes in Non-Cash Working Capital

(in millions)	1989	1988
Decrease (increase) in current assets		
Accounts receivable	$ (5.8)	$72.3
Inventories	63.2	(52.9)
Prepaid expenses	(5.1)	1.9
Increase (decrease) in current liabilities		
Accounts payable	66.0	36.8
Taxes payable	9.5	(39.9)
Long-term debt due within one year	4.9	3.7
Working capital relating to acquisitions, divestitures and unusual items	(169.9)	13.1
Net increase (decrease) in cash	$(37.2)	$35.0

7. Inventories

(in millions)	1989	1988
Finished and in process	$224.5	$243.6
Materials and supplies	97.5	133.1
Containers	22.7	31.2
	$344.7	$407.9

32

8. Other Assets

(in millions)	**1989**	1988
Investments in partly-owned businesses (note 9)	**$ 86.8**	$ 54.8
Investments in and advances to other companies	**47.2**	65.9
Loans to employees under share purchase plans (note 12)	**21.5**	14.1
Goodwill, licences, trademarks and other proprietary rights	**363.6**	438.5
Unamortized debt financing expense	**8.7**	8.6
	$527.8	$581.9

Partly-owned businesses are companies and partnerships in which the Company has significant influence and are accounted for using the equity method of accounting.

Investments in other companies are carried at the lower of cost and net realizable value. Income is recognized when dividends are received.

Goodwill and other proprietary rights are being amortized by charges to earnings over the lesser of their estimated useful lives and forty years. Amortization expense was $19.2 million in 1989 and $20.4 million in 1988.

9. Partly-Owned Businesses

Investments in partly-owned businesses include the following:

Canada	% Equity Interest
BCL Entertainment Corp.	45.0
Supercorp Entertainment	50.0
Canada Malting Co. Limited	19.9
Auscan Closures Canada and Company, Limited	50.0
Toronto Blue Jays Baseball Club	45.0
McGavin Foods Limited (50% voting)	60.0
Allelix Crop Technologies	30.0

United States	
International Talent Group (ITG)	50.0

Trinidad	
Catelli-Primo Limited	46.4

During the year, Allelix Inc. was reorganized into three separate entities. John Labatt continues to hold a 30% interest in Allelix Crop Technologies, formerly the Agriculture division of Allelix Inc.

10. Non-Convertible Long-Term Debt

(in millions)	**1989**	1988
Sinking fund debentures		
6½% Series E to mature October 1, 1989	**$ 0.1**	$ 0.1
7⅜% Series F to mature April 15, 1992	**1.4**	1.6
9½% Series G to mature September 1, 1990	**9.8**	10.5
8½% Series H to mature March 1, 1993	**10.4**	12.4
9¼% Series I to mature March 15, 1994	**13.3**	14.5
11⅜% Series J to mature October 1, 1999	**32.0**	33.0
9½% debentures to mature January 21, 1992	**100.0**	100.0
10½% debentures to mature July 30, 1995	**119.0**	123.0
10⅜% debentures to mature April 21, 1998	**100.0**	100.0
Note issuance facility	**59.5**	—
Bank term loan to mature June 30, 2003 at discounted amount	**27.0**	28.2
	472.5	423.3
Other long-term liabilities	**75.3**	68.9
	547.8	492.2
Less portion due within one year included in current liabilities	**15.5**	10.6
	$532.3	$481.6

During the year, the Company arranged a U.S.$50.0 million floating rate note issuance facility with a consortium of financial institutions. Under this facility, which provides access to the Euro-Short-Term Paper Market for a minimum of eight years, funds can be raised at market interest rates through the issue of unsecured notes.

The above balances include long-term debt of $253.3 million at April 30, 1989 and $206.8 million at April 30, 1988, denominated in United States dollars translated at the rate of exchange at the balance sheet date.

Maturities and sinking fund requirements for the years ending April 30, 1990, through 1994 are; $15.5 million; $22.0 million; $115.9 million; $95.9 million; and $14.8 million, respectively.

The sinking fund debentures are secured by a floating charge on the undertaking, property and assets of John Labatt Limited. At April 30, 1989, the Company had satisfied all of the covenants under the trust deed relating to the sinking fund debentures.

11. Convertible Debentures

The convertible debentures are reported under the heading of convertible debentures and shareholders' equity on the balance sheet to reflect the permanent nature of this capital. This presentation is supported by the long maturities, the low initial interest rates, an indication by many of the holders of these debentures that they intend to convert in the future and the Company's intention to ultimately have them converted to equity. The convertible debentures are unsecured obligations and are subordinated to all other indebtedness of the Company.

Particulars of the convertible debentures are as follows:

(in millions)	1989	1988
1983 adjustable rate debentures to mature June 16, 2003	$ 40.2	$ 41.1
1986 adjustable rate debentures to mature February 28, 2006	124.2	124.6
1987 adjustable rate debentures to mature April 1, 2007	125.0	125.0
	$289.4	$290.7

The 1983 adjustable rate convertible debentures pay a minimum interest rate of 6% and are convertible, at the holder's option, on or before the earlier of the last business day prior to either redemption or June 16, 2003, into common shares of the Company at a conversion price of $11.25 per share unless the Company fixes an interest rate of 6½%, whereupon the conversion price becomes $13.4375 per share. The debentures are redeemable at par plus accrued interest.

The 1986 adjustable rate convertible debentures pay a minimum interest rate of 6% and are convertible, at the holder's option, on or before the earlier of the last business day prior to either redemption or February 27, 2006, into common shares of the Company at an initial conversion price of $17.875 per share until February 28, 1990 and, thereafter, if the Company fixes an interest rate of 7%, at a conversion price of $20.00 per share. The debentures are redeemable at par plus accrued interest after February 28, 1990 and at any time prior to this date, at 106% of par plus accrued interest if at least 85% of the original principal amount of the debentures has been converted.

The 1987 adjustable rate convertible debentures pay a minimum interest rate of 5% and are convertible, at the holder's option, on or before the earlier of the last business day prior to either redemption or March 31, 2007, into common shares of the Company at an initial conversion price of $27.00 per share until April 1, 1992 and, thereafter, if the Company fixes an interest rate of 6%, at a conversion price of $30.00 per share. The debentures are redeemable at par plus accrued interest after April 1, 1992 and at any time prior to this date, at 105% of par plus accrued interest if at least 85% of the original principal amount of the debentures has been converted. On April 1, 2007, the Company has the option to retire any debentures then outstanding by issuing common shares of equivalent fair market value to the debenture holders.

12. Share Capital

Authorized and issued

The authorized capital stock of the Company is as follows:

4,000,000 preferred shares issuable in series, of which 300 consist of a series designated as "Series 1 Preferred Shares".

Common shares of no par value in unlimited amount.

Preferred Shares

During the year, the Company issued by private placement 300 Series 1 Preferred Shares for $150 million. The dividend rate on the shares is fixed at 7.85% per annum, payable quarterly until March 31, 1994. The dividend rate for subsequent periods will be established by negotiation between the Company and the holders of the Series 1 Preferred Shares or, if no agreement is reached, by a bid solicitation procedure involving investment dealers or, if no bids are accepted, by a monthly auction procedure. The shares are redeemable by the Company on or after March 31, 1994 at par plus any accrued and unpaid dividends.

Common Shares

The changes in issued and fully paid common shares of the Company are as follows:

(in millions)	1989		1988	
	Shares	**Amount**	Shares	Amount
Issued and out-standing, beginning of year	**73.79**	**$258.0**	72.73	$244.2
Issued under employee share purchase and option plans	**0.72**	**13.0**	0.64	8.7
Issued as a result of debenture conversions	**0.10**	**1.3**	0.40	4.7
Issued under share-holder dividend reinvestment plan and stock dividend election program	**0.02**	**0.4**	0.02	0.4
	0.84	**14.7**	1.06	13.8
Issued and out-standing, end of year	**74.63**	**$272.7**	73.79	$258.0

Shares available for share purchase and option plans

Details of unissued common shares for allotment to employees under share purchase or option plans as of April 30, 1989 are as follows:

Unissued common shares designated for allotment under By-Law No. 3 (1987)		3,000,000
Less:		
Issued	581,082	
Under option	120,000	
Reserved for employee share purchase plan maturing in July 1989	427,329	1,128,411
Shares available for issue		1,871,589

Shares under option to employees under By-Law No. 3 and previous By-Laws as of April 30, 1989, are as follows:

Plan	Number of shares	Price per share	Expiry date	
1979 Share option	20,000	$ 5.44	December	1989
1983 Share option	42,000	10.75	October	1993
1984 Share option	8,000	9.71	June	1994
1985 Share option	121,603	13.59	June	1995
1986 Share option	60,500	22.23	December	1996
1987 Share option	90,000	22.68	November	1997
1988 Share option	30,000	22.17	March	1999
	372,103			

Of the 372,103 shares under option there are 51,603 under option to officers of the Company. Under these plans, the individuals are entitled to purchase the shares over periods of up to 10 years.

The following schedule sets out details of the loans to employees for shares purchased:

(in millions)	1989	1988
Officers	**$16.8**	$10.5
Other employees	4.7	3.6
	$21.5	$ 14.1
Number of shares	**1.4**	1.2

13. Leases

Operating leases

The Company has entered into long-term operating leases, substantially all of which will be discharged within 10 years. Fixed rental expense for 1989 was $23.9 million ($20.8 million in 1988). Future annual fixed rental payments for years ending April 30 are as follows:

(in millions)	
1990	$21.9
1991	19.3
1992	17.4
1993	12.5
1994	10.3

In aggregate, fixed rental payments for subsequent years amount to $23.4 million.

Capital leases

Assets leased by the Company under agreements which transfer substantially all of the benefits and risks of ownership of the assets to the Company are accounted for as capital leases. The total fixed assets acquired under capital leases at the end of the year were not material.

14. Pension Plans

The Company has retirement programs which provide benefits based on employee years of service and in some instances, employee earnings. Based on the most recent actuarial valuations, using the accrued benefit method and management's best estimates, the Company's pension plan funded status is as follows:

(in millions)	
Estimated present value of pension plan obligations	$334.0
Pension plan assets at market value	$334.0

15. Acquisitions and Divestitures

During the year, the Company made the following business acquisitions and divestitures:

Labatt Brewing Company

Effective April 30, 1989, the Company sold the Canadian wine business which operates four wineries across Canada.

Effective November 2, 1988, the Company purchased a 50% interest in International Talent Group (ITG), a rock artist talent agency in New York City.

Labatt Food Company

Effective April 30, 1989, the Company sold Catelli, the retail packaged food processing business operating primarily in Canada.

Effective December 31, 1988, the Company purchased a 50.5% interest in a wheat starch and gluten company in Bordeaux, France.

16. Segmented Financial Information

Information by class of business

The classes of business are as follows:

Labatt Brewing Company comprises the brewing activities in Canada and the United States, the sale of Canadian-made beers in the United States and overseas, and the marketing in the United Kingdom of lager produced and distributed under agreements with U.K. brewers.

Labatt Food Company comprises the production and sale of dairy products, food products and fruit juices, primarily in Canada and the United States.

Partly-owned businesses are not allocated to the business segments.

The segmented reporting has been changed this year to conform with the two distinct operating companies structure established last year.

The following is a summary of key financial information by business segment for the years ended April 30, 1989 and 1988.

36

Information by class of business

(in millions)	1989		1988	
	Gross sales	**Depreciation & Amortization**	Gross sales	Depreciation & Amortization
Brewing Company	**$1,818.1**	**$ 43.2**	$1,632.6	$ 38.9
Food Company	**3,606.1**	**83.8**	3,474.4	75.4
	$5,424.2	**$ 127.0**	$5,107.0	$ 114.3
	Capital expenditures		Capital expenditures	
Brewing Company	**$ 78.6**		$ 74.6	
Food Company	**159.8**		117.9	
	$ 238.4		$ 192.5	
	Contribution	**Assets employed**	Contribution	Assets employed
Brewing Company	**$ 157.5**	**$ 516.1**	$ 140.1	$ 527.3
Food Company	**105.8**	**1,110.4**	154.6	1,308.3
	263.3	**1,626.5**	294.7	1,835.6
Unusual items	**(9.0)**		—	
Interest	**(69.4)**		(66.9)	
Earnings before income taxes	**$ 184.9**		$ 227.8	
Cash receivable on divestitures		**315.2**		—
Short-term investments		**200.0**		200.0
Investments in partly-owned businesses		**86.8**		54.8
Current liabilities other than bank advances and short-term notes		**528.0**		447.6
Total assets per consolidated balance sheet		**$2,756.5**		$2,538.0

Information by geographic segment

The Company operates principally in the geographic areas of Canada and the United States. Geographic segmentation is determined on the basis of the business location where the sale originates.

On the following page is a summary of key financial information by geographic segment for the years ended April 30, 1989 and 1988.

37

Information by geographic segment

(in millions)	1989		1988	
	Gross sales	**Depreciation & Amortization**	Gross sales	Depreciation & Amortization
Canada	$3,398.9	$ 77.0	$3,136.4	$ 69.6
United States	2,025.3	50.0	1,970.6	44.7
	$5,424.2	$ 127.0	$5,107.0	$ 114.3

	Capital expenditures		Capital expenditures	
Canada	$ 166.6		$ 127.8	
United States	71.8		64.7	
	$ 238.4		$ 192.5	

	Contribution	**Assets employed**	Contribution	Assets employed
Canada	$ 231.8	$ 843.6	$ 232.8	$ 958.5
United States	31.5	782.9	61.9	877.1
	263.3	1,626.5	294.7	1,835.6
Unusual items	(9.0)		—	
Interest	(69.4)		(66.9)	
Earnings before income taxes	$ 184.9		$ 227.8	
Cash receivable on divestitures		315.2		—
Short-term investments		200.0		200.0
Investments in partly-owned businesses		86.8		54.8
Current liabilities other than bank advances and short-term notes		528.0		447.6
Total assets per consolidated balance sheet		$2,756.5		$2,538.0

17. Related Party Transactions

In the normal course of business, the Company entered into transactions with affiliates and partly-owned businesses on competitive commercial terms similar to those with unrelated parties. These transactions did not have a material impact on reported net earnings.

At April 30, 1989 the Company held $158.0 million ($158.0 million at April 30, 1988) of marketable securities of affiliates.

The total income earned on these marketable securities during the year was $12.5 million ($12.3 million in 1988).

18. Subsequent Event

In June 1989, Labatt Brewing Company announced its 70% equity investment in a new Italian-based brewing company which will combine the brewing businesses of Birra Moretti S.p.A. and Prinz Brau, S.p.A.

Glossary

Accelerated depreciation A type of depreciation method that writes off a relatively larger amount of the asset's cost nearer the start of its useful life than does the straight-line method *(p. 409)*.

Account The detailed record of the changes that have occurred in a particular asset, liability or owner equity during a period *(p. 43)*.

Account format of the balance sheet Format that lists the assets at the left with liabilities and owner equity at the right *(p. 149)*.

Account payable A liability that is not written out. Instead, it is backed by the reputation and credit standing of the debtor *(p. 16)*.

Account receivable An asset, a promise to receive cash from customers to whom the business has sold goods or services *(p. 15)*.

Accounting The system that measures business activities, processes that information into reports and financial statements, and communicates the findings to decision makers *(p. 4)*.

Accounting cycle Process by which accountants produce an entity's financial statements for a specific period *(p. 131)*.

Accounting information system The combination of personnel, records and procedures that a business uses to meet its need for financial data *(p. 227)*.

Accounts receivable turnover Ratio of net credit sales to average net accounts receivable. Measures ability to collect cash from credit customers *(p. 808)*.

Accrual-basis accounting Accounting that recognizes (records) the impact of a business event as its occurs, regardless of whether the transaction affected cash *(p. 90)*.

Accrued expense An expense that has been incurred but not yet paid in cash *(p. 98)*.

Accrued revenue A revenue that has been earned but not yet received in cash *(p. 100)*.

Accumulated depreciation The cumulative sum of all depreciation expense from the date of acquiring a plant asset *(p. 97)*.

Acid-test ratio Ratio of the sum of cash plus short-term investments plus net current receivables to current liabilities. Tells whether the entity could pay all its current liabilities if they came due immediately. Also called the quick ratio *(p. 806)*.

Adjusted trial balance A list of all the ledger accounts with their adjusted balances *(p. 103)*.

Adjusting entry Entry made at the end of the period to assign revenues to the period in which they are earned and expenses to the period in which they are incurred. Adjusting entries help measure the period's income and bring the related asset and liability accounts to correct balances for the financial statements *(p. 93)*.

Aging of accounts receivable A way to estimate bad debts by analysing individual accounts receivable according to the length of time they have been due *(p. 334)*.

Allowance for doubtful accounts A contra account, related to accounts receivable, that holds the estimated amount of collection losses. Also called Allowance for uncollectible accounts *(p. 331)*.

Allowance for uncollectible accounts Another name for Allowance for doubtful accounts *(p. 331)*.

Allowance method A method of recording collection losses based on estimates prior to determining that the business will not collect from specific customers *(p. 330)*.

Amortization Expense that applies to intangible assets in the same way depreciation applies to plant assets and depletion applies to natural resources *(p. 421)*.

Appropriation of retained earnings Restriction of retained earnings that is recorded by a formal journal entry *(p. 642)*.

Articles of incorporation The document issued by the federal or provincial government giving the incorporators permission to form a corporation *(p. 573)*.

Articles of partnership Agreement that is the contract between partners specifying such items as the name, location and nature of the business, the name, capital investment and duties of each partner, and the method of sharing profits and losses by the partners. Also called the partnership agreement *(p. 532)*.

Asset An economic resource a business owns that is expected to be of benefit in the future *(p. 15)*.

Auditing The examination of financial statements by outside accountants, the most significant service that public accountants perform. The conclusion of an audit is the accountant's professional opinion about the financial statements *(p. 10)*.

Authorization of stock Provision in the articles of incorporation of a corporation that gives the issuing jurisdiction's permission for the corporation to issue (that is, to sell) a certain number of shares of stock *(p. 580)*.

Average cost method Inventory costing method based on the average cost of inventory during the period. Average cost is determined by dividing the cost of goods available for sale by the number of units available *(p. 368)*.

Bad debt expense Another name for Uncollectible accounts expense *(p. 329)*.

Balance sheet List of an entity's assets, liabilities and owner equity as of a specific date. Also called the statement of financial position *(p. 23)*.

Balancing the ledgers Establishing the equality of (a) total debits and total credits in the general ledger, (b) the balance of the accounts receivable control account in the general ledger and the sum of individual customer accounts in the accounts receivable subsidiary ledger, or (c) the balance of the accounts payable control account in the general ledger and the sum of individual creditor accounts in the accounts payable subsidiary ledger *(p. 250)*.

Bank collection   Collection of money by the bank on behalf of a depositor *(p. 288)*.

Bank reconciliation   Process of explaining the reasons for the difference between a depositor's records and the bank's records about the depositor's bank account *(p. 288)*.

Bank statement   Document for a particular bank account showing its beginning, and ending balances and listing the month's transactions that affected the account *(p. 286)*.

Batch processing   Computerized accounting for similar transactions in a group or batch *(p. 232)*.

Beginning inventory   Goods left over from the preceding period *(p. 365)*.

Board of directors   Group elected by the shareholders to set policy for a corporation and to appoint its officers *(p. 575)*.

Bond discount   Excess of a bond's maturity (par) value over its issue price *(p. 656)*.

Bond indenture   Contract under which bonds are issued *(p. 655)*.

Bond premium   Excess of a bond's issue price over its maturity (par) value *(p. 656)*.

Bond sinking fund   Group of assets segregated for the purpose of retiring bonds payable at maturity *(p. 668)*.

Bonds payable   Groups of notes payable (bonds) issued to multiple lenders called bondholders *(p. 653)*.

Bonus   Amount over and above regular compensation *(p. 452)*.

Book value of a plant asset   The asset's cost less accumulated depreciation *(p. 97)*.

Book value of stock   Amount of owners' equity on the company's books for each share of its stock *(p. 591)*.

Book value per share of common stock   Common shareholders' equity divided by the number of shares of common stock outstanding *(p. 815)*.

Budgeting   Setting of goals for a business, such as its sales and profits, for a future period *(p. 11)*.

Bylaws   Constitution for governing a corporation *(p. 575)*.

Callable bonds   Bonds that the issuer may call or pay off at a specified price whenever the issuer wants *(p. 669)*.

Canada (or **Quebec**) **Pension Plan**   All employees and self-employed persons in Canada (except in Quebec where the pension plan is the Quebec Pension Plan) between 18 and 70 years of age are required to contribute to the Canada Pension Plan administered by the Government of Canada *(p. 455)*.

Capital   Another name for the owner equity of a business *(p. 15)*.

Capital cost allowance   Depreciation allowed for income tax purposes by Revenue Canada; the rates allowed are called capital cost allowance rates *(p. 409)*.

Capital deficiency   Debit balance in a partner's capital account *(p. 552)*.

Capital expenditure   Expenditure that increases the capacity or efficiency of an asset or extends its useful life. Capital expenditures are debited to an asset account *(p. 423)*.

Capital lease   Lease agreement that transfers substantially all of the benefits and risks of ownership from the lessor to the lessee *(p. 672)*.

Capital maintenance   Income may be earned by a company only after capital is maintained. Capital may be defined as financial capital or operating capability *(p. 721)*.

Capital stock   A corporation's capital from investments by the shareholders. Also called Share capital *(p. 577)*.

Cash-basis accounting   Accounting that records only transactions in which cash is received or paid *(p. 90)*.

Cash disbursements journal   Special journal used to record cash disbursements by cheque *(p. 242)*.

Cash equivalent   Highly liquid short-term investments that can be converted into cash with little delay *(p. 750)*.

Cash flows   Cash receipts and cash payments (disbursements) *(p. 747)*.

Cash receipts journal   Special journal used to record cash receipts *(p. 237)*.

Central processing unit (CPU)   The brain of a computer. It performs mathematical and logical operations and controls the other components of the computer system *(p. 863)*.

Certified General Accountant (CGA)   A professional accountant who earns this title through a combination of education and experience and the passing of national exams in certain subjects. *(p. 7)*.

Certified Management Accountant (CMA)   A professional accountant who earns this title through a combination of education, experience, and acceptable scores on national written examinations *(p. 7)*.

Chartered Accountant (CA)   A professional accountant who earns this title through a combination of education, experience, and an acceptable score on a written four-part national examination *(p. 7)*.

Chairperson of the board   Elected person on a corporation's board of directors, usually the most powerful person in the corporation *(p. 575)*.

Change in accounting estimate   A change that occurs in the normal course of business as a company alters earlier expectations. Decreasing uncollectible account expense from 2 percent to 1 1/2 percent of sales and changing the estimated useful life of a plant asset are examples *(p. 503)*.

Change in accounting principle   A change in accounting method, such as from the FIFO method to the LIFO method for inventories and a switch from an accelerated depreciation method to the straight-line method *(p. 503)*.

Chart of accounts   List of all the accounts and their account numbers in the ledger *(p. 59)*.

Cheque   Document that instructs the bank to pay the designated person or business the specified amount of money *(p. 286)*.

Cheque register   Special journal used to record all cheques issued in a voucher system *(p. 303)*.

Closing entries   Entries that transfer the revenue, expense, and owner withdrawal balances from these respective accounts to the capital account *(p. 145)*.

Closing the accounts   Step in the accounting cycle at the end of the period that prepares the accounts for recording the transactions of the next period. Closing the accounts consists of journalizing and posting the closing entries to set the balances of the revenue, expense, and owner withdrawal accounts to zero *(p. 142)*.

Collection method   Method of applying the revenue principle by which the seller waits until cash is received to record the sale. This method is used only if the receipt of cash is uncertain *(p. 498)*.

Commission   Employee compensation computed as a percentage of the sales that the employee has made *(p. 452)*.

Common-size statement   A financial statement that reports only percentages (no dollar amounts); a type of vertical analysis *(p. 799)*.

Common stock   The most basic form of capital stock. In describing a corporation, the common shareholders are the owners of the business *(p. 579)*.

Comparability principle   Specifies that accounting information must be comparable from business to business and that a single business's financial statements must be comparable from one period to the next *(p. 496)*.

Completed-contract method Method of applying the revenue principle by a construction company by which all revenue earned on the project is recorded in the period when the project is completed *(p. 500)*.

Conservatism Concept that underlies presenting the gloomiest possible figures in the financial statements *(p. 374)*.

Consignment Transfer of goods by the owner (consignor) to another business (consignee) who, for a fee, sells the inventory on the owner's behalf. The consignee does not take title to the consigned goods *(p. 367)*.

Consistency principle A business must use the same accounting methods and procedures from period to period *(p. 372)*.

Consolidation method for investments A way to combine the financial statements of two or more companies that are controlled by the same owners *(p. 711)*.

Constant dollars Dollars that are restated using the consumer price index so that they have the same purchasing power as the dollars to which they are being compared *(p. 719)*.

Consumer price index A price index published monthly by Statistics Canada that tracks the movement of consumer prices over time and indicates changes in the purchasing power of the dollar *(p. 719)*.

Contingent liability A potential liability *(p. 343)*.

Contra account An account with two distinguishing characteristics: (1) it always has a companion account and (2) its normal balance is opposite that of the companion account *(p. 97)*.

Contra asset An asset account with a credit balance. A contra account always has a companion account and its balance is opposite that of the companion account *(p. 97)*.

Contract interest rate Interest rate that determines the amount of cash interest the borrower pays and the investor receives each year. Also called the Stated interest rate *(p. 657)*.

Control account An account whose balance equals the sum of the balances in a group of related accounts in a subsidiary ledger *(p. 236)*.

Controlling (majority) interest Ownership of more than 50 percent of an investee company's voting stock *(p. 711)*.

Convertible bonds Bonds that may be converted into the common stock of the issuing company at the option of the investor *(p. 670)*.

Convertible preferred stock Preferred stock that may be exchanged by the preferred shareholders, if they choose, for another class of stock in the corporation *(p. 590)*.

Copyright Exclusive right to reproduce and sell a book, musical composition, film, or other work of art. Issued by the federal government, copyrights extend 50 years beyond the author's life *(p. 422)*.

Corporation A business owned by shareholders that begins when the federal government or provincial government approves its articles of incorporation. A corporation is a legal entity, an "artificial person," in the eyes of the law *(p. 12)*.

Cost accounting The branch of accounting that determines and controls a business's costs *(p. 10)*.

Cost method for investments The method used to account for short-term investments in stock and for long-term investments when the investor holds less than 20 percent of the investee's voting stock. Under the cost method, investments are recorded at cost and reported at the lower of their cost or market value *(p. 706)*.

Cost of a plant asset Purchase price, sales tax, purchase commission and all other amounts paid to acquire the asset and to ready it for its intended use *(p. 404)*.

Cost of goods sold The cost of the inventory that the business has sold to customers, the largest single expense of most merchandising businesses. Also called Cost of sales *(p. 183)*.

Cost of sales Another name for Cost of goods sold *(p. 183)*.

Cost principle States that assets and services are recorded at their purchase cost and that the accounting record of the asset continues to be based on cost rather than current market value *(p. 497)*.

Coupon bonds Bonds for which the owners receive interest by detaching a perforated coupon (which states the interest due and the date of payment), from the bond and depositing it in a bank for collection *(p. 654)*.

CPP Abbreviation for Canada Pension Plan *(p. 455)*.

CPU Abbreviation of Central processing unit *(p. 863)*.

Credit The right side of an account *(p. 47)*.

Credit memorandum Document issued by a seller to indicate having credited a customer's account receivable account *(p. 246)*.

Creditor The party to a credit transaction who sells a service or merchandise and obtains a receivable *(p. 327)*.

Cumulative preferred stock Preferred stock whose owners must receive all dividends in arrears before the corporation pays dividends to the common shareholders *(p. 588)*.

Current asset An asset that is expected to be converted to cash, sold, or consumed during the next twelve months, or within the business's normal operating cycle if longer than a year *(p. 148)*.

Current liability A debt due to be paid within one year or one of the entity's operating cycles if the cycle is longer than a year *(p. 149)*.

Current portion of long-term debt Amount of the principal that is payable within one year *(p. 447)*.

Current ratio Current assets divided by current liabilities *(p. 805)*.

Current value Present cost of replacing an asset's particular service potential or usefulness *(p. 720)*.

Date of record Date on which the owners of stock to receive a dividend are identified *(p. 613)*.

Days' sales in receivables Ratio of average net accounts receivable to one day's sales. Tells how many days' sales remain in Accounts Receivable awaiting collection *(p. 808)*.

Debentures Unsecured bonds, backed only by the good faith of the borrower *(p. 655)*.

Debit The left side of an account *(p. 47)*.

Debit memorandum Business document issued by a buyer to state that the buyer no longer owes the seller for the amount of returned purchases *(p. 248)*.

Debt ratio Ratio of total liabilities to total assets. Tells the proportion of a company's assets that it has financed with debt *(p. 810)*.

Debtor The party to a credit transaction who makes a purchase and creates a payable *(p. 327)*.

Declaration date Date on which the board of directors announce the intention to pay a dividend. The declaration creates a liability for the corporation *(p. 613)*.

Default on a note Failure of the maker of a note to pay at maturity. Also called Dishonour of a note *(p. 343)*.

Deferred income taxes The reconciling amount that results when different amounts are added to or deducted from income for tax purposes and for financial reporting purposes. Occurs when Income tax allocation is used *(p. 857)*.

Deferred revenue Another name for Unearned revenue *(p. 578)*.

Deficit Debit balance in the retained earnings account *(p. 578)*.

Defined benefits pension plan Benefits to be paid to the employee upon retirement are specified *(p. 675)*.

Defined contribution pension plan The contribution to the plan is defined and the benefits to be paid to the employee depend on what is available at retirement *(p. 675)*.

Depletion That portion of a natural resource's cost that is used up in a particular period. Depletion expense is computed in the same way as units of production depreciation *(p. 420)*.

Deposit in transit A deposit recorded by the company but not yet by its bank *(p. 288)*.

Depreciation Expense associated with spreading (allocating) the cost of a plant asset over its useful life *(p. 96)*.

Direct method Format of the operating activities section of the statement of changes in financial position that lists the major categories of operating cash receipts (collections from customers and receipts of interest and dividends) and cash disbursements (payments to suppliers, to employees, for interest and income taxes) *(p. 751)*.

Direct write-off method A method of accounting for bad debts by which the company waits until the credit department decides that a customer's account receivable is uncollectible and then records uncollectible account expense and credits the customer's account receivable *(p. 329)*.

Disclosure principle Holds that a company's financial statements should report enough information for outsiders to make knowledgeable decisions about the company *(p. 501)*.

Discounting a note payable A borrowing arrangement in which the bank subtracts the interest amount from the note's face value. The borrower receives the net amount *(p. 444)*.

Discounting a note receivable Selling a note receivable before its maturity *(p. 342)*.

Dishonour of a note Another name for Default on a note *(p. 343)*.

Disk drive Computer input device that reads data and instructions from magnetic disks *(p. 863)*.

Diskette Thin 5¼ inch or 3½ inch diameter round magnetic disk enclosed in a square plastic envelope. Also called a Floppy diskette *(p. 863)*.

Dissolution Ending of a partnership *(p. 532)*.

Dividend yield Ratio of dividends per share of stock to the stock's market price per share *(p. 815)*.

Dividends Distributions by a corporation to its shareholders *(p. 578)*.

Dividends in arrears Cumulative preferred dividends that the corporation has failed to pay *(p. 588)*.

Donated capital Special category of shareholders' equity created when a corporation receives a donation (gift) from a donor who receives no ownership interest in the company *(p. 586)*.

Declining-balance (DB) method See Accelerated depreciation *(p. 409)*.

Double taxation Corporations pay their own income taxes on corporate income. Then, the shareholders pay personal income tax on the cash dividends that they receive from corporations *(p. 575)*.

Doubtful account expense Another name for Uncollectible account expense *(p. 329)*.

Earnings per share (EPS) Amount of a company's net income per share of its outstanding common stock *(p. 631)*.

Economic dependence A company that is dependent on another company as its supplier or customer *(p. 508)*.

Effective interest rate Another name for market interest rate *(p. 657)*.

Electronic fund transfer System that accounts for cash transactions by electronic impulses rather than paper documents *(p. 305)*.

Ending inventory Goods still on hand at the end of the period *(p. 366)*.

Entity An organization or a section of an organization that, for accounting purposes, stands apart from other organizations and individuals as a separate economic unit. This is the most basic concept in accounting *(p. 13)*.

Entry price The amount of cash required to buy an asset that is similar to the asset being valued *(p. 720)*.

EPS Abbreviation of Earnings per share of common stock *(p. 631)*.

Equity A legal and economic claim to the assets of a business. Equities are divided between outsider claims (liabilities) and insider claims (owner equity or capital) *(p. 15)*.

Equity method for investments The method used to account for investments in which the investor can significantly influence the decisions of the investee. Under the equity method, investments are recorded initially at cost. The investment account is debited (increased) for ownership in the investee's net income and credited (decreased) for ownership in the investee's dividends *(p. 709)*.

Estimated residual value Expected cash value of an asset at the end of its useful life. Also called Residual value, Scrap value and Salvage value *(p. 407)*.

Estimated useful life Length of the service that a business expects to get from an asset, may be expressed in years, units of output, miles or other measures *(p. 407)*.

Exit price The net amount of cash that would be received from selling the asset *(p. 720)*.

Expense Decrease in owner equity that occurs in the course of delivering goods or services to customers or clients *(p. 19)*.

Extraordinary item A gain or loss that is infrequent, not typical of the business and does not depend on a management decision *(p. 630)*.

Extraordinary repair Repair work that generates a capital expenditure *(p. 423)*.

FIFO The First-in, first-out inventory method *(p. 368)*.

Financial accounting The branch of accounting that provides information to people outside the business *(p. 12)*.

Financial statements Business documents that report financial information about an entity to persons and organizations outside the business *(p. 22)*.

Financing activity Activity that obtains the funds from investors and creditors needed to launch and sustain the business. A section of the statement of changes in financial position *(p. 749)*.

First-in, first-out (FIFO) method Inventory costing method by which the first costs into inventory are the first costs out to cost of goods sold. Ending inventory is based on the costs of the most recent purchases *(p. 368)*.

FOB destination Terms of a transaction that govern when the title to the inventory passes from the seller to the purchaser — when the goods arrive at the purchaser's location *(p. 367)*.

FOB shipping point Terms of a transaction that govern when the title to the inventory passes from the seller to the purchaser — when the goods leave the seller's place of business *(p. 367)*.

Franchises and licenses Privileges granted by a private business or a government to sell a product or service in accordance with specified conditions *(p. 422)*.

Fringe benefits Employee compensation, like health and life insurance and retirement pay, which the employee does not receive immediately in cash *(p. 453)*.

Gain An increase in owner equity that does not result from a revenue or an investment by an owner in the business *(p. 511)*.

Generally accepted accounting principles (GAAP) Accounting guidelines, formulated by the CICA's Accounting Standards Committee, that govern how businesses report their financial statements to the public *(p. 9)*.

General journal Journal used to record all transactions that do not fit one of the special journals *(p. 233)*.

General ledger Ledger of accounts that are reported in the financial statements *(p. 234)*.

Going-concern concept Accountants' assumption that the business will continue operating in the foreseeable future *(p. 494)*.

Goods available for sale Beginning inventory plus net purchases *(p. 365)*.

Goodwill Excess of the cost of an acquired company over the sum of the market values of its net assets (assets minus liabilities) *(p. 423)*.

Gross margin Excess of sales revenue over cost of goods sold. Also called Gross profit *(p. 176)*.

Gross margin method A way to estimate inventory based on a rearrangement of the cost of goods sold model: Beginning inventory + Net purchases = Cost of goods available for sale. Cost of goods available for sale − Cost of goods sold = Ending inventory. Also called the Gross profit method *(p. 377)*.

Gross pay Total amount of salary, wages, commissions, or any other employee compensation before taxes and other deductions are taken out *(p. 453)*.

Gross profit Excess of sales revenue over cost of goods sold. Also called Gross margin *(p. 176)*.

Gross profit method Another name for the gross margin method of estimating inventory cost *(p. 377)*.

Hardware Equipment that makes up a computer system *(p. 230)*.

High-low method Method of separating a mixed cost into its variable and fixed components *(p. 896)*.

Holding gain (loss) The gain (loss) that arises from holding an item in inventory when the cost of the item increases *(p. 727)*.

Horizontal analysis Study of percentage changes in comparative financial statements *(p. 794)*.

Imprest system A way to account for petty cash by maintaining a constant balance in the petty cash account, supported by the fund (cash plus disbursement tickets) totalling the same amount *(p. 298)*.

Income from operations Gross margin (sales revenue minus cost of goods sold) minus operating expenses. Also called Operating income *(p. 191)*.

Income statement List of an entity's revenues, expenses, and net income or net loss for a specific period. Also called the Statement of operations *(p. 23)*.

Income summary A temporary "holding tank" account into which the revenues and expenses are transferred prior to their final transfer to the capital account *(p. 145)*.

Income tax A general-purpose tax levied on the income of a taxpayer. Entirely separate from all other taxes, it is the federal government's largest source of revenue *(p. 843)*.

Incorporators Persons who organize a corporation *(p. 575)*.

Indirect method Format of the operating activities section of the statement of changes in financial position that starts with net income and shows the reconciliation from net income to operating cash flows. Also called the Reconciliation method *(p. 766)*.

Inflation Decrease in the purchasing power of the dollar *(p. 719)*.

Information system design Identification of an organization's information needs, and development and implementation of the system to meet those needs *(p. 11)*.

Installment method Method of applying the revenue principle in which gross profit (sales revenue minus cost of goods sold) is recorded as cash is collected *(p. 498)*.

Intangible asset An asset with no physical form, a special right to current and expected future benefits *(p. 403)*.

Integrated software Computer program that includes modules handling different functions. Coordinates the output of the various modules *(p. 864)*.

Interest The revenue to the payee for loaning out the principal, and the expense to the maker for borrowing the principal *(p. 339)*.

Interest-coverage ratio Another name for the Times-interest-earned ratio *(p. 810)*.

Interest period The period of time during which interest is to be computed, extending from the original date of the note to the maturity date *(p. 339)*.

Interest rate The percentage rate that is multiplied by the principal amount to compute the amount of interest on a note *(p. 339)*.

Internal auditing Auditing that is performed by a business's own accountants to evaluate the firm's accounting and management systems. The aim is to improve operating efficiency and to ensure that employees follow management's procedures and plans *(p. 11)*.

Internal control Organizational plan and all the related measures adopted by an entity to meet management's objectives of discharging statutory responsibilities, profitability, prevention and deletion of fraud and error, safeguarding of assets, reliability of accounting records, and timely preparation of reliable financial information *(p. 229)*.

Inventory cost Price paid to acquire inventory — not the selling price of the goods. Inventory cost includes its invoice price, less all discounts, plus sales tax, tariffs, transportation fees, insurance while in transit, and all other costs incurred to make the goods ready for sale *(p. 367)*.

Inventory turnover Ratio of cost of goods sold to average inventory. Measures the number of times a company sells its average level of inventory during a year *(p. 807)*.

Investing activity Activity that increases and decreases the assets that the business has to work with. A section of the statement of changes in financial position *(p. 749)*.

Invoice Seller's request for payment from a purchaser. Also called a bill *(p. 177)*.

Journal The chronological accounting record of an entity's transactions *(p. 49)*.

Last-in, first-out (LIFO) method Inventory costing method by which the last costs into inventory are the first costs out to cost of goods sold. This leaves the oldest cost — those of beginning inventory and the earliest purchases of the period — in ending inventory (p. 369).

LCM rule The Lower-of-cost-or-market rule (p. 375).

Lease Rental agreement in which the tenant (lessee) agrees to make rent payments to the property owner (lessor) in exchange for the use of the asset (p. 672).

Leasehold Prepayment that a lessee (renter) makes to secure the use of an asset from a lessor (landlord) (p. 422).

Ledger The book of accounts (p. 43).

Lessee Tenant in a lease agreement (p. 672).

Lessor Property owner in a lease agreement (p. 672).

Leverage Another name for Trading on the equity (p. 813).

Liability An economic obligation (a debt) payable to an individual or an organization outside the business (p. 15).

LIFO The Last-in, first-out inventory method (p. 369).

Limited liability No personal obligation of a shareholder for corporation debts. The most that a shareholder can lose on an investment in a corporation's stock is the cost of the investment (p. 574).

Liquidation The process of going out of business by selling the entity's assets and paying its liabilities. The final step in liquidation of a business is the distribution of any remaining cash to the owners (p. 549).

Liquidation value of stock Amount a corporation agrees to pay a preferred shareholder per share if the company liquidates (p. 592).

Liquidity Measure of how quickly an item may be converted to cash (p. 148).

Long-term asset An asset other than a current asset (p. 148).

Long-term investment Separate asset category reported on the balance sheet between current assets and plant assets (p. 678).

Long-term liability A liability other than a current liability (p. 149).

Loss A decrease in owner equity that does not result from an expense or a distribution to an owner of the business (p. 511).

Lower-of-cost-or-market (LCM) rule Requires that an asset be reported in the financial statements at the lower of its historical cost or its market value (current replacement cost or net realizable value) (p. 375).

Mainframe system Computer system characterized by a single computer (p. 230).

Maker of a note The person or business that signs the note and promises to pay the amount required by the note agreement. The maker is the debtor (p. 339).

Management accounting The branch of accounting that generates confidential information for internal decision makers of a business, such as top executives (p. 12).

Marginal income The income earned by a taxpayer that puts the taxpayer into the next (higher) tax bracket. For example, in Ontario, marginal income would be income above $28,275 or $56,549 (p. 848).

Marginal income tax rate The higher rate of tax paid on a marginal dollar of income (p. 848).

Market interest rate Interest rate that investors demand in order to loan their money. Also called the Effective interest rate (p. 657).

Market value of stock Price for which a person could buy or sell a share of stock (p. 591).

Marketable security Another name for short-term investment, one that may be sold any time the investor wishes (p. 705).

Matching principle The basis for recording expenses. Directs accountants to identify all expenses incurred during the period, measure the expenses and match them against the revenues earned during that same span of time (p. 92).

Materiality concept States that a company must perform strictly proper accounting only for items and transactions that are significant to the business's financial statements (p. 509).

Maturity date The date on which the final payment of a note is due. Also called the due date (p. 339).

Maturity value The sum of the principal and interest due at the maturity date of a note (p. 339).

Menu List of options for choosing computer functions (p. 865).

Menu-driven Type of computer software that offers a list of options for doing various functions (p. 865).

Microcomputer A computer small enough for each employee (work station) to have his or her own (p. 231).

Minicomputer Small computer that operates like a large system but on a smaller scale (p. 231).

Minority interest A subsidiary company's equity that is held by shareholders other than the parent company (p. 714).

Monetary asset Asset whose value is stated in a fixed number of dollars. This amount does not change, regardless of changes in the purchasing power of the dollar (p. 724).

Monetary liability Liability stated in a fixed number of dollars. This amount does not change, regardless of changes in the purchasing power of the dollar (p. 725).

Monitor Computer output device that resembles a television and allows the user to view data being processed and to receive messages from the program being run (p. 863).

Mortgage Borrower's promise to transfer the legal title to certain assets to the lender if the debt is not paid on schedule (p. 671).

Multiple-step income statement Format that contains subtotals to highlight significant relationships. In addition to net income, it also presents gross margin and income from operations (p. 196).

Mutual agency Every partner can bind the business to a contract within the scope of the partnership's regular business operations (p. 532).

Net earnings Another name for Net income or Net profit (p. 19).

Net income Excess of total revenues over total expenses. Also called Net earnings or Net profit (p. 19).

Net loss Excess of total expenses over total revenues (p. 19).

Net monetary assets Excess of monetary assets over monetary liabilities (p. 725).

Net monetary liabilities Excess of monetary liabilities over monetary assets (p. 725).

Net pay Gross pay minus all deductions, the amount of employee compensation that the employee actually takes home (p. 453).

Net profit Another name for Net income or Net earnings (p. 19).

Net purchases Purchases less purchase discounts and purchase returns and allowances (p. 181).

Net sales Sales revenue less sales discounts and sales returns and allowances (p. 183).

Nominal account Another name for a Temporary account — revenues and expenses — that are closed at the end of the period. In a proprietorship the owner withdrawal account is also nominal (p. 144).

Nominal dollars Dollars stated in terms of current purchasing power. The antonym is Constant dollars (p. 719).

Nonmonetary asset Asset whose price may change when the purchasing power of the dollar changes, such as inventory, land, buildings and equipment *(p. 725)*.

Non-refundable tax credit Another name for a Tax credit *(p. 853)*.

Non-sufficient funds cheque A "hot" cheque, one for which the payer's bank account has insufficient money to pay the cheque *(p. 288)*.

Note payable A liability evidenced by a written promise to make a future payment *(p. 16)*.

Note receivable An asset evidenced by another party's written promise that entitles you to receive cash in the future *(p. 15)*.

NSF cheque A non-sufficient funds cheque *(p. 288)*.

Off-balance-sheet financing Acquisition of assets or services with debt that is not reported on the balance sheet *(p. 674)*.

On-line processing Computerized accounting for transaction data on a continuous basis, often from various locations, rather than in batches at a single location *(p. 232)*.

Operating activity Activity that creates revenue or expense in the entity's major line of business. Operating activities affect the income statement. A section of the statement of changes in financial position *(p. 749)*.

Operating capability (capital) The ability of an organization to provide a particular level of production of goods or provision of services *(p. 722)*.

Operating expenses Expenses, other than cost of goods sold, that are incurred in the entity's major line of business: rent, depreciation, salaries, wages, utilities, property tax and supplies expense *(p. 191)*.

Operating income Another name for Income from operations *(p. 191)*.

Operating lease Usually a short-term or cancelable rental agreement *(p. 672)*.

Ordinary repair Repair work that creates a revenue expenditure, which is debited to an expense account *(p. 424)*.

Organization cost The costs of organizing a corporation, including legal fees, taxes and charges by promoters for selling the stock. Organization cost is an intangible asset *(p. 587)*.

Other expense Expense that is outside the main operations of a business, such as a loss on the sale of plant assets *(p. 191)*.

Other receivables A miscellaneous category that includes loans to employees and branch companies, usually long-term assets reported on the balance sheet after current assets and before plant assets. Other receivables can be current assets *(p. 328)*.

Other revenue Revenue that is outside the main operations of a business, such as a gain on the sale of plant assets *(p. 191)*.

Outstanding cheque A cheque issued by the company and recorded on its books but not yet paid by its bank *(p. 288)*.

Outstanding stock Stock in the hands of a shareholder *(p. 576)*.

Owner's equity The claim of an owner of a business to the assets of the business. Also called Capital *(p. 15)*.

Par value Arbitrary amount assigned to a share of stock *(p. 580)*.

Parent company An investor company that owns more than 50 percent of the voting stock of a subsidiary company *(p. 711)*.

Participating preferred stock Preferred stock whose owners may receive (that is, participate in) dividends beyond the stated amount or stated percentage *(p. 589)*.

Partnership A business with two or more owners *(p. 12)*.

Partnership agreement Another name for the Articles of partnership *(p. 532)*.

Patent A federal government grant giving the holder the exclusive right for 17 years to produce and sell an invention *(p. 422)*.

Payee of a note The person or business to whom the maker of a note promises future payment. The payee is the creditor *(p. 339)*.

Payroll Employee compensation, a major expense of many businesses *(p. 452)*.

Pension Employee compensation that will be received during retirement *(p. 674)*.

Percentage of completion method Method of applying the revenue principle by a construction company by which revenue is recorded as the work is performed *(p. 500)*.

Periodic inventory system The business does not keep a continuous record of the inventory on hand. Instead, at the end of the period the business makes a physical count of the on-hand inventory and applies the appropriate unit costs to determine the cost of the ending inventory *(p. 379)*.

Permanent accounts The assets, liabilities and capital accounts. These accounts are *not* closed at the end of the period because their balances are not used to measure income. Also called a Real account *(p. 144)*.

Perpetual inventory system The business keeps a continuous record for each inventory item to show the inventory on hand at all times *(p. 380)*.

Petty cash Fund containing a small amount of cash that is used to pay minor expenditures *(p. 298)*.

Plant asset Long-lived assets, like land, buildings and equipment, used in the operation of the business *(p. 96)*.

Postclosing trial balance List of the ledger accounts and their balances at the end of the period after the journalizing and posting of the closing entries. The last step of the accounting cycle, the postclosing trial balance ensures that the ledger is in balance for the start of the next accounting period *(p. 147)*.

Posting Transferring of amounts from the journal to the ledger *(p. 50)*.

Preferred stock Stock that gives its owners certain advantages over common shareholders, such as the priority to receive dividends before the common shareholders and the priority to receive assets before the common shareholders if the corporation liquidates *(p. 579)*.

Prepaid expense A category of miscellaneous assets that typically expire or get used up in the near future. Examples include prepaid rent, prepaid insurance, and supplies *(p. 94)*.

Present value Amount a person would invest now to receive a greater amount at a future date *(p. 656)*.

President Chief operating officer in charge of managing the day-to-day operations of a corporation *(p. 575)*.

Price/earnings ratio Ratio of the market price of a share of common stock to the company's earnings per share *(p. 814)*.

Principal amount The amount loaned out by the payee and borrowed by the maker of a note *(p. 339)*.

Printer The printer prints out information stored in the central processing unit *(p. 863)*.

Prior period adjustment Correction to retained earnings for an error of an earlier period is a prior period adjustment *(p. 634)*.

Private accountant Accountant who works for a single business, such as a department store or Northern Telecom *(p. 7)*.

Program Set of instructions that tell the computer what to do *(p. 861)*.

Progressive tax A tax where the rates of tax increase as income increases. For example, income tax *(p. 846)*.

Promissory note   A written promise to pay a specified amount of money at a particular future date *(p. 339)*.

Proprietorship   A business with a single owner *(p. 12)*.

Proxy   Legal document that expresses a shareholder's preference and appoints another person to cast the vote *(p. 575)*.

Public accountant   Accountant who serves the general public and collects fees for work, which includes auditing, income tax planning and preparation, management consulting and bookkeeping *(p. 7)*.

Purchase discount   Reduction in the cost of inventory that is offered by a seller as an incentive for the customer to pay promptly. A contra account to purchases *(p. 179)*.

Purchase returns and allowances   Decrease in a buyer's debt from returning merchandise to the seller or from receiving from the seller an allowance from the amount owed. A contra account to purchases *(p. 180)*.

Purchases   The cost of inventory that a firm buys to resell to customers in the normal course of business *(p. 177)*.

Purchases journal   Special journal used to record all purchases of inventory, supplies and other assets on account *(p. 242)*.

Purchasing power gain (or loss)   A purchasing power gain occurs during inflation because a company is able to pay its liabilities with dollars that are cheaper than the dollars borrowed. A purchasing power loss occurs during inflation when a creditor receives dollars that are worth less than the dollars lent *(p. 724)*.

Quick ratio   Another name for the Acid-test ratio *(p. 806)*.

Rate of return on common shareholder's equity   Net income minus preferred dividends, divided by average common shareholders' equity. A measure of profitability. Also called Return on common shareholders' equity *(p. 812)*.

Rate of return on net sales   Ratio of net income to net sales. A measure of profitability. Also called Return on sales *(p. 811)*.

Rate of return on total assets   The sum of net income plus interest expense divided by average total assets. This ratio measures the success a company has in using its assets to earn a profit. Also called Return on assets *(p. 812)*.

Real account   Another name for a Permanent account — asset, liability and capital — that is *not* closed at the end of the period *(p. 144)*.

Receivable   A monetary claim against a business or an individual, acquired mainly by selling goods and services and by lending money *(p. 327)*.

Reconciliation method   Another name for the indirect method of formatting the operating activities section of the statement of changes in financial position *(p. 766)*.

Redemption value of stock   Price a corporation agrees to pay for stock, which is set when the stock is issued *(p. 591)*.

Registered bonds   Bonds for which the owners receive interest cheques from the issuing company *(p. 654)*.

Regressive tax   A tax which is a fixed percentage and which is not levied on the basis of ability to pay; thus individuals with high incomes pay a smaller proportion of their income in taxes than do individuals with low incomes. For example, sales tax *(p. 848)*.

Relative-sales-value method   Allocation technique for identifying the cost of each asset purchased in a group for a single amount *(p. 405)*.

Reliability principle   Requires that accounting information be dependable (free from error and bias). Also called the Objectivity principle *(p. 496)*.

Report format of the balance sheet   Format that lists the assets at the top, with the liabilities and owner equity below *(p. 149)*.

Residual value   Same as Estimated residual value *(p. 407)*.

Retail method   A way to estimate inventory cost based on the cost of goods sold model. The retail method requires that the business record inventory purchases both at cost and at retail. Multiply ending inventory at retail by the cost ratio to estimate the ending inventory's cost *(p. 378)*.

Retained earnings   A corporation's capital that is earned through profitable operation of the business *(p. 577)*.

Return on assets   Another name for Rate of return on total assets *(p. 812)*.

Return on common shareholders' equity   Another name for Rate of return on common shareholders' equity *(p. 812)*.

Return on sales   Another name for Rate of return on net sales *(p. 811)*.

Revenue   Increase in owner equity that is earned by delivering goods or services to customers or clients *(p. 18)*.

Revenue Canada rate   The maximum depreciation rate, also called the Capital cost allowance rate, that Revenue Canada allows a taxpayer to use in calculating depreciation expense, also called capital cost allowance, in determining taxable income *(p. 409)*.

Revenue expenditure   Expenditure that merely maintains an asset in its existing condition or restores the asset to good working order. Revenue expenditures are expensed (matched against revenue) *(p. 424)*.

Revenue principle   The basis for recording revenues, tells accountants when to record revenue and the amount of revenue to record *(p. 91)*.

Reversing entry   An entry that switches the debit and the credit of a previous adjusting entry. The reversing entry is dated the first day of the period following the adjusting entry *(p. 882)*.

Salary   Employee compensation stated at a yearly, monthly or weekly rate *(p. 452)*.

Sales discount   Reduction in the amount receivable from a customer, offered by the seller as an incentive for the customer to pay promptly. A contra account to Sales revenue *(p. 182)*.

Sales journal   Special journal used to record credit sales *(p. 234)*.

Sales method   Method of applying the revenue principle in which revenue is recorded at the point of sale. This method is used for most sales of goods and services *(p. 498)*.

Sales returns and allowances   Decrease in the seller's receivable from a customer's return of merchandise or from granting the customer an allowance from the amount the customer owes the seller. A contra account to Sales revenue *(p. 182)*.

Sales revenue   Amount that a merchandiser earns from selling inventory before subtracting expenses *(p. 182)*.

Salvage value   Another name for residual value or estimated residual value *(p. 407)*.

Segment of a business   A distinguishable component of a company *(p. 628)*.

Serial bonds   Bonds that mature in installments over a period of time *(p. 654)*.

Service charge   Bank's fee for processing a depositor's transactions *(p. 288)*.

Share capital   Another name for Capital stock *(p. 577)*.

Shareholder   A person who owns the stock of a corporation *(p. 12)*.

Shareholders' equity   Owners' equity of a corporation *(p. 577)*.

Short-term note payable   Note payable due within one year, a common form of financing *(p. 444)*.

Single-step income statement   Format that groups all revenues together and then lists and deducts all expenses together without drawing any subtotals *(p. 196).*

Slide   An accounting error that results from adding one or more zeroes to a number, or from dropping a zero. For example, writing $500 as $5,000 or as $50 is a slide. A slide is evenly divisible by 9 *(p. 151).*

Software   Set of programs or instructions that cause the computer to perform the work desired *(p. 151).*

Specific cost method   Inventory cost method based on the specific cost of particular units of inventory *(p. 368).*

Spreadsheet   Integrated software program that can be used to solve many different kinds of problems. An electronically prepared work sheet *(p. 151).*

Stable monetary unit concept   Accountants' basis for ignoring the effect of inflation and making no adjustments for the changing value of the dollar *(p. 495).*

Stated capital   The value assigned by the Board of Directors of a corporation to a share of no-par stock at the time of its issue and thus its issue price *(p. 577).*

Stated interest rate   Another name for the Contract interest rate *(p. 657).*

Statement of changes in financial position   Reports cash receipts and cash disbursements classified according to the entity's major activities: operating, financing and investing *(p. 747).*

Statement of financial position   Another name for the Balance sheet *(p. 23).*

Statement of operations   Another name for the Income statement *(p. 23).*

Statement of owner's equity   Summary of the changes in the owner equity of an entity during a specific period *(p. 23).*

Stock   Shares into which the owners' equity of a corporation is divided *(p. 574).*

Stock dividend   A proportional distribution by a corporation of its own stock to its shareholders *(p. 613).*

Stock split   An increase in the number of outstanding shares of stock coupled with a proportionate reduction in the book value per share of stock *(p. 616).*

Stock subscription   Contract that obligates an investor to purchase the corporation's stock at a later date *(p. 582).*

Straight-line method   Depreciation method in which an equal amount of depreciation expense is assigned to each year (or period) of asset use *(p. 407).*

Subsequent event   An event that occurs after the end of a company's accounting period but before publication of its financial statements and which may affect the interpretation of the information in those statements *(p. 504).*

Subsidiary company   An investee company in which a parent company owns more than 50 percent of the voting stock *(p. 711).*

Subsidiary ledger   Book of accounts that provides supporting details on individual balances, the total of which appears in a general ledger account *(p. 236).*

Tax avoidance   Structuring of business transactions in order to pay the least amount of income tax at the latest possible time permitted by the law *(p. 859).*

Tax credit   Amount that is subtracted directly from the amount of tax owed to the government. Also called Non-refundable tax credits *(p. 851).*

Tax evasion   Illegal activity designed to reduce tax *(p. 859).*

Tax return   Document on which each taxpayer reports income and shows the computation of income tax *(p. 848).*

Taxable income   Earnings amount on which the income tax is based. It is the figure that is multiplied by the tax rate to compute the amount of income tax *(p. 846).*

Temporary accounts   The revenue and expense accounts which relate to a particular accounting period are closed at the end of the period. For a proprietorship, the owner withdrawal account is also temporary. Also called a Nominal account *(p. 144).*

Term bonds   Bonds that all mature at the same time for a particular issue *(p. 654).*

Time and a half   Overtime pay computed as 150 percent (1.5 times) the straight-time rate *(p. 452).*

Time period concept   Ensures that accounting information is reported at regular intervals *(p. 494).*

Times-interest-earned ratio   Ratio of income from operations to interest expense. Measures the number of times that operating income can cover interest expense. Also called the Interest-coverage ratio *(p. 810).*

Trade discount   A purchase discount that provides a lower price per item the larger the quantity purchased *(p. 180).*

Trademarks and trade names   Distinctive identifications of a product or service *(p. 422).*

Trading gain (loss)   The gain (loss) that arises from the sale of an item from inventory *(p. 727).*

Trading on the equity   Earning more income than the borrowed amount, which increases the earnings for the owners of a business. Also called Leverage *(p. 677).*

Transaction   An event that affects the financial position of a particular entity and may be reliably recorded *(p. 16).*

Transposition   An accounting error that occurs when digits are flip-flopped. For example, $85 is a transposition of $58. A transposition is evenly divisible by 9 *(p. 151).*

Treasury stock   A corporation's own stock that it has issued and later reacquired *(p. 618).*

Trial balance   A list of all the ledger accounts with their balances *(p. 54).*

UI   Abbreviation of Unemployment Insurance *(p. 455).*

Uncollectible account expense   Cost to the seller of extending credit. Arises from the failure to collect from credit customers *(p. 329).*

Underwriter   Organization that purchases the bonds from an issuing company and resells them to its clients, or sells the bonds for a commission, agreeing to buy all unsold bonds *(p. 654).*

Unearned revenue   A liability created when a business collects cash from customers in advance of doing work for the customer. The obligation is to provide a product or a service in the future. Also called Deferred revenue *(p. 100).*

Unemployment Insurance   All employees and employers in Canada must contribute to the Unemployment Insurance Fund which provides assistance to unemployed workers *(p. 455).*

Units-of-production (UOP) method   Depreciation method by which a fixed amount of depreciation is assigned to each unit of output produced by the plant asset *(p. 408).*

Unlimited personal liability   When a partnership (or a proprietorship) cannot pay its debts with business assets, the partners (or the proprietor) must use personal assets to meet the debt *(p. 533).*

Useful life   Same as Estimated useful life *(p. 407).*

Vertical analysis   Analysis of a financial statement that reveals the relationship of each statement item to the total, which is the 100 percent figure *(p. 797).*

Voucher   Document authorizing a cash disbursement *(p. 299).*

Voucher register   Special journal used to record all expenditures in a voucher system, similar to but more comprehensive than the purchases journal *(p. 301).*

Voucher system   A way to record cash payments that enhances internal control by formalizing the process of approving and recording invoices for payment *(p. 299).*

Wages   Employees' pay stated at an hourly figure *(p. 452).*

Wasting assets   are plant assets that are natural resources *(p. 403).*

Withheld income tax   Income tax deducted from employees' gross pay *(p. 453).*

Work sheet   A columnar document designed to help move data from the trial balance to the financial statements *(p. 132).*

Workers' compensation   A provincially administered plan which is funded by contributions by employers and which provides financial support for workers injured on the job *(p. 456).*

Working capital   Current assets minus current liabilities, measures a business's ability to meet its short-term obligations with its current assets *(p. 805).*

Index

Check Figures for Problems

13-1A Total assets, $152,620
13-2A 1.d. Warner, $30,000; Deitmer, $27,000; Mullaney, $24,000
13-3A 4. Lake's capital at ⅛ interest, $30,000; 5. Lake's capital at 15% interest, $34,500
13-4A 5. Debit Golden, Capital, $29,000
13-5A 1.d. Disbursement of cash to partners: Yagoda, $3,100; Kelly, $2,400; Dobbs, $0
13-6A Disbursements to: Morales, $6,000; Goldberg, $8,000
13-1B 2. Total assets, $111,600
13-2B 1.d. Hogan, $42,500; Stanford, $37,500; Reichlin, $52,000
13-3B 3. Newton's capital at ⅛ interest, $60,000; 5. Newton's capital at 10% interest, $34,000
13-4B 5. Debit Herron, Capital, $60,600
13-5B 1.d. Disbursement of cash to partners: Monet, $0; Dixon, $14,625; Palma, $5,375
13-6B Disbursements: Bell, $2,625; Pastena, $1,375
DP 1 No check figure
DP 2 No check figure

14-1A Total shareholders' equity, $91,000
14-2A Total shareholders' equity: Beliveau, $155,000; Monroe, $585,000
14-3A Total shareholders' equity, $221,570
14-4A Total pref. dividends to pay before paying common dividends, $29,449,156
14-5A 2. 19X3 dividends: Preferred, $2,000; Common, $32,000
14-6A Book value per share: Preferred, $28.20; Common, $7.16
14-7A Total assets, $683,000
14-1B Total shareholders' equity, $177,500
14-2B Total shareholders' equity: Baker, $94,000; Wang, $397,000
14-3B Total shareholders' equity, $324,320
14-4B Total yearly pref. dividends to pay before paying common dividends, $209,556
14-5B 2. 19X3 dividends: Preferred, $42,500; Common, $222,500
14-6B Book value per share: Preferred, $56.45; Common, $4.80
14-7B Total assets, $378,000
DP 1 Total shareholders' equity: Plan 1, $405,200; Plan 2, $380,200
DP 2 No check figure
FSP No check figure

15-1A No check figure
15-2A Total shareholders' equity, Dec. 31, 19X2, $808,700
15-3A Total shareholders' equity, Dec. 31, 19X6, $321,500; Total shareholders' equity, Dec. 31, 19X7, $339,600
15-4A Earnings per share, $3.25; Total shareholders' equity, Sept. 30, 19X6, $618,000
15-5A Retained Earnings balance, Dec. 31, 19X3, $114,000; Earnings per share, $.30

15-6A 2. Debit to Retained Earnings, $28.3 mil.; 2. Debit to Retained Earnings, $0.8 mil.; 1. Credit to Common Stock, $8 mil.
15-7A Earnings per share for net income, $.97; Total shareholders' equity, $420,000
15-1B No check figure
15-2B Total shareholders' equity, Dec. 31, 19X4, $565,400
15-3B Total shareholders' equity, Dec. 31, 19X8, $443,000; Total shareholders' equity, Dec. 31, 19X9, $513,000
15-4B Total shareholders' equity, June 30, 19X5, $509,000
15-5B Retained Earnings balance, June 30, 19X4, $194,000; Earnings per share, $7.85
15-6B 2. Debit to Retained Earnings, $1.3 mil.; 2. Debit to Retained Earnings, $107.8 mil.; 1. Credit to Common Stock, $3.2 million.
15-7B Earnings per share for net income, $2.89
DP 1 No check figure
DP 2 No check figure
FSP No check figure

16-1A 2. Interest Expense, $112,500
16-2A Interest expense for one year, $54,500
16-3A 3. Dec. 31, 19X3, bond carrying value, $105,262
16-4A Sept. 30, 19X5, debenture carrying value, $108,958
16-5A Dec. 31 Interest Expense, Dr. $43,500 (on bonds); Dr. $7,290 (on lease liability)
16-6A No check figure
16-7A 2. Long-term investment in bonds, $486,350; 3. Short-term investment in bonds, $485,000
16-1B 2. Interest Expense, $80,000
16-2B Interest expense for one year, $25,950
16-3B 3. Dec. 31, 19X3, bond carrying value, $45,128
16-4B July 31, 19X5, debenture carrying value, $166,350
16-5B Dec. 31 Interest Expense, Dr. $93,000 (on bonds); Dr. $10,230 (on lease liability)
16-6B No check figure
16-7B Dec. 31, Interest Revenue Cr. $600 (Long-term Investment in bonds)
DP 1 Plan A EPS, $1.26; Plan B EPS, $1.29; Plan C EPS, $1.05
DP 2 No check figure
FSP No check figure

PV-1 3. $112,472; 4. $89,364
PV-2 Dec. 31, 19X2, bond carrying value, $476,049
PV-3 Dec. 31, 19X2, bond carrying value, $4,584,909
PV-4 Dec. 31, Depr. Exp., $3,562; Interest Exp., $2,619
PV-5 Cost (present value) of bond investment, $462,350